ISCARIOTh quierat denumero
duodecim etabiitetconlocutusest
principibussacerdotum quomodotraderet
eum etgauisisunt etconstitueruntei
pecuniam dare etconfessusest
etquaerebatoportunitatemuttraderetei
sineturba: uenitautem diespaschae
inquaoportebatimmolaripascha etmisit
petrumetiohanendicens
euntesparatenobis
pascha utmanducemus adilli
dixerуntei ubibispramenus
tibi adilledixitecce introeuntibus
uobis inciuitatemobuiabit
uobis homobaiulansuascellumaquae
qui sequiminieumindomumubiintro
ierit etdicitis patrifamiliaedomus
dicitmacister ubiest diuersorium
ubipascha cum discipulismeosedam
illeuobis ostendet superioremdomum
stratumibiparate
abientesautem inueneruntsicutdixeratillis
etparauerunt pascha etcum
fuithora recubuit et
apostolicumillo etdixitadeos
concupiscentiaconcupiuihocpascha
manducareuobiscumpriusquampatiar
dicoenimuobis iamnonmanducabo
abeo usquequonobmedatur
inregnodei etaccipiens
calicem benedicens dixit
accipithoc etpartiminiuobis
dicoenimuobisamodo nonbibam

M 2

hermeneia

**Hermeneia
—A Critical
and Historical
Commentary
on the Bible**

Luke 3

A Commentary
on the Gospel of Luke 19:28—24:53

by
François Bovon

Translation by
James Crouch

Edited by
Helmut Koester

**Fortress
Press**   Minneapolis

Luke 3
A Commentary on the Gospel of Luke 19:28—24:53

The Payne and Semitica fonts used to print this work are available from Linguist's Software, Inc., PO Box 580, Edmonds, WA 98020-0580 USA.Tel. 425-775-1130. www.linguistsoftware.com.

Cover and interior design by Kenneth Hiebert
Typesetting and page composition by
The HK Scriptorium

Library of Congress cataloging-in-publication data is available #795757104

The paper used in this publication meets the minimum requirements of American National Standard for Information Sciences—Permanence of paper for Printed Library Materials, ANSI Z329.48–1984.

Manufactured in the U.S.A.

16   15   14   13   12   1   2   3   4   5   6   7   8   9   10

The Author

François Bovon is Frothingham Professor of the History of Religion at Harvard Divinity School. He received his appointment to Harvard in 1993, where he was chair of the New Testament Department from 1993–98, resuming the chair again in 2001. A native of Switzerland, for twenty-six years he was Professor of New Testament and Christian Origins at the Divinity School of the University of Geneva, where he was also dean from 1976–79, and continues as an honorary professor.

He received his baccalaureate degree and licentiate in theology from the University of Lausanne, and his Th.D. from the University of Basel. He has also received an honorary doctorate from the University of Uppsala, Sweden.

His research has focused on the Gospel of Luke and Acts of the Apostles, as well as noncanonical Acts of the Apostles. His major publications include *De Vocatione Gentium* (1967), *Exegesis: Problems of Method and Exercises in Reading* (editor, 1978), *Les Actes Apocryphes des Apôtres* (editor, 1981), *Luke the Theologian* (1987), *New Testament Traditions and Apocryphal Narratives* (1995), *Écrits apocryphes chrétiens I* (editor with Pierre Geoltrain, 1997), *Acta Philippi* (1999), and *The Apocryphal Acts of the Apostles* (editor, 1999). He is also interested in the history of interpretation and critical editions of new early Christian texts in Greek, traveling regularly to the Vatican Library, the monastery libraries on Mount Athos, Greece, and the monastery of St. Catherine (Sinai) for this research.

Endpapers

The endpapers of this volume show folios from the bilingual Codex Bezae (D; fifth century), which contains the Greek text and the Latin translation of the Gospels and Acts on facing pages. The front endpapers show Luke 22:3-18 and the back endpapers show Luke 22:18-32, including the shorter version of the Lord's Supper in Luke 22:19b-20. Photographs of folios 271v, 272r, 272v, 273r courtesy of the Cambridge University Library.

Contents

The name *Hermeneia*, Greek ἑρμηνεία, has been chosen as the title of the commentary series to which this volume belongs. The word *Hermeneia* has a rich background in the history of biblical interpretation as a term used in the ancient Greek-speaking world for the detailed, systematic exposition of a scriptural work. It is hoped that the series, like its name, will carry forward this old and venerable tradition. A second, entirely practical reason for selecting the name lies in the desire to avoid a long descriptive title and its inevitable acronym, or worse, an unpronounceable abbreviation.

The series is designed to be a critical and historical commentary to the Bible without arbitrary limits in size or scope. It will utilize the full range of philological and historical tools, including textual criticism (often slighted in modern commentaries), the methods of the history of tradition (including genre and prosodic analysis), and the history of religion.

Hermeneia is designed for the serious student of the Bible. It will make full use of ancient Semitic and classical languages; at the same time, English translations of all comparative materials—Greek, Latin, Canaanite, or Akkadian—will be supplied alongside the citation of the source in its original language. Insofar as possible, the aim is to provide the student or scholar with full critical discussion of each problem of interpretation and with the primary data upon which the discussion is based.

Hermeneia is designed to be international and interconfessional in the selection of authors; its editorial boards were formed with this end in view. Occasionally the series will offer translations of distinguished commentaries which originally appeared in languages other than English. Published volumes of the series will be revised continually, and eventually, new commentaries will replace older works in order to preserve the currency of the series. Commentaries are also being assigned for important literary works in the categories of apocryphal and pseudepigraphical works relating to the Old and New Testaments, including some of Essene or Gnostic authorship.

The editors of *Hermeneia* impose no systematic-theological perspective upon the series (directly, or indirectly by selection of authors). It is expected that authors will struggle to lay bare the ancient meaning of a biblical work or pericope. In this way the text's human relevance should become transparent, as is always the case in competent historical discourse. However, the series eschews for itself homiletical translation of the Bible.

The editors are heavily indebted to Fortress Press for its energy and courage in taking up an expensive, long-term project, the rewards of which will accrue chiefly to the field of biblical scholarship.

The editor responsible for this volume is Helmut Koester, John H. Morison Research Professor of Divinity and Winn Research Professor of Ecclesiastical History at Harvard Divinity School.

Peter Machinist   *Helmut Koester*
For the Old Testament   For the New Testament
Editorial Board   Editorial Board

One of my doctoral students said to me recently: "I have just read one of your articles, and do you know what?" "What?" I replied. She explained: "When it was published I had not even been born." That's what happens to someone who in the United States is called a "senior scholar."

The "senior scholar" I am began this commentary in the seventies. The invitation was extended to me by Eduard Schweizer during a trip of the Studiorum Novi Testamenti Societas to Israel. The professor in Zurich, who along with Rudolf Schnackenburg edited the Evangelisch-Katholischer Kommentar zum Neuen Testament, wanted me to take over the Gospel according to Luke for this ecumenical collection. At the same time, Philippe H. Menoud of the Université de Neuchâtel died; he had been entrusted with the Third Gospel and the Acts of the Apostles for the Commentaire du Nouveau Testament. Colleagues from the Commentaire du Nouveau Testament then advised me to take over the Gospel of Luke from my Neuchâtel colleague and to leave to others the Epistle to the Hebrews, for which I was to write the commentary.

Any serious commentary has excursuses. As a student I loved to educate myself by reading such syntheses. Unfortunately, the analysis of the various pericopes, the examination of Luke's language, the criticism of the sources reworked by the evangelist, and especially the history of interpretation have taken my complete attention. I no longer found the time to compose these concentrations of knowledge and wisdom, and I regret it.

I have always had a passion for the history of Christianity, Church History as it was called in those days, ever since I sat on the benches of the Vinet auditorium in the Old Academy of Lausanne where Henri Meylan introduced us to Ambrose of Milan, the discoverer of the relics of Saint Protasius and Saint Gervasius, whose cult reached the shores of Lake Geneva at Saint-Prex and the Rhone River in Geneva (see in the city the medieval church of Saint-Gervais). The history of exegesis and the history of the reception of the Gospel texts have occupied my spirit with increasing intensity. The readers will discover here unexpected interpreters, such as an Emperor Charlemagne who asked his advisor Alcuin about Jesus' attitude toward wearing the sword. They will also discover original interpretations—that, for example, of Severus of Antioch in the East in the seventh century and Johann Albrecht Bengel in Germany in the eighteenth century who give a more anthropological than christological meaning to the ascension of Jesus. In their view the Risen One did not need an ascension. If, according to Luke 24:50-53, he nevertheless ostensibly went to heaven, it was for the sake of the believers, who, following the Master, are invited to pass from death to new life, from their suffering to their ascension.

James E. Crouch, to whom I owe my gratitude, has accepted the task of composing the index of passages that concludes this volume. Other cumulative indexes to the three volumes of this commentary in English are in preparation by Fortress Press and will be made available through the Fortress website at www.fortresspress.com/bovon.

At the end of this last volume, I cannot avoid thanking everyone who has helped me. First, Bertrand Bouvier, who has advised me on many points of Greek philology and literature. Second, Jim Crouch, the translator of the volume in English, whose competence and precision have no limits. Third, Helmut Koester, who has been the scholarly editor of my commentary on Luke. Despite his age and his health, he was eager to bring this work to completion in English for the Hermeneia series. Fourth, Neil Elliott from Fortress Press, who took care of the publication. I felt his training and his skill in New Testament studies.

Former students (Benjamin Dunning, Susanna Drake, Brent Landau, Jon Stokes, David Kaden, Simon Lee, Taylor Petrey, and Cavan Concannon), as well as recent students (Jung Hyun Choi, Matthew Sullivan, Geoffrey Smith, Matthew Ketchum, and Eunyung Lim), have worked with me on the project. They have demonstrated competence and perseverance, and they can be assured of my gratitude. The same is true of the librarians of the Andover Library (Harvard Divinity School), in particular Michelle A. Gauthier, Renata Z. Kalnins, Gloria J. Korsman, Donna M. Maguire, Bernadette C. Perrault, Laura K. Whitney, and Steven M. Beardsley, along with the secretaries Kathy Lou, Matthew Turner, Cole Gustafson, Hayfa Abduljaber, and Robin Lee. Finally, Henry Mottu and Eldon Jay Epp have followed the birth of this commentary with interest and faithfulness. I thank them.

Cambridge, Massachusetts
May, 2012

Reference Codes

BiBh — Bible Bhashyam
BibLeb — Bibel und Leben
BibTh — Biblical theology
BiH — Biblische Handbibliothek
BiKi — Bibel und Kirche
BiRe — Bible Review
BiSe — Biblical Seminar
BiTr — Bible Translator
BJRL — Bulletin of the John Rylands University Library of Manchester
BLit — Bibel und Liturgie
BLTS — Bulletin. Lutheran Theological Seminary
BN — Biblische Notizen
Bonaventure
  Comm. Luc. — Commentarius in Evangelium S. Lucae
B. Qam. — See under Rabbinic Writings
BR — Biblical Research
Bruno de Segni
  Comm. Luc. — Commentarius in Lucam
BSABR — Bibliotheca Sacra and American Biblical Repository
BSac — Bibliotheca Sacra
BSRel — Biblioteca di scienze religiose
BTB — Biblical Theology Bulletin
BTF — Bangalore Theological Forum
BTS — Bible et Terre Sainte
BVC — Bible et vie chrétienne
BW — Biblical World
BWANT — Beiträge zur Wissenschaft vom Alten und Neuen Testament
ByZ — Byzantinische Zeitschrift
BZ — Biblische Zeitschrift
BZNW — Beihefte zur Zeitschrift für die neutestamentliche Wissenschaft und die Kunde der älteren Kirche
CAB — Cahiers d'archéologie biblique
Cassiodorus
  Exp. Ps. — Expositio psalmorum
CAT — Commentaire de l'Ancien Testament
Cath(M) — Catholica. Münster
CB — Cultura biblica
CBFV — Cahiers bibliques de Foi et Vie
CBiPa — Cahiers de Biblia Patristica
CBQ — Catholic Biblical Quarterly
CBrug — Collationes Brugenses
CCCM — Corpus Christianorum. Continuatio mediaevalis
CCen — Christian Century
CCER — Cahiers du Cercle Ernest-Renan
CCSG — Corpus Christianorum. Series Graeca
CCSL — Corpus Christianorum. Series Latina
C.E. — Common Era
CFi — Cogitatio fidei
ChiSt — Chicago Studies
ChrTo — Christianity Today

CivCatt — Civiltà cattolica
Clement of Alexandria
  Paed. — Paedagogus
  Strom. — Stromata
ClR — Classical Review
CNT — Commentaire du Nouveau Testament
col(s). — column(s)
Comp. — Compostellanum. Compostela
ConB — Coniectanea biblica
ConBNT — Coniectanea biblica, New Testament
ConNT — Conjectanea Neotestamentica
Const. Ap. — Constitutio apostolica
CoTh — Collectanea Theologica
CQR — Church Quarterly Review
CRB — Cahiers de la Revue Biblique
CrozQ — Crozer Quarterly
CrSt — Christianesimo nella storia
CSCO — Corpus scriptorum Christianorum orientalium
CScR — Christian Scholar's Review
CSEL — Corpus scriptorum ecclesiasticorum Latinorum
CSion — Cahiers Sioniens
CTh — Cahiers theologiques
CThM — Calwer theologische Monographien
CThMi — Currents in Theology and Mission
CTM — Concordia Theological Monthly
CuBi — Cultura biblica
Cyprian
  Fort. — Ad Fortunatum
  Test. — Testimonia
Cyril of Alexandria
  Serm. Luc. — Sermons from Cyril's *Commentarii in Lucam*
Cyril of Jerusalem
  Hom. cat. — Catechetical Lecture
DACL — Dictionnaire d'archéologie chrétienne et de liturgie
Dio Cassius
  Hist. rom. — Historia Romana
Diogenes Laertius
  Vit. Phil. — Vitae philosophorum
DBM — Deltion biblikon meleton
DBSup — Dictionnaire de la Bible, Supplément
Did. — Didache
Did. Apost. — Didascalia Apostolorum
Div — Divinitas
DRev — Downside Review
DThC — Dictionnaire de théologie catholique
DtPfrBl — Deutsches Pfarrerblatt
ed(s). — editor(s), edited by, edition
EdF — Erträge der Forschung
EDNT — Horst Balz and Gerhard Schneider, eds., *Exegetical Dictionary of the New Testament* (3 vols.; Grand Rapids: Eerdmans, 1990–93)
EeV — Esprit et Vie

EeV.P	*Esprit et Vie—deuxième partie: prédication*	Gregory Nazianzus	
		Or. Theol.	*Theological Orations*
EHPhR	Études d'histoire et de philosophie religieuses	Gregory of Nyssa	
EHS.T	Europäische Hochschulschriften, Theologie (Reihe 23)	*Hom. in Ascensionem*	*Homilia in Ascensionem*
		Gregory the Great	
EKKNT	Evangelisch-katholischer Kommentar zum Neuen Testament	*Hom. Ev.*	*Homiliae in Evangelia*
		Hom. Ez.	*Homiliae in Ezechielem*
		Moral. in Iob	*Moralia in Librum Iob*
EKKNTV	*Evangelisch-katholischer Kommentar zum Neuen Testament Vorarbeiten*	*Serm.*	*Sermones*
		GuL	*Geist und Leben*
EKL	*Evangelisches Kirchenlexikon*	Haymo of Auxerre	
EL	*Ephemerides liturgicae*	*Comm. Is.*	*Commentarius in Isaiam*
Ep. apost.	*Epistula apostolorum*	HeB	*Homiletica en Biblica*
Ep. Arist.	*Epistle of Aristeas*	Hermas	
Ephraem the Syrian		*Sim.*	*Similitudes*
Comm. Diat.	*Commentary on the Diatessaron*	*Vis.*	*Visions*
Epiphanius		Herodotus	
Schol.	*Scholia*	*Hist.*	*Historiae*
EpRe	*Epworth Review*	HeyJ	*Heythrop Journal*
ER	*Ecumenical Review*	Hilary of Poitiers	
EstBib	*Estudios bíblicos*	*Comm. Matt.*	*Commentarius in Matthaeum*
EstEcl	*Estudios eclesiásticos*	Hippolytus of Rome	
EstTeol	*Estudios teológicos*	*Comm. Daniel*	*Commentarium in Danielem*
ESW	*Ecumenical Studies in Worship*	*Noetus*	*Against the Heresy of One Noetus*
ET	English Translation	HNT	Handbuch zum Neuen Testament
EtB	Études bibliques	Homer	
EThL	*Ephemerides theologicae lovanienses*	*Il.*	*Iliad*
		Od.	*Odyssey*
EThR	*Études théologiques et religieuses*	*HPR*	*Homiletic and Pastoral Review*
EThS	Erfurter theologische Schriften	HSoed	*Horae Soederblomianae*
		HThK	Herders theologischer Kommentar zum Neuen Testament
EThSt	Erfurter theologische Studien		
EuA	*Erbe und Auftrag*		
Euripides		*HTR*	*Harvard Theological Review*
Alc.	*Alcestis*	HTS	Harvard Theological Studies
Andr.	*Andromache*	*HUCA*	*Hebrew Union College Annual*
Eusebius		*IBSt*	*Irish Biblical Studies*
Dem. evang.	*Demonstratio evangelica*	ICC	International Critical Commentary
Hist. eccl.	*Historia ecclesiastica*		
Euthymius Zigabenus		*IER*	*Irish Ecclesiastical Record*
Comm. Luc.	*Commentarius in Lucam*	Ignatius	
Comm. Matt.	*Commentarius in Matthaeum*	*Eph.*	*Letter to the Ephesians*
EvTh	*Evangelische Theologie*	*Rom.*	*Letter to the Romans*
Exp	*Expositor*	*Smyrn.*	*Letter to the Smyrnaeans*
ExpT	*Expository Times*	*Trall.*	*Letter to the Trallians*
FB	Forschung zur Bibel	*Imm*	*Immanuel*
FC	Fathers of the Church	*Int*	*Interpretation*
FoRe	*Forum Religion*	IP	Instrumenta patristica
frg(s).	fragment(s)	Irenaeus of Lyon	
FRLANT	Forschungen zur Religion und Literatur des Alten und Neuen Testaments	*Adv. haer.*	*Adversus haereses*
		Dem.	*Demonstration of the Apostolic Preaching (Epideixis)*
FTS	Frankfurter theologische Studien	*ITQ*	*Irish Theological Quarterly*
GCS	Griechische christliche Schriftsteller	*ITS*	*Indian Theological Studies*
		JAC	*Jahrbuch für Antike und Christentum*
GöMisz	*Göttinger Miszellen*		
Gos. Pet.	*Gospel of Peter*	JAC.E	*Jahrbuch für Antike und Christentum—Ergänzungsband*
Gos. Thom.	*Gospel of Thomas*		
Greg	*Gregorianum*	*JBL*	*Journal of Biblical Literature*

JEH	*Journal of Ecclesiastical History*	LO	Lex Orandi
Jerome		LOS	London Oriental Series
Comm. Is.	*Commentarii in Isaiam Prophetam*	*LouvSt*	*Louvain studies*
Comm. Matt.	*Commentariorum in Evangelium*	*LQ*	*Lutheran Quarterly*
	Matthaei	LSJ	H. G. Liddell, R. Scott, and H.
Epist.	*Epistulae*		S. Jones, *A Greek-English Lexicon*
Vir. ill.	*De viris illustribus*		(9th ed. with revised supplement;
JETS	*Journal of the Evangelical Theological*		Oxford: Clarendon, 1996)
	Society	*LThK*	*Lexikon für Theologie und Kirche*
JJS	*Journal of Jewish Studies*	Lucian of Samosata	
JK	*Junge Kirche*	*Fug.*	*Fugitivi*
JLW	*Jahrbuch für Liturgiewissenschaft*	*Bis Acc.*	*Bis Accusatus*
John Chrysostom		*Peregr. Mort.*	*De morte Peregrini*
Hom. de sacra	*Homiliae de sacra Pentecoste*	*LumVie*	*Lumière et vie*
Pentecoste		*LV*	*Lumen vitae*
Hom. Matth.	*Homiliae in Matthaeum*	*LV(B)*	*Lumière et vie. (Bruges)*
Josephus		*LV(L)*	*Lumière et vie (Lyon)*
Ant.	*Antiquities of the Jews*	LXX	Septuagint
Bell.	*Bellum Judaicum*	*m.*	*See under* Rabbinic Writings
JR	*Journal of Religion*	John Maldonat	
JRomS	*Journal of Roman Studies*	*In Luc.*	*Comentarii in quatuor evangelistas:*
JSJ	*Journal for the Study of Judaism in*		*In Lucam et Joannem*
	the Persian, Hellenistic, and Roman	*Mart. Pol.*	*Martyrdom of Polycarp*
	Period	*MD*	*La Maison-Dieu*
JSJSup	Supplements to the Journal	MdB	Le Monde de la Bible
	for the Study of Judaism in the	*MHG Wa*	*See under* Rabbinic Writings
	Persian, Hellenistic, and Roman	*MKQ*	*Mankind Quarterly*
	Period	MNAW	Mededeelingen der Koninklijke
JSNT	*Journal for the Study of the New*		Akademie van Wetenschappen
	Testament	*MoTh*	*Modern Theology*
JSNTSup	Journal for the Study of the New	MR	Mythes et Religions
	Testament Supplement Series	ms(s)	manuscript(s)
JSPE	*Journal for the Study of the*	*MScRel*	*Mélanges de science religieuse*
	Pseudepigrapha	MT	Masoretic Text
JTS	*Journal of Theological Studies*	*MTh*	*Melita Theologica*
Jub.	*Jubilees*	*MThZ*	*Münchener theologische Zeitschrift*
Jud	*Judaica*	MTS	Marburger Theologische Studien
Justin Martyr		n(n).	note(s)
1 Apol.	*Apologia*	NABPR	National Association of Baptist
Dial.	*Dialogus cum Tryphone Judaeo*		Professors of Religion
De resurr.	*De resurrectione*	*NCI*	*Nouvelles chrétiennes d'Israël*
KatBl	*Katechetische Blätter*	*NedThT*	*Nederlands theologisch tijdschrift*
KBANT	Kommentare und Beiträge zum	*Neot*	*Neotestamentica*
	Alten und Neuen Testament	n.F.	Neue Folge (= New Series)
KD	*Kerygma und Dogma*	NHC	Nag Hammadi Codex
KEK	Kritisch-Exegetischer Kommentar	NICNT	New International Commentary
	über das Neue Testament		on the New Testament
Ketub.	*See under* Rabbinic Writings	NIGTC	The New International Greek
KIT	Kleine Texte für Vorlesungen und		Testament Commentary
	Übungen	*NKZ*	*Neue kirchliche Zeitschrift*
KRB	Kleine Reihe zur Bibel	*NovT*	*Novum Testamentum*
KP	*Der kleine Pauly* (Stuttgart: Alfred	NovTSup	Novum Testamentum
	Drückenmüller, 1969)		Supplements
KT	Kaiser Traktate	*NRSV*	*New Revised Standard Version*
ktl.	καὶ τὰ λοιπά (= "etc."; with	*NRTh*	*La nouvelle revue théologique*
	abbreviated Greek titles)	n.s.	New Series
Lat	*Lateranum*	NSTh	Nouvelle série théologique
LCL	Loeb Classical Library	NTAbh	Neutestamentliche
LD	Lectio divina		Abhandlungen
LiBi	Lire la Bible		

NTG	*The New Testament in Greek*, vol. 3: *The Gospel According to Luke* (ed. American and British Committees of the International Greek New Testament Project; 2 vols.; Oxford: Clarendon, 1984–87)		*PLS*	*Patrologiae cursus completus, series Latina: Supplementum* (5 vols.; Paris: Garnier, 1958–74)
			Plato	
			Leg.	*Leges*
			Phaed.	*Phaedo*
NThS	*Nieuwe theologische studien*		*Resp.*	*Respublica*
NTS	*New Testament Studies*		*Symp.*	*Symposion*
NTTS	New Testament Tools and Studies		Pliny the Elder	
NV	*Nova et vetera*		*Nat. hist.*	*Naturalis Historia*
NZSTh	*Neue Zeitschrift für systematische Theologie*		Plutarch	
			Sept. sap. conv.	*Septem sapientium convivium*
OBO	Orbis biblicus et orientalis		*De sera num. vind.*	*De sera numinis vindicta*
OLB	Orte und Landschaften der Bibel		*Def. Orac.*	*De defectu oraculorum*
OLP	*Orientalia lovaniensia periodica*		*Mor.*	*Moralia*
OrChrA	Orientalia Christiana Analecta		PNTC	Pelican New Testament Commentaries
Origen			PO	Patrologia Orientalis
Cels.	*Contra Celsum*		PoTh	Point théologique
Comm. Joh.	*Commentarius in Johannem*		*P.Oxy.*	*See under* papyri
Comm. Matt.	*Commentarius in Matthaeum*		PrPe	*Priest and People*
Comm. Rom.	*Commentarii in Epistulam ad Romanos*		*PRSt*	*Perspectives in Religious Studies*
Comm. ser. Matt.	*Commentarium series in evangelium Matthaei*		PS	Patrologia Syriaca
			Ps.-Clem. Hom.	*Pseudo-Clementine Homilies*
Hom. Ex.	*Homiliae in Exodum*		*Ps.-Clem. Rec.*	*Pseudo-Clementine Recognitions*
Hom. Gen.	*Homiliae in Genesim*		Pseudo-Origen	
Hom. Lev.	*Homiliae in Leviticum*		*Comm. Matt.*	*Commentarius in Matthaeum*
Hom. Luc.	*In Lucam Homiliae*		Pseudo-Philo	
Mart.	*Exhortatio ad martyrium*		*Ant. Bibl.*	*Liber Antiquitatum Biblicarum*
Princ.	*De principiis*		*PSV*	*Parole spirito e vita*
ÖTBK	Ökumenischer Taschenbuch-Kommentar		PTMS	Princeton Theological Monograph Series
papyri			QD	Questiones disputatae
P.Cair.Zenon	*Zenon Papyri*		*QLP*	*Questions liturgiques et paroissiales*
P. Lond.	*Greek Papyri in the British Museum*		*QR*	*Quarterly Review*
P.Oxy.	*Oxyrhynchus Papyri*		*QuLi*	*Questions liturgiques*
par(r.)	parallel(s)		Qumran	
ParO	*Parole de l'Orient*		1QH	*Thanksgiving Hymns* from Qumran Cave 1
PaVi	*Parole di vita*		1QS	(*Rule of the Community*) *Manual of Discipline* from Qumran Cave 1
PEQ	*Palestine Exploration Quarterly*			
PETSE	Papers of the Estonian Theological Society in Exile		4QMMT	*The Halakhic Letter* from Qumran Cave 4
PG	J.-P. Migne, *Patrologiae cursus completus, series graeca* (162 vols.; Paris: Migne, 1857–86)		CD	Cairo Genizah text of the Damascus Document
Philo of Alexandria			Rabbinic Writings	
Abr.	*De Abrahamo*		*ᶜAbod. Zar.*	*ᶜAboda Zara*
Fug.	*De fuga et inventione*		*ʾAbot R. Nat.*	*ʾAbot de Rabbi Nathan*
Leg. Gaj.	*Legatio ad Gaium*		*b.*	Babylonian Talmud (followed by the name of the tractate)
Plant.	*De plantatione*			
Sacr.	*De sacrificiis Abelis et Caini*		*Bar.*	*Baraita*
Vit. Mos.	*De vita Mosis*		*B. Qam.*	*Baba Qamma*
Photius			*Exod. Rab.*	*Exodus Rabbah*
Bibl.	*Bibliotheca*		*Gen. Rab.*	*Genesis Rabbah*
Pindar			*Ketub.*	*Ketubot*
Ol.	*Olympionikai*		*Lev. Rab.*	*Leviticus Rabbah*
PJT	*Pacific Journal of Theology*		*m.*	Mishna (followed by the name of the tractate)
PL	J.-P. Migne, *Patrologia latina cursus completus, series Latina* (217 vols.; Paris: Migne, 1844–64)			

MHG Wa	Writings*Midrash ha-Gadol (Leviticus Rabbha)*	*SBLSP*	*Society of Biblical Literature Seminar Papers*
Pesaḥ.	*Pesaḥim*	SBS	Stuttgarter Bibelstudien
Pesiq. R.	*Pesiqta Rabbati*	SBT	Studies in Biblical Theology
Sanh.	*Sanhedrin*	SC	Sources chrétiennes
Šeqal.	*Šeqalim*	*ScEc*	*Sciences ecclésiastiques*
Tanḥ.	*Tanḥuma*	*ScEs*	*Science et esprit*
Yeb.	*Yebamot*	SCJ	Studies in Christianity and Judaism
RAC	*Reallexikon für Antike und Christentum*	*Scr*	*Scripture*
RAECE	*Revue archéologique de l'Est et du Centre-Est*	*ScrVict*	*Scriptorium Victoriense*
		SDM	Scripta et documenta
RB	*Revue biblique*	*SE*	*Sacris erudiri*
RCatT	*Revista catalana de teologia*	*SEÅ*	*Svensk exegetisk årsbok*
RDN	*Revue diocésaine de Namur*	*SémBib*	*Sémiotique et bible*
RdT	*Rassegna di teologia*	Seneca the Elder	
REA	*Revue des études anciennes*	*Contr.*	*Controversiae*
REB	*Revista eclesiástica brasileira*	SESJ	Suomen Eksegeettisen Seuran julkaisuja
RechBib	Recherches bibliques		
REJ	*Revue des études juives*	SH	Subsidia hagiographica
RestQ	*Restoration quarterly*	SHAW.PH	Sitzungsberichte der Heidelberger Akademie der Wissenschaften—Philosophisch-Historische Klasse
RevAg	*Revista agustiniana*		
RevBib	*Revista biblica*		
RevExp	*Review and Expositor*		
RevScRel	*Revue des sciences religieuses*	SJ	Studia Judaica
RevThom	*Revue thomiste*	*SJT*	*Scottish Journal of Theology*
RGG	Kurt Galling, ed., *Religion in Geschichte und Gegenwart* (7 vols.; 3d ed.; Tübingen: Mohr Siebeck, 1957–65)	SNTSMS	Society for New Testament Studies Monograph Series
		SNTU	*Studien zum Neuen Testament und seiner Umwelt*
RHPhR	*Revue d'histoire et de philosophie religieuses*	*SO*	*Symbolae osloenseis*
RHR	*Revue de l'histoire des Religions*	SPAW	Sitzungsberichte der preussischen Akademie der Wissenschaften
RIDA	*Revue internationale des droits de l'antiquité*	SPAW.PH	Sitzungsberichte der preussischen Akademie der Wissenschaften — Philosophisch-Historische Klasse
RivB	*Rivista biblica*		
RL	Religion and Literature	SPB	Studia Post-Biblica
RNT	Regensburger Neues Testament	SQS	Sammlung ausgewählter kirchen- und dogmengeschichtlicher Quellenschriften
RRéf	*Revue réformée*		
RSLR	*Rivista di storia e letteratura religiosa*		
RSPhTh	*Revue des sciences philosophiques et théologiques*	*SR*	*Studies in Religion/Sciences religieuses*
RSR	*Recherches de science religieuse*	SRivBib	Supplementi alla Rivista biblica
RThL	*Revue théologique de Louvain*	*ST*	*Studies in Theology*
RThPh	*Revue de théologie et de philosophie*	StANT	Studien zum Alten und Neuen Testament
RTK	Roczniki Teologiczno-Kanoniczne		
Rupert of Deutz		StAnt	Studia Antoniana
Comm. Ioh.	*Commentaria in euangelium sancti Iohannis*	StBL	Studies in Biblical Literature
		StD	Studies and Documents
In Gen.	*In Genesim*	*StEv*	*Studia Evangelica*
SacDoc	*Sacra doctrina*	*StGra*	*Studia Gratiana*
Sanh.	See under Rabbinic Writings	*StMor*	*Studia moralia*
SANT	Studien zum Alten und Neuen Testament	*StMiss*	*Studia missionalia*
		StNT	Studien zum Neuen Testament
SBA	Studies in Biblical Archaeology	*StPat*	*Studia Patavina*
SBB	Stuttgarter biblische Beiträge	*StPatr*	*Studia Patristica*
SBL	Society of Biblical Literature	Str-B	Hermann L. Strack and Paul Billerbeck, *Kommentar zum Neuen Testament aus Talmud und Midrasch*
SBLDS	Society of Biblical Literature Dissertation Series		

	(2d. ed.; 4 vols.; Munich: Beck, 1956)
StT	Studi e testi
StTh	*Studia Theologica*
StZ	*Stimmen der Zeit*
s.v.	*sub verbo* or *sub vocem* under the word or entry
Tacitus	
Ann.	*Annals*
T. Adam	*Testament of Adam*
T. Abr.	*Testament of Abraham*
T. 12 Patr.	*Testaments of the Twelve Patriarchs*
T. Benj.	*Testament of Benjamin*
T. Gad	*Testament of Gad*
T. Jud.	*Testament of Judah*
TAPA	*Transactions of the American Philological Association*
TBT	*The Bible Today*
TCSPCK	Theological Collections. SPCK
TDNT	Gerhard Friedrich and Gerhard Kittel, eds., *Theological Dictionary of the New Testament* (trans. Geoffrey W. Bromiley; 10 vols.; Grand Rapids: Eerdmans, 1964–76)
TeKo	*Texte und Kontexte*
Tertullian	
Adv. Marc.	*Adversus Marcionem*
Adv. Prax.	*Adversus Praxeam*
Apol.	*Apologeticum*
Bapt.	*De baptismo*
Cor.	*De corona militis*
Idol.	*De idololatria*
Mon.	*De monogamia*
Or.	*De oratione*
TFT.S	Theologische Faculteit Tilburg—Studies
ThA	Theologische Arbeiten
ThBei	*Theologische Beiträge*
ThBl	*Theologische Blätter*
ThD	*Theology Digest*
Theodore of Mopsuestia	
Comm. Luc.	*Commentary on Luke*
Theol	*Theology* (London)
Theophylactus	
Enarr. Luc.	*Enarrationes in Lucam*
ThF	Theologische Forschung
ThG(B)	*Theologie der Gegenwart (Bergen-Enkheim)*
ThGl	*Theologie und Glaube*
ThH	Théologie historique
ThHKNT	Theologischer Handkommentar zum Neuen Testament
ThLZ	*Theologische Literaturzeitung*
ThR	*Theologische Rundschau*
ThRv	*Theologische Revue*
ThStK	*Theologische Studien und Kritiken*
ThTo	*Theology Today*
ThV	*Theologische Versuche*

ThViat	*Theologia viatorum*
ThZ	*Theologische Zeitschrift*
TJT	*Toronto Journal of Theology*
TRE	*Theologische Realenzyklopädie*
TRev	*Theologische Revue*
TS	*Theological Studies*
TSAJ	Texte und Studien zum antiken Judentum
TTh	*Tijdschrift voor Theologie*
TThZ	*Trierer theologische Zeitschrift*
TTK	*Tidsskrift for teologi og kirke*
TU	Texte und Untersuchungen zur Geschichte der altchristlichen Literatur
TW	Theologie und Wirklichkeit
TynB	*Tyndale Bulletin*
v(v).	verse(s)
VC	*Vigiliae Christianae*
VCSup	Supplements to Vigiliae Christianae
VD	*Verbum Domini*
v.l.	*varia lectio*
VMStA	Veröffentlichungen des Missionspriesterseminars St. Augustin bei Bonn
VoxTh	*Vox theologica*
VR	*Vox reformata*
VSpir	*Vie spirituelle*
VT	*Vetus Testamentum*
WA	Martin Luther, *Kritische Gesamtausgabe* (= Weimar edition)
WThJ	*Westminster Theological Journal*
WUNT	Wissenschaftliche Untersuchungen zum Neuen Testament
Xenophon	
Hist. Graec.	*Historia Graeca (Hellenica)*
Yeb.	*See under* Rabbinic Writings
ZBK	Zürcher Bibelkommentare
ZDPV	*Zeitschrift des deutschen Palästina-Vereins*
ZKG	*Zeitschrift für Kirchengeschichte*
ZKTh	*Zeitschrift für katholische Theologie*
ZKW	*Zeitschrift für Kunstwissenschaft*
ZNW	*Zeitschrift für die neutestamentliche Wissenschaft*
ZThK	*Zeitschrift für Theologie und Kirche*

2. Short Titles of Commentaries, Studies, and Articles Often Cited

Except for commentaries, secondary literature found in only one section of this work is not included in this list of Short Titles. To avoid burdening an already long list of short titles, these works are listed with full bibliographical information at the beginning of their respective sections and then cited in the footnotes with easily recognizable short titles.

All commentaries on Luke, and occasional dictionaries, are short-titled in this list and only with the name of the author.

When the English translation of a foreign language work is based on an edition earlier than the one cited in this commentary, both the commentary and this list continue to cite the foreign language edition.

Aland, *Synopsis*
Kurt Aland, ed., *Synopsis Quattuor Evangeliorum: Locis parallelis evangeliorum apocryphorum et Patrum adhibitis* (3d ed.; Stuttgart: Württembergische Bibelanstalt, 1965).

Aletti, *Art de raconter*
Jean-Noël Aletti, *L'art de raconter Jésus Christ: L'écriture narrative de l'évangile de Luc* (Paris: Seuil, 1989).

Alexandre, *Dictionnaire*
Charles Alexandre, *Dictionnaire grec-français composé sur un nouveau plan* (Paris: Hachette, 1888).

Amphoux, "Chapitre 24."
Christian-Bernard Amphoux, "Le chapitre 24 de Luc et l'origine de la tradition textuelle du Codex de Bèze (D.05 du NT)," *Filologia Neotestamentaria* 4 (1991) 21-48.

Bachmann, *Tempel*
Michael Bachmann, *Jerusalem und der Tempel: Die geographisch-theologischen Elemente in der lukanischen Sicht des jüdischen Kultzentrums* (BWANT 109; Stuttgart: Kohlhammer, 1980).

Bailly
Anatole Bailly, *Dictionnaire grec-français . . .* (2d ed.; Paris: Hachette, 1897).

Bammel, "Trial"
Ernst Bammel, "The Trial before Pilate," in Ernst Bammel and C. F. D. Moule, eds., *Jesus and the Politics of His Day* (Cambridge: Cambridge University Press, 1984) 403–12, 425–51.

Bammel and Moule, *Jesus and the Politics of His Day*
Ernst Bammel and C. F. D. Moule, eds., *Jesus and the Politics of His Day* (Cambridge: Cambridge University Press, 1984).

Barth, *Church Dogmatics*
Karl Barth, *Church Dogmatics* (Edinburgh: T. & T. Clark, 1936–1977).

Bengel, *Gnomon*
Johann Albert Bengel, *Gnomon of the New Testament* (trans. Charlton T. Lewis and Marvin R. Vincent; 2 vols.; Philadelphia: Perkinpine & Higgins, 1860–62).

Bengel, *Gnomon* (G)
Quotations not appearing in the ET are cited according to the German edition: Johann Albrecht Bengel, *Gnomon. Auslegung des Neuen Testaments in fortlaufenden Anmerkungen*, vol. 1 (trans. C. F. Werner; 7th ed.; Stuttgart: Steinkopf, 1959).

Benoit, *Exégèse et théologie*
Pierre Benoit, *Exégèse et théologie* (4 vols.; Paris: Cerf, 1961–83).

Benoit, *Passion and Resurrection*
Pierre Benoit, *The Passion and Resurrection of Jesus Christ* (trans. Benet Weatherhead; New York: Herder & Herder, 1970).

Bernardini
R. P. Bernardini, ed., *Bonaventure, Opera Omnia*, vol. 7: *Commentarius in Evangelium S. Lucae* (Quaracchi: Collegium S. Bonaventurae, 1882–1902).

Bertram, *Leidensgeschichte*
Georg Bertram, *Die Leidensgeschichte Jesu und der Christuskult* (FRLANT 32; Göttingen: Vandenhoeck & Ruprecht, 1922).

Betz, *Abraham unser Vater*
Otto Betz, Martin Hengel, and Peter Schmidt, eds., *Abraham unser Vater: Juden und Christen im Gespräch über die Bibel: Festschrift für Otto Michel zum 60. Geburtstag* (Arbeiten zur Geschichte des Spätjudentums und Urchristentums 5; Leiden: Brill, 1963).

Bieler, *ΘΕΙΟΣ ΑΝΗΡ*
Ludwig Bieler, *ΘΕΙΟΣ ΑΝΗΡ: Das Bild des "göttlichen Menschen" in Spätantike und Früchristentum* (1935–36; reprinted Darmstadt: Wissenschaftliche Buchgesellschaft, 1967).

Black, *Aramaic Approach*
Matthew Black, *An Aramaic Approach to the Gospels and Acts, with an Appendix on the Son of Man by Geza Vermes* (3d ed.; Oxford: Clarendon, 1967).

Black, "Arrest and Trial"
Matthew Black, "The Arrest and Trial of Jesus and the Date of the Last Supper," in A. J. B. Higgins, ed., *New Testament Essays: Studies in Memory of Thomas Walter Manson, 1893–1958* (Manchester: Manchester University Press, 1959) 19–33.

Blinzler, *Prozess*
Josef Blinzler, *Der Prozess Jesu: Das jüdische und das römische Gerichtsverfahren gegen Jesus Christus auf Grund der ältesten Zeugnisse dargestellt und beurteilt* (3d expanded ed.; Regensburg: Pustet, 1960). [The English translation of 1959 is based on an older German edition.]

Bock
Darrell L. Bock, *Luke* (2 vols.; BECNT; Grand Rapids: Baker, 1994–96).

Bornkamm, *Jesus*
Günther Bornkamm, *Jesus of Nazareth* (trans. Irene McLuskey and Fraser McLuskey with James M. Robinson; New York: Harper, 1960).

Bossuyt and Radermakers
Philippe Bossuyt and Jean Radermakers, *Jésus, Parole de la grâce: Selon St. Luc* (2 vols.; Brussels: Institut d'études théologiques, 1981).

Bovon, "Effet"
François Bovon, "Effet de réel et flou prophétique dans l'œuvre de Luc," in *A cause de l'Evangile: études sur les Synoptiques et les Actes: offertes au P. Jacques Dupont, O.S.B. à l'occasion de son 70e anniversaire* (LD 123; Paris: Cerf, 1985) 349–59 (reprinted in idem, *Révélations*, 65–74).

Bovon, *Last Days*
François Bovon, *The Last Days of Jesus* (trans. Kristin Hennessy; Louisville: Westminster John Knox, 2006).

Bovon, "Lukan Story of the Passion"
François Bovon, "The Lukan Story of the Passion of Jesus (Luke 22–23)," in idem, *Studies in Early Christianity* (WUNT 161; Tübingen: Mohr Siebeck, 2003) 74–105.

Bovon, *Luke the Theologian*
François Bovon, *Luke the Theologian: Fifty-Five Years of Research (1950–2005)* (2d rev. ed.; Waco, Tex.: Baylor University Press, 2006).

Bovon, *L'œuvre*
François Bovon, *L'œuvre de Luc: Études d'exégèse et de théologie* (LD 130; Paris: Cerf, 1987).

Bovon, "Salut."
François Bovon, "Le salut dans les écrits de Luc: Essai," *RThPh* 3. Reihe 23 (1973) 296–307; reprinted in idem, *L'œuvre*, 165–79.

Bovon, *Révélations*
François Bovon, *Révélations et écritures: Nouveau Testament et littérature apocryphe chrétienne. Recueil d'articles* (MdB 26; Geneva: Labor et Fides, 1993).

Bovon, *Studies*
François Bovon, *Studies in Early Christianity* (Tübingen: Mohr Siebeck, 2003).

Bovon, *Traditions*
François Bovon, *New Testament Traditions and Apocryphal Narratives* (trans. Jane Haapiseva-Hunter; PTMS 36; Allison Park, Pa.: Pickwick, 1995).

Bovon et al., *Écrits apocryphes chrétiens*
François Bovon, Pierre Geoltrain, and Jean-Daniel Kaestli, eds., *Écrits apocryphes chrétiens* (2 vols.; Bibliothèque de la Pléiade 442; Paris: Gallimard, 1997).

Brandon, *Trial*
S. G. F. Brandon, *The Trial of Jesus of Nazareth* (New York: Stein & Day, 1968).

Braun, *Tertullien. Contre Marcion*
René Braun, *Tertullien. Contre Marcion: Introduction, texte critique, traduction et notes* (5 vols.; SC 365, 368, 399, 456, 483; Paris: Cerf, 1990–2004).

Brock, *Mary Magdalene*
Ann Graham Brock, *Mary Magdalene, the First Apostle: The Struggle for Authority* (HTS 51; Cambridge, Mass.; Harvard Divinity School, 2003).

Brown, *Death of the Messiah*
Raymond E. Brown, *The Death of the Messiah: From Gethsemane to the Grave. A Commentary on the Passion Narratives of the Four Gospels* (2 vols.; New York: Doubleday, 1994).

Brown, *New Testament Essays*
Raymond E. Brown, *New Testament Essays* (Milwaukee: Bruce, 1965).

Brown, *Apostasy*
Schuyler Brown, *Apostasy and Perseverance in the Theology of Luke* (AnBib 36; Rome: Pontifical Biblical Institute, 1969).

Büchele, *Tod Jesu*
Anton Büchele, *Der Tod Jesu im Lukasevangelium: Eine redaktionsgeschichtliche Untersuchung zu Lk 24* (FTS 26; Frankfurt: Knecht, 1978).

Bultmann, *History*
Rudolf Bultmann, *The History of the Synoptic Tradition* (trans. John Marsh; rev. ed.; New York: Harper & Row, 1976).

Bultmann, *John*
Rudolf Bultmann, *The Gospel of John* (Philadelphia: Westminster, 1971).

Burger, *Davidssohn*
Christoph Burger, *Jesus als Davidssohn: Eine traditionsgeschichtliche Untersuchung* (FRLANT 98; Göttingen: Vandenhoeck & Ruprecht, 1970).

Cadbury, *Style*
Henry J. Cadbury, *The Style and Literary Method of Luke* (1920; HTS 6; reprinted New York: Kraus Reprint, 1969).

Caird
George Bradford Caird, *The Gospel of St. Luke* (PNTC; Harmondsworth: Penguin, 1963).

Calvin, *Harmony*
David W. Torrance and Thomas F. Torrance, eds., *Calvin's Commentaries*, vols. 1–3: *A Harmony of the Gospels Matthew, Mark, and Luke* (trans. A. W. Morrison and T. H. L. Parker; Grand Rapids: Eerdmans, 1959–).

Casalegno, *Tempio*
Alberto Casalegno, *Gesú e il tempio: studio redazionale di Luca-Atti* (Brescia: Morcelliana, 1984).

Catchpole, *Trial*
David R. Catchpole, *The Trial of Jesus: A Study in the Gospels and Jewish Historiography from 1770 to the Present Day* (SPB 18; Leiden: Brill, 1971).

Clivaz, *L'ange et la sueur de sang*
Claire Clivaz, *L'ange et la sueur de sang (Lc 22,43-44) ou comment on pourrait bien encore écrire l'histoire* (Biblical Tools and Studies 7; Leuven: Peeters, 2010).

Conzelmann, *Theology*
Hans Conzelmann, *The Theology of St. Luke* (trans. Geoffrey Buswell; 1961; reprinted Philadelphia: Fortress Press, 1982).

Creed
John Martin Creed, ed., *The Gospel according to St. Luke: The Greek Text with Introduction, Notes, and Indices* (London: Macmillan, 1930).

Daube, *Rabbinic Judaism*
David Daube, *The New Testament and Rabbinic Judaism* (Jordan Lectures in Comparative Religion 2; London: Athlone, 1956).

Delebecque, *Évangile*
Edouard Delebecque, *Évangile de Luc* (1976; reprinted Paris: Klincksieck, 1992).

Delorme, "Procès"
Jean Delorme, "Le procès de Jésus ou la parole risquée (Lc 22,54—23,25)," in idem and Jean Duplacy, eds., *La Parole de grâce: Études lucaniennes à la mémoire d'Augustin George* (essays reprinted from

RSR 69; Paris: Recherches de science religieuse, 1981) 123–46.

Derrett, *Law*
J. Duncan M. Derrett, *Law in the New Testament* (London: Darton, Longman & Todd, 1970).

Derrett, *Studies*
J. Duncan M. Derrett, *Studies in the New Testament* (6 vols.; Leiden: Brill, 1977–95).

Dibelius, *Botschaft und Geschichte*
Martin Dibelius, *Botschaft und Geschichte: Gesammelte Aufsätze* (2 vols.; Tübingen: Mohr, 1953, 1956).

Dibelius, *Tradition*
Martin Dibelius, *From Tradition to Gospel* (trans. Bertram Lee Woolf; 2d ed.; Cambridge: Clarke, 1971).

Dietrich, *Petrusbild*
Wolfgang Dietrich, *Das Petrusbild der lukanischen Schriften* (BWANT 5/14; Stuttgart: Kohlhammer, 1972).

Dillon, *Eye-Witnesses*
Richard J. Dillon, *From Eye-Witnesses to Ministers of the Word: Tradition and Composition in Luke 24* (AnBib 82; Rome: Biblical Institute Press, 1978).

Dinkler, *Petrusdarstellungen*
Erich Dinkler, *Die ersten Petrusdarstellungen: Ein archäologischer Beitrag zur Geschichte des Petrusprimates* (Marburger Jahrbuch für Kunstwissenschaft 11; Marburg: Verlag des Kunstgeschichtlichen Seminars der Philipps-Universität Marburg, 1939; actually published in 1941 with vol. 12, 1939) 1–79.

Dömer, *Heil*
Michael Dömer, *Das Heil Gottes: Studien zur Theologie des lukanischen Doppelwerks* (BBB 51; Cologne/Bonn: Hanstein, 1978) 99–106.

Donahue, "Trial of Jesus"
John R. Donahue, "From Crucified Messiah to Risen Christ: The Trial of Jesus Revisited," in Arthur E. Zanonni, ed., *Jews and Christians Speak of Jesus* (Minneapolis: Fortress Press, 1994) 93–121.

Dupont, *Évangiles synoptiques*
Jacques Dupont, *Études sur les évangiles synoptiques* (ed. Franz Neirynck; 2 vols.; BEThL 70A, 70B; Louvain: Louvain University Press/Peeters, 1985).

Dupont, *Nouvelles études*
Jacques Dupont, *Nouvelles études sur les Actes des Apôtres* (LD 118; Paris: Cerf, 1984).

Dupont-Sommer and Philonenko, *Écrits intertestamentaires*
André Dupont-Sommer and Marc Philonenko, eds., with the collaboration of Daniel A. Bertrand, *La Bible: Écrits intertestamentaires* (Paris: Gallimard, 1987).

Dussaut, "Triptyque"
Louis Dussaut, "Le triptyque des apparitions en Luc 24 (analyse structurelle)," *RB* 94 (1987) 161–213.

Eckey
Wilfried Eckey, *Das Lukasevangelium: Unter Berücksichtigung seiner Parallelen* (2 vols.; Neukirchen-Vluyn: Neukirchener Verlag, 2004).

Ehman, "Luke 23:1-49"
John W. Ehman, "Luke 23:1-49," *Int* 52 (1998) 74–76.

Ehrman, *Corruption*
Bart D. Ehrman, *The Orthodox Corruption of Scripture: The Effect of Early Christological Controversies on the Text of the New Testament* (New York: Oxford University Press, 1993).

Erasmus, *Paraphrasis*
Desiderius Erasmus of Rotterdam, *Paraphrasis in N. Testamentum,* in P. Vander, ed., *Opera omnia,* vol. 7 (Leyden, 1706; facsimile reprint London: Gregg, 1962).

Ernst
Josef Ernst, *Das Evangelium nach Lukas: Übersetzt und erklärt* (RNT 3; Regensburg: Pustet, 1977).

Ernst, "Schriftauslegung"
Josef Ernst, "Schriftauslegung und Auferstehungsglaube bei Lukas," *ThGl* 60 (1970) 360–374; reprinted in idem, *Schriftauslegung: Beiträge zur Hermeneutik des Neuen Testaments und im Neuen Testament* (Munich: Schöningh, 1972) 177–92.

C. A. Evans
Craig A. Evans, *Luke* (New International Biblical Commentary 3; Peabody, Mass.: Hendrickson, 1990).

C. F. Evans
Christopher Francis Evans, *Saint Luke* (TPI New Testament Commentaries; Philadelphia: Trinity Press International, 1990).

Evans, *Tertullian: Adversus Marcionem*
Ernest Evans, trans., *Tertullian: Adversus Marcionem* (2 vols.; Oxford Early Christian Texts; Oxford: Clarendon, 1972)

Feldkämper, *Der betende Jesus*
Ludger Feldkämper, *Der betende Jesus als Heilsmittler nach Lukas* (VMStA 29; St. Augustin: Steyler, 1978).

Finegan, *Überlieferung*
Jack Finegan, *Die Überlieferung der Leidens- und Auferstehungsgeschichte Jesu* (BZNW 15; Giessen: Töpelmann, 1934).

Fitzmyer
Joseph A. Fitzmyer, *The Gospel according to Luke: Introduction, Translation, and Notes* (2 vols.; AB 28, 28A; Garden City, N.Y.: Doubleday, 1981, 1985).

Five Gospels
Robert W. Funk, Roy W. Hoover, and the Jesus Seminar, *The Five Gospels: The Search for the Authentic Words of Jesus: New Translation and Commentary* (New York: Macmillan, 1993).

Flender, *Heil*
Helmut Flender, *Heil und Geschichte in der Theologie des Lukas* (BEvTh 41; Munich: Kaiser, 1965).

Geldenhuys
Norval Geldenhuys, *Commentary on The Gospel of Luke* (Grand Rapids: Eerdmans, 1951).

George, *Études*
  Augustin George, *Études sur l'œuvre de Luc* (Sources bibliques; Paris: Gabalda, 1978).
George, "Sens."
  Augustin George, "Le sens de la mort de Jésus," in idem, *Études sur l'oeuvre de Luc* (Sources bibliques; Paris: Gabalda, 1978) 185–212 (originally published in *RB* 80 [1973] 186–217).
Giblin, *Destruction*
  Charles Homer Giblin, *The Destruction of Jerusalem according to Luke's Gospel: A Historical-Typological Moral* (AnBib 107; Rome: Biblical Institute Press, 1985).
Gnilka, *Markus*
  Joachim Gnilka, *Das Evangelium nach Markus* (2d ed.; 2 vols.; EKKNT 2; Neukirchen-Vluyn: Neukirchener Verlag, 1986).
Godet
  Frédéric Godet, *A Commentary on the Gospel of St. Luke* (trans. E. W. Shalders; 4th ed.; 2 vols.; Edinburgh: Clark, 1881, 1890).
Goulder, *New Paradigm*
  Michael D. Goulder, *Luke: A New Paradigm* (2 vols.; JSNTSup 20; Sheffield: JSOT Press, 1989).
Grangaard, *Conflict*
  Blake R. Grangaard, *Conflict and Authority in Luke 19:47 to 21:4* (Studies in Biblical Literature 8; New York: Lang, 1999).
Grass, *Ostergeschehen*
  Hans Grass, *Ostergeschehen und Osterberichte* (4th ed.; Göttingen: Vandenhoeck & Ruprecht, 1970).
Green, "Demise."
  Joel B. Green, "The Demise of the Temple as Cultural Center in Luke-Acts: An Exploration of the Rending of the Temple Veil," *RB* 101 (1994) 495–515.
Green
  Joel B. Green, *The Gospel of Luke* (NICNT; Grand Rapids: Eerdmans, 1997).
Grotius, *Annotationes*
  Hugo Grotius, *Annotationes in Novum Testamentum, editio nova*, vol. 1: *Quatuor Evangelia et explicationem Decalogi continens* (ed. Christian Ernst von Windheim; Leipzig: Ioannem Carolum Tetzschnerum, 1755).
Grundmann,
  Walter Grundmann, *Das Evangelium nach Lukas* (2d ed.; ThHKNT 3; Berlin: Evangelische Verlagsanstalt, 1961).
Guillaume, *Luc interprète*
  Jean-Marie Guillaume, *Luc interprète des anciennes traditions sur la résurrection de Jésus* (EtB' Paris: Gabalda, 1979).
Haenchen, *Acts*
  Ernst Haenchen, *The Acts of the Apostles: A Commentary* (Philadelphia: Westminster, 1971).
Haenchen, *Weg Jesu*
  Ernst Haenchen, *Der Weg Jesu: Eine Erklärung des Markus-Evangeliums und der kanonischen Parallelen* (Berlin: Töpelmann, 1966) 372–79.

Hahn, *Titles*
  Ferdinand Hahn, *The Titles of Jesus in Christology: Their History in Early Christianity* (trans. H. Knight and G. Ogg; New York: World, 1969).
Harnack, *Marcion*
  Adolf von Harnack, *Marcion, das Evangelium vom fremden Gott: Eine Monographie zur Geschichte der Grundlegung der katholischen Kirche* (2d ed.; TU 45; 1924; reprinted Darmstadt: Wissenschaftliche Buchgesellschaft, 1985). [Cited by the German edition with *, because the ET does not include the extensive appendices.]
Hoffmann, "Graben"
  Paul Hoffmann, "Der garstige breite Graben: Zu den Anfängen der historisch-kritischen Osterdiskussion," in idem, *Tradition und Situation: Studien zur Jesusüberlieferung in der Logienquelle und den synoptischen Evangelien* (NTAbh n.F. 28; Münster: Aschendorff, 1995) 341–72.
Horsley and Hanson, *Bandits*
  Richard A. Horsley and John S. Hanson, *Bandits, Prophets, and Messiahs: Popular Movements at the Time of Jesus* (New Voices in Biblical Studies; Minneapolis: Winston, 1985).
Hug, *Finale*
  Joseph Hug, *La finale de l'Évangile de Marc (Mc 16,9-20)* (EtB; Paris: Gabalda, 1978).
Jeremias, *Parables*
  Joachim Jeremias, *The Parables of Jesus* (trans. Samuel Henry Hooke; 2d rev. ed.; New York: Scribner, 1972).
Jeremias, *Sprache*
  Joachim Jeremias, *Die Sprache des Lukasevangeliums: Redaktion und Tradition im Nicht-Markusstoff des dritten Evangeliums* (KEK Sonderband; Göttingen: Vandenhoeck & Ruprecht, 1980).
Johnson
  Luke Timothy Johnson, *The Gospel of Luke* (Sacra Pagina 3; Collegeville, Minn.: Liturgical Press, 1991).
Jülicher, *Gleichnisreden*
  Adolf Jülicher, *Die Gleichnisreden Jesu* (2d. ed.; 2 vols.; Tübingen: Mohr Siebeck, 1910).
Just
  Arthur A. Just, *Luke* (2 vols.; Concordia Commentary; St. Louis: Concordia, 1996, 1997).
Just, *Luke*
  Arthur A. Just, *Luke* (Ancient Christian Commentary on Scripture. New Testament 3; Downers Grove, Ill.: InterVarsity, 2003).
Kaestli, *L'eschatologie*
  Jean-Daniel Kaestli, *L'eschatologie dans l'œuvre de Luc: Ses caractéristiques et sa place dans le développement du Christianisme primitif* (NSTh 22; Geneva: Labor et Fides, 1969).
Karris, *St. Bonaventure's Commentary*
  Robert J. Karris, *St. Bonaventure's Commentary on the Gospel of Luke, Chapters 17–24* (Works of St. Bonaventure 8.3; St. Bonaventure, N.Y.: Franciscan Institute, St. Bonaventure University, 2004).

Kingsbury, *Conflict*
Jack Dean Kingsbury, *Conflict in Luke: Jesus, Authorities, Disciples* (Minneapolis: Fortress Press, 1991).

Kinman, "Eschatology."
Brent Kinman, "Lucan Eschatology and the Missing Fig Tree," *JBL* 113 (1994) 669–78.

Klauck, *Allegorie*
Hans-Josef Klauck, *Allegorie und Allegorese in synoptischen Gleichnistexten* (NTAbh n.s. 13; Münster: Aschendorff, 1978).

Klein, *Rekonstruktion and Interpretation*
Günter Klein, *Rekonstruktion and Interpretation: Gesammelte Aufsätze zum Neuen Testament* (BEvTh 50; Munich: Kaiser, 1969).

Klein, "Verleugnung"
Günter Klein, "Die Verleugnung des Petrus: Eine traditionsgeschichtliche Untersuchung," *ZThK* 58 (1961) 285–328; reprinted in idem, *Rekonstruktion und Interpretation*, 49–98.

Kloppenborg, "Exitus"
John S. Kloppenborg, "Exitus clari viri: The Death of Jesus in Luke," *TJT* 8 (1992) 106–20.

Klostermann
Erich Klostermann, *Das Lukasevangelium* (HNT 2.1; Tübingen: Mohr Siebeck, 1919).

Kümmel, *Promise*
Werner Georg Kümmel, *Promise and Fulfillment: The Eschatological Message of Jesus* (trans. Dorothea M. Barton; London: SCM, 1957).

Lagrange
Marie-Joseph Lagrange, *Évangile selon Saint Luc* (7th ed.; EtB; Paris: Gabalda, 1948).

Lampe
G. W. H. Lampe, *A Patristic Greek Lexicon* (Oxford: Clarendon, 1961).

Leenhardt, *Sacrement*
Franz Leenhardt, *Le sacrement de la Sainte Cène* (Série théologique de l'"Actualité Protestant"; Neuchâtel: Delachaux & Niestlé, 1948).

Léon-Dufour, *Études*
Xavier Léon-Dufour, *Études d'Évangile: Parole de Dieu* (Paris: Seuil, 1965).

Léon-Dufour, *Résurrection*
Xavier Léon-Dufour, *Résurrection de Jésus et message pascal* (Parole de Dieu; Paris: Seuil, 1971).

L'Eplattenier
Charles L'Eplattenier, *Lecture de l'évangile de Luc* (Paris: Desclée, 1982).

Liberto, "Fear"
David Liberto, "To Fear or Not to Fear? Christ as Sophos in Luke's Passion Narrative," *ExpT* 114 (2003) 219–23.

Lietzmann, "Prozess Jesu"
Hans Lietzmann, "Der Prozess Jesu," *SPAW.PH* 14 (1931) 313–22; reprinted in idem, *Kleine Schriften*, vol. 2: *Studien zum Neuen Testament* (ed. Kurt Aland; TU 68; Berlin: Akademie-Verlag, 1958) 251–63.

Linder, "Destruction"
Ammon Linder, "The Destruction of Jerusalem Sunday," *SE* 30 (1987–88) 253–92.

Linnemann, *Studien*
Eta Linnemann, *Studien zur Passionsgeschichte* (FRLANT 102; Göttingen: Vandenhoeck & Ruprecht, 1970).

Linnemann, "Verleugnung"
Eta Linnemann, "Die Verleugnung des Petrus," *ZThK* 63 (1966) 1–32.

Lohfink, *Himmelfahrt*
Gerhard Lohfink, *Die Himmelfahrt Jesu: Untersuchungen zu den Himmelfahrts- und Erhöhungstexten bei Lukas* (StANT 26; Munich: Kösel, 1971).

Lohse, *Geschichte*
Eduard Lohse, *Die Geschichte des Leidens und Sterbens Jesu Christi* (1st printing of the paperback edition; Gütersloh: Mohn, 1979). [The ET is based on an older German edition.]

Loisy
Alfred Loisy, *L'Évangile selon Luc* (Paris: Émile Nourry, 1924).

Luther, *Evangelien-Auslegung*
Evangelien-Auslegung, part 3: *Markus und Lukasevangelium* (ed. Erwin Mülhaupt; Göttingen: Vandenhoeck & Ruprecht, 1938–54).

Luz, *Matthew 1–7*
Ulrich Luz, *Matthew 1–7* (trans. James E. Crouch; Hermeneia; Minneapolis: Fortress, 2007).

Luz, *Matthew 8–20*
Ulrich Luz, *Matthew 8–20* (trans. James E. Crouch; Hermeneia; Minneapolis: Fortress, 2001).

Luz, *Matthew 21–28*
Ulrich Luz, *Matthew 21–28* (trans. James E. Crouch; Hermeneia; Minneapolis: Fortress, 2005).

Maier
Gerhard Maier, *Lukas-Evangelium* (2 vols.; Neuheusen-Stuttgart: Hanssler, 1991–92).

Malina and Neyrey, "Conflict"
Bruce J. Malina and Jerome H. Neyrey, "Conflict in Luke-Acts: Labelling and Deviance Theory," in Jerome H. Neyrey, ed., *The Social World of Luke-Acts: Models for Interpretation* (Peabody, Mass.: Hendrickson, 1991) 97–122.

Manicardi, "Parola"
Ermenegildo Manicardi, "L'ultima parola di Gesú secondo Luca e il racconto della morte di Stefano in Atti," in Rinaldo Fabris, ed., *La Parola di Dio cresceva (At 12,24): scritti in onore di Carlo Maria Martini nel suo 70. compleanno* (SRivBib 33; Bologna: EDB, 1998) 251–70.

Marshall
I. Howard Marshall, *The Gospel of Luke: A Commentary on the Greek Text* (NIGTC; Grand Rapids: Eerdmans, 1978).

Masson, *Vers les sources*
Charles Masson, *Vers les sources d'eau vive: Études d'exégèse et de théologie du Nouveau Testament* (Lausanne: Payot, 1961).

Matera, "Jesus before Pilate"
  Frank J. Matera, "Luke 23:1-25: Jesus before
  Pilate, Herod, and Israel," in Frans Neirynck,
  ed., *L'Évangile de Luc — The Gospel of Luke* (2d ed.;
  BEThL 32; Leuven: University Press/Peeters, 1989)
  535–51.
Mekkattukunnel, "Proof"
  A. G. Mekkattukunnel, "Further Proof for the Unity
  of Luke-Acts," *BiBh* 29 (2003) 221–29.
Metzger, *Textual Commentary* (1st ed.)
  Bruce M. Metzger, *A Textual Commentary on the Greek
  New Testament: A Companion Volume to the United Bible
  Societies' Greek New Testament* (New York: United
  Bible Societies, 1971).
Metzger, *Textual Commentary* (2d ed.)
  Bruce M. Metzger, *A Textual Commentary on the Greek
  New Testament: A Companion Volume to the United
  Bible Societies' Greek New Testament* (2d ed.; Stuttgart:
  United Bible Societies, 1994).
Meynet
  Roland Meynet, *L'Évangile de Luc* (Rhétorique sémi-
  tique 1; Paris: Lethielleux, 2005).
Meynet, *Évangile*
  Roland Meynet, *L'évangile selon Saint Luc: Analyse
  rhétorique* (2 vols.; Paris: Cerf, 1988).
Meynet, *Guide*
  Roland Meynet, *Avez-vous lu saint Luc? Guide pour la
  rencontre* (LiBi 88; Paris: Cerf, 1990).
Meynet, *Parole*
  Roland Meynet, *Quelle est donc cette parole? Lecture
  "rhétorique" de l'évangile de Luc (1–9, 22–24)* (2 vols.;
  LD 99; Paris: Cerf, 1979).
Moulton-Milligan, *Vocabulary*
  James Hope Moulton and George Milligan, *The
  Vocabulary of the Greek New Testament: Illustrated
  from the Papyri and Other Non-Literary Sources* (1930;
  reprinted Grand Rapids: Eerdmans, 1974).
Mülhaupt
  Erwin Mülhaupt, ed., *D. Martin Luthers Evangelien-
  Auslegung* (3d ed.; 5 vols.; Göttingen: Vandenhoeck
  & Ruprecht, 1957).
Neirynck, *Evangelica*
  Frans Neirynck, *Evangelica: Gospel Studies =
  Evangelica: Études d'évangile: Collected Essays* (ed.
  Frans van Segbroeck; 3 vols.; BEThL 60, 99, 150;
  Leuven: Peeters, 1982).
Neirynck, *L'Évangile de Luc — The Gospel of Luke*
  Frans Neirynck, ed., *L'Évangile de Luc —The Gospel of
  Luke* (2d ed.; BEThL 32; Leuven: University Press/
  Peeters, 1989).
Nestle-Aland (27th ed.)
  Eberhard Nestle, ed., *Novum Testamentum
  Graece* (27th ed.; rev. Kurt Aland; Stuttgart:
  Württembergische Bibelgesellschaft, 1993).
Neyrey, "Absence"
  Jerome H. Neyrey, "The Absence of Jesus'
  Emotions—The Lucan Redaction of Lk 22,39-46,"
  Bib 61 (1980) 153–71.

Neyrey, *Passion*
  Jerome H. Neyrey, *The Passion according to Luke:
  A Redaction Study of Luke's Soteriology* (New York:
  Paulist, 1985).
Nolland
  John Nolland, *Luke* (3 vols.; Word Biblical
  Commentary 35A–C; Dallas: Word, 1989–93).
NTG
  The New Testament in Greek, vol. 3: *The Gospel
  According to Luke* (ed. American and British
  Committees of the International Greek New
  Testament Project; 2 vols.; Oxford: Clarendon,
  1984, 1987).
Origenes Werke
  Origenes Werke (GCS; 12 vols.; Leipzig: Hinrichs,
  1899–1955).
Parker, *Living Text*
  D. C. Parker, *The Living Text of the Gospels*
  (Cambridge: Cambridge University Press, 1997)
  148–57.
Parrot, *Holy Sepulchre*
  André Parrot, *Golgotha and the Church of the Holy
  Sepulchre* (trans. Edwin Hudson; SBA 6; London:
  SCM, 1957).
Payne Smith, *Cyril*
  Cyril of Alexandria, *Commentary on the Gospel of
  St. Luke* (trans. Robert Payne Smith; 2 vols.; 1859;
  reprinted New York: Studion, 1983).
Pelletier, "Tradition"
  André Pelletier, "La tradition synoptique du 'voile
  déchiré' à la lumière des réalités archéologiques,"
  RSR 46 (1958) 161–80.
Petzke, *Sondergut*
  Gerd Petzke, *Das Sondergut des Evangeliums nach
  Lukas* (Zürcher Werkkommentare zur Bibel;
  Zurich: Theologischer Verlag, 1990).
Phillips, *Paraphrase*
  Jane E. Phillips, *Desiderius Erasmus, Paraphrase on
  Luke* (Toronto: University of Toronto Press, 2003).
Plummer
  Alfred Plummer, *A Critical and Exegetical Commentary
  on the Gospel according to St. Luke* (5th ed.; ICC;
  Edinburgh: T. & T. Clark, 1922).
Popkes, *Christus Traditus*
  Wiard Popkes, *Christus Traditus: Eine Untersuchung
  zum Begriff der Dahingabe im Neuen Testament* (Zurich:
  Zwingli, 1967).
Prete, *Opera*
  Benedetto Prete, *L'opera di Luca: Contenuti e prospet-
  tive* (Turin: Leumann, Elle di ci, 1986).
Prete, "Preghiere"
  Benedetto Prete, "Le preghiere di Gesù al Monte
  degli Ulivi e sulla Croce nel racconto lucano della
  passione," in Associazione biblica italiana, ed., *Gesù
  e la sua Morte* (Brescia: Paideia, 1984) 75–96.
Price, *Widow*
  Robert M. Price, *The Widow Traditions in Luke-Acts:
  A Feminist-Critical Scrutiny* (SBLDS 155; Atlanta:
  Scholars Press, 1997).

Prigent, *Fin de Jérusalem*
Pierre Prigent, *La fin de Jérusalem* (CAB 17; Neuchâtel: Delachaux et Niestlé, 1969).

Quesnel et al, *Nourriture et repas*
Michel Quesnel, Yves-Marie Blanchard, and Claude Tassin, eds., *Nourriture et repas dans les milieux juifs et chrétiens de l'antiquité: Mélanges offerts au professeur Charles Perrot* (LD 178; Paris: Cerf, 1999).

Radl
Walter Radl, *Das Lukas-Evangelium* (EdF 261; Darmstadt: Wissenschaftliche Buchgesellschaft, 1988).

Radl, *Paulus und Jesus*
Walter Radl, *Paulus und Jesus im lukanischen Doppelwerk: Untersuchungen zu Parallelmotiven im Lukasevangelium und in der Apostelgeschichte* (Europäische Hochschulschriften 23/49; Frankfurt a. M.: Lang, 1975).

Radl, "Sonderüberlieferungen"
Walter Radl, "Sonderüberlieferungen bei Lukas? Traditionsgeschichtliche Fragen zu Lk 22,67f; 23,2 und 23,6-12," in Karl Kertelge, ed., *Der Prozess gegen Jesus* (QD 112; Freiburg i. B.: Herder, 1988) 131–47.

Réau, *Iconographie*
Louis Réau, *Iconographie de l'art Chrétien* (3 vols. in 6; Paris: Presses universitaires de France, 1955–59), vol. 2: *Iconographie de la Bible*.

Rehkopf, *Sonderquelle*
Friedrich Rehkopf, *Die lukanische Sonderquelle: Ihr Umfang und Sprachgebrauch* (WUNT 5; Tübingen: Mohr Siebeck, 1959).

Reiling and Swellengrebel, *Translator's Handbook*
J. Reiling and J. L. Swellengrebel, *A Translator's Handbook on the Gospel of Luke* (Helps for Translators 10; Leiden: Brill, 1971).

Renan, *Life*
Ernest Renan, *The Life of Jesus* (1902; reprinted New York: Modern Library, 1927).

Rese, *Motive*
Martin Rese, *Alttestamentliche Motive in der Christologie des Lukas* (StNT 1; Gütersloh: Mohn, 1969).

Reuss, *Lukas-Kommentare*
Joseph Reuss, *Lukas-Kommentare aus der griechischen Kirche: Aus Katenenhandschriften gesammelt und herausgegeben* (TU 130; Berlin: Akademie-Verlag, 1984).

Rigaux, *Dieu l'a ressuscité*
Béda Rigaux, *Dieu l'a ressuscité: Exégèse et théologie biblique* (Gembloux: Duculot, 1973).

Ringe
Sharon H. Ringe, *Luke* (Westminster Bible Companion; Louisville: Westminster John Knox, 1995).

Robinson et al., *Critical Edition of Q*
James M. Robinson, Paul Hoffmann, and John S. Kloppenborg, eds., *The Critical Edition of Q: Synopsis including the Gospels of Matthew and Luke, Mark and Thomas with English, German, and French Translations of Q and Thomas* (Hermeneia. Supplements; Minneapolis: Fortress Press, 2000).

Roloff, *Kerygma*
Jürgen Roloff, *Das Kerygma und der irdische Jesus: Historische Motive in den Jesus-Erzählungen der Evangelien* (Göttingen: Vandenhoeck & Ruprecht, 1970).

Rosenblatt, "Crucifixion"
Samuel Rosenblatt, "The Crucifixion of Jesus from the Standpoint of the Pharisaic Law," *JBL* 75 (1956) 315–21.

Rudberg, "Verhöhnung"
Gunnar Rudberg, "Die Verhöhnung Jesu vor dem Hohenpriester," *ZNW* 24 (1925) 307–9.

Russ, "Vermächtnis"
Rainer Russ, "Das Vermächtnis des gekreuzigten Herrn: Jesu letzte Worte im Evangelium nach Lukas (Bilder von Dieter Groß)," *BK* 50 (1995) 128–35.

Sabourin
Leopold Sabourin, *L'Évangile de Luc: Introduction et commentaire* (Rome: Gregorian University Press, 1985).

Sauget, "Nouvelles homélies"
Joseph M. Sauget, "Nouvelles homélies du Commentaire sur l'Évangile de s. Luc de Cyrille d'Alexandrie dans leur traduction syriaque," in *Symposium Syriacum 1972* (OrChrA 197; Rome: Pont. Institutum Orientalium Studiorum, 1974) 439–56.

Schanz
Paul Schanz, *Commentar über das Evangelium des heiligen Lucas* (Tübingen: Fues, 1883).

Schenke, *Studien*
Ludger Schenke, *Studien zur Passionsgeschichte des Markus: Tradition und Redaktion in Markus 14,1-42* (FB 4; Würzburg: Echter, 1971).

Schiller, *Iconography*
Gertrud Schiller, *Iconography of Christian Art*, vol. 2: *The Passion of Jesus Christ* (trans. Janet Seligman: Greenwich, Conn.: New York Graphic Society, 1971).

Schlatter
Adolf Schlatter, *Das Evangelium des Lukas: Aus seinen Quellen erklärt* (Stuttgart: Calwer, 1931).

Schmid
Josef Schmid, *Das Evangelium nach Lukas* (3d ed.; RNT; Regensburg: Pustet, 1955).

Schmithals
Walter Schmithals, *Das Evangelium nach Lukas* (ZBK.NT 3.1; Zurich: Theologischer Verlag, 1980).

Schneemelcher, *New Testament Apocrypha*
Wilhelm Schneemelcher, ed., *New Testament Apocrypha* (rev. ed.; English translation edited by R. McL. Wilson; 2 vols.; Louisville: Westminster John Knox, 1991, 1992).

Schneider
Gerhard Schneider, *Das Evangelium nach Lukas* (2d ed.; 2 vols.; ÖTBK 3.1–2; Gütersloh: Mohn, 1984).

Schneider, *Lukas*
Gerhard Schneider, *Lukas, Theologe der Heilsgeschichte: Aufsätze zum lukanischen Doppelwerk* (BBB 59; Königsstein: Hanstein, 1985).

Schneider, *Passion Jesu*
  Gerhard Schneider, *Die Passion Jesu nach den drei älteren Evangelien* (BiH 11; Munich: Kösel, 1973).

Schniewind, *Parallelperikopen*
  Julius Schniewind, *Die Parallelperikopen bei Lukas und Johannes* (1914; reprinted Hildesheim: Olms, 1958).

Schramm, *Markus-Stoff*
  Tim Schramm, *Der Markus-Stoff bei Lukas: Eine literarkritische und radaktionsgeschichtliche Untersuchung* (SNTSMS 14; Cambridge: Cambridge University Press, 1971).

Schürmann, *Abschiedsrede*
  Heinz Schürmann, *Quellenkritische Untersuchung des Lukanischen Abendmahlsberichtes Lk 22, 7-38*, Part 3: *Jesu Abschiedsrede, Lk 22, 21-38* (NTAbh 20.5; Münster: Aschendorffsche Buchdruckerei, 1957).

Schürmann, *Einsetzungsbericht*
  Heinz Schürmann, *Quellenkritische Untersuchung des lukanischen Abendmahlsberichtes Lk 22, 7-38, Part 2: Der Einsetzungsbericht, Lk 22, 19-20* (NTAbh 20.4; Münster: Aschendorff, 1955).

Schürmann, *Paschamahlbericht*
  Heinz Schürmann, *Quellenkritische Untersuchung des lukanischen Abendmahlsberichtes Lk 22, 7-38, Part 1: Der Paschamahlbericht, Lk 22 (7-14) 15-18* (NTAbh 19.5; Münster: Aschendorff, 1953).

Schürmann, *Traditionsgeschichtliche Untersuchungen*
  Heinz Schürmann, *Traditionsgeschichtliche Untersuchungen zu den synoptischen Evangelien* (KBANT; Düsseldorf: Patmos, 1968).

Schürmann, *Ursprung*
  Heinz Schürmann, *Ursprung und Gestalt: Eröterungen und Besinnungen zum Neuen Testament* (KBANT; Düsseldorf: Patmos, 1970).

Schweizer
  Eduard Schweizer, *Das Evangelium nach Lukas: Übersetzt und erklärt* (NTD 3; Göttingen: Vandenhoeck & Ruprecht, 1982).

Senior, *Passion*
  Donald Senior, *The Passion of Jesus in the Gospel of Luke* (Wilmington, Del.: Glazier, 1989).

Sherwin-White, *Roman Society*
  A. N. Sherwin-White, *Roman Society and Roman Law in the New Testament* (1963; reprinted Grand Rapids: Baker, 1978).

Smith and Taussig, *Many Tables*
  Dennis E. Smith and Hal Taussig, *Many Tables: The Eucharist in the New Testament and Liturgy Today* (Philadelphia: Trinity Press International, 1990).

Smyth, *Greek Grammar*
  Herbert Weir Smyth, *Greek Grammar* (1916; rev. Gordon M. Messing; reprinted Cambridge, Mass.: Harvard University Press, 1984).

Spicq, *Lexicon*
  Ceslas Spicq, *Theological Lexicon of the New Testament* (trans. and ed. James D. Ernest; 3 vols.; Peabody, Mass.: Hendrickson, 1994).

Sterling, "*Mors Philosophi*"
  Greg Sterling, "*Mors Philosophi:* The Death of Jesus in Luke," *HTR* 94 (2001) 383–402.

Swanson, *Manuscripts*
  Reuben J. Swanson, ed., *New Testament Greek Manuscripts: Luke* (Pasadena, Calif.: William Carey International University Press, 1995).

Sylva, *Reimaging*
  Dennis D. Sylva, ed., *Reimaging the Death of the Lukan Jesus* (Athenäums Monografien: Theologie 73; Frankfurt: Hain, 1990).

Talbert, *Reading*
  Charles H. Talbert, *Reading Luke: A Literary and Theological Commentary on the Third Gospel* (New York: Crossroad, 1982).

Tannehill
  Robert C. Tannehill, *Luke* (ANTC; Nashville: Abingdon, 1996).

Taylor, *Passion Narrative*
  Vincent Taylor, *The Passion Narrative of St. Luke: A Critical and Historical Investigation* (SNTSMS 19; Cambridge: Cambridge University Press, 1972).

Taylor, *Third Gospel*
  Vincent Taylor, *Behind the Third Gospel: A Study of the Proto-Luke Hypothesis* (Oxford: Clarendon, 1926).

Theissen, *Miracle Stories*
  Gerd Theissen, *Miracle Stories of the Early Christian Tradition* (trans. F. McDonagh; Philadelphia: Fortress Press, 1983).

Tiede
  David Lenz Tiede, *Luke* (Augsburg Commentary on the New Testament; Minneapolis: Augsburg, 1988).

Trautmann, *Handlungen*
  Maria Trautmann, *Zeichenhafte Handlungen Jesu* (FB 37; Würzburg: Echter, 1980).

Trilling, *Christusverkündigung*
  Wolfgang Trilling, *Christusverkündigung in den synoptischen Evangelien: Beispiele gattungsgemässer Auslegung* (BiH 4; Munich: Kösel, 1969).

Trimaille, "Manger et boire"
  Michel Trimaille, "'Manger et boire' dans l'oeuvre de Luc," in Michel Quesnel, Yves-Marie Blanchard, and Claude Tassin, eds., *Nourriture et repas dans les milieux juifs et chrétiens de l'antiquité: Mélanges offerts au professeur Charles Perrot* (LD 178; Paris: Cerf, 1999) 121–37.

Tsutsui, "Evangelium Marcions"
  Kenji Tsutsui, "Das Evangelium Marcions: Ein neuer Versuch der Textrekonstruktion," *AJBI* 18 (1992) 67–132.

Untergassmair, "Sinndeutung"
  Franz Georg Untergassmair, "Thesen zur Sinndeutung des Todes Jesu in der lukanischen Passionsgeschichte," *ThGl* 70 (1980) 180–93.

van Iersel, *Sohn*
  Bastiaan Martinus Franciscus van Iersel, *"Der Sohn" in den Synoptischen Jesusworten: Christusbezeichnung der Gemeinde oder Selbstbezeichnung Jesu?* (NovTSup 3; Leiden: Brill, 1961).

van Tilborg and Counet, *Jesus' Appearances*
  Sjef van Tilborg and Patrick Chatelion Counet, *Jesus' Appearances and Disappearances in Luke 24* (Biblical Interpretation Series 45; Leiden: Brill, 2000).

van Unnik, *Sparsa Collecta*
  Willem C. van Unnik, *Sparsa Collecta: The Collected Essays of W. C. van Unnik* (3 vols.; NovTSup 29–31; Leiden: Brill, 1973–83).

Vicent Cernuda, "Barrabás"
  Antonio Vicent Cernuda, "Pro Barrabás, contra Jesús!" *EstBib* 59 (2001) 29–46.

Walter, "Tempelzerstörung"
  Nikolaus Walter, "Tempelzerstörung und synoptische Apokalypse," *ZNW* 57 (1966) 38–49.

Weinert, "Temple"
  Francis D. Weinert, "The Meaning of the Temple in Luke-Acts," *BTB* 11 (1981) 85–89.

Wellhausen
  Julius Wellhausen, *Das Evangelium Lucae* (Berlin: Reimer, 1904).

Westcott and Hort, *New Testament*
  Brooke Foss Westcott and Fenton John Anthony Hort, *The New Testament in the Original Greek* (2 vols.; 1881; reprinted Graz: Akademische Druck- und Verlagsanstalt, 1974).

Wiefel
  Wolfgang Wiefel, *Das Evangelium nach Lukas* (ThHKNT 3; Berlin: Evangelische Verlagsanstalt, 1988).

Wilkinson, "Words"
  John Wilkinson, "The Seven Words from the Cross," *SJT* 17 (1964) 69–82.

Winter, *On the Trial*
  Paul Winter, *On the Trial of Jesus* (rev. and ed. T. A. Burkill and Geza Vermes; SJ 1; Berlin: de Gruyter, 1974).

Zehnle, "Death"
  Richard Zehnle, "The Salvific Character of Jesus' Death in Lucan Soteriology," *TS* 30 (1969) 420–44.

Zorell, *Lexicon*
  Francisco Zorell, *Novi Testamenti Lexicon Graecum* (Paris: Lethielleux, 1911).

Commentary

The Royal Procession (19:28-40)

Bibliography

Baarlink, H., "Friede im Himmel: Die lukanische Redaktion von Lk 19,38 und ihre Deutung," *ZNW* 76 (1985) 170–86.

Bauer, Walter, "The 'Colt' of Palm Sunday (Der Palmesel)," *JBL* 72 (1953) 220–29, reprinted in idem, *Aufsätze und kleine Schriften* (ed. Georg Strecker; Tübingen: Mohr Siebeck, 1967) 109–21.

Blenkinsopp, Joseph, "The Oracle of Judah and the Messianic Entry," *JBL* 80 (1961) 55–64.

Burger, Christoph, *Jesus als Davidssohn: Eine traditionsgeschichtliche Untersuchung* (FRLANT 98; Göttingen: Vandenhoeck & Ruprecht, 1970) 112–14.

Buth, Randall, "Luke 19:31-34, Mishnaic Hebrew, and Bible Translation: Is κύριοι τοῦ πώλου Singular?" *JBL* 104 (1985) 680–85.

Catchpole, David R., "The 'Triumphal' Entry," in Ernst Bammel and C. F. D. Moule, eds., *Jesus and the Politics of His Day* (Cambridge: Cambridge University Press, 1984) 319–34.

Davies, T. L., "Was Jesus Compelled?" *ExpT* 42 (1930–31) 526–27.

del Agua Pérez, Agustín, "Deras cristológico en el relato lucano de la entrada de Jesús en Jerusalén: Lc 19,28-40," in A. Vargas-Machuca and Gregorio Ruiz, eds., *Palabra y Vida: Homenaje a José Alonso Díaz en su 70 Compleaños* (Publicaciones de la Universidad Pontificia Comillas de Madrid, Serie I, Estudios 28; Teología I, 15; Madrid: Universidad Pontificia Comillas de Madrid, 1984) 177–88.

Derrett, J. Duncan M., "Law in the New Testament: The Palm Sunday Colt," *NovT* 13 (1971) 241–58, reprinted in idem, *Studies in the New Testament* (6 vols.; Leiden: Brill, 1977–95) 2:165–83.

Doeve, Jan W., "Purification du Temple et desséchement du figuier: Sur la structure du 21ème chapitre de Matthieu et parallèles (Marc 11,1—12,12, Luc 19,28—20,19)," *NTS* 1 (1954–55) 297–308.

Duff, Paul Brooks, "The March of the Divine Warrior and the Advent of the Greco-Roman King," *JBL* 111 (1992) 55–71.

Fernández Marcos, Natalio, "La unción de Salomón y la entrada de Jesús en Jerusalén: 1 Re 1,33-40/ Lc 19,35-40," *Bib* 68 (1987) 89–97.

Frayn, R. S., "Was Jesus Compelled?" *ExpT* 43 (1931–32) 381–82.

Frenz, Albrecht, "Mt 21,5-7," *NovT* 13 (1971) 259–60.

Fuchs, Albert, "Die Agreements der Einzugsperikope Mk 11,1-10 par Mt 21,1-9 par Lk 19,28-38," *SNTU* 23 (1998) 215–27.

George, Augustin, *Études sur l'oeuvre de Luc* (Sources bibliques; Paris: Gabalda, 1978) 274–76.

Idem, "La royauté de Jésus selon l'évangile de Luc," *ScEc* 14 (1962) 57–69.

Gruber, Mayer I., "The Meaning of Biblical Parallelism: A Biblical Perspective," *Prooftexts: A Journal of Jewish Literary History* 13 (1993) 289–93.

Guy, Laurie, "The Interplay of the Present and Future in the Kingdom of God (Luke 19:11-44)," *TynB* 48 (1997) 119–37.

Haenchen, Ernst, *Der Weg Jesu: Eine Erklärung des Markus-Evangeliums und der kanonischen Parallelen* (Berlin: Töpelmann, 1966) 372–79.

Hahn, Ferdinand, *The Titles of Jesus in Christology: Their History in Early Christianity* (trans. H. Knight and G. Ogg; New York: World, 1969) 83–84.

Kinman, Brent, *Jesus' Entry into Jerusalem: In the Context of Lukan Theology and the Politics of His Day* (AGJU 28; Leiden: Brill, 1995) 184–202 (bibliography).

Idem, "Parousia, Jesus' 'A–Triumphal' Entry, and the Fate of Jerusalem (Luke 19:28-44)," *JBL* 118 (1999) 279–94.

Idem, "'The Stones Will Cry Out' (Luke 19–40)—Joy or Judgment?" *Bib* 75 (1994) 232–35.

Kuhn, Heinz-Wolfgang, "Das Reittier Jesu in der Einzugsgeschichte des Markusevangeliums," *ZNW* 50 (1959) 82–91.

Linder, Ammon, "The Destruction of Jerusalem Sunday," *SE* 30 (1987–88) 253–92.

Mariadasan, Varuvel, *Le triomphe messianique de Jésus et son entrée à Jérusalem: Étude critico-littéraire des traditions évangéliques (Mc 11:1-11, Mt 21:1-11, Lc 19,28-38, Jn 12:12-16* (Tindivanam: Catechetical Centre, 1978).

Martin, Albert William, "The Interpretation of the Triumphal Entry in the Early Church" (Ph.D. diss., Vanderbilt University, 1971).

Mastin, Brian A., "The Date of the Triumphal Entry," *NTS* 16 (1969–70) 76–82.

Meikle, James, "Was Jesus Compelled?" *ExpT* 43 (1931–32) 288.

Patsch, Hermann, "Der Einzug Jesu in Jerusalem: Ein historischer Versuch," *ZThK* 68 (1971) 1–26.

Petuchowski, Jakob J., "'Hoshi'ah Na' in Psalm CXVIII 25—A Prayer for Rain," *VT* 5 (1955) 266–71.

Rese, Martin, *Alttestamentliche Motive in der Christologie des Lukas* (StNT 1; Gütersloh: Mohn, 1969) 196–99.

Rilliet, Frédéric, "Une homélie syriaque sur la fête des Rameaux attribuée à Jean Chrysostome," *ParO* 8 (1977–78) 151–216.

Idem, "La louange des pierres et le tonnerre: Luc 19,40 chez Jacques de Saroug et dans la patristique syriaque," *RThPh* 117 (1985) 293–304.

Ruiz, Gregorio, "El clamor de las piedras (Lc 19,40—Hab 2,11): El Reino choca con la ciudad injusta en la fiesta de Ramos," *EstEcl* 59 (1984) 297–312.

Samuel, O., "Die Regierungsgewalt des Wortes
Gottes: Eine Betrachtung zu Luk. 19,29-40," *EvTh*
3 (1936) 1–3.

Schniewind, Julius, *Die Parallelperikopen bei Lukas und
Johannes* (1914; reprinted Hildesheim: Olms, 1958)
26–28.

Spurin, Richard, "Why Did Jesus Go to Jerusalem?,"
ExpT 106 (1994–95) 178–79.

Tatum, W. Barnes, "Jesus' So-Called Triumphal
Entry: On Making an Ass of the Romans," *Forum:
Foundations and Facets* n.s. 1 (1998) 129–43.

Trautmann, Maria, *Zeichenhafte Handlungen Jesu* (FB
37; Würzburg: Echter, 1980) 347–78.

28 **After he had said this, he went ahead, up to
Jerusalem.ᵃ 29/ When he came near to Bethphage and Bethany, toward the mount called
the Mount of Olives, it happened that he sent
two of the disciples 30/ and said to them,ᵇ "Go
into the village that lies before us; when you
enter it you will find a young assᶜ on which
no one has ever sat. Untie it and bring it here.
31/ And if anyone asks you, 'Why do you untie
it,' you shall say that its master needs it."
32/ And when those who had been sent were
going, they found it to be as he had told them.
33/ While they were untying the young ass, its
owners said to them, "Why are you untying
the ass?" 34/ They answered, "Because its
master needs it." 35/ Then they led it to Jesus,
and when they had thrown their garments on
the young ass, they helped Jesus mount it.
36/ While he rode ahead,ᵈ they spread their
garments on the way. 37/ When he drew near
to the foot of the Mount of Olives, the whole
multitude of disciples began to praise God
with a loud voice for all the mighty deeds they
had seen. 38/ They said,ᵉ "Blessed is the king
who comes in the name of the Lord. Peace in
heaven and glory in the highest."**

39 **Some of the Pharisees from the crowd called to
him, "Master,ᶠ rebuke your disciples." 40/ He
answered them, "I tell you: If these are silent,
the stones will cry out."**

a   Literally: "And having said this, he went on ahead up toward
Jerusalem."
b   Literally: "saying" (without "to them")
c   Literally: "foal/colt," "young one," "young ass."
d   Literally: "While he strode ahead."
e   Literally: "saying."
f   Or: "Teacher" (Greek διδάσκαλε). In vv. 31-34 the Greek
word is κύριος, "master," which can also mean "Lord,"
"Mister," "owner."

Synchronic Analysis

One senses already the presence of the city of Jerusalem (vv. 28, 41-44)—still, however, from a distance. Thus, the event in question is an approach to (see vv. 29, 37, 41) rather than an entry into the city. (The verb "to enter" does not appear until v. 45, and there it refers to the temple.)[1] What takes place during this approach, in the outlying villages of Bethphage and Bethany (vv. 29-30), at the foot of the legendary Mount of Olives (vv. 29, 37)? Various marginal happenings are mentioned. Later they will turn out to be major events, but at the moment their immediate significance remains unclear and ambiguous. After Jesus' primary destination, Jerusalem, is reported (v. 28), mention is made of a special intention. Its importance ("his master needs him," v. 34) but not its significance is underscored. It involves taking possession

1   See C. F. Evans, *Saint Luke* (TPI New Testament Commentaries; Philadelphia: Trinity Press International) 677; and Darrell L. Bock, *Luke* (2 vols.; BECNT; Grand Rapids: Baker, 1994, 1996) 2:1546. Doeve ("Purification") is of the opinion that the pericopae of 19:28—20:19 have been arranged according to the midrashic method.

of a young ass (vv. 29-34). This action, arranged by Jesus, leads to further preparations in which the disciples take the initiative.[2] They took off their garments, laid some of them on the ass as a saddle, and helped Jesus mount it. Then they spread some of the others on the ground in the place of a red carpet.[3] While this is happening, Jesus remains quiet and passive (from v. 32 to v. 39).

The main action begins with a brief summary (v. 37a). The disciples present, described as a "multitude" ($\pi\lambda\hat{\eta}\vartheta o\varsigma$—translated here as "multitude of disciples"), are the only persons involved. They express their joy over Jesus' miracles by thanking God with praise and by blessing the hero with words of Scripture and a liturgical formula (vv. 37b-38).[4]

Later the readers learn that a crowd of people ($\check{o}\chi\lambda o\varsigma$) is present. They also hear a challenge of the Pharisees that appears to involve a complaint, which, however, is not further explained (v. 39). Jesus, again active and speaking, silences them by giving his approval to the praise, which appears to be at the same time both staged and spontaneous (v. 40).

In summary, the readers are present for four brief actions that follow one another in rapid sequence without any detailed commentary:

Vv. 28-34: Once the readers are reminded of the opening situation, two disciples take possession of a young ass.

Vv. 35-36: The disciples help Jesus mount the ass.

Vv. 37-38: The multitude of disciples erupts in praise.

Vv. 39-40: Some Pharisees try to intervene. Jesus silences them.[5]

Diachronic Analysis

Using a synoptic comparison, we are able to establish a hypothesis to explain how the evangelist brought together the traditional materials available to him, and we can discover the redactional features with which Luke put his own imprint on them. The report he has reproduced has a parallel in John as well as in Mark and Matthew.[6]

Three of Luke's details are found only in the Fourth Gospel:[7] the recollection of Jesus' miracles imprinted on the disciples' memory (v. 37; John 12:16), the title "king" given to Jesus (v. 38; John 12:13), and the Pharisees' negative reaction (v. 39; John 12:19). Thus, Luke shares with John several recollections of Jesus' last days.[8]

Luke and Matthew share the following, primarily grammatical, details: the aorist of the verb "to approach," where Mark uses the present (v. 29; Matt 21:1);[9] the aorist "he sent," where Mark has the historical present (v. 29; Matt 21:1); the omission of $\alpha\dot{v}\tau o\hat{v}$ ("his" after the word "disciples" (v. 29; Matt 21:1); the present participle $\lambda\acute{e}\gamma\omega\nu$ (v. 30; Matt 21:2), where Mark has the present indicative; the use (twice) of the verb "lead to" ($\check{\alpha}\gamma\omega$), where Mark uses the verb "bring to" ($\varphi\acute{e}\rho\omega$, vv. 30, 35; Matt 21:2, 7); "that" ($\check{o}\tau\iota$) after "you shall say" (v. 31; Matt 21:3); the observation that the disciples did as Jesus had instructed them (v. 32; Matt 21:6);[10] the absence of the words "tied outside near a gate where the street turns" (Mark 11:4; see v. 32 and Matt 21:6); the absence of "blessed is the kingdom of our father David that comes" (Mark 11:10; see v. 38 and Matt 21:9).

---

2 Patsch ("Einzug," 15–16) cites the case of a contemporary of Jesus and the apostles: "Rabbi Jochanan ben Zakkai once rode toward Jerusalem on an ass, and his disciples followed him" (*b. Ketub.* 66b *Bar.*; Str-B 2:414; this according to the Munich MS. In the Bamberg MS he leaves Jerusalem). The Talmud (*Talmud Bavli* [Steinsaltz ed.; New York: Random House, 1994], vol. 11, tractate *Ketubot*, part 5, p. 18) chooses the reading "he leaves Jerusalem"; see also the parallel passage in *Sifre Devarim* 31.14 §305 (130a).

3 By contrast, Marie-Joseph Lagrange (*Évangile selon saint Luc* [7th ed.; EtB; Paris: Gabalda, 1948] 499) thinks that other people spread their garments on the ground.

4 See Lagrange, 499; and C. F. Evans, 680.

5 See the slightly differing schematic portrayal in Bock, 2:1551.

6 The report does not appear in the *Gospel of Thomas*. According to Rese (*Motive*, 196–99), the connections between 19:36-40 and the Gospel of John are not that close.

7 See Schniewind, *Parallelperikopen*, 26–28.

8 There are also a number of agreements between Matthew and John, esp. the quotation from Zech 9:9.

9 The reference to Bethphage does not appear in all manuscripts of Mark. If it should be the case that it was not original, then the existence of this small village in Luke and Matthew constitutes another minor agreement.

10 On these small agreements, see Andreas Ennulat,

In my opinion, however, these observations do not justify positing a literary relationship between the First and Third Gospels.[11] It is quite possible that both evangelists improved Mark, their common source, in the same way. They may also have been able to remember having heard an orally transmitted form of the report. To imagine, as another hypothesis does, that alongside Mark both of them draw on a Deutero-Mark[12] is a solution that is both complicated and improbable.[13]

The connections between Luke and Mark are consistent with a close relationship between the two Gospels. Luke appears as a *rewriter* who improves Mark's style, narration, and ideas. Nevertheless, in doing so he retains what is essential in his source's narratives down to the smallest details of many of its expressions.[14] Along with Mark, he names Bethany and calls attention to the Mount of Olives (v. 29; Mark 11:1); he mentions only a single animal (Matthew famously speaks of an ass and a colt in exact fulfillment of the prophecy of Zech 9:9); he disregards the quotation from Zech 9:9; in the same order and with the same words he describes what the two disciples do (vv. 32-35). In addition to the minor agreements between Matthew and Luke already mentioned, one can also observe differences between Luke and Mark: Luke omits the words "and he will send it back here immediately" (Mark 11:3b). He fails to mention the branches that had been cut (Mark 11:8). He readily repeats Jesus' direction and location (v. 37a). Twice he avoids mentioning "Hosanna" (Mark 11:9-10). He offers a new formula—"Peace in heaven and glory in the highest" (v. 38b)—in place of the second "Hosanna" shout ("Hosanna in the highest," Mark 11:10c). He ends by

inserting a brief exchange between the Pharisees and Jesus (vv. 39-40). We can explain most of the Lukan narrative by assuming that Luke is critically faithful to Mark. For the features unique to the Third Gospel we are indebted here to its redactor's initiative. It is probable, however, that Luke did not fabricate Jesus' statement about the stones that cry out (v. 40). It is, rather, an early, free-floating logion, which the evangelist (in v. 39) came to adopt and deliberately and carefully to quote (v. 40). Thus, I doubt that we have here the influence of Luke's special material.[15]

Matthew and John develop their sources in the direction of a messianism that is the fulfillment of biblical prophecies, but Luke, who at this point follows Mark, understands Jesus' ride as an act that symbolizes the imminent or realized kingdom.[16] Since the episode in which the ass is found can be understood only in terms of the LXX text of Zechariah and corresponds to a motif found in the literature of Greek aretalogies, it is not possible to give it an early date. It is even less possible to regard it as historical. It is an acceptable introduction, which, however, is not indispensable for the main narrative.[17] The procession of Jesus, who is praised by the disciples while riding on an ass, constitutes a literary unit that quite satisfies the criteria of form criticism.[18] Honored first as one of the joyful pilgrims to whom Psalm 117 [118] refers, the historical Jesus becomes after Easter the impulse for the first Christologies. In this episode he becomes as the Risen One, the Son of David, who makes an appearance to his city as a conqueror and demonstrates his kingship to the impatient multitudes.

Die "Minor Agreements": Untersuchungen zu einer offenen Frage des synoptischen Problems (WUNT 2/62; Tübingen: Mohr Siebeck, 1994) 245–52.

11 Contra Michael D. Goulder, *Luke: A New Paradigm* (2 vols.; JSNTSup 20; Sheffield: JSOT Press, 1989) 2:685–88.

12 That is the hypothesis of Fuchs, "Agreements."

13 There are various agreements between Matthew and Mark. It is, for example, the multitude and not necessarily the disciples who offer praise (Matt 21:8-9; Mark 11:8-10). See also the double Hosanna-shout (Matt 21:9; Mark 11:9-10).

14 For a good comparison between Mark and Luke, see Joseph A. Fitzmyer, *The Gospel according to Luke: Introduction, Translation, and Notes* (2 vols.; AB 28, 28A; Garden City, N.Y.: Doubleday, 1981, 1985)

2:1242–43, who also discovers connections between Luke and John in this pericope (John 12:12-16).

15 Contra Patsch, "Einzug," 8–9; and Schramm, *Markus-Stoff*, 148; in agreement with Mariadasan, *Triomphe*. Kim Paffenroth (*The Story of Jesus according to L* [JSNTSup 147; Sheffield: Sheffield Academic Press, 1997] 32–33, 65 n. 243, and 95 n. 154) is uncertain.

16 On the Lukan theme of royalty, so emphatically present here and qualified as that of Jesus, see p. 9 below and n. 39.

17 The secondary character of the search for the ass is emphasized by Rudolf Bultmann, *The History of the Synoptic Tradition* (trans. John Marsh; rev. ed.; New York: Harper & Row, 1976) 261.

The episode has been compared to the visitations that Greek, Roman, or Jewish rulers, princes, or governors made to their capitals and cities.[19] The local citizens prepared these triumphal entrances. They decorated the streets; dressed in white, they went outside the city walls to meet the hero, the victorious general, or the magistrates who constituted the highest authority. They organized speeches as well as the reception.[20] Long before the ancient model was applied to Palm Sunday, it had been—a fact too often overlooked—used to portray in advance the parousia of the Son of Man. Using it for the entry into Jerusalem meant that one adapted the model in such a way that, as a prelude to the passion, it should not be confused with a triumphal entry of a political or military nature. Nor should it be mistaken for a religious parousia that, since Jesus was still a mortal human being, was not to be portrayed as a triumph. Thus the ambiguous character of the episode: the ass is both a sign of kingship and a mark of humility—a sign of an insignificant kingship in the age of Tiberius and Pilate, and at the same time a living but fragile metaphor of a solemn heavenly enthronement. Luke, but also each of the other three evangelists, is thinking of the peace that is "in heaven," because the demons of oppression still dwell on earth. Luke takes the story that is still moving toward its conclusion and attaches it to the "promise–fulfillment"

typology that extends from the Scriptures to the present moment.[21]

Commentary

■ **28** According to Luke, Jesus comes from Jericho (18:35; 19:1) and, going ahead (ἔμπροσθεν) of the others, makes his way toward Jerusalem. Verse 28 offers one of the formulaic summaries (cf. 9:51; 13:22; 17:11) that accompany the Travel Narrative.[22] The words Jesus had just spoken (ταῦτα, "this") are the parable of the pounds, to which is added the journey of the prince who set out to obtain his royal crown (19:12-14).

■ **29-34** "And it happened" (καὶ ἐγένετο) serves to mark a new episode. Jesus now approaches two villages. In spite of two scholarly hypotheses, we do not know the exact location of Bethphage (literally, "the house of wild figs").[23] The village of Bethany (probably the "house of Anania") lay 2.7 kilometers east of Jerusalem on the eastern slopes of the Mount of Olives. The fourth evangelist locates Mary, Martha, and Lazarus in this village (John 11:1, 18; 12:1). We should not confuse it with the Bethany "beyond the Jordan" mentioned in John 1:28.[24] When Luke speaks of the "mountain named the Mount of Olives," he is thinking of readers who are not familiar with the geography of Palestine.[25] By defining it exactly

18 According to Tatum ("Entry"), Jesus wanted not to give a messianic sign but to challenge the Romans, to remind them of God's power, finally "making an ass out of the Romans" (p. 131). Trautmann (*Handlungen*, 347–78) is of the opinion that there lies at the beginning of the narrative an event that attracted attention, but it was an event that did not come from the intention of Jesus. On this occasion he did not want to give a prophetic sign. Mastin ("Date") suggests that Jesus' entry into Jerusalem took place in autumn, probably at the feast of the Dedication of the Temple.

19 See Duff, "March," 55–71; Kinman, *Entry*, 25–47; idem, "Parousia," 280–84. Fernández Marcos ("Entrada") insists that there are connections between the entries into Jerusalem of Jesus (19:35-40) and Solomon (1 Kgs 1:33-40).

20 See Lucien Cerfaux, *Christ in the Theology of St. Paul* (trans. Geoffrey Webb and Adrian Walker; New York: Herder & Herder, 1959) 32–33; Kinman, *Entry*, 25–47.

21 On this adaptation, see Hans Conzelmann, *The*

Theology of St. Luke (trans. Geoffrey Buswell; 1961; reprinted Philadelphia: Fortress Press, 1982) 74; and Kinman, *Entry*, 91–122, who emphasizes the nontriumphal aspect of this entry.

22 Note the motif of proceeding (πορεύομαι) up (ἀναβαίνω) toward the holy city as well as the use of the imperfect to indicate continuous action.

23 On Bethphage, see Fitzmyer, 2:1247. Lagrange (p. 498) writes: "We continue to believe that, in climbing the Mount of Olives on the old road that passed the hollow located between the Victoria-Augusta hospice and the village of et Tor, Jesus left Bethany quite far to his left. Thus even though it was closer to Jerusalem, the village of Bethphage had to be mentioned before that of et Tor." Origen (*Hom. Luc.* 27.1) is of the opinion that Bethphage means "house of the jawbone."

24 On Bethany, see Fitzmyer, 2:1248. Origen (*Hom. Luc.* 27.1) declares that Bethany means "house of obedience."

25 Mark writes simply "Mount of Olives." On this four-kilometer-long mountain, lying to the east of Jerusa-

as "in the direction of the mountain" ($\pi\rho\grave{o}\varsigma$ $\tau\grave{o}$ $\acute{o}\rho o\varsigma$) Luke shares Mark's understanding that the two villages lie on a slope of the Mount of Olives.

Jesus' command to the two disciples he had chosen ("two *of the* disciples") seems to be easy to carry out and at the same time insurmountably difficult. The paradox emphasizes the divine man's miraculous fore-knowledge,[26] which is confirmed by the cautious words ("you shall say that the master needs it"). In antiquity it was primarily military and political authorities who impounded provisions or mounts. Even in those cases when impoundment is mentioned to benefit rabbis, we would miss the miraculous dimension the evangelist suggests to us if we were to place Jesus' action in this category.[27] Instead, we must consider that the evangelist understands Jesus as a "king" ($\beta\alpha\sigma\iota\lambda\epsilon\acute{v}\varsigma$, v. 38) who makes use of his title "Master" or "Lord" ($\kappa\acute{v}\rho\iota o\varsigma$, vv. 31, 34) and requisitions the animal he needs.[28] The concept of need was important for legitimating and carrying out impoundments (cf. Mark 2:25 par. Luke 6:3). Since Jesus is a poor Galilean, the contrast is especially conspicuous.

Even if it is true that, without any distinguishing characteristic, $\pi\hat{\omega}\lambda o\varsigma$ usually means "foal/colt," on occasion, even without further modification, it means the "young" of various animals—for example, a "young ass." If we assume that Zechariah's prophecy lies behind the Synoptic episode, it can only mean the young offspring

of a she-ass. Matthew understood it this way (21:4), and we can assume that Mark and Luke did also.[29]

Why is it important that the young ass has never been ridden? It preserves the reference to Zech 9:9 (LXX) in which the young ass is "new." Doubtless its purpose is also to underscore Jesus' messianic privilege.[30] That the young ass will be "bound" is not only obvious; it may also be biblical. Judah's famous oracle (Gen 49:11), which first-century C.E. readers interpreted messianically, shows that the hero "binds" his ass to the vine. In the middle of the second century Justin Martyr compared the two texts (*1 Apol.* 32.1.5–6), and in his narration of the episode of the palm branches he points out that the young ass was tied to a grape vine.[31]

Luke here pits the Lord against the owners of the young ass, the "Lord" ($\kappa\acute{v}\rho\iota o\varsigma$, vv. 31 and 34) against the "masters" ($\kappa\acute{v}\rho\iota o\iota$, v. 33). Why does the ass have more than one owner? Is Luke influenced here by Mark, who says "some of the ones standing there"? Does he think the ass was common property? Is there a Semitism here where a grammatical plural sometimes can serve to designate a reality in the singular? Does he want to allegorize and, as Paul does in 1 Cor 8:6, contrast Christ, the sole Lord, with the numerous heathen "lords" called deities? It is difficult to answer these questions, and the plural form remains an enigma.[32]

---

lem beyond the Kidron Valley and running from north to south, with its three summits of which traditionally the middle one is considered to be the Mount of Olives, see Fitzmyer, 2:1248. The word $\acute{\eta}$ $\acute{\epsilon}\lambda\alpha\acute{\iota}\alpha$ means olive tree as well as olive. Instead of $\acute{\epsilon}\lambda\alpha\iota\hat{\omega}\nu$ (genitive plural) one can also read $\acute{\epsilon}\lambda\alpha\iota\acute{\omega}\nu$ (nominative masculine singular: "olive grove"); see Lagrange, 498.

26   On such a superhuman power, see Ludwig Bieler, $\Theta EIO\Sigma$ $ANHP$: *Das Bild des "göttlichen Menschen,"* in idem, *Spätantike und Frühchristentum* (1935–36; reprinted Darmstadt: Wissenschaftliche Buchgesellschaft, 1967) 87–94; Rosa Söder, *Die apokryphen Apostelgeschichten und die romanhafte Literatur der Antike* (Würzburger Studien zur Altertumswissenschaft 3; 1932; reprinted Stuttgart: Kohlhammer, 1969) 65–67.

27   The Hebrew Bible already indicates the rights of a king, in particular, the right to requisition an ass (1 Sam [LXX 1 Kgdms] 8:16). This system was called $\grave{\alpha}\gamma\gamma\alpha\rho\epsilon\acute{\iota}\alpha$, derived from a term that

originally designated the organization of the Persian couriers. The verb $\grave{\alpha}\gamma\gamma\alpha\rho\epsilon\acute{v}\omega$ means "to requisition," "to subject to forced labor," "to force." Concerning the case of a rabbi, see *b. Yoma* 35b (Soncino translation, 163–64); Derrett, "Colt."

28   The $\acute{o}\tau\iota$ (vv. 31 and 34) in fact introduces a direct discourse. It functions as does a colon.

29   The famous article by Bauer ("Colt"), which argues in favor of "foal/colt," has been criticized by Kuhn, "Reittier." In the attempt to remain faithful to the letter of Zech 9:9, Matthew puts Jesus simultaneously on the female ass and her young ass (Matt 21:7). See Gruber, "Parallelism," 291–92; Frenz, "Mt 21,5-7."

30   See here Kuhn, "Reittier," 86–91.

31   See also *Ps.-Clementine Rec.* 1.49–50; 5.10.14; *Hom.* 3.72.2; Blenkinsopp, "Oracle."

32   It may be that with this plural Luke simply wants to designate who the owners of the ass are (the farmer, his wife, his children, his servants . . .). Nevertheless, on the plural $o\acute{\iota}$ $\kappa\acute{v}\rho\iota o\iota$ (v. 33), Buth ("Transla-

■ **35-36** It is obvious: the double action of laying the clothes on the ass and having Jesus sit on it expresses, on the one hand, the desire to provide a saddle, a somewhat ostentatious gesture,[33] and, on the other hand, the will to welcome the visitor as a prince or dignitary.[34] The improvised and yet theatrical aspect of the scene is noteworthy: the disciples must act "as if." To this point Jesus has traveled by foot. By having him mount an ass, one attributes to him a special—for Luke, a royal—role. The Lukan Jesus does not refuse this honor.[35]

■ **37-38** As if he wanted to emphasize a new, decisive stage, Luke makes a point of repeating the location: "at the foot of the Mount of Olives." Then in his own words he mentions praising God for the mighty deeds at which the disciples and the multitude had marveled and blessing the Christ who comes (a messianic expression) in the name of the Lord (here meaning God).

The interaction between theology and Christology deserves attention: *God* receives the praise, for he is the source of *Jesus'* intervention. It is God who permitted the deeds and words of his Son to be effective. Thus, one praises God for the "mighty deeds" ($\delta\upsilon\nu\acute{\alpha}\mu\epsilon\iota\varsigma$).[36] For Luke, salvation is not only a hearing of the words; it

is also a seeing of God's great deeds ($\epsilon\hat{\iota}\delta o\nu$, "they have seen," translated "they had seen").[37] There is no doubt that on this day what is essential of the Father's activity takes place through the Son (see also 5:26; 7:35; 13:13).

Following Mark, in v. 38 Luke quotes, without citing, Ps 117 (118):26. He gives the verse a messianic significance ("he who comes" is no longer a simple pilgrim).[38] He does not hesitate to give Jesus the title $\beta\alpha\sigma\iota\lambda\epsilon\acute{\upsilon}\varsigma$ ("king," "emperor"), for in his view, as in that of the evangelist John, Jesus' kingship is not of this world (which is not to say that there are no social and political effects here below).[39]

Luke confirms this interpretation with a doxology that is different from the one in the birth narrative. At the beginning of his ministry, Jesus came to bring peace on earth (2:14) through the good that he would bring about with words and deeds (see Acts 10:38). At the end of his ministry Jesus establishes through his passion and his resurrection—here Luke is similar to Ephesians (Eph 2:14-18)—cosmic peace "in heaven." He is praised for this, and the Father too is praised in him. In this central point as well, Luke is not far removed from John.[40]

---

tion") refers in particular to Exod 21:29 and 36, where the plural is used for the singular (the text speaks of the owner of an ox). The LXX translates it as singular, $\acute{o}$ $\kappa\acute{\upsilon}\rho\iota o\varsigma$ $\alpha\mathring{\upsilon}\tau o\hat{\upsilon}$, "its owner." In Acts 16:16 the plural $o\acute{\iota}$ $\kappa\acute{\upsilon}\rho\iota o\iota$ in a Greek context doubtless represents a real plural. On Luke's insistence in presenting Jesus here as the Lord, see Hahn, *Titles*, 84.

33   The verb $\grave{\epsilon}\pi\iota\rho\acute{\iota}\pi\tau\omega$ ("to throw" [his clothes]) indicates the brisk gesture of impatience. The expression $\acute{\rho}\acute{\iota}\pi\tau\omega$ $\tau\grave{\alpha}$ $\grave{\iota}\mu\acute{\alpha}\tau\iota\alpha$ is found in Plato, e.g., *Resp.* 5.473E.

34   When Jesus' intimates learn of his anointing at the hands of the prophet sent by Elisha, they spread their garments before the feet of the one whom they from that time on celebrate as king (2 Kgs [LXX 4 Kgdms] 9:13). On the day of his coronation, David's heir, Solomon, rode on a young ass (1 Kgs [LXX 3 Kgdms]1:32-40). See Fernández Marcos, "Entrada."

35   From a historical point of view, I imagine that Jesus, a popular pilgrim and recognized as a prophet, agreed to ride on a young ass and to receive acclamation. Psalm 117 (118) could be understood in a nonmessianic way: even if associated with the feast of Tabernacles it could take on an eschatological

coloring in ancient Judaism. See Robert Martin-Achard, *Essai biblique sur les fêtes d'Israël* (Geneva: Labor et Fides, 1974) 75, 83–88, and 92.

36   Elsewhere Luke has mentioned the divine $\delta\acute{\upsilon}\nu\alpha\mu\iota\varsigma$, which permits Jesus to fulfill his function as physician and thaumaturge. See 5:17 and 8:46. He uses the term in the plural with reference to miracles in 10:13; here in 19:37; Acts 2:22; 8:13; and 19:11.

37   On this Lukan connection among "praise," "see," and "miracles," see Mariadasan, *Triomphe*, 19. See also 2:30; and vol. 1 of this commentary, 101–3, on 2:29-32.

38   The readers remember that the numerous miracles of Jesus are mentioned (7:21-22) as a response to the question of John the Baptist ("Are you the one who is to come?" 7:19-20).

39   George, "Royauté"; idem, *Études*, 274–76; del Agua Pérez, "Entrada," 182–88; Kinman, "Parousia," 284–89. On the text $\acute{o}$ $\grave{\epsilon}\rho\chi\acute{o}\mu\epsilon\nu o\varsigma$ $\acute{o}$ $\beta\alpha\sigma\iota\lambda\epsilon\acute{\upsilon}\varsigma$, see Bruce M. Metzger, *A Textual Commentary on the Greek New Testament: A Companion Volume to the United Bible Societies' Greek New Testament* (2d ed.; Stuttgart: United Bible Societies, 1994) 144–45.

40   On $\delta\acute{o}\xi\alpha$ in Luke, see esp. 9:32; 24:26. On the interpretation of the doxology and the different hypoth-

■ **39-40** In contrast to what happens in Mark and Matthew, the multitude plays no great role. It is the Pharisees who intervene. They oppose the disciples in a confrontation with which Luke has already made us familiar (cf. 5:30; 6:2; etc.). Even if a similar opposition appears in the Gospels of Matthew (21:14-16) and John (12:19), what Luke here describes takes on a special coloration: Jesus is told to reprimand his disciples.[41]

Jesus solemnly ("I tell you") states that the situation is extraordinary; it deserves to be taken seriously. If the disciples were forced to keep silent,[42] the stones would cry out. Luke, for whom stones are symbols of death and silence,[43] had already had John the Baptist say that the all-powerful God could raise children of Abraham from these stones (3:8). Here he puts a similar affirmation in Jesus' mouth, an affirmation that has been interpreted in different ways. The prophet Habakkuk speaks of stones and beams that in a crisis or a tragic event could speak. If the sinner (oppressor, plunderer, thief) continues his evil deeds, the evil will come back on him. "Indeed, the stone in the wall will cry out, and the rafter in the framework will answer him" (Hab 2:11). If I understand it correctly, the house refuses to carry out the criminal intentions of the evil person. Thus, the stone and the beam rebel by speaking the truth and by bearing witness to God's judgment. Likewise, the stones will cry out the truth here, even if it is not certain that the Lukan verse alludes to the verse in Habakkuk.[44] It is more likely that they speak of the Son's legitimacy and the Father's wisdom than that they announce the destruction of Jerusalem or denounce injustice.[45] The motif of the stones that cry out, suggested here in Luke's proverb-like sentence, also appears in certain religious, mythological, and literary texts of antiquity.[46]

History of Interpretation

The Christian liturgy of the first centuries cited Luke's two-volume work to justify the festivals of Pentecost and the Ascension.[47] To establish and inaugurate Palm Sunday, however, it chose to go back to the Gospel of Matthew, thus celebrating Jesus' triumphal entry into the holy city of Jerusalem.[48]

In his polemical work against Marcion, Tertullian ignores Luke's account of the entry into Jerusalem (*Adv. Marc.* 4.37–38).[49] By contrast, we have received a short sermon of Origen in its Latin version that is dedicated to the young ass (*Hom. Luc.* 37). As one would expect, the

---

eses regarding its origin, see Baarlink ("Friede"), who thinks that peace had provisionally retired into heaven.

41 On the redactional character of v. 39, see Diachronic Analysis above.

42 The word $\dot{\epsilon}\acute{\alpha}\nu$ followed by the future is irregular. The subjunctive of numerous manuscripts ($\sigma\iota\omega\pi\acute{\eta}\sigma\omega\sigma\iota\nu$) is a correction by purists. In that era the conjunction $\dot{\epsilon}\acute{\alpha}\nu$ followed by the indicative gradually becomes more prevalent (1 Thess 3:8; 1 John 5:15), but this construction from the pen of an author such as Luke is still astonishing.

43 One does not give one's children stones to eat (11:11).

44 See Ruiz ("Clamor"), who agrees with the reference. The stones, anxious because of the fate that awaits them (the destruction of the city of Jerusalem), will cry out against the injustice. It is a question neither of a shout of praise nor of the noise created by the destruction of Jerusalem.

45 The manuscripts ℵ (= 01) and B (= 03) support the future active $\kappa\rho\acute{\alpha}\xi ουσιν$. The manuscript 1241 has the subjunctive aorist $\kappa\rho\acute{\alpha}\xi ωσιν$, D (= 05) the future middle $\kappa\rho\acute{\alpha}\xi ονται$. A, W, Θ, Ψ, and $f^{1, 13}$, as well as the majority of the witnesses of the Byzantine period, have the future perfect $\kappa\epsilon\kappa\rho\acute{\alpha}\xi ονται$, which would be unique in the New Testament.

46 Kinman ("Stones"), who is not aware of the study cited in the preceding note, thinks that the cry of the stones is a cry of joy. He cites an interesting parallel from Cicero (*Against Piso* 52), who says that on his return from exile in the year 57 B.C.E. the very walls, the buildings, and the temple proclaimed the joy of Rome.

47 See Robert Cabié, *La Pentecôte: L'évolution de la Cinquantaine pascale au cours des cinq premiers siècles* (Bibliothèque de Liturgie; Tournai: Desclée, 1965) 182, 197.

48 See Mariadasan, *Triomphe,* 3:56, 65. On pp. 57–62 this author quotes or mentions a series of Christian texts from late antiquity related to the narrative or the festival of the palm branches. I was not able to look at A. W. Martin, "Interpretation." On the celebration of the festival of the Branches in late antiquity, especially in Jerusalem, see H. Leclercq, "Rameaux" ("Dimanche des")," *DACL* 14.2 (1948) cols. 2060–64.

49 Tertullian (*Adv. Marc.* 4.37–38) passes directly from the parable of the pounds (19:11-27) to the next polemic beginning in 20:1.

preacher believes in "a sense that lies deeper than the meaning of the simple narrative" (37.1).[50] The mount on which Jesus rides represents the human soul. Untying the ass shows that the human being is delivered from the forces of evil and is entrusted to the Lord, who needs him. The disciples, that is, the apostles, lay their clothes, that is, their works, on the ass. These works become the believers' attire. The clothes on the ground represent the doctrine and the life of the apostles whom the faithful imitate. Origen closes by saying that he prays to God that the disciples' praise may never end and that in no case would their work of love grow cold.[51]

In his commentary on the *Diatessaron*, Ephraem of Syria expresses the opinion that the disciples' praise was interrupted at Jesus' death. Then it was the stones that praised Jesus by delivering up the dead they had contained (Matt 27:51-53). Along with this literal interpretation, Ephraem is also familiar with a figurative one: the stones that cry out represent the Gentiles who have come to faith. Two centuries later James of Sarug rejoices at the praise in the mouth of the disciples, whom he compares with children. Then he connects the stones that could have cried out with a great thunder, doubtless with the thunder the crowd thinks it hears according to John 12:29. For those who need proofs for their faith he concedes that the literal sense (the crashing of the tombs that open on Good Friday; Matt 27:51-53) is still possible.[52]

As is his custom, Albert the Great organizes the Lukan material carefully (*Evang. Luc.* 19:28-40 [580–89]). In his view, vv. 28-40 can be subdivided into four sections: the seizure of the young ass, the placing of Jesus on the ass, the eruption into song, and the rejection of the grievance. He uses the term "preparation" to describe the approach to Jerusalem. He begins with the literal sense before moving to the figurative (*secundum mysterium*). He speaks of certain spiritual explanations without accepting all of them. The two disciples who were sent to untie the ass are Philip, the evangelist of Samaria, and Peter, who converted the Roman centurion, Cornelius. Following John Chrysostom, Albert mentions the ten reasons why the ass represents the nation of the Gentiles. The statement "the Lord needs it" speaks more of the spiritual than the literal sense: "more in view of the mystery than of the means of transport" (*magis ad mysterium quam ad vehiculum*)! In its literal sense the procession involves three realities: the veneration of the believers, the envy of the evil persons, and their refutation. The veneration itself is divided into three parts: the clothing cast off from the bodies ready for martyrdom, the expressed praise, and the confession of royal dignity. Thus, the commentary gives a clear and consistent account of the

50 A modern allegory from the pen of O. Samuel, "Regierungsgewalt": The Jesus entering Jerusalem is the Word of God in action.

51 See also Ambrose of Milan *Exp. Luc.* 9.1-16: Jesus goes up to the temple not made with human hands. Next follows the text of Matthew that mentions the female ass and her foal. The sense of the scene in which the owners deliver the young ass to the Lord corresponds to that given by Origen. The same is true for the interpretation of the clothes of Christ, who straddles the mount. Ambrose himself is responsible for the interpretation of the bridle that restricts the ass (Albertus Magnus *Evang. Luc.*). It symbolizes the heavenly Word. See Cyril of Alexandria *Serm. Luc.* 130 (Robert Payne Smith, *A Commentary upon the Gospel according to S. Luke, by S. Cyril, Patriarch of Alexandria, Now First Translated into English from an Ancient Syriac Version* [2 vols.; Oxford: Oxford University Press, 1859; reprinted New York: Studion, 1983] 2:601–6): The entry into Jerusalem takes place at a time when Jesus prepares to liberate the entire world. It offers the opportunity to give a sign. Riding a young ass, Jesus shows that the nations soon will be summoned to the gospel, while the mother ass represents disobedient Israel. The young ass moves from the country to the city, from pagan uncouthness to Christian civility. See also the Venerable Bede *Luc. Exp.* 5.1834–2020.

52 Ephraem Syrus, *Commentaire de l'Évangile Concordant ou Diatessaron* (trans. L. Leloir; SC 121; Paris: Cerf, 1966) 315–16; James [Jacob] of Sarug, "Sur le dimanche des Hosannas 43–45," in: Jaques de Saroug, *Six homélies festales en prose* (ed. Frédéric Rilliet; PO 43.4; Turnhout: Brepols, 1986) 606–9. See also Rilliet ("Louange"), who provides additional Syrian and Greek patristic references to Luke 19:40.

wording of the text and at the same time decodes it in order to bring to light the figurative sense.[53]

Calvin, who rejects some of the above-mentioned allegories, insists on the theatrical character of the event.[54] Thus, Jesus "wanted to show by a solemn ceremony the nature of His Kingdom." In a certain sense the instruction he gave was "ridiculous," his equipment "a sign of terrible and shameful poverty," and the action he carried out seemed to be exposed deliberately "to the mockery of all men." Nevertheless, there is wisdom in all these things. Jesus referred to the prophet Zechariah, bore witness about his kingdom, and let it be understood "that it has nothing to do with earthly empires." "Christ's lowly condition" should not keep the believers from "seeing in this spectacle His spiritual Kingdom"—on the contrary.[55]

Conclusion

We should avoid referring to the Lukan narrative (19:28-40) as the story of the "palm branches" or of the "entry into Jerusalem," for it neither mentions palm branches nor does it tell of a triumphal entry into the city. As with the story of the transfiguration, it lifts a veil. At the beginning of the humiliation it reveals the paradox of Jesus' kingship. Neither the Pharisees, nor the cautious crowd, nor the disciples will be moved at the passion by the memory of this suspected dignity. When he dies, Jesus will be alone. Yet his Easter exaltation will confirm the prophetic and symbolic value of his royal procession approaching the holy city.

---

53 See also the *Glossa ordinaria* (*PL* 114:329–30) and Bruno of Segni *Comm. Luc.* 2.46 (*PL* 165:438–40), who directs attention to v. 40 and to vv. 41-46.

54 Jean Calvin, *Calvin's Commentaries,* vols. 1–3: *A Harmony of the Gospels* (ed. David W. Torrance and Thomas F. Torrance; trans. A. W. Morrison and T. H. L. Parker; Grand Rapids: Eerdmans, 1959) 2:291.

55 See also Martin Luther, *Evangelien-Auslegung*, part 3: *Markus und Lukasevangelium* (ed. Erwin Mülhaupt; Göttingen: Vandenhoeck & Ruprecht, 1938–54) 895–902; Desiderius Erasmus of Rotterdam, *Paraphrasis in N. Testamentum*, in *Opera omnia*, vol. 7 (ed. P. Vander; Leyden: Vander, 1706; facsimile reprint London: Gregg, 1962) 432–34.

Jerusalem Fails to Recognize the Visitation, and Jesus Restores the Temple (19:41-48)

Bibliography: Verses 41-44

Aus, Roger David, *My Name Is "Legion": Palestinian Judaic Traditions in Mark 5, 1-20 and Other Gospel Texts* (Studies in Judaism; Dallas: University Press of America, 2003) 209–52.

Borg, Marcus J., *Conflict, Holiness & Politics in the Teachings of Jesus* (Studies in the Bible and Early Christianity 5; New York: Mellen, 1984) 201–21.

Idem, "Luke 19:42-44 and Jesus as Prophet?" *Forum* 8 (1992) 99–112.

Buse, Ivor, "The Cleansing of the Temple in the Synoptics and in John," *ExpT* 70 (1958–59) 22–24.

Cantrell, Richard A., "The Cursed Fig Tree: Luke and a Difficult Text," *TBT* 29 (1991) 105–8.

Dupont, Jacques, "Il n'en sera pas laissé pierre sur pierre (Marc 13,2; Luc 19,44)," *Bib* 52 (1971) 301–20, reprinted in idem, *Études sur les évangiles synoptiques* (ed. Franz Neirynck; 2 vols.; BEThL 70A, 70B; Louvain: Louvain University Press and Peeters, 1985) 1:434–55. Cited here according to the reprint.

Gaston, Lloyd, *No Stone on Another: Studies in the Significance of the Fall of Jerusalem in the Synoptic Gospels* (NovTSup 23; Leiden: Brill, 1970) 12, 66, 244, 355–60.

Kinman, Brent, "Lucan Eschatology and the Missing Fig Tree," *JBL* 113 (1994) 669–78.

Kühschelm, Roman, "Verstockung als Gericht: Eine Untersuchung zu Joh 12,35-43; Lk 13,34-35; 19,41-44," *BLit* 57 (1984) 234–43.

Linder, "Destruction."

Méhat, André, "Les écrits de Luc et les événements de 70: Problèmes de datation," *RHR* 209 (1992) 149–80.

Osten-Sacken, Peter von der, "Jesu Weinen über sein Volk: Predigt über Lukas 19,41-44," in Erhard Blum, Christian Macholz, and Ekkehard W. Stegemann, eds., *Die Hebräische Bibel und ihre zweifache Nachgeschichte: Festschrift für Rolf Rendtorff zum 65. Geburtstag* (Neukirchen-Vluyn: Neukirchener Verlag, 1990) 555–59.

Reicke, Bo, "Synoptic Prophecies on the Destruction of Jerusalem," in David Edward Aune, ed., *Studies in New Testament and Early Christian Literature: Essays in Honor of Allen P. Wikgren* (NovTSup 33; Leiden: Brill, 1972) 121–34.

Sandnes, Karl Olav, "Jesus som profet," *TTK* 60 (1989) 95–109.

Bibliography: Verses 45-48

Bachmann, Michael, *Jerusalem und der Tempel: Die geographisch-theologischen Elemente in der lukanischen Sicht des jüdischen Kultzentrums* (BWANT 109; Stuttgart: Kohlhammer, 1980) 132–70, 273–89.

Barrett, C. K., "The House of Prayer and the Den of Thieves," in E. Earle Ellis and Erich Grässer, eds., *Jesus und Paulus: Festschrift für Werner George Kümmel zum 70. Geburtstag* (Göttingen: Vandenhoeck & Ruprecht, 1975) 13–20.

Baumann, Georg, "Die lukanische Interpretation der Zerstörung Jerusalems," *NovT* 6 (1963) 120–27.

Casalegno, Alberto, *Gesù e il tempio: studio redazionale di Luca-Atti* (Brescia: Morcelliana, 1984).

Chance, J. Bradley, *Jerusalem, the Temple, and the New Age in Luke-Acts* (Macon, GA: Mercer University Press, 1988).

Conzelmann, *Theology*, 75–78.

Dawsay, James M., "Confrontation in the Temple: Luke 19:45—20:47," *PRSt* 11 (1984) 153–65.

Idem, "The Origin of Luke's Positive Perception of the Temple," *PRSt* 18 (1991) 5–22.

Idem, "Was Ur-Markus the Source for Lk 19:45—20:47?" *MTh* 42 (1991) 95–110.

Derrett, J. Duncan M., "The Zeal of the House and the Cleansing of the Temple," *DRev* 95 (1977) 79–94.

Eppstein, Victor, "The Historicity of the Gospel Account of the Cleansing of the Temple," *ZNW* 55 (1964) 42–58.

Evans, Craig A., "Jesus' Action in the Temple: Cleansing or Portent of Destruction," *CBQ* 51 (1989) 237–70.

Gaston, *No Stone* (see above), 102–19, 338–39 and passim.

Giblin, Charles Homer, *The Destruction of Jerusalem according to Luke's Gospel: A Historical-Typological Moral* (AnBib 107; Rome: Biblical Institute Press, 1985) 47–56.

Haenchen, *Weg Jesu*, 382–89.

Hahn, *Titles*, 155–57.

Hamilton, Neill Q., "Temple Cleansing and Temple Bank," *JBL* 83 (1964) 365–72.

Hengel, Martin, "Between Jesus and Paul: The 'Hellenists,' the 'Seven' and Stephen (Acts 6,1-15; 7,54—8,3)," in idem, *Between Jesus and Paul: Studies in the Earliest History of Christianity* (trans. John Bowden; Philadelphia: Fortress Press, 1983) 1–29.

Hiers, Richard H., "Purification of the Temple: Preparation for the Kingdom of God," *JBL* 90 (1971) 82–90.

Jeremias, Joachim, "Zwei Miszellen: 1. Antik-Jüdische Münzdeutungen. 2. Zur Geschichtlichkeit der Tempelreinigung," *NTS* 23 (1977) 177–80.

Lukito, Daniel Lucas, "The Cleansing of the Temple: An Analysis of the Intention of Jesus," *Stulos: Theological Journal* 1 (1993) 31–42.

Manson, T. W., "The Cleansing of the Temple," *BJRL* 33 (1950–51) 271–82.

Mendner, Siegfried, "Die Tempelreinigung," *ZNW* 47 (1956) 93–112.

Oakman, Douglas E., "Cursing Fig Trees and Robbers' Dens: Pronouncement Stories within a Social-Systemic Perspective. Mark 11:12-25 and Parallels," *Semeia* 64 (1994) 253–72.

Riley, Gregory J., *Resurrection Reconsidered: Thomas and John in Controversy* (Minneapolis: Fortress Press, 1995) 127–56.

Rius-Camps, Josep, "Origen lucano de la pericope de la mujer adultera (Jn 7,53—8,11)," *Filologia Neotestamentaria* 6.12 (1993) 149–75.

Roloff, Jürgen, *Das Kerygma und der irdische Jesus: Historische Motive in den Jesus-Erzählungen der Evangelien* (Göttingen: Vandenhoeck & Ruprecht, 1970) 89–110.

Roth, Cecil, "The Cleansing of the Temple and Zechariah 14,21," *NovT* 4 (1960) 174–81.

Schmidt, Francis, *How the Temple Thinks: Identity and Social Cohesion in Ancient Judaism* (trans. J. Edward Crowley; BiSe 78; Sheffield: Sheffield Academic Press, 2001).

Schnider, Franz, and Werner Stenger, *Johannes und die Synoptiker: Vergleich ihrer Parallelen* (BiH 9; Munich: Kösel, 1971) 26–53.

Schramm, *Markus-Stoff*, 149.

Söding, Thomas, "Die Tempelaktion Jesu," *TThZ* 101 (1992) 36–64.

Trautmann, *Handlungen*, 78–131.

Trocmé, Étienne, "L'expulsion des marchands du Temple," *NTS* 15 (1968–69) 1–22.

Waal, C. van der, "The Temple in the Gospel according to Luke," *Neot* 7 (1963) 49–59.

Weinert, Francis David, "The Meaning of the Temple in the Gospel of Luke" (Ph.D. diss., Fordham University, 1979).

Idem, "The Meaning of the Temple in Luke-Acts," *BTB* 11 (1981) 85–89.

41 When he drew near, he saw the city, wept over it 42/ and said, "If this day even you had been able to recognize what leads to peace[a] . . . But now it is hidden from your eyes. 43/ Because days will come upon you when your enemies will raise up a rampart around you and surround you and will press you from all sides; 44/ and they will dash you and your children in you to the ground; and they will not leave one stone on another in you, because you did not recognize the time[b] of your visitation."[c]

45 When he had entered the temple, he began to drive out the sellers, 46/ saying to them, "It is written: My house shall be a house of prayer but you have made of it a den of robbers."

47 And he was teaching daily in the temple; but the chief priests and the scribes—that is, the leaders of the people—sought to destroy him.[d] 48/ And they did not know[e] what to do, for all the people hung on him and were all ears.

a Literally: "the things concerning peace."
b Another possible translation: "the opportunity" or "the favorable moment."
c That is: "the visitation you received."
d Or: "to kill him."
e Literally: "they did not find."

Analysis

Luke gives a coherent account: While Jesus is approaching Jerusalem riding on his young ass, he receives the acclamation of the disciples. Then he refutes the Pharisees' criticism (19:28-40). He weeps over the city and drives the sellers out of the temple before, to the surprise of the authorities and to the joy of the people, he teaches regularly in the sacred area (19:41-48). The priests, the scribes, and the elders ask him where he gets his authority. Jesus evades the question (20:1-8) before telling a final parable, the parable of the murderous vine-dressers

(20:9-18). Luke is thinking of a sojourn of several days, but he mentions only a single entering (directly into the Temple, 19:45).[1]

Compared with this logical development, Mark's text, which I assume served as Luke's source, is surprising in the complicated way it moves Jesus from one location to another and in the appearance of the puzzling pericope concerning the barren fig tree. After the episode of the young ass (Mark 11:1-10), Jesus enters the holy city, where he simply looks around before spending the night in Bethany: day 1 (Mark 11:11). On the next day, after cursing the fig tree, he returns to the city, drives the sellers from the temple, and leaves the city for the night: day 2 (Mark 11:2-19). On the next morning, after he has verified that the fig tree has dried up, he again enters the city and converses with the authorities, who ask him about the source of his authority. Jesus proceeds with the parable of the murderous vine-dressers: thus the third day (Mark 11:20—12:12).[2]

Some commentators think that, in addition to Mark, Luke is familiar with an account earlier than or parallel to the Second Gospel, an account he prefers because of its greater coherence.[3] It is a daring hypothesis, because, except for the episode of the fig tree, to which I will return, the differences between Luke and Mark deal with the seams and not the events themselves. Thus, Luke always feels free to examine Mark's redactional arrangement and sometimes to reorganize the sequences according to his own logic.[4]

According to the hypothesis I am assuming, the evangelist rearranges Mark's text, eliminating the pericope of the barren fig tree (Mark 11:12-14 and 20-25) for two reasons: (a) He has already given a parable about a fig tree (13:6-9), and he fears monotony. (b) He is uncertain about this puzzling episode and Jesus' stern, almost unjust attitude.[5]

If Luke omits one literary unit, he adds another, very appropriate unit: the lament over Jerusalem (19:41-44), which he regards as a counterpart to the disciples' praise (19:38) and as an echo of the Pharisees' rebuke (19:39). It is important to compare this lament with some of Luke's other passages: the quarrel with Jerusalem (13:34-35), the announcement of Jerusalem's ruin (21:20-24), and the lamentation spoken to the daughters of the holy city (23:27-31).[6] Verses 41-44 of Luke 19 contain redactional elements,[7] but they come essentially from Luke's special material. Apart from the introduction Luke drafted (v. 41), they constitute an oracle of woe. They describe a punishment that the city could have avoided. Jerusalem should have realized this (v. 42 and v. 44c). In their insistence on this point, the beginning and end of the oracle play off of one another without tedious repetition. There was the fortunate day ("on this day," v. 42; "the [favorable] time," v. 44), which offered an opportunity of peace ($\tau\grave{\alpha}\ \pi\rho\grave{o}\varsigma\ \epsilon\grave{\iota}\rho\acute{\eta}\nu\eta\nu$, "that leads to peace," v. 42), a decisive visit ($\acute{\eta}\ \grave{\epsilon}\pi\iota\sigma\kappa\sigma\pi\acute{\eta}\ \sigma\sigma\upsilon$, "your visitation," v. 44). In her spiritual blindness the city wasted it all: "But now it is hidden from your eyes" (v. 42). This state-

---

1   On this unit, see Conzelmann, *Theology*, 74–78; Dawsey, "Origin," 10–13, 16–21. Bibliography on the expulsion of the sellers from the temple is in Trocmé, "Expulsion," 1 n. 5; Fitzmyer, 2.1268; John Nolland, *Luke* (3 vols.; WBC 35A–C; Dallas: Word, 1989–93) 3:929, 933–34, 939.

2   The studies on this Markan unit are innumerable. See, e.g., Haenchen, *Weg Jesu*, 389–405.

3   Dawsey, "Confrontation," 156–60; idem, "Ur-Markus"; idem, "Origin."

4   See Conzelmann, *Theology*, 74–94. On the pre-Markan and pre-Johannine condition of various episodes, see Schnider and Stenger, *Johannes*, 26–53, esp. 40–41.

5   Can one say Luke did not like Mark's "sandwiches"? In 8:40-56 he preserves the way Mark combines the two miracles (Mark 5:21-43). On Luke's omission of the episode of the barren fig tree, see Kinman

("Eschatology"), who proposes theological reasons: Luke does not despair of Israel's future. See also Cantrell ("Fig Tree"), who thinks that, since the episode of the unfruitful fig tree is reminiscent of Jer 8:10-13, Luke replaced it with the lament of vv. 41-44, which fulfills the same accusing function as Jeremiah's passage.

6   The first text comes from Q, the second from Mark, the third from the special material. On the links between 19:43-44 and 23:27-31, see Dupont, "Pierre sur pierre," 447–52.

7   E.g., $\grave{\epsilon}\gamma\gamma\acute{\iota}\zeta\omega$ ("to draw near"), $\sigma\upsilon\nu\acute{\epsilon}\chi\omega$ ("to hold together"), $\grave{\alpha}\nu\vartheta'\ \grave{\mathring{\omega}}\nu$ ("instead of the fact that"), $\acute{\eta}\ \grave{\epsilon}\pi\iota\sigma\kappa\sigma\pi\acute{\eta}$ ("the visitation"). See Joachim Jeremias, *Die Sprache des Lukasevangeliums: Redaktion und Tradition im Nicht-Markusstoff des dritten Evangeliums* (KEK Sonderband; Göttingen: Vandenhoeck & Ruprecht, 1980) 281–82.

ment, which is an accusation, leads to the mention of the punishment: "The days will come" (as a contrast to the past "day"), when the enemies, who remain anonymous, will besiege, capture, and completely destroy the city without sparing its inhabitants. In this well-structured oracle one recognizes the parataxis of Semitic style (see the many "ands"), as well as the omnipresence of the second person singular personal pronoun, sometimes in its accented form and sometimes in its enclitic form (σύ, σου, σέ, σου, σοι, σε, σε, σε, σου, σοί, σοί, σου).[8] The literary quality of the piece, characteristic of Luke's special material,[9] is evident in the equilibrium of the whole (see the outline below), in the precision of the military vocabulary, in the feeling of regret expressed,[10] and in the inexorable character of the punishment. This "you" that is challenged here can only be the holy city. The description of the attack it suffers corresponds to every siege in antiquity (see, e.g., Josephus *Bell.* 6.1.3 §§24–28); to those described in the Hebrew Scriptures,[11] beginning with that of Jerusalem in 586 B.C.E.;[12] and then to the attack that led to the fall of Jerusalem in 70 (see Josephus *Bell.* book 5). This oracle of woe belongs to a well-established genre of Old Testament prophetic literature. It is less an apophthegm than an oracle of judgment clothed in a lament and provided with a brief introduction (see, e.g., Mic 6:3-5).[13] One can present it graphically, in its literal content, in the following manner:

V. 42: If even you had recognized this day also [literally, also *you*] the (ways that lead) to peace!

V. 43: But in reality they were hidden from your eyes [literally, "from the eyes of *you*"].
Because the days will come on *you*,
and they will raise up your enemies [literally, "the enemies of *you*"],
a rampart against *you*,
and they will surround (you), *you*,
and they will press (you), *you*,
from all sides

V. 44: and they will dash (you) to the ground, *you*,
and (your) children in *you* [literally, "the children of *you*"].
And they will leave no stone on another in *you*,
because you did not recognize the time of your visitation [literally, "the visitation of *you*"].[14]

Verses 45-46 briefly mention Jesus' action in driving the sellers from the temple and then offer a (mixed) quotation from Isa 56:7 and Jer 7:11.[15] Our analysis of the details will explain that Luke, who follows Mark here, has his reasons for abbreviating the text.

Luke ends the unit with a transitional summary[16] that emphasizes Jesus' teaching in the temple (v. 47a) before he contrasts the desire of the leaders to eliminate Jesus (v. 47b) with the protection that the people provide the Master simply by admiring Jesus' word (v. 48). Here Luke

8   Noted by Dupont, "Pierre sur pierre," 445; and Méhat, "Écrits," 164–67.

9   On these verses, see Gerd Petzke, *Das Sondergut des Evangeliums nach Lukas* (Zürcher Werkkommentare zur Bibel; Zurich: Theologischer Verlag, 1990) 172–74. Borg ("Prophet") is of the opinion that Jesus was a sage and a prophet. Verses 42-44 can reflect an authentic lamentation of Jesus.

10   Note the aposiopesis in v. 42a. See Méhat, "Écrits," 164–67.

11   See Jer 29:3; 37:33; Ezek 4:1-3, 21-22; see also Jeremiah 27–29; 52:4-5; 1 Sam [LXX 1 Kgdms] 23:8; 2 Kgs [LXX 4 Kgdms] 6:14; 25:1-2; Ezek 26:8; 1 Macc 15:13-14; Josh 7:9. The list is taken from Méhat, "Écrits," 165. See Dupont, "Pierre sur pierre," 445–46.

12   On the connections between 19:41-44 and the description of the fall of Jerusalem in 586 B.C.E., see C. H. Dodd, "The Fall of Jerusalem and the Abomination of Desolation," *JRomS* 37 (1947)

47–53; reprinted in idem, *More New Testament Studies* (Grand Rapids: Eerdmans, 1968) 69–83.

13   On this literary genre in the Hebrew Bible, see Claus Westermann, *Basic Forms of Prophetic Speech* (trans. Hugh Clayton White; Philadelphia: Westminster, 1967) 169–76, 202–3. Bultmann (*History*, 36) classes the passage as an apophthegm. Barrett ("House," 18) rejects this view.

14   Méhat, "Écrits," 164; Dupont, "Pierre sur pierre," 445; idem, *Les trois apocalypses synoptiques: Marc 13; Matthieu 24–25; Luc 21* (LD 121; Paris: Cerf, 1985) 120–27.

15   Without the words "for all nations." On the reasons for omitting these words see below, p. 20.

16   Note the use of the imperfect and, in the first case, even the periphrastic imperfect.

rewrites Mark 11:18. Thus, the two units 19:45-46 and 47-48 take up again two successive units of Mark.[17]

Commentary

■ **41-42** The verb "to draw near" (ἐγγίζω) has played an important role since Jesus arrived from Jericho (vv. 28-29). Here, as elsewhere, Luke gives special importance also to seeing.[18] When he sees the city, Jesus weeps.[19] The verb κλαίω is stronger than δακρύω ("to shed tears") and designates here a real wailing.[20] In other circumstances[21] Jesus would have acted, protected, or healed. Here he resorts to no divine δύναμις (see 5:17; 8:46). His mission is no longer to intervene; now it is to verify the failure and to deliver God's judgment. More than anywhere else Luke's Jesus stands in the line of the prophets of Israel. Because Israel did not want to acknowledge God's plan for it, its enemies will prevail with unrelenting severity. It is something the Master must say, but he does so not without profound regret.[22]

Jesus' final sentence remains incomplete.[23] It involves an aposiopesis, a rhetorical construction used by Israel's prophets.[24] Charged with emotion, the sentence expresses a helpless regret: Oh! If the city had only been able to recognize! It is a question not of the intellectual knowledge favored by the Greeks but of an existential comprehension such as that cherished by the Hebrews.[25] "On this day": God's presence is always contextual in Israel; it is bound to a life plan included in the time of salvation and of perdition. "Even you" (καὶ σύ)[26] emphasizes the responsibility of the comprehending subject.

The expression "the things that lead to peace" (τὰ πρὸς εἰρήνην) is vague. It may be that the plural (τά) indicates that God has offered Jerusalem various occasions to attain peace. This "peace" means not only the silence of weapons;[27] it also means the harmonious relation with God—the "peace in heaven" that has just been mentioned (v. 38), which comes about with or without the approval of the holy city. Israel's Messiah, whose birth the Christmas angels celebrated in song with words of peace ("and peace on earth," 2:14), brings this peace to reality. This peace established by Christ is real and is not to be confused with the Jewish messianic hope or with the Roman imperial power. It is not limited to heaven. After the ascension the disciples of Christ will proclaim it to the entire world. They will try to live it and to get others to live it.[28]

For the present (νῦν, "now") these peace efforts are not in vain, but they are not recognized. Indeed, the "now" belongs to the past of Jesus, of the temple, and of the passion, but as the "today" of Deuteronomy (Deut 4:38-40) and the "today" of Jesus' inaugural proclama-

---

17   See Schramm, *Markus-Stoff*, 149. The details of the literary relationship between Luke and Mark are presented below in the interpretation.

18   E.g., at the death of the son of the widow (7:13) or in the parable of the Good Samaritan (10:31-33). Note there the three "having seen" (ἰδών) as here (v. 41).

19   It can only be Jerusalem, just as for Byzantines it could only be Constantinople. This is the source of the name Istanbul. The Turks have taken over the term from the Greek expression εἰς τὴν πόλιν ("into the city").

20   Alfred Plummer, *A Critical and Exegetical Commentary on the Gospel according to St. Luke* (5th ed.; ICC; Edinburgh: T&T Clark, 1922) 449. It is the attitude of the widow of Nain at the death of her only son (7:11-13). In addition, in John 11:35 Jesus sheds tears (δακρύω) at the death of his friend, Lazarus. Luke 19:41 and John 11:35 are the only two times where it is said of Jesus that he shed tears.

21   See the connection between Jesus' looking and his active compassion in 7:13.

22   On the genre of the piece see n. 13 above.

23   There are several text-critical problems in vv. 41-48. They are well presented and resolved in Plummer, 449–55; and Metzger, *Commentary* (2d ed.), 145.

24   For an Old Testament example of an aposiopesis, see Exod 32:32. In the New Testament, see Luke 22:42 ("Father, if you will, take this cup from me . . ."); John 6:62; 12:27; BDF §482.

25   On γινώσκω, see BAGD, s.v.; Walter Schmithals, "γινώσκω," *EDNT* 1:248–51.

26   Grammatically, one can also translate as "also you," but then one has the difficulty of understanding with whom Jesus is comparing Jerusalem. By translating as "even you" one discreetly recalls the privileges of the holy city.

27   Even though vv. 43-44 describe the opposite with military terms.

28   On peace in Luke, see José Comblin, "La paix dans la théologie de saint Luc," *EThL* 32 (1956) 439–60; François Bovon, *Luke the Theologian: Fifty-Five Years of Research (1950–2005)* (2d rev. ed.; Waco, Tex.: Baylor University Press, 2006) 209.

tion in Nazareth (4:21), this νῦν becomes present in the decisions taken in the church and in the synagogue.

God manifests himself and hides himself. He rejects compelling obviousness. He has made himself visible in the person and in the acts of Jesus (see v. 37). Alas, the right to close one's eyes belongs to human freedom.[29] As a result, revelation grows dim. Nevertheless, the day will come when what is hidden will be revealed and will become irrefutably obvious (12:2).[30] Before that distant day, however, there is, in the short term, the threatening days of calamity (vv. 43-44).

■ **43-44** "The days will come" is a common expression in prophetic and apocalyptic literature.[31] The future tense allows no hesitation: the future belongs to God and is proclaimed by the prophets he authorizes. Since these days will come "over [upon] you," Jesus wept "over it" (v. 41).

A description of the siege of Jerusalem follows. Her enemies surprise her[32] by building a "palisade" (χάραξ).[33] This machinery makes it possible to "surround" the city[34] and to "press" it on all sides.[35] The description is brief and eloquent. It appears to be inspired by Scripture, in particular by Isa 29:3 LXX: "and I, like David, will encircle you, and will raise a palisade around you and set up towers around you" (καὶ κυκλώσω ὡς Δαυὶδ ἐπὶ σὲ καὶ βαλῶ περὶ σὲ χάρακα καὶ θήσω περὶ σὲ πύργους). Luke, who doubtless is familiar with the siege of Jerusalem by Titus in 70,[36]

prefers the biblical language over historical reporting. Speaking of the future (as seen by Jesus), he dispenses with details and precise descriptions.

If v. 43 describes the siege of the city, v. 44 tells of its capture with the two common elements, the fate of the inhabitants and the destiny of the buildings. Both involve inexorable cruelty.[37] The inhabitants[38] will be crushed[39] and the city razed. In chap. 21 Luke will present a different prophecy about the fall of Jerusalem. In his view, the two descriptions complement each other and are not quite identical. This one comes from Luke's special material, the other from the Gospel of Mark.[40] In chap. 21, Luke omits one of Mark's expressions—the statement that one stone will not be left on another (Mark 13:2). Doubtless he wants to avoid repeating the almost identical sentence of the special material, which he quotes here about the entire city.[41] While Luke 21, following Mark 13, mentions a number of events that will take place before the fall of the city, Luke 19 moves directly from the time of Jesus to the destruction of Jerusalem. The text is concerned here not with the unfolding of a history but with the logical contrast between the rejected offer and the disastrous consequences of this refusal. The two expressions, side by side yet different, eloquently suggest: "If even you had been able to recognize . . ." (v. 42) and "because you did not recognize . . ." (v. 44).

For Luke, καιρός ("time") is eminently positive. It is the valuable opportunity offered by God. The same is

---

29 On ἐκρύβη ἀπὸ ὀφθαλμῶν σου, see Jer 16:17 LXX.

30 See vol. 2 of this commentary on Luke 12:2.

31 J. A. Bengel (noted by Plummer, 451) pointed out the contrast: Dies, multi, quia unum diem non observas ("many days, because you do not observe the one day"). See Johann Albert Bengel, *Gnomon of the New Testament* (trans. Charlton T. Lewis and Marvin R. Vincent; 2 vols.; Philadelphia: Perkinpine & Higgins, 1860, 1862) 1:502. For the Latin, see J. A. Bengel, *Gnomon Novi Testamenti* (secundum editionem tertiam, 1773; Berlin: Ludov. Frid. Fues, 1855) 183.

32 On παρεμβάλλω, "insert," "insinuate," "introduce," see BAGD, s.v. The verb often suggests an element of surprise.

33 On the term, which initially means "stake, post" (Latin *vallum*), then "palisade" (Latin also *vallum*), "the palisade and the small earthwork" that is erected to elevate it (*vallum* and *ager*), finally "fortified line," see Plummer, 451; and BAGD, s.v.

34 On περικυκλῶ, see BAGD, s.v.

35 On συνέχω, "hold together," "contain," "press," "compress," see BAGD, s.v.

36 See Pierre Prigent, *La fin de Jérusalem* (CAB 17; Neuchâtel: Delachaux et Niestlé, 1969) 36–46.

37 Like that of the king's enemies at the end of the parable of the pounds (19:27).

38 Since the city is seen as a mother, the τέκνα are not the children but the inhabitants of Jerusalem. The usage is common. See Joel 2:23; Zech 9:13; Bar 4:19, 21, 25; 1 Macc 1:38; Matt 23:37; Luke 13:34; Gal 4:25.

39 The verb ἐδαφίζω means literally "to reduce to the level of the ground" (ἔδαφος, "ground"), "to demolish," "to level," "to throw to the ground," sometimes "to fling against the earth violently."

40 On Luke 21:20-24, see the commentary below.

41 On the connections between Mark 13:2 and Luke 19:44, see Dupont, "Pierre sur pierre."

true of "visitation" (ἐπισκοπή). It is the arrival and the favorable presence of God's envoy. The attentive readers recall the evangelist's grateful and nostalgic love of these terms. The theme of the visit appeared already in the infancy stories[42] and the one about the favorable time at the beginning of the Galilean ministry.[43] Unfortunately, here the positive moment rooted in God comes up against the negative forces of human beings.

■ **45-46** Most historians of primitive Christianity accept the authenticity of Jesus' action against the temple and its leadership.[44] Mark has preserved the memory of an action of Jesus that suggests that it was an effort at reform (this action refers to Jesus' refusal to let people carry the cultic vessels [Mark 11:16]). The violence directed against the sellers[45] does not call into question the religious function of the sanctuary. As the Fourth Gospel has made clear, it was intended as a prophetic act, an expression of zeal for the Lord.[46] In a rare instance, Jesus' action is stronger than his words. Before acting, the Master doubtless remembers Zech 14:21: "There will no longer be a merchant in the house of the Lord of hosts on that day."[47] Jesus' words are based on Scripture. They are a mixed quotation combining a line from Isa 56:7 LXX (ὁ γὰρ οἶκός μου οἶκος προσευχῆς κληθήσεται) and an expression from Jer 7:11 (σπήλαιον λῃστῶν).[48] The attack is directed less against the temple than against those who have diverted its mission

for their own profit. The money collected for the temple tax was kept there (Exod 30:13-16). This tax was to be paid in the form of the sanctuary's shekel; in those days that meant in shekels from Tyre that had been declared to be sacred. Since not everyone had these shekels, a system of exchange was essential, and it proved to be quite useful. Obviously, the exchange was profitable for the money changers, who earned their livelihood in this way and used the profit (see *m. Šeqal.* 1.7) to protect themselves against possible losses. There were also markets on the Mount of Olives, in particular for buying the animals for the sacrifices. In the year 30 (probably the year in which Jesus carried out the temple cleansing and was crucified), in a dispute with the high priest the Sanhedrin lost the right to meet in the temple precincts. The group then was welcomed on the Mount of Olives by market vendors, the family of Bene Hanan. Perhaps by way of reprisal, perhaps to simplify the pilgrims' journey, Caiaphas, the high priest at that time, authorized the opening of a market in one of the temple courts (probably in the Court of the Gentiles).[49] Thus, animals had begun to be sold only recently in the sacred precinct when Jesus opposed it. Nothing indicates, however, that Jesus sided with the Sanhedrin against the high priest. Coming from the country, he was shocked by the customs in the capital city. As a prophet, he wanted to render "to God the things that are God's" (20:25).[50]

---

42 On ἐπισκοπή and ἐπισκέπτομαι, see vol. 1 of this commentary, 72, on 1:68; 76 on 1:78; 273–74 on 7:16.

43 On καιρός, see vol. 2 of this commentary on 12:54-56. In 4:16-21 the opportune time is called the "favorable/acceptable year" (4:19).

44 Defenders of the historicity are, e.g., Trocmé, "Expulsion," 13–20; Söding, "Tempelaktion," 56–59; Oakman, "Fig Trees," 268.

45 See the "Zealot" interpretation of a revolutionary Jesus from Reimarus to Brandon. Lukito ("Cleansing," 34) introduces this interpretation without himself accepting it.

46 On this act as a prophetic sign see Trautmann, *Handlungen*, 129–32; Schnider and Stenger, *Johannes*, 37–49.

47 On the act that is more important than the quotation, see Barrett, "House," 18. On the reference to Zech 14:21, see Roth ("Cleansing"), who is of the opinion that in Jesus' day there were two interpretations of this oracle in circulation. According to the

first, at the end of time there would be no more vendors in the temple. According to the second, all foreigners would have access to the temple. According to Barrett ("House," 19–20), Jesus may have remembered Mal 3:1-3.

48 On the mixed quotation, see Roth, "Cleansing," 176–77. According to Barrett ("House," 19), the mixed quotation must have been added secondarily to the original narrative.

49 For information on the connections between the business dealings in the temple and the agrarian society, see Eppstein, "Historicity." See also Oakman, "Fig Trees," 263–66; and Barrett, "House," 17. On the date of the episode, see Manson, "Cleansing." Haenchen (*Weg Jesu*, 382–83) provides concrete information on the temple and its activities. On the money one was permitted to bring into the temple, see Jeremias, "Zwei Miszellen," 179–80.

50 On Jesus' provincial anger, see Renan, *La vie de Jésus* (Paris: Lévy, 1863), 147–60, 210–11, 222 (Eng. trans. *The Life of Jesus* [1902; repr., New York: Modern

The first Christians maintained a connection to the temple, but there is no text indicating that they continued the practice of blood sacrifices. They came to the temple as a place of prayer and of practical evangelistic activity. Luke supports this image and projects it into the life of Jesus (in 19:45—21:38 Jesus concentrates his activity in the temple). He describes Jesus' disciples after the ascension as active in the temple (24:52). It is in the temple that Peter and the other apostles pray and preach the risen Jesus (Acts 3:1).[51]

The so-called Hellenists in primitive Christianity made a decisive move when they spiritualized the idea of the temple and criticized the sacred building in Jerusalem (see Acts 6:13; 7:47-50).[52] Then Jesus' statements about the fall of the temple (Mark 13:2 par.; 14:58 par.; 15:29 par.; Luke 13:35; 19:44; John 2:19-21) took on the appearance of true prophecies. Stephen and his friends were persecuted in large part because of their hostility to the temple made with human hands. When he wrote his Gospel, Mark interpreted the cleansing of the temple as a prophecy that predicted its disappearance (whence comes the episode of the barren fig tree that frames the account on both sides).[53]

Luke concedes that a vigorous cult concentrated in Jerusalem no longer exists in his day, but he maintains that for the time of Jesus and the first Christians there was a legitimate temple in the holy city. He fears, however, a Zealot reading of the event that would characterize Jesus as a revolutionary.[54] That Jesus is "king" ($\beta\alpha\sigma\iota\lambda\epsilon\acute{v}\varsigma$, v. 38) is theologically valid for the evangelist, but it is only in the figure of the Suffering Servant that his kingdom is of this world. Only a brief sentence remains from Mark's already concise narrative (v. 45).[55] Mark said that the temple must be a house of prayer "for all peoples" according to the quotation of Isa 56:7. Luke and Matthew omit these words. Are they following a version of Mark that differs from our present copy? I think rather that the two evangelists shorten Isaiah's prophecy willfully and for the same reasons. Speaking after 70, the year of the destruction of the temple, they realize that this sanctuary can no longer serve "all peoples" as a place of prayer.[56] They also tell themselves that in their day it is the Christian church that has become the only place open for the prayers of all peoples.[57]

As for the robbers ($\lambda\eta\sigma\tau\alpha\acute{\iota}$) from the Jeremiah quotation, they represent first of all the merchants who exploit

Library, 1927] 206–12 [chap. 12], 274, 283) (sometimes with expressions of hostility toward Judaism). According to Oakman ("Fig Trees," 264–68), Jesus wants the temple really to be for everybody; with his action Jesus wants to bring the Jews to repentance. According to Söding ("Tempelaktion," 59–61, 63), his message of the kingdom unsettles the temple. For Lukito ("Cleansing," 38–40), Jesus shows his messianic identity. According to Dawsey ("Confrontation," 155), Jesus binds his teaching, understood as an instrument, with the cleansing of the temple. According to Roloff (*Kerygma*, 89–110), who offers both principal interpretations (criticism of the temple and universal opening), the pericope gives an account of a prophetic act of Jesus, who wants to bring about Israel's conversion. According to Hiers ("Purification"), by cleansing the temple Jesus wanted to prepare Israel for the kingdom of God.

51   On the attitude of the Jerusalem church toward the temple, see Trocmé, "Expulsion," 13. There are a number of studies of Luke's conception of the Jerusalem temple: Weinert, "Meaning of the Temple in the Gospel of Luke"; Bachman, *Tempel;* Casalegno, *Tempio;* Chance, *Jerusalem.* To these monographs one must add van der Waal, "Temple"; and Dawsey, "Origin."

52   Marcel Simon, *St. Stephen and the Hellenists in the Primitive Church* (New York: Longmans, Green, 1958). For a different opinion, see Hengel, "Hellenists," 18. Since then the Christian community (1 Cor 3:17) or the body of believers (1 Cor 6:19) represent the true temple of God.

53   On the barren fig tree, which gives meaning to the temple episode, as well as on the omission of this incident, see Cantrell, "Fig Tree"; Kinman, "Eschatology."

54   See Burger, *Davidssohn*, 112–14.

55   See Trocmé, "Expulsion," 6–7; and Trautmann, *Handlungen*, 98–101. In contrast to Mark, Luke neglects the buyers and money changers. Nor does he mention the sellers of doves.

56   On the mixed quotation and the absence of the words "for all peoples," see Trocmé, "Expulsion," 6; and Barrett, "House," 17–19.

57   On the church as a place of prayer for all peoples, see Eph 2:11-12.

their inordinate privileges. But for those who had followed the course of the Jewish revolt, "robbers" was also, in the eyes of the Roman conquerors, a disrespectful way of referring to the Zealots,[58] those partisans of violence against the occupier who, in the last months of the siege, had made the temple their landmark.

■ **47-48** For Luke, following Mark, Jesus' act was directed principally at the leaders responsible for the temple ($\dot{v}\mu\epsilon\hat{\iota}\varsigma$ $\delta\acute{\epsilon}$, "but you," v. 46). It is understandable that an attitude and language such as Jesus used, even if tempered, would have greatly irritated the temple personnel. That the temple police, a squad of husky Levites, did not intervene and that the Roman troops quartered close to the temple in Antonia did not lift a finger show that the incident was a minor event[59] (the prophets always chose the small to interpret the large[60]). Even its small scale, however, does not keep the scene from being shocking for the spectators. Since only one high priest served at a time, the plural $\dot{a}\rho\chi\iota\epsilon\rho\epsilon\hat{\iota}\varsigma$ refers to the group of professional priests who lived in Jerusalem and who occupied the responsible posts in the temple organization.[61]

According to Mark and Luke, these men, along with the scribes, want to take Jesus' life.[62] What is the expression "the leaders of the people," absent from Mark, doing here? It can designate the third group of the Sanhedrin, the "elders," whom Luke will mention by name in the first verse of the next chapter (20:1). If we give the "and" ($\kappa\alpha\acute{\iota}$) an epexegetical—that is, explicative—sense,[63] it can also indicate the sense of the terms "chief priests" and "scribes" for readers who have little familiarity with the earlier Jewish realities. Then the two groups constitute "the leaders of the people."[64]

No matter how powerful they might be, these men did not dare mount a frontal attack on Jesus. The *vox populi* in Rome, Athens, or Jerusalem carried weight.[65] And if, as Luke said, all the people were hanging on Jesus' every word, it was better to wait and not to attract the attention of the Roman authorities, who would not be eager to challenge a unanimous popular mood. These are the facts as Luke gives them. By and large he follows Mark's description, as does Matthew.[66] Only John, who depends on other traditions, puts the episode at the beginning

58   Josephus emphasizes this title of the Jewish patriots. Cf. George Wesley Buchanan, "Brigands in the Temple," *HUCA* 30 (1959) 169–77; Roth, "Cleansing," 176–80; Prigent, *Fin de Jérusalem*, 9–10; Barrett, "House," 15–17. It appears that the Christians in the capital city did not support the revolt. Eusebius of Caesarea (*Hist. eccl.* 3.5.3) reports that they fled from the capital city to Pella, but the historicity of this report is a matter of controversy among scholars. See Jürgen Wehnert, "Die Auswanderung der Jerusalemer Christen nach Pella—historisches Faktum oder theologische Konstruktion? Kritische Bemerkungen zu einem neuen Buch," *ZKG* 102 (1991) 231–55.

59   This is the classic argument of the opponents of a revolutionary Jesus. See Oscar Cullmann, *Jesus and the Revolutionaries* (trans. Gareth Putam; New York: Harper & Row, 1970); Martin Hengel, *Was Jesus a Revolutionist?* (trans. William Klassen; Philadelphia: Fortress Press, 1971).

60   On the smallness of the sign compared with the largeness of the reality and on the sacramental *signum* vis-à-vis God's *res*, see Louis-Marie Chauvet, *Symbol and Sacrament: A Sacramental Reinterpretation of Christian Existence* (Collegeville, Minn.: Liturgical Press, 1995) 346–47 (on the symbolic economy of sobriety).

61   On the idea of the high priest, see Albert Vanhoye,

Old Testament Priests and the New Priest: According to the New Testament (trans. J. Bernard Orchard; Studies in Scripture; Petersham, Mass.: St. Bede's Publications, 1986) 1–59, esp. 8–14. Note the use of the term in the singular and in the plural in the Fourth Gospel. Even if the fourth evangelist gives the impression that there had been two high priests at one time (John 18:19, 22; 11:49-51; 18:13, 24), he wants to say that only one was active and that the other, although retired, had kept his title.

62   They "seek" to kill Jesus. On the verb $\zeta\eta\tau\acute{\epsilon}\omega$, which can be used in a good or a bad sense, see vol. 2 of this commentary on 11:9. In any event, Luke sees a great deal of energy in this searching.

63   On the epexegetical $\kappa\alpha\acute{\iota}$, see BDF §442.9.

64   It is customary for Luke, a good pedagogue. One finds it also in Luke 22:67 and 70 (the title "Son of God" in v. 70 explains the enigmatic title Messiah [v. 67] for non-Jews).

65   Even in trials, see $\dot{\epsilon}\kappa\beta\acute{o}\eta\sigma\iota\varsigma$. See the perhaps excessive thesis of Jean Colin, *Les villes libres de l'Orient gréco-romain et l'envoi au supplice par acclamations populaires* (Latomus 82; Bruxelles-Berchem: Latomus, 1965); François Bovon, *The Last Days of Jesus* (trans. Kristin Hennessy; Louisville: Westminster John Knox, 2006) 50.

66   On Mark's redaction, see Söding, "Tempelaktion," 39–41; and Joachim Gnilka, *Das Evangelium nach*

of Jesus' ministry (John 2:14-17), depicts a more aggressive Jesus armed with a whip and reawakens the memory of the zeal as the disciples remember it (Ps 68 [69]:10 is quoted in John 2:17). Alongside the report of the temple purification (John 2:13-22), the evangelist John[67] also includes a notice about the destruction and rebuilding of the temple theologically identical with the body of Jesus.[68]

History of Interpretation

Origen raises the question about Christ's tears (*Hom. Luc.* 38). He sees them as the application of the beatitude "Blessed are you who weep." In the course of his life, Jesus corroborated each of the beatitudes. Indeed, Jerusalem represents the earthly city whose destruction constituted a divine punishment. Above all, however, it represents the capital of human souls. Jesus weeps especially for those who are besieged by various sins.[69]

The Christian West also reflects on Christ's tears and relates them to the beatitudes. Augustine writes, "Blessed are those who weep; you imitate him who wept over Jerusalem" (*Virginit.* 28).[70] Gregory the Great gives

Jesus' lament a moral sense: As the Master wept over Jerusalem, likewise preachers are to mourn the human life burdened with sins (*Hom. Ez.* 1.2.19).[71] For his part, the Venerable Bede remembers that Jesus wept in his life. He wept at the death of Lazarus (John 11:35) and here (Luke 19:41). As he wept over Lazarus before he raised him, relatives and neighbors must also weep over the sins of their parents and friends (*In Luc.* 2.1516–20).[72] An anonymous commentator, probably writing in Ireland in the eighth century, indicates that Jesus never laughed. It is fitting, therefore, that Christians share his tears. As for Jerusalem, the city has no peace, because it lacks faith in Christ (Anonymous *Comm. Luc.* 19:41-44).[73]

Bonaventure compares Jesus' tears with the divine condescension mentioned in the Old Testament (e.g., Deut 4:7). He wept, therefore, on behalf of his people (*pro nobis*). He drew near to Jerusalem with his body and with his heart. In a figurative sense Jesus wept for the people's sins—sins that encircle them and throw them to the ground. Against these attacks the believers must build a fortress in which Christ comes to dwell (*Comm. Luc.* 19.63–75).[74]

Calvin thinks in clearly universal terms.[75] Since Christ

Markus (2d ed.; 2 vols.; EKKNT 2; Neukirchen-Vluyn: Neukirchener Verlag, 1986) 2:127–28. On Matthew's redaction, see Ulrich Luz, *Matthew: A Commentary* (trans. James E. Crouch; 3 vols.; Hermeneia; Minneapolis: Fortress Press, 2002–7) 3:6. On Christian rereadings of the temple cleansing, see Söding, "Tempelaktion," 63–64; Oakman, "Fig Trees," 254.

67   On the episode in John, see Jürgen Becker, *Das Evangelium des Johannes, Kapitel 1–10* (ÖTBK 4.1; Gütersloh: Mohn, 1979) 120–27; Mendner, "Tempelreinigung."

68   Rius-Camps ("Origen") tries to demonstrate that the pericope of the adulteress (John 7:53—8:11), a late addition to the Gospel of John, is actually Lukan and belongs to the section on the temple (Luke 19:47—21:38). Plummer (455) is aware of the attempt to locate the episode in this period. This was already the opinion of Renan (*Life*, 311–12).

69   See also Cyril of Alexandria, *Serm. Luc.* 131; Payne Smith, *Cyril*, 2:607–12. There are two Greek fragments: Joseph Reuss, *Lukas-Kommentare aus der griechischen Kirche: Aus Katenenhandschriften gesammelt und herausgegeben* (TU 130; Berlin: Akademie-Verlag, 1984) 195, frgs. 293 and 294. Cyril offers an exegesis of Luke 19:41-48 that is very hostile toward

Jews. In the process he makes use of various oracles of Jeremiah, especially Jer 6:19. If Jesus weeps over Jerusalem, it is because he wishes that the city were happy, living in peace with God, and thus offering him faith. Nowhere have I sensed that Origen influenced Cyril.

70   CSEL 41:265.

71   CCSL 142:29–30; see also Gregory's *Hom. Ev.* 39, devoted to Luke 19:41-47 (*PL* 76:1293–1301).

72   In commenting on Luke 19:41-47, Bede (*In Luc.* 5.2021–2197) extensively quotes Gregory the Great's second homily mentioned in the previous note.

73   CCSL 108C, 94–95. Rupert of Deutz (*In Gen.* 6.45; CCCM 21:417) explains that when Jesus weeps he expresses his feelings and his human nature. An exegetical tradition announces that the enemies of v. 43 are Vespasian and Titus. See Gregory (n. 71 above), Anonymous (*Comm. Luc.* 19.41–44), and Thomas Aquinas *Catena Aurea* 19.5 (p. 261).

74   Bonaventure, *Opera omnia*, vol. 7: *Commentarius in Evangelium S. Lucae* (ed. R. P. Bernardini; Quaracchi: Collegium S. Bonaventurae, 1881–1902) 495–501.

75   Calvin, *Harmony*, 2.295–3.10. My remarks refer to 2.295–97.

wants to bring salvation to everyone, beginning with the lost sheep of the house of Israel, he grieves when faced with the sullen inhabitants of Jerusalem. Like the medieval theologians, Calvin interprets these tears as an expression of human feelings. An experienced rhetorician, he notices Jesus' emotion even as far as the interruption in the thread of his discourse (the above-noted

aposiopesis in v. 42). As a friend of Hebrew thought, he conceives of "peace" (v. 42) in the fullness of well-being.[76]

Over the centuries preachers and theologians have respected Jesus' tears and been attentive to the unhappy people who let the divine offer escape. All of them try to apply the message to the present by locating Jesus' adversaries in the history of nations or in the fate of individuals.[77]

---

76 Erasmus (*Paraphrasis*, 435–37) also notes the aposiopesis. He supplements it in an interesting way: If you had been able to recognize your day as I have recognized it . . . He adds: The next day will no longer be yours; it will be that of the Romans. Martin Luther, in his sermon from August 16, 1528 (WA 27:304–11; Erwin Mülhaupt, ed., *D. Martin Luthers Evangelien-Auslegung* [5 vols.; 3d ed.; Göttingen: Vandenhoeck & Ruprecht, 1957] 3:341–47), retains the literal sense of a punishment of Jerusalem. Yet, because the Gospel always serves as an example, he envisages a figurative sense: The Jerusalem authorities are the bishops and all the princes who

are hostile toward the reformation and who bring Germany to ruin.

77 Linder ("Destruction") takes as his starting point the festival of the Ninth of Ab, when the Jews remember the fall of Jerusalem. He then examines the origin and the development of the Sunday on which Christians have observed this event since late antiquity. The date of this Sunday was established in summer, between the festival of Saint Peter and Saint Paul on June 29 and that of Saint Laurence on August 10. Since the middle of the eighth century, Luke 19:41-47 has gradually become the liturgical reading.

Questions without Answer (20:1-8)

Bibliography

Brock, Ann Graham, *Mary Magdalene, the First Apostle: the Struggle for Authority* (HTS 51; Cambridge, MA: Harvard Divinity School, 2003) *passim*.

Burchard, Christoph, "Fußnoten zum neutestamentlichen Griechisch, II," *ZNW* 69 (1978) 143–57, esp. 146–49.

Chilton, Bruce, and Jacob Neusner, *Types of Authority in Formative Christianity and Judaism* (London: Routledge, 1999).

Fuchs, Albert, "Die Frage nach der Vollmacht Jesu: Mk 11,27-33 par Mt 21,23-27 par Lk 20,1-8," *SNTU* 26 (2001) 27–58.

Grangaard, Blake R., *Conflict and Authority in Luke 19:47 to 21:4* (Studies in Biblical Literature 8; New York: Lang, 1999) 63–77.

Haenchen, *Weg Jesu*, 392–96.

Kingsbury, Jack Dean, *Conflict in Luke: Jesus, Authorities, Disciples* (Minneapolis: Fortress Press, 1991).

Kremer, Jacob, "Jesu Antwort auf die Frage nach seiner Vollmacht," *BibLeb* 9 (1968) 128–36.

Mussies, G., "The Sense of ΣΥΛΛΟΓΙΖΕΣΘΑΙ at Luke 20,5," in T. Baarda, A. F. J. Klijn, and W. C. van Unnik, eds., *Miscellanea Neotestamentica* (2 vols.; NovTSup 48; Leiden: Brill, 1978) 2:59–76.

Roloff, *Kerygma*, 93–95, 101–2.

Schramm, *Markus-Stoff*, 149–50.

Shae, Gam Seng, "The Question on Authority of Jesus," *NovT* 16 (1974) 1–29.

---

1 **Now it happened that on one of these days, when he was teaching the people in the temple and preaching the good news, the chief priests and scribes with the elders encountered him 2/ and spoke to him saying,ª "Tell us with what authorityᵇ you do all these things or who it is who gave you this authority?" 3/ He answered them: "I also have a question for you.ᶜ Tell me: 4/ The baptism of John—was it from heaven or from human beings?" 5/ They reasoned and said,ᵈ "If we say from heaven, he will say, why did you not believe him?" 6/ But if we say from human beings, all the people will stone us, for they are convinced that John is a prophet. 7/ They answered that they did not know the origin.ᵉ 8/ And Jesus said to them, "Neither will I tell you by what authority I do these things."**

a   Literally: "and said to him saying."
b   Literally: "in what authority."
c   Literally: "I also will ask you something" (or: a word, λόγος).
d   Or: "They reasoned among themselves, saying."
e   Literally: "And they answered they did not know whence."

Jesus' ministry had begun with a series of disputes with the scribes and the Pharisees (5:17—6:11). It concludes with a series of disputes with the scribes and chief priests, and then with the Sadducees (20:1—21:38). The apostles' missionary activity will elicit the same opposition (Acts 3:1—5:42). The proclamation of the gospel (see εὐαγγελιζομένου, v. 1) sets loose waves of hostility.[1]

Analysis

Jesus' only sojourn in Judea and Jerusalem that Luke depicts begins in a striking manner. The evangelist first expresses a christological truth: The Master, riding on his young ass, deserves the title "king" (19:38). Then Luke draws an ecclesiological consequence: The

---

1   See Jean Zumstein, "L'apôtre comme martyr dans les Actes de Luc," *RThPh* 112 (1980) 371–90.

"people" of God (λαός, 19:48; 20:6, 45) appear in sharp relief next to the blind Jewish authorities.

The question of authority (20:1-8) provokes the first of these disputes. It is followed by a polemical parable (20:9-19), the problem of tax paid to Caesar (20:20-26), a discussion about the resurrection (20:27-40), a question from Jesus about the Son of David (20:41-44), and a final warning (20:46-47).[2]

All these events, as also the apocalyptic discourse of chap. 21, take place in the temple. Luke creates a final phase of activity, or more precisely of teaching (the verb διδάσκω is used several times: 19:47; 20:1, 21; 21:37; 23:5), and emphasizes that it takes place in the environs of the Jerusalem sanctuary.[3]

The episode dealing with authority takes place against the background alluded to in 19:47-48 and recalled here in v. 1a: Jesus teaches the people daily in the temple. The point of departure is indicated by the expression "now it happened . . . on one of these days" (v. 1a). It consists of the intervention of the authorities (v. 1b), who ask Jesus a double question about his authority and its origin (v. 2). For his part (κἀγώ, "I also"), Jesus responds by posing a question to his interrogators (v. 3): What about the authority of John the Baptist (v. 4)? The opponents then talk among themselves (vv. 5-6) and finally acknowledge

their ignorance and refuse to answer (v. 7), whereupon the Master also refuses to discuss the matter any further (v. 8).[4]

Here in schematic form is the structure of the brief dialogue of the deaf conversation partners:

Vv. 1-2: Intervention and question of the authorities
Vv. 3-4: Jesus' answer in the form of a question
Vv. 5-6: The authorities' reflection
V. 7:   Admission of the authorities' ignorance
V. 8:   Jesus' refusal to answer[5]

The episode belongs to the three-part tradition. Exegetes generally agree that it circulated only in this tradition. Thus, Matthew and Luke inherited it from Mark.[6] Even Tim Schramm concedes that Luke depends only on Mark here.[7] The evangelist obviously permitted himself to revise his source. The adjustments he makes appear from the very beginning. The opening indicated above ("it happened . . . on one of these days," v. 1) is characteristic of his narrative style.[8] He makes a point of specifying that Jesus' teaching goes along with the communication of the good news (v. 1).[9] The double question of the notable persons (v. 2) coincides with Mark's text.[10] Luke reworks the first part of Jesus' answer by simplifying it (v. 3).[11] One might say he leaves the second

2   Several scholars (e.g., Plummer, 455; and Fitzmyer, 2:1271) comment on the sequence. Charles H. Talbert (*Reading Luke: A Literary and Theological Commentary on the Third Gospel* [New York: Crossroad, 1982], 185–87) is of the opinion that 19:45—21:38 and 22:1—24:53 constitute two sections that have parallels at the end of Acts.

3   It is to the credit of Hans Conzelmann (*Theology*, 75–78, 164) that he has called attention to this redactional change. The same is true of the above-mentioned activity of the apostles (Acts 3:1—5:42).

4   There is a certain narrative tension, for if the authorities declare they do not know, Jesus considers that he does not want to answer.

5   For further examples of the subdivision, see Roland Meynet, *L'évangile selon Saint Luc: analyse rhétorique* (2 vols.; Paris: Cerf, 1988) 1:185; 2:191; and Grangaard, *Conflict*, 66, 69.

6   I find only two minor agreements between Luke and Matthew: ἐρωτήσω and κἀγώ (v. 3; Matt 21:24). They are not enough to shake the hypothesis of an exclusive dependence on Mark. See Nolland, 3:942.

7   I. Howard Marshall (*The Gospel of Luke: A Com-*

mentary on the Greek Text [NIGTC; Grand Rapids: Eerdmans, 1978] 723) errs here. What Schramm (*Markus-Stoff*, 149–50) says is that if Luke depends here solely on Mark, that does not exclude the possibility that there was a similar narrative in a parallel tradition.

8   See n. 21 below.

9   It is difficult to know whether Luke was thinking of two complementary activities (teaching and evangelizing) or of a certain kind of "teaching" that coincided with the "proclamation of the gospel." In the latter case, the καί before εὐαγγελιζομένου is epexegetical. If teaching is mentioned often, proclaiming the gospel is rare. I lean toward the first of these options.

10 Luke simply changes the aorist indicative ἔδωκεν ("gave") into an aorist participle ὁ δούς ("the one who has given") and eliminates the redundant ἵνα ταῦτα ποιῇς ("that you may do these things"; Mark 11:28).

11 He prefers ἐρωτῶ to ἐπερωτῶ (which is not necessarily an improvement, since Mark's verb may suggest a question to be added to the ques-

part intact (v. 4).[12] He copies the first hypothesis with no change ("if we say, 'from heaven,'" Mark 11:31), replacing in the introduction (v. 5) the verb διαλογίζομαι with the verb συλλογίζομαι.[13] He rewrites the second hypothesis, characterized in the Second Gospel with a harsh anacoluthon.[14] The sentence flows more naturally (he describes the people as "convinced that," while Mark writes that the people "held that") and expresses the leaders' risk (stoning).[15] In v. 7 Luke states precisely that they did not know "whence"; they did not know the "origin" (Mark says simply they did not know; 11:33). As for the final sentence (v. 8), it is identical in the two Gospels.[16]

Primarily two exegetes have tried to explain the origin of the episode. Rudolf Bultmann ingeniously observes a change in meaning between v. 30 and vv. 31-32 in Mark 11. Here the issue is the opposition between God and human beings in general; there it is the opposition between God and the people not empowered by God in particular. He especially emphasizes rabbinic parallels, controversies in which a rabbi responds to a question by asking a question. Finally, he expresses the opinion that the verb πιστεύω, "believe" (Mark 11:31), reflects a Christian perception that is more Hellenistic than Semitic. Thus, he suggests a distinction between two stages in the development of the tradition of this episode. A first version (without vv. 31-32) corresponds to the rabbinic disputes better than the second. A second version added the content of vv. 31-32 and in so doing changed the sense of the words of the Jewish leaders. Nevertheless, according to Bultmann, even the first version of the development does not necessarily reflect a historical event. It may

correspond to concerns of the early church, a dispute between Jesus' disciples and those of John the Baptist.[17]

Gam Seng Shae takes up the question.[18] He first defines which are the redactional elements of the Markan version. There are not many: Mark 11:27a and 32b. Then, moving from the written phase back to the oral phase, he subdivides the oral phase into at least two periods. Originally the disciples of Jesus, facing the disciples of John the Baptist, told of a rabbinic-style dispute in four parts: (a) The opponents: Who gave this authority? (b) Jesus: Is John's baptism from heaven or from humans? (c) The opponents: from heaven. (d) Jesus: My authority also is from heaven. This (authentic) dispute could have taken place at any time and was tied neither to the entry into Jerusalem nor to the cleansing of the temple. In the question (Mark 11:28) "these things" and "this" designated all of Jesus' ministry and not a particular action. Later the episode was reinterpreted in light of the bonds between the early church and the temple. Its hook was the recollection of the cleansing of the temple, and it was understood as an eminently christological text (Jesus was no longer put on the same level with John the Baptist, and he began to score points when facing the Jerusalem authorities). At that time the first Christians had to justify their attitude toward the temple, and they too were asked about the source of their authority (Acts 4:7). Their best argument was the reference to Jesus' attitude in a similar situation in the story of the episode in its revised form.

Personally, I also think that one can distinguish between two stages in the oral phase. In the first stage one is told about a dialogue that was going nowhere—a dialogue between Jesus and the Jewish opponents who

---

tion already asked). He consciously states κἀγώ ("and also I," "for my part"). He removes the ἕνα ("one") before λόγον and changes the imperative from "and answer me" to "and tell me." Finally, by eliminating "and I will tell you by what authority I do these things" he loses what appears to him to be an obvious clarification but gains in conciseness.

12   Luke omits the repetition of the imperative "answer me" (Mark 11:30).

13   The interpretation will return to this relatively important change. See the commentary on 20:5-6 below.

14   "But shall we say 'from human beings'? . . . they feared the crowd" (Mark 11:32).

15   Mark emphasized: "really a prophet" (Mark 11:32). Luke says simply: "a prophet" (v. 6).

16   Luke prefers the aorist εἶπεν ("he said") to Mark's historical present λέγει ("he says"; Mark 11:33).

17   See Bultmann, *History*, 19–20.

18   See Shae, "Question." In reading this otherwise remarkable article, one does not understand why the author moves from a positive response of the opponents to a refusal to answer and from a positive Jesus to a hesitant Jesus.

themselves had a certain religious authority. The dialogue did not necessarily take place in Jerusalem, and it was associated neither with the entry into the holy city nor with the cleansing of the temple. In contrast to Shae, however, I am of the opinion that the historical Jesus had the rhetorical skill to evade the question and to avoid giving any answer at all (careful as he was not to make a show of his prophetic consciousness, especially before people of a hostile disposition). It is because of this same skill that the early Christians did not forget the episode.

A second oral phase associated the incident with the last period of Jesus' ministry. Unlike the christological reserve of the historical Jesus, Christian memory intensifies the opposition between Jesus and, in its view, the heart of Israel's religious power, the Sanhedrin, represented by the three groups priests, scribes, and elders. Jesus' authority is taken for granted. With enthusiasm it is asserted that it comes from God. The Sanhedrin's ignorance, more pretended than real, becomes an indication of impotence, a sign of its inability.

Commentary

■ **1** This first verse reflects Luke's style and intentions. The expression "now it happened" is characteristic of a new event in the life of Jesus.[19] "On one of these days" is not necessarily a Semitism. It can be a narrative style appropriate at that time[20] that was popular with Luke (cf. 5:17; 8:22).[21] Jesus continues the teaching begun in Galilee (4:15, 30; 5:17) and carried on in Judea (19:45). The temple gives a special connotation to what the Master has to say. Luke suggests a continuity of the biblical message, a legitimate hermeneutic of the Holy Scriptures, and an actualization of Israel's institutions that is in keeping with God's plan and the approach of the kingdom of God. The addition of the explanation "and proclaimed the good news" directs the readers' attention to this theological program.[22]

Then the official representatives of Judaism, against whom Luke directs his entire work, confront Jesus and his plan.[23] The three groups[24] are presented judiciously. Such was indeed the composition of the Great Sanhedrin.

It is not easy to understand why Luke never says simply, "the chief priests, the scribes, and the elders." One time he says, "the chief priests and scribes, that is to say, the leaders of the people," omitting the elders (19:47). Here he says, "the chief priests and the scribes with the elders" (v. 1). At any event, this official delegation[25] asks Jesus a question. His teaching in the temple will have been interrupted by such questions (see 20:21, 27; 21:7),

---

19   Since the first chapter of the Gospel, the reader has been accustomed to this and similar formulas (see 1:5, 8; 2:1, 15, etc.).

20   Even if it is known in Syriac, one does not find it in the Hebrew Bible, in the intertestamental literature, or in the LXX. On the other hand, it is current in the Greek Christian literature even independent of Lukan influence. One cannot declare it to be "non-Greek." Burchard ("Fußnoten," 146–49) holds this opinion against Plummer (225), Schramm (*Markus-Stoff*, 84, 96–97), and others. Nevertheless, Burchard (147) explains: "It remains conceivable that the Syntagma, although correct in Greek, actually has been executed according to a Semitic pattern." It is to be noted that the manuscripts vary between ἐν μιᾷ τῶν ἡμερῶν, which I retain, even if I must translate it as "on one of *these* days," and ἐν μιᾷ τῶν ἡμερῶν ἐκείνων.

21   See vol. 1 of this commentary, 318, on 8:22.

22   From the Galilean period Luke has established a connection between the teaching and the proclamation of the good news. Cf. 4:31, 43.

23   On ἐφίσταμαι ("approach," "appear") see 2:9; Acts 4:1; 6:12; Marshall, 109. See also vol. 1 of this commentary, 87, on 2:9.

24   On the composition of the Sanhedrin, see Bo Reicke, *The New Testament Era: The World of the Bible from 500 B.C. to A.D. 100* (trans. David E. Green; Philadelphia: Fortress Press, 1968) 142–52; and Eduard Lohse, "συνέδριον," *TDNT* 7 (1971) 860–71. Many manuscripts have "priests" instead of "chief priests." Some scholars (see the list of names in Fitzmyer, 2:1274) prefer this reading. I hold to "chief priests," since it is possible that the writers corrected the text thinking there had been only one high priest and did not realize the term could refer to the most important priests.

25   See Kremer, "Antwort," 130. To be precise, Luke does not speak of a delegation. Like the popular storytellers, he includes the entire Sanhedrin in his attack.

so much so that one could speak on this matter of a "day of questions."[26]

■ **2** The question is about the ἐξουσία of Jesus. In Greek the term designates freedom granted, authority, and power.[27] The nature of this quality, conferred by a higher power, depends on the social milieu, the institutional framework, and the civilization in which it is exercised.[28] Here it is a question of spiritual, prophetic authority, since Jesus was not part of the establishment.[29] Recognizing true prophets and denouncing false prophets have accompanied the life of the people of Israel from ancient times. One thinks of the struggle between Jeremiah and Hananiah (Jeremiah 28).[30] The criteria for recognizing and denouncing have never had a rational objectivity (that would be from below, from the human level). They can only belong to the order of things recognized in faith (coming from God, from above). They can be the contents of the message (one had to beware of the prophets of happiness and peace; see Jer 4:10; 6:14; 14:13; 23:17) or the messenger's moral attitude (an argument well into the time of the early Christians, in particular of the *Didache* [11.6-12]). In addition to the divine, thus legitimate, or the human, thus suspect, origin, it is necessary also to specify the application and the extent of this "authority" (ἐξουσία). The Lukan context suggests linking it to preaching and teaching (of the prophets, the sages, or the rabbis). It is concerned neither with the cultic function of the priest nor with the sociopolitical function of the elder.[31] In this prophetic and didactic framework Jesus' authority often created a problem, and various New Testament traditions preserved the memory of such debates (Mark 2:1-12 par.; Luke 11:15-23; 13:14-17). Sometimes, but less frequently, it was explicitly the question of messianic authority that was raised, particularly during Jesus' passion (see Mark 14:61 par. Matt 26:63 par. Luke 22:67).[32] More than the Synoptics, the Gospel of John is concerned with the question of Jesus' authority (John 2:18-22; 5:11-30; 6:36-54; 8:37-47; 17:2). The apostolic authority lies in the extension of Jesus' authority (see Mark 2:18-28; 6:7; 13:34).[33] It will also be expanded in the period when various kinds of ministry are evolving in the ancient church. Added to it will be the right to celebrate the sacraments and to lead the life of the ecclesial community.[34]

■ **3-4** In keeping with the oral tradition of their communities, the evangelists preserved the memory of a Jesus who, refusing to answer immediately, chooses the tactic of the counterquestion. This behavior eliminates the surprise effect and makes it possible to avoid revealing oneself immediately. Far from being seen as something negative, it was regarded as legitimate and even honorable among the rabbis[35] and also among the philosophers.[36]

Jesus, in turn,[37] asks a question.[38] He refers to John the Baptist, whose activity certainly did not take place

26 See Plummer (455, 445), who thinks, although cautiously, that it is a question of April 4 in the year 30.

27 On ἐξουσία in the Greek world, see Werner Foerster, "ἔξεστιν κτλ.," *TDNT* 2 (1964) 562–63.

28 The Latin world carefully distinguished among the qualities of the *imperium*, originally military, bestowed on the general; the *potestas*, by nature political, residing in the senate and the magistrates; and the *auctoritas*, of a personal nature, given to an outstanding leader or to the emperor. See François Bovon, *New Testament Traditions and Apocryphal Narratives* (trans. Jane Haapiseva-Hunter; PTMS 36; Allison Park, Pa.: Pickwick, 1995) 133–35, 224.

29 On ἐξουσία in Israel, see Werner Foerster, "ἔξεστιν κτλ.," *TDNT* 2 (1964) 564–66.

30 See André Neher, *Jérémie* (Paris: Librairie Plon, 1960) 117–21.

31 On authority in Israel, see Roland de Vaux, *Ancient Israel: Its Life and Institutions* (trans. John McHugh; 2d ed.; London: Darton, Longman & Todd, 1973).

32 With respect to 20:1-8, Kremer ("Antwort," 135)

insists on the testimony this passage delivered about Jesus' supreme authority.

33 See Chilton and Neusner, *Types of Authority;* and Brock, *Mary Magdalene*. Nolland (3:944) summarizes the situation well: "Jesus trades question for question, implicitly suggesting that he will somehow build his answer to their question on their answer to his question."

34 On this topic, see Jürgen Roloff and Knut Schäferdick, "Amt," *TRE* 2 (1978) 509–52.

35 See Str-B 1:861; Bultmann, *History*, 20; Shae, "Question," 13–14.

36 As Plato's dialogues attest, Socrates practiced this technique in order to stimulate the questioner's thinking. The Sophists, the Stoics, and the Cynics also made use of it.

37 This κἀγώ, which both Luke and Matthew have, underscores Jesus' right to ask questions of the highest authority of Judaism in that day.

38 Is there a difference between ἐρωτῶ (Luke) and ἐπερωτῶ (Mark)? Does the term λόγος designate

in Jerusalem and belonged to the past. This reference to John the Baptist would have been astonishing to the mind of the first Christians, but it was not surprising coming from the lips of Jesus. It recalls his beginnings at the side of the Baptist and the importance of his own baptism. Elsewhere he is located at John's side, although with a significant difference (7:31-35). He acknowledged the prophetic importance of the precursor's ministry (7:24-28).[39] Thus, he made an honest attempt finally to get an admission from the authorities—the recognition of the Jewish authorities of the prophet whom Herod had caused to be put to death. Should they grant this acknowledgment, he is prepared to ally himself with John in order to claim the same kind of authority. In my judgment, the question in v. 4 reflects a reaction of the historical Jesus.[40]

■ **5-6** The embarrassment of the three groups, who at the beginning of the oral tradition probably were distinguished by their silence, now comes to expression, but it does so in the voice of the early Christians.[41] Those Christians, speaking from an encampment of their own choosing, accuse the Sanhedrin of closing itself off from God's intervention on behalf of the people (and they are thinking as much of the rejection of Jesus as of that of John) or of cowardice, since the Jewish leaders fear "all the people" (who understood John and acknowledged

without reserve the validity of his prophetic ministry).[42] In his reading of the events, Luke goes even further than Mark: He imagines that the people will go so far as to stone the Sanhedrin.[43] In so doing he draws more on his romantic imagination than on legal or historical probability.[44]

One point deserves attention: Mark mentions a dialogue, even a dispute, among the members of the Sanhedrin (he uses the verb $\delta\iota\alpha\lambda o\gamma\acute{\iota}\zeta o\mu\alpha\iota$). Luke prefers a different verb ($\sigma\upsilon\lambda\lambda o\gamma\acute{\iota}\zeta o\mu\alpha\iota$). Since the time of the Vulgate, which understands these two verbs as synonyms, exegetes have neglected the difference between the one and the other formulation.[45] We are indebted to G. Mussies for noting this difference and giving us the correct significance of the verb that Luke uses.[46] What we have here is not a more or less vehement debate but a reflected calculation, an established accounting, a continuous reasoning, a balanced reflection. In contrast to $\delta\iota\alpha\lambda o\gamma\acute{\iota}\zeta o\mu\alpha\iota$, the relatively rare verb $\sigma\upsilon\lambda\lambda o\gamma\acute{\iota}\zeta o\mu\alpha\iota$ has a philosophical connotation (which we have inherited in the term "syllogism"). Here is a significant use of the verb with respect to Diogenes of Sinope: "It was his custom to reason ($\sigma\upsilon\nu\epsilon\lambda o\gamma\acute{\iota}\zeta\epsilon\tau o$) as follows: Everything belongs to the gods. Those who are wise are the friends of the gods. Now among friends everything is shared. Thus everything belongs to those who are wise."[47]

the outward form (a question) or the content (some matter)? See n. 11 above.

39 See vol. 1 of this commentary, 283–84, 285–88, on 7:24-28 and 31-35.

40 The *Five Gospels* of the Jesus Seminar offers a different opinion (Robert W. Funk, Roy W. Hoover, and the Jesus Seminar, *The Five Gospels: The Search for the Authentic Words of Jesus. New Translation and Commentary* [New York: Macmillan, 1993]).

41 Kremer ("Antwort," 135) draws a clear distinction between the level of the historical Jesus and that of the first Christians who report the episode.

42 Günther Bornkamm (*Jesus of Nazareth* [trans. Irene McLuskey and Fraser McLuskey with James M. Robinson; New York: Harper, 1960] 50) writes: "The decision concerning John and his baptism of repentance is also the decision concerning Jesus and his mission." Luke 7:29-30 has already contrasted two opposing Jewish attitudes toward John the Baptist: one positive, that of the people and the tax collectors, the other negative, that of the scribes and the Pharisees.

43 Luke uses the compound verb $\kappa\alpha\tau\alpha\lambda\iota\vartheta\acute{\alpha}\zeta\omega$, which is rare and appears only in Christian authors, perhaps influenced by Luke. See G. W. H. Lampe, *A Patristic Greek Lexicon* (Oxford: Clarendon, 1961) s.v.; and Fitzmyer, 2:1275–76.

44 There were cases of legal or illegitimate stonings. The difference between $\kappa\alpha\tau\alpha\lambda\iota\vartheta\acute{\alpha}\zeta\omega$ and the simple $\lambda\iota\vartheta\acute{\alpha}\zeta\omega$ ("to stone") may be that in the end the one who is stoned collapses ($\kappa\alpha\tau\acute{\alpha}$, "downward"). In Acts 7:58, in connection with the stoning of Stephen, Luke uses the verb $\lambda\iota\vartheta o\beta o\lambda\hat{\omega}$, "to attack by throwing stones," "to stone."

45 Doubtless yielding to the reflex to harmonize, the Vulgate expresses the $\delta\iota\epsilon\lambda o\gamma\acute{\iota}\zeta o\nu\tau o$ of Mark 11:31 and the $\sigma\upsilon\nu\epsilon\lambda o\gamma\acute{\iota}\sigma\alpha\nu\tau o$ of Luke 20:5 with the same verb, *cogitabant*. See Mussies, "Sense," 73.

46 Mussies, "Sense."

47 Ibid., 59, 76.

■ 7-8 Luke does not say whether Jesus' opponents are honest. Doubtless he is of the opinion that they are not. Had they wanted to run the risk of being honest and of acknowledging the signs of John the Baptist, according to the evangelist they would have dared to admit (a) that they knew the source[48] of the Baptist's authority and (b) that they located him near God in heaven. Luke obviously adopts a Baptist—and, above all, a Christian—outlook. It is therefore not astonishing that he had Jesus say that he refused to answer, since Jesus himself had not received the answer he expected.

Finally, we find on the lips of Jesus the expression his questioners used at the beginning: $\tau\alpha\hat{\upsilon}\tau\alpha$ $\pi o\iota\hat{\omega}$ in v. 8 takes up $\tau\alpha\hat{\upsilon}\tau\alpha$ $\pi o\iota\epsilon\hat{\iota}\varsigma$ of v. 2. In the context of chaps. 19 and 20 "these things" ($\tau\alpha\hat{\upsilon}\tau\alpha$) are the symbolic actions of the entry into Jerusalem and especially the expulsion of the merchants from the temple. Yet for Luke these signs are but the last, perhaps the most ambitious and most shocking, of a long series of signs and words. In the prayer that the Lukan Jesus addressed to the Father, there was also the question of a $\tau\alpha\hat{\upsilon}\tau\alpha$, at the same time both precise and vague (10:21).[49] On the one hand, God, the Father, in his "good pleasure" ($\epsilon\grave{\upsilon}\delta o\kappa\acute{\iota}\alpha$) reveals, through his Son, $\tau\alpha\hat{\upsilon}\tau\alpha$ (that is, his plan of salvation), to the little ones, that is, to his people. On the other hand, Jesus, the Son, in the name of his Father, fulfills $\tau\alpha\hat{\upsilon}\tau\alpha$, that is, the signs about the plan of salvation, and he speaks words about this divine economy. In Luke's eyes, this complementarity of the Father's plan and the realization of this plan by the Son constitute the strength of Christian faith. Yet because of its very power and its exclusivity, the plan of salvation arouses the opposition of those who see God's intention inscribed in other realities and communicated in other mediums, principally the law or the temple.

History of Interpretation

In a difficult passage Tertullian draws his inspiration from the episode in Luke 20:1-8 to apply it to Marcion, who, inwardly divided, does not know whether he must identify John the Baptist with God the creator or God the savior (*Adv. Marc.* 4.38.1–2).

Cyril of Alexandria sees in the question posed to Jesus a way of fleeing from the truth, a rejection of light, in a word, sin (*Serm. Luc* 133).[50] Augustine of Hippo sees this question in terms of John 1:29 (lamb of God) and comes to the conclusion that Christ acts with the authority of the lamb, who bears the sins of the world (*Tract. in Ioh.* 5.14).[51] The Venerable Bede understands the scene as a case of intentionally withholding religious knowledge on the part of Jesus (*In Luc.* 5.2222–35). Following Augustine (*Tract. in Ioh.* 35.2),[52] whom he quotes, Bede places the episode in a typological relationship with Psalm 131 (132):17-18: John the Baptist embodies the lamp prepared for God's anointed, and Jesus' opponents represent the psalm's enemies, covered with shame. He quotes John 16:12 on this subject ("you cannot bear everything I have yet to say to you"), then Matt 7:6 ("do not throw pearls before the swine").[53]

Without always admitting it, medieval exegesis often relies on patristic exegesis.[54] Without any scruples at all, it insists on the guilt of Jesus' opponents.

Calvin explains why the Jewish leaders ask about authority instead of doctrine: "They dispute His calling and commission," because "they had previously failed in their attacks many times."[55] The reformer has no more regard for Jesus' opponents than do the exegetes of antiquity and the Middle Ages:[56] "Their dealings show perversity and evil." How can they doubt Jesus' divine calling when from it they had seen so many miracles?

---

48   Compared with Mark 11:33, which does not have $\pi o\vartheta\acute{\epsilon}\nu$, Luke firmly holds to the Baptist's authority.

49   See vol. 2 of this commentary, on 10:21.

50   Payne Smith, *Cyril*, 2:621; Reuss, *Lukas-Kommentare*, 198 (frg. 302). The Syriac text, which I paraphrase only partially, corresponds to the Greek fragment: $o\dot{\iota}$ $\delta\grave{\epsilon}$ $\varphi\epsilon\acute{\upsilon}\gamma o\upsilon\sigma\iota$ $\tau\grave{\eta}\nu$ $\dot{\alpha}\lambda\acute{\eta}\vartheta\epsilon\iota\alpha\nu$ $\kappa\alpha\grave{\iota}$ $\delta\upsilon\sigma\sigma\epsilon\beta o\hat{\upsilon}\tau\nu\epsilon\varsigma$ $o\grave{\upsilon}$ $\kappa\alpha\tau\alpha\pi\epsilon\varphi\rho\acute{\iota}\kappa\alpha\sigma\iota\nu$ ("The others flee the truth and, filled with impiety, they are not at all horrified").

51   CCSL 36:48–49.

52   CCSL 36:318.

53   The gloss is based on Bede. It also uses the quotations from John 16:12 and Matt 7:6; *Glossa Ordinaria*, Luke 20:4-8 (*PL* 114:331).

54   See, e.g., Bonaventure *Comm. Luc.* 20.1-9 (Bernardini, 501–3) and Albertus Magnus *Evang. Luc.* 20.1-8 (599–603).

55   Calvin, *Harmony*, 3:11–12.

56   Martin Luther shares this opinion. Jesus' reaction is not mild; it is "sharp and harsh," because the Jews' question was "an arrogant question" (*Evangelien-Auslegung*, 924–25).

Jesus' counterquestion is "to convict them out of their own mouths of impudent pretense to ignorance on a subject they well understood." Why add other proofs on behalf of Jesus than those already given by John the Baptist? Finally, Calvin defends Jesus, who had not "intended His example to encourage the sophist's device of silencing truth." He is delighted by the alternative "from human beings" or "from God," because from that we know "that no kind of teaching or sacred sign may be accepted in our worship unless evidently sent by God."[57]

Conclusion

The Lukan Christ succeeded in attracting the attention of the Jewish authorities and in upsetting them. He has become a personality with whom the most powerful people must deal. By means of his rhetorical skill and power, he has embarrassed them and even rendered them mute. Thus, his authority of divine origin, like that of John the Baptist, manifested itself on the human level in a brilliant manner.

The chief priests, the scribes, and the elders, the heart of national power, have broken with the people who earlier defended the Baptist and now support Jesus. For Luke, this moment confirms the separation between divine truth and the ignorance of the Jewish leaders, which is more pretended than real. The true prophetic line empowered by God is opposed to Israel's religious and political leaders. The following parable will indicate where this opposition leads. For now, the λαός, "the people," still have confidence in Jesus, the faithful keeper of the divine message.

The faith inspired by Jesus Christ encourages each person to surrender one's self-assurance, to acknowledge that one's a-priori stances are relative, and to open oneself to question. Will Luke's readers accept this challenge?[58]

---

57 According to Erasmus (*Paraphrasis*, 437), Jesus' opponents claim, *Nobis ignotus es, nulla potestate publica praeditus es*, "For us you are an unknown, you are equipped with no public authority." We find the same hostility toward the Jews as we find in Luther and Calvin: An impious thought (*ab impio cogitatione;* col. 437) is the father of the question.

Erasmus notes ingeniously that, had Jesus' opponents answered honestly, they would have lost some of their authority before the people (*Si respondissent verum, periclitabatur apud populum illorum auctoritas;* col. 438).

58 See Kremer, "Antwort," 135–36.

The Parable of the Murderous Winegrowers (20:9-19)

Bibliography

Almeida, Yván, *L'opération sémantique des récits-paraboles: Sémiotique narrative et textuelle, herméneutique du discours religieux* (BCILL 13; Louvain: Peeters, 1978) 153–95.

Arnal, William E., "The Parable of the Tenants and the Class Consciousness of the Peasantry," in Stephen G. Wilson and Michael Desjardins, eds., *Text and Artifact in the Religions of Mediterranean Antiquity: Essays in Honour of Peter Richardson* (SCJ 9; Waterloo, Ont.: Wilfrid Laurier University Press, 2000) 135–57.

Baarda, Tjitze, "'The Cornerstone': An Aramaism in the Diatessaron and the Gospel of Thomas?" *NovT* 37 (1995) 285–300.

Bammel, Ernst, "Das Gleichnis von den bösen Winzern (Mk 12,1-9) und das jüdische Erbrecht," *RIDA* 3, series 6 (1959) 11–17.

Baumgarten, Joseph M., "4Q500 and the Ancient Conception of the Lord's Vineyard," *JJS* 40 (1989) 1–6.

Berder, Michel, *La pierre rejetée par les bâtisseurs: Psaume 118,22-23 et son emploi dans les traditions juives et dans le Nouveau Testament* (EtB n.s. 31; Paris: Gabalda, 1996).

Black, Matthew, "The Christological Use of the Old Testament in the New Testament," *NTS* 18 (1971–72) 1–14.

Idem, "The Parables as Allegory," *BJRL* 42 (1959–1960) 273–87.

Blank, Josef, "Die Sendung des Sohnes: Zur christologischen Bedeutung des Gleichnisses von den bösen Winzern Mk 12,1-12," in Joachim Gnilka, ed., *Neues Testament und Kirche: Für Rudolf Schnackenburg* (Freiburg: Herder, 1974) 11–41.

Brooke, George J., "4Q500 1 and the Use of Scripture in the Parable of the Vineyard," *Dead Sea Discoveries* 2 (1995) 268–94.

Brown, Raymond E., *New Testament Essays* (Milwaukee: Bruce, 1965) 254–64.

Bruce, F. F., "New Wine in Old Wine Skins: III. The Corner Stone," *ExpT* 84 (1973) 231–35.

Cahill, Michael, "Not a Cornerstone! Translating Ps 118, 22 in the Jewish and Christian Scriptures," *RB* 106 (1999) 345–57.

Carlston, Charles E., *The Parables of the Triple Tradition* (Philadelphia: Fortress Press, 1975) 40–45, 76–81, 178–90.

Crossan, John Dominic, "The Parable of the Wicked Husbandmen," *JBL* 90 (1971) 451–65.

Dehandschutter, B., "La parabole des vignerons homicides (Mc 12,1-12) et l'évangile selon Thomas," in M. Sabbe, ed., *L'Évangile selon Marc: Tradition et rédaction* (BEThL 34; Leuven: Leuven University Press, 1974) 203–19.

Derrett, J. Duncan M., "Allegory and the Wicked Vinedressers," *JTS* n.s. 25 (1974) 426–32.

Idem, "The Parable of the Wicked Vinedressers," in idem, *Law in the New Testament* (London: Darton, Longman & Todd, 1970) 286–312.

Dodd, C. H., *The Parables of the Kingdom* (rev. ed.; New York: Scribner, 1961) 96–98.

Dombois, Hans, "Juristische Bemerkungen zum Gleichnis von den bösen Weingärtnern (Mk. 12,1-12)," *NZSTh* 8 (1966) 361–73.

Doran, Robert, "Luke 20:18: A Warrior's Boast?" *CBQ* 45 (1983) 61–67.

Drury, John, "The Sower, the Vineyard and the Place of Allegory in the Interpretation of Mark's Parables," *JTS* 24 (1973) 367–79.

Evans, Craig A., "Jesus' Parable of the Tenant Farmers in Light of Lease Agreements in Antiquity," *JSPE* 14 (1996) 65–83.

Idem, "On the Vineyard Parables of Isaiah 5 and Mark 12," *BZ* 28 (1984) 82–86.

Feldman, Asher, *The Parables and Similes of the Rabbis* (2d ed.; 1927; reprinted Folcroft, Pa.: Folcroft Library Editions, 1975) 125–49.

Feldmeier, Reinhard, "Heil im Unheil: Das Bild Gottes nach der Parabel von den bösen Winzern (Mk 12,1-12 par)," *ThBei* 25 (1994) 5–22.

Gozzo, Serafino M., *Disquisitio critico-exegetica in parabolam Novi Testamenti de perfidis vinitoribus* (StAnt 2; Rome: Pontificium Athenaeum Antonianum, 1949).

Grangaard, *Conflict*, 77–98.

Haenchen, *Weg Jesu*, 396–405.

Hengel, Martin, "Das Gleichnis von den Weingärtnern Mc 12,1-12 im Lichte der Zenonpapyri und der rabbinischen Gleichnisse," *ZNW* 59 (1968) 1–39.

Hester, James D., "Socio-Rhetorical Criticism and the Parable of the Tenants," *JSNT* 45 (1992) 27–57.

Horne, Edward H., "The Parable of the Tenants as Indictment," *JSNT* 71 (1998) 111–16.

Hubaut, Michel, *La parabole des vignerons homicides* (CRB 16; Paris: Gabalda, 1976).

Jeremias, Joachim, "Der Eckstein," *Angelos* 1 (1925) 65–70.

Idem, *The Parables of Jesus* (trans. Samuel Henry Hooke; 2d rev. ed.; New York: Scribner, 1972) 70–77.

Jülicher, Adolf, *Die Gleichnisreden Jesu* (2 vols.; Tübingen: Mohr Siebeck, 1910) 2:385–406.

Kingsbury, *Conflict*, 59–61, 98–101.

Idem, "The Parables of the Wicked Husbandmen and the Secret of Jesus' Divine Sonship in Matthew: Some Literary-Critical Observations," *JBL* 105 (1986) 643–55.

Klauk, Hans-Josef, *Allegorie und Allegorese in synoptischen Gleichnistexten* (NTAbh n.s. 13; Münster: Aschendorff, 1978) 286–316.

Idem, "Das Gleichnis vom Mord im Weinberg (Mk 12,1-12; Mt 21,33-46; Lk 20,9-19)," *BibLeb* 11 (1970) 118–45.

Kloppenborg, John S., "Egyptian Viticultural Practices and the Citation of Isa 5:1-7 in Mark 12:1-9," *NovT* 44 (2002) 134–59.

Idem, *The Tenants in the Vineyard: Ideology, Economics, and Agrarian Conflicts in Jewish Palestine* (WUNT 195; Tübingen: Mohr Siebeck, 2006).

Kümmel, Werner Georg, "Das Gleichnis von den bösen Weingärtnern (Mk 12,1-9)," in *Aux sources de la tradition chrétienne: Mélanges offerts à M. Maurice Goguel à l'occasion de son soixante-dixième anniversaire* (Neuchâtel/Paris: Delachaux & Niestlé, 1950) 120–31; reprinted in idem, *Heilsgeschehen und Geschichte: Gesammelte Aufsätze* (2 vols.; MTS 3/16; Marburg: Elwert, 1965, 1978) 1:207–17.

Le Bas, Edwin E., "Was the Corner Stone of Scripture a Pyramidion?" *PEQ* 78 (1946) 103–15.

Idem, "Zechariah's Climax to the Career of the Corner-Stone," *PEQ* 83 (1951) 139–55.

Idem, "Zechariah's Enigmatical Contribution to the Corner-Stone," *PEQ* 82 (1950) 102–22.

Léon-Dufour, Xavier, "La parabole des vignerons homicides," *ScEc* 17 (1965) 365–96; reprinted in idem, *Études d'Évangile* (Paris: Seuil, 1965) 303–44.

Lowe, Malcolm, "From the Parable of the Vineyard to a Pre-Synoptic Source," *NTS* 28 (1982) 257–63.

Maiburg, Ursula, "Christus der Eckstein: Ps 118,22 und Jes 28,16 im Neuen Testament und bei den lateinischen Vätern," in Ernst Dassmann, ed., *Vivarium: Festschrift Theodor Klauser zum 90. Geburtstag* (JAC.E 11; Münster: Aschendorff, 1984) 247–56.

Marcus, Joel, "The Intertextual Polemic of the Markan Vineyard Parable," in Graham N. Stanton and Guy G. Stroumsa, eds., *Tolerance and Intolerance in Early Judaism and Christianity* (Cambridge: Cambridge University Press, 1998) 211–27.

Merli, Dino, "La parabola dei vignaioli infedeli (Mc. 12,1-12)," *BeO* 15 (1973) 97–107.

Milavec, Aaron, "The Identity of 'The Son' and 'The Others': Mark's Parable of the Wicked Husbandmen Reconsidered," *BTB* 20 (1990) 30–37.

Montefiore, Hugh, "A Comparison of the Parables of the Gospel according to Thomas and of the Synoptic Gospels," *NTS* 7 (1960–61) 220–48.

Newell, Jane E., and Raymond R. Newell, "The Parable of the Wicked Tenants," *NovT* 14 (1972) 226–37.

Orchard, J. Bernard, "J. A. T. Robinson and the Synoptic Problem," *NTS* 22 (1975–76) 346–52.

Puig i Tàrrech, Armand, "La paràbola dels vinyaters homicides (Lc 20,9-19) en el context de Lc-Ac," *RCatT* 16 (1991) 39–65.

Quispel, Gilles, "L'Évangile selon Thomas et le Diatessaron," *VC* 13 (1959) 87–117; reprinted in idem, *Gnostic Studies* (2 vols.; Istanbul: Nederlands Historisch-Archaeologisch Instituut in het Nabije Oosten, 1974–75) 2:31–55.

Rese, *Motive*, 171–73.

Ricœur, Paul, "The Bible and Imagination," in idem, *Figuring the Sacred: Religion, Narrative and Imagination* (trans. David Pellauer; Minneapolis: Fortress Press, 1995) 144–66.

Robinson, J. A. T., "The Parable of the Wicked Husbandmen: A Test of Synoptic Relationships," *NTS* 21 (1974–75) 443–61.

Schoedel, William R., "Parables in the Gospel of Thomas: Oral Tradition or Gnostic Exegesis?" *CTM* 43 (1972) 548–60.

Schottroff, Willy, "Das Gleichnis von den bösen Weingärtnern (Mk 12,1-9 parr.): Ein Beitrag zur Geschichte der Bodenpacht in Palästina," *ZDPV* 112 (1996) 18–48.

Schrage, Wolfgang, *Das Verhältnis des Thomas-Evangeliums zur synoptischen Tradition und zu den koptischen Evangelienübersetzungen: Zugleich ein Beitrag zur gnostischen Synoptikerdeutung* (Berlin: Töpelmann, 1964) 137–45.

Schramm, *Markus-Stoff*, 150–67.

Silva, Rafael, "La parábola de los renteros homicidas," *Comp.* 15 (1970) 319–53.

Snodgrass, K. R., "The Parable of the Wicked Husbandmen: Is the Gospel of Thomas Version the Original?" *NTS* 21 (1975) 142–44.

Idem, *The Parable of the Wicked Tenants: An Inquiry into Parables Interpretation* (WUNT 27; Tübingen: Mohr, 1983).

Idem, "Recent Research on the Parable of the Wicked Tenants: An Assessment," *Bulletin for Biblical Research* 8 (1998) 187–216.

van Iersel, Bastiaan Martinus Franciscus, *"Der Sohn" in den Synoptischen Jesusworten: Christusbezeichnung der Gemeinde oder Selbstbezeichnung Jesu?* (NovTSup 3; Leiden: Brill, 1961) 124–45.

Weiser, Alfons, *Die Knechtsgleichnisse der synoptischen Evangelien* (SANT 29; Munich: Kösel, 1971) 49–57.

Weren, W. J. C., "De parabel van de wijnbouwers (Lc 20, 9-19)," in B. M. F. van Iersel, ed., *Parabelverhalen in Lucas: Van Semiotiek naar Pragmatiek* (Tilburg: Tilburg University Press, 1987) 251–80.

9	And he began to tell the people this parable. A man[a] planted a vineyard and let it out to winegrowers. Then he went to another country for a long time. 10/ At the appropriate time he sent a servant to the winegrowers that they should give him some of the fruit of the vineyard. But after the winegrowers had beaten him, they sent him away empty-handed.[b] 11/ Then he decided to send still another servant. But this one too, after they had beaten and disgraced him, they sent away empty-handed. 12/ Then he decided to send a third. But this one also, after they had wounded him, they threw out. 13/ Then the lord of the vineyard said, "What shall I do? I will send my beloved son. Maybe they will respect him." 14/ When they saw him, the winegrowers debated with one another saying, "This is the heir. Let us kill him so the inheritance will be ours." 15/ And after they had thrown him out of the vineyard, they killed him. What then will the lord of the vineyard do to them? 16/ He will come and make the winegrowers perish and give the vineyard to others. When they heard these words they said, "Not on your life!" 17/ Looking at them sharply, he said to them, "How is it then with this word of scripture:[c] The stone which the builders rejected has become the cornerstone?[d] 18/ Whoever falls on this stone will be broken in pieces, and on whomever it falls it will crush."
19	The scribes and the chief priests, in that very hour, tried to lay hands on him. But they feared the people, for they knew that he had told this parable against them.[e]

a Literally: "a human being."
b Literally: "sent him away empty."
c Literally: "this that is written."
d Literally: "the head of the corner."
e Or: "at them."

The tragic history of this vineyard raises formidable questions for all who comment on it. The Lukan version, close to that of the *Gospel of Thomas*, is brilliant in its simplicity and its logic. Must we see it as a version independent of, perhaps even older than, Mark? Are we dealing with a parable, or is it rather an allegory of God's misadventures with the people? Working back from the allegorizing versions of the Gospels, can one recreate the oral version of an original parable? Can what appears to modern readers to be artificial and improbable have been probable and useful in Israel in Jesus' day? Were the quotations that serve as an appendix (vv. 17-18) added to the account by the early Christians, or were they part of Jesus' message from the very beginning? These are the main kinds of interrelated questions that modern exegetes passionately discuss.[1]

---

1 Along with the monographs by Gozzo (*Disquisitio*), Hubaut (*Parabole*), Snodgrass (*Tenants*), and Kloppenborg (*Tenants*), see Jülicher (*Gleichnisreden* 2:385–406); Kümmel, ("Gleichnis"); Dodd (*Parables*, 93–98); Jeremias (*Parables*, 70–77); Léon-Dufour ("Vignerons"); Klauck (*Allegorie*, 286–316).

Synchronic Analysis

Since the approach to Jerusalem, Luke insists on the special links that connect Jesus with the "people" (19:47—20:1; 20:9; cf. 20:6, 19). The Master teaches, and this teaching here takes the form of a parabolic story.[2] After Jesus had been interrupted by the chief priests and their assistants (20:1-8), here he takes up again the thread of his lesson. Indirectly the parable shows a similarity to the course of Jesus' life, which has just arrived at a new stage. According to the evangelist, upon his arrival in Jerusalem Jesus immediately encountered the opposition of the Jewish authorities (19:39, 47-48; 20:1-2, 19).[3] Luke regards the narrative as an announcement of the topic and as a prophecy. In this case the parabolic story performs the same function as the anointing at Bethany at the beginning of Mark's passion narrative (14:3-9). Jesus alludes to what threatens him and demonstrates that his foreknowledge and his obedience go together.

Three brief events (v. 9) set the narrative in motion: (a) the planting of the vineyard; (b) the contract made with the tenant winegrowers; and (c) the master's departure. Everything appears to be simple. Three double clauses express the following events: the successive, unsuccessful sending of three servants (vv. 10-12). Everything becomes complicated. Then, introduced by a question ($\tau\acute{\iota}$ $\pi o\iota\acute{\eta}\sigma\omega$; "What shall I do?" v. 13), comes the central episode, the sending of the son who is not "respected" (vv. 13-15a). The owner remains impotent. The story closes with this man's decision (vv. 15b-16a). This final part begins with a question that resembles that of v. 13: "What then will he do . . .?" ($\tau\acute{\iota}$ $o\mathring{\upsilon}\nu$ $\pi o\iota\acute{\eta}$-$\sigma\epsilon\iota$ . . . ; v. 15b). The owner shows that he is all-powerful.[4]

Then the evangelist mentions the effect of the story on the hearers, which, in turn, provokes a reply from Jesus. The people refuse to accept the decision of the owner of the vineyard (v. 16b), but Jesus counters with a scriptural passage that confirms the truth of his parable (vv. 17-18).

In a narrative conclusion, Luke maintains his distinction between the authorities and the people. To be sure, the people's reaction to the biblical quotation is not mentioned, but the hostility of the scribes and the chief priests, still restrained by the strong popular pressure, is clearly visible (v. 19).

In condensed form:
1. Setting in motion: establishing the plan (v. 9)
2. Unsuccessful attempts to collect rent (vv. 10-12)
3. Central episode: sending the son (vv. 13-15a)
4. The owner's decision (vv. 15b-16a)
5. Final dialogue (vv. 16b-19)

Diachronic Analysis

It is possible that Luke sometimes knows of or finds a simpler and less allegorical form of the story than that of Mark.[5] It seems difficult to allow, however, that he does not depend here on Mark, from whom he takes over so many formulations literally (e.g., $\mathring{\eta}\rho\xi\alpha\tau o$, "he began," v. 9; $\kappa\alpha\grave{\iota}$ $\mathring{\epsilon}\xi\acute{\epsilon}\delta\epsilon\tau o$ $\alpha\mathring{\upsilon}\tau\grave{o}\nu$ $\gamma\epsilon\omega\rho\gamma o\hat{\iota}\varsigma$, "and let it out to winegrowers," v. 9). In the course of the narrative one finds only one or two characteristic expressions of the special material: the inner monologue ("What shall I do?" v. 13),[6] the repeated sending ($\kappa\alpha\grave{\iota}$ $\pi\rho o\sigma\acute{\epsilon}\vartheta\epsilon\tau o$ . . . $\pi\acute{\epsilon}\mu\psi\alpha\iota$, "and he decided still to send," vv. 11, 12). The Lukan peculiarities appear to be either omissions

---

These pages had already been written when I received John S. Kloppenborg's work. I did so with thanks. As much as possible I have tried to take this remarkable monograph into account in the footnotes of my commentary. I note here and now that this scholar presents and criticizes numerous modern as well as old interpretations.

2   In addition to the text of Isaiah 5, there is an interesting targum on Isaiah 5 that, along with various Jewish stories and parables, contains some parallels to the Gospel account. See J. F. Stenning, *The Targum of Isaiah* (Oxford: Clarendon, 1949) 16–17; *b. Sanh.* 91ab; *Tanḥ.* קדושים (Buber 38a, 57); *Exod. Rab.*15.19; 30.17; Str-B 1:867–77; Hubaut, *Parabole*, 77–79; Snodgrass, *Tenants*, 21–26.

3   Puig i Tàrrech, "Vinyaters"; Carlston, *Parables*, 76; Klauck, "Weinberg," 127, 144.

4   On the structure of the narrative leading to a climax see Puig i Tàrrech, "Vinyaters," 43; Snodgrass, *Tenants*, 55.

5   For a history of the transmission of the parable that often differs from my reconstruction, see Hubaut, *Parabole*, 105–14; Snodgrass, *Tenants*, 41–71; Kloppenborg, *Tenants*, 271–77. Van Iersel (*Sohn*, 140) offers a presentation of the original form of the parable.

6   The literary origin of this question is uncertain. Luke can draw his inspiration from the next words in Mark's text (Mark 12:9: $\tau\acute{\iota}$ [$o\mathring{\upsilon}\nu$] $\pi o\iota\acute{\eta}\sigma\epsilon\iota$, "what will he [now] do"), from the thoughts of the master

(e.g., in the initial description of the vineyard in v. 9) or stylistic or logical improvements (e.g., in the sending of the servants in vv. 10-12). Of course, it may be that the Markan version that Luke reworks is different from, more compact than, the Markan version we know. How, furthermore, are we to explain Luke's similarities to the *Gospel of Thomas* logion 65?[7] It is true that the *Thomas* logion may follow Luke, but it may also be familiar with a pre-literary version of Mark, Luke's special material, or an oral tradition. It is a difficult decision. I lean toward the following solution: Luke follows Mark, but he also knows and on occasion is inspired by a parallel version, one that may come from his special material.[8] For its part *Thomas* must be based on an orally transmitted version and on Luke.[9]

In the first part (v. 9), Luke follows his customary practice of preferring the singular "parable"

($παραβολή$) over Mark's plural, and he chooses the sequence subject–verb–direct object ("A man planted a vineyard"; Mark offers the sequence object–subject–verb). Like *Thomas,* he ignores the work of preparing the vineyard, which in Mark is clearly influenced by Isaiah 5. If I do not know why Luke acts as he does, I at least understand that the length of the master's absence is important to him (he adds $χρόνους$ $ἱκανούς$, "a long time," v. 9). *Thomas* mentions neither the absence nor its duration.

In the second part (vv. 10-12), Luke composes a crescendo. With the first envoy he repeats what Mark says: The servant is *beaten*,[10] then sent back *with empty hands*.[11] The sad fate of the second envoy[12] is that he is beaten, *insulted*, and sent back with empty hands (Mark, who also mentions the insulting, appears to add that the head is wounded).[13] As for the third envoy, in Mark he is killed,

---

of the vineyard in Isa 5:4-5, or from his special material, which is fond of inner dialogue (see n. 39 below).

7 These connections were examined as soon as the *Gospel of Thomas* was discovered. See Quispel, "Évangile"; Montefiore, "Comparison," 226–27, 236–38 (*Gos. Thom.* uses an independent and primitive version); Schrage, *Thomas–Evangelium,* 137–45 (the version of the *Gos. Thom.* is a mixed form made up of elements from the Synoptic versions); Crossan, "Husbandmen" (the version of the *Gos. Thom.* is closer to the original than are the Synoptic versions); Dehandschutter, "Vignerons" (*Gos. Thom.* 65 is an adaptation of Luke 20:9-19); Schoedel, "Thomas," 557–60 (compared to Luke, *Gos. Thom.* is secondary); Snodgrass, "Husbandmen" and *Tenants,* 111 (against the priority accorded to *Gos. Thom.* 65); Baarda, "Cornerstone."

8 By contrast, Black ("Allegory," 280–81) thinks that Luke follows his source (S^{Lk} or Q) and occasionally is influenced by Mark. Schramm (*Markus-Stoff,* 166) concludes his analysis by saying that Luke combines here Mark and a traditional parallel version, which has traits older than Mark's version. A rigorous analysis of Luke's re-reading of Mark comes from the pen of Kloppenborg (*Tenants,* 201–18).

9 Various scholars have imagined the parable as it actually came from the mouth of Jesus. According to Crossan ("Husbandmen," 464–65), Jesus tells the shocking story of a successful murder (the punishment was not yet part of the story) in order to encourage all to seize their chance in times of crisis. Hester ("Tenants") thinks that Jesus originally

wanted to incite the tenant farmers to revolt against the large landowners who deliberately ignore the Hebrew concept of inheritance. Lowe ("Vineyard") supposes that in its primitive, pre-Matthean form the parable referred to John the Baptist as the "son" and not to Jesus. Horne ("Indictment") disagrees with Hester ("Tenants") and thinks that Jesus' hearers, who themselves were peasants and winegrowers, asked who had the right interpretation of the Mosaic Law about the distribution of land. The lord of the vineyard is God, and the homicidal winegrowers represent the priestly class. The Newells ("Parable," 226, 235–37) suggest that the parable attacks the brutal methods of the Zealots, who took the life and goods of their adversaries, especially those who were foreigners. Kloppenborg (*Tenants,* 350–51) goes back to a form of the parable earlier than the Gospels of Mark and *Thomas* and concludes "that a reading of the 'originating structure' of the parable as critical of wealth inheritance, and status is the most coherent one." I do not think that was the point of the parable.

10 Luke changes the parataxis from two coordinated verbs to an aorist participle ("after they had beaten him") and a main clause ("they sent him away").

11 In vv. 10-11 $κενόν$ means the hands were empty, empty-handed.

12 $ἕτερος$ does not mean only the other of two but also, as here, another of several. Mark has $ἄλλος,$ "any other."

13 The text of Mark 12:4 is poorly attested. The manuscripts waver between $ἐκεφαλαίωσαν$, which usually means "to summarize," and a *hapax legome-*

36

in Luke only wounded, thus reserving the supreme pain for the son. Matthew is aware of only two successive sendings. In his case they are groups of envoys (Matt 21:34-36; it may be that he is thinking of older and newer prophets). *Thomas*, like Matthew, also knows of only two sendings prior to that of the son, but, as with Mark and Luke, he mentions only a single envoy each time.

In the third part (vv. 13-15a), the one whom Luke calls here "the lord of the vineyard" (ὁ κύριος τοῦ ἀμπελῶνος)[14]—Luke gets this designation later in Mark (Mark 12:9 par. Luke 20:15)—wonders what he should do. He decides to send his "beloved son." The readers recognize the allusion to the christological designation.[15] This is one of the few places where Luke amplifies Mark's allegorizing, continuing the allegorizing effort by inverting two verbs. The son is thrown out of the vineyard *before* he is killed, just as Jesus, condemned in the city, will perish outside the walls (Heb 13:12-13; Mark: "They killed him and threw him out of the vineyard"). For the rest of the story Luke is content to improve Mark's style. The tenants "discussed among themselves" (Mark: they "said to themselves"). They fomented their plot "so the inheritance may be ours" (Mark: "and the inheritance will be ours").

In the fourth part (vv. 15b-16a), Luke takes over Mark's text with no changes. Such unusual agreement is a weighty argument against the thesis that Luke took over a parallel story in its entirety. For his part, the author of the *Gospel of Thomas* is not familiar with the last part of the parable. He ends it with the murder of the son and concludes with one of his favorite exhortations: "He who has ears, let him hear!" (see *Gos. Thom* 8, 21, 63, 96, etc.).

From its very beginning—a beginning I locate more in the time of the early church[16] than during the life of Jesus—the parabolic story of the murderous winegrowers and the rejected son (בֵּן [*bēn*] in Hebrew) was accom-

panied, interpreted, and supplemented by a scriptural reference to the stone (אֶבֶן [*'eben*] in Hebrew). Such an addition was felt to be necessary, not only to underscore the agreement of Jesus' teaching with that of Scripture but also to add a reference or an allusion to the resurrection of him whom death could not hold fast (see Acts 2:24).[17] Mark 12:10-11, which Matt 21:42 follows to the letter, quotes Ps 117 (118):22-23 according to the LXX. For some inexplicable reason, Luke quotes only v. 22 of the psalm and omits the words "This is the Lord's doing; it is wonderful in our eyes."[18] No less difficult to explain is the saying that Luke adds immediately to the quotation of the psalm: "Whoever falls on this stone will be broken in pieces, and on whomever it falls it will crush" (v. 18). The *Gospel of Thomas*, which contains a compact and not very allegorical form of the parable, also continues with a logion that is certainly independent but immediately follows the parable: "Jesus said, 'Show me the stone the builders rejected; it is the cornerstone.'" Thus, the author of the apocryphal Gospel is aware of the relationship between the parable and the quotation from Psalm 117 (118). Clearly the early Christians were concerned to connect the parable and the scripture theologically, especially to use the stone as a covert way of speaking of the son. They did not all do it the same way, but all of them emphasized that the rejection of the son (and the stone) was not the last word of the story. Where the parable ends according to an ecclesiological logic (the vineyard is given to "others," v. 16), the reference to scripture directs one's attention to Christology. Luke's v. 18, coming after the scripture quotation, undoubtedly reflects a theological intention that in the final analysis returns to the ecclesiological program: Just as the winegrowers in their hostility to the "son" ultimately lose the vineyard, so those who oppose the "stone" will finally be defeated. In fact, Luke joins ecclesiology to Christology: the constitution and survival of God's people depend on the relation

---

non totius Graecitatis ἐκεφαλίωσαν, whose sense we guess to be "to hit on the head." See Hubaut, *Parabole*, 33–35; BDF §108.1, n. 1.

14   *Gospel of Thomas* 65 has "the master."

15   See 3:22: "You are my beloved son"; 9:35: "This is my chosen Son." Van Iersel (*Sohn*, 129–30) brings the parable's Christology closer to texts such as Acts 7:51-52 and Heb 1:1-2; Acts 13:57; John 1:11; 3:16; and Luke 11:45-51.

16   See Haenchen, *Weg Jesu*, 400; Merli, "Parabola," 104.

17   Feldmeier ("Heil," 7–8) contrasts the story's horror and the regard for the stone.

18   Luke quotes Ps 117 (118):22 a second time in Acts 4:11, where he also omits v. 23. Cf. Schramm, *Markus-Stoff*, 151.

established to the "stone," that is, to the "son." Thus, from the very beginning the parabolic story appears to have contained allegorical features, which tended to be especially intense in Mark and Matthew.[19]

Commentary

■ **9** A "man" (ἄνθρωπος—in Matthew this man is an οἰκοδεσπότης, a "house owner"; in *Thomas* the owner is a good man) planted a vineyard. The cultivation of a vineyard was different from that of grain or olive trees.[20] It required special care. Sometimes it was surrounded by a wall and equipped with a well or cistern; sometimes it could also contain a shelter for tools. The vines liked stony ground and needed little water. The work was thankless for the first few years, because one had to wait until the fourth or fifth year before harvesting grapes. Unlike today's seedlings, vines in that day were not grafted. Certain areas, such as the Plain of Jezreel, were more conducive than others to cultivating vines. In theory, only vines were cultivated on a plot of land, but occasionally a fruit tree, such as the fig tree of 13:6, could cohabit with the vines. As is known, businessmen who were city dwellers often bought vineyards and rented them to tenant farmers. We even know the conditions of such transactions. The tenant farmers could pay the rent for the vineyard in kind or in cash. One example is the case of a finance minister of King Ptolemy II Phila-delphus (285–246 B.C.E.) by the name of Apollonius, who owned a vineyard in Beth-Anath in Galilee. This man had an agent named Zenon, who undertook a long voy-age of inspection for his master. A year and a half later another agent, named Glaukias, visited his master's property, accompanied by Melas, the manager of the field.[21] A papyrus provides us with the report of his inspection:

> Once I had arrived at Beth-Anath and had summoned Melas, I visited the plantation and all the rest. It seems to me that he [i.e., Melas] has done adequate and satisfactory work. He said that the vineyard contained 80,000 plants. He also has built a cistern and a rather sizeable dwelling. He had me taste the wine, and I could not tell if it was from Chios or was local.

In the light of this document, there is nothing surprising about the beginning of the parable. The situation is plausible, and the hearers are at ease.

Since the days of the prophet Isaiah, the vineyard, of great value to every landowner, could serve as a meta-phor.[22] The love-smitten poet, for example, could use it, as is the case in the Song of Songs, to describe his beloved (see Cant 1:6; 2:13, 15; 6:11; 7:8-10, 13; 8:11-12). The prophet could also use this metaphor to portray the existence of the one and multifarious people. The readers of Isaiah knew that well. The manuscripts from the Dead Sea have demonstrated that at the time of Jesus the vineyard served as a metaphor for the chosen people (see 4Q500 1).[23] The first Christians, following Jesus, also understood the vineyard in this way.

It is impressive to note that the verb "to produce," "to entrust for a work," "to let out" (ἐκδίδωμι) utilized by

---

19   Certain exegetes have correctly insisted that the distinction between parable and allegory is fluid. See Black, "Allegory"; Brown, *New Testament Essays*, 254–64; Snodgrass, *Tenants*, 13–26; Klauck, *Allegorie*. Feldmeier ("Heil," 9–15) wants us to respect the difference. Although Jülicher (*Gleichnisreden*, 2:406) regarded the passage as an allegory created after Easter by the early Christians, Dodd (*Parables*, 93–98) and Jeremias (*Parables*, 70–76) tried to move from the allegorizing versions of the Gospels back to a parabolic story given by the historical Jesus. See Hengel, "Zenonpapyri," 1–9; Crossan, "Hus-bandmen," 455 ("clearly an allegory"); Kümmel, "Gleichnis," 131 ("a valuable witness for the early church's view of history"). Kloppenborg (*Tenants*, 50–70) concludes that the allegorical elements are

secondary, since they do not appear in the version of *Gos. Thom.* 65.
20   On the cultivation of a vineyard in antiquity in Palestine, see Feldman, *Parables*, 125–49; and Klop-penborg, *Tenants*, 278–349, 355–586.
21   Hengel ("Zenonpapyri," 11–16, 19–31) describes the socioeconomic situation of the region, the system of tenant farming, and in particular the organiza-tion of a viticultural estate. He cites numerous documents, among them the papyrus I quote here (*P.Lond.* VII 1948 inv. 2661). See also Kloppenborg, *Tenants*, 367–70.
22   Klauck, *Allegorie*, 298–300; Hubaut, *Parabole*, 16–26.
23   Baumgarten, "Vineyard"; Brooke, "Use."

the Synoptic Gospels, was used as a technical term for placing a field or a vineyard in tenant farming.[24]

It is understandable that the master's departure is mentioned, since the story is about a large landowner who from time to time comes to visit his lands.[25] It also is an appropriate image for defining the situation of God, who appears to be absent from the world, even though it is God's creation, or of Christ, exalted to the right hand of the Father, whose return is certain, even though its date is not known. Throughout his entire work Luke has no illusions: he reckons with the delay of the parousia. In the similar part of the parable of the minas, he underscored the departure of an $\mathring{\alpha}\nu\theta\rho\omega\pi\sigma\varsigma$ to a distant land (19:12).

■ **10** Mark had already used the term "convenient moment" or "suitable time" ($\kappa\alpha\iota\rho\acute{o}\varsigma^{26}$). Luke stays with this expression, which is appropriate for him. In the life of a vineyard it can refer to the time after the few years needed to produce the first grapes. We should note in passing that the master does not expect to receive the entire harvest, only some of the fruit ($\mathring{\alpha}\pi\grave{o}\ \tauo\hat{v}\ \kappa\alpha\rhoπο\hat{v}\ \tauo\hat{v}\ \mathring{\alpha}μπελ\hat{\omega}νος$, "from the fruit of the vineyard"). Yet even this part is refused him. The servant he had sent[27] returns beaten and $\kappa\epsilon\nu\acute{o}\varsigma$, literally "empty." What thus

far has been a likely story becomes from this point on enigmatic.[28]

The refusal to pay is still understandable (the wine-growers can cite a thousand reasons),[29] but that one would beat the owner's messenger goes beyond the realm of probability. Even if in that time the situation in Galilee was unstable,[30] the author slips here surreptitiously from the image to christological reality. Following the Deuteronomistic line, he is thinking of the fate experienced by the prophets whom God sent (see 13:34).[31]

■ **11** The verbal form $\pi\rho\sigma\acute{\epsilon}\theta\epsilon\tauo$, followed by an infinitive, is unusual in classical Greek. It is found in the LXX, however, to reproduce a Hebrew expression יסף [qal or hiphil + infinitive]) that means that one continues or repeats an action. For example, "Pharaoh . . . continued to sin" ($\Phi\alpha\rho\alpha\grave{\omega}\ . . . \pi\rho\sigma\acute{\epsilon}\theta\epsilon\tauo\ \tauo\hat{v}\ \mathring{\alpha}μαρτάνειν$, Exod 9:34). Luke uses this construction in Acts 12:3: "He also arrested Peter" ($\pi\rho\sigma\acute{\epsilon}\theta\epsilon\tauo\ \sigmaυλλαβεῖν\ \kappa\alpha\grave{\iota}\ \Pi\acute{\epsilon}\tau\rhoον$). Thus, the master sent someone else, another servant.[32] Understanding the text this way, however, ignores the master's intention, his decision and his determination. Thus, I would translate: "Then he decided to send still another servant." Unlike some exegetes, I am reluctant to speak here of a "Semitism" and to see in this "Semitism"

24 BAGD, s.v. $\mathring{\epsilon}\kappa\delta\acute{\iota}\delta\omega\mu\iota$; Hubaut, *Parabole*, 27; Schottroff, "Bodenpacht," 33. On the socioeconomic situation in Palestine, the cultivation of vineyards, and especially the inheritance problems, see Bammel, "Gleichnis"; Derrett, "Parable"; Dombois, "Bemerkungen"; Hengel, "Zenonpapyri"; Derrett, "Allegory"; Snodgrass, *Tenants*, 31–40; Evans, "Tenant" (good analysis of the term $\gamma\epsilon\omega\rho\gamma\acute{o}\varsigma$, "peasant," "tenant farmer"); Schottroff, "Bodenpacht" (important for everything dealing with tenant farming).

25 The verb $\mathring{\alpha}\pi\sigma\delta\eta\mu\hat{\omega}$ initially means "to be absent from the country," "to travel abroad," then "to travel, "to be absent." It is difficult to sense what nuance Luke gives this verb.

26 Using the dative to indicate the point in time in response to the question "when?" is correct. See BDF §200. The absence of the article is not unusual; see BDF §255.

27 On the role of the servants (who represent for the evangelists the prophets), their mission, and their sufferings, see Weiser, *Knechtsgleichnisse*, 49–57.
On the theological range of the verb $\mathring{\alpha}\pi\sigma\sigma\tau\acute{\epsilon}\lambda\lambda\omega$, which is especially appropriate for defining the prophetic mission, see Hubaut, *Parabole*, 28.

28 See Kümmel, "Gleichnis," 122–23; van Iersel, *Sohn*, 141–42; Haenchen, *Weg Jesu*, 399.

29 Hengel ("Zenonpapyri," 26–27) reports a similar, unfruitful effort. According to a letter that a certain Alexander sent to a certain Oryas, Zenon tries to recover the amount of a debt. To do so he sends Straton, his subordinate, who, ill-served by the weak local authority, cannot carry out his assignment and is even driven out of the village ($\mathring{\epsilon}\gamma\beta\alpha\lambda\epsilon\hat{\iota}\nu$ for $\mathring{\epsilon}\kappa\beta\alpha\lambda\epsilon\hat{\iota}\nu$, the same verb as in Luke 20:12). It is *P.Cair.Zenon* 26–27. See also Kloppenborg, *Tenants*, 364–67.

30 See Dodd, *Parables*, 93–94, and those who share his opinion, such as Jeremias, *Parables*, 74–76.

31 The parable doubly reflects a prophetic conscience: by the presence of the envoys and the insistence on the oracle of woe, which concludes it. See Feldmeier ("Heil," 15–16), who refers to Isa 5:1-7; 2 Chr 36:15-16; and *Pesiq. R.* 26/129a. On the connection $\delta\sigma\hat{v}\lambda\sigma\varsigma$– prophet, which he finds obvious, see Brown, *New Testament Essays*, 257.

32 See BAGD, s.v. $\pi\rho\sigma\tau\acute{\iota}\theta\eta\mu\iota$ 1c; BDF §435; Black, "Allegory," 281.

the indication of a version prior to Mark. Based on Acts 12:3, I would speak rather of a "Septuagintalism" and of Luke's effort (or that of his special material, if that is where he got his inspiration on this point) to align his prose with that of the Jewish sages of Alexandria.

While Mark is content with the verb "to send" (ἀποστέλλω), Luke alternates between ἀποστέλλω (v. 10) and πέμπω ("to send," vv. 11-12). He makes a point of avoiding monotony and regards these two verbs as synonyms.

This second[33] servant is not only "beaten," like the first, but also "dishonored." Luke does not tell us what the nature of the insults is,[34] but they must have constituted an attack on the servant's moral respectability or physical integrity. One thinks of the apostle Paul, who speaks of the "more honorable" or "less honorable" parts of the body (1 Cor 12:23). It may be that the poor servant was stripped naked or even underwent some sort of sexual mistreatment.[35]

■ **12** The fate of the third servant is worse than that of both of the others: he is wounded.[36] The blows that had merely landed on the skin of the first two servants here penetrate the flesh of the third. The verb τραυματίζω ("to wound") suggests that blood was flowing. Furthermore, the servant is not only "sent back" (ἐξαπέστειλαν, vv. 10-11); he is "driven out," "expelled" (ἐξέβαλον).

Like Mark's version, Luke's speaks of three rejected envoys. The version of *Thomas* knows only two, corresponding to Matthew's two waves of envoys.[37] How are we to explain this divergence? *Thomas* and Matthew apply to the latter the literary rule of three cases, while Mark and Luke apply it only to the servants and treat the fate of the son separately.[38] It may be that different christological sensitivities account for this divergence. Mark and Luke reflect a "higher" Christology and refuse simply to insert the Son into the succession of the prophets (in this point their version of the parable could be secondary).

■ **13** The "lord of the vineyard" wonders what he should do.[39] He decides to send (πέμπω again; Mark: ἀποστέλλω) his beloved son.[40] Sending the heir can be easily explained: the owner probably has neither the time nor the desire to travel. The son will be able to speak not only with a knowledge of the facts but especially with legitimate authority.[41] The verb "to respect" (ἐντρέπομαι, which initially means "to retreat into oneself," then "to reflect," "to let oneself move," "to feel respect") is surprising, but it is in fact quite appropriate. The servants had been scorned; the son, endowed with his father's honor, should be respected.[42] "Perhaps" (ἴσως), found only in Luke and *Thomas*,[43] calls attention to the allegory, because from the perspective of social reality the master can only expect respect, at the very least with regard to himself and his son. Why does Luke ignore Mark's adverb "finally" (ἔσχατον, Mark 12:6)? Is he not usually interested in references to the temporality of the plan of salvation? Presumably he wants to avoid any connection between the sending of the Son and the end of time.

---

33 Mark 12:4: "Then he sent another servant to them; this one they wounded in the head and insulted."

34 On ἀτιμάζω, see BAGD, s.v.; Weiser, *Knechtsgleichnisse*, 54; Hubaut, *Parabole*, 35.

35 See Étienne Trocmé, *L'Evangile selon saint Marc* (CNT 2; Geneva: Labor et Fides, 2000) 298.

36 The verb τραυματίζω (here and in Acts 19:16) and the substantive τραῦμα (Luke 10:34) are used in the New Testament only by Luke. In the LXX, especially Isa 53:5, the terms from this family of words can designate the fate of the prophets. See Weiser, *Knechtsgleichnisse*, 56–57.

37 The Syriac versions try to reduce the number of envoys to two in order to harmonize with Matthew. This is the case with the Sinaitic Syriac version, which omits Mark 12:4, as well as the Syriac Cureton version, which omits Luke 20:12. See Snodgrass, "Husbandmen," 143.

38 See Black, "Allegory," 282; Robinson, "Husbandmen," 447–48.

39 The inner dialogue (cf. 12:17; 15:17) is characteristic of the special material. See vol. 2 of this commentary on 12:17.

40 As is appropriate in classical Greek, in following the substantive with the adjective Luke repeats the definite article: τὸν υἱόν μου τὸν ἀγαπητόν. Thus, the emphasis is on the son; see BDF §270.1, esp. n. 2.

41 See Hengel, "Zenonpapyri," 30–31.

42 Hubaut (*Parabole*, 42–43) notes that the verb ἐντρέπομαι appears in the LXX in contexts in which God requires repentance from his people (Lev 26:41; 2 Kgs [LXX 4 Kgdms] 22:19; 2 Chr 7:14; 12:7, 12; 30:11; 34:27; 36:12); see also Exod 10:3.

43 ἴσως is a *hapax legomenon* in the New Testament. The use of this adverb here must be to prevent the criticism that God, in spite of divine omniscience,

■ **14-15a** Identical in their sense, the texts of Mark and Luke are different in their form. Luke offers a superior composition, because he more elegantly mentions a discussion among the winegrowers and establishes a clearer cause-and-effect connection between the son's murder and the inheritance of the vineyard.

Some commentators have tried to claim that there was a legal logic behind the winegrowers' behavior—that they would have believed that by killing the heir they could become owners of the property. Admittedly, there is a law according to which those who cultivate the land are regarded as the legitimate owners if the owner neglects his property and does not appear for three years. Here, however, the owner is concerned about his vineyard, and he is not close to dying. As the story is told, it clearly emphasizes the foolish attitude of the winegrowers.[44] Even if local justice has sympathy for the place's winegrowers, it must accuse them for their ill-treatment of the servants and especially for the assassination of the son.[45]

■ **15b-16a** Twice (vv. 10-11) the winegrowers "sent back" the servants with empty hands. Twice (v. 12 and v. 15) they "expelled" someone—first the third servant, then the son. In other words, the son is not allowed to set foot on his father's land, nor is he permitted to lay claim to his right as heir. He will be killed outside the vineyard. Are the winegrowers trying to avoid a curse that would

be placed on the ground if blood were shed on it? Mark, who locates the assassination before the expulsion, had not thought of that. It is more likely that there is an allegorical reason for this change of order. If the son's death points to the crucifixion of Christ, it must take place outside the walls of the holy city, thus outside the vineyard.[46]

Attention is focused exclusively on the relationship between the owner and the winegrowers.[47] The story says practically nothing about what the servants did,[48] or the son. The son in particular appears to be passive, submissive to the father and at the same time subject to the mercy of the winegrowers.[49]

The text says nothing about the father's feelings, his grief or his anger. It concentrates exclusively on what he does. Having been seen as powerless to this point, he suddenly awakens, self-confident and master of his decisions. He makes three decisions: He will come,[50] have the winegrowers put to death, and retake his vineyard in order to give it to others. That the lord of the vineyard has the right of life and death over its farmers does not correspond, I presume, to Jewish, Greek, or Roman law in antiquity. The narrator and his hearers are navigating here in allegorical water. Each reader understands that the story is about God and God's judgments.

The concept of the "others" attracts attention. From the very beginning of the Gospel, Luke knows that no city has the right to lay claim to Jesus. He is also

would have been mistaken; see Snodgrass, *Tenants*, 52–53. Like Léon–Dufour ("Vignerons," 338), I think that on certain points Matthew has preserved traces of the original parable better than Mark or Luke.

44 Derrett ("Parable," 296–308) mistakenly tries to standardize what Ricœur ("Imagination," 155) calls the parable's "narrative extravagance" and to make us believe that in those days one could become an owner simply through assassination.

45 In antiquity, leaving a dead person without burial represents the most extreme cruelty and barbarism; see Kümmel, "Gleichnis," 123.

46 See Robinson, "Husbandmen," 449. The Venerable Bede (*In Luc.* 5.2327–43) already makes this connection.

47 Derrett ("Parable," 289–95) examines this relationship from a legal point of view (to be used prudently in light of the author's sometimes too active imagination). On identifying the servants with the

scriptural prophets, see Weiser, *Knechtsgleichnisse*, 49, 55.

48 *Gospel of Thomas* 65 grants the first servant a certain weight: "He sent his servant so that the workers might give him the fruit of the vineyard. They seized his servant and beat him, almost killing him. The servant went back and told his master. His master said, 'Maybe they did not recognize him.'"

49 A remarkable analysis of the Christology of the "son" in the parable comes from the pen of Blank, "Sendung." This post-Easter (but not yet influenced by Hellenism) Christology is quite old, for in the earliest form of the parable it includes the son in the line of the prophets.

50 The readers remember the action of God, who comes to punish Israel's bad shepherds (Jer 23:2; Ezek 34:10). The verb ἔρχομαι is not used in these passages, but it is present in several apocalyptic and messianic texts (see Hab 2:3; Dan 7:13; vol. 1 of this commentary, 281–82, on 7:18-23).

obligated to "other" cities (4:43). In the course of the chapters the "others" can be the Samaritans, the tax collectors, or the Gentiles. In Acts the author will insist on these "others" who receive the promises and demonstrate a higher level of hearing (Acts 13:46; 18:6; 28:28). For Luke the "others" are, above all, Christians, especially Gentile Christians. Since they are here the future winegrowers responsible for the vineyard, it may be that he is thinking in particular of the persons responsible for the church, of the apostles and then of the pastors of the communities.[51] That had probably not always been the case. The thought may initially have been of Jesus' disciples, called to replace the authorities of the people, then of the Jewish Christians replacing the Jews. In any event, the Christian tradition has rethought and expanded the concept of the people of God. The author of the Gospel of John writes, "I sent you to reap that for which you did not labor. Others have labored, and you have entered into their labor" (John 4:38). Later he mentions, in addition to the Jews, others—Greeks introduced by Philip; they too want to see Jesus. The Johannine Jesus by no means rejects this request (John 12:20-26). Paul offers his gospel first to Israel, then to the nations (Rom 1:16). The Letter to the Ephesians thinks about this relationship between the Jews and the Gentiles and regards the latter as "having been alienated from citizenship in Israel" (Eph 2:12).

The story ends here.[52] It says nothing about how this terrible plan is carried out. The "doom" pronounced on the winegrowers is expressed by the verb Luke uses elsewhere to describe the risk of death incurred by the disciples in the storm (8:24: $\dot{\alpha}\pi\acute{o}\lambda\lambda\upsilon\mu\iota$, "to lose," "to cause to perish"). Paul also resorts to it in an important passage to refer to those who pass up the offer of salvation (1 Cor 1:18). As for the "gift" of the vineyard to others, it is expressed by the verb Luke uses elsewhere to speak of God's generosity: "to give" ($\delta\acute{\iota}\delta\omega\mu\iota$, 11:3, 9, 13; 12:32; 19:13). This verb also has a central theological importance in the Gospel of John (see, e.g., John 1:12, 17; 3:16, 27, 34; 6:11, 27; etc.).

■ **16b-18** Luke likes to include dialogues. He imagines that the hearers react indignantly. He does not specify here who they are. Initially it must be the people who are presented as Jesus' conversation partners in v. 9. Then it must be the Jewish authorities who are not far away (20:1-8) and who evidently feel that the image of the winegrowers is directed at them.

Jesus confronts them with his look and his word.[53] This word is scriptural and, as at decisive moments (see Acts 28:25-28), it is the agreement between the message of scripture and the teaching of Jesus that assures Luke's Christian position. The scriptural passage, quoted already by Mark and later in Acts, is v. 22 of Ps 117 (118).[54] It is a principal scriptural witness for the early Christians. Doubtless the passage was used initially by Aramaic-speaking believers, since it makes a play on the words "son" (בֵּן) and "stone" (אֶבֶן).[55] With the reversal it also was able to account for the failure of the cross (the stone rejected by the architects)[56] and to emphasize the providential character of the resurrection (the stone

---

51 The prophetic writings (Jer 23:1-4; Ezek 34:1-31) already speak of the divine judgment on Israel's bad shepherds and of the coming of God, who will care for his people and then will install another or other shepherds. On these "others," see Kümmel, "Gleichnis," 127–28: the vineyard represents not Israel but the kingdom of God. The "others" represent the eschatological people of God, the Christians, Jews, and Gentiles among whom this eschatological gift is presently deposited (Merli, "Parabola," 100).

52 In *Gos. Thom.* 65 the story ends with the murder of the son.

53 The dative αὐτοῖς can refer to ἐμβλέψας ("he is looking at them"), to εἶπεν ("he is speaking to them"), or more probably, as is Luke's custom, to both ("he looks at them and he speaks to them").

54 See also Isa 28:16. On the quotation from Psalm 117 (118) and the metaphor of the stone, see Jeremias,

"Eckstein"; Le Bas, "Corner Stone"; Rese, *Motive*, 171–73; Bruce, "Stone"; Hubaut, *Parabole*, 61–66; Maiburg, "Eckstein" (the author draws a distinction between a christological sense and then an ecclesiological sense of the biblical quotation; after that she brings a rich collection of quotations from the Latin fathers, most of whom take over the ecclesiological interpretation); Baarda, "Cornerstone"; Berder, *Pierre*; Cahill, "Cornerstone" (Ps 117 [118]:22 is about neither a cornerstone nor a keystone but the stone located visibly at the crown).

55 See already John Lightfoot (1602–1675), *A Commentary on the New Testament from the Talmud and Hebraica, Matthew–1 Corinthians* (4 vols.; 1859; reprinted Grand Rapids: Baker, 1979) 2:435; Snodgrass, *Tenants*, 113–18.

56 The verb ἀποδοκιμάζω, translated as "to reject,"

that became the cornerstone).[57] Other biblical texts that speak of the "stone" serve to complete the image. The stone is also a stumbling block that announces the hardening of Israel. In chap. 2, Luke has already referred discreetly to this text, Isa 8:14. He has Simeon say, "Behold, this child is destined for the falling and the rising of many in Israel, and for a sign of contradiction" (2:34). The word "stone," functioning as a hook, allows the statement to call to mind this additional meaning of stone, not found in Ps 117 (118):22.[58] Yet it does so only partially. It speaks only of the unhappy human contacts with this stone (not of the "raising up" announced in 2:34). In this case one wonders whether v. 18 has not been influenced by Dan 2:34-35 (the apocalyptic stone that destroys the statue with the clay feet).[59]

Two cases, both negative, are considered: (a) if someone falls on the stone, it has the last word; (b) if the stone falls on someone, the stone will still have the upper hand. The alternative of 2:34, which, along with the disastrous fall still offered a favorable outcome, vanishes. In addition, the images that the saying evokes make sense only allegorically: (a) those who believe they can cast on the stone all the weight of their fall ($\pi\hat{\alpha}\varsigma$ $\dot{o}$ $\pi\epsilon\sigma\grave{\omega}\nu$ $\dot{\epsilon}\pi\grave{\iota}$ $\dot{\epsilon}\kappa\epsilon\hat{\iota}\nu o\nu$ $\tau\grave{o}\nu$ $\lambda\acute{\iota}\vartheta o\nu$) will find themselves broken ($\sigma u\nu\vartheta\lambda\alpha\sigma\vartheta\acute{\eta}\sigma\epsilon\tau\alpha\iota$),[60] and (b) those who will have the misfortune to see the stone falling on them ($\dot{\epsilon}\varphi'$ δ' $\ddot{o}\nu$ $\pi\acute{\epsilon}\sigma\eta$), will feel how it crushes them ($\lambda\iota\kappa\mu\acute{\eta}\sigma\epsilon\iota$ $\alpha\dot{u}\tau\acute{o}\nu$).[61] The entire statement is puzzling. Luke does not say that the scriptural quotation ended with the previous verse. Nor does he claim that the sentence comes from scripture. He also does not claim that he is the author of this proverbial saying. Is it then a fragment of the special material, a free-floating saying, a quotation from an apocryphal book or a passage from a collection of *testimonia*?[62] Numerous manuscripts of Matthew know the statement and transmit it in Matt 21:44, after the quotation from Psalm 117 (118). It is preceded there by an introduction attributing it to Jesus (and not to scripture) along with a comment explaining that "the kingdom of God will be taken from you and given to a people producing its fruits" (Matt 21:43). The presence of the statement in these manuscripts of Matthew is doubtless due to the influence of Luke.[63] It is not a statement to be attributed to the Sayings Source.[64]

■ **19** Luke ends the pericope by returning to Mark's text (Mark 12:12) and writing it in his style: The Jewish leaders (see 19:47-48; 20:1; only the scribes and chief priests are named, not the elders) seek to arrest Jesus. The verb "to seek" ($\zeta\eta\tau\acute{\epsilon}\omega$), which comes from Mark, makes it possible for Luke to express the movement of the human will, which, depending on the passage, can be positive (see 11:9) or, as here, negative. For fear of the people, the leaders hesitate to act. (Luke replaces Mark's "the crowd" ($\ddot{o}\chi\lambda o\varsigma$) with "the people" ($\lambda\alpha\acute{o}\varsigma$, a term he likes because of its ecclesiastical connotation.)[65] They have understood ($\ddot{\epsilon}\gamma\nu\omega\sigma\alpha\nu$) that the parable was meant

means precisely "to reject after an examination," "to repel/spurn after a test," "to disapprove."

57 On the "stone" in *Gos. Thom.* 66, see Baarda ("Cornerstone"), who comes to the following conclusion: One cannot say here that the *Gospel of Thomas* is prior to the Synoptic tradition or that there is a relationship between the apocryphal Gospel and the *Diatessaron*. It is also not advisable to speak of Semitism in connection with *Gos. Thom.* 66.

58 On v. 18, see Bornkamm, "$\lambda\iota\kappa\mu\acute{\alpha}\omega$," *TDNT* 4 (1967) 280–81; Rese, *Motive*, 171–73; Doran, "Boast"; Snodgrass, *Tenants*, 65–71, 105 n. 143.

59 See Black, "Use," 11–14.

60 On $\sigma u\nu\vartheta\lambda\hat{\omega}$ ("to press," "to crush") see BAGD, s.v.

61 On $\lambda\iota\kappa\mu\hat{\omega}$ ("to winnow," "to crush," "to trample"), see BAGD, s.v. In Dan 2:44 the verb is read according to Theodotion's version.

62 See Rese, *Motive*, 173. In my opinion, Luke regards this statement as a quotation from scripture. It is

an indication of how freely he deals with the sacred text.

63 See Bornkamm, "$\lambda\iota\kappa\mu\acute{\alpha}\omega$," *TDNT* 4 (1967) 281 n. 7; Metzger, *Commentary* (2d ed.), 47. Luz (*Matthew 21–28*, 36 n. 11) differs, thinking this verse belongs to the text of Matthew.

64 The *Five Gospels* of the Jesus Seminar (378) and James M. Robinson and his colleagues (*The Critical Edition of Q: Synopsis Including the Gospels of Matthew and Luke, Mark and Thomas with English, German, and French Translations of Q and Thomas* [Hermeneia Supplements; Minneapolis: Fortress Press, 2000) pay scarcely any attention to Luke 20:18 and its parallels in some manuscripts of Matt 21:44. The Jesus Seminar is satisfied to regard this sentence as the product of early Christianity.

65 Puig i Tàrrech, "Vinyaters," 54–59.

for them.[66] Even if it was addressed to the people, it was aimed at their leaders, who did not cultivate the vineyard on behalf of the Lord.

History of Interpretation

The earliest reception of the parable in the *Shepherd of Hermas* is curious. In a vigorous passage, the Shepherd explains to Hermas that true fasting is not the ascetic exercise to which he is compelled but the practice of virtue; it thus consists of moral and not ritual obedience (*Hermas, Sim.* 5.1.1–5). To explain what he means, the Shepherd tells a parable, which—and that is what is interesting about the passage—is simply a positive version of the parable of the murderous winegrowers (*Hermas, Sim.* 5.2.1–11). The slave to whom the vineyard is entrusted fulfills his function here to perfection. He even goes to such lengths as to dig out the weeds. On his return the master is delighted with the results, discusses it with his son, frees the slave, and wants to make him co-heir with his son. Before he has time to do so, the master learns of another of his slave's good deeds: he shared with his companions the food his master had sent for him.[67]
One more reason to grant him the promised freedom. In an optimistic way, this text describes for us what the vineyard of the Lord can become in the hands of the "others," the new winegrowers—how the Christian life takes place and how pastoral ministry is practiced. It also reminds us that obedience opens the way to freedom.

The latter is not, as with Paul (see Rom 7:24—8:2; 2 Cor 3:17; Gal 5:1), a gift to those who believe on the basis of an efficacious act of God; it is given to those who keep the commandments with a pure heart.[68]

At the time when the parable of the winegrowers attracted the attention of Hermas, Marcion completely ignored it and even eliminated it from his gospel, undoubtedly because it assumed too strong a continuity between the prophets of old and the Son of the new covenant.[69]

In response to Valentinus, but also to Marcion, Irenaeus recalls the parable of the murderous winegrowers. He interprets it in terms of the plan of salvation before concluding, "One and the same God Father planted the vineyard, led the people out, sent the prophets, sent his Son, and entrusted his vineyard to other winegrowers who bring the fruits to him in their time" (*Adv. haer.* 4.36.2).

Two centuries later[70] Ambrose expresses a special interest in the vineyard of the parable (*Exp. Luc.* 9.23–33). The vineyard (*vinea*) represents the house of Israel. It has been planted by God, who since then has watched over it with great care. Thus, it has been "defended, equipped, prepared" (24). Attracted by the text of John 15, Ambrose then says that Christ is the winestock (*vitis*), and the Christians are the branches. He describes the work in the vineyard and the growth of the plants and fruits with expressions reminiscent of Virgil. Moreover, inspired by the *Georgica*, he describes the grape harvest

---

66   Following the *verba dicendi*, Luke often replaces the simple dative with πρός + accusative. In this case, one must translate, "because they knew he had directed this parable to them." But πρός followed by the accusative can also contain an idea of hostility, which is the case here. In this case, it is necessary to understand, "because they knew it was against them he had directed this parable."

67   This ending appears to be redundant. It is doubtless necessary to read the passage as the confluence of two stories. The first ended with the adoption of the slave as son (the more allegorical version) and the other with the shared meal (the less allegorical version). See Martin Dibelius, *Der Hirt des Hermas* (HNT Ergänzungsband 4; Tübingen: Mohr Siebeck, 1923) 564–65.

68   On this passage of Hermas, see the commentaries by Norbert Brox, *Der Hirt des Hermas* (KEK Ergän-

zungsband 7; Göttingen: Vandenhoeck & Ruprecht, 1991) 301–12; and Carolyn Osiek, *Shepherd of Hermas: A Commentary* (Hermeneia; Minneapolis: Fortress Press, 1999) 168–72.

69   See Adolf von Harnack, *Marcion, Das Evangelium vom fremden Gott: Eine Monographie zur Geschichte der Grundlegung der katholischen Kirche* (2d ed.; TU 45; 1924; reprinted Darmstadt: Wissenschaftliche Buchgesellschaft, 1985) 228*; Kenji Tsutsui, "Das Evangelium Marcions: Ein neuer Versuch der Textrekonstruktion," *AJBI* 18 (1992) 67–132, here 119.

70   No sermon or commentary from Origen on the Lukan version of the parable has come down to us. On his interpretation of Matthew's version, see Luz, *Matthew 21–28*, 38–39. Origen appears to be one of the few who interpreted the vineyard as the human heart and who understood the parable as an illustration of individual existence.

and the pressing of the grapes by the winegrowers with bare feet.[71] But he does not forget the abused servants— the prophets and Israel's other faithful such as Jeremiah, Isaiah, and especially Naboth.[72]

Cyril of Alexandria stresses other aspects of the parable (*Serm. Luc.* 134).[73] In addition to the judgments against Israel and its leaders, whom unfortunately almost all ancient Christian authors associated with the winegrowers,[74] the bishop of Alexandria is interested in the figure of the master of the vineyard. In his opinion, the fact that the owner is absent for a long time requires an explanation. Since God had revealed himself to Moses in the burning bush, he no longer manifested himself visibly. That does not mean that he ignored his people. That he sent a series of servants, the prophets, proves as much. Finally, how does one explain the master's question, "What shall I do?" According to Cyril, it expresses not the inability of an incompetent person but the reflection in which, for example, a physician engages when faced with a previously incurable disease.[75]

The Venerable Bede—like many others, he follows Jerome on this point[76]—brings the parable of the murderous winegrowers close to that of the workers sent to the vineyard (Matt 20:1-16) (*In Luc.* 5.2236–2387). He develops an interpretation that, in spite of certain differences in the details (e.g., in the identification of the servants sent), has become normative. The owner is God. The vineyard represents Israel. That the master goes away should not be taken literally; it means that God gives people a free will. No fruit comes from Israel except that produced by the envoys. The first to bring fruit was Moses, the second David, and the third the choir of the prophets, as is demonstrated by the law of Moses, the Psalms of David, and the prophetic oracles, which one can still read today. With Jerome's assistance, Bede exonerates God. That the master of the vineyard asks "What shall I do?" (v. 13) is again due to the divine will to protect human freedom.[77] The son's inheritance reverts finally to "others," to the church consisting primarily of Gentiles. The death of the son outside the vineyard corresponds to Jesus' death outside the walls of Jerusalem. The prophecy of Psalm 117 (118):22 has been fulfilled, thanks to the preaching directed to the Gentiles, who, along with the Jews who have become Christians, constitute a city of believers, a temple for God. Whoever stumbles against the stone, that one sins without losing the possibility of repentance. Whomever the stone strikes, that is the person who denies Christ, refuses to repent, and is condemned.

The Christian exegesis of the parable was firmly set in late antiquity. It is characterized by a number of constant elements: the reference to God's plan of salvation, which has been resisted by Israel's repeated disobedience; the christological interpretation of the son and his fate; the

---

71 See Gabriel Tissot's notes (*Traité sur l'Évangile de S. Luc*) on Ambrose's *Expositio evangelii secundum Lucam* (2d ed.; SC 45, 52; Paris: Cerf, 1971–76) 2:152.

72 A fragment of Apollinaris of Laodicea explains the various servant sendings: the first at the time of Elijah; the second at the time of Amos, Hosea, and Isaiah; and the third at the time of Jeremiah, Ezekiel, and Daniel. He then tries to harmonize the three sendings of Mark and Luke with the two sendings of Matthew. See frg. 8 in Reuss, *Lukas-Kommentare*, 6. Thomas Aquinas (*Catena aurea* 20.2.267) quotes a fragment from Basil of Caesarea, who sees in the question of v. 15 (the master wonders what he will do) a sign of the customary benevolence of God, who does not deal severely before he has given a warning, and a fragment from Eusebius of Caesarea, who brings the stone of Luke 20:17-18 closer to Daniel's vision, probably to the vision of Daniel 2. It concerns Jesus' human body.

That it is thrown without the use of a hand speaks of Jesus' modest and virginal birth.

73 See Payne Smith, *Cyril*, 2:623–29. There are four Greek fragments of this sermon in Reuss, *Lukas-Kommentare*, 198–200 (frgs. 303–6).

74 Cyril finds summarized in this parable the entire history of the children of Israel. He accuses them of apostasy and idolatry.

75 The "other" winegrowers, who in the final analysis receive the responsibility for the vineyard, represent the apostles and the ministers of the new covenant. As for the cornerstone, it connects two sections of wall, symbolizing Christ, who unites Jews and Gentiles in himself (Eph 2:15-16 is then quoted).

76 See Jerome *In Matth.* 21:33 (*PL* 26.156–57) whom he follows and the *Glossa ordinaria* Luke 20.9 (*PL* 114.331) and Bonaventure *Comm. Luc.* 20.12 (Bernardini, 504) who follow him.

77 Bede again quotes Jerome *Comm. Matt.* 21.37-38 (*PL* 26:157).

identification of the church or its ministers with the "other" winegrowers; the harmonization of the differences among the Synoptic Gospels (especially concerning the number of envoys); the interpretation *in bonam partem* of the features of the master of the vineyard that might be disturbing (his departure, v. 9; his uncertainty, v. 13); the absence of a distinction between the winegrowers (who are responsible for the vineyard) and the vineyard (the people), which often leads to an uncontrolled attack on the "Jews"; the lack of precision in the interpretation of the "others"—sometimes it is the church made up of Jews and Gentiles, sometimes it is the nations who are happy to be able to turn to Christ. The medieval interpretations[78] down to the modern period[79] of which I am aware change this image little. Not until the rise of the historical-critical methods do the first doubts appear. Does not the parable reflect the time when the church is building its own identity? Should it not, therefore, go back to the earliest epochs of Christianity rather than to the time of the historical Jesus?[80] Moreover, is not the allegorical genre it adopts quite different from the parables[81] that are characteristic of the Nazarene?[82]

Conclusion

The parabolic story belongs to the prophetic genre of an attack on Israel's leaders. It speaks of the human violence that responds to God's efforts on behalf of the people. It also describes the ultimate divine intervention, the sending of the Son, which marks a turning point—the transfer of responsibility to new leaders.

As is the case with any comparison, the text is not unambiguous. In the eyes of some interpreters, the winegrowers can include the entire nation, responsible before its God. From this perspective, the nature of the vineyard changes. Instead of the image of the people, it becomes the image of the divine possessions, even the kingdom of God (see Matt 21:43). That cannot have been the original meaning.

The quotation from Ps 117 (118):22 does not permit us to see in the narrative a rejection of Israel in favor of the nations. Christ the cornerstone brings the two peoples together. As a consequence, here too the nature of the vineyard necessarily changes: the vineyard corresponds to the believers who come from Israel and the nations. In this regard Paul speaks of the two olive trees, the natural olive tree and the grafted olive tree (Rom 11:16-24). That the text does not push the allegory that far suggests another, historical and parenetic, conclusion. The early Christians who tell this story recall Jesus' struggle on behalf of a true leadership in Israel and look forward to authentic leaders for the church of their day. God reserves the freedom to criticize his ordinary servants with the message of his extraordinary envoys.[83]

---

78 See *Glossa ordinaria* Luke 20:9-19 (*PL* 114:331–32); Albertus Magnus *Evang. Luc.* 20.9-19 (602–10); Bonaventure *Comm. Luc.* 20.10–25 (Bernardini, 503–9); Thomas Aquinas *Catena aurea* 20.2–3 (265–68).

79 See Erasmus, *Paraphrasis*, 438–40; Luther, *Evangelien-Auslegung*, 927–30. Calvin (*Harmony*, 3:14–23) tries to read the parable not without an existential implication: It would be wrong to see in it only a single, objective description of the history of salvation without realizing that the parable can be applied to the church at any time; see Luz, *Matthew 21–28*, 39.

For elements of the history of patristic and medieval interpretation, see Silva, "Parábola," 322–26.

80 For Jülicher (*Gleichnisreden*, 2:406) the parable, down to its smallest detail, can be understood only as the "product of early Christian theology."

81 See ibid., 2:402–5.

82 See now in critical perspective the history of interpretation that Kloppenborg (*Tenants*, 7–21) has released.

83 This distinction is important for Calvin (*Harmony*, 3:18–20).

Caesar's Denarius and God's Domain (20:20-26)

Bibliography

Abel, Ernest L., "Jesus and the Cause of Jewish National Independence," *REJ* 128 (1969) 247–52.

Abrahams, Israel, "Give unto Caesar," in idem, *Studies in Pharisaism and the Gospels* (Series 1) (Cambridge: Cambridge University Press, 1917) 62–65.

Barraclough, Ray, "Jesus' Response to Reputation—A Study of Mark 12:14 and Parallels," *Colloquium* 28 (1996) 3–11.

Barrett, C. K., "The New Testament Doctrine of Church and State," in idem, *New Testament Essays* (London: SPCK, 1972) 1–19.

Bea, Agostino, "'Date a Cesare quel che è di Cesare e a Dio quel che è di Dio,'" *CivCatt* 109 (1958) 572–83.

Bori, Pier Cesare, "Date a Cesare quel che è di Cesare . . . (Mt 22, 21): Linee di storia dell'interpretazione antica," *CrSt* 7 (1986) 451–64.

Bornkamm, Günther, *Jesus of Nazareth* (trans. Irene McLuskey and Fraser McLuskey with James M. Robinson; New York: Harper, 1960) 121–24.

Brandon, S. G. F., *The Trial of Jesus of Nazareth* (New York: Stein & Day, 1968) 66–68.

Bünker, Michael, "'Gebt dem Kaiser, was des Kaisers ist!'—aber: was ist des Kaisers? Überlegungen zur Perikope von der Kaisersteuer," in Luise Schottroff and Willy Schottroff, eds., *Wer ist unser Gott: Beiträge zu einer Befreiungstheologie im Kontext der "ersten" Welt* (Munich: Kaiser, 1986) 153–72.

Cassidy, Richard J., *Jesus, Politics, and Society: A Study of Luke's Gospel* (Maryknoll, N.Y.: Orbis, 1978) 55–61.

Castelli, Enrico, "Hermeneutik und Kairos," in Franz Theunis, ed., *Kerygma und Mythos 6.7: Geschichte, Zeugnis und Theologie* (Hamburg-Bergstedt: Reich, 1976) 60–64.

Cullmann, Oscar, *Dieu et César: le procès Jésus, Saint Paul et l'Autorité, L'Apocalypse et l'Etat totalitaire* (Civilisation et Christianisme; Paris: Delachaux & Niestlé, 1956) 20–25.

Cuvillier, Élian, "Marc, Justin, Thomas et les autres: Variations autour de la péricope du denier à César," *EThR* 67 (1992) 329–44.

Dawsey, James M., "Entre César e Deus (Lc 20,20-26)," *REB* 44 (1984) 391–93.

Derrett, J. D. M., "Luke's Perspective on Tribute to Caesar," in Richard J. Cassidy and Philip J. Scharper, eds., *Political Issues in Luke–Acts* (Maryknoll, N.Y.: Orbis, 1983) 38–48.

Idem, "Render to Caesar," in idem, *Law in the New Testament* (London: Darton, Longman, & Todd, 1960) 313–38.

Giblin, Charles Homer, "'The Things of God' in the Question Concerning Tribute to Caesar (Lk 20:25; Mk 12:17; Mt 22:21)," *CBQ* 33 (1971) 510–27.

Goppelt, Leonhard, "The Freedom to Pay the Imperial Tax (Mk 12, 17)," *StEv* 2 (TU 87), 1964, 183–94.

Idem, "Die Freiheit zur Kaisersteuer (zu Mk. 12,17 und Röm 13,1-7)," in Georg Kretschmar and Bernhard Lohse, eds., *Ecclesia und Res Publica* (Kurt Dietrich Schmidt zum 65. Geburtstag; Göttingen: Vandenhoeck & Ruprecht, 1961) 40–50.

Groupe de Dole, "L'impôt à César (Luc 20,20-26)," *SémBib* 18 (1980) 8–15.

Haenchen, *Weg Jesu*, 406–9.

Hart, Henry St. John, "The Coin of 'Render unto Caesar . . .' (A Note on Some Aspects of Mk 12:13-17; Mt 22:15-22; Lk 20:20-26)," in Ernst Bammel and C. F. D. Moule, eds., *Jesus and the Politics of His Day* (Cambridge: Cambridge University Press, 1984) 241–48.

Howgego, C. J., *Ancient History from Coins* (London: Routledge, 1995).

Kennard, J. Spencer, *Render to God: A Study of the Tribute Passage* (New York: Oxford University Press, 1950) (not accessible to me).

Lapide, Pinchas, "Soll man dem Kaiser Steuer zahlen? Jesus und die Politik," *Neue Zürcher Zeitung*, February 18–19, 1984, 69–70.

Loewe, H. M. J., *"Render unto Caesar": Religious and Political Loyalty in Palestine* (Cambridge: Cambridge University Press, 1940).

Owen-Ball, David T., "Rabbinic Rhetoric and the Tribute Passage (Mt 22:15-22; Mk 12:13-17; Lk 20:20-26)," *NovT* 35 (1993) 1–14.

Petzke, Gerd, "Der historische Jesus in der sozialethischen Diskussion. Mk 12,13-17 par," in Georg Strecker, ed., *Jesus Christus in Historie und Theologie: Neutestamentliche Festschrift für Hans Conzelmann zum 60. Geburtstag* (Tübingen: Mohr Siebeck, 1975) 223–35.

Radici Colace, Paola, "L'uomo = nummus nella teologia Agostiniana dell'imago Dei," *Studi tardoantichi* 8 (1989) 401–17.

Rist, Martin, "Caesar or God (Mark 12:13-17)? A Study in Formgeschichte," *JR* 16 (1936) 317–31.

Salin, Edgar, "Jesus und die Wechsler," in Arye Ben-David, *Jerusalem und Tyros: Ein Beitrag zur palästinensischen Münz- und Wirtschaftsgeschichte (126 a.C.–57 p.C.)* (Kleine Schriften zur Wirtschaftsgeschichte 1; Tübingen: Mohr Siebeck, 1969) 49–55.

Schramm, *Markus-Stoff*, 168–70.

Sevenster, J. N. "Geeft den Keizer, wat des Keizers is, en Gode, wat Gods is," *NedThT* 17 (1962–63) 21–31.

Stauffer, Ethelbert, "The Story of the Tribute Money," in idem, *Christ and the Caesars: Historical Sketches* (Philadelphia: Westminster, 1955) 112–37.

Stock, Augustine, "Render to Caesar," *TBT* 62 (1972) 929–34.

Tagawa, Kenzo, "Jésus critiquant l'idéologie théocratique: Une étude de Marc 12,13-17," in *Reconnaissance à S. de Dietrich* (CBFV; Paris: Foi et Vie, 1971) 117–25.

Ukpong, Justin S., "Tribute to Caesar, Mk 12:13-17 (Mt 22:15-22; Lk 20:20-26)," *Bibel Bhashyam* 21 (1995) 147–66.

Vanbergen, P. "L'impôt dû à César," *LV(B)* 50 (1960) 12–18.

Völkl, Richard, *Christ und Welt nach dem Neuen Testament* (Würzburg: Echter, 1961) 112–15.

Weir, T. H., "Luke XX. 20," *ExpT* 28 (1916–17) 426.

20 In their effort to keep him under surveillance they sent spies who pretended to be fair in order to catch him in his words so that they could deliver him to the jurisdiction and authority of the governor. 21/ They asked him saying, "Master, we know that you speak and teach with uprightness and that you do not regard the person but that you teach the way of God according to the truth. 22/ Are we permitted to pay tribute to Caesar or not?" 23/ He saw through their cunning and said to them, 24/ "Show me a denarius. Whose image and inscription does it bear?" They said, "Caesar's." 25/ He said to them, "So then, give back to Caesar what is Caesar's and to God what is God's." 26/ And they were not able to catch him in his words in front of the people, and, admiring his answer, they were silent.

Since Jesus entered the temple, the religious authorities have formed a hostile front and tried to bring down the Master with their questions. The first issue, the problem of the tax (vv. 20-26), is of great importance, and by responding to the question Jesus, whose cause Luke supports, accepts a significant risk.

Even though the dialogue is abbreviated and the final sentence easy to understand, the pericope has led to contradictory interpretations. Some have read in Jesus' answer a criticism of the Zealots, who with their religious enthusiasm and their violent hostility toward the Romans sought to establish or restore God's power.[1] By contrast, others have discovered in it the opinion of an inflammatory Jesus, who was hostile toward the imperialistic might of the Romans and critical of the Jewish collaborators.[2] Still others have seen in it only irony and in this irony a skillful refusal to discuss the subject,[3] since, in fact, the problem of taxes and duties is not important when

---

1 A good presentation of this hypothesis, even if he does not accept it, comes from the pen of Fitzmyer (2:1292–93).

2 See Brandon, *Trial*, 66–68; Abel, "Independence." According to Tagawa ("Idéologie"), Jesus attacks not the Zealots but the Jewish theocrats. In effect, he is refusing to let religion become the opiate of the people. According to Ukpong ("Caesar," 166), "Jesus' statement on the tribute question was not a direct answer to the question asked nor a practical directive but a statement of principle indicat-

ing that the question had to be answered in the light of Caesar's claim vis-à-vis God's claim on the Jewish people. It was for the interlocutors to draw the conclusion themselves, which in effect was that payment of the tribute was not lawful."

3 See Cuvillier, "Marc," 333. According to Giblin ("Caesar," 510) and Fitzmyer (2:1292), Søren Kierkegaard, Martin Dibelius, and Albert Schweitzer are on the list of those who hold the "ironic" interpretation. I do not share Robert C. Tannehill's opinion: "This witty reply minimizes the

the end of the world is near and the kingdom of God is imminent. Finally, others have found in it a theological structure that contrasts political power with God's authority.[4]

Analysis

A three-pronged approach makes it possible to determine the sense of this passage: a synchronic analysis of the biblical text in its literary context; a diachronic analysis of the oral tradition from its origins to its written form and then to its canonical and noncanonical repetitions; finally, a sociohistorical analysis of the first century C.E.

Since the account of the approach to Jerusalem (Luke 19:28-40), Luke has resumed his use of the Gospel of Mark. In fact, he follows his model in the pericopes that precede and follow this passage: the question of authority (Luke 20:1-8 par. Mark 11:27-33), the parable of the murderous winegrowers (Luke 20:9-19 par. Mark 12:1-12), the question of the resurrection (Luke 20:27-40 par. Mark 12:18-27), the identity of the Messiah (Luke 20:41-44 par. Mark 12:35-37a), and so on. In addition, nothing in the contents or in the formulations of vv. 20-26 betrays the presence of another source.[5] The minor agreements between Luke and Matthew are insignificant and coincidental.[6]

Luke keeps the structure Mark gave this unit.

a. Introduction: Sending the informers (v. 20)
  b. vocal intervention of these men; initial flattery (v. 21) and insidious question (v. 22)
    c. Jesus' reaction in which he ascertains (v. 23) and questions (v. 24a)
  d. Response of the inquisitors (v. 24b)
    e. Jesus' decisive and final statement (v. 25)
f. conclusion emphasizing Jesus' success (v. 26)[7]

The introduction (v. 20) replaces Mark's Pharisees and Herodians[8] with informants whom Luke describes in moral terms. They are so hypocritical that they boast of their honesty. The harmful intention of these people is described in a less picturesque way than in Mark, who uses the verb $\dot{\alpha}\gamma\rho\epsilon\acute{\upsilon}\omega$, "to catch by hunting or fishing." In Luke they are simply hoping "to seize" Jesus ($\dot{\epsilon}\pi\iota\lambda\alpha\mu\beta\acute{\alpha}\nu o\mu\alpha\iota$). Luke clarifies their ulterior motive: they hope to deliver Jesus finally to what Luke grandiosely calls "the power and the authority of the governor."[9] The evangelist changes the first words these agents say in Mark only formally. "You are true" (Mark 12:14) becomes "you speak and teach with uprightness" (v. 21). The too vague "You do not let yourself be influenced by anyone," literally, "you are not concerned with anything [or 'anybody']" (Mark 12:14) disappears, and "you do not take into account people's condition" (Mark 12:14) is replaced by the biblical expression "you do not regard the person."[10] The last part of this *captatio benevolentiae* (Mark 12:14) is perfectly suitable for Luke; he keeps it without

---

importance of the issue being raised" (*Luke* [ANTC; Nashville: Abingdon, 1996] 293).

4 On various interpretations and their defenders, see Bea, "Cesare," 573–74; Derrett, "Render," 313; Giblin, "Caesar," 510–14; Petzke, "Diskussion," 226–27; Ukpong, "Caesar," 148–53; Fitzmyer, 2:1292–93.

5 Cf. Schramm, *Markus-Stoff,* 168–70.

6 Verse 21: $\delta\iota\delta\acute{\alpha}\sigma\kappa\epsilon\iota\varsigma$ ("you teach"; see Matt 22:16); v. 22: the repetition of the question is avoided (see Matt 22:17); v. 24: $\delta\epsilon\acute{\iota}\xi\alpha\tau\epsilon$ ("show"; see Matt 22:19 [$\dot{\epsilon}\pi\iota\delta\epsilon\acute{\iota}\xi\alpha\tau\epsilon$]); v. 25: the imperative $\dot{\alpha}\pi\acute{o}$-$\delta o\tau\epsilon$ ("return") precedes $\tau\grave{\alpha}\ K\alpha\acute{\iota}\sigma\alpha\rho o\varsigma$ ("what is Caesar's"; see Matt 22:21).

7 A good analysis of the Lukan redaction is in Giblin, "Caesar," 517–20.

8 The Pharisees play scarcely any role in the events that take place in Jerusalem, and there is no reason to mention the Herodians here, since Luke's readers know little about them.

9 Manuscript D = 05 (Codex Bezae), the Latin manuscript e (fifth century, preserved in Trent), and the Syriac so-called Curetonian version have only "the governor" instead of "the jurisdiction and authority of the governor."

10 See Deut 10:17; Dan 2:8 LXX; Sir 35:12-13; Rom 2:11; 1 Pet 1:17; Jas 2:1. At a decisive point of his work Luke attributes this quality to God: in Peter's speech to the first Gentile convert, the centurion Cornelius (Acts 10:34-35). The divine impartiality must have been a constant element in Christian catechesis.

any change: "But you teach the way of God according to the truth" (v. 21). With two exceptions, the same is true of the question with which the informers hope to bring Jesus down: "Are we permitted to pay tribute to Caesar or not?" (v. 22). The two exceptions are these: Luke prefers the Greek term for "tribute" ($\phi\acute{o}\rho o\varsigma$) over the Latin loanword for "tax" ($\kappa\hat{\eta}\nu\sigma o\varsigma$).[11] In addition, he regards as redundant the repetition of the question he reads in the Gospel of Mark: "Should we pay or not pay?" (12:14).

In his own description of Jesus' original reaction, the evangelist makes the following changes: For him Jesus "observes," "reflects," or "considers" ($\kappa\alpha\tau\alpha\nu o\acute{e}\omega$, v. 23) while according to Mark he simply "knows" ($o\hat{\iota}\delta\alpha$, Mark 12:15). What he observes is their "deceit" or "malice" ($\pi\alpha\nu o\nu\rho\gamma\acute{\iota}\alpha$)[12] and not their hypocrisy ($\acute{\upsilon}\pi\acute{o}\kappa\rho\iota\sigma\iota\varsigma$, Mark 12:15); to that he had already called attention in v. 20 ($\acute{\upsilon}\pi o\kappa\rho\iota\nu o\mu\acute{e}\nu o\upsilon\varsigma$, "who pretended").

The evangelist simplifies Jesus' initiative. He does not think it is necessary to say, "Why are you trying to trap me?" (Mark 12:15),[13] and he does not wait to get the denarius before asking what is on the coin (v. 24; see Mark 12:15-16).

In Luke, the decisive dialogue (vv. 24-25) resembles the conversation in Mark (12:16-17) so much that one could well mistake the one for the other. There is, at the most, a stylistic difference here or there.[14] As one would expect, Luke, who out of respect changes little in the words of Jesus, is not at all reluctant to change the narrative part (the staging or, as here, the conclusion). Verse 26 is a free, Lukan variation of Mark's abrupt ending ("And they marveled at him," Mark 12:17). Noteworthy is the skillful *inclusio* (the verb $\acute{e}\pi\iota\lambda\alpha\mu\beta\acute{a}\nu o\mu\alpha\iota$ ["seize, catch," v. 20] reappears in v. 26 with an elegant variation:

$\acute{\rho}\hat{\eta}\mu\alpha$ ["word"] instead of $\lambda\acute{o}\gamma o\varsigma$ ["talk, remark, word"] and the mention of the success of Jesus who with his "answer" ($\acute{a}\pi\acute{o}\kappa\rho\iota\sigma\iota\varsigma$) reduced his adversaries to silence ($\acute{e}\sigma\acute{\iota}\gamma\eta\sigma\alpha\nu$, "they were silent").

In spite of these numerous differences in detail, Luke's account corresponds to that of Mark. The same is true of Matthew, who also has followed Mark. We have here a unit one cannot dismantle. The question, showing the denarius, and Jesus' final statement constitute an apophthegm, which quickly began to circulate among the early Christians.[15]

The three Synoptic Gospels unanimously disparage Jesus' questioners for political or moral reasons. The same is true of a noncanonical Gospel fragment, the *Papyrus Egerton* 2. Published in 1935, this papyrus presents the same episode as the Synoptic Gospels, but it offers a completely different ending. It emphasizes the controversy and portrays an accusing Jesus. Instead of the response, "Render to Caesar what is Caesar's," *Papyrus Egerton* 2 describes an angry Jesus who, quoting the prophet Isaiah, condemns the people who honor God only with their lips. The author of this fragment found in the oral tradition a polemical version of the episode and kept of it only the judgment.[16]

The text of *Gos. Thom.* 100 is even shorter than that of Mark; it does not condemn Jesus' conversation partners at all. It furthermore presents a scenario different from that of the Synoptics. The conversation partners take the initiative by showing Jesus a (here golden) coin. Strictly speaking, they do not ask him a question; they remind him of the reality. In substance, they say that the Romans and their emperor require us to pay taxes. Jesus reacts as he does in the Synoptic Gospels, teaching that they

---

11   On $\kappa\hat{\eta}\nu\sigma o\varsigma$, see BAGD, s.v.

12   Infected by Matthew, a number of witnesses of Luke offer here the term $\pi o\nu\eta\rho\acute{\iota}\alpha$ ("maliciousness," "ruse," "cunning").

13   Influenced by Matthew and Mark, the scribes of many manuscripts insert these words here in v. 23 in Luke's text. See the critical apparatus of Nestle-Aland (27th ed.).

14   As is his practice, Luke offers here $\tau\acute{\iota}\nu o\varsigma$ $\acute{e}\chi\epsilon\iota$ + accusative (v. 24) instead of $\tau\acute{\iota}\nu o\varsigma$ + the implied verb "to be" (Mark 12:16); $\pi\rho\acute{o}\varsigma$ + accusative after a *verbum dicendi* (v. 25) (Mark has the dative after the verb "to say," Mark 12:17). In addition, $\tau o\acute{\iota}\nu\upsilon\nu$,

"thus," "well," before the imperative "render" can contain a suggestion of irony.

15   See Bultmann, *History*, 26, 48; Giblin, "Caesar," 514–17; Haenchen, *Weg Jesu*, 407. Following David Daube, Owen-Ball ("Tribute") is of the opinion that the pericope's literary genre corresponds to a rabbinic pattern called "the pattern of forensic interrogation."

16   On *Papyrus Egerton* 2, see Daniel A. Bertrand, "Fragments évangéliques," in François Bovon, Pierre Geoltrain, and Jean-Daniel Kaestli, eds., *Écrits apocryphes chrétiens* (2 vols.; Bibliothèque de la Pléiade 442; Paris: Gallimard, 1997) 1:412–16.

should give to Caesar what is due him and to God what belongs to him. What is original in the *Gospel of Thomas* is the way the statement continues; it consists of three terms rather than of two. The third, christological element is: "and give me what is due me."[17] Undoubtedly, the *Gospel of Thomas* is based here not on the Synoptic Gospels but on a parallel oral version. In certain points this version is less developed than that of the Synoptic Gospels (the conversation partners are not yet treated unfavorably). In other ways, it is more developed. The coin has become a gold piece, and the Christology is firmly established in the sentence.[18]

Justin Martyr, who relates the episode in an apologetic context, undoubtedly also makes use of an oral form of the episode (*1 Apol.* 17.2). He has just affirmed that Christians pay their taxes. By doing so, he adds, they respect the teaching of their Master: "Because at this time some came to ask him if it was necessary to pay tribute to Caesar, and he answered: Tell me, whose image is on the coin?—They said, Caesar's, and he answered: Then give Caesar what is Caesar's and God what is God's." As in the *Gospel of Thomas*, with Justin Jesus' questioners are not evil-minded, and their question is legitimate. In addition, only the image is mentioned, not the inscription. As for the formulations, they do not follow any particular Gospel. The vocabulary is sometimes reminiscent of Matthew ($\nu\acute{o}\mu\iota\sigma\mu\alpha$ ["money"], Matt 22:19; "therefore" ($o\mathring{v}\nu$) after the imperative "give," Matt 22:21), sometimes of Luke ($\phi\acute{o}\rho o\varsigma$ ["tribute"], Luke 20:22, admittedly in the plural in Justin). Like the author of the *Gospel of Thomas*, Justin transmits an oral version

of the episode that begins with a legitimate question that Jews as well as Christians would ask. I am not convinced by the hypothesis that the *Gospel of Thomas* and Justin Martyr changed the story to exonerate Jesus' questioners, who initially were hostile to the Master.[19] From the perspective of form criticism, one would say that both the hostility of the conversation partners in the canonical Gospels and the christological addition to the reply in the *Gospel of Thomas* are secondary elements.[20]

Thus, it seems that the episode circulated in two forms: the form behind the Synoptic Gospels and the form one might find behind Justin and *Thomas*. The latter was unaware of or ignored the polemic and kept only Jesus' teaching. These two forms of the narrative had their roots in the different ways the same episode was remembered. It is probably historically true that Jesus had been asked whether one was obligated to pay taxes to the Romans or not. Then each one remembered how the Master got out of the situation brilliantly by using a coin and making a concise statement evoking God and Caesar. Without forgetting the origin of the episode, some people—from Mark, through Luke, to the *Papyrus Egerton* 2—emphasized the initial question posed to Jesus, a question that quickly was understood to be a test, then a trap. Others—from *Thomas* to Justin—underscored the quality of Jesus' answer, on which they conferred a universal ethical scope.

The historian of antiquity understands why there were some among the first Christians who could think of the initial question as a trap.[21] For centuries Israel had experienced a foreign power in its land and had looked

---

17   On *Gos. Thom.* 100, see Bertil Gärtner, *The Theology of the Gospel according to Thomas* (trans. Eric J.Sharpe; New York: Harper, 1961) 32–33; Richard Valantasis, *The Gospel of Thomas* (New York: Routledge, 1997) 180–81.

18   Concerning logion 100 of the *Gospel of Thomas*, I do not think it is necessary to set God against Jesus and to see in God the demiurge, understood negatively (contra Cuvillier, "Marc"). Most exegetes incorrectly regard the entire version of the episode in the *Gospel of Thomas* as a secondary reading of the original Synoptic form.

19   On this point my interpretation differs from that of Cuvillier, "Marc," 341–42.

20   Cuvillier ("Marc") examines the six versions of this episode and concludes that the three noncanonical

versions are forms of the "reception" of the three canonical versions.

21   See the important article by Abrahams ("Caesar," 62–65), which shows well that the problem posed to Jesus was old and topical. He refers to Jer 29:7; Dan 8:16; Qoh 8:2 and cites Johanan ben Zakkai (a rabbi of the first century C.E.), Samuel of Nehardea (165–257 C.E.), and the rabbi Nahum ben Simai, who was famous for his holiness because he had never looked at the image on a coin. See also Stauffer, "Tribute Money," 115–32; Cullmann, *César*, 11–26; Derrett, "Render," 316–23; Lapide, "Steuer." Finally, see Bea ("Cesare," 574–77), who adds other references: Dan 2:21, 37-38; 4:14, 29; Wis 6:1-11; *1 Enoch* 46:5; *2 Bar.* 82:9; 1 Clem. 4.5; 14.1; 60.4; 61.1; 1 Tim 2:1-2; Rev 13:1-8. Goppelt

---

for ways of preserving its faith (which originally made little or no distinction between religious and political areas) in spite of the occupation. Since the law had been written at a time when the question had not yet arisen, the prophetic books, and especially the Writings, sought an acceptable solution of God's requirements and the constraints of the foreign sovereigns. The search for a solution did not take place without trials or dissensions. A minority in Israel argued for a faith without compromise: one had to resist foreign occupation, refuse to pay tribute, and try to drive out the aggressor by means of armed struggle. Judas of Gamala began his resistance by refusing to pay any tax to the Romans.[22] He is but the best-known example of an attitude that flares up any time oppression becomes intolerable. Another minority did not avoid contact with the occupation forces. It is not too much of an exaggeration to say that this option resembled what during the Second World War was called collaboration. Various aristocratic and priestly families did not hesitate to play this card. Theological reflection, in particular of the Pharisees, opens a third way of interpretation, which finally becomes normative in Israel and then in the church of the first centuries. It is important to distinguish between God's authority and that of the prince. As long as political power limits its ambitions to the realm of this world, believers can and indeed must accept it. On the other hand, as soon as it exceeds its rights and demands unconditional submission, or even religious veneration, believers must criticize it and organize nonviolent resistance. Thus, martyrs mark the limits of political power with their blood. Yet, before blood flows, the religious community has time "to give back to Caesar what is Caesar's." By asking Jesus about the tax owed to the Roman occupier, Jesus' questioners thus raise a well-known, delicate, and controversial subject of burning topicality. They were not wrong to ask the question, and their intention was not necessarily perverse.[23]

Commentary

■ **20** Luke, who is skillful and resolute in introducing the theme, chooses language that is precise and even unusual. The rare (it appears only here in the entire New Testament) substantive adjective ἐγκάθετος ("agent," "informer") enables him to lay out the situation: there are people confronting Jesus, "the scribes and the chief priests" (v. 19), who "observe," "watch," "spy on" him (these are the nuances of the verb παρατηρέω).[24] They do this from a distance and in the shadows by making use of "agents," "informers." Formerly one would have referred to them as "people who lie in wait or waylay"; today one might even call them "undercover informants" (these are the possible translations of ἐγκάθετος). These men dare to approach Jesus. Luke reproaches them not only for their visible expression of opposition to Jesus but also for hiding their criminal intention (to deliver an innocent man)[25] under the cover of righteousness. Thus, this alleged morality will be used to achieve the worst kind of political goal. These people will distort the Master's teaching and accuse him before Pilate of refusing to pay taxes to Caesar (23:2).[26] Luke anticipates here Jesus' arrest and announces that Jesus will appear

---

("Kaisersteuer") does not give enough attention to the Jewish roots of the solution Jesus adopts.

22   See Josephus *Bell.* 2.8.1 §118; Acts 5:37; Origen *Comm. Matt.* 17.25 (*Origenes Werke* [12 vols.; GCS; Leipzig: Hinrichs, 1899–1955] 10:655).

23   See Derrett, "Render," 316; Barrett, "State," 7–8.

24   Edouard Delebecque (*Évangile de Luc* [1976; reprinted Paris: Klincksieck, 1992] 126) translates παρατηρήσαντες with the words *de leur aguet* ("from ambush, furtively"). D = 05 (Codex Bezae) and Θ = 038 (Codex Koridethi), perhaps along with the Old Latin witnesses, have "having taken some distance" (ἀποχωρήσαντες) instead of παρατηρήσαντες ("having watched"). W = 032 (Freer Codex) offers ὑποχωρήσαντες ("having withdrawn"). The Syriac (called the Sinai and Cureton) versions have simply "after that."

25   Numerous manuscripts offer εἰς τό ("in view of") instead of ὥστε ("so that").

26   Some exegetes, incorrectly, think that the accusation against Jesus was valid and that, even if he said to give Caesar and God what was coming to them, he in fact refused to pay his taxes; see Brandon, *Trial*, 66–68. Richard A. Horsley (*Jesus and the Spiral of Violence: Popular Jewish Resistance in Roman Palestine* [San Francisco: Harper & Row, 1987] 306–17) is of the opinion that Mark, and perhaps Luke as well, portrayed Jesus as someone who was hostile to the payment of taxes.

before the Roman governor. We will come across the verb "to deliver" ($\pi\alpha\rho\alpha\delta\iota\delta\omega\mu\iota$) again on the lips of Jesus when Judas kisses him (22:48) and the fact of the delivery to the governor after the Sanhedrin has met (23:1). As for the words "jurisdiction and authority ($\dot{\epsilon}\xi o\upsilon\sigma\iota\alpha$)," they anticipate the terrible expression in the garden of the Mount of Olives: "But this is your hour, and the power ($\dot{\epsilon}\xi o\upsilon\sigma\iota\alpha$) of darkness" (22:53).

■ **21** Without v. 20, the *captatio benevolentiae* of v. 21 appears to be honest.[27] In fact, similar to a Johannine saying with diverse meanings,[28] the hypocritical compliment actually speaks the truth. Jesus is a "master" ($\delta\iota\delta\dot{\alpha}\sigma\kappa\alpha\lambda o\varsigma$),[29] who "teaches" ($\delta\iota\delta\dot{\alpha}\sigma\kappa\omega$, twice)[30] "the way of God" ($\tau\dot{\eta}\nu$ $\dot{o}\delta o\nu$ $\tau o\hat{\upsilon}$ $\vartheta\epsilon o\hat{\upsilon}$) "uprightly" ($\dot{o}\rho\vartheta\hat{\omega}\varsigma$)[31] and "according to the truth" ($\dot{\epsilon}\pi$ ' $\dot{\alpha}\lambda\eta\vartheta\epsilon\dot{\iota}\alpha\varsigma$)[32] "without respect of the person" ($o\dot{\upsilon}$ $\lambda\alpha\mu\beta\dot{\alpha}\nu\epsilon\iota\varsigma$ $\pi\rho\dot{o}\sigma\omega\pi o\nu$).[33] Is there a better definition of Jesus' ministry? This description, which would be appropriate for the best rabbi and would fit well with the most learned Greek philosopher (does Plato not say tirelessly that Socrates was the best master and that he taught the truth with uprightness?), especially proclaims the truth about Christ. As the evangelist often says, Jesus revealed "God's plan" ($\dot{\eta}$ $\beta o\upsilon\lambda\dot{\eta}$ $\tau o\hat{\upsilon}$ $\vartheta\epsilon o\hat{\upsilon}$), and the movement that arose from his teaching represents "God's way" ($\dot{\eta}$ $\dot{o}\delta\dot{o}\varsigma$ $\tau o\hat{\upsilon}$ $\vartheta\epsilon o\hat{\upsilon}$).[34]

■ **22** In a Hebraic context, "it is allowed" refers to the authority of the law. If the question is raised, however, it is because the divine commands are silent on this subject or are ambiguous. That it is a question here of permission implies that believers are not in conscience obligated to pay tribute to Caesar.

With Augustus, the word $K\alpha\hat{\iota}\sigma\alpha\rho$ evolved from a proper name (the *cognomen* or first name of Julius Caesar) to an honorific title. In Luke's day every reader understood that they were speaking of the Roman emperor. While Mark and Matthew use the term "tax" ($\kappa\hat{\eta}\nu\sigma o\varsigma$, Latin *census*), Luke prefers the term "tribute" ($\varphi\dot{o}\rho o\varsigma$), which has the double advantage of being Greek and of indicating that at issue here is a tax paid to a foreign power, "tribute." By contrast, the Greek word ($\kappa\hat{\eta}\nu\sigma o\varsigma$) indicates a direct, personal tax imposed after a counting of the population, thus the Latin word *census* for such a tax. Luke's word ($\varphi\dot{o}\rho o\varsigma$) has a broader meaning. It indicates the "tribute" an occupied land owes an occupying power. Sometimes its scope is limited to the individual sphere. Then it suggests a payment, a tenant lease, a rent, or a tax.[35]

■ **23-24** Luke maintains the scene's polemical atmosphere. As an omniscient narrator, he knows and states that Jesus is aware of his questioners' malice and that he asks them to show him a denarius. Several kinds of currency were in circulation in that day. The people who lived in Judea liked to use the shekel of Tyre in their daily transactions. The Jesus of the canonical Gospels asks for a "denarius," because he knows that the Romans require that the tax be paid in Roman currency.[36] In that day, the denarius was a silver coin. While the coins minted in honor of Augustus were still in circulation, the most common coins were those minted in Lyon over the course of a quarter century bearing the effigy of Tiberius. Tiberius appears in profile on the front of the coin with the inscription (TI CAESAR DIVI AUG F AUGUSTUS —

---

27   As the Groupe de Dole ("César," 12) says, "Liars can tell the truth, even when they are lying."

28   See the inadvertent prophecy of the high priest in John 11:49-50.

29   On $\delta\iota\delta\dot{\alpha}\sigma\kappa\alpha\lambda o\varsigma$ as a christological title, see Hahn, *Titles*, 73—78.

30   On $\delta\iota\delta\dot{\alpha}\sigma\kappa\omega$, see Karl Heinrich Rengstorf, "$\delta\iota\delta\dot{\alpha}\sigma\kappa\omega$ $\kappa\tau\lambda$.," *TDNT* 2 (1964) 135–48.

31   On $\dot{o}\rho\vartheta\hat{\omega}\varsigma$, see 7:43 and vol. 1 of this commentary, 296 n. 50.

32   On $\dot{\alpha}\lambda\dot{\eta}\vartheta\epsilon\iota\alpha$, see Hans Hübner, "$\dot{\alpha}\lambda\dot{\eta}\vartheta\epsilon\iota\alpha$," etc. *EDNT* 1 (1990) 57–60.

33   On the God who is no respecter of persons, see François Bovon, *De Vocatione Gentium: Histoire de l'interprétation d'Act 10, 1—11, 18 dans les six premiers siècles* (BGBE 8; Tübingen: Mohr Siebeck, 1967) 212–24.

34   On $\beta o\upsilon\lambda\dot{\eta}$ $\tau o\hat{\upsilon}$ $\vartheta\epsilon o\hat{\upsilon}$, see Luke 7:30; Acts 2:23; 4:28; 13:36; 20:27; and on $\dot{o}\delta\dot{o}\varsigma$ $\tau o\hat{\upsilon}$ $\vartheta\epsilon o\hat{\upsilon}$, see Luke 1:76; 3:4; Acts 9:2; 13:10; 18:25-26. See also Jacques Dupont, *Le discours de Milet: Testament pastoral de Saint Paul (Actes 20,18-36)* (LD 32; Paris: Cerf, 1962) 119–25.

35   See Konrad Weiss, "$\varphi\dot{\epsilon}\rho\omega$ $\kappa\tau\lambda$.," *TDNT* 9 (1974) 78–83. On capitation, the personal, direct tax (head tax), see Stauffer, "Tribute Money," 115–32.

36   The ancient sources admittedly do not say explicitly that the head tax imposed on the Jews by the Romans had to be paid in Roman money. Undoubtedly it was taken for granted. On this tax, see E. Mary Smallwood, *The Jews under Roman Rule from Pompey to Diocletian: A Study in Political Relations* (2d ed. 1981; reprinted Leiden/Boston: Brill, 2001) 151. On Roman money, especially the denarius, see

Tiberius Caesar divi Augusti filius Augustus); on the reverse side a woman, undoubtedly representing Livia as Pax, is sitting on a throne with the abbreviation "great pontiff," which always refers to the emperor (*pontifex maximus,* abbreviated PONTIF MAXIM). As dishonest as they are, the questioners cannot ignore what is obvious. With a single word they answer: "Caesar's."

■ **25** The expression τοίνυν is justified here because of the mocking superiority it implies: "Well, give to Caesar what is Caesar's. . . ." Why must one "render [give back]" (ἀπόδοτε) instead of "give"?[37] The Roman currency meant that there were advantages to the Roman order. The circulation of this money went hand in hand with a certain economic stability and a certain political peace.[38] The Roman authorities sought to convince their subordinates of the advantages of a submissive attitude. Luke's Jesus would not deny that.[39] It is also possible that this verb has an opposite function: Give him his coins back, and then we're even. If the first interpretation emphasizes the speaker's integration into the Roman system, the second suggests keeping one's distance. That the position defended by Jesus and the evangelists leads to contradictory interpretations undoubtedly is caused by this verb's ambiguity. Before we try to remove this ambiguity, let us first of all say that Jesus called forth the admiration of his hearers and then that of his disciples. With his answer, which was to become proverbial, he extracted himself from the difficulty admirably. Had he answered "no," he would have spoken like a Zealot who was hostile toward the Romans. If his answer had been "yes," he would have appeared to be, if not a collaborator, at least a conformist who was unable to ignite the religious enthusiasm of his compatriots.

The word order also deserves attention. The sentence reaches its high point at the conclusion; given the movement of the sentence, its essential part is "Give (back) to God what is owed him" (καὶ τὰ τοῦ θεοῦ τῷ θεῷ).[40] God must indeed be served first; honor and allegiance belong to him. Jewish literature and the earliest Christian writings (1 Cor 7:33-34) mention τὰ τοῦ κυρίου, "the things of the Lord," in contrast to τὰ τοῦ κόσμου, "the things of the world" and compete in repeating this priority of the first commandment. Sometimes such a service rendered to the creator is even described as an exclusive service;[41] Luke 16:13 contrasts every other obligation with obedience to God. Here, by contrast, much as the summary of the law adds the love of neighbor to the love of God, the Gospel saying speaks of serving God in connection with the social reality of networks and obligations.[42]

■ **26** The questioners would have liked to "catch" Jesus, but the subtlety of his words protects him from being tripped up by what he says. Luke, who without hesitation sides with Jesus, delights in noting the inability (οὐχ ἴσχυσαν, "they were not able") of the people he had disqualified from the very beginning. The conclusion of the episode underscores Jesus' triumph: left speechless,

---

Derrett, "Render," 329–33; Hart, "Coin." My thanks to Matteo Campagnolo for his assistance on this subject.

37 Bornkamm (*Jesus,* 122) is of the opinion that one should not attribute any particular connotation to this verb, which was used at that time to say "to pay" taxes. In the same sense, see Petzke, "Diskussion," 230. Stauffer ("Tribute Money," 132–33) offers a contrary opinion.

38 See Barrett, "State," 8.

39 Even when he knows of the character of the foreign power of the Roman Empire and the polytheism that characterized its official religion, Stauffer ("Tribute Money," 134) is able to write: "The *Imperium Caesaris* is the way and the *Imperium Dei* the goal of history." In my understanding, the concepts "way" and "goal" are foreign to this statement of Jesus.

40 See Barrett, "State," 8–9. The expression τά with the genitive has been examined carefully by Giblin, "Caesar," 520–21 (it refers not only to "things" but also to "duties").

41 The LXX often uses ἀποδίδωμι ("give [back]") in a religious context in the sense of "fulfilling one's duties to God" (see Stauffer, "Tribute Money," 132–33).

42 Derrett ("Render," 324–28) thinks that, as is appropriate, Jesus uses scripture to solve the problem. Even if he does not quote the passage, Jesus is thinking of Qoh 8:2 ("I [i.e., I say to you]. Obey the command of the king, and do not be in a hurry to withdraw from it because of the divine oath . . ."). Owen-Ball ("Tribute") thinks that the image refers to Gen 1:26 (*imago Dei*) and the inscription to Exod 13:9 ("It will be to you a sign on the hand and a memorial between the eyes, so that the law of the

his opponents are even forced to admire the Master's response (ἀπόκρισις).[43]

History of Interpretation

This answer became so famous that a German historian of the nineteenth century could say that of Jesus' entire teaching these words have had the greatest impact on the course of history.[44]

From the second century on the memory of the apophthegm made it possible for Christians to order their civil responsibility vis-à-vis Roman power with a clear conscience. As Justin says, Christians agree to pay their taxes (1 Apol. 17.1–4). Other authors add that they resist imperial power only when it crosses the limit the Creator has assigned it.[45] When it claims religious authority and demands to be venerated as holy, it becomes idolatrous and encounters the decided opposition of the partisans of Christ.[46]

Tertullian brings the episode of the denarius closer to the question asked Jesus about his authority (Luke 20:1-8) (Adv. Marc. 4.38.1–3).[47] In both cases Jesus avoids the trap and turns the situation in his favor. The African then asks himself: What does Jesus mean by these "things of God"? To understand this, one must consider the parallel that Jesus draws with the coin. Just as an image and an inscription occupy the two sides of the coin, so the human creature is with the image and the likeness of God. It bears the name God has given it, and shares in God's essence (materia). To render to God what belongs to God is to affirm that human beings belong to God and must also return to God.[48]

The catena literature, in two fragments difficult to translate,[49] preserved the view of Apollinaris of Laodicea (fourth century), which one can summarize in six points: (1) The questioners set a trap that confronts Jesus with a deadly alternative (to support the oppression of the people or to provoke his own arrest). (2) The description of Jesus from the lips of his adversaries (v. 21) merits attention because of the accuracy of the terms used. (3) There was a man, Judas the Galilean, who refused to submit to the emperor and to pay taxes to the Romans. (4) The Savior—this is the christological title used—unmasked his questioners and called for a coin. (5) This answer was convincing and admirable. (6) In spite of its ambiguity, the answer admitted, on the one hand, the legitimacy of paying taxes and, on the other hand, ordered right behavior vis-à-vis God.

Lord may be in your mouth"). Stock ("Caesar," 929) thinks of Isa 45:1-6 (Cyrus, God's anointed) as a possible Old Testament counterpart to "render to Caesar . . ."

43   As a matter of fact, Jesus' saying is less original than it appears to be. One could cite various Jewish parallels; see Str-B 1:885; see also the Sentence of Sextus 20: τὰ μὲν τοῦ κόσμου τῷ κόσμῳ, τὰ δὲ τοῦ θεοῦ τῷ θεῷ ἀκριβῶς ἀποδίδου, "Render with exactitude to the world what belongs to the world and to God what is God's." See Henry Chadwick, ed., The Sentences of Sextus: A Contribution to the History of Early Christian Ethics (Texts and Studies, n.s. 5; Cambridge: Cambridge University Press, 1959) 14.

44   This statement of Leopold von Ranke ("Ursprung des Christentums," in idem, Zeitbilder und Charakteristiken [Berlin: Deutsche Bibliothek, 1918] 28) is frequently quoted by exegetes; see Bea, "Cesare," 572; Sevenster, "Keizer," 21; Petzke, "Diskussion," 226, n. 13.

45   See Passio sanctorum Scilitanorum in Gustav Krüger and Gerhard Ruhbach, eds., Ausgewählte Märtyrerakten [4th ed.; SQS n.F. 3; Tübingen: Mohr Siebeck, 1965] 29): Donata dixit: Honorem Caesari quasi Caesari; timorem autem Deo ("Donata said: We accord honor to Caesar as Caesar, but we fear God"); Theophilus of Antioch Ad Autolycum 1.11; Tertullian Apol. 28.3–33.4; Hippolytus of Rome Comm. Dan. 3.20–25, 31; Hugo Rahner, Kirche und Staat im frühen Christentum: Dokumente aus acht Jahrhunderten und ihre Deutung (Munich: Kösel, 1961) 42–57; Bori, "Date."

46   One is reminded of the episode mentioned by Eusebius of Caesarea (Hist. eccl. 3.20.4): Jesus' cousins, of Davidic descent, are brought before Domitian in Rome as messianic pretenders. When the emperor learns that they pay their taxes, he releases them. The example is cited by Stauffer, "Tribute Money," 135–36.

47   See also Tertullian Idol. 15.3–4; Jerome Comm. Matt. 22.15–22 (PL 26:162–63); Giblin, "Caesar," 511 n. 8.

48   It is appropriate to mention Origen's interpretation here: Hom. Luc. 39.4–6 and Comm. Matt. 17.25–28 (Origenes Werke 10:652–63).

49   See Reuss, Lukas-Kommentare, 6–7 (frgs. 9–10). The first five points are summarized in frg. 9, the sixth in frg. 10.

The attention paid to the image and Tertullian's parallelism between the emperor's effigy and the image of God reappear in the comments of Ambrose (*Exp. Luc.* 10.34–36).[50] Contrasting the two worlds, the preacher of Milan affirms that Christ and his disciples are created not in the image of the emperor but in the image of God. Opening a new course, he advocates asceticism, arguing that one must pay taxes as long as one is attached to this world. One can avoid the burden of the public treasury only by abandoning its goods and by renouncing the world!

During the Middle Ages, Jesus' statement, along with Rom 13:1-7 and 1 Pet 2:13-17, served as an important scriptural basis for the theological principles that regulated the relations between state and church. One can see its influence in the decisions of the Fourth Lateran Council or in the writings of Thomas Aquinas.[51] In a speech in 1958, Pope Pius XII summarized the traditional Roman Catholic position: church–state relations vary from country to country, yet Jesus' statement and the teaching of the apostles contain the principles that must regulate any relationship between the state and the church.[52]

The Protestant Reformation did not modify this recourse to "Render to Caesar what is Caesar's and to God what is God's." Initially Luther reacted vehemently against Jesus' adversaries, saying that instead of flattering Jesus with fine words and before asking about the tax for Caesar they would have done better to produce good deeds and not set a trap for him. The reformer observes in particular that Jesus takes his adversaries at their word and tells them the truth by calling attention above all to their hypocrisy. As a true teacher, Christ helps them come up with the good answer. They must give back to Caesar what they would rather keep from him and must give to God what they had hidden from him. What happened to Jesus' questioners in that day can be repeated among Christians today. Doctrinally, Luther says, this story can teach us to distinguish between the kingdom of the world and the kingdom of Jesus Christ. If political authority were intrinsically bad, Jesus would not have invited people to "give to Caesar what is Caesar's." Luther quotes here Rom 13:1 ("every authority comes from God") and encourages everyone to respect the *Stände* ("social categories," "states"). That there are examples of bad governments does not justify condemning political authority as such. As for "giving to God what is God's," it designates faith in God and love of neighbor. No political authority has the right to prohibit this religious practice. To keep the command to "give to God what is God's" means at baptism to renounce the devil and his pompous ceremonies.[53]

Calvin confirms Luther's interpretation:

A clear distinction is set out here between the spiritual and civil government, that we should know ourselves to be under no external constraint from holding a clear conscience in the sight of God. . . . The doctrine goes further. Every man has a duty as far as he is called to render to his fellow man. . . . Obedience to leaders and magistrates is always linked to the worship and fear of God, but if in return the leaders usurp the rights of God they are to be denied obedience as far as possible short of offence to God.[54]

Conclusion

It has been said that Jesus' answer avoids the question and prohibits a political reading of the episode. It has also been said that the doctrine of two kingdoms ignores Jesus' eschatological expectation and runs the risk of subordinating the spiritual to the political realm. Finally, the claim has been made that the biblical passage, as the theologians of the Middle Ages and the Reformation have interpreted it, makes it possible to justify the

50   Like Tertullian, Ambrose mentions in this context the episode in which Jesus' authority is disputed (Luke 20:1-8).

51   Fourth Lateran Council (1215), Constitution 42, *De saeculari iustitia*, in Norman P. Tanner, ed., *Decrees of the Ecumenical Councils* (2 vols.; Washington, D.C.: Georgetown University Press, 1990) 1:253.

52   See Bea, "Cesare," 582–83.

53   Luther, *Evangelien-Auslegung*, 939–46.

54   Calvin, *Harmony*, 3:23–27 (the quotations come from 26 and 27).

political and social false paths of a state that is eager to control the church.[55] It is true that the Bible is unable to prevent the abuses that have come with its success. It seems doubtful, however, that a reading that is constant from Justin through Thomas Aquinas to Calvin falsifies the sense of a text that is so obvious.

Even if the distinction between the economic and religious domains does not escape the modern readers of v. 25, the symbolic range of the coin mentioned in v. 24 often remains veiled. Unlike modern readers, however, earlier readers immediately recognized this semantic load.[56] It was impossible to mention the emperor's image and the titles by which he was known without thinking, by symmetry, of the image of God and the names corresponding to his person.[57] The image was not a fiction, nor were the words merely convention. To give the priority to $\tau\grave{\alpha}$ $\tauο\hat{\upsilon}$ $\vartheta\epsilon ο\hat{\upsilon}$ ("that which is God's") was to be in contact with the Creator and to reveal in one's own humanity the features of the image of God. It was also to uncover the emperor's ideological abuses (his claim to be "Son of God") and to limit political power to the establishment of peace and justice.

---

55 The fear of such excesses is understandable in light of the experience with the National Socialists during the Third Reich. One detects it in the works of Bornkamm (*Jesus*, 120–24) and Petzke ("Diskussion," 234–35).

56 Modernity begins with the Renaissance. The sixteenth-century commentators I have read appear to be insensitive to the problem of the image.

57 Tertullian, one of the first interpreters of this text, reacts positively to the concept of "image," and in his interpretation of this passage alludes to Gen 1:26 (*imago Dei*) (see above under "History of Interpretation").

In Dispute with the Sadducees
(20:27-40)
Bibliography

Anderson, John, "A Look at Implicit Information in Rabbinical Argumentation," in *Notes on Translation* 13, no. 3 (1999) 13–14.

Aune, David E., "Luke 20:34-36: A 'Gnosticized' Logion of Jesus?" in Hermann Lichtenberger, ed., *Geschichte–Tradition–Reflexion: Festschrift für Martin Hengel zum 70. Geburtstag*, vol. 3: *Frühes Christentum* (Tübingen: Mohr Siebeck, 1996) 187–202.

Bartina, Sebastián, "Jesús y los saduceos: 'El Dios de Abraham, de Isaac y de Jacob' es 'El que hace existir' (Mt 22,23-33; Mc 12,18-27; Lc 20,27-40; Hebr 11,13-16)," *EstBib* 21 (1962) 151–60.

Baumbach, Günther, "Der sadduzäische Konservatismus," in Johann Maier and Josef Schreiner, eds., *Literatur und Religion des Frühjudentums: Eine Einführung* (Würzburg: Echter, 1973) 201–13.

Bianchi, Ugo, "The Religio-historical Relevance of Luke 20:34-36," in R. van den Broek and M. J. Vermaseren, eds., *Studies in Gnosticism and Hellenistic Religions: Presented to Gilles Quispel on the Occasion of His 65th Birthday* (Études préliminaires aux religions orientales dans l'Empire romain 91; Leiden: Brill, 1981) 31–37.

Brock, Sebastian P., "Early Syrian Asceticism," *Numen* 20 (1973) 1–19.

Bultmann, *History*, 26, 49.

Burrows, Millar, "Levirate Marriage in Israel," *JBL* 59 (1940) 23–33.

Carton, Gilles, "Comme des anges dans le ciel," *BVC* 28 (1959) 46–52.

Charpentier, Étienne, "Tous vivent pour lui: Lc 20,27-38," *AsSeign* NS 63 (1971) 82–94.

Cohn-Sherbok, Daniel M., "Jesus' Defence of the Resurrection of the Dead," *JSNT* 11 (1981) 64–73.

Daalen, D. H. van, "Some Observations on Mark 12,24-27," *StEv* 4 [TU 102] (1968) 241–45.

Daube, David, *The New Testament and Rabbinic Judaism* (London: Athlone, 1956) 158–63.

Downing, F. Gerald, "The Resurrection of the Dead: Jesus and Philo," *JSNT* 15 (1982) 42–50.

Dreyfus, François, "L'argument scripturaire de Jésus en faveur de la résurrection des morts (Marc, XII, 26-27)," *RB* 66 (1959) 213–24.

Eijk, Ton H. C. van, "Marriage and Virginity, Death and Immortality," in Jacques Fontaine und Charles Kannengiesser, eds., *Epektasis: Mélanges patristiques offerts au Cardinal Jean Daniélou* (Paris: Beauchesne, 1972) 209–35.

Ellis, E. Earle, "Jesus, the Sadducees and Qumran," *NTS* 10 (1963–64) 274–79.

Ferrar, W. J., "A Note on Lk 20,39," *ExpT* 30 (1918–19) 39.

Fletcher-Louis, Crispin H. T., *Luke-Acts: Angels, Christology and Soteriology* (WUNT 2/94; Tübingen: Mohr Siebeck, 1997) 78–86, 219–22.

Flusser, David, "The Sons of Light in Jesus' Teaching and in the New Testament," in *Biblical Archaeology Today: Proceedings of the International Congress on Biblical Archaeology, Jerusalem, April 1984* (Jerusalem: Israel Exploration Society, 1985) 427–28.

Frank, Suso, *ΑΓΓΕΛΙΚΟΣ ΒΙΟΣ: Begriffsanalytische und begriffsgeschichtliche Untersuchung zum "Engelgleichen Leben" im frühen Mönchtum* (BGAM 26; Münster: Aschendorff, 1964).

George, Augustin, "Les Anges," in idem, *Études sur l'oeuvre de Luc* (Sources bibliques; Paris: Gabalda, 1978) 149–83, esp.180–83.

Grangaard, *Conflict*, 111–28.

Gundry, Robert Horton, *The Use of the Old Testament in St. Matthew's Gospel* (NovTSup 18; Leiden: Brill, 1967) 20–22.

Haenchen, *Weg Jesu*, 409–12.

Hahn, *Titles*, 75–82.

Janzen, J. Gerald, "Resurrection and Hermeneutics: On Exodus 3.6 in Mark 12.26," *JSNT* 23 (1985) 43–58.

Kilgallen, John J., "The Sadducees and Resurrection from the Dead: Luke 20, 27-40," *Bib* 67 (1986) 478–95.

Kingsbury, *Conflict*, 26–27, 98–101, 106, 149 and passim.

Le Moyne, Jean, *Les Sadducéens* (EtB; Paris: Gabalda, 1972) 123–27, 129–35.

Levenson, Jon Douglas, *Resurrection and the Restoration of Israel: The Ultimate Victory of the God of Life* (New Haven: Yale University Press, 2006).

Main, Emmanuelle, "Les Sadducéens et la résurrection des morts: Comparaison entre Mc 12, 18-27 et Lc 20, 27-38," *RB* 103 (1996) 411–32.

Manns, Frédéric, "La technique du Al Tiqra dans les évangiles," *RevScRel* 64 (1990) 1–7.

Meyer, Rudolf, "Σαδδουκαῖος," *TDNT* 7 (1971) 35–54.

Montanti, C., "Lc. 20,34-36 e la filiazione divina degli uomini," *BeO* 13 (1971) 255–75.

Mudiso Mbâ Mundla, Jean-Gaspard, *Jesus und die Führer Israels: Studien zu den sog. Jerusalemer Streitgesprächen* (NTAbh 17; Münster: Aschendorff, 1984) 71–109, 299–305.

Müller, Karlheinz, "Jesus und die Sadduzäer," in Helmut Merklein and Joachim Lange, eds., *Biblische Randbemerkungen: Schülerfestschrift für Rudolf Schnackenburg zum 60. Geburtstag* (Würzburg: Echter, 1974) 3–24.

Neirynck, Frans, "La matière marcienne dans l'évangile de Luc," in *L'Évangile de Luc—The Gospel of Luke*, 67–111, 304–5.

Odeberg, Hugo, "Ἰακώβ," *TDNT* 3 (1965) 191–92.

Prete, Benedetto, "L'insegnamento di Gesù sulla risurrezione dei morti nella formulazione di Lc 20,27-40," *RevBib* 41 (1993) 429–51.

Rigaux, Beda, *Dieu l'a ressuscité: Exégèse et théologie biblique* (Gembloux: Duculot, 1973) 24–39.

Robinson, Bernard P., "'They Are as Angels in Heaven': Jesus' Alleged Riposte to the Sadducees (Mark 12:18-27; parr. Mt 22:23-33; Lk 20:27-40)," *NBl* 78 (1997) 530–37.

Schramm, *Markus-Stoff*, 170–71.

Schubert, Kurt, "Die Entwicklung der Auferstehungslehre von der nachexilischen bis zur frührabbinischen Zeit," *BZ* 6 (1962) 177–214.

Schwankl, Otto, *Die Sadduzäerfrage (Mk. 12,18-27 parr): Eine exegetisch-theologische Studie zur Auferstehungserwartung* (BBB 66; Frankfurt: Athenäum, 1987).

Strawson, William, *Jesus and the Future Life: A Study in the Synoptic Gospels* (London: Epworth, 1959) 203–10.

Suhl, Alfred, *Die Funktion der alttestamentlichen Zitate und Anspielungen im Markus-Evangelium* (Gütersloh: Mohn, 1965) 67–72.

Trowitzsch, Michael, "Gemeinschaft der Lebenden und der Toten. Lk 20,38 als Text der Ekklesiologie," *ZThK* 79 (1982) 212–29.

Wiles, Maurice, "Studies in Texts: Lk 20.34-36," *Theology* 60 (1957) 500–502.

27 **But some Sadducees, those who say there is no resurrection, approached him and questioned him 28/ saying, "Master, Moses wrote for us: 'If a man who has a wife but no children dies, let his brother take her for a wife[a] and raise up offspring[b] for his brother.' 29/ Once there were seven brothers; the first took a wife and died without children. 30/ And the second 31/ and the third took her and likewise all seven left no children and died. 32/ Finally, the woman also died. 33/ The woman, therefore, whose wife will she become in the resurrection? For the seven had her as a wife."**

34 **And Jesus said to them, "The children[c] of this age marry and are given in marriage, 35/ but those who are considered worthy to reach that age and the resurrection from the dead neither marry nor are given in marriage. 36/ For they can no longer die, for they are equal to angels and are children of God, being children of the resurrection. 37/ That the dead are raised, Moses also revealed in the episode of the bush[d] when he says, 'the Lord is the God of Abraham, and the God of Isaac, and the God of Jacob.' 38/ God is not the God of the dead but of the living, since all live from him."[e]**

39 **Some of the scribes answered and said, "Master you have spoken well." 40/ For they did not dare to question him further.**

a   Literally: "takes the wife."
b   Literally: "seed," "sperm."
c   Literally: "sons"; also twice in v. 36.
d   Literally: "at the bush."
e   Or: "for him."

It is important to understand this text in its double, narrative and theological, logic. To do so, we must compare it with the parallel accounts of Mark (12:18-27) and Matthew (22:23-33) and seek the origin of the episode by combining synchronic and diachronic readings.[1] The work, however, does not end there; we must also evaluate the range of the doctrinal issues in the controversy. The discussion begins with a reference to the Law of Moses from which the Sadducees seek to apply a commandment about marriage to a reality referred to twice as ἀνάστασις ("resurrection," vv. 27, 33). It continues with a series of assertions from Jesus about the ordinance of marriage or non-marriage in "this time" and in "that time," the time of the ἀνάστασις (the word "resurrection" appears again in vv. 35 and 36). The Master's reply ends with a brief scriptural proof that leads from the Law of Moses to the identity of God who inspired it (vv. 37-38). On a single page Luke leads his readers from an ancient example to the new reality of the resurrection, from humankind to the children of the resurrection, from one word of Moses to another, from one image of God to another.

Analysis

The Sadducees replace the agents sent by the scribes and the chief priests (20:19-20) in order to question Jesus (v. 27). They present him with a test case, first citing the rule (v. 28), then offering an example (vv. 29-32), finally formulating their question (v. 33).

Jesus' response takes place in two stages. Without arguing, the Master begins by affirming that in "this time" people marry but that those who are the recipients of "that time" do not (note the present tense of the indicative in vv. 34-35). Then he explains his statement (note γάρ, "for") rather than the case submitted to him; v. 36. Continuing to "forget" the woman and the seven brothers, he concentrates finally on the biblical roots of the resurrection of the dead by enigmatically[2] juxtaposing a quotation from Exodus 3 (v. 37) and a personal assertion, which he briefly justifies (v. 38). The episode ends with the compliments of some and the intimidated silence of others (vv. 39-40). The result in schematic form is:

V. 27   arrival of the group of Sadducees,
Vv. 28-33   their intervention
     a) v. 28 recall of the levirate commandment
     b) vv. 29-32 story of the woman and the seven brothers
     c) v. 33 question directed to Jesus
Vv. 34-38   Jesus' reply
     a) vv. 34-36 contrast between "this time" and "that time"
     b) vv. 37-38 Moses' revelation and Jesus' thesis
Vv. 39-40   congratulations of the scribes and silence of the others.[3]

This controversy is the last of a series that began with Jesus' entry into the temple (19:45). The series was interrupted by a parable of Jesus (20:9-19), and it will be followed by a question from Jesus (the Son of David, 20:41-44), an episode observed in passing (the widow and her pittance, 21:1-4), and a final question directed to Jesus about the date of the destruction of the temple (in 21:7 the same verb, ἐπερωτῶ is used as in 20:21 and 20:27). Even if the sequence of received and asked questions cannot be fitted exactly into a precise rabbinic literary genre,[4] it does correspond to the practices of dialogue and polemic of the schools of ancient

---

1   See Strawson, *Jesus*, 203–10; Charpentier, "Tous"; Rigaux, *Dieu l'a ressuscité*, 24–39; Kilgallen, "Sadducees"; Mudiso Mbâ Mundla, *Jesus*, 71–109, 299–305; Schwankl, *Sadduzäerfrage*, 14–62 (survey of research) and 442–65 (Lukan redaction); Prete, "Insegnamento."

2   See Frank Kermode, *The Genesis of Secrecy: On the Interpretation of Narrative* (Cambridge, Mass.: Harvard University Press, 1979) 2–3.

3   For a similar scheme, see Bock 2:1618; Meynet (*Évangile*, 1:188–89; 2:192–93) offers a different structure.

4   Daube (*Rabbinic*, 158–63) thinks that the Synoptic tradition, especially Matthew and Mark, merged the memories of Jesus into a rabbinic schema representative of four types of questions. Daube's hypothesis has been taken over by a number of people and criticized by some; see Mudiso Mbâ Mundla, *Jesus*, 303–5; Le Moyne, *Sadducéens*, 123–24. After a meticulous examination, Cohn-Sherbok ("Defence") concluded that Jesus followed neither any of the Hillel's seven exegetical rules nor the thirty-two rules later composed by Eliezar ben Jose, the Galilean. Thus, the Nazarene had received no rabbinical training.

Judaism.[5] This observation explains why the conversation partners, instead of contradicting Jesus openly, prefer to ask a question.

Most exegetes are of the opinion that Luke took over Mark's account and that he has rewritten the text, improving the style, clarifying the positions, and directing attention to the sense given. The dependence on Mark is especially clear at the beginning of the story, the arrival and the intervention of the Sadducees (vv. 27-33).[6] The improvements include the following:[7] "Some Sadducees" instead of "Sadducees" (Mark 12:18); these men "approach" ($\pi\rho\sigma\epsilon\lambda\vartheta\acute{o}\nu\tau\epsilon\varsigma$, v. 27) instead of "come to him" ($\check{\epsilon}\rho\chi\nu\tau\alpha\iota \ldots \pi\rho\grave{o}\varsigma \alpha\grave{v}\tau\acute{o}\nu$, Mark 12:18); they "oppose" ($o\grave{\iota} \, \grave{\alpha}\nu\tau\iota\lambda\acute{\epsilon}\gamma\nu\tau\epsilon\varsigma$, v. 27[8]) instead of "they say" ($o\check{\iota}\tau\iota\nu\epsilon\varsigma \, \lambda\acute{\epsilon}\gamma\nu\sigma\iota\nu$, Mark 12:18); the brothers die "without children" ($\check{\alpha}\tau\epsilon\kappa\nu\varsigma$, v. 29; see also $o\grave{v} \, \kappa\alpha\tau\acute{\epsilon}\lambda\iota\pi\nu \, \tau\acute{\epsilon}\kappa\nu\alpha$, "they left no children," v. 31) instead of "without seed" ($\sigma\pi\acute{\epsilon}\rho\mu\alpha$, Mark 12:20, 21, 22);[9] "whose wife will she become in the resurrection?" is better than "whose wife will she be?" (Mark 12:23).

The dependence on Mark is visible also in the last part of Jesus' intervention (vv. 37-38): the same subject matter, the resurrection of the dead; the same reference to the episode of the burning bush; the same mention of the God of Abraham, of Isaac, and of Jacob (Mark 12:26-27). Verses 37-38 of Luke 20, however, contain certain improvements that go beyond the formal framework.[10] The evangelist ignores the "book," the reading and the "bush" understood as the title of a pericope (Mark 12:26). He is interested in the voice of Moses,[11] for it "reveals" ($\grave{\epsilon}\mu\acute{\eta}\nu\nu\sigma\epsilon\nu$ in v. 37 is Lukan) the identity of God.[12] To this first change, which relates to the communication of the truth, Luke adds a second, which relates to the content of the truth. It seems that he is referring less to Exod 3:6 than to Exod 3:15: it is not the question of an "I" who reveals one of his titles but of a voice who declares the God of Abraham, of Isaac, and of Jacob to be Lord. If Luke is thinking of the statement of Exod 3:15 in its entirety, along with the context of the burning bush, he knows that, unlike in Exod 3:6, God has already communicated his true name (Exod 3:14): YHWH, rendered in the LXX, Luke's Bible, as $\kappa\acute{v}\rho\iota\varsigma$, "Lord." He also knows that the statement Moses is to make has been dictated to him by God. Here is the complete text of Exod 3:15 according to the LXX: "And God said again to Moyses, 'Thus you will speak to the sons of Israel, "The Lord, the God of your fathers, God of Abraam and God of Isaak and God of Iakob, has sent me to you." This is an

---

5   See, e.g., Ellis, "Sadducees." Le Moyne (*Sadducéens*, 123–25), among others, refers to the "account of *b. Sanh.* 90b where Rabbi Gamaliel II (around the year 90 C.E.) is questioned by the Sadducees about the scriptural proof for the resurrection" (125).

6   For good Synoptic comparisons, see Mudiso Mbâ Mundla, *Jesus*, 74–81; Rigaux, *Dieu l'a ressuscité*, 24–31; Fitzmyer, 2:1299.

7   In these verses there are also some differences that do not represent improvements (is one to attribute them to Luke or to the Markan text Luke had at his disposal?): $o\grave{\iota}$ instead of $o\check{\iota}\tau\iota\nu\epsilon\varsigma$ (Mark 12:18), $\grave{\epsilon}\pi\eta\rho\acute{\omega}\tau\eta\sigma\alpha\nu$, aorist, instead of the imperfect $\grave{\epsilon}\pi\eta\rho\acute{\omega}\tau\omega\nu$ (Mark 12:18), $\check{\epsilon}\chi\omega\nu \, \gamma\nu\nu\alpha\hat{\iota}\kappa\alpha$ (emphasis on the earlier situation) instead of $\kappa\alpha\tau\alpha\lambda\acute{\iota}\pi\eta \, \gamma\nu\nu\alpha\hat{\iota}\kappa\alpha$ (emphasis on the situation at the time of death; Mark 12:19); a rearrangement of the brief descriptions of the successive deaths (Mark 12:20-22); $\check{v}\sigma\tau\epsilon\rho\nu$ instead of $\check{\epsilon}\sigma\chi\alpha\tau\nu \, \pi\acute{\alpha}\nu\tau\omega\nu$ (Mark 12:22).

8   To be sure, the text is not certain. The variant $\lambda\acute{\epsilon}\gamma\nu\tau\epsilon\varsigma$ (as in Mark) is also well attested; see the critical apparatus in Nestle-Aland (27th ed.).

9   If Luke keeps $\sigma\pi\acute{\epsilon}\rho\mu\alpha$ ("seed") in v. 28, it is because it is part of the scriptural text that Mark quotes (to be sure, the text of Deut 25:5 LXX is somewhat different, but it does contain the word).

10   The rewriting of the beginning of this section can be attributed to grammatical improvements: "That the dead are raised, Moses also revealed in the episode of the bush when he says . . ." (v. 37) instead of "As for the fact that the dead are to be raised, did you not read in the book of Moses, in the account of the burning bush, how God said to him . . ." (Mark 12:26).

11   In Stephen's speech in Acts 7:38, the Law of Moses is understood not as a written text but as a collection of living oracles that God spoke to Moses.

12   Luke adds $\grave{\omega}\varsigma \, \lambda\acute{\epsilon}\gamma\epsilon\iota$ ("when he says"), which grammatically refers to Moses. By contrast, the Markan parallel explicitly designates God as the subject of the of the proposition: $\pi\hat{\omega}\varsigma \, \epsilon\check{\iota}\pi\epsilon\nu \, \alpha\grave{v}\tau\hat{\omega} \, \grave{o} \, \vartheta\epsilon\grave{o}\varsigma \, \lambda\acute{\epsilon}\gamma\omega\nu$, "how God said to him" (Mark 12:26). One can wonder whether, apart from the grammar, Luke did not also regard God as the true subject of this verb "to speak," $\lambda\acute{\epsilon}\gamma\epsilon\iota$.

everlasting name of mine and a memorial of generations to generations.'"[13]

There is a third substantial change. To Jesus' doctrinal statement ("God is not the God of the dead but of the living," v. 38),[14] which he has taken over from Mark 12:27a, Luke adds a short commentary: "Because all live from him." In so doing he eliminates the criticism that the Markan Jesus directed to the Sadducees: "You are completely wrong" (Mark 12:27b). Luke's concern is to underscore not the human error but the message of God, which, as will be seen, is life-giving truth.

As always, Luke takes liberties when beginning or ending an episode. If at the beginning of the pericope he changed little (v. 27), at the end he intervenes vigorously (vv. 39-40). He indeed feels the need to create the ending himself. He does it first of all by making use of a literary process that German-language exegetes call the *Chorschluss*,[15] that is, the cry of admiration from the spectators or the congratulations of the hearers.[16] The "scribes," of whom it has not been said that they had disappeared from the scene,[17] concede that they have been convinced by Jesus' arguments. Luke undoubtedly thinks that these scribes are of the Pharisaic inclination and that they share Jesus' opinion about the resurrection.[18] Understanding what is going on, they congratulate him with a formula that would be appropriate for Greek philosophical as well as for talmudic agreement: διδάσκαλε, καλῶς εἶπας, "Teacher, you have spoken well!" Luke is concerned to remind the readers that Jesus' message, and later that of the Christians, causes a parting of the ways. Even if the division into two groups is not explicit here, it is probable. The scribes of v. 39 are not the same people as the Sadducees of v. 27. To the approval of those who are convinced he adds as a counterpoint the disappointment of those who are obstinate (see Luke 4:22, 28-29; Acts 28:24-25). These are the people—Luke is undoubtedly thinking primarily of the Sadducees—who, defeated rhetorically and theologically, no longer dare to face their adversary (v. 40).[19]

Verses 34-36 are still to be analyzed. I have left them to the end, because one can be undecided about them. On the one hand, one can say that Luke has only the one source, Mark, at his disposal and that, if vv. 34-36 diverge to such a degree from Mark, it is because Luke felt obligated to intervene here vigorously. On the other hand, one can say that Luke has a parallel version here that he prefers over the Markan formulation. In favor of the first assumption is its simplicity and the fact that Luke is reluctant to mix two sources in the same episode. One must grant the other assumption that the vocabulary and the doctrinal categories of these verses are not characteristic of Luke. The expressions "children of this age" and "children of the resurrection" have a Semitic tonality.[20] The three *hapax legomena* ἰσάγγελοι ("equal to angels"), ἄτεκνος ("without children"), and γαμίσκομαι ("to be given in marriage," "marry" [for a woman]) also attract

---

13 English translation by Larry J. Perkins in Albert Pietersma and Benjamin G. Wright, eds., *A New English Translation of the Septuagint* (New York: Oxford University Press, 2009).

14 Luke changes the word order. He begins with θεός, adds a δέ, and continues with the verb and its negation, οὐκ ἔστιν. Mark 12:27: οὐκ ἔστιν θεός. In Luke 20:38, as in Mark 12:27, θεός is used without the article, since it has an attributive function.

15 "Chorus," "chorus of acclamation." See Martin Dibelius, *From Tradition to Gospel* (trans. Bertram Lee Woolf; 2d ed.; Cambridge: Clarke, 1971) 53, 58, 71, 75. Gerd Theissen (*Miracle Stories of the Early Christian Tradition* [trans. F. McDonagh; Philadelphia: Fortress Press, 1983] 70) avoids the term, because it does not make it possible to distinguish between admiration and acclamation.

16 There is a good example of a *Chorschluss* in 5:26; see vol. 1 of this commentary, 184, on 5:26.

17 They have been present since 19:47; their presence is recalled in 20:19.

18 In Acts 23:6-9 Luke states explicitly that the subject of the resurrection divides the Sadducees and Pharisees. By contrast, this theme brings the Pharisees closer to Paul, just as here in Luke 20:39 it brings the scribes closer to Jesus.

19 In his redaction of v. 40 (the intimidated opponents) Luke is influenced by Mark 12:34b, the end of the following pericope in that Gospel (Mark 12:28-34, the greatest commandment). Luke omits the pericope here, since he has included its essence in an earlier passage (Luke 10:25-28). That such displacements were possible is clear from a reading of the Gospel of Matthew, which uses Mark 12:34b as the conclusion of the following literary unit, the question about the Son of David (Matt 22:46).

20 See Fitzmyer, 2:1305, 1101.

our attention.[21] The presence of two different forms of the verb "to be given in marriage, to marry" (γαμίζομαι and γαμίσκομαι) suggests a double origin (the first verb from Mark, the second from the other source).[22] The special theology of these verses looks to a present reality that Mark resolutely fixes in the future and supports, in the final analysis, the hypothesis of a parallel version.[23] It is true that Luke usually avoids combining heterogeneous elements, but sometimes, as here, he also offers an alternate version of Jesus' words.[24]

Personally, I am convinced by these last arguments, and I hold to the hypothesis that the origin of vv. 34b-36[25] is independent of Mark. I do not think that these verses belong to Q. Nor does one find them in the *Gospel of Thomas*. They must come from the evangelist's special material or from an independent tradition of free-circulating sentences such as one finds in some patristic literature.[26] Let us note the principal differences between Luke 20:34b-36 and Mark 12:24b-25. The double error of which Jesus, according to Mark, accuses the Sadducees (they know neither the Scriptures nor the power of God; Mark 12:24b) disappears, as the words "you are quite wrong" (Mark 12:27b) are absent further down in Luke 20:38. Luke's version contrasts two eons and recalls what takes place in "this time" (v. 34b). It specifies that only those who are worthy (v. 35a) will take part in the resurrection. To the absence of marriage in the resurrection it adds a positive aspect: the impossibility of dying (v. 36a). It prefers "equal to angels" (ἰσάγγελοι, v. 36a) to the expression "like angels" (Mark 12:25b). Finally, it gives the "children of the resurrection" the title "children of God" (v. 36b). As we will see in our exegesis, it is probable that Luke added explanations to the traditional unit he takes over here (vv. 34b-36).

As I said, most exegetes accept that the entire account, except for vv. 34b-36, is dependent on Mark. Yet readers should remember that there are other solutions to the Synoptic Problem. According to some, Luke could depend on Matthew or Proto-Matthew.[27] For this pericope an original solution has been suggested recently, which I, however, do not find convincing.[28] According to Emmanuelle Main, Jesus' argumentation, as the Gospel of Luke reports it, would correspond perfectly to the debates among rabbis as they were held in the first century of the Common Era, while that of the Gospel of Mark would no longer have much in common with such argumentation. There Jesus shamelessly displays his christological power as victorious Lord and no longer makes the effort to reason. Therefore, Luke would offer here the original and authentic, "the best," version of the episode,[29] while Mark would reflect more the later discussion that Christians would have with their Jewish opponents.

---

21   See Montanti, "Filiazione," 262–63.
22   It should be noted, however, that the text is not certain at these places and that some manuscripts read γαμίσκονται in Mark 12:25 and γαμίζονται in Luke 20:34. See esp. Kurt Aland, ed., *Synopsis Quattuor Evangeliorum: Locis parallelis evangeliorum apocryphorum et Patrum adhibitis* [3d ed.; Stuttgart: Württembergische Bibelanstalt, 1965] 384 and *NTG* 2:145.
23   See the commentary below on vv. 34b-36.
24   See Montanti, "Filiazione," 268; Schramm, *Markus-Stoff*, 170–71; Mudiso Mbâ Mundla, *Jesus*, 71, 78. Rejecting this hypothesis and favoring an exclusive dependence on Mark are Neirynk, "Matière," esp. 166–67; Rigaux, *Dieu l'a ressuscité*, 33–34 (cautiously); Gerhard Schneider, *Das Evangelium nach Lukas* (2d ed.; 2 vols.; ÖTBK 3.1-2; Gütersloh: Mohn, 1984) 2:404–5; Fitzmyer, 2:1299; Schwankl, *Sadduzäerfrage*, 461.
25   In its simplicity v. 34a sounds exactly like Mark 12:24a. Yet on two points Luke changes his source.

He avoids the asyndeton by adding a καί ("and"), and he prefers εἶπεν ("he said") over ἔφη ("he said," "he says"). Luke is also very close to Mark in v. 35b (see Mark 12:25a).
26   Justin Martyr knows these words of Jesus. Either he has them from Luke 20:34b-36, or he knows them as independent logia. See Justin *Dial.* 81.4; see also Justin *De resurr.* 3, whose authenticity is uncertain; Maurice Geerard, *Clavis Patrum Graecorum*, vol. 1 (Turnhout: Brepols, 1983) no. 1081; texts are in Aland, *Synopsis*, 385.
27   William R. Farmer (*The Synoptic Problem: A Critical Analysis* [New York: Macmillan, 1964]) defends the Two-Gospel hypothesis, according to which Luke used Matthew while Mark, the shortest Gospel, is the youngest and used the other two Synoptic Gospels. Goulder (*New Paradigm*, 2:697–701) is of the opinion that Luke used Matthew as well as Mark.
28   I summarize briefly Main's thesis ("Sadducéens") here.
29   Main, "Sadducéens," 430.

Finally, a word on Matthew.[30] In general, the first evangelist operates as does Luke. He takes over Mark's text and improves and clarifies it, but he does so less readily and with less literary care. Matthew especially remains faithful to Mark where Luke (vv. 34b-36) departs from him. Sometimes Matthew corrects Mark in the same way Luke does, resulting in some minor agreements, but they are not important enough to cause an exegetical headache. Matthew and Luke give their preference to the verb "to approach" ($\pi\rho\sigma\acute{\epsilon}\rho\chi\omega\mu\alpha\iota$) and to the aorist "they questioned" ($\acute{\epsilon}\pi\eta\rho\acute{\omega}\tau\eta\sigma\alpha\nu$, Matt 22:23 par. Luke 20:27). Neither of them likes "last of all," "after all of them" ($\acute{\epsilon}\sigma\chi\alpha\tau\sigma\nu$ $\pi\acute{\alpha}\nu\tau\omega\nu$, Mark 12:22; see $\acute{\upsilon}\sigma\tau\epsilon\rho\sigma\nu$ . . . $\pi\acute{\alpha}\nu\tau\omega\nu$, "finally, after them all," Matt 22:27, and $\acute{\upsilon}\sigma\tau\epsilon\rho\sigma\nu$, "then," "finally," Luke 20:32). They both evoke the Word of God rather than a verse of Scripture (Matt 22:31-32 and Luke 20:37). They both eliminate "you are quite wrong" ($\pi\sigma\lambda\grave{\upsilon}$ $\pi\lambda\alpha\nu\hat{\alpha}\sigma\vartheta\epsilon$) that in Mark 12:27b completes Jesus' response (Matt 22:32; Luke 20:38). They both are concerned to end the episode with a conclusion that, although different from one another, is of their own making (Matt 22:33; Luke 20:39-40).

Commentary

■ **27** The new questioners are not anonymous here; they are a group of Sadducees.[31] Josephus, the Dead Sea Scrolls, the New Testament, and the rabbinic writings are our principal sources of information about them.[32]

As their name indicates, they refer to Zadok, one of the most important priests active during David's reign.[33] Thanks to the reform of Josiah (ca. 623 B.C.E.), the king's descendants impose a priestly dynasty on Jerusalem, which manages to reduce in importance the priests outside the capital, the future Levites (see Ezek 44:10-14; 40:46; 43:19; 48:11). The prophet Ezekiel transmits an oracle of God in favor of the "sons of Zadok" (Ezek 44:15). Gradually a hierarchy is constituted with the system of a single high priest consecrated for life (the title "high priest" appears at this time). According to 1 Chr 5:29-41 (6:1-15) and 6:35-38 (6:50-53), these Zadokite priests also claim to be "sons of Aaron" through their ancestor Phinehas, the son of Eleazar and grandson of Aaron. They then manage to marginalize another group of priests who also claim, but through Ithamar, to be sons of Aaron. By the time Jesus ben Sirach writes Ecclesiasticus, the monopoly of the Zadokite priests is undisputed.[34] From that time on, political conflicts, quarrels among the Zadokites themselves, persecutions, emigrations to Egypt, and retreats to the desert mark the decline of the Zadokites and give rise to irreconcilable personal ambitions.[35] In Herod's day the chief priests active in Jerusalem claim hereditary links to the Zadokites, as do the pious men who took refuge in the desert of Judah and formed the Qumran community. In spite of the political changes from the Seleucids through the Maccabees, the Hasmoneans, and the Herodians to the Romans, there was always a priestly aristocracy in Jeru-

---

30   See Luz, *Matthew 21–28*, 68–69.

31   On the Sadducees, see Meyer, "$\Sigma\alpha\delta\delta\sigma\nu\kappa\alpha\hat{\imath}\sigma\varsigma$"; Le Moyne, *Sadducéens*; Baumbach, "Konservatismus"; Müller, "Sadduzäer" (allusions to Sadducees in New Testament in places other than the explicit texts).

32   I share the opinion of James VanderKam and Peter Flint (*The Meaning of the Dead Sea Scrolls: Their Significance for Understanding the Bible, Judaism, Jesus, and Christianity* [San Francisco: Harper, 2002] 250–52), who conclude that the Dead Sea Scrolls are of an Essene rather than a Saducean origin. Nevertheless, Essenes and Sadducees both claimed a Zadokite origin. See also Meyer, "$\Sigma\alpha\delta\delta\sigma\nu\kappa\alpha\hat{\imath}\sigma\varsigma$," 38–40.

33   See 2 Sam [LXX 2 Kgdms] 15:24-37; 17:15; 19:11-12. He became the chief of the priests at the time of Solomon, for whom he had taken sides and whom on David's orders he anointed king (1 Kgs [LXX 3 Kgdms] 1:32-40). It is true that there are

other Zadoks from whom our Sadducees could have derived their name: *'Abot de Rabbi Nathan* (5) reports that at the beginning of the second century B.C.E. Antigonus of Soko had two disciples, Zadok and Boethus. According to rabbinic sources, the Sadducees and Boethusians go back to these founding persons. In addition, according to Josephus (*Ant.* 18.1.1 §4), when Quirinius was the governor in 7 B.C.E. it was a Pharisee by the name of Zadok who helped Judas the Galilean launch the Zealot movement. See Meyer, "$\Sigma\alpha\delta\delta\sigma\nu\kappa\alpha\hat{\imath}\sigma\varsigma$," 36–43; Baumbach, "Konservatismus," 202–4.

34   The Hebrew manuscript B of Cairo intercalates a psalm here (Sir 51:12) that was not translated into Greek. Its characteristic line is: "Praise him who chose the sons of Zadok as priests, for his love is eternal."

35   On the troubled times of the Maccabees and Hasmoneans, see Meyer, "$\Sigma\alpha\delta\delta\sigma\nu\kappa\alpha\hat{\imath}\sigma\varsigma$," 36–44.

salem with conservative tendencies to which the name Zadokites—Sadducees in Greek—remained attached.[36] They believed that God intervened little in the world and that human beings were entirely responsible. They distrusted oral tradition and acknowledged as sacred Scripture only the law God had entrusted to Moses. They did not believe in the resurrection of the dead.[37]

Luke mentions the Sadducees here in the Gospel and at the beginning and end of the book of Acts (Acts 4:1-2; 5:17; 23:6-8). On several occasions he presents them as resolute opponents of the resurrection and contrasts them with Jesus, then with Paul. In Acts he also mentions their opposition to angels and spirits. The tableau Luke portrays is coherent, and on the central point of the resurrection he repeats Mark's opinion (as Matthew also does) and concurs in the view of Josephus as well as that of the rabbinic sources.[38]

■ **28** They do not hesitate to call him "master/teacher."[39] There is no reason to suspect flattery or hypocrisy in this title. The Sadducees are engaged in an intellectual and academic debate. Compared with other disputes (e.g., 18:18), the question (v. 33) emerges only after a long introduction (vv. 28-32). They begin by quoting what "Moses has written for us," that is to say, a passage of the Pentateuch (the only sacred Scripture in the eyes of the Sadducees). One will notice the "for us," which designated the nation of Israel as the perpetual recipient of the written law. The Sadducees sought out a text that in their day had scarcely any relevance any longer. Modern scholars doubt that the levirate commandment was still practiced at the time. It is, nevertheless, Holy Scripture that is being debated, and the Sadducees believe that it is as authoritative for Jesus as it is for them.[40] It is a debate within Judaism. The heirs of the Pharisees, the rabbis of the Amoraic period, will continue to pay attention to the levirate regulation.[41] If Luke, who is certainly open to Christian universalism and the Gentile nations, does not ignore the rule, it is because he respects the Jewish origins of Jesus and the church and preserves the Scriptures with devotion and fidelity. The quotation, however, is not exact. It is a compilation of elements from Deut 25:5 and Gen 38:8 according to the LXX.[42] To understand this rule we must recall four fundamental realities of Hebrew society: (a) the importance of the family, the members of which generally lived together;[43] (b) polygamy permitted for men; (c) priority given to the needs of men rather than to those of women; (d) the importance of descendents to ensure the continuation of the name. The levirate system established by the law is not primarily for the purpose of protecting the widow; it is to ensure an

---

36   See Baumbach, "Konservatismus," 203–4: "Thus from the middle of the second pre-Christian century we can speak of the Sadducees as the status party [*Standespartei*] of the high-priestly nobility in Jerusalem."

37   See Meyer, "Σαδδουκαῖος," 46–51.

38   Luke likes the verb ἐπερωτῶ and uses it eighteen times (2:46; 3:10, 14; 6:9; 8:9, 30; 9:18; 17:20; 18:18; 20:21, 27, 40; 22:64; 23:6, 9; Acts 1:6; 5:27; 23:34). The people who ask questions can be well-intentioned or malicious. They can be disciples, crowds, soldiers, political or religious authorities, Pharisees or Sadducees, even Jesus himself. The question can come from interest, uneasiness, suspicion, or hostility. If one asks questions, it is to learn something, but this knowledge can either enrich the spirit of the disciples or give arguments to a judge who faces a decision.

39   The agents of the scribes and Pharisees challenged Jesus with this same title, διδάσκαλε ("master, teacher," 20:21). On this title, see Bovon, *Luke the Theologian*, 204–5.

40   In its vocabulary the story of the Sadducees is influenced not only by the levirate law but also by the story of Tamar. Genesis 38 tells the story of Er, the son of Judah, who married Tamar and died childless. After Er's death, Judah said to Onan, his second son, "Go to your brother's wife and act with her as the close relative of the deceased and raise up a lineage for your brother" (Gen 38:8). What Onan did to void producing a descendant who would not be his is well known. When a third brother, Shelah, was not given in marriage to Tamar, she took revenge on her father-in-law, Judah. See Janzen, "Resurrection," 46–47; Mudiso Mbâ Mundla, *Jesus*, 85: For the Sadducees, only the objective and literal sense of the text had authority.

41   See Burrows, "Levirate"; Fitzmyer, 2:1305; Main, "Sadducéens," 415–17.

42   The conjunction ἐάν followed by an aorist subjunctive introduces an eventuality; ἵνα followed by an aorist subjunctive has here the value of an imperative; see BDF §387 (3).

43   Deuteronomy 25:5 begins by mentioning the "brothers who live together," which in those days was the ideal family life. See vol. 2 of this commentary, on 15:12.

alternative solution that can provide descendants for the man without leaving the family circle. In Jesus' day, as monogamy gradually was imposed, the system of levirate marriage gradually fell into disuse.[44] Still, the law remained with all its authority.

■ **29-33** To test the applicability of a law one must have concrete cases, real life situations, examples. The Sadducees choose the example of seven brothers that with its breadth is certainly impressive but also artificial.

Moreover, it may be that the Sadducees chose this example in a time when other Jewish movements celebrated the memory of the seven brothers of the Maccabean period. Indeed, people have noticed similarities between this pericope and *4 Maccabees*, which venerates the courage of the seven brothers and their mother.[45]

That the woman never had children is a necessary part of the narrative so the story can reach its final configuration: Seven men had the same wife, and now all of them, including the woman, have died. These are the only two things that matter. Left out of consideration here are the marital relations of the various brothers, who were not necessarily unmarried when they took their brother's wife to produce descendants for him after he had died. Also not considered is that one had to grant the widow protection, especially the widow who was childless.

Modern readers are struck by the androcentrism inherent in the Mosaic commandment and the Sadducees' account. The man decides: it is he who "takes" the woman and who "has" a woman. It goes without saying that what is expected of her is that she give birth to a child, especially a male child. When in v. 33 she becomes the grammatical subject of the sentence, it is simply to clarify whose wife—one is tempted to say, whose object—she will be at the resurrection of the dead. The turning point the story takes with Jesus' intervention changes this perspective by evoking a life that in time will be liberated from the constraints of marriage. Still, Jesus' answer does not refer primarily to this aspect. On the one hand, it makes a distinction between the "times"

and, on the other hand, while referring to God, manifests the nature of the ἀνάστασις, the so-often mentioned "resurrection."

Luke uses—and he is the only evangelist to do so—the adjective ἄτεκνος ("who has no children," "without children") to describe the man's situation at his death. The expression sounds better to Greek ears than does the Semitic formula "without leaving a descendant" (literally, "seed") of Mark 12:20. For attentive readers it also has a legal connotation. If at the end of the narrative (v. 31) Luke resorts to the expression οὐ κατέλιπον τέκνα ("left no children"), he does so under the influence of Mark, who writes of the second brother "without leaving a descendant" (μὴ καταλιπὼν σπέρμα, literally, "seed"; Mark 12:21; Mark himself is influenced by the biblical text he quotes: καὶ καταλίπῃ γυναῖκα, "by leaving a woman"; Mark 12:19).

In reading these verses I am struck by the importance attached to certain terms and themes: the man, the woman, the children, death, and the lack of children. Yet at the very beginning there is also the word ἀνάστασις, first from the pen of the narrator (v. 27), then on the lips of the Sadducees (v. 33), finally from the mouth of Jesus (vv. 35 and 36). The connection between this term and the scriptural text, as well as the scenario that is erected, appears in the biblical quotation itself. There one reads that the levirate system is imposed with a precise objective "so that he raises up offspring" (ἵνα . . . ἐξαναστήσῃ σπέρμα, v. 28). Why, wonder and ask the Sadducees, should we speak of a "resurrection" other than the one described, proposed, or imposed by the law? Thus, lying behind the Sadducees' question[46] and in the Gospel pericope is the issue of the definition of the "resurrection." It is also a quarrel between ancient and modern, because the Sadducees hold to the old system of real life on this earth and in this time. What comes after death belongs to the impersonal and powerless world of the shades, the lifeless domain of Sheol. The only thing one can do, the only thing their God can think to do to limit the havoc, is to ensure the succession of human generations. You

---

44 Fitzmyer (2:1304) points out, however, that Josephus (*Ant.* 4.8.23 §§254–56) speaks of the system as if it were still applied.

45 See Le Moyne, *Sadducéens*, 126. Bock (2:1620) refers to Tob 3:8; 6:10-12; 7:11-13 as an example of a chain of marriages.

46 The verb of this question is uncertain: γίνεται ("becomes") or ἔσται ("will be"). Both are well attested, but ἔσται is probably influenced by the parallel in Mark 12:23. Therefore, I hold to γίνεται.

live on in your children. It is they who will bear your name. And if that happens, the only people who benefit are the men, fathers and sons.

If one reads v. 33 attentively, one understands the skepticism of the Sadducees. If there is a different "resurrection" from that offered by the law, then the system envisaged becomes nonsensical and impossible. At the time of the aforesaid resurrection, these seven men will not all be able to have the same woman. Whether the Sadducees are thinking of polygamy or monogamy does not matter, because here one would have a case— unimaginable—of polyandry. As if they wanted to underscore this implicit impossibility,[47] they follow their question with the redundant words: "For the seven had her as a wife" (v. 33b).

■ **34-36** In my judgment, the introduction, "And Jesus said to them" ($\kappa\alpha\grave{\iota}$ $\epsilon\hat{\iota}\pi\epsilon\nu$ $\alpha\mathrm{\mathring{v}}\tauο\hat{\iota}\varsigma$ $\mathring{o}$ $\mathring{I}\eta\sigmaο\hat{v}\varsigma$), is a Lukan resumption and modification of the Markan parallel (Mark 12:24a).[48] It has been suggested that it also could be the beginning of the tradition independent of Mark that Luke quotes here. It is true that, after the *verba dicendi*, the evangelist prefers $\pi\rho\acute{o}\varsigma$ followed by the accusative. I would answer that, since he sometimes uses the dative in such cases, he could well have kept the $\alpha\mathrm{\mathring{v}}\tauο\hat{\iota}\varsigma$ that Mark had suggested. Moreover, as is the case with free-floating logia, the independent tradition probably conveyed sentences without any introductory formula, or at least without mentioning anonymous recipients.

Let us first consider Jesus' statements (vv. 34b-36) as an independent unit. This unit is composed of two parts. The first, vv. 34b-35, contrasts in a symmetrical and antithetic way the two "times" and especially the two human categories, the great majority on the one side, the righteous or the elect on the other. One will note an element that says the same thing twice and disturbs this symmetry: the words "and the resurrection from the dead" ($\kappa\alpha\grave{\iota}$ $\tau\hat{\eta}\varsigma$ $\mathring{\alpha}\nu\alpha\sigma\tau\acute{\alpha}\sigma\epsilon\omega\varsigma$ $\tau\hat{\eta}\varsigma$ $\mathring{\epsilon}\kappa$ $\nu\epsilon\kappa\rho\hat{\omega}\nu$, v. 35).[49] This redundancy probably comes from Luke, whose twofold objective is to bind the logia more closely to the controversy over the resurrection and to clarify for his readers the sense of the expression "at that time."

The form of the second part of the unit, v. 36, is less harmonious. In fact, it contains in its first half two successive statements, each one accompanied by "for" ($\gamma\acute{\alpha}\rho$); "for they can no longer die," and "for they are equal to angels. . . ." Furthermore, in its second half Jesus' assertion, with its repetition of the verb "to be," also is not distinguished by its elegance: "and are children of God, being children of the resurrection." In my opinion, here too we must reckon with an editorial effort on Luke's part, which, in trying to achieve clarity, robs the sentence of some of its vigor and temperance. I suggest, therefore, that the words "for they can no longer die" and the expression "they are children of God" come from the evangelist. With this double insertion Luke wanted to prevent misunderstandings and to enlighten spirits. Indeed, the first statement supplies in advance the meaning of the unusual adjective $\mathring{\iota}\sigma\acute{\alpha}\gamma\gamma\epsilon\lambdaο\iota$ ("equal to angels"). The second qualifies the sense of the Semitic formula "being children of the resurrection."

What did these statements attributed to Jesus originally mean? They take over the Jewish contrast between the two eons, "this time" and "that time." Yet they do not necessarily understand these eras as successive periods,[50] nor do they understand them in a timeless manner as the designation of two domains, of two concurrent reigns, of two spaces rather than two times. I would suggest that, in keeping with the eschatology one can attribute to the historical Jesus and a number of early Christians, these statements speak of two periods that partly overlap. "That time" has already begun in "this time" (see Luke 16:8). In support of this hypothesis I can cite the

---

47   To understand well what is at issue in this dispute one must admit what Anderson ("Look," 13) says: "Implicitness was functioning as a prominence marker."

48   On these verses, see Wiles, "Studies"; Montanti, "Filiazione"; Bianchi, "Relevance"; Aune, "Logion."

49   In v. 34 good witnesses such as the Codex Bezae (D = 05), some Old Latin manuscripts, and certain versions (the Syriac in particular) offer a longer text. Before "marry and are given in marriage" they have the words "are begotten and beget." Accord-ing to Wolfgang Wiefel (*Das Evangelium nach Lukas* [ThHKNT 3; Berlin: Evangelische Verlagsanstalt, 1988] 342), this could be the original text of Luke. The absence of these words in most Greek manuscripts would result from an effort to assimilate Luke's text to that of Mark (I would say rather of Matthew and Mark).

50   Leopold Sabourin (*L'Évangile de Luc: Introduction et commentaire* [Rome: Gregorian University Press, 1985] 323) is of the opinion that Luke is thinking of two successive periods.

67

grammatical time, the present indicative, of all the main verbs of vv. 34b-36. I also note that, in spite of the precise details in "when they rise from the dead" (Mark) and "in the resurrection" (Matthew), the tradition retained by Mark and then by Matthew does not necessarily suggest two successive periods, because the present indicative is used here as well (Mark 12:25 par. Matt 22:30).

The case of marriage, which one enters or in which one is involved with others, is only one of a number of examples of human life. Luke 17:27 mentions it along with eating and drinking. Luke 17:28 mentions feeding, commerce, agriculture, and building; Luke 17:34-35 sleeping and working. These activities are not criticized, but neither are they valued. What gives the language a negative coloring and passes judgment on the people engaged in the activities are the expressions "of this time" here (v. 34), "in the days of Noah" (Luke 17:26) and "in the days of Lot" (Luke 17:28).

To characterize the other group the sentence uses καταξιῶ, a verb with a moral connotation (there is nothing similar to it in the parallel of Mark 12:25).[51] One can understand the aorist passive participle καταξιωθέντες in two ways. If the emphasis is on human passivity, it retains the idea of the gracious intervention of God; if the emphasis is on the ethical tone, the participle retains the reward given to ethical virtue. We cannot decide on the basis of the participle itself; the author of this sentence certainly did not contrast God's share and the human share. For him it is a matter of a happy relationship in the framework of the covenant, of a human response in faith and deed to the divine initiative.

In this case the verb τυγχάνω (here in the aorist infinitive τυχεῖν) does not have the meaning "to reach by accident"; it means rather "to reach" or "to attain." Greek authors sometimes use this verb in an ethical framework. In the tragedy *The Persians*, Aeschylus writes ὅσοι δὲ λοιποὶ κάτυχον σωτηρίας and in *Prometheus Bound*, τούτου τυχεῖν οὐκ ἠξιώθην αὐτός.[52]

How are we to understand the words "they neither marry nor are given in marriage"?[53] Let us first of all note that in v. 34 "to be given in marriage" is expressed by the verb γαμίσκομαι, and that in v. 35 it is expressed by the verb γαμίζομαι.[54] This difference is surprising, and I offer the following explanation: in v. 34 γαμίσκομαι is the verb of the independent tradition, while in v. 35 Luke, who quotes this tradition, is influenced by the parallel of Mark 12:25, which has γαμίζομαι.

The statement means first of all that for the elect the conditions of life differ radically from those of the common run of people.[55] It then suggests that these conditions apply not only to a future after death or at the end of time but also to a present that can be described as eschatological in anticipation. Finally, it implies an ascetic determination and obligation. As Paul says in a parallel passage that is striking in its similarities (1 Cor 7:32-34), those who have welcomed the new times and who have been welcomed in them, no longer worry about this world but trust entirely in the Lord. Must we go

51   See Kilgallen, "Sadducees," 482; Prete, "Insegnamento," 431, 440–41; Bock, 2:1622–23; J.-B. Frey, "La vie dans l'au-delà dans les conceptions juives au temps de Jésus-Christ," *Bib* 13 (1932) 129–68. On p. 153 Frey refers to a Jewish epitaph in Rome in honor of a woman named Regina and summarizes it thus: "The husband expresses his certainty that she who is now lying in the tomb *will live again*, that she *will return to the light, that she will rise for the age promised to those who are* worthy of it" (italics from Frey). Main ("Sadducéens," 423 n. 43) called this epitaph to my attention.

52   "All the others who have attained salvation . . . ," that is to say, who have escaped death (Aeschylus *Pers.* 508). "I myself was not judged worthy to attain that," namely, compassion (Aeschylus *Prom.* 239–40). See also Pindar *Ol.* 2.85–86.

53   Jesus' answer contradicts the hope of certain rabbis who expected the resurrection to be a time of mar-velous fruitfulness with countless childbirths; see Str-B 4.2:890–91; and van Daalen, "Observations," 241.

54   I understand these verbs as the result of the authority of the father who gives his daughter in marriage. See J. Reiling and J. L. Swellengrebel, *A Translator's Handbook on the Gospel of Luke* (Helps for Translators 10; Leiden: Brill, 1971) 653; Tannehill, 295. Joel B. Green (*The Gospel of Luke* [NICNT; Grand Rapids: Eerdmans, 1997] 721) thinks that the woman cooperates by agreeing to the marriage.

55   Tertullian (*Mon.* 10.5–6) is of the opinion that this verse does not mean that abolishing the sexual relationships will involve the separation of the couple. Thus, there will be a spiritual intimacy. In my judgment, the biblical text does not say that explicitly. See Carton ("Anges," 51–52), who quotes Tertullian's text.

further and, like the bearers of this tradition, conceive of a decidedly encratic community that rejects marriage and its consequences or its implications, such as sexuality and procreation? If we take the text literally, we must answer yes. It may also be, however, that the author of these words, Jesus or an early Christian prophet, is simply playing with the words and expressing a preference. Paul prefers celibacy, but he does not impose it on everyone. It is "as if" one does not marry or is not given in marriage. It is also possible that the text presupposes a practice identical to that of the Syrian church of the first centuries:[56] After accepting Christian faith and receiving baptism, the believers should not change their marital status. Thus, there is no Christian celebration of marriage, but neither does one dissolve the existing marriages. It is a way of respecting the apostle's injunction: "Let each person remain before God in the condition (κλῆσις) in which one was called" (1 Cor 7:20).

"For they are equal to angels."[57] It would be good to know what the author of this statement understands with the word "angel." Based on the information found in the Jewish writings of antiquity, angels had the following characteristics. They are beings who are close to God, created by God, but foreign to the material world. If they have a body at all, it is completely different from the bodies of human beings or animals. In addition, the angels are not defined by gender; they are not limited by the male–female distinction.[58] Although they are created,

that is, marked by a beginning, they have no need to fear an end or to hope for it. As Luke says of the people who are like them, "they can no longer die" (v. 36). Their origin and their existence depend on God, the king, whose court they represent. They facilitate the relationship with a deity who is increasingly understood as distant and transcendent. As their name indicates, they are the "envoys," the "messengers" of God when he wants to come to human beings to inform them, to admonish them, to protect them, to punish them, or to prepare for them a future dictated by the divine economy. When they are not on a mission, they take part in the worship of God, fulfilling in heaven the task human beings try to fulfill on earth, in the temple, or in their assemblies. These are the beings the author envisions when he says, "for they are equal to angels" (v. 36).

The Markan parallel has the words "but they are as angels in heaven" (12:25b). Are the two formulations equivalent? By resorting to the exceptional adjective ἰσάγγελος, the author of the statement undoubtedly wanted to be more precise. He is speaking not of a resemblance, whose degree and nature would remain unspecified, but of an equality.[59] "Those who are considered worthy to reach that age" join, because of that very dignity, the rank of angels in the midst of God's creation. This elevation certainly does not leave them

---

56 See Brock, "Asceticism."

57 Kilgallen ("Sadducees," 485 n. 17) presents a series of modern interpretations of this expression. See also Montanti, "Filiazione," 272; Robinson, "Angels." See 2 Bar. 51:10 and 1 Enoch 104:6.

58 See Carton ("Anges," 51) and Mudiso Mbâ Mundla (Jesus, 91), who quote 1 Enoch 15:6-7. In this passage the angels are certainly male, but God does not give them women, because their nature is spiritual and their residence is in heaven.

59 It is possible that Luke is the creator of the adjective ἰσάγγελος; see Lagrange, 516, and Plummer, 469–70. The idea that the believers who have died or have been raised are like angels is neither new nor unique to the evangelists. Aune ("Logion," 193) offers the following parallels. Philo of Alexandria (Sacr. 1.5) affirms that at his death Abraham inherited immortality and became equal to the angels (ἴσος ἀγγέλοις γεγονώς); 2 Bar. 51:10 promises the righteous a future similar to that of angels and

stars, as we have seen above (n. 57); 1 Enoch 15:6 points out that in their spiritual and heavenly residences angels have no need of wives. As Lagrange (516) indicates, later, in the fifth century of the Common Era, the Neoplatonist Hierocles (Commentarius in aureum carmen 4.3) explains a verse of Pythagoras as follows: "This word commits us to honor the men who (by virtue of their wisdom) have taken their place among the divine generations, those who are equal to the daemons and to the angels, and are similar to the famous heroes" (τοὺς ἰσοδαίμονας καὶ ἰσαγγέλους καὶ τοῖς ἀγανοῖς ἤρουσιν ὁμοίους), in F. G. A. Mulloch, ed., Fragmenta philosophorum Graecorum, vol. 1 (Paris: Didot, 1883) 425. The term also appears in the Gospel of Judas 5.13 (p. 40), where from the mouth of Jesus the author attacks people who claim it for themselves.

unchanged. Without being identical to the angels (equal does not mean identical), they became like them in at least two regards: They are no longer divided into men and women, and they no longer run the risk of dying. Personally, I am of the opinion that the theology of these statements is not far removed from that of the apostle Paul. He is convinced that death entered the world because of Adam and that sin is universal (Rom 5:12-21). In his view, in Jesus Christ sin and death are defeated at the same time. Those who believe in the gospel of Jesus Christ become new creatures. They rediscover the glory that Adam lost in the fall (Rom 3:23). In the resurrection (which begins with the renewal of the νοῦς [Rom 12:2] but which, because of death, is not yet completed), the transformed or resuscitated beings will be "spiritual bodies" (1 Cor 15:44 in the singular). That is to say, they will be like the angels, persons whose bodies will not suffer corruption but will be quickened by the Spirit without experiencing death.

At the end of v. 36 Luke moves to another level and indicates who God's friends are. The first expression ("children of God")[60] is part of Israel's religious vocabulary. In the LXX, as well as in the Jewish and then Christian literature, it indicates various realities—in the plural of angels or the people of the covenant, in the singular of the present king or the coming king, the Messiah. As is known, Hebrew theology understood the relationships between God and human beings in terms not of procreation but of adoption. The expression υἱοὶ θεοῦ shares this conviction. What the "children of that age" have become, they became by an act of divine will and not because of nature, by a juridical decision and not a biological process. Yet, when God is involved in establishing this new relationship—this adoption—it goes without saying that the juridical act goes beyond any legal framework. The adoption is more than a forensic act. From now on the "children of God" share in the divine life.[61] It

is this transformation that evokes the second expression, "children of the resurrection." The Semitism "children of" designates a relationship and a dependence. These "children," that is, these human beings, come from this regenerating act expressed in the term ἀνάστασις, "resurrection." They depend on it; they rejoice in it; and they participate in it.

Thus, the evangelist[62] preferred the version parallel to the Markan text. He chose this independent response for a precise reason: it morally characterizes the blessed beneficiaries of resurrection. On the one hand, in his eyes καταξιωθέντες explains the choice of the elect; on the other, their quasi-angelic existence corresponds to the rigorous orientation he gives the Christian message. Even when he prefers these statements to the Markan parallel, however, he must correct them somewhat. "Correct" is undoubtedly too strong a word; "interpret" is better. As the rest of his work attests, for Luke "resurrection" belongs to the future, even if the kingdom of God has drawn near and, for believers, has already arrived to a certain extent in the figure of Christ, in the formulation of the Word of God, and because of the presence of the Holy Spirit. If the received tradition insisted on a resurrection in the present that was still to show itself in the future, the Lukan redaction underscores the future of a resurrection of which the first effects can already be felt. The evangelist has these convictions in his heart when he specifies that "that age" is the time of "the resurrection from the dead," that those who have become like angels can no longer die,[63] and that the "children of the resurrection" are the "children . . . of God."

Four concluding remarks:

1. Originally, the tradition taken over in vv. 34b-36 was independent of the controversy with the Sadducees; the latter was limited to the resurrection, its existence. The tradition used here and the Lukan redaction are interested in the nature of the resurrection, what it is.

---

60 The words καὶ υἱοί εἰσιν ("and they are the sons," translated as "children") are missing from Codex Bezae (D = 05), some Old Latin witnesses (it), and the Syriac Sinai version. Wiefel (342) regards them as a gloss. I keep them because they appear in almost all Greek manuscripts (with minor variations). See Reuben J. Swanson, ed., *New Testament Greek Manuscripts: Luke* (Pasadena, Calif.: William Carey International University Press, 1995) 346; and Nestle-Aland's apparatus (27th ed.).

61 According to Montanti ("Filiazione"), vv. 34-36 understand divine sonship as an eschatological reality.

62 See Carton, "Anges," 49–50; Kilgallen, "Sadducees."

63 On this phrase and its survival in antiquity, see Bianchi, "Relevance."

2. I translated the term *υἱοί*, which appears three times, as "children." It is my opinion that the author included "daughters" when he used the masculine "sons."

3. It is not the first time the Gospel of Luke promises the believers the status of children of God. One is reminded that the expression appears in the Sermon on the Plain. In 6:35 we read: "And you will be children [literally, 'sons'] of the Most High."

4. I have commented on the androcentric and patriarchal character of the LXX quotations and of the example of the seven brothers. Without combating it directly, Jesus opposes it indirectly by saying that believers are beings like the angels, that is, equal among themselves.

■ **37-38** In these verses Luke returns to his primary source, the Gospel of Mark.[64] Here Mark mentions a second answer of Jesus. The first showed that the Mosaic levirate rule could apply only to life on this earth and that things would be different at the time of the resurrection of the dead. The second confronts the question of the resurrection, more precisely the scriptural roots of this doctrine.[65] I will limit my interpretation to Luke's reworking of the Markan version.

The Sadducees were mistaken with their biblical reference. According to Luke, Moses did indeed speak about resurrection, which should silence the objections of the Sadducees, but he did so at another place. He had even "revealed" it. (I know that *μηνύω* can mean simply "to indicate," but when speaking about Moses, God, and the law the author compels the meaning "to reveal," a meaning that is quite possible in Greek.) He revealed it *ἐπὶ τῆς βάτου*,[66] that is, at the time of the episode of the burning bush.[67]

"He" says. Grammatically the pronoun refers to Moses, but behind this human subject there must be the divine subject. This revelatory "saying" mentions the God of Abraham, Isaac, and Jacob. Luke and Mark agree on this point.[68] But where Mark refers to Exod 3:6 and begins with "I" (*ἐγώ*), Luke names the "Lord" (*κύριος*), that is, the very person of God, the equivalent of God's proper name, YHWH, in the Hebrew Bible. In so doing, he refers to Exod 3:15, the verse immediately following the well-known revelation of God's proper name: "I am who I am" (Exod 3:14).[69]

Thus, this God who comes to reveal his name is also the God of the patriarchs. One will note that the formula is solemn and repetitive: "The God of Abraham, and the God of Isaac, and the God of Jacob"—that is to say, the God of Israel, who is faithful to each generation. Yet is it not a tautology to say that God is God? If the statement says more than God is God, it is not a tautology. An erudite and convincing study has demonstrated that the common expression God of Abraham, of Isaac, and of Jacob designates God not so much as the one worshiped by the patriarchs but as the God who has charge of Abraham, Isaac, and Jacob.[70] It is in this sense and this sense only that the biblical quotation is true. The underlying reasoning is as follows: if God protected the patriarchs, if he cares for his people, he will not stop doing it. Consequently, the patriarchs, dead though they may be, are not abandoned to the shades of Sheol. Thanks to God's faithfulness, they will live again.[71] Such thinking would not have been possible a few centuries earlier, but in the time of Jesus and the first Christians the ancient solution, still maintained by the Sadducean minority, no longer

---

64 On these verses, see Dreyfus, "Argument"; Bartina, "Saduceos"; Suhl, *Funktion*, 67–72; Gundry, *Use*, 20–22; Downing, "Resurrection"; Manns, "Technique."

65 Based on the parallels in *4 Macc.* 7:19 and 16:25, some have thought that Jesus is demonstrating the immortality of the soul; see, on the contrary, Norval Geldenhuys, *Commentary on the Gospel of Luke* (Grand Rapids: Eerdmans, 1951) 511–12.

66 Mark has the masculine ὁ βάτος. Luke prefers the more common female ἡ βάτος. See BAGD, s.v.

67 I indicated above that with these words Mark is thinking of the *pericope* of the burning bush; Luke, it seems to me, imagines more the *episode* of the burning bush.

68 See Downing ("Resurrection"), who compares the usage in the Synoptic Gospels and in Philo of Alexandria (*Abr.* 50–55; *Fug.* 55–59): "At least one Jewish near-contemporary of Jesus found himself bound by an interpretation of Exodus 3:6 and 15-16 that took the words to mean that God had related himself so closely to mortal men as to raise awkward and inescapable questions about mortality as such."

69 See Kilgallen, "Sadducees," 487–94.

70 I am referring here to Dreyfus, "Argument"; Bartina ("Saduceos") takes over this demonstration.

71 See Heb 11:11 and 13-16, verses that also see a relationship between the patriarchs and the coming world. See also *T. Jud.* 25:1.

satisfies the doctrinal exigencies of those who have experienced persecution and martyrdom.[72]

Several exegetes have observed that the text invoked by Jesus had never been cited by Jewish authors to support the resurrection.[73] That is hardly surprising: Jesus did not take part in the scholastic and rabbinic world. He knew it from the outside, which, despite everything else, gives the debate a scholarly twist, yet he could not, nor did he want to, follow their requirements and rules.

I have been speaking of Jesus, but of course the authenticity of the exchange is not guaranteed.[74] Even if it is probable that he had a confrontation with the Sadducees, the arguments of the historical Jesus could well have gone in directions other than those the evangelists trace. Nevertheless, it seems probable to me that Jesus replied by limiting the applicability of the Law of Moses while mentioning the new conditions of those who rise from the dead. In addition, it is not out of the question that he added an argument from Scripture (especially since the text cited is original and unexpected).[75] That he concluded with a final logion is also probable, because it is so vivid and, moreover, is reminiscent of another statement ascribed to him ("Let the dead bury the dead," 9:60). Yet, when we admit the authenticity of all of these elements,[76] we are left with a redundant unit (I count some two answers of Jesus), and that contradicts the rule of form criticism that the simplest form is the earliest form. Thus, it may be that already at the Markan level, or perhaps even earlier, our pericope has merged two episodes from the life of Jesus: a controversy with the Sadducees that ended with a reference to the resurrection, a time when marriage would be excluded, and a dispute about the resurrection in which Jesus emerged victorious by referring to the God of the exodus.[77]

Jesus' final statement, "God is not the God of the dead but of the living," says openly what is only implicit in the quotation of Exodus 3.[78] Thus, while solving the enigma, it puts forth another. While it is elegant and legitimate to say that God is the God of the living and not of the dead, that does not answer the question about the countless people who have died, ultimately of everyone. Such an elliptical answer solves the problem only with an implicit argument.[79] With his name[80] God is related to "being"; by his nature he is attached to "living." He is indeed the creator, and he continues to be the protector and savior of Israel. Moreover, in Hebrew the verb "to live" is very

---

72 On the development of the belief in the resurrection of the dead, see Schubert, "Auferstehungslehre"; Pierre Grelot, "La résurrection de Jésus et son arrière-plan biblique et juif," in Paul de Surgy, ed., *La résurrection du Christ et l'exégèse moderne* (LD 50; Paris: Cerf, 1969) 17–53; Charpentier, "Tous," 85–88; Rigaux, *Dieu l'a ressuscité*, 3–22; Schwankl, *Sadduzäerfrage*, 141–300; C. F. Evans, 712–14. On Levenson (*Resurrection*), see the next note.

73 See, e.g., Philippe Bossuyt and Jean Radermakers (*Jésus, Parole de la grâce: Selon St. Luc* [2 vols.; Brussels: Institut d'études théologiques, 1981] 2:433), who note that the rabbis favor Deut 11:9 and 32:39. Cohn-Sherbok ("Defence," 70–71) introduces a number of rabbinic texts that, following Jewish exegetical rules, prove the resurrection from other passages of the Pentateuch. Levenson (*Resurrection*) advocates the thesis that the belief in resurrection is rooted in the faith of Israel from ancient times. He writes (p. x): "I argue that the expectation of the resurrection of the dead was a weight-bearing beam in the edifice of rabbinic Judaism."

74 Bultmann (*History*, 26, 49) thinks that the Synoptic episode reflects a controversy of the primitive church rather than a debate involving the historical Jesus; see also Haenchen, *Weg Jesu*, 411.

75 On the idea that Jesus was original and little influenced by the rabbis see Cohn-Sherbok, "Defence." On the connections made by some of the Dead Sea writings between the realm of death and the eschatological hope rooted in Scripture, see Ellis ("Sadducees," 277–79), who calls attention in particular to 1QH 3.19–22; 6.29–30, 34.

76 Van Daalen ("Observations," 243–45) notes that Jesus' answer is theocentric rather than christocentric.

77 Haenchen (*Weg Jesu*, 410) notes that there is in Mark 12:26 par. Luke 20:37 a "new beginning"; similarly, before him Bultmann, *History*, 26, 49. Rigaux (*Dieu l'a ressuscité*, 34–36) cites the defenders and opponents of the secondary character of Mark 12:26-27 par. Luke 20:37-38).

78 Ellis ("Sadducees," 275–76) regards the words πάντες γὰρ αὐτῷ ζῶσιν as a Lukan gloss, as a pesher, as a contemporizing commentary.

79 See Anderson, "Look."

80 See Bartina, "Saduceos," 154–55; Kilgallen, "Sadducees," 488–90.

close to the verb "to be," which is present even in the name of God. The philologists even tell us that in Jesus' day the two verbs were pronounced in the same way.[81] Whoever says "God" also says "the Giver of Life."[82] And since in Israel and for Christians death is not "natural," God can only be against it. And that is the resurrection faith, more precisely, the faith in the resurrection from the dead (one notes ἐκ νεκρῶν in v. 35; see also Mark 12:26 par. Matt 22:31). It is this underlying reflection that the theologian Luke is concerned to put at the end of Jesus' logion (neither Mark nor Matthew took the trouble to do so). With a single phrase he explains to his readers what Jesus wants to say when he speaks of the God of the living and not of the dead; for, he says, "all live from him."[83] Nevertheless, Luke does not completely satisfy us. We would like to know who in his eyes are these πάντες, these "all." We would also like to know what the function of the dative αὐτῷ is. Does it mean "from him" or "for him"?[84] The rest of Luke's entire work invites us not to neglect the universalism of salvation or the fullness of a God who at the same time is origin and destination, cause and finality.

■ **39-40** The scribes (Luke is thinking of the scribes of a Pharisaic inclination, who agree with the resurrection) applaud.[85] The audience, however, is divided. The others, undoubtedly the Sadducees who had initiated the debate, have lost their arrogant assurance, but they are not convinced. They simply do not "dare" to ask him any more questions. The final word, according to Luke, is that they have nothing more to say. They are silent.[86]

History of Interpretation

Menander and Cerdon are scarcely more than names to us, and for the most part the works of Marcion and Tatian have been lost. Nevertheless, the historian can affirm this much: in the second century there were a number of Christian movements associated with these names that rejected marriage as a purveyor of death, preached chastity, and imposed on all believers "who are considered worthy to reach that age" a literal, immediately valid interpretation of Luke 20:34-36 and a spiritual interpretation of the resurrection of the dead. One thinks, for example, of the theological position of Menander that Eusebius of Caesarea describes (in order, of course, to oppose it). It recalls the statement of Luke 20:34-36 and finds there the *worthiness* of the elect (the same verb καταξιῶ), the *received gift* of salvation, and the *impossibility of death that follows it*.[87] As the entrance to the new life, baptism makes eschatology present so that the spiritualized resurrection begins immediately.[88] The ancient witnesses show that this reading of Luke 20:34-

81 See Manns, "Technique," 6.
82 See Carton, "Anges," 50; Haenchen (Weg Jesu, 410–11), who refers to Pss 6:5-6; 29 (30):9b-10; 113B (115):17; Jer 38:18; Deut 12:2-3.
83 On this comment of Luke, see Kilgallen, "Sadducees," 491–94.
84 Delebecque (Évangile, 127) translates in an interesting way: car tous ont la vie liée à lui, "for all have life related to him."
85 Talbert (Reading, 195) notes that v. 39 becomes— I would note paradoxically—the occasion of a twofold critique of the scribes: of their theology (20:41-44) and of their lifestyle (20:45-47; 21:1-4).
86 To the exegetical and theological dimensions of the episode recognized by biblical scholars, Janzen ("Resurrection") adds a hermeneutical dimension. Jesus does, indeed, establish an analogy between the time of the patriarchs, that of Moses, and that of later generations that is to be understood hermeneutically. He also reproaches the Sadducees, at least in Mark and Matthew, for not understanding the Scriptures.
87 διὰ τοῦ μεταδιδομένου πρὸς αὐτοῦ βαπτίσματος, οὗ τοὺς καταξιουμένους ἀθανασίαν ἀίδιον ἐν αὐτῷ τούτῳ μεθέξειν τῷ βίῳ, μηκέτι θνήσκοντας, "after having received baptism from him, those who were deemed worthy of it would partake, even in this life, of everlasting immortality and would never die" (Eusebius Hist. eccl. 3.26.2). Two centuries earlier, Irenaeus of Lyon (Adv. haer. 1.23.5) had presented Menander in a similar way and had insisted on the impossibility of dying after baptism. See Aune, "Logion," 198.
88 See also Acts of Paul and Thecla 12: "And Demas and Hermogenes said to him: 'Who this man is, we do not know. But he deprives young men of wives and maidens of husbands, saying: "Otherwise there is no resurrection for you, except ye remain chaste and do not defile the flesh, but keep it pure"'" (translation, Wilhelm Schneemelcher, New Testament Apocrypha [English translation edited by R. McL. Wilson; rev. ed.; 2 vols.; Louisville: Westminster John Knox, 1991–92] 2:241). Clement of Alexandria (Strom 3.48.1) attacks encratic Christians who "as

36 (or the freely circulating logia that Luke collects) asserted itself especially in Syria, even outside heretical circles.[89] It is understandable that in other places and in more orthodox communities the church's authors made a point of projecting Luke's vv. 34-36 into the future and of using them polemically.[90]

At the beginning of the third century Tertullian referred to Marcion's interpretation (*Adv. Marc.* 4.38). The African is careful to say that Jesus answered precisely the question the Sadducees asked. With this unexpected remark he is ready to criticize Marcion who has (a) added a reference to the God of "that time" to the text of Luke 20:35 and (b) made a distinction between the God of "this time," who supports marriage, and the God of "that time," who champions virginity.[91] If Marcion were right, and if his text of Luke were the correct one, Jesus would not have answered the Sadducees' question and would not have been guilty. Since in Tertullian's eyes that is an impossibility, Marcion is wrong!

In the middle of the third century, Origen preached on Luke 20:27-40 (*Hom. Luc.* 39). He avoids, no doubt intentionally, the Lukan formulation of vv. 34-36 as too compromised by the encratic interpretation. He quotes, indeed, Matt 22:29-30, while quickly insisting on the future of the promise and the real transformation of the believers: "Those who will be as angels will certainly be angels." He concludes this point with a twofold observation. (a) "Here below, because of death, there must be marriages and children, but where immortality reigns there is no need for marriage or sons." The point is polemical: Origen refuses to anticipate the future situation of the kingdom. (b) Always hostile toward those who oppose marriage, he claims to have found nowhere in Scripture a prohibition of this institution (39.2).[92] In the following paragraph (39.3), Origen indicates that in his eyes the Sadducees' error was that they understood materially the promises of God, which relate to the heavenly world. One must understand the promised descendants or the Jerusalem foretold by the prophets in a spiritual sense. Thus, Jesus is right when he criticizes the Sadducees for their ignorance of the Scriptures (a claim, I repeat, made not by Luke but by Matthew and Mark). Origen spends no more time on this passage. For reasons not clear to me, he moves to the question of the tax owed to Caesar, which, however, in the three Synoptic Gospels precedes the Sadducees' question.[93]

A fragment preserved in a Greek catena of Luke and attributed to Apollinaris of Laodicea (fourth century) preserved a polemical explanation of the Markan formula "as God's angels in heaven" (12:25, the parallel to Luke 20:36).[94] If I understand it accurately, the author thinks that the resurrection of the dead will be an act

---

they claim, . . . have already attained the state of resurrection, and for that reason repudiate marriage." See also the *Epistle of Pseudo-Titus* 10 (*PLS* 2:1532; Schneemelcher, *New Testament Apocrypha,* 2:53–74). I am relying here on Aune, "Logion," 195.

89 See Brock, "Asceticism," 5–6; Bianchi, "Relevance," 34–35; Aune, "Logion."

90 See Aune, "Logion," 197.

91 See Harnack, *Marcion,* 229*; and Tsutsui, "Evangelium Marcions," 120, who regards the sense of v. 35 in Marcion's gospel as not very clear. On Marcion's interpretation of Luke 20:34-36, see also Aune, "Logion," 198–99. According to Marcion, these verses justify an ascetic baptismal practice. Rejecting marriage and procreation, he still expected a resurrection not of the flesh but of a spiritual body, similar in form to that of the angels.

92 It is not clear to me whether those with whom Origen is in dialogue here, who ask "Where . . . is it written that neither man nor woman should marry?" are friends or enemies.

93 See also Origen *Comm. Matt.* 17.29–36 (*Origenes Werke,* 10.663–703).

94 It is fragment 11 of the edition of Reuss (*Lukas–Kommentare,* 7). A sentence of this fragment (about the multitude of angels and resurrected persons, which does not increase) is found in a fragment attributed, apparently incorrectly, to Cyril of Alexandria that Payne-Smith (*Cyril,* 2:638–39) translates in a footnote (n. 8). It is so interesting that I offer his translation here: "And just as the angelic multitude is vast, but does not increase by generation, but remains as it was created, so also is it with the risen saints. Nor is there any longer need of marriage: for here indeed after Adam lost through sin the grace of immortality, the succession of race is maintained by the procreation of children; and God provided by His foreknowledge this resource from the very beginning; for when He made man, He made them male and female. We shall be therefore superior to our present condition, by having put off corruption, and receiving a superior body, one, that is, which

of creation by God and not a natural process (οὐκ ἐκ φυσιολογίας, "not according to the laws of nature"). Then he turns to the Marcionites and Valentinians, who, he says, apply Jesus' promise only to the soul. On the resurrection of bodies he says that the Sadducees and Jesus discussed the subject.

In the ascetic and monastic literature of the fourth century, encratic literature enjoys, not without some changes, a renewal of attention. The authors of treatises on virginity and the defenders of the monastic virtues are eager to quote the Gospel of Luke.[95] Luke 20:34-36 serves as one of their proof-texts. Without wanting to impose virginity on everyone, they do not reserve the fulfillment of Jesus' words for the eschatological future. It is the ascetics and the monks who here below are already "equal to angels" (ἰσάγγελοι). It is the virgins who are "considered worthy to reach that age." It is the spiritual ones who are the "children of God" and the "children of the resurrection." In a way "they can no longer die." At the end of time these men and these women also regain the status of humanity before the fall, Adam's first and glorious condition.

In the same epoch, Jerome is astonished by Jesus' final answer (*Comm. Matt.* 22.31–33).[96] He is amazed that the quotation from Exodus 3 hardly appears to him to apply to the problem of the resurrection. He finally understands that Jesus chose a passage from the law, because he remembers (something Cyril of Alexandria will forget) that the Sadducees did not acknowledge the canonical authority of the prophetic books.

The brief remarks of Ambrose (end of the fourth century) are offensive in their exacerbated allegorical character and their anti-Semitism (*Exp. Luc.* 9.37–39). The bishop of Milan goes so far as to give the example put forth by the Sadducees, "the most detestable faction of the Jews," a spiritual sense (referring to 2 Cor 3:6, he asks, "Doesn't the letter kill?"). The woman represents the unfruitful synagogue. Neither should the brothers be understood literally. If I understand correctly, collectively they represent Christ, the true brother who will "gather from the dead people of the Jews the knowledge of the divine worship as a wife, and will have descendants in the person of the apostles" (9.38). If they love and obey, God's people "will have in the resurrection this celestial union in which no bodily defilement will shame their modesty; rather, the gifts of divine grace will enrich them" (9.39).

Sermon 136 of Cyril (fifth century) is devoted in its entirety to Luke 20:27-38.[97] Drawing on Acts 23:8, the patriarch of Alexandria presents the Sadducees as narrow opponents of the resurrection. "For we affirm, that the hope of the whole world is the resurrection from the dead, of whom Christ was the first-born and first-fruits." As for the Sadducees, in their folly they resist the inspired Scriptures. Either because he did not know, or because he was pretending not to know, that the scriptural canon of the Sadducees was limited to the Pentateuch, Cyril turns to the company of the prophets for help. Thus, he composes a chain of scriptural proofs gathered from the prophetic books and the psalms: Hos 13:14; Jer 23:16; Isa 25:8; Wis 1:14; Ps 103 (104):29-30 (amazingly, he does not include Dan 12:2). He alternates between these Old Testament quotations and quotations from the New Testament (1 Cor 15:56; Rom 7:7; 4:15; 2 Pet 1:21; 1 Cor 15:42). These quotations prepare for the following principal argument: once Christ has blotted out the sin that leads to death and corruption, those realities disappear, the tears dry, and the lamentations are silent. Cyril understands in a moral (and not ascetic) way the opposition between the "children of this world," the sinners, and the "children of God," the righteous, who live honorably according to the divine election. What characterizes the first group is not marriage but—a very orthodox perspective—the lusts of the flesh. Those

---

has regard only to the things of the Spirit, and the mind [νοῦς], which now urges us into vice, will not then even exist, the Creator maintaining us in conformity to His own will, by the influence of the Holy Ghost, as certainly he does the holy angels also."

95 See Cyprian *De habitu virginum* 22: "When you persevere in chastity and virginity, you are equal to the angels." This passage is quoted by Carton, "Anges," 51. See also Gregory of Nyssa *De opificio hominis* 17

(*PG* 44:188–89); for a French translation by Jean Laplace, with notes by Jean Daniélou, see *Grégoire de Nysse, La création de l'homme* (SC 6; reprinted Paris: Cerf, 2002) 162–65.

96 *PL* 26:164–65; Bartina, "Saduceos," 151–52; Dreyfus, "Argument."

97 Payne-Smith, *Cyril*, 2:635–39. The quotations come from 636 and 639 of this translation.

who do not allow themselves carnal pleasures are like the holy angels. They are judged to be worthy of a glory that Cyril promises for the future. Continuing his interpretation of the text of Luke, the patriarch explains the biblical quotation of Exod 3:6 (he tends here toward the formulation of Matthew and of Mark). God, he says in a convincing way, would not be the God of Abraham, Isaac, and Jacob, if he permitted the patriarchs to die forever. He is, rather, the God of the living who will involve them and "all who are upon the earth" in the resurrection. Without saying it, he is probably thinking of a universal resurrection before the last judgment rather than a universal salvation ($\grave{\alpha}\pi o\kappa\alpha\tau\acute{\alpha}\sigma\tau\alpha\sigma\iota\varsigma$ $\pi\acute{\alpha}\nu\tau\omega\nu$). The sermon concludes with an evocation of this resurrection, which it affirms with New Testament testimonies such as John 11:25 ("I am the resurrection and the life") and 1 Cor 15:52 (he will raise the dead "suddenly, in the twinkling of an eye, at the last trumpet").[98]

In the sixteenth century, Erasmus describes, as do many others, the differences between the Sadducees and the Pharisees and presents their question, which he regards as absurd (*Paraphrasis*, 441–42). He then summarizes Jesus' position, notes that in this age people die and are born, and that marriage is not a matter of happiness but of necessity. For him, happiness is reserved for those who will be judged worthy to participate in the coming age, an age from which death will be excluded and in which marriage will be rendered unnecessary. He then explains the reference to Exodus 3. If the Sadducees were right, God's claim to be the God of the patriarchs would be illegitimate. To illustrate his point he makes use of the traditional image of the seed that dies before it reappears and gives rise to a tree. Such a transformation is the business not of impotent human beings but of God alone.

Luther explains the differences among the Jewish sects, adding Essenes, whom he calls *Essäer*, to the Pharisees and Sadducees.[99] He regards the episode as a strange story[100] and is surprised that people in high places are so ignorant of the resurrection. He is also astonished at how reserved Jesus is in his answer.[101] Following Matthew's text, he emphasizes their incomprehension of the Scriptures and of the power of God (Matt 22:29). Then he speaks of the resurrection and affirms that in that time the differences between the sexes will continue to exist but that the marital relations will disappear and give way to a very different life.[102] He explains why Jesus chose a text from the Pentateuch rather than from the prophets (because of the Sadducees' limited canon) and presents a reasoning one also finds in Calvin: As a husband has a wife, a father a son, and a master a servant, so God must have living persons as believers.[103] God regards death as the sleep of an infant in its cradle. For God, those who rest in their tombs are not dead. It is not enough to say that the soul lives on, for Abraham is not merely a soul. It is not difficult for God to awaken soul and body. One will remember the importance Luther attributes to the right understanding of the Scriptures.[104]

For his part, Calvin emphasizes God's grandeur and the comfort that the resurrection hope brings.[105] It is

---

98   As an example of medieval interpretation, see the pages Bonaventure devotes to these verses (*Comm. Luc.* 20.35–45; Bernardini, 512–16). They are available in English translation in Robert J. Karris, *St. Bonaventure's Commentary on the Gospel of Luke, Chapters 17–24* (Works of St. Bonaventure 8.3; St. Bonaventure, N.Y.: Franciscan Institute, Bonaventure University, 2004), 1931–44.

99   Luther, *Evangelien-Auslegung*, 948–51.

100 "Eine seltsame Geschichte" (ibid., 948).

101 "Mich wundert, dass Christus nicht besser sie abgewuscht hat, wie Er oft den Pharisäern gethan," "I am surprised that Christ did not do a better job of brushing them off, as he often did to the Pharisees" (ibid., 949).

102 "Aber es wird dort ein geistlich, himmlisch Leben sein und werden die Auserwählten gleich sein wie die Engel Gottes im Himmel," "But there will be a spiritual, heavenly life and the elect will be as the angels of God in heaven" (ibid., 949–50).

103 "Denn Er ist nicht ein gemalter noch geschnitzter Gott; auch nicht ein Gaukelgott; sondern ein natürlicher, wahrer, ewiger, allmächtiger Gott," "For he is not a painted God or carved God, nor is he a phantom God; he is a natural, true, eternal, almighty God" (ibid., 950).

104 Lagrange (517) cites an interpretation from the same period, that of Luther's adversary, the Catholic theologian Cajetan.

105 Calvin, *Harmony*, 3:27–33. "The godly find extraordinary comfort" and "the [infinite] power of God" are mentioned on p. 30, the Papists on pp. 29–30, the example and the arguments on soul and body on pp. 29–30, the theology of the apostle Paul

clear that Pauline theology is used here as a hermeneutical framework for Calvin's Gospel Harmony (adoption, faith, the Holy Spirit, the life that is still hidden). Calvin makes his polemic relevant by repeatedly including the "Papists" in his comments. He shares with Luther certain of his examples (father–children, king–subjects, thus God–the living) and certain arguments (bodies and souls belong together). Attentive to the nuances of each Gospel, he appreciates that Luke explains the life of angels by the absence of death. Indeed, he fears that the humans raised from the dead will be too much like the angels in heaven. In his defense, he notes that the enemies of the truth characterized by separation can marshal their forces when Satan—who, of course, is not mentioned in the biblical text—brings them together. As a jurist he well understands and explains the levirate law and its practical applications.

Luke 20:38, "God is not the God of the dead but of the living," with its editorial precision, "since all live from him," attracted the attention of Karl Barth from the beginning of his ministry to the last days of his life. On Easter Sunday, 1916, the young pastor of Safenwil preached on Luke 20:38, and on December 9, 1968, the day before his death, the old professor quoted this verse on the last page that he wrote.[106] This verse also occupies the theologian of Basel when he writes the introduction to his *Protestant Theology in the Nineteenth Century* and in volumes I/2 and IV/1 of his *Church Dogmatics*. This verse helps him with his Easter sermon: The parishioners of Safenwil, he preaches, believe in life; they cannot not believe in it. But a word of caution: the dead people of the village are not resting only in the cemetery; they are present also in the church. Thus the difference between the living and the dead must be qualified on two levels,[107] because from a human point of view death comes to all, and from God's point of view all are called to life. Only God gives life, because he is the God of the living. Jesus Christ, the Risen One, constitutes the Easter community.

Throughout his entire life Barth emphasized the ecclesiological character of Luke 20:38. The church has its existence from God. If all the faithful live in him or for him, "there is no past in the Church, so there is no past in theology."[108] The voice of the theologians of earlier times belongs to the present: one needs to know how to hear it.[109] The church embraces the visible church and the invisible church, the church militant and the church triumphant, in short, the church of the living and the dead.[110] Luke 20:38 is an ecclesiological text, because it speaks of the "living" and of "all" who receive life from God. It is a text that, with its insistence on God, serves Barth well when he draws the contours of the church. It is also important to him when he underscores the role of preaching and that of the confession of faith.[111]

Conclusion

Luke 20:27-40 baffles the readers and transposes them to another world, another time, that of the scriptural debates of Jewish antiquity. Without being, like

especially on pp. 31–32, the Lukan nuances on p. 31 ("they will no longer die," v. 36) and p. 32 ("for all live unto him," v. 38), the active Satan on pp. 28–29.

106 Karl Barth, *Gesamtausgabe*, vol. 1: *Predigten, 1916* (ed. Hermann Schmidt; Zurich: Theologischer Verlag, 1998) 168–75; idem, *Final Testimonies* (trans. Geoffrey W. Bromiley; Grand Rapids: Eerdmans, 1977) 60. See also the photograph (absent in this ET) between p. 64 and p. 65 in the German edition of this work (*Letzte Zeugnisse* [Zurich: EVZ-Verlag, 1969]). I am following here the noteworthy *Habilitations–Probevorlesung* of Trowitzsch, "Gemeinschaft."

107 See Trowitzsch, "Gemeinschaft," 215.

108 Karl Barth, *Protestant Theology in the Nineteenth Century: Its Background and History* (Valley Forge, Pa.: Judson, 1973) 17.

109 "Augustine, Thomas, Luther, Schleiermacher and all the others are not dead; they are alive. They continue to speak and want to be heard as living voices as sure as we know that we, and they with us, are in the Church"(ibid., quoted in Trowitzsch, "Gemeinschaft," 217–18).

110 See Trowitzsch, "Gemeinschaft," 219–21.

111 See ibid., 212–13.

the scribes, a professional exegete, the Lukan Jesus still can read the texts and give a convincing answer to the Sadducees. He initially explains the "how" of the resurrection (a life like that of the angels, vv. 34-36) before demonstrating with a quotation from the Law of Moses the "that," its existence (vv. 37-38).[112]

These verses also transpose us, especially, into another world, another time, that of the resurrection. It offers a "great consolation" (Calvin) to all who have lost a loved one, to all who suffer. For them the continuing life of the deceased is rooted in God's being and not in an uncertain human survival attached to memories, merits, or even to the immortality of the soul.[113] In a picturesque and rigorous style vv. 34-36 speak emphatically both of the life offered by the resurrection and of the radiance of "that age" into the existence in "this age."

---

112 On the connections between the two parts of Jesus' answer, see Kilgallen, "Sadducees," 494 n. 40.

113 Charpentier ("Tous," 93–94) is of the opinion that Mark and Matthew follow an Old Testament line to which Psalm 16 bears witness: God loves human beings too much to give them up to death. Luke follows a different line that is present in Psalm 72 (73): The believers love God too much for their relationship to end with their death. Fred B. Craddock (*Luke* [Louisville: Westminster John Knox Press, 1990] 238) thinks that the first argument (vv. 34-36) comes from reason, the second (vv. 37-38) from the authority of Scripture; see also Charles L'Eplattenier, *Lecture de l'évangile de Luc* (Paris: Desclée, 1982) 229–30.

Messiah—Son of David—Lord
(20:41-47)
Bibliography

Burger, *Davidssohn*, 114–16.

Chilton, Bruce, "Jesus ben David: Reflections on the Davidssohnfrage," *JSNT* 14 (1982) 88–112.

Cullmann, Oscar, *The Christology of the New Testament* (London: SCM, 1963) 117–33.

Daube, David, *The New Testament and Rabbinic Judaism* (Jordan Lectures in Comparative Religion 2; London: Athlone, 1956) 158–69.

Derrett, J. Duncan M., "'Eating up the houses of widows': Jesus' Comment on Lawyers?" *NovT* 14 (1972) 1–9.

Dupont, Jacques, *Nouvelles études sur les Actes des Apôtres* (LD 118; Paris: Cerf, 1984) 210–95.

Fitzmyer, Joseph A., "The Contribution of Qumran Aramaic to the Study of the New Testament," *NTS* 20 (1974) 382–407, esp. 386–91.

Idem, "The Son of David Tradition and Mt 22: 41-46 and Parallels," in idem, *Essays on the Semitic Background of the New Testament* (Sources for Biblical Study 5; Missoula, Mont.: Scholars Press, 1974) 113–26.

Flender, Helmut, *Heil und Geschichte in der Theologie des Lukas* (BEvTh 41; Munich: Kaiser, 1965) 43.

France, Richard T., *Jesus and the Old Testament: His Application of Old Testament Passages to Himself and His Mission* (Downers Grove, Ill.: InterVarsity Press, 1971) 100–102, 163–69.

Friedrich, Gerhard, "Messianische Hohepriesterwartung in den Synoptikern," *ZThK* 53 (1956) 265–311, esp. 286–89.

Gagg, Robert Paul, "Jesus und die Davidssohnsfrage: Zur Exegese von Markus 12, 35–37," *ThZ* 7 (1951) 18–30.

Grangaard, *Conflict*, 124–59, 161–85.

Hahn, *Titles*, 104–7, 170–71, 240–78.

Hay, David M., *Glory at the Right Hand: Psalm 110 in Early Christianity* (Nashville: Abingdon, 1973) 104–21.

van Iersel, *Sohn*, 171–73.

Idem, "Fils de David, et Fils de Dieu," in Édouard Massaux et al., eds., *La Venue du Messie: Messianisme et eschatologie* (RechBib 6; Bruges: Desclée de Brouwer, 1962) 113–32, esp.121–23.

Keck, Fridolin, *Die öffentliche Abschiedsrede Jesu in Lk 20,45–21,36: Eine redactions- und motivgeschichtliche Untersuchung* (FB 25; Stuttgart: Katholisches Bibelwerk, 1976) 36–46.

Kingsbury, *Conflict*, 98–101 and passim.

Lindars, Barnabas, *New Testament Apologetic: The Doctrinal Significance of Old Testament Quotations* (London: SCM, 1961) 45–51.

Lohse, Eduard, "υἱὸς Δαυίδ," *TDNT* 8 (1972) 478–88.

Idem, "Der König aus Davids Geschlecht: Bemerkungen zur messianischen Erwartung der Synagoge," in Otto Betz et al., eds., *Abraham unser Vater: Juden und Christen im Gespräch über die Bibel: Festschrift für Otto Michel zum 60. Geburtstag* (Arbeiten zur Geschichte des Spätjudentums und Urchristentums 5; Leiden: Brill, 1963) 337–45.

Lövestam, Evald, "Die Davidssohnfrage," *SEÅ* 27 (1962) 72–82.

Meyer, Eduard, *Ursprung und Anfänge des Christentums* (3 vols.; 1921; reprinted Darmstadt: Wissenschaftliche Buchgesellschaft, 1962) 2:446.

Michaelis, Wilhelm, "Die Davidssohnschaft Jesu als historisches und kerygmatisches Problem," in Helmut Ristow und Karl Matthiae, eds., *Der historische Jesus und der kerygmatische Christus: Beiträge zum Christusverständnis in Forschung und Verkündigung* (Berlin: Evangelische Verlagsanstalt, 1961) 317–30.

Neugebauer, Fritz, "Die Davidssohnfrage (Mark xii. 35-37 Parr.) und der Menschensohn," *NTS* 21 (1975) 81–108.

Rengstorf, Karl Heinrich, "Die στολαί der Schriftgelehrten: Eine Erläuterung zu Mark. 12, 38," in Otto Betz et al., eds., *Abraham unser Vater: Juden und Christen im Gespräch über die Bibel: Festschrift für Otto Michel zum 60. Geburtstag* (Arbeiten zur Geschichte des Spätjudentums und Urchristentums 5; Leiden: Brill, 1963) 383–404.

Rese, *Motive*, 173–74.

Sande Bakhuyzen, Willem Hendrik van de, *Der Dialog des Adamantius* (GCS 4; Leipzig: Hinrichs, 1901) 198–201.

Schneider, Gerhard, "Die Davidssohnfrage (Mk 12, 35-37)," *Bib* 54 (1972) 65–90. Reprinted in idem, *Jesusüberlieferung und Christologie: Neutestamentliche Aufsätze, 1970–1990* (NovTSup 67; Leiden: Brill, 1992) 307–32.

Schramm, *Markus-Stoff*, 171.

Schwarz, G., "'Die Häuser der Witwen verzehren'? (Markus 12, 40/Luke 20, 47)," *BN* 88 (1997) 45–46.

Suhl, Alfred, "Der Davidssohn im Matthäus-Evangelium," *ZNW* 59 (1968) 57–81.

Wrede, William, "Jesus als Davidssohn," in idem, *Vorträge und Studien* (Tübingen: Mohr Siebeck, 1907) 147–77, esp. 170–71.

41	Then he said to them, "How can they say[a] the Messiah is the Son of David? 42/ For David himself says in the book of Psalms: The Lord said to my Lord, Sit to my right side 43/ until I make your enemies a stool under your feet.[b] 44/ Thus David calls him Lord, so how is he his son?"[c]
45	And while all the people were listening, he said to his disciples, 46/ "Beware of the scribes, who want[d] to go around in long robes and who love[e] greetings in public places and the best seats in the synagogues, and the chief places at dinners, 47/ who devour the houses of widows and pretend[f] to make long prayers. These people will receive an even more severe punishment."

a   Or: "one says."
b   Or: "footstool."
c   The Greek manuscripts are not aware of capital letters beginning proper names and titles. Here in vv. 41-44, one can hesitate to capitalize Messiah, Son of David, Lord, and Son.
d   Or: "desire," "like," "hold with."
e   Or: "have the practice of."
f   Literally: "Appear to pray." The word $\pi\rho\acute{o}\phi\alpha\sigma\iota\varsigma$ means at the same time "cause" (simulated or apparent), "pretext," "excuse," "motive." Thus, one could also translate "pray for this reason," but this translation is less probable.

Verses 41-44 and 45-47 are two short literary units that for practical reasons are taken together in this commentary. The first intercalates a biblical quotation between two questions dealing with the Messiah.[1] The second constitutes a warning. The "scribes," here challenged, there put on display, connect the two units.[2] They are also connected to the preceding unit (v. 39). For its part, the word "widow" ensures continuity between these pericopes and what follows in Luke 21:1-4 (the widow's offering).

Analysis

Luke continues with his new reading of the Gospel of Mark. He remains faithful to its sequence, even when he runs the risk of repeating himself, something he does

not like to do.[3] He regularly improves its writing and occasionally changes the meaning.[4]

As he likes to do in his introductory remarks, Luke freely summarizes a sentence of Mark in three words (v. 41a). He is more precise than Mark about the people to whom the question is directed ("them," i.e., the "scribes" of v. 39), but he omits Jesus' teaching in the temple, which Mark mentions (12:35a). That is surprising, since elsewhere the evangelist insists on that time of teaching in the area of the sanctuary (see 19:47; 21:37; 22:53).[5] As is his custom, the evangelist then respects Jesus' words even in their form: the first question (v. 41b) corresponds to the formulation of Mark 12:35b.[6]

In the introduction to the scriptural quotation (v. 42a par. Mark 12:36a) Luke prefers to insert "for" ($\gamma\acute{\alpha}\rho$)[7] and to give the reference ("in the book of Psalms")

1   A noteworthy survey of scholarship, especially in German language exegesis, is in Schneider, "Davidssohnfrage," 66–81.

2   However, Luke does not avoid a point of tension. In v. 39 the scribes share Jesus' opinion about the resurrection. In vv. 45-47, by contrast, they are subjected to Jesus' criticism.

3   In 11:46 he has already soundly criticized the scribes, whom he calls there the "lawyers," following the Sayings Source (see the parallel in Matt 23:4). Here he somewhat mechanically follows Mark. See Lagrange, 518–19. According to Schramm (*Markus-Stoff*, 171), Luke follows Mark, except in v. 46, where he reproduces another tradition.

4   For a good synoptic comparison of vv. 41-44 with

Mark 12:35-37a, see Rese, *Motive*, 173–74; Burger, *Davidssohn*, 114–16; and Neugebauer, "Davidssohnfrage," 82–84. Keck (*Abschiedsrede*, 36–46) precisely analyzes Luke's new reading of Mark 12:37b-40 in vv. 45-47.

5   See Conzelmann, *Theology*, 77–78.

6   Two of the differences do not change the meaning: an infinitive clause in Luke instead of Mark's declarative clause with $\acute{o}\tau\iota$; the word order ($\upsilon\acute{\iota}\grave{o}\varsigma$ $\Delta\alpha\upsilon\acute{\iota}\delta$ $\acute{\epsilon}\sigma\tau\iota\nu$, Mark; $\epsilon\grave{\iota}\nu\alpha\iota$ $\Delta\alpha\upsilon\grave{\iota}\delta$ $\upsilon\acute{\iota}\acute{o}\nu$, Luke). The third, an omission ("the scribes" as the subject of the verb "they say"), changes the circumstances of this statement: Since it is more vague, the statement becomes more general.

7   Countless manuscripts read $\kappa\alpha\grave{\iota}$ $\alpha\grave{\upsilon}\tau\acute{o}\varsigma$ ("and he

instead of the divine mediation ("in the Holy Spirit"). This last change goes beyond the literary level and poses a question to the theologian (we will return to this point in the interpretation). With one exception, the quotation itself from Psalm 109 (110):1 (vv. 42b-43 par. Mark 12:36b) corresponds to Mark's quotation. The change ($\dot{\upsilon}\pi o\pi\acute{o}\delta\iota o\nu$, "footstool," instead of $\dot{\upsilon}\pi o\kappa\acute{a}\tau\omega$, "under") can be explained by Luke's concern to follow as much as possible the text of the LXX.

In recalling Jesus' second question (v. 44 par. Mark 12:37), Luke says essentially the same thing as Mark, but he does so more elegantly. He avoids repeating "David himself" ($\alpha\dot{\upsilon}\tau\grave{o}\varsigma\ \Delta\alpha\upsilon\acute{\iota}\delta$), ensures the connection with "therefore" ($o\mathring{\upsilon}\nu$), knowingly prefers "calls" rather than "says," and replaces "from where" ($\pi\acute{o}\vartheta\epsilon\nu$) with "how" ($\pi\hat{\omega}\varsigma$).[8]

The evangelist shares these last two corrections with Matthew. For the rest, Matthew went his own way by creating a real dialogue between Jesus and the Pharisees (Matt 22:42 specifies that it is about the Messiah), while Mark and Luke limit themselves to what Jesus says. Finally, Matthew makes a point of creating a conclusion for the conversation he created (22:46). He uses here Mark's conclusion from the previous pericope, which he had intentionally omitted at that place (Mark 12:34b).

Mark concludes the episode on the Son of David with the statement "And the large crowd heard him gladly" (12:37b). Luke knows these words and uses them (while reformulating them) as an introduction to the next unit, the warning (vv. 45-47).[9]

With a genitive absolute Luke focuses attention on "the people"[10] and the "disciples," creating a scene reminiscent of that of the Sermon on the Plain (6:17). Having been listeners, the scribes now become the subjects of the discourse. The "people" (Luke prefers this positive term to Mark's inconstant[11] "crowd") are listening, but the warning is directed primarily to the disciples.[12]

In Jesus' energetic warning (vv. 46-47), Luke stays with Mark's text. Yet he cannot keep from changing the banal "look at" ($\beta\lambda\acute{\epsilon}\pi\epsilon\tau\epsilon$, Mark 12:38) to "beware" ($\pi\rho o\sigma\acute{\epsilon}\chi\epsilon\tau\epsilon$, a verb that, as we will see in the interpretation, is valued by the Christian parenesis of the time). He also makes a point of avoiding an awkwardness of Mark (a zeugma, to be precise)[13] while inserting the verb "to love" before the reference to the greetings. Finally, he changes two present participles (Mark 12:40) into a relative clause in the present indicative: "they who devour . . . and . . . pray" ($o\mathring{\iota}\ \kappa\alpha\tau\epsilon\sigma\vartheta\acute{\iota}o\upsilon\sigma\iota\nu$ . . . $\kappa\alpha\grave{\iota}$ . . . $\pi\rho o\sigma\epsilon\acute{\upsilon}\chi o\nu\tau\alpha\iota$, v. 47). By doing this he does not modify the ideas of duration and of repetition in the present tense, which are conveyed both by the indicative and by the participle.[14]

Most synoptic comparisons end here, since their authors are prejudiced by the idea of a scriptural canon. There is, however, an important parallel that is scarcely younger than the Gospels of Luke or Matthew. It is in the

---

himself"; the selected text reads $\alpha\dot{\upsilon}\tau\grave{o}\varsigma\ \gamma\acute{\alpha}\rho$). See here the apparatus in Nestle-Aland (27th ed.).

8   The manuscripts waver in the word order ($\kappa\acute{\upsilon}\rho\iota o\nu$ $\alpha\dot{\upsilon}\tau\acute{o}\nu$ or $\alpha\dot{\upsilon}\tau\grave{o}\nu\ \kappa\acute{\upsilon}\rho\iota o\nu$ and $\alpha\dot{\upsilon}\tau o\hat{\upsilon}\ \upsilon\acute{\iota}\acute{o}\varsigma$ or $\upsilon\acute{\iota}\grave{o}\varsigma$ $\alpha\dot{\upsilon}\tau o\hat{\upsilon}$), but this does not affect the meaning; see here the apparatus in Nestle-Aland (27th ed.).

9   One finds a condensed analysis of these verses in Keck, *Abschiedsrede*, 36–46.

10   Luke keeps the idea of a great number, but, as is his custom, he prefers $\pi\hat{\alpha}\varsigma$ ("all") to the $\pi o\lambda\acute{\upsilon}\varsigma$ ("many") of Mark 12:37b.

11   Keck (*Abschiedsrede*, 39–40) correctly points out that at his trial the "crowd" will turn against Jesus; see 22:6, 47, 52; 23:4-5, 48.

12   It is undoubtedly because he introduces the "disciples" that Luke regards the words "in his teaching" (Mark 12:38a) as useless and pleonastic.

13   One speaks of zeugma when a verb is connected to two objects or subjects but relates to only one of

them; see BDF §479 (2); Herbert Weir Smyth, *Greek Grammar* (1916; rev. Gordon M. Messing; reprinted Cambridge, Mass.: Harvard University Press, 1984) §3048. On the elimination of this zeugma, see Keck, *Abschiedsrede*, 44.

14   It is difficult to define the literary genre of vv. 41-44. Mark and Luke quote sentences of Jesus that include a biblical quotation, while Matthew transforms these sentences into a controversy. Often the rabbis in solving problems asked themselves questions and, of course, quoted biblical passages. See Daube, *Rabbinic Judaism*, 158–63, from whom, however, we will not take over the entire scheme; Lohse, "$\upsilon\acute{\iota}\grave{o}\varsigma\ \vartheta\epsilon o\hat{\upsilon}$," 484–85. As for vv. 45-47, they are both parenetic and polemical sentences; see Bultmann (*History*, 113–14), who holds especially to the polemical orientation of these sentences. Gagg ("Jesus") thinks that vv. 41-44 initially represented a controversy, whose beginning, an attack on Jesus,

Epistle of Barnabas, a pseudepigraphic writing from the beginning of the second century.[15] In chap. 12 we read:

> See again Jesus, not as son of man, but as Son of God, but manifested in a type in the flesh. Since therefore they are going to say that the Christ is David's son, David himself prophesies, fearing and understanding the error of the sinners, "The Lord said to my Lord sit thou on my right hand until I make thy enemies thy footstool." And again Isaiah speaks thus, "The Lord said to Christ my Lord, whose right hand I held, that the nations should obey before him, and I will shatter the strength of Kings." See how David calls him Lord and not son! (*Barn.* 12.10-11)[16]

Although this passage of the *Epistle of Barnabas* is obscure in places, it permits a number of observations. In contrast to the Synoptic Gospels, Jesus is not the author of these reflections. The problems are clearly Christian, post-Easter—which could be the case in the Synoptic Gospels as well. In addition, a second quotation from Isaiah (45:1) accompanies that from Psalm 109 (110). The first Christian theology is constructed by using the Scriptures. Probably in opposition to certain Jewish Christians, the author of the epistle understands Jesus not as a human being (a "son of a man") but as a divine being (a "Son of God") incarnate ("appeared in flesh"). As in the Synoptic Gospels, the text refers to a contrary theological view according to which the Messiah is David's son. The author attacks not this formula as such but an unspecified interpretation, which results from the error of the sinners. It is to counter this error in advance that the prophet David has spoken Psalm

109 (110):1.[17] Isaiah too expresses himself in the same sense. In a symmetrical conclusion of the last verse of our pericope (Luke 20:44), David calls the Messiah "Lord" (glory, exaltation, and power thus accompany him) and not "Son," which would imply limitation and submission. The passage from the epistle is not aware of the style of the questions, but the structure of the words is identical to our passage. The Christian scriptural argument responds to the initial opinion of the adversaries. Then to this argument a conclusion is added that makes use of its best part. Undoubtedly the *Epistle of Barnabas* depends not on the Gospels but on an oral tradition that parallels the Synoptic tradition.[18] This parallel is suggestive of a messianic and christological controversy between Jews and Christians, or between rival Christian groups. This quarrel is centered on the title "Son of David" and, consequently, on the nature of messianism and Christology. The appeal to Scripture asserts itself as the most obvious solution. The bearers of the Synoptic tradition, like the author of the *Epistle of Barnabas*, derive from the scriptural passages a Christology that brings the Messiah closer to God. This Christology underscores the lordship and rejects the Messiah's subordination.[19]

Commentary

■ **41** When he writes "Then he said to them," Luke is thinking of Jesus and the "scribes," whom he has just mentioned.[20] Indeed, the scribes of a Pharisaic tendency set a great value on the Davidic origin of the Messiah.[21] The "how" ($\pi\hat{\omega}\varsigma$) that introduces the question is significant. The issue is not "why" these people call the Messiah "Son of David" but "how" they interpret this title.[22] There

---

was truncated. According to Gagg, what Jesus is trying to achieve is not a christological clarification but the end of the debate!

15 *Barnabas* 12.10-11 has not been completely neglected in Synoptic studies; see Fitzmyer, "Tradition," 125–26; Hay, *Glory*, passim.

16 English translation by Kirsopp Lake in the LCL, *Apostolic Fathers*, 1:387. See also Pierre Prigent and Robert A. Kraft, eds., *Epître de Barnabé* (SC 172; Paris: Cerf, 1971) 172–75.

17 The quotation corresponds to that of Luke, and both are identical to the text of the LXX (except that the LXX has a definite article before the first $\kappa\acute{\nu}\rho\iota o\varsigma$, which a manuscript of Barnabas imitates).

18 See Helmut Koester, *Synoptische Überlieferung bei den Apostolischen Vätern* (TU 65; Berlin: Akademie-Verlag, 1957) 157.

19 See the invaluable notes in Prigent and Kraft, *Epître de Barnabé* (n. 16 above).

20 Although one might hesitate in this regard if one thinks that v. 40 refers implicitly to Sadducees.

21 *Psalms of Solomon* 17:21 uses the title "Son of David" for the Messiah. The *Psalms of Solomon*, which date from the first century B.C.E., are, in my judgment, Pharisaic in their orientation. See also the fifteenth of the Eighteen Benedictions; Chilton, "David," esp. 100; Fitzmyer, "Tradition," 119–22.

22 In those days the Pharisees were not the only Jews

are important reasons for thinking that they were hoping for a final human liberator who was descended from the family of David.[23] It is this opinion that the text wants to test, to correct, and to contradict.[24]

■ **42-43** This control and this correction are carried out with the help of a scriptural quotation. What counts for Luke is the biblical character of the quotation; thus, he prefers the expression "in the book of Psalms." The evangelist doubts neither King David's prophetic charisma nor the inspiration and the canonicity of his psalms.[25] Since, however, proof is limited to David's role on the human level, Luke obviously avoids speaking here of the earlier presence of the Holy Spirit in the person of the king and singer.[26]

The quotation from Ps 109 (110):1 is the most widely used quotation in the New Testament.[27] Its success comes from the twofold advantage it brings. It makes it possible to see God and the Messiah side by side, and it compares one to the other, a Lord and another Lord, which corresponds to the new Christian creed (see, e.g., 1 Cor 8:6).[28] Sitting at the right hand also makes it possible to express Jesus' resurrection in terms of exaltation and power. This appeal to Ps 109 (110):1 is part of an apologetic effort. Faced with the criticisms of the scribes, the Christians offer what is essential: the resurrection and the Easter exaltation as legitimation of Jesus' messiahship.[29]

One of the Jewish criticisms was related to the origin of the Messiah. The Gospel of John mentions this objection: Can a Nazarene be descended from David? He must at all costs come from Judea (John 7:40-44). In their own way the infancy gospels (Luke 1–2; Matthew 1–2) as well as Jesus' genealogy (Luke 3:23-38; Matt 1:1-17) respond to the same objection by including Jesus in David's family and by locating his birth in Bethlehem.[30] Jesus' Davidic character is also part of the earliest christological formulas, since the expression "descended from David" ($\dot{\epsilon}\kappa \ \sigma\pi\dot{\epsilon}\rho\mu\alpha\tau\sigma\varsigma \ \Delta\alpha\nu\dot{\iota}\delta$) appears in the brief credo with which Paul begins the Epistle to the Romans (Rom 1:3).[31]

The book of Acts also bears witness to this quarrel over interpretation. Relying there on traditions he respects, Luke relates Jesus to David and David to Jesus. David found grace before God (Acts 7:46; 13:22). This grace, in fact a threefold grace, permitted him to become a king beloved of God, to be assured of a messianic descendant, and to achieve the status of prophet. And it is here that the Christian hermeneutic playfully deals with the difficulties: David's respectability appears (somewhat like that of John the Baptist)[32] in a realistic humility. David realized that his messianic descendant would be elevated to a level higher than his own—that the resurrection would make this descendant stronger

---

to look for a Davidic Messiah. According to the Dead Sea writings, the Essenes shared this hope but also looked for a priestly Messiah. See 1QS 9.10–11; CD 12.23; 4Q174 (*Florilegium*); 4Q175 (*Testimonia*).

23   Many manuscripts, in fact the majority, offer $\nu\dot{\iota}\grave{o}\nu$ $\Delta\alpha\nu\grave{\iota}\delta \ \epsilon\hat{\iota}\nu\alpha\iota$, while Sinaiticus (‎א = 01), Vaticanus (B = 03), Parisinus (L = 019), the minuscule 579, and some others contain the order retained by Nestle-Aland (27th ed.), $\epsilon\hat{\iota}\nu\alpha\iota \ \Delta\alpha\nu\grave{\iota}\delta \ \nu\iota\acute{o}\nu$. This difference does not affect the meaning.

24   On David, Davidic messianism, and the Son of David in Luke-Acts, see Cullmann, *Christology*, 117–33; Lövestam, "Davidssohnfrage"; Lohse, "König"; Lohse, "$\nu\iota o\grave{\iota} \ \Delta\alpha\nu\acute{\iota}\delta$"; Hahn, *Titles*, 240–78; Fitzmyer, "Tradition"; Burger, *Davidssohn*, 107–52; Chilton, "David." On the title Messiah, see Hahn, *Titles*, 136–228.

25   On Luke's use of Scripture, see Bovon, *Luke the Theologian*, 87–121.

26   This all the more, since in Acts 2:33 the divine gift of the Spirit is explicitly reserved to Jesus Christ.

27   On the Christian use of Ps 109 (110):1, see Dupont,

Nouvelles études, 210–95; Hahn, *Titles*, 104–7; Hay, *Glory*. On the Lukan use, see Rese, *Motive*, 173–74.

28   On the title $\kappa\acute{\nu}\rho\iota o\varsigma$ ("Lord"), see Fitzmyer, "Contribution," 386–91; Hahn, *Titles*, 68–135.

29   Lohse ("$\nu\iota\grave{o}\varsigma \ \Delta\alpha\nu\acute{\iota}\delta$," 483) correctly shows that for Luke, especially in Acts, it is the resurrection that makes of Jesus, David's *son*, Jesus, David's *Lord*.

30   Burger (*Davidssohn*, 115), Lohse ("$\nu\iota\grave{o}\varsigma \ \Delta\alpha\nu\acute{\iota}\delta$," 485), Lövestam, ("Davidssohnfrage," 74–82), and Hay (*Glory*, 115–16) invite us to read anew these texts and those of Acts dealing with David in order to understand the sense Luke gives to Jesus' questions.

31   The affirmation does not lose its topical relevance. In Pauline circles it is taken up again in a writing of the following generation, 2 Tim 2:8. Here too it refers to a faith formula.

32   See John 3:30: "That one must increase, and I must decrease."

than death, would open the gates of heaven to him, and would bestow the Holy Spirit on him.[33]

■ **44** Here the scriptural quotation benefits the Synoptic Jesus. Initially this benefit consists of an observation: "Thus David calls him Lord." (The αὐτόν, "him," can only refer to the Messiah, the χριστός of v. 41, the object of the dispute.) The text presupposes here that Psalm 109 (110) is messianic and that the "my Lord" addressed here represents the Messiah. It goes without saying, although the early Christians refuse to consider this possibility, that other interpretations of this psalm are possible.

Verse 44 continues with a question. A number of exegetes regard the question as rhetorical and believe that it is expecting a negative answer—no, the Messiah cannot be the Son of David.[34] Admittedly, the text is difficult, and the commentaries enumerate as many as eight different interpretations.[35] Because of the repetition of "how" (πῶς), however, I cannot see here a rejection of the title.[36] The interrogative adverb favors the choice of the best interpretation. Therefore, the question is not rhetorical; it corresponds to an invitation to christological reflection. In its own way, it implicitly draws the christological consequences from the quotation. Many readers are astonished by the text's reserve.[37] At the time when the evangelists copy it, why end with a question? If the oldest Synoptic tradition does not affirm—as the Pauline

credo is not reluctant to do it—that Jesus the Messiah is Son of David according to the flesh, it is because the tradition wants to make a point of respecting the epochs.[38] As long as the resurrection has not yet taken place, Jesus' relation to the messianic titles remains enigmatic. Of course, the Lukan text remains only moderately reserved. With the help of Psalm 109 (110), Luke *explicitly* affirms the Messiah's lordship while *implicitly* suggesting that the Messiah in question is none other than Jesus. Elsewhere in his work Luke uncovers the solution of the enigma: At the beginning of the Gospel he includes Jesus in David's family by way of Joseph (1:27; 2:4; 3:23, 31), promises him "the throne of David" (1:32), declares him to be a "horn of salvation . . . in the house of David, his servant" (1:69), and lets him be born in Bethlehem, the city of David (2:4). Thus, there is no reason for doubt: According to Luke, in his human identity Jesus is the Son of David.[39] But no matter how honorable he may be, David—following the example of Elizabeth, who calls Mary "the mother of my Lord" (1:43)—must bow before one who is greater than he: "my Lord" (Ps 109 [110]:1). Acts underscores this when it contrasts David's mortality with Jesus' resurrection:

Brothers, I may say to you with confidence: "The patriarch David is dead, he was buried, and today his tomb is still with us here. But he was a prophet and knew

---

33   For Lövestam ("Davidssohnfrage," 73), what is at issue in vv. 41-44 is the relationship between the Messiah's lordship and his Davidic sonship.

34   See Wrede, "Davidssohn"; Meyer, *Ursprung*, 2:446; Bultmann, *History*, 136–37; Suhl, "Davidssohn," 57–59. For his part, Schneider ("Davidssohnfrage," 83–85) finds that the text is strict about the title Son of David. Hay (*Glory*, 118 n. 51) calls attention to the dialogue on orthodox faith known as the *Dialogue of Adamantus* 4.46 (*PG* 11:1849; pp. 198–201 in the edition of van de Sande Bakhuyzen) a passage in which an interlocuter, Megethius, who represents the Marcionite opponent, argues, based on our passage (Mark 12:35-37parr.), that Jesus is not the Son of David.

35   See Nolland, 3:971. Fitzmyer ("Tradition") arranges the interpretations in three categories: (a) Jesus denies that the Messiah must be a son of David; (b) the Messiah must be more than the Son of David; (c) Jesus implicitly refers here to the Son of Man. Van Iersel (*Sohn*, 171–73) thinks that, thanks to the

quotation of Ps 109 (110):1, a second aspect of the Christology is clarified alongside the title Son of David, at least in Matthew's case, namely, that of the Son of God.

36   To understand the πῶς of v. 44, Burger (*Davidssohn*, 115–16) calls attention to Acts 2:34-36.

37   In the form of a question the passage harmonizes biblical verses and apparently contradictory scriptural categories such as Messiah, Son of David, and Lord. This was quotidian work for the scribes in Israel. See Daube, *Rabbinic Judaism*, 158–63; Fitzmyer, "Tradition," 124–26.

38   See Burger, *Davidssohn*, 116.

39   According to Cullmann (*Christology*, 133), Jesus did not deny his descent from David; he merely rejected the theological interpretation of a nationalistic and political Messiah, Son of David. According to Lövestam ("Davidssohnfrage," 81), this position of Jesus is also that of the Christians who transmitted the pericope.

that God had sworn an oath to him that someone descended from him, of the fruit of his loins, would sit on his throne. He thus foresaw the resurrection of Christ and said in this connection that he was not abandoned to the abode of death nor did his flesh see corruption. This Jesus God raised up, of which we all are witnesses. Exalted to the right hand of God, he has thus received from the Father the promised Holy Spirit and has poured it out, as you see and hear." (Acts 2:29-33)[40]

I have been interpreting the passage from the perspective of the early Christians, in particular from Luke's point of view.[41] There are many exegetes, however, who raise the question of the historicity of the episode in the life of Jesus.[42] Those who argue in favor of authenticity do so mainly on the basis of the ambiguity of Jesus' answer. The Christians, they claim, would have had no scruples about explicitly using the christological titles. With some hesitation I side with those who doubt the authenticity of the episode, and I do so for three primary reasons: (1) The articulation of the christological titles Messiah (or Christ), Son of David, and Lord poses a Christian, post-Easter problematic.

(2) In its Hebrew formulation Ps 109 (110):1 does not offer the same possibilities as in its Greek formulation in the LXX. The Hebrew does not place two Lords side by side but two persons with different names. The first is God, designated by his proper name, the Tetragrammaton YHWH; the second is Adonai, "my Lord," a royal designation.[43] (3) The independent tradition attested by the *Epistle of Barnabas* reflects a debate among Christians, not a discussion between Jesus and his conversation partners.

■ **45-47** Following Mark, Luke attaches to this elevated doctrinal statement a down-to-earth warning.[44] As is often the case in Jewish literature of that time, the connections are made by hook-words and not by logical reasoning. It is undoubtedly the word "scribes" and the dialogue with these questioners that caused these verses to be located here. Since Luke may have sensed that this transition was artificial, he changed (as I already noted) the Markan conclusion of the previous pericope into an elegant introduction: "All the people" (a nod in the direction of those who like the expression and the reality of the "people of God") listen to Jesus. Luke's readers know how profitable it is to "listen to" what Jesus says (6:47 and 7:1).[45] Jesus himself directs his discourse to his disciples[46] (which, in

---

40 The title Son of David or the thesis of a Davidic descent does not disappear from the postapostolic literature: see *Did.* 9.2; Ignatius *Eph.* 18.2; *Rom.* 7.3; *Smyrn.* 1.1; *Trall.* 9.1 (for the human side of Jesus Christ); Justin Martyr *Dial.* 43.1; 45.4; 100.3; 120.2; *Asc. Isa.* 11.2; see Lohse, "υἱὸς Δαυίδ," 487–88. The *Ps.-Clem. Hom.* 18.13 establish a sharp contrast between the titles Son of God and Son of David; see Hay, *Glory*, 118 n. 51. According to Hegesippus (see Eusebius *Hist. eccl.* 2.23.13–14), in the martyrdom of James, the brother of the Lord confesses the Son of Man while the converts respond with the title Son of David; see Hay, *Glory*, 120.

41 Hay (*Glory*, 121) surmises that the early Christians remembered the argument about the Son of David because they liked to make use of Ps 109 (110):1. Neugebauer ("Davidssohnfrage," 83) is of the opinion that the Lukan reading of the pericope moves in the direction of a christological edifying of the community. On p. 84 he places the pericope precisely between the questions put to Jesus and his execution. On pp. 88–89 he is of the opinion that Jesus reacts here not only against the Messiah's genealogy but against the entire messianology. On pp. 92–95 he reflects on the word "son" contained in the chris-

tological titles Son of David, Son of God, and Son of Man, explaining that the term corresponds to an eschatological expectation, designates an individual reality, and supports the development of analogies.

42 See Gagg, "Jesus"; Cullmann, *Christology*, 130–33; Michaelis, "Davidssohnschaft"; Chilton, "David," esp. 90–92 (authenticity is not to be excluded).

43 See Fitzmyer, "Contribution," 389–90 (even if there is no evidence for an Aramaic text of Ps 109 [110]:1 that uses מָרֵא ["Lord"] twice, we cannot exclude the possibility that the play on words of the LXX and the New Testament does not rest on an Aramaic form).

44 Keck (*Abschiedsrede*, 11 and passim) argues that a long farewell speech of Jesus begins here and extends to 21:36. In my opinion the evangelist sets here an exaggerated caesura between 20:44 and 20:45. Against Keck's hypothesis, see Nolland, 3:975.

45 See vol. 1 of this commentary, 254 and 260, on 6:47 and 7:1; Keck, *Abschiedsrede*, 38. See also the importance of hearing the Christian message at the end of Acts (28:22-28); Dupont, *Nouvelles études*, 469, 473–77.

46 Some manuscripts, such Vaticanus (B = 03) and

Luke's eyes, indicates priority rather than exclusiveness). The pair people–disciples symbolically represents the Christian community and its leaders.

Jesus' discourse, like that of the church, has parenetic elements. In Luke's day, the moral regulations multiplied. Here they take the form of a warnng ($\pi\rho o\sigma\acute{\epsilon}\chi\omega$ $\grave{\alpha}\pi\acute{o}$, "to refrain").[47] The church is urged to be prudent. The parenesis, however, is accompanied by polemic. While speaking to the disciples, Luke's Jesus attacks the scribes outside the community.

Polemic is part of the religious arsenal of antiquity. One builds one's own identity by disparaging the identity of the "other." The Christian community derives its unity not by dissociating itself from Judaism, since, of course, its origins are Jewish, but by setting itself apart from the other branches of the multifaceted Judaism of that day.

Jesus condemns three attitudes: the pride expressed by arrogance and a haughty behavior; the avarice expressed by the exploitation of the weak, who actually should be protected; and the hypocrisy that resorts to religion in order to beguile or to impress.

The word $\sigma\tau o\lambda\acute{\eta}$[48] (from the verb $\sigma\tau\acute{\epsilon}\lambda\lambda\omega$, "to send," "to prepare," "to equip," "to decorate") indicates a garment that in certain circumstances or social conditions is appropriate.[49] It can be a festive dress (see Job 30:13 LXX) or a functional garment.[50] It can also be the special garment worn by the victorious soldier

(Josephus *Vita* 334), by the king in his office and dignity (see 1 Macc 6:15), or especially by the priests exercising their office (2 Macc 3:15). Let us not forget that, for the Greeks, Oriental people were characterized by their long, trailing robes.[51] Luke has already used the word when speaking about the return of the prodigal son.[52]

Here the garment ($\sigma\tau o\lambda\acute{\eta}$) is a solemn robe that must correspond to particular occasions or the social group of the scribes. In any case, wearing it in public gives great satisfaction.[53] To go further and to see here a garment intended to celebrate the Sabbath, a garment that the scribes wanted to impose on everyone, is perhaps an interpretation that the text in its brevity does not encourage.[54]

Jesus' quarrel describes concretely the scribes' daily life and thereby opens a sociological window. The daily conduct ($\pi\epsilon\rho\iota\pi\alpha\tau\epsilon\hat{\iota}\nu$, "to walk") leads these gentlemen "into the public places" ($\grave{\epsilon}\nu\ \tau\alpha\hat{\iota}\varsigma\ \grave{\alpha}\gamma o\rho\alpha\hat{\iota}\varsigma$), where they enjoy the exaggerated salutations ($\grave{\alpha}\sigma\pi\alpha\sigma\mu o\acute{\upsilon}\varsigma$, "greetings") of the flatterers. "In the synagogues" they are sensitive to protocol and its privileges. They treasure the "foremost seats" ($\pi\rho\omega\tau o\kappa\alpha\vartheta\epsilon\delta\rho\acute{\iota}\alpha\varsigma$). "At the banquets" ($\grave{\epsilon}\nu\ \tau o\hat{\iota}\varsigma\ \delta\epsilon\acute{\iota}\pi\nu o\iota\varsigma$) to which they are invited they arrange it so they can enjoy the "first places" or the "first couches" ($\pi\rho\omega\tau o\kappa\lambda\iota\sigma\acute{\iota}\alpha\varsigma$).

As if this fourfold form of arrogance were not enough, Jesus adds, in a double relative clause, the twofold charge of exploiting widows[55] and religious hypocrisy. It may be

---

the Codex of Bezae (D = 05), read simply "to the disciples." See the apparatus on this passage in Nestle-Aland (27th ed.).

47   On this verb, see Keck, *Abschiedsrede*, 42–44.

48   Curiously, the Syriac Sinai and Curetonian versions must have read $\grave{\epsilon}\nu\ \sigma\tau o\alpha\hat{\iota}\varsigma$ ("in the porticoes") in their Greek texts, while the Greek manuscripts have $\grave{\epsilon}\nu\ \sigma\tau o\lambda\alpha\hat{\iota}\varsigma$ ("in robes").

49   In a remarkable way, Rengstorf ("Schriftgelehrten") portrays the word in Greek, Hellenistic Jewish, and early Christian literature; its Hebrew equivalents (the term $\sigma\tau o\lambda\acute{\eta}$ even made its way into Rabbinic Hebrew as a loanword); and the development of the costume in Israel (especially from the possession of one garment to two garments, the second, cleaner and more beautiful, was reserved for the Sabbath).

50   According to Rengstorf ("Schriftgelehrten," 392–94), the garment is neither the Jewish *tallith*, nor the Greek and Roman dress of the popular philosophers. There is, moreover, uncertainty about what the *tallith* actually was. According to some (e.g.,

Daube), it was a solemn coat reserved for pious and learned men. According to others (e.g., Rengstorf), it was an outer garment worn by everyone, men and women. As for the philosopher's coat, it was called ὁ $\tau\rho\acute{\iota}\beta\omega\nu$, literally, the worn or coarse coat.

51   See Alexandre, s.v. Bertrand Bouvier informs me that the banal meaning of $\sigma\tau o\lambda\acute{\eta}$ in modern Greek is "uniform."

52   See vol. 2 of this commentary on 15:22.

53   See Nolland, 3:976.

54   I distance myself here from Rengstorf's final hypothesis ("Schriftgelehrten").

55   Schwarz ("Witwen") thinks that the expression "to devour the houses of the widows" is difficult. He assumes that it comes from a mistranslation of the Aramaic. The original would have meant that the scribes went so far as to sleep with the widows (אכל "to eat," can be understood as a euphemism for "to have sexual relations with").

that these two charges illustrate in inverse order and in negative form the double command of love (see 10:27; see also 1:75).[56]

In Israel the widow[57] was the fragile person weakened by the death of her husband whom God requires Israel to protect.[58] Here, however, the rhetoric functions well: it is precisely this social category that, instead of being protected, is threatened by the exactions of the scribes.[59] The author of this model attack offers no proof of his allegation,[60] nor does he provide details.

The portrait of the scribes at prayer offers no more nuance.[61] It resembles the vitriolic description of the Pharisee of the parable (18:9-14) and portrays the scribes as two-faced. One of the faces is directed toward God, but instead of demonstrating humility, contrite for their faults and trusting in God, the scribes show their hypocrisy. The other face turns to human beings. Instead of interceding on behalf of their brothers and sisters in danger, and instead of joining them in fellowship in a worship filled with spirit, love, and truth, the scribes use their show of piety to gain admiration and respect and even to enrich themselves.[62]

The criticism leads to judgment ($\kappa\rho\iota\mu\alpha$), which here is equivalent to "a punishment," a "condemnation." The punishment corresponds to justice: it will be in proportion to the offense. When the abuses are more serious, the punishment will be worse ($\pi\epsilon\rho\iota\sigma\sigma\acute{o}\tau\epsilon\rho\sigma\nu$, "more severe," literally "more abundant"). Luke is thinking here of the eschatological judgment.[63]

Unlike Matthew, who gathers the invectives of Q and Mark into one chapter (23), Luke keeps them separate. He presented some in chap. 11 (11:37-52) and transmits the others, much more briefly, here (20:45-47) against the scribes.[64] This division does not avoid repetitions. One need only compare 11:43, which comes from Q (see Matt 23:6-7), with 20:46, which comes from Mark (12:38-39):

---

56   In view of the grammatical structure of v. 47, it has been suggested that the practice of long prayers went hand in hand with exploiting widows. By showing their piety in public, the incriminated scribes hope to be seen in a good light and to be given the guardianship of the widows; see Derrett, "Widows," 5.

57   On the widows in Israel and especially in Luke, see Robert M. Price, *The Widow Traditions in Luke-Acts: A Feminist-Critical Scrutiny* (SBLDS 155; Atlanta: Scholars Press, 1997).

58   Derrett ("Widows") explains that in Israel, according to the testamentary provisions of a deceased husband or father or the arrangements of the legal authorities, a guardian or manager (Greek $\grave{\epsilon}\pi\acute{\iota}\tau\rho\sigma\pi\sigma\varsigma$) could be appointed to deal with the widow's affairs. These persons, who had to be trustworthy and sometimes were required to take an oath, were paid for their services. One could suspect all sorts of things. It was sometimes said expressly that such and such a person "ate and drank" or "dressed" at the expense of the widowed victim. See already Isa 1:23; 10:2; and esp. *b. Giṭ.* 52b.

59   The verb $\kappa\alpha\tau\epsilon\sigma\vartheta\acute{\iota}\omega$ ("to devour") can be used in a figurative sense; see Anatole Bailly, *Dictionnaire grec-français* . . . (2d ed.; Paris: Hachette, 1897) s.v.; Nolland, 3:976. Paul uses it in Gal 5:15, where he exhorts the faithful not to bite or devour one another. See Otto Michel, "$\hat{\sigma}\hat{\iota}\kappa\sigma\varsigma$ $\kappa\tau\lambda$.," *TDNT* 5 (1967) 128–29.

60   The misuse of money is one of the charges most readily made by antiquity's polemicists. Paul, who paid his own expenses, defends himself vigorously against the accusation. See 1 Cor 9:10-11; 2 Cor 8:20-21; 2 Cor 9:4-5, 12; 2 Cor 11:7-11; 2 Cor 12:14-18; Phil 4:10-20. Simon Magus was similarly accused, this time by the Christian Luke (see Acts 8:18-24). The evangelist does not spare the Pharisees from this charge (see 16:14 and this commentary on 16:14-15) or, here in v. 47, the scribes.

61   On the word $\pi\rho\acute{o}\varphi\alpha\sigma\iota\varsigma$, see n. f above on the translation of v. 47. As for $\mu\acute{\alpha}\kappa\rho\alpha$, it is a neuter plural of the adjective $\mu\alpha\kappa\rho\acute{o}\varsigma$, $\acute{\alpha}$, $\acute{o}\nu$ ("long") and functions here as an adverb. It modifies the verb "to pray": their devotions are interminable.

62   Codex Bezae (D = 05) brings the two actions mentioned in v. 47 closer: the long prayers are part of the scribes' strategy to devour the widows' houses. It offers the reading "by devouring the houses of the widows under the cover of long prayers." See Nestle-Aland's apparatus (27th ed.) here. Derrett's interpretation ("Widows," 5) points in the same direction.

63   See the mention of the last judgment, called $\kappa\rho\acute{\iota}\sigma\iota\varsigma$, in 11:31 and 32 and the verb $\kappa\alpha\tau\alpha\kappa\rho\acute{\iota}\nu\omega$, "condemn," that accompanies it. Without indicating an eschatological judgment, the word $\kappa\rho\acute{\iota}\mu\alpha$ reappears in 23:40 and 24:20.

64   In his chap. 23, Matthew places a curse on the scribes and the Pharisees with one wave of the hand.

Luke 11:43	Luke 20:46
"Woe to you Pharisees, because you love the first seat in the synagogues and the greetings in the public places."	"Beware of the scribes, who want to walk around in robes and who like greetings in the public places and the first seats in the synagogues and the first places at banquets."

It is a favorite subject with Luke. One is concerned about good manners, especially the correct behavior during banquets.[65] This morality is in no way eschatological. It is similar to Plutarch's advice in the *Moralia* and anticipates the admonitions of Clement of Alexandria in the *Paedagogus*.[66]

As chap. 14 demonstrates, Luke's severity is not directed only at the "others," the people who are not part of the Christian community. Luke does not exclude the risk of backsliding in the church. The abuses cited can threaten anyone. It is also important to beware of the "scribes" within the Christian community, even within oneself.

History of Interpretation

A century ago William Wrede drew a distinction between a liberal and an orthodox reading of this pericope.[67] The

liberals, among whom he counted himself, are of the opinion that Jesus here refuses the title Son of David. The orthodox, on the other hand, claim that behind Jesus' question is the opinion that the Messiah is more than the Son of David. Is he not the Son of God?

According to Wrede's criteria, the exegesis I have developed up to this point belongs to the orthodox interpretations. In fact, the reading of Christian theologians from the patristic period to the Reformation confirms this reading. From Tertullian's time (*Adv. Marc.* 4.38.10),[68] but also with an Ambrose (*Exp. Luc.* 10.1–5)[69] or a Cyril of Alexandria (*Serm. Luc.* 137),[70] the pericope points to the sense of the title Son of David and its connections with the title Lord. These exegetes and preachers unanimously accept the title Son of David, but they apply it to the human side, more precisely to the human nature of Christ.

This view remains dominant during the Middle Ages and into the Renaissance.[71] One finds it in the writing of Erasmus, the moralist[72] who, unlike the theologians, is more attracted to the explanation of the polemical warning of vv. 45-47 (*Paraphrasis*, 442–43). One finds

---

65 See Luke 14:7-11 and vol. 2 of this commentary on those verses.

66 See Plutarch *Mor.* 612C–748D (= *Quaestiones conviviales*); Clement of Alexandria *Paed.* 2.1, 4.

67 Wrede, "Davidssohn," 167–68. Suhl ("Davidssohn," 58) called my attention to this distinction.

68 The issue is specifying the relation between Son of David and Lord. Since Jesus is Lord and Son of God, Tertullian says in passing to Marcion, he cannot destroy the Creator! Jesus had accepted the title Son of David from the blind man without batting an eye (18:38-39). Here he attacks the tradition that keeps the scribes from acknowledging that he is also the Lord, the Lord of David.

69 The bishop of Milan is aware that the episode places us in the time before the passion. In this moment Jesus includes the belief in his messiahship and his lordship. Ambrose explains vigorously the connections between the Father and the Son, then takes up the question of the Son of David: "The error here is not that one recognizes him as Son of David but that one does not believe he is the Son of God. The true faith is not one of the two but both

the one and the other." Then, using both Testaments, Ambrose proves that "Christ is at the same time God and man, one in two natures and not a double."

70 Payne Smith, *Cyril*, 2:640–44. There are two Greek fragments, published by Reuss, *Lukas–Kommentare*, 202–3 (frgs. 314–15). Here Jesus reveals the mystery of his person. To receive him it is necessary to have faith, which is the beginning of understanding. Emmanuel is both David's Son and David's Lord. The connection between these two realities is the heart of the mystery that is to be understood. The preacher makes Jesus' adversaries contemporary. Today they are those who divide Christ into two sons (meaning, I assume, the Nestorians). For Cyril, Christ is Son of David in his incarnation. If he came down into our circumstances, it was to effect our salvation. In his divine glory, nature, and sovereignty, he is David's Lord.

71 For the Middle Ages, see as an example the *Glossa ordinaria* 20.41–47 (*PL* 114:333–34).

72 In a time when no one was able to answer the question, v. 44, Jesus was content *per aenigma significasse*

it also in Luther's preaching,[73] where he discusses it in terms of the opposition between law and grace and meditates extensively on the enemies of Christ mentioned in Ps 109 (110):1. Finally, one recognizes it in Calvin's *Harmony of the Gospels,* which accuses Satan of accepting Jesus, David's son, only as a simple human being without divine nature.[74] The same Calvin also—already, one might say—knows the mentality of a scholar. He is aware of the Synoptic Problem. Luke, for example, adds sentences here (vv. 45-47), "which Matthew retained in their proper place." In his opinion, "we have often seen the Evangelists as occasion required collecting various sayings of Christ into one group." A good prince, he concedes in connection with another pericope, "If any care to follow the conjecture that Christ said the same things more than once, I have no great objection."

Conclusion

The content of vv. 41-44 is, using the modes of question and quotation, doctrinal. In dialogue with the Jewish theology of the scribes, the early Christians who transmit these verses, and Luke in particular, question an interpretation of the Messiah that sees him as a human being of Davidic stock. By quoting Ps 109 (110):1 they are able to elevate the status of the Messiah while refusing to limit him to the human sphere and thus bringing him as close as possible to God. He is Lord, David's Lord. The speeches of Acts make clear that, for Luke, it is the resurrection that brought about this transformation. From now on Jesus is at the right hand of the Father. In the infancy narratives and Jesus' genealogy, the evangelist explains how the Davidic sonship is to be understood.

The content of vv. 45-47 is, using the modes of parenesis and polemic, ethical. They pillory the "scribes," who, as members of the people of Israel, can be found in the Christian community. To seem rather than to be, to be driven by power rather than by service, to have rather than to be, to exploit rather than to protect, to pretend to pray rather than to communicate with God—such are the grievances. The spectators of this pillorying are the disciples and all the people; that is, in Luke's eyes they are the Christian leaders and all the people of the church.

---

divinam naturam, "to indicate the divine nature with an enigma" (Erasmus *Paraphrasis,* col. 442). Erasmus then extensively analyzes the malice, the ambition, and the greed of Jesus' adversaries, this breed of histrionic bunglers.

73 Luther, *Evangelien–Auslegung,* 957–61. At the quotation in v. 41 Luther introduces the question of the law. From the law the scribes know only the double commandment of love. They are not aware that they are not able to accomplish it. They will really love God and their neighbor only by recognizing Christ and knowing who he is, because he is the only human being who has fulfilled the law. It is as a true man that he is David's Son. He is even more, as he explains with the quotation of Ps 109 (110):1. The opponents understand, incorrectly, that the power of the Messiah sitting on David's throne is a reign of this world (*nur weltlich regieren,* 957). To know Christ is not only to describe who he is; it is also to know his ministry and his work.

74 Calvin, *Harmony,* 3:41–54; quotations from 46 and 71.

A Widow: An Example or a Victim? (21:1-4)

Bibliography

Arlandson, James Malcolm, *Women, Class, and Society in Early Christianity: Models from Luke-Acts* (Peabody, Mass.: Hendrickson, 1997) 172–75.

Aufhauser, Johannes B., *Buddha und Jesus in ihren Paralleltexten* (KIT 157; Bonn: Marcus & E. Weber, 1926) 13–16.

Blass, F., "On Mark 12, 42 and 15,16," *ExpT* 10 (1898–99) 185–87, 286–87.

Clemen, Carl, *Religionsgeschichtliche Erklärung des Neuen Testaments: Die Abhängigkeit des Ältesten Christentums von nichtjüdischen Religionen und philosophischen Systemen* (2d ed.; Giessen: Töpelmann, 1924) 251–53.

Degenhardt, Hans-Joachim, *Lukas, Evangelist der Armen: Besitz und Besitzverzicht in den lukanischen Schriften. Eine traditions- und redaktionsgeschichtliche Untersuchung* (Stuttgart: Katholisches Bibelwerk,1965) 93–97.

Faber, Georg, *Buddhistiche und Neutestamentliche Erzählungen: Das Problem ihrer gegenseitigen Beeinflussung* (Leipzig: Hinrichs, 1913) 55–57.

Flückiger, Felix, "Die Redaktion der Zukunftsrede in Mark 13," *ThZ* 26 (1970) 395–409.

Gaston, Lloyd, "Sondergut und Markusstoff in Luk. 21," *ThZ* 16 (1960) 161–72.

Grangaard, *Conflict*, 168–85.

Hass, Hans, *"Das Scherflein der Witwe" und seine Entsprechung im Tripitaka* (Leipzig: Hinrichs, 1922).

Howgego, C. J., *Ancient History from Coins* (London: Routledge, 1995).

Kingsbury, *Conflict*, 6, 32, 126.

Lee, G. M., "The Story of the Widow's Mite," *ExpT* 82 (1971) 344.

Malina, Bruce J., and Jerome H. Neyrey, "Conflict in Luke-Acts: Labelling and Deviance Theory," in Jerome H. Neyrey, ed., *The Social World of Luke-Acts: Models for Interpretation* (Peabody, Mass.: Hendrickson, 1991) 97–122.

Malipurathu, T., "The Praxis of Poverty from the Lucan Perspective: The Example of the Poor Widow (Lk 21,1-4)," *BiBh* 21 (1995) 167–83.

Price, *Widow Traditions*, xl.

Ramsay, W. M., "On Mark 12,42," *ExpT* 10 (1898–99) 232, 336.

Roller, Otto, *Münzen, Geld und Vermögensverhältnisse in den Evangelien* (Karlsruhe: Fidelitas, 1913) 33–35.

Schramm, *Markus-Stoff*, 171, 186.

Sebastian, V., "Jesus' Teaching on Offering, Lk 21,1-4," *BiBh* 22 (1996) 110–19.

Simon, L., "Le sou de la veuve, Marc 12/41-44," *EThR* 44 (1969) 115–26.

Simonetti, Manlio, "Origene e la povera vedova: Commento a Giovanni XIX, 7-10 (40-58)," *RSLR* 27 (1991) 476–81.

Sperber, Daniel, "Mark xii 42 and Its Metrological Background: A Study in Ancient Syriac Versions," *NovT* 9 (1967) 178–90.

Walter, Nikolaus, "Tempelzerstörung und synoptische Apokalypse," *ZNW* 57 (1966) 38–49.

Weinert, "Temple."

Wright, Addison G., "The Widow's Mites: Praise or Lament?—A Matter of Context," *CBQ* 44 (1982) 256–65.

1 When he looked up he saw the rich putting[a] their offerings in the treasury. 2/ He also saw an indigent[b] widow who put two pennies[c] in it. 3/ And he said, "Truly I say to you, this poor widow put in more than all the others; 4/ for all of these gave to the offerings out of their excess,[d] but out of her lack[e] she gave everything she had to live."[f]

a   Literally: "throwing."
b   Or "poor," or perhaps "needy."
c   Literally: "two leptas."
d   I retain a literal translation here.
e   Here too I translate literally.
f   Literally: "everything she had" or "all the life she had."

In the last twenty years, two diametrically opposed interpretations have been proposed.[1] According to the first, older interpretation, Jesus compares the widow[2] to the rich people, then praises her. According to the second, modern interpretation, Jesus compares the widow to the scribes of the previous pericope (20:45-47) and, in the form of a lament, underscores the degree to which she has been religiously exploited. The alternative is the following question: Is the poor woman blessed, or is woe pronounced on the temple's wealthy exploiters?

---

1   For a presentation of the various interpretations that have been proposed, see Wright, "Lament," 257–59; Fitzmyer, 2:1320–21.

2   On the idea of the widow in Luke, see 7:12; vol. 1 of this commentary (271), on 7:12b; see also commentary on 20:45-47; Price, *Widow Traditions*, esp. ix–xli.

Analysis

After controversies, parables, questions, and warnings (19:47—20:47), here is a narrative episode that ends in a double saying of Jesus. A long apocalyptic discourse (21:5-28), a parable—that of the fig tree, which promises fruit (21:29-33)—and a final warning (21:34-36) follow the episode of the widow. What connects all these pericopes is not their literary genre but their relationship to the temple, in which Jesus has been teaching (19:47) since he entered Jerusalem (19:29-40) and drove out the sellers (19:45-46). The literary genre of controversy continues to dominate, but the series of disputes is interrupted by other genres. Thus, we have found a parable, that of the murderous winegrowers (20:9-10), and here we have an apophthegm.

Luke did not invent this sequence, even though he gives more attention to the temple than does his predecessor.[3] Since the approach to Jerusalem (19:28), Luke has been following Mark's sequence faithfully.[4] Matthew follows the same practice but with greater freedom. Here, for example, Matthew parts company with Mark by, for reasons some exegetes try to fathom, omitting the anecdote about the widow.[5]

Consistent in his literary practices, Luke respects Mark's order without being afraid to revise it.[6] Instead of sitting ($\kappa\alpha\grave{\iota}$ $\kappa\alpha\theta\acute{\iota}\sigma\alpha\varsigma$), Jesus looks up to see those around him ($\grave{\alpha}\nu\alpha\beta\lambda\acute{\epsilon}\psi\alpha\varsigma$ $\delta\acute{\epsilon}$). Instead of contemplating ($\grave{\epsilon}\theta\epsilon\acute{\omega}\rho\epsilon\iota$), he sees ($\epsilon\hat{\iota}\delta\epsilon\nu$), that is to say, he catches people in the actual deed. To describe what he sees, Luke avoids Mark's transition (from the general, the "crowd," to the particular, the "widow," by way of the group of the "rich") in order to set up a contrast between the "rich" and the "poor widow."[7] While he uses the technical term "treasury" ($\gamma\alpha\zeta o\varphi\upsilon\lambda\acute{\alpha}\kappa\iota o\nu$, we would say "poor box"), he avoids the unfortunate repetition of the word (Mark 12:41) by omitting that Jesus sat opposite this "treasury."[8] What the passers by throw "into the treasury" are "their offerings," while the parallel text speaks of "copper coins" or "much" money. In Luke's text the widow is not at first "poor" ($\pi\tau\omega\chi\acute{\eta}$) but "needy," "wretched" ($\pi\epsilon\nu\iota\chi\rho\acute{\alpha}$) when Jesus speaks she is $\pi\tau\omega\chi\acute{\eta}$, as in Mark). Luke prefers the direct object (Jesus sees the rich people, then the widow) rather than the indirect question "how" people throw in their money (Mark 12:41). Luke keeps the "two copper coins,"[9] but he omits Mark's explanation that they "equal a quadrans."[10] To avoid distraction, he eliminates the reference to the disciples (Mark 12:43a)

---

3 See Weinert, "Temple"; Bovon, *Luke the Theologian*, 363 n. 23, 640.

4 He parts company with Mark in only three brief instances. He omits the cursing of the fig tree (Mark 11:20-26) and the discussion of the greatest commandment (Mark 12:28-34) in order to keep from repeating himself (see 10:25-28). He also inserts a warning (21:34-46) from his own special material in preference to the final parable of the doorkeeper (Mark 13:33-37).

5 See Simon ("Sou," 122–24), who thinks that Matthew and his church are shocked by an episode that in the final analysis turns out to be absurd (see n. 43 below). For a different explanation, see Luz, *Matthew 21–28*, 158.

6 See the synoptic comparison in Degenhardt, *Lukas*, 94–95 esp. n. 37; Simon, "Sou," 116–18; Marshall, 750–52; Fitzmyer, 2:1320; Arlandson, *Women*, 172–73.

7 On the "disappearance" of the crowd, see Marshall, 771.

8 The expression "to throw in the treasury" appears twice in Mark (12:41, 43).

9 Luke adds a more precise designation of the place: the widow deposits these two pennies "there" ($\grave{\epsilon}\kappa\epsilon\hat{\iota}$).

10 There has been a great deal of controversy over Mark's explanation. Some commentators—W. M. Ramsay (two short articles), in particular—think that Mark felt obliged to explain the two Oriental leptas to a Roman audience. Therefore, the Gospel of Mark must have originated in Rome! For the argument to be convincing, the quadrans would have to be unknown, or at least not well known, in the East. Even if the empire's eastern cities, principalities, or provinces did not issue their currencies in gold coins, and seldom in silver coins, they had a practical monopoly on small coins. According to these authors, small bronze Roman coins, among them the quadrans, did not reach the empire until the second, and especially in the third, century. For other scholars—Friedrich Blass (two short articles) in particular—the quadrans was known in the Orient in the first century, and Mark's explanation has nothing to say about where the Gospel would have been written.

and gives Jesus' words with his customary fidelity. He merely avoids the loanword "amen" (he replaces it with "truly") and the redundancy "who are putting something in the treasury" (Mark 12:43b). Other details: Luke prefers to say "all these" instead of "all," to repeat the word "offering" ("to the offerings"), to replace abstract reality (ὑστέρησις) with concrete reality (ὑστέρημα) to indicate the "lack," and he undertakes a final change of order: He places the emphasis on the "goods" or the "life" (which I have translated as "everything she had to live") instead of leaving them in weak apposition. One can see that the synoptic comparison shows more similarities than dissimilarities. The differences can be explained primarily by Luke's effort to improve the Gospel's language for his cultured readers. They may also be explained by the concern to bring about semantic displacements. Luke's characterization of the widow or the term he chooses to describe the offerings slightly change the sense of the episode inherited from Mark. Simplifying the scenery and reducing the number of people involved support a comparison and a contrast.

We have here a short episode that underscores Jesus' wisdom, the kind of text one customarily calls an apophthegm.[11] What counts in such stories is the decisive word of the Master. Unlike other cases, here the setting is an essential part of the saying of Jesus; it is not a story created by the early Christians to serve as the framework for a traditional word of Jesus.[12] The solemnity of the saying, introduced by "truly I say to you," does not necessarily imply that Jesus' words must have a kerygmatic or apocalyptic content. They constitute rather a valuable diagnosis, a wise observation such as a philosopher might make, even a judgment inspired by a prophet that runs counter to popular opinion.[13] From a form-critical

perspective these words of Jesus do not have the characteristics of the lament.[14]

Even if the location in the temple area is fundamental to the episode, it is unlikely that the series of events as they are given by Mark and then Luke and Matthew is old or even that it corresponds to historical reality. It may be true that Mark and Luke place the criticism of those who exploit widows alongside the portrayal of the widow with the two pennies, but that does not mean that the two episodes originally were related. Thus, we should not look to the literary context to discover the meaning of the unit at the stage of its oral tradition. Independent of its literary context, the pericope cannot imply a criticism of the temple or a criticism of the exploitation of widows. The exegesis will let us know if in its written and redactional form the text brings a change of meaning, namely, a radical transformation of a wisdom or prophetic saying into a lament over a poor woman and oppressive priests.

Formally, the Lukan version of the story is subdivided as follows:

Vv. 1-2 With a glance Jesus makes a twofold observation:

    V. 1 the offering of the rich

    V. 2 the offering of the widow

Vv. 3-4 With a word Jesus makes a twofold appreciation:

    V. 3 the widow's act (ascertaining the fact)

    V. 4a the act of the rich

V. 4b   the value judgment on the widow's act

The text thus consists of two parts, each of which is subdivided.[15] I do not see how one can speak here of a concentric structure.[16] We have a parallel and antithetic structure with a skillful inversion: The look passes from the rich to the widow, the voice passes from the widow to

---

11   See Bultmann, *History*, 32–33. English-language exegetes speak of a "pronouncement story"; Fitzmyer, 2:1320.

12   Dibelius (*Tradition*, 261) suggests this hypothesis with some hesitation.

13   Occasionally Jesus spoke wisdom sayings. To say that it was not possible for him to resemble a philosopher, as Wright ("Lament," 260) does, comes from a *petitio principii*.

14   Note the difference in style between our passage and, for example, the lament in 19:41-44. I disagree here with those who, following Wright ("Lament"),

think that Jesus' saying represents a lament. On the lament, see Claus Westermann, *Basic Forms of Prophetic Speech* (trans. Hugh Clayton White; Philadelphia: Fortress Press, 1967) 202–3.

15   See the various attempts to structure the text; Meynet, *Évangile*, 1:190, 2:195–96; Sebastian, "Offering," 111–12; Malipurathu, "Poverty," 179; Arlandson, *Women*, 174.

16   Malipurathu ("Poverty," 179) and Sebastian ("Offering," 109) both use this or a similar expression, even if this latter author also notes the antithetic parallelism.

the rich, only to return cleverly to the widow, the main character.[17] This process facilitates the reading by avoiding a back and forth, and it focuses the attention on the person of the woman. The center of interest is thus in the center of the text.

Such paradoxical stories (the generous giver is not what one thinks) circulate in all cultures. I cite here as examples three parallels that exegetes have long since discovered, one from India, another from Greece, the third from Israel.[18] The first comes from Indian Buddhism, probably from the first or second century C.E. A poor widow begs for food during a religious celebration. Unfortunately, she has nothing to offer in return, until she remembers that she had found two coins on a manure pile. The priest then begins to sing a hymn in honor of the widow, while she sings of her hope of a full reward.[19] The second parallel is a fragment of a lost tragedy of Euripides, *Danae*: "More than once I see poor people who are wiser than the rich and who give offerings to the gods with their weak hands [if we read $\mu\iota\kappa\rho\hat{\alpha}$ $\chi\epsilon\iota\rho\hat{\iota}$]; yet they are more pious than those who sacrifice oxen."[20] The third parallel is a passage from *Leviticus Rabbah:* A poor woman brought only a handful of flour as an offering. That irritated the priest, who was think-

ing how he could divide this offering between what was to be given to God and what was to be kept for food for the clergy. When scolded in a dream, the priest learns not to scorn one who has offered her own life.[21] All of these parallels admire the virtue of the poor when compared with the attitude of the rich, and not one of them laments the sad fate that religion could impose on those who are destitute.

Commentary

■ **1-2** Did the Lukan Jesus look down in discouragement at the end of the preceding warning?[22] Even if he did, the fact is that he looks up at this moment and sees those who are tossing in their alms. Like other religions, Judaism had developed the system of giving offerings. They could be gathered in the temple, as is the case here, in support of the temple worship.[23] They could also be collected outside the temple for social relief, in particular, to aid widows and orphans.[24] Rabbinic literature indicates that there were thirteen trumpet-shaped offering chests in the temple for collecting the gifts (*m. Šeqal.* 6.5–6).[25] One of them carried the legend "Gold for the cover of the arch." If the system had already reached this level of organiza-

17 One thinks of other Lukan contrasts between rich and poor, beginning with the beatitudes and the woes (6:20-26) and the rich man and poor Lazarus (16:19-31).
18 On these parallels, see Fitzmyer, 2:1320.
19 There is a presentation of the text in Clemen, *Erklärung*, 251–53; Faber, *Erzählungen*, 55–57; Haas, "*Scherflein*," 106–16; Aufhauser, *Buddha*, 13–16. Bultmann (*History*, 33) sees an influence of the Buddhist story on the Gospel story. Degenhardt (*Lukas*, 96, esp. n. 43) has serious reservations. We should not exclude the possibility that the Gospel influenced the Buddhist account. In that case the Buddhist story would be part of the "reception history" (*Wirkungsgeschichte*). The links between Buddhism and primitive Christianity should be reconsidered; the influences, if there are any, can go in both directions.
20 Euripides, *Danae*, frg. 327, in Richard Kannicht, ed., *Tragicorum Graecorum Fragmenta*, 5.1 *Euripides* (Göttingen: Vandenhoeck & Ruprecht, 2004) 379. One sees other parallels as early as J. J. Wettstein, *Novum Testamentum Graecum* (1751; reprinted Graz: Akademische Druck und Verlagsanstalt, 1962)

1:618–19. See Lee ("Story") who emphasizes the more thematic than formal relationship between our passage and the fragment of Euripides. See also Fitzmyer, 2:1320.
21 *Leviticus Rabbah* 107a or 3.5; *Midrash Rabbah*, vol. 4: *Leviticus*, chaps. 1–19 (3d ed.; trans. J. Israelstam; London: Soncino, 1983) 40–41. See Str-B 2:45–46; Fitzmyer, 2:1320; C. F. Evans, 728–29 (who refers to Josephus *Ant.* 6.7.4 §149 and *Lev. Rab.* 107a or 3.5).
22 See Sebastian, "Offering," 113.
23 On the system of offerings collected in the temple, see Str-B 2:37–45.
24 In calling attention to the tension between "Hebrews" and "Hellenists," Luke refers to this second system, which the Christians borrowed from their Jewish fellow countrymen (Acts 6:1). On the Jewish system of aid to the poor, see Degenhardt, *Lukas*, 23–26; Bovon, *Luke the Theologian*, 444.
25 See *Mishnayot: Die sechs Ordnungen der Mischna. Hebräischer Text mit Punktation, deutscher Übersetzung und Erklärung* (Victor Goldschmidt Ausgabe, 3d ed.; Basel, 1968) 2:284–86; Str-B 2:37–42.

tion, it may have been this offering chest into which the rich deposited their alms.[26] None of the offering chests appears to have been intended for an offering as modest as that of the widow. Thus, she must have put her two pennies[27] in one of the six offering chests intended for the "voluntary offerings." If, according to the evangelists, Jesus knows how much the widow gave, it is not because of the designation of the chests; it is because of his supernatural knowledge as a divine man.[28]

What exactly does the word γαζοφυλάκιον mean, a term known to the Synoptic tradition, the Gospel of John (John 8:20), Josephus, and a few other Hellenistic Jewish authors?[29] Etymologically it refers to a space where one keeps (φυλάσσω) the treasure (γάζα, a word that comes from Persia, where it means the imperial treasure). But what space is it? It can be a particular building (an impression Mark gives when he locates Jesus "opposite" the γαζοφυλάκιον) or all of the offering chests that can be placed in any given building. Luke is less clear than Mark, since he writes: "who put their offerings in the treasury" (τοὺς βάλλοντας εἰς τὸ γαζοφυλάκιον τὰ δῶρα αὐτῶν) and two lines farther on "they put into the gifts" (ἔβαλον εἰς τὰ δῶρα). By using the word γαζοφυλάκιον the evangelist is probably thinking of one of these offering chests, such as the one that was found in Delos, in the first sanctuary of the Egyptian gods, the Serapeion A.[30] Neither Mark nor Luke thus appears to distinguish among the various chests. In short, for the Jewish readers of Greek, the γαζοφυλάκιον means a room or a building reserved for storing and guarding the offerings.

The first meaning of the verb βάλλω is "to throw." In Greek, however, the semantic field of the verb does not coincide with that of the English verb "to throw." Sometimes in Greek this verb serves to indicate the gesture or action of those who "put" their money into the strongbox, "invest" in their savings, "pay" their debts, or "give" their offerings. Thus, the use of the verb here is not surprising.[31]

On the other hand, what strikes the exegete is the frequency of the use of this verb: five times in a few lines! Do these repetitions represent an awkwardness on the part of the narrator or are they intentional? I rather believe, following Pascal (*Pensées* 1.48), that the repetitions are not at all unfortunate. The readers should not be distracted by a variety of verbs. It is always the same gesture. What does change are those who do it, what the act implies for them, and the amount they give.

Luke does avoid, however, another of Mark's repetitions, that of the adjective "poor" (πτωχή). Where it stands alone, Luke prefers the less common adjective πενιχρός. In Greek there is, however, at least in their origin, a difference between these two adjectives. The former refers to the person who has nothing and can do nothing except cower in shame and, sometimes, beg.[32] The second refers to one who must work to earn a living, then to the person who is needy, destitute, poor, or a beggar. (The verb πένομαι means initially "to work," "to toil" to earn one's living, then "to be poor.")[33] In fact, there are two adjectives that come from this root, the less common πενιχρός and the second, more common, πένης. It is difficult to know precisely why Luke avoids πτωχός and why he prefers πενιχρός over πένης. In Luke's day πενιχρός expressed poverty more than the need to work. By using πενιχρός along with πτωχός Luke wants to avoid monotony, yet it may be that with the adjective πενιχρός he also wants to suggest discreetly that this widow works to survive.[34]

26 C. F. Evans (728) observes correctly that Luke puts the word "rich" at the end of the sentence out of his concern for their pomposity.

27 On λέπτον ("coin"), see 12:59; Blass, "Mark" (two short articles) and Ramsay, "Mark" (two short articles); Degenhardt, *Lukas*, 95. See n. 10 above.

28 Jesus' omniscience has just been alluded to in connection with the requisition of the ass (19:30-36); see Bieler, ΘΕΙΟΣ ΑΝΗΡ, 87–91.

29 On γαζοφυλάκιον, see Str-B 2:37–45; Plummer, 475; Degenhardt, *Lukas*, 95.

30 See Philippe Bruneau and Jean Ducat, *Guide de Délos* (Ecole française d'Athènes; Paris: Boccard, 1965) 138.

31 See LSJ, s.v., and BAGD, s.v. Nevertheless, Cyril of Alexandria prefers the verb προσφέρω, see frg. 316, line 2, in Reuss, *Lukas-Kommentare*, 204.

32 See Simon, "Sou," 117.

33 Aristophanes *Plutus* 552–53, cited by Fitzmyer, 2:1322: "The life of a poor person (πτωχός) is to live having nothing at all, whereas the life of a needy person (πένης) is to live sparingly and dependent on toil."

34 On the adjective πενιχρός, see Plummer, 475; on poverty in Luke, see Malipurathu, "Poverty"; Degenhardt, *Lukas*, 96–97; Bovon, *Luke the Theologian*, 442–48.

■ **3-4** In a solemn manner Jesus notes that in a sense the widow gives more than all the others. Jesus' saying thus has a double energy. It observes, then it values; it settles first on the facts, then on the interpretation. It first extricates a human reality from the suffocating silence society imposes on it—a society that looks at external appearances and respects the rich because of their wealth. It then expresses a truth (ἀληθῶς λέγω ὑμῖν, "truly I say to you," v. 3) on lack and abundance, on the wealth of the poor woman and the gift of her life (v. 4b).[35] By contrast, it implicitly disparages the gifts that come from abundance and excess.

Before going further, I would like to present here the interpretation of Addison G. Wright that has been affirmed by numerous and well-known exegetes.[36] Wright begins by asserting that most of the traditional interpretations are dictated more by the piety and the morality of the Christian churches than by historical-critical rigor.[37] He then is of the opinion that at no time does the text try to congratulate the widow or to emphasize the value of her action. Finally, based on the previous context he sees a thematic relationship between the accusation of exploiting widows (19:47) and the case of this poor widow. She would have interiorized the requirements of a rapacious religion that wants to grow rich on the backs of poor people. Here Jesus would denounce the temple (whose destruction he will predict in 21:6). I have already indicated above that the literary genre of the episode does not support Wright's ingenious hypothesis. To what I said there I add that, according to both the tradition and the redaction the contrast is between the rich and the poor widow[38] and not between the widow and gloomy exploiters.

Beyond the obvious reality that there are poor people who are more generous than rich people, Luke, following Mark and tradition (going back to Jesus?), develops a topic that is a favorite with him, sharing goods and the gift of oneself. He is not thinking here of the nature of the temple, for which he has sympathies as well as reservations. As in the beatitudes, he begins with the rich, whose wealth is not impugned. What he is really interested in is the widow's existence. He knows, of course, that Jewish and Christian moral teachings both seek to protect widows. Yet, again, that is not what is at stake in the episode. Here the widow is regarded not as the object of a necessary solicitude but as an ethical subject. To be sure—and it is here that we move from the human to the divine point of view—the widow's act is exaggerated (she will have nothing more to live on), absurd (the temple can do quite well without these two pennies), and even impossible (how can one give what one does not have? how can she take something from her "lack," ὑστέρημα, v. 4?). That is just it: according to Luke, who has said it with regard to riches (one is to abandon all riches; 12:33; 14:33), Christian existence is neither reasonable nor achievable. That does not matter. By giving everything she has, her whole life (βίος has the two meanings) (see 8:43; 15:12, 30),[39] the widow attracts Jesus' attention. This Jesus loves her; it is not, as some exegetes would have it, that the temple functionaries embitter him.[40] By attracting Jesus' attention, it is as if she "comes to him" or "hears his words" (6:47), as if she gets eternal life.

35   See Wiefel, 346; Roland Meynet, *Avez-vous lu saint Luc? Guide pour la rencontre* (LiBi 88; Paris: Cerf, 1990) 231; Maier, 2:516; Malipurathu, "Poverty"; Fred B. Craddock, *Luke* (Louisville: Westminster John Knox Press, 1990) 242.

36   Wright, "Lament"; see also Fitzmyer, 2:1320–21; David Lenz Tiede, *Luke* (Augsburg Commentary on the New Testament; Minneapolis: Augsburg, 1988) 354; C. A. Evans, 306–7; Green, 728–29; Sharon H. Ringe, *Luke* (Westminster Bible Companion; Louisville: Westminster John Knox, 1995) 250. For his part, L'Eplattenier (233–35) thinks that both readings, the old and the modern, are possible.

37   Wright ("Lament," 257–59) first lists five variations of the traditional interpretation: (1) The true measure of a gift is what one has left over. (2) What counts is the spirit in which the act is done. (3) It is a question here of giving everything. (4) Pious offerings must correspond to how much one has. (5) Giving alms is a duty. In his opinion, the only defensible variant (which in the final analysis he does not support) is the first one. He thinks it is the only one justified by the text.

38   See Arlandson, *Women*, 173–74. For a sociological approach to this contrast, see Malina and Neyrey, "Conflict."

39   See Fitzmyer, 2:1322; C. F. Evans, 729.

40   Obviously, one thinks of the virtue of the widow of Zarephath (1 Kgs [LXX 3 Kgdms] 17:8-16), who first serves God and the man of God before she thinks of herself and her son.

Luke does not associate salvation only with redemption by the cross and resurrection. He also attaches it to Jesus' ministry and to the attitude of his conversation partners toward him. As Christ who was rich became poor in order to enrich poor human beings (2 Cor 8:9), so the widow profited from her need and created abundance from her poverty. If the verb βάλλω ("to throw," "to pour") occurs frequently, the vocabulary of want[41] and that of abundance are also present and active in early Christianity. The widow has given "more." She took from her "lack." She offered everything she had, in a sense her entire life.[42] Luke draws here not only a lesson of morality but also a lesson of theology.[43]

History of Interpretation

In what has come down to us of his work,[44] Origen does not say much about the widow's offering,[45] but one passage deserves our attention. In his *Commentary on the Gospel of John* Origen reproaches Heracleon for remaining dumb before the evangelist's comment: Jesus "spoke these words at the place called the Treasury while he was teaching in the Temple" (John 8:20). Origen is especially concerned to draw a spiritual message from this verse by connecting it with the episode of the widow (the word γαζοφυλάκιον in both places invites him to make the connection).[46] The temple must be understood in a spiritual sense: it is the church. The offerings of silver represent the abilities of the Christians that they use for the edification of the church. Drawing on the parable of the talents in Matt 25:14-30, Origen observes that these abilities are not uniformly distributed. Jesus, looking at the people passing by, is obviously the divine Word who observes the human beings at their work. To be sure, the rich give much, but it is much less than they could give. The poor widow went to the limit of her abilities, and she gave everything to the church. (The two coins represent the theoretical and practical acts.) Returning to John's text,[47] Origen claims that with his divine words Jesus himself makes his contribution to the edification of the

---

41 C. F. Evans (728) wonders whether the thought does not become paradoxical here: the widow gave what she did not have.

42 Malipurathu ("Poverty," 182–83) notices the revolutionary character of the pericope that praises the unconditional love and offers a radical plan of action.

43 Bossuyt and Radermakers (2:434) go so far as to write: "This oppressed and generous woman simply becomes the living image of Jesus." Maier (2:515) draws the same parallel. In an original, risky, and enigmatic article, Simon ("Sou") offers two possible interpretations. What he calls the weak hypothesis: The death of the temple and the end of the religion ("which permits the rich person to be religiously rich"; 121). What he calls the strong hypothesis: Because the widow establishes no relationship to her neighbor, accomplishes an act that cannot be repeated, is in the final analysis absurd, without finality and without morality, the account describes the death of the subject and the birth of the word.

44 The first patristic references to the story of the generous widow include the following: Irenaeus *Adv. haer.* 4.18.2: In the new economy offerings will be given by free persons and not by slaves. It is more than the tithe; one's entire life is offered to the Lord. Thus, "the poor widow here cast her entire subsistence into God's treasury." Clement of Alexandria (*Strom.* 4.6.35.3) thinks that the intention is more important than the gift itself. In view of the rich and the poor widow the Savior "declared that this widow gave more than all others, because the rich man gave to the treasury from his excess, and the widow from her poverty." See also Cyprian of Carthage (*De opere et eleemosynis* 15): The widow remembers the divine precepts; she has the honor to be praised by the judge before the last judgment. She who lacks everything is rich in works. What counts is not the abundance of the gift but the intention behind it. In the *Symposium* (9.4 §248), Methodius of Olympus gives the widow of the Gospels as an example who, in fact, is a combination of the woman who finds her coin by sweeping diligently (Luke 15:8-10) and the widow of our passage.

45 Origen *Hom. Gen.* 1.8 and *Comm. Matt.* 15.21: In these two passages Origen notes that the value of the gift depends on the intention with which one gives it. For this material on Origen I am following Simonetti ("Origene"). He gives these references on 479.

46 Simonetti, "Origene."

47 Simonetti ("Origene," 477) detects here "the combined interpretation of the Johannine passage and the episode of the widow."

church (see *Comm. Joh.* 19.7.2 §40–19.8 §52).[48] For their part, the believers also participate. Having praised the widow, Origen—and this is surprising—expresses some reservations about her. Why, he wonders, is she so poor? It is because—the theologian continues to speak on the spiritual level—in religious matters her understandings were too simplistic (ἁπλούστερον περὶ τῶν θείων φρονοῦσαν). Since, as is well known, Origen rejects any determinism, he presupposes the widow's own responsibility.[49]

To my knowledge such an original interpretation remains isolated in late antiquity.[50] Cyril of Alexandria offers a more representative patristic exegesis (*Serm. Luc.* 138).[51] Following the literary genre of the episode there, he stays with the moral rather than the allegorical interpretation. Creating a network of scriptural quotations,[52] Cyril celebrates the virtue of all who are generous and who go so far as to give of themselves. These are the people whom Jesus observes and rewards as a judge of their performances. In return, Cyril praises Christ, the arbitrator, for his unsurpassable kindness. He looks not so much at those who at the time are otherwise engaged in the temple but at those who are involved in giving their offerings. The preacher invites his hearers, following Jesus, to reflect on the competition among compassionate people and to admire in particular the gift of the woman who, according to him, constantly begged. Cyril also tries to persuade the rich among his hearers who dare to disagree. (This gives us an expressive image of the economic situation of the rich in that day.) He makes

use here of the wisdom of Paul (2 Cor 8:12) that no one is expected to achieve the impossible; he merely encourages the rich to be generous and the poor to do what they can. The Omniscient One is able to recognize one's willingness and intention. He crowns the simple and generous people with a higher honor. Indeed, the person who gives sows for the harvest, for rich blessings.[53]

Finally, I mention Erasmus (*Paraphrasis,* 444) and Calvin, because they both expand the view, as does Wright.[54] They are not content with contrasting the rich and the widow, as Luke does. They associate them with the scribes, the Pharisees, and the priests.[55] Erasmus in particular reproaches them not only for their greed (he is undoubtedly thinking of 16:14) but also for exploiting the people (he is thinking certainly of 20:45-47). By requiring almsgiving under the cover of religion they are forcing people, and especially the poor, to do something they require neither of their children nor of their relatives. Thus—this is an original argument—they contradict the Law of Moses (without acknowledging it, Erasmus is thinking of Mark 7:8-13), which instructed children to support their aged parents before giving their mite to God.[56] With their viciousness the priests embezzled the money in the chests and used it primarily for their own profit, for their own luxury. The kinship with Wright's arguments ends here, for both Erasmus and Calvin interpret Jesus' sayings in the traditional sense.[57]

---

48 Origen does not mention here the redemptive work of the cross.

49 Simonetti ("Origene," 478–81) sees here in the background the doctrine of the preexistence of the souls. Is he right?

50 In his *Exp. Luc.* 10.6, Ambrose of Milan does not comment on the episode of the widow, because he says, he spoke about it in his work on the widows. Indeed, we can read his commentary in *De viduis* 5.27–32. See Franco Gori, ed., *Sant' Ambrogio, Opere Morali* 2.1: *Verginità e vedovanza. Introduzione, traduzione, note e indici* (Milan/Rome: Biblioteca Ambrosiana–Città nuova, 1989) 268–77.

51 See Payne–Smith, *Cyril,* 2:645–49. There is also a Greek fragment (316) edited by Reuss, *Lukas-Kommentar,* 204.

52 Matt 5:7; Prov 25:2; Matt 25:40; Prov 19:17; Job 35:7-8; Jas 2:13; 2 Cor 8:12; Jas 1:27; Isa 52:6; Deut 15:7-8; Luke 6:38; 2 Cor 9:7; Deut 15:10; Rom 12:8; 2 Cor 9:6-7, 8.

53 The idea appears also in Luther, *Evangelien-Auslegung,* 981: "It means: scatter abroad, seize it, God loves a cheerful giver. Thus God is faithful to give in abundance to all kinds of good works, says S. Paul."

54 Calvin, *Harmony,* 3:72. See n. 14 above and the commentary on vv. 3-4.

55 Calvin, *Harmony,* 3:72: "As for the sacred offerings of that time it is likely that they were not expended on rightful uses, yet as the legal cult still flourished Christ did not reject them."

56 For Wright ("Lament," 260–61) this Mosaic regulation is a good reason for attacking the traditional interpretation.

57 See, e.g., Calvin, *Harmony,* 3:72: "Men's offerings are not to be reckoned at their outward value, but only by the motive of the heart." From that the reformer

Conclusion

After the warning and the criticism (20:45-47), Luke changes the subject (21:1-4). He pierces the deceptive appearances to come to the heart of the truth.[58] The widow went the way on which Jesus would like to take his disciples. She risked losing something in order to become something, recognized her want in order to make something from it. She puts the verb "to have" in the past tense. Jesus offers her the verb "to be" as a future reality.

---

draws a lesson for the poor ("that they consecrate themselves") and for the rich ("it is not enough for their generosity to exceed that of the poor").

58   See Arlandson, *Women*, 175.

Bibliography

Achtemeier, Elizabeth, "Luke 21, 25-36," *Int* 48 (1994)
401–4.

Aejmelaeus, Lars, *Wachen vor dem Ende: Die traditions-
geschichtlichen Wurzeln von 1 Thess 5:1-11 und Lukas
21:34-36* (SESJ 44; Helsinki: Kirjapaino Raamat-
tutalo, 1985).

Bartsch, Hans-Werner, *Wachet aber zu jeder Zeit! Ent-
wurf einer Auslegung des Lukasevangeliums* (Hamburg-Bergstedt: Reich, 1963) 118–23.

Str-B 2:255–56.

Bloomquist, L. Gregory, "Rhetorical Argumentation
and the Culture of Apocalyptic: A Socio-Rhetorical Analysis of Luke 21," in Stanley E. Porter and
Dennis L. Stamps, eds., *Rhetorical Interpretation
of Scripture* (JSNTSup 180; Sheffield: Sheffield
Academic, 1999) 173–209.

Bovon, *Luke the Theologian*, 1–85.

Braumann, Georg, "Die lukanische Interpretation der Zerstörung Jerusalems," *NovT* 6 (1963)
120–27.

Idem, "Das Mittel der Zeit: Erwägungen zur Theologie des Lukasevangeliums," *ZNW* 54 (1963)
117–45.

Bridge, Steven L., *Where the Eagles Are Gathered: The
Deliverances of the Elect in Lukan Eschatology* (JSNT-
Sup 240; London: Sheffield Academic, 2003)
115–80.

Buzzard, Anthony F., "Luke's Prelude to the Kingdom
of God: The Fall of Jerusalem and the End of
Age—Luke 21:20-33," *A Journal from the Radical
Reformation: A Testimony of Biblical Unitarianism* No.
4 (1995) 32–43.

Carroll, John T., *Response to the End of History: Eschatology and Situation in Luke-Acts* (SBLDS 92; Atlanta:
Scholars Press, 1988).

Conzelmann, Hans, "Geschichte und Eschaton nach
Mc 13," *ZNW* 50 (1959) 210–21.

Cotter, Anthony C., "The Eschatological Discourse,"
CBQ 1 (1939) 125–32, 204–13.

Del Agua Pérez, Agustín, "Derás Lucano de Mc 13 a
la luz de su 'teología del Reino': Lc 21,5-36," *EstBib*
39 (1981) 285–313.

Drury, John, "'Let the reader understand!' Mark
13.14," *Modern Believing* n.s. 39 (1998) 4–9.

Dupont, Jacques, "Les épreuves des chrétiens avant
la fin du monde (Lc 21,5-19)," *AsSeign* 64 (1969)
77–86; reprinted in idem, *Évangiles synoptiques*,
2:1117–27.

Idem, *Les trois apocalypses synoptiques: Marc 13; Matthieu
24–25; Luc 21* (LD 121; Paris: Cerf, 1985).

Elliott, John H., "Temple versus Household in Luke-
Acts: A Contrast in Social Institutions," in Jerome
H. Neyrey, ed., *The Social World of Luke-Acts: Models
for Interpretation* (Peabody, Ma.: Hendrickson,
1991) 211–40.

Fee, Gordon D., "A Text-Critical Look at the Synoptic
Problem," *NovT* 22 (1980) 12–28.

Feuillet, André, "Le discours de Jésus sur la ruine du
Temple d'après Marc XIII et Luc XXI, 5-36," *RB*
55 (1948) 481–502; 56 (1949) 61–92.

Idem, "Loi de Dieu, Loi du Christ et Loi de l'Esprit
d'après les Épîtres pauliniennes," *NovT* 22 (1980)
29–65.

Flückiger, Felix, "Luk. 21,20-24 und die Zerstörung
Jerusalems," *ThZ* 28 (1972) 385–90.

Idem, "Die Redaktion der Zukunftsrede in Mark 13,"
ThZ 26 (1970) 395–409.

Fusco, Vittorio, "Le discours eschatologique lucanien:
'Rédaction' et 'composition' (Lc 21,5-36 et Mc
13,1-37)," in Camille Focant, ed., *The Synoptic
Gospels* (BEThL 110; Louvain: Leuven University
Press/Peeters, 1993) 311–55.

Galbiati, Enrico, "L'avvento liberatore (Luca 21,25-
33)," *BeO* 3 (1961) 222–24.

Gaston, Lloyd H., "Sondergut und Markus-Stoff in
Luk 21," *ThZ* 16 (1960) 161–72.

Geiger, Ruthild, *Die lukanischen Endzeitreden: Studien
zur Eschatologie des Lukas-Evangeliums* (EHS.T
23.16; Bern: Lang, 1973).

George, Augustin, "Tradition et rédaction chez Luc:
La construction du troisième évangile," in I. de
la Potterie, ed., *De Jésus aux Évangiles* (BEThL 25;
Louvain/Paris: Duculot, 1967) 100–129; reprinted
in idem, *Études*, 14–41.

Hartman, Lars, *Prophecy Interpreted: The Formation of
Some Jewish Apocalyptic Texts and of the Eschatological Discourse Mark 13 par.* (Lund: Gleerup, 1966)
226–35.

Jeremias, *Parables*, 29, 93, 119–20, 170–71.

Jülicher, *Gleichnisreden* 2.3–11.

Kaestli, Jean-Daniel, *L'eschatologie dans l'oeuvre de Luc:
Ses caractéristiques et sa place dans le développement du
Christianisme primitif* (NSTh 22; Geneva: Labor et
Fides, 1969) 41–57.

Kay, James F., "Redemption Draws Near: Luke 21:25-
36," *CCen* 114, no. 32 (1997) 1033.

Keck, Fridolin, *Die öffentliche Abschiedsrede Jesu in Lk
20, 45—21,36: Eine redaktions- und motivgeschichtliche Untersuchung* (FB 25; Stuttgart: Katholisches
Bibelwerk, 1976).

Kinman, "Eschatology."

Koester, Craig, "The Origin and Significance of the
Flight to Pella Tradition," *CBQ* 51 (1989) 90–106.

Koester, Helmut, "Συνέχω, συνοχή," *TDNT* 7 (1971)
877–87.

Kümmel, Werner Georg, *Promise and Fulfillment: The
Eschatological Message of Jesus* (trans. Dorothea M.
Barton; London: SCM, 1957) 95–104.

Künzi, Martin, *Das Naherwartungslogion Markus 9,1 par: Geschichte seiner Auslegung, mit einem Nachwort zur Auslegungsgeschichte von Markus 13, 30 par.* (BGBE 21; Tübingen: Mohr Siebeck, 1977).

Lambrecht, Jan, "Die Logia-Quellen von Markus 13," *Bib* 47 (1966) 321–60.

Idem, "Die 'Midrasch-Quelle' von Mk 13," *Bib* 49 (1968) 254–70.

Idem, "Redactio sermonis eschatologici," *VD* 43 (1965) 278–87.

Lauras, Antoine, "Le commentaire patristique de Lc. 21,25-33," *StPatr* 7 (TU 92; Berlin: Akademie-Verlag, 1966) 503–15.

Maddox, Robert, *The Purpose of Luke-Acts* (FRLANT 126; Göttingen: Vandenhoeck & Ruprecht, 1982) 115–23, 149–50.

Mahoney, Matthew, "Luke 21:14-15: Editorial Rewriting or Authenticity?" *ITQ* 47 (1980) 220–38.

Malina and Neyrey, "Conflict."

Manson, T. W., *The Sayings of Jesus: As Recorded in the Gospels according to St. Matthew and St. Luke* (1949; reprinted Grand Rapids: Eerdmans, 1979) 323–37.

Mattill, A. J., *Luke and the Last Things: A Perspective for the Understanding of Lukan Thought* (Dillsboro: Western North Carolina Press, 1979) passim.

McNicol, Allan J., "The Composition of the Synoptic Eschatological Discourse," in David L. Dungan, ed., *The Interrelations of the Gospels* (BEThL 95; Louvain: Leuven University Press/Peeters, 1990) 157–200.

Idem, David L. Dungan, and David B. Peabody, eds., *Beyond the Q Impasse: Luke's Use of Matthew. A Demonstration by the Research Team of the International Institute for Gospel Studies* (Valley Forge, Pa.: Trinity Press International, 1996) 257–71.

Meyer, Rudolf, *Der Prophet aus Galiläa: Studie zum Jesusbild der drei ersten Evangelien* (1940; reprinted Darmstadt: Wissenschaftliche Buchgesellschaft, 1970) 6–19.

Morgen, Michèle, "Lc 17,20-37 et Lc 21,8-11.20-24. Arrière-fond scripturaire," in C. M. Tuckett, ed., *The Scriptures in the Gospels* (BEThL 131; Louvain: Leuven University Press, 1997) 307–26.

Nicol, W., "Tradition and Redaction in Luke 21," *Neot* 7 (1973) 61–71.

Nielsen, Anders E., *Until It Is Fulfilled: Lukan Eschatology according to Luke 22 and Acts 20* (WUNT 126; Tübingen: Mohr Siebeck, 2000) 212–42.

O'Neill, J. C., "The Six Amen Sayings in Luke," *JTS* 10 (1959) 1–9.

Otto, Randall E., *Coming in the Clouds: An Evangelical Case for the Invisibility of Christ at His Second Coming* (Lanham, Md.: University Press of America, 1994).

Pedersen, Sigfred, "Zum Problem der vaticinia ex eventu (eine Analyse von Mt 21,33-46 par.; 22,1-10 par.)," *StTh* 19 (1965) 167–88.

Perez Fernandez, M., "'Prope est aestas' (Mc 13,28; Mt 24,32; Lc 21,29)," *VD* 46 (1968) 361–69.

Perkins, Pheme, "If Jerusalem Stood: The Destruction of Jerusalem and Christian anti-Judaism," *Biblical Interpretation* 8 (2000) 194–204.

Perrot, Charles, "Essai sur le discours eschatologique (Mc 13,1-37; Mt 24,1-36; Lc 21,5-36)," *RSR* 47 (1959) 481–514.

Petzke, *Sondergut*, 174–75.

Potterie, Ignace de la, "Les deux noms de Jérusalem dans l'Évangile de Luc," *RSR* 69 (1981) 57–70; reprinted in J. Delorme et J. Duplacy, eds., *La Parole de grâce: Études lucaniennes à la mémoire d'Augustin George* (Paris: Recherches de science religieuse, 1981).

Prieur, Alexander, *Die Verkündigung der Gottesherrschaft: Exegetische Studien zum lukanischen Verständnis von βασιλεία τοῦ Θεοῦ* (WUNT 2/89; Tübingen: Mohr Siebeck, 1996) 273–80.

Salas, Antonio, *Discurso escatológico: Estudio de Lc . 21,20-36* (El Escorial, Spain: Biblioteca "La Ciudad de Dios," 1967).

Sperber, Daniel, "Mark 12, 42 and Its Metrological Background: A Study in Ancient Syriac Versions," *NovT* 9 (1967) 178–90.

Stenschke, Christoph W., *Luke's Portrait of Gentiles Prior to Their Coming to Faith* (WUNT 2/108; Tübingen: Mohr Siebeck, 1999) 59.

Swanson, *Manuscripts*, 350–61.

Tannehill, Robert C., "Homiletical Resources: Gospel Lections for Advent," *QR* 2 (1982) 9–14.

Idem, "Israel in Luke-Acts: A Tragic Story," *JBL* 104 (1985) 69–85.

Taylor, Vincent, "A Cry from the Siege: A Suggestion Regarding a Non-Marcan Oracle Embedded in Lk 21,20-36," *JTS* 26 (1925) 136–44.

Tyson, Joseph B., "The Jewish Public in Luke-Acts," *NTS* 30 (1984) 574–83.

Verheyden, Josef, "The Source(s) of Luke 21," in Frans Neirynck, ed., *L'Évangile de Luc—The Gospel of Luke* (2d ed.; BEThL 32; Leuven: Leuven University Press/Peeters, 1989) 491–516.

Wainwright, Arthur W., "Luke and the Restoration of the Kingdom to Israel," *ExpT* 89 (1977–78) 76–79.

Walter, "Tempelzerstörung."

Wehnert, Jürgen, "Die Auswanderung der Jerusalemer Christen nach Pella—historisches Faktum oder theologische Konstruktion? Kritische Bemerkungen zu einem neuen Buch," *ZKG* 102 (1991) 231–55.

Willimon, William H., "Take Heed to Yourselves: Luke 21:25-36," *CCen* 103, no. 37 (1986) 1085–86.

Winter, Paul, "The Treatment of His Sources by the Third Evangelist in Luke 21–24," *StTh* 8 (1954) 138–73.

Zmijewski, Josef, *Die Eschatologie-Reden des Lukas-Evangeliums: Eine traditions- und redaktionsgeschichtliche Untersuchung zu Lk 21,5-36 und Lk 17,20-37* (BBB 40; Bonn: Hanstein, 1972).

Idem, "Die Eschatologie-Reden Lk 21 und Lk 17: Überlegungen zum Verständnis und zur Einordnung der lukanischen Eschatologie," *BibLeb* 14 (1973) 30–40.

5 **And to some who were saying that the temple was decorated with beautiful stones and votive monuments he declared, 6/ "These things you see, the days will come when nothing will be left of them, stone upon stone, that will not be destroyed."**

7 **And they questioned him again: "Master, when will that be, and what will be the sign when it is about to happen?" 8/ And he said, "See to it that you are not led astray, for many will come in my name saying, 'It is I' and 'The time has drawn near.' Do not go after them. 9/ But when you hear talk of wars and disturbances, do not be afraid, for these things must happen first; the end will not happen immediately."**

10 **Then he said to them, "One people will rise up against another people and one kingdom against another kingdom; 11/ and there will be great earthquakes and from place to place famines and pestilences and terrifying events, and great signs will come from the heavens.**

12 **"Before all of that, however, they will lay their hands on you and persecute you, delivering you to the synagogues and prisons and taking you to appear before kings and governors for the sake of my name. 13/ That will lead you to testify. 14/ So put it in your hearts not to worry in advance about your defense.[a] 15/ Because I myself will give you a mouth and wisdom which none of your opponents will be able to resist or contradict.**

16 **"And you will be delivered up even by parents, brothers, relatives, and friends, and they will put some of you to death. 17/ You will be hated by everyone because of my name. 18/ But not a hair of your head will be lost. 19/ By persevering you will gain your souls.**

20 **"But when you see Jerusalem surrounded by armed troops, you will know that its desolation has drawn near. 21/ Then let those who live in Jerusalem flee to the mountains, and those who live in its midst go out, and those who live in the countryside, let them not enter the city.[b] 22/ For these are the days of retribution so that everything that has been written will be fulfilled. 23/ Woe to those who**

a Literally: "to defend you."
b Literally: "enter it."

are pregnant[c] and to those who are nursing children in those days! For there will be great distress on the land and anger against this people. 24/ And they will fall by the sharpness[d] of the sword and will be taken into captivity among all the nations, and Jerusalem will be trodden under foot by the nations until the times of the nations are fulfilled.

25 "And there will be signs in the sun and the moon and the stars, and on the earth a fearful reaction among the nations made helpless by the crash and waves of the sea, 26/ and human beings exhausted by fear and waiting for things that will come upon the inhabited earth, for the powers of the heavens will be shaken. 27/ And then they will see the Son of Man coming on a cloud with great power and glory. 28/ When these things begin to happen, stand erect and lift your heads, because your deliverance draws near."

29 Then he told them a parable: "See the fig tree and all the trees. 30/ When they have already burst forth, you see from yourselves and know that the summer is already near. 31/ Thus you also, when you see these things happening, you know that the kingdom of God is near. 32/ Truly I say to you that this generation will not pass away until all has taken place. 33/ Heaven and earth will pass away, but my words will not pass away.

34 "Take heed to yourselves that your hearts not be weighed down with drunkenness, intoxication, and earthly cares and that that day not come upon you unexpectedly, 35/ like a snare. For it will come upon everyone living on the face of the whole earth. 36/ Watch and make your requests at every moment, that you have the strength to escape these things that are going to happen and to stand before the Son of Man."

37 During the days he was teaching in the temple, and at night he went out and dwelled on the mountain called the Mount of Olives. 38/ And early in the morning all the people came to him in the temple to hear him.

c   Literally: "who have in their belly."
d   Literally: "by the mouth."

As in the other two Synoptic Gospels, Jesus gives a major address here shortly before his passion.[1] In Luke it is the last public teaching[2] of the Master, who reserves for his last meal the final chance to speak to his disciples (22:14-38). The theme of this talk to the people is the last things. Faithful to primitive Christian tradition, the evangelist places this theme at the end of his work.[3] He follows here one of his models, Mark, whom he continues to read anew.[4]

This passage poses formidable problems, the thorniest of which is related precisely to the connections between Luke and Mark.[5] It is certain that Luke knows and uses the parallel passage in Mark: he follows its position, its order, and its contents. On several points, however, he deviates from his model, either because he wants to express a personal opinion or because he feels the need to quote a parallel document. The alternative becomes complicated, because one must raise the question of the unity of the verses that are neither Markan nor Lukan. Are they scattered sayings of Jesus that the evangelist collected here because they have a common set of themes,[6] or do they come from an apocalyptic speech of Jesus parallel to that in Mark?[7]

Synchronic Analysis

As a literary unit, the apocalyptic speech is clearly delimited. It follows the apophthegm about the widow's mite

1 Cotter ("Discourse") attempts to prove the authenticity of Jesus' eschatological discourse attested by the three Synoptic Gospels. He argues against R. H. Lightfoot (*History and Interpretation in the Gospels* [London: Hodder & Stoughton, 1935] 94), whom he quotes on p. 126: "In the discourse we may see, reflected as it were in a mirror, the travail, the perplexity and the unconquerable hope of early Christianity." In Cotter's opinion, on the contrary, the unanimity of the Greek manuscripts, the versions, and the patristic quotations confirm the historicity of the discourse.

2 On this point Luke changes the perspective of Mark, who makes the disciples Jesus' questioners; see Mark 13:1, 3. On this Jewish public, see Tyson ("Jewish Public"), who, referring to Aristotle's *Poetics* (13.6), emphasizes the pattern of the abrupt reversal. Here the people are still friendly to Jesus. That will change in the scene of the arrest (22:47-53). Tannehill ("Tragic Story") emphasizes the tragic end of the people of Israel and Jerusalem in Luke-Acts.

3 Paul does the same thing: He puts his apocalyptic texts at the end of his epistles (see 1 Thess 4:13—5:11 and 1 Corinthians 15). Mark serves as an example for Matthew and Luke (see Mark 13; Matthew 24–25; and Luke 21). The book of the Apocalypse itself found its place at the end of the New Testament.

4 The previous pericopes also followed the Markan arrangement; see Luke 20:1—21:4 par. Mark 11:27—12:44.

5 Manson (*Sayings*, 323) writes, "This second speech (Lk. 21:5-36) runs parallel to Mk. 13 and Mt. 24, and the relation of Lk. to Mk. presents one of the most complicated and difficult problems in the criticism of the Gospels." Fitzmyer (2:1323) shares this opinion.

6 In addition to Mark and Matthew, whose second apocalyptic discourse of Jesus is usually regarded as parallel, as well as Luke's other apocalyptic passages, which sometimes deal with the same subjects (12:35-53; 13:23-30, 34-35; 17:20-35; 19:41-44), we must take into account the apocalyptic traditions attested in the New Testament epistles (Rom 14:10; 2 Cor 5:10; 1 Thess 4:16; 2 Thess 2:3-4, 8-10), the *Didache* (10.5; 16.3–5, 7), the *Epistle of Barnabas* (4.3; 15.5), Justin Martyr (*Dial.* 35.3; 82.1–2), the *First Epistle of Clement* (23.3–4), the *Second Epistle of Clement* (6.7), the *Shepherd of Hermas* (*Herm. Vis.* 4.1.1–2.5), and the *Gospel of Thomas* (§11). The text of most of these parallels is printed in Aland's *Synopsis* (396–418) following the various sections of the apocalyptic discourse.

7 For a discussion of the works of Zmijewski (*Eschatologie-Reden*), Geiger (*Endzeitreden*), and Kaestli (*L'eschatologie*), see Bovon, *Luke the Theologian*, 24–28, 62–66. In "Lk 21 und Lk 17" Zmijewski has summarized his position. Bloomquist ("Argumentation") undertakes a fourfold approach: (1) Innertextual Analysis (he is sensitive to the speech's progression, its repetitions, its beginning and ending, suggesting that one not neglect what precedes it). (2) Intertextual Analysis (choosing among reference, recitation, recontextualization, and reconfiguration, he selects this last term: Luke reconfigures Mark). (3) Sociocultural Texture: According to Luke, Jesus' teaching is "subcultural." (4) Ideological Texture: Luke contradicts the imperial ideology of Augustus, starting from the periphery (Jerusalem) against the center (Rome). I have reservations about the conclusions (207–9). To say that the heart

(21:1-4) and immediately precedes the account of the passion (22:1—23:56). It is introduced by a brief dialogue. Some people (τινές) express their admiration for the beauty of the Jerusalem temple (v. 5). Jesus baffles them by announcing that these stones they admire are going to fall (v. 6; note the hook-word λίθος, which connects v. 6 to v. 5). The people move the conversation along by asking a double question. Accepting Jesus' pessimistic prognosis, they ask him about the date (πότε) of this catastrophe and the nature of a harbinger (τί τὸ σημεῖον, v. 7). Jesus replies by beginning his long apocalyptic talk (ὁ δὲ εἶπεν, "and he said," v. 8). Even if later, on two occasions,[8] introductions interrupt this address, the crowd never disturbs its flow with an objection. Still, the sequence hardly appears logical, since Jesus does not directly answer the double question of v. 7. Using the imperative and the second person plural, he begins by warning his hearers not to let themselves be impressed by messianic pretenders (v. 8) or by the sounds of war (v. 9). From that point on the theme of war serves as a hook. There will be wars; great catastrophes—natural, economic, even supernatural; and "signs from heaven" (vv. 10-11), but that will not be the end (ἀλλ' οὐκ εὐθέως τὸ τέλος, "but not immediately the end," v. 9b).

Suddenly the speech takes a new turn (v. 12). Again Jesus speaks a challenging "you," which this time appears to point to the Christian community and no longer to the crowd of hearers. In several prophetic sentences Jesus predicts persecutions, gives advice, and makes promises (vv. 12-19).[9] Then, without warning, he turns again to the theme of war, which he limits here to a particular history, to the siege and fall of Jerusalem (vv. 20-24). Less parenetic than what preceded, this last paragraph abandons the second person plural[10] and is more descriptive than prescriptive. The historical events it portrays correspond no less to the fulfillment of scriptural prophecies (v. 22). There the "nations" are contrasted with "Jerusalem," yet mysteriously Jesus grants these invaders a time, actually "times," that will be fulfilled (v. 24).

In vv. 25-28 the speech takes up again the term and the theme of "signs," which had been mentioned in v. 11. The catastrophe is more cosmic than ever, yet it does not last forever. It must leave space for, "then" (τότε), the arrival of the Son of Man. The text underscores the visibility of this arrival ("And then they will see . . . ," v. 27). This paragraph, which is also descriptive, nevertheless ends with a double imperative in the second person plural. Jesus invites his hearers to rise up and lift their heads at the approach of their deliverance (v. 28).

With an apparently inconsistent logic, the text continues with the parable of the fig tree (vv. 29-31).[11] In itself clear, the parable says that the fig tree that comes into leaf ushers in the summer. Jesus then makes it easy for the readers who are invited to learn the lesson: "Thus you also, when you see these things happening, you know that the kingdom of God is near" (v. 31). Following Mark, Luke hangs here two independent sentences. The first, which refers to an imminent eschatological fulfillment (v. 32), is a doublet of 9:27. The second refers to the perpetuity of Jesus' statements (v. 33). With its reference to the passing character of heaven and earth, this phrase recalls a sentence of Q, Luke 16:17 par. Matt 5:18.

Alternating again between indicative and imperative, vv. 34-36, the conclusion of the address, invite the hearers and readers to vigilance. Written in a style that recalls the morality of the age, these verses are clearly different from the other parenetic passages of the speech.

Finally, Luke closes this apocalyptic chapter with a narrative summary in the imperfect (vv. 37-38). He first mentions that Jesus spends these days teaching in the temple and these nights on the Mount of Olives (v. 37). Then he speaks of "all the people," who join the Master each morning to hear him. The conspiracy of the chief priests and the scribes (22:1-2) as well as Satan's subversion of the heart of Judas (22:3) will suddenly threaten this harmonious fellowship.[12]

---

of the discourse concerns what is permitted and that the barriers must be destroyed seems to me to be vague and imprecise.

8   "Then he said to them" (v. 10); "then he told them a parable" (v. 29).

9   On vv. 5-19 and its structuring, see Dupont, "Épreuves."

10   Jesus, however, does not completely avoid giving advice; see v. 21.

11   Actually, it is a second parable about a fig tree. Luke 13:6-9 already presented a parable about the fig tree that does not bear fruit.

12   Maddox (*Purpose*, 115–23, 149–50) is of the opinion that, compared to Luke 17, Luke 21 is more

Diachronic Analysis

In the introduction in the form of a dialogue (vv. 5-6), Luke depends only on Mark.[13] He changes the identity of Jesus' conversation partners by eliminating the reference to the disciples; he waits until the Last Supper for a final message to them (22:15-46). He maintains the contrast between the beauty of the place and its catastrophic future, but he reformulates all of it in his own words. The verb $\kappa o \sigma \mu \omega$ ("to put in order," "to adorn") is appropriate here. The term $\dot{\alpha} \nu \dot{\alpha} \vartheta \eta \mu \alpha$ ("gift," "ex-voto," "votive monument") is preferable to the vague $o \dot{\iota} \kappa o \delta o \mu \dot{\eta}$ ("building"). $\Theta \epsilon \omega \rho \hat{\omega}$ ("to regard, contemplate") better reflects the admiration of the temple visitors than does $\beta \lambda \epsilon \pi \omega$ ("to look at"). That "the days will come" underscores the chronological problem. Luke prefers the future "will be left" ($\dot{\alpha} \varphi \epsilon \vartheta \dot{\eta} \sigma \epsilon \tau \alpha \iota$) and "will be destroyed" ($\kappa \alpha \tau \alpha \lambda \nu \vartheta \dot{\eta} \sigma \epsilon \tau \alpha \iota$).

Luke refuses to understand the apocalyptic speech as an esoteric teaching. He thus eliminates Mark's distinction between a public appearance coming out of the temple (Mark 13:1) and the private stay on the Mount of Olives ($\kappa \alpha \tau' \iota \delta \iota \alpha \nu$, "privately," Mark 13:3). He retains, however, the sequence of questions[14] and answers that follow (vv. 7-11) and is satisfied to rewrite the remarks in his own style and vocabulary. He inserts a vocative "Master" (v. 7), a title he puts in the mouth of Jesus' questioners who are not his disciples. He replaces the rich "to fulfill, achieve, complete" ($\sigma \upsilon \nu \tau \epsilon \lambda \hat{\omega}$, Mark 13:4) with the common "to happen" ($\gamma \iota \nu o \mu \alpha \iota$, v. 7), perhaps because from now on he wants to remove the link between the fall of the temple and the fulfillment of the end. In order to show that Jesus does indeed answer the question that has been asked, he makes specific the deceitful eschatological message of the false envoys of Christ. To Mark's ambiguous "I am" he adds the words "and: the time is at hand" (v. 8b). "Do not go after them" (v. 8c) forms the counterpart to "see to it that you are not led astray" (v. 8a). For that reason he can omit the words "and they will lead many astray" (Mark 13:6). He mentions the "disturbances" ($\dot{\alpha} \kappa \alpha \tau \alpha \sigma \tau \alpha \sigma \iota \alpha \iota$, v. 9) rather than the sounds of war, thus adding inner instability to the external

---

interested in the historical events. He also offers a division of the discourse into nine parts (vv. 5-7, 8-9, 10-11, 12-19, 20-24, 25-27, 28, 29-33, 34-36). He thinks that, according to Luke, there will not be much time between the fall of Jerusalem and the end of time. He is especially interested in vv. 12-19 (the time of persecutions corresponding to the period covered by the book of Acts).

13   From the pen of Conzelmann ("Geschichte") comes a remarkable presentation of Mark's editorial and theological work that opens the way for Luke. Mark combines Christology and eschatology and makes room for the time of the church between Easter and the parousia. In a very informative article, Fusco ("Discours") presents a twofold analysis of both Luke's redaction and his composition. He concludes that Luke has no source other than Mark. According to Nicol ("Tradition"), Luke used Mark and traditional elements (vv. 11b, 18, 21b, 22, 23b, 24, 25, 26a, 34-36). Except for vv. 34-36, which come from the West, these traditional elements come from Palestine. Even if the fall of Jerusalem is historical and not eschatological, and although the speech exhorts the church at great length, Luke brings closer together Israel's history, that of the church, and eschatology. Bartsch (*Wachet*, 118–23) thinks that Luke separates the death of Jesus and the end of time but still maintains the imminence

of the parousia (see v. 32). Verheyden ("Source[s]") gives an excellent study of the sources behind Luke 21. He himself is of the opinion that Mark is Luke's primary source and affirms: "In determining the non-Markan material, we are far from a pre-Lukan gospel draft" (513). There is also a bold reconstruction of the origins of Jesus' apocalyptic discourse from Perrot ("Essai"). First there was an Aramaic preaching of Jesus in what originally may have been two distinct blocks: The destruction of the temple, the decisive sign, and the date form the first block; the time of distress, the cosmic catastrophe, the arrival of the Son of Man, and the unforeseeable date constitute the second block. Finally, the link between the two blocks is established as follows: "The preaching about the catastrophe becomes a song of victory" (502). This preaching was translated into Greek (with some final improvements: the addition of Mark 13:9-13 and the transposition of Mark 13:21-23 from the end to the middle of the speech). It was then adopted and adapted by each evangelist. Luke, for example, felt free in rereading the work and may have been inspired by a second source. Unlike Lambrecht ("Logia-Quellen"), I do not believe Q is present in Mark 13.

14   The verb $\dot{\epsilon} \pi \epsilon \rho \omega \tau \hat{\omega}$ ("to ask," "to interrogate," "to question") that Mark uses (Mark 13:3) is appropriate for him, and he keeps it (v. 7).

wars.[15] "For these things must happen" ($\delta\epsilon\hat{\iota}$ $\gamma\grave{\alpha}\rho$ $\tau\alpha\hat{\upsilon}\tau\alpha$ $\gamma\epsilon\nu\acute{\epsilon}\sigma\vartheta\alpha\iota$, v. 9) is clearly better than "it is necessary to happen" without a grammatical subject in Mark 13:7. The addition of "first" ($\pi\rho\hat{\omega}\tau o\nu$) confirms Luke's interest in chronology; the choice of "not about" ($o\dot{\upsilon}\kappa$ $\epsilon\dot{\upsilon}\vartheta\acute{\epsilon}\omega\varsigma$, instead of $o\ddot{\upsilon}\pi\omega$, "not yet," Mark 13:7) is a reminder of the Lukan rejection of imminence.

Why does Luke feel obligated to introduce the reference to future wars with the words, "then he said to them" (v. 10)? It is not enough to say that these words simply repeat the contents of v. 9. It should rather be acknowledged that Luke here remembers that the origin of these sentences is independent of Mark. By adding this introduction Luke is indeed getting ready to quote a source other than Mark. The second half of v. 11, missing in Mark (as well as in Matthew), appears to reflect neither Luke's intention nor his style. I suggest, therefore, that all of v. 11 comes from a source other than Mark. Luke prefers this variant for various reasons: it includes the classical homonymous play on words, "famines and pestilences" ($\lambda\iota\mu o\grave{\iota}$ $\kappa\alpha\grave{\iota}$ $\lambda o\iota\mu o\acute{\iota}$); it signals from this moment the signs from heaven that, in his eyes, will precede the arrival of the Son of Man (vv. 25-27); it favorably omits the words "these things are the beginning of the birth pangs" ($\mathring{\alpha}\rho\chi\grave{\eta}$ $\mathring{\omega}\delta\acute{\iota}\nu\omega\nu$ $\tau\alpha\hat{\upsilon}\tau\alpha$, Mark 13:8), which establish a link between the political events ($\tau\alpha\hat{\upsilon}\tau\alpha$, "these events") and "the end of time" (the metaphor $\mathring{\omega}\delta\acute{\iota}\nu\epsilon\varsigma$, "birth pangs"). Another indication that vv. 10-11 are not Lukan is the fact that nowhere else does Luke use the word $\varphi\acute{o}\beta\eta\tau\rho o\nu$.

In vv. 12-19 as well Luke does more than simply revise Mark. He continues to rewrite his second source, probably his own special material, from which he introduced the quotation in v. 10. This speech from the special material runs parallel here with the text of the Second Gospel. Some arguments supporting this hypothesis are the following: it is difficult to imagine that Luke writes v. 12, whose laborious syntax is worse than that of Mark 13:9, or that between vv. 13 and 14 he eliminates the proclamation of the gospel to the Gentiles (Mark 13:10),

a subject that in the book of Acts is close to his heart, and that in v. 18 he adds a providential protection that contradicts the real threat of persecution. To be sure, the sequence of the sentences corresponds to that of Mark, but the formulation of their contents changes at every moment. While Lukanisms may appear here or there,[16] they are not enough to explain the differences. As is the case in the Markan parallel, the special material probably also regarded the disciples as Jesus' hearers (indeed, the persecution is directed against the Christian community). Among the number of differences from Mark, one will reckon the expression "before all of that" (v. 12; in Luke's eyes this is a fortunate substitute that removes from the historical events the eschatological connotation that the metaphor of the "birth pangs" gives the Markan formulation in Mark 13:8). Different from Mark also are the clarification that it is a special pleading ($\mathring{\alpha}\pi o\lambda o\gamma\eta\vartheta\hat{\eta}\nu\alpha\iota$, "to defend oneself," translated in v. 14 as "your defense"); the assurance that Jesus himself ($\mathring{\epsilon}\gamma\acute{\omega}$, "I," v. 15) will inspire his disciples; the omission of the Holy Spirit (Mark 13:11b) that Luke had already mentioned in this role in 12:12; the addition of the statement about the hair (v. 18), and the different wording of the promise to all who persevere (v. 19).

What is true for vv. 12-19 is still true for vv. 20-24. The differences between Mark and Luke are too obvious to be explained simply by assuming a redactional revision of the Second Gospel by the third evangelist. The biblical expression (Dan 12:11; 11:31; 9:27 LXX) "the abomination of desolation" (Mark 13:14) becomes the siege of Jerusalem, which announces that "its desolation" has drawn near (v. 20).[17] The appeal to the readers of Mark 13:14 disappears. The flight to the mountains of Judea, mentioned in both documents, is accompanied in the special material by a series of details (vv. 21b-22), the most interesting of which associates the fall of Jerusalem with the application of a righteousness whose scriptural character is underscored. Luke's source ignored, or at least neglected, Mark's concrete details about those who are surprised on their housetop or at work in the field

---

15   Why does Luke choose $\mu\grave{\eta}$ $\pi\tau o\eta\vartheta\hat{\eta}\tau\epsilon$ (Mark and Matthew have $\mu\grave{\eta}$ $\vartheta\rho o\epsilon\hat{\iota}\sigma\vartheta\epsilon$)?

16   The list of relatives and friends who turn against the believers (v. 16) appears to be redactional. The word $\gamma o\nu\epsilon\hat{\iota}\varsigma$ reminds one of 18:29; $\sigma\upsilon\gamma\gamma\epsilon\nu\epsilon\hat{\iota}\varsigma$ of 1:36; $\varphi\acute{\iota}\lambda o\iota$ of 15:6 and 9. See the list in 14:26.

17   The term $\mathring{\epsilon}\rho\acute{\eta}\mu\omega\sigma\iota\varsigma$, which the two sources share, goes back to Daniel (Dan 8:13, etc.).

(Mark 13:15-16). Luke also has every reason to omit them, since he has quoted the Q equivalent in 17:31. The special material also omitted the precaution about winter (Mark 13:18), but it does mention pregnant women or nursing mothers (v. 23a par. Mark 13:17). Was this oracle of woe identical in Mark and in Luke's special material? Perhaps Luke lets himself be contaminated here by Mark. The description of the final tribulation, understood in both places as catastrophic, differs in its wording (vv. 23b-24 and Mark 13:19-20): here "distress" (ἀνάγκη), there "tribulation" (θλῖψις); here an omission, there a reference to the history of the world from the creation until today; here a sentence about the fall of Jerusalem and the disasters it will involve (v. 24), there mention of the divine kindness that shortens the tribulations of the elect (Mark 13:20). When I read the list of these differences and weigh their importance, I come to the conclusion that Luke's version is more than an editorial reworking of Mark. It represents a variant of the apocalyptic speech of the Second Gospel. As an additional argument, I make note of the rhythmic, almost poetic character of vv. 20-24 in Luke. Nowhere else does the third evangelist give this literary form to his revisions.[18]

Luke does not make use of vv. 21-23 of Mark 13. In chap. 17, following the Sayings Source (Q; Luke 17:23), he has already used the equivalent of the first sentence, and he regards the second as a repetition of what he has already said (v. 8), with the exception that in Mark 13:22 the pretenders do bad things with their "signs," while in v. 8 they mislead with their words.

Finally, the special material and the Gospel of Mark mention, each in its own way, the appearance of final apocalyptic signs. According to both documents, these signs will be celestial and will be concerned with the sun, the moon, and the stars. According to the special material—it is less important for Mark—the terrestrial repercussions (καὶ ἐπὶ τῆς γῆς, "and on the earth," v. 25) of these heavenly phenomena will be terrible. Here below, it will be the sea, a negative force in Hebrew literature, which will be churned up. From that time the "nations" (v. 24 predicted the end of their "times") will gather in "a fearful reaction among the nations" (συνοχὴ ἐθνῶν) "made helpless" (ἐν ἀπορίᾳ), while there are human beings "exhausted by fear and waiting" (ἀποψυχόντων . . . ἀπὸ φόβου καὶ προσδοκίας). "And then they will see[19] the Son of Man coming on a cloud with great power and glory" (v. 27). While Mark closes with the gathering of the elect from the four winds (13:27), the special material ends with an exhortation to the faithful. When the events begin to unfold, it will be time to raise oneself up, because the redemption will be at hand (v. 28).

With a new narrative introduction ("Then he told them a parable") Luke indicates that he is changing his source (v. 29). In fact, he returns to the Markan text and carefully follows Mark's form of the parable. Nevertheless, he permits himself some stylistic improvements (a description of the vegetation and a repetition of the adverb "already," v. 30) and especially the insertion of two themes: the imprecise imminence (Mark 13:29) becomes the imminence of the βασιλεία τοῦ θεοῦ, the "kingdom of God" (v. 31), and the ignorance of the day and the hour, which even the "Son" shares (Mark 13:32), must be removed, since it will be mentioned later in the two-volume work (Acts 1:7) and will implicate only humans. The parable, which circulated independently, later provided the material for an exhortation in the *First Epistle of Clement* (1 Clem. 23.3–4; see also 2 Clem. 11.2–3).

From a form-critical point of view, one must distinguish among the parable (v. 30), the lesson that follows it (v. 31), and the sentences attached to it (vv. 32-33). The parable and the lesson existed independently in their oral stage. As the prophet Amos had already done (Amos 8:1-2), the speaker plays with the homophony between "summer" (קַיִץ) and "end" (קֵץ).[20] There is no reason to think that the first speaker was not the historical Jesus. The early Christians treasured this parable for its eschatological message. To be more explicit, they first added the sentence about "this generation" that "will not pass away" and then—without seeing anything in it other than a confirmation or authentication—that about the perpetuity of Jesus' words.[21] They concluded their

---

18   See Manson, *Sayings*, 328–29.

19   The visibility will be complete; everyone, men and women, believers and unbelievers, will be present.

20   See Perez Fernandez, "Aestas," 364–67.

21   One finds in the *Gospel of Thomas* (§11) a counterpart to v. 33: "Jesus said: 'This heaven will pass away, and the one above it will pass away. The dead are not alive, and the living will not die.'"

interpretation with an explanation or a correction that Luke omits: in fact, no one knows the time of the end (Mark 13:32).

Then once again Luke abandons Mark. He probably does not repeat the parable of the doorkeeper, because it seems to him to resemble the beginning of the parable of the pounds (19:12-13) and those about the servants (12:35-40, 41-46). In v. 36, however, he does not dismiss Mark's beginning imperative, ἀγρυπνεῖτε ("be watchful," Mark 13:33). He offers a short moral teaching, which begins with προσέχετε δὲ ἑαυτοῖς ("take heed to yourselves," v. 34). This exhortation (vv. 34-36) has no Synoptic equivalent. With its vocabulary, its intonation, and its orientation it is reminiscent of early Christian catechesis[22] and the passages in which Luke expresses his moral concern (see, e.g., 8:11-15 or 3:10-14). Our analysis of the details will indicate whether we should attribute these three verses to the evangelist or to his special material.

There is no question about vv. 37-38. It is a narrative conclusion in the form of a generalizing overview in the imperfect. The evangelist is certainly the author of these few lines.

After a great deal of hesitation I have decided the following: in keeping with his customary practice, Luke alternates between his sources, here between Mark and his own special material: vv. 5-9 (Mark), vv. 10-28 (S^Lk), vv. 29-33 (Mark), vv. 34-36 (S^Lk or Luke himself).[23] In comparison, Matthew copies Mark's text accurately, inserting various sayings and parables from Q (Matt 24:37-50; 25:14-30) and adds two otherwise unknown apocalyptic texts, the parable of the virgins (Matt 25:1-13) and the one of the last judgment (Matt 25:31-46).

It is not my intention to write the prehistory of the two sources Luke uses here. Various hypotheses have been put forth on this subject:[24] Christian appropriation of a Jewish apocalypse,[25] Mark's use of various sources (an apocalypse, missionary sayings, and a prophecy about the temple),[26] editorial grouping of scattered sayings.[27] It is more useful to discover the parallels between this apocalyptic address and certain passages in the epistles. There one finds a concern that the early Christians shared: to think existentially and communally about the connections between Jesus and the end of time. In both kinds of texts one finds a common eschatological impatience and a refusal of any apocalyptic speculation. 1 Thess 5:1-3, Acts 1:6-8, Rev 3:3; and the Synoptics (Mark 13:18-32 par.) are the diverse and independent witnesses of this early Christian teaching that looks for the Day of the Lord, underscores its imminence, and insists on

---

22 See below in the interpretation of vv. 34-36 the parallels one reads in the epistles.

23 As a comparison, see the positions adopted by Manson (*Sayings*, 323–37), Taylor ("Siege"), and Fitzmyer (2:1326–30). Contrary to the general opinion of his day, Gaston ("Sondergut") thinks that Luke makes use of a Proto-Luke, which connected in a sequence the essential elements of 19:41-44, 47-48; 21:5-7, 20, 21b-22, 23b-24, 10-11, 25-26, 28, 37-38 (for his reconstruction of the source, see pp. 171–72). Hartman (*Prophecy*, 226–35) is of the opinion that, in addition to Mark, Luke used a second source with apocalyptic and midrashic characteristics.

24 See Nolland, 3:984–86.

25 This is the old hypothesis of Timothée Colani, *Jésus-Christ et les croyances messianiques de son temps* (Strasbourg: Truttel & Wurtz, 1864).

26 This is the hypothesis of Flückiger, "Redaktion." See also the complicated pages of Winter, "Treatment": if one separates Mark 13 from Luke 21, only scattered parts are left. From the time of Caligula (39–40 c.e.) Luke received from intermediaries

such as Mark, Q, and the special material a loose apocalyptic sheet. Luke uses it, thanks to Q, in chap. 17 and, along with Mark, in chap. 21. There is, moreover, a relation between Luke 21:21b and the oracle preserved by Eusebius of Caesarea in *Hist. eccl.* 3.5.2–3 (exhortation to flee Jerusalem during the siege). According to C. Koester ("Pella"), it is not impossible, although by no means certain, that Luke knew the tradition about Pella. See also Wehnert ("Auswanderung"), who examines the thesis of Jozef Verheyden (*De vlucht van den Christenen naar Pella: onderzoek van het getuigenis van Eusebius en Epiphanius* [Brussels: AWLSK, 1988]) and comes to an opposite conclusion from that author. According to Wehnert, the tradition about Pella rests on a historical substrate.

27 This is the hypothesis of Bultmann (*History*, 122–23, 125, 323) as well as Kümmel (*Promise*, 95–104), according to whom Mark 13 contains three kinds of sentences. The eschatological sayings go back to the historical Jesus; others, apocalyptic, come from Judaism or Jewish Christianity; finally, still others reflect the experience of the primitive church.

its unpredictability. To such a catechesis one owes the recollection and the reminder of a Christian apocalyptic that depends on the sayings of the Lord and adapts them to the community's reality (e.g., the experience of the fall of Jerusalem, Luke 21:20-24), while emphasizing the agreement of the facts or the prophecies with the Scriptures (see the reference to Daniel in Mark 13:14, 26 par., the quotation from Isa 13:10 added by Matt 24:29, and the mention of "everything that has been written" in the source of Luke 21:22).[28]

Commentary

■ **5-6** The word ἱερόν refers to "the temple area" and thus designates a space larger than the sanctuary itself (ναός).[29] According to various ancient authors, among them Josephus,[30] the beauty of the Jerusalem temple and its surroundings was legendary.[31] At this moment Jesus' conversation partners are expressing a feeling of admiration for something made by human hands and not so much their piety for the place where one meets the divine. To be sure, by predicting the destruction of the temple Jesus contradicts them, but he is speaking about the same reality as they. While in 19:43-44 he had already predicted the fall of Jerusalem, here in v. 6 he is speaking of the holiest part of the city.[32] In both places there will not be left "stone on stone."

Various streams of the Gospel tradition convey this kind of oracle of woe in different forms. In the earlier passage the oracle of Jesus is attached (19:43-44) with which he will be reproached during his trial (Mark 14:58; 15:29).[33] The Gospel of John is aware of this same prophecy in a different form (John 2:19-22). Historically, it is probable that, as here (Luke 21:5-6), Jesus predicted the destruction of the temple without saying it would be rebuilt (Mark 14:58; 15:29; John 2:19-22). He also, as here, probably spoke in the passive (third person) rather than in the active form (first person, Mark and John; the latter also uses the second person).[34] Nevertheless, Jesus' words, even in the form reported by Luke, had to be shocking. How would admirers of Notre-Dame in Paris react if they heard that "no stone will be left on another"? If Jesus' prophecy was remembered, it was for two reasons: (a) Some early Christians (the Hellenists; see Stephen's testimony reported by Luke in Acts 6:14) followed Jesus here, but they interpreted this apocalyptic prophecy[35] as the criticism of an obsolete religious institution. (b) History confirmed Jesus' intuition. The Jewish revolt was crushed by the Romans, who, as is known, captured and destroyed Jerusalem and its temple in 70 C.E.

According to Kümmel, the eschatological message of the historical Jesus does not depend on the apocalyptic message.

28 On the connections between Luke 21 and the Scripture, see Morgen, "Arrière-fond scripturaire." Del Agua Pérez ("Derás") regards Luke 21 as a *derash*, a homiletic commentary that makes Mark 13 current. This updating is necessary because the Lukan Christians lead a different life, and the resurrection imposes changes on Jesus' message. It places Jesus in the light of Scripture, adapts the apocalyptic data, allegorizes the parables, and chooses a homiletic tone.

29 Elliott ("Temple") offers an interesting contrast between temple and house. The temple stops being perceived in a positive light; only the house integrates the values of the Gospel.

30 On the destruction and the lost beauty of the Jerusalem temple, see Josephus *Bell.* 6.4.5–8 §§249–67; Fitzmyer, 2:1331.

31 The manuscript tradition of v. 5 varies between ἀναθήμασιν and ἀναθέμασιν. Originally synonyms, the first term kept its positive meaning, while the second came to take on a negative meaning (preserved in our word *anathema*), a sense that is hardly appropriate here. See the Nestle-Aland apparatus on this verse. The question is: Are these ἀναθήματα votive monuments or votive gifts: buildings or objects? On ἀνάθημα in the sense of "ex-voto," see Hippolyte Delehaye, *Les origines du culte des martyrs* (2d ed.; SH 20; Brussels: Société des Bollandistes, 1933) 114–15.

32 Conzelmann (*Theology*, 75–78, 198–99) thought he could distinguish between the temple, the place where Jesus preached, and the city of Jerusalem, the place of the passion. Justifiably, George ("Construction," 25–28) opposes this hypothesis by pointing out that chap. 21 identifies the destiny of the temple with the fate of Jerusalem.

33 For Mark (Mark 14:57) the testimony is false; Luke's version of Jesus' trial is not aware of this grievance.

34 See Meyer, *Prophet*, 16–18.

35 The words ἐλεύσονται ἡμέραι ("the days will come," v. 6), give the oracle an apocalyptic character.

Luke understands this oracle not simply as a pessimistic statement (*sic transit gloria mundi*) but as the prophetic expression of the will of God. That means for him the end of blood sacrifices.

■ **7-9** Jesus' questioners[36] ask him[37] a twofold question. The first, πότε ("When?"), takes up the question in 17:20; the second, that of the σημεῖον ("sign"), recalls that of 11:16. In Israel, the demand for a sign often reveals a lack of confidence in God, although the God of the patriarchs is not stingy in offering signs to those who put their trust in him. According to the apostle Paul, the quest for signs characterizes the religious efforts of the Jews (1 Cor 1:22). Thus, the questioners want to be equipped to face the future as Jesus describes it.

Their twofold request is not directly rejected by Jesus, but neither is it approved. There are bad teachers of whom one should be wary. Verse 8 refers polemically to Christian prophets who "will come"—and who no doubt had already come in Luke's day—"in my name." They will be numerous, thus threatening. They will say, "It is I" (literally, "I am"). This formula, which comes from Mark, is enigmatic. One can understand it in three ways. In an absolute sense, it actualizes the identity of God himself, the Tetragrammaton.[38] Applied to Jesus as a form of recognition, it connects the Nazarene to the Messiah (see the answer Jesus gives the high priest in Mark

14:62: "I am he"). When connected with the testimony of Christ and regarded as elliptic, it expresses authority and inspiration. Was it not said that Montanus claimed, "I am the Father, and the Son, and the Paraclete"?[39] Unlike Matthew, who chooses the second possibility (he adds "I am the Messiah"; Matt 24:5), Luke chooses the third solution. Thinking of false messengers, he is suspicious of their apostolic claim and their apocalyptic message. By adding "the time has drawn near," he expresses his hostility toward a wing of early Christianity that claims to have the apocalyptic calendar. Luke is certainly thinking that these people should not be followed. The expression "Do not go after them" is not trite. Whether taken in a good or a bad sense, since the time of the Hebrew Bible it has expressed the strongest religious commitment.[40] There is a solid, albeit implicit, connection between Jesus' answer and the question of the listeners. These illegitimate witnesses can offer only a false date and improper signs. Then only the true voice of Jesus resounds. There will be wars and revolutions. You should not fear them (μὴ πτοηθῆτε)[41] and should not follow the false messengers (μὴ πλανηθῆτε . . . μὴ πορευθῆτε . . .). The expression "wars and disorders" continues the announcement of v. 6 and prepares for the broad description of vv. 20-24. These events must happen. The δεῖ ("it is necessary") incorporates this

---

36   Codex Bezae (D = 05), influenced by the parallels in Mark and Matthew, explains that these questioners are οἱ μαθηταί, "the disciples." In the same way, it replaces "when it is about to happen" with τῆς σῆς ἐλεύσεως, "of your coming." See the Nestle-Aland apparatus (27th ed.) here.

37   The vocative διδάσκαλε is characteristic of Jesus' questioners, who admire him without having decided to follow him. By calling him "Master" and not "Prophet," they put themselves in this part of the conversation on the level of the interpretation of prophecy.

38   On the absolute ἐγώ εἰμι, see John 8:24, 58; Rudolf Bultmann, *The Gospel of John* (Philadelphia: Westminster, 1971) 225 n. 3, 327 n. 4; Eduard Schweizer, *Ego Eimi . . . : Die religionsgeschichtliche Herkunft und theologische Bedeutung der johanneischen Bildreden, zugleich ein Beitrag zur Quellenfrage des vierten Evangeliums* (FRLANT 56; Göttingen: Vandenhoeck & Ruprecht, 1939); Alain de Libera and Emilie Zum Brunn, eds., *Celui qui est: Interprétations juives et chrétiennes d'Exode 3,14* (Paris: Cerf, 1986).

39   On the oracle of Montanus, see Kurt Aland, "Bemerkungen zum Montanismus und zur frühchristlichen Eschatologie," in idem, *Kirchengeschichtliche Entwürfe* (Gütersloh: Mohn, 1960) 105–48, esp. 143–44.

40   On this adherence, expressed in terms of walking or of movement, see, e.g., (a) in the Hebrew Bible: Deut 6:14; 13:5; Judg 2:12, 19; 1 Kgs (LXX 3 Kgdms) 18:21; Jer 7:9; (b) in the New Testament: Matt 10:38; 1 Pet 2:10; (c) in Luke and Acts: Luke 1:6; Acts 9:31.

41   The verb πτοῶ, which is not very frequent, means "to terrify," "to frighten." In the New Testament it appears only here and in 24:37, both times in its passive form. Codex Bezae (D = 05), as well as the Latin manuscript q (sixth–seventh century), prefers the more common verb φοβηθῆτε ("do not fear"); see the Nestle-Aland apparatus (27th ed.) on this verse.

catastrophe in the plan of God, who rules not only the end but also the beginning and the middle of history. When Luke rejects the imminence of the end and historicizes certain events that others regarded as apocalyptic, he is not turning his back on eschatology; he is organizing it according to what he believes is God's design. The Jewish war (and undoubtedly he would say all the wars of all history) escapes neither the control nor the will of God. It even unfolds according to the Scriptures (v. 22). That it is part of God's history with his people, however, does not mean that it has ultimate value or even that it is a "sign" of the end. The year 70 is "not yet" (Mark); it is "not immediately" (Luke) the end.[42]

■ **10-11** Luke introduces here a long quotation from his special material. He provides it with the short introduction, "then he said to them." The Gospel does bring "the nations" (τὰ ἔθνη; see 24:47 and often in Acts) together in a promising plurality of forgiveness and unity, but here it keeps them separated—they even oppose one another (ἔθνος ἐπ᾽ ἔθνος, v. 10). Two peoples[43] or two kingdoms face off against each other[44] like fighting animals.[45] The

hostility is such that it can result only in defeat for both of them. The text then mentions three other disasters: earthquakes (σεισμοί), famines (λιμοί), and epidemics (λοιμοί).[46] Such lists are not unusual in apocalyptic literature.[47]

Less common is the combination of φόβητρα ("terrifying events") and σημεῖα ("signs"). The first word reflects the earth and fear;[48] the second, the heaven and divine messages.[49]

■ **12-19** Of the apocalyptic calamity, which strikes everyone, the text separates the tests that come down ἐφ᾽ ὑμᾶς ("on you"), that is, on the Christian community.[50] The great blows may still lie in the future, but the lesser persecutions have already started. Luke says it clearly: πρὸ δὲ τούτων πάντων ("before all of that," v. 12). It is not easy to know from what the first-century Christians suffered: social marginalization, bureaucratic vexations, denunciation to the local or Roman authorities, lawsuits, and lynching?[51] It is also possible that some of them gave their persecutors the sticks with which they wanted to be beaten. In any case, in its variety the early Chris-

---

42   On τέλος, see Samuel Ngayihembako, *Les temps de la fin: Approche exégétique de l'eschatologie du Nouveau Testament* (MdB 29; Geneva: Labor et Fides, 1994) passim.

43   On ἔθνος ("people," "nation"). see Nikolaus Walter, "ἔθνος etc.," *EDNT* 1 (1990) 381–83; Denise Kimber Buell, *Why This New Race: Ethnic Reasoning in Early Christianity* (New York: Columbia University Press, 2005).

44   The verb ἐγείρω is used also in Mark 13:22 par. Matt 24:24; Matt 24:11. It initially means "to awaken," "to awake," then "to erect," "to excite."

45   Luke 11:17-18 alludes to the case of a divided kingdom whose fall is certain.

46   The term σεισμός is frequently used for an "earthquake" (it is known that a horrible earthquake destroyed Laodicea and Colossae in 60/61 C.E.). The word λιμός means "hunger," then "famine" (Acts 11:28 mentions a famine during the time of the emperor Claudius; there were indeed a number of famines between 46 and 48 C.E. in various parts of the empire). As for λοιμός, it refers to the "plague" and other contagious diseases. On these terms, see BAGD, s.vv. By reversing the word order, a number of manuscripts relate the words "from place to place" to the earthquakes and not to the famines and plagues; see the apparatus in Nestle-Aland (27th ed.) on Luke 21:11.

47   See BAGD, s.v. λιμός 2.

48   On φόβητρον (or φόβηθρον), something unusual that causes fear, a "terrifying event," see James Hope Moulton and George Milligan, *The Vocabulary of the Greek New Testament: Illustrated from the Papyri and Other Non-Literary Sources* (1930; reprinted Grand Rapids: Eerdmans, 1974) s.v.

49   The word order at the end of v. 11 (καὶ ἀπ᾽ οὐρανοῦ — ἔσται) changes depending on the manuscripts. In addition, Old Latin manuscripts, as well as some Syriac versions, add (under the influence of Matt 24:20?) the equivalent of καὶ χειμῶνες ("and the storms").

50   Braumann ("Mittel," 140–45) is of the opinion that the delay of the parousia is not the problem Luke has to solve here. The problem is the present suffering of the church, which it solves through its own reflection about time: In spite of the persecutions, the Christian community is on God's side and can with confidence await the parousia, the delay of which is acknowledged.

51   See Jacques Moreau, *La persécution du christianisme dans l'Empire romain* (MR; Paris: Presses universitaires de France, 1956); Pierre Maraval, *Les persécutions des chrétiens durant les quatre premiers siècles* (BHC 30; Paris: Desclée, 1992).

tian literature testifies to the phenomenon of persecution or at the very least reveals the conviction of being oppressed. The spectrum ranges from the Paul of the epistles to the John of the Apocalypse by way of the Synoptic Gospels, the Acts of the Apostles, the First Epistle of Peter and that of Clement.[52] There is a common vocabulary in these passages, especially in ours: ἐπιβάλλω τὰς χεῖρας ἐπί . . . ("to lay hands on"); διώκω ("to pursue," "to persecute"); παραδίδωμι εἰς . . . ("to deliver to"); ἀπάγομαι ἐπί . . . ("to be led away to appear before"). There are the names of authorities—βασιλεύς ("king" or "emperor"); ἡγεμών ("governor")—as well as the places where the arrests take place, the investigations are done, or the punishments are meted out, here "synagogues" and "prisons" (v. 12). For Luke and his fellow believers the persecution has only one honorable origin: adherence to the name of Jesus.[53] It also leads to a first result, witnessing, εἰς μαρτύριον (v. 13).

It is a moment for which one must prepare, just as a defendant prepares a defense with the help of an attorney. One's attitude in preparing the testimony must entail every precaution: θέτε οὖν ἐν ταῖς καρδίαις ὑμῶν ("so put it in your hearts," v. 14). The counsel, however, is paradoxical. The best preparation, Jesus says, is not to prepare; one's concern must be not to be concerned (v. 14). Still, Luke does not recommend improvising any more than does Mark or Matthew. He demands that one not be concerned (μὴ προμελετᾶν, "not to worry in advance," v. 14)[54] so that the ἐγώ of Christ can intervene. The risen Jesus, serving as advocate through

his Holy Spirit, will not take the place of the Christian defendant, but such an "attorney," a παράκλητος, will "give you a mouth and wisdom" (v. 15). Therefore, "none" of the opponents of the earth (note the alliteration ἀντιστῆναι—ἀντειπεῖν—ἀντικείμενοι) "will be able" to say anything against you or against the wisdom that Jesus will have placed on your lips. Your defense will be thoroughly prepared.[55]

A second wave describes more precisely the tragic origin of the opposition (vv. 16-19): family and friends. In 12:52-53 the reader has already learned that Jesus' message will create divisions in the family, for example, the father against his son and the son against his father. Here it is because of their commitment that the disciples are threatened by their own family and even by the circle of their friends.[56] The vocabulary speaks of extreme violence: They "will be delivered" and "will be led to death"[57] by those who usually guarantee protection and well-being. It is certainly not a question of murder,[58] but of death sentences as a result of denunciations by members of the family. The verb θανατῶ ("to lead to death," "to condemn to death") comes after παραδίδωμι ("to deliver"). Jesus, who has demanded that they "hate" their family (14:26), notes that hatred causes hatred. Since they have burned their bridges, the Christians have caused their own rejection: "You will be hated by everyone because of my name" (v. 17). As in v. 12, it is the commitment to the "name" of Jesus, thus the situation as disciples of Christ, that is the cause of the hostility and hatred.[59]

---

52   See, among other places, 1 Thess 2:14-16; Gal 1:13; 2 Tim 3:11; Matt 10:17; 23:34; Luke 11:49; Acts 4:3; 5:17-18; 7:54-60; 8:3; 9:15; 13:50; 14:5, 19; 1 Pet 1:6; 3:13-17; 4:12-19; Rev 1:9; 2:3, 13; Ignatius *Rom.* 2.1–8.3; *1 Clem.* 5–6; vol. 2 of this commentary on 12:11-12.

53   On the "name of Jesus," see François Bovon, "Names and Numbers in Early Christianity," *NTS* 47 (2001) 278–80.

54   Instead of μὴ προμελετᾶν, Codex Bezae (D = 05) prefers μὴ προμελετῶντες, thus avoiding two consecutive infinitives. See the apparatus of Nestle-Aland (27th ed.) here.

55   On the verb ἀπολογοῦμαι, see vol. 2 of this commentary on 12:11-12; BAGD, s.v. Luke uses the verb also in Acts 19:33; 24:10; 25:8 and 26:1-2, 24. He has already employed it in 12:11. Each time it appears in a legal context.

56   Luke has accustomed us to such lists; see n. 16 above.

57   The elliptical construction θανατώσουσιν ἐξ ὑμῶν (v. 16) is impressive in its arbitrariness, perhaps even in its violence: They will strike at random, simply hitting into the group. On the ellipses, see Smyth, *Greek Grammar*, §3022.

58   The verb would be ἀποκτείνω ("to kill").

59   There is no difference in meaning or in range between "for the sake of my name" (v. 12) and "because of my name" (v. 17); it is simply a way to vary the wording.

Is it necessary to make a distinction between hatred expressed (14:26) and hatred experienced (here in v. 17)? One often justifies the former by regarding it as the opposite of an irrefutable preference and condemns the second as an unjust retribution. Luke moves in this direction by distinguishing two kinds of hatred. The first is metaphorical and expresses the social intransigence to which commitment to the gospel leads; the second is real and indicates the hostility, also social, that any vigorous belief arouses.

Luke places an unconditional divine protection alongside this explosion of violence. As I have said, the indirect parallels of Mark 13:13 and Matt 24:9b-14 do not know this stamp of confidence: "But not a hair of your head will be lost" (v. 18). How is this paradox to be explained? Let us begin by understanding v. 18 as an isolated statement. Following the Sayings Source, Luke has already referred to the divine providence in these terms: "But even the hairs of your head are numbered. Fear not" (12:7 par. Matt 10:30). In addition, at the end of Acts he has Paul reassure the crew of the vessel in danger by saying, "Thus I urge you to take some food for your safety. Once again, not one of you will lose a hair of his head" (οὐδενὸς γὰρ ὑμῶν θρὶξ ἀπὸ τῆς κεφαλῆς ἀπολεῖται, Acts 27:34). With this expression Luke takes up a biblical idiom that we first meet in 1 Sam (LXX 1 Kgdms) 14:45 on the lips of the people who save Jonathan from the threat of death by his father Saul, who thinks it is his duty to make Jonathan atone for a mistake made in Israel's victory over the Philistines: "Not one hair of his head will fall to the ground." One finds the same expression in 2 Sam (LXX 2 Kgdms) 14:11, when King David assures the woman of Tekoa of his protection. In 1 Sam (LXX 1 Kgdms) 1:52 it is Solomon who uses a similar expression to promise Adonijah his justice and his protection: "If he acts as an honest man, not one of his hairs will fall to the ground." Thus, in all of these texts this vigorous and emphatic expression refers to God's physical protection in this life. The example of Samson, betrayed by Delilah (Judg 16:15-31), reminds us that in Israel's symbolism the loss of hair was equivalent to a loss of vital energy and divine support. Luke is thinking here of God's eschatological protection in the kingdom or after death. Viewed in the long term, only Providence counts in Luke's eyes. This interpretation, doubly metaphorical (from hair to life and from life to eternal life) is confirmed by the following verse: κτήσασθε τὰς ψυχὰς ὑμῶν ("you will gain your souls," v. 19).[60] Another Lukan verse, 9:25, plays with the categories of loss and gain and helps us understand this expression. It is not a question of getting what one does not have but of establishing forever one's property rights.[61] That does not happen without "perseverance" (ὑπομονή, v. 19).[62] The Lukan paragraph on persecutions (vv. 12-19) thus has two peaks: a promise (life) and an injunction (perseverance). What is needed is the ὑπομονή, in the sense of perseverance, of determination, of the will toward and against everything,[63] in order to overcome the resistance and to reunite with God, with whom the contact will never have been broken. This Lukan conviction is maintained throughout the entire two-volume work: from the parable of the sower

---

60 The manuscript tradition wavers between κτήσεσθε (indicative future), which I retain, and κτήσασθε (imperative aorist). Marcion appears to have read σώσετε ("you will save"). See the apparatus of Nestle-Aland (27th ed.) here; Harnack, *Marcion*, 231*, Tsutsui, "Evangelium Marcions," 121.

61 Elsewhere Luke uses the verb κτῶμαι in the literal sense of "to acquire" (18:12; Acts 1:18; 8:20; 22:28). On this verb, see BAGD, s.v.

62 In Mark 13:13 par. Matt 24:13, the equivalent of "to gain one's soul" is "to be saved." These two Gospels give this promise an ethical note while using the same word family as Luke. They use the verb ὑπομένω ("to persevere"). On salvation in Luke, see Bovon, *Luke the Theologian*, 273–328, 642.

63 On ὑπομονή here, see Dupont, "Épreuves," 1125–26; on Luke, see 8:15 and vol. 1 of this commentary, 311 on 8:8 and 15. See also Francisco Zorrell's definition (*Novi Testamenti Lexicon Graecum* [Paris: Lethielleux, 1911], s.v.: In NT sic vocatur illa virtus qua homo, calamitatibus, vexationibus, tentationibus nullis fractus, in fide ac pietate forti animo perdurat ("In the NT this is what the virtue is called by which the human being, unbroken by calamities, tortures, temptations, endures with courage in faith and piety").

at the beginning of the Gospel ($\kappa\alpha\rho\pi o\phi o\rho o\hat{v}\sigma\iota\nu\ \dot{\epsilon}\nu$ $\dot{v}\pi o\mu o\nu\hat{\eta}$, "they bear fruit in perseverance," 8:15) to the teaching of Paul in Acts ($\dot{\epsilon}\pi\iota\sigma\tau\eta\rho\dot{\iota}\zeta o\nu\tau\epsilon\varsigma\ \tau\grave{\alpha}\varsigma\ \psi\upsilon\chi\grave{\alpha}\varsigma$ $\tau\hat{\omega}\nu\ \mu\alpha\vartheta\eta\tau\hat{\omega}\nu,\ \pi\alpha\rho\alpha\kappa\alpha\lambda o\hat{\upsilon}\nu\tau\epsilon\varsigma\ \dot{\epsilon}\mu\mu\dot{\epsilon}\nu\epsilon\iota\nu\ \tau\hat{\eta}\ \pi\dot{\iota}\sigma\tau\epsilon\iota$ $\kappa\alpha\grave{\iota}\ \ddot{o}\tau\iota\ \delta\iota\grave{\alpha}\ \pi o\lambda\lambda\hat{\omega}\nu\ \vartheta\lambda\dot{\iota}\psi\epsilon\omega\nu\ \delta\epsilon\hat{\iota}\ \dot{\eta}\mu\hat{\alpha}\varsigma\ \epsilon\dot{\iota}\sigma\epsilon\lambda\vartheta\epsilon\hat{\iota}\nu\ \epsilon\dot{\iota}\varsigma$ $\tau\grave{\eta}\nu\ \beta\alpha\sigma\iota\lambda\epsilon\dot{\iota}\alpha\nu\ \tau o\hat{\upsilon}\ \vartheta\epsilon o\hat{\upsilon}$, "They strengthened there the heart of the disciples and exhorted them to persevere in the faith. We must, they said, pass through many afflictions to enter the kingdom of God," Acts 14:22).

■ **20-24** Following his source, a source different from Mark, Luke relates here the capture of Jerusalem,[64] and he does so in language that is more military than religious.[65] The holy city will be "surrounded by armed troops" (v. 20), then "trodden under foot by the nations" (v. 24). Its inhabitants "will fall by the sharpness[66] of the sword and will be taken into captivity among all the nations" (v. 24).[67] Such a description is far removed from the perspective of Mark, who is inspired by the prophetic book of Daniel (Dan 9:27; 11:31; 12:11) and mentions the attack on the temple, "the abomination of desolation" (Mark 13:14). The Lukan text strictly maintains the historical character of the fate of Jerusalem. It also expresses its geographical aspect, mentioning twice (vv. 20 and 24) that this will happen in "Jerusalem," thus "on the earth" (v. 25). This destiny represents the realization of Jesus' prophetic predictions of coming

wars (vv. 9 and 10). It is also expressed in general terms whose abstract character paradoxically underscores the specific and personal impact: $\dot{\epsilon}\rho\dot{\eta}\mu\omega\sigma\iota\varsigma$ ("depopulation," "abandonment," "desolation," "devastation," v. 20); $\dot{\epsilon}\kappa\delta\dot{\iota}\kappa\eta\sigma\iota\varsigma$ ("legal proceedings," "revenge," "retribution," "punishment," v. 22)[68]; $\dot{\alpha}\nu\dot{\alpha}\gamma\kappa\eta\ \mu\epsilon\gamma\dot{\alpha}\lambda\eta$ ("great need," "heavy blows,"[69] "tragic fate," "great distress," v. 23); $\dot{o}\rho\gamma\dot{\eta}$ (not "anger" as a reaction of one's mood but "anger" as an expression of the judgment of God as sovereign judge, v. 23).[70]

This appreciation is accompanied by a first, more precise definition that reminds us of Luke's interest in time: "these days" (v. 22) or "those days" (v. 23)[71] will themselves precede other days, the "times of the nations" (v. 24). A second, further definition then emphasizes that this dark destiny is deserved. At issue is "*its* desolation" (v. 20), the fate reserved for "this people" (v. 23). A third definition is that this "retribution" will correspond to the will of God that has been known of old and has even found written expression ($\pi\dot{\alpha}\nu\tau\alpha\ \tau\grave{\alpha}\ \gamma\epsilon\gamma\rho\alpha\mu$-$\mu\dot{\epsilon}\nu\alpha$, "everything that has been written," v. 22). A fourth explanation then says, without being eschatological, that the historical capture of Jerusalem corresponds to God's plan and constitutes a stage leading to the end and to the ultimate "deliverance" (v. 28).[72] The approach of the one ($\ddot{\eta}\gamma\gamma\iota\kappa\epsilon\nu\ \dot{\eta}\ \dot{\epsilon}\rho\dot{\eta}\mu\omega\sigma\iota\varsigma\ \alpha\dot{\upsilon}\tau\hat{\eta}\varsigma$, "its desolation has drawn

---

64 On vv. 20-24, see Taylor, "Siege"; Braumann, "Zerstörung"; Pedersen, "Problem"; Flückiger, "Zerstörung"; Fee, "Look," 17–23; Wainwright, "Restoration"; C. Koester, "Pella"; Wehnert, "Auswanderung."

65 With de la Potterie ("Jérusalem," 66–67), one will note, however, that here in v. 20 Luke chooses Ἰερουσαλήμ to designate the city. Different from the Hellenized form ($\tau\grave{\alpha}$ and $\dot{\eta}$ Ἱεροσόλυμα), this Semitic form (treated in Greek as an unchangeable feminine) underscores the holy character of the City of David, which remains the place where God's redemptive plan will be realized.

66 Literally, "by the mouth of the sword" or "at the mouth of the sword." What is the mouth of the sword if not its lips, thus its two sharp edges? On this dative instrumental, see BDF §195 (1).

67 One can compare this description with that of 19:43-44. The contents are similar, but one must contrast the different vocabulary: $\pi\alpha\rho\epsilon\mu\beta\dot{\alpha}\lambda\lambda\omega$ $\chi\dot{\alpha}\rho\alpha\kappa\alpha$—$\kappa\upsilon\kappa\lambda\hat{\omega}$; $\dot{\epsilon}\chi\vartheta\rho o\dot{\iota}$—$\sigma\tau\rho\alpha\tau\dot{o}\pi\epsilon\delta\alpha$; $\sigma\upsilon\nu\dot{\epsilon}\chi\omega$— $\pi\alpha\tau\hat{\omega}$; $\delta\alpha\phi\iota\hat{\omega}$—$\pi\dot{\iota}\pi\tau\omega\ \sigma\tau\dot{o}\mu\alpha\tau\iota\ \mu\alpha\chi\alpha\dot{\iota}\rho\eta\varsigma$.

68 On $\dot{\epsilon}\kappa\delta\dot{\iota}\kappa\eta\sigma\iota\varsigma$, see vol. 2 of this commentary on 18:7a.

69 This is the [French] translation of Delebecque, *Évangile*, 131: *lourde fatalité*.

70 With 3:7 this is the only time $\dot{o}\rho\gamma\dot{\eta}$ is used in Luke-Acts. It corresponds to Pauline usage in, e.g., 1 Thess 1:10 or Rom 1:18.

71 "These days" ($\dot{\eta}\mu\dot{\epsilon}\rho\alpha\iota\ldots\ \alpha\hat{\upsilon}\tau\alpha\iota$) and "those days" ($\dot{\epsilon}\nu\ \dot{\epsilon}\kappa\epsilon\dot{\iota}\nu\alpha\iota\varsigma\ \tau\alpha\hat{\iota}\varsigma\ \dot{\eta}\mu\dot{\epsilon}\rho\alpha\iota\varsigma$) are the same days, but the first time they are considered in their immediacy and the second time in their distance, imaginatively toward the future and historically toward the past.

72 This problematic of history and eschatology has been dealt with by a number of authors in the previous generation. It is enough to mention the names of Hans Conzelmann, Helmut Flender, Ruthild Geiger, Josef Zmijewski, Jean-Daniel Kaestli, and A. J. Mattill. See Bovon, *Luke the Theologian*, 1–85. According to Walter ("Tempelzerstörung"), Luke understands the entire address as an answer to the question of the time of the fall of the temple. Luke

near," v. 20) will precede the other (ἐγγίζει ἡ ἀπο-λύτρωσις ὑμῶν, "your deliverance draws near," v. 28). The attitudes that the history calls forth resemble those characteristic of the end of time (flight and untimely displacements, v. 21). The verbs πίμπλημι ("to fill up, fulfill, accomplish," v. 22 [referring to Scripture] and "to fulfill, accomplish," v. 24 [referring to the time of the nations]) also include the fate of Jerusalem in the prophecy–fulfillment pattern.[73]

We turn now to the fate of the city and the lot of its inhabitants. It is true that Scripture knows and describes the siege and fall of various cities, among them Jerusalem, which succumbed to the blows of Nebuchadnezzar (2 Kings [LXX 4 Kingdoms] 25 and 2 Chronicles 36). In describing the future, the speaker of vv. 20-24 was able to begin with these descriptions. Nevertheless, the passage sounds too real to be only a single prophecy; it is also a description as seen from recent history. What Luke writes of the fall of Jerusalem, of the siege, of the armies surrounding the cities, the attempts to flee, the confused movements caused by panic, the fate of expectant women and young mothers, the massacres, and the removals of the population, all of these things resemble the descrip-

tion of Josephus too much not to reflect the experience of the drama of the year 70.

Two final points must be mentioned. (1) Along with this entire description one should not forget the prescriptive and the apodictic elements.[74] In v. 21 three imperatives offer the possibility of escaping the drama. All three invite people to break every connection to the city: by fleeing to the mountains,[75] by abandoning the city,[76] or by giving up reentering the city.[77] The reference to this commandment[78] serves less to show a way out of the dilemma than to emphasize the desperate measures to which people are driven at this time. In v. 23 it is no longer even an imperative; it is a declaration and a lament: how they will pity those who on other occasions radiate joy! The expectant women and the young mothers, bearing new life, will be—indeed in prophetic anticipation already are and in historical retrospective still are—to be pitied (see Isa 54:1). The initial οὐαί of the curses (6:24-26) is repeated several times in the Gospel.[79] As a decisive warning it resounds here in v. 23 once again (see 11:42, 43, 44, 46, 52; 17:1).

(2) A great deal of ink has been spilled over the enigmatic expression "the times of the nations."[80] In order to

historicizes the event and detaches it from the end of time. Here we are not far from Conzelmann's position. More recently, Perkins ("Destruction") has tried to imagine how history would have continued had the Romans not destroyed Jerusalem in 70 C.E. The anti-Judaism of the Gospels could not have developed, and the Christian church, even while integrating the Gentiles into its midst, would have remained a Jewish sect.

73 On the verbs πίμπλημι and πληρῶ see vol. 1 of this commentary on 1:15, 20, 57; 2:6; 4:21, 36 n. 56; 40 n. 97; 69, 85, 154.

74 There are variant readings of the imperative aorist γνῶτε in v. 20: γινώσκετε (indicative or imperative present) and γνώσεσθε (indicative future); see the apparatus of Nestle-Aland (27th ed.). See Green, 732: "Thematically, Jesus' discourse underscores the faithful hand of God in the series of events to unfold and the call for a concomitant human faithfulness."

75 Do the inhabitants of Jerusalem belong to the οἱ ἐν τῇ Ἰουδαίᾳ or not? They undoubtedly form part of it, and the expression designates all the inhabitants of Judea.

76 Codex Bezae (D = 05), as well as several manuscripts of the Vulgate, precede the imperative

ἐκχωρείτωσαν ("let them go out") with the negative particle μή ("let them not go out"), doubtless under the influence of the third imperative ("let them not enter the city"); see the apparatus of Nestle-Aland (27th ed.).

77 The words οἱ ἐν μέσῳ αὐτῆς indicate more those who are in the inner city at the time of the siege than the regular inhabitants of the capital. Similarly, the words οἱ ἐν ταῖς χώραις indicate those who at that time are outside the walls, in the countryside.

78 One must compare v. 21 with 17:31. In both places the reference is to the risk of certain movements, here in the city, there in the country. While here it is a question of fleeing the city, there it is a question of leaving the house.

79 See Morgen, "Arrière-fond scripturaire," 321: "Instead of an apocalyptic passage predicting the future, the prophetic words put in Jesus' mouth in Luke 21 are of a different literary genre that is directed more toward a theological meditation on the past."

80 These words are not found in Codex Bezae (D = 05). It is thus not clear in this manuscript what the subject of the verb "are fulfilled" is.

understand it, one should isolate it neither from the verb πληρῶ ("fulfill"), which rules it, nor from the literary context of vv. 21-24. Jerusalem will not only be taken; it will also be "trodden under foot," πατουμένη. The scope of this present passive participle is not limited to the fall of the holy city. It includes the length of the occupation to which the "nations"—that is, the foreign nations, more precisely the Romans—will subject it. The temporal subordinate clause becomes clear: Jerusalem's humiliation,[81] its desolation, will be limited. It will end with the fulfillment of the "times of the nations." Luke, who likes ambiguities, especially when they deal with the future, who thus follows the practice of prophetic haziness,[82] is thinking here of both the end of Roman power and the massive conversion of the Gentiles. More than many other sentences this temporal subordination confirms in a sparkling way the Lukan understanding of salvation-history.

■ **25-28** After having kept the readers[83] for a while in the historical area, Luke leads them here into the apocalyptic area.[84] Two events will take place there: (a) First, heaven and earth will indicate with significant shocks that the end is imminent; (b) then the Son of Man will appear to all of restless humanity. Then—such is the invitation—the Christian community, attentive, will rise up and rejoice in the day of its deliverance. The first point is the more fully developed. It is divided into two parts: in heaven and on the earth.

Verse 11 had already proclaimed the signs of the heaven. To this point one has had to wait for them (v. 12), because Luke refuses to speed up history for the sake of eschatology. Now they take place not directly in the sky but in the three celestial bodies known to ancient science: the sun, the moon, and the stars. That is to say, they will occur by day as well as by night. By day the sun will be veiled; by night the moon and the stars, abruptly or for a longer time, will gain in luminous intensity. The ancients liked to believe that heavenly signs, whose appearance certain people knew how to analyze, predicted or accompanied major events in the lives of individuals and nations. In particular, the prophets of Israel had laid the groundwork: "I will give wonders in heaven and on the earth, blood, fire, columns of smoke. The sun will change into darkness and the moon into blood with the coming of the great and formidable day of the Lord" (Joel 3:3-4).

On earth, human beings also react to the signs of heaven. The term συνοχή means "coherence," "contraction," "hindrance," "impediment," "anguish." In 2 Cor 2:4, the only other place where it occurs in the New Testament, Paul uses it with the sense of "anguish." Helmut Koester has shown that συνοχή was used in antiquity to express anxious reactions to astronomical phenomena. For Luke, what matters here is not a human answer to an apocalyptic event but fear in view of disturbing signs in the stars.[85]

As for ἐν ἀπορίᾳ, I have translated it as "helpless." The nations are probably brought together, but in any case they are afraid of the ocean. From time immemorial, Israel, a people of peasants and not of sailors, has lived in fear of floods.[86] Here this fear becomes panic in the face of the "rumbling" (τὸ ἦχος)[87] and the "heaving"

---

81 The verb πατῶ, which literally means "to press with the feet," often also has a figurative meaning, "to insult," "to scorn," "to humiliate." See BAGD, s.v.

82 See François Bovon, "Effet de réel et flou prophétique dans l'oeuvre de Luc," in *A Cause de l'Evangile: études sur les Synoptiques et les Actes, offertes au P. Jacques Dupont, O.S.B. à l'occasion de son 70e anniversaire* (LD 123; Paris: Cerf, 1985) 349–59. The anonymous Irish author of the eighth century (*Comm. Luc.* 21, 14 [CCSL 108C, 95]) understands the expression as a reference to the salvation of the nations by faith.

83 On vv. 25-28, see Galbiati, "Avvento"; Tannehill, "Resources"; E. Achtemeier, "Luke 21:25-36"; Kay, "Redemption"; Stenschke, *Gentiles*, 59.

84 According to Helmut Flender (*Heil und Geschichte in der Theologie des Lukas* [BEvTh 41; Munich: Kaiser,

1965] 103–5), Luke wants to connect the fall of Jerusalem (eschatology of the past) with the end of time (eschatology of the future). Contra Conzelmann (*Theology*, 130), there is no caesura between v. 24 and v. 25.

85 See Koester "συνέχω, συνοχή," 877–87.

86 On the fear of the sea felt by the people of Israel, see vol. 1 of this commentary, 317–21, on 8:22-25.

87 There is ὁ ἦχος ("sound," "echo," "clamor"), which Luke uses in Acts 2:2 (the "sound of the trumpet"). Here there is the synonym τὸ ἦχος (genitive ἤχους), which must be understood in the literal sense of noise, obviously an alarming rumbling. Codex Bezae (D = 05), as with many manuscripts of the Byzantine text, has ἠχούσης (present participle of the verb ἠχῶ) instead of ἤχους. It is thus the "sea

($\sigma\acute{\alpha}\lambda o\varsigma$, translated as "crash and waves")[88] of the "sea" ($\vartheta\acute{\alpha}\lambda\alpha\sigma\sigma\alpha$). It is enough to think of Ps 64 (65):8: "Who stills the roaring of the seas, the roaring of their waves, and the rumbling of the peoples,"[89] and of Isa 24:19: "The earth is broken, the earth is burst asunder, it is violently shaken."

Then a genitive absolute brings a new source of anxiety, the fear of the future. This cascade of expressions confirms the avalanche of unforeseen events and the fear they cause. The people are "exhausted" (literally, they "lose their breath of life,"[90] "their soul") from "fear" ($\varphi\acute{o}\beta o\varsigma$)[91] and "waiting" ($\pi\rho o\sigma\delta o\kappa\acute{\iota}\alpha$).[92] They fear what "will happen," literally, "what will come upon[93] the inhabited earth" ($o\grave{\iota}\kappa o\upsilon\mu\acute{e}\nu\eta$).[94] These fears are entirely justified. Indeed, a cosmic shock is to be expected. The passive form of the verb $\sigma\alpha\lambda\epsilon\acute{\upsilon}\omega$ (in v. 25 one already had the substantive $\acute{o}$ $\sigma\acute{\alpha}\lambda o\varsigma$, "the shock," "the heaving") has its usual meaning, "to be agitated" (speaking initially about the anchored boats shaken by the waves). Here it is not only the waves of the sea or the earthly elements that are shaken but "the powers of the heavens" (the expression appears to go back to Isa 34:4). The verb $\sigma\alpha\lambda\epsilon\acute{\upsilon}\omega$ has taken on an apocalyptic coloring, as one sees when reading one of the few apocalyptic passages of the epistle to the Hebrews:

. . . of him whose voice shook the earth then but who now has made this proclamation: One last time I will make not only the earth tremble but also the heaven. The words one last time proclaim the removal of everything that takes part in the world's instability so that what cannot be shaken remains" ($o\hat{\upsilon}$ $\acute{\eta}$ $\varphi\omega\nu\grave{\eta}$ $\tau\grave{\eta}\nu$ $\gamma\hat{\eta}\nu$ $\acute{e}\sigma\acute{\alpha}\lambda\epsilon\upsilon\sigma\epsilon\nu$ $\tau\acute{o}\tau\epsilon$, $\nu\hat{\upsilon}\nu$ $\delta\grave{e}$ $\acute{e}\pi\acute{\eta}\gamma\gamma\epsilon\lambda\tau\alpha\iota$ $\lambda\acute{e}\gamma\omega\nu\cdot$ $\acute{e}\tau\iota$ $\acute{\alpha}\pi\alpha\xi$ $\acute{e}\gamma\grave{\omega}$ $\sigma\epsilon\acute{\iota}\sigma\omega$ $o\grave{\upsilon}$ $\mu\acute{o}\nu o\nu$ $\tau\grave{\eta}\nu$ $\gamma\hat{\eta}\nu$ $\grave{\alpha}\lambda\lambda\grave{\alpha}$ $\kappa\alpha\grave{\iota}$ $\tau\grave{o}\nu$ $o\grave{\upsilon}\rho\alpha\nu\acute{o}\nu$. $\tau\grave{o}$ $\delta\grave{e}$ $\acute{e}\tau\iota$ $\acute{\alpha}\pi\alpha\xi$ $\delta\eta\lambda o\hat{\iota}$ $\tau\grave{\eta}\nu$ $\tau\hat{\omega}\nu$ $\sigma\alpha\lambda\epsilon\upsilon o\mu\acute{e}\nu\omega\nu$ $\mu\epsilon\tau\acute{\alpha}\vartheta\epsilon\sigma\iota\nu$ $\acute{\omega}\varsigma$ $\pi\epsilon\pi o\iota\eta\mu\acute{e}\nu\omega\nu$, $\acute{\iota}\nu\alpha$ $\mu\epsilon\acute{\iota}\nu\eta$ $\tau\grave{\alpha}$ $\mu\grave{\eta}$ $\sigma\alpha\lambda\epsilon\upsilon\acute{o}\mu\epsilon\nu\alpha$). (Heb 12:26-27)[95]

Here in v. 26, as in Heb 12:26-27, it is the heaven that is shaken,[96] and not only the heaven as part of the visible creation but also the invisible "powers" that inhabit it.[97] Thus, the cosmos will be violently shaken. The apocalyptists imagine a kind of anti-creation, not a disappearance by fire such as the Stoics expected, an $\acute{e}\kappa\pi\acute{\upsilon}\rho\omega\sigma\iota\varsigma$,[98] but a universal catastrophe from which only God can derive an eschatological profit by sending the Son of Man.

The first Christians share various ideas about the end of time.[99] The most common image is that of the Son of Man. Influenced by Daniel's vision (in Dan 7:13), the believers reckon with the sudden, flashing, and visible appearance of the risen Messiah on the clouds of heaven.

that thunders." See the apparatus of Nestle-Aland (27th ed.) on this text and BAGD, s.v.

88 On $\sigma\acute{\alpha}\lambda o\varsigma$, see Zorell, s.v. and BAGD, s.v.

89 See also Ps 45 (46):3-4; 88 (89):10; Wis 5:22; Jonah 1:15.

90 $\grave{\alpha}\pi o\psi\acute{\upsilon}\chi\omega$ $\grave{\alpha}\pi\acute{o}$ plus the genitive with the causal sense. The verb was used already by Homer in *Od.* 24.348 to describe Laertes, who fainted away when he recognized his son, Ulysses. It is remarkable that this verb appears only here in the New Testament.

91 On $\varphi\acute{o}\beta o\varsigma$, see Horst Balz, "$\varphi\acute{o}\beta o\varsigma$, etc.," *EDNT* 3 (1993) 432–34.

92 In the entire New Testament $\pi\rho o\sigma\delta o\kappa\acute{\iota}\alpha$ appears only here and in Acts 12:11. Luke likes to use the verb $\pi\rho o\sigma\delta o\kappa\hat{\omega}$. On the waiting, see vol. 1 of this commentary, 39, on 1:21.

93 Luke uses the verb $\acute{e}\pi\acute{e}\rho\chi o\mu\alpha\iota$ eight times, but this is the only time he resorts to the present participle as a substantive.

94 On $o\grave{\iota}\kappa o\upsilon\mu\acute{e}\nu\eta$, used by Luke in 2:1; 4:5, and here in v. 26, see vol. 1 of this commentary, 83, 143, on 2:1 and 4:5.

95 On Heb 12:26-27, see Harold W. Attridge, *The Epistle to the Hebrews: A Commentary on the Epistle to the Hebrews* (Hermeneia; Philadelphia: Fortress Press, 1989) 380–82.

96 There are other occurrences in Luke-Acts: Luke 6:38, 48; 7:24; Acts 2:35; 4:31; 16:26; 17:13. See Horst Balz, "$\sigma\alpha\lambda\epsilon\acute{\upsilon}\omega$, etc.," *EDNT* 3 (1993) 224. It is sometimes difficult to say whether the verb is to be understood in the strict or the figurative sense.

97 Since the works of Heinrich Schlier and Oscar Cullmann, on the heavenly $\delta\upsilon\nu\acute{\alpha}\mu\epsilon\iota\varsigma$, one must refer to the works of Walter Wink, especially to *The Powers That Be: Theology for a New Millennium* (New York: Doubleday, 1999).

98 See the earlier conjecture by Frank Olivier on 2 Pet 3:10 that today is generally rejected: *Essais dans le domaine du monde gréco-romain antique et dans celui du Nouveau Testament* (Geneva: Droz, 1963) 127–52.

99 Along with the coming of the Son of Man, one must announce the arrival of the Day of the Lord (1 Thess 5:1-3; 2 Pet 3:11-13). The two concepts are often combined, as is already the case in 1 Thess 4:13—5:3. Another concept appears, e.g., in Ignatius of Antioch, who is not aware of the coming of

This arrival, mentioned here in v. 27, comes together with the judgment on the nations and the redemption of the chosen people. Even if the title "Son of Man" does not appear there, it is the description in Rev 19:11-16 that best suggests to modern readers what the first Christians hoped for in their imagination: the glorious arrival of a worldwide king, surrounded by his angelic forces, who comes from heaven to restore justice and peace (see also Rev 1:7 and 14:14). The apostle Paul shares this hope, as a summary of his preaching (1 Thess 1:9-10)[100] and an apocalyptic description (1 Thess 4:13—5:2) attest. Following the apostle, the Pastoral Epistles refer to this event with the term "appearance" (ἐπιφάνεια), thus emphasizing the visibility of the parousia (1 Tim 6:14; 2 Tim 4:1, 8; Titus 2:13). 2 Thessalonians 2:8 confirms this (τῇ ἐπιφανείᾳ τῆς παρουσίας αὐτοῦ, "by the appearance of his arrival"). Mark, and especially Matthew, and their communities, also are waiting for this parousia (Mark 13:26; 14:62; Matt 16:27; 19:28; 24:30; 25:31). The term παρουσία, which initially means "presence," then "coming," appears in various primitive Christian writings to indicate this eschatological event.[101]

Luke himself does not hesitate to mention the title "Son of Man" or to allude to his ultimate arrival. Beginning in 5:24[102] he uses the term "Son of Man," and in 9:26 he mentions his arrival for the first time (already including the concept of "glory" and the presence of the "holy angels"). He confirms his belief in the parousia (even if he does not use the term) in his first apocalyptic speech, in which he mentions "one of the days" or "the days of the Son of Man" (17:22, 26).

What distinguishes the second coming from the first is the power and the glory. Like his co-religionists, Luke establishes a contrast between Jesus' coming from the crib to the cross, characterized by weakness and suffering, and the coming of the Son of Man after the resurrection, characterized by power and glory. For him, the Jesus who was raised at Easter and entered into his glory (24:26) sits at the right hand of the Father, where he stays (22:69). Later he will come[103] (21:27).[104] With Mark and Matthew, Luke shares the presence of the cloud as well as the reference to the power and the glory (see Mark 13:26; Matt 24:30).[105]

This paragraph ends with an exhortation written in an elegant style and with a select vocabulary (v. 28). Here the Lukan Jesus challenges his disciples and gives them a command, which is also a promise. The words "when these things begin to happen" refer to the arrival of the Son of Man and beyond that to the cosmic signs (v. 25). To avoid any confusion, Luke—or his source—uses the verb ἄρχομαι, "to begin."[106] The signs are at the beginning, the Son of Man at the end.

The "you" of the Christian community resolutely distinguishes itself from the "them," that is to say, from

---

100   Curiously, Paul uses here the title Son and not Son of Man. The apostle probably realizes that the expression Son of Man could be misunderstood by Greeks not used to the biblical categories. This view also lies behind his great chapter on the resurrection (see esp. 1 Cor 15:23-25 and 51-52).

101   See Matt 24:3, 27, 37, 39; 1 Cor 15:23; 1 Thess 2:19; 3:13; 4:15; 5:23; 2 Thess 2:1, 8; Jas 5:7-8; 2 Pet 1:16 (?); 3:4, 12; 1 John 2:28. One also finds the terms συντέλεια [τοῦ] αἰῶνος ("fulfillment of time," Matt 13:39, 49; 24:3) and παλιγγενεσία ("regeneration," Matt 19:28). See also *Did.* 16.3-8; *Barn.* 4.9; Justin *Dial.* 35.3 and 82.1–2.

102   On the title "Son of Man" in Luke, see vol. 1 of this commentary, 183 n. 31, on 5:21-24.

103   On the messianic and eschatological character of the verb "to come," see vol. 1 of this commentary, 282, on 7:19-20.

the Son of Man or the Day of the Lord and claims that the individual meets God immediately after death (see, e.g., Ignatius *Eph.* 12.2).

104   Acts 7 poses a special problem, since the Son of Man rises up to receive the first martyr, Stephen, at his death. Luke undoubtedly harmonizes here the collective concept of the parousia with his hope of an individual eschatology at death. See Bovon, *Luke the Theologian*, 205–6.

105   Following Dan 7:13, Mark and Matthew use the plural "clouds." If Luke uses the singular here, it may be because of his faithfulness to his source or to narrative logic. In the account of the ascension, Jesus is lifted up on a cloud (Acts 1:10), and the angel promises the disciples that their master will return "in the same way" (Acts 1:11). Revelation 14:14-15 also has the singular, while Rev 1:7 has the plural. 1 Thessalonians 4:17 carries the plural, but there one has the removal of the believers at the time of the parousia.

106   He does not need to use this verb in the parallel sentences of vv. 31 and 32. Let us add that various witnesses, among them two, Codex Bezae (D = 05) and the minuscule 13, read ἐρχομένων ("when

the rest of the "humans" (ἄνϑρωποι). The latter will be horrified when the signs appear (v. 26). For their part, the disciples will demonstrate their special relation to the God of history and his messianic mediator by having courage (v. 28). They will straighten themselves and lift up their heads, while the others will faint away. In 13:11 Luke used the verb ἀνακύπτω in a literal sense: Thanks to Jesus, the bent-over woman, who cannot "straighten herself," is restored.[107] The recovery of this daughter of Abraham is admittedly physical, but it is no less a deliverance exemplary of any redemption: "and immediately she was straightened, and she glorified God" (καὶ παραχρῆμα ἀνωρϑώϑη καὶ ἐδόξαζεν τὸν ϑεόν, 13:13).[108] The verb ἀνακύπτω is the opposite of συγκύπτω ("to bend, bow down," "to bend over") in 13:11 or of κατακύπτω ("to stoop," "to bend over," "to bow the head") in John 8:6-11, the story of the adulteress. Reading the passages where the verb παρακύπτω ("to stoop", "to look at more closely") appears (see 1 Pet 1:12) shows that sometimes one should not be reluctant to understand these verbs figuratively. By "standing erect" here (v. 28) the believers will not only see (something the human beings will also do); they also will prepare to take part in the happiness of the kingdom. They will prepare themselves first of all by lifting up their bodies, the humiliation, oppression, and persecution of which have been described in vv. 12-19. Then they will prepare

themselves by "raising" or "lifting the head,"[109] and by daring to look, not fearing to face, not turning aside.[110]

Hope can be renewed, because what is coming no longer causes fear: "because your deliverance draws near" (διότι ἐγγίζει ἡ ἀπολύτρωσις ὑμῶν). Of note here are (1) the verb "to approach, draw near," whose eschatological meaning is common;[111] (2) the present tense, which underscores that it is imminent; and (3) the term "deliverance" (ἀπολύτρωσις), which is unusual in Luke, undoubtedly coming from the source he used, but along with "salvation" (σωτηρία) and "visitation" (ἐπισκοπή) is part of the New Testament vocabulary of salvation. In order to recall what Luke expects salvation to be—personal and social deliverance, the renewal of body and soul, the end of iniquity and oppression, the establishment of justice and peace, as well as the reversal of conditions—one must go back to the Magnificat (1:46-55), the beatitudes (6:20-26), the mission instructions (10:6-11), and the parable of the rich man and the poor Lazarus (16:19-31). The word ἀπολύτρωσις is made up of λύτρον, which designates the "ransom" paid, and the preposition ἀπό ("out of," "of"). In Greek the term defines the redemption, then the freedom, of a captive or a prisoner of war, once the ransom has been paid.[112] Although not very frequent, the term takes on a religious coloring, especially in the Hellenistic Jewish literature.[113] In the writings of the apostle Paul the term

---

these things will come," literally, "arriving"), doubtless under the influence of ἐρχόμενον ("arriving," translated "coming") of the previous line. This participle, followed by the infinitive γίνεσϑαι, does not give a satisfying meaning; see the apparatus of Nestle-Aland (27th ed.) on this text.

107 It is probably an error that some manuscripts, the Freer Codex of Washington (W = 032), that of the Great Laura on Mt. Athos (Ψ = 044), and the family of minuscules f¹ read ἀνακαλύψατε ("reveal, uncover") instead of ἀνακύψατε ("stand erect"). The scribes responsible for this variant probably imagined that up to that point the human beings had covered their faces (as a sign of mourning?).

108 See vol. 2 of this commentary on 13:11-17.

109 In the New Testament the verb ἐπαίρω ("to lift," "to hoist," "to raise") can be followed with words in the accusative such as "the eyes" (6:20), "the hands" (for blessing, 24:50; for prayer, 1 Tim 2:8), "your heads" (here, v. 28), "the voice" (Luke 11:27; Acts 2:14), or even "the heel" (John 13:18).

110 It is neither rare nor surprising that in Greek the expression "to lift the head" is used in the figurative sense and that it expresses recovered courage and awakened hope. On the parallels in Hebrew, see Str-B 2:255–56.

111 See, e.g., 10:9, 11; 21:8; Rom 13:12; Heb 10:25; Jas 5:8; 1 Pet 4:7; on the verb, see Detlev Dormeyer, "ἐγγίζω, etc.," EDNT 1 (1990) 370–71.

112 On ἀπολύτρωσις, see Léopold Sabourin, Rédemption sacrificielle, une enquête exégétique (Studia; Paris: Desclée de Brouwer, 1961); Karl Kertelge, "ἀπολύτρωσις," EDNT 1 (1990) 138–40. The technical term for the emancipation of a slave is ἀπελευϑέρωσις, but an inscription from Cos attests that ἀπολύτρωσις could be used for the sacred manumission of a slave; see BAGD, s.v.

113 See Ceslas Spicq, Theological Lexicon of the New Testament (trans. and ed. James D. Ernest; 3 vols.; Peabody, Mass.: Hendrickson, 1994) 2:423–29; BAGD, s.v.

means redemption, which he does not need to explain (Rom 3:24).[114] The New Testament texts use the term with various nuances:[115] (a) the total eschatological liberation brought about by Christ (here as well as in Rom 8:23; Eph 1:14; 4:30); (b) the status of the liberated person (Col 1:14; Eph 1:7); (c) by metonymy, the person of Christ the redeemer (1 Cor 1:30).[116]

■ **29-33** Luke rejoins Mark here and introduces[117] a parable.[118] In fact, the parable itself (v. 30) is followed immediately by a lesson drawn from it (v. 31). It is a genuine parable (*Gleichnis*), which convinces by the regularity and universality of the lived experience, rather than a parabolic story (*Parabel*), which surprises by its unusual character.[119] As is often the case, the parable refers to nature and to the farmer's experience. The fig tree occupies a by no means negligible place in the Gospel tradition, especially in Luke.[120] The evangelist, of whom one assumes that he comes from the city, simpli-

fies Mark's precise description ("as soon as the branches become tender," Mark 13:28) and replaces it with the general assertion "when they have already burst forth" (v. 30).[121] Then Luke again takes over Mark literally: "You know that the summer is near."[122] He adds, however, an adverb that is dear to his heart, "already" (ἤδη, "that the summer is already near"), which he had already used in the subordinate clause. In an apocalyptic context this double "already" (ἤδη) is significant. It does not serve a realized eschatology such as that advocated by Paul's adversaries (see 1 Cor 4:8); it is used rather in the service of a salvation history, which concentrates the presence of the signs in the end-time.[123] The parable thus confirms the speech's final exhortation: "Thus you also, when you see these things happening, know[124] that the kingdom of God is near" (v. 31).

---

114 See also the important use of the term in Hebrews. It appears only once, but in the heart of the epistle (Heb 9:15).

115 It is the distribution established by Zorell (*Lexicon*, s.v.), but in a different order.

116 If my hypothesis is accepted, by following his source rather than the Gospel of Mark since v. 10, Luke has omitted important sections on the divine shortening of the days (Mark 13:18-20) and the appearance of false Christs and prophets (Mark 13:21-23).

117 The introduction in v. 29a is purely redactional. It drops the verb "learn" and adds in a rather pedantic way "and all the trees."

118 On the Lukan use of παραβολή, see vol. 1 of this commentary, 307–8, on 8:4, 5a and 9-11.

119 Jülicher (*Gleichnisreden*, 2:3–11) puts the parable of the fig tree at the beginning of his interpretation of the parables. From Jesus' mouth it announced, in his opinion, the imminence of the end and of the parousia. Jeremias (*Parables*, 119–20) thinks that from Jesus' mouth it announced the imminence of the time of salvation and that it was in the writing of the Christians that it spoke of the apocalyptic catastrophe.

120 See 13:6-9; Mark 11:13-14, 20-21; 13:28; John 1:49-51. Luke is not aware of the strange episode of the cursed fig tree (Mark 11:13-14, 20-21). Kinman ("Eschatology") describes the various explanations that exegetes give for this absence. His own explanation is that Luke, full of hope for Israel, could not tolerate an episode that appears to leave no chance

for this nation. In a sermon on the other Lukan parable of the fig tree (13:6-9), Peter Chrysologus (fifth century) stated that vv. 30-31 of Luke 21 designate the nation of Israel, which, like a sterile fig tree, bears only leaves but nevertheless predicts the future, Christ (*Sermo* 106.4; CCSL 24A:660). An old German sermon goes even further in this direction: When the Jews are converted to the gospel, the last day will be at hand (*Sermo* 3, in Anton Emanuel Schönbach, ed., *Altdeutsche Predigten* [1886–91; reprinted Darmstadt: Wissenschaftliche Buchgesellschaft, 1964] 11).

121 On προβάλλω, see Spicq, *Lexicon*, 3:177–78. Following his tendency to generalize, Luke adds the words "and all the trees." This addition is unfortunate here, because the point of the parable depends on a peculiarity of the fig tree. Unlike, e.g., the olive tree, it loses its leaves in winter.

122 On this expression, see Perez Fernandez, "Aestas."

123 Codex Bezae (D = 05) has a somewhat different text here: ὅταν προβάλωσιν τὸν καρπὸν αὐτῶν, γινώσκεται ἤδη ὅτι ἐγγὺς τὸ θέρος ἐστίν ("When they have sent forth their fruit, one knows ['you know,' if one corrects to γινώσκετε] that the summer is already near"). Other, especially Latin, witnesses have a related text. See the apparatus of Nestle-Aland (27th ed.) here. In v. 31 one must read γινώσκετε with Nestle-Aland (27th ed.), even though various manuscripts have γινώσκεται. We should remember that γινώσκεται ("it is known,"

In v. 32 Luke quotes a saying of Jesus that undoubtedly underscores the imminence ("this generation will not pass away"). Since he keeps the "Amen" ($\dot{\alpha}\mu\dot{\eta}\nu$), which he often drops as a $\lambda\dot{\epsilon}\xi\iota\varsigma\ \beta\alpha\rho\beta\alpha\rho\iota\kappa\dot{\eta}$,[125] he also keeps and accommodates himself to this archaic sentence. The sentence has its parallel in Mark 9:1 (there the subject is explicitly the arrival of the kingdom of God, which comes in power).[126] What is most shocking for Luke, who is reading the tradition, is the mention of "this generation." If we do not want to admit that the evangelist, who has often resisted suggestions of imminence, contradicts himself, we must say that he probably interprets the expression "this generation" to mean "this age."[127] What remains for Luke is the interaction of history and eschatology, the believers' unceasing attention to the future, and the hope of a kingdom of God whose coming is assured.[128]

As if he wanted to confirm that Jesus is right and that even his prophetic words are firm, Luke quotes a sentence that is known in Matthew in another context (Matt 5:18): "Heaven and earth will pass away, but my words will not pass away" (v. 33). The sentence is ambitious in the extreme and must reflect more the conviction of the early Christians than Jesus' own feelings. It is a way of putting the new teaching, that of Jesus, if not above at least on the level of the old teaching, that of Moses, regarded as inspired, even eternal.[129]

From a form-critical point of view we must consider that the parable (vv. 29b-30) never existed without the symmetrically matching interpretation (v. 31)[130] and that they circulated together independently (somewhat like the comments about the weather in 12:54-56). As is often the case, an isolated statement of Jesus (v. 32 on "this generation") was added to this unit to facilitate or confirm the meaning given to the parable and its interpretation. At this stage, the bearers of the tradition hoped for the imminent arrival of the kingdom of God. Finally, there is the rule according to which sentences are connected by means of identical words: The verb "to pass away" ($\pi\alpha\rho\dot{\epsilon}\rho\chi\omega\mu\alpha\iota$) permitted here another sentence of Jesus (v. 33, on "my words," where this verb appears twice) to be connected to v. 32. That v. 33 deals with eschatology only indirectly scarcely matters. It is introduced not as a commentary on the parable; it serves rather on the level of the statement to authenticate the speaker and to sanction his message.

■ **34-36** These three verses belong to that moral teaching of Jesus for which there is no Synoptic parallel. It would be misleading simply to emphasize the ethical character of this material and without reservation to approximate it to the moral philosophy of an Epictetus. The counsel and the commandments that these phrases contain are designed neither to ensure calm happiness nor to promote the development of the soul. Rather, they are to

---

"one knows") was and still is pronounced the same way as $\gamma\iota\nu\dot{\omega}\sigma\kappa\epsilon\tau\epsilon$ ("you know" or "know").

124 The form $\gamma\iota\nu\dot{\omega}\sigma\kappa\epsilon\tau\epsilon$ can be either a present indicative ("you know") or a present imperative ("know"). Against Fitzmyer (2:1351), I choose the indicative.

125 On the Lukan sentences with $\dot{\alpha}\mu\dot{\eta}\nu$, see O'Neill ("Amen Sayings," 9), who concludes: "The Amen sayings bind up two things: God's plan of salvation in history, and the call to a Christian life within that setting. . . . The Amen sayings are a guide to ordinary Christians."

126 See Künzi, *Naherwartungslogion*.

127 It is improbable that the semantic possibilities of $\pi\dot{\alpha}\nu\tau\alpha$, "all things," permit Luke to limit its content to persecutions, which the disciples have already experienced (vv. 12-19).

128 Mattill (*Last Things*) concedes that certain Lukan texts presuppose a delay of the parousia but thinks that the evangelist maintains the idea of imminence. He writes (p. 6): "The Gospel of Luke is probably the most apocalyptic of all four Gospels."

Then (p. 9): "From first to last in his two volumes he gives expression to a passionate longing for the consummation." Finally (p. 10): "The new age will soon come with the return of Christ." Personally, I do not think Luke believes in the imminence of the parousia. On the opinion of Maddox (*Purpose*, 121–22), see n. 12 above.

129 Many manuscripts have the subjunctive aorist $\pi\alpha\rho\dot{\epsilon}\lambda\vartheta\omega\sigma\iota\nu$ instead of the indicative future $\pi\alpha\rho\epsilon\lambda\epsilon\dot{\upsilon}\sigma\upsilon\tau\alpha\iota$ (second occurrence); see the apparatus of Nestle-Aland (27th ed.). The subjunctive aorist in a main clause can have the meaning of an indicative future; see BDF §363.

130 Two details are not symmetrical: (a) the double $\dot{\eta}\delta\eta$ ("already") of the parable is missing from the interpretation; but (b) there, as if to compensate, "seeing" is mentioned ($\dot{\iota}\delta\eta\tau\epsilon$, "you see," v. 31).

prepare the hearers for a decisive future of which no one knows the time when it will take place. One can make up for this ignorance only by constant vigilance. It is true that the author of these sentences is concerned with moral anthropology and that he knows the vocabulary of human passions, but he uses this knowledge in the service of a speech that is strongly determined by the believing existence as well as by the expectation of the parousia.[131]

In order to demonstrate this eschatological concern, it is enough to point out the expression "that day" (v. 34), the risk of surprise ($αἰφνίδιος$, "sudden," translated "unexpectedly," v. 34; the word $παγίς$, "snare," v. 35), the universality of God's ultimate power ("upon everyone living . . . ," v. 35), the threatening character ("that you have the strength to escape," v. 36) of the last events ("these things that are going to happen", v. 36), and the reality of the last judgment ("to stand before the Son of Man," v. 36).

Two ethical verbs, however, dominate the construction: "take heed to yourselves" (v. 34) and "watch . . . at every moment" (v. 36). Such imperatives are not surprising to the readers of the Synoptic tradition, especially of the Gospel of Luke. One need only recall $προσέχετε$ . . . $ἑαυτοῖς$ in 12:1 and 17:3[132] and $ἀγρυπνεῖτε$ in Mark 13:33.[133] These verbs exhort not only an attitude worthy of God but also a lifestyle in keeping with the salvation history that will reach its end.

Verse 34 defines this ethical choice in terms that disavow neither the Jewish moralists nor the Greek philosophers of the period. The believers' hearts should not be weighed down, should not grow heavy;[134] that is, they should not be diverted from their spiritual purpose. The verb $βαρῶ$ suggests the troubles of a difficult digestion,[135] which is confirmed by the terms $κραιπάλη$ and $μέθη$. The first word is rare (the French word *crapule*, "debauchery, drunkenness" comes from it) and indicates first the vapors of the wine, then the excesses of the second term: the "drunkenness" that leads to violence, then "alcoholism."[136] The second, more common term indicates the drinking, then the state of one who has drunk too much, "intoxication."[137] These terms, which initially one must understand literally, unfold a broader meaning. They speak of a dissolute life of excess (such as Luke implies about the rich man of the parable; 16:19). People who devote themselves to such carousing are fixated on the material existence. Moreover, by neglecting what for the author of this passage constitutes the essence, they are assailed by the "earthly cares." For such people the Day of the Lord, "that day," will be a surprise ($ἐπιστῇ ἐφ' ὑμᾶς αἰφνίδιος$, "will come on you unexpectedly") and will catch them in a "snare" ($παγίς$, "net," "trap," "snare," anything that stops or holds).[138] This description of the risks incurred by the careless believers[139] is reminiscent, on the one hand, of the Lukan parable of the sower (8:14) and, on the other, of the early Christian catechetical warnings such as the apostle Paul in particular expresses (1 Cor 7:32-33; 1 Thess 5:2-11; Rom 13:13). The Pauline parenesis of 1 Thessalonians 5 works on two levels, the material

---

131 On these verses, see Petzke, *Sondergut*, 174–75. Mattill (*Last Things*, 105–6) deservedly calls attention to the parallels of these verses in Isa 24:17-20 LXX.

132 The expression appears already in the LXX (e.g., in the singular, Gen 24:6; Exod 10:28; 34:12). One finds it also in Plutarch *Sept. sap. conv.* 4 (*Mor.* 150B). In 12:1 and 20:46 the verb is followed by the preposition $ἀπό$, a construction that is not classical and appears to be a Semitism (or a Septuagintalism); here it is followed by a subordinate clause introduced by $μήποτε$ and the subjunctive aorist. See Zorell, *Lexicon*, s.v.; and BDF §370 (2).

133 The verb $ἀγρυπνῶ$ is rather rare in the New Testament (still, see Eph 6:18; Heb 13:17). The apostle Paul, who does not use it, resorts instead to the substantive $ἀγρυπνία$ ("sleeplessness," "vigilance," "insomnia," 2 Cor 6:5; 11:27).

134 See in this context the use of the verb $βαρῶ$ in Plato *Symp.* 203B.

135 The verb $βαρῶ$ occurs in the New Testament in Luke 9:32 par. (for sleep); 2 Cor 1:8 (for difficulties); 2 Cor 5:4 (for the thought of imminent death); 1 Tim 5:16 (for the widows supported by relatives instead of the church community).

136 If we accept that the author of these verses takes Isa 24:17-20 LXX as a starting point, we will not be surprised to read the verb $κραιπαλῶ$ ("to have a heavy head after being intoxicated") in v. 20 of the prophetic book.

137 Paul uses the plural form of $μέθη$ in Rom 13:13 and Gal 5:21.

138 On $παγίς$, which also appears in Rom 11:9 in a quotation from Ps 68 (69):23-24 according to the LXX, see Zorell, *Lexicon*, s.v.; BAGD, s.v.

139 The word order and the corresponding punctuation vary according to the manuscripts. Some witnesses attach the words $ὡς παγίς$ ("like a trap") to the following words and displace the $γάρ$ ("because") by

reality and the spiritual reality. Drunkenness, sleep, and night are at one and the same time the visible face and the figurative component of sin and the denial of God (1 Thess 5:7). On the other hand, fasting and vigilance, as concrete expressions, serve well as the armor of faith and love and as the helmet of the hope of salvation (1 Thess 5:8). In Pauline terms, the exhortation of Luke 21:34-36 encourages the believers not to remain in darkness but to become "children of the light" (1 Thess 5:4-5).

As is the case with many early Christian apocalyptic texts, our passage emphasizes more the irruption of the divine world into human history than the progression of the faithful toward the kingdom. The "day" "will come" ($\dot{\epsilon}\varphi\dot{\iota}\sigma\tau\eta\mu\iota$) or "will come in" ($\dot{\epsilon}\pi\epsilon\iota\sigma\dot{\epsilon}\rho\chi\sigma\mu\alpha\iota$), and all these events "will occur" ($\tau\dot{\alpha}\ \mu\dot{\epsilon}\lambda\lambda\sigma\nu\tau\alpha\ \gamma\dot{\iota}\nu\epsilon\sigma\vartheta\alpha\iota$).

The text also emphasizes the unforeseeable character of the end. Everything will happen unexpectedly. The guilty will be in danger of being caught in the trap just as it is said elsewhere that the day of the Son of Man or the Son of Man himself will come unexpectedly, like a thief (1 Thess 5:2; 2 Pet 3:10; Rev 3:3; see also Matt 24:43-44; Luke 12:39). This certainty repeats the one expressed in 12:35-40 (one's loins must be girded and lamps lit while waiting for the Master's return, the hour of which

no one knows)[140] and in 12:41-46 (the parable of the two servants).

Three expressions still deserve attention because of their unusual character. (a) Instead of saying simply "human beings," v. 35 mentions "everyone living on the face of the whole earth."[141] As if he could put himself in the place of God or of the gods, the author contemplates the entire earth and sees there the small human beings scattered everywhere. (b) In v. 36 vigilance[142] is accompanied by constant prayer: "make your requests[143] at every moment."[144] This requirement repeats that of 18:1 and is close to what the apostle Paul says to the Christians of Thessalonica: $\dot{\alpha}\delta\iota\alpha\lambda\epsilon\dot{\iota}\pi\tau\omega\varsigma\ \pi\rho\sigma\sigma\epsilon\dot{\nu}\chi\epsilon\sigma\vartheta\epsilon$ ("pray without ceasing," 1 Thess 5:17),[145] with the exception that Paul emphasizes the duration of prayer and Luke, its favorable occasions. (c) This vigilance and this prayer make it possible for the believers to avoid the final catastrophe, which a parallel text (Mark 14:38) calls $\pi\epsilon\iota\rho\alpha\sigma\mu\dot{\sigma}\varsigma$, the last "test" or "temptation." To do so one needs power, moral energy, and even physical resistance ($\kappa\alpha\tau\iota\sigma\chi\dot{\nu}\omega$, "to be strong," "to have power," "to be stronger than").[146] The verb $\dot{\epsilon}\kappa\varphi\epsilon\dot{\nu}\gamma\omega$ ("to flee," "to escape," "to manage to avoid") should make one think not of a cowardly flight but of a successful escape.[147] In

---

inserting it between $\pi\alpha\gamma\dot{\iota}\varsigma$ and $\dot{\epsilon}\pi\epsilon\iota\sigma\epsilon\lambda\lambda\epsilon\dot{\nu}\sigma\epsilon\tau\alpha\iota$ ("will come upon, happen"). The result reads: "that that day does not come on you unexpectedly, for it will happen like a trap. . . ."

140　The other two Synoptics share this opinion. See, e.g., Mark 13:33-37 (the parable of the doorkeeper); Matt 24:43-44 (the Son of Man like a thief); Matt 25:13 (the conclusion of the parable of the virgins).

141　The verb $\kappa\dot{\alpha}\vartheta\eta\mu\alpha\iota$ means initially "to sit," then "to assist, to be present," then finally, as here, "to inhabit" (see also Acts 2:2); for $\pi\rho\dot{\sigma}\sigma\omega\pi\sigma\nu$ as the "face" or the "surface" of the earth, see 12:56 and Acts 17:26.

142　In a related passage (Mark 13:33-37) Mark uses two almost synonymous verbs that Luke employs here in v. 36: $\gamma\rho\eta\gamma\sigma\rho\hat{\omega}$ ("to watch") and $\dot{\alpha}\gamma\rho\upsilon\pi\nu\hat{\omega}$ ("not to sleep," "to be awake"). See finally Matt 26:41 par. Mark 14:38: $\gamma\rho\eta\gamma\sigma\rho\epsilon\hat{\iota}\tau\epsilon\ \kappa\alpha\dot{\iota}\ \pi\rho\sigma\sigma\epsilon\dot{\nu}\chi\epsilon\sigma\vartheta\epsilon$, "watch and pray."

143　On $\delta\dot{\epsilon}\sigma\mu\alpha\iota$ ("to be deficient," "to ask," "to beseech") see vol. 1 of this commentary, 385, on 9:38 (Luke's most common word for prayer is $\pi\rho\sigma\sigma$-$\epsilon\dot{\nu}\chi\sigma\mu\alpha\iota$).

144　The sense of $\kappa\alpha\iota\rho\dot{\sigma}\varsigma$ can be trivialized, but it can also maintain its nuance of "opportune moment."

The anonymous Irish author from the eighth century (*Comm. Luc.* 21:36; CCSL 108C:95) thinks of "four times" (undoubtedly the four seasons) and of all the ages of life.

145　See also 1 Thess 1:2 and 2:13 as well as Rom 12:12 and 1 Pet 4:7.

146　Luke uses $\kappa\alpha\tau\iota\sigma\chi\dot{\nu}\omega$ also in 23:23. There is an interesting and well established variant reading: $\dot{\iota}\nu\alpha\ \kappa\alpha\tau\alpha\xi\iota\omega\vartheta\hat{\eta}\tau\epsilon$ ("so that you are considered worthy"). It is attested by Codex Alexandrinus (A = 02), Codex Ephraemi Rescriptus (C = 04), Codex Bezae (D = 05), Codex Koridethi (Θ = 038), the minuscule family f^{13}, a large number of Byzantine witnesses, the Latin and Syriac versions. In spite of the weight of these witnesses, this variant is probably secondary, because of its insistence on the moral worth of those who will be redeemed in the future.

147　On the use of $\dot{\epsilon}\kappa\varphi\dot{\nu}\gamma\omega$ in early Christian literature, see Zorell, *Lexicon*, s.v.; BAGD, s.v. In the literal sense: Acts 16:27; 19:16. In the figurative sense: Rom 2:3; 2 Cor 11:33; 1 Thess 5:3; Heb 2:3; 12:25.

an intriguing passage the epistle to the Hebrews (6:18) confers on Christians the title "those who have fled for refuge" in God, "the refugees" (οἱ καταφυγόντες). This title, obviously to be understood in a good sense, designates the believers as those who have known how to escape temptations, to withstand the tests, and finally to prepare to meet their Lord (here, v. 36: "to stand[148] before the Son of Man").[149] These remarks, taken as a whole, suggest that Luke is the author of these sentences and that they do not come from the special material.

■ **37-38** Luke closes with a summary that he himself has written and whose vocabulary is choice and precise.[150] Instead of the καθ᾽ ἡμέραν, "each day," of 19:47, Luke prefers here the plural with the accusative of duration: "the days" (τὰς ἡμέρας), to which he contrasts "the nights" (τὰς δὲ νύκτας). These temporal expressions thus embrace the entire life of Jesus in this last period.[151]

Luke confirms what he has said and repeated since Jesus' entrance into the holy city. The Master teaches there and dispenses his teaching in the temple.[152] Jesus' daily presence on the sacred grounds and his exit from the city in the evening are traditional data confirmed by three different witnesses: Mark 11:15, 19, 27 par. Matt 21:12, 17, 23; John 8:1-2; and here, vv. 37-38.[153] John's parallel is especially interesting. It is part of the non-Johannine pericope of the adulteress (John 7:53—8:11). It contains the same information as Luke but does not appear to have any literary dependence. All in all, these three testimonies doubtless constitute solid historical information about a practice of Jesus.

From a literary point of view, vv. 37-38 fulfill a double function. On the one hand, thanks to a summary statement, they make it possible for the evangelist to give a general significance to a specific teaching. On the other, they conclude the first part of Jesus' stay in Jerusalem and, along with 19:47-48, form a clear inclusion.

Stylistically, Luke drafted these two sentences carefully, doubtless under the inspiration of the LXX. For the sojourn at night he makes use of the verb αὐλίζομαι, which the Greeks use to speak of nights spent away from home, often in the open air (literally, "in a courtyard," αὐλή).[154] For the arrival of the people in the morning he uses the verb ὀρθρίζω (rather than the more ancient ὀρθρεύω, "to be early," "to rise early," "to arrive early in the morning"; ὄρθρος is "daybreak," "dawn").[155] In short, this is the essence[156] of what Luke wants to present: Jesus

---

148 Instead of the passive infinitive σταθῆναι (which here replaces the intransitive form στῆναι), Codex Bezae (D = 05), most Old Latin witnesses, and the Syriac versions, have στήσεσθε, the future form (in the second person plural) of the middle or intransitive. Thus, the future state of the elect is emphasized: "And you will present yourselves upright before the Son of Man."

149 The anonymous Irish author of the eighth century (*Comm. Luc.* 21:36; CCSL 108C:96) says: "He who can stand upright before God does not yield before the abyss of the one who is condemned to death."

150 Delebecque (*Évangile*, 133) remarks on the literary quality of these two verses.

151 According to Delebecque (*Évangile*, 133), although I do not know if he is right: "The plural contains an emotion that is underscored by the plural of 'night.' They are Jesus' last days, the days are limited."

152 See 19:45, 47-48; 20:1; 21:5-6. On the temple in Luke, see vol. 1 of this commentary, 100–101, on 2:25-28, and vol. 2 of this commentary on 18:10; Bovon, *Luke the Theologian*, 363 n. 23, 640.

153 Matthew 21:17 mentions Bethany and not the Mount of Olives for the night. In this context Matthew uses the same verb, αὐλίζομαι, with the primary meaning "to bivouac."

154 According to Delebecque (*Évangile*, 133), the verb αὐλίζομαι is "very classical" and "has two applications, one rural and one military, and . . . [in] the *Odyssey* and Herodotus refers either to flocks of birds who spend the night outside or to soldiers who bivouac." In my judgment, it is also easy to apply it to people who, quite simply, spend the night away from home (see Tob 4:14; 6:11; 9:5; Judg 19:6 [according to B = 03, Vaticanus]).

155 On this verb, see the suggestive note from Delebecque, *Évangile*, 133: "The only example of the verb ὀρθρίζω in the NT, but there are several examples in the Septuagint (especially in Cant 7:11-12, where the verbs ὀρθρίζω and αὐλίζομαι follow one another . . .)."

156 The family of minuscules *f*[13] adds here, between 21:38 and 22:1, the pericope of the adulteress that the majority of witnesses insert in John 7:53—8:11.

teaches in the temple and spends the night on the Mount of Olives; the people, eager "to hear him,"[157] go up to the temple at the break of day.[158]

History of Interpretation

When, as is his custom, Tertullian opposes Marcion's interpretation of Luke 21:5-38, he rejects the distinction between two gods and demonstrates the convergence between Jesus' teaching and the prophecies of the Old Testament (*Adv. Marc.* 4.39).[159] The first thrust, difficult to understand, concerns the expression "in my name" (v. 8). Tertullian's Jesus has the right to express himself thus, because it is God the creator who has called him that way and who gave Christ the name of Jesus.[160] Since he is foreign to God the creator, Marcion's Christ is subject to criticism. Is he not impudent when he who usurps his name warns against those who will come "in his name"? The second thrust relates to vv. 9-19. Tertullian has no trouble quoting the prophets of the Old Testament who anticipated the oracles of Jesus about the coming signs and future persecutions.[161] While he notes that the sufferings will precede the signs, he enriches his reflections about the persecutions with the experience of the martyrs of his day. That God fills his witnesses with wisdom when they have to speak is something Tertullian knows from Scripture (Balaam, Numbers 22–24, and Moses, Exod 4:10-12)[162] and from contemporary history: "Where indeed do we find wisdom that is greater and more impossible to contradict than in a simple and clear confession in the name of a martyr 'strong by means of God,' which is the translation of 'Israel'?" (4.39.7).[163] After he has mentioned the cosmic catastrophes (vv. 20-26) and the coming of the Son of Man (vv. 27-31),[164] in a third thrust Tertullian vigorously contradicts Marcion. It would be disastrous to attribute the catastrophes to the God of old and the promises to the God of salvation. Prophets and apostles agree that one God is behind both kinds of oracles. Tertullian writes: "And it will become obvious that your Christ makes no promises higher than those of my Son of Man" (4.39.12). Misfortunes will happen to the Gentiles, happiness to the elect. These disasters will come before the parousia; the age of joy will follow. Tertullian finds confirmation of his views in the parable of the fig tree (vv. 29-32) and concludes by referring to the warnings (vv. 32-35) and Luke's final summary (vv. 37-38).

Ambrose of Milan understands that there is a literal meaning to the fall of the temple, the persecutions, and the cosmic signs, but he prefers to look for the allegorical sense of the verses he explains (*Exp. Luc.* 10.6–45). In doing so he often substitutes an individual perspective for a universal scene, a present spiritual care for a cosmic and eschatological concern. The temple is destroyed by the enemy, but the temple can designate the synagogue, "which collapses in ruins when the church emerges" (10.6). The sanctuary can also refer to the temple that is in each human being. In the bishop's eyes, the apocalyp-

---

157 Hearing is the attitude of those who make a point of knowing the gospel message and adhering to it. See esp. 8:15 and Acts 28:28; Dupont, *Nouvelles études*, 473–77.

158 The anonymous eighth-century Irish author (*Comm. Luc.* 21, 14 [CCSL 108C:96]) interprets the morning spiritually. It is the moment to listen to the truth when the ignorance of the night is dissipated.

159 Apparently Marcion's Gospel did not include Luke 20:45-47; 21:1-4; or 21:21-24. Thus, following his method, Tertullian does not deal with these verses. For the fourth book of *Adversus Marcionem* one now has available the edition of Claudio Moreschini and the French translation as well as the notes from René Braun, *Tertullien, Contre Marcion* (5 vols.; SC 365, 368, 399, 456, 483; Paris: Cerf, 1990–2004), vol. 4.

160 On this name change, see Tertullian *Adv. Marc.* 3.15–16.

161 In this chap. 39 Tertullian quotes Zech 9:15-16; Isa 44:5; 50:4; Pss 9:19; 115:6 (116:15); Zech 6:14; Joel 3:3-4; Hab 3:9, 12; Dan 7:13-14; Ps 2:8; Hab 3:13.

162 These two examples are found in inverse order as references to the same text of Luke 21:14-15 in Cyprian *Fort.* 10. (Undoubtedly one should read Balaam and not Balaac in Braun's translation.)

163 This conviction that God puts words of wisdom on the lips of his martyrs becomes traditional. One finds it in the Venerable Bede *Expositio Actuum apostolorum* 6.10 (CCSL 121:33).

164 Tertullian (*Adv. Marc.* 4.39.11) rightly connects the coming of the Son of Man with the journey of the prince to claim his kingship in the parable of the pounds (19:12).

tic program is less interesting than Christ's invasion of the soul: "It is to me that Christ must come; it is for me that his advent must take place" (10.7). Ambrose notices that the questions addressed to Jesus vary from one Gospel to the next. "Luke decided that one would know enough about the end of the world if one were informed about the coming of the Lord" (10.9). Nevertheless, Ambrose feels able to refer to the atmosphere of the end of the world that reigns around him (he mentions the Huns, the Alani, the Taifales, the Samartians, and the Goths).

He prefers to speak of the war against covetousness and passions; to say "that the gospel is proclaimed so that this age will be destroyed!" (10.14); to describe the various kinds of Antichrists (10.15–21); to explain the "disagreements of the texts" (10.23) about pregnant women;[165] to speculate about the winter and the Sabbath;[166] to interpret the cosmic signs of v. 25 in a spiritual sense (end of religion) (10.36–37).[167] In short, the coming of the Son of Man will be realized in the entire universe as it is already realized in him who receives Christ into his heart (10.39).[168]

Cyril of Alexandria devotes a sermon to Jesus' apocalyptic address (*Serm. Luc.* 139).[169] In it he admires the divine knowledge of the one who predicts the transformation of a creation of which he was the architect. He points out that Jesus scorns the temple and the respect given to it and compares—so Cyril imagines—the human building with the heavenly abodes (he is undoubtedly thinking of John 14:2). The bishop of Alexandria notes the tension between the earthly starting point (the beauty of the temple) and the goal (the end of the world). He is of the opinion that it was the hearers who gave the conversation a different turn by mistaking Jesus' answer. They imagined that the prediction of the fall of the temple referred to the consummation of the universe. Thinking in modern categories, according to Cyril Jesus then agreed to move from history to eschatology (Cyril refuses to include the ruin of Jerusalem in the apocalyptic calendar).

According to the bishop of Alexandria, Jesus then invites people to be wary of false messiahs. They will be able only to imitate the first coming of Christ,[170] the one characterized by humility and incarnation.[171] Yet what the faithful now must await is the second coming of the Messiah, which will be characterized by the visible realities of glory and power. Then Christ, according to Cyril, offers signs of the end of the world.[172] When, after that,

---

165 A blessing or, as here in v. 23, a curse. The solution lies in distinguishing between good and bad pregnant women, the latter being weighted down—an allusion to v. 34?—"weary of virtues and heavy because of vices" (*Exp. Luc.* 10.23).

166 Does Ambrose refer suddenly to Matt 24:20 par. Mark 13:18, or does he read this sentence in his Gospel of Luke? (*Exp. Luc.* 10.33).

167 In §37 he writes: "For the heavenly sun becomes smaller or grander for me according to my faith." In the same paragraph he thinks that the church is to Christ as the moon is to the sun (and there are eclipses because of the vices of the flesh!).

168 Ambrose then speaks about the "powers of the heaven" (v. 26), the "clouds" (v. 27), and the "fig tree" (v. 29) (*Exp. Luc.* 10.39–45).

169 The text quoted at the beginning is limited to vv. 5-13 of Luke 21. The extant Greek fragments (Reuss, *Lukas-Kommentar*, 204–6, frgs. 317–24) correspond to two-thirds of the sermon. Verses 37-38 appear with vv. 1-6 of Luke 22 at the beginning of sermon 140. The bishop derives the following threefold teaching from Luke 21:5-38: (a) Jesus then proclaimed the reality beyond the shadow of the law; (b) the people liked to listen to him, because his word was powerful; (c) Jesus lodged on the Mount of Olives, far from the noise of the city, which is an example for those who want to live quietly (is he thinking of the monks?).

170 According to frg. 318 (Reuss, *Lukas-Kommentare*, 204), these false messiahs will come τὸ αὐτοῦ πρόσωπον ἑαυτοῖς περιπλάττοντες, "by taking his face for themselves." They will wear the mask of Christ (πρόσωπον also means mask). They will try to pass for him; they will ape him.

171 The Syriac text then mentions 1 Cor 2:8, but the quotation does not appear in frg. 318 (Reuss, *Lukas-Kommentare*, 205).

172 While the Syriac translation speaks of imminence, frg. 319 (Reuss, *Lukas-Kommentare*, 205) is satisfied to speak about a sign of the consummation of the world. This difference between the thought of the Greek-speaking theologian of Alexandria and that of his translator rooted in the Syriac tradition is significant.

the Master begins to speak again about the fall of Jerusalem and the persecution of Christians, he is "mixing his themes."[173] Faithful to Luke, Cyril is concerned to distinguish between what belongs to history and what concerns the end of time. He emphasizes that in v. 25 Jesus returns to the theme of eschatology.[174] When he comes as the Son of Man, he will improve everything, renewing creation and ushering in the resurrection of the dead.

With the exception of Ambrose, the Latin Christian authors of late antiquity and the Middle Ages do not feel obligated to give an allegorical interpretation to Jesus' apocalyptic speech.[175] They retain the literal meaning, remembering the historical fall of Jerusalem and sometimes referring to the testimony of Josephus.[176] They establish a relationship between certain predictions of Jesus and the catastrophes that fall on the world in their day without necessarily seeing in them signs of an imminent end. They emphasize the role of judge that the Son of Man will play and, when they are preachers,[177]

challenge their flocks to prepare themselves morally by scorning the world and looking forward to the coming redemption.[178]

Here, in essence, is the message of Gregory the Great in the two sermons he devoted to this chapter of Luke.[179] In *Homily* 1, for example, he exhorts his hearers to be ready and notes that the creation is aging just as the human body ages,[180] denounces the plagues of the world, expresses the opinion that present misfortunes[181] predict the coming catastrophes,[182] insists on the severity of the last judgment, invites them (with 1 John 2:15) to hate the world, and understands the exhortation "lift your heads" to mean "rejoice in your hearts" or "in your spirits," because, he says, in Scripture the "head" often designates the "spirit" (*mens*).[183]

In the centuries of late antiquity and the Middle Ages, v. 19 gained a great deal of attention: "By persevering you will gain your souls" (*in patientia vestra possidebitis animas vestras*).

---

173 *Τὸν λόγον κεράννυσι* (frg. 319; Reuss, *Lukas-Kommentare*, 205); the Syriac is translated as, "He mixes the accounts together in both parts of the narrative" (Payne Smith, *Cyril*, 2:652).

174 *εἶτα μεθίστησι πάλιν τοὺς λόγους ἐπὶ τὸν τῆς συντελείας καιρόν*, "then he again transfers his comments to the time of the consummation" (frg. 322; Reuss, *Lukas-Kommentare*, 206); see Payne Smith, *Cyril*, 2:653.

175 I thank in particular Eva Tobler, who was my assistant in Geneva and brought to my attention a list of Latin texts relating to Luke 21:5-38.

176 See the Venerable Bede *In Luc.* 6.102–8.

177 Luke 21:25-33 was the Gospel text for the second Sunday of Advent. When did this practice begin?

178 The commentary of the Venerable Bede (*In Luc.* 6.40–401) goes in this same direction. He states in particular that the temple of stones had to fall so that the spiritual temple, Christ, could be established (6.40–62). He then points to Simon the Magician as the first Antichrist (6.77–81). Finally, he sometimes quotes authors whom he venerates without naming them, such as here Jerome or Gregory the Great.

179 Under discussion are sermons 1 and 35 of *Homiliae in Evangelia* (*PL* 76:1077–81, 1259–65). For an English translation, see Gregory the Great, *Forty Gospel Homilies* (trans. David Hurst; Cistercian Studies Series 123; Kalamazoo, MI: Cistercian Publications, 1990) 15–20, 301–11. In sermon 35, delivered to the people and not to monks on the occasion of the

birthday of an anonymous saint, Gregory follows the biblical text closely. To be noted are (a) Gregory calls his hearers' attention to a textual variant (in v. 11 "storms" instead of "signs"); and (b) the signs, namely, the disasters, will come as punishments for the sins committed.

180 Sermon 3, an old German sermon published by Schönbach (*Altdeutsche Predigten*, 9), which, by the way, mentions Gregory the Great a bit later, takes over this comparison.

181 Gregory mentions the hurricane that two days earlier had uprooted fruit-bearing trees, destroyed houses, demolished churches, and killed people. While he thinks one still must wait for the heavenly signs, he notices that already in his day the air is getting worse and he remembers that the barbarian invasions were preceded by fire in the sky, signs of the human blood that was going to be shed.

182 The old German sermon 77, published by Schönbach (*Altdeutsche Predigten*, 183–84), understands the signs as messages preceding the eternal punishments inflicted on the sinners.

183 The same sermon (Schönbach, *Altdeutsche Predigten*, 184) understands v. 28 similarly: The believer must direct his spirit toward heaven so that at the end of days Christ will come to help him.

The word ὑπομονή ("perseverance," "endurance," "determination," "patience") was thus rendered by the Latin *patientia*. Many people regarded this Christian quality as the most valuable and decisive virtue. It certainly was the most indispensable in these times of uncertainty and upheavals. Augustine thinks that Jesus formulates in this v. 19 a promise by connecting patience to hope (*Enarr. Ps.* 118, *Serm.* 15.2).[184] Gregory the Great says that having this patience is to live in perfection and to rule over all the movements of the spirit.[185] Cassiodorus declares that by patience, the guardian of faith, one bears all the world's oppressions and is victorious over the devil (*Exp. Ps.* 32.20).[186]

Among the medieval commentaries[187] I single out for special attention Bonaventure's long, studious pages. For him vv. 5-6 confirm a truth of faith: the true homeland of believers is in heaven. The disciples are still attached to their perceptions and are mistaken for three reasons: they confound what is small and what is large and thus ignore Isa 66:1 ("heaven is my throne . . ."); they take the image for reality and thus ignore Acts 17:24-25 (God does not live in human dwellings); they think that what is transitory is eternal and thus ignore 1 Cor 7:31 (the image of this world is passing away). In reality, Jesus gives notice of the destruction of Jerusalem ("by Titus and Vespasian, forty-two years after the passion of the Lord,"

a delay that God offered Israel for repentance) (Bonaventure *Comm. Luc.* 7.11).[188]

Obedient to his passion for organization, Bonaventure follows by enumerating three ways of erring (vv. 8-11): heresies, wars, and epidemics.[189] For each category he finds numerous scriptural arguments. Referring to vv. 16-17, he makes a distinction between public and private persecutions (from outside and from within the family, if one follows Gregory the Great *Serm.* 1).[190] With many others, and quoting Gregory again, he is interested in the victorious patience mentioned in v. 19. Jerusalem surrounded (v. 20)—Bonaventure allegorizes here and understands the matter *spiritualiter*—is the *insurrectio perversorum contra ecclesiasticam pacem*, "the revolt of the wicked against the peace of the church" (*Comm. Luc.* 7.30).[191] This partial presentation of Bonaventure's exegesis should suffice. Let us simply note how the theologian defuses the time bomb contained in v. 32: "this generation" refers not to Jesus' contemporaries but to the race of mortals.

In his *Paraphrasis* on Luke 21 (444–48), Erasmus alternates between the first person of Jesus and the third person of the interpreter. Often he stays with the literal and historical meaning: Jerusalem was destroyed and Christians were persecuted. Sometimes he explains in his way what the apocalyptic speech had left in the shadows.

---

184 CCSL 40:1711. Elsewhere Augustine interprets this verse in the contexts of salvation, the resurrection, or patience. In *Tract. in Ioh.* 52.11 (CCSL 36:450), he justifies John 12:32 with Luke 21:19: Christ draws to himself the entire human being (the Latin has *omnia* and not *omnes*, "everything" and not "all"). In his opinion, Luke 21:18 also confirms this interpretation ("not a hair of your head will be lost"). See also *Civ.* 22.12–14 (CCSL 48:831–33). This last passage makes one think that Luke 21:18 was used on both sides of the controversies over the resurrection of the flesh. See finally *Pat.* 7–8 [6–7] (*PL* 40:613–14): by patience you will gain your souls (Luke 21:19), not dwellings. And the promise about the hair (Luke 21:18) will encourage the martyrs.

185 Gregory the Great *Moral. in Iob* 5.16.33 (CCSL 143:241); see also idem, *Serm.* 35.4, 9 (*PL* 76:1261–62, 1264–65).

186 CCSL 97:291–92. The anonymous Irish author of the eighth century (*Comm. Luc.* 21.19 [CCSL 108C:95]) comments thus on v. 19: "Because patience is the circle that contains all virtues."

187 See also Bruno de Segni, *Comm. Luc.* 2.47 (*PL* 165.440–43) and Thomas Aquinas *Catena aurea*, 273–81. In *Comm. Ioh.* 12.490–92 on John 16:4, Rupert of Deutz (CCCM 9:675) holds that Luke 21:18-19 supports the promise of the Johannine Christ (John 16:4a) and serves as comfort for times of oppression. Thomas of Chobham (*Summa de arte praedicandi* 4.716–36 [CCCM 82:111]) answers a *vulgaris questio* and, using v. 18, explains what will happen to hair at the time of the resurrection (there will be just enough for decency!).

188 Bernardini, 524.

189 Exegetical traditions were established: Simon the Magician is regarded as the first of the false envoys; the Jewish historian Josephus is cited in connection with the fall of Jerusalem; and Gregory the Great serves as an authority in matters of interpretation.

190 *PL* 76:1259.

191 Bernardini, 530.

The temple had been admired by Jews and foreigners. It was replaced by the temple of the soul, whose worship is gratuitous and whose ornaments are the virtues. He goes on to imagine that, because of the reaction of the disciples (v. 7), Jesus decided to keep them in a constant state of preparation by holding their attention with ambiguous comments. This is the first time we have come across this argument in the history of interpretation. It serves to explain the illogical sequence of the address (v. 8, e.g., does not answer the question of v. 7). Mixing several things, Jesus speaks at one and the same time of Christian persecutions for the sake of the gospel, the fall of Jerusalem, and the end of the world,[192] whose date remains unknown.[193] In the judgment of Erasmus, however, Jesus' teaching is, above all, moral, for what is essential is being worthy[194] of the kingdom.[195]

Because he preaches salvation by grace and by the faith that overcomes fear, Martin Luther reads the apocalyptic speech paradoxically. Since humanity is divided into believers and unbelievers, the latter ignore not only God but also the imminent judgment God prepares and the irrefutable signs he sends. The true Christians, freed from the fear of divine punishment, do not need these signs, but the signs nevertheless exist and Scripture gives notice of them or calls them to memory. How then are we to understand them, and how are we to read the apocalyptic address? Faithful to the lectionary that he shares with the Catholic tradition, the reformer preaches on Luke 21:25-33 on the second Sunday in Advent (December 10, 1531).[196]

The Christians, even the true ones, are still fragile (*simul justi et peccatores*). Explaining the apocalyptic passages to them is thus not useless.[197] A text from Scripture such as Luke 21 is still useful and, when understood well, does not exploit the fear it might engender. On the contrary, it serves—Luther does not stop repeating it—to comfort and encourage the faithful. Most of the signs mentioned[198] have already taken place and have lost their frightening quality.[199] As for those that are still to come, they cannot intimidate the true believers. The

---

192 Without appearing to depend on him, like Gregory the Great (see references above, n. 185), Erasmus (*Paraphrasis*, 445) establishes a parallel between the symptoms of a disease that affects the human body and the signs that precede the end of the world.

193 I have not come close to summarizing the entire paraphrase of Erasmus, who devotes an entire paragraph to each verse. Significantly, there is only one exception, and it concerns v. 32 ("this generation"). I suppose that, like many others, the humanist was embarrassed and thus did not paraphrase and comment on this statement of Jesus.

194 In v. 36 Erasmus reads not κατισχύσητε ("that you have the strength") but, with the Vulgate and the *textus receptus*, καταξιωθῆτε ("that you be judged worthy") See the note by Jane E. Phillips (*Desiderius Erasmus, Paraphrase on Luke* [Toronto: University of Toronto Press, 2003] 182 n. 28). The humanist's interest in personal ethics does not keep him from describing precisely the earthly catastrophes and the cosmic signs.

195 Another humanist (Hugo Grotius, *Annotationes in Novum Testamentum, editio nova*, vol. 1: *Quatuor Evangelia et explicationem Decalogi continens* [ed. Christian Ernst von Windheim; Leipzig: Ioannem Carolum Tetzschnerum, 1755] 891–99) is modern in the quality of his philological remarks but is still old in his lack of source criticism and a historical perception of the Lukan text. On the word παγίς in v. 35

he refers to Isa 24:17 (Hebrew and Greek). With regard to the command to watch (v. 36), he is of the opinion that Christ recommends two things (note the play on words he draws from the parallel in Matt 26:41 [it is necessary here to correct the reference]): προσοχὴν καὶ προσευχήν ("prudence and prayer"). As an exegete who is a believer, he thinks that these exhortations of Jesus are addressed to "us."

196 Martin Luther, "Predigt über Lucä 21,25-33, von der Zukunft Christi und denen vorgehenden Zeichen des Jüngsten Tages," in idem, *Sämtliche Schriften*, ed. Johann Georg Walch (Halle: Gebauer, 1941) 7:1356–85. See the critical edition and the introduction to this sermon in WA 34.2:459–82, 604–6. The sermon was published immediately in Wittenberg in 1532.

197 Luther divides the biblical passage into two parts. In his opinion, the text first lists the signs of the coming of the Lord and then exhorts people to understand them as a consolation.

198 One can understand the signs literally, but we are not forbidden—quite the contrary—to understand them also in a figurative sense; see Luther, "Predigt von der Zukunft Christi," 8 (cols. 1361–62).

199 Ibid., 5–6 (cols. 1360–61).

signs foretelling punishments are indeed for the infidels. The Christians can be happy that they will escape them. And if they appear, it means that the end of time is near, a new reason for the Christians to rejoice about them.[200] Furthermore, the biblical text itself invites us to "lift your heads, because your deliverance draws near" (v. 28).[201] For this reason Luther dares to say that his sermon consists of "sweet sugar" and is "a charming and joyful sermon."[202] Since the message of the apocalyptic address amounts to saying, "thy kingdom come," whoever longs for the end of time is faithful to the Lord's Prayer, the creed, and the Decalogue.[203] Because he mixes levels, Luther is astonished by the parable of the fig tree (vv. 29-30). How can this so optimistic image (vegetation, summer) fit with such sad events (disasters of creation, winter)? Christ introduces his own rhetoric and uses "a strange language and new grammar."[204] I do not understand why, but Luther forgets that the story of the fig tree, a metaphor for the arrival of the Son of Man, is not on the same level as the sudden appearance of the cosmic signs.[205]

John Calvin explains Jesus' apocalyptic address by arranging Matthew 24–25, Mark 13, and Luke 21 synoptically.[206] He has no problem in looking at the differences, and on occasion he even wonders if in a given passage it is Christ or the evangelist who is expressing himself.[207] He takes the literal and historical sense quite seriously.[208]

Christ takes leave of the temple before erecting a new one that is "far more splendid."[209] The disciples are far too human and simply admire appearances.[210] Therefore, Scripture does not stop correcting our meaning by calling our attention to the transitory appearance of the world. Concerning the external beauty of the Jerusalem temple, the reformer, following exegetical tradition, does not fail to return to Josephus.[211] Following theological tradition, he explains the fall of the temple as God's vengeance, a "terrible example,"[212] against the people who had rejected the Son. He is aware of the delay of the parousia[213] and thus exhorts people to have patience (the word flows unceasingly from his pen), and he accuses the disciples of having confused the fulfillment of the kingdom with its beginning.[214] Between the two, between the ascension and the day of redemption, there is the long human story: "a long and sad epic of woes," "a maze of evil."[215] The disciples' mistake was that they "confused the two, as though the temple could not be put down without the ruin of the whole earth."[216] In other words, the end of Jerusalem must be separated from the apocalyptic scenario. By doing this, Jesus opens, according to Calvin, a wide area for the proclamation of the gospel, for the life of the church, for its spiritual combat during the persecutions, for testing how durable it is in time, for its practice of charity.[217] Calvin finds in the expression

---

200 Luther's belief in the imminence of the end appears occasionally as, e.g., in the "Predigt von der Zukunft Christi," 23 (cols. 1372–73).

201 Ibid., 18–20 (cols. 1368–70).

202 Ibid., 3 (col. 1359, listed in error as page 1361).

203 Ibid., 25–28 (cols. 1374–77).

204 Ibid., 32–33 (cols. 1380–82).

205 There are several other sermons of Luther on Luke 21; I recall also the pages of the *Adventspostille* of 1522, WA 10.1.2:93–120; Mülhaupt, 3:353–71, 372–77; Luther's *Evangelien-Auslegung*, 981–1001.

206 Calvin, *Harmony*, 3:73–118.

207 Ibid., 3:86. Elsewhere (80) he notes, "Luke in slightly different words . . . ," then reassures himself: ". . . gives the same sense." Later (91) he expresses the opinion that Luke often moves sentences to integrate them in a new context.

208 Calvin (*Harmony*, 3:78) insists that Jesus' predictions about war were fulfilled during the Jewish revolt of 66–70. Then the Christians were not to be afraid (Matt 24:6 par. Luke 21:9).

209 Calvin, *Harmony*, 3:74.

210 Calvin (*Harmony*, 3:74) is not reluctant to say that the Catholics of his day regard the papacy in the same way.

211 Ibid., 3:74, 78. ("The reader may find the rest in Josephus").

212 Ibid., 3:74.

213 For Calvin (*Harmony*, 3:83) Jesus wants to say, "The end of the age will not come until I have long tested my church with hard and wearisome temptations." "Christ did not then appear."

214 Ibid., 3:76.

215 Ibid., 3:83, 77.

216 Ibid., 3:83.

217 Calvin (*Harmony*, 3:76) notes the risks the church must face during this long period, false doctrines and scandals, but he also mentions charity, then the proclamation of the gospel (3:82).

"mouth and wisdom" of Luke 21:15 a stylistic device: "I interpret the two terms as linked by hypallage."[218] Calvin further explains at length how, according to Matthew and Mark, Jesus quoted and understood the prophecy of Daniel 7 about the Son of Man, which involves him in difficult apocalyptic calculations.[219] It does not help to comfort oneself by referring to the parallel words of Luke, who mentions not the "abomination of desolation" but "Jerusalem surrounded" (v. 20), since "he [Luke] is not meaning to say the same thing but something different."[220] Still further, when he comments on the parable of the fig tree, Calvin gives it an unusual meaning: As the trees in winter appear to be dead but nevertheless are preparing for summer's blooming, so the church, which today appears to be "weak and feeble," is nevertheless "gathering strength." Calvin quotes here 2 Cor 4:16 (the outer man is decaying, but the inner man renews himself).[221] Finally, on v. 32 ("this generation will not pass away") Calvin comments that Christ, who emphasized duration, cannot suddenly contradict himself by mentioning imminence. Christ "simply teaches that in one generation events would establish all he had said. Within fifty years the city was wiped out. . . ."[222] This confidence in the truth of Christ's words (v. 33) goes hand in hand with ignorance about the time of the end. Calvin remarks: "Note that the uncertainty of the time of Christ's coming (which for the most part induces idleness in men) ought to be a stimulus to our attention and watchfulness."[223]

Conclusion

Even if somehow he blends various documents or if he rewrites Mark's often confused speech, Luke neverthe-less expects this chapter to be read as a whole, and he is convinced that it reflects the words of Jesus. What coherence then does Luke give to this page of his Gospel?

There the future dominates the present. It will bring an end to the current order of things (vv. 5-6). It is, however, not easy to prepare for the future. The greatest risk lies in succumbing to the idea that what is to come is imminent (vv. 7-8). Menacing calamities will happen, but they will not represent the end (vv. 9-11). From now on, and even before these events, Christians will undergo persecutions; yet though subjected to harsh blows by human power they will be protected by God (vv. 12-19). Then follows, as a war predicted by Jesus and noted by Luke as a fact, the capture of Jerusalem by foreigners whose empire will not be without an end (vv. 20-24). Their time will come to an end. Then, and only then, the cosmic signs predicted in v. 11 will appear. They will be the last things, because the coming of the Son of Man—in 12:40 and 17:30 Luke has already told his readers about it so that they are informed—will put an end to their appearance (vv. 25-28).

If the readers have not understood this message, a parable will help. The kingdom will be at hand (only) when these signs have unfolded, just as the summer is near when the leaves sprout and the fruit of the fig tree ripens (vv. 29-31). All of that relates to this generation and the life of each person (v. 32). It is Jesus who says this, and his word is infallible (v. 33). Thus, in this waiting for the end, one can only live vigilantly and with ethical dignity (vv. 34-36). This was, according to the evangelist, the teaching of Jesus in which the people were greatly interested (vv. 37-38).

218 Ibid., 3:81.
219 Ibid., 3:86. He specifies that "Christ chose [in the book of Daniel] only what suited his purpose" and he "tweaks their [the disciples'] ears . . . and bids them read the passage themselves with attention."
220 Ibid.
221 Ibid., 3:97.
222 Ibid.
223 Ibid., 3:103. John Maldonat (*In Luc.*, cols. 1177–78 [on Luke 21]) points out that he discussed the apocalyptic address in connection with Matthew 24 (cols. 489–508). He comments in detail on each word, often referring to the church fathers, and is of the opinion that Jesus answers the disciples' questions. In so doing, however, he alternates between the fall of Jerusalem and the parousia and separates them from one another.

The Satanic Plot (22:1-6)

Bibliography

Boyarin, Daniel, *Dying for God: Martyrdom and the Making of Christianity and Judaism* (Figurae; Stanford: Stanford University Press, 1999) 93–126.

Brown, Schuyler, *Apostasy and Perseverance in the Theology of Luke* (AnBib 36; Rome: Pontifical Biblical Institute, 1969) 82–97.

Colautti, Federico M., *Passover in the Works of Josephus* (JSJSup 75; Leiden: Brill, 2002) 174–84.

Dugmore, Clifford William, "A Note on the Quartodecimans," *StPatr* 4 (TU 79; Berlin: Akademie, 1961) 411–21.

Hein, Kenneth, "Judas Iscariot: Key to the Last-Supper Narratives?" *NTS* 17 (1970–71) 227–32.

Jonge, M. de, "Judas Iskarioth, de verrader I," *HeB* 18 (1959) 149–56, 178–81.

Idem, "Judas Iskarioth, de verrader II: Problemen rondom de Nieuw-Testamentische verhalen," *HeB* 19 (1960) 38–45.

Idem, "Judas Iskarioth, de verrader III: De mens Judas," *HeB* 19 (1960) 69–80.

Klauck, Hans-Josef, *Judas, ein Jünger des Herrn* (QD 111; Freiburg i. B.: Herder, 1987).

Kübler, Mirjam, *Judas Iskariot: Das abendländische Judasbild und seine antisemitische Instrumentalisierung im Nationalsozialismus* (Schriften der Hans Ehrenberg Gesellschaft 15; Waltrop: Spenner, 2007).

Meynet, *Guide*, 88–92.

Niemand, Christoph, "Zur Funktion der Judasgestalt in den Evangelien: Materialien und Anregungen zur Diskussion eines problematischen Befundes," *Protokolle zur Bibel* 1 (1992) 85–99.

Preisker, Herbert, "Der Verrat des Judas and das Abendmahl," *ZNW* 41 (1942) 151–55.

Schenke, Ludger, *Studien zur Passionsgeschichte des Markus: Tradition und Redaktion in Markus 14,1-42* (FB 4; Würzburg: Echter, 1971) 12–66, 119–50.

Schramm, *Markus-Stoff*, 182–84.

Schwarz, Günther, *Jesus und Judas: Aramaistische Untersuchungen zur Jesus–Judas–Überlieferung der Evangelien und der Apostelgeschichte* (BWANT 123; Stuttgart: Kohlhammer, 1988) esp. 176–82.

Segal, Judah Benzion, *The Hebrew Passover: From the Earliest Times to A.D. 70* (LOS 12; London: Oxford University Press, 1963).

Senior, Donald, *The Passion of Jesus in the Gospel of Luke* (Wilmington, Del.: Glazier, 1989) 40–48.

Turner, H. E. W., "The Chronological Framework of the Ministry," in D. E. Nineham et al., eds., *Historicity and Chronology in the New Testament* (TCSPCK 6; London: SPCK, 1965) 59–74, esp. 68–74.

Wambacq, Benjamin N., "Pesah-Massôt," *Bib* 62 (1981) 499–518.

Zerafa, P., "Passover and Unleavened Bread," *Ang* 41 (1964) 235–50.

1 The feast of the unleavened breads, called the Passover, drew near. 2/ And the chief priests as well as the scribes sought in what manner[a] they could get rid of him, because they feared the people. 3/ Then Satan entered Judas, the one called Iscariot, who was[b] one of the Twelve. 4/ And he went away and discussed with the chief priests and the officers in what manner he might deliver him to them. 5/ They were glad, and they came to an agreement with him about how much money they would give him.[c] 6/ As for him, he gave his word.[d] He sought an opportunity to deliver him to them without the knowledge of the crowd.[e]

a   Literally: "how"; see also v. 4.
b   Literally: "being."
c   Another possible translation: "they came to an agreement among themselves about how much money they would give him" (in this case $αὐτῷ$ goes only with $δοῦναι$).
d   Literally: "And he engaged himself," "and he promised."
e   Another possible translation: "apart from the crowd." The meaning of "without trouble" is unlikely.

Analysis

In the previous chapter (Luke 21) Luke let Jesus speak in the temple area. At the beginning of this chapter (Luke 22) he calls attention to other characters, to his opponents, and is interested in the sacred calendar, that is, he is more concerned about time than about space. Thus, vv. 1-6 take place as the Passover approaches, while vv. 7-13 will be placed at the beginning of the festival.[1]

Verses 1-6 describe an encounter, a conversation, and an agreement. After the evangelist has indicated that the festival is at hand, he mentions the plan of the leaders of the people.[2] Then Judas—precisely which Judas is explained—leaves the Master and goes away from the group of the Twelve to which he belongs. He goes to the other camp and comes to an agreement with his new partners. Luke twice indicates not only the plan but also "the manner" in which it will be carried out ($\tau\grave{o}$ $\pi\hat{\omega}\varsigma$, vv. 2, 4). The conversation results in an agreement that fills one party, Israel's leaders, with joy and commits the other party, Judas. Not all is settled, however. One certainly intends to lay hands on "him" (Jesus' name is not mentioned, either because of the evangelist's reserve or because of the conspirators' dissimulation) with the help of someone close to him who will be paid for his service, but they need to find the right occasion. For the moment, an exact date and hour cannot be determined, because they do not know where Jesus will go to celebrate the Passover.

Nevertheless, the story progresses. It moves from "they sought" ($\grave{\epsilon}\zeta\acute{\eta}\tau o\upsilon\nu$) of the chief priests and the scribes (v. 2) to "he sought" ($\grave{\epsilon}\zeta\acute{\eta}\tau\epsilon\iota$) of Judas (v. 6), from the general plan to the details of its execution. The driving force of the story here is neither divine providence nor human will. It comes, Luke says explicitly, from an intervention of Satan who enters Judas (v. 3). Verse 3 appears at a diabolical juncture between the purposes of the leaders (vv. 1-2) and the traitor's commitment (vv. 4-6).

Other symmetries appear. The nearness of the festival requires preparations whose sacred normality contrasts with the irregularity of the plot. Verses 7-13 are devoted to these preparations for the Passover. At the very beginning of the festival (v. 7), Jesus' initiative is expressed in a command given to the disciples. In order for it to be realized, it too requires an encounter, a conversation, and an agreement. Sent by the master, the two disciples, Peter and John, meet the owner of the house and make arrangements to reserve the room for the celebration. While Satan supports the plot against Jesus, it is Jesus who ensures the successful preparations of the feast (the repeated reference to the preparation in vv. 8-9 and 12-13 corresponds to the repeated negative requirement of vv. 2 and 6).

At the beginning of the passion narrative Luke again takes up and adapts the Gospel of Mark.[3] Verses 1-2 parallel Mark 14:1-2, and vv. 3-6 correspond to Mark 14:10-11.[4] In v. 1 Luke prefers the idea of approaching ($\H{\eta}\gamma\gamma\iota\zeta\epsilon\nu$, "drew near") to Mark's more precise "after two days." By elevating the style of the sentence, he chooses, perhaps unfortunately, to identify the festival of unleavened breads with the Passover. In v. 2 he elegantly simplifies the text, avoiding the arrest by cunning and the verb "to kill." As we have seen, he emphasizes the "how"[5] and makes use of a verb that often appears in Acts: "to do away with," "to make disappear" ($\grave{\alpha}\nu\alpha\iota\rho\hat{\omega}$).[6] Yet he discreetly makes use of the motif of cunning by evoking the fear of the people.

In v. 3 the evangelist intervenes vigorously in Mark's narrative. Following a tradition he shares with John

---

1   Meynet (*Guide*, 89–92) is of the opinion that Luke 22:1-53 forms a sequence whose beginning (vv. 1-7) and ending (vv. 47-53) parallel each other. He calls it "Jesus' testament." At the beginning Judas is the betrayer; at the end the apostles are. In my opinion, in vv. 49-51 the disciples are not guilty of betrayal; they simply behave badly. Moreover, vv. 52-53, which refer to the Jewish authorities, cannot be subsumed under the title "the apostles betray their master." What is true is that the plot is fomented in vv. 1-6 and carried out in vv. 47-53. Senior (*Passion*, 40, 42) observes that Luke tries here to include the readers in the mood of the passion by means of short and rapid notes.

2   Note the imperfect $\grave{\epsilon}\zeta\acute{\eta}\tau o\upsilon\nu$, which underscores the authorities' intention and insistence.

3   What is left of the *Gospel of Peter* is mainly a long fragment that begins with Jesus' appearance before Pilate. Thus, we do not know what this Gospel contained parallel to Luke 22:1-6.

4   Schramm (*Markus-Stoff*, 182–83) gives a good analysis of the traditional elements from Mark and of Luke's editorial elements.

5   See Schneider, 2:440.

6   On this verb, see Plummer, 490. Codex Bezae (D = 05) prefers the verb $\grave{\alpha}\pi\acute{o}\lambda\lambda\upsilon\mu\iota$ ("to lose").

133

(see John 13:2, 27; 6:70-71),[7] he is convinced that Judas acted under the influence of Satan.[8] He also changes the composition of the opposing group. While the general plan came from the chief priests and the scribes (v. 2), two of the three groups of the Sanhedrin,[9] its details are worked out by the chief priests and the "officers" (v. 4; Mark knows nothing about the presence of the στρατηγοί, who were not part of the Sanhedrin). In addition, two expressions from Mark 14:11 (ἀκούσαντες, "they, after they had heard," that is, "this news," and ἐπηγγείλαντο, "they promised") find no favor in Luke's eyes. The first omission is understandable (simply hearing makes Israel's leaders passive), but it is not clear why Luke does not like the idea of promising. Admittedly, the verb he puts in its place, συντίθημι, is perfectly appropriate. A Lukan peculiarity is also the verb ἐξομολογῶ, here with the meaning "to commit, to keep one's word." Like Matthew,[10] Luke prefers the substantive "opportunity, favorable occasion" (εὐκαιρία) rather than Mark's adverb "opportunely," "at the right moment" (εὐκαίρως). By adding "unbeknownst to the crowd" in a subordinate clause with an infinitive, Luke refers to the fear of the crowd, which he had omitted earlier when Mark mentioned it in 14:2.[11]

Mark's passion narrative inserts the anointing at Bethany (14:3-9) between the mention of the plan (14:1-2) and the fomenting of the plot (14:10-11). Luke reads this pericope in his copy of Mark but ignores it. One can offer three reasons for this omission: (a) The relationship between this story and another action told earlier in Luke 7:36-50 is too pronounced; the evangelist is worried about the monotony of what could appear to be repetitious. (b) Since for Luke the proclamation of the gospel does not begin until after Jesus' resurrection, one should not give an account here of Jesus' oracle contained in the Markan version of the anointing (14:9: "Truly I say to you, wherever the gospel will be proclaimed . . ."). (c) The old passion narrative that Mark himself uses had no anointing in Bethany. By omitting it here Luke returns to the traditional account.[12]

Commentary

■ **1-2** Originally, Passover and the feast of unleavened bread were two different annual celebrations. The first, a one-day festival celebrated during the first month of the year on the fourteenth of Nisan, was followed immediately by the second, which lasted one week.[13] The first

---

7   Neither Luke nor John calls the devil Satan by his own choice. That they do so here is due to the influence of a common tradition. See Schramm, *Markus-Stoff,* 182–83.

8   The exegetes and historians try to reconstruct the reasons why Judas betrayed his master. Was he disappointed that Jesus had not tried to establish the kingdom of God on earth concretely? Had he lost faith in his master? Had he succumbed to the temptation of the money? see Bock, 2:1704; Klauck, *Judas;* Raul Niemann, ed., *Judas, wer bist Du?* (Gütersloh: Mohn, 1991); Hyam Maccoby, *Judas Iscariot and the Myth of Jewish Evil* (London: Halban, 1992); William Klassen, *Judas: Betrayer or Friend of Jesus?* (Minneapolis: Fortress Press, 1996).

9   The third group was made up of Israel's "elders." Several copyists have sensed the tension between v. 2 and v. 4 with regard to the people hostile to Jesus. Some have solved it by adding the "scribes" to the list in v. 4, while others simply eliminated the reference to the "officers." Still others have specified that they were the "temple officers." See the apparatus of Nestle-Aland (27th ed.) on this text and Swanson, *Manuscripts,* 363.

10   This "minor agreement" between Matthew and Luke, as well as the choice of Ἰσκαριώτης (Mark has Ἰκαριώθ), does not justify erecting literary connections between the two evangelists. By contrast, Goulder (*New Paradigm,* 2:720–21) believes they are important and concludes: "The coincidence of hapax is due to Luke's reminiscence of Matthew." I do not believe that at all.

11   Thus, the people are not part of the plot; moreover, they still have a favorable attitude toward Jesus. They will turn against him only at the time of the decisive scene before Pilate (23:13-25) in what Robert C. Tannehill (*The Narrative Unity of Luke-Acts: A Literary Interpretation* [2 vols.; Philadelphia: Fortress Press, 1986, 1990] 1:164) calls a "drastic shift."

12   This is the view of Fitzmyer (2:1373) and, more cautiously, of Schneider (2:440).

13   The text I accept along with Nestle-Aland's 27th ed. had the imperfect ἤγγιζεν ("drew near"). The aorist ἤγγισεν ("had drawn near") is attested by Codex Bezae (D = 05), a Paris manuscript from the eighth century (L = 019), and all or some of the Old Latin witnesses (it).

featured the Passover meal and recalled the delivery from Pharaoh, especially the decisive night when Egypt's firstborn were massacred and Israel's firstborn were spared, literally, "passed over," by the destroying angel.[14] The second also celebrated the exodus, particularly the absence of bread baked with yeast during the crossing of the desert. Both of them celebrated, and still celebrate, God's saving initiative with his people. Since they were linked together, they were often mixed in a single designation.[15] Luke in any case confuses them.[16]

That the passion of Jesus took place at the Passover season rests on a solid historical basis.[17] Even Jewish tradition preserves the memory of it.[18] The oldest patristic witnesses about the Christian Easter festival confirm that Jesus died and was raised in spring at the time of the Jewish Passover. Some Christians, the famous Quartodecimans, even demanded that the Christian festival should coincide with the Jewish Passover and be celebrated on the fourteenth of Nisan. They were finally the losers in a dispute in the second century C.E. in which for the first time the churches of the West opposed the churches of the East.[19]

The Jewish Passover brought together the Jewish families that had come to Jerusalem as pilgrims. The lambs' throats were cut in the temple area, but the meals were eaten in the houses in the city. The atmosphere of religious euphoria and some of the Jewish traditions encouraged the spirits to celebrate not only the initial liberation but also the final delivery. It is understandable,

therefore, that the authorities would avoid exciting the crowd by intervening openly.

■ **3** Luke chooses the language of possession rather than that of demonic inspiration, thus giving more force to the event. Satan literally enters the person of Judas.[20] Thus, according to the evangelist, Jesus' destiny transcends the rivalry of human groups and becomes the stakes in a wager between the devil and God. At the end of the face-to-face confrontation in the desert, Satan had been forced to retreat (4:1-13), but he had not abandoned his plans.[21] Here he renews the attack in a roundabout way. Contrary to the opinion of Conzelmann, who speaks of "a period free from Satan,"[22] Satan remained vigilant throughout Jesus' ministry (see 22:28); there never was a time when he was absent.

Satan's intrusion does not appear to relieve Judas of his responsibility.[23] Luke is able to maintain human responsibility no matter who is the owner of the premises, God or Satan (see 16:13).

Since Judas is a common name and there are two Judases among the Twelve (6:16), a surname is not out of order. The Gospels know the Semitic form Ἰσκαριώθ (Luke 6:16; Mark 14:1) or the Hellenistic form Ἰσκαριώτης (v. 3 here and Matt 26:14). Various hypotheses have been proposed on this subject. Judas could be a man (שׁיא in Hebrew) from the village of Kerioth mentioned in Josh 15:25 and Jer 48:24 but in no contemporary New Testament document, or he could be a revolutionary who hid his dagger under his robe, one of

14 See Exod 12:1-20; 23:15; 34:18; Lev 23:5-8; Num 28:16-25; Deut 16:1-8, 16; 2 Chr 35:16-19; Joachim Jeremias, "πάσχα," *TDNT* 5 (1967) 896–904; Wambacq, "Pesah-Massôt"; Bock, 2:1702.
15 Josephus blends them in *Ant.* 3.10.5 §249; 14.2.1 §21; 17.9.3 §213; *Bell.* 2.1.3 §1. See Lagrange, 538.
16 Luke mentions the Passover in 2:41 and Acts 12:4. In Acts 12:3 and 20:6 he refers to this feast with the name the "days of unleavened bread." In connection with 22:1, Grotius (*Annotationes*, 899) speaks of a synecdoche, saying that Luke applied the name Passover, which lasted one day, to the entire feast, which was extended over eight days.
17 See Fitzmyer (2:1369), who also refers to patristic texts, and C. F. Evans (771–74), who compares the Synoptics with John and with the kerygmatic formulas, which know no date.
18 See the *baraita Sanhedrin* 43a (a *baraita* represents an

old tradition "outside" the Mishna but accepted into the Talmud), which declares that Jesus (Yeshu) was a magician who was hanged on the day before the Passover; Bovon, *Last Days*, 21.
19 See Odo Casel, "Art und Sinn der ältesten christlichen Osterfeier," *JLW* 14 (1934) 10–14.
20 See the excursus on the devil in vol. 1 of this commentary, 141–42.
21 Lagrange (539) writes with finesse: "Satan appears on stage again as one could expect it after 4:13. We have here an indication of how carefully Luke composes." See also Wiefel, 358–59.
22 Conzelmann, *Theology*, 28.
23 Lagrange (539) notes here: "Judas accepts it (only in Luke), which underscores his free choice and his culpability."

the Sicarii who violently resisted the Roman occupation (the term Sicarii comes from the Latin *sicarius*, which means "dagger." He would thus be the man with the dagger). Or it could be a post-Easter, Aramaic surname: the man of deceit. Luke does not explain this surname any more than do Mark and Matthew.[24] Following Mark, he emphasizes another aspect: Judas's membership in the group of the Twelve.[25] In 6:16 the evangelist mentions Judas's betrayal, and here, in 22:3, he calls attention to the apostleship. In Acts 1:15-17 both data are combined, the betrayal and the membership in the group of the Twelve.

■ **4-6** It is terrible: Judas goes away ($\dot{\alpha}\pi\epsilon\lambda\vartheta\acute{\omega}\nu$) from Jesus and the Twelve.[26] No psychological detail is provided; only the movement of his body speaks. This movement from one place to another means that Judas changes camps. Luke had predicted it in 6:16 ($\dot{o}\varsigma$ $\dot{\epsilon}\gamma\acute{\epsilon}\nu\epsilon\tau o$ $\pi\rho o\delta\acute{o}\tau\eta\varsigma$, "who became a traitor"). Is there some nuance in the redactional choice of the verb $\sigma\upsilon\lambda$-$\lambda\alpha\lambda\acute{\epsilon}\omega$? The simple $\lambda\alpha\lambda\acute{\epsilon}\omega$ means "to converse," "to discuss." Positively it can indicate divinely inspired speaking,[27] negatively useless babbling. The compound form, used four times by Luke (4:36; 9:30; 22:4; Acts 25:12), derives its connotation only from its linguistic context. Here it is the guilty intention that changes the sense from "to converse" to "to plot."

The title "chief officer" ($\sigma\tau\rho\alpha\tau\eta\gamma\acute{o}\varsigma$) is well chosen, since it refers to the temple police. The plural, on the other hand, is surprising[28] because, as Acts indicates (4:1; 5:24, 26), there was only one chief officer of the temple guard ($\dot{o}$ $\sigma\tau\rho\alpha\tau\eta\gamma\grave{o}\varsigma$ $\tau o\hat{\upsilon}$ $\dot{\iota}\epsilon\rho o\hat{\upsilon}$). Luke must be thinking here of the chiefs of the various units.[29]

One must make a distinction between "to deliver" and "to betray."[30] Even if Judas's act was an act of betrayal and if in 6:16 Iscarioth has been designated as a future betrayer, twice here (vv. 4 and 6) the verb $\pi\alpha\rho\alpha\delta\acute{\iota}\delta\omega\mu\iota$ is used, which means "to deliver," "to hand over," "to transmit" ($\pi\alpha\rho\acute{\alpha}\delta o\sigma\iota\varsigma$ is the "tradition"). "To betray" is $\pi\rho o\delta\acute{\iota}\delta\omega\mu\iota$ (originally, this verb means "to give in advance," "to distribute"). Luke is writing the story of the one who has delivered Jesus to death, but since the vocabulary of tradition goes back as far as the origins of Christianity and is rooted in Judaism, the evangelist feels that the verb $\pi\alpha\rho\alpha\delta\acute{\iota}\delta\omega\mu\iota$ is rich in its ambiguity. By relating the drama of the passion, he too "delivers" Jesus to future generations. Judas delivered him with a betrayal; Luke in his book, delivers him according to a tradition.

Remaining with the story: the response to the verb "to deliver" ($\pi\alpha\rho\alpha\delta\acute{\iota}\delta\omega\mu\iota$) is the verb "to give" ($\delta\acute{\iota}\delta\omega\mu\iota$). The agreement that results from the "conversation" ($\sigma\upsilon\lambda\lambda\alpha\lambda\acute{\epsilon}\omega$) consists of a trade: Judas "will deliver" Jesus to the authorities; the chiefs "will give" money to Iscarioth.[31] There is more than satisfaction in the air; there is joy ($\dot{\epsilon}\chi\acute{\alpha}\rho\eta\sigma\alpha\nu$, "they were glad").[32] On Judas's part there is also a commitment, a solemn agreement ($\dot{\epsilon}\xi o$-

---

24 See C. C. Torrey, "The Name 'Iscariot,'" *HTR* 36 (1943) 51–62; Bertil Gärtner, *Die rätselhaften Termini Nazoräer und Iskariot* (HSoed 4; Lund: Gleerup, 1957) 40–42; Fitzmyer, 1:620; John P. Meier, *A Marginal Jew: Rethinking the Historical Jesus*, vol. 3 (New York: Doubleday, 2001) 210–11, 258–59; vol. 1 of this commentary, 210, on 6:14-16.

25 On the Twelve, see vol. 1 of this commentary, 208–11, on 6:12-16; John P. Meier, "The Circle of the Twelve: Did It Exist during Jesus' Public Ministry?" *JBL* 116 (1997) 635–72; Ann Graham Brock, *Mary Magdalene, the First Apostle: The Struggle for Authority* (HTS 51; Cambridge, Mass.: Harvard Divinity School, 2003) 145–55.

26 See Senior (*Passion*, 47), who refers to Acts 1:25.

27 On Luke's use of $\lambda\alpha\lambda\acute{\epsilon}\omega$, see vol. 1 of this commentary 59, 92, 355–56, on 1:45; 2:17-18; and 9:10-11.

28 One sees something similar in Luke and the other evangelists in their use of "chief priests" in the plural. The fact is that there was only one chief

priest. It is probable, however, that the title took on a wider usage and that it gradually included the chief priests of earlier years and/or the group of the principal priests of Jerusalem.

29 On the term $\sigma\tau\rho\alpha\tau\eta\gamma\acute{o}\varsigma$ and its Hebrew and Aramaic equivalents with Jewish authors, see BAGD, s.v.; Plummer, 490–91; Lagrange, 539; Fitzmyer, 2:1375.

30 See Evans, 776. Tannehill (310) is wrong when he translates $\pi\alpha\rho\alpha\delta\acute{\iota}\delta\omega\mu\iota$ as "betray" (as does the NRSV), even if he mentions that the primary sense is "to deliver."

31 Erasmus (*Paraphrasis*, 449) summarizes well: *Illi polliciti sunt pecuniam, hic operam* ("These [the Jewish leaders] promised the money, that one [Judas] the work"). On the role of the money, see Fitzmyer, 2:1375; and François Bovon, *Studies in Early Christianity* (WUNT 161; Tübingen: Mohr Siebeck, 2003) 83.

32 Plummer (491) comments on the verb $\dot{\epsilon}\chi\acute{\alpha}\rho\eta\sigma\alpha\nu$

μολόγησεν), which will precede his act.[33] In the ancient church the *exhomologesis* becomes the public confession of sin, yet the verb originally indicates various speaking acts: "to confess," "to acknowledge," "to promise." Its appearance in the active form is unusual. Luke may be understanding it in the sense of "giving his formal agreement" (etymologically the simple ὁμολογέω means "to speak the same language," "to agree").[34]

The nature of the agreement gives the entire vocabulary of this episode a negative connotation, yet each term, taken alone, can have a good meaning. That is true even of the final εὐκαιρία (καιρός is the "time" or the "favorable moment," the "occasion"; see 4:13). Naturally, the prefix εὐ- is positive. We thus have here a "good occasion," an "opportunity." It is good, of course, only from the point of view of Jesus' adversaries or, on a second level, from the ultimate theological point of view (was it not opportune that Jesus died for his own people?).[35]

History of Interpretation

Tertullian is of the opinion that as the master of his destiny Jesus himself chose the date of his passion. By doing this he incorporated his fate into the typological movement of revelation. By dying at Passover, he declared that he died as the lamb whose blood brought salvation. Thus, the law looked forward to his passion, and he himself wanted to carry out this symbol. In addition, Tertullian points out that Jesus could have been handed over by one of his opponents. He was betrayed by one of his own in order to fulfill the scriptural text (Ps 40 [41]:10) that says that the psalmist's friend has lifted his heel against him (*Adv. Marc.* 4.40.1–2). With these two commentaries Tertullian continues his fight against Marcion, who set

the Old and New Testaments against one another and interpreted them as the plans of two different gods.

In his commentary on Luke (*Comm. Luc.* 22.3.1–7),[36] Bonaventure divides the Gospel into three parts: the incarnation, the proclamation, and the passion. The third part begins here. This beginning is itself subdivided into two sections: the events that immediately precede the passion, then those that are concurrent with it. Four episodes make up the antecedents: the wicked machinations of the betrayer in our verses (vv. 1-6), the institution of the altar sacrament (22:7-23), the instruction of the disciples (22:24-38), and the garden scene (22:39-46). To explain various verses Bonaventure uses the harmony of the Gospels and is inspired by the agreements between the Old and New Testaments. The "two days" of Matt 26:2 permit him to establish that the day of Judas's betrayal was Wednesday, the day of Mercury, the god of commerce! The Gospel of John enables him to note the parallel between the passing of the Passover and the passion of Jesus (John 13:1), or to say that it was not Judas who selected the date (John 7:30; 10:18). The medieval doctor Erasmus then observes the contradiction between the priests' holiness in the Scripture and their meanness in the story of the passion.[37] Like many other theologians both before and after him, he is uneasy about Satan's intrusion into the heart of Judas. He refuses to understand v. 3 as an indication of determinism: Satan could only encourage Judas to hand Jesus over. (He entered him *non per illapsum essentiae, sed per suggestionem nequitiae*, "not to cause the downfall of his being, but to suggest his perversity.")

Erasmus's *Paraphrasis* (448–49) poses various questions following the order of the verses. It presents the meaning and the etymology of the two festivals (v. 1) and

---

("they were glad") in a way that I would say is typically British: "It was wholly unexpected, and it simplified matters enormously."

33 The words καὶ ἐξομολόγησεν are missing from part of the manuscript tradition, in particular from the original text of Sinaiticus (א* = 01*), Codex Ephraem (C = 04), N (= 022), most Old Latin witnesses, the Sinaitic Syriac version (sy^s), as well as from Eusebius of Caesarea; see the apparatus of Nestle-Aland (27th ed.) here and Swanson, *Manuscripts*, 363.

34 See BAGD, s.v.; and Lampe, s.v.

35 Bonaventure (*Comm. Luc.* 22.3.7 [Bernardini, 542])

thinks that there are three kinds of delivering: the Father delivers his Son (Rom 8:32); the Son delivers himself (Eph 5:25); and, finally, the betrayer delivers Jesus (Matt 26:23).

36 Bernardini, 540–42.

37 Bock (2:1703) speaks here of irony: "In the midst of this holiday season that celebrates life, the leadership schemes to end the life of one who comes to bring life."

emphasizes the determining role that God plays even in the criminal actions of men (v. 2), then the action of Satan (v. 3), who tempts Jesus at the beginning of the Gospel "personally" (*per se*) and at the end "through his ministers and agents" (*per suos ministros et organa*). He notes artfully that the one who hands Jesus over is close to him in function but an enemy in his attitude.

Grotius is uneasy about the wills involved at the time of Judas's betrayal. He recognizes the role of Satan, who in this particular case confirms the general rule of Ephesians (the prince of the power of the air at work on the rebellious sons, Eph 2:2).[38] He also remembers that nothing happens without God's agreement. He hesitates, however, to attribute an external necessity to Judas that would whitewash him. He demonstrates that the passion narrative raises metaphysical problems whose difficulty is reflected in the commentator's sentence.

Conclusion

By omitting the pericope of the anointing in Bethany, Luke brought the murderous intention of vv. 1-2 closer to the successful plot of vv. 4-6, tying them together with a reference to Satan (v. 3). As a result, one of the two camps, that of the adversaries of Jesus, whose intentions thus far had not taken concrete form,[39] is ready for the impending duel. For his part, Jesus, surrounded by his own people and following an antithetic symmetry, makes his own preparations for the Passover (vv. 8-9, 11-13), his last Passover before the kingdom of God comes (v. 16).

---

38 Grotius, *Annotationes*, 899–900.
39 See 4:28-29; 6:11; 7:30; 11:53-54; 13:31; 19:47-48; 20:1, 19; Fitzmyer, 2:1374.

Bibliography

Arnott, Arthur G., "The First Day of the Unleavened. Mt 26:17, Mk 14:12, Lk 22:7," *BiTr* 35 (1984) 235–38.

Benoit, Pierre, "La date de la Cène," *RB* 65 (1958) 590–94; reprinted in idem, *Exégèse et théologie* (4 vols.; Paris: Cerf, 1961–83) 1:255–61. Review of Annie Jaubert, *La date de la Cène* (see below).

Str-B, 1:987–989; 4:41–76.

Black, Matthew, "The Arrest and Trial of Jesus and the Date of the Last Supper," in A. J. B. Higgins, ed., *New Testament Essays: Studies in Memory of Thomas Walter Manson, 1893–1958* (Manchester: Manchester University Press, 1959) 19–33.

Blinzler, Josef, "Qumran-Kalender and Passionschronologie," *ZNW* 49 (1958) 238–51.

Braun, Herbert, *Qumran und das Neue Testament* (2 vols.; Tübingen: Mohr Siebeck, 1966) 2:43–54.

Brown, Raymond E., "The Problem of Historicity in John," in idem, *New Testament Essays* (Milwaukee: Bruce, 1965) 143–67, esp.160–67.

Bultmann, *History*, 263–64.

Chenderlin, Fritz, "Distributed Observance of the Passover: A Preliminary Test of the Hypothesis," *Bib* 57 (1976) 1–24, esp. 13–14.

Dalman, Gustaf, *Jesus-Jeshua: Studies in the Gospels* (trans. Paul P. Levertoff; 1929; reprinted New York: Ktav, 1971) 106–20.

Delorme, Jean, "Jésus a-t-il pris la dernière cène le mardi soir?" *AmiCl* 67 (1957) 218–23, 229–34.

Edanad, Antony, "Institution of the Eucharist according to the Synoptic Gospels," *BiBh* 4 (1978) 322–32.

Foster, John, "'Go and Make Ready' (Luke xxii.8, John xiv.2)," *ExpT* 63 (1951–52) 193.

Green, Joel B., "Preparation for Passover (Luke 22:7-13): A Question of Redactional Technique," *NovT* 29 (1987) 305–19.

Haenchen, *Weg Jesu*, 474–75.

Jacob, René, *Les péricopes de l'entrée à Jérusalem et de la préparation de la cène: Contribution à l'étude du problème synoptique* (Église nouvelle—Église ancienne 3: Études bibliques 2; Paris: Beauchesne, 1973).

Jankowski, Gerhard, "Passah und Passion: Die Einleitung der Passiongeschichte bei Lukas," *TeKo* 13 (1982) 40–60.

Jaubert, Annie, "Le calendrier des Jubilés et de la secte de Qumrân: Ses origines bibliques," *VT* 3 (1953) 250–64.

Eadem, "Le calendrier des Jubilés et les jours liturgiques de la semaine," *VT* 7 (1957) 35–61.

Eadem, *La date de la Cène: Calendrier biblique et liturgie chrétienne* (EtB; Paris: Gabalda, 1957).

Eadem, "La date de la dernière Cène," *RHR* 146 (1954) 140–73.

Jeremias, *Sprache*, 286.

Le Déaut, Roger, *La nuit pascale: Essai sur la signification de la Pâque juive à partir du Targum d'Exode XII 42* (AnBib 22; Rome: Institut biblique pontifical, 1963).

Leenhardt, Franz, *Le sacrement de la Sainte Cène* (Série théologique de l'"Actualité Protestante"; Neuchâtel: Delachaux & Niestlé, 1948).

MacMillan, H., "The Man Bearing a Pitcher of Water: Luke xxii. 10," *ExpT* 3 (1891–92) 58–60.

Robbins, Vernon K., "Last Meal: Preparation, Betrayal, and Absence," in Werner H. Kelber, ed., *The Passion in Mark: Studies on Mark 14–16* (Philadelphia: Fortress Press, 1976) 21–40.

Ruckstuhl, Eugen, *Chronology of the Last Days of Jesus: A Critical Study* (trans. Victor J. Drapela; New York: Desclee, 1965).

Sabbe, Maurits, "The Footwashing in Jn 13 and Its Relation to the Synoptic Gospels," *EThL* 58 (1982) 279–308.

Schenke, *Studien*, 152–98.

Schramm, *Markus-Stoff*, 183.

Schürmann, Heinz, "Der Abendmahlsbericht Lk 22,7-38 als Gottesdienstordnung, Gemeindeordnung, Lebensordnung," in idem, *Ursprung und Gestalt: Erörterungen und Besinnungen zum Neuen Testament* (KBANT; Düsseldorf: Patmos, 1970) 108–50.

Idem, "Der Dienst des Petrus and Johannes," *TThZ* 60 (1951) 99–101; reprinted in idem, *Ursprung*, 274–76.

Idem, *Quellenkritische Untersuchung des lukanischen Abendmahlsberichtes Lk 22, 7-38, Part 1: Der Paschamahlbericht: Lk 22, (7-14.)15-18* (NTAbh 19.5; Münster: Aschendorff, 1953).

Senior, *Passion*, 49–53.

Smith, Dennis E., and Hal Taussig, *Many Tables: The Eucharist in the New Testament and Liturgy Today* (Philadelphia: Trinity Press International, 1990).

Sterling, Greg, "*Mors Philosophi:* The Death of Jesus in Luke," *HTR* 94 (2001) 383–402.

Taylor, Vincent, *Behind the Third Gospel: A Study of the Proto-Luke Hypothesis* (Oxford: Clarendon, 1926) 34–35.

Wanke, Joachim, *Beobachtungen zum Eucharistieverständnis des Lukas auf Grund der lukanischen Mahlberichte* (EThS 8; Leipzig: St. Benno, 1973) 61–62.

Winter, P. "Luke 22, 7-18," *VoxTh* 26 (1955–56) 88–91.

Zerwick, Maximilian, "Praehistoria textus sacri — cui bona?" *VD* 36 (1958) 154–60.

7 The day of unleavened breads arrived, when one had to sacrifice the Passover lamb. 8/ And he sent Peter and John, saying to them, "Go and prepare the Passover for us so that we may eat it." 9/ But they said to him, "Where do you want us to prepare it?" 10/ He said to them, "Behold, when you enter the city, you will meet a man carrying an earthenware jar of water. Go with him to the house he will enter. 11/ Then you will say to the owner of the house, 'The Master has us say to you,[a] "Where is the room where I am to eat Passover with my disciples?"' 12/ That man will then show you a large, prepared upper room. Make your preparations there." 13/ They went away[b] and found it as he had told them, and they prepared the Passover. 14/ And when the hour had come, he sat at table, and the apostles with him.

a   Literally: "says to you."
b   Literally: "Thus having gone."

While adverse forces dominated the previous scene (22:1-6), here (vv. 7-14) it is favorable elements, Jesus and his own people, who are in the center of the picture. Although he is never mentioned by name, in this moment Jesus is the Master (ὁ διδάσκαλος) of knowledge and power. What he knows and organizes refers to the Jewish festival of Passover.

Synchronic Analysis

The obligation mentioned in v. 7 (ἔδει, "one had to") is discharged in v. 14 ("he sat at table, and the apostles with him"). Between the two there is the joint effort of the Master and his disciples: Jesus directs (v. 8), then—following Augustine's formula—he gives what he has commanded (vv. 10-12). The disciples, who initially question themselves and him (v. 9), then carry out his command without stumbling (v. 13). Graphically the result is:

V. 7	The duty to be celebrated is not yet ready to be carried out.
V. 8	Jesus wants to fulfill this duty with the help of his disciples.
V. 9	Peter and John question Jesus.
Vv. 10-12	Jesus gives the answer.
V. 13	The disciples carry out the Master's command.
V. 14	The duty to be celebrated is ready to be carried out.

Thus, there are three levels: first, that of religion, Scripture, or God, who provided for the liturgical celebration of Passover (vv. 7, 14). Then there is the level of Jesus, who enables the exercise of religion (vv. 8, 10-12). Finally, there is the level of the community, which, with its questioning, hearing, and obedience, puts the Master's plan into practice and thus measures up to God's expectation (vv. 9, 13).[1]

---

1   Three things lead me to include v. 14 with this literary unit: (a) the thematic relationship between v. 14 and v. 7; (b) the new departure made by v. 15; and (c) the fact that Luke follows Mark to v. 14 and then his own special material from v. 15. Meynet (*Guide*, 95) also gives attention to the structure of this literary unit. He puts v. 10, the sign of recognition, in the middle, notes that vv. 9 and 11 contain similar questions, and underscores the importance of the verb "to prepare," which vv. 8-9 and 12-13 mention symmetrically. Bock (2:1709) divides the text as follows: v. 7, the beginning situation; vv. 8-12, instructions relating to the meal: (a) sending; (b) question; (c) instruction; v. 13, carrying out the instructions. In addition, he believes that the episode corresponds to a historical memory that is, moreover, emotionally charged. See also Talbert, *Reading*, 206.

Our presentation of this structure remains incomplete as long as we do not underscore the density of the vocabulary. The previous pericope mentioned the nearness of the festival, while this pericope emphasizes its arrival, mentioning it four times (vv. 7-8, 11, and 13). Furthermore, as with all special occasions, the Passover requires preparations: the text also uses the verb "to prepare" four times. The last two references in vv. 12-13 correspond to the first two in vv. 8-9. Taken together, they frame the account and determine its thematic.

Diachronic Analysis

There is no doubt that Luke continues to follow the Gospel of Mark here.[2] The statistics prove[3] that he is depending on his model, and if on occasion he distances himself from Mark, it is to define something more precisely or to improve the style.[4]

In v. 7 Luke does not bother to calculate the days (he speaks of "the day," where Mark speaks of the "first day"; Mark 14:12), yet he makes a point of creating expectation by mentioning the duty to be fulfilled. He says "one had to sacrifice the Passover lamb," while Mark is content to say that they "sacrificed the Passover lamb" (14:12). In v. 8 Luke does not hesitate to change his source in order to establish Jesus as the leader: It is the Master who takes the initiative in sending the disciples into the city, while in Mark 14:12 it is the disciples who first express their concern. Without explaining why, Luke makes a point of indicating which two disciples are sent as scouts. He gives the names of Peter and John, whose common

activity Acts confirms (Acts 3:1, 11; 4:13, 19; 8:14). While respecting his source, Luke does not forget the disciples' question (v. 9),[5] which, moreover, is essential to the story, since it serves as a springboard. Jesus' answer, the length and precision of which are intentional (vv. 10-12), corresponds to that formulated in the Gospel of Mark down to the details of syntax and vocabulary.[6] At the most one can note that Luke, who likes the preposition σύν, prefers the verb συναντάω over ἀπαντάω when speaking of the providential encounter.[7] Since sometimes he can be inattentive, he also neglects the etymology of the word οἰκοδεσπότης ("owner," literally, "master of [the] house") and adds a genitive, "of the house," that is superfluous in Greek (v. 11). Since the adjective "ready" (ἕτοιμον) is not attested in all the manuscripts of Mark (14:15), it may be that Luke did not find it in his source. It is also possible that he regarded it as unnecessary. "As he had told them" (v. 13) is an improvement over Mark's "as he told them" (14:16). In v. 14 two redactional touches deserve notice: instead of "evening" (Mark 14:17), Luke speaks of the "hour," a term that appears again in v. 53. In addition, as he sometimes does (see 6:13; 9:10), he designates the Twelve as already being the "apostles" (v. 14).[8]

One wonders whether the changes the evangelist makes in the Gospel of Mark, his source for this passage, result simply from his editorial will or whether they are also dictated by a parallel version. The question arises, because it must be conceded that Luke alternates in drawing from various sources. The following pericopes come from his special material and require some sort

---

2   See Schramm, *Markus-Stoff*, 183; Schneider, 2:441; Wiefel, 360; Goulder (*New Paradigm*, 2:720) writes: "At least it is agreed by almost everyone that Luke begins by following Mark."

3   Taylor (*Third Gospel*, 34–35) estimates that Luke here takes over some 65.2 percent of Mark's vocabulary. Schürmann (*Paschamahlbericht*, 75) is even more exact. He calculates that Luke shares 50 of the 106 words in Mark 14:12-18a, chooses equivalent words for 20 others, and differs from the Second Gospel on only 36 occasions. Thus, for him Luke 22:7-14 is an editorial repetition of Mark.

4   Fitzmyer (2:1376–77) gives a good survey of the connections between Luke and his sources.

5   Well noted by Lagrange, 541.

6   Luke generally respects the traditional form of

Jesus' sayings. That is not the case in Matthew's parallel (Matt 26:18).

7   He uses this verb in 9:37. Luke's love for verbs formed with the preposition σύν ("with") appears clearly in 15:6. See vol. 2 of this commentary on 15:5-6. Some manuscripts choose a third possibility, ὑπαντάω, while Codex Bezae (D = 05) maintains Mark's verb ἀπαντάω; see the apparatus of Nestle-Aland (27th ed.) here.

8   The manuscripts go various ways here. Most have "the apostles"; some, under the influence of Matt 26:20 and Mark 14:17, have "the Twelve"; some others, combining the two variants, write "the twelve apostles"; finally, still others, faithful to Mark 14:12 and Matt 26:17-19, retain "his disciples." See the apparatus of Nestle-Aland (27th ed.).

of introduction. Thus, we cannot exclude the possibility that Luke is inspired by a second source of information. One cannot prove it, however,[9] because the differences from the Second Gospel all have Lukan features: The pair "Peter and John" and the title "apostles" are characteristic of Luke's two-volume work.

All are struck by the connection between the miraculous discovery of the young ass in the account of the entry into Jerusalem (Mark 11:1-11) and the no less miraculous discovery of the room Jesus and his disciples need for the Passover meal (Mark 14:12-17).[10] Mark, whom Luke follows in both cases (19:28-38 and here, vv. 7-14), is not afraid to relate the two episodes using the same narrative structure and the same vocabulary.[11] It is obvious that, in order to record one of the episodes, Mark is inspired by the other. Yet the doublet character, which this redactional choice confers on the two accounts, did not disturb Luke, who does not hesitate to integrate both of them into his work. Why he does so has been debated. Some think that the prophet Samuel's prescience in announcing to Saul a number of imminent signs that do not fail to occur (beginning with the mules that were found), in 1 Samuel 9–10, must have inspired the early Christians. Others think that such cases of prescience are part of popular folklore.

Ludger Schenke is probably alone in his conclusion, based on his meticulous investigation, according to which the miraculous discovery of the upper room was, from a form-critical perspective, originally an isolated legend with no relationship to the Last Supper and whose *Sitz im Leben* was a room in Jerusalem venerated by the early Christians.[12] Rudolf Bultmann, followed by Gerhard Schneider, thinks, rather, that it is about a legendary development that from its origin was used to introduce the account of Jesus' last meal with his disciples.[13]

An unavoidable final observation: Although inexplicable, there is an occasional convergence in the passion narrative between the Gospels of Luke and John. It appears here in the use of the word "hour." This term that is characteristic of the Fourth Gospel appears there, as in Luke 22:14, at the beginning of the passion. John speaks of the "hour" in which the Son must leave this world to return to his Father, and he does so without relating it to the Passover feast (John 13:1).

Commentary

■ **7** As v. 1 showed, Luke, in following Mark, is interested in Jewish customs, but he does not describe them accurately.[14] The slaughter of the Passover lamb, which strictly speaking was not a sacrifice, took place not on the first day of unleavened bread but on the previous evening, the day before Passover, that is, the afternoon before the evening Passover meal.[15]

---

9 I share Schneider's question as well as his hesitation (2:442).

10 See Jacob, *Péricopes*, 15–27. He thinks that Mark has two sources at his disposal in describing the preparation for the Lord's Supper (see also the appendix, Église nouvelle—Église ancienne 3: Études bibliques 2, 127) and that Luke is not content simply to copy Mark; at every moment he uses Mark by putting his personal imprint on him. Jacob (80–81) specifies that, in addition to Mark, Luke knows the second source Mark uses, 1 Samuel 9–10. For the entry into Jerusalem it establishes a typology between King Saul, who has not yet been rejected, and Jesus. For the preparation of the Passover meal it brings Samuel in his priestly function closer to Jesus.

11 Schürmann's portrayal (*Paschamahlbericht*, 121) of the parallels between the two accounts is convincing.

12 Schenke, *Studien*, 152–98, esp. 181–94. According to

Schenke, it is the Markan redaction that emphasized the Passover feast and attached the episode to Jesus' passion.

13 Bultmann, *History*, 263–64; Schneider, 2:441–42.

14 Two text-critical remarks need to be made about v. 7: (a) the so-called Western text (Codex Bezae [D = 05], many Old Latin manuscripts, the Sinaitic and Curetonian Syriac versions) speak about the "day of Passover" and not about the "day of unleavened bread." Yet this reading does not eliminate the chronological difficulty; (b) the best manuscripts are uncertain about the presence of the proposition ἐν ("in") before the dative relative pronoun ᾗ. The preposition is not necessary. The dative designating a moment is classical. One can imagine a popular use of the preposition that the purists have eliminated—or the opposite!

15 See Lagrange (540), however, who suggests: "But since Luke, like Josephus, had followed the practice of calling the feast of unleavened bread the Pass-

Various authors have described the preparations for the festival,[16] no one with more precision than Gustaf Dalman.[17] Originally, not only was the throat of the Passover lamb cut in the temple area, but it was eaten there as well. In time, there was not enough room in the temple, and the entire city became the necessary sacred space. Thus, Jesus, who spent the nights on the Mount of Olives (21:37), had to find a place within the city walls to celebrate the Passover. The inhabitants of Jerusalem were prepared to make space available to the pilgrims. They were even expected to perform this service free of charge.

In fact, people living in Jerusalem were not to regard themselves as owners. The holy city belonged to God and then, vicariously, to the entire nation. Thus, to make a room available was to acknowledge these rights of God and the people. This religious tradition explains the owner's willingness. The guests expressed their gratitude by giving the hide of the slaughtered lamb to the owner of the place. In Luke's view, the miracle lies not in this willingness but in the supernatural knowledge about what may have been the last free room!

The Samaritans had maintained the original requirement and ate the Passover standing and in haste. The Jews had adapted the command. They were to share the meal, well situated and lying down in order to show that they were no longer slaves but free. They had adopted the shape of the Greek and Roman *triclinium*. In the case of Jesus and his disciples, the latter occupied the two long sides (five people on each side), and two of them were located next to Jesus at the end of the table. The couches, formed from large cushions, could be arranged on the ground or raised on a wooden frame.

The lamb's throat was to be cut "between two evenings." The afternoon, after the daily sacrifice had been offered, was the time for slaughtering the lambs. The book of *Jubilees* (49:10-12) and the historian Josephus (*Bell.* 6.9.3 §523) imply that this slaughter was held between 2:30 and 5:00 o'clock.[18] Neither Luke nor the other evangelists pay attention to this action. They speak about the Passover that one eats but never explicitly refer to the lamb or its slaughter. Is this so that they can better allude to the new meal, the Lord's Supper?

■ **8** Luke names the two whom Jesus sends. Does he choose Peter and John, the future spokespersons of the Jerusalem church, to stress how important their task is or, instead, to indicate that the apostolic authority is exercised in the most modest tasks? It is difficult to say.[19] It is, however, not difficult to notice that, while Luke takes over from Mark the verb ἀποστέλλω ("to send"), he is the only one who ends the episode by qualifying Jesus' companions in this solemn moment as ἀπόστολοι, the "ones sent," the "apostles" (v. 14).

Luke likes the vocabulary of "preparation." In a sense, the kingdom of God is still in preparation. To be sure, Christians, following the example of the old Simeon, have already seen in the person of Jesus the salvation that God has "prepared" before the world (2:31). Yet one continues to wait, as chap. 21 has eloquently pointed out. Moreover, here it is a question of indirect preparations for the kingdom, since the subject is the preparation of the Jewish Passover, which will serve as a framework

---

over, he could name the day of unleavened bread the day of preparation for the Passover, all the more so that leavened bread was to disappear on that day." For the biblical references to the Passover celebration, see above, n. 14 on 22:1-6.

16 Fitzmyer (2:1377–82) gives clear answers to the following three questions: (1) Was Jesus' last supper a Passover meal? Answer: That is the claim of the Synoptic Gospels, especially of Luke. (2) What about the Johannine tradition that places the Last Supper on the evening before Passover? Answer: All the Gospels have theological reasons for choosing the date they appoint. (3) Do the Synoptic Gospels and the Gospel of John make use of different calendars (the hypothesis of Annie Jaubert, *Date*)? Fitzmyer's answer here is no. In the same sense Bock (2:1710)

says, "The use of popular idiom is more likely than a calendrical difference."

17 Dalman, *Jesus-Jeshua*, 106–20; see also C. F. Evans, 778. One finds the most useful information in the tractate *Pesaḥim* (5) of the Mishnah.

18 See also Exod 12:6; Lev 23:5; Num 9:3, 5; Deut 16:6.

19 Plummer (492) made his choice: "The treason of Judas might lead Jesus to select two of his most trusted Apostles." Senior (*Passion*, 52) is of the opinion that, by carrying out their mission, Peter and John serve as a model of what the disciples later will have to be. Jesus himself will give the example at the time of the Last Supper. Tannehill (311) writes soberly: "The apostles, who will be the church's first leaders, must act like table servants."

for the Last Supper of Jesus. This will become the first example of a new Christian rite, which itself will look forward to the banquet of the kingdom.

■ **9** In spite of, or rather because of, Jesus' initiative, the disciples' question as Mark formulates it remains legitimate. They say in effect: Good, but where will we find the place?[20]

■ **10-12** Jesus' answer constitutes the heart of the episode. It speaks only of human realities, but it does so with a precision that prepares for the miraculous encounter, the providential synchronism.[21] In those days it was often said that, except for his own flask, a man does not carry water; he leaves this work to women. The text in fact does not care about the gender of the person mentioned. In Luke, as in Mark, it is a "human being" (ἄνθρωπος) and not a "man" (ἀνήρ) whom the envoys will find. A κεράμιον is obviously a clay vase, probably baked in a kiln, although water stays fresh better in porous earthenware jars hardened in the sun. In its construction the expression "water jar" (κεράμιον ὕδατος) is reminiscent of "alabastar jar filled with ointment" (ἀλάβαστρον μύρου) in 7:37.[22] The first word designates the container; the second, with the genitive, specifies the contents.

Once the disciples have met the water carrier, they will follow him until he reaches his destination.[23] Yet they do not speak to him,[24] for only the master of the house will be able to say if he has a free room and if he is prepared to put it at the disposal of the embarrassed group.[25] In this moment the account wavers. Jesus, who is not a beggar, becomes a person of power. The title "the teacher," "the Master" (ὁ διδάσκαλος) suggests as much. Moreover, he has not waited to this point to speak with authority. From the first exchange his words are full of authority. Note the present tense: "The Master has us say to you." The question to be addressed to the owner of the house will not be a hesitant request. The host has no choice but to yield to the demands of the other master.[26] Jesus requires a "room" (κατάλυμα), a term we have met and explained in the infancy narrative (2:7, where I translated it as "roadhouse" ["a place where one can stop and unharness a mount or draught animal . . . a provisional place to spend the night"]).[27] Verse 12 specifies that this room will be an "upper chamber" (ἀνάγαιον) located upstairs in the house. It will have good dimensions (μέγα, "large") and will be "prepared" (ἐστρωμένον). This last participle implies that the room in question will be ready and the wide couches they need will be there. The verb στρώννυμι, of which we have here the perfect passive participle, actually means "to spread out." The only other place where Luke uses the verb, Acts 9:34, contains the expression στρῶσον σεαυτῷ (for which one must imply a direct object τὴν κλίνην, "the couch"), which means "spread out [the couch] for yourself," with the meaning "make your bed." What is meant is that the carpets were unrolled or spread out to welcome the guests. To be sure, some translators have

---

20 Some manuscripts add σοι ("for you"), while others, doubtless influenced by Matt 26:17, have σοι φαγεῖν τὸ πάσχα ("for you to eat the Passover"). See the apparatus in Nestle-Aland (27th ed.) on this text.

21 With Schneider (2:442), I opt for Jesus' prescience and the prophetic, supernatural power he had over the servant and then over the owner of the house. Several exegetes think that, even if Jesus directs the operation, he does not do so in a miraculous way: He could have made arrangements in advance with the master of the house. See the possibilities suggested by Plummer, 492–93; C. F. Evans, 777; and Tannehill, 311.

22 See already Plummer (492), who suggests that the water was certainly not for the purpose of baking unleavened bread, but to permit the participants to wash their hands before the meal. And why could it not have been used for drinking?

23 Without these variants changing the sense, the manuscripts differ with regard to the subordinate relative clause. According to some it is introduced by εἰς ἥν ("in which"); according to others, by οὗ ("where"), οὗ ἐάν or οὗ ἄν ("wherever").

24 "You will say" (ἐρεῖτε) is an indicative future. It functions as an imperative. The negation οὐ in the future is sometimes used as a negative imperative (as in the Decalogue). The future without negation is more rare; see Plummer, 493.

25 Plummer (492) observes correctly: "Evidently the ἄνθρωπος is not the head of the household, but a servant or slave." The master of the house is mentioned in the following verse: ὁ οἰκοδεσπότης.

26 Senior (*Passion*, 52) observes rightly: "The whole thrust of the scene underscores Jesus' command of the situation."

27 See vol. 1 of this commentary, 86, on 2:7b.

preferred the meaning "to furnish." It seems, however, that the verb στρώννυμι suggests soft objects such as fabrics, blankets, mattresses, carpets rather than hard objects such as furniture.[28]

■ **13** Such is the demonstration of Jesus' divine knowledge and power that the emissaries find everything just as their master had announced. Probably[29] the episode never existed independently,[30] but it nevertheless had a special function—to show that Jesus is master of his destiny and that he is concerned to respect the religion of his people even when other people, the Jewish leaders, are so concerned about fomenting their plot that they forget the principles of their religion.[31]

■ **14** This serves as a transitional verse, since it not only shows the success of Jesus' prophetic power,[32] but also leads into the scene of the Last Supper. The title "apostles," which Luke substitutes for the "Twelve" of Mark 14:17, gives the scene an ecclesiastical solemnity. This meal will have not only a liturgical value but also a soteriological scope. The term ὥρα ("hour"), which refers to the Jewish Passover, also enriches itself as the first Lord's Supper.[33]

History of Interpretation

Ambrose of Milan is interested here not in the time but in the place (*Exp. Luc.* 10.46–48). That this space is elevated reflects the virtue of the one who offers hospitality.

Jesus knows this in advance, a sign of his divine majesty. As a sign of his humility he chooses a poor, anonymous, simple father of a family (Ambrose does not make a distinction between two persons). In addition, the water in the amphora raises the admiration of the preacher, who praises its kindnesses. In the literal sense, the water gives life to nature; in the figurative sense, it regenerates the universe. This emphatic praise is accompanied by an unexpected cry from the heart: "May it please God to allow me to carry the jug of water . . . !" (10.47).[34]

In his homilies on Luke, Cyril of Alexandria explains the meaning of the Jewish Passover and the etymology of the word Φασέκ, which means "passage" (διάβασις) (*Serm. Luc.* 141).[35] As a Christian theologian, he adds that the disciples of Christ also need "to pass." They need to pass from the love of the flesh (φιλοσαρκία) to asceticism (ἐκράτεια). He then explains that Jesus' strategy was to keep Judas from being informed too early and from betraying too quickly. He follows by attributing symbolic value to the upper room, to the water taken there, as well as to the vase that contains it.

The Venerable Bede criticizes the ambitious people who desire beautiful residences and, inspired by the deficiency that has plagued the disciples, he recalls that the Son of Man had no place where he could lay his head (*In Luc.* 6.476–530). The water in the jar makes it possible for the theologian to suggest moving from the figura-

28 BAGD, s.v.; and Moulton-Milligan, *Vocabulary*, s.v., explain well the verb στρωννύω or στρώννυμι and offer judiciously selected examples. In the account of the entry into Jerusalem it is, according to Mark 11:8 and Matt 21:8, "clothing" that the crowd spreads like a red carpet under the feet of Jesus perched on his young ass. My interpretation appears to be confirmed by the spiritual commentary of Theophylactus cited below in n. 39.

29 With Bultmann, *History*, 263–64; and Schneider, 2:441–42.

30 Contra Schenke, *Studien*, 181–94.

31 Tannehill (311) and Sabourin (339) are of the opinion that the episode emphasizes another aspect, the secrecy. They are following an old interpretation according to which Jesus acted secretly so that Judas would not know the place of the Passover gathering too soon. Talbert (*Reading*, 206) is right when he says that the fulfillment of Jesus' prophecy (v. 13) will inspire confidence in the readers.

32 Jean-Noël Aletti (*L'art de raconter Jésus Christ: L'écriture narrative de l'Évangile de Luc* [Paris: Seuil, 1989] 157) makes a general observation. In the passion narrative, the Gospels of Matthew and Mark refer to the psalms of supplication, while Luke presents a Jesus who is much calmer, whose attitude returns to the psalms of trust.

33 Senior (*Passion*, 53) suggests a different contrast that is also valid: "But that 'hour' belonged not only to the power of darkness; it was also the moment in which the death of the Son of Man would being life to the world."

34 This praise of water entered the Milanese liturgy and, in a slightly different form, the so-called Mozarabic liturgy. See the note from Gabriel Tissot in Ambrose's *Évangile de Luc*, vol. 2 (SC 52bis) 172 n. 1.

35 See Payne Smith, *Cyril*, 2:659–66; frgs. 326–28 in Reuss, *Lukas-Kommentare*, 207–8.

tive to the real, from the Passover to the redemption in Christ, to baptism and to the Lord's Supper.[36]

Bonaventure does not avoid the question of the date, and he rejects the solution of the "Greeks," who follow the Johannine chronology of the passion (*Comm. Luc.* 22.3.8–20).[37] With precision Ulrich Luz has presented this difference of opinion between West and East, which, on the one side, led to the Western host from unleavened bread such as Jesus shared at the time of an actual Passover meal and, on the other side, to bread with leaven, which the Orthodox do not hesitate to use in their liturgy (since Jesus celebrated his Last Supper before the Passover meal).[38] Bonaventure tries to extricate himself from the difficulty by distinguishing between the two meanings given the word "Passover," claiming that the Last Supper reflects the image and the crucifixion reflects the reality and the truth. Is he finally able to extricate himself from the dilemma? (*Comm. Luc.* 22.3.10). I am not sure that he is.

Three other aspects merit attention. The medieval doctor underscores the role assigned to Peter and John. One of them, Peter, knows; the other, John, loves. The first calls to faith, the second to love. By faith the believers chew the word, by love they take it into their body. This double portrait, composed from various passages of the Gospels, reminds each person that it is necessary to prepare seriously before approaching the table of the Lord (*Comm. Luc.* 22.3.11). Further, Bonaventure reflects on the spiritual meaning of the city and, within

the city, of the house with its upper room. The city, with its solid foundations, its beauty, and the amenities it offers, is none other than the church, while the upper room represents the soul, which rises toward contemplation (22.3.15). Finally, concerning v. 14, which brings together Jesus and his apostles, the medieval theologian alludes to the emotional sphere. In this verse (22.3.20), he writes, "is shown Christ's wonderful intimacy with his disciples."[39]

Erasmus (*Paraphrasis,* 449–50) remains bound here to the medieval exegesis and the symbolic meaning it gave to the Passover and the elements mentioned. He insists on the ecclesiological scope of everything that happens and does not avoid a conclusion hostile to the Jews: "You note the beginning of the church and the end of the synagogue."[40]

As many both before and after him, Calvin is concerned to harmonize the Synoptic and Johannine chronologies.[41] It is also important to him to present a Jesus who is rigorously faithful to the regulations of the Law of Moses. In addition, he gives his commentary a personal and theological note: the disciples needed this testimony of the absolute power of Christ before facing the suffering and death of their master. "It is worth our while today to overcome the scandal of the cross to know that as the very hour of death was upon Him, the glory of Godhead appeared in Christ along with the weakness of the flesh."[42] Like Ambrose, Calvin does not hesitate to bring the message up to date and to say of the disciples who

---

36 I quote lines 503–4: *Aqua quippe lavacrum gratiae, amphora mensuram perfectam significat,* which I understand as follows: "Water means the purification grace offers, the amphora means its perfect measurement." This is an allusion to the statement in the Sermon on the Plain relating to measure (Luke 6:38) that Ambrose quotes in his homily (*Exp. Luc.* 10.47).

37 Bernardini, 542–45; trans. Karris, *St. Bonaventure's Commentary,* 2034–44.

38 Luz, *Matthew 21–28,* 354–57.

39 Theophylactus (*Enarr. Luc.* 22.7–13 [*PG* 123:1064–66]) summarizes the episode, gives the meaning of Passover (following many others), calculates the date, and comes to the conclusion that Jesus sent Peter and John on Thursday morning. Like Bonaventure, he meditates on the symbolic role each apostle plays. Finally, based on the verb στρών-

νυμι ("spreading out"), he works out a spiritual meaning, saying that everything that is distorted must be straightened out. Euthymius Zigabenus (*Comm. Luc.* 7–14 [*PG* 129.1076–77]) makes more basic remarks. The difference in meaning between ἐγγίζω ("to approach," v. 1) and ἔρχομαι ("to come," v. 7), which he renders with πλησιάζω ("to bring near," "to draw nearer," the second verb indicating a stronger imminence) makes it possible for him to take up again the question of the chronology and to explain the two days of Matt 26:2 par. Mark 14:1 and the first day of Matt 26:17 par. Mark 14:12.

40 The quotation appears in the last lines of col. 449. See Phillips, *Paraphrase,* 186–89.

41 Calvin, *Harmony,* 3:126–29.

42 Ibid., 3:127.

had carried out Jesus' command: "We must keep to this rule, if we wish our faith to be approved, to be satisfied by this command alone, to go at God's bidding, to expect the success He promises, and not to be over anxious."[43]

In the commentary of Luz, readers will find examples of the modern exegesis of this Synoptic passage, particularly in its Matthean formulation, which is much less miraculous than the versions of Mark and Luke.[44]

---

43 Ibid., 3:128.
44 Luz, *Matthew 21–28*, 352–53.

Bibliography

Aland, Kurt, "Die Bedeutung des 𝔓⁷⁵ für den Text des Neuen Testaments: Ein Beitrag zur Frage der 'Western Non-Interpolations,'" in idem, *Studien zur Überlieferung des Neuen Testaments and seines Textes* (AzNTT 2; Berlin: de Gruyter, 1967) 155–72, esp. 160, 164–65.

Amphoux, Christian-Bernard, "Le dernier repas de Jésus. Lc 22,15-20 par," *EThR* 56 (1981) 449–54.

Backhaus, Knut, "Hat Jesus vom Gottesbund gesprochen?" *ThGl* 86 (1996) 343–56.

Bacon, B. W., "The Lukan Tradition of the Lord's Supper," *HTR* 5 (1912) 322–48.

Bahr, Gordon J., "The Seder of Passover and the Eucharistic Words," *NovT* 12 (1970) 181–202.

Bammel, Ernst, "𝔓⁶⁴⁽⁶⁷⁾ and the Last Supper," *JTS* 24 (1973) 189–90.

Bastiaens, Jean C., *Interpretaties van Jesaja 53. Een intertextueel onderzoek naar de lijdende Knecht in Jes 53 (MT/LXX) en in Lk 22:14-38, Hand 3:12-26, Hand 4:23-31 en Hand 8:26-40* (TFT.S 22; Tilburg: Tilburg University Press, 1993).

Bate, H. N., "The 'Shorter Text' of St Luke xxii 15-20," *JTS* 28 (1927) 362–68.

Beck, Norman A., "The Last Supper as an Efficacious Symbolic Act," *JBL* 89 (1970) 192–98.

Benoit, Pierre, "The Accounts of the Institution and What They Imply," in Jean Delorme et al., eds., *The Eucharist in the New Testament: A Symposium* (trans. E. M. Stewart; London: Chapman, 1964) 71–101.

Idem, "Luc xxii, 19b-20," *JTS* 49 (1948) 145–47.

Idem, "Le récit de la cène dans Lc xxii, 15-20: Etude de critique textuelle et littéraire," *RB* 48 (1939) 357–93; reprinted in idem, *Exégèse et théologie* (4 vols.; Paris: Cerf, 1961–83) 1:163–209.

Billings, Bradly S., "The Disputed Words in the Lukan Institution Narrative (Luke 22:19b-20): A Sociological Answer to a Textual Problem," *JBL* 125 (2006) 507–26.

Idem, *Do This in Remembrance of Me: The Disputed Words in the Lukan Institution (Luke 22.19b-20). An Historico-Exegetical, Theological and Sociological Analysis* (Library of New Testament Studies 314; London: T. & T. Clark, 2006).

Black, M., "The 'Fulfilment' in the Kingdom of God," *ExpT* 57 (1945–46) 25–26.

Blakiston, H. E. D., "The Lucan Account of the Institution of the Lord's Supper," *JTS* 4 (1902–3) 548–55.

Bonsirven, Joseph, "Hoc est corpus meum: Recherches sur l'original araméen," *Bib* 29 (1948) 205–19.

Bornkamm, *Jesus*, 160–62.

Bösen, Willibald, *Jesusmahl, eucharistisches Mahl, Endzeitmahl: Ein Beitrag zur Theologie des Lukas* (SBS 97; Stuttgart: Katholisches Bibelwerk, 1980).

Box, G. H., "The Jewish Antecedents of the Eucharist," *JTS* 3 (1901–2) 357–69.

Idem, "St Luke xxii 15,16," *JTS* 10 (1908–9) 106–7.

Burkitt, F. C., "On Luke xxii 17-20," *JTS* 28 (1926–27) 178–81.

Burkitt, F. C., and A. E. Brooke, "St Luke xxii 15,16: What Is the General Meaning?" *JTS* 9 (1907–8) 569–72.

Carpinelli, Francis Giordano, "Do This as My Memorial" (Luke 22:19): Lukan Soteriology of Atonement," *CBQ* 61 (1999) 74–92.

Christie, W. M., "Did Christ Eat the Passover with His Disciples? Or, The Synoptics versus John's Gospel," *ExpT* 43 (1931–32) 515–19.

Cohn-Sherbok, Dan, "A Jewish Note on τὸ ποτήριον τῆς εὐλογίας," *NTS* 27 (1980–81) 704–9.

Cooper, John C., "The Problem of the Text in Luke 22:19-20," *LQ* 14 (1962) 39–48.

Cullmann, Oscar, "La signification de la Sainte–Cène dans le christianisme primitif," *RHPhR* 16 (1936) 1–22.

Cullmann, Oscar, and F. J. Leenhardt, *Essays on the Lord's Supper* (trans. J. G. Davies; ESW 1; Atlanta: John Knox, 1958).

Delebecque, Edouard, *Études grecques sur l'Évangile de Luc* (Collection d'études anciennes; Paris: Belles Lettres, 1976) 123–65.

Descamps, Albert, "Les origines de l'Eucharistie" (1970), in idem, *Jésus et l'Église: Études d'exégèse et de théologie* (BEThL 77; Leuven: University Press, 1987) 455–96.

Du Plessis, L. J., "The Saving Significance of Jesus and His Death on the Cross in Luke's Gospel—Focussing on Luke 22:19b-20," *Neot* 28 (1994) 523–40.

Eagar, A. R., "St. Luke's Account of the Last Supper: A Critical Note on the Second Sacrament," *Exp* 7,5 (1908) 252–62, 343–61.

Epp, Eldon Jay, "The Disputed Words of the Eucharistic Institution (Luke 22,19b-20): The Long and Short of the Matter," *Bib* 90 (2009) 407–16.

Feld, Helmut, *Das Verständnis des Abendmahls* (EdF 50; Darmstadt: Wissenschaftliche Buchgesellschaft, 1976).

Feneberg, Rupert, *Christliche Passafeier und Abendmahl: Eine biblisch-hermeneutische Untersuchung der neutestamentlichen Einsetzungsberichte* (StANT 27; Munich: Kösel, 1971).

Fitzmyer, Joseph A., "Papyrus Bodmer XIV: Some Features of Our Oldest Text of Luke," *CBQ* 24 (1962) 170–79, esp. 177.

Flusser, David, "The Last Supper and the Essenes," *Imm* 2 (1973) 23–27.

Fuller, Reginald H., "The Double Origin of the Eucharist," *BR* 8 (1963) 60–72.

Geerlings, Jacob, *Family 13, The Ferrar Group: The Text according to Luke* (StD 20; Salt Lake City: University of Utah Press, 1961).

Ghiberti, Giuseppe, "Gesù e la sua morte secondo i racconti della Cena: Alcune interpretazioni del XX secolo," in Associazione biblica italiana, ed., *Gesù e la sua morte* (Brescia: Paideia, 1984) 129–53.

Ginn, Richard J., *The Present and the Past: A Study of Anamnesis* (PTMS 20; Allison Park, Pa.: Pickwick, 1989).

Goetz, Karl Gerold, "Zur Lösung der Abendmahlsfrage," *ThStK* 108 (1937) 81–123.

Goguel, Maurice, *L'eucharistie: Des origines à Justin Martyr* (Paris: Fischbacher, 1910).

Goosens, Werner, *Les orgines de l'eucharistie sacrement et sacrifice* (Gembloux: Duculot, 1931).

Gregg, David W. A., "Hebraic Antecedents to the Eucharistic Anamnèsis Formula," *TynB* 30 (1979) 165–68.

Hagemeyer, Oda, "Tut dies zu meinem Gedächtnis! (I Kor 11,29f; Lk 22,19)," in Lothar Lies, ed., *Praesentia Christi: Festschrift Johannes Betz zum 70. Geburtstag* (Düsseldorf: Patmos, 1984) 101–17.

Hahn, Ferdinand, "Die alttestamentlichen Motive in der urchristlichen Abendmahlsüberlieferung," *EvTh* 27 (1967) 337–74.

Idem, "Zum Stand der Erforschung des urchristlichen Herrenmahls," *EvTh* 35 (1975) 553–63.

Higgins, A. J. B., "The Origins of the Eucharist," *NTS* 1 (1954–55) 200–209.

Holtzmann, Oscar, "Zu Lukas 22,20," *ZNW* 3 (1902) 359.

Hook, N., "The Dominical Cup Saying," *Theol* 77 (1974) 625–30.

Jeremias, Joachim, *The Eucharistic Words of Jesus* (trans. Norman Perrin; New York: Scribner, 1966) 97–100, 138–203, and passim.

Idem, *New Testament Theology* (New York: Scribner, 1971) 12, 31, 137, 190, 248, 288–292.

Idem, *Sprache*, 286–88.

Idem, "This Is My Body . . . ," *ExpT* 83 (1972) 196–203.

Idem, "Zur Exegese der Abendmahlsworte Jesu," *EvTh* 7 (1947–48) 60–63.

Kaestli, *L'eschatologie*, 58–59.

Kenyon, Frederick G., and S. C. E. Legg, "The Textual Data," in Roderic Dunkerley, ed., *The Ministry and the Sacraments* (New York: Macmillan, 1937) 271–86, esp. 285–86.

Kertelge, Karl, "Die soteriologischen Aussagen in der urchristlichen Abendmahlsüberlieferung and ihre Beziehung zum geschichtlichen Jesus," *TThZ* 81 (1972) 193–202.

Kilmartin, Edward J., *The Eucharist in the Primitive Church* (Englewood Cliffs, N.J.: Prentice-Hall, 1965).

Kilpatrick, G. D., "Luke xxii. 19b-20," *JTS* 47 (1946) 49–56.

Klauck, Hans-Josef, *Herrenmahl und hellenistischer Kult: Eine religionsgeschichtliche Untersuchung zum ersten Korintherbrief* (NTAbh n.s. 15; Münster: Aschendorff, 1982).

Idem, *The Religious Context of Early Christianity: A Guide to Graeco-Roman Religions* (trans. Brian McNeil; Edinburgh: T. & T. Clark, 2000) 327–30, 492–97.

Klawans, Jonathan, "Was Jesus' Last Supper a Seder?" *BiRe* 27, no. 5 (2001) 24–33.

Kosmala, Hans, "Das tut zu meinem Gedächtnis," *NovT* 4 (1960–61) 81–94; reprinted in idem, *Studies, Essays, and Reviews* (3 vols.; Leiden: Brill, 1978) 2:59–72.

Kuhn, Karl-Georg, "The Lord's Supper and the Communal Meal at Qumran," in Krister Stendahl, *The Scrolls and the New Testament* (New York: Harper, 1957) 65–93.

Kurz, William S., "Luke 22:14-38 and Greco-Roman and Biblical Farewell Addresses," *JBL* 104 (1985) 251–68.

Lambert, J. C., "The Passover and the Lord's Supper," *JTS* 4 (1902–3) 184–93.

LaVerdiere, Eugene A., *Dining in the Kingdom of God: The Origins of the Eucharist in the Gospel of Luke* (Chicago: Liturgy Training Publications, 1994).

Idem, "A Discourse at the Last Supper," *TBT* 71 (1974) 1540–48.

Lebeau, Paul, "La parole eschatologique de Jésus à la Cène (Mt. 26,29) dans l'exégèse patristique," *StPatr* 7 [TU 92] (1966) 515–23.

Idem, *Le vin nouveau du royaume: Étude exégétique et patristique sur la parole eschatologique de Jésus à la Cène* (Bruges: Desclée de Brouwer, 1966).

Le Déaut, Roger, "Goûter le calice de la mort," *Bib* 43 (1962) 82–86.

Leenhardt, *Sacrement*.

Légasse, Simon, "Jésus devant le Sanhédrin," *RThL* 5 (1974) 170–97.

Idem, "La Passion comme 'coupe.' Essai sur la genèse d'une métaphore," in Michel Quesnel, Yves-Marie Blanchard, and Claude Tassin, eds., *Nourriture et repas dans les milieux juifs et chrétiens de l'antiquité: Mélanges offerts au professeur Charles Perrot* (LD 178; Paris: Cerf, 1999) 173–79.

Lemoine, Bernadette, "Étude comparée des quatre récits de la Cène," *EL* 108 (1994) 52–72.

Leonard, P. E., "Luke's Account of the Lord's Supper against the Background of Meals in the Ancient Semitic World and More Particularly Meals in the Gospel of Luke" (Diss., Manchester, 1976).

Léon-Dufour, Xavier, "'Faites ceci en mémoire de moi' Lc 22,19; 1 Cor 11, 25," *Christus* 24 (1977) 200–208.

Idem, "Jésus devant sa mort à la lumière des textes de l'institution eucharistique et des discours d'adieu," in Jacques Dupont, ed., *Jésus aux origines de la christologie* (BEThL 40; Leuven: Leuven University Press, 1975) 141–68.

Idem, "Das letzte Mahl Jesu und die testamentarische Tradition nach Lk 22," *ZKTh* 103 (1981) 33–55.

Idem, "Prenez! 'Ceci est mon corps pour vous,'" *NRTh* 104 (1982) 223–40.

Idem, *Sharing the Eucharistic Bread: The Witness of the New Testament* (trans. Matthew J. O'Connell; New York: Paulist, 1987) 87–90, 230–47.

Lohmeyer, Ernst, "Vom urchristlichen Abendmahl," *ThR* n.s. 9 (1937) 168–227; 10 (1938) 81–99.

Macina, Menahem, "Fonction liturgique et eschatologique de l'anamnèse eucharistique (Lc 22,19; 1 Co 11,24.25)," *EL* 102 (1988) 3–25.

Magne, Jean, "Les paroles sur la coupe," in Joël Delobel, ed., *Logia: Les Paroles de Jésus—The Sayings of Jesus: Mémorial Joseph Coppens* (Leuven: Leuven University Press, 1982) 485–90.

Marcos, José Luis Espinel, *La Eucaristía del Nuevo Testamento* (2d ed.; Salamanca: San Esteban, 1997).

Margerie, Bertrand de, "Hoc facite in meam commemorationem" (Lc 22,19b): Les exégèses des Pères préchalcédoniens (150–451)," *Div* 28 (1984) 43–69, 137–49.

Marshall, I. Howard, *Last Supper and Lord's Supper* (Grand Rapids: Eerdmans, 1981).

Marxsen, Willi, *The Beginnings of Christology: Together with the Lord's Supper as a Christological Problem* (Philadelphia: Fortress Press, 1979) 87–122.

McGowan, Andrew, *Ascetic Eucharists: Food and Drink in Early Christian Ritual Meals* (New York: Oxford University Press, 1999).

Meier, John P., "The Eucharist at the Last Supper: Did It Happen?" *ThD* 42 (1995) 335–51.

Merklein, Helmut, "Erwägungen zur Überlieferungsgeschichte der neutestamentlichen Abendmahlstraditionen," *BZ* 21 (1977) 88–101, 235–44; reprinted in idem, *Studien zu Jesus und Paulus* (2 vols.; WUNT 43, 105; Tübingen: Mohr Siebeck, 1987, 1998) 1:157–80.

Merx, Adalbert, *Die Evangelien des Markus und Lukas nach der Syrischen im Sinaikloster gefundenen Palimpsesthandschrift* (Berlin: Reimer, 1905) 441–48.

Metzger, Bruce M. *A Textual Commentary on the Greek New Testament: A Companion Volume to the United Bible Societies' Greek New Testament* (New York: United Bible Societies, 1971) 173–77; idem, *Textual Commentary* (2d ed.), 147–50.

Meynet, *Guide*, 94–96.

Monks, George G., "The Lucan Account of the Last Supper," *JBL* 44 (1925) 228–60.

Muhlack, Gudrun, *Die Parallelen von Lukas-Evangelium und Apostelgeschichte* (TW 8; Bern: Lang, 1979) 89–105.

Nestle, Eb., "Zu Lc 22,20," *ZNW* 7 (1906) 256–57.

Idem, "Zu Lukas 22,20," *ZNW* 3 (1902) 252.

Neyrey, Jerome H., *The Passion according to Luke: A Redaction Study of Luke's Soteriology* (New York: Paulist, 1985) 12–17.

Nock, Arthur Darby, *Early Gentile Christianity and Its Hellenistic Background* (New York: Harper & Row, 1964).

Parker, D. C., *The Living Text of the Gospels* (Cambridge: Cambridge University Press, 1997) 148–57.

Parker, Pierson, "Three Variant Readings in Luke-Acts," *JBL* 83 (1964) 165–70.

Patsch, Hermann, *Abendmahl und historischer Jesus* (CThM 1; Stuttgart: Calwer, 1972) 89–103.

Penn, Michael, "Ritual Kissing, Heresy and the Emergence of Christian Orthodoxy," *JEH* 54 (2003) 625–40.

Pesch, Rudolf, *Das Abendmahl und Jesu Todesverständnis* (QD 80; Freiburg: Herder, 1978) 24–30.

Idem, "Das Abendmahl und Jesu Todesverständnis," in Karl Kertelge, ed., *Der Tod Jesu: Deutungen im Neuen Testament* (QD 74; Freiburg: Herder, 1976) 137–87.

Idem, "Das Evangelium in Jerusalem: Mk 14,12-26 als ältestes Überlieferungsgut der Urgemeinde," in Peter Stuhlmacher, ed., *Das Evangelium und die Evangelien* (WUNT 28; Tübingen: Mohr Siebeck, 1983) 113–55.

Idem, "The Last Supper and Jesus' Understanding of His Death," *BiBh* 3 (1977) 58–75.

Idem, *Wie Jesus das Abendmahl hielt: Der Grund der Eucharistie* (Freiburg: Herder, 1977) 33–46.

Petzer, J. H., "Luke 22:19b-20 and the Structure of the Passage," *NovT* 26 (1984) 249–52.

Petzer, Kobus, "Style and Text in the Lucan Narrative of the Institution of the Lord's Supper (Luke 22.19b-20)," *NTS* 37 (1991) 113–29.

Petzke, Gerd, *Das Sondergut des Evangeliums nach Lukas* (Zurich: Theologischer Verlag, 1990) 176–80.

Porporato, F. X., "Hoc facite in meam commemorationem: Lc. 22, 19; 1 Cor. 11, 24.25," *VD* 13 (1933) 264–70.

Idem, "De lucana pericopa 22,19b-20," *VD* 13 (1933) 114–22.

Quesnel, Michel, Yves-Marie Blanchard, and Claude Tassin, eds., *Nourriture et repas dans les milieux juifs et chrétiens de l'antiquité: Mélanges offerts au professeur Charles Perrot* (LD 178; Paris: Cerf, 1999) passim.

Quesnell, Quentin, "The Women at Luke's Supper," in Richard J. Cassidy and Philip J. Sharper, eds., *Political Issues in Luke-Acts* (Maryknoll, N.Y.: Orbis, 1983) 59–79.

Radl, Walter, *Das Lukas-Evangelium* (EdF 261; Darmstadt: Wissenschaftliche Buchgesellschaft, 1988) 7–33, 113–32.

Idem, "Sonderüberlieferungen bei Lukas? Traditionsgeschichtliche Fragen zu Lk 22,67f; 23,2 und 23,6-12," in Karl Kertelge, ed., *Der Prozess gegen Jesus* (QD 112; Freiburg i. B.: Herder, 1988) 131–47.

Réau, Louis, *Iconographie de l'art Chrétien* (3 vols. in 6; Paris: Presses universitaires de France, 1955–59), vol. 2: *Iconographie de la Bible*, part 2, 406–26.

Rese, Martin, "Zur Problematik von Kurz- and Langtext im Lk xxii.17ff," *NTS* 22 (1975–76) 15–31.

Reumann, John, "The Last and the Lord's Supper," *BLTS* 62 (1982) 17–39.

Richardson, R. D., "The Place of Luke in the Eucharistic Tradition," *StEv* 1 [TU 73] (1959) 663–75.

Roloff, Jürgen, "Anfänge der soteriologischen Deutung des Todes Jesu (Mk. x. 45 und Lk. xxi. 27)," *NTS* 19 (1972–73) 38–64.

Schäfer, Karl Th., "Zur Textgeschichte von Lk 22,19b.20," *Bib* 33 (1952) 237–39.

Schenke, *Studien*, 286–347.

Schenker, Adrian, *Das Abendmahl Jesu als Brennpunkt des Alten Testaments: Begegnung zwischen den beiden Testamenten: Eine bibeltheologische Skizze* (BiBe 13; Fribourg, Switzerland: Schweizerisches Katholisches Bibelwerk, 1977).

Schiller, Gertrud, *Iconography of Christian Art*, vol. 2: *The Passion of Jesus Christ* (trans. Janet Seligman; Greenwich, Conn.: New York Graphic Society, 1971) 24–41.

Schlosser, Jacques, *Le Règne de Dieu dans les dits de Jésus* (2 vols.; EtB; Paris: Gabalda, 1980) 1:419–747.

Schürmann, Heinz, "Abendmahl, letztes, A. Jesu," *LThK* 1 (1957) 26–31.

Idem, "Der Abendmahlsbericht Lk 22,7-38 als Gottesdienstordnung, Gemeindeordnung, Lebensordnung," in idem, *Ursprung und Gestalt: Eröterungen und Besinnungen zum Neuen Testament* (KBANT; Düsseldorf: Patmos, 1970) 108–50.

Idem, "Die Gestalt der urchristlichen Eucharistiefeier," *MThZ* 6 (1955) 107–31; reprinted in idem, *Ursprung*, 77–99.

Idem, "Das Herrenmahl im Neuen Testament," *ThLZ* 79 (1954) 577–92.

Idem, "Lk 22,19b-20 als ursprüngliche Textüberlieferung," *Bib* 32 (1951) 364–92, 522–41; reprinted

in idem, *Traditionsgeschichtliche Untersuchungen zu den synoptischen Evangelien* (KBANT; Düsseldorf: Patmos, 1968) 159–92.

Idem, "Lk 22,42a das älteste Zeugnis für Lk 22,20," *MThZ* 3 (1952) 185–88; reprinted in idem, *Traditionsgeschichtliche Untersuchungen*, 193–97.

Idem, *Quellenkritische Untersuchung des lukanischen Abendmahlsberichtes Lk 22, 7-38*, Part 1: *Der Paschamahlbericht, Lk 22, (7-14.) 15-18*; Part 2: *Der Einsetzungsbericht, Lk 22, 19-20*; Part 3: *Jesu Abschiedsrede, Lk 22, 21-38* (NTAbh 19.5, 20.4, 20.5; Münster: Aschendorff, 1953, 1955, 1957).

Idem, "Die Semitismen im Einsetzungsbericht bei Markus und bei Lukas," *ZKTh* 73 (1951) 72–77.

Schwank, B., "Das ist mein Leib, der für euch hingegeben wird (Lk 22,19)," *EuA* 59 (1983) 279–90.

Schweitzer, Albert, *The Problem of the Lord's Supper according to the Scholarly Research of the Nineteenth Century and the Historical Accounts*. Vol. 1 of *The Lord's Supper in Relationship to the Life of Jesus and the History of the Early Church* (1901; trans A. J. Mattill, Jr.; ed. John Reumann; Macon, Ga.: Mercer University Press, 1982).

Schweizer, Eduard, "Abendmahl," *RGG* 1:10–21.

Idem, "Rezension von H. Schürmann, Der Einsetzungsbericht Lk. 22, 19 bis 20," *ThLZ* 81 (1956) 217–19.

Idem, "Rezension von H. Schürmann, Der Paschamahlbericht," *ThLZ* 80 (1955) 156–57.

Shepherd, W. H., "A Tradition-Historical Reconstruction of the Development of the Eucharist from the Last Supper to Its Attestation in First Century C.E. Hellenistic Christianity" (Diss., McGill University, Montréal, 1987).

Smith and Taussig, *Many Tables*.

Smith, M. A., "The Lukan Last Supper Narrative," *StEv* 6 [TU 112] (1973) 502–9.

Snodgrass, Klyne, "Western Non-Interpolations," *JBL* 91 (1972) 369–79.

Sparks, H. F. D., "St. Luke's Transpositions," *NTS* 3 (1956–57) 219–23.

Speier, Solomon, "Das Kosten des Todes-Kelches' in Targum," *VT* 13 (1963) 344–45.

Stemberger, Günter, "Pesachhaggada und Abendmahlsberichte des Neuen Testaments," *Kairos* 29 (1987) 147–58.

Ström, Åve V., Gerhard Delling, Georg Kretschmar, Erwin Iserloh, and Albrecht Peters, "Abendmahl III," *TRE* 1 (1977) 43–145.

Suharyo, Ignatius, *Ecclesiological Implications of the Lucan Last Supper Narrative* (Rome: Pontificia Università Urbaniana, 1981).

Sweetland, Dennis M., "The Lord's Supper and the Lukan Community," *BTB* 13 (1983) 23–27.

Sykes, Marjorie H., "The Eucharist as 'Anamnesis'," *ExpT* 71 (1959–60) 115–18.

Throckmorton, Burton H., Jr., "The Longer Reading of Luke 22:19b-20," *ATR* 30 (1948) 55–56.

Traets, C., "Les paroles sur la coupe pendant la prière eucharistique: Trois considérations bibliques et liturgico-pastorales (II)," *QuLi* 77 (1996) 213–28.

Trimaille, Michel, "'Manger et boire' dans l'œuvre de Luc," in Michel Quesnel, Yves-Marie Blanchard, and Claude Tassin, eds., *Nourriture et repas dans les milieux juifs et chrétiens de l'antiquité: Mélanges offerts au professeur Charles Perrot* (LD 178; Paris: Cerf, 1999) 121–37.

Van Cangh, Jean-Marie, "Le déroulement primitif de la Cène (Mc 14, 18-26 et par.)," *RB* 102 (1995) 193–225.

Vööbus, Arthur, "A New Approach to the Problem of the Shorter and Longer Text in Luke," *NTS* 15 (1968–69) 457–63.

Idem, *The Prelude to the Lukan Passion Narrative* (PETSE 17; Stockholm: ETSE, 1968).

Wanke, Joachim, *Beobachtungen zum Eucharistie-verständnis des Lukas auf Grund der lukanischen Mahlberichte* (EThS 8; Leipzig: St. Benno, 1973).

Weren, W. J. C., "The Lord's Supper: An Inquiry into the Coherence in Luke 22,14-18," in Hans Jörg auf der Maur, Leo Bakker, Annewies van de Bunt, Joop Waldram, eds., *Fides sacramenti, sacramentum fidei: Studies in Honour of Pieter Smulders* (Assen: Van Gorcum, 1981) 9–26.

Westcott, Brooke Foss, and Fenton John Anthony Hort, *The New Testament in the Original Greek* (2 vols.; 1881; reprinted Graz: Akademische Druck- und Verlagsanstalt, 1974) vol. 2: *Introduction, Appendix*, 63–64 (in the appendix).

Ziesler, J. A., "The Vow of Abstinence: A Note on Mark 15:25 and Parallels," *Colloquium: The Australian and New Zealand Theological Review* 5 (1972) 12–14.

Idem, "The Vow of Abstinence Again," *Colloquium: The Australian and New Zealand Theological Review* 6 (1973) 49–50.

15	Then he said to them, "With all my desire I have wanted[a] to eat this Passover with you before my passion.[b] 16/ Indeed, I say to you I will not eat it[c] until it is fulfilled in the kingdom of God." 17/ And after he had taken[d] a cup and given thanks, he said, "Take this and divide it among yourselves. 18/ Indeed, I say to you that from now on I will not drink[e] of the fruit of the vine until the kingdom of God comes."	a	Literally: "With desire I desired." It is a formula in Semitic style (see Gen 2:17).
		b	Literally: "before I suffer."
		c	Literally: "I really do not eat it."
		d	Literally: "having received."
		e	Literally: "I really do not drink."
19	And after he had taken a loaf[f] and had given thanks, he broke it and gave it to them, saying, "This is my body, which is given for you. Do this in memory of me." 20/ And likewise the cup after supper, saying, "This cup is the new covenant in my blood, which is shed for you."[g]	f	Or: "bread."
		g	Verses 19c-20 are not included in some manuscripts; see the commentary.

Luke,[1] who has mentioned the Passover on several occasions (vv. 1, 7, and 13-14), never explicitly tells us whether Jesus and his people have eaten this sacred, miraculously prepared meal. He probably believes it, since he includes the diners (v. 14) and even mentions the table (v. 21).

Synchronic Analysis

As with any ritual, scarcely anything is told about this Passover meal. What is important is the unforeseen event that takes place during the liturgical routine.

---

1 The bibliography at the beginning of this pericope represents only a sample of the existing literature. I have consulted the most recent works: LaVerdiere, *Eucharist*; Marcos, *Eucharistía*; and McGowan, *Ascetic Eucharists*. While LaVerdiere emphasizes the complementarity of the first rituals, the centripetal forces, and the respect in those days for tradition, by contrast Smith and Taussig (*Many Tables*) underscore the diversity, the absence of an authoritative origin, and the assimilation of the early Christians to the ancient pattern of fellowship meals. While LaVerdiere is interested in theology, Smith and

The unexpected belongs completely to Jesus, who by word and gesture creates the event. In v. 15 the Master addresses his disciples (εἶπεν πρὸς αὐτούς, "he said to them"). In vv. 16 and 18 Luke says twice that he speaks to them (λέγω γὰρ ὑμῖν, "indeed, I say to you"). In vv. 17, 19, and 20, he speaks three more times to them (εἶπεν, "he said"; λέγων, "saying"). Along with this abundance of words there is an economy of gestures: in v. 17 Jesus seizes the cup; in v. 19 he takes the bread, breaks it, and distributes it.

It is not easy to connect these verses. Verse 15 opens the speech by focusing attention on the present Passover ("this Passover"). While v. 16 looks to the eschatological future in which the Passover will be "fulfilled in the kingdom of God," it speaks above all of the time that extends from the present to the end. It will be a time of paschal abstinence for Jesus. Note the first person singular: οὐ μὴ φάγω, "I will not eat."

Verse 17 mentions an action and a word. Jesus takes the cup to give it to his disciples, and he invites them to share it. Note the second person plural and the expression "among you." Thus, the disciples' table fellowship (v. 17) corresponds to Jesus' paschal abstinence (v. 16).

Verse 18 corresponds to v. 16. It says the same thing about drinking that v. 16 says about eating. It is the same abstinence that is imposed on Jesus until the arrival of the kingdom.

Verse 19 corresponds to v. 17 and speaks of the same communal sharing. It speaks here of the bread, while v. 17 mentioned the cup.

Just as the somewhat isolated v. 15 introduced Jesus' words, v. 20, separated by the supper, concludes this action of the Master.

There are, in my view, three implied poles that stand in tension with one another in these verses: that of the time, that of the people, that of the elements.

V. 15: Jesus between this Passover and his imminent passion
V. 16: Jesus between now and the kingdom of God: without the Passover
V. 17: "You" from now on: with the cup
V. 18: Jesus between now and the kingdom of God: without the wine
V. 19: "You" from now on: with the bread
V. 20: "You" from now on: with the cup

Three verses deal with Jesus' fate (vv. 15, 16, 18), three with the fate of the disciples (vv. 17, 19, 20). Three refer to food (vv. 15, 16, 19), three to drink (vv. 17, 18, 20). One verse mentions the exact present moment (v. 15), two the ultimate future (vv. 16, 18), three the intermediate time, the continuous present (vv. 17, 19, 20).[2]

Diachronic Analysis

According to my hypothesis, Luke leaves Mark here in order to rejoin his second source, his special material. He will follow it until v. 38 (the episode of the two swords) before returning to the Second Gospel (the episode of Gethsemane).

Verses 15 (the last Passover) and 17 (the first cup) have no Synoptic parallel. Verse 16, and especially v. 18, can certainly be compared with Mark 14:25, a verse that is placed after and not before the words of institution. As Heinz Schürmann has shown, however, it is hardly likely that Luke is inspired here by Mark.[3] It is more probable that each of the two sources, the special material and Mark, contained a word about the apocalyptic hope for the kingdom of God.

As for vv. 19-20, there are a number of reasons for bringing them closer to 1 Corinthians 11 than to Mark 14. With the bread Luke, like Paul, uses the verb "I give thanks" (εὐχαριστῶ, v. 19a), while the two other Syn-

Taussig make full use of the scientific study of religion. The two works do have, however, one point in common. They correctly insist that Luke 22:15-20 must be included first in the meals of Jesus and then in those of the early Christians. Trimaille ("Manger et boire") offers a good examination of the expression "eating and drinking" and also remembers all of the meals mentioned in Luke-Acts. See also the first section of the article "Abendmahl," in the *TRE* 1 (1977) 43–89, authored by Ström, Delling, and Kretschmar. From an exegetical and historical per-

spective, one will always refer to Goguel (*Eucharistie*), from an exegetical and theological perspective, to Leenhardt (*Sacrement*).
2 Léon-Dufour (*Sharing*, 87–90, 230–47) is of the opinion that the Lukan text belongs to the literary genre of the testament. He is not wrong, even if he does not adequately note that Luke's text is not only a farewell speech.
3 Schürmann, *Paschamahlbericht*, 123; "Abendmahlsbericht."

optics use "I bless" (εὐλογέω). Both, Luke and Paul, qualify the body by saying it "is given for you" (v. 19c), an explanation absent in Mark and Matthew. They also transmit—and they are the only ones to do so—the command to remember Jesus (v. 19d). Neither of them feels the need to include verbs in connection with the cup (Mark and Matthew mention no fewer than four: to take, to give thanks, to give, to drink). Yet each of them makes a point of inserting the comment on the cup after the meal (20a); each also speaks of the "new covenant in my blood," while Mark and Matthew use the expression "my blood of the covenant." While the four witnesses speak of shed blood, Luke differs from the other two Synoptics, who have the formula "for many." He says "for you" (Paul remains silent here) as, like Paul, he had already said about the bread (v. 19c).

Although he concedes that a special source lies behind Luke 22:15-20, Joachim Jeremias has spent a great deal of energy demonstrating that the original text lies behind the Gospel of Mark.[4] Schürmann, on the other hand, has expended great effort trying to show that it lies behind the Lukan version.[5] Both of them are driven by the passion, inherited from romanticism, to arrive at the naturally pure and solidly historical origin. A generation after their still significant work, I take into account the diversity of early Christianity and its first two capitals, Jerusalem and Antioch, and I pose the

hypothesis that the Markan and Matthean version of the Eucharist corresponds to the liturgy of the fellowship of the Twelve, whose beginnings lie in Jerusalem. I locate the Lukan and Pauline version in Antioch, a community founded by the Hellenists (it is known how much Paul is indebted to this group, which, based on the book of Acts, I call the Seven). In support of my hypothesis I cite the double tradition of the miracle of the multiplication of the loaves. The feeding of the five thousand ends with enough bread to fill twelve baskets (an allusion to the later ministry of the Twelve, Mark 6:30-44); that of the four thousand ends with enough surplus bread to fill seven baskets (portions intended for the future ministry of the seven Hellenists, Mark 8:1-10).

Before we go further, we must mention an important text-critical problem that has divided the spirits for more than a century.[6] Codex Bezae (D = 05)[7] and several Old Latin witnesses do not contain vv. 19cd (they end with "this is my body") and 20 (they begin again with "but behold, the hand . . . ," v. 21).[8] This short text, which one can call "Western," also receives some support from the Old Syriac Curetonian version, which is unaware of v. 20.[9] Illustrious scholars, beginning with B. F. Westcott and F. J. A. Hort, have suggested that the short text corresponds to Luke's original text and that subsequently this text was contaminated by the First Epistle to the Corinthians (1 Cor 11:24-25).[10] In their view the reason

---

4 Jeremias, *Eucharistic Words*, 160–64.

5 Schürmann, *Einsetzungsbericht*, 131–32, 151–53.

6 The problem is presented well by Metzger, *Commentary* (1st ed.), 173–77; and Fitzmyer, 2:1387–88.

7 See Frederick H. Scrivener, *Bezae Codex Cantabrigiensis: being an exact copy, in ordinary type, of the celebrated uncial Graeco–Latin manuscript of the four Gospels and Acts of the Apostles / written early in the sixth century and Presented to the University of Cambridge by Theodore Beza, A.D. 1581* (Facsimile; 1864; reprinted Pittsburgh: Pickwick, 1978) 249–50.

8 These are the Old Latin manuscripts a, d, ff², i, and l. They are valuable manuscripts of the fourth (a), fifth (d, ff², and i), and eighth (l) centuries. The fifth-century manuscripts b and e also have a short text, but with an inversion: they do not have vv. 19cd and 20, but they contain v. 19ab before vv. 17-18. See Adolf Jülicher, ed., *Das Neue Testament in altlateinischer Überlieferung nach den Handschriften herausgegeben* (2d ed. by Walter Matzkow and Kurt Aland; Berlin: de Gruyter, 1976) 243.

9 The Syriac Curetonian version omits v. 20 and contains the following order: vv. 19, 17, 18. The Syriac Sinaitic version has a long text but in a peculiar order: vv. 19, 20a ("and after the supper"), vv. 17, 20b ("this is my blood, the new covenant"; the cup is not mentioned), 18. The Peshitta knows vv. 19-20 but is not aware of vv. 17-18. The same is true of several manuscripts of the Coptic Bohairic version.

10 See Westcott and Hort, *New Testament*, 2:63–64. In the edition itself (vol. 1, *Text*, 177) the two editors set the verses in question in double brackets. In their opinion they did not form part of Luke's original text. Reading Fitzmyer (2:1388) makes it possible to appreciate how influential the decision of Westcott and Hort was on other editors of the New Testament as well as on many exegetes. Missing from Nestle until the 25th edition, the long text is included again as of the 26th edition.

for this interpolation was clear: the readers of Luke's original text felt the absence of the traditional words of institution. Their opponents based their arguments on the quantity and the quality of the Greek manuscripts that contain the long text. In particular, the oldest and most famous, such as the Bodmer Papyrus XIV–XV ($\mathfrak{p}^{75}$), Codex Vaticanus (B = 03), and Codex Sinaiticus (א = 01) all attest the long text.[11] It appeared to them that there was a second reason for choosing the long text: It is the *lectio difficilior*, since the long text has an awkward double reference to the cup (in vv. 17 and 20).[12]

The history of research has swung like a pendulum. The advocates of the short text held sway during the first half of the twentieth century, and their opponents during the second half. At present the advocates of the short text have retaken the field: Bart D. Ehrman and D. C. Parker prefer it.[13] This tendency is due to the fact that contemporary scholarship gives greater attention to the so-called Western text of Acts and the Gospel of Luke. While earlier decisions were made according to a chronological rule, scholarship today gives more respect to geographical data. It is quite possible that there were different forms of the same text in different areas.[14] Scholars have also become more modest, more resigned, even more skeptical. They have abandoned the effort to find the original text and are satisfied with the oldest forms to which they have access.[15] Instead of arguing over whether the Western or the Egyptian text is older, they concede that there are two venerable forms attested as early as the second century of the Common Era. Shall we accept the opinion of these scholars, give up finding the original text of Luke, and say that these two forms of Luke 22 are of equal value and correspond to two contemporary forms of Luke-Acts? I would be inclined to that view if the Greek manuscripts were better distributed. Yet their number and their weight tip the balance in favor of the long text. The remaining difficulty, as Joseph A. Fitzmyer, an advocate of the long text admits, is how to explain the origin of the short text.[16] With its double reference to the cup (vv. 17 and 20) the long text is certainly redundant, as the advocates of the long text concede. But why did the scribes of the short text omit the traditional liturgical formula (vv. 19b-20), which they certainly knew, rather than the unusual statement of v. 17? That is peculiar. Some have thought of the arcane discipline according to which the written words of institution were not to be seen by pagan eyes.[17] Was the omission really caused by an excess of veneration? And why was the censorship exerted only on certain copies of a single Gospel? The argument is hardly convincing. One thing appears certain: the presence of two cups in the long text is awkward. Why does one cup appear already

---

11 Several old versions must be added to these countless manuscripts: the Vulgate, the Syriac versions (with the exception of the Curetonian, the Sinaitic, and the Peshitta), the Coptic (except for a few manuscripts of the Bohairic version), the Armenian, and Georgian versions; see Metzger, *Commentary* (1st ed.), 173–74. We must also add the witness of Christian authors of the second century: Marcion, who retained at least part of vv. 19 and 20, Tatian, and perhaps Justin; see Benoit, "Récit," 164–66 (in the collected works).

12 The other forms of the text (see Metzger, *Commentary* [1st ed.], 174; and Fitzmyer, 2:1388) all appear to depend on these two basic forms. Metzger (p. 175) offers a slightly adapted table drawn up by F. G. Kenyon and S. E. C. Legg ("The Textual Data," in Roderic Dunkerley, ed., *The Ministry and the Sacraments* [London: SCM, 1937] 284–85), who give in Greek six different forms of Luke 22:17-20. See also Adalbert Merx (*Die vier kanonischen Evangelien nach ihrem ältesten bekannten Texte: Übersetzung und Erläuterung der syrischen im Sinaikloster gefundenen*

Palimpsesthandschrift, vol. 2/2: *Die Evangelien des Markus und Lukas* [Berlin: Reimer, 1905] 441–48), who also provides the text of several versions.

13 Bart D. Ehrman, *The Orthodox Corruption of Scripture: The Effect of Early Christological Controversies on the Text of the New Testament* (New York: Oxford University Press, 1993) 197–209; Parker, *Living Text*, 148–57.

14 See the introduction in vol. 1 of this commentary, 6–7, and the suggestive study by Christian-Bernard Amphoux, "Les premières éditions de Luc," *EThL* 67 (1991) 312–27; 68 (1992) 38–48.

15 See Eldon Jay Epp, "The Multivalence of the Term 'Original Text' in New Testament Textual Criticism," *HTR* 92 (1999) 245–81.

16 Fitzmyer, 2:1388. Recently Billings ("Disputed Words") has suggested that the scribes eliminated vv. 19b-20 from Luke 22 after the persecutions, in particular those of Lyon and Vienna. They wanted to spare the Christians from the charge of cannibalism.

17 See Metzger, *Commentary* (1st ed.), 176.

in v. 17, if according to the traditional command it will have to be mentioned again in v. 20? The order of the short text, which is not encumbered by this presence of two cups, is nevertheless surprising when it locates the cup before the bread. It is true that in the *Didache* (9.2–3) and elsewhere there is such an unusual sequence,[18] yet there the cup is introduced only after the meal (v. 15). As one can see, the arguments cancel one another, and no solution is really convincing.

If one assumes, as I do, that Luke has a second source alongside Mark, one can try to delineate its contours. As Rudolf Bultmann has well noted,[19] it begins with a biographical character (Jesus considers his own passion). Moreover, as the references to the kingdom of God (vv. 16 and 18) and to the cup (v. 17) suggest, it is strongly focused on eschatology. Yet the biographical and eschatological components do not prevent communal and liturgical elements. The tradition underscores the presence of the disciples (note the repeated "you") and gives them liturgical support in the absence of their hero (the shared meal, v. 16, and the passed cup, v. 17).

What about the rest of the story (vv. 19-20)? It is probable that Luke's special source or Luke himself combined two traditions—the biographical, of which I just spoke (vv. 15-18), and the liturgical, which unfolds the words of institution (vv. 19-20).[20] This kind of telescoping of the traditions would explain the double presence of the cup. But since the first occurrence of the cup (v. 17) is framed by sentences that look toward the future of the kingdom (vv. 16, 18), the person responsible for bringing this material together preserved it all the more readily, as the second (v. 20) directs attention toward the past of the cross. Consideration of the Gospels of Mark and Matthew also suggests that there were two traditions. After recalling the Lord's Supper, they both transmit a saying on waiting for the kingdom (Mark 14:15 par. Matt 26:29).[21] I am aware, of course, of the conjectural character of my hypothesis. I know that the idea of a biographical legend advocated by Bultmann[22] has been rejected by Jack Finegan and Pierre Benoit.[23] I also know that when the hypothesis was taken over by Jeremias and Schürmann, the two learned men were criticized by Gerhard Schneider and Hermann Patsch.[24] One must expect opposition.

Commentary

■ **15** It is unusual in the Gospels that Jesus expresses his desires. Here he does it openly, and he does so with a Semitic formula that doubles the verb ($\dot{\epsilon}\pi\iota\vartheta\upsilon\mu\dot{\epsilon}\omega$) with a substantive from the same root ($\dot{\epsilon}\pi\iota\vartheta\upsilon\mu\dot{\iota}\alpha$).[25] Even if the ancient expression of "desire" ($\dot{\epsilon}\pi\iota\vartheta\upsilon\mu\dot{\iota}\alpha$) is not to be confused with the modern outbreak of the *libido* since Freud, there is nevertheless an anthropological continuity between the two. The ancients employed $\dot{\epsilon}\pi\iota\vartheta\upsilon\mu\dot{\iota}\alpha$ with a multiplicity of meanings, which the linguistic context had to direct in the right channels. It could be a bad desire, an expression of covetousness, or a good desire, the demonstration of a lively will. Luke, of whom it is incorrectly said that he is not concerned to emphasize Jesus' feelings, has mentioned another formulation of this desire. In his statement about the baptism that will constitute his death, the Lukan Jesus uses a different verb "I am pressed" ($\sigma\upsilon\nu\dot{\epsilon}\chi o\mu\alpha\iota$), which indicated the course of his life until his death: "and how I am pressed until it is accomplished" (12:50).

---

18 See already 1 Cor 10:16; Metzger, *Commentary* (1st ed.), 174 n. 1.

19 Bultmann, *History*, 266.

20 Meynet (*Guide*, 96) almost overemphasizes the contrast between the old Passover and the new covenant.

21 See Gnilka (*Markus*, 2:240–43, 246–47), who appears not to mention the hypothesis of the two traditions.

22 Bultmann, *History*, 266.

23 Jack Finegan, *Die Überlieferung der Leidens- und Auferstehungsgeschichte Jesu* (BZNW 15; Giessen: Töpelmann, 1934) 11; Benoit, "Récit," 186–200 (in the collected works).

24 Schneider, 2:444; and Patsch, *Abendmahl*, 93–94.

25 One finds the same formula in Gen 31:30 LXX. On this kind of expression, see BDF §198 (6); and Fitzmyer, 2:1395–96. The Greek, it is true, is also aware of the etymological figure $\nu\dot{o}\tau\omega$ $\nu o\sigma\epsilon\dot{\iota}\nu$ ("to be reached by a disease"). Claire Clivaz emphasizes Jesus' legitimate desire (*L'ange et la sueur de sang [Lk 22,43-44]: ou comment on pourrait bien encore écrire l'histoire* [Biblical Tools and Studies 7; Leuven: Peeters, 2010]).

The statement does not explain why it was so important for Jesus to eat this Passover with his disciples before his passion. The rest of the text, however, gives the explanation. For him it will be a last opportunity; for them it will be a first celebration.

■ **16-18** Twice, in v. 16 and v. 18, Jesus emphasizes his abstinence, which will be due to his absence: "I will not eat" (οὐ μὴ φάγω, v. 16) and "I will not drink" (οὐ μὴ πίω, v. 18) are not simply two negative forms of the future. These subjunctive aorists with a double negation are strong formulas ("the most definite form of negation regarding the future")[26] more than wishes, almost oaths or incantations. Deep in the knowledge of God, Jesus assures his disciples and himself that he will die and that from now on nothing will matter for him except that the kingdom take root.[27]

Verse 16 makes the meaning specific: today's Passover has its value, but it has not yet reached its fullness.[28] Even though it has been wanted by God since the time of the exodus, even though it is respected by Jesus, the Passover is no less a human ritual, a sign that looks forward to the hoped-for reality, an imperfect celebration awaiting fulfillment. The theological structure on which Jesus' words are based corresponds to the ideas of the Epistle to the

Hebrews, according to which the Day of Atonement must be repeated annually because of its imperfection, while the death of Jesus has a once-and-for-all eschatological perfection.[29]

Without referring explicitly to the cup, also without saying which of the four Jewish Passover cups he is using, Jesus says clearly in v. 18, as in v. 16, that he will be absent beginning with his death and until the kingdom comes.

Wedged between these two looks into the future (vv. 16 and 18), v. 17 mentions a prophetic gesture accompanied by an imperative saying. What Jesus now is doing, the disciples will have to do (by implication from now until the inbreaking of the kingdom of God): Take[30] a cup[31] and share it. Why? To experience solidarity (note εἰς ἑαυτούς, "among you"), to make up for Jesus' absence (Jesus' "I" disappears from the sentence), and to wait for the future, encouraged by the symbolic, strengthening, and festive[32] force of the wine.[33] Verses 16-18, as is also the case with Mark 14:25 par. Matt 26:29, attest that the Eucharist of the first Christians was not only a memorial of the death of Jesus but also a joyful anticipation of the end. The juxtaposition of these two aspects in Luke 22:15-20 indicates that, in the evangelist's day, they belonged together. The prehistory of the pericope sug-

---

26 BDF §365.
27 On the kingdom of God, see the excursus in vol. 2 of this commentary at 13:18. It would be wrong to identify the realization of the kingdom with the resurrection of Christ or the establishment of the church. The expression ἡ βασιλεία, with or without τοῦ θεοῦ, will appear again in 22:29-30 and 23:51, then in the book of Acts (e.g., Acts 1:3; 28:23).
28 The subject of the verb πληρωθῇ ("be fulfilled") is αὐτό ("this"), which refers to τοῦτο τὸ πάσχα in v. 15. The verb πληρόω ("to fulfill") flows freely from Luke's pen. He uses it to speak of the fulfillment of Scripture (Luke 4:21; 24:44), of the fulfillment of a time or of times (Luke 21:24; Acts 7:23; 9:23), and of all that fills the heart or the life of a human being or a people (Luke 2:40; Acts 2:28; 5:28; 13:25, 52). Luke usually uses this verb to emphasize the realization of God's plan (Luke 1:20; 9:31; 24:44). See vol. 1 of this commentary, 154 n. 27 on 4:20b-21.
29 The theme of fulfillment, present in v. 16, is absent from v. 18. Thus, in spite of their relationship v. 16 and v. 18 are not completely symmetrical.
30 The verb δέχομαι initially means "to receive," "to welcome," then, as here, "to take" (see Eph 6:17: καὶ τὴν περικεφαλαίαν τοῦ σωτηρίου δέξασθε, "and take the helmet of salvation"). Further on, in the same v. 17 and then in v. 19, Luke refers to the bread with the verb λαμβάνω, which initially means "to take," then "to receive." Are we to perceive different nuances in the use of these two verbs? It is likely that Jesus asked for a cup and then in some sense "received" it (v. 17).
31 Note the absence of the definite article: "a cup." The definite article τό ("the") added by some manuscripts (principally Codex Alexandrinus [A = 02] and Codex Bezae [D = 05]) gives the account a liturgical flavor ("the" cup one knows from the ritual).
32 See Lebeau, *Vin nouveau*, 33–52. This entire book is devoted to Jesus' eschatological saying on the cup, v. 18, and its parallels in Mark 14:25 and Matt 26:29.
33 Why, just like his Synoptic companions (Mark 14:25; Matt 26:29), does Luke speak of "the fruit of the vine" (τὸ γένημα τῆς ἀμπέλου) and not of the wine (οἶνος)? We must say initially that τὸ γένημα is a new word from the Hellenistic period that is

gests that originally they were different traditions. Verses 15-18 recall the eschatological nature of one of the traditions and vv. 19-20, the commemorative character of the other.[34]

■ **19-20** That Jesus accompanies his action and his words with a prayer ($\varepsilon\dot{\upsilon}\chi\alpha\rho\iota\sigma\tau\acute{\eta}\sigma\alpha\varsigma$, "after he had given thanks"), means that the present moment as well as the future moments are religious and henceforth constitute a ritual.

Christian exegetes are quite often of the opinion that the new ritual "replaces" the Passover. It must be said to them that Luke does not use this verb and that, on the contrary, in Acts he shows Christians who are eager to fulfill their Jewish religious duties.[35] Thus, we must imagine that ceremonies were added rather than substituted, even though, if one reflects systematically, it is well known that the addition of a new element of necessity modifies a given structure.

One can regard vv. 15-18 as a unit (vv. 15-16: eat–eat; vv. 17-18: share–drink), but one is also struck by the symmetries between vv. 16 and 18, on the one hand (Jesus will abstain), and vv. 17 and 19, on the other (the disciples will eat and drink). This contrast between what awaits Jesus and the apostles, however, is not symmetrical, since the food precedes the drink for Jesus and follows it for the disciples. There appears to be a history of diverse traditions behind the text. This fact is confirmed by the last parallel between v. 19 (bread) and v. 20 (cup). A number of symmetrical elements are confirmed by the Pauline parallel (1 Cor 11:24-25), and yet the beginning of v. 20 appears lame and elliptical. The beginning of v. 17 forms a better parallel with the beginning of v. 19. Nevertheless, I find in vv. 15-18 a biographical tradition

directed toward the kingdom and a second, liturgical tradition in vv. 19-20 confirmed by Paul in 1 Cor 11:24-25.

The readers of the Gospel recall the account of the miracle of the loaves and fishes, where they have read the formula, "Then taking the five loaves and the two fish and looking up to heaven, he blessed them and broke them and gave them to the disciples to set before the crowd" (Luke 9:16). Thus, they are not surprised that the bread appears here, broken and distributed, after an act of thanksgiving.

The astonishment comes from the sentence "This is my body, which is given for you." "This" can refer only to the bread. The bread corresponds to the body, represents the body, is "my body." None of the Jewish meals known to us contains a similar formula. Nor are the suggested Greek parallels any more appropriate. The atmosphere may be that of the Passover, but what takes place here is not the Passover. The evangelist, who is drawing here on his church's ritual, is of the opinion that in the Lord's Supper the bread recalls Jesus' act and represents the presence of Christ. This body of Christ, which Luke imagines as risen, he also conceives as crucified. Although the bread, even when broken, is hardly suggestive of a violent death, it is distributed to the participants as the body of Jesus that "is given for you." Luke knows his church's creed and knows that Jesus' death can be considered from different angles. From one perspective it corresponds to the high point of human malice; from another angle it represents the realization of God's plan of redemption. Luke is reserved about the expiatory nature of Jesus' death. It may be that he fears that it will make the believers passive and the irresponsible recipients of cheap grace. Yet he does not hesitate to acknowl-

---

derived from the verb $\gamma\acute{\iota}\nu o\mu\alpha\iota$ ("to become"). It designates what plants produce. It should not be confused with the old word $\tau\grave{o}\ \gamma\acute{\varepsilon}\nu\nu\varepsilon\mu\alpha$, which comes from the verb $\gamma\varepsilon\nu\nu\acute{\alpha}\omega$ ("to beget/generate") and indicates baby animals. Sometimes, however, the scribes substituted one word for the other; see Moulton-Milligan, *Vocabulary*, s.v. $\gamma\acute{\varepsilon}\nu\eta\mu\alpha$; and BAGD, s.vv. $\gamma\acute{\varepsilon}\nu\eta\mu\alpha$ and $\gamma\acute{\varepsilon}\nu\nu\eta\mu\alpha$. It should be said also that the expression is biblical (Isa 32:12; see Deut 22:9; Hab 3:17) as Ulrich Luz has well noted (*Matthew 21–28*, 382 n. 104).

34   The emphasis on fellowship is all the more marked when one recognizes that at the time of the Passover meal each person had his/her own cup. See

Leenhardt, *Sacrement*, 15. In this moment Jesus invites his disciples to share the same cup.

35   It is amazing that in v. 19 Luke speaks of $\ddot{\alpha}\rho\tau o\varsigma$ (normally bread with leaven) after having mentioned in vv. 1 and 7 the feast of unleavened bread ($\tau\grave{\alpha}\ \ddot{\alpha}\zeta\upsilon\mu\alpha$). Jeremias (*Eucharistic Words*, 62–66) is of the opinion that $\ddot{\alpha}\rho\tau o\varsigma$ can be used for the unleavened bread one consumes at Passover. Above all, I think that Luke "forgets" here Jesus' historical Passover meal and thinks only of the liturgical Lord's Supper of the Christians. On the elements of the Eucharist, bread and wine, but also milk and honey, even bread and water, see McGowan, *Ascetic Eucharists*.

edge the biblical tradition of the expiatory suffering of the righteous person. He takes it over in the context of Jesus' passion and will use it again in Paul's speech to the elders of Ephesus intended only for Christians (Acts 20:28).

While in the previous tradition (vv. 15-18) the disciples' present faced the future of the kingdom, this tradition (vv. 19-20) recalls the past of the passion. The anamnesis is as necessary as the prolepsis. The τοῦτο ("this") that is to be remembered (v. 19c) is undoubtedly more wide-reaching than the τοῦτο of "this is my body" (v. 19b). It includes the entire Lord's Supper and not only the bread. The memory is not the nostalgia and melancholy of a past that is over and done with; in keeping with the Jewish concept of the active memory of the history of salvation, it is the realization in the present of the divine benefits. In the form of a narrative Luke is saying that in its saving components Jesus' passion becomes present in the ritual.

Verse 20, which Luke separates from v. 19 with an evening meal, repeats the same truth by mentioning the cup.[36] What meal is it that has taken place between the two? The Passover meal? The presence of the words "after the supper" (μετὰ τὸ δειπνῆσαι) is dictated by the liturgical tradition that influences the narrative.

In Luke's day the early Christians were aware of being the people of the end of time. They made the prophecy of Jeremiah 31 about the new covenant their own. They understood the death of their Lord as an atonement (v. 19) and as a covenant sacrifice (v. 20). Thus, they are not merely spectators of an end; they are also the participants of a beginning. This new beginning does not mean that the old is rejected. On the contrary, in keeping with the economy of salvation, it is highly valued. That a cup can represent a covenant is possible only if it is recognized that the wine it contains is shed just as the blood of the victim was shed at the foot of the altar. That the wine is drunk causes a telescoping of images—here the wine is shed; there it is drunk. In the worship of the Lukan community the content of the cup was certainly drunk, but a

distinction was made between this act and the presentation of the cup, an effective sign of the new covenant.

Grammatically, the construction of v. 20 resembles that of v. 19, but its elements are more extensive: "this cup" of v. 20 corresponds to the "this" of v. 19; "the new covenant in my blood, which is shed for you" corresponds to the "my body, which is given for you." The longer formula here is not only heavy; it is also awkward. The words "shed for you" (τὸ ὑπὲρ ὑμῶν ἐκχυννόμενον), which speak of blood, are neuter, just as the word αἷμα ("blood") is neuter, yet they are in the nominative or accusative case, while the word blood is in the dative (ἐν τῷ αἵματί μου, "in my blood"). "The new covenant" (ἡ καινὴ διαθήκη) is in the nominative, but it is feminine. Roland Barthes has said that transgression begins in grammar. Let us say that the Christian innovation begins in the subversion of the grammatical order, unless Luke attaches "which is shed for you" (τὸ ὑπὲρ ὑμῶν ἐκχυννόμενον) to "this cup" (τοῦτο τὸ ποτήριον). That is not very likely, since that could create a tension with vv. 17-18. Finally, in spite of the waves this anacoluthon raises, the meaning is clear. The cup here constitutes the new covenant that is established in the blood of Jesus, and this blood has been shed for you.

One finds here, as in v. 19, a play between the first person singular (μου) and the second person plural (ὑμῶν). The fellowship is not only established among "you"; it is also created between "you" and "me." The interplay of "I" and "you" in vv. 15-18 had not yet created a fellowship between Christ and his church.

The reference to the cup is explained within the framework of the meal, especially of the paschal meal. One should not forget, however, the metaphorical range accorded it. To the divine judgment to which the Old Testament writings allude (Ezek 23:31-34; Jer 25:15-16, 27-28) is added death in the later Jewish literature. In the *Testament of Abraham,* the last enemy presents himself with the words: "I am the bitter cup of death." Twice the *Targum Neofiti I* uses the expression "to taste the cup of death," and the Rainer fragment of the *Apocalypse of Peter*

---

36   The adverb ὡσαύτως ("likewise") appears in the fourth position, while in 1 Cor 11:25 it comes first. Schürmann (*Einsetzungsbericht,* 34–36) is of the opinion that this difference could have an implication for the meaning. One could understand the Lukan formulation to be saying that Jesus also took the cup after the supper (i.e., the bread had also been taken after the supper).

announces to the apostle that he will have to drink this cruel chalice.[37] The image is also obviously present in the Gospels, when Jesus wishes to avoid "this cup" (Luke 22:42 parr.) or when he tells the disciples that they too will have to drink it (Mark 10:38-39 par. Matt 20:22-23; Luke does not have this passage). Here in v. 20 "this cup" corresponds exactly to the death of Jesus.

Once again the Lukan Jesus has practiced commensality with his disciples.[38] As was often the case (see 7:36-50; 14:1-24), during the meal he propounds a teaching that was not without relationship to the food. Here the institution of the Lord's Supper is inserted into the last meal; thus, the liturgical future has its roots in the historical event.[39]

The resulting story, which influences the readers and their theological thought, is amazingly rich.[40] It touches the meaning of unexpected events such as Jesus' brutal death; the emptiness left by the Master's absence; the communion of the disciples, who do well to rely on one another; the demarcation between insiders and outsiders; and the sharing of spiritual and eschatological goods.

History of Interpretation

In his commentary on Matthew, Ulrich Luz presents the history of interpretation of the story of the Last Supper, placing the emphasis on the development of its artistic representations and on the debates on the subject at the time of the Reformation.[41] Thus, it is not expedient to repeat here what he has done so well. It is desirable, however, to find some commentaries occasioned by Luke's own statements in the Gospel, principally in vv. 15-18.

With reference to v. 15, Tertullian emphasizes the knowledge and will of Jesus, who knows when he must suffer and why this time is providential. The Master is not, as Marcion would like to have him, hostile toward the Passover. It is a festival that belongs to him and that he definitely wants to celebrate.[42] In the African's eyes Jesus is like the paschal lamb whose blood is the bearer of salvation, and he wants to turn the symbol into reality. Jesus' desire is focused on the essence of the harmony between the Testaments and on the realization of salvation. To underscore this divine plan, Tertullian does not hesitate to repeat several times the verbs to wish (*concupio* and *concupisco*) and even to speak once of Jesus' intense feeling (*ideo et adfectum suum ostendit*, "this is why he also showed his feeling"). He specifies in addition that "it would have been unworthy of God to wish for something foreign to him"[43]

37   *Testament of Abraham* (long recension) 16.12: ἐγώ εἰμι τὸ πικρὸν τοῦ θανάτου ποτήριον; *Targum Neofiti* Gen 40:23 and Deut 32:1; *Apoc. Pet.* 14.4 (Rainer fragment); see also *Asc. Isa.* 5.13 and *Mart. Pol.* 14.2; Légasse, "Métaphore"; Le Déaut, "Calice"; Speier, "Kosten."

38   Various authors correctly connect the Last Supper with other meals that Jesus and/or his disciples share in Luke-Acts; see n. 1 above. See in particular vol. 2 of this commentary on 14:1-24 and the bibliography on the three literary units found there.

39   On the sacred meals in the various religions of antiquity, see the notable works by Klauck: *Herrenmahl,* and *Religious Context,* 42–54, 68–80.

40   See in Smith and Taussig (*Many Tables,* 89–108) the presentation of what the historians of religion from Emile Durkheim to Jonathan Z. Smith have said about the sacred meals. See also Quesnel, *Nourriture et repas.*

41   Luz, *Matthew 21–28,* 352–53, 354–57, 365–78.

42   Jesus' wish is not to destroy the Law but to preserve it: *O legis destructorem, qui concupierat etiam pascha servare!* "O the destroyer of the Law, he who had wished even to preserve the Passover!" *Adv. Marc.* 4.40.1.

43   *Adv. Marc.* 4.40.1 and 3. Since Marcion eliminated v. 16 from his Gospel and seems to have eliminated vv. 17-18 (see Harnack, *Marcion,* 233*), Tertullian begins with the words of institution (vv. 19-20) in order to fight against Marcion's docetism (*Adv. Marc.* 4.40.3–6). It is a matter of true bread and a true cup, he writes, because the elements refer to a real body and real blood. The irony, the rhetorical zest, and Tertullian's logic, which is pushed to absurdity, make this passage difficult to understand. As one can imagine, the African's explanation of "this is my body" in the sense of "that is to say, the form of my body" (*id est figura corporis mei*) has led to commentaries; see the bibliography in René Braun, *Tertullien, Contre Marcion: Introduction, texte critique, traduction et notes* (5 vols.; SC 365, 368, 399, 456, 483; Paris: Cerf, 1990–2004) 4:499.

Unlike Tertullian, Cyril of Alexandria limits Jesus' desire to the occasion and to the unexpected.[44] The Master wants at any cost to keep Judas from having him arrested before the Passover, which would make impossible any typological connection. In addition, Cyril connects the two sayings of Jesus (vv. 15-16) to their realization in the church and not to the end of time. In his eyes God's reign is more a spiritual than an eschatological reality. It is equivalent to "the justification by faith" (τὴν ἐν πίστει δικαίωσιν) and manifests itself in the sacraments of the church.

The Venerable Bede examines vv. 15-18 carefully in order to give a full account (*In Luc.* 6.531–92). Jesus' desire refers to a Passover whose typological value expresses to the world the mysteries of his passion. In an original manner the author refers to the book of Joshua, to the passage that describes the first Passover celebrated after the arrival of the Israelites in Canaan, the passage that also marks the end of the miraculous manna (Josh 5:10-12). What attracts Bede in the episode of the book of Joshua is the concept of transition: from the manna to the food of the country, from Moses to Joshua, from uncircumcision to circumcision. In the same way, Jesus' desire is at the appointed moment to pass from the ceremonies imposed by the law to the mysteries of his body and his blood. Thus, Jesus swore not to eat of the Passover anymore until it was fulfilled in the church (Bede identifies the reign of God with the church). The cup of v. 17 thus refers to the old Passover, which Jesus in his desire intended to bring to an end. Verse 18 can mean simply that Jesus will not eat between this last meal and the day of his resurrection (Bede here quotes Acts 10:41: "We who ate and drank with him after his resurrection from the dead"). It more logically means, however, that Jesus refuses to celebrate the Passover any longer. Every-thing that appears fleshly in the law must henceforth be transferred into a spiritual order. Like many others in the East and West of Christendom in that day, Bede, with his interpretation, deprives Jews of the right to observe their own rituals. There is no room for a double interpretation of the Mosaic commandments. Only the figurative meaning of Exodus 12 (the account of the introduction of the Passover) is essential.[45]

Theophylactus —he had not read Joachim Jeremias!—asks the question: Since the Passover meal is eaten standing up, why did Jesus lie down (v. 15)? (*Enarr. Luc.* 22.14–20).[46] One can suppose, he says, that the Master, once the Passover meal was over, sat informally at the table to eat something else (the author does not seem to subscribe completely to this explanation, but he gives no other). As Jesus "desires" to share this last meal, so he also desires to converse with his disciples. Travelers about to leave on a journey know the value of these last talks. Yet Jesus wishes—one finds again the argument of Cyril of Alexandria—to impart to his disciples the great mysteries of the new covenant.

It is with Theophylactus and Euthymius Zigabenus (*Comm. Luc.* 22.16–18; and esp. *Comm. Matt.* 26.29)[47] that one finds the most precise explanation of vv. 16 and 18. It is given in particular in the commentary of Zigabenus on Matth 26:19, thus a parallel text to which he refers in his commentary on Luke. The hour at which Jesus will again eat will be the hour of his resurrection (Acts 10:41 is quoted as it is in Bede). As a resurrected person, Jesus did not need to eat. If he does, it is so that people will not think he is a phantom (an allusion to Luke 24:37-43). As for the kingdom, it is neither usurped nor is it anachronistic at the time of the resurrection. The resurrection is indeed the moment in which all power is conferred on Jesus Christ.[48]

---

44 Cyril of Alexandria *Serm. Luc.* 141. See Payne Smith, *Cyril*, 2:662–63; Reuss, *Lukas-Kommentare*, 208 (frg. 328).

45 In condensed form, Bede's interpretation becomes part of the *Glossa ordinaria* (*PL* 114:337–38). One can imagine its later success. See, e.g., the formulation in Bonaventure's *Comm. Luc.* 22.3.21 (Bernardini, 545): "Now Christ wanted to eat it because the image was excluded and the truth was introduced."

46 *PG* 123:1068–69.

47 *PG* 129:1077, 669, respectively.

48 In his two works (*Vin nouveau*, 185–234, and "Parole eschatologique") the erudite exegete Paul Lebeau has presented in an exhaustive way what remains of the patristic interpretation of v. 18. For some of the ancient writers as well as for modern exegetes, the statement refers to the eschatological arrival of the kingdom (for Justin Martyr [*Dial.* 51] in a millenarian way; for Titus of Bostra [*Scholia Luc.* 22.16] in a typological way; see Joseph Sickenberger, *Titus von Bostra, Studien zu dessen Lukashomilien* [TU 21; Leipzig: Hinrichs, 1901] 241–42). For others it was

The exegetes of the Renaissance and the Reformation continue to interpret the passage theologically, and they too emphasize the transition from the Old to the New Testament. They also adorn their remarks with historical and philological comments. In particular, one can note accents due to confessional positions. The Protestants underscore Jesus' submission to the Mosaic regulations; the Catholics, the incomparable value of the new ritual.[49] Thus, Erasmus writes that Jesus rejoiced to see this time arrive because he will be refreshed by the salvation of the people. Then he states that the paschal lamb, slaughtered annually, represents the type of Jesus' death. This is why the truth is now present and the shadow will disappear (*Paraphrasis*, 450).

For his part, Calvin is of the opinion that the evangelists do not always respect the chronological order of the events (Luke places the naming of the traitor after the meal, while Mark and Matthew locate it before the meal). He does assume, however, that Judas was present at the Lord's Supper. He then worries about the double reference to the cup in Luke before consoling himself by saying that Jesus "repeated the action once more." Indeed, the ritual of the Jewish sacrifices suggests the historicity of the first cup (Calvin refers to Ps 114–15 [116]:13). The second, Christian cup is part of the "new mystery, whose order is different from the paschal lamb." Nor is it impossible, according to Calvin, that this double reference is "a repetition, (as the Evangelists do sometimes say the same thing twice)." In the eyes of the reformer, what counts is that Jesus scrupulously followed the Law of Moses.[50] For his part, with his philological comments and his relevant quotations from Philo, Josephus, Virgil, and Origen, Hugo Grotius brings us into the modern age.[51]

Conclusion

The Passover is reminiscent of a transition. According to Luke, for the last time Jesus celebrated the exodus from Egypt and called attention to the redemption of Israel. By himself passing through death and experiencing

---

realized at the time of the resurrection and in the meals the risen Christ took with his disciples (thus for Ephraem the Syrian [*Comm. Diat.* 19.5], who quotes Acts 10:41 on this subject as the Venerable Bede and Euthymius Zigabenus also do; see above). Finally, for others it is achieved in the life of the church (thus Jerome *Epist.* 120.2). Origen, who knows and partly defends the eschatological interpretation of Matt 26:29 (the parallel of Luke 22:18), emphasizes the Christian spiritualization of eating and drinking as the fulfillment of the Old Testament; see Origen *Comm. Rom.* 5.1 and *Comm. ser. Matt.* 86. The anonymous Irish author (*Comm. Luc.* 22.15–17 [CCSL 108C:94]) interprets vv. 15 and 17 in three concise and expressive sentences: "That is to say that the desire desires from its desire; that is to say that he desires the New Testament from the Old one." Then: "He shows that the Old Testament Passover is different from the Passover of his passion." Finally: "This cup is the consummation of the Old Testament."

49 That does not prevent Calvin (*Harmony*, 3:133) from writing: "This should pass without any debate: That legal figures were abolished, and a new Sacrament was here brought forward by Christ."

50 Calvin, *Harmony*, 3:128–39; quotations from 132. Calvin proves his historical consciousness by wondering (132) whether the contemporary practice of keeping bread in reserve under the tablecloth is a modern practice or if it goes back to antiquity. In his interpretation of vv. 19-20 he emphasizes the community of believers and attacks the celebration of the Mass by the priest alone (133). He also says that it is Christ, not a human being, who invites to the communion. It is also important to agree about the consecration; there is no change of substance (134). To say that the bread is his body is to make use of sacramental language and to use the rhetorical form of metonymy, that is, the transmutation of the name (134). Calvin attributes his theory of the signs to Augustine (134–35). After quarreling with the "Papists" and their transubstantiation, he attacks, without naming them, the Lutherans and their consubstantiation (he also does not use this word) (135). In his eyes, what counts is moving from the sign to the reality and admiring that in the Lord's Supper, by the presence of the Holy Spirit, there is in true faith fellowship with the Lord, sharing in his flesh and blood (136). The sacrament and its signs are necessary, because the risen Christ is no longer on earth; he is sitting at the right hand of God (136).

51 Grotius, *Annotationes*, 900–903. On 900 Grotius notes that the expression ἐπιθυμίᾳ ἐπεθύμησα ("with all my desire I have wanted") has its parallel in the LXX (Gen 31:30; Num 11:4). The famous lawyer also makes a text-critical comment on v. 17.

resurrection, he will wait for the kingdom of God, which will be established in power at the end of time. Then he will take part in the final Passover. This last Passover will have been fulfilled (v. 16). It will no longer be a ritual. It will be more than a Lord's Supper or a Eucharist. It will be the messianic and eschatological festival (14:24), the time of the reunion and the fullness (see Rev 21:4).

While he is waiting, Jesus leaves his disciples a new ritual, of which nothing suggests that it puts the other ritual in the shadow. This Lord's Supper or Eucharist is a communion with the double characteristic of looking back, toward the death of Christ as an act of redemption and establishment of a new covenant, and ahead, to the kingdom and its joyful banquet.

Bibliography

Arens, Eduardo, *The ΗΛΘΟΝ-Sayings in the Synoptic Tradition: A Historical-Critical Investigation* (OBO 10; Freiburg, Switzerland: Universitätsverlag, 1976) 117–61.

Argyle, A. W., "Luke xxii. 31f," *ExpT* 64 (1952–53) 222.

Baarda, Tjitze, "'Als hij die bedient' Luc 22,27: Marginalia bij een woord van Jezus in het verhaal van het avondmaal in het evangelie van Lucas," in H. H. Grosheide et al., eds., *De knechtsgestalte van Christus: Studies door collega's en oud-leerlingen aangeboden aan H. N. Ridderbos* (Kampen: Kok, 1978) 11–22.

Baladrón, F. Morell, "El relato de la pasión según san Lucas: De Streeter a Brown: 70 años de investigación de la composición de Lc 22–23 [2a parte]," *EstBib* 54 (1996) 79–114, 225–60.

Bammel, Ernst, "Das Ende von Q," in Otto Böcher and Klaus Haacker, eds., *Verborum veritas: Festschrift für Gustav Stählin zum 70. Geburtstag* (Wuppertal: Brockhaus, 1970) 39–50.

Bartsch, Hans-Werner, "Jesu Schwertwort, Lukas xxi.35-38. Überlieferungsgeschichtliche Studie," *NTS* 20 (1973–74) 190–203.

Berger, Klaus, "Der 'brutale' Jesus: Gewaltsames in Wirken und Verkündigung Jesu," *BiKi* 51 (1996) 119–27.

Bischinger, Michael, "Die Zwei Schwerter-Theorie. Exegese. Geschichtliche Untersuchung über die Interpretation von Lk 22,35-38" (diss., Vienna, 1971); inaccessible to me.

Bösen, Willibald, *Jesusmahl, Eucharistisches Mahl, Endzeitmahl: Ein Beitrag zur Theologie des Lukas* (SBS 97; Stuttgart: Katholisches Bibelwerk, 1980) 134–39.

Botha, F. J., "ὑμᾶς in Luke xxii. 31," *ExpT* 64 (1952–53) 125.

Bovon, François, "Effet," 349–59.

Idem, "L'importance des médiations dans le projet théologique de Luc," *NTS* 21 (1974–75), 23–39; reprinted in idem, *L'œuvre de Luc: Études d'exégèse et de théologie* (LD 130; Paris: Cerf, 1987) 181–203.

Idem, "Le salut dans les écrits de Luc: Essai," *RThPh* 3. Reihe 23 (1973) 296–307; reprinted in idem, *L'oeuvre*, 165–79.

Brock, *Mary Magdalene*, 19–40.

Brown, Raymond E., Karl P. Donfried, and John Reumann, eds., *Peter in the New Testament: A Collaborative Assessment by Protestant and Roman Catholic Scholars* (1973; reprinted Eugene, Ore.: Wipf & Stock, 2002) 119–25.

Brown, S., *Apostasy*, 62–63.

Brunet, G., "Et aussitôt le coq chanta," *CCER* 108 (1979) 9–12.

Casey, Maurice, "The Original Aramaic Form of Jesus' Interpretation of the Cup," *JTS* 41 (1990) 1–12.

Christensen, J., "Le Fils de l'homme s'en va, ainsi qu'il est écrit de lui," *ST* 10 (1956–57) 28–39.

Clark, Kenneth Willis, "The Meaning of κατακυριεύειν," in J. K. Elliott, ed., *Studies in New Testament Language and Text: Essays in Honour of George D. Kilpatrick on the Occasion of His Sixty-fifth Birthday* (NovTSup 44; Leiden: Brill, 1976) 100–105.

Clarke, William K. L., "The Use of the Septuagint in Acts," in F. J. Foakes Jackson and Kirsopp Lake, eds., *The Beginnings of Christianity* (5 vols.; London: Macmillan, 1920–33) 2:104.

Clivaz, Claire, "Douze noms pour une main: Nouveaux regards sur Judas à partir de Lc 22.21-2," *NTS* 48 (2002) 400–416.

Cohen, Richard, *By the Sword: A History of Gladiators, Musketeers, Samurai, Swashbucklers, and Olympic Champions* (New York: Random House, 2002).

Crossan, John Dominic, *In Fragments: The Aphorisms of Jesus* (San Francisco: Harper & Row, 1983) 202–4, 285–95.

Cullmann, Oscar, *Jesus and the Revolutionaries* (New York: Harper & Row, 1970) 47–50.

Danker, Frederick W., *Benefactor: Epigraphic Study of a Graeco-Roman and New Testament Semantic Field* (St. Louis: Clayton, 1982) 102.

Idem, "The Endangered Benefactor in Luke-Acts [22,25]," *SBLSP* 15 (1981) 39–48.

Delobel, Joël, "The Sayings of Jesus in the Textual Tradition: Variant Readings in the Greek Manuscripts of the Gospels," in idem, ed., *Logia: Les Paroles de Jésus—The Sayings of Jesus: Mémorial Joseph Coppens* (Leuven: Leuven University Press, 1982) 431–57.

Derrett, J. Duncan M., "History and the Two Swords," in idem, *Studies in the New Testament* (6 vols.; Leiden: Brill, 1977–95) 3:193–99, 200–214.

Dietrich, Wolfgang, *Das Petrusbild der lukanischen Schriften* (BWANT 5/14; Stuttgart: Kohlhammer, 1972) 116–39.

Dupont, Jacques, "Le logion des douze trônes (Mt 19,28; Lc 22,28-30)," *Bib* 45 (1964) 355–92; reprinted in idem, *Études sur les évangiles synoptiques* (ed. Franz Neirynck; 2 vols.; BEThL 70A, 70B; Louvain: Louvain University Press and Peeters, 1985) 2:706–43.

Evans, Craig A., and James A. Sanders, *Luke and Scripture: The Function of Sacred Tradition in Luke-Acts* (Minneapolis: Fortress Press, 1993) 38–44, 154–85, 200–212.

Feldkämper, Ludger, *Der betende Jesus als Heilsmittler nach Lukas* (VMStA 29; St. Augustin: Steyler, 1978) 17–47, 94–116, 206–49, 270–98, 315–37.

Feuillet, A., "Le logion sur la rançon," *RSPhTh* 51 (1967) 365–402.

Finlayson, S. K., "The Enigma of the Swords," *ExpT* 50 (1938–39) 563.

Foerster, Werner, "Lukas 22, 31f," *ZNW* 46 (1955) 129–33.

Fridrichsen, Anton, "Scholia in Novum Testamentum, 1: Luk. 22:31," *SEÅ* 12 (1947) 124–31.

Galot, J., "Le pouvoir donné à Pierre," *EeV* 98 (1988) 33–40.

George, Augustin, "La royauté de Jésus selon l'évangile de Luc," *ScEc* 14 (1962) 57–69.

Gillman, John, "A Temptation to Violence: The Two Swords in Luke 22:35-38," *LouvSt* 9 (1982–83) 142–53.

Gormley, Joan P., "The Final Passion Prediction: A Study of Luke 22:35-38" (Ph.D. diss., Fordham University, 1974).

Gounelle, Rémi, "A propos des volailles cuites qui ont chanté lors de la passion du Christ," in *Recherches Augustiniennes* [Paris] 33 (2002) 19–63.

Guillet, Jacques, "Luc 22,29: Une formule johannique dans l'évangile de Luc?" *RSR* 69 (1981) 113–22.

Gundry, Robert H., "The Narrative Framework of Mt 16,17-19: A Critique of Cullmann's Hypothesis," *NovT* 7 (1964–65) 1–9.

Hahn, *Titles*, 153–55.

Hall, S. G., "Swords of Offence," *StEv* I (TU 73; Berlin: Akademie-Verlag, 1959) 499–502.

Hobhouse, S., "And He That Hath No Sword, Let Him . . . Buy One" (Luke xxii. 35-38)," *ExpT* 30 (1918–19) 278–80.

Hoffmann, Paul, "'Dienst' als Herrschaft oder 'Herrschaft' als Dienst?" *BiKi* 50 (1995) 146–52.

Hoffmann, Paul, and Volker Eid, *Jesus von Nazareth und eine christliche Moral: Sittliche Perspektive der Verkündigung Jesu* (QD 66; Freiburg i. B.: Herder, 1975) 100–105, 186–230.

Hoffmann, Paul, and Christoph Heil, *Die Spruchquelle Q: Studienausgabe Griechisch und Deutsch* (Darmstadt: Wissenschaftliche Buchgesellschaft, 2002) 145.

Jones, D. L., "The Title παῖς in Luke–Acts," *SBLSP* (1982) 217–26.

Joüon, Paul, "Notes philologiques," *RSR* 18 (1928) 345–59, esp. 355.

Klein, Günter, "Die Berufung des Petrus," *ZNW* 58 (1967) 1–44, esp. 39–44; reprinted in idem, *Rekonstruktion und Interpretation: Gesammelte Aufsätze zum Neuen Testament* (BEvTh 50; Munich: Kaiser, 1969) 11–48.

Idem, "Die Verleugnung des Petrus: Eine traditionsgeschichtliche Untersuchung," *ZThK* 58 (1961) 285–328; reprinted in idem, *Rekonstruktion und Interpretation*, 49–98.

Knoch, Otto, "Tut das zu meinem Gedächtnis! (Lk 22,23-27; 2 Kor 11,24f): Die Feier der Eucharistie in den urchristlichen Gemeinden," in Josef Schreiner, ed., *Freude am Gottesdienst: Festschrift für Josef G. Plöger zum 60. Geburtstag* (Stuttgart: Katholisches Bibelwerk, 1983) 31–42.

Kurz, William S., *Farewell Addresses in the New Testament* (Zacchaeus Studies. New Testament; Collegeville, Minn.: Liturgical Press, 1990) 207–35.

Idem, "Luke 22:14-38 and Greco-Roman and Biblical Farewell Addresses," *JBL* 104 (1985) 251–68.

Lampe, G. W. H., "The 'Two Swords' (Luke 22:35-38)," in Ernst Bammel and C. F. D. Moule, eds., *Jesus and the Politics of His Day* (Cambridge: Cambridge University Press, 1984) 335–51.

Larkin, William J., Jr., "Luke's Use of the Old Testament as Key to His Soteriology," *JETS* 20 (1977) 325–35.

Larrabe, J. L., "Confirma en la fe a tus hermanos (Lc 22,32): Magisterio y teólogos en la Iglesia," *Lumen* 31 (1982) 273–99.

Lattey, Cuthbert, "A Note on Cockcrow," *Scr* 6 (1953) 53–55.

LaVerdiere, Eugene A., "A Discourse at the Last Supper," *TBT* 71 (1974) 1540–48.

Lecler, Joseph, "L'argument des deux glaives (Luc xxii,38) dans les controverses politiques du Moyen Age: ses origines et son développement," *RSR* 21 (1931) 299–339; 22 (1932) 151–77, 280–303.

Lee, R. E., "Luke xxii. 32," *ExpT* 38 (1926–27) 233–34.

Lehmann, Martin, *Synoptische Quellenanalyse und die Frage nach dem historischen Jesus: Kriterien der Jesusforschung untersucht in Auseinandersetzung mit Emanuel Hirschs Frühgeschichte des Evangeliums* (BZNW 38; Berlin: de Gruyter, 1970) 103–6, 148–52.

Linnemann, Eta, *Studien zur Passionsgeschichte* (FRLANT 102; Göttingen: Vandenhoeck & Ruprecht, 1970) 70–108.

Eadem, "Die Verleugnung des Petrus," *ZThK* 63 (1966) 1–32.

Lohfink, Gerhard, *Die Sammlung Israels: Eine Untersuchung zur lukanischen Ekklesiologie* (SANT 39; Munich: Kösel, 1975) 79–84.

Lull, David J., "The Servant-Benefactor as a Model of Greatness (Luke 22:24-30)," *NovT* 28 (1986) 289–305.

Martin, Troy, "Time and Money in Translation: A Comparison of the Revised Standard Version and the New Revised Standard Version," *BR* 38 (1993) 55–73.

Maurer, Christian, "Knecht Gottes und Sohn Gottes im Passionsbericht," *ZThK* 50 (1953) 1–38.

McDowell, E. A., "Exegetical Notes," *RevExp* 38 (1941) 44–48.

Minear, Paul S., "A Note on Luke xxii 36," *NovT* 7 (1964–65) 128–34.

Minnerath, Roland, *Jésus et le pouvoir* (PoTh 46; Paris: Beauchesne, 1987) 119–38.

Moulder, W. J., "The Old Testament Background and the Interpretation of Mark x. 45," *NTS* 24 (1977–78) 120–27.

Munck, Johannes, "Discours d'adieu dans le Nouveau Testament et dans la littérature biblique," in *Aux sources de la tradition chrétienne: Mélanges offerts à M. Maurice Goguel à l'occasion de son soixante-dixième anniversaire* (Neuchâtel: Delachaux & Niestlé, 1950) 155–70.

Napier, T. M., "The Enigma of the Swords," *ExpT* 49 (1937–38) 467–70.

Idem, "The Enigma of the Two Swords (Luke xxii. 35-38)," *ExpT* 51 (1939–40) 264.

Nave, Guy D., Jr., *The Role and Function of Repentance in Luke-Acts* (Academia Biblica 4; Leiden: Brill, 2002).

Nelson, Peter K., "The Flow of Thought in Luke 22.24-27," *JSNT* 43 (1991) 113–23.

Idem, *Leadership and Discipleship: A Study of Luke 22:24-30* (SBLDS 138; Atlanta: Scholars Press, 1994).

Idem, "Luke 22:29-30 and the Time Frame for Dining and Ruling," *TynB* 44 (1993) 351–61.

Idem, "The Unitary Character of Luke 22.24-30," *NTS* 40 (1994) 609–19.

Olley, John W., "God on the Move—A Further Look at Kataluma in Luke," *ExpT* 103 (1992) 300–301.

Ott, Wilhelm, *Gebet und Heil: Die Bedeutung der Gebetsparänese in der lukanischen Theologie* (SANT 12; Munich: Kösel, 1965) 75–81.

Petzke, *Sondergut*, 180–84.

Pickar, Charles H., "The Prayer of Christ for Saint Peter," *CBQ* 4 (1942) 133–40.

Piovanelli, Pierluigi, "Livre Du Coq," in François Bovon, Pierre Geoltrain, and Jean-Daniel Kaestli, eds., *Écrits Apocryphes Chrétiens* (Paris: Gallimard, 1997) 2:135–203.

Popkes, Wiard, *Christus Traditus: Eine Untersuchung zum Begriff der Dahingabe im Neuen Testament* (Zurich: Zwingli, 1967) 134–42, 174–81, 217–19.

Prast, Franz, *Presbyter und Evangelium in nachapostolischer Zeit: Die Abschiedsrede des Paulus in Milet (Apg. 20,17-38) im Rahmen der lukanischen Konzeption der Evangeliumsverkündigung* (FB 29; Stuttgart: Katholisches Bibelwerk, 1979) 223–62.

Prete, Benedetto, "Confirma fratres tuos," *SacDoc* 15 (1970) 181–218.

Idem, *Il primato e la missione di Pietro: Studio esegetico-critico del testo di Lc. 22,31-32* (SRivBib 3; Brescia: Paideia, 1969).

Idem, "Il senso di ἐπιστρέψας in Luca 22,32," in *San Pietro: Atti della xix settimana biblica* (Brescia: Paideia, 1967) 113–35.

Quecke, Hans, ". . . euch wie Weizen zu mahlen (Luk 22.31 sahid): Zu den Koptischen Verben sok und sike," *GöMisz* 29 (1978) 101–4.

Radl, Walter, *Paulus und Jesus im lukanischen Doppelwerk: Untersuchungen zu Parallelmotiven im Lukasevangelium und in der Apostelgeschichte* (EHS.T 49; Frankfurt a. M.: Lang, 1975) 40–62, 174–262, 298–387.

Rasmussen, Larry, "Luke 22:24-27," *Int* 37 (1983) 73–76.

Refoulé, François, "Primauté de Pierre dans les évangiles," *RSR* 38 (1964) 1–41.

Rehkopf, Friedrich, *Die lukanische Sonderquelle: Ihr Umfang und Sprachgebrauch* (WUNT 5; Tübingen: Mohr Siebeck, 1959).

Reinach, Salomon, "Les deux épées," *RAECE* 4/19 (1912) 435.

Idem, "Encore les deux épées," *RAECE* 5/10 (1919) 370–71.

Rese, Martin, "Die 'Stunde' Jesu in Jerusalem (Lukas 22,1-53): Eine Untersuchung zur literarischen und theologischen Eigenart des lukanischen Passionsbericht" (Habilitationsschrift, Münster i. W., 1970).

Rickards, Raymond R., "Luke 22:25: They Are Called 'Friends of the People,'" *BibTh* 28 (1977) 445–46.

Robinson et al., *Critical Edition of Q*, 558–61.

Roloff, Jürgen, "Anfänge der soteriologischen Deutung des Todes Jesu (Mk. x. 45 and Lk. xxii. 27)," *NTS* 19 (1972–73) 38–64.

Idem, *Apostolat, Verkündigung, Kirche: Ursprung, Inhalt und Funktion des kirchlichen Apostelamtes nach Paulus, Lukas und den Pastoralbriefen* (Gütersloh: Mohn, 1965) 186–87.

Idem, *Exegetische Verantwortung in der Kirche: Aufsätze* (ed. Martin Karrer; Göttingen: Vandenhoeck & Ruprecht, 1990) 134–42, 181–206, 343–66.

Schenke, *Studien*, 199–285.

Schlatter, Adolf, *Die beiden Schwerter Lukas 22,35-38: Ein Stück aus der besonderen Quelle des Lukas* (BFCTL 20/6; Gütersloh: Bertelsmann, 1916).

Schlosser, Jacques, "La genèse de Luc, xxii, 25-27," *RB* 89 (1982) 52–70.

Schneider, Gerhard, "Jesus vor dem Synedrium," *BibLeb* 11 (1970) 1–15; reprinted in idem *Lukas, Theologe der Heilsgeschichte: Aufsätze zum lukanischen Doppelwerk* (BBB 59; Königsstein: Hanstein, 1985) 158–72.

Idem, "'Stärke deine Brüder!' (Lk 22,32): Die Aufgabe des Petrus nach Lukas," *Catholica* 30 (1976) 200–206; = Albert Brandenburg and Hans Jörg Urban, eds., *Petrus und der Papst* (Münster: Aschendorff, 1977) 36–42; reprinted in idem, *Lukas*, 146–52.

Schulz, Siegfried, *Q—Die Spruchquelle der Evangelisten* (Zurich: Theologischer Verlag, 1972) 330–36.

Schürmann, *Abschiedsrede*.

Schwarz, Günther, *Jesus und Judas: Aramaistische Untersuchungen zur Jesus–Judas–Überlieferung der Evangelien und der Apostelgeschichte* (BWANT 123; Stuttgart: Kohlhammer, 1988) 110–15, 162–75.

Idem, "κύριε, ἰδοὺ μάχαιραι ὧδε δύο," *BN* 8 (1979) 22.

Sellew, Philip, "The Last Supper Discourse in Luke 22:21-38," *Forum* 3, no. 3 (1987) 70–95.

Sloan, Ian, "The Greatest and the Youngest: Greco-Roman Reciprocity in the Farewell Address, Luke 22:24-30," *SR* 22 (1993) 63–73.

Stauffer, Ethelbert, "Abschiedsreden," *RAC* 1 (1950) 29–35.

Idem, *New Testament Theology* (trans. John Marsh; New York: Macmillan, 1955) 344–47.

Steen, Norman Bruce, "The Interpretation of Jesus' Sword-Saying in Luke 22:35-38" (Diss., Calvin Seminary, 1981).

Sterling, "*Mors Philosophi.*"

Sutcliffe, Edmund F., "'Et tu aliquando conversus,' St. Luke 22,32," *CBQ* 15 (1953) 305–10.

Tannehill, Robert, "A Study in the Theology of Luke-Acts," *ATR* 43 (1961) 195–203.

Taylor, Vincent, *The Passion Narrative of St. Luke: A Critical and Historical Investigation* (SNTSMS 19; Cambridge: Cambridge University Press, 1972) 59–61.

Thompson, James, "The Odyssey of a Disciple (Luke 22,31-34)," *RestQ* 23 (1980) 77–81.

Thomson, P., "ἐπιστρέφω (Luke xxii. 32)," *ExpT* 38 (1926–27) 468.

Tiede, David L., "The Kings of the Gentiles and the Leader Who Serves: Luke 22:24-30," *Word and World* 12 (1992) 23–28.

Tierney, Brian, "A Scriptural Text in the Decretales and in St. Thomas: Canonistic Exegesis of Luke 22,32," *StGra* 20 (1976) 363–77.

Tobin, William J., "The Petrine Primacy: Evidence of the Gospels," *LV* 23 (1968) 27–70.

Trimaille, "Manger et boire," 121–37.

Vogler, Werner, *Judas Iskarioth: Untersuchungen zu Tradition und Redaktion von Texten des Neuen Testaments und ausserkanonischer Schriften* (ThA 42; Berlin: Evangelische Verlagsanstalt, 1983) 43–47, 79–81.

Vööbus, Arthur, *The Prelude to the Lukan Passion Narrative: Tradition-, Redaction-, Cult-, Motif-Historical and Source-Critical Studies* (PETSE 17; Stockholm: ETSE, 1968) 29–40.

Walter, Nikolaus, "Die Verleugnung des Petrus," *ThV* 8 (1977) 45–61, esp. 50–53.

Western, W., "The Enigma of the Swords," *ExpT* 50 (1938–39) 377.

Idem, "The Enigma of the Swords, St. Luke xxii, 38," *ExpT* 52 (1940–41) 357.

Wickert, Ulrich, "'Und wenn du dermaleinst dich bekehrst, so stärke deine Brüder': Der Bischof von Rom und die Einheit der Christen," *Cath(M)* 30 (1976) 269–94.

Wright, W. F., "Studies in Texts," *Theol* 44 (1942) 296–300.

21	"But behold, the hand of the one who betrays me is with me at the table,[a] 22/ for the Son of Man goes as it has been ordained, but woe to that person[b] by whom he is betrayed." 23/ And they began to argue among themselves who of them might be about to do this.	a Literally: "on the table." b Literally: "that human being." c Another translation: "which of them seemed to be greater." d Literally: "reign over them." e Another translation: "claim to be."
24	But there was also a dispute among them about which of them was to be regarded[c] as the greatest. 25/ He said to them, "The kings of the nations are their sovereigns,[d] and those who have authority over them are called[e] benefactors. 26/ But with you it is not so. Instead, let the greatest among you become like the youngest, and the one who governs as the one who serves. 27/ For who is greater, the one who lies at the table or the one who serves? Is it not the one who is at the table? But I am in your midst as the one who serves.	

28	"But you, you are the ones who have stayed with me in my ordeals. 29/ I thus grant the kingdom for you as my father had granted it for me, 30/ so that you eat and drink at my table in my kingdom, and you will sit on thrones judging the twelve tribes of Israel.
31	"Simon, Simon, behold Satan has laid claim to you in order to sift you like grain.f 32/ But I have asked for you that your faith not fail. And you, once you have changed,g strengthen your brothers." 33/ And he said to him, "Lord, I am ready to go with you, even to prison and even to death." 34/ But he said, "I tell you, Peter, the cock will not have crowedh today until you have denied three times that you know me."
35	Then he said to them, "When I sent you out without a purse and bag and sandals, were you lacking anything?" They answered, "Nothing." 36/ Then he said to them, "But now, whoever has a purse, take it, likewise a bag, and whoever does not have a sword, let him sell his coat and buy one. 37/ For I say to you that this thing that has been written must be fulfilled in me, namely, 'and he was reckoned with the lawless men,' because thus what concerns me has its fulfillment."i 38/ They said, "Lord, here are two swords."j He said to them, "It is enough."

f   Another translation: "to shake you in the sieve."
g   Another translation: "when you have turned back."
h   Literally: "will not sound."
i   Literally: "Because the thing concerning me has an end."
j   Literally: "Lord, behold, here, two swords."

The readers of the Gospel have long known that the life of Jesus is coming to an end. The author has just reminded them of it by portraying the Passover as a last supper ("before my passion," v. 15). Thus, the conversation that takes place in this hour is a final conversation.

Synchronic Analysis

Death always gives an undeniable importance and authority to a person's last words. Plato's *Phaedo* retains the memory of Socrates' farewell;[1] the Bible transmits Moses' spiritual testament.[2] The Greek parallels evoke the past; are concerned about a future characterized by the absence of the philosopher or the political figure; think of continuity, of honor, and of what is to be done; reflect finally on life after death. The Hebrew parallels share all of these concerns, but they often see things from God's point of view. They speak of the plan the Lord puts into practice, the covenant he has made with the entire nation, and the defense that people must make to the deity in the face of history's cruelty. In spite of numerous sketches and many enumerations of parallel texts, it is not possible to define strictly a precise genre or to list their essential elements. The New Testament contains various farewell speeches, the best known of which are those of Jesus in the Gospel of John (John 13–17) and Paul in the Acts of the Apostles (Acts 20:18-35). Since Luke and Acts constitute one work written by the same author, it goes without saying that the exegete will look at this speech.[3] The reader notices that the

1   To the final chapters of the *Phaedo* one can add other examples: Plutarch *Vita, Cato minor* 66–70; Plutarch *Vitae, Otho* 15–17; Diogenes Laertius *Vitae, Epicurus* 15–22; see Kurz, "Luke 22," 261.

2   To Deuteronomy (Deut 28:69—30:2) one can add Tobit 14 and the *Testaments of the Twelve Patriarchs.*

Kurz ("Luke 22") calls special attention to 1 Macc 2:49-70 and 1 Kgs 2:10 as parallels to Luke 22.

3   On Acts 20:18-35 see Stauffer, *New Testament Theology*, 344–47; Munck, "Discours d'adieu," 155–70; Jacques Dupont, *Le discours de Milet: Testament pastoral de Saint Paul (Actes 20, 18-36)* (LD 32; Paris:

Lukan Paul gradually justifies his past by recalling his efforts, announces the unavoidable fate to which he subjects himself, exhorts the elders to care for the flock that cannot survive without shepherds, anticipates the dangers that threaten the community. Then Christ's witness entrusts his hearers to the deity before reiterating all the merits of his ministry, and he ends his farewell homily by quoting a saying of Jesus. If the Lukan Paul insists on his innocence and the value of his ministry (Acts 20:18-21, 26-27, 31, 33-35), it is because it has to be defended. The tone of Jesus' last conversation in Luke 22:14-38 is quite different. If there are defendants, they are the disciples and not the Master: Judas of course (vv. 21-23), then all the disciples (vv. 24-27), finally Peter (vv. 31-34). Unlike Acts 20, Luke 22 contains no recollection of the ministry of Jesus, nor does it speculate about the impending death. Attention is paid almost exclusively to the disciples (one is not yet speaking about the communities of believers and the believers whom the Twelve will lead to Christ). For Judas it is a case of guilty failure that the divine foreknowledge describes as "economic" necessity (vv. 21-23). For the disciples the future opens on a certain type of authority, namely, that which is the opposite of power: service (vv. 24-27).[4] An eschatological promise corresponds to this injunction: the invitation to the kingdom's banquet and the promise of final magistracy (vv. 28-30).[5] For Peter it will be a way of ups and downs, of a detour and a return, finally of a conversion and a comfort that he can give to others (vv. 31-34). The alternating particular and general lead finally to an enig-matic thought—that of the two swords—that is intended for everyone (vv. 35-38).

Concerning Luke 22:15-38, the exegetes are right to speak of a "farewell,"[6] but they are probably wrong to speak of a farewell "speech." We have here rather a final conversation. Even if Jesus conducts it in a masterly way, the Twelve intervene on several occasions (vv. 23, 33, 35c, 38a). Luke himself alternates between narrative passages and the words exchanged at the table.[7] Nine times he introduces new comments by Jesus and three times sentences by the disciples.[8] Such a presentation corresponds to a dialogue. This conversation has its rhythm and its themes. It speaks first of the immediate future, Jesus' final fate (vv. 21-23); then it uncovers the disciples' future in the church (vv. 24-27) before opening their eschatological horizon (vv. 28-30). Finally it returns the attention to the present and the apostolic mission (vv. 31-34 and 35-38).

Diachronic Analysis

If one examines the style of this pericope and the sequence of its elements, one sees rough transitions.[9] The transition from the Lord's Supper to the designation of the traitor is jarring. It consists only of the expression "but behold" ($\pi\lambda\dot{\eta}\nu$ $\dot{\iota}\delta o\acute{\upsilon}$, v. 21). To be abrupt, it is abrupt. To be sure, the reality is also harsh: the arrest follows hard on the heels of the Last Supper (vv. 47-54). The second transition is done gently. The new element is introduced with the formula $\dot{\epsilon}\gamma\dot{\epsilon}\nu\epsilon\tau o$ $\delta\dot{\epsilon}$, "now it came

---

Cerf, 1962); Rudolf Pesch, *Die Apostelgeschichte* (2 vols.; EKK 5; Neukirchen-Vluyn: Neukirchener Verlag, 1986) 2:196–208; C. K. Barrett, *A Critical and Exegetical Commentary on the Acts of the Apostles* (2 vols.; ICC; Edinburgh: T. & T. Clark, 1994, 1998) 2:961–84.

4   Fitzmyer (2:1412) makes a good observation. After vv. 21-23, which show how far the treason of a close relation can go, it is logical that one thinks of the other extreme: Who is the best? (vv. 24-27). He writes: "This seems to be the logic in the Lucan collocation of the parts of the discourse."

5   Nelson ("Character") regards vv. 24-30 as a coherent unit: the great ones, A (vv. 24-25), must become servants, B (vv. 26-27); the servants, B´ (v. 28), will become great, A´ (vv. 29-30). He is of the opinion that this schema expresses a unifying symbolism:

the death and resurrection of Jesus constitute a pattern that the disciples are to imitate.

6   See Schlatter, *Schwerter;* Schürmann, *Abschiedsrede;* Prete, *Primato;* Kurz, "Luke 22"; idem, *Farewell Addresses;* Nelson, *Leadership;* idem, "Character."

7   Verses 14, 17a, 19a, 20a, 23a, and 24 are narrative.

8   With reference to Jesus, see vv. 15a, 17b, 19a, 20a, 25a, 34a, 35a, 36a, and 38b. (One must add the three times when Jesus says that he is speaking, thus where he seizes the word—vv. 16a, 18a, and 37a). See, with reference to the disciples, vv. 33a, 35c, and 38a (one must add v. 23b, where the style is indirect).

9   See the report on Lukan research and Luke's sources in the passion narrative from the pen of Baldarón, "Relato."

to pass" (v. 24), translated as "but there was," which the evangelist used in his Gospel when he wanted to pass from one episode to the other (as in 6:12). A formal relationship also facilitates the juxtaposition of vv. 21-23 and 24-27. The reference to the traitor ends with the question: "who of them might be about to do this?" (τὸ τίς ἄρα εἴη ἐξ αὐτῶν ὁ τοῦτο μέλλων πράσσειν, v. 23); and the subject of the argument is also similarly formulated as a question: "which of them was to be regarded as the greatest" (τὸ τίς αὐτῶν δοκεῖ εἶναι μείζων, v. 24). Observing the contents of these two units, however, one cannot avoid recognizing that their themes are different: the betrayal of the leader, on one hand, the desire to control his companions, on the other. The following transition is no better. One can approve the formal structure of alternating the personal pronouns: v. 26 "you," v. 27 "I," v. 28 "you" again, then v. 29 "I," and v. 30 "you." Yet in considering the content of vv. 24-30, one can only wonder at the diversity of the themes. The subject of mutual service among disciples is abruptly abandoned on behalf of the solidarity with the afflicted Master. Of course, one can say that there is a connection and that the same ethical requirement underlies the attitudes that complement one another, and one can add that vv. 29-30 speak of the reward that is promised with this virtue. Still, it is not very coherent. The topic is scarcely mentioned before it is abandoned and the perspective narrows. Suddenly the Master—we are not told why—addresses only one of his disciples. Although he had spoken about the betrayer in the third person, he speaks to Simon in the second person. He offers a reminder of something of which the disciple seems not even to be aware. Satan appears to be truly awakened. He has laid claim to the disciples, beginning with Simon (v. 31), as he had earlier taken possession of Judas (v. 3). For his part Jesus has not remained inactive; he has displayed the power of his prayer. As a result Simon will not lose faith, and he will effect his conversion (with these two complementary terms Luke defines the essence of Christian existence). This will be only the beginning point. The imperative "strengthen" (στήρισον) dominates vv. 31-33. One is

astonished, however, by the unexplained combination of the kingdom (vv. 29-30) and the church (v. 32), all the more so as Peter's final fate returns to the foreground (vv. 33-34). A short dialogue reveals the unconscious self-assurance of the apostle, whom the Master reprimands. Why, finally, is the spokesman of the Twelve called by turns Simon (v. 31) and Peter (v. 33)? Is it an allusion to 6:14? In vv. 35-38 one moves, if not from one shore to the other, at least from the singular "you" to the plural "you," from the immediate to the distant future, from denying to militancy. Here again the readers notice an abrupt change of orientation.

As we have seen, we have in this pericope not a farewell speech but a final dialogue. It should be added that the dialogue does not progress according to the logic of a Plato. It resembles more a museum room in which are hanging, discreetly framed, the sayings of the Master. If a literary antecedent must be sought, one should turn to the collections of sentences and proverbs.

I pose the thesis that at the end of the episode of the miraculous discovery of the upper room Luke abandoned one of his sources, the Gospel of Mark, and from that point on (v. 14) has rejoined his second source, the special material.[10] Even those who assume the existence of a parallel source admit the influence of Mark here or there in our pericope. Heinz Schürmann, for example, thinks that in the reference to the betrayer (vv. 21-23) and Peter's boastfulness (vv. 33-34) Luke is following Mark and not the special source.[11] Others are of the opinion that in the following unit about power and service (vv. 24-27) Luke also makes use of Mark but of a passage prior to the passion narrative (Mark 10:41-45), a passage he had earlier neglected (see Luke 18:31-43).[12] Personally, I do not make this concession. Verses 21-23 may relate the same thing as Mark 14:18-21, but they are written in a different way. When one puts Mark 14:18-21 and Luke 22:21-23 side by side in parallel columns, one is compelled to see two independent formulations. Luke speaks of the hand, Mark of one of the Twelve; Luke of the table, Mark of the dish; Luke of what has been ordained, Mark of what has been written. The bearers of

---

10 With Schürmann (*Abschiedsrede*, 139–40), at the conclusion of an analysis of more than one hundred pages.

11 Schürmann, *Abschiedsrede*, 3–35.

12 See Fitzmyer, 2:1411–14 (the relationship of vv. 24-26 to Mark 10:42-44 may be clear, but determining the relationship of v. 27 to Mark 10:45 is delicate).

Mark's tradition and those of the special source remember Jesus' premonition and a sentence that evokes both the fate of the Son of Man and the curse on the one who does the crime, but they transmit their memory independently of one another.[13]

One need only compare Mark and Matthew to understand what a literary dependence is. On the question of the betrayal (Mark 14:18-21 par. Matt 26:21-25) as well as the dispute about greatness (Mark 10:41-45 par. Matt 20:24-28) Matthew draws abundantly from Mark. By contrast, Luke makes use of a different account of the passion. Dependent on historical memory, its sequence differs little from that of Mark, but its statements have few common elements. I can imagine that if Luke did not follow Mark in chap. 18 (true greatness), it is because he knew that an episode parallel to Mark 10:41-45 was going to emerge from his second source in the course of the passion narrative. For this reason, following his technique of alternating material, Luke does not part company with his special source during all of vv. 15-38. He takes from Mark neither the designation of the betrayer (vv. 21-23) nor the invitation to service (vv. 24-27). Nor does he take from Q the statement about the twelve thrones (vv. 28-30). As Matt 19:28 suggests, this statement probably existed in the Sayings Source, but Luke prefers the version of his source, which contains the contrast, not found in Matthew and Q, between persevering in the trials and glory in the kingdom.[14]

As we have seen, in vv. 31-34 the special material knows the same episodes as the tradition preserved in Mark (Peter's arrogance and the prophecy about the cock). It also preserved—as the only source to do so—a command addressed only to Simon Peter. Our detailed analysis will make it possible to show what change Luke makes in the tradition he takes up again. It appears that Luke's redaction is stronger in v. 32 than in v. 31.[15]

The announcement of the denial (vv. 33-34) is like the designation of the betrayer. The narratives in Mark and the special material are parallel, but each account tells the story in different terms. In Mark, Peter speaks a double oath: that he will not stumble and that he will die with Jesus (14:29, 31ab). In Luke, he speaks only one oath: that he is prepared to accept prison and even death (v. 33). Luke does not mention the night to which Mark calls attention. The cock crows twice here (Mark) and once there (Luke). In Mark (14:31c) the other disciples echo Peter's words; in Luke they do not intervene.

It is easy to say that the episode of the two swords (vv. 35-38) appears only in Luke. It is more difficult to decide whether it comes from the special material or is the fruit of Luke's editorial activity.[16] On one hand, there are numerous redactional elements. First, the vocabulary: ἄτερ ("without"), νῦν ("now"), τὸ γεγραμμένον ("what is written"), δεῖ ("it is necessary"), τελῶ ("to fulfill" in the passive), τὸ περὶ ἐμοῦ ("what concerns me").[17] In addition, the references in the text to the missionary address (10:4) appear to reflect an intention of the evangelist. Finally, the prophetic haziness, that is, the sentence's ambiguity, seems to be typically Lukan.[18] On the other hand, there are also non-Lukan elements in these verses,[19] the most obvious being the reference itself to the missionary address. Curiously, Jesus refers not to the instructions given to the Twelve (9:3), as he should have done in the circumstances, but to those given to the Seventy (10:3).

The recourse to the special material also creates a difficulty, because the reference is to 10:3, to the missionary address, which originates in Q! To complicate the

---

13   On v. 23, Rehkopf (*Sonderquelle*, 21–27) suggests that the expression συζητεῖν πρὸς ἑαυτούς ("to argue among themselves") is traditional. Luke would have written more correctly συζητεῖν πρὸς ἀλλήλους ("to argue, one with the others"). This is undoubtedly not the opinion of the numerous interpreters who think that Luke follows only Mark and, under the double pressure of his imagination and a few isolated memories, gives him a new turn. See, among many others, Rese, "Stunde," 95–100, 131–34.

14   Most scholars choose a different solution. On the most recent reconstruction of Q, see Robinson et

al., *Critical Edition of Q*, 558–61. These authors are of the opinion that these verses constituted the conclusion of the Sayings Source. See also Hoffmann and Heil, *Spruchquelle*, 112–13, 145.

15   On these verses, see esp. Prete, *Primato*, 57–73.

16   See already Alfred Loisy, *L'Évangile selon Luc* (Paris: Émile Nourry, 1924) 521. Fitzmyer (2:1428–31) lines up with those who see a tradition behind these verses, and he cites those who share his opinion.

17   See Fitzmyer, 2:1429.

18   See Bovon, "Effet," 349–59.

19   See Taylor, *Passion Narrative*, 67–68.

matter, the episode of the two swords not only refers to the past; it speaks too of another, future episode that also implies a sword, the one in which Peter cuts off the ear of the servant of the high priest (vv. 49-51). Luke treats this episode, however, in a manner more reminiscent of John 18:10-11 than of Mark 14:47! Finally, it must be said that v. 37 merits special treatment. It is not an indispensable part of the unit about the two swords, and, introduced as it is with "for I say to you" ($\lambda\acute{\epsilon}\gamma\omega\ \gamma\grave{\alpha}\rho\ \acute{\upsilon}\mu\hat{\iota}\nu$), it must have had an independent existence.

To sum up: The description of the tableaux to which Luke invites us here (vv. 21-38) has its organizer—the author of the special source, whose passion narrative was so similar to that of Mark that without any loss Luke could pass from one to the other. That is what he does here, even if he is not ignorant of Mark's parallels to certain episodes. Yet the special material's greater richness induces him to prefer it to the Markan text. Except for a certain amount of editorial retouching, vv. 21-38 come from the special source.

Commentary

■ **21-23** As in v. 4 and v. 6, the verb "to deliver, to hand over" ($\pi\alpha\rho\alpha\delta\acute{\iota}\delta\omega\mu\iota$) is used (vv. 21, 22).[20] This "delivery," which is to become "tradition," is more important than the "betrayal" ($\pi\rho o\delta\acute{\iota}\delta\omega\mu\iota$). The "hand" is a metonym of the person and of that person's active will. The "hand" can save as well as lead to death. Essential to life, it also expresses personal identity.[21] Judas, whose name (v. 3) is omitted, belongs to the group; more precisely, he has a

personal relationship with its chief "with me" ($\mu\epsilon\tau'\ \acute{\epsilon}\mu o\hat{\upsilon}$, v. 21).[22] For the ancients, as for people today, commensality ($\acute{\epsilon}\pi\grave{\iota}\ \tau\hat{\eta}\varsigma\ \tau\rho\alpha\pi\acute{\epsilon}\zeta\eta\varsigma$, "at the table")[23] expresses social and emotional relationships, established or anticipated.

The early Christians had to find a justification for the abominable thing that Judas was doing. A sentence whose subject is the solemn "Son of Man" does the job.[24] That Jesus goes ($\pi o\rho\epsilon\acute{\upsilon}\epsilon\tau\alpha\iota$) to his fate corresponds to Luke's Christology.[25] The evangelist agrees with God's first defenders, who say that this fate of the Messiah corresponds to the divine plan. In Acts, Luke will use the same verb, "to fix, ordain" ($\acute{o}\rho\acute{\iota}\zeta\omega$), and the composite "to fix in advance" ($\pi\rho oo\rho\acute{\iota}\zeta\omega$).[26] The "hand" of the lawless people is mentioned also in one of these parallels (Acts 2:23); in another, the hand of God (Acts 4:28). Without greater reflection on the matter, for Luke the hand of Judas and the hand of God are joined together. The plan of the one has taken human form in the conspiracy of the other. The parallels in Mark and Matthew explain this divine "economy" by referring to the Scriptures (Mark 14:21; Matt 26:24). Luke will also soon quote it (v. 37). That, however, by no means removes the paradox. Jesus' death is a human crime as well (see the schema of contrasts in Acts in, e.g., Acts 4:10). The Judas who is ordained by God's foreknowledge has earned the laments: The $o\grave{\upsilon}\alpha\acute{\iota}$ ("woe unto") is reminiscent of the woes of the beatitudes (Luke 6:24-26).[27] The betrayal is like the crucifixion. There are two sides to the same act: the positive side, the beatitude, which corresponds to God's plan (doubtless because of the saving fruit this death constitutes), and the negative side, the curse,

20   See Popkes, *Christus Traditus*, 134–42, 174–81, 217–19.
21   See vol. 1 of this commentary, 201–5, on 6:6-10.
22   "With me" is found in Mark 14:20 and Matt 26:23. The hand appears in Matt 26:23 and, implicitly, in Mark 14:20. These words must have belonged to the passion narrative that the early Christians recounted.
23   The use of $\acute{\epsilon}\pi\acute{\iota}$ with the genitive and the definite article $\acute{\eta}$ correspond to current language; see the examples cited by BAGD, s.v. (for movement one use with the accusative).
24   On the title "Son of Man" in Luke, see vol. 1 of this commentary, 183, n. 31 on 5:21-24. The article by Gerhard Schneider mentioned in that footnote is included in Schneider, *Lukas*, 89–113.
25   See the Lukan summary reports in 9:51; 13:22 ($\delta\iota\alpha\pi o\rho\epsilon\acute{\upsilon}o\mu\alpha\iota$); 17:11. Mark 14:21 and Matt 26:24 use the verb $\acute{\upsilon}\pi\acute{\alpha}\gamma\omega$, "to go away."
26   The simple verb appears on the lips of Peter (Acts 2:23) and Paul (Acts 17:26, 31), the compound $\pi\rho oo\rho\acute{\iota}\zeta\omega$, whose meaning is little different, on the lips of the early Christians in prayer (Acts 4:28).
27   The relationship even includes the connection $\pi\lambda\grave{\eta}\nu\ o\grave{\upsilon}\alpha\acute{\iota}$ ("but woe").

which corresponds to the human plot.[28] A person is identified with each side: Jesus, the Son of Man ($\upsilon\dot{\iota}\dot{o}\varsigma$ $\tau o\hat{\upsilon}$ $\dot{\alpha}\nu\vartheta\rho\dot{\omega}\pi o\upsilon$) and the "human being" ($\dot{\alpha}\nu\vartheta\rho\omega\pi o\varsigma$), the "person" of Judas.[29] No evangelist was willing to live with the paradox. Mark explains the curse (14:21c); Matthew takes over the explanation and adds a short dialogue between Jesus and Judas (26:24c-25). Luke continues by mentioning the question the disciples asked among themselves (v. 23).[30] One needs the genius of a Karl Barth and the sensitivity of a dialectical theologian to express the mystery of an absolute divine power that puts up with and even makes use of human malice.

■ **24-27** The following episode[31] corresponds well to a "dispute" ($\varphi\iota\lambda o\nu\epsilon\iota\kappa\dot{\iota}\alpha$), even if the first meaning of the word were "desire to win."[32] The term is well chosen. Unlike the Synoptic parallel (Mark 10:35-45), nothing here indicates that James and John (or their mother, Matt 20:20!) are behind this crisis. The text is imprecise, saying only that tension erupts among the disciples. After the worst is described (vv. 24-25), here the best is demanded (vv. 26-27). The comparative, "greater," "better" ($\mu\epsilon\dot{\iota}\zeta\omega\nu$),[33] understood in the sense of "better" than the others, came to designate "the best" of all, "the greatest," "the strongest."

Some have wanted to see no criticism of political power in v. 25, since the benefactors, as their name indicates, wanted only good and the book of Acts applies the verb of this family of words to Jesus himself (Acts 10:38).[34] That is an incorrect understanding of the usage of language, of the intentions of the benefactors,[35] and of the exercise of power. On language, the same term can be understood in a good or a bad sense; Satan can "rule" as well as Christ! On benefactors, antiquity's patrons were generally forced into the role by the pressure of the social system of the day. They profited from it by gaining clients and by enhancing their reputation. On the exercise of power, it is true that kings and authorities can rule by practicing justice, but that is never guaranteed in advance. In no case can they humble themselves enough to offer themselves in sacrifice, nor can they love enough to be servants by giving up their authority.

To be sure, it would be an exaggeration to understand the verb $\kappa\upsilon\rho\iota\epsilon\dot{\upsilon}\omega$ in the sense of exerting excessive power or an abuse of power, but it would be equally wrong to confuse ancient monarchies with modern democracies. One easily understands the title $\beta\alpha\sigma\iota\lambda\epsilon\dot{\upsilon}\varsigma$, which legally designates a king or an emperor, but in popular language it can indicate all kinds of potentates. Less easy to understand is the presence of the participle "those who have authority." One often finds the $\dot{\epsilon}\xi o\upsilon\sigma\dot{\iota}\alpha\iota$ in the lists

---

28   Instead of the classical $\mu\dot{\epsilon}\nu$ . . . $\delta\dot{\epsilon}$, Luke uses the rougher $\mu\dot{\epsilon}\nu$ . . . $\pi\lambda\dot{\eta}\nu$. Furthermore, the text of this v. 22 has variants. The most important: the words $\ddot{o}\tau\iota$ $\dot{o}$ $\upsilon\dot{\iota}\dot{o}\varsigma$ $\mu\dot{\epsilon}\nu$ correspond to $\kappa\alpha\dot{\iota}$ $\dot{o}$ $\mu\dot{\epsilon}\nu$ $\upsilon\dot{\iota}\dot{o}\varsigma$ in many manuscripts, beginning with Alexandrinus (A = 02).

29   Christensen ("Fils de l'homme") emphasizes the contrast between the departure of the Son of Man and the betrayal of Judas. He is furthermore of the opinion that a passage from the book of Ezekiel clarifies the Lukan verse. Ezekiel 12 tells of the departure in exile of the prophet, called "son of man," who by night, encumbered with his baggage, leaves the company of the godless people. The early Christians would have seen in this passage a prophecy of Jesus' fate.

30   The philologist admires the literary quality of v. 23. One finds there various Lukan ingredients: the use of the verb $\ddot{\alpha}\rho\chi o\mu\alpha\iota$ with the meaning "to begin," the preposition $\pi\rho\dot{o}\varsigma$ ("intended for"), translated as "among," the use of the neuter article $\tau\dot{o}$ followed by a clause, the indirect question expressed by an optative ($\epsilon\ddot{\iota}\eta$), the Hellenistic use of $\mu\dot{\epsilon}\lambda\lambda\omega$ with

the present infinitive (classical: future infinitive), and the Christian understanding of a divine plan (see BAGD, s.v., $\mu\dot{\epsilon}\lambda\lambda\omega$, 1c$\delta$).

31   In a completely Lukan manner it is introduced with $\dot{\epsilon}\gamma\dot{\epsilon}\nu\epsilon\tau o$ $\delta\dot{\epsilon}$ ("but there arose, happened").

32   According to the etymology: $\varphi\dot{\iota}\lambda o\varsigma$ ("friend") and $\nu\dot{\iota}\kappa\eta$ ("victory"). The two orthographies coexist, but the correct orthography must be $\varphi\iota\lambda o\nu\iota\kappa\dot{\iota}\alpha$, see Moulton-Milligan, *Vocabulary*, s.v.

33   The form is classical. The popular form $\mu\epsilon\iota\zeta\dot{o}\tau\epsilon\rho o\varsigma$ appears as soon as the comparative value of $\mu\epsilon\dot{\iota}\zeta\omega\nu$ is no longer understood (see 3 John 4). The superlative sense of this comparative is well attested; see BAGD, s.v. $\mu\dot{\epsilon}\gamma\alpha\varsigma$, 2b$\alpha$.

34   See the surprising article by Lull, "Servant-Benefactor."

35   On the term $\epsilon\dot{\upsilon}\epsilon\rho\gamma\dot{\epsilon}\tau\eta\varsigma$, see Fitzmyer, 2:1417; BAGD, s.v.; Paul Veyne, *Le pain et le cirque: Sociologie historique d'un pluralisme politique* (Univers historique; Paris: Seuil, 1976); Richard P. Saller, *Personal Patronage under the Early Empire* (New York: Cambridge University Press, 1982).

of powers,[36] but why do we have here the participial form of the verb? The concept of "authority" (ἐξουσία) is not unexpected, since it often appeared along with that of "power" (δύναμις) in order to designate power as a recognized power. Along with his *imperium* and his *potestas*, the Roman emperor appreciated his *auctoritas*.[37] Here, alongside the kings whose power is noted (κυριεύω, "to reign, to rule"),[38] are, probably on a lower level, all who exercise authority over these nations (note the genitive τῶν ἐθνῶν, "of the nations" and the double αὐτῶν, which keep the power and authority grounded). Whether καλοῦνται is passive or middle is a matter of controversy: "are they called" or "do they call themselves"?[39] As is often the case, Luke does not bother to clarify the matter, since, all things considered, the two go together. Those who pay for the restoration of the Barker Center of Harvard University are happy to be called patrons, and their gift is the reason for this designation. I imagine that they do everything they can to welcome this praise.

Luke is no more precise when he writes the following ellipse: ὑμεῖς δὲ οὐχ οὕτως. Is it an indicative: "with you it is not so," or an imperative: "as for you, it is not to be so"? It is necessary to maintain the ambiguity of the text, which, like the beatitudes, describes a situation and imposes an attitude. The Christian community does not make use of the criteria of political society; indeed, it should not use them.[40] Verse 26 makes explicit the imperative (γινέσθω, "let become"), v. 27 the indicative (εἰμί, "I am"). What gives the text its power is that the imperative is deployed in an ecclesial context and the indicative in a christological reality. This distinction is underscored with the words "the youngest" (νεώτερος), and the "responsible" person, the "one who leads" (ἡγούμενος). Luke uses the first term in Acts 5:6, probably to describe a group of young Christians (young in age and by virtue of their recent conversion).[41] The second term appears in Hebrews to indicate, if not a ministry, at least an ecclesial responsibility. "Remember," writes the author "your leaders" (μνημονεύετε τῶν ἡγουμένων ὑμῶν, Heb 13:7). He says that these responsible persons have proclaimed the Word of God.[42] By subverting the human system of authority and the exercise of power, the Jesus of Luke (who must reflect the historical Jesus here) requires that the person at the top lower himself. In this sense there is a double demand, for this movement, this inversion, is difficult to bring about. The inverse is not necessary now. It will take effect only in the kingdom (vv. 28-30), where the humblest will rule and will judge Israel.

For the present, here below in the church, it is the christological model that dominates: "But I am in your midst as[43] the one who serves" (v. 27b). And so that will be clear, since the setting is a meal, the distinction is made between the one who has taken his place at the table (the ἀνακείμενος, the guest seated at the table[44]) and the active servant (twice Luke chooses ὁ διακονῶν, "the one who serves," over διάκονος "the servant," because he knows that there are inactive and incompetent servants; 12:45-46). This servant Christology casts light on life in the church, as a number of pericopes have already suggested. Jesus frequently referred to the image of the "servant": 12:35-40, 41-46, 47-48; 17:7-10.[45] Luke, who is concerned to establish this christological founda-

---

36 Romans 8:38; 1 Cor 15:24; Eph 1:21; 3:10; 6:12; Col 1:13, 16; 2:10, 15; 1 Pet 3:22.

37 See François Bovon, *Révélations et écritures: Nouveau Testament et littérature apocryphe chrétienne: Recueil d'articles* (MB 26; Geneva: Labor et Fides, 1993) 132.

38 On κυριεύω and κατακυριεύω, used by the parallels Mark 10:42 and Matt 20:25, see Clark, "Meaning."

39 See Fitzmyer, 2:1416–17.

40 In my view the biblical text does not justify what Fitzmyer (2:1417) writes: "Jesus's injunction must be rightly understood; he does not eliminate distinction or rank in Christian life. . . . His words are not to be understood in an egalitarian sense. . . ."

41 A few verses later (Acts 5:10), apparently with no reason, Luke changes and makes use of the word νεανίσκοι ("young men").

42 For centuries and still today, ὁ ἡγούμενος, the *hegumen* (also *hegumenos, igumen*) is the monk who is in charge of a Greek Orthodox monastery.

43 With Schlosser ("Genèse," 67–68) we must understand the ὡς here in the sense of "as" and not "as an example of."

44 In spite of the reservations of the Atticists (Phrynichus 187 [191], 79), the verb ἀνάκειμαι is frequently used with the meaning of "being at the table"; see BAGD, s.v.; and Schürmann, *Abschiedsrede*, 81-82.

45 See the valuable study of Alfons Weiser, *Die Knechtsgleichnisse der synoptischen Evangelien* (SANT 29; Munich: Kösel, 1971).

tion for the church's ministry, is not influenced by Mark's soteriological parallel (10:45), even though he is familiar with it.[46] He prefers to stay with his own tradition, even if the Christology of service to which it bears witness is less forceful than the Christology of redemption of Mark 10:45. He has nothing against atonement. He is simply giving his undivided attention to the Christ who offers himself as a model to his church, and especially to the persons in charge of it.[47]

■ **28-30** In the context of Judas's betrayal and Peter's denial, the assertion of the disciples' solidarity is an intrusion. This positive note seems to "forget" Judas and to anticipate Peter's transformation (v. 32b). In Acts, Peter will belong to the collective of the Twelve, while Judas will be excluded from it (Acts 1:15-26). Once this identification and this realization of the "you" are made, the intrusion offers a welcome touch of color. After he has commanded the disciples to serve in the church (vv. 26-27), Jesus promises them a kingdom and announces a banquet (vv. 29-30).

Verse 28 bears editorial marks, either those of the author of the special source or of Luke himself. The verb "to remain," "to persevere" (διαμένω) appears another time in Luke-Acts, in connection with Zechariah and his deafness (1:22). The term "test," "temptation" (πειρασμός) occurs in the plural in Acts in a similar context. In Acts 20:19 it is Paul who bids farewell and speaks of his trials. One remembers also the end of the temptation story (Luke 4:13), when the devil ended every "temptation" (πειρασμός) and withdrew to wait for his hour. This hour comes in 22:3 when he reappears to enter into Judas. Contrary to the opinion of Hans Conzelmann,[48] Luke does not think that Jesus is free of temptations between these two moments. The expression ἐν τοῖς

πειρασμοῖς μου proves it. It is simply that the temptations at the beginning and end were the most intensive and the most dramatic.

Verses 29-30 recall a former affirmation: "Do not fear, little flock, your Father was well pleased to give you the kingdom" (12:32).[49] Remembering the trials is today's response to the earlier fear. The Father's role in relation to the kingdom is proclaimed. The role of Christ, absent in 12:32, is doubly emphasized here. It is no longer "your Father" but "my Father" who is the master of the kingdom, and he gives it not directly, but through his Son as mediator (διατίθεμαι, "I grant"). Is there an interest in the times of these events? The Father's action is expressed in the aorist "he has granted" (διέθετο) that of the Son in the present tense. Is it a present referring to a continuing reality (Christ's faithfulness) or a present referring to an immediate future (beginning with the resurrection or the ascension)? I lean toward the first option: The Son's permanent offer responds to the disciples' perseverance. Did chap. 10 not say that the kingdom had already come near to you (10:9b)? Did not chap. 17 affirm that in the person of Jesus the kingdom was "in your midst," "in the space that is yours" (17:21b)? The "as" (καθώς) is important. At issue is the continuity of salvation history and the harmony between God's world and that of creation. God entrusted his power to the Son, who will share it with his people.[50]

As is often the case in the biblical tradition, the kingdom and Luke's reception of it are understood as a banquet (14:24) anticipated and symbolized by Jesus' meals with his disciples or with sinners (5:29-32; 7:34-35; 15:2; 19:5-7; 22:14). The expression "at my table" connects this future of the kingdom with the present of the Lord's Supper (v. 21).[51] People have wondered about the

---

46 There is an unexpected parallel in the Matthean speech against the Pharisees: "The one who is greatest among you will be your servant" (Matt 23:11). Ulrich Luz (*Matthew 21–28*, 98) is of the opinion that it acts here as a shortened redactional doubling of Matt 20:26.

47 Schlosser ("Genèse") thinks, on the contrary, that vv. 25-27 are a strongly edited new reading of Mark 10:42-45 and that they originate in no other source.

48 Conzelmann, *Theology*, 80–83.

49 See vol. 2 of this commentary, the analysis and interpretation, on 12:32.

50 Guillet ("Formule johannique") adds v. 29 to the

already long list of parallels between the Gospel of Luke and the Gospel of John. He is thinking of John 15:9; 15:12; or 20:21. He calls attention to καθώς, "which establishes not a simple comparison, but a comparison between relations" (114). He cites Olivier de Dinechin, "Καθώς: la similitude dans l'évangile selon saint Jean," *RSR* 58 (1970) 195–236. It would be a mistake to detach v. 29 from v. 30 or to separate v. 29 from v. 28; the alternation "I"—"you" is an indication of the connection among these three verses and of their internal coherence.

51 See Oscar Cullmann, *La foi et le culte de l'Église primitive* (Bibliothèque théologique; Neuchâtel:

connection between the Father's kingdom and that of the Son. In my opinion, they refer less to different realities than to different periods. If we compare our passage with 1 Cor 15:23-28, we discover that the early Christians wondered about the "order" ($\tau\acute{\alpha}\gamma\mu\alpha$) of the last events: When death has been destroyed, Christ the king will finally give power back to his Father.[52] "Eating" and "drinking" have always expressed the essence of a meal.[53]

The parallel of Matt 19:28, which probably comes from Q, also speaks of the end of the times, the reign of the Son, and the function of judge granted to the Twelve. Thus, we are dealing with a very early hope of the first Christians. This hope is connected with the conviction that they are Israel (see Gal 6:16) and with the memory of the judges who formerly led the nation. Thus, the function described by the verb "to judge" ($\kappa\rho\acute{\iota}\nu\omega$) is not only legal; it also includes executive power.[54] This power will not be exerted independently of the competence of the Son, who in the parable in Matt 25:34 is represented as the eschatological "king" and in the kerygmatic formulas as the judge ($\kappa\rho\iota\tau\acute{\eta}\varsigma$) of the living and the dead (Acts 10:42). In the days of Jesus and the apostles, the image of the throne took on a spiritual import (one thinks of celestial powers, "thrones," alongside the other forces, all of which were understood as threatening God's authority)[55] or an apocalyptic import (one waits for God and his angels ultimately to exert the power represented by the thrones).[56]

■ **31-34** Jesus speaks to one of the Twelve.[57] This disciple carries his old Semitic name, Simon, and one knows him since the miraculous catch of fish (5:4, 5, 8, 10) and the call to be an apostle (6:14).[58] From the beginning Luke has instructed his readers that this disciple has another name, a new name, a surname of sorts, "Peter" (5:8), that he received from Jesus (6:14). Furthermore, the evangelist used this new name a few lines earlier (22:8) and will again make use of it later (22:34). The tradition of the double name Simon Peter is largely attested in the New Testament (see, e.g., Matt 16:16). Yet before he was called "Peter," which is a Greek form, this new name was Cephas, which is the Semitic form (it is attested by the apostle of the Gentiles in 1 Cor 1:12; 3:22; 9:5; 15:5; Gal 1:18).[59] Paul makes it clear (Gal 2:8-14) and John affirms (John 1:42) that the Semitic term Cephas is translated into Greek as Peter.[60]

Delachaux & Niestlé, 1963). This author rigorously draws a distinction between the two realities.

52 It must be admitted that 1 Cor 15:23-28 is difficult to understand. See Wolfgang Schrage, *Der erste Brief an die Korinther* (EKK 7/4; Neukirchen-Vluyn: Neukirchener Verlag, 2001) 150–231.

53 On eating and drinking in Luke, see Trimaille, "Manger et boire."

54 I share the opinion of Fitzmyer (2:1419), who also refers to Ps 121 (122):4-5 and to the replacement of Judas by Matthias (Acts 1:15-26).

55 This is why the Christians expect their destruction (1 Cor 15:24) or subjection (Eph 1:20-21).

56 On the throne of God, see Matt 23:22; Acts 2:30; Heb 12:2; Rev 4:2; on the throne of Christ, Matt 25:31; Acts 3:21; on the throne of God's assistants, Rev 4:4 and 11:16. In a number of texts Christ is called upon to share the throne with God (Rev 3:21; 5:6; 22:1), which calls particular attention to the problematic of the reign of God and the reign of Christ mentioned above (see above and n. 51). On the symbolism of the throne, see G. Cope, "Throne Symbolism in the New Testament," *StEv* 3 [TU 88] (1964) 178–82.

57 On vv. 31-32, see the study by Prete (*Primato*), where the tradition history, the literary structure, the historical context, the vocabulary, the redactional elements, and the doctrinal range are studied in turn. See also Foerster ("Lukas") and Pickar ("Prayer"), who observes that Jesus' words are divided into three parts (vv. 31, 32a, 32b).

58 There are other Simons mentioned in the New Testament. To avoid confusion they are always precisely identified. To stay with Luke, there are Simon the Zealot (6:15; Acts 1:13), Simon the Pharisee (7:40, 43, 44), Simon the Magician (Acts 8:9; here the presentation differs somewhat: Luke speaks of "a certain man called Simon," making it impossible to confuse this new person with Simon Peter), and finally Simon the tanner (Acts 10:6, 17, 32).

59 I have a friend from the German-speaking part of Switzerland who has been living a long time in French Switzerland. I continue to call him Peter, even though he prefers to be called Pierre.

60 The Greek *Martyrdom of Peter* as well as the Greek Rainer fragment of the *Apocalypse of Peter* refer to the apostle as Peter. See Léon Vouaux, *Les Actes de Pierre: Introduction, textes, traduction et commentaire* (Les apocryphes du Nouveau Testament; Paris: Letouzey et Ané, 1922) 398–467; and M. R. James,

The repetition of a name in the vocative is not unusual in Semitic languages. Luke, or his tradition, makes use of this process in 6:46 ("Lord, Lord") and in 10:41 ("Martha, Martha").[61] It appears again in Acts 9:4 ("Saul, Saul"). It expresses regard and affection, sometimes with a nuance of remonstrance.

Simon Peter is challenged as a person responsible for and/or representing the Twelve. The readers remember that at the transfiguration Luke presented "Peter and those who were with him" (9:32). In Acts they will discover Peter's leading role.[62]

Satan becomes especially active again at the end of the Gospel. He has entered Judas (22:3), and he lays claim to the disciples. By claiming the apostles he acts as a public prosecutor who at God's court has the task of prosecuting the guilty. The evangelist uses here the verb "to claim" ($\dot{\epsilon}\xi\alpha\iota\tauο\hat{υ}μαι$), which appears only here in the New Testament but is well attested in Greek literature, in both its active and middle forms. In the active it means "to ask," "to claim"; in the middle, as here, "to claim for oneself."[63] It is exactly the attitude Satan adopts when he appears before God to "claim" Job and when God places Job at Satan's mercy (Job 1:6-12; 2:1-6; to be sure, the verb $\dot{\epsilon}\xi\alpha\iota\tauο\hat{υ}μαι$ does not appear here in the LXX, but the reality is there).[64]

Satan doubtless claims the disciples ("you") from God in order to subject them to the test of the sieve.[65] This "sifting" can be understood in two ways. The grain can pass through the sieve, which catches the largest waste, or it can retain the grain and let the straw and other impurities pass through.[66] Luke used the same kind of metaphor in his portrayal of John the Baptist (3:17). There it is "the stronger one" who, with his fan in hand, cleans his floor and gathers the grain ($\sigmaῖτος$, the same word as here).[67] The verb $\sigma\iota\nu\iota\dot{α}\zeta\omega$ is late and probably has the same meaning as $\sigma\dot{η}\vartheta\omega$, "to sift," "to filter."[68] It appears to come from the word $\sigma\iota\nu\dot{ι}ον$, which must mean the "screen," the "sieve." If one brings these terms closer to $\sigmaῖνος$ ("injury," "damage") this sifting cannot take place without a certain violence. This is the way the Christian writers understood it: "to shake," "to disturb," then "to try," "to test."[69]

The grain is seen in a positive light, as is suitable for Jesus' disciples and friends. Without going so far as the metaphor of the grain of wheat that dies (John 12:24), the comparison, by making use of the rare verb "to sift" ($\sigma\upsilon\nu\iota\dot{α}\zeta\omega$), mentions a trial in which a person might be defeated. Since the previous verse (v. 28) has affirmed the disciples' continuing victory during the ministry of Jesus, the reference here cannot be to the same tests or

"The Rainer Fragment of the Apocalypse of Peter," *JTS* 32 (1931) 270–71. The Latin text of the *Acts of Peter* (*Actus Vercellenses* 33) has the following curious explanation that makes sense only in Latin: "My name is Peter [*Petrum*], because Christ the Lord found it good to call me 'ready for everything' [*paratum*]." See Vouaux, *Actes de Pierre*, 364–65. In the patristic age some authors, probably offended by the conflict between Paul and Cephas in Antioch (Gal 2:11-14), assumed that among the early Christians there were other people called Cephas in addition to Simon Peter. See Hans Dieter Betz, *Galatians: A Commentary on Paul's Letter to the Churches in Galatia* (Hermeneia; Philadelphia: Fortress, 1979) 95–97, 102–12.

61   See vol. 1 of this commentary, 253 n. 57, on 6:46; and vol. 2 on 10:41.

62   See Oscar Cullmann, *Peter: Disciple, Apostle, Martyr: A Historical and Theological Study* (2d ed.; Philadelphia: Westminster, 1962); Dietrich, *Petrusbild*; Bovon, *Luke the Theologian*, 388–91; Brock, *Mary Magdalene*, 19–40.

63   See Bailly, s.v.

64   See Prete, *Primato*, 80. On Job 1, see Samuel Terrien, *Job* (CAT 13; Neuchâtel: Delachaux & Niestlé, 1963) 54–56, 58–59; Wiefel, 374.

65   Petzke (*Sondergut*, 181) thinks (wrongly, in my opinion) that Satan's presence relieves Peter of a good part of his responsibility.

66   See Foerster ("Lukas," 130–31), who chooses here the first method and cites Sir 27:4: "When a sieve is shaken, the refuse remains; so a man's filth remains in his thoughts."

67   See vol. 1 of this commentary, 126–27, on 3:17. Pickar ("Prayer," 135) is of the opinion that "the stronger one" in 3:17 is Christ and composes this striking formula: "Our Lord used a fan and winnowed to get rid of the chaff, but Satan a fan and winnowed to get rid of the wheat."

68   See LSJ, s.v.; Prete (*Primato*, 81–82) brings the meaning closer to that of the verb $\lambda\iota\kappa\mu\hat{\omega}$ ("to crush," Matt 21:44 par. Luke 20:18) and recalls Amos 9:9-10 (Israel will be shaken).

69   See Lampe, s.v.

to the same period. This testing probably refers to the behavior of Jesus' closest companions during the passion of their Master. It is known that the Gospels were concerned about this matter and had divided opinions. Mark and Matthew do not hesitate to describe them as cowards who fled (Matt 26:31 par. Mark 14:27, then Matt 26:56 par. Mark 14:50). Luke tends to spare them by remaining discreet.

The Master adds that, to thwart Satan's efforts, he has prayed that Peter's faith not disappear.[70] This statement confirms the framework of a trial, which presupposes Jesus' words—a trial at God's court. On the one hand, Satan "demanded" and obtained the right to test Peter. On the other, Jesus, regarded in his divine greatness more than in his precarious humanity, "requested" as an attorney, and it was granted to him that Peter's faith finally would prevail.[71] The time of the trial is not given, but it lies in the past (see the two aorist verbs). The judge, God the Father, is not mentioned, nor is his judgment explicitly given.[72] Why?

The denial (v. 34) is not part of the loss of faith (v. 32); it is part of the test (v. 31). Since there will be immediate repentance, not without Jesus' help (22:61-62), the continuity of Peter's life of faith is assured. He will return to himself as well as to God. Jesus can already proclaim it: "once you have changed" ($\dot{\epsilon}\pi\iota\sigma\tau\rho\dot{\epsilon}\psi\alpha\varsigma$).[73] The figure of Peter is representative of humanity. The underlying anthropology lays out the fall and the restoration. Without offering an easy consolation, it includes men and women in an existence stretched between the threat of an active evil and salvation by a risky faith. According to Luke, the double activity of Satan and Christ does not fix life in a determinism that frees people from their own culpability. Human responsibility still exists, but it can rejoice in the support of God and his Messiah. Jesus "turned" to Peter ($\sigma\tau\rho\alpha\varphi\epsilon\dot{\iota}\varsigma$, 22:61). The participle is from $\sigma\tau\rho\dot{\epsilon}\varphi\omega$, the verb that is present also in Peter's "once you have changed" ($\dot{\epsilon}\pi\iota\sigma\tau\rho\dot{\epsilon}\psi\alpha\varsigma$, v. 32). The text understands faith as the essential sign of the refound life. It is the faith to which the Acts of the Apostles is devoted. Yet it remains a human, and thus fragile, reality, a perishable good about which the Lukan Jesus is concerned: "When the Son of Man comes, will he find faith on the earth?" (18:8).[74]

Simon Peter not only represents human beings; he is also the main person responsible for the community. The Italian exegete Benedetto Prete does not hesitate to speak here about the "primacy" of Peter. Let us say that Jesus' sentence presupposes the apostle's pastoral function and defines its main mission. Simon Peter will fulfill his ministry by strengthening his brothers and sisters.[75] At the very least, the idea of primacy is ambiguous, because today it cannot ignore Roman pontifical claims. It is also made questionable by the term "brothers,"

---

70 On Jesus' prayer for Peter, see Pickar, "Prayer." On $\delta\dot{\epsilon}o\mu\alpha\iota$ ("to pray," "to request") see Prete, *Primato*, 84. On $\dot{\epsilon}\kappa\lambda\epsilon\dot{\iota}\pi\omega$ in an intransitive sense, "to be wanting," "to disappear," see 16:9 and vol. 2 of this commentary on 16:9; Prete, *Primato*, 86–87. On Peter's $\pi\dot{\iota}\sigma\tau\iota\varsigma$, Peter's faith, see Prete, *Primato*, 87–90.

71 See Pickar, "Prayer," 135 (with reference to Satan: "The use of the aorist here implies success in the demand") and 136 (with reference to Jesus: "The prayer of Christ for Peter was efficacious").

72 Many of the biblical parallels quoted by modern authors on vv. 31-34 had already been cited by medieval authors; see the numerous quotations in Bonaventure's commentary, *Comm. Luc.* 22.1–45 (Bernardini, 552–53); he calls attention in succession to Matt 16:16 (Peter's privilege), Zech 3:1 (Satan's presence), Job 1:6 (Satan's role), Sir 27:4 (sieve), Rom 15:1 (supporting the weak), Prov 18:19 (according to the Vulgate, brother supported by a brother), 1 Cor 15:57 (our victory in Christ), 1 Pet

5:10 (God will strengthen you after the test), Rom 1:11-12 (desire to be comforted), Job 4:4 (judgments that redress, make right), John 13:36-37 (Peter today and tomorrow), Ps 102 (103):14 and Ps 93 (94):11 (God knows us), Prov 28:26 (the fool and the wise).

73 On this aorist participle, which is intransitive here, see BAGD, s.v., and Prete, *Primato*, 91–93; Pickar, "Prayer," 137–40. Sutcliffe ("Aliquando") gives five ways of understanding this participle. He chooses the fifth, which is different from mine: "and do thou in turn confirm thy brethren," that is, strengthen your brothers as I have strengthened you. Grotius (*Annotationes*, 908) had anticipated this solution; see below, at the end of the "History of Interpretation" of this section.

74 See vol. 2 of this commentary on 18:8b.

75 In the *Phaedo*, shortly before his death Socrates exhorts his disciples to be strong (*Phaed.* 117E).

178

which, unlike "children," eliminates the paternal image from the line of authority.[76] For Luke, the Christian community does not survive without persons in charge (the reality principle excludes the euphoric utopias of the enthusiasts). Yet these ministers, who do not exist prior to the community[77] and who express their authority in service (22:26-27), do not constitute a society separate from the people of the church. Nor do they structure themselves hierarchically. Peter does not have the primacy portrayed in the works of art of the Middle Ages, dressing him, the fisherman of Galilee, in episcopal and pontifical clothing with the tiara.[78] As *primus inter pares* Peter is here the responsible brother, who, along with others, will be the leader in the church of Jerusalem before going away to another place (a discreet allusion to his death, Acts 12:17).[79]

The term "brother" and the absence of "sister" are explained by the presence of the Twelve. They also reflect the customs of the time, which, unfortunately, often ignore the presence of women. In one's interpretation, however, understanding ἀδελφοί inclusively as brothers and sisters is not forbidden.[80]

The verb "to strengthen" (στηρίζω) belongs to the characteristic vocabulary of the church's ethic.[81] In a time when the life of faith is threatened by waiting and its accompanying weariness, by the inner threats that shake the energies of believers, and by outer pressures that question one's Christian identity, one must strive to stay the course. Thus, the leaders' responsibility is to comfort, to encourage, and to strengthen. For his part, God shares in this task. He strengthens the hearts just as he established the universe.[82] There is an implicit analogy between creation and redemption. Rooted in the moral vocabulary of Judaism,[83] the verb "to strengthen" is applied by Paul to the personal discipline of the faithful (see Rom 1:11; 1 Thess 3:2, 13). Its usage is current in the Christian writings at the end of the first century. One finds it in the Deutero-Pauline letters, the Catholic

---

76 In the Latin correspondence found recently at Vindolanda in the north of England during the excavations of a Roman camp next to Hadrian's wall, the people doing the writing greet one another with the words "brother" or "sister," even though they are not connected by family ties. See Alan K. Bowman, *Life and Letters on the Roman Frontier: Vindolanda and Its People* (London: British Museum, 2003) 134–35; and Anthony Birley, *Garrison Life at Vindolanda: A Band of Brothers* (Stroud: Tempus, 2002) 106–11. On ἀδελφοί as the designation of the members of the community in the New Testament, especially in Luke (6:41-42; Acts 1:15-16; 6:3, etc.), see BAGD, s.v.

77 See Jacques Dupont, "Les ministères de l'Église naissante d'après les Actes des apôtres," in *Ministères et célébration de l'Eucharistie: Sacramentum 1* (Studia Anselmiana 61; Rome: Anselmiana, 1973) 94–148; Jean Delorme, ed., *Le ministère et les ministères selon le Nouveau Testament* (Parole de Dieu; Paris: Seuil, 1974), esp. the articles by Annie Jaubert on the community and Augustin George on Luke-Acts; Bovon, *Luke the Theologian*, 407–25.

78 See, e.g., the altarpiece of Saint Peter by Martin de Soria (Aragon), active from 1471 to 1487, preserved at the Museum of Fine Arts in Boston. See the *Illustrated Handbook: Museum of Fine Arts* (Boston: Museum of Fine Arts, 1976) 262–63.

79 Schneider ("Stärke") thinks, contrary to Oscar Cullmann ("Πέτρος, Κηφᾶς," TDNT 6 [1968]

100–112), that Luke's image of Peter differs from those of Matthew and Mark. According to Luke, Peter's ministry involves more than encouraging the brothers. Moreover, according to Acts, after the apostle has disappeared, others, especially Paul, will feel called to strengthen the communities. In addition, Peter is not simply the beginning point of the church and its first leader; he is also a missionary. His sudden disappearance means that others will continue his task, especially that of encouraging the brothers. Pickar ("Prayer") notes that here, as in Matt 16:16 and John 21:15-19, Christ is especially concerned for Peter. Picker includes all of the apostles and the believers in this concern of Jesus.

80 This is what the *NRSV* does when it encounters the vocative ἀδελφοί ("brothers").

81 See Günther Harder, "στηρίζω, κτλ.," TDNT 7 (1971) 653–57; Gerhard Schneider, "στηρίζω etc.," EDNT 3 (1993) 276; Prete, *Primato*, 93–94.

82 The verb στηρίζω can also express the stability and the organization of the universe, created and "established" by God. See *1 Clem.* 33.3; also *1 Clem.* 8.5 on God's intention.

83 In the LXX, see, e.g., Ps 50 (51):14 סמך, a Hebrew equivalent of στηρίζω, takes on an ethical importance in the writings of Qumran. See 1QS 4.5; 8.3; 1QH 1.35; 2.9. In the rabbinic writings this verb is the technical term for the ordination of rabbis; see *b. Sanh.* 14; *b. ʿAbod. Zar.* 8b; Harder, "στηρίζω," 655.

Epistles, and the writings of the Apostolic Fathers.[84] Luke uses the compound verb ἐπιστηρίζω four times in Acts (14:22; 15:32, 41; 18:23), where it confirms the meaning given here.[85] Just as in earlier days material nourishment, bread, strengthened the hearts of the Israelites and prepared them for action (see Judg 19:5), today in the same way the apostolic word (Luke 22:32) and the gift of the Spirit (Rom 1:11) support the faith of the Christians. The verb "to strengthen" (στηρίζω) and the term "brothers and sisters" (ἀδελφοί), as well as the context of Luke 22:31-32, suggest a post-Easter perspective.[86] Luke accepts Peter's leadership[87] just as Matthew does in the famous statement "You are Peter" (16:18).[88]

The transition from vv. 31-32 to vv. 33-34 is abrupt, even if in the two paragraphs Jesus is speaking only with Simon Peter. In fact, Luke appears to change the subject here, since he first quotes Peter's arrogant statement. Based on its contents, the wording of the special source—since that is what we are reading here—contains information found in the three canonical Gospels. Peter's mistaken diagnosis in overestimating himself is vigorously corrected by Jesus who refers to the crowing of the cock.

It is a lovely program, very Christian, that Peter draws. "Being ready" is for Luke a Christian virtue,[89] all the more so that it is accompanied by a christological touch, "with you."[90] Going also corresponds to the essence of Christianity,[91] understood by Luke in Acts (Acts 9:2) as the "way."[92] Tribulation and martyrdom (here "prison" and "death") are the lot of the apostle, then for the evangelist, of the faithful.[93] But—and this is important—ethics is not something that takes place externally. Without a new heart there is no courageous attitude. Prior to the passion of the "prince of life" (Acts 3:15) Peter's courageous ambitions are unrealistic and unrealizable. Only after the fall and the repentance (22:54-62), the passion of the Messiah, the visit to the empty tomb (24:12), the personal then collective appearances of the Risen One (24:34; 24:36-49), the ascension (24:50-53; Acts 1:9-11) and Pentecost (Acts 2:1-13) will Simon, now definitely having become Peter, find the valor of faith, this Christian παρρησία, this right to the word and this apostolic authority to preach the Christian kerygma (Acts 2:29; 4:13, 29).[94] For now, one will not have to wait long to see Peter's beautiful dreams collapse. The "today" (σήμερον), which can mean for Luke the actualization of salvation (4:21), becomes here the inexorable cipher that marks the time of the fall.[95]

Originating in India, the cock came first to Persia, then rather early to Greece, where it is called "the

---

84   See 2 Thess 2:17; 3:3; Jas 5:8; 1 Pet 5:10; 2 Pet 1:12; *1 Clem.* 13.3; 35.5; Ignatius *Eph.* 12.1; *Phld.*, prescript.

85   Luke also knows the literal and cosmic sense mentioned above in n. 82: "a great chasm has been established" (16:26). He knows as well the biblical expression "to set his face" (9:51).

86   See Schneider, "στηρίζω" (above, n. 81) col. 660.

87   See Brock, *Mary Magdalene*, 21 n. 6, 164. Verse 32 is also compared with 2 Sam 15:18-22: David speaks to Ittai the Gittite, who says that he is ready to follow the king for life or death, and counsels him to take care of his brothers and not to follow him. Ittai insists on going with him, and David finally permits it.

88   See Ulrich Luz, *Matthew 8–20* (trans. James E. Crouch; Hermeneia; Minneapolis: Fortress Press, 2001) 353–77.

89   See 12:40, and vol. 2 of this commentary on that verse.

90   See 11:23; 22:28; 23:43; and vol. 1 of this commentary, 254–56, on 6:47-49. See also 6:3-4, where the expression is applied to David's companions.

91   The verb πορεύομαι ("to go") is characteristic already of the Jewish believing existence (1:6), of Jesus' life of faith (9:51, 53; 13:33; 17:11; 22:22), and finally of the circumstances of the Christians (Acts 18:6; 20:22; 22:21). In Rom 6:4 Paul uses the verb περιπατέω ("to move around," "to go") to indicate the Christian life as a going in newness of life.

92   See Bovon, *Luke the Theologian*, 362–64.

93   See 6:22; 9:23-26; 11:49-51; 14:25-27; 21:12-19; Acts 7:51—8:1; 14:22; Bovon, *Luke the Theologian*, 436–42.

94   See Bovon, *Luke the Theologian*, 228–30, 325–28, 388–91.

95   On σήμερον ("today") in Luke, see vol. 1 of this commentary, 153–54, on 4:20b-21.

Persian bird."[96] When it arrived in Palestine is uncertain. The Hebrew Bible mentions it seldom, if at all.[97] Rabbinic texts bear witness to a certain hostility toward it. Some laws proscribe raising it in Jerusalem; others forbid priests in Israel from possessing it (*m. B. Qam.* 7.7; *b. B. Qam* 79).[98] Still, the Gospels do not hesitate to reveal its presence in Jesus' day (see Mark 14:30, 68, 72, par.).

Everyone knows that the crowing of the cock proclaims the morning. Plato attests it in the *Symposium* (223C).[99] The Latins call the third watch of the night (approximately midnight until 3:00 A.M.) the *gallicinium*, the "song of the cock"; then the word comes to mean "from the crowing of the cock." The Greeks copy their neighbors and, in the Hellenistic age, create the word "song of the cock" (ἀλεκτοροφωνία)."[100] Thus, for the ancients the crowing of the cock scans the day.

Legends preserved in various languages (among them Greek, Latin, Coptic, and Ethiopic) have developed around the cock of Jesus' last night. Common to these various accounts is the story that Jesus raised from the dead a roasted cock that had been brought to the table at the Last Supper. Restored to life, the cock announces the passion of the Lord.[101]

Even apart from these apocryphal books, for the Christian consciousness there is no denial of Peter without the presence of the cock. The canonical Gospels all mention it.[102] In the patristic age it becomes the witness of the fall of the first among the apostles and the preview of Jesus' prophetic power. It also marks the hour of repentance and bitter tears. Far from being an ornamental addition, the cock is an important character in the passion of Jesus. The patrons and sculptors of the first Christian sarcophagi (fourth century) confirm this view. They acknowledge this creature's important role by placing it at Peter's side at the top of a column.[103]

On the vocabulary of confession and denial, readers may refer to 12:8-9 and the commentary on those verses.[104] Here (22:54-62) Peter will be the example of denial; in the Acts of the Apostles he will exemplify the proclamation of the Gospel and the confession of faith.[105]

■ **35-38** The conversation goes on. After the aside with Peter, it again becomes general. Once again Luke shows Jesus' virtue.[106] Instead of being concerned with himself,

---

96 The classical prose form was ὁ ἀλεκτρυών; the poetic form was ὁ ἀλέκτωρ, but in time it became prosaic; see LSJ, s.v. On the cock in antiquity, see M. S. Enslin, "Hahn," *BHH* 2 (1964) 625–26.

97 The LXX mentions ἀλέκτωρ only in Prov 30:31 (24:66). The Hebrew Bible has זַרְזִיר here, but its meaning is not certain. This word could indicate the cock; see Ludwig Koehler and Walter Baumgartner, *The Hebrew and Aramaic Lexicon of the Old Testament* (5 vols.; Leiden: Brill, 1994–2000) 1:281. The Vulgate uses *gallus* in Isa 22:17; Job 38:36; and Prov 30:31. The Latin text of Tob 8:11 has *circa pullorum cantum* to indicate the hour the cock crows, but nothing like it appears in the LXX at this passage, and there is no fragment of this passage from Qumran. I am grateful to Fitzmyer (2:1427) for much of this information, and he gives further details.

98 See Brunet, "Coq"; Fitzmyer, 2:1427.

99 One also remembers that, according to Plato (*Phaed.* 118A), when Socrates was about to die he asked that one discharge a debt he owed by giving a cock to Asclepios.

100 See Mark 13:35 and Matt 26:34 v.l.; BAGD, s.v.; Martin, "Time and Money," 55–69.

101 See Gounelle, "Volailles"; Piovanelli, "Livre du Coq."

102 Mark 14:30, 68, 72; Matt 26:34, 74-75; Luke 22:34, 60-62; John 13:38; 18:27.

103 See Erich Dinkler, *Die ersten Petrusdarstellungen: Ein archäologischer Beitrag zur Geschichte des Petrusprimates* (Marburger Jahrbuch für Kunstwissenschaft 11; Marburg: Verlag des Kunstgeschichtlichen Seminars der Philipps-Universität Marburg, 1939; actually published in 1941 with vol. 12, 1939).

104 See vol. 2 of this commentary, on 12:8-9.

105 Luke 12:9 uses the verb ἀρνοῦμαι for the behavior of the person who first denies and ἀπαρνοῦμαι for the one who as a second person responds. Here the evangelist or his source uses ἀπαρνοῦμαι for the denial three times. Although the simple and compound verbs are both attested in the Gospel, only the simple verb is used in Acts. It is difficult to determine what nuance the composite verb might bring. Perhaps it underscores the total character of the denial. The simple verb also appears to be used more often for the rejection of a thing and the composite verb for the denial of a person. For the two verbs, see BAGD, s.vv.

106 See Sterling, "*Mors Philosophi*."

in this hour that actually is his hour, the Master's interest turns, once again, to his disciples. He is concerned about their future fate after Easter rather than their present role during the passion. One could say that he turns his attention to their professional rather than their personal future. And Jesus' injunctions are more about a missionary than a pastoral future, since they envisage the travels of the itinerant preachers and take into account the dangers the most humble of them will encounter on the way.

In any case, the equipment is important, whether it is for the worker, the soldier, or the traveler. Like the best intention, the best training is not enough. Such worldly wisdom applies also to the gospel. Among the early Christian authors, Luke is probably the one who is most concerned about the tools that are needed for the task. These practical concerns are part of a broader Lukan reflection about mediations.[107] Luke's God needs human beings; he has no hands but theirs. And people do not preach the gospel in a disembodied way. Since they are of flesh and blood, they need bags for their journeys, food for their meals, and even swords to repel the brigands.

Thinking of time, the evangelist distinguishes between periods, a period of peace and a period of war.[108] The memories he evokes refer, of course, to the past, but the instructions he puts in Jesus' mouth make sense only for the future. Thus, the present is the time during which the future is constructed on the knowledge of the past. As we have seen, the reference is to the sending of the Seventy in Luke 10 and not the sending of the Twelve in Luke 9. Even if he speaks here to the Twelve, it is likely that the Lukan Jesus does not make a mistake.

He makes rather a subtle point. Luke is thinking that what awaits the Christian preachers is less the mission in Israel (of the Twelve, Luke 9) than the evangelization of the world (the Seventy, Luke 10).

What vv. 35-38 affirm is that different times require different equipment. While Jesus was alive, the disciples were protected by the presence of their Master. Their mission corresponded more to military maneuvers than to a war. The equipment Jesus authorized then was reduced to a minimum. After Easter, when the Lord has been taken into heaven, things will be different. Then serious things will begin. The risks will be real, and it will be necessary to have the best equipment.

Thus, these four enigmatic verses[109] also have their obvious side. For a brief moment Luke opens a window on his concept of history.[110] What was valid at the time of the historical Jesus will not be applicable at the time of the risen Christ. Modern exegetes are wrong when they are surprised at the ethical and ecclesial differences they find between the Gospel and Acts. Luke is neither Mark nor John. The Lukan Gospel is primarily point of reference, secondarily transparency. One can understand the present situation of the believers only by keeping an eye on Acts while reading the Gospel. As Calvin will think, here more Lukan than Pauline, the Risen One is absent because of the ascension. It is thus important to make the indispensable provisions for this hard time that is the church's time. While nothing was missing in Jesus' presence (v. 35), there is the risk that everything could be missing in his absence. Thus, one must get what is absolutely necessary. The sword ($\mu\acute{\alpha}\chi\alpha\iota\rho\alpha$) becomes welcome.[111] One must even sacrifice one's coat for it (no

---

107 See Bovon, "Médiations."

108 See Petzke, *Sondergut*, 182.

109 Lampe ("Swords") analyzes these verses adroitly and in dialogue with a number of exegetes. He begins (p. 335) by observing: "The idea that Luke 22:36-8 really presents Jesus as acting like an officer 'checking' his men's weapons before battle is bizarre." He further says (p. 337) justifiably that there must have been compelling reasons to sell one's coat and to buy a sword, since it was also used by the poor as a cover. He concludes (pp. 350–51) by arguing that a literal interpretation of v. 38 cannot do justice to the entire Lukan account. Derrett ("Swords") is of the opinion that the idea of the sword comes from Ezekiel 21 and that the repetition

of the word "sword" in this chapter of the prophet (Ezek 21:14) explains the presence of the two swords in the Gospel. My response is that Ezekiel 21 speaks of a single sword—the sword in the hands of the God who is coming to punish his people.

110 Conzelmann (*Theology*, 81–83, 186 n. 1, 232 and passim) emphasizes the importance of vv. 35-36, especially the $\dot{\alpha}\lambda\lambda\dot{\alpha}$ $\nu\hat{\nu}\nu$ ("but now"). Minear ("Note") is of the opinion that this expression opens Jesus' passion, not the time of the church.

111 On the difference between $\mu\acute{\alpha}\chi\alpha\iota\rho\alpha$ ("large knife," "cutlass," "short sword"), a kind of "saber," and $\dot{\rho}o\mu\varphi\alpha\acute{\iota}\alpha$ ("heavy sword," "sword") see vol. 1 of this commentary, 105, on 2:33-35. There is a third term, $\xi\acute{\iota}\varphi o\varsigma$ ("short sword," "dagger"), which does

doubt there is some rhetorical exaggeration here). Then the disciples show two swords. Is that a good thing? Are they wrong? What does Luke's Jesus want to say when he concludes "that is enough"? Does he want to suggest that by taking the word "sword" literally they are mistaken or that, indeed, two swords will be enough for the group?[112]

Later one of the disciples cuts off the ear of an attacker that Jesus immediately heals. Even if the episode of the two swords does refer to the past (Luke 10), it is also illuminated by the future (22:49-51). In v. 49 the disciples ask Jesus about the use of force. The impetuous disciple does not wait for Jesus' answer: he intervenes *manu militari*. That Jesus replaces the severed ear is an answer, admittedly nonverbal but quite visible, to the disciples' question. At least in this hour of passion there is no question of using force, of drawing one's sword. How will things be after the resurrection? Doubtless the same. There is no report of any Christian missionary who carried a weapon or drew his weapon out of its scabbard. The enigma of "that is enough" is absorbed into the miracle of the ear that is saved. By inviting his disciples "to buy a sword," the Lukan Jesus resorts to a "figure of speech." Thus, "that is enough" interrupts a talk that threatens to be derailed. It goes without saying that other interpretations are possible and have been proposed.

Verse 37 is very surprising, less because of its contents than because of its position. What is it doing here? I imagine that it underscores the disciples' awkwardness. Since Jesus has said what he had to say to them (v. 36), he risks speaking about himself (v. 37). His statement is christologically, soteriologically, and scripturally heavy. It is also exceptional, since elsewhere Luke hardly ever

emphasizes the scope of the sacrifice on the cross (see Luke 22:19-20; Acts 20:28).[113] As a result, the disciples should be paying attention. Instead, they are stuck on outward appearances and worried about their fate. They come back to the question of the swords (v. 38). Many things escape them, and they completely misunderstand. By saying "that is enough" Jesus cuts short the discussion.

The statement of v. 37 is peculiar to Luke, but the evangelist is not its creator. He lays out a traditional sentence. One concludes as much from the Isaiah quotation, which does not correspond to the text of the LXX[114] to which Luke usually refers.[115] One also deduces it from the doctrinal position that the quotation constructs. We are not accustomed to such a conception from Luke. What is this construction? The Scripture is determinative, especially a prophetic text, which is fulfilled in Jesus' day. That is perfectly Lukan. The words "what is written" ($\tau\grave{o}$ $\gamma\epsilon\gamma\rho\alpha\mu\mu\acute{\epsilon}\nu o\nu$), "must" ($\delta\epsilon\hat{\iota}$), "being finished" ($\tau\epsilon\lambda\epsilon\sigma\vartheta\hat{\eta}\nu\alpha\iota$, translated as "be fulfilled") and "end" ($\tau\acute{\epsilon}\lambda o\varsigma$, translated as "has its fulfillment") are by no means surprising coming from Luke. The same thing is true of the christological reference to the first person singular ($\dot{\epsilon}\nu$ $\dot{\epsilon}\mu o\acute{\iota}$, "in me," $\pi\epsilon\rho\grave{\iota}$ $\dot{\epsilon}\mu o\hat{\upsilon}$, "about me," translated as "what concerns me"). The quotation from Isa 53:12 is striking by its newness. It comes from the fourth of the servant poems. The context reassures Luke. He who is counted among the godless is none other than the servant of God. The book of Acts will develop further the reference to Isaiah 53 (in the conversation between Philip and the Ethiopian eunuch, Acts 8:32-33) and the reference to the servant (Acts applies the title $\pi\alpha\hat{\iota}\varsigma$, "servant," to Jesus on several occasions; 3:13, 26; 4:27,

---

not appear in the New Testament. On these three terms, see BAGD, s.vv. Luke prefers $\mu\acute{\alpha}\chi\alpha\iota\rho\alpha$; $\dot{\rho}o\mu\varphi\alpha\acute{\iota}\alpha$ appears only once (2:35) and $\xi\acute{\iota}\varphi o\varsigma$ never. Contrary to what I said in vol. 1, 105, the short sword was not necessarily curved. See Helga Weippert, "Dolch und Schwert," in Kurt Galling ed., *Biblisches Reallexikon* (2d ed.; Tübingen: Mohr Siebeck, 1977) 57–62. See Cohen, *By the Sword*. Sometimes in antiquity travelers (Jesus and his disciples were walking from Galilee to Jerusalem) carried a weapon to defend themselves on the way, if necessary, against brigands.

112 Schwarz ($\kappa\acute{\upsilon}\rho\iota\epsilon$) thinks he can solve the enigma of v. 38 by resorting to an Aramaic original. The word אלמ means both "goal" ($\tau\acute{\epsilon}\lambda o\varsigma$ from Jesus' mouth,

v. 37) and sword ($\mu\acute{\alpha}\chi\alpha\iota\rho\alpha$ from the mouth of the disciples, v. 38). Jesus sees that there is a misunderstanding and, since time is pressing, he stops the discussion ("it is enough," v. 38).

113 Bovon, "Salut."

114 See Martin Rese, *Alttestamentliche Motive in der Christologie des Lukas* (StNT 1; Gütersloh: Mohn, 1969) 154–64; David W. Pao, *Acts and the Isaianic New Exodus* (WUNT 2/130; Tübingen: Mohr Siebeck, 2000) 5–6.

115 See Traugott Holtz, *Untersuchungen über die alttestamentlichen Zitate bei Lukas* (TU 104; Berlin: Akademie-Verlag, 1968) 166.

30). With this unusual appeal to Isaiah Luke initially emphasizes Christ's participation in guilty humanity. In his eyes, Jesus sided with the sinners and tax collectors, the prostitutes and the godless. Yet this "he was reckoned"[116] with the ἄνομοι, literally, those who are "lawless," goes beyond companionship. Even if the idea is only implied, the brief quotation calls attention to the redemption of the godless. Isaiah 53 explicitly affirms it, as does the recent institution of the Lord's Supper (Luke 22:19-20). Inspired by the tradition he has received, Luke discreetly suggests that Jesus' death, as much as it may be the suffering of a martyr, also belongs to the category of the expiatory sacrifice for the sins of the people.

History of Interpretation

The length of the pericope and the number of commentaries make it impossible to present the entire history of interpretation. For the verses that have a Synoptic parallel, vv. 21-23 and 24-27, I refer to the paragraphs on *Wirkungsgeschichte* (History of Interpretation) of Joachim Gnilka and Ulrich Luz.[117] For the rest I will offer selections.[118]

In his struggle against Marcion, Tertullian pauses at v. 22, the woe against Judas. In the words of a modern translator and interpreter, "the woe against Judas cannot accord with a very good God. By letting his disciple choose how he will commit the crime, Christ opens himself to the objections Marcion makes against the creator in the case of Adam and his error: He did not know, or could not know, or did not want to know."[119] Then the African rebukes Marcion for his interpretation of vv. 33-34 (we do not know what happened to the other verses from the pen of the merchant from Pontus).[120] Jesus' words to Peter, as well as those about the betrayer,

display a divine speaker in whom anger and love dwell together. Thus, the Christ is not simply good, as Marcion would like for him to be. The one God of the two Testaments expresses at one and the same time his grace and his jealousy (*Adv. Marc.* 4.41.1–2).[121]

Curiously, Ambrose passes immediately from the preparation for the Passover to Jesus' farewell without stopping at the account of the Lord's Supper (*Exp. Luc.* 10.49–55). He then quotes v. 29 ("I grant the kingdom for you as my father had granted it for me") and, thinking of the "as" (*sicut*) of this verse, he notes the analogies. Human beings cannot compete with Jesus, who is equal to the Father, but they can approach a resemblance if they renounce this world. Christ is the *plena imago dei* ("the plenary image of God"); the believers can be *ad imaginem dei* ("near the image of God"). This thesis makes it possible for the Milanese bishop to call attention to Holy Communion, which is not earthly food but the access to eternal life. It also enables him to teach his hearers that "the twelve thrones have not been created to receive our bodies that they sit on them." Everything is spiritual: the judgment of the apostles who are sitting on their thrones, as well as the moral attitude of the believers who avoid any argument about priority. Ambrose makes no excuses for the disciples. They were wrong to argue (vv. 24-27), just as Peter was guilty for strutting about (v. 33) and then denying (vv. 34, 54-60). But these bad examples come from the sinful human condition; they are not the last word. Peter wept and repented (vv. 61-62); "Thus I do not reproach him for having denied; I congratulate him for having wept. One is the fact of our common condition; the other the sign of virtue." And Ambrose exhorts his audience to be converted and to keep themselves from the world. By emphasizing the analogies and the imitation, the bishop of Milan

---

116 It is the same verb with the same form (ἐλογίσθη) that is used for the imputation of faith to justice in Gen 15:6, cited by Paul on several occasions (Gal 3:6; Rom 4:3).

117 Luz, *Matthew 21–28*, 361–63 (revealing the betrayer); Gnilka, *Markus*, 2:105–7; and Luz, *Matthew 8–20*, 545–46 (dispute among the disciples).

118 Sutcliff's article ("Aliquando") presents various interpretations of v. 32 (Jesus' exhortation to Peter) given through the centuries and offers a number of references.

119 Braun, *Tertullien. Contre Marcion*, 4:503 n. a.

120 See Harnack (*Marcion*, 233*), who points out that vv. 21-30, with the exceptions of v. 22b, are not attested, and that vv. 35-38 were eliminated by Marcion.

121 Here I try to say clearly what is expressed in a rhetorical and complicated manner by Tertullian. For his part, Origen favors the figurative sense of v. 36 (buying a sword); see Origen *Comm. Matt.* 15.2; *Hom. Lev.* 7.5; see Lecler, "L'argument" (first installment)," 301.

skillfully articulates the relationship among the Father, the Son, and the disciples in vv. 29-30 and compares it with the example of service that Jesus personally offers in v. 27. The believers of yesterday and today will be lifted to God's level if they descend to the level where Christ placed himself as a servant.

Ambrose then devotes a page to the episode of the two swords, which raises more questions than it answers. With all modesty he offers his explanations only with caution. The use of the sword is permitted only in self-defense, not for vengeance. Jesus himself neither avenged nor defended himself. "He preferred to sacrifice himself." Perhaps it is necessary, Ambrose suggests, to understand the passage in a spiritual sense: To sell one's garment is to give up one's life; to buy a sword is to receive the word of God (Ambrose must be thinking of Heb 4:12). This spiritual meaning is confirmed by v. 37, where Christ is described as a servant. Still, Ambrose asks himself, why two swords? Perhaps to call attention to the two Testaments. And why the words "it is enough"? "To make it clear that nothing is lacking for the person who is strengthened by the teaching of the two testaments." Thus, only allegory rescues Ambrose from his dilemma.[122]

There is an anonymous Irish commentary on Luke, dating from around 780–785, which draws on Ambrose, Augustine, Gregory the Great, and the Venerable Bede.[123] It is short, and some of its formulations are quite vivid.[124] Thus, the author explains the repetition of Simon's name with the double affirmation: *pro dolore et pro amore*, "for pain and love." Or on the image of the sieve he writes, "so that those who are approved and those who are rejected appear clearly." As for Jesus'

prayer for Peter, in reality it refers to the entire church, because Christ is the head of all the members. Jesus cannot keep Peter from doubting, but he is able to ensure that the apostle's faith does not remain weak forever. In commenting on "strengthen your brothers," the author says: "It now is clear that he prays for Peter for the following reason: This one was himself worthy to strengthen the other brothers." If in v. 35 Jesus mentions "the shortage of present things," he does so in his opinion because of the "blessing to come." And on v. 36 the anonymous author remains faithful to his contrasts and distinguishes between the "life according to the flesh" and the "power of the Holy Spirit." His comment on v. 37 is curious: "It is as if he has said: Be manly by means of your works through me and through the Holy Spirit. Buy for yourself, because I will soon remove my physical presence from you." He easily and assertively solves the enigma of the two swords: "Here it is the question of the dignity of the body and the soul." Referring to "it is enough," he says, "What is 'enough' for the will of God is what must be accomplished by the body and the soul."

Usually one does not find emperors and kings among the exegetes of the New Testament.[125] There are, however, exceptions: the emperors Charlemagne and Henry IV and King Edgar of England. In their dialogues, even in their controversies with bishops and popes, they laid claim to v. 38 of Luke 22.

Charlemagne asks: How can Jesus, who reproaches Peter for having cut off the ear of Malchus (John 18:10-11; Matt 26:51-52; Luke 22:60-61), recommend the purchase of swords (v. 36)? To this justifiable question Alcuin gives an allegorizing answer: the two swords represent temporal power and spiritual power. And in

---

122 According to Cyril of Alexandria (*Serm. Luc.* 145; cf. Payne Smith, *Cyril*, 2:681–82) and frg. 339 (Reuss, *Lukas-Kommentare*, 214), the Lord predicted the Jewish war, while the disciples misunderstood him and referred his words to his imminent passion. According to Cyril, Jesus almost had a smile on his face when he said, "it is enough." Concerning the two swords (v. 38), John Chrysostom (*Hom. Matt.* 84.1; *PG* 58:751–52) thinks of the two knives used to cut the paschal lamb; see Lecler, "L'argument" (first installment), 301.

123 Bede (*In Luc.* 6.674–875) is especially interested in the exercise of the church's ministry, which is different from power in the world. The author of

Quaestiones Veteris et Novi Testamenti 75 (the work circulated under Augustine's name; *PL* 35:2273) is of the opinion that, while praying for Peter, Christ also prayed for the others; Pickar ("Prayer," 136) refers to this passage.

124 Anonymous *Comm. Luc.* 22:21–38 (CCSL 108C:96).

125 I am following here the remarkable article of Lecler, "L'argument," published in three installments.

another letter he adds in an imperial-papist way: And both swords are in your hands, Sire![126]

As a matter of fact, for a long time there was no such interpretation, either in the East[127] or the West.[128] In his sixth Novella, the emperor Justinian made a distinction between temporal power and spiritual power, but he did not yet refer to Luke 22:36-38.[129] Only gradually does the allegorical sense of the two swords, referring to the two powers, develop. Edgar, the king of England (tenth century) addresses himself to the Archbishop of Canterbury and to his prelates, saying in substance: I have the sword of Constantine, and you have the sword of Peter.[130] In 1076, the German emperor Henry IV, angry over what he regarded as the offense of Hildebrand (Pope Gregory VII), wrote to the German bishops, citing Luke 22:38 as his authority.[131] During this controversy, known as the investiture controversy, it is primarily the advocates of conciliation who make use of the statement about the two swords as a way out of the dilemma: To each his sword! As a result the allegorical interpretation that sees two powers behind the two swords becomes widespread, and from the twelfth century on it is the common interpretation.[132]

Conciliation and harmony could have triumphed had it not been for the intervention of Saint Bernard, who decided that the two swords were granted only to the pope.[133] Is it not the disciples who said to Jesus, "Lord, here two swords" (v. 38)? From that time on the axiom *papa habet utrumque gladium* ("the pope has both swords") becomes emblematic. The canonists, followed later by the theologians, impose this view while providing further essential clarification. If the sword of spiritual power is entrusted to the church to use (*ad usum*, "for the use"), the sword of temporal power is given her so she may place it in the hands of the emperor or king (*ad nutum*, "for the consent").[134] This is why at a coronation the pope gives the emperor the sword of temporal power. While earlier official documents made a clear distinction between the powers, several popes, especially Gregory IX and Innocent IV, do not hesitate to lay claim to this interpretation. The bull *Unam sanctam* of Pope Boniface VIII from November 18, 1302, defends this (for him) advantageous allegory.[135] This exegesis continued to be successful until the seventeenth century, in spite of the criticisms made beginning in the fourteenth century by John of Paris, Dante, Marsilius of Padua, and William of Occam.[136]

Resistance from the political power was to be expected. They did not hesitate, and they were supported by the intellectual efforts of the legal experts of the various courts. The defenders of the princes pointed out Justinian's distinction between the powers[137] and sug-

---

126 Alcuin *Epistulae* 136, 171 (Ernst Dümmler, ed., *Epistolae variorum Carolo Magno regnante scriptae* [Monumenta Germaniae historica. Epistolae IV; Berlin: Weidmann, 1895] 205–6, 282); see Lecler, "L'argument" (first installment), 299–300, 304–5.

127 Lecler ("L'argument" [first installment], 301) summarizes the interpretations of Origen, Chrysostom, and Cyril of Alexandria; see above, nn. 121 and 122.

128 According to Lecler ("L'argument" [first installment], 305), in the West the interpretation of Ambrose and Bede was repeated until the tenth century.

129 See Hugo Rahner, *Church and State in Early Christianity* (trans. Leo Donald Davis; San Francisco: Ignatius, 1992) 204–5.

130 Lecler, "L'argument" (first installment), 306.

131 Lecler ("L'argument" [first installment], 307–8) refers to Ludwig Weiland, ed., *Monumenta Germaniae historica: Constitutiones et Acta*, vol. 1 (Hannover: Impensis Bibliopolii Hahniani, 1893) 112–13.

132 Lecler, "L'argument" (first installment), 309.

133 See Bernard of Clairvaux *De consideratione* 4.3.7

(*PL* 182:776); Lecler ("L'argument" [first installment], 312–13) is of the opinion that Bernard was influenced by Hugo of St. Victor. John of Salisbury (*Polycratus* 4.3 [*PL* 199.516]), who is also dependent on Hugo, advocates the same position.

134 See also Jean Montaigne *De parlamentis* 2 n. 15 in *Tractatus universi juris* (Venice, 1584–86) Tome 16, folie 177^{v}, who writes: "The church has the pure property of secular jurisdiction, the emperor is only the usufructuary." Quoted by Lecler, "L'argument" (first installment), 319.

135 See Heinrich Denzinger, *Enchiridion symbolorum: definitionum et declarationum de rebus fidei et morum* (ed. Karl Rahner; 31st ed.; Freiburg i. B.: Herder, 1957) 219.

136 See Lecler, "L'argument" (first installment), 339. For example, Dante Alighieri (*De monarchia* 3.9 [ed. Karl Witte; Vienna: Braumüller, 1874] 112–16) rejects the allegorical meaning. Holding to the literal sense, he understands the two swords as defensive weapons.

137 See above, n. 129.

gested returning to an interpretation of Luke 22:38 that preceded the adventuresome commentaries of Bernard of Clairvaux.[138]

To complicate matters, Peter's reprehensible attack on the servant of the high priest led to differing interpretations. Some accuse the prince of the apostles of having misused temporal power.[139] Others, fewer in number, think of a misuse of spiritual power.[140]

Few modern readers remember these interpretations, the political and practical effects of which were felt throughout medieval Europe.[141] Various exegetes recall them,[142] however, including Father Lagrange, who cites the bull of Boniface VIII. Yet he does so to justify the pope who authored it. He writes that its interpretation is limited to the bull of 1302 and has nothing of the infallibility of the definition. What Lagrange calls to mind, however, is only that the swords and powers are equal and not the papal claim to the two swords.

It is interesting to read Calvin's comments on the same verses about the two swords.[143] Yet what does he say before that about the responsibility given Peter (vv. 31-32)?[144] He notes, first of all, the difference between Matthew and Mark on the one hand and Luke on the other. In his opinion "in Luke's words there is richer teaching," since the other two Synoptics limit

themselves to the narrative while the third evangelist sees their theological scope behind the historical reality of the facts.[145] If one may dare to say it, it is the metahistorical mention of Satan that suggests this remark to Calvin. Basing his comments on Eph 6:12, the reformer recalls that the believers are always confronted by the Evil One and those whom he calls "the spiritual forces."[146] Remembering this is even more necessary, given the human tendency to be careless, since "Satan has drawn up these forces to lay siege on you and makes the occasion suit his purpose of undermining your faith" and since "all temptations, wherever they come from, are fabricated in the workshops of that foe."[147] It is significant that, after he has emphasized the disciples' disloyalty, he thinks of their repentance "in the holy protection of God" and forgets the pastoral responsibility that had been given to Peter.[148]

Calvin recovers his energy to explain the verses of Luke that have no parallels in the left-hand column of his harmony or synopsis. His commentary on vv. 35-38 anticipates some four centuries in advance my own interpretation.[149] My membership in the Reformed tradition may well explain why, even before having read Calvin, I would have come to an interpretation that corresponds to his: "The whole of Christ's saying," he writes, "is that

138 Lecler, "L'argument" (first installment), 327–30.

139 Thus Geoffrey of Bath (or Babion), according to Lecler, "L'argument" (first installment), 310.

140 Thus Robert Pulleyn, according to Lecler, "L'argument" (first installment), 320.

141 The second and third installments of Lecler's article ("L'argument") continue the history of the interpretation of Luke 22:38 from the fourteenth to the seventeenth century, thus including the period of the Reformation. Noteworthy is the renewed attention given to Luke 22:38 at the time of the quarrel between Pope Boniface VIII, mentioned above, and the king of France, Philippe the Beautiful. One must also mention the opposition of the Protestants to the allegorical exegesis of the two swords. In their judgment the pope's temporal claims can only come from the Evil One. See below, n. 152.

142 Lagrange, 558; Plummer, 507 n. 1; Schneider, 2:455; Fitzmyer, 2:1434; Petzke, *Sondergut*, 183; Bock, 2:1749 n. 34.

143 Before that, see Erasmus (*Paraphrasis*, 451–54), whose comments, equitably applied to various verses, underscore the salient points. He thinks, for

example (col. 454), that the disciples showed the two swords in the same way they had showed the two fish before the miracle of the loaves and fish (9:12-17). Then he returns to the position of Ambrose, for whom the two swords represent the two Testaments.

144 Calvin, *Harmony,* 3:140–43.

145 Ibid., 3:140.

146 Ibid.

147 Ibid., 3:141. Calvin inserts some comments here on the verb "to sift." "The simile of sifting does not entirely fit in at all points." It would be wrong to mix v. 32 with 3:17 (comparing it with the "fan or sieve, for the chaff to be driven from the wheat"). The word here means "simply to blow about or shake up with force." Satan is not at all thinking of purifying the disciples by sifting them. Thus, the image is not completely appropriate. Calvin does not hesitate to be critical. All the same, he concludes that the misfortune of the trial to which the disciples will succumb will, thanks to God's help, in some way lead to their conversion and their faith.

148 Ibid.

149 Ibid., 3:144–45.

He has spared the disciples thus far in not putting any burden upon them beyond their capacity. He reminds them of His earlier gentleness, so that now they can prepare themselves more eagerly for harder conflict."[150] Jesus initially protected his disciples; "mere beginners," he held them "in shady and quiet corners" so they would become hardened for the struggle.[151] The disciples, being boys, are called here to grow up and become men. They must learn how to do without and to be armed for the spiritual struggles that await them. It is thus essential to be well equipped. The orders given the twelve apostles are actually intended for all believers. It is sad to notice, remarks Calvin, that although Jesus is so clear, the disciples are still confused. How is it that, after being called to carry their cross, the disciples seize their sword? This weakness of the disciples may be easy to understand, but the same cannot be said for Luke's statement. Does he want to say that the disciples have what they need to defend themselves or that they are not adequately equipped? Like Ambrose, Calvin acknowledges that v. 38 remains enigmatic.[152]

In his *Annotationes,* Grotius gives special attention to the divine plan mentioned in v. 22.[153] This is not surprising when one recognizes that Grotius was a Protestant, even if he rejected the strict Calvinistic orthodoxy. This plan of God does not need human action to be realized. Judas, Herod, and Pilate play their role only with God's approval, yet this God does not compel them to bad deeds; he is content to permit them to intervene. God is not the origin of evil; human responsibility remains. Grotius criticizes other positions and seeks support from numerous ancient authors: Justin, Clement of Alexandria, Cyprian, Salvianus, Chrysostom, Origen, and Irenaeus. They file by in an impressive procession. On v. 32, the other verse that attracts his special attention,[154] Grotius is concerned about Peter's faith rather than

about his later ministry. He thinks that this faith will be tested but will not die. Distinguishing, along with Aristotle, between state (or condition) and energy, he affirms that Peter's faith lost some of its energy but that the state of this faith, although shaken, was not destroyed. He does not understand the participle ἐπιστρέψας as referring to a conversion, but, finding in it a Semitism (see Ps 84 [85]:7), he sees it as a way of saying "anew." Grotius appears to understand "anew" in the sense of "in your turn." Peter must encourage his brothers in the same way that Jesus has just prayed for him. Why is Grotius so concerned about Peter's faith? Because he refuses to say that Peter had previously lost his faith. But why does he worry about it?

Conclusion

What Luke gives us in these verses is not a farewell speech but a final conversation. For this section he draws on his special source rather than on Mark. Although it is the evening before Jesus' suffering and death, the exchange of words deals more with the future of the Christian community of the disciples, thus with ecclesiology, than with the Master's imminent fate, with Christology. As he says in v. 27, he who will soon be condemned puts his own fate in the background and fulfills his ministry of self-denial and service. He urges his fallible followers to organize themselves on a model different from the all-too-human model of the power of the strongest (vv. 24-26). Only service comparable with his own service will give them access to the kingdom, its festive table, and its seats of honor (vv. 28-30). A particular mission is entrusted to Peter: not to command but to strengthen (vv. 31-32). The principle of reality escapes neither Jesus nor Luke, his spokesperson. The community—the church—will consist not of innocent but of

---

150 Ibid., 3:144.

151 Ibid.

152 Calvin ends his commentary on vv. 35-38 with a bitter denunciation of the bishops who, based on the saying about the two swords, claim for themselves two powers, temporal and spiritual. Before Calvin, beginning in 1518 Luther had identified the pope as the Antichrist and had rejected the Roman claim of the two powers. See Luther, "Von dem Papsttum zu Rom" (1520), WA 6:308.

153 Grotius, *Annotationes*, 903–9.

154 Curiously, Grotius, the jurist, makes no allusion here to the allegorical application of the two swords (v. 38) to temporal and spiritual powers.

guilty people who have been forgiven (vv. 23 and 33-34), and its leaders will inherit their leadership with dirty hands that have been washed *in extremis* (vv. 31-32). The approaching time will be serious; the training exercises and great maneuvers will give way to actual, although spiritual, hand-to-hand combat. The Christian life states its requirements: material, adequate equipment (vv. 35-38).

Jesus' Last Prayer
(22:39-46)
Bibliography

Aland, Kurt, "Alter und Entstehung des D-Textes im Neuen Testament. Betrachtungen zu $\mathfrak{p}^{69}$ und 0171," in Ramon Roca-Puig und Sebastià Janeras, eds., *Miscellània Papirològica Ramón Roca-Puig en el seu vuitantè aniversari* (Barcelona: Fundació Salvador Vives Casajuana, 1987) 37–61; reprinted in idem, *Supplementa zu den Neutestamentlichen und den kirchengeschichtlichen Entwürfen* (Berlin: de Gruyter, 1990) 72–96.

Ambruster, Carl J., "The Messianic Significance of the Agony in the Garden," *Scr* 16 (1964) 111–19.

Arthus, Maurice, and Victor Chanson, "Les sueurs de sang," *RevThom* 6 (1898) 673–96.

Aschermann, Harmut, "Zum Agoniegebet Jesu, Lc. XXII, 43sq.," *ThViat* 5 (1953–54) 143–49.

Aus, Roger David, *The Wicked Tenants and Gethsemane: Isaiah in the Wicked Tenants' Vineyard, and Moses and the High Priest in Gethsemane. Judaic Traditions in Mark 12:1-9 and 14:32-42* (University of South Florida International Studies in Formative Christianity and Judaism 4; Atlanta: Scholars Press, 1996) 65–159.

Baarda, Tjitze, "Luke 22:42-47a: The Emperor Julian as a Witness to the Text of Luke," *NovT* 30 (1988) 289–96.

Bagatti, Bellarmino, Michele Piccirillo, and Albert Prodomo, *New Discoveries at the Tomb of the Virgin Mary in Gethsemane* (trans. L. Sciberras; Jerusalem: Franciscan Printing Press, 1975).

Barbour, Robin S., "Gethsemane in the Tradition of the Passion," *NTS* 16 (1969–70) 231–51.

Bate, H. N., "Luke xxii 40," *JTS* 36 (1935) 76–77.

Beck, B., "Gethsemane in the Four Gospels," *EpRe* 15 (1988) 57–65.

Benoit, Pierre, *The Passion and Resurrection of Jesus Christ* (trans. Benet Weatherhead; New York: Herder & Herder, 1970) 1–23.

Bertram, Georg, *Die Leidensgeschichte Jesu und der Christuskult* (FRLANT 32; Göttingen: Vandenhoeck & Ruprecht, 1922) 43–49.

Best, Ernest, *The Temptation and the Passion: The Markan Soteriology* (SNTSMS 2; Cambridge: Cambridge University Press, 1965).

Bishop, E. F. F., "A Stone's Throw," *ExpT* 53 (1941–42) 270–71.

Black, Matthew, "The Cup Metaphor in Mark xiv.36 and Parallels," *ExpT* 59 (1947–48) 195.

Blaising, Craig A., "Gethsemane: A Prayer of Faith," *JETS* 22 (1979) 333–43.

Boman, Thorleif, "Der Gebetskampf Jesu," *NTS* 10 (1963–64) 261–73.

Bonnington, Mark, "The Obedient Son: Jesus in Gethsemane," *Anvil* 16 (1999) 41–48.

Bornkamm, Günther, "Sohnschaft und Leiden," in Walter Eltester, ed., *Judentum, Urchristentum, Kirche: Festschrift für Joachim Jeremias* (BZNW 26; Berlin: Töpelmann, 1960) 188–98.

Bovon, François, "The Lukan Story of the Passion of Jesus (Luke 22–23)," in idem, *Studies in Early Christianity* (WUNT 161; Tübingen: Mohr Siebeck, 2003) 74–105.

Boyarin, Daniel, *Dying for God: Martyrdom and the Making of Christianity and Judaism* (Figurae; Stanford: Stanford University Press, 1999) 93–126.

Brown, Raymond E., *The Death of the Messiah: From Gethsemane to the Grave. A Commentary on the Passion Narratives of the Four Gospels* (2 vols.; Anchor Bible Reference Library; New York: Doubleday, 1994) 1:110–234.

Brun, Lyder, "Engel und Blutschweiss: Lc 22,43-44," *ZNW* 32 (1933) 265–76.

Carle, Paul-Laurent, "L'agonie de Gethsémani: Enquête exégétique et théologique du Père Feuillet," *Div* 21 (1977) 429–32.

Clivaz, *L'ange et la sueur de sang.*

Eadem, "The Angel and the Sweat like "Drops of Blood" (Lk 22:43-44): $\mathfrak{p}^{69}$ and f^{13}," *HTR* 98 (2005) 419–40.

Colunga, Alberto, "La agonía de Jesús en Getsemani," *CuBi* 16 (1959) 13–17.

Cowe, S. P., "Christological Trends and Textual Transmission: The Pericope of the Bloody Sweat (Luke 22:43-44) in the Armenian Version," in Shahe Ajamian and Michael E. Stone, eds., *Text and Context: Studies in the Armenian New Testament, May 22–28, 1992* (University of Pennsylvania Armenian Texts and Studies 13; Atlanta: Scholars Press, 1994) 35–48.

Cranfield, C. E. B., "The Cup Metaphor in Mark xiv.36 and Parallels," *ExpT* 59 (1947–48) 137–38.

Cullmann, Oscar, *Immortality of the Soul or Resurrection of the Dead? The Witness of the New Testament* (London: Epworth, 1958) 19–27.

Daube, David, "A Prayer Pattern in Judaism," *StEv* 1 [TU 73] (1973) 539–45.

Derrett, J. Duncan M., "Sleeping at Gethsemane," *DRev* 114 (1996) 235–45.

Dibelius, Martin, "Gethsemane," *CrozQ* 12 (1935) 254–265; reprinted in idem, *Botschaft und Geschichte: Gesammelte Aufsätze* (2 vols.; Tübingen: Mohr, 1953, 1956) 1:258–71.

Duplacy, Jean, "La préhistoire du texte en Lc 22,43-44," in Eldon Jay Epp and Gordon D. Fee, eds., *New Testament Textual Criticism: Its Significance for Exegesis. Essays in Honour of Bruce M. Metzger* (New York: Oxford University Press, 1981) 77–86; reprinted in idem, *Études de critique textuelle du*

Nouveau Testament (ed. Joël Delobel; BEThL 78; Leuven: Leuven University Press, 1987) 349–85.

Ehrman, Bart D., *The Orthodox Corruption of Scripture: The Effect of Early Christological Controversies on the Text of the New Testament* (New York: Oxford University Press, 1993) 187–94.

Ehrman, Bart D., and Mark A. Plunkett, "The Angel and the Agony: The Textual Problem of Luke 22:43-44," *CBQ* 45 (1983) 401–16.

Feuillet, André, *L'agonie de Gethsémani: Enquête exégétique et théologique suivie d'une étude du 'Mystère de Jésus' de Pascal* (Paris: Gabalda, 1977) 13–141, 144–61.

Idem, "Le récit lucanien de l'agonie de Gethsémani (Lc xxii. 39-46)," *NTS* 22 (1975–76) 397–417.

Fillion, L.-Cl., "L'ange et la sueur de sang à Gethsémani," in idem, *Essais d'exégèse: exposition, réfutation, critique, mœurs juives* (Lyon: Delhomme et Briquet, 1884) 101–27.

Fuchs, Albert, "Gethsemane: Die deuteromarkinische Bearbeitung von Mk 14:32-42 par Mt 26:36-46 par Lk 22:39-46," *SNTU* Serie A 25 (2000) 23–75.

Galizzi, Mario, *Gesù nel Getsemani (Mc 14, 32-42, Mt 26, 36-46, Lc 22, 39-46)* (BSRel 4; Zurich: Pas, 1972).

Gamba, G. G., "Agonia di Gesù," *RivB* 16 (1968) 159–66.

Gerhardsson, Birger, *The Testing of God's Son (Matt. 4:1-11): An Analysis of an Early Christian Midrash* (ConBNT 2; Lund: Gleerup, 1966).

Goppelt, Leonhard, "ποτήριον," *TDNT* 6 (1968) 148–58.

Green, Joel B., "Jesus on the Mount of Olives (Luke 22,39-46): Tradition and Theology," *JSNT* 26 (1986) 29–48.

Harder, C., "Unterrichtsentwurf über Mk 14:32-42: Jesus in Gethsemane," in Rolf Bohnsack, Hayo Gerdes, Hellmut Heeger, eds., *Gottes Wort in der evangelischen Unterweisung: Religionspädagogische Beispiele und didaktische Erörterungen. Festschrift für Gerhard Bohne zu seinem 70. Geburtstag* (Berlin: Die Spur, 1965) 105–12.

Harnack, Adolf, "Probleme im Text der Leidengeschichte Jesu," *SPAW* 11 (1901) 251–55.

Héring, Jean, "Simples remarques sur la prière à Gethsémané: Matthieu 26.36-46; Marc 14.32-42; Luc 22.40-46," *RHPhR* 39 (1959) 97–102.

Idem, "Zwei exegetische Probleme in der Perikope von Jesus in Gethsemane (Markus XIV 32-42; Matthäus XXVI 36-46; Lukas XXII 40-46)," in *Neotestamentica et Patristica: Eine Freundesgabe, Herrn Professor Dr. Oscar Cullmann zu seinem 60. Geburtstag überreicht* (NovTSup 6; Leiden: Brill, 1962) 64–69.

Hobart, William Kirk, *The Medical Language of St. Luke* (1882; reprinted Grand Rapids: Baker, 1954) 79–86, 168–70.

Holleran, J. Warren, *The Synoptic Gethsemane: A Critical Study* (AnGr 191; Rome: Università gregoriana, 1973) 83–103, 170–98, 214–20.

Holzmeister, Urban, "Exempla sudoris sanguinei (Lc. 22,44)," *VD* 18 (1938) 73–81.

Keen, W. W., "The Bloody Sweat of Our Lord," *Baptist Quarterly Review* 14 (1892) 169–75.

Idem, "Further Studies on the Bloody Sweat of our Lord," *BSac* 54 (1897) 469–83.

Kelber, Werner H., "Mark 14,32-42: Gethsemane. Passion Christology and Discipleship Failure," *ZNW* 63 (1972) 166–87.

Kiley, Mark, "Lord, Save My Life" (Ps 116:4) as Generative Text for Jesus' Gethsemane Prayer (Mark 14:36a)," *CBQ* 48 (1986) 655–59.

Korn, Joachim Hans, ΠΕΙΡΑΣΜΟΣ: *Die Versuchung des Gläubigen in der griechischen Bibel* (BWANT 72; Stuttgart: Kohlhammer, 1937) 76–87.

Kruger, Hennie, "Die twee swaarde (Luk. 22:35-53), 'n poging tot verstaan," *Nederduitse gereformeerde teologiese tydskrif* 27 (1986) 191–96.

Kuhn, Karl Georg, "Jesus in Gethsemane," *EvTh* 12 (1952–53) 260–85.

Idem, "New Light on Temptation, Sin and Flesh in the N.T.," in Krister Stendahl, ed., *The Scrolls and the New Testament* (New York: Harper, 1957) 94–113.

Larkin, William J., "The Old Testament Background of Luke XXII.43-44," *NTS* 25 (1978–79) 250–54.

Léon-Dufour, Xavier, *Face à la mort: Jésus et Paul* (Parole de Dieu 18; Paris: Seuil, 1979) 73–100, 320.

Idem, "Jésus à Gethsémani: Essai de lecture synchronique," *ScEs* 31 (1979) 251–68.

Idem, "Jésus face à la mort menaçante," *NRTh* 100 (1978) 802–21.

Idem, "Passion: La Passion selon saint Luc," *DBSup* 6 (1960) 1176–79.

Lescow, Theodor, "Jesus in Gethsemane," *EvTh* 26 (1966) 141–59.

Idem, "Jesus in Gethsemane bei Lukas und im Hebräerbrief," *ZNW* 58 (1967) 215–39.

Linnemann, *Studien*, 34–40, 178–79.

Lods, Marc, "Climat de bataille à Gethsémané," *EThR* 60 (1985) 321–31.

Lönartz, Michael, "De sudore sanguinis" (Diss., Bonn, 1850).

Madigan, Kevin, "Ancient and High-Medieval Interpretations of Jesus in Gethsemane: Some Reflections on Tradition and Continuity in Christian Thought," *HTR* 88 (1995) 157–73.

Makridis, V., *"καὶ ἐγένετο ὁ ἱδρὼς αὐτοῦ ὡσεὶ θρόμβοι αἵματος καταβαίνοντες ἐπὶ τὴν γῆν. ἐξηγητικὴ συμβολὴ εἰς Λουκ. 22,44,"* *DBM* n.s. 2 (1981) 45–62.

Metzger, *Commentary* (2d. ed.), 151.

Moffatt, J., "Exegetica: Luke xxii. 44," *Exp* 7/8 (1914) 90–92.

Mohn, Werner, "Gethsemane (Mk 14,32-42)," *ZNW* 64 (1973) 194–208.

Murphy-O'Connor, Jerome, "What Really Happened at Gethsemane?" *BiRe* 14, no. 2 (1998) 28–39, 52.

Murray, P., "The Prayers of Jesus in Luke's Passion Narrative," *Emmanuel* 107 (2001) 88–95, 105–6.

Neyrey, Jerome H., "The Absence of Jesus' Emotions—The Lucan Redaction of Lk 22,39-46," *Bib* 61 (1980) 153–71.

Ott, Wilhelm, *Gebet und Heil: Die Bedeutung der Gebetsparänese in der lukanischen Theologie* (SANT 12; Munich: Kösel, 1965) 82–90.

Paton, W. R., "Agônia (Agony)," *ClR* 27 (1913) 194.

Rabeau, G., "Agonie du Christ," *Catholicisme* 1 (1948) 226–28.

Radl, Walter, *Paulus und Jesus im lukanischen Doppelwerk: Untersuchungen zu Parallelmotiven im Lukasevangelium und in der Apostelgeschichte* (EHS.T 49; Frankfurt am Main: Lang, 1975) 159–68.

Robinson, B. P., "Gethsemane: The Synoptic and Johannine Viewpoints," *CQR* 167 (1966) 4–11.

Ruprecht, Louis A., "Mark's Tragic Vision: Gethsemane," *RL* 24 (1992) 1–25.

Sabbe, Maurits, "The Arrest of Jesus in John 18:1-11 and Its Relation to the Synoptic Gospels: A Critical Evaluation of A. Dauer's Hypothesis," in Marinus de Jonge, ed., *L'Évangile de Jean: Sources, rédaction, théologie* (BEThL 44; Gembloux: Duculot, 1977) 203–34.

Saunderson, Barbara, "Gethsemane: The Mission Witness," *Bib* 70 (1989) 224–33.

Schenke, *Studien*, 461–560.

Schneider, Gerhard, "Engel and Blutschweiss (Lk 22, 43-44): 'Redaktionsgeschichte' im Dienste der Textkritik," *BZ* 20 (1976) 112–16; reprinted in idem, *Lukas, Theologe der Heilsgeschichte: Aufsätze zum lukanischen Doppelwerk* (BBB 59; Königsstein: Hanstein, 1985) 153–87.

Schürmann, Heinz, "Lk 22,42a das älteste Zeugnis für Lk 22,20?" *MThZ* 3 (1952) 185–88; reprinted in idem, *Traditionsgeschichtliche Untersuchungen zu den synoptischen Evangelien* (KBANT; Düsseldorf: Patmos, 1968) 193–97.

Skard, Eiliv, "Kleine Beiträge zum Corpus Hellenisticum Novi Testamenti," *SO* 30 (1953) 100–103.

Smith, Craig A., "A Comparative Study of the Prayer of Gethsemane," *IBSt* 22 (2000) 98–122.

Smith, Harold, "Acts xx. 8 and Luke xxii. 43," *ExpT* 16 (1904–5) 478.

Soards, Marion L., "Understanding Luke 22:39," *BT* 36 (1985) 336–37.

Stanley, David Michael, *Jesus in Gethsemane: The Early Church Reflects on the Suffering of Jesus* (New York: Paulist, 1980) 188–222.

Sterling, *"Mors Philosophi."*

Strobel, August, "Die Psalmengrundlage der Gethsemane-Parallele Hbr 5,7ff," *ZNW* 45 (1954) 252–66.

Surkau, Hans Werner, *Martyrien in jüdischer und frühchristlicher Zeit* (FRLANT 54; Göttingen: Vandenhoeck & Ruprecht, 1938) 90–100.

Taylor, Joan E., "The Garden of Gethsemane: Not the Place of Jesus' Arrest," *BARev* 21 (1995) 26–35.

Tostengard, Sheldon, "Luke 22:39-46," *Int* 34 (1980) 283–88.

Trémel, Y. B., "L'agonie de Jésus," *LumVie* 13 (1964) 79–103.

Tsutsui, "Evangelium Marcions," 124.

Vacant, Alfred, "Agonie du Christ: Interprétation et conséquences théologiques du récit," *DThC* 1 (1930) 619–21.

Van Lopik, T., "Once Again: Floating Words, Their Significance for Textual Criticism," *NTS* 41 (1995) 286–91.

Idem, "Tekstkritiek: telt het wegen of weegt het tellen?," *NedThT* 45 (1991) 101–6.

Weissenrieder, Annette, and Friederike Wendt, "'Warum schlaft ihr?' Überlegungen zum Jüngerbild in Lk 22,39-46 im Lichte ikonographischer und medizinhistorischer Quellen," in Annette Weissenrieder, Friederike Wendt, and Petra von Gemünden, eds., *Picturing the New Testament: Studies in Ancient Visual Images* (Tübingen: Mohr Siebeck, 2005) 96–126.

Wild, Edith, "Histoire de l'exégèse de la péricope de Gethsémani" (Diss., Strasbourg, 1975).

39 Then once outside, he went as was his custom[a] to the Mount of Olives, and the disciples
followed him. 40/ When he had come to this
place, he said to them, "Pray that you not
enter into temptation." 41/ And he went away
from them about a stone's throw, knelt, and
prayed[b] 42/ saying, "Father, if you will, remove
this cup from me; nevertheless, let not my
will but yours be done." 43/ Then an angel
appeared to him from heaven who strengthened him. 44/ And in agony he prayed even
more intensely; and his sweat became as
clots of blood falling to the ground.[c] 45/ And
once he had gotten up from prayer he went to
the disciples and found them sleeping from
sorrow. 46/ He said to them, "What! Are you
sleeping? When you have gotten up, pray so
that you will not come into temptation."

a   Literally: "according to the custom."
b   Another translation: "He began to pray," if one understands
    the action of the imperfect as inchoative.
c   Verses 43-44 are not attested by all manuscripts; see below, at
    the end of the Diachronic Analysis.

Synchronic Analysis

Jesus leaves the house (ἐξελθών, "once outside," v. 39)
that had given him shelter one last time (22:10-14). In
spite of the circumstances, he goes, accompanied by his
disciples, to the Mount of Olives, continuing the custom
he had established (21:37). Instead of resting there, however, he invites the disciples to pray and, as an example,
starts to pray for himself. He expresses his desire in the
form of an imperative (παρένεγκε, "remove," v. 42), yet
he twice subjects it to the will of his Father (εἰ βούλει,
"if you will," and τὸ θέλημά σου, "your will," v. 42). This
hope for a coming together of the wills, this "please" with
its double connotation (my desire and your approval),
once it is expressed, does not remain unanswered. As
one knows since Job (chaps. 38–42),[1] however, God does
not always answer human beings as they would like. The
cup does not disappear as if by the wave of a magic wand,
and a very human fear grips the Son (v. 44, coming
hard on the heels of v. 43, underscores the reality of a
deep darkness). Yet the Father is not locked in silence.

He sends an angel to comfort him who cannot escape
his fate. Rising up (ἀναστάς, "once he had gotten up,"
v. 45, corresponds to θεὶς τὰ γόνατα, "knelt," v. 41), the
Master renews contact with the disciples. Unfortunately,
his followers were unable to accomplish (v. 45) what
he had done (to stay awake and pray).[2] Thus, his question to them is a thinly veiled complaint. Then, in light
of the task that has not been accomplished, the Master
reiterates his command (v. 46 repeats v. 40). Unlike
Jesus, however, the disciples will have to pray standing
up (ἀναστάντες, "rise up," v. 46) perhaps to keep from
falling asleep.

   The literary unit I have just summarized is skillfully
connected to the text that precedes it. It is the last night
after the last meal, and it takes place outside, after the
evening spent inside.[3] These verses (39-46) are also connected to what follows. They form the preparation for
the testing, the armed vigil before the physical and spiritual combat of the passion. As the story of the temptations (4:1-13) preceded the ministry, the life of Jesus, the
story of the Mount of Olives precedes the martyrdom,

---

1   See Roland de Pury, *Job ou l'homme révolté* (5th ed.;
    Essais bibliques 4; Geneva: Labor et Fides, 1982)
    42–51.
2   Lods ("Bataille") emphasizes the metaphor of com-
    bat, which determines the portrayal of the episode
    of the Mount of Olives.
3   Is this a reflection of Israel's double existence,
    initially nomadic, then settled, a reflection lived

liturgically during the Passover night (once they
had arrived in Jerusalem, the pilgrims willingly
"camped out" on the Mount of Olives after they had
eaten the Passover meal in a house in the city)?

the death of Jesus. Yet the way the unit (vv. 39-46) is joined to what goes before and what follows varies. The calm rhythm of v. 39 still offers a quiet transition from the Passover to the Mount of Olives, while the sharp tone of v. 47 signals an abrupt change. In fact, in reading the genitive absolute ("while he was still speaking," v. 47) one understands that the intrusion of the crowd and the intervention of Judas interrupt the conversation between Jesus and his disciples.

The scene itself (vv. 39-46) is artfully constructed: a chiastic composition emphasizes a twofold problem, subsumed under the category of prayer, which touches the disciples and concerns Jesus.[4] Verses 39-40a ensure the literary transition and note the change of location. Verse 40b, like v. 46, contains Jesus' injunction to his disciples; these two verses enclose the pericope and constitute an inclusion.[5] Verses 41-44 deal with Jesus in his dialogue with God. The first of these verses describes in detail Jesus' movement and action. The second (v. 42) recalls the Son's cautious (see the two reservations, ϵi, "if," and $\pi\lambda\acute{\eta}\nu$, "however") if daring (the command given to God) word to his Father. The third (v. 43) makes use of the vocabulary of the epiphanies to express the divine response. The fourth (v. 44), which, from a human perspective, has shocked many readers, underscores in a narrative way that the response from on high was not literally a granting of the request. As for v. 45, it serves as a counterpart to v. 41, but it is also similar to vv. 39-40a in the way it provides a transition. There is, however, a difference: It is here a different transition, not the long distance from the house to the Mount of Olives but in the other direction, the distance of a stone's throw. These verses (39-40a and 45) lead, however, to the same result, to the nearness, which makes the conversation possible.

One can represent this unit's plan graphically as follows:

Vv. 39-40a   Movement of Jesus and his disciples to a new place
    V. 40b Instruction to the disciples
        V. 41 Jesus' movement
           V. 42 Jesus' prayer
              V. 43 Heavenly response
           V. 44 Jesus' situation
        V. 45 Jesus' movement
    V. 46 Instruction to the disciples

Diachronic Analysis

The comparison of the Gospel of Luke and that of Mark reveals a large number of differences.[6] Consequently, I come to the same conclusion that I drew from the two previous pericopes (22:14-20; 22:21-38): The differences do not reflect a Lukan rewriting of the Markan material; they are to be explained rather by the third evangelist's use of another source. The block of material borrowed from this other source extends from 22:15 to 22:46.[7]

Here is the list of these differences.[8] Verse 39: Luke and Mark both say that after the Last Supper Jesus and his disciples leave the house and go to the Mount of Olives (v. 39 par. Mark 14:26). The relationship stops there, because Mark notes that the group is singing while going out and adds a quotation from Scripture (about expelling the shepherd, Zech 13:7), a prediction (Jesus will go before his disciples into Galilee), and the announcement of Peter's denial (Mark 14:26-31). Luke knows nothing of any of this or, in the case of the denial, has included it earlier (22:31-34). In addition, as is often the case at the beginning or end of a pericope, the evangelist emphasizes with a typically Lukan vocabulary that Jesus moved from one place to another and the disciples followed (v. 39). He does not mention the "place of Gethsemane" (Mark 14:32a).

---

4   Ehrman (*Corruption*, 191) also finds a chiasm, but he does so by excluding vv. 43-44.

5   See Nolland, 3:1081.

6   A comparison with the Gospel of Matthew leads to the same result, since on this passage the First Gospel carefully reproduces his source, Mark.

7   Green ("Mount of Olives") holds the view that Luke here uses Mark and a parallel tradition. By so doing the evangelist presents Jesus as the servant of the Lord. Holleran (*Gethsemane*, 198) comes to the conclusion that Luke takes over a source different from Mark. He would have inserted into this source vv. 43-44, which come from still another source known to the Fourth Gospel and Hebrews.

8   They have often been described. Fitzmyer's presentation (2:1437) is especially clear; see also Benoit, *Passion and Resurrection*, 15–17; Holleran, *Gethsemane*, 174–86.

Verse 40: Only Luke reports the group's arrival at its destination and immediately mentions the command to pray given to the disciples. He does not speak of an invitation to sit (Mark 14:32b), nor of the selection of the three disciples Peter, James, and John, nor of the fear that Jesus feels and confesses (Mark 14:33-34; the fear will appear later in Luke, in v. 44, in a different form).

Verse 41: In words different from Mark, Luke expresses the movement of Jesus, who withdraws and assumes the position appropriate for prayer. Nothing corresponds to Mark 14:35b (". . . that, if possible, this hour might pass from him").

Verse 42: As is often the case, the similarity among the Gospels is most obvious in connection with the sayings of Jesus. Luke, however, who does not have a fetish for the original language, omits the Aramaic word ʾabbā and correctly uses the vocative ($\pi\acute{\alpha}\tau\epsilon\rho$, "father").[9] The request itself is expressed with the same imperative and the same image of the cup,[10] although the wording of the reservation is different. It is doubled in Luke; for once he uses the Attic form $\beta o\acute{\upsilon}\lambda\epsilon\iota$ and speaks in more abstract words of God's will than does Mark.[11]

Verses 43-44: These two verses have no parallel in Mark (or in Matthew). Jesus' condition, which Luke describes by mentioning sweat and drops of blood, is only remotely similar to the words Mark risks in describing feelings ("he began to feel fear and distress," Mark 14:33b).

Verse 45: While Mark and Luke agree that after his prayer Jesus found the disciples sleeping, they express it differently. Luke writes carefully ("once he had gotten up from prayer"; Mark does not make the effort to describe the movement); Luke stays with the past tense ("he found"; Mark makes use of the historical present) and invokes the verb $\kappa o\iota\mu\hat{\omega}\mu\alpha\iota$ ("to sleep"; Mark prefers the synonym $\kappa\alpha\vartheta\epsilon\acute{\upsilon}\delta\omega$). Luke is the only one who provides an (admittedly curious) explanation for the disciples' sleep: "from sorrow" ($\grave{\alpha}\pi\grave{o}\ \tau\hat{\eta}\varsigma\ \lambda\acute{\upsilon}\pi\eta\varsigma$).

Verse 46: The question of the disappointed or indignant Jesus is addressed to the entire group (in Mark it is addressed only to Peter). It consists of only two words, "What! Are you sleeping?" ($\tau\acute{\iota}\ \kappa\alpha\vartheta\epsilon\acute{\upsilon}\delta\epsilon\tau\epsilon$), while it is expanded in Mark: "You did not have the strength to watch one hour!" (14:37b). Luke uses another verb, "to be stretched out," "to sleep" ($\kappa\alpha\vartheta\epsilon\acute{\upsilon}\delta\omega$) and thus avoids a repetition, which does not appear to bother Mark. To the question Luke adds a final command, which connects with the one placed at the beginning of the pericope (v. 40b).

Luke's account stops here (v. 46), while Mark's goes on. Mark emphasizes vigilance ("watch and pray," Mark 14:38a) before quoting the famous sentence, missing from Luke: "The spirit is willing, but the flesh is weak" (Mark 14:38b). Mark continues by mentioning the scenario twice (14:39-41a) and Jesus' final words ("It is enough. The hour has come. Behold, the Son of Man is delivered into the hands of sinners. Rise up! Let us go! Behold, he who betrays me has arrived"; Mark 14:41b-42).[12]

The comparison should not be limited to the Synoptic tradition, for there are also parallels between the Synoptic Gospels and the Gospel of John.[13] The author of the Fourth Gospel certainly knows the Gethsemane tradition. Along with the Synoptics, he acknowledges that Jesus was disturbed by the idea of death ("Now my soul is troubled"; John 12:27a), but unlike the Synoptics he rejects the idea that the Master sought to avoid martyrdom ("And what shall I say? Father, save me in

---

9   Mark 14:36 follows the popular practice of using the nominative with the article as vocative ($\dot{o}$ $\pi\alpha\tau\acute{\eta}\rho$, "the Father," "Father").

10 $\pi\alpha\rho\acute{\epsilon}\nu\epsilon\gamma\kappa\epsilon$ . . . $\grave{\alpha}\pi$ $\grave{\epsilon}\mu o\hat{\upsilon}$ ("remove from me") and $\tau\grave{o}\ \pi o\tau\acute{\eta}\rho\iota o\nu$ ("the cup"). Luke places the demonstrative $\tau o\hat{\upsilon}\tau o$ ("this") before, Mark after, the mention of the cup.

11 Luke uses a formula that includes the word $\vartheta\acute{\epsilon}\lambda\eta\mu\alpha$ ("will"). "Nevertheless, let not my will but yours be done." One finds a shorter version of the formula in Acts (Acts 21:14).

12 On the history of the tradition before Mark, see Kuhn ("Gethsemane"), who concludes that the sec-

ond evangelist fuses two stories, one of which is centered on Christology (Mark 14:32, 35, 40, 41), the other on ethics (Mark 14:33-34, 36-38). Following Kuhn, Lescow ("Lukas") is of the opinion that Luke emphasizes the ethical and existential range of the second story. On the prehistory of the pericope, see also Mohn, "Gethsemane"; Kelber, "Gethsemane."

13 See Robinson ("Gethsemane"), who tends to underscore the differences between the Synoptic and Johannine versions. He thinks that John understands the garden (John 18:1) as the rediscovered paradise.

this hour? But it is precisely for this hour that I came"; John 12:27b). It is important to call attention to this attitude of John, for it confirms the reservations that many Christians, happy to rely on a strong Christ, over time expressed about a helpless Jesus. By choosing his own source, Luke also avoided taking over Mark's two disquieting verbs: "greatly frightened" (ἐκθαμβεῖσθαι) and "distressed" (ἀδημονεῖν, Mark 14:33). Without, however, going as far as John, Luke does not eliminate the episode, but he is doubly cautious, stressing that Jesus did not want anything that was opposed to God's will (v. 42). While this allusion to the Gethsemane episode appears in chap. 12 of John, thus before the farewell addresses, later in chap. 18 there is a reference to Jesus leaving the city and crossing the Kidron. The fourth evangelist indeed begins the passion narrative with these words: "After he had spoken these things, Jesus went out with his disciples beyond the brook Kidron, where there was a garden he entered with his disciples" (John 18:1). In this way he connects the farewell evening in the house with the walk to the Mount of Olives. This sequence corresponds to that of Luke or rather to that of his special source, which combines the upper room (22:14-38) and the Mount of Olives (22:39-46) by leaving out the conversation with the disciples (Mark 14:26-31).[14]

Luke is the only one of the canonical Gospels that mentions the beneficial appearance of an angel and the physical symptoms of Jesus' psychic tension (vv. 43-44), but it is not the only one if we extend the synoptic comparison beyond the New Testament canon.[15] Indeed, we have known for some fifty years that a Jewish-Christian Gospel offered the same information. A *Historia passionis*

Domini, a Latin text of an anonymous medieval German author,[16] points out: "But how the angel strengthened Christ in the struggle of prayer that is reported in the Gospel of the Nazarenes. Anselm mentions the same thing in his lament: 'Be strong, Lord, because now comes the time where the human race, sold in Adam, must be redeemed by your suffering.'"[17] The reference to Anselm's work[18] is not as enigmatic as it appears, and the reference to an apocryphal Gospel is certain. This medieval document, which to my knowledge still has not been published, bears witness that Luke was not the only Gospel to mention an angelic intervention during the episode on the Mount of Olives. At least one other Gospel shared this information and went even further: it quoted the angel's words. By mentioning the "time" that "comes," these remarks are reminiscent of the Gospel of John (see John 12:27, 31; 4:23; 5:25), and they recall the Pauline epistles with the doctrinal view of redemption (see 1 Cor 15:22, 45; Gal 3:13; Rom 5:12-21). To be sure, we must be cautious, because it is only probable, although not certain, that the noncanonical Gospel quoted in the Middle Ages is the one that circulated in the second century of the Common Era. Moreover, it is possible, although hardly probable, that it depends directly on Luke (in this case it would be part of the history of the text's reception and not of its tradition history). I think it is more likely that, like the entire pericope, the two verses (43-44) belonged to Luke's special material and that the author of the *Gospel of the Nazarenes* is inspired here by this source rather than by the Gospel of Luke.[19] As a consequence, both the Gospel of Luke and the *Gospel of the Nazarenes* would be witnesses of a very

14   On the parallels between Luke and John in this passage, see Schniewind, *Parallelperikopen*, 32–33; Wiefel, 378.

15   See Philipp Vielhauer and Georg Strecker, "Jewish-Christian Gospels," in Schneemelcher, *New Testament Apocrypha*, 1:151, 163; A. F. J. Klijn, *Jewish-Christian Gospel Tradition* (VCSup 17; Leiden: Brill, 1992) 142–44, 23.

16   It is B. Bischoff who discovered this text. He shared this text with Philipp Vielhauer and A. F. J. Klijn. Both of them refer to an exchange of letters with Bischoff, indicating the folios, the age, and the origin of the manuscript, but not its identity and location. Where is this "theological collection" that probably comes from northern Germany and dates from the fourteenth–fifteenth centuries?

17   It is folio 32ʳ of the manuscript. Klijn (*Jewish-Christian Gospel Tradition*, 143) and Aland (*Synopsis*, 457) provide the Latin text. The *Synopsis* speaks of the *Gospel of the Hebrews* (this confusion between these two Judeo-Christian Gospels is well known).

18   On the same page Klijn thinks that it could be a reference to a *Planctus*, sometimes attributed to Anselm. Claire Clivaz has helped me find it: it is a work sometimes called *Planctus* and sometimes *Dialogus beatae Mariae et Anselmi de Passione Domini*. The unauthentic work belongs to the spurious works of Anselm of Canterbury. Our passage is accessible in the edition of this text in chap. 1, *PL* 159.273.

19   See Bovon, "Lukan Story of the Passion," 98–99.

old tradition.[20] When Hebrews dramatizes Jesus' prayers and tears (Heb 5:7), it is likely based on the same tradition.[21] In the middle of the second century, Justin Martyr also was aware of the episode, but he says explicitly that he has it from the apostles' memoirs, thus from the Gospels, most probably from Luke (*Dial.* 103.8). He is then the first witness of the reception (*Wirkungsgeschichte*) of these verses. Somewhat later, if we can believe Ephraem's commentary (*Comm. Diat.* 20.11), Tatian, who in his time was a student of Justin, incorporated the bloody sweat into the *Diatessaron*.

We come now to the problem that has made this pericope famous among textual critics. Do vv. 43-44 belong to the text of Luke or not? External criticism, which examines the nature, the number, and the age of the manuscript evidence, is divided.[22] Without needing to mention all of the witnesses, let us say that some of the oldest and best known attest these verses, others do not. 𝔓[75], the Bodmer papyrus, does not know them, while ℵ (= 01), the Codex Sinaiticus, does. A (= 02), Alexandrinus, and B (= 03), Vaticanus, remain silent; a first corrector of Sinaiticus also omits them. D (= 05), Codex Bezae, and 0171, a very old uncial fragment from about the year 300, are witnesses of their presence.[23] What is certain is that both forms of the text, the short and the long, are attested in the middle of the second century. One could say that the Alexandrine text is hostile and that the Western text is favorable to their presence,[24] but that is a simplification. It is certain, however, that these verses are scarcely known in the communities of Egypt in the second through the fourth centuries, while they are quite well known in Syria. Marcion may bear witness to the short text, Justin Martyr to the long text.[25] In the fourth century, Epiphanius of Salamis provided the valuable

20 The Coptic papyrus Strassburg 5–6, which Stephen Emmel recently attached to the *Gospel of the Savior*, contains on the recto of the first folio a prayer of Jesus that combines the themes of the high-priestly prayer of John 17 and the prayer of Gethsemane and on the verso an account of Gethsemane with a reference to the passion; the statement "the spirit is willing . . ."; the tears of the apostles; and a speech of Jesus, who encourages and exhorts his disciples. In what is extant it mentions neither the visit of the angel nor the drops of blood. See Daniel A. Bertrand, "Fragments évangéliques," in Bovon et al., *Écrits apocryphes chrétiens*, 1:427–28. According to Bertrand, the two folios date from the fifth–sixth centuries, and the text could date from the third century. Among the agrapha is an indirect one preserved by Tertullian *Bapt.* 20.2 (see n. 84 below): "I believe that because they had fallen asleep the disciples were tempted to abandon the Lord at the moment of his arrest . . . even though previously there had been the word that no one would enter the Kingdom of Heaven without having been tempted." Tertullian does not say explicitly that this word of Jesus was stated in Gethsemane. In the *Gospel of Nicodemus*, Latin recension A, chap. 20, Satan, who speaks there with Hell, refuses to give Jesus the title of Son of God and uses the episode on the Mount of Olives, in particular the statement "My soul is deeply grieved to death" (Matt 26:38), to limit Jesus' identity to that of a simple human being. See Rémi Gounelle and Zbigniew Izydorczyk, *L'Évangile de Nicodème, ou, Les actes faits sous Ponce Pilate (recension latine A): suivi de La lettre de Pilate à*

l'empereur Claude (Apocryphes 9; Turnhout: Brepols, 1997) 188.

21 See Erich Grässer, *An die Hebräer* (EKK 17/1; Neukirchen-Vluyn: Neukirchener Verlag, 1990) 265–67, 296–305, 312–14; Strobel, ("Psalmengrundlage"), who refers to Psalms 114 and 115 of the LXX (= Psalm 116).

22 Ehrman and Plunkett ("Angel," 401–3), Wiefel (377–78), and C. F. Evans (182–83) offer a clear presentation of the witnesses, the "external evidence." Some manuscripts read these verses at another place, following Matt 26:39. Duplacy ("Préhistoire," 78) summarizes the problem well: "Were our verses added to the text no later than 150, or were they eliminated before 200–250 at the latest?"

23 Fragment 0171 begins with v. 44. See Aland, "Alter und Entstehung," 37–61; Kurt Aland and Barbara Aland (*The Text of the New Testament: An Introduction to the Critical Editions and to the Theory and Practice of Modern Textual Criticism* [trans. Erroll F. Rhodes; Grand Rapids: Eerdmans, 1989] 63) offer a photograph of it (v. 44 is at the bottom of what remains of the left-hand column; v. 45 and the following verses are in the right-hand column). I thank Eldon Jay Epp for his help in understanding the nature and the presentation of this fragment. Claire Clivaz tells me that there is an Old Latin witness, a (Vercelli, fourth century), that contains vv. 43-44.

24 Thus Ehrman and Plunkett, "Angel," 402.

25 On Marcion, see Harnack, *Marcion*, 234*; Tsustui, "Evangelium Marcions," 124. On Justin, see the preceding paragraph.

information that some advocates of the divinity of the Son rejected these verses (*Ancoratus* 31.4–5).[26] Modern critics are understandably divided. Some think that these verses were added to underscore the human nature of Christ at a time when docetism was threatening (as Ignatius of Antioch inserts the adverb ἀληθῶς, "truly," in the confessional formula to emphasize the reality of the passion).[27] Others think that these verses were quickly offensive in a century (the second) in which the believers found their comfort in the lordship of a Son, the divine Word.

The internal criticism is also not easy to deal with. A great deal has been made of the chiastic structure of the pericope,[28] although one can find a chiasm here with or without these verses. People have also analyzed the vocabulary with contrasting results. Some terms and expressions correspond to Lukan usages;[29] others are singular in the New Testament (the three terms ἀγωνία, "struggle," "anguish"; ἱδρώς, "sweat"; θρόμβος, "clots of blood," "drops" are all *hapax legomena* in the New Testament).[30] Finally, the theology of these verses has been questioned. Some have said that Luke softens Mark's text, emphasizes the Son's docile obedience, and, later, omits Jesus' cry of abandonment (Mark 15:34). Thus, he could not have presented such a fragile, human Messiah.[31] Others have noted that Luke changes the passion narrative to make it conform to the stories of martyrdom.[32] It is not unusual that the martyrs, even if they finally die, receive comfort from heaven during their torment. In Acts 7:56-57 did not Stephen see how he was received by the Son of Man at the moment of his agony? All things considered, I am of the opinion that Luke did not create the episode nor was he ignorant of it. As I have said, the block 22:15-46 comes from Luke's

special material and contained vv. 43-44. It may be that Luke was reluctant to include them. Although he probably is not afraid to underscore Jesus' human nature (in the Gospel [24:46] and in Acts [17:3] he is quite willing to speak of the suffering of the one he calls the suffering Messiah [παθητός ὁ χριστός, Acts 26:23]), he does balk at acknowledging a discord between the Father's will and that of the Son. That, however, is not the issue in vv. 43-44. The tension between the two wills, that of God and that of Jesus, appears instead in the prayer itself in v. 42, and Luke tries to minimize it. Here it is a question of an angelic intervention, and Luke does not disdain that.[33] It is also here a question of the external marks of an internal situation, the visible signs of an invisible reality, and Luke is the champion of such external signs (one thinks of the Holy Spirit in the form of a dove at the time of the baptism where the evangelist says it appeared bodily; 3:22).[34]

We still need to explain why these verses are missing in so many good manuscripts. Must we detect Marcion's influence there?[35] Four clues will put us on the right track: (a) the view of Epiphanius, who, as we have seen, called attention to various advocates of the divinity of Christ who rejected these signs of humanity; (b) then the fate of *Sinaiticus* (א = 01), which originally had these verses and then lost them because a scribe no longer supported them; (c) then the tendency of a tradition from Mark that emphasized Jesus' humanity and abandonment leading up to John, who, as we have seen, explicitly rejects the Son's request to his Father (John 12:27); finally, (d) the evidence of Christian art, which for centuries did not dare to portray Christ on the cross or, if it was risked, as is done by the artist of the wooden gate of the church of the Santa Sabina in Rome (fifth

26   Cited and translated in Ehrman and Plunkett, "Angel," 404–5.

27   E.g., Ignatius *Trall.* 9.1; see also the note from Pierre Thomas Camelot in *Ignace d'Antioche, Polycarpe de Smyrne, Lettres, Martyre de Polycarpe* (SC 10; 1969; reprinted Paris: Cerf, 1998) 100 n. 4.

28   Ehrman, *Corruption*, 191–92.

29   On the vocabulary of vv. 43-44, see Holleran, *Gethsemane*, 92–101.

30   Ibid., 96.

31   This is the opinion of Ehrman (*Corruption*, 190) and of Ehrman and Plunkett ("Angel," 411).

32   See Dibelius, "Gethsemane."

33   See, e.g., 1:11, 26-28; 2:9; 24:4; Acts 12:7.

34   See vol. 1 of this commentary, 128–29, on 3:22; and Bovon, *Luke the Theologian*, 16, 229, 237 n. 30.

35   Bate ("Luke xxii, 40") notes a variant attested by Sinaiticus (א = 01) and several other witnesses but which does not appear here in the 27th edition of Nestle-Aland: the infinitive προσεύχεσθαι ("to pray") instead of the imperative προσεύχεσθε ("pray"). He thus suggests replacing the direct speech with the indirect in v. 40.

century), portrayed him as alive, impassive, with the arms outstretched as in prayer or a blessing.[36] All of these representations point in the same direction. One did not need to be docetic to be disconcerted by the episode of Gethsemane and Jesus' all-too-obvious struggle against death.[37]

Commentary

■ **39** The reference to 21:37 is beyond doubt. By specifying that Jesus remains faithful to his customary behavior, Luke suggests that the threats coming from Judas's betrayal do not divert him from his ministry, his vocation, his destiny.[38] Thus, Judas will have no trouble finding him, because Jesus is not going to try to flee. By remaining faithful to the verb "to go," the evangelist recalls that Jesus' mission is accomplished by going a way and respecting its stages. By retaining the verb "to follow" to describe the disciples' attitude, he insists on the expected obligation and the conformity that is expected between the believers' existence and the example of Christ. Without being able to detect how much of the pericope is traditional, we can say that, as is often the case in the introductions and the staging, Luke's imprint is decisive here. The style and the vocabulary prove it.[39]

■ **40** The editorial signs are, however, less obvious in v. 40.[40] Furthermore, there is a thematic contrast with the

preceding verse. According to the "custom" (v. 39), the group should have rested. But Jesus does not even think of doing that. He proposes, rather, that they watch and devote the night to prayer (v. 40). As the readers know, Jesus prays at every important moment of his life.[41] This prayer of Jesus (vv. 41-45) is framed here by an invitation that he addresses twice to his disciples (vv. 40, 46). This double invitation actualizes—the readers remember this also—the request of the Lord's Prayer, "and lead us not into temptation" (11:4).[42] Yet there is the same term ($\pi\epsilon\iota\rho\alpha\sigma\mu\acute{o}\varsigma$) as "test" and as "temptation." Beforehand one does not know if the coming event is a "test" that one overcomes or a "temptation" to which one succumbs. Prayer does not keep the "test" from happening—the case of Jesus will prove it—but it implores God, who is able to keep the "test" from becoming an irresistible "temptation." By choosing the second person plural over the first person, the Lukan Jesus underscores the disciples' responsibility. The Master cannot take the place of his disciples here.[43] There are extraordinary tests, which it is better to avoid so that they do not become the temptation that makes one fall. This is why Jesus gives his instruction before he goes to set an example (vv. 41-44).

■ **41** Once again Luke underscores the dignity of Jesus, here with the emphatic expression "and he" ($\kappa\alpha\grave{\iota}\ \alpha\grave{\upsilon}\tau\acute{o}\varsigma$), which Joachim Jeremias regards as christological.[44] Jesus distances himself from the group of his disciples. The

---

36   The crucifixion was seldom represented during the first centuries of Christian art.

37   Among the many who favor the Lukan authenticity of vv. 43-44 are the following: Brun, "Engel"; Benoit, *Passion and Resurrection*, 17–18; Duplacy, "Préhistoire"; Feuillet, *Agonie*, 397–98; Senior, *Passion*, 87. Among those who reject the Lukan authenticity of vv. 43-44 are Metzger, *Commentary* (2d ed.), 151; and Ehrman and Plunkett, "Angel." Sabourin (351) wavers.

38   On the location of the episode, see Taylor, "Gethsemane," who is of the opinion that Jesus spent the night not in the open air in a garden but in a cave where oil was pressed, the cave of Gethsemane. On the historicity, see Saunderson ("Gethsemane"), who thinks that the naked young man (Mark 14:51-52) may have been a witness of the scene.

39   See above, 194, esp. n. 8.

40   The expression $\dot{\epsilon}\pi\grave{\iota}\ \tau o\hat{\upsilon}\ \tau\acute{o}\pi o\upsilon$, "at this place" (without movement), is found nowhere else in Luke-Acts. The similar expression $\dot{\epsilon}\pi\grave{\iota}\ \tau\grave{o}\nu\ \tau\acute{o}\pi o\nu$, "to

this place" (with movement), appears twice (19:4; 23:33), in passages I attribute to the special source.

41   See 3:21; 6:12; 9:18, 28-29; 11:1; 23:34; vol. 1 of this commentary, 129, on 3:21-22, and 206, on 6:12; Monloubou, *Prière*, 57–61. In v. 41 the manuscripts waver between the imperfect $\pi\rho o\sigma\eta\acute{\upsilon}\chi\epsilon\tau o$ ("he was praying"), which Nestle-Aland (27th ed.) accepts, and the aorist $\pi\rho o\sigma\eta\acute{\upsilon}\xi\alpha\tau o$ ("he prayed").

42   See vol. 2 of this commentary, on 11:4. Héring ("Probleme") takes from Loisy the idea that Jesus originally asked his disciples to pray so that he himself would not fall into temptation.

43   On $\pi\epsilon\iota\rho\alpha\sigma\mu\acute{o}\varsigma$ in Luke, see vol. 1 of this commentary, 138, on 4:1-13; vol. 2, on 11:4; Brown (*Apostasy*) and my criticism in *Luke the Theologian*, 439–42; Korn, $\Pi EIPA\Sigma MO\Sigma$, 76–86; Heinrich Seesemann, "$\pi\epsilon\hat{\iota}\rho\alpha\ \kappa\tau\lambda$.," *TDNT* 6 (1968) 23–36.

44   Jeremias (*Sprache*, 37–38) notes: "In most cases it is the Christology that sets the tone" (p. 37). See vol. 1 of this commentary, 167, on 5:1. Neyrey ("Absence") gives a good presentation of Jesus, the courageous

well-chosen verb ἀποσπῶ is linguistically superior to its Markan parallel; it means "to pull away," "to withdraw." Luke uses it in the active form in Acts 20:30 and, as here, in the passive form in Acts 21:1 (with the idea of painful separation): "After we had been separated from them."[45] The passive aorist (ἀπεσπάσθη) has an intransitive meaning and indicates an action that is concluded: Jesus "withdrew from them."[46] He went about a stone's throw from them.[47] It is not an unusual expression; one finds it in Thucydides (*Peloponnesian War* 5.62.2).[48] The exegetes who are concerned to save the authenticity of Jesus' words think that with this remark Luke is emphasizing Jesus' proximity.[49] The exegetes who are not interested in the matter are of the opinion that the distance was too far for anything to be heard.[50] In reality, the expression says more about what is seen than about what is heard. According to Luke, the disciples were able to see Jesus kneeling and praying. The medieval artists knew quite well how to represent the right distance. Even if the liturgical practice were to stand while praying (18:13; Matt 6:5),[51] it was not unheard of for Jews to kneel in exceptional circumstances.[52] Here the posture underscores the intensity of the supplication and the humility of the one who is praying. One finds it in Acts (9:40; 20:36; 21:5) and in the epistles (Eph 3:14). It was customary not for praying to God or the gods, but for petitioning sovereigns or suzerains (see, e.g., 1 Chr 29:20 LXX; 3 Kgdms 8:54). When God is understood as a Lord, then the knees bend before him (see Isa 45:23), as one sees in the Philippian hymn (Phil 2:10).

■ **42** Jesus speaks to God as to a father, as to his Father.[53] He risks asking. The "cup" is a well-known, common, and yet ambiguous metaphor: punishment, destiny, death?[54] "Punishment" is scarcely probable, because the Lukan Jesus has never given the impression that he is guilty.[55] "Destiny" emphasizes duration too much, the time here being when one watches for a brief[56] and singular event. "Suffering" or "death" is the right choice, even if it will come with unjust violence, since we are dealing with a man who is still young.[57] This interpretation is justified,

---

hero. I do not, however, share his interpretation of ἀγωνία as "combat."

45 See BAGD, s.v.; Feuillet, *Agonie*, 399.

46 See BDF §313; G. B. Caird, "The Glory of God in the Fourth Gospel: An Exercise in Biblical Semantics," *NTS* 15 (1968–69) 265–77, esp. 268.

47 The accusative is correct in designating a distance; see Daniel B. Wallace, *Greek Grammar beyond the Basics: An Exegetical Syntax of the New Testament* (Grand Rapids: Zondervan, 1996) 201–2; the same is true of ὡσεί to designate approximation; see BAGD, s.v. ὡσεί, 2.

48 See *T. Gad* 1:3 (family α). See also Homer *Il.* 3.12; Gen 21:16 (the distance of a bowshot).

49 Thus Feuillet, *Agonie*, 400.

50 C. F. Evans, 809.

51 The so-called *Amida* prayer, the essence of the synagogue worship, means etymologically the prayer one pronounces while standing.

52 See Solomon, who by turns stood and knelt (2 Chr 6:12-13). There were, it seems, rules for the common mortals, for the priest, and for the king. There were also positions in addition to standing or kneeling, such as bowing or lying. See Str-B 2:259–61.

53 Aus (*Gethsemane*) and Kiley ("Lord") think that Ps 114 (116):4 lies behind Jesus' prayer. On the invocation "Father" in Luke, see vol. 2 of this commentary, on 11:2a (the Lord's Prayer).

54 On ποτήριον ("goblet," "cup"), see Cranfield,

"Cup"; Black, "Cup"; Goppelt, "πίνω κτλ.," *TDNT* 6:148–58. The term is seldom used metaphorically in Greek literature. The corresponding Hebrew term כּוֹס, on the other hand, is used frequently in Hebrew literature, and the image is common in the civilizations of the ancient Near East. See, e.g., Isa 51:17, 22-23; Ezek 23:31-34; Jer 25:15-16, 17, 27-28; Ps 74 (75):9; Hab 2:16; *Ps. Sol.* 8.14-15; Rev 14:10; 17:4. The author of the Apocalypse also uses the word φιάλη ("bowl," "cup") in Rev 15:7; 16:1; 21:9. There this term often expresses God's anger and judgment. The idea is that the cup contains a poison that is so deadly or a wine so strong that it robs you of your ability, delivers you to the enemy, or puts you in a disastrous situation.

55 Nevertheless, Goppelt ("πίνω," 152–53) comes finally to this understanding: the cup of Luke 22:44 parr. indicates Jesus' fate, not the sad fate, but the judgment that God pronounces on human sin and that Christ will undergo. In my opinion Goppelt projects a Pauline doctrine onto the Synoptic tradition.

56 The use of the cup with the meaning of destiny or fate is rare. See Ps 15 (16):5-6.

57 The image of the cup is hardly used in the Hebrew Bible to express suffering or death apart from the condemnation of a court, but the sense is essential here. It must be a question of a usage that developed in the course of time. See Pseudo-Philo *Ant.*

all the more so since elsewhere the Master[58] has compared martyrdom to a cup.[59] No human being, full of plans and wishes, wants to cease to exist. For a long time there has existed in antiquity—Tertullian and others bear witness to it—a general fear of death.[60] Here Jesus unequivocally displays his membership in the race of mortals.

He also shows that he is responsible and anxious to harmonize his will with that of the deity. Luke insists, more than Mark or Matthew, on this filial obedience. As we have seen in the analysis, Luke initially expresses this reservation that Jesus gives his request with the typically Athenian formula, "if you will" (ϵi $\beta o\acute{\nu}\lambda\epsilon\iota$).[61] As if God could not have heard, the Lukan Christ repeats himself and cannot be any more explicit: "Nevertheless, let not my will but yours be done."

Nothing indicates that the Jesus of Luke has superhuman knowledge here. Although Luke has implied that Jesus had predicted his passion and on two occasions his resurrection (Luke 9:22; 18:33), the threatening danger, like a wave that sweeps everything from its path, makes one forget any changes the future would bring. Robin Barbour emphasizes not only the human aspect that the Gospel narrative confers on Jesus but also the theological necessity that this feeling of distress was historical.[62]

Along with a subjective concept of redemption, the Christology of Luke opens the way to Christians' faith and life. They too will call God Father (or Mother), will live their earthly existence in a faith that knows the fear of death, and will take their will upon themselves by submitting it in prayer to the will of God. Thus, the disciples appeared to be unable (v. 45) to continue to accompany him (v. 39) to this point (v. 42). They will need the proclamation of Easter (24:23-27, 36-43, 44-48) and the Spirit of Pentecost (Acts 2:1-4, 14-36) to change them and to set them on the path of obedience and following the model of Jesus.

■ **43** Neither Jewish nor Christian tradition disdains human life in favor of an easy afterlife. Around the beginning of the Common Era, about the time a theology of martyrdom develops as a result of harsh experiences,[63] the bravest and the holiest vigorously express a refusal to die. As an example[64] I choose the account of the death of Abraham in the long version of the *Testament of Abraham*.[65] Abraham does not think of the death

Bibl. 50.6 ("I drank the cup of my tears"); *T. Abr.* (long recension) 1:3 and passim (see the commentary on v. 43 below).

58 Mark 10:38-39: "'Can you drink the cup I will drink or be baptized with the baptism with which I will be baptized?' They said to him: 'We can.' Jesus said to them: 'The cup I will drink you will drink, and with the baptism with which I will be baptized you will be baptized.'" These verses, known also by Matthew (Matt 20:22-23), are missing from Luke (see vol. 2 of this commentary, on 18:15-17 and 18:35-43).

59 The meaning is attested also in *Asc. Isa.* 5:13 and various rabbinic texts; see Goppelt, "$\pi\iota\nu\omega$," 152 n. 39 (above, n. 54). It will be further extended under the influence of the Gospels. When he was about to die, Polycarp offered the following prayer: "I bless you for making me worthy of this day and hour that I may receive a share among the number of the martyrs in the cup ($\tau\tilde{\omega}$ $\pi o\tau\eta\rho\acute{\iota}\omega$) of your Christ . . ." (*Mart. Pol.* 14.2; trans. Bart Ehrman, *The Apostolic Fathers*, vol. 1 [LCL] 387).

60 Tertullian *De testimonio animae* 4.1–11. I thank André Schneider, who called this text to my attention and even translated it for me. See also Heb 2:15 ($\varphi\acute{o}\beta\omega$ $\vartheta\alpha\nu\acute{a}\tau o\upsilon$, "through fear of death"); and the references in Harold W. Attridge, *The Epistle to the Hebrews: A Commentary on the Epistle to the Hebrews* (Hermeneia; Philadelphia: Fortress Press, 1989) 98 n. 165.

61 See Smyth, *Greek Grammar* §628; BDF §27.

62 Barbour, "Gethsemane," 251. Bonnington ("Obedient Son") thinks, on the contrary, that the text emphasizes less the suffering or the anguish than Jesus' obedience.

63 See Boyarin, *Dying for God.*

64 See also the *Apocalypse of Sedrach* 9–15 and the *Greek Apocalypse of Ezra* 6.

65 See Francis Schmidt, *Le Testament grec d'Abraham: Introduction, édition critique des deux recensions grecques, traduction* (TSAJ 11; Tübingen: Mohr Siebeck, 1986). Opinions about the date of this work and its two recensions vary greatly. The dates vary from the first to the fifth centuries of the Common Era. See Albert-Marie Denis et al., *Introduction à la littérature judéo-hellénistique* (2 vols.; Turnhout: Brepols, 2000) 1:197–98. For the English translation of the long recension from which (with the exception of 20:5) the following excerpts come, see E. P. Sanders in James H. Charlesworth, ed., *The Old*

that God is preparing for him. To soften the torments, the Creator demands that Death appear in the guise of a benevolent archangel. In view of the enthusiastic greeting with which the patriarch receives him, Death abandons the lie and tells him what cup he must drink.[66] Abraham rejects him in a sentence that recalls Jesus' supplication: "Leave, leave me, because I want to rest on my couch" ($\mathring{\alpha}\pi\epsilon\lambda\vartheta\epsilon$, $\mathring{\alpha}\pi\epsilon\lambda\vartheta\epsilon$ $\mathring{\alpha}\pi$ $\mathring{\epsilon}\mu o\hat{v}$, $\mathring{o}\tau\iota$ $\vartheta\acute{\epsilon}\lambda\omega$ $\mathring{\alpha}\nu\alpha$-$\pi\alpha\acute{\upsilon}\epsilon\sigma\vartheta\alpha\iota$ $\mathring{\epsilon}\nu$ $\tau\hat{\eta}$ $\kappa\lambda\acute{\iota}\nu\eta$ $\mu o\upsilon$) (T. Abr. [long recension] 16:2). Death then explains to Abraham that he adapts the beauty or ugliness of his appearance to the degree of virtue or vice of those he must look after. Abraham then insists on seeing his ugliness. Death accepts and reveals his various faces. "And he showed him also another face, of a fierce, storm-tossed sea and a fierce, turbulent river and a frightening three-headed dragon and a mixed cup of poisons" (long recension 17:16). These appearances frighten the patriarch's servants so much that seven of them perish (although at the end they will escape unscathed). A second and then a third time Abraham rejects Death's advances before he becomes finally indifferent. Then Death explains the various faces to him, and Abraham presents a new request to him. In vain; he feels his life force leaving and his spirit in distress. He beseeches Death for the last time, and "then a liquid ($\mathring{\iota}\delta\rho\acute{\omega}\varsigma$) oozed from his eyes, similar to clots of blood ($\vartheta\rho\acute{o}\mu\beta o\iota$ $\alpha\mathring{\iota}\mu\alpha\tau o\varsigma$)" (long recension 20:5).[67] His son Isaac and his wife, Sarah, hover around him. Then, when the deceived patriarch kisses the hand of Death, his soul adheres to the hand and leaves the body of Abraham.

This example shows at least two things: (a) that the most prominent members of the people of Israel could fear death, something that could be of comfort to the frightened, common mortals; (b) that God comes to help those who face the last passage, something that can encourage everyone who sooner or later must face the same terminal date. To this parallel that can be drawn between the death of Abraham and the death of Jesus[68] we must, however, add a difference. Jesus submits much more easily and quickly to the inexorable will of God.[69] It is remarkable, although scarcely ever mentioned, that Abraham and Jesus have the same physical symptoms (sweat and clots of blood). This unusual similarity requires an explanation. A probable literary relationship could go in either direction and would be interesting either way. If it should go from the Testament of Abraham to the Gospel, it says something about what the evangelist has read. If it should go from the Gospel to the Testament, it offers a new witness for the textual problem mentioned above. Whatever the answer to this question might be, the parallel underscores the common fraternity of human beings in the face of death: fear is experienced bodily.[70]

An angel appears to Jesus. It is not the angel of Death disguised as an angel of light. Luke does not deal with such subtleties. He appears ($\mathring{\omega}\varphi\vartheta\eta$) as God can appear to Abraham in Ur of the Chaldees (Acts 7:2) or to Moses on Sinai. Other angels are sent: one to Zacharias (the same verb, $\mathring{\omega}\varphi\vartheta\eta$, 1:11), another to Mary ($\mathring{\alpha}\pi\epsilon\sigma\tau\acute{\alpha}\lambda\eta$, "he was sent," 1:26), others (called $\mathring{\alpha}\nu\delta\rho\epsilon\varsigma$, "men," 24:4) to the women who had run to the tomb, finally another to Peter in prison ($\mathring{\epsilon}\pi\acute{\epsilon}\sigma\tau\eta$, "was standing there," "happened," Acts 12:7). The angel delivers no message; he communicates a power. While the woman with the flow

Testament Pseudepigrapha (2 vols.; Garden City, N.Y.: Doubleday, 1983, 1985) 1:882–95.

66 "I am the bitter cup of death," $\mathring{\epsilon}\gamma\acute{\omega}$ $\epsilon\mathring{\iota}\mu\iota$ $\tau\grave{o}$ $\pi\iota\kappa\rho\grave{o}\nu$ $\tau o\hat{v}$ $\vartheta\alpha\nu\acute{\alpha}\tau o\upsilon$ $\pi o\tau\acute{\eta}\rho\iota o\nu$ (T. Abr. [long recension] 16:12).

67 There are differences among the manuscripts, one reads "his face" instead of "his eyes," others hesitate about the word "drops." See Schmidt, Le Testament d'Abraham (above, n. 65), 164–67, critical apparatus.

68 Some have preferred to compare Jesus' fate with that of Socrates; see Cullmann, Immortality, 19–27. Larkin ("Background") thinks that the fate of Jesus resembles that of Daniel: both are comforted by an angel and can see that God's will is carried out in their lives. See esp. Dan 10:18 according to the version of Theodotion.

69 Along with the similar elements, this time with Mark and Matthew, one could also mention that Jesus prays three times and that Abraham begs Death three (or even four) times to leave him.

70 Several exegetes refer to examples from the reality of wars and imprisonments. Thus Benoit writes: "A priest, who assisted one of his brethren shot by the Germans in 1914, told me that he could understand this sweating of blood by a man in good health at the moment of execution" (Passion and Resurrection, 18 n. 2).

of blood received the healing energy from Jesus (Luke 8:43-48; it is the word δύναμις, "power," that is used in v. 46), here it is Jesus who needs the divine comfort. The angel again gives Jesus power: ἐνισχύων (the present participle indicates that this transfer of power took some time). The angel gives Jesus what Peter will transmit to his brothers and sisters ("strengthen your brothers," στήρισον τοὺς ἀδελφούς σου, 22:32). The hearers will have these words fresh in their ears.

■ **44** One expects the reverse order: first the human ἀγωνία, then the divine comfort. Life does not consist of happy endings. The angel of the olive garden is not an *angelus ex machina*. God's presence is real, but it does not eliminate the struggle.

The meaning of ἀγωνία is controversial. The Greek word ἀγών indicates "competition," "struggle." Among the authors of the classical period, such as Pindar (*Ol.* 2.53) or Herodotus (*Hist.* 2.91), ἀγωνία has no other meaning. In the Hellenistic and then in the Roman epoch, however, ἀγωνία indicates less the reality of the struggle than the spirit of the one who is facing a conflict, a trial, or death (see Philo *Plant.* 175). The word can be rendered with "interior distress," "anguish," with the various degrees of intensity these terms can imply. Moreover, the verb ἀγωνιῶ undergoes the same evolution. In the New Testament age it means "being anxious," and one uses another verb, ἀγωνίζομαι, to say "to be involved in a competition," "to fight."[71] It is not likely that ἀγωνία designates here an exterior "struggle." It is improbable that it expresses the victory of an inner "struggle."[72] In no case does the Greek word correspond to the sense some modern dictionaries give "agony": "the struggle preceding death." It corresponds to the

French usage at the end of the sixteenth century: *angoisse* ("anguish," "distress"),[73] and that is the sense it has kept in modern Greek.

The vocabulary becomes more precise without requiring that we detect the hand of a physician here. The term ἱδρώς indicates sweat (Plato speaks of "dry" sweats, to contrast them with the perspiration produced by a bath [*Phaed.* 239C]).[74] The ancients knew the unusual phenomenon of a perspiration that was colored by the blood. Aristotle knows that there is such a thing as haematidrosis.[75] The Jewish romance *Joseph and Aseneth* gives an example.[76] One would have said (ὡσεί, "as") θρόμβοι of blood. The word θρόμβος can have two meanings—the clot and the drop. I do not know why I think of clots rather than drops. How did the medieval artists picture them? To the best of my knowledge, the artists of Christian antiquity did not dare to represent this scene. Drops or clots, this sweat of blood falls to the ground. The help "from heaven" (v. 43) does not abolish the humanity, which returns "to the ground" (v. 44).[77]

■ **45** Clots or drops, that is the only thing that falls to the ground. Jesus stands up and surrenders. The power delivered by the angel has its effect. He goes back to his disciples (the distance of a "stone's throw" is not far) and is surprised (is it really a surprise for him?) to find them sleeping. Luke makes an excuse for them: they are numb "from sadness" (ἀπὸ τῆς λύπης), an expression one finds already in the LXX (Isa 50:11: ἐν λύπῃ κοιμηθήσεσθε, "you will fall asleep in sadness"). People usually say that sadness keeps you from sleeping, yet I also know that a great misfortune, a grief overwhelms you. Then sleep becomes a refuge and a last protection. The word λύπη initially expresses "sorrow," "grief," "sadness," or

---

71   See Diogenes Laertius *Vit. Phil.* 7.112–13; see also Tannehill, 324.

72   Contra Gamba, "Agonia"; Galizzi, *Getsemani*, 20–23, 202–3; Neyrey, "Absence," 161–65. Neyrey thinks of the victorious struggle against sadness.

73   *Petit Robert*, s.v. (*Le nouveau Petit Robert: Dictionnaire alphabétique et analogique de la langue française* [Paris: Dictionnaires Le Robert, 1996]).

74   See Bailly, s.v.

75   Arisotle *Hist. an.* 3.19: γίγνεται γὰρ ἰχωροειδές, καὶ διαρροῦται οὕτως ὥστε ἤδη τινὲς ἴδισαν αἱματώδη ἱδρῶτα, "If it becomes too fluid, they fall ill, because then the blood becomes ichor-like, and it gets so thin that cases have been known in which

blood-like sweat has been observed" (trans. A. L. Peck, LCL).

76   *Joseph and Aseneth* 4.11: "And when Aseneth heard these words from her father, plenty of red sweat poured over her face, and she became furious with great anger, and looked askance at her father with her eyes, and said . . ." (trans. C. Burchard in James H. Charlesworth, ed., *The Old Testament Pseudepigrapha* [2 vols.; Garden City, N.Y.: Doubleday, 1983] 2:207).

77   On vv. 43-44, see Makridis, "ὁ ἱδρώς."

"affliction." It further indicates a "painful condition," a "difficult situation," or, finally, a "physical pain." We should retain the first meaning. Sorrow overwhelms them, because they sense that death is going to take their Master from them.

■ **46** Jesus refuses to feel sorry for them. Like him, they are to stand up; the prayer he offered his Father, that they were unable to speak, is to enable them to face the situation. With this inclusion (v. 46 recalls v. 40) and with this invitation the literary unit ends.[78] The way the narrative continues keeps us from knowing whether this time the disciples did what Jesus commanded. Probably not, since the crowd and Judas interrupt Jesus' comments (22:47a), and Peter will not find his spiritual energy before he denies his master (22:54-62).

History of Interpretation

Justin Martyr is the first witness of our text (*Dial.* 97.3–106.4).[79] In chap. 103 of the *Dialogue with Trypho* he demonstrates that the sufferings mentioned in Psalm 21 (22) are prophecies of the passion of Christ. He states in particular that v. 15 of the psalm ("All my bones are poured out and scattered like water; my heart has become like wax melting in the midst of my belly") predicts Jesus' prayer on the Mount of Olives and his arrest: "For in the memoirs of the Apostles and their successors, it is written that His perspiration poured out like drops ($\vartheta\rho\acute{o}\mu\beta o\iota$ without the word $\alpha\H{\iota}\mu\alpha\tau o\varsigma$) as He prayed and said: 'If it is possible, let this cup pass from me.' His heart and bones were evidently quaking, and his heart was like wax melting in his belly, so that we may understand that

the Father wished his Son to endure in reality these sufferings for us, and may not declare that, since he was the Son of God, he did not feel what was done and inflicted upon Him" (103.8).[80]

Three brief comments: (1) Since Justin emphasizes here the apostolic origin and authority of the Gospel, it is probably because he knew that the verses in question appeared in neither Matthew nor Mark, and perhaps he knew Luke's short version as well as the long. (2) In this passage Justin not only argues against Trypho the Jew; he also attacks in passing the Docetists of any stripe who deny the sufferings of Jesus (see in particular the adverb "really," "truly," $\alpha\lambda\eta\vartheta\H{\omega}\varsigma$). (3) What is especially close to Justin's heart is the correspondence between the scriptural text and the history Jesus lived.

Irenaeus of Lyon is also familiar with the detail of the blood sweat (*Adv. haer.* 3.22.2; 4.35.3).[81] He uses it twice against the Valentinians in a chain of episodes from the life of Jesus that underscore his humanity and his function as the new Adam.[82]

Marcion may have neglected the Gethsemane scene, since Tertullian does not mention it in chap. 41 of book 4 of *Adversus Marcionem*.[83] Tertullian does refer to it, however, in his treatise on prayer, when he explains the petition of the Lord's Prayer, "Lead us not into temptation." Satan is the tempter; God merely puts us to the test. The petition of the Lord's Prayer is confirmed by the command Jesus gives his disciples in Gethsemane. In spite of this order the disciples succumbed to temptation and abandoned their Lord. Tertullian concludes that the last petition of the Lord's Prayer, "but deliver us from the

---

78 Senior (*Passion*, 84–89) emphasizes the role of prayer in facing evil and death.

79 The reader will find a short presentation and a selection of patristic texts in English translation in Arthur A. Just, *Luke* (2 vols.; Concordia Commentary; St. Louis: Concordia, 1996, 1997) 340–44. Luz (*Matthew 21–28*, 398–408) and Gnilka (*Markus*, 2:265) provide valuable information about the other Synoptics. I did not have access to the unpublished dissertation by Edith Wild, "Histoire de l'exégèse."

80 I added the words in parentheses (translation of Thomas B. Falls in FC).

81 In *Dem.* 75, Irenaeus relies on v. 42 and its synoptic parallels without quoting it, when he says that

Jesus' passion corresponded to the will of God the Father.

82 Clement of Alexandria (*Paed.* 1.46.1; *Strom.* 4.75.1) mentions the cup Jesus had to drink. The way he explains in the *Paedagogus* the meaning of milk and blood, without referring to the drops of blood, can lead one to assume that his specimen of Luke did not contain vv. 43-44.

83 See Harnack, *Marcion*, 234*. Tsutsui ("Evangelium Marcions") is right to recommend caution and to say that the presence of vv. 43-44 is simply not attested in Marcion. Tertullian's silence, however, justifies concluding that these verses probably were absent from Marcion's gospel.

evil one," confirms the meaning one must give to "lead us not into temptation."[84]

Around 180, Celsus expressed an interest in the Gethsemane episode. If Jesus is God, he could feel neither the fear of death nor physical pain. This is the point of view of the pagan philosopher. If he suffered and begged God to save him from this cup, he cannot be God. This is the point of view that Celsus attributes to the thinking Jew. Origen contradicted the views expressed by Celsus and gave his interpretation of the scene in his *Contra Celsum* (2.24–25). He renounced the esoteric explanation intended for the perfect people and contented himself with an elementary explanation: Jesus' prayer, an expression of his humanity, bears witness chiefly to Jesus' submission to the will of God. In his final hours, Jesus proves his firmness of heart by revealing the spirit he mentions in the expression "the spirit is willing, but the flesh is weak" (Matt 26:41).[85]

It is the cup that interests Origen in his *Exhortatio ad martyrium* (29).[86] He thinks that every martyrdom is called a "cup," as the Gospel (Gethsemane episode) and Psalm 115 (116) prove. In an original way Origen notes that this psalm brings the death of the saints (v. 6 [v. 15]) close to the "cup of salvation" (v. 4 [v. 13]).

At the same time, in the first half of the third century, Hippolytus of Rome also mentions the blood sweat of Luke 22:44 in his satirical writing against Noetus

(18.2). He is the first to refer along with it to v. 43, the help brought to Jesus by the angel (which he mentions *after* having mentioned the blood sweat). Thus, when he concludes that Christ the comforter himself had need of comfort, Hippolytus follows the exegetical line of Justin and Irenaeus, who cite the Lukan Gethsemane episode to call to mind the incarnation of the Son.[87]

Thus, during these first centuries, the Gethsemane episode was drawn into the controversies about the incarnation and Jesus' human nature. In addition, it served parenetic ends: one was to follow the example of Jesus and not that of the disciples.[88]

In the fourth century, Christian literature becomes so extensive that I cannot go beyond some samples.[89] I have chosen Ephraem the Syrian, whose commentary on Tatian's *Diatessaron* devotes a number of pages to the scene of Jesus on the Mount of Olives (*Diat.* 20.1–11). Jesus' sorrow was real, and it reflects the human reality of the Master, who is not ashamed to admit it. Nevertheless, it is disturbing, and Ephraem looks for various ways to explain it. The request to remove the cup was directed to God to protect those who would have to live with its consequences (Origen knew this explanation[90]). Another explanation is that this fear "comes over him so that his nature would be manifest as Adam's son on whom, according to the word of the apostle, 'death reigns'" (20.4). A third explanation is that Jesus identi-

---

84 Tertullian (*Or.* 8.5–6; see also *Bapt.* 20.1–2) (based more on Matt 26:41 par. Mark 14:38 than on Luke 22:40 or 46, which is quoted) compares (by contrasting) the believers preparing for baptism and the disciples in the Garden of Gethsemane (see n. 20 above). Finally, see Tertullian *Adv. Prax.* 27.11, the passage in which the author makes a distinction in the one "persona" Jesus between God and the human being, then sets out a stereotypical list of allusions to Jesus' human character (the words *anxia usque ad mortem*, "[Jesus' flesh] anxious until death," may refer to v. 44).

85 Without repudiating it, Origen mentions in §25 another explanation: Jesus prayed to the Father not for himself but so that people would avoid the disasters, which would be sure to come with his passion. See also the interpretation of Gethsemane in Origen's *Comm. Matt.* 26.36–46 (Werke 11; GCS 38; 204–16).

86 I am thankful to Just (*Luke*, 341) for this reference.

87 See Ehrman and Plunkett, "Angel," 406–7.

88 According to the indexes I have consulted, Cyprian appears to have had no particular interest in the episode of Gethsemane.

89 There are various Greek homilies of late antiquity on Matt 26:39, the parallel to Luke 22:42: John Chrysostom *Hom. Matt.* 83 or 84 (*PG* 58:746–52); Pseudo-Chrysostom, "In illud, Pater, si possibile . . ." (*PG* 61:751–56); Amphilochius of Iconium *Oratio* 6, "In illud, Pater, si possibile . . ." (CCSG 3:139–52); Basil of Seleucia *Oratio* 32, "In illud, Pater, si possibile . . ." (*PG* 85:349–60); Severian of Gabala, "In illud, Pater, transeat a me calix ist (Matth., xxvi, 39)" (Ch. Martin, ed., "Note sur l'Homélie de Sévérien de Gabala: In illud: Pater, transeat a me calix ist [Matth., xxvi, 39]," *Le Muséon* 48 [1935] 311–21; and Johannes Zellinger, *Studien zu Severian von Gabala* [Münsterische Beiträge zur Theologie 8; Münster: Aschendorff, 1926] 9–21).

90 See n. 85 above.

205

fied with the disciples' feelings so that he could serve as an example to them (20.7).[91] A last explanation is that Jesus "was afraid in order to deceive death; he wanted to incite it, to devour it, and soon to reject it" (20.7). At the heart of Ephraem's thinking is the contrast between the two Adams. Commenting on the blood sweat, he notes, "'His sweat was as drops of blood,' says the evangelist. He perspired to heal Adam's sickness. 'In the sweat of your face, God says, you will eat your bread' (Gen 3:19). And he remained in prayer in this garden in order to lead Adam back to the garden that once had been his" (20.11).[92]

At the other end of the ancient world, Ambrose of Milan meditates in a personal way on the mystery of the Mount of Olives (*Exp. Luc.* 10.56–63). A clear distinction between the two natures of Christ[93] eliminates the fears that disturbed Ephraem. The Latin bishop does not want to excuse Jesus. On the contrary, he congratulates him for "having taken over my feelings" (10.56). In this intro-spective way, which anticipates Luther's message and makes one think of Bach's chorales, he exclaims:

Thus it was for me he was afflicted, although there was no reason for him to suffer affliction. And laying aside the enjoyment of his eternal divinity, he lets himself be overwhelmed by the lassitude of my infirmity. He took my sorrow to give me his joy. In our footsteps he descended into the anguish of death, wanting to lead us back to life in his footsteps. I thus do not hesitate to speak about sorrow, because I preach the cross. (*Exp. Luc.* 10.56)

It goes without saying that this reverence for the weak-ness of Jesus does not reflect a concession to Arianism. Ambrose explicitly rejects an Arian interpretation of the episode (10.56).[94]

In a last gasp of paganism the emperor Julian adopts an attitude that is reminiscent of that of Celsus in his attack on the Christians. In an extant fragment of his treatise *Against the Galileans* he writes:

Furthermore, Jesus prays in such language as would be used by a pitiful wretch who cannot bear misfor-tune with serenity, and though he is a god is reassured by an angel. And who told you, Luke, the story of the angel, if indeed this ever happened? For those who were there when he prayed could not see the angel; for they were asleep. Therefore when Jesus came from his prayer he found them fallen asleep from their grief and he said: "Why do ye sleep? Arise and pray," and so forth.[95]

In the fifth century, Cyril of Alexandria, like Ephraem the Syrian a century earlier, questions the fear of death

---

91 This last explanation is in turn subdivided: the believers learn from Jesus how not to glorify them-selves about death before the hour, to pray in order to avoid temptation, to be free of the fear of death by receiving Jesus' comfort.

92 The *Liber Graduum*, written in Syriac at the begin-ning of the fourth century, refers twice to the prayer of Jesus, to the comfort brought by the angel, and to the clots of blood (*Sermo* 18.3 and *Sermo* 20.8 [*PS* 3:435–40, 543–48]). The author's concern is to invite Christians to the prayerful struggle in tears against sin, a level of spiritual growth following the example of Christ, whose prayer was heard and who achieved perfection (Heb 5:7-9). I am indebted for this double reference to Dr. Emmanuel Papoutsakis, whom I thank.

93 "As a human being he resists death; as God he maintains the sentence" (*Exp. Luc.* 10.59).

94 In *De Trinitate* 10.27–29 and 36–43, Hilary of Poitiers meditates at great length from an anti-Arian perspective on the Gethsemane narrative. He refers to vv. 43-44 of Luke 22, knowing that they are missing in various Greek and Latin manuscripts. On the christological risks Hilary takes, see Madi-gan, "Ancient and High-Medieval Interpretations," 162–63.

95 Trans. Wilmer Care Wright, *The Works of the Emperor Julian*, vol. 3 (LCL 157; Cambridge, Mass.: Har-vard University Press, 1913) 431. See Christopher Gérard, *L'empereur Julien, Contre les Galiléens: Une imprécation contre le christianisme: introduction, traduc-tion, et commentaire* (Brussels: Ousia, 1995) 72. Neumann designates it fragment 7 (Karl Johannes Neumann, *Iuliani Imperatoris Librorum contra Christia-nos quae supersunt Insunt Cyrilli Alexandrini fragmenta Syriaca* (Leipzig: Teubner, 1880). The fragment was preserved by Theodore of Mopsuestia *Comm. Luc. Fragmenta* (*PG* 66:723–24). See Baarda, "Julian."

that overcomes Christ on the Mount of Olives.[96] His Christology underscores the divinity of the Word just as does in a later century the mosaic of the church Sant' Apollinare Nuovo in Ravenna. Jesus' fear and weakness in this moment surprise Cyril.[97] To acknowledge them he resorts to the concept of mystery, a mystery he reveals to his hearers.[98] According to him, such an attitude of Jesus can be explained only by the divine economy that wanted the incarnation of the Word.[99] Even here Jesus' fear is not a reluctance to suffer but the expression of his concern for his disciples and his people. "And tell me, which wine grower, when his vineyard is abandoned and devastated, does not agonize over it?"[100] Did Jesus not shed tears over Jerusalem?[101]

As an oversimplification, one can say that the Jewish Christians, the followers of Paul of Samosata, the Arians, the Nestorians, and even the Chalcedonians appreciated, or at least tolerated, vv. 43-44. The Docetists, the Nicaeans, and the Monophysites scarcely liked them at all; they either put up with them or tried to ignore them. In the seventh century, as the last consequence of the christological quarrels, the conflict ignited over the energy of Christ, then over his will or his wills. In the time when monothelitism was ascendant, Maximus the Confessor paid with his life for his defense of the two natures, then of the two wills, of Christ. Monothelitism was finally defeated, and dyothelitism emerged victorious from the sixth ecumenical council, the Council of Constantinople (680–681). The Gethsemane episode played a major role there, because in a sense both wills of Jesus are expressed—that of his tempted human nature and that of his divine nature, the nature that conforms to that of the Father.[102]

In the time of the Venerable Bede,[103] at the beginning of the eighth century, the practice of exegetical borrowing had already begun (Bede *In Luc.* 6.876–954). In his exegesis of Luke 22:39-46, Bede quotes Jerome and Gregory the Great. He thus mixes tradition with innovation. Belonging to tradition are the reflection on the place to which Jesus retreats, all the more easy to find since it was well known; the relationship between Jesus' command (v. 46) and the petition of the Lord's Prayer (11:4); the comment on Jesus' solitude; the interpretation of Jesus' sorrow, which is a sorrow "for us"; finally, the idea that nearing death is a struggle. To the innovation I attribute the allegorical interpretation of the walk to the Mount of Olives: It means that the disciples, who at the Last Supper were initiated into the mysteries of the body and blood of Jesus and who at the time of the crucifixion would be baptized into his death, must still be invested with the supreme seal of the Holy Spirit. I also attribute to Bede the two parts of the prayer of Jesus (v. 42), which reflect his two natures: the request corresponds to his humanity, the filial obedience to his divinity.[104]

---

96 Cyril preached two sermons on the Mount of Olives episode. The first is devoted to the fear that tests Jesus; the second to the prayer that Jesus gives as an example while at a distance from his disciples. It also deals with the voluntary and involuntary character of Jesus' passion. See Cyril of Alexandria *Serm. Luc.* 146, 147; cf. Payne Smith, *Cyril,* 2:683–92. Fragments of these sermons are frgs. 340–44 in Reuss, *Lukas-Kommentare,* 214–16.

97 In the first sermon he wonders on several occasions why Jesus was afraid; see Payne Smith, *Cyril,* 2:684–85.

98 See the beginning of the first sermon (Payne Smith, *Cyril,* 2:683–84).

99 Ibid., 684, 686.

100 Ibid., 685.

101 Ibid., 686.

102 See Maximus the Confessor *Opuscula Theologica et Polemica* 6 (*PG* 91:61–68); Maximus the Confessor, *Opuscules théologiques et polémiques,* introduction by Jean-Claude Larchet, translation and notes by Emmanuel Ponsye (Sagesses chrétiennes; Paris: Cerf, 1998) 43–49, 142–44; see also Maximus the Confessor, *L'agonie du Christ,* introduction by François-Marie Léthel (Les Pères dans la foi 64; Paris: Migne, 1996); Lods, "Bataille," 428–29.

103 Just (*Luke,* 343, 342) quotes in English translation a difficult passage from Gregory of Nazianzus (*Or. Theol.* 30.12) on the same will that the Father and Son have and another passage from John Damascene (beginning of the eighth century) (*On the Orthodox Faith* 3.18), which discusses the human will and the divine will, both of which are present in Jesus Christ and are at the time active in Gethsemane. On the Latin and especially the medieval patristic interpretation of Gethsemane, see Madigan, "Ancient and High-Medieval Interpretations."

104 The anonymous Irish *Comm. Luc.* 22:41–44 (CCSL 108C:96–97) (end of the eighth century) makes only three comments on the episode: the first, with perhaps an allegorical or tropological meaning, analyzes the stone's throw; the second concerns the

The presence or the absence of vv. 43-44 appears to have caused intense debates in Armenia.[105] From the eighth through the thirteenth centuries the manuscripts waver; some contain these verses, others do not. Those that do contain them do so in various forms. Some have only v. 43, thus not v. 44. Others neglect the comfort that the angel brought as well as the drops of blood but emphasize that Jesus prayed "with power."[106] The marginal note of a manuscript from the middle of the thirteenth century that includes vv. 43-44 explains, "this passage is in the Gospels of the Franks, the Syrians and the Greeks, but not of the Alexandrians. And the Gospel of the Armenians appears to have been translated from the latter, because the passage in question does not appear in the Armenian Gospels. Yet all the commentators refer to it; they quote it and explain it. And, having found it in my model, I myself made a copy of it."[107]

As S. P. Cowe has shown,[108] the vacillations of the Armenian manuscript tradition could not be separated from this church's theological quarrels and the international political situation of that day. A dissident theologian, Yovhannés Mayragomecʿi (seventh century) holds the view that the flesh of Christ corresponds to that of Adam before and not after the fall. It thus knew no human passions. It was impossible for Christ to know fear, since that was considered to be a passion. As the great authority Gregory the Illuminator attests, vv. 43-44 are not part of the Gospel. He never speaks of them. They must have been added under Nestorian influence.[109]

The repudiation of the position of Mayragomecʿi by Tʿéodoros (seventh century) must be seen against the background of the victory of the emperor Heraclius against the Persians and the return of Byzantine influence to the Armenians. Tʿédoros gives a reading different from that of Gregory the Illuminator and thinks that vv. 43-44 belong to the Gospel.[110]

Before we leave Armenia, let us say that the presence or absence of our verses in the Armenian manuscripts is related to the hypothesis that the Bible was translated into Armenian in two stages. This hypothesis, as well as the sequence of the texts (did the presence or the absence of vv. 43-44 come first?), is debated by the scholars.[111] In any event, the vacillations of the Armenian manuscripts, which resemble those of the Greek and Syriac manuscripts, correspond to doctrinal opinions that favor either the humanity or the divinity of Jesus.[112]

In the thirteenth century, Bonaventure understood by counting (*Comm. Luc.* 22.51–58).[113] Just as four pericopes precede the passion itself,[114] there are seven conditions for successful prayer that are strung together in these verses. (1) The prayer must be secret (v. 39). (2) It is accompanied by the anxiety provoked by imminent

---

appearance of the angel (even if in his flesh Jesus is comforted by a visible angel, in his spirit he is of an invisible majesty); the third refers to the blood sweat that makes clear that Jesus gives his blood of his own free will and that he does not suffer less than the others.

105 On this subject, see Cowe, "Christological Trends"; and before him Duplacy, "Préhistoire," 83.

106 These comments are dependent on Cowe ("Christological Trends," 47), who has examined extensively the critical apparatus of Zohrab's edition of the Armenian Bible.

107 This manuscript, codex 558 of the Chester Beatty collection in Dublin, was commissioned by Catholicos Konstandin Barjrberdcʿi and thus probably comes from the scriptorium at Hromkla; see Cowe, "Christological Trends," 46.

108 Cowe, "Christological Trends," 41, 47.

109 Ibid., 38–41.

110 Ibid., 41–43.

111 Ibid., 43–44.

112 In *The Disputation of Sergius the Stylite with a Jew* 7.7, the author, who in the eighth century wrote in Syriac, made this enigmatic pronouncement: "If the Son sought help from an angel, in the same way the Father laid a curse upon Meroz because they did not come to the help of the Lord . . ." (trans. A. P. Hayman, *The Disputation of Sergius the Stylite against a Jew* [CSCO 339; Scriptores Syri 153; Louvain: Secretariat du Corpus SCO, 1973] 18). The curse of Meroz goes back to the Song of Deborah (Judg 5:23). The meaning is probably that there was a weakness of the Son as there was a weakness of the Father. For this reference I am indebted to Dr. Emmanuel Papoutsakis, who has also given me other references as well as bibliographical references.

113 Bernardini, 555–58.

114 See above, "History of Interpretation" on 22:1–6.

danger (v. 40). (3) It is expressed in humility (Jesus kneels, v. 41).[115] (4) It is done with discernment, knowingly (this is how I understand the term *discretio*), as Jesus' prayer proves (v. 42). (5) Strength is not lacking, nor is the comfort the angel brings (v. 43). (6) It comes from a context of anguish (v. 44). (7) The prayer is lucid, just as Jesus acts discreetly in going to the disciples to see if they are awake (v. 45). To this principal enumeration he adds two secondary enumerations, that of the seven gifts of blood Jesus made (beginning with circumcision and ending with the thrust of the spear) and that of the Master's three prayers (according to Matthew and Mark). Such calculations reassure or delight the medieval doctor, who, by the way, like the entire Christendom of his day, could conceive of Jesus' dread only as a fear on our behalf. "The angel appears," he writes, "to comfort; not because of his weakness, but for our comfort." As had been the case in antiquity, the establishment of a strong Christology made a weak humanity of Jesus unthinkable.[116]

Since the Reformation was not primarily related to Christology, the interpretations of Erasmus (*Paraphrasis*, 454–55) and Luther,[117] then those of Calvin[118] and Maldonatus,[119] are not basically opposed to one another. One and all are still characterized by the evolution of piety, which, coming from the background of an almighty Christ opens itself, in the fourteenth century, to the mysteries of the Son of God. This *Christus dolorosus* stands behind many explanations.

In the time of the Enlightenment, the dogma of the two natures wavered among independent thinkers, then among the Protestants. Then the fear and the suffering of Christ really become his. With the "Eloi, eloi, lama sabachthani" of Mark 15:34, the drops of blood and the fear become examples of Jesus the man. His vacillation generally evokes admiration. Does he not overcome his legitimate apprehension with a heroic resignation? On the other hand, these expressions of his weakness provoke sarcastic comments from those who defend the figure of the strong man.

The enlightened and critical spirits of the nineteenth century, followed as they would be by the defenders of the liberal theology, are among the admirers. Ernest Renan, in his famous *Vie de Jésus*, writes two significant pages about Jesus on the Mount of Olives.[120] On the one hand, he summarizes the various versions of the episode

---

115 Bonaventure gives two allegorical meanings to the stone's throw (the cornerstone moves away for a brief time and immediately returns; every praying person must tear oneself away from the appetites of the flesh).

116 Plummer (511) quotes a statement from Bernard of Clairvaux in which the medieval theologian says that Jesus "prayed not only with his eyes but, so to speak, with all of his parts, so that his entire body, which is the Church, is purified by the tears of his entire body" (*Dominica Palmarum, Sermo* 3.4 [*PL* 183: 262]).

117 Luther, *Evangelien-Auslegung*, 1154–59. Luther acknowledges Jesus' fear, even if he thinks it is no small thing to admit that the Son of God had such a feeling. He then raises what is for him the decisive question: How does the Gethsemane episode benefit Christians? The answer is threefold: The biblical scene shows, first of all, the weight of sin. In the second place, it teaches where to find consolation: at the place where death, once the punishment for sin, has become the cure for sin. In the third place, it urges people to pray when testing comes into their life.

118 Calvin, *Harmony*, 3:146–54. The Geneva reformer notes the Lukan characteristics. He knows the questions that the episode has raised with the exegetes, who are captivated by the divine glory of Christ. He has an appreciation for the commentary of Ambrose of Milan, and he quotes Cyril of Alexandria. He attributes the fear to Jesus' human nature. Since, contrary to common mortals, Jesus is without sin, he chose God's will over his own. There were—as Karl Barth would develop—two reasons for his fear: death as separation and transition and death as judgment and punishment in view of redemption. Calvin meditates on the changing—we would say psychological—attitude of Jesus and the real conditions of the prayer. Against the monothelite heretics of the past, he is convinced that there were in Jesus two wills, just as he had two natures—one human, which, as if he had been dazzled by the intrusion of death, had forgotten his redemptive mission, the other divine, which remembered God's immutable plan.

119 Maldonat (*In Luc.* 22:38 [149]) refers to the explanation of the scene on the Mount of Olives that he gives in his commentary on Matthew.

120 Ernest Renan, *Vie de Jésus*, 236–37 (English translation from the The Modern Library translation of 1927, *The Life of Jesus*, chap. 23, "Last Week of Jesus," 333–35.)

by harmonizing them; on the other, he interprets them as narrative according to the line I have just laid out. I cite some characteristic extracts: "A deep melancholy appears, during these last days, to have filled the soul of Jesus, who was generally so joyous and serene. All the narratives agree in relating that before his arrest he underwent a short experience of doubt and trouble; a kind of anticipated agony. . . . His soul was sad even unto death; a terrible anguish weighed upon him; but resignation to the divine will sustained him." While momentarily overcome with distress ("the enormous weight of the mission he had accepted pressed cruelly on Jesus"), he comes to himself heroically. Renan expresses this image of the superior human being[121]—one says this pointedly—in the old categories of patristic Christology. "Human nature asserted itself for a time. Perhaps he began to hesitate about his work. . . . It is certain at least that his Divine nature soon regained the supremacy."

This interpretation of a heroic Jesus was subjected to Nietzsche's criticism. In his *Antichrist,* the philosopher explicitly challenges Renan. "M. Renan, that buffoon *in psychologicis,* has introduced the two most inappropriate terms possible into his introduction of the Jesus type: the concept of *genius* and the concept of the *hero* ('héros'). But if anything is unevangelical it is the concept of the hero."[122]

The reaction of dialectical theology was different. In the famous pages on his doctrine of redemption, Karl Barth renews an old interpretation, without explicitly saying so, of Calvin in particular.[123] The episode of the Mount of Olives expresses the difficulty and the hardness of the matter: He who has come down from heaven must be delivered into the hands of sinners. Does that have to happen? Jesus (in a prayer!) calls all of that into question. According to Barth, who without saying it contradicts Martin Dibelius, the manifest fear of Jesus has nothing to do with the martyr's. And the theologian from Basel contrasts the account of the temptations in which Jesus is victorious with that of Gethsemane, in which he becomes weak. He may be finished with Satan, but Satan is not finished with him. Not only is Satan against him, but the world he has come to save abandons him. Even the disciples leave him (the church sleeps!). Barth sees at the center of the pericope neither the enigma of the world nor that of evil, but the enigma of God. It is the *Gottesfrage,* the question of God, in particular the theodicy question. God is absent. God does not answer (Barth must perform an exegetical sleight of hand to make believable that the angel's help does not correspond to an answer from God). To be more precise, at this instant God hides behind Satan (my image, not Barth's); God's will coincides with that of Satan (Barth's expression). At first Jesus refuses this monstrosity, then he discovers that it represents the only means of overcoming evil, of expiating sin, of offering redemption. It is by arranging for Jesus' death, by abandoning him to death, that God gains the victory over death and reduces it to nothing. Jesus understands this. Thus, if he is afraid, it is less because he fears life's end, which each human being faces one day, than because he must undergo a death that is unique, since only it can offer the world redemption. This distinction, which I have found in Calvin, represents a Reformed interpretation of the passion of Christ that undoubtedly owes more to Paul than to Luke. The cup that Jesus had to drink was not so much the symbol of death as it was the expression of the wrath of God.

Conclusion

On the one side there are the sleeping disciples, who try to escape from the anxieties. On the other there is Jesus, who is sleepless, tormented by fear.

---

121 A little further on (ibid., 246; trans., 344), at the beginning of the chapter "Arrest and Trial of Jesus," Renan recalls the Gethsemane episode: "Overawing his friends by his inherent greatness, he watched and prayed."

122 Friedrich Nietzsche, *The Anti-Christ: Attempt at a Critique of Christianity* (trans. Walter Kaufmann in *The Portable Nietzsche* [1954; reprinted New York: Viking, 1968] 600). I have discovered that Ruprecht ("Tragic Vision," 13–16) also refers to Nietzsche.

123 Barth, *Church Dogmatics* (Edinburgh: T. & T. Clark, 1936–1977) 4/1, 264–73; see also 3/3, 500 (angels play almost no role in the life of Jesus; Luke 22:43 is an exception); and 3/4, 401 (the fear of death [Luke 22:44] is mentioned in connection with the problem of suicide; Jesus did not surrender his life as something that had no value).

At the beginning and at the end of the narrative (vv. 39-40 and 45-46) Luke gives his attention to the fate of the disciples. At the beginning they follow; then they grow tired. Their bodies are heavy with sadness. Jesus charges them to awaken and pray. Only this twofold attitude—such is the implicit but obvious message—will end their sadness and restore them to Jesus' side. Whether they respond favorably or not to the command remains doubtful.

For his part, Jesus moves away from his disciples, without saying or knowing that he is breaking away body and soul. He wants to beseech and to convince his Father without saying or knowing that God will stay absent and silent. Thus, in the center of the episode Jesus remains alone. For Luke, however, God's silence is not total. Admittedly, God does not answer in person, and his answer does not correspond to the request. After all, an angel is sent. Even though he does not take away the cup, he does give him the power to drink it. Furthermore, the action does not take place without struggle: body and soul Jesus suffers. He is confused by the anguish and tortured in his flesh. The blood that clots outside his veins or arteries expresses the intensity of his fear physically. Jesus shares completely in the human condition. Still, he does not interrupt the play. Indeed, in the following episode he regains all his energies and asserts himself, without violence but with the determination that God gave him by granting his request without satisfying it.[124]

Christians have been thinking about this passage since antiquity. At first they were surprised that their Lord had to experience such a testing; then they understood that Jesus' humanity had a function in God's "economy." Did he not have to die so that he could become "the prince of life" ($\acute{o}$ $\mathring{\alpha}\rho\chi\eta\gamma\grave{o}\varsigma$ $\tau\mathring{\eta}\varsigma$ $\zeta\omega\mathring{\eta}\varsigma$, Acts 3:15)? The way goes from Christmas to Good Friday, and the distance is not long.

---

124 This exegesis was already finished when I became aware of the remarkable doctoral dissertation of Claire Clivaz, which I followed with interest: *L'ange et la sueur de sang*. Although we are in accord about the Lukan origin of vv. 43-44, which thus are not an interpolation, we do not agree on the meaning to be given to the Greek word $\mathring{\alpha}\gamma\omega\nu\acute{\iota}\alpha$. Clivaz advocates the meaning *lutte* ("struggle"). Whatever the meaning that should be given this word, the exegete from the Canton of Vaud presents with talent the framework of the "struggle" in which the pericope is written.

The Arrest of Jesus (22:47-53)

Bibliography

Benoit, *Passion and Resurrection*, 15–18, 42–45.

Black, "Arrest and Trial."

Brandon, S. G. F., *The Trial of Jesus of Nazareth* (New York: Stein & day, 1968) 116–25.

Dauer, Anton, *Die Passionsgeschichte im Johannesevangelium: Eine traditionsgeschichtliche und theologische Untersuchung zu Joh 18, 1-19, 30* (StANT 30; Munich: Kösel, 1972) 49–61.

Dibelius, Martin, "Judas und der Judaskuss," *DtPfrBl* 43 (1939) 727–28; reprinted in idem, *Botschaft und Geschichte: Gesammelte Aufsätze* (2 vols.; Tübingen: Mohr Siebeck, 1953, 1956) 1:272–77.

Doeve, J. W., "Die Gefangennahme Jesu in Gethsemane: Eine traditionsgeschichtliche Untersuchung," *StEv* 1 [TU 73] (1959) 458–80.

Donahue, John R., "From Crucified Messiah to Risen Christ: The Trial of Jesus Revisited," in Arthur E. Zanonni, ed., *Jews and Christians Speak of Jesus* (Minneapolis: Fortress Press, 1994) 93–121.

Ford, J. Massyngberde, *My Enemy Is My Guest: Jesus and Violence in Luke* (Maryknoll, N.Y.: Orbis, 1984) 120–21.

Goulder, *New Paradigm*, 2:744–47.

Green, Joel B., *The Death of Jesus: Tradition and Interpretation in the Passion Narrative* (WUNT 2/33; Tübingen: Mohr Siebeck, 1988) 18–77, 264–68.

Hall, S. G., "Swords of Offence," *StEv* 1 [TU 73] (1959) 499–502.

Joüon, Paul, "Luc 22, 50-51, τὸ οὖς τοῦ ὠτίου," *RSR* 24 (1934) 473–74.

Linnemann, *Studien*, 41–69.

Matera, Frank J., *Passion Narratives and Gospel Theologies: Interpreting the Synoptics through Their Passion Stories* (New York: Paulist, 1986) 150–69, 119–223.

Quispel, Gilles, "The Gospel of Thomas and the Trial of Jesus," in T. Baarda et al., eds, *Text and Testimony: Essays on New Testament and Apocryphal Literature in Honour of A. F. J. Klijn* (Kampen: Kok, 1988) 193–99.

Rehkopf, *Sonderquelle*, 31–85.

Rice, George E., "The Role of the Populace in the Passion Narrative of Luke in Codex Bezae," *AUSS* 19 (1981) 147–53.

Rostovtzeff, M., "οὖς δεξιὸν ἀποτέμνειν," *ZNW* 33 (1934) 196–99.

Sabbe, Maurits, "The Arrest of Jesus in John 18:1-11 and Its Relation to the Synoptic Gospels: A Critical Evaluation of A. Dauer's Hypothesis," in Marinus de Jonge, ed., *L'Évangile de Jean: Sources, rédaction, théologie* (BEThL 44; Gembloux: Duculot, 1977) 203–34.

Schneider, Gerhard, *Die Passion Jesu nach den drei älteren Evangelien* (BiH 11; Munich: Kösel, 1973).

Idem, "Die Verhaftung Jesu: Traditionsgeschichte von Mk 14,43-52," *ZNW* 63 (1972) 188–209; reprinted in idem, *Jesusüberlieferung und Christologie: Neutestamentliche Aufsätze, 1970–1990* (NovTSup 67; Leiden: Brill, 1992) 236–57.

Senior, *Passion*, 89–93.

Taylor, *Passion Narrative*, 72–76.

Tyson, Joseph B., *The Death of Jesus in Luke-Acts* (Columbia: University of South Carolina Press, 1986) 15–38, 120–60.

Watson, Alan, *The Trial of Jesus* (Athens: University of Georgia Press, 1995) 64.

47	**While he was still speaking, behold a crowd, and one called Judas, one of the Twelve, came before them, and he approached Jesus to kiss him. 48/ But Jesus said to him, "Judas, do you betray the Son of Man with a kiss?"[a]**
49	**And when those around him saw what was going to happen, they said, "Lord, shall we strike with the sword?" 50/ And one of them struck the servant of the high priest and cut off his right ear. 51/ Jesus answered, "Let it happen until this point." Then he touched the ear and cured him.**
52	**Then Jesus said to those who had come out against him, the chief priests, the officers of the temple, and the elders, "You have come out with swords and clubs as against a robber! 53/ When I was with you daily in the temple, you did not lift a hand against me, but this is your hour and the power of darkness."**

a   Another translation: "Judas, you betray the Son of Man with a kiss!"

In this passage, which Christian tradition has entitled "the arrest of Jesus," the arrest itself is missing. It will be mentioned only in passing in a subordinate participial clause, at the beginning of the next pericope (v. 54).[1] Luke obviously avoids the verb "to seize" ($\kappa\rho\alpha\tau\acute{\epsilon}\omega$), which Mark uses four times (14:44, 46, 49, 51). This silence does not mean, however, that the readers are to forget the dangers threatening Jesus. On the contrary, in these verses Luke reminds them of the dangers: the delivered Son of Man (v. 48), the option of armed resistance (v. 49), the blow struck at the servant's ear (v. 50), the presence of swords and clubs (v. 52), and the expression "lift a hand against me" (v. 53). These negative recollections form the background of a positive reality that takes place in the foreground. Jesus' authority is expressed in three ways. (a) Judas does not have time to plant his kiss (v. 47) before Jesus reproves him (v. 48);[2] (b) the hesitating disciples (v. 49) and then the overzealous companion (v. 50) are rebuffed with an enigmatic word and a healing act of the Master (v. 51); (c) the adversaries who are intruding are humbled by a word of Jesus that reveals their cowardice and their malice (vv. 52b-53).

Analysis

According to the hypothesis I have posed, Luke alternates between his sources more than he combines them. Since the beginning of chap. 22, he has followed first Mark (22:1-14) and then his own special source (22:15-46). Here he again rejoins Mark and follows him faithfully until the appearance before Pilate (22:47—23:5).

There is no doubt about Luke's dependence on Mark in these vv. 47-53, and that is admitted by most exegetes.[3] That does not mean that Luke blindly reproduces his source.[4] He rewrites it as he thinks best. At the beginning he follows it closely (v. 47),[5] but he saves the reference to the swords and the clubs until the end (v. 52) in order to avoid Mark's unfortunate repetition (14:43 and 48). He is silent about the function of the kiss in Mark 14:44; it is Jesus rather than the narrator who explains it. Moreover, this transfer did not proceed without modification. Instead of serving to recognize Jesus at night and in the middle of the group, the kiss shows the contrast between the affection it presupposes and the hostility that comes with it here (to betray the Son of Man, v. 48). Since the words of Jesus, who understands and controls the situation, are more important than the actions of the adversaries, what Judas does (Mark 14:45) does not even need to be mentioned. Luke speaks only of Judas's intention (v. 47b). As I said earlier, the arrest itself (Mark 14:46) disappears as such and survives only discreetly at the beginning of the following episode ($\sigma\upsilon\lambda\lambda\alpha\beta\acute{o}\nu\tau\epsilon\varsigma$ $\alpha\mathring{\upsilon}\tau\acute{o}\nu$, "having seized him," v. 54). Luke makes use of the Markan episode of the cut-off ear (Mark 14:47), but since it expresses what for him is a principle—the refusal of any armed resistance[6]—he introduces the incident with a general question from the disciples (v. 49). Everyone recognizes the redactional character of this sentence. Noteworthy are the classical expression "those around him" ($o\mathring{\iota}$ $\pi\epsilon\rho\mathring{\iota}$ $\alpha\mathring{\upsilon}\tau\acute{o}\nu$), which we find in Acts (Acts 13:13, $o\mathring{\iota}$ $\pi\epsilon\rho\mathring{\iota}$ $\Pi\alpha\mathring{\upsilon}\lambda o\nu$, "those around Paul");[7] the use of the future participle ($\tau\grave{o}$ $\mathring{\epsilon}\sigma\acute{o}\mu\epsilon\nu o\nu$, "what was

1   See C. F. Evans, 814; Senior, *Passion*, 93.

2   See Senior, *Passion*, 90.

3   For example, Fitzmyer, 2:1448. Schneider (*Passion Jesu*, 43–55) carefully compares the Lukan redaction with that of the Gospel of Mark; he finds that v. 53b is not Markan, comes from the tradition, and belongs to the special material; and he thinks, finally, that Luke and John have additions and omissions in common.

4   There are various opinions about the prehistory of the pericope as Mark gives it. For Doeve ("Gefangennahme"), there is behind Mark a traditional unit of Aramaic origin that each evangelist expands in his own way. For Linnemann (*Studien*, 41–69), there are three small independent units: (a) a biographical apophthegm (Mark 14:43, 48-49); (b) the account of Jesus' arrest as arranged by

Judas (Mark 14:44-46); and (c) the mention of the disciples' reaction (Mark 14:47, 50-52). According to Schneider ("Verhaftung"), we have here a short primitive account that grew over time (e.g., with the episode of the ear that was cut off).

5   The wording of the beginning of v. 47 corresponds exactly to that of Mark 14:43, which Matt 26:47 also accurately repeats. Nevertheless, Luke's new reading omits the $\kappa\alpha\mathring{\iota}$ $\epsilon\mathring{\upsilon}\vartheta\acute{\upsilon}\varsigma$ ("and at once"), which is typical of Mark but which Luke dislikes here, as he does elsewhere. In the story of Cornelius, Luke will begin a section in a similar way (Acts 10:44); see Plummer, 511.

6   See Ford, *My Enemy Is My Guest*, 120–21; Senior, *Passion*, 91.

7   Here are three references to Josephus from Adolf Schlatter (*Das Evangelium des Lukas: Aus seinen*

going to happen"), which appears only here in the New Testament; the christological title "Lord" ($\kappa\acute{\upsilon}\rho\iota\epsilon$), which, as is known, is a favorite of Luke;[8] and the recourse to questions in the midst of a didactic dialogue, a process that is part of the third evangelist's literary technique. As always, Jesus restores health. The Lukan Messiah cannot tolerate here the damage his disciples have done. Jesus heals the wounded person (v. 51),[9] not without at the same time expanding the lesson ($\dot{\epsilon}\hat{\alpha}\tau\epsilon$, "let it happen," is plural and responds more to the question from the group [v. 49] than to the individual attack [v. 50]). Let us add that in Mark the intemperate act is designed to effect the release of Jesus, who has just been arrested, while in Luke it is to prevent the imminent arrest.

The third evangelist drastically shortens the end of the episode. He eliminates the flight of the disciples (Mark 14:50), because he has a high regard for the Twelve and wants to keep them in Judea to be witnesses for the day of the resurrection. (Luke will also change the command of Christ, preserved in Mark, to go before him to Galilee, Mark 16:7; cf. Luke 24:6.)[10] He also omits the episode of the naked young man (Mark 14:51-52), perhaps because he does not understand its significance. According to Luke, the attention must be focused on Jesus, who is threatened, rather than on one of his disciples whom they try to arrest. Furthermore, why does he neglect the reference to the Scriptures (Mark 14:49)? Is it because he has already mentioned them (v. 37) or because he prefers the voice of Jesus (v. 53b) to that of the ancient prophets? It is difficult to say.

The literary unit ends with an addition not known to the Markan parallel (14:48-49): "But this is your hour and the power of darkness" (v. 53b). Is this Johannine-sounding wording Lukan, or is the evangelist concerned to attach a traditional sentence here as a general conclusion? It may be that the interpretation of the details will enable us to answer this question.

To sum up, Luke takes here a Markan passage and reworks it according to his plan. He probably does not make use of another source[11] but knows oral traditions that John also uses.[12] In a narrative style that connects the episodes Mark has presented several well-known actions of Jesus' companions or adversaries: the behavior of Judas (14:43-46); the move of the aggressive disciple (14:47); the act of the crowd that arrests Jesus (14:43, 48-49); the flight of the disciples (14:50); the adventure of the naked young man (14:51-52). Luke, in the form of a conversation inserted into a concrete situation, turns his attention to Jesus and describes him as having a knowledge that in three ways[13] overshadows his adverse fate:

(a) Jesus unmasks the disconcerting intention of Judas, who is approaching (vv. 47-48)
(b) Jesus heals the wounded person and prohibits violence (vv. 49-51)
(c) Jesus denounces the cowardice of the opponents and proclaims the tragic nature of the present hour (vv. 52-53)

Quellen erklärt [Stuttgart: Calwer, 1931] 436): *Vita* 58 §303, which uses a similar formula in connection with an attack the historian himself has experienced in the synagogue of Tiberias: ὡς δ᾽ εἶδον οἱ σὺν ἐμοὶ τὸ γινόμενον, "My companions, seeing what was happening" (trans. Thackeray, LCL, 113); *Bell.* 1.7.2 §144 and 5.7.4 §324, two passages that make use of the expression οἱ περί with the accusative.

8   See Bovon, *Luke the Theologian*, 214–18.
9   On Jesus as a physician and thaumaturge, see vol. 1 of this commentary, 177, on 5:12-16.
10   See Schneider, *Passion Jesu*, 54–55.
11   With Schneider, 2:460; contra Rehkopf (*Sonderquelle*, 31–85), who thinks that Luke follows a particular source to which he adds elements taken from Mark, and Taylor, *Passion Narrative*, 72–76.

12   With Sabourin, 352. The links between Luke and John, particularly the pre-Johannine tradition, have been examined by Dauer, *Passionsgeschichte*, 49–61. He arrives at the following conclusion: The differences between Luke and Mark are due to Lukan redaction and not to the presence of another source or a parallel tradition. As for the source used by the evangelist John, it is based on the Synoptic Gospels, here on Mark and Luke, and not on a tradition independent of the Synoptics. It is on this point that I disagree with Dauer.
13   Tannehill (325) also divides the pericope into three parts, and he too emphasizes the dominant role of Jesus. Wiefel (380) also writes: "Thereby Jesus stands in the foreground as the leading person." Fitzmyer (2:1447, 1449) goes in the same direction. Rehkopf (*Sonderquelle*, 31) sees four different parts:

From a literary point of view, the pericope is part of the passion narrative and never did have an autonomous existence.[14] Historically, Jesus' arrest is an event whose authenticity Paul already attests: "the Lord Jesus, in the night when he was handed over . . ." (1 Cor 11:23).[15]

Commentary

■ **47-48** The plot made a short time earlier (22:1-6) begins to take place. The evangelist had told of the uncertainty of the chief priests and the scribes and of their twofold question about "the how" ($\tau\grave{o}$ $\pi\hat{\omega}\varsigma$, translated as "in what manner," 22:2, 4). Judas rescues them here from their awkward situation by approaching Jesus to kiss him.

The arrival of the adversaries (v. 47) interrupts the conversation between Jesus and his disciples.[16] These adversaries form a large group that Luke, following Mark, calls the "crowd" ($\check{o}\chi\lambda o\varsigma$).[17] Unlike Mark, however, Luke refers to these many opponents by explaining that Judas "goes before" them ($\pi\rho o\acute{e}\rho\chi o\mu\alpha\iota$).[18] Like Mark, in a solemn way he calls Judas "one of the Twelve," the group that has been well known since 6:13,[19] and

thus underscores how serious the betrayal is.[20] When he says—and he is the only one to do so here[21]—$\acute{o}$ $\lambda\epsilon\gamma\acute{o}$-$\mu\epsilon\nu o\varsigma$ $\emph{Ἰούδας}$, it is not to say "a man called Judas," nor is it to mention a surname, as was the custom (but which presupposes a name that is missing here);[22] it is to recall that the narrative had only recently mentioned him twice (22:3, 21-22) and to call attention to his sinister notoriety.[23]

The verb $\varphi\iota\lambda\acute{e}\omega$, which initially means "to love," in the way that two "friends" ($\varphi\acute{\iota}\lambda o\iota$) love each other, also designates, beyond the feeling and the relationship, the signs of affection one gives. The word $\varphi\acute{\iota}\lambda\eta\mu\alpha$ can mean the "kiss" or the "hug." Depending on the particular location and the social context, the $\varphi\acute{\iota}\lambda\eta\mu\alpha$ can mean a gesture of affection, of love, or of respect. Here it is the respect an inferior gives to a superior person, such as that of the orthodox believer who kisses the ring of his bishop or the hand of his priest or that of the Jewish student who kisses his rabbi.[24] Judas wants to give the impression that he respects and honors his Master. In this case, the kiss is given at the moment when the two persons meet each other.[25]

Luke evidently remembers what he has just written.[26]

(a) the arrival of the group, v. 47a; (b) the kiss of Judas, vv. 47b-48; (c) the sword blow, vv. 49-51; (d) the word of Jesus to his adversaries, vv. 52-53.

14 C. F. Evans (814) writes: "The story will have been shaped by the passion of which it was a part."

15 Bock (2:1765–66) even tries to maintain the historicity of the miracle.

16 On the verb $\lambda\alpha\lambda\acute{e}\omega$ ("to pronounce inarticulate sounds," "to babble," "to speak," "to converse") and its sometimes religious significance in Luke, see H. Jaschke, "$\lambda\alpha\lambda\epsilon\hat{\iota}\nu$ bei Lukas," *BZ* 15 (1971) 109–14.

17 Influenced by Matt 26:47, Codex Beza (D = 05) and the Syriac Sinaitic and Curetonian versions add to the word "crowd" the adjective $\pi o\lambda\acute{v}\varsigma$, a "large" crowd.

18 On $\pi\rho o\acute{e}\rho\chi o\mu\alpha\iota$, a characteristically Lukan word, see BAGD, s.v. Some manuscripts, such as the Papyrus Bodmer $\mathfrak{p}^{75}$) and another, uncial manuscript Γ (= 036) support the variant $\pi\rho o\sigma\acute{\eta}\rho\chi\epsilon\tau o$, "he advanced" (the verb can be followed by the accusative in order to say, "to go toward someone"). Another variant, attested by Codex Beza (D = 05), the family f^1, ms 2542 (first hand), and several others, is $\pi\rho o\hat{\eta}\gamma\epsilon\nu$ ("he went ahead").

19 On the Twelve, see vol. 1 of this commentary, 206–11, on 6:12-16.

20 Dauer (*Passionsgeschichte*, 56–57) accurately notes that the identity of Judas in this passage corresponds to Luke's description at the beginning of the book of Acts (Acts 1:16).

21 See Matt 26:14 in the context of the plot to kill Jesus.

22 See Col 4:11: "Jesus, who is called Justus."

23 With C. F. Evans, 816.

24 Commentators like to cite Gen 27:26; 2 Sam (LXX 2 Kgdms) 15:5; 20:9; Prov 7:13; Luke 7:45; 15:20; Rom 16:16, biblical passages where kisses are mentioned. See Gustav Stählin, "$\varphi\iota\lambda\acute{e}\omega$ $\kappa\tau\lambda$.," *TDNT* 9 (1974) 118–27, 138–41; C. F. Evans, 816–17.

25 Various Greek, Latin, and Syriac manuscripts bring the Lukan text closer to that of Mark 14:44 and especially to that of Matt 26:48 by adding at the end of v. 47: "Because he gave them this sign: The one I will kiss, it is he." In particular the witnesses are Codex Beza (D = 05), the uncial manuscript from Tbilisi known as Codex Koridethi (Θ = 038), the family f^{13}, the ms 700, all Greek minuscule manuscripts, the Latin manuscripts aur, b, c, r¹, and two Syriac translations, the Peshitta and the Harclean; see the apparatus in Nestle-Aland (27th ed.).

26 As Goulder (*New Paradigm*, 2:744–45) points out, Luke could also have been inspired by Mark 14:41,

In the material from his special source the betrayal was the equivalent of a delivery (the verb παραδίδωμι, "to transmit," "to deliver," has already appeared four times [see 22:4, 6, 21, 22]), and it is as the Son of Man (ὁ υἱὸς τοῦ ἀνθρώπου, 22:22) that Jesus is going to suffer.[27]

■ **49-51** "That Judas hurries ahead of the other members of his group makes it possible for the disciples to recognize quickly what is going to happen."[28] Indeed, Jesus' defenders, literally, "those who were around him," realize what is imminent. Luke uses the future neuter participle as a substantive "what was going to happen" (τὸ ἐσόμενον), which one finds also in the writings of Sirach and the historian Josephus.[29] The participle ἰδόντες ("seeing") is well chosen: The future is so clear that it is obvious. The question emerges in the form of a deliberative future (πατάξομεν, "we will strike"?) introduced by "if" (εἰ). This way of speaking, common in Luke,[30] is not classical but it has its roots in the LXX.[31] The evangelist omits here the verb "to strike," "to upset" (παίω) that Mark uses when the ear is struck (14:47). He chooses instead (twice, vv. 49 and 50) "to hit," "to beat" (πατάσσω), a verb that Mark used earlier (14:27) in a passage that Luke has omitted (the quotation from

Zech 13:7: "I will hit the shepherd . . ."). When I reread the New Testament passage where this verb appears (Acts 7:24; 12:7, 23; Rev 11:6; 19:15), I note that with its concrete character πατάσσω can mean here a quickly struck blow. Luke will use "to strike" (παίω) later in the first mocking scene (22:64). By using the verb πατάσσω here in an absolute sense (without a direct object)[32] and adding the qualifying "with a sword,"[33] the evangelist puts in the mouth of the apostles a question not of immediate concern but of general interest. The issue is nothing less than armed resistance. Even if he had left hazy what may have been the symbolic meaning of the two swords in the earlier episode (22:36-38),[34] here he deprives the word "sword" of any metaphorical sense and emphasizes that Jesus takes a clear position. Without ambiguity the Master contradicts his impulsive disciple[35] and teaches the others by word and deed. In Luke's eyes the ἐᾶτε ἕως τούτου was not ambiguous.[36] It is our limited knowledge of the Greek of that day that makes us stumble.[37] The exegetes waver. Some translate: "Let it happen up to this point," that is to say, do not prevent the arrest and the entire passion. Others see a double command: "Leave [things as they are]! thus far,

---

which he did not quote: ἰδοὺ παραδίδοται ὁ υἱὸς τοῦ ἀνθρώπου, "behold, the Son of Man is delivered."

27 One could not stand the simplicity of Mark, for whom Jesus remains silent during the kiss of Judas. Thus, Matthew has Jesus say: "Comrade, this is why you are here," i.e., "Friend, do that for which you have come" (Matt 26:50). John, like Luke, has Jesus take the initiative and engage in dialogue with his opponents and ask them whom they are seeking (John 18:4). The answer ἐγώ εἰμι ("I am," or "I am he") gives rise to interesting theological reflection (John 18:5-8).

28 Lagrange, 564.

29 Sirach 48:25 (in the plural); Josephus (*Vita* 13 §73), who speaks about those who were not able to see what was going to happen (also in the plural); Schlatter, 436. Two old uncial manuscripts, Codex Beza (D = 05) and 0171 (the fragment mentioned above, p. 197 n. 23 on 22:39-46), some other Greek and various Latin and Syriac manuscripts bear the aorist participle τὸ γενόμενον, "what had happened," or its equivalent.

30 Luke 13:23; Acts 1:6; 7:1; 19:2; 21:37; 22:25; 26:23 (twice); see Fitzmyer, 2:1448, 1450–51.

31 See, e.g., Gen 17:17; 44:19; Amos 3:3-6; 6:12; BDF §440 (3); Fitzmyer, 2:1451.

32 It is the first usage indicated by LSJ, s.v. πατάσσω, I.

33 Luke follows the LXX practice and uses the preposition ἐν ("in") in an instrumental sense "with," "by"; see BAGD, s.v. ἐν, 5. The word μάχαιρα designates a "short sword" and any kind of "knife"; see above, p. 182 n. 111, on 22:21-38. Because of the redactional verse 49 and connections between this episode and that of the two swords (22:35-38), I think that, in Luke's view, the disciple used a weapon and not a knife that had been used to slay the Passover lamb.

34 See the commentary above on 22:35-38.

35 Only the fourth evangelist says that it was Peter and that the servant of the high priest was called Malchus (John 18:10-11).

36 The verb ἐάω means "to leave," "to permit," "to abandon," "to let go." It is difficult, if not impossible, to translate the imperative ἐᾶτε with "stop," as some would like to do.

37 The difficulty does not date from today. As early as the beginning of the fifth century, Augustine (*De cons. evang.* 3.5.17) knew two interpretations, which I summarize as follows: "Leave it! No further!" (accepting Peter's violent act) and "Let it hap-

[but no farther]."[38] Finally, still others: "Let me go so far [and heal the wounded person]."[39] What is clear is that the Jesus of Luke dissociates himself from his disciples, responds to their general question with a negative answer, and, with the miraculous healing, repairs what the unhappy disciple had done.[40] I hold to the first translation: "Let it happen to this point" (the τοῦτο, literally "this," probably refers to τὸ ἐσόμενον, "what is going to happen").

Adding deed to word, the Lukan Jesus—and he is the only one who does this—for the last time draws on his δύναμις, his "power" of divine origin (see 6:19; 8:46) and heals the ear simply by touching it.[41] For Luke, the miracle expresses Jesus' opposition to all armed resistance.[42]

The usual term for the ear is οὖς (v. 50). Grammatically both τὸ ὠτίον (Matt 26:51) and τὸ ὠτάριον (Mark 14:47) are diminutives (in time the diminutives, popular in common usage, lose their semantic diminutive value). Luke uses different Greek words for "ear," first οὖς (v. 50),[43] then ὠτίον (v. 51). Why does he change?

To avoid repetition? To give "this poor, small ear" an emotional connotation? To specify that what was struck or cut off was the "outer ear"? To follow the tendency in that day to use ὠτίον rather than ὠτός for the genitive?[44] I hold to this last hypothesis and refuse to see here a significant difference between the two terms.[45] That Luke and John speak of the "right" ear (v. 50; John 18:10) is one of the many examples of a relationship between the two Gospels in the passion narrative. I am thinking here less of a literary dependence than of the influence of a single oral tradition.[46] Let us remember that the right side was regarded as the more honorable. In addition, the four Gospels have retained the victim's social and professional status: he was "a slave" or "servant" (δοῦλος, which can be used in a flattering way) of the high priest.[47]

■ **52-53** In the popular literature, the kings themselves arrest the prisoners and execute them. In the literary texts, the kings have the guilty persons arrested and order them put to death. Here it is the popular Mark who respects the authorities and states that the troop comes

---

pen and let me be arrested" (Peter's violent act is rejected). Augustine accepts this latter solution. See Lagrange, 564–65.

38 In its revised edition of 1935 the [French] Louis Segond version of the Bible translates, *Laissez, arrêtez!* ("Leave off, stop!")

39 Such are by and large the options suggested by C. F. Evans, 819.

40 Rostovtzeff ("Οὖς") calls attention to a comparable incident that took place in 183 B.C.E. in Tebtunis in Egypt (Tebtunis papyri 3, 793, col. 11, frg. 1, verso 3). According to Rostovtzeff, only a good fencer can limit his blow to cutting off an ear. Thus, such a blow, which is more a matter of honor than it is life-threatening, has a symbolic value. That it was the right ear adds to the shame. See Arthur S. Hunt and J. Gilbart Smiley, eds., *The Tebtunis Papyri*, vol. 3, part 1 (London: Frowde, 1933) 240–41, 244.

41 On the verb ἅπτομαι ("to touch") used frequently in Luke in a context of healing (6:19; 7:14, 39; 8:45-47; 18:15), see vol. 1 of this commentary, 271–73, 294–95, and 337–40, on 7:13-15; 7:38; and 8:43-48.

42 According to Hall ("Swords"), Mark 14:47 suggests that if Jesus does not condemn the act of his disciple he falls under the *lex Julia majestatis*. That is intolerable for Luke, who is convinced that Jesus is innocent of any sedition.

43 The verbal form ἀφεῖλεν (second aorist active of

ἀφαιρέω, "to remove," "to take away," "to detach from") implies that the ear, more precisely the outer ear, was cut off by the blow of the sword.

44 See the two pages of Joüon, "Luc." This author doubts that Luke, who elsewhere expresses neither disgust nor sadness when confronted with the passion of Jesus, should suddenly give an emotional connotation to the ὠτίον of v. 51. He also points out that ὠτίον refers less to a "small ear" than to the "outer ear." See also BDF §111 (3). It may be that the popular language of the day was more likely to use ὠτίον for the genitive than ὠτός, which Joüon calls the anomalous form.

45 Codex Beza (D = 05) and the Old Latin witnesses tell about the healing (end of v. 51) in a somewhat different way: καὶ ἐκτείνας τὴν χεῖρα ἥψατο αὐτοῦ καὶ ἀπεκατεστάθη τὸ οὖς αὐτοῦ, "and after he stretched out the hand, he touched him, and his ear was restored." The form ἀπεκατεστάθη presents a double augment, on which see Smyth, *Greek Grammar* §451.

46 In 6:6 Luke had specified that the withered hand (Mark 3:1-6) was in fact the right hand.

47 On the idea of "servant" in Luke, see 12:41-46 and vol. 2 on 12:21-46.

"from the chief priests, the scribes, and the elders" (14:43), and it is the cultivated Luke who confronts Jesus directly with the chief priests, the officers of the temple, and the elders themselves.[48]

As we have seen, Luke brings together here what Mark has said in two different places (14:43 and 48-49): the list of the hostile authorities and Jesus' caustic remark. Among the authorities, he replaces the "scribes" with the "officers of the temple."[49] Indeed, he uses here a title, "officer" ($\sigma\tau\rho\alpha\tau\eta\gamma\acute{o}\varsigma$), which he had introduced in 22:4 and which he will use again in Acts ($\acute{o}$ $\sigma\tau\rho\alpha\tau\eta\gamma\grave{o}\varsigma$ $\tauο\hat{υ}$ $\acute{\iota}\epsilon\rhoο\hat{υ}$, "the officer of the temple," Acts 4:1).[50] If Mark is thinking of the tripartite division of the Sanhedrin, Luke is thinking more of the organization of the temple and, probably, of the city.[51] In v. 52 Luke is not announcing the arrival of a second group but specifying the identity of those who, according to v. 47, had already arrived: $\pi\alpha\rho\alpha\gamma\acute{\iota}\nuο\mu\alpha\iota$ does not mean "to come later"; it means simply "to be present," "to arrive."[52] That this verb is fol-

lowed here by the preposition "upon," "against" ($\acute{\epsilon}\pi\acute{\iota}$) indicates hostility (one usually speaks of coming $\pi\rho\acute{o}\varsigma$ ("to," "near") someone, e.g., 7:4; Acts 20:18).[53]

The Lukan Jesus, who expresses himself here in the same way the Markan Jesus does,[54] directs a reproach to those who came to arrest him. In fact, it is a double reproach. On the one hand, these people wrongly regard Jesus as a "brigand" ($\lambda\eta\sigma\tau\acute{\eta}\varsigma$), even though every day he had publicly demonstrated his innocuous character. On the other hand, they act in secret so that they do not have to confront the crowd that is ready to defend Jesus. The first objection deals with the use of violence ("with swords and clubs");[55] the second, with deceit (the coward benefits from the night; see the word "darkness" at the end of v. 53 and perhaps, by contrast, the reference to the "day"[56] at the beginning of the same verse).[57]

We need to define more precisely the meaning of the word $\lambda\eta\sigma\tau\acute{\eta}\varsigma$. A $\lambda\eta\sigma\tau\acute{\eta}\varsigma$ is not merely a simple "thief" ($\kappa\lambda\acute{\epsilon}\pi\tau\eta\varsigma$, 12:33, 39). He is a "brigand" who does not

---

48   John 18:3 and 12 mention, on the one hand, a cohort and, on the other, servants or attendants sent by the chief priests and the Pharisees. The fourth evangelist is undoubtedly thinking of a Roman cohort. He also increases the miraculous element, since both the soldiers and the civilians collapse in fear when Jesus, whose omniscience is explicitly mentioned, reveals his identity (John 18:4-8).

49   In Luke 9:22, on the other hand, the evangelist accepts the list of Mark 8:31, which comprises, although in a different order, the same three categories as that of Mark 14:43.

50   See the analysis and commentary above on 22:4-6.

51   See Francis Schmidt, *How the Temple Thinks: Identity and Social Cohesion in Ancient Judaism* (trans. J. Edward Crowley; Biblical Seminar 78; Sheffield: Sheffield Academic, 2001) 98–113; he gives a lively description of the activities of the people in charge of the temple.

52   This is the sense Luke gives to this verb, which he frequently uses. See, e.g., 7:4; Lagrange, 565.

53   It should be noted that many manuscripts read $\pi\rho\acute{o}\varsigma$ ("to") and not $\acute{\epsilon}\pi\acute{\iota}$ ("against"). See the apparatus of Nestle-Aland (27th ed.) on this verse; and Plummer, 513.

54   Only the obvious differences: Luke avoids the verb $\kappa\rho\alpha\tau\acute{\epsilon}\omega$, "to seize," "to arrest" (Mark 14:49) and substitutes for it the milder expression "to stretch out the hands" (v. 53). In the same sense, he omits

the words $\sigma\upsilon\lambda\lambda\alpha\beta\epsilon\hat{\iota}\nu$ $\mu\epsilon$ ("to seize me," Mark 14:48). In addition, he prefers to precede the main clause with a genitive absolute (v. 53), while Mark is satisfied with a parataxis (Mark 14:49). Luke also avoids following the verb "to be" with the preposition $\pi\rho\acute{o}\varsigma$ ("toward," "among," Mark 14:49) and correctly says "to be" $\mu\epsilon\tau\acute{\alpha}$ ("with," v. 53). Why does he fail to refer to Jesus' teaching activity ($\delta\iota\delta\acute{\alpha}\sigma\kappa\omega\nu$, "teaching," Mark 14:49)?

55   The word $\xi\acute{\upsilon}\lambdaο\nu$ means "wood" and indicates anything that is made of wood: "board," "rough-hewn wood," "beam," "post," "gallows," "cross," sometimes "stick." Lucian of Samosata (*Fug.* 14; *Bis Acc.* 24) uses the expression $\pi\alpha\tau\acute{\alpha}\sigma\sigma\omega$ $\tau\hat{\omega}$ $\xi\acute{\upsilon}\lambda\omega$ ("to beat with a stick"); Charles Alexandre, *Dictionnaire grec-français composé sur un nouveau plan* (Paris: Hachette, 1888) s.v.

56   The expression $\kappa\alpha\vartheta$ $\acute{\eta}\mu\acute{\epsilon}\rho\alpha\nu$ means "each day," "every day," "daily."

57   It is probably no accident that the temple is mentioned twice in vv. 52-53. Jewish identity and one's fidelity to God were proven in relation to the temple. On the temple in Luke-Acts, see Conzelmann, *Theology*, 75–78, 164–65; Klaus Balzer, "The Meaning of the Temple in the Lukan Writings," *HTR* 58 (1965) 263–77; Bachmann, *Tempel;* Casalegno, *Tempio.*

hesitate to resort to violence to achieve his ends. Moreover, in Luke's day, the term had taken on a particular significance. For the Roman occupiers and the Jewish authorities concerned about political stability, it designated those who disturbed the public order: both those they regarded as revolutionaries and those they saw as terrorists. Thus, the Jewish historian Josephus, who finally lines up with the Romans, the stronger side, refers to the Jewish patriots who tried to throw off the yoke of the occupier as "brigands," "robbers." It is possible, even probable, that the two thieves crucified at the same time as Jesus were not simple criminals. By calling them $\lambda\eta\sigma\tau\alpha\acute{\iota}$, Mark (15:27) and Matthew (27:38) most likely are thinking of revolutionaries, since crucifixion, a Roman punishment, was applied in particular to those who disturbed public order and threatened the security of the state.[58]

There is no doubt that Barabbas was a revolutionary, since the evangelist Mark says of him that he was a rebel, an agitator (15:7). It is not useless to mention the instability that reigned then in Palestine, the direct or indirect oppression from Rome, and the widespread wish among the Jews to restore the land to God.[59] From the perspective of *Realpolitik* one can understand why the Jerusalem authorities wanted to limit the damage by discreetly removing Jesus, whose activity, even if it was not violent and was free of political ambition, challenged the people and provoked upheavals. The evangelists, especially Luke, had a completely different conviction. They are present at what they regard as the triumph of evil: "but this is your hour" ($\dot\alpha\lambda\lambda'$ $\alpha\ddot\upsilon\tau\eta$ $\dot\epsilon\sigma\tau\grave\iota\nu$ $\dot\upsilon\mu\hat\omega\nu$ $\dot\eta$ $\ddot\omega\rho\alpha$). Not only must Jesus' defenders let things run their course ($\dot\epsilon\hat\alpha\tau\epsilon$, "let it happen," v. 51), not only Jesus, who miraculously healed the amputated ear and thus demonstrated his supernatural power, but God himself withdraws. He leaves the

field to the opponents: "But this is your hour."[60] And this hour will make it possible for the countervailing power to be active. The word $\dot\epsilon\xi o\upsilon\sigma\acute\iota\alpha$ has here more the sense of power than of authority. It is literally what is allowed ($\ddot\epsilon\xi\epsilon\sigma\tau\iota\nu$), thus what God lets happen.[61]

Biblical symbolism puts light on the side of God. Thus, the countervailing power displays itself at night. Luke puts the artisans of passion in the darkness ($\sigma\kappa\acute o\tau o\varsigma$). Even though the Fourth Gospel does not offer a parallel to v. 53b, the Johannine character of this sentence has often been noted. It is true that the idea of "hour" and the image of "darkness" are categories that are prominent in the Fourth Gospel, but various Synoptic parables as well as Pauline exhortations make use of the same symbolic world. Jesus and his disciples, the apostles and the believers belong to the light;[62] the world and the powers of evil are of the night. The decisive hour, the eschatological turning point, leaves its mark on all early Christians. For the present, the power of darkness is stronger than human powers. Luke believes that Satan, who had tempted Jesus (4:1-13), comes again, worms his way into Judas (22:3), strains the disciples through a sieve (22:31), and delivers Jesus to the powerful people of this world (v. 53). Paul and John also affirm this decisive participation of the devil in the death sentence of Jesus.[63] Luke thinks less of the evil that the Jews do than of that committed by those who hold political power.

History of Interpretation

In the second century, the text underwent two attacks. On the one side, Marcion, who ordinarily did not spare the disciples of Jesus, was disturbed by the blow with the sword. He simply removed vv. 49-51 from his Gospel.[64]

---

58 Luke calls them "criminals/evildoers," $\kappa\alpha\kappa o\hat\upsilon\rho\gamma o\iota$, in truth a vague term (23:32, 33, 39).

59 See Richard A. Horsley and John S. Hanson, *Bandits, Prophets, and Messiahs: Popular Movements at the Time of Jesus* (New Voices in Biblical Studies; Minneapolis: Winston, 1985).

60 The concept of "hour" is Johannine (see, e.g., John 2:4), yet Mark uses it in 14:41 in the Gethsemane story. It may be that Luke was influenced by this Markan verse, which he did not quote.

61 On $\dot\epsilon\xi o\upsilon\sigma\acute\iota\alpha$, see Bock, 2:1773, who refers to Luke 4:6; 23:7; Eph 6:12; Col 1:13.

62 See Matt 5:14 ("You are the light of the world"); Matt 25:1-13 (the virgins carry their lighted lamps in the night); Mark 13:33-35 (watching in the night); 1 Thess 5:4-8 (Christians are children of the light).

63 See 1 Cor 2:8 and John 14:30. Luke has Paul say that he was sent by God "to open their eyes so that they may turn from darkness to light ($\dot\alpha\pi\grave o$ $\sigma\kappa\acute o\tau o\upsilon\varsigma$ $\epsilon\grave\iota\varsigma$ $\varphi\hat\omega\varsigma$), from the power of Satan to God ($\kappa\alpha\grave\iota$ $\tau\hat\eta\varsigma$ $\dot\epsilon\xi o\upsilon\sigma\acute\iota\alpha\varsigma$ $\tau o\hat\upsilon$ $\Sigma\alpha\tau\alpha\nu\hat\alpha$ $\dot\epsilon\pi\grave\iota$ $\tau\grave o\nu$ $\vartheta\epsilon\acute o\nu$)" (Acts 26:18).

64 See Plummer, 513; Harnack, *Marcion*, 234*; Tsutsui, "Evangelium Marcions," 124.

On the other side, the pagan philosopher Celsus had no confidence in the Christians' Gospels. He was of the opinion that Jesus had fled in a shameful way and had hidden in order to avoid arrest (see Origen *Cels.* 2.10).[65]

At the beginning of the third century, Tertullian dealt at least twice with this episode in the life of Christ. In his *Contra Marcionem* he demonstrates that Jesus is not only the manifestation of the unknown God, the good God; he is also the portrait of the righteous God of the Old Testament. Indeed, the beginning of Jesus' passion reveals both his love of others and his punitive justice. One must take seriously the words spoken to Judas, "woe to that person by whom he is betrayed" (Luke 22:22), and one must realize the judgment Christ makes against Peter (Luke 22:33-34).[66] Tertullian ends his paragraph thinking of the kiss that the Son receives from Judas. Jesus was not the only one who was unloved; God the Father was also loved by his people only with their lips (an allusion to Isa 29:13) (*Adv. Marc.* 4.41.1–2). In *De Oratione* 18, the African speaks of the kiss of peace. He teaches us that the kiss of peace was not given on the day of Passover, that is to say, on Good Friday. By refusing this act on this day, Christians avoided confusing it with the kiss of Judas. In the same paragraph he speaks against those who omit the kiss of peace on other days of fasting as well.[67]

A few years later Origen would respond to Celsus and would defend the historical truth of the Gospels, saying that Jesus sought neither to hide, nor to flee, nor to avoid martyrdom (*Cels.* 2.10).

In the fourth century, Ambrose reflected on these verses for the spiritual benefit of his Milanese audience (*Exp. Luc.* 10.63–71). Like a juggler, he tosses in the air various Bible verses dealing with kisses (which one still finds in modern commentaries)[68] by contrasting, for example, the kiss of enemies (Prov 27:6) with the kiss of friends (Cant 1:2). The kiss of Judas was hypocritical, since under the cover of affection it caused bloodshed. Then he speaks of the healing of the wounded servant. If Jesus preferred to heal by deed rather than by word, it was to remind that he was the Creator. With various refrains Ambrose makes a point of avoiding christological misinterpretations and, without explicitly saying it, of contradicting Jews and Arians. The kiss of Judas, like the passion itself, touched only the human nature of Jesus Christ (which is why Jesus uses the title Son of Man in v. 48). Jesus cannot be criticized for accepting the kiss of Judas. He did it not from hypocrisy but because he refused to flee. Finally, Ambrose turns without charity to the adversaries of Christ. They understood so little of the patience and the compassion of Jesus that they arranged for the death of the righteous man. This attack from Ambrose feeds on an allegorical interpretation of the severed ear. The Jews lost the ear, while the church can listen to the Word of God. Finally, we note that Ambrose, like most Christian authors of antiquity, was not content to explain a single Gospel at a time. His exposition of the Gospel of Luke mentions, for example, the name of Peter, yet it is only the Gospel of John who thus names the disciple who drew his sword from the sheath (John 18:10-11).[69]

Ephraem the Syrian regarded the *Diatessaron* as the canonical Gospel on which to comment. What he retains of the episode of the arrest of Jesus from his harmony of the Gospels (*Comm. Diat.* 20.12–13) is this: the Romans[70] arrest Jesus with the help of Judas. The day will come (doubtless Ephraem is thinking of the fall of Jerusalem) when the Romans will avenge Jesus. Even if he expresses a patient affection toward Judas, Jesus still takes back from him—an interesting observation—the Holy Spirit he had conferred on him (speaking of Matt 13:12: "But he who does not have, even what he has will be taken

---

65 Plummer, 511.
66 Tertullian regards the denial (22:54-62) as the punishment Christ inflicts on Peter (22:34) for having made the arrogant statement "Lord, I am ready to go with you, even to prison and even to death" (22:33).
67 Plummer, 512.
68 For example, Bock 2:1768 n. 3, even if the ancient list and the modern list are not completely equal.
69 Since Peter had received from Christ the right

to bind and to loose (Matt 16:19), he was simply exerting this right when he cut off the servant's ear. According to Ambrose, this ear's hearing was really bad!
70 It is likely because of the cohort mentioned in John 18:3 and 12 that Ephraem grants the Romans such an important place in his commentary.

away"). Later Jesus responds to violence with a healing, and Ephraem gives an allegorical meaning to the restoration of the ear. It returns to its elevated position in the body. Still later, Christ will kindly raise up the crowd that had fallen abruptly at his feet (a notion the *Diatessaron* owes to John 18:6). Nevertheless, even this much grace is not enough. Ephraem is troubled by Jesus' adversaries, who did not know to seize the occasion and who responded to love with hatred. Finally, like others, Ephraem underscores Jesus' rejection of any armed resistance. He has this beautiful formula: that one whose word is a sword (he is probably thinking of Isa 49:2; Eph 6:17; Heb 4:12; Rev 1:16; 19:15) has no need of a sword.

In the fifth century, Cyril of Alexandria devoted his 148th homily on Luke to the arrest of Jesus.[71] One finds here many of the elements we raised in Ambrose. In those days there was a Christian interpretation of the Gospels that was common to many people. Among the points we have not yet seen are the following: On the connection between the arrest and the scene on the Mount of Olives, Cyril points out that in his own way Judas was not able to watch and pray as Jesus had commanded (22:40, 46). On the surprising ὁ λεγόμενος ("called") coupled with the name of Judas (v. 47), Cyril suggests that Judas is so guilty that Luke, deep in sadness, cannot pronounce this name without "wearing gloves." Judas represents the extremes: he had received all the honors of an apostle, but then he lost everything, including the hope of eternal life. The entire passion story depends on the will of Christ, who arranges it.

Satan is behind Judas, but even he could not have done anything had he not received the divine permission. The "hour" (v. 53) between Good Friday and Easter is short and imminent. The "darkness (v. 53) is a way of speaking about Satan (2 Cor 4:4 is quoted). For Jesus it was not enough to refuse armed resistance; he gave the believers of all times a model of nonviolent ethics.[72]

At the beginning of the eighth century, the Venerable Bede inherited centuries of Christian interpretation. Ambrose, Jerome, and Augustine are his reference points and his sources. This inheritance does not keep him from expressing his own opinion and from formulating his questions (*In Luc.* 6.974–1072). While he is not the first to establish a parallel between Peter, who draws his sword, and Phinehas, who stabs with his spear (Num 25:6-15),[73] and to defend Jesus for taking so long to answer (v. 51) the disciples' question (v. 49),[74] he does think Matthew is right in locating the chief priests in the court of Caiaphas rather than Luke, who places them behind Judas on the Mount of Olives. He justifies Luke, however, for a theological and literary reason. By saying that these authorities immediately followed Judas, he denies them any loophole and deprives them of any excuse for their action. Along with allegorical gyrations, relating, for example, to the right side (v. 50) and the left, he gives the healing of the ear a spiritual meaning: the novelty of the Spirit replaces the age of the letter.[75]

I will end this history here, in which I have emphasized the exegesis of the text more than the general history of its interpretation. I have before me the com-

71 See Payne Smith, *Cyril*, 2:693–97.
72 Like other church fathers, Cyril sprinkles his explanation of Luke with remarks that relate to the characteristics of Matthew and John.
73 See already Ambrose *Exp. Luc.* 10.66.
74 See already Augustine *De cons. evang.* 3.5.17 (*PL* 34:1167; see n. 37 above); Lagrange, 564–65. The Venerable Bede (*In Luc.* 6.1011–12) takes up the statement of Augustine: *Sed non putuerunt etiam simul dici, quae simul fieri potuerunt*, "but they [these events] could not be spoken at the same time they could happen."
75 The anonymous Irish *Comm. Luc.* 22.53 (CCSL 108C:97) is interested only in v. 53 and devotes no more than four lines to it, yet these lines are important. He says of the "hour" that "it is the hour of your freedom," which, if I read him correctly, precedes "my hour." Good Friday belongs to the sinful human beings and to the forces of evil, which are free to act. Easter will belong to God and his Christ. The anonymous author then speaks of the "darkness," which he sets at the moment the sun goes down. His proof is the eclipse of the sun at the time of the crucifixion. Euthymius Zigabenus (*Comm. Luc.* 22.53 [*PG* 129:1085]) also expresses his opinion about the "hour." It is the hour, he says, when you received from God the power to act against me; see Plummer, 513–14.

mentary of Bonaventure (*Comm. Luc.* 22.59–66),[76] the paraphrase of Erasmus (455–56),[77] the annotations of Grotius.[78] The limits I am imposing on this survey for practical reasons by no means imply disdain for the interpretations of the Middle Ages, the Renaissance, or the Reformation. With the commentary of Ulrich Luz one can fill in some of the gaps.[79]

Conclusion

Luke does not express the horror or the revolt that the tragic situation he describes provokes in him, nor does he emphasize Jesus' patience and benevolence. As Luke describes him, Jesus is not offended. At most he explains to Judas what he is doing (v. 48b). He would rather restore the physical integrity of the wounded servant than become exhausted with criticisms of his undisciplined disciples (v. 51). Then he brings to light what is made in obscurity, and he has no need of an extensive accusation directed against the chief priests and their assistants (vv. 52-53). Thus, the strength of the passage lies in the light it casts on remote areas. The text would be weaker if the fire of revenge were to respond to the penetrating violence. The evangelist can only note what happens. Jesus can only submit. God himself can only let it happen. It is truly the hour of others, the powers of darkness. But the hour will pass, and the darkness of the night will give way to the light of the day.

---

76 Bernardini, 558–61.

77 Erasmus calls attention to the space separating Judas from the group, which follows him and states that in time of war one gives signs of recognition such as the kiss here. See the translation of Phillips, *Paraphrase*, 200–202.

78 Grotius (*Annotationes*, 911) sees behind the question of v. 49 an uncertainty between what nature dictates (resistance) and what teaching inculcates (patience).

79 Luz, *Matthew 21–28*, 412–14.

Peter's Denial and the Mocking Scene (22:54-65)

Bibliography

Benoit, Pierre, "Les outrages à Jésus prophète (Mc xiv 65 par.)," in *Neotestamentica et Patristica: Eine Freundesgabe, Herrn Professor Dr. Oscar Cullmann zu seinem 60. Geburtstag überreicht* (NovTSup 6; Leiden: Brill, 1962) 92–110.

Birdsall, J. Neville, "τὸ ῥῆμα ὡς εἶπεν αὐτῷ ὁ Ιησούς· Mark xiv. 72," *NovT* 2 (1957) 272–75.

Boyd, W. J. Peter, "Peter's Denial—Mark xiv.68; Luke xxii.57," *ExpT* 67 (1955–56) 341.

Delorme, Jean, "Le procès de Jésus ou la parole risquée (Lc 22,54—23,25)," in *La Parole de grâce: Études lucaniennes à la mémoire d'Augustin George* (ed. J. Delorme and J. Duplacy; Paris: Recherches de science religieuse, 1981) 123–46; essays reprinted from *RSR* 69 (1981).

Dietrich, *Petrusbild*, 139–57.

Dinkler, *Petrusdarstellungen*.

Evans, Craig A., "'Peter Warming Himself': The Problem of an Editorial 'Seam,'" *JBL* 101 (1982) 245–49.

Flusser, David, "Who Is It That Struck You?" *Imm* 20 (1986) 27–32.

France, Richard T., "Jésus devant Caiphe," *Hokhma* 15 (1980) 20–35.

Klein, "Verleugnung."

Lampe, G. W. H., "St. Peter's Denial," *BJRL* 55 (1972–73) 346–68.

Lehmann, Martin, *Synoptische Quellenanalyse und die Frage nach dem historischen Jesus: Kriterien der Jesusforschung untersucht in Auseinandersetzung mit Emanuel Hirschs Frühgeschichte des Evangeliums* (BZNW 38; Berlin: de Gruyter, 1970) 106–12.

Linnemann, "Verleugnung."

Masson, Charles, "Le reniement de Pierre: Quelques aspects de la formation d'une tradition," *RHPhR* 37 (1957) 24–35; reprinted in idem, *Vers les sources d'eau vive: Études d'exégèse et de théologie du Nouveau Testament* (Lausanne: Payot, 1961) 87–101.

Mayo, C. H., "St. Peter's Token of the Cock Crow," *JTS* 22 (1921) 367–70.

McEleney, Neil J., "Peter's Denials—How Many? To Whom?" *CBQ* 52 (1990) 467–72.

Miller, David L., "ἐμπαίζειν: Playing the Mock Game (Luke 22:63-64)," *JBL* 90 (1971) 309–13.

Murray, G., "St. Peter's Denials," *DRev* 103 (1985) 296–98.

Nauerth, Claudia, "Hahn," *RAC* 13 (1986) 360–72.

Neirynck, Frans, "Τίς ἐστιν ὁ παίσας σε· Mt 26,68/Lk 22,64 (diff. Mk 14,65)," *EThL* 63 (1987) 5–47.

Pesch, Rudolf, "Die Verleugnung des Petrus: Eine Studie zu Mk 14,54.66-72 (und Mk 14,26-31)," in Joachim Gnilka, ed., *Neues Testament und Kirche: Für Rudolf Schnackenburg* (Freiburg i.B.: Herder, 1974) 942–62.

Rudberg, Gunnar, "Die Verhöhnung Jesu vor dem Hohenpriester," *ZNW* 24 (1925) 307–9.

Schneider, Gerhard, *Verleugnung, Verspottung und Verhör Jesu nach Lukas 22, 54-71: Studien zur lukanischen Darstellung der Passion* (StANT 22; Munich: Kösel, 1969) 73–104, 105–34, 211–20.

Soards, Marion L., "'And the Lord Turned and Looked Straight at Peter': Understanding Luke 22:61," *Bib* 67 (1986) 518–19.

Idem, "A Literary Analysis of the Origin and Purpose of Luke's Account of the Mockery of Jesus," *BZ* 31 (1987) 110–16.

Unnik, W. C. van, "Jesu Verhöhnung vor dem Synedrium (Mk 14.65 par.)," *ZNW* 29 (1930) 310–11; reprinted in idem, *Sparsa Collecta: The Collected Essays of W. C. van Unnik* (3 vols.; NovTSup 29–31; Leiden: Brill, 1973–83) 1:3–5.

Vanhoye, Albert, "L'intérêt de Luc pour la prophétie en Lc 1,76; 4,16-30 et 22,60-65," in F. van Segbroeck et al., eds., *The Four Gospels 1992: Festschrift Frans Neirynck* (3 vols.; BEThL 100; Leuven: Leuven University Press, 1992) 2:1529–48.

54 After they had arrested him they led him away and brought him into the house[a] of the high priest. Peter followed at a distance. 55/ Lighting a fire in the middle of the courtyard, they sat down together. Peter sat in their midst. 56/ Then a maid, seeing him as he sat near the light and gazing at him, said, "This man was also with him."[b] 57/ But he denied it with these words: "Woman, I do not know him." 58/ A little later another saw him and said, "You are also one of them." But Peter said, "Man, I am not." 59/ Then about an hour later someone else insisted, "In truth, this one was also with him, for indeed he is a Galilean."

a Another translation: "the palace."

b Another translation: "And wasn't this one a member of his party?"

60/ But Peter said, "Man, I do not know what you are saying." And in the very instant while he was still speaking, the cock crowed. **61/** When the Lord turned, he looked at Peter, and Peter remembered the word of the Lord when he had said to him that today, before the cock crows, you will have denied me three times. **62/** And he went outside and wept bitterly.[c]

63   The men who were holding Jesus captive mocked him and beat him. **64/** And when they had covered him with a veil, they questioned him: "Prophesy," they said, "which one of us has hit you?"[d] **65/** And they spoke many other insults against him.

c   It is not certain that this verse was originally part of the Gospel of Luke; see below, the diachronic analysis and the commentary on v. 62.

d   The aorist participle παίσας comes from the verb παίω ("to strike") and not, as I believed initially, from the verb παίζω ("to play").

The exegetes regard "and he" (καὶ αὐτός), which appears elsewhere (e.g., 6:20), as an expression of a high Christology.[1] I would suggest, on the other hand, that the accusative "him" (αὐτόν) sometimes functions in Luke as a sign of submission, of humiliation, of a low Christology. Three successive episodes use this pronoun with the accusative to express how Jesus became the plaything of his opponents: in v. 54 men seize "him"; in v. 63 they hold "him" captive; in 23:1 they lead "him" to Pilate. From the subject of his life Jesus has become its object.[2] Nevertheless, as it was at the arrest (22:47-53), this object (αὐτόν) at a certain level remains a subject, the master of knowledge and foreknowledge (v. 61).

By contrast, Peter appears in the same hour as the one who does not know, who does not want to know (vv. 57, 60). The traditional title, "the denial of Peter," is time-honored, and I have kept it. One can add that this denial makes it possible to speak of three temptations of Peter (in antithetic symmetry with the three temptations of Jesus, 4:1-13).[3] Finally, one must say that this negative side also has a positive side. The crowing of the cock confirms the prophecy (v. 60); Jesus' look provokes a memory (v. 61); and Peter's awakened awareness opens the chapter of conversion, of faith, and of mission (vv. 61-62).

Synchronic Analysis

Luke imposes a clear linearity on the sequence of the events. In the night, Jesus is arrested as arranged by Judas (22:47-53), after which he is led to the palace of the high priest (22:54a).[4] While he is waiting for his case to be judged the next morning, he is denied by his disciple Peter (22:54b-62), and he is ridiculed by his guards (22:63-65). In the morning he is taken to the court of the Jewish authorities to be questioned (22:66-71). He will then be turned over to the Roman governor (23:1).

The simplicity of this sequence does not reflect the historical events; it is the result of a literary construction. Mark, who is entitled to the same trust and who deserves the same suspicion, offers a different order of events. Furthermore, the logic of a trial needs no superfluous events such as Peter's denial. By turning his attention to the principal disciple (vv. 54b-56), the evangelist diverts it from the Master. While it is right to say that the passion narrative, unlike the controversy or miracle stories, constitutes a connected account,[5] it is good to add that the various episodes, which are not essential to its development, serve as welcome digressions and call attention to characters other than Jesus (Judas, Peter, Herod, etc.).[6]

---

1   See vol. 2 of this commentary, on 17:11.
2   See Bovon, "Lukan Story of the Passion," 76–77.
3   See Fitzmyer (2:1460), who suggests that the maid and the two men play the role of Satan, the tempter.
4   Senior (*Passion*, 94) notes the strong connection Luke makes between Peter's denial and the preceding material (the prayer not to succumb to temptation [v. 46] and the "sifting" of the disciples [v. 31]).
5   See Dibelius, *Tradition*, 178–80.
6   See Bovon, "Lukan Story of the Passion," 74–75.

In its first sentence v. 54 mentions, finally, Jesus' arrest and—as an essential complement—the first place he was confined. In its second sentence it introduces Peter and describes what he does.

Verses 55-62 are divided into three courses, according to a well-known narrative rule.[7] The maidservant interrupts Peter's rest. She does not speak directly to him, but she does speak loudly enough that he can hear (vv. 55-57). Then a little later another character challenges him directly (v. 58), and, finally, an hour later still another person (vv. 59-60a). These three attacks, which take place over the course of several hours, put in motion the threefold denial, which "at the very moment" (παραχρῆμα) arouse the crowing of the cock. Jesus looks at Peter, and the disciple remembers (vv. 60b-62). Peter then leaves, weeping tears of repentance. He will not reappear until Easter, when he runs to the tomb (24:12).

The anonymous power, called in v. 53 the power of darkness, reappears like a monster of the deep. "They" have arrested Jesus (v. 54); "they" will make sport of him until the early morning hours (vv. 63-65).

Diachronic Analysis

Scholars have proposed various hypotheses to explain the origin of these verses. Since Luke's narrative sequence differs from that of Mark, and since the Lukan redaction of the betrayal includes a number of unique characteristics, for some scholars it is probable that Luke is using here a pericope of his special material into which he inserts Markan details.[8] The many elements that Luke shares with the second evangelist encourage others to retain only one source, Mark, and to attribute to Luke and his literary talent those things that differ from Mark's narration.[9] It is a difficult decision. Vincent Taylor,[10] who elsewhere defends the hypothesis of a second source, is content here with a Markan origin.[11] I. Howard Marshall, who argues in his commentary for Markan influence, tends here toward a dependence on the special source.[12] The hypotheses can be multiplied and refined. Some suggest that Luke depends on Mark and on oral tradition.[13] I have no difficulty joining this solution, while recalling my general hypothesis that the sources alternate.[14] Luke follows Mark from the arrest to the appearance before Pilate (Luke 22:47—23:5), which is not to say that he is insensitive to the oral tradition, that he rejects any detail he reads in his own source, or that he does not exercise a right to his personal opinion. (Indeed, he does not agree that there was a night meeting of the Sanhedrin.)

Luke shares the following elements with Mark: the presence of Peter, who, once in the court, warms himself by the fire; the three comments, which lead to the threefold denial; the observation a maidservant makes at the beginning; the first denial, whose versions in Luke and Mark are identical word for word; the contents of the second remark (see the ἐξ αὐτῶν, "of them," "of their number," and the verb "to be"); certain details of the third (ἐπ' ἀληθείας, "in truth," Luke; ἀληθῶς, "truly," Mark; the word "Galilean"); the wording of the third denial, the essence of which in Luke is influenced by Mark's second denial (Peter claims that he does not understand); the immediate crowing of the cock after the third reply. These elements appear to me to justify speaking of Luke's literary dependence on Mark.[15]

7   See C. F. Evans, 823.

8   For example, Walter Grundmann, *Das Evangelium nach Lukas* (2d ed.; ThHKNT 3; Berlin: Evangelische Verlagsanstalt, 1961) 415–16; David R. Catchpole, *The Trial of Jesus: A Study in the Gospels and Jewish Historiography from 1770 to the Present Day* (SPB 18; Leiden: Brill, 1971) 160–74.

9   For example, Fitzmyer (2:1456–57), who nevertheless thinks that the special source influenced the mocking scene (vv. 63–65).

10   Taylor, *Third Gospel*, 48–49.

11   Fitzmyer (2:1456–57) draws up a list of people who defend the Markan origin and a list of the advocates of a parallel source.

12   Marshall, 839–40. Consistent with his hypothesis, Schlatter (436–37) is of the opinion that Luke here follows his special source, which offers a good succession of the facts without any major changes.

13   See vol. 1 of this commentary, 6–8.

14   The special material also offers an account of the denial. I have attributed the prediction of the denial to the special material (22:33-34); see above, the diachronic analysis of 22:21-38.

15   Bock (2:1775–76) lists the differences among the Synoptic Gospels related to the sequence of the episodes, notes with Josef Ernst (*Das Evangelium nach Lukas: Übersetzt und erklärt* [RNT 3; Regensburg: Pustet, 1977] 612–17) that in the denial only 69 of

In addition, several features of the Third Gospel are explained by an editorial logic and a concern to speak well. Luke, who never simply copies automatically, makes a point of writing with elegance and precision, something our exegesis will clearly show. I give here only one or two examples. Luke does not like the πρὸς τὸ φῶς of Mark 14:54 to say "near the fire" (here he uses the word πῦρ, "fire") in v. 55 and reserves Mark's expression for later in v. 56, where he gives it its actual meaning, "near the light"). Since Luke likes to refer to women and men side by side,[16] he keeps the "maidservant" only the first time (v. 56; see the vocative γύναι, "woman," in v. 57) and the second time substitutes a man in her place (vocative ἄνθρωπε, "human being," "man," v. 58). Thinking it will be a long time until the Sanhedrin convenes, since it can meet only by day (22:66), Luke mentions the "hour" between the second and the third denial (v. 59). As time passes, the opinion of the people grouped around the fire becomes stronger, and the verb διϊσχυρίζομαι ("to affirm," "to insist," v. 59) is a good choice. Luke is of the opinion that only one crowing of the cock is enough (v. 60); he does not understand why Mark speaks of a double crowing (14:30, 72). It may be that as an urban man he does not know that the cry of the first cock arouses the other gallinaceous birds. Finally, as one who can handle pathos,[17] Luke adds to the crowing of the cock the look of the Lord, which awakens Peter's memory and repentance (v. 61a).

Luke prefers to present the episode of the denial in one piece (vv. 54-62), while Mark introduces it (14:54), then interrupts it with a trial before the Sanhedrin by night followed by mocking (14:55-56), then finally takes it up again (14:66-72). This choice makes it possible for Luke easily to simplify Mark, who has the Sanhedrin meet twice (Mark 14:55-64; 15:1), and to locate the court session in the morning, as is appropriate (Luke 22:66-71).

It appears that the third evangelist completely reformulated the mocking scene, vv. 63-65, which he knows from Mark 14:65.[18] He removes the humiliating spitting, avoids the verb κολαφίζω ("to slap," regarded as vulgar or foreign?), and finally substitutes a general formula adapted for a summary with the imperfect ("And they spoke many other insults against him") for the specific statement of Mark 14:65.

For this pericope, as for several others of the passion cycle, synoptic work must deal with four voices. Along with the others, the Gospel of John is in circulation (John 18:15-27). The fourth evangelist is familiar with the scene of the threefold denial, which, like Mark, he interrupts to insert a legal hearing, here a dialogue with the high priest. In addition, he includes many details not known by Luke, Mark, and Matthew.[19] Unlike the authors of the other passion accounts, John and Luke do not appear to have shared here information not found in Mark and Matthew.[20] What about the connections between Luke and Matthew? In general, Matthew has a greater respect for Mark's order and wording, and he accepts Mark's so-called sandwiching or intercalation, that is, the insertion of two episodes (the appearance

---

the 263 words correspond to those of Mark, and along with John Martin Creed (*The Gospel according to St. Luke: The Greek Text with Introduction, Notes, and Indices* [London: Macmillan, 1930] 275–76) offers the major differences among the Synoptics.

16 See 2:25 and 36; 13:19 and 20; 15:4 and 8; C. F. Evans, 825; vol. 2 of this commentary, on 15:8-10.

17 See C. F. Evans, 827. I differ with those who think that Luke makes a point of resisting the expression of feelings. Neyrey ("Absence") is one of them.

18 Schneider (2:464) and Fitzmyer (2:1458) are of the opinion that Luke depends here on his special source and not on Mark.

19 John draws a distinction between two characters he names, Annas and Caiaphas. He indicates that Caiaphas was the high priest that year. He recalls the prophecy of Caiaphas (it is expedient that one man should die for the people; John 11:49). Along with

Peter he mentions a companion, "another disciple," who was known to the high priest. He explains the fire by saying that it was cold, and he emphasizes that Peter needed to be warm. Matthew also knows the name Caiaphas (Matt 26:3, 57).

20 At most, one can say that Luke is not unaware of the names of the high priests Annas and Caiaphas, but he mentions them not here but at the beginning of the Gospel (3:2) and in Acts (Acts 4:6). In Luke 3:2 the two men appear to share the high priesthood (note the singular ἐπὶ ἀρχιερέως, "under the high priest"). In Acts 4:6 it is Annas and not Caiaphas who appears to hold this office. See Plummer (515), who thinks that Annas and Caiaphas shared the same residence. According to Lagrange (568), Luke was thinking of Annas when he wrote the word high priest (v. 54).

before the Sanhedrin followed by the mocking scene, Matt 26:59-68) into another (Peter's denial, Matt 26:58, 69-75); he also takes over the expression ἀπὸ μακρόθεν to say "from afar" (Matt 26:58), the precision at "the court of the high priest" (Matt 26:58), and the reference to the curses and oaths (Matt 26:74).[21]

It is necessary, however, to point out a certain number of *minor agreements* that Matthew and Luke have against Mark. Some are explained by a common concern to clarify or simplify: Both evangelists are happy to end the threefold denial with a single crowing of the cock (vv. 60-61 and Matt 26:74-75, already earlier v. 34 and Matt 26:34); both prefer the imperfect "followed" to the aorist "had followed" when describing Peter's behavior (v. 54 and Matt 26:58); both substitute ἐκάθητο ("he sat," v. 55 and Matt 26:58) for the periphrastic form ἦν συγκαθή-μενος ("he was sitting," Mark 14:54). Correctly, both follow the verb of remembering with the genitive (v. 61 and Matt 26:75). The two following agreements are more curious: Matthew and Luke both end the denial scene with words not found in Mark: "And he went outside and wept bitterly" (v. 62 and Matt 26:75). The two evangelists also have the exact same wording of the torturers' questions: "Prophesy, which one of us has hit you?" (v. 64 and Matt 26:68); Mark 14:65 is satisfied with the imperative "Prophesy!" The first—if one dares to say—major *minor agreement* might be explained in the following way. Verse 62 is attested neither by all the witnesses nor by all the versions. It seems to be absent in the very old fragment of uncial 0171 (ca. 300)[22] as well as in many Old Latin manuscripts.[23] It could be that the Lukan text was contaminated by this well-known statement from Matthew.[24] To be precise, the expression of Mark 14:72, "and rushing out he wept" (καὶ ἐπιβαλὼν ἔκλαιεν) is not easy to understand. It may be that a more understandable, parallel expression was necessary in the oral tradition that Matthew and Luke, independently of each other, decided to follow. As for the second case, it is still mysterious, but it is not enough to establish that Luke was based on Matthew.[25]

Along with the Synoptic Problem of the relationships among the Gospels, the commentaries raise the question of the historicity of the episodes related.[26] While the question is legitimate at a certain level, it should not influence the literary analysis. For many, from Frédéric Godet to Darrell L. Bock, there is a strong desire to harmonize the Gospels, and it is accompanied by a desire to save the historicity of every episode and every detail.[27] One thus arrives at two preliminary interrogations of Jesus during the night followed by a trial the next morning before the Sanhedrin.[28] Peter's denial took place after the first hearing (Matthew and Mark) but before the second (Luke). One also states that the cock crowed once (Matthew and Luke), but that this cock immediately awakened his neighbor, who also started to crow (Mark).[29] Let's be serious. This is no way to solve the historical question. As they are, the Gospels are irreconcilable, and we will never know the precise course of Jesus'

---

21 The agreements between Mark and Matthew are much more numerous than the simple examples I give; see Luz, *Matthew 21–28*, 453–54.

22 Fragment 0171 is difficult to read. One cannot be absolutely certain that v. 62 is missing.

23 See Adolf Jülicher, *Itala: Das Neue Testament in alt-lateinischer Überlieferung nach den Handschriften*, vol. 3: *Lucas-Evangelium* (Berlin: de Gruyter, 1954) 254; Plummer, 517; C. F. Evans, 828; and Bock, 2:1804–5. In the Westcott and Hort edition (*New Testament*, vol. 1: *Text*, 178) the verse is placed in double brackets. See Metzger, *Commentary* (2d ed.), 151; *NTG* 2:198.

24 This is the opinion, for example, of Grundmann (417), Ernst (615, with caution), and Catchpole, *Trial*. Others, such as Fitzmyer (2:1465), Bock (2:1804–5), and Luz (*Matthew 21–28*, 454) think differently, claiming that the manuscript evidence, especially from Greek witnesses, is too weak.

25 Contra Goulder, *New Paradigm*, 2:750.

26 See, e.g., Marshall, 840; Fitzmyer, 2:1453–56; Bock, 2:1775–77.

27 Frédéric Godet, *A Commentary on the Gospel of St. Luke* (trans. E. W. Shalders; 4th ed.; 2 vols.; Edinburgh: Clark, 1890) 2:311–19; and Bock (2:1775–77), who concludes: "A probable sequence can be established, and historicity need not be doubted" (1777).

28 Thus Godet, 2:311–16; Plummer, 514–15; Bock, 2:1779–80.

29 If one begins, the others will follow. Leo Tolstoi knew that. He writes in *War and Peace* (trans. Richard Pevear and Larissa Volokhonsky; New York: Knopf, 2007) 917: "A cock crowed far away, others responded nearby."

last hours. The essential things are certain: Jesus' arrest; his appearance before a Jewish authority; then the trial in the court of Pilate, the Roman governor, which ends with a death sentence and an execution.[30] These events are confirmed by other sources: Acts, the epistles, and even by some Jewish and Roman documents.[31]

Is Peter's denial historical?[32] As one sees in Luke, the early Christians tended to admire the apostles. Thus, it is difficult to imagine that they invented or disseminated the story of such an apostasy.[33] Even if we cannot know all the details, it appears to be certain that Peter was one of the last to flee (note the contrast between the verb "to flee," Mark 14:50 par. Matt 26:56 and the verb "to follow," Mark 14:54 par. Matt 26:58 par. Luke 22:54) and that he did not do it without having abandoned his Master. There appear to be three reasons why the early Christians were not able to deny the memory of this event (they were quite capable of forgetting an event when it was to their advantage to forget).[34] The first is apologetic:

When an event is so well known (let us not forget that the four Gospels know it), it is better to explain it than to keep silent about it or deny it.[35] Therefore, they decided to affirm that Christ had predicted the event (Mark 14:29-31 par. Matt 26:33-35 par. Luke 22:33-34). The second explanation refers to the structure of the Christian life, which consists of sins, followed by repentance, conversion, faith, and a new existence (see Acts 2:37-38; Rom 6:1-11).[36] The life of Peter in general and the threefold denial in particular offered an excellent illustration of this structure, which furthermore corresponded to Jesus' fate: on Good Friday a plaything of human malice and at Easter a recipient of divine mercy (see the contrast schematic, which Luke places in the midst of Peter's apostolic preaching in Acts, e.g., 2:22-24; 3:13-15; 4:10; 10:39-40).[37] The third explanation carries more of a risk, and I base it on an observation made in connection with the *Acts of Peter*.[38] It has been suggested that certain episodes of this work originated in the quarrels in the patristic period

---

30   The literature on the trial of Jesus and its historical problems is immense. See especially Josef Blinzler, *Der Prozess Jesu: Das jüdische und das römische Gerichtsverfahren gegen Jesus Christus auf Grund der ältesten Zeugnisse dargestellt und beurteilt* (3d expanded ed.; Regensburg: Pustet, 1960) (the English translation of 1959 is based on an older German edition); Brown, *Death of the Messiah;* Bovon, *Last Days.*

31   For a short critical and chronological presentation of these sources, see Bovon, *Last Days,* 3–24.

32   A presentation of the arguments for and against is in Marshall, 840. See the studies of Lampe, "Denial"; Klein, "Verleugnung"; Linnemann, "Verleugnung"; Pesch, "Verleugnung."

33   It is important to Klein ("Verleugnung") to remember this, although he admits the anti-Petrine tendencies of certain streams of primitive Christianity.

34   See Bovon, *Studies,* 11–13.

35   Lagrange (569) maintains that the evangelists wanted to spare the leading apostle and at the same time to respect the historical truth. Wiefel (382–83) notices the interest the early Christians had in this episode. In a subtle, not to say specious, commentary, Ambrose of Milan (*Exp. Luc.* 10.74–92) tends to minimize Peter's fault by saying that the apostle did not deny the Son of God; he only acknowledged that he did not know the man Jesus. It is essential to show that if Peter sinned, he did so against the Son of Man and not against the Holy Spirit (Luke

12:10). Thus, he is able to receive forgiveness. Cyril of Alexandria (*Serm. Luc.* 149) rejects this kind of interpretation and rightly observes that it is prejudicial against the reality of the incarnation; see Payne Smith, *Cyril,* 2:698–99. Celestino Corsato (*La Expositio Euangelii secundum Lucam di sant' Ambrogio: ermeneutica, simbologia, fonti* [Studia ephemeridis Augustinianum 43; Rome: Institutum Patristicum Augustinianum, 1993] 177–278) has demonstrated that Ambrose and Cyril were inspired more by the commentary on Luke authored by Origen than by the latter's homilies, which are only partly preserved.

36   Schneider (2:466) thinks that the expression "the word of the Lord" (v. 61) establishes this bridge between the historical episode and the situation of the church. Ambrose of Milan (*Exp. Luc.* 10.90–91) emphasizes the exemplary character of the life of the apostle Peter, especially his tears, which the Christians are to imitate.

37   See Jürgen Roloff, *Neues Testament* (Neukirchener Arbeitsbücher; Neukirchen-Vluyn: Neukirchener Verlag, 1977) 185–86.

38   See Gérard Poupon, "Les Actes de Pierre et leur remaniement," in *Aufstieg und Niedergang der römischen Welt* 2.25.6 (Berlin: de Gruyter, 1988) 4363–83.

(between rigorists and persons who were more lax) over repentance and forgiveness. I pose the hypothesis that, vis-à-vis the rigorists of the first century of the Common Era as they appear in the Epistle to the Hebrews (6:1-8), the defenders of the Synoptic tradition, by preserving and transmitting the episode of Peter's denial, wanted to say that forgiveness is always possible for the one who repents. Is not the apostle Peter the best example?[39] On the other hand, there are some who emphasize the personal responsibility of the sinner who is called to repentance (see Acts 2:5, 16, 21-22; 3:3, 19); others suggest that the process of $\mu\epsilon\tau\acute{a}\nu\omega\iota\alpha$, of "conversion," of "repentance," was impossible without divine assistance. Even if he underscores the human part,[40] Luke belongs to this last group. According to his formulation, God offers $\mu\epsilon\tau\acute{a}\nu\omega\iota\alpha$ (Acts 11:18) as an opportunity that the human will must grasp. This theological motif is editorially inserted here in narrative form. Before Peter's tears there is the Lord's look at him (vv. 61-62).[41]

Commentary

■ **54** The verb $\sigma\upsilon\lambda\lambda\alpha\mu\beta\acute{a}\nu\omega$ is a good choice, because, as on this occasion, it can take on the precise and legal sense "to arrest" a suspect or a criminal. Luke uses it with this meaning in Acts (in the active, 1:16; 12:3; in the passive, 23:27).[42] Readers also note Luke's respect for Jesus:

the evangelist mentions the arrest only in passing, by means of a participle.

The juxtaposition of the two principal verbs ($\mathring{\eta}\gamma\alpha\gamma\sigma\nu$ $\kappa\alpha\grave{\iota}$ $\epsilon\mathring{\iota}\sigma\acute{\eta}\gamma\alpha\gamma\sigma\nu$) appears to be an unfortunate repetition. Yet it may be that both are necessary, the first having the legal sense "to lead," the second the topographic meaning "to bring" to a place.[43]

The word $\sigma\mathring{\iota}\kappa\acute{\iota}\alpha$ ("house") can mean more than a simple house. It can mean a large residence, a palace. Flavius Josephus leads one to believe that the palace of the high priest was located on the western hill of the city of Jerusalem (the temple being, of course, on the eastern hill) (*Bell.* 2.17.6 §426).[44]

That Peter "follows" is positive,[45] but that he does it "from afar," "at a distance" ($\mu\alpha\kappa\rho\acute{o}\vartheta\epsilon\nu$)[46] awakens suspicion. If he keeps his distance, does that not mean that he is already afraid? Thus, this adverb is used as a marker.

■ **55** This verse sets the stage. It mentions first the fire, then those around it. The two verbs used confirm Luke's predilection for compound verbs. Nevertheless, the first one is rare, and Luke uses it awkwardly. In time the original sense of the verb $\acute{a}\pi\tau\omega$ ("to tie," "to attach," "to suspend") expanded to mean "to light" a fire, a lamp (since one prepared the fire by "weaving together" brush and pieces of wood?). Luke gives almost the same meaning to the compound $\pi\epsilon\rho\iota\acute{a}\pi\tau\omega$ ("to light around" "to light"; the meaning of the prefix $\pi\epsilon\rho\iota$- appears to be

---

39 This is undoubtedly the same intention the fourth-century Christians had who commissioned the sarcophagi representing Peter accompanied by the cock. See Dinkler, *Petrusdarstellungen*, 75–79 and passim; Nauerth, "Hahn," 369.

40 See Bovon, *L'œuvre*, 170–71.

41 On this look, see C. F. Evans, 827.

42 Luke also uses it in the middle voice in Acts 26:21 with the same meaning as the active. Even if Mark and Matthew use $\kappa\rho\alpha\tau\acute{\epsilon}\omega$ ("to seize") to describe Jesus' arrest (e.g., Mark 14:46 par. Matt 26:50), they still put $\sigma\upsilon\lambda\lambda\alpha\mu\beta\acute{a}\nu\omega$ on Jesus' lips to speak about what is happening to him (Mark 14:48 par. Matt 26:55). John 18:12 also uses this verb. See Zorell, *Lexicon*, s.v.; C. F. Evans, 822.

43 See C. F. Evans, 822. Lagrange (568) has suggested another distinction: The simple verb means that one brings Jesus into the city (let us not forget that for Luke the arrest takes place on the Mount of Olives), while the compound verb means that one leads him into the residence of the high priest.

There is a final interpretation, that of Plummer, 515: The first verb emphasizes that Jesus is moved away from a place; the second, that he is brought to another place. In any event, the verb $\epsilon\mathring{\iota}\sigma\acute{a}\gamma\omega$ ("to bring into") is a word Luke likes; see Jeremias, *Sprache*, 296.

44 Wiefel, 383. The word $\sigma\mathring{\iota}\kappa\acute{\iota}\alpha$, followed by a genitive, is often used to designate one's property or residence; see Acts 10:32 or 18:7.

45 Ambrose of Milan (*Exp. Luc.* 10.72) is of the opinion that this following was a sign of devotion and piety. The denial will serve to prove that Peter shares the lot common to humanity. His repentance will show his faith.

46 C. F. Evans (824) says that Luke gives $\mu\alpha\kappa\rho\acute{o}\vartheta\epsilon\nu$ the meaning "at a distance" and $\acute{a}\pi\grave{o}$ $\mu\alpha\kappa\rho\acute{o}\vartheta\epsilon\nu$, which he reads in Mark, the meaning "from a distance." I think rather that $\acute{a}\pi\grave{o}$ $\mu\alpha\kappa\rho\acute{o}\vartheta\epsilon\nu$ was originally pleonastic. Over time, the people who used this expression forgot the significance of the suffix -$\vartheta\epsilon\nu$, which indicates the origin.

weakened), even if this sense is scarcely attested for the compound, which normally means "to attach around," "to attach," "to suspend," then "to get for somebody."[47] The fire is built in the middle of the court, and the people sit around it (sometimes the verb συγκαθίζω is transitive, as in Eph 2:6; sometimes, as here, it is intransitive with the meaning "to sit together."

Luke focuses the attention: in the middle of the palace there is a "court" (αὐλή),[48] and in the middle of the court a fire. People are sitting around the fire, and Peter is in the middle of the people.[49] The two participial verbs περιαψάντων and συγκαθισάντων function as genitive absolutes, but Luke does not follow the classical rule. He does not connect them with an explicit subject, and, above all, he does not leave them in their independence, since he connects them to the genitive αὐτῶν of the expression "in their midst." Luke—let us not forget it—writes in the Roman period, and many of his contemporaries take the same liberties with the ancient grammatical norms as he does. Instead of holding him strictly to the rules, let us rather admire the description of the place and the situation he has composed with Mark's materials (Mark 14:54, 66).

■ **56** It is not insignificant that it is a[50] "maidservant" who is interested in Peter.[51] While Jesus does not fal-

ter before the high priest, the highest authority, Peter becomes irresolute when confronted by a being who in that day represents weakness and submission, a woman and a maidservant. The look of the "Lord" (κύριος) will be a response to the look of this "maidservant" (παιδίσκη).[52] Peter, who should be independent, lets himself be influenced by others. The glance of the maidservant is described by two verbs: the first, "seeing" (ἰδοῦσα), comes from Mark 14:67; the second, "gazing at" (ἀτενίσασα), is characteristic of Luke.[53]

Mark says twice that Peter was warming himself by the fire (14:54, 67). Each time Luke avoids this reference that is prejudicial to the main disciple of Jesus, who is suffering at the same time, and Luke replaces it with the neutral verb, "to sit" (κάθημαι, vv. 55, 56).[54]

While Mark uses μετά followed by the genitive to say "with," Luke prefers here σύν with the dative. When used with the verb "to be," this expression can have the nuance of "to be of the party of."[55] "This one" (οὗτος) referring to Peter, has a pejorative connotation. Unlike in Mark, in Luke the grievance is expressed in the third person singular.[56]

■ **57** The verb ἀρνοῦμαι is strong.[57] It means "to deny," "to repudiate," "to refuse," "to disavow." Luke 12:9 ("But whoever denies me before men") showed that Israel's

---

47 On περιάπτω, see Moulton-Milligan, *Vocabulary*, s.v. As if they were avoiding the problem, most Greek manuscripts read ἀψάντων and attach an αὐτῶν to συγκαθισάντων, thus making the text give the normal reading "to light" and presenting a correct genitive absolute. See here the apparatus in Nestle-Aland (27th ed.). This has the air of a stylistic improvement.

48 On αὐλή, see vol. 2 of this commentary, on 11:21.

49 Without fearing a repetition of the preceding verse (v. 54), Luke adds the name of Peter to make explicit the subject of the verb "sat." Mark, justifiably, did not think that was necessary (14:54b).

50 The indefinite τις accompanying a name is characteristic of Luke's style; see 1:5; Jeremias, *Sprache*, 296.

51 Luke already used the word παιδίσκη once in the plural in 12:45. See BAGD, s.v. On Hagar as a παιδίσκη, see Franz Mussner, *Der Galaterbrief: Auslegung* (HThK 9; Freiburg i. B.: Herder, 1988) 316–34.

52 Luke will not fail to notice that the second person

to challenge Peter will not do so without having looked at him (ἰδὼν αὐτόν, v. 58).

53 See 4:20; Acts 1:10; 3:4, 12; 6:15; 7:55; 10:4; 11:6; 13:9; 14:9; 23:1. Except for 2 Cor 3:7, the verb appears nowhere else in the New Testament. According to Zorell, *Lexicon*, s.v., it is attested in Polybius and Epictetus. See Lagrange, 568.

54 One must make a distinction between κάθημαι ("to sit"), καθέζομαι, a more recent verb that has the same meaning (see 2:46), and καθίζω, transitive "to set," or intransitive "to sit down," which we have found in v. 55 in its compound συγκαθίζω.

55 At the time of the third denial Luke will use μετά ("with"). See the commentary on v. 59 below.

56 The expression πρὸς τὸ φῶς ("near the light") comes from Mark, from his first description (Mark 14:54) and not from the exact parallel of this verse (Mark 14:67).

57 See Tannehill, 326–27. Thus, Peter is guilty. Fitzmyer (2:1461) points out that at the time of the miraculous catch of fish, when facing Jesus, Peter

religious language and Jesus' contemporary use of it had given the word a wide-ranging sense.[58] Denial is the opposite of confession (ὁμολογῶ), and it refers to the attitude of those who refuse to put their confidence in God and who reject the messengers who speak to them. This is the meaning that Luke's Christian readers give to v. 57. The pagan readers read a refusal in that verse: He denied him, locating the fault on the moral rather than the theological plane. The words "Woman, I do not know him,"[59] constitute the predicted denial, representing in reality a lie, but a lie that speaks the truth of the moment. Those who have read the Gospel remember here another word, a cruel and final word of the Master, who refuses to open the gate of the kingdom and who does not know those who knock at the gate (13:25). Here, as there, the rupture appears to be consummated.[60]

■ 58 Peter's answer does not satisfy the audience. Another person also looks at Peter (ἰδών, "having seen"), does not believe the lie, and repeats the assertion of his companion: "You are also one of them" (Καὶ σὺ ἐξ αὐτῶν εἶ). Peter's answer differs in form, but the content is the same.[61] "Man, I am not." In Mark it is the same maidservant who argues (14:69), while Luke prefers to

change characters and to attribute the second assertion to a man[62] after that from a woman (an alternation, which, as we have seen, that he likes).[63]

■ 59 Whereas the first two comments occurred one after the other, the second happened "after a short while" (μετὰ βραχύ, v. 58[64]), an entire hour separates the second from the third occurrence. By contrast, Mark makes only one reference to time and brings the second and third denials closer together with the expression "after a little while" (μετὰ μικρόν). By saying "then about[65] an hour later,"[66] Luke, who is aware of no interrogation and nighttime trial, waits for morning and prepares for the crowing of the cock.[67]

The evangelist takes other liberties compared to his source, Mark. It is not "the ones standing by" (Mark 14:70) who challenge Peter but, shortly after the maidservant, another individual (ἕτερος, "another"), and finally a third (ἄλλος τις, "someone else," v. 59). Before he speaks, this last person concentrates his energies (the verb διϊσχυρίζομαι, "to insist," contains the word ἰσχύς, "force"). Luke chooses this verb to underscore the insistence of the third speaker, insistence that is noted also with the expression "in truth" (ἐπ' ἀληθείας).[68]

---

referred to himself as an ἀνὴρ ἁμαρτωλός ("a sinful man").

58   See vol. 2 of this commentary, on 12:8-9.

59   Boyd ("Denial") contradicts Matthew Black (*An Aramaic Approach to the Gospels and Acts, with an Appendix on the Son of Man by Geza Vermes* (3d ed.; Oxford: Clarendon, 1967). The Markan and Lukan forms of Peter's first denial cannot be two different translations of the same Aramaic original.

60   Senior (*Passion*, 96–97) correctly notes that with his refusal Peter denies at one and the same time his relation to Jesus, his membership in the group of the Twelve, and his identity as a disciple.

61   In making the second comment, Luke is inspired by the beginning of Mark's third observation (Mark 14:70).

62   Luke sometimes uses ἄνθρωπος ("human being") with the meaning of ἀνήρ ("man"). It is what he does when, as in 2:25; 13:19; and 15:4, he gives an example of a man beside that of a woman. Although he readily uses the vocative plural ἄνδρες (see, e.g., Acts 2:14; 17:22), he does not use the vocative singular (ἄνερ), and he replaces it, as here in v. 58 and v. 60, with ἄνθρωπε (see also 5:20).

63   See nn. 16 and 62 above.

64   Luke appears to be inspired by the μετὰ μικρόν ("after a little while") of Mark 14:70 and to move it from the third to the second denial.

65   Luke likes to indicate the approximate character of a time. To do this he adds ὡς (e.g., 8:42) or, as here and in 3:23, ὡσεί; see Zorell, *Lexicon*, s.v. ὡς, IV, 5a, and s.v. ὡσεί, 3; Jeremias, *Sprache*, 297. According to Grotius (*Annotationes*, 911), ὡσεί often suggests that more is implied than is said. That would mean here: "at least an hour."

66   In the active voice, the classical verb διΐστημι means "to separate," "to set aside," "to divide." The middle form διΐσταμαι (aorist διέστην) has the intransitive meaning "to separate," "to disjoin." Here an hour, literally, has separated from the previous hour and is, therefore, past. Luke uses the verb again in 24:51 and in Acts 27:28. These are the only places it is used in the New Testament; see Plummer, 516.

67   For Wiefel (383), Luke wants to point out that the denial was not a brief incident.

68   The ἀληθῶς of Mark 14:70 is well chosen, since the adverb is used when it is a matter of checking whether a fact is true. The expression ἐπ' ἀληθείας is also appropriate, but perhaps for another reason.

The man is convinced that he is right and implies that Peter is wrong, that he has been lying. While Mark had chosen the direct address for the first and third occurrences, Luke retains an indirect attack for the first (v. 56) and the third time (v. 59) and chooses a direct address in the second person singular for the second reaction (v. 58). The unhappy Peter is subjected to a veritable crossfire. Of course, the three remarks are believed by all the bystanders. To mark the links between Jesus and Peter, Luke, who had used "with" (σύν) in v. 56, resorts here to a different Greek term for "with" (μετά) perhaps under the influence of Mark 14:67 (first interrogation). For the first time, one of Peter's questioners offers an explanation in support of his opinion:[69] "And he is indeed a Galilean." Unlike Matthew, who notes differences between ways of speaking or accents (λαλιά, Matt 26:73), Luke does not tell us on what this statement is based. It may well be the way the disciple talks; it could also be the way he dresses.[70]

■ 60 Luke spares Peter (Mark said that he cursed and swore; 14:71) by writing simply, "But Peter said." In addition—another moderation—Luke's Peter says he does not understand, while in Mark Peter claims not to know "the man about whom you speak," a rather disagreeable way of referring to Jesus. Nevertheless, as he often does in this pericope, to express himself Luke resorts to a sentence from Mark that appears elsewhere, in fact in the first answer (Mark 14:68). Peter persists. Twice (vv. 57

and 60) he yells that he does not know Jesus, that he does not know what they are talking about. Only negations! Three times "not" (οὐκ, vv. 57, 58, 60) for a threefold denial.[71]

Jesus' comments end in v. 47. Here in v. 60 it is those of Peter that are ended with the same formula (ἔτι λαλοῦντος αὐτοῦ, "while he was still speaking").[72] Luke has accustomed us to the adverb παραχρῆμα ("the same moment," "at once," "immediately") and to the role played by expressions of haste or suddenness to mark a divine intervention or the realization of a predestined plan.[73] That the cock crows at daybreak is only normal, but that Peter ends his threefold denial at this precise moment foreseen by Christ is not normal; it is for Luke part of God's plan in history.

■ 61 Those who frequent law courts know that groups are waiting in the corridors, that paths cross and looks are exchanged between those who are leaving a session and those who are waiting outside. That is what happens here. To show that Jesus is elsewhere occupied but that he does not forget the fate of his disciple, Luke uses the participle στραφείς ("when he turned"). There is no need to tell us what occupies Jesus at the moment. The readers know that he has lost his freedom of movement. What they learn is that Jesus uses his last remaining right, the right to turn his head[74] and look[75] at his disciple.[76] The evangelist does not describe this look. All that one can say is that Jesus is concerned not about

It underscores the speaker's sincerity—here that of the man who is insistent and sincerely believes he is right.

69 Luke again takes an idiom from Mark: the joining of the two conjunctions καὶ γάρ (Mark 14:70), literally, "for indeed."

70 On Galilean speech see Matt 26:73; Luz, *Matthew 21–28*, 455. Luke mentions "Galilee" on several occasions (see 1:26; 2:4, 39; 3:1; 4:14, 31; 5:17; 8:26; 17:11; 23:5, 49, 55; 24:6). He will also refer to this region in Acts, although more discreetly (Acts 9:31; 10:37; 13:31). The evangelist used the term "Galilean" in 13:1 and 2 in connection with Pilate's victims, and he will use it again in 23:6 in connection with Jesus.

71 Augustine of Hippo (*Sermo* 285.3 [*PL* 38.1294–95]) brings the threefold denial closer to the threefold "do you love me?" that the risen Christ asks the apostle (John 21:15-17); see Just, *Luke*, 349–50. The

same comparison is in Ambrose of Milan, *Exp. Luc.* 10.90.

72 Only the order of the words is different, avoiding a hiatus. In v. 47 we read ἔτι αὐτοῦ λαλοῦντος.

73 Note the haste with which Mary goes to Elizabeth in 1:39; see vol. 1 of this commentary, 57–58, on 1:39-40. One finds παραχρῆμα frequently in Luke, especially to call attention to the sudden character of the miracle that has occurred: see 1:64; 4:39; 5:25; 8:44, 47, 55; 13:13; 18:43; 19:11 (in the last text the event is not a miracle, but the [wrongly expected] appearance of the kingdom of God).

74 Luke makes use of the same participle in 7:9. On στρέφω and ἐπιστρέφω and their middle-passive, see Bovon, *Luke the Theologian*, 314–20.

75 On ἐμβλέπω, see LSJ, s.v.; and BAGD, s.v.

76 In his *De Passione Sermo* 3, viz. 41 (54).5 (SC 74:60–63), Leo the Great emphasizes the importance of this look. This look penetrates Peter and invites him

himself but about his disciple. Does he reveal sadness? Or does his look contain a reproach? Or does he want to be right? We do not know. Luke merely shows the effect the look produces.

Indeed, Peter does immediately remember the word of Jesus. His reaction corresponds to the Christian attitude that Luke describes throughout his double work. In the Gospel, Luke calls to mind that the word of God is to be heard, not to be forgotten but to be lived.[77] When Jesus turns to him, Peter also turns to his Lord, since "he remembered the word of the Lord." More important than a physical movement, it is a matter of an inner reversal (see ἐπιστρέψας, "once turned around," "once converted," v. 32). With this "conversion" (μετάνοια) the apostle appears to be the model of the believer. And Luke is concerned to make clear that the one who speaks the word to Peter, then looks at him, is not simply "Jesus," but "the Lord" (the title ὁ κύριος, "the Lord," appears here twice).[78] Jesus' word is remembered (v. 61) in a way that corresponds better to the parallel in Mark (14:72) than to the prediction itself in its Lukan wording (v. 34).[79] That is because Luke earlier followed his own source and here he conforms to the Second Gospel.[80]

■ 62 It is quite difficult to say whether this verse originally was part of the Gospel of Luke. I lean toward the view that it was contaminated from Matt 26:75b. This Matthean conclusion of the story shows externally the spiritual work going on internally in Peter. The tears indicate the repentance (Ambrose of Milan *Exp. Luc.*

10.87–90). That they are bitter (πικρῶς, "bitterly") is explained by the horror of the sin that has just been committed. That Peter "went outside," indicates that he cannot hold his feelings in any longer. From then on he is on the way to forgiveness and the new life.

The commentaries are often exhaustive in Synoptic comparison and historical reconstructions. In the process their authors forget what is essential: a phenomenology or a psychology of denial. Spouses can reject one another; they can separate; but they cannot pretend that they do not know each other. The denial belongs to a larger, less-intimate social framework than the family. It belongs to the group, the band, the association, the party. What is it really about? It is a quick decision made in a crisis situation, a reflexive self-protection[81] stemming more from panic than from calculation—a decision made more from impulse than from reflection, which consists in "letting down" someone whom one previously has "held up." Such an abrupt change, for which the abandoned person is not responsible, is morally shocking to everyone. From a distance and for the observer it is a reflection of cowardice, selfishness, injustice, and ingratitude.[82] Close at hand and for the interested party it involves survival in a situation marked by injustice and violence. In this sense, what is remarkable about Peter's repentance is that it happens when the violence has not yet reached its peak. Apart from the fact that Peter has come to himself, his attitude still is shameful and is the occasion for reproach and criticism. To say it differently:

---

to turn to the one who is looking at him. See Just, *Luke*, 349.

77 See, e.g., 6:47; 8:15, 21; 11:28; also vol. 1 of this commentary, 254–56 and 315–16, on 6:47-49 and 8:19-21.

78 On the title ὁ κύριος ("the Lord") in Luke, see vol. 1 of this commentary, 88–89, on 2:11; Bovon, *Luke the Theologian*, 214–18.

79 Even though one of them normally means "to deny" and the other "to refuse," "to disown," Luke follows Mark in giving about the same meaning to the simple verb ἀρνοῦμαι (v. 57, as well as 12:9) that he gives to the compound verb ἀπαρνοῦμαι (here in v. 61, as well as 12:9). In 9:23 the manuscripts waver between the two forms; see vol. 1 of this commentary, 366, on 9:23.

80 The Markan use of ὡς ("as," "when") pleases Luke, who likes this usage; see Jeremias, *Sprache*, 298.

81 Cyril of Alexandria (*Serm. Luc.* 149) notes that the

fear of death is stronger than any human endurance. It will be vanquished only after the victory over death constituted by the redemption of Good Friday and the resurrection on the day of Easter; Payne Smith, *Cyril*, 2:699.

82 Augustine of Hippo (*Epist.* 265.2 [*PL* 33:1086]) draws a distinction between Peter and the penitents who sit patiently on the benches of his church. The apostle is not as guilty as they, because he sinned before he had received the gift of the Holy Spirit, before the resurrection of Christ and Pentecost, while they were baptized and received the Spirit before they foundered in evil. See Just, *Luke*, 349. Cyril of Alexandria (*Serm. Luc.* 149) is wary of such a distinction: When he denied Jesus, had Peter not already shared the body of Christ at the Last Supper? The patriarch of Alexandria prefers to emphasize the power of the temptation and the God who forgives; Payne Smith, *Cyril*, 2:700–701.

Peter's repentance is disappointing in the sense that it took three successive denials, the crowing of the cock, and the look of the Master for it finally to happen. Let those who have never been faint-hearted and who have always demonstrated their civil courage cast the first stone at him (John 8:7).

■ **63-65** Luke inserts here a scene of mocking that the other two Synoptic Gospels place at the end of the night hearing before the Sanhedrin (Mark 14:65 par. Matt 26:67-68), a hearing that he himself does not know at this place. Mark, Matthew, and John have a second such scene in the context of the trial before Pilate (Mark 15:16-20a par. Matt 27:27-31a par. John 19:2-3). Luke is unaware of this second scene,[83] because he is following there his special source (from 23:6 to 23:43). It may also be that he does not want to give a negative image of the Romans. The first insults lie in a Jewish framework. With their deeds and words the torturers accuse Jesus of being a false prophet. The later insults are to be explained in a Roman context. The governor's soldiers ridicule Jesus' royal pretensions.[84]

As I have said,[85] Luke rewrote the episode that Mark had told. He clarifies the identity of those who attack Jesus: They are "the men who were holding him captive."[86] He uses the verb ἐμπαίζω (v. 63), which suggests mocking more than torture (cf. the word παῖς, "child"). It happens that the play involves making fun of someone.

The amusement degenerates into cruelty. It is the verbs δέρω and παίω that indicate that the serious mocking was accompanied by blows. Let us not forget that the first sense of δέρω is "to skin." In Luke's day, however, it evolved from "to beat until flayed" to simply "to beat" (Mark, whom Luke is adapting, speaks of spitting and slapping). When toying with Jesus, these men[87] cover his face.[88] Then they put him to the test by giving him the rules of the cruel game: "prophesy" (προφήτευσον; all three Synoptics have this verb).[89] One would expect the imperative "guess!" (μάντευσαι), but it is Jesus' prophetic ministry that is challenged by derision, not his talents as a soothsayer.

W. C. van Unnik recalls that Pollux's work (*Onomasticon* 9.113, 129) contains the description of two children's games.[90] The rules of the first game require that the child close his eyes and guess who touches him. Those of the second game say that the child must cover his eyes with his hands and guess with which hand his companion slapped him. There must have been such games from time immemorial.[91] It is the narrative function of these games, more than the social reality, that is important to the evangelists, especially to Luke. By playing these games the opponents question Jesus' prophetic mission.[92] Throughout the Gospel, however, Luke has emphasized the Nazarene's prophetic charisma.[93] Here, as elsewhere,[94] he emphasizes that many in Israel rejected this

---

83 Well observed by Lagrange, 567, 570.

84 See Benoit, *Passion and Resurrection*, 92; Bovon, *Last Days*, 39, 51.

85 See the diachronic analysis above.

86 The verb συνέχω means "to hold together," "to compress," "to hold connected [in chains]," "to hold captive." The present participle underscores the duration of the action. I am not sure that Lagrange (570) is right when he says that συνέχω with the meaning of "to arrest" by the police, "to hold in prison" is rare. The French scholar cites a papyrus from Magdola and 1 Macc 13:15. See P. Jouquet and G. Lefebure, "Papyrus de Magdola," in *Mélanges Nicole: Recueil de mémoires de philologie classique et d'archéologie offerts à Jules Nicole à l'occasion du XXXe anniversaire de son professorat* (Geneva: Kündig, 1905) 281–88; see also J. H. Moulton and G. Milligan ("Lexical Notes from the Papyri," *Exp*, 8th series, 9 [1911] 278–79), who cite other examples.

87 Luke likes to use the plural ἄνδρες ("men"); see, e.g., 7:20 and n. 62 above.

88 On this point, by mentioning the face, Mark is more precise than Luke. It is, indeed, the eyes that need to be covered. Luke is satisfied to say, "when they had covered him with a veil." The verb περικαλύπτω is not rare; see Alexandre, s.v.

89 Rudberg ("Verhöhnung") calls attention to a passage of Diodorus of Sicily (*Bibliotheca historica* 34–35.2), which illustrates that in antiquity one could humiliate with an opposite. A master ridicules the predictions of his slave who claims to be a prophet.

90 Van Unnik, "Verhöhnung."

91 The reader will always read with profit the book of Johan Huizinga, *Homo ludens: A Study of the Play-Element in Culture* (1949; reprinted London: Routledge & Kegan Paul, 1980) 89–93, 107–8.

92 Thus, they choose to use the verb προφητεύω ("to prophesy," v. 64).

93 See 4:24; 7:16, 39; 9:8, 19; 13:33; 24:19; Bovon, *Luke the Theologian*, 201–3.

94 One finds the strongest expression of this rejection

messenger of God, this prophet inspired by the Holy Spirit. Luke is neither the first nor the only one to celebrate the misunderstood prophets. In fact, in Israel the true prophets always had to confront the false prophets (see Jeremiah 28).[95] The biblical writings provide several examples of truly offended prophets.[96] In 1 Kgs (LXX 3 Kgdms) 22:24-28, for example, the prophet Micaiah, son of Imlah, dares to proclaim the word of God and to announce the defeat of Ahab, in spite of the contrary opinion of the four hundred false prophets who predict victory—an opinion that, of course, the king wants to hear. Therefore, the prophet must experience jeers and insults: "Then Zedekiah son of Chenaanah came up to Micaiah, slapped him on the cheek, and said, 'Which way did the spirit of the Lord pass from me to speak to you?'" (1 Kgs [LXX 3 Kgdms] 22:24).[97] The famous description of the Suffering Servant (Isa 52:13—53:12) certainly has in mind the fate of the true prophet. In the book of Zechariah, the prophet pays the price for his faithfulness: "'Awake, O sword, against my shepherd, against the man who is my associate,' says the Lord of hosts. 'Strike the shepherd, that the sheep may be scattered; I will turn my hand against the little ones'" (Zech 13:7).[98]

The Greeks and Romans, who bowed down before the victorious heroes, also respected the wise and the philosophers, who at the risk of suffering chose values other than success or power.[99] Plato describes the judgment against Socrates, and Seneca admires pain endured with serenity.[100] The Greek and Roman readers of the Gospel did not automatically side with the strongest. Some of them recognized the power of Jesus, the ridiculed prophet.

Luke wants to conclude the account:[101] He summarizes the attitude of the guards with a general formula. They, he writes, say all kinds of insults against Jesus.[102] The verb βλασφημέω does not necessarily imply an attack against God; it can mean "to insult," "to offend."[103] Nevertheless, toying with the prophet has a religious basis, and Luke understands Jesus to be God's spokesman (see 10:16).[104] Furthermore, in Acts 26:11 the verb βλασφημέω means to deny his Lord or his God, "to slander God," "to blaspheme." It is also interesting to note that, according to the accounts of the Acts of the Apostles, the disciples undergo the same insults as their Master. Luke makes use of the same present participle,

in Acts 7:51-53, from the mouth of Stephen; see Senior, *Passion*, 98.

95 On the misunderstood prophets in the Hebrew Bible, see Gerhard von Rad, *Old Testament Theology* (trans. D. M. G. Stalker; 2 vols.; New York: Harper & Row, 1962, 1965) 2:17, 31–32, 72–76, 203–5, 273–75 and passim.

96 The greatest prophets, Moses, Elijah, Jeremiah, and Ezekiel, all suffered for their message (see Exod 17:4; 32:32; 1 Kings [LXX 3 Kingdoms] 19; Jer 8:18-23; Ezek 4:4-8; Neh 9:26).

97 See Mordechai Cogan, *1 Kings: A New Translation with Introduction and Commentary* (AB 10; New York: Doubleday, 2001) 492–93, 496–98.

98 See André Lacocque, *Zacharie 9–14* (CAT 11c; Neuchâtel: Delachaux & Niestlé, 1981) 196–97.

99 See Hans Dieter Betz, *Paul's Apology, II Corinthians 10–13, and the Socratic Tradition* (Center for Hermeneutical Studies in Hellenistic and Modern Culture 2; Berkeley, Calif.: The Center, 1975).

100 See esp. Plato *Apology of Socrates* and *Phaedo;* Seneca *De ira* 2.32.1–34.5; Sterling, "*Mors Pholosophi*," esp. 384–90.

101 With this intention Luke uses a general formula much as he had described the preaching of John

the Baptist: πολλὰ μὲν οὖν καὶ ἕτερα παρακαλῶν εὐηγγελίζετο τὸν λαόν, "So, with many other exhortations, he proclaimed the good news to the people" (3:18). Bonaventure (*Comm. Luc.* 22.77 [Bernardini, 563]) understood this point well: *Et quia non est possible narrare omnia convicia Christo illata, ideo, ut concludat omnia in summa quadam, subdit . . .*, "And because it is not possible to tell all the insults inflicted on Christ, he adds, summarizing the whole. . . ."

102 Applying a process with which he is familiar, Luke understands the accusative ἕτερα πολλά ("many other things") as the direct object of two verbs at the same time, βλασφημοῦντες ("insulting") and ἔλεγον ("they spoke"). The verb λέγω is not usually followed by the preposition εἰς ("toward," here "against"), but the other verb, βλασφημοῦντες, is often followed by εἰς, and it brings the preposition along with it. My translation is finally: "And they spoke many other insults against him."

103 On the Lukan use of the verb βλασφημέω, see vol. 2 of this commentary, on 12:10.

104 Bovon, *L'œuvre*, 224–28.

βλασφημοῦντες, to describe the attitude of the opponents of the Christians (Acts 13:45; 18:6; 19:37).

History of Interpretation

In the footnotes of the preceding pages I have called attention to the interpretation of various ecclesiastical authors of late antiquity.[105] Thus, I am satisfied here[106] to read the pages Calvin devotes to this episode in his *Harmony of the Gospels*.[107] The reformer acknowledges the diversity among the Gospels (the attitude of the humanist influenced by the Renaissance), but he promises to harmonize the divergent facts (the attitude of the theologian embedded in the tradition of the church). Calvin the historian is of the opinion that in that day the Jews had lost the right of capital punishment but that they still had the right "to a secondary court of discipline." The theologian finds it horrible that in the heart of religion one conspires against God. This drama was beneficial for humanity, however, because "by His bonds we are loosed from the tyrannical power of the devil and from the guilt which in God's sight kept us prisoner." As a modern exegete, he notes that "the evangelists were not too exact about the time sequence." As a man of the church, he writes: "Peter's fall, here described, brilliantly mirrors

our own infirmity.[108] His repentance, in turn, is a memorable demonstration for us of God's goodness and mercy. The story of one man contains teaching of general, and indeed prime, benefit for the whole church." Of the two sides of repentance to which the Venerable Bede calls attention,[109] Calvin the reformer emphasizes the one that makes divine love shine. The psychologist observes that it takes little to break a man ("but, at the voice of a young woman, he is scared") and that the higher one is, the more careful one must be not to fall. Then Calvin harmonizes the statements of the Gospels. He concludes that the second charge had to come from a group, since Mark keeps the role of the "chamber maid" and Matthew and Luke speak of a different person! About the crowing of the cock, he asserts that once the animal started to raise his voice, he did not stop. More seriously, he recognizes that, as long as the Holy Spirit had not been poured out, even the greatest apostles allow Satan "to work his power on us with violence." Thus, in order to keep from falling—Calvin insists again—one needs God's help through the Holy Spirit. Involved in the polemic of the Reformation, he thinks that Peter did not merit forgiveness. He received it "from the kind fatherly affection of God." About Jesus' look at Peter—Calvin notes that it is a Lukan touch—he is of the opinion that

---

105 See, moreover, the Venerable Bede *In Luc.* 6.1073–1187. This author gives the fire lit in the court an allegorical meaning. It is the fire of affection and the fire of avarice. He has respect for Jesus' prediction (v. 34), but he also is careful not to diminish Peter's guilt. He associates Peter's sin with the night and his repentance with the morning. The cock plays the part of the Master who invites one to vigilance and to resistance to sin. God's mercy accompanies Peter's penitence. It is Jesus' look at Peter that expresses this mercy of God (Bede refers to Ps 12 [13]:3-4). The insults fulfill the prophecy of Micah 4:14 (5:1): "With a rod they strike the ruler of Israel upon the cheek." Finally, the veil that hides Jesus' head alludes, for Bede, to the one with which Moses covered himself.

106 I am also looking at the pages of Bonaventure *Comm. Luc.* 22.67–77 (Bernardini, 560–64) and the two columns of Erasmus, *Paraphrasis*, 456–57. Bonaventure retains four elements: *Petri tepiditas in formidando, fragilitas in negando, pietas Domini in recipiendo, et fidelitas Petri in redeundo*, "Peter's tepidity when he is afraid, his weakness when he denies, the

compassion of the Lord when he restores Peter, and the faithfulness of the latter when he comes to himself" (561). Erasmus notes in particular about v. 56 (intervention of the maidservant): *Non hoc actum est fortuito, sed ita placuit divinae dispensationi*, "That did not happen by accident; it corresponded to a divine dispensation" (456).

107 Calvin, *Harmony*, 3:163–64, 169–73. The first three quotations come from 163–64, the next two from 169–70, the last three from 172–73.

108 Passing from Peter to the Christians, Calvin comments further on about the threefold denial: "whence it appears how slippery and steep is the slope on which we fall."

109 See n. 105 above.

it was a special glance (he explains that Jesus had also seen Judas coming). It is the look that represents grace: "With the turning of his eyes on Peter, there went the secret power of the Spirit."[110]

Conclusion

From the moment when Jesus had predicted the imminent denial (v. 34) and had formulated the oracle of the final conversion (v. 32), Luke could no longer suppress the terrible incident. The evangelist demonstrated his courage by refusing to retract the threefold denial of the apostle he venerates. Earlier I indicated why the early Christians had not renounced this cumbersome memory.[111] Luke, who shared these reasons, had others as well. He emphasizes on the negative side Peter's denial, on the positive side Jesus' courage. This threefold sin, a catastrophic event, clarifies the following stage, the repeated confession to Christ that the believers make in the Acts of the Apostles. For Luke, Christian existence is less a progression than a transformation. In the course of his literary work the evangelist illustrates this doctrinal schema: Peter as well as Paul had both passed from darkness into light (Acts 26:18), from denial or persecution to faith and preaching. Luke believes and bears witness that for such upheavals to be possible God's intervention must prepare the way, accompanied then by human decisions. The evangelist presents himself as the theologian of God's plan. There is, however, no unilateral action of the Lord without human participation. Jesus' look (v. 61) is accompanied by Peter's awakening consciousness (vv. 61-62). Luke 22:54-62 is the story of a conversion. That Jesus himself did not yield at the time of the insults (vv. 63-65) is part of the redemptive action he undertook during his ministry, carried out in his passion, and completed in his resurrection.

---

110 In *De cons. evang.* 3.6.26 (*PL* 34:1172–73), Augustine of Hippo explains the look Jesus gives Peter in this crucial moment. Bonaventure (*Comm. Luc.* 22.72 [Bernardini, 562]) refers to this commentary of Augustine and thus demonstrates the existence of an exegetical tradition.

111 See the diachronic analysis above.

Jesus' Appearance before the Sanhedrin (22:66-71)

Bibliography

Benoit, *Passion and Resurrection*, 93–114.

Black, "Arrest and Trial."

Blinzler, Josef, "Geschichtlichkeit and Legalität des jüdischen Prozesses gegen Jesus," *StZ* 147 (1950–51) 345–57.

Idem, *Prozess*, 95–174.

Idem, "Das Synedrium von Jerusalem and die Strafprozessordnung der Mischna," *ZNW* 52 (1961) 54–65.

Bovon, *Last Days*, 34–38.

Idem, "Lukan Story of the Passion."

Brown, *Death of the Messiah*, 1:311–560.

Browne, Gerald M., "Ad CG II 7,139:20," *BASP* 15 (1978) 191–93.

Büchsel, Friedrich, "Die Blutgerichtsbarkeit des Synedrions," *ZNW* 30 (1931) 202–10.

Idem, "Noch einmal: Zur Blutgerichtsbarkeit des Synedrions," *ZNW* 33 (1934) 84–87.

Burkill, T. Alec, "The Trial of Jesus," *VC* 12 (1958) 1–18.

Cantinat, Jean, "Jésus devant le Sanhédrin," *NRTh* 75 (1953) 300–308.

Catchpole, David R., "The Problem of the Historicity of the Sanhedrin Trial," in Ernst Bammel, ed., *The Trial of Jesus: Cambridge Studies in Honour of C. F. D. Moule* (SBT 2/13; Naperville, Ill.: Allenson, 1970) 47–65.

Idem, *Trial*, 153–220.

Cohn, Haim, *The Trial and Death of Jesus* (New York: Ktav, 1977).

Danby, Herbert, "The Bearing of the Rabbinical Criminal Code on the Jewish Trial Narratives in the Gospels," *JTS* 21 (1919–20) 51–76.

Delorme, Jean, "Le procès de Jésus ou la parole risquée (Lc 22,54—23,25)," in *La Parole de grâce: Études lucaniennes à la mémoire d'Augustin George* (Paris: Recherches de science religieuse, 1981) 123–46; essays reprinted from *RSR* 69 (1981).

Derrett, J. Duncan M., "Midrash in the New Testament: The Origin of Luke 22:67-68," *StTh* 29 (1975) 147–56; reprinted in idem, *Studies in the New Testament* (6 vols.; Leiden: Brill, 1977–95) 2:184–93.

Dibelius, Martin, "Das historische Problem der Leidensgeschichte," *ZNW* 30 (1931) 193–201; reprinted in idem, *Botschaft und Geschichte: Gesammelte Aufsätze* (2 vols.; Tübingen: Mohr, 1953, 1956) 1:248–57.

Donahue, John R., *Are You the Christ? The Trial Narrative in the Gospel of Mark* (SBLDS 10; Missoula, Mont.: Scholars Press, 1973) 5–102, 139–87.

Idem, "Trial of Jesus."

Duplacy, Jean, "Une variante méconnue du texte reçu: '. . . *H AΠΟΛΥΣΗΤΕ*' (Lc 22, 68)," in J. Blinzler, O. Kuss, and F. Mussner, eds., *Neutestamentliche Aufsätze: Festschrift für Prof. Josef Schmid zum 70. Geburtstag* (Regensburg: Pustet, 1963) 42–52; reprinted in idem, *Études de critique textuelle du Nouveau Testament* (ed. Joël Delobel; BEThL 78; Leuven: University Press/Peeters, 1987) 25–38.

Feuillet, André, "Le triomphe du Fils de l'homme d'après la déclaration du Christ aux Sanhédrites (Mc., xiv, 62; Mt., xxvi, 64; Lc., xxii, 69)," in Édouard Massaux, ed., *La venue du Messie: Messianisme et eschatologie* (RechBib 6; Bruges: Desclée de Brouwer, 1962) 149–71.

Flender, Helmut, *Heil und Geschichte in der Theologie des Lukas* (BEvTh 41; Munich: Kaiser, 1965) 44–46.

Fricke, Weddig, *The Court-Marshall of Jesus: A Christian Defends the Jews against the Charge of Deicide* (trans. Salvator Attanasio; New York: Grove Weidenfeld, 1990).

Genest, Olivette, *Le Christ de la Passion: Perspective structurale. Analyse de Marc 14,53—15,47, des parallèles bibliques et extra-bibliques* (Recherches: Théologie 21; Tournai: Desclée, 1978).

Gnilka, Joachim, "Die Verhandlungen vor dem Synhedrion und vor Pilatus nach Markus 14,53—15,5," *EKKNTV* 2 (1970) 5–21.

Goguel, Maurice, "A propos du procès de Jésus," *ZNW* 31 (1932) 289–301.

Goulder, M. D., "On Putting Q to the Test," *NTS* 24 (1977–78) 218–34, esp. 226–30.

Gourgues, Michel, *À la droite de Dieu: Résurrection de Jésus et actualisation du Psaume 110:1 dans le Nouveau Testament* (EtB; Paris: Gabalda, 1978) 143–61.

Grant, Frederick C., "On the Trial of Jesus: A Review Article," *JR* 44 (1964) 230–37.

Greene, Glenn Roger, "The Portrayal of Jesus as Prophet in Luke-Acts" (Diss., Southern Baptist Theological Seminary, Louisville, 1975).

Heil, John Paul, "Reader-Response and the Irony of Jesus before the Sanhedrin in Luke 22:66-71," *CBQ* 51 (1989) 271–84.

Herranz Marco, Mariano, "El proceso ante el Sanhedrín y el ministerio público de Jesús," *EstBib* 34 (1975) 83–111.

Horsley and Hanson, *Bandits*.

Husband, Richard Wellington, *The Prosecution of Jesus: Its Date, History and Legality* (Princeton: Princeton University Press, 1916).

Jaubert, Annie, "Les séances du Sanhédrin et les récits de la Passion," *RHR* 166 (1964) 143–69; 167 (1965) 1–33.

Jeremias, Joachim, "Zur Geschichtlichkeit des Verhörs Jesu vor dem Hohen Rat," *ZNW* 43 (1950–51) 145–50.

Juel, Donald, *Messiah and Temple: The Trial of Jesus in the Gospel of Mark* (SBLDS 31; Missoula, Mont.: Scholars Press, 1977).

Kempthorne, Renatus, "The Marcan Text of Jesus' Answer to the High Priest (Mark xiv 62)," *NovT* 19 (1977) 197–208.

Kilgallen, John J., "Jesus' First Trial: Messiah and Son of God (Luke 22, 66-71)," *Bib* 80 (1999) 401–14.

Kilpatrick, George Dunbar, *The Trial of Jesus* (London: Oxford University Press, 1953) 1–21.

Kolping, Adolf, "'Standrechtlich gekreuzigt': Neuere Überlegungen zum Prozess Jesu," *TRev* 83 (1987) 265–76.

Lamarche, Paul, "La déclaration de Jésus devant le Sanhédrin," in idem, *Christ vivant: Essai sur la christologie du Nouveau Testament* (LD 43; Paris: Cerf, 1966) 147–63.

Légasse, Simon, "Jésus devant le Sanhédrin: Recherche sur les traditions évangéliques," *RThL* 5 (1974) 170–97.

Lietzmann, Hans, "Bemerkungen zum Prozess Jesu," *ZNW* 30 (1931) 211–15.

Idem, "Der Prozess Jesu," SPAW.PH 14 (1931) 313–22; reprinted in idem, *Kleine Schriften,* vol. 2: *Studien zum Neuen Testament* (ed. Kurt Aland; TU 68; Berlin: Akademie-Verlag, 1958) 251–63.

Linnemann, *Studien,* 70–135.

Linton, Olof, "The Trial of Jesus and the Interpretation of Psalm cx," *NTS* 7 (1960–61) 258–62.

Lührmann, Dieter, "Markus 14.55-64: Christologie und Zerstörung des Tempels im Markusevangelium," *NTS* 27 (1980–81) 457–74.

Matera, Frank J., "Luke 22,66-71: Jesus Before the ΠΡΕΣΒΥΤΕΡΙΟΝ," in Frans Neirynck, ed., *L'Évangile de Luc—The Gospel of Luke* (2d ed.; BEThL 32; Leuven: Leuven University Press/Peeters, 1989) 517–33.

Idem, "The Trial of Jesus: Problems and Proposals," *Int* 45 (1991) 5–16.

McLaren, James S., *Power and Politics in Palestine: The Jews and the Governing of Their Land, 100 BC–AD 70* (JSNTSup 63; Sheffield: JSOT Press, 1991) 188–93.

Meyer, Franz E., "Einige Bemerkungen zur Bedeutung des Terminus 'Synhedrion' in den Schriften des Neuen Testaments," *NTS* 14 (1967–68) 545–51.

Plevnik, Joseph, "Son of Man Seated at the Right Hand of God: Luke 22,69 in Lucan Christology," *Bib* 72 (1991) 331–47.

Quispel, Gilles, "The Gospel of Thomas and the Trial of Jesus," in Tjitze Baarda et al., eds., *Text and Testimony: Essays on New Testament and Apocryphal Literature in Honour of A. F. J. Klijn* (Kampen: Kok, 1988) 193–99.

Rese, *Motive,* 199–200.

Rosenblatt, Samuel, "The Crucifixion of Jesus from the Standpoint of the Pharisaic Law," *JBL* 75 (1956) 315–21.

Rudberg, "Verhöhnung."

Schneider, Gerhard, "Gab es eine vorsynoptische Szene 'Jesus vor dem Synedrium'"? *NovT* 12 (1970) 22–39.

Idem, "Jesus vor dem Synedrium," *BibLeb* 11 (1970) 1–15; reprinted in idem, *Lukas, Theologie der Heilsgeschichte: Aufsätze zum lukanischen Doppelwerk* (BBB 59; Königsstein: Hanstein, 1985) 158–72.

Idem, "Das Verfahren gegen Jesus in der Sicht des dritten Evangeliums (Lk 22,54—23,25): Redaktionskritik und historische Rückfrage," in Karl Kertelge, ed., *Der Prozeß gegen Jesus* (QD 112; Freiburg i. B.: Herder, 1988) 111–30.

Schubert, Kurt, "Die Juden and die Römer," *BLit* 36 (1962–63) 235–42.

Idem, "Das Verhör Jesu vor dem Hohen Rat," in Josef Sint, ed., *Bibel und zeitgemässer Glaube,* vol. 2: *Neues Testament* (Klosterneuburg: Klosterneuburger Buch- und Kunstverlag, 1967) 97–130.

Sloyan, Gerard Stephen, *Jesus on Trial: the Development of the Passion Narratives and Their Historical and Ecumenical Implications* (Philadelphia: Fortress Press, 1973).

Sterling, "*Mors Philosophi.*"

Taylor, *Passion Narrative,* 77–80.

Tyson, Joseph B., "The Lukan Version of the Trial of Jesus," *NovT* 3 (1959) 249–58.

Unnik, W. C. van, "Jesu Verhöhnung vor dem Synedrium (Mk 14.65 par.)," *ZNW* 29 (1930) 310–11; reprinted in idem, *Sparsa Collecta: The Collected Essays of W. C. van Unnik* (3 vols.; NovTSup 29–31; Leiden: Brill, 1973–83) 1:3–5.

Valentin, Patrick, "Les comparutions de Jésus devant le Sanhédrin," *RSR* 59 (1971) 230–36.

Walaskay, Paul W., "The Trial and Death of Jesus in the Gospel of Luke," *JBL* 94 (1975) 81–93.

Winter, Paul, "Luke XXII 66b-71," *StTh* 9 (1955) 112–15.

Idem, "Marginal Notes on the Trial of Jesus," *ZNW* 50 (1959) 14–33, 221–51.

Idem, *On the Trial of Jesus* (rev. and ed. T. A. Burkill and Geza Vermes; Studia Judaica 1; Berlin: de Gruyter, 1974).

Idem, "The Trial of Jesus and the Competence of the Sanhedrin," *NTS* 10 (1963–64) 494–99.

Zeitlin, Solomon, *Who Crucified Jesus?* (New York: Harper & Brothers, 1942).

66   **When the day dawned, the assembly of the elders of the people gathered, chief priests and scribes. One led him to their Sanhedrin[a] 67/ saying, "If you are the Messiah,[b] tell us." But he said to them, "If I told you, you would not believe me. 68/ And if I ask the question, you would not answer me.[c] 69/ From now on the Son of Man will sit at the right hand of the power of God." 70/ They all said, "Then you are the Son of God?"[d] He said to them, "It is you who say that I am." 71/ Then they said,[e] What further testimony do we need? For we ourselves have heard the words[f] from his mouth."**

a   Another translation: "to their session" or "to the room where they met."
b   Other translations: "If it is you the Messiah" and "Are you the Messiah?"
c   Literally: "you would not answer."
d   Another translation: "Are you then the Son of God?"
e   Another translation: "But they said."
f   Literally: "For we ourselves have heard it from his mouth."

According to the evangelist, the power of darkness (22:53) continues to act. The opposition to Jesus that originated much earlier (6:11) was organized at the beginning of the festival (22:1-6), and the elaborate plan began to be carried out on the Mount of Olives (22:47-53). After he was arrested the previous evening,[1] Jesus spent the night in the house of the high priest (22:54). Early in the morning (22:66), an official meeting of the authorities is held. Luke will give a report of it here (22:67-71) before telling about the appearance before Pilate.[2]

The logic of this plot actually should have led to a spectacular confrontation between Jesus and the leaders of his people, to a clear opposition between opponents who have irreconcilable convictions. Yet in spite of the views of several commentators,[3] the text remains obscure. Jesus does not say who he is,[4] and the Sanhedrin pronounces no sentence.[5] Although Jesus' personality is discussed and two concepts of the Messiah clash,[6] these stakes remain veiled. The opposition is obvious, but the precise issues of the disagreement remain unspoken.

Analysis

Verse 66 provides the information that an official authority will deal with the one who is waiting in the house of the high priest. Verses 67-71 present the hearing that Jesus then undergoes. Two questions lead to two answers of different lengths, one long (vv. 67b-69), the other short (v. 70b). The gathering has the last word (v. 71) and is ready for the next stage, the appearance before Pilate (23:1). From judges who conduct an examination or an inquest (vv. 67-71) they become accusers when they appear before the Roman governor (23:2). An examination or an inquest is usually carried out by only one or two persons. By presenting a large assembly Luke gives this stage the solemnity of a trial.

Two solutions are possible for the exegete who is looking for the origin of this passage. According to the first solution, Luke is relying on his own special source.[7] Indeed, the sequence of the episodes and the contents of the literary unit differ from the Gospel of Mark. The trial takes place on the day after Peter's denial and the

---

1   That is certain, even if the hour is not specifically stated. The meal took place in the evening (22:14), and the cock crowed early in the morning, at the end of the night (22:60).
2   C. F. Evans correctly writes: "This could be said to be the crucial section of the passion narrative, indeed of the Gospel. For it treats of the final confrontation of Jesus with Israel. . . . Yet the synoptic accounts of so vital a matter . . . are so brief and compressed as to be problematic at almost every point" (830–31).
3   See, e.g., Sabourin, 358; and Tannehill, 330–31.
4   Unlike in Mark 14:62, where the evangelist has him say that he is the Messiah.
5   Unlike Mark 14:64 and Matt 26:65-66.
6   See Lagrange, 573; Sabourin, 357; Goulder, *New Paradigm*, 2:753.
7   This is the hypothesis retained by Schlatter, 436–38; Catchpole, *Trial*, 153–220; Tyson, "Version."

mocking scene, while in Mark it is held during the night at the same time as the denial (14:53-72, which uses the so-called "sandwich" technique or intercalation). The Lukan text is not aware of the episode of the false witnesses (Mark 14:56-61a); it duplicates the tribunal's question (Mark 14:61; v. 67a and v. 70a), emphasizes a Jesus who avoids clear answers (vv. 67b-69 and v. 70b), prefers the seating of the Son of Man over his arrival (Mark 14:62b), and says nothing of the tearing of the priests' vestments (Mark 14:63a), the charge of blasphemy (Mark 14:64a), and the last judgment (Mark 14:64b). These are many differences. If we add that the text of Luke may contain some non-Lukan elements[8] and shares with John Jesus' skepticism about the dialogue (vv. 67b-68),[9] we will agree that the hypothesis is defensible.

According to the other hypothesis, these differences are to be explained by Luke's redactional purposes.[10] Luke freely rewrites what Mark, his primary source for the narrative parts, gives him.[11] Our interpretation of the details will show that Luke's theology is behind many of the changes he makes in Mark's text, the most important of which concerns the christological dialogue.[12] Luke gives the question of the Jewish authorities twice in order to make it possible for Jesus to redefine the title "Messiah" in transcendent terms ("Son of God" not by adoption but in reality). The sentence about the Son of Man sitting at God's right hand, inserted between the two questions, provides the theological and scriptural argument for this demonstration.[13] The Lukan Jesus never explicitly says that he is this character, but what he implies is convincing. The authorities are not mistaken there. They need no further testimony to pursue the charge against Jesus.

One can waver between these two hypotheses. Since the differences from Mark are easily explained from Luke's point of view and since Luke follows Mark in the following episode (Jesus before Pilate, 23:1-5), I maintain my hypothesis that large blocks of material come alternatively from Mark and the special source. From Jesus' arrest to his appearance before Pilate (22:47—23:5), Luke follows and adapts the Gospel of Mark.

Commentary

■ **66** While it is obvious that Luke confers solemnity on the occasion, he does so in a way that is ambiguous for modern readers. What does he mean exactly by the word πρεσβυτέριον, a word that he is one of the first to use?[14] Etymologically the term means "assembly of the elders," but for such an assembly the Greeks had the term γερουσία.[15] Luke knows that the "elders" or "presbyters" were one of the three groups making up the Jerusalem Sanhedrin. This is probably why he makes use of the term πρεσβυτέριον ("assembly of the elders"). Since he

8   See Schneider, "Synedrium," 164–66 (cited according to the collection).
9   On the parallel with John 10:24-25, see the commentary below on v. 67.
10 Three authors who think that here Luke depends on Mark are Lietzmann, "Prozess Jesu," 251–55 (cited according to the collection); Eduard Lohse, *Die Geschichte des Leidens und Sterbens Jesu Christi* (Gütersloh: Mohn, 1979) 69–73; and C. F. Evans, 830–33.
11 Goulder (*New Paradigm*, 2:753) explains the sequence of the Lukan pericopes in the following way: "It is topically and liturgically convenient to have the Denial material together at cockcrow, and the Trial matter together at dawn." In the same paragraph he states his opinion that Luke omits here certain details in order to use them later in connection with Stephen (Acts 6:11-14).
12 Fitzmyer (2:1461–62) remarks with astonishment that the Lukan version of the trial is less anti-Jewish than its parallel in the Gospel of Mark. He also notes that the absence of witnesses and the lack of any reference to the destruction of the temple make vague the charges against Jesus.
13 C. F. Evans (832) rightly thinks that many of the Synoptic differences in this pericope come from the differences in christological matters.
14 In Acts 22:5 Luke will use it a second time. In Luke's day the author of 1 Timothy is the first to use the term to define the group of "elders" or "presbyters" of a Christian church (1 Tim 4:14); see C. F. Evans (834), who thinks that it is simply an accident that this term does not appear in Greek prior to Luke. On the vocabulary and the syntax of v. 66, see Lagrange, 571.
15 Josephus (*Ant.* 12.3.3 §142) describes this institution with the expression ἡ γερουσία καὶ οἱ ἱερεῖς καὶ οἱ γραμματεῖς ("the assembly of the elders, the priests, and the scribes"). On the words πρεσβυτέριον, γερουσία, and συνέδριον see C. F. Evans, 834.

also knows that two other groups belong to it and that one of them in particular has been active against Jesus, he adds "chief priests and scribes" (the coordinating τέ καί connects these two groups to one another rather than to the preceding word, the well-known πρεσβυτέριον).[16] Grammatically, this expression, "chief priests and scribes" (without the definite article), is in apposition, but it appears to be rather flexible in Luke so that he can mention the three groups of the Sanhedrin. As for the word συνέδριον, it is usually used to speak about the Sanhedrin, but it can also mean the meeting of this official assembly.[17] The following αὐτῶν appears awkward only if the members of the Sanhedrin are the subject of the verb, "they led" (ἀπήγαγον),[18] but it is better to give this verb an impersonal subject, "one led him." One led him before "their Sanhedrin" (τὸ συνέδριον αὐτῶν), that is to say, the Sanhedrin that these groups constitute. The verb "to lead" implies that the meeting was held somewhere other than in the house of the high priest to which Jesus initially had been brought (v. 54). Finally, it could be that συνέδριον here means the place where they met. Such a sense is found in other documents.[19]

Various recent historical studies have analyzed the nature and the function of the Sanhedrin.[20] They have shown that the Mishna tractate *Sanhedrin* gives an idealized image of the institution. In the first century were there two legal bodies, a Great and a Small Sanhedrin? Was there a βουλή ("a council"), as in the Hellenistic cities alongside a συνέδριον? Was this συνέδριον an authority that met regularly, or did it come together only when circumstances required? In my opinion there was in Jesus' day an authority called συνέδριον ("Sanhedrin" in Hebrew), made up of elders, priests, and scribes;[21] the extent of their prerogatives remains, alas, obscure. This body appears to have had certain political and legal powers. On one point the Gospels are in agreement: This council was able to refer Jesus to Pilate to accuse him.

■ **67** Mark lets the trial begin by introducing witnesses who put forth a statement of Jesus about the destruction of the temple (14:57-61a). Since Mark is not clear about what they say,[22] Luke prefers to omit this cumbersome testimony.[23]

No disciple attended the meeting of the Sanhedrin; everything the Gospels write on this subject is based on a partisan reconstruction.[24] Nevertheless, the charges leveled against Jesus had to be in circulation. The *titulus*,

---

16   For the most part Luke uses the enclitic τε followed by καί; see 2:16; 12:45; 21:11; etc. (always in the Gospel); Plummer, 518.

17   See, e.g., John 11:47. On the presence of the word in inscriptions and Josephus, see Fitzmyer, 2:1466.

18   A number of manuscripts have ἀνήγαγον ("they made [him] go up"), which could have the legal sense "they referred [him]," instead of ἀπήγαγον ("they led" [translated "one led"]); see the apparatus of Nestle-Aland (27th ed.) on this text. Grotius (*Annotationes*, 912) prefers ἀνήγαγον, because in his opinion the Sanhedrin held its meeting in a higher portico. Xenophon (*Hist. Graec.* 3.3.11) and Josephus (*Ant.* 12.10.1 §390) use ἀνάγω in the legal sense; see BAGD, s.v. ἀνάγω, 2.

19   See BAGD, s.v. συνέδριον, 3. Lagrange (571) rejects this hypothesis.

20   See McLaren, *Power and Politics*; Donahue, "Trial of Jesus," 96–97; Bovon, *Last Days*, 34–38.

21   In addition to the Gospels, Josephus also attests the tripartite structure of the Sanhedrin; see n. 15 above.

22   From the beginning Mark speaks of false testimony, even though the statement of these people corresponds to a saying of Jesus that is making the rounds of various circles: the temple will be destroyed, and another, not made with human hands, will be built. What is false in their statement is the ἐγώ ("I"); Jesus had never claimed that he himself would destroy the temple; see Mark 14:57–58 par. Matt 26:61; John 2:19-22; Mark 15:29 par. Matt 27:40; Mark 13:2 par. Matt 24:2 par. Luke 21:6; Acts 6:14; John 4:21-23; Benoit, *Passion and Resurrection*, 99–104.

23   It has been correctly stated that Luke was familiar with the Markan episode of the false witnesses but that he wanted to conceal it. According to Schneider (2:468), Jesus' answer to the second question, in his opinion a positive answer, makes mentioning the witnesses useless. It has also been noted that at the end of the pericope Luke replaced the word "witnesses" (Mark 14:63) with the word "testimony" (v. 71). On the other hand, it has not been pointed out sufficiently that Luke probably borrowed the word "testimony" from two earlier verses of Mark (Mark 14:55-56).

24   Schneider ("Synedrium") offers a good methodological approach by prefacing the historical investigation with a rigorous analysis of the sources.

the inscription attached to the cross, shows that Pilate condemned Jesus for a political reason. This is the way the governor reacted against anything he regarded as a threat to public order and to Roman authority. While Christian sources know that the Jewish authorities played a role in the fate of Jesus and tend to emphasize it, Jewish and Roman sources sometimes note the responsibility of the local courts and sometimes that of the Roman power. An old rabbinic text thinks that Jesus' hanging was a Jewish affair, while Tacitus speaks only of Pilate.[25] The oldest Christian document, Paul's first letter to the Thessalonians, places a great emphasis on Israel's responsibility (1 Thess 2:14-16). The predictions of the passion do not ignore Jesus' scene before the Sanhedrin (Luke 9:22 par. Mark 8:31 par. Matt 16:21), nor do they forget his appearance before the Romans (Luke 18:32-33). In my view, it is certain that Jesus first appeared before a Jewish court, which immediately turned him over to Roman authority.[26]

Luke is certain that the Sanhedrin asked[27] about Jesus' messiahship,[28] and, unlike Mark but in agreement with Matt 26:64, he thinks that Jesus avoids a direct answer.[29] To express this evasiveness Luke makes use of a traditional saying (about which John testifies that it was in circulation) and adapts it to his needs: "The Jews surrounded him and said to him, 'How long will you keep us in suspense? If you are the Christ, tell us openly!' Jesus answered them, 'I told you, and you do not believe'" (John 10:24-25).[30] It is not the first time that Jesus evades difficulty in a controversy. The best-known precedent is the time Jesus responded with silence when he was asked about authority (20:1-8). Today's question (v. 67) is not much different from yesterday's question (20:2).[31] Here, as there, Luke thinks that the question is a trap and that the Master was right not to be drawn into it.[32] In fact, the end of the Gospel and the entire book of Acts confirm that most of Israel did not "believe" that Jesus was the Messiah.[33] It has been said that a messianic claim constituted neither a blasphemy nor an error that would lead to death. That is right from the Jewish point of view, but, given the royal implications of any messianic claim, it was quite different for the Romans. Since Jesus' fate could not avoid the occupier's control, it is not surprising that the Jewish authorities raised the question of Jesus' messianic identity. Nor was the question unimportant for Israel as well, because false pretenders were to be exposed, just as were false prophets or the priests of iniquity. The question was on which side was the true and on which side the false.[34]

25 It is a *baraita* of the tractate *Sanhedrin* 6.1 or, according to another division, *b. Sanh.* 43a; Tacitus *Ann.* 15.44; see Bovon, *Last Days*, 21–22.

26 On the relation between the divergent accounts of the Gospels and historical reality, see Bock (2:1791–94), who by harmonization and addition tries to preserve the historicity of most of the information given by the evangelists.

27 According to Lagrange (572), there is "something engaging and confidential" about the words "tell us."

28 Cyril of Alexandria (*Serm. Luc.* 150) is astonished that the Jewish authorities asked the question. Do not the prophetic writings as well as Jesus' miracles answer the question? See Payne Smith, *Cyril*, 2:705.

29 The subordinate clause "if you are the Messiah" is a hypothetical question in a real case (thus the indicative and the absence of ἄν), unlike a hypothetical question in possible cases (with ἄν and the subjunctive) in vv. 67b and 68. See Smyth, *Greek Grammar* §§2289–2301. Another possibility is that εἰ could introduce a subordinate interrogative. One would then translate "are you the Christ?" The sense would not be much different. Bock (2:1794–

95) is undoubtedly wrong to act as if these two uses were independent of each other.

30 The commentators also refer to an Old Testament precedent, Jer 38:14-15 [LXX 45:14-15], which is more formal than thematic.

31 See the commentary above on 20:2. One thinks also of Jesus' enigmatic remarks on the Messiah Son of David, 20:41-44. As C. F. Evans (837) notes, the style is more reminiscent of a discussion than of an interrogation. Cyril of Alexandria (*Serm. Luc.*, 150) also refers to these two other texts that show the same attitude of Jesus; see Payne Smith, *Cyril*, 2:705–6.

32 Ambrose of Milan (*Exp. Luc.* 10.97) congratulates Jesus for not answering, for he is convinced that "the best cause is that which is justified without being defended."

33 Twice here Luke uses οὐ μή followed by a verb in the aorist subjunctive. It is a question of expressing energetically the possibility of failure; see BDF §365.

34 On the question of the true and false prophet, the true and false Messiah, the true and false high priest, see Gottfried Quell, *Wahre und falsche Propheten: Versuch einer Interpretation* (BFCTh

■ **68** It is understandable that some Latin manuscripts omit v. 68,[35] since this verse simply confirms Jesus' reserved attitude (v. 67b). Still, the repetition is not useless. On the formal level it gives Jesus' answer a rhetorical dimension,[36] and on the thematic level it reverses the roles. Although he is being questioned, Jesus presumes that he can begin to ask questions.[37] The defendant already sees himself as judge. The following verse will continue along this line, since a function of the Son of Man is to judge human beings. What the evangelist John shows in the light of day,[38] Luke implies: The judge is not who we think.[39]

■ **69** It is not the first time that Jesus has surprised people by resorting to the title "Son of Man."[40] When Peter confesses that Jesus is the Messiah, the latter announces the cruel fate of the Son of Man (9:22 par.; see also 9:44). When he mentions the events of the end of time, he predicts the arrival of the Son of Man on the clouds (21:27 par. Mark 13:26 par. Matt 24:30). The reader understands, but the Sanhedrin hears and is surprised[41]—surprised initially, because after having avoided any explanation (vv. 67b-68) Jesus nevertheless gives an answer; then surprised because nothing in the sentence indicates that Jesus is this Son of Man. But it is the readers who matter. They have known for a long time that Jesus, modest and glorious, is the Son of Man predicted by the prophet Daniel. Thus, Jesus, who has just refused to give a direct answer to a malicious question, announces to all who are willing to hear it in faith that the Son of Man, who shares the human condition (7:34), enjoys divine authority (5:24), and has agreed to follow the path that leads to death (18:31-33), will soon be exalted.[42] Luke uses the Markan parallel (14:62) as his inspiration, but he boldly reworks the prophecy. He does

---

46.1; Gütersloh: Bertelsmann, 1952); James E. Brenneman, *Canons in Conflict: Negotiating Texts in True and False Prophecy* (New York: Oxford University Press, 1997).

35 The reference is to e, an Old Latin manuscript (fifth century) preserved at Trent in Italy as well as some manuscripts of the Vulgate; see the apparatus of Nestle-Aland (27th ed.) on the text. Marcion appears to have omitted it too; see Harnack, *Marcion*, 234*; Wiefel, 385.

36 C. F. Evans (836) notes the literary quality of the four equal proposals that make up Jesus' answer in vv. 67b and 68. He also notes that the verb "to say" in the answer repeats the "tell us" of the question (v. 67a).

37 Lagrange (572) recalls that Jesus had earlier posed the question about the Messiah (20:41); see also Tannehill (329): "Note the reference to Jesus as questioner in verse 68"; Bock (2:1796): "By appearances Jesus is subject to the judgment of the leadership, but ironically he says that in reality they are judged by him."

38 In the scene structured so well in John 18:28—19:16 the evangelist announces—certainly *sub contrario*—Jesus' kingship (19:3) and declares that Pilate installs the defendant on the seat of judgment (19:13; many exegetes, however, understand the verb $\kappa\alpha\vartheta\acute{\iota}\zeta\omega$, "to seat," in the intransitive sense of "to sit").

39 At the end of v. 68 the text is not secure. Some manuscripts add $\mu o\iota$ ("to me") to the verb "to answer." Still others—the variant is more important—also add $\mu o\iota$ but make it follow the words $\mathring{\eta}$ $\mathring{\alpha}\pi o\lambda\acute{\upsilon}\sigma\eta\tau\epsilon$, which gives: "You would not answer me or you would release me" or "You would neither answer me nor release me" (the translation is difficult). Although it is attested by Codex Alexandrinus (A = 02), Codex Bezae (D = 05), the Freer Codex (W = 032), a manuscript from Athos (Ψ = 044), the family of minuscules f^{13}, and the Byzantine tradition, this long reading must be secondary. Indeed, it disturbs the balance of Jesus' two sentences (v. 67b and v. 68) and introduces a new element (Jesus' release); see Metzger, *Commentary* (2d ed.), 152; Fitzmyer, 2:1467; and especially Duplacy ("Variante"), who, by contrast, advocates the long reading.

40 Tannehill (329) comments that in this v. 69 Jesus introduces a new element, namely, that the suffering Son of Man will receive messianic power after the events that are presently taking place.

41 Catchpole (*Trial*, 140–41) presents several Jewish texts that bring clarity to our passage. One of them in particular, *b. Sanh.* 38b, reports on an incident that must have happened at the beginning of the second century of the Common Era. Various rabbis were opposed to Rabbi Aqiba, who held the opinion that David would have his place at the right hand of God. It was their judgment that this presence would profane the Shekinah, the presence of God, and would constitute blasphemy (see *m. Sanh.* 6.4); see also Bock, 2:1798.

42 Here the opinion of Cyril of Alexandria, *Serm. Luc.* 150; see Payne Smith, *Cyril,* 2:707: Because they show their ignorance and do not understand the mystery, the members of the Sanhedrin learn from Jesus—in the saying on the Son of Man (v. 69)—

not like the verb "you will see" addressed to the adversaries,[43] whereas he wants those who read the Gospel in faith to hear. He also avoids this verb, because what is important to him here is not the parousia but the Easter exaltation. Luke thus eliminates the verb "you will see" and in the same move eliminates the reference to "coming with the clouds of heaven" (Mark 14:62). He keeps the sitting at the right hand of God. Unlike the parousia, the exaltation has the advantage of already having happened[44] (because of the formula ἀπὸ τοῦ νῦν, "from now on," the future "will be" [ἔσται has the value of an immediate future]).[45] It is not visible, as the parousia will be, but it calls forth the certainty that encourages, and that is enough for faith.

■ **70** Even if they do not agree with it, the members of the Sanhedrin unanimously (πάντες, "all")[46] follow the argument. They said to themselves: He doesn't want to admit it openly, but even if he does not speak of the Son of Man inappropriately, he is inordinately ambitious. He is a charismatic who believes in his prophetic gift and—who knows—in his messianic future. Thus they ask their second question: "So you are the Son of God?" That is

the narrative logic. Even more important, however, is the christological logic.[47]

The evangelist is aware of the ambiguities of the term "Messiah,"[48] a term familiar to Jews but foreign to Greeks. Doubling the question initially has a didactic function. By repeating the question and by formulating it in terms of "Son of God," Luke the teacher facilitates the task of his questioners. Moreover, the evangelist is familiar with this process and makes use of it at critical moments of his work. In particular, he has used it when defining precisely the love of one's enemies (6:27-28, compared with Matt 5:44).[49]

But there is more here than an effort to explain things for Greeks; there is also a doctrinal desire. According to Luke, Jesus' adversaries are thinking of a Davidic Messiah with political ambitions, a leader who wants to call Israel to insurrection against the Romans. There were, indeed, such seditious leaders, and Luke, like Josephus, knows some of them.[50] That is why the Jesus movement creates fear and the authorities go so far as to denounce the Master to Pilate (23:1-5). While he reiterates the question, Luke absolutely makes a point of

---

that they have only a little time left to exert their power: until the hour of the cross. After that there will be the reign of the Son of Man. The Venerable Bede (*In Luc.* 6.1211–20) and then Bonaventure (*Comm. Luc.* 22.82 [Bernardini, 564] interpret v. 69 on the Son of Man and his exaltation with the help of the Philippian hymn (Phil 2:6-11). This must be an exegetical tradition of the West.

43 He replaces it with the future of the verb to be: ἔσται, "he will be."

44 Fitzmyer (2:1463) writes that the Lukan version "has divested the answer of some of its apocalyptic stage props."

45 John Albert Bengel (*Gnomon of the New Testament* [trans. Charlton T. Lewis and Marvin R. Vincent; 2 vols.; Philadelphia: Perkinpine & Higgins, 1860, 1862] 1:520) comments as follows: "This itself was his path to glory." Plummer (518) quotes it in its more concise Latin version: *Hoc ipsum erat iter ad gloriam.* See also Fitzmyer (2:1467) and Schneider (2:469), according to whom Luke understands the expression "from now on" in salvation-historical terms: it refers to the time of the church, when the Son of Man is exalted beyond death.

46 The word πάντες is unique to Luke; the other evangelists do not underscore this unanimity. See, however, Mark 14:64.

47 See Schneider, 2:470.

48 On ὁ χριστός in Luke, see Bovon, *Luke the Theologian*, 212–14, 532–36; and vol. 1 of this commentary, 89, on 2:11.

49 See vol. 1 of this commentary, 234–39, on 6:27-28.

50 Without necessarily having been leaders, there are Barabbas (23:18-19) and the two thieves at the cross (23:33, 39-43); more serious leaders of sedition were Theudas and Judas the Galilean (Acts 5:36-37). For our purposes it matters little that Luke is mistaken in the chronology (in reality Judas preceded Theudas). The historian Josephus knows these latter two characters, as well as others who claimed to be the Messiah and who wanted to claim leadership during the Jewish revolt of the years 66–70 C.E. See Josephus *Ant.* 20.5.5 §§97–99; 18.1.1 §§4–10; 20.5.2 §102; Bo Reicke, *The New Testament Era: The World of the Bible from 500 B.C. to A.D. 100* (trans. David E. Green; Philadelphia: Fortress Press, 1968) 112, 136–37, 176, 204–6, 258–60; Prigent, *Fin de Jérusalem*, 18–21; Horsley and Hanson, *Bandits*, 88–134.

avoiding misunderstanding: Jesus is the Messiah,[51] but it is necessary to understand the significance of the term. He is the "Son of God" on the other side of death. The sitting occurs not in the palace at the right hand of the temple; it is the heavenly exaltation at the right hand of the Father (see 24:51; Acts 2:33; 3:19-21; 7:55-56). In the account of the annunciation, Luke had given the same christological argument. After the prediction of the Davidic Messiah (1:30-33), the angel had described to Mary the divine identity of the child she would bear. It was the same Son-of-God title that made possible the transition from one meaning of the concept of Messiah to another (1:35).[52]

It is not easy to sense the nuance that Luke gives to Jesus' second answer. Does the Nazarene congratulate the Sanhedrin, or does he once again refuse to answer? In my opinion, the evangelist initially confirms Jesus' reserve in vv. 67-68: "It is you who say that[53] I am,"[54] I did not say anything. But then he implies that if the Sanhedrin, hostile as it is, proclaims it to be true, then it must be true. Thus, there is ambivalence between a refusal and an agreement. In fact, even if one chooses the agreement, the words "I am it," in Greek ἐγώ εἰμι, literally, "I am," are also ambiguous, since they mean either "that is right" or that the divine title, the absolute "I am," can be applied to Jesus.[55]

■ **71** The members of the Sanhedrin[56] intervene finally, because they think they have heard Jesus make an admission in his own words. But they heard "It is you who say that I am" (v. 70b) in the sense of "you are right to say so," and the phrase about the Son of Man (v. 69)

as referring to the speaker. They do not need external[57] evidence.[58] To express this conclusion Luke remains close to his source, Mark 14:63b, even if he conceals the charge of blasphemy and does not explicitly mention the decision against Jesus (Mark 14:64).

History of Interpretation

I am interested in limiting this historical investigation[59] to what may well be one of the oldest disputes over the interpretation of a Lukan passage—that between Tertullian (*Adv. Marc.* 4.41.3–5) and Marcion. Marcion's position, which we can reconstruct only from the statements of his opponents, can be summarized as follows: At this time Christ did not reveal his identity to the Sanhedrin, "because . . . he had to be able to suffer" (*Adv. Marc.* 4.41.3).[60] According to Marcion, the Savior's suffering had to proceed, even if it were not going to be real agony. This position calls to mind what the apostle Paul says in First Corinthians: "We speak God's wisdom, secret and hidden, which God decreed before the ages for our glory. None of the rulers of this age understood this; for if they had, they would not have crucified the Lord of glory" (1 Cor 2:7-8). It also approximates what is said about the coming of the Savior to human beings in the *Ascension of Isaiah* (10:16-31), the *Epistula Apostolorum* (13–14), and the *Pistis Sophia* (7.11–15; this text emphasizes the final ascension through the spheres more than the descent). In order for the divine plan to be realized, the Son had to descend through the heavenly spheres to manifest himself on the human level without being recognized

---

51   Luke continues to repeat it in Acts (see already Acts 2:36, then, e.g., 9:20-22).

52   See vol. 1 of this commentary, 51–52, on 1:30-35; Sabourin, 357; Kilgallen, "First Trial," 402–3, 410, 413–14.

53   Plummer (519) correctly thinks that the ὅτι of v. 70b must have the declaratory sense of "that" rather than the meaning of "because."

54   In Euripides' tragedy *Hippolytus* (352), the nurse asks Phaedra for the name of the man she loves. When the nurse suggests it is Hippolytus, Phaedra answers: "You are the one who says it, not I" (σοῦ τάδ᾽, οὐκ ἐμοῦ κλύεις, literally, "You understand that from you, not from me").

55   The absolute ἐγώ εἰμι ("I am"), reserved for God, has its roots in the introduction of the Lord in Exod 3:14. It appears in the Gospel of John (8:58).

56   Mark is more concrete; he includes the scene in which the high priest tears his clothing (14:63a).

57   Even if he has training as a rhetorician, Luke is not interested in showing his competence in legal matters. He wants to make understandable the result achieved and not the procedure followed.

58   On the concept of witnessing and witnesses in Luke-Acts, see Bovon, *Luke the Theologian*, 416–19.

59   In the previous notes I called attention to some comments of Ambrose of Milan, of Cyril of Alexandria, of the Venerable Bede, and of Bonaventure. See above, nn. 28, 31, 32, and 42.

60   Trans. Ernest Evans, *Tertullian: Adversus Marcionem*, (2 vols.; Oxford Early Christian Texts; Oxford: Clarendon, 1972) 2:497.

by the angels stationed on each of the seven overarching heavens.

Tertullian's position awakens a double interest both by the aggressive spirit he exerts against his opponent and by the lively attention he brings to the text of the Gospel. First of all, he maintains ironically that Marcion's interpretation leads to a contradiction: How could the good God be so cruel as voluntarily to put the Jewish leaders in ignorance? Then he expresses the opinion that the motive described by Marcion is not accurate. Even if Jesus had answered them openly and revealed his true identity, by Jesus' own words (v. 67) his opponents would not have believed him, and they would have continued to seek his death. In any event, since, according to Marcion, the true identity of the Savior was that he was a different God, the members of the Sanhedrin, committed to their own God, would not have tolerated such a claim and, according to Tertullian, they would have unhesitatingly sent Christ to his martyrdom.

The African then says delicately what in his eyes is the true reason for Jesus' hesitation: Displaying his identity at this time would serve no good purpose, since his conversation partners, who "ought to have known who he was from his works which were in fulfillment of the scriptures," wanted to extort a confession from him (*Adv. Marc.* 4.41.3).[61] Christ's discretion is legitimate and honorable; he does not force himself on people, and he wants to be personally recognized. Sensing the nuances of the Gospel text, Tertullian then gives an account of the Son of Man in v. 69. In his opinion, Jesus does not leave his questioners empty-handed. He does not want to force on them what is obvious from the evidence, yet he suggests to them who he is. This crutch he gives them is the statement about the Son of Man (v. 69). Tertullian knows his Bible, and he refers the statement to the prophecy of Daniel (7:13) and to the Psalms (109 [110]:1). He notes, moreover, that the members of the Sanhedrin follow the line of reasoning and draw the essential conclusion: they introduce the title "Son of God" (v. 70a). In the eyes of the African, Jesus' answer (v. 70b) to this second intrusion is initially a new way of refusing to be engaged. And yet—Tertullian is not at all lacking in finesse—Jesus also approves of the opinion of his opponents. The analysis of the second duel between Jesus and the Jewish leaders finally leads Tertullian to his ultimate criticism addressed to Marcion: When they say "Son of God," the Jewish notables are thinking of their God (and not of Marcion's unknown God). If in the end Jesus approves of what they say, it is because he too accepts that there is only one God. Finally, we must take the statement "Then you are the Son of God" as an assertion and not as a question (*Adv. Marc.* 4.41.5). Tertullian does not doubt that the members of the Sanhedrin understood what Jesus implied: Christ's identity is obvious when we read the Scripture and take seriously his work.

Conclusion

As long as Christ has not ascended to the right hand of God, the confrontation between Jewish faith and Christian faith cannot take place openly. It is in the book of Acts that Luke will bring the two ways into face-to-face confrontation. For the time being questions alternate with equivocations and interrogations with suggestions. Who is Jesus? Is he the Messiah? Is he thus the Son of God? Does the Son of Man clarify the debate? These questions and their curious responses provoke faith and reinforce incredulity. Believing readers side with Jesus. They confess him to be the Messiah, the Son of God in the Christian sense. They recognize him as the Son of Man. Their position is strengthened by the agreement between the prophecies of Scripture and their fulfillment in the ministry of Jesus. Yet the narrative does not portray believers who accept the words of Jesus; it speaks of the opposition the Master encounters.

---

61   Trans. Evans, *Tertullian*.

Jesus before Pilate
(23:1-5)

Bibliography

Aletti, *Art de raconter*, 155–76.

Bailey, John Amedee, *The Traditions Common to the Gospels of Luke and John* (NovTSup 7; Leiden: Brill, 1969) 64–77.

Bammel, Ernst, "The Trial before Pilate," in idem and C. F. D. Moule, eds. *Jesus and the Politics of His Day* (Cambridge: Cambridge University Press, 1984) 403–12, 425–51.

Blinzler, *Prozess*, 175–204.

Borse, Udo, "Die geschichtliche Absicherung (Lk 23,5-16) des christologischen Psalmwortes (Ps 2,1s/LXX) und seiner Auslegung (Apg 4,25-28)," *SNTU* 26 (2001) 129–38.

Brown, *Death of the Messiah*, 1:627–35, 665–759.

Colin, Jean, "Sur le procès de Jésus devant Pilate et le peuple," *REA* 67 (1965) 159–64.

Ehman, John W., "Luke 23:1-49," *Int* 52 (1998) 74–76.

Finegan, *Überlieferung*, 25–27.

Garnsey, Peter, "The Criminal Jurisdiction of Governors," *JRomS* 58 (1968) 51–59.

George, Augustin, "Le sens de la mort de Jésus," in idem, *Études sur l'oeuvre de Luc* (Sources bibliques; Paris: Gabalda, 1978).

Heil, John Paul, "Reader-Response and the Irony of the Trial of Jesus in Luke 23:1-25," *ScEs* 43 (1991) 175–86.

Heusler, Erika, *Kapitalprozess im lukanischen Doppelwerk: Die Verfahren gegen Jesus und Paulus in exegetischer und rechtshistorischer Analyse* (NTAbh n.s. 38; Münster: Aschendorff, 2000).

Horvath, Tibor, "Why Was Jesus Brought to Pilate?" *NovT* 11 (1969) 174–84.

Irmscher, Johannes, "σὺ λέγεις (Mark xv.2—Matt. xxvii.11—Luke xxiii.3)," *Studii Clasice* 2 (1960) 151–58.

Kastner, Karl, *Jesus vor Pilatus: Ein Beitrag zur Leidensgeschichte des Herrn* (NTAbh 4/2–3; Münster: Aschendorff, 1912) 64–78.

Kwaak, Hans van der, *Het proces van Jezus: Een vergelijkend onderzoek van de beschrijvingen der evangelisten* (Assen: Van Gorcum, 1969).

Léon-Dufour, Xavier, "Passion," *DBSup* 6 (1960) 1419–92.

Lietzmann, "Prozess Jesu," 313–22.

Matera, Frank J., "Luke 12:1-25: Jesus before Pilate, Herod, and Israel," in Frans Neirynck, ed., *L'Évangile de Luc—The Gospel of Luke* (2d ed.; BEThL 32; Leuven: Leuven University Press/Peeters, 1989).

Neagoe, Alexandru, *The Trial of the Gospel: An Apologetic Reading of Luke's Trial Narratives* (Cambridge: Cambridge University Press, 2002).

Radl, "Sonderüberlieferungen," 131–47.

Robinson, William C., *The Way of the Lord: A Study of History and Eschatology in the Gospel of Luke* (diss., Basel; Eng. trans. published privately, 1962) 43–56 (German: Hamburg: Reich, 1964, pp. 30–36).

Schneider, *Passion Jesu*, 83–94.

Idem, "The Political Charge against Jesus," in Bammel and Moule, *Jesus and the Politics of His Day*, 403–14.

Vicent Cernuda, Antonio, "Nacimiento y verdad de Jesús ante Pilato," *EstBib* 50 (1992) 537–51.

Idem, "Pro Barrabás, contra Jesús!" *EstBib* 59 (2001) 29–46.

---

1 **Then the entire multitude of them arose and led him before Pilate. 2/ They began to accuse him with these words: "We found this individual[a] perverting our nation, forbidding paying taxes to Caesar, and saying he was Christ King." 3/ Pilate questioned him saying, "Are you the king of the Jews?"[b] He answered thus: "You say it."[c] 4/ Pilate said to the chief priests and to the crowd, "I find no guilt in this man." 5/ But they insisted, saying that he agitates the people, teaching throughout all Judea,[d] beginning in Galilee even to this place.**

a   Literally: "this one."
b   Or: "Is this you, the king of the Jews?"
c   Or: "You are the one who says it."
d   On the necessity of giving an extensive meaning to this term "Judea," see the commentary below on 23:5.

Luke, who regards Christ as the "judge of the living and the dead" (Acts 10:42), has him appear here before Pilate, the judge of the temporal power of that age. In addition to the dramatic abasement of a judge in the role of the accused, there is the unbearable paradox of the divine delivered to the human.[1] Although these tensions are present, they remain hidden. Yet the structure of Luke's entire Gospel and Acts expresses them and gives an accounting of them.

Analysis

The few verses analyzed here form the link of a chain.[2] With the following events, the appearance before Herod (23:6-12), Pilate's conversation with the Jewish authorities (23:13-16), and the decision of the indecisive Pilate (23:18-25), they constitute a literary unit in which the Roman governor is the main figure. In addition, the appearance before Pilate cannot be explained without what precedes it: the meeting of the Sanhedrin (22:66-71), which logically continues the making of the plot (22:1-6) and the arrest (22:47-53).[3] If we remember the intensity of Jesus' dialogue with his disciples in the upper room and in the garden on the Mount of Olives, we can see the progression from Jesus' presence among his own, his new community (22:7-46), to his confrontation with the authorities of Israel, his community of origin (22:47-

71), and his meeting with Pilate, the representative of Rome's worldwide power (23:1-25).

The appearance before Pilate proceeds according to a logic that respects both the narrative requirements and the Roman procedural rules.[4] Jesus is brought by his adversaries (v. 1); they accuse him (v. 2); the judge turns to the accused to question him (v. 3a); the latter responds, admittedly evasively (v. 3b); the judge expresses his opinion (v. 4); this opinion, that the accused is innocent, provokes renewed opposition on the part of the accusers (v. 5). The evangelist thinks that the trial is not closed, and he gives it an unexpected turn. Roman law knows the *remissio*,[5] and it is a remission, admittedly a temporary delay, that Pilate offers. The mention of Jesus' ministry in Galilee (v. 5) reminds him that Herod, the prince of Galilee, is in Jerusalem during these holidays, so he decides to let Jesus appear before him (vv. 6-7).[6]

We must compare the Lukan version of the trial before Pilate with those of the other Gospels. Mark's arrangement and, following him, that of Matthew have neither the logic nor the elegance of the Lukan account. Following a morning meeting of the Sanhedrin, about which no details are given, the Jewish authorities bring Jesus to Pilate after they have bound him (Mark 15:1 par. Matt 27:1-2).[7] Without a charge made here, Pilate immediately asks Jesus about his possible royal identity.

---

1 See John Calvin's interpretation presented below at the end of the "History of Interpretation" of this pericope.

2 Matera ("Jesus before Pilate," 535) speaks of "an extended trial composed of four scenes" (before the Sanhedrin, before Pilate, before Herod, and again before Pilate).

3 According to Talbert (*Reading*, 212), 22:39—23:25 is a unit, and this unit is part of a larger whole made up of 22:1—23:56. According to Meynet (*Guide*, 104, and *Évangile*, 1:215 and 2:224–29), it is 22:54—23:25 that constitutes a unit, and it is in the form of a chiasm:
Peter abandons Jesus (22:54-62)
 The guards toy with Jesus (22:63-65)
  Before the Sanhedrin (22: 66-70)
   Verdict (22:71)
  Before the governor (23:1-5)
 Herod toys with Jesus (23:6-12)
All abandon Jesus (23:13-25).

Personally, I do not think that Luke is particularly concerned to emphasize v. 71 in chap. 22.

4 See Bovon, *Last Days*, 44–46.

5 On this *remissio*, see Bammel, "Trial," 423.

6 Meynet (*Évangile*, 2:227) is of the opinion that, after the introduction in v. 1, the trial before Pilate, vv. 2-5, "is constructed concentrically." Verses 2 and 5 (Jewish accusations) correspond to each other, as do vv. 3a and 4 (Pilate's words). Verse 3b, the statement of Jesus, who, according to Meynet, accepts the royal title, occupies the center of the literary unit.

7 Matthew (and he is the only one who does it) intercalates here the episode of the death of Judas (27:3-10). Luke is familiar with a completely different version of this account, and at the beginning of the book of Acts he puts it in Peter's mouth (Acts 1:16-20).

Jesus' answer is identical in the three Synoptic Gospels: Σὺ λέγεις, "you say it" or "you are the one who says it" (v. 3 par. Mark 15:2 par. Matt 27:11). The rest of the account in Mark and Matthew differs from that of Luke. The charges of the Jewish authorities then rain down on Jesus before Pilate questions the defendant again, indeed, two more times. Jesus remains silent both times, which does not fail to surprise Pilate (Mark 15:3-5 par. Matt 27:12-14). According to the hypothesis I hold in this commentary, Luke does not know Matthew, but he does know Mark. What is his attitude here? Two solutions have been proposed. According to the first, Luke does not tolerate Mark's logical awkwardness well, and he restores the narrative logic that conforms with the ordinary course of a Roman trial and writes the entire narrative in his style and with his words.[8] What he respects in Mark because it is central in his eyes is Pilate's first question ("Are you the king of the Jews?") and Jesus' answer ("You say it"). Except for a few details, Luke's v. 3 corresponds to Mark 15:2. According to the second solution, Luke depends here on his special source, which in its own way tells of Jesus' appearance before Pilate.[9] Various arguments speak for this hypothesis. There are considerable differences between the vocabularies of the Lukan and Markan versions. To be sure, Luke likes to improve Mark's prose, but he seldom does so in such proportions (of the eighty-nine words in the passage, Luke shares only twenty of them with Mark).[10] The narrative sequence is also different. If the beginnings resemble one another here and there (after the meeting of the Sanhedrin, Jesus is brought before Pilate),[11] only Luke logically mentions the charges brought against Jesus (v. 2). After the core of the short exchange between Pilate and Jesus that the two have in common (v. 3), the accounts diverge. Luke is not aware of Pilate's new questions, Jesus' silence in response, and the governor's final surprise. Mark, on the other hand, does not know Pilate's declaration of Jesus' innocence or the new grievances brought by the Jewish authorities (relating to Jesus' itinerant teaching).

It is difficult to decide. After great hesitation I choose an editorial reworking of Mark. The vocabulary of these verses is indeed Lukan and does not make one think of the characteristics of the special source.[12] Staying for the moment with v. 1,[13] when one thinks of the participle ἀναστάν ("arose"), of ἅπαν ("entire"), of τὸ πλῆθος ("the multitude"), or of the thematic arrangement of the complaints made about Jesus—the seduction of the people, Jesus' teaching, the risk of sedition—all arguments made against the Christians in the book of Acts,[14] one will admit that Luke begins with and improves the Gospel of Mark. According to the hypothesis of alternating sources that I follow,[15] one sees that at the end of the episode (v. 5) Luke stops copying Mark and, beginning with the Herod episode (v. 6), continues with his special source. He was also astute enough to mention Galilee in connection with the ministry of Jesus (v. 5), thus creating a welcome transition to the Herod episode (v. 6).

Since it is unlikely that the Gospel of John knows the Synoptics,[16] any agreement between this writing and the Gospel of Luke must have a different explanation. What links are there? On the one hand, the Fourth Gospel goes its own way and works out as an equivalent

---

8   See Creed, 279–80; Schneider, 2:471; Fitzmyer, 2:1472; Radl, "Sonderüberlieferungen"; Wiefel, 388. Matera ("Jesus before Pilate") is a vigorous advocate of Luke's dependence on Mark, and on Mark alone.

9   See Taylor, *Passion Narrative*, 86–87, 89. For Taylor, v. 3 is a Markan insertion in a non-Markan episode. Even if he does not defend it, Matera ("Jesus before Pilate," 536–37) clearly portrays this hypothesis and the exegetes who support it.

10   See Ernst, 621.

11   Luke does not say that Jesus is bound when he arrives at Pilate's court (Mark 15:1 par. Matt 27:2). This silence can come from Luke's source or from an intention of the evangelist (a reluctance to humiliate Jesus; the defendant has freedom of movement as long as Pilate's sentence is not pronounced).

12   See Fitzmyer, 2:1471–72.

13   In v. 2 one notes the verbs ἄρχομαι ("to begin"), κωλύω ("to hinder," "to forbid"); in v. 4 the use of πρός ("to") after the verb λέγω ("to say"); in v. 5 the use of κατά and the adjective ὅλος (see 4:14; 8:39).

14   See Matera ("Jesus before Pilate," 539), who refers to Acts 17:6-7 and 24:5. Bammel ("Trial," 425–26) refers to the connections between the text of Luke and the situation of Christianity at the time the evangelist was writing.

15   See Bovon, "Lukan Story of the Passion," 92–97.

16   On the other hand, there is a tendency these days to admit a literary dependence of the Fourth Gospel on the other three; see Raymond E. Brown, *An Introduction to the Gospel of John* (ed. Francis J. Maloney; New York: Doubleday, 2003) 94–104.

of the trial before Pilate the episode of Barabbas and the mocking, a complex and structured scene contrasting the "inside" of the praetorium and the "outside," where the Jews are (John 18:28—19:16).[17] The theological discussion between Pilate and Christ takes place inside; the haggling between the Jews and Pilate takes place outside. In the center of the chiastic composition, John 19:1-3, at an unspecified place, probably the threshold, Jesus receives the crown of thorns and the title of king of the Jews. For John, the soldiers who mock Jesus without knowing it speak the truth hidden behind the opposing appearances.

On the other hand, however, the Fourth Gospel shares more than one element with the Synoptics, and especially with Luke. Concerning the pericope with which we are at present concerned, we must call attention to Pilate's question, which is identical to the question reported by the Synoptics,[18] and to Jesus' answer, which is clarified and amplified in the Fourth Gospel (John 18:34-38a). We must especially note Pilate's declaration of Jesus' innocence, which John alone shares with Luke (John 18:38b). In fact, in both works Pilate expresses his opinion that Jesus is innocent three times (John 18:38b;

19:6b, 12a and Luke 23:4, 14-15, 22).[19] That the passion narratives circulated independently of one another prevented neither the similarities nor the influences. Both communities, the Lukan and the Johannine, emphasized Pilate's favorable opinion of Jesus and especially underscored the Jewish authorities' lack of intelligence.[20]

Even if he confers a religious dimension on his work, Luke does not abandon the historical perspective. He believes that what he reports should be about actual events. Thus, the modern reader, especially today's historian, asks: Can we trust Luke historically? Since I have dealt with this question elsewhere,[21] I will limit myself to my conclusion: Jesus underwent a Roman punishment, crucifixion,[22] and it was a Roman authority, the governor Pilate, who imposed this punishment on him. Wearing the title "prefect,"[23] Pilate, about whose strong and even violent character there is ample evidence,[24] quickly understood the risk of disorders that the Galilean preacher Jesus could generate. As the emperor's representative, the governor of this procuratorial province had great freedom of action. His justice was administrative; it was not bound by the *ordo*, the "order," of the Roman judicial courts. This *cognitio extra ordinem*—examination,

---

17   See Josef Blank, "Die Verhandlung vor Pilatus: Joh 18,28—19:16 im Lichte johanneischer Theologie," *BZ* 3 (1959) 60—81.

18   See Fitzmyer, 2:1475.

19   The third time, John 19:12, Pilate expresses his opinion implicitly, wanting to release his prisoner. On the possible connections between Luke and John, see Ernst, 621.

20   The *Gospel of Peter* cannot be used here as a point of comparison. The main Greek extant fragment does not begin until the end of the hearing with Pilate. Here is the beginning: "But of the Jews none washed their hands, neither Herod nor any one of his judges. And as they would not wash, Pilate arose. And then Herod the king commanded that the Lord should be marched off, saying to them, 'What I have commanded you to do to him, do ye'" (*Gos. Pet.* 1–2; trans. Christian Maurer in Schneemelcher, *New Testament Apocrypha*, 1:223).

21   See Bovon, *Last Days;* previously Blinzler, *Prozess*, 175–262; Catchpole, *Trial*, 221–60; Bammel ("Trial") is finally of the opinion—wrongly, in my judgment—that in fact historically it was the Jewish authorities and not Pilate who condemned Jesus; Lagrange (576) defends the historicity of Jesus' trial

against what he calls "the neo-mythical school." Horvath ("Why") asks why Jesus was not stoned as Stephen was. In his opinion the Jewish authorities wanted to give the Nazarene a final chance to demonstrate with a sign his messianic authority before the Roman governor.

22   Along with Bammel ("Trial," 441–42), I concede that Jewish authorities occasionally condemned guilty people to be crucified, but it is difficult to see that in this case the Sanhedrin, the religious and political authorities, did not respect the norms given by the Law of Moses—norms that are not aware of punishment by crucifixion.

23   It is later that the governor of a procuratorial province such as Judea receives the title "procurator." See Bovon, *Last Days*, 25 n. 1.

24   On Pilate, see Jean-Pierre Lemonon, *Pilate et le gouvernement de la Judée: Textes et monuments* (EtB; Paris: Gabalda, 1981); Blinzler, *Prozess*, 194–96; Warren Carter, *Pontius Pilate: Portraits of a Roman Governor* (Collegeville, MN: Liturgical Press, 2003).

accusation, and judgment apart from the *ordo*—explains why Pilate could hear this trial and conclude it so quickly.[25] On the other hand, Pilate's hesitation mentioned in the Gospels is not credible. It is to be attributed to the Christians, who after the Jewish revolt and the fall of Jerusalem in 70 C.E. emphasize the politically inoffensive character of the religious movement that their Master had launched. It is they as well who are responsible for the negative description of the Jewish authorities. The latter thought they would be well advised to refuse to recognize Jesus' authority and to maintain calm in the city that could be especially tense during the religious holidays. An anti-Roman, revolutionary wind arose regularly, and it often blew out of Galilee.[26]

Commentary

■ **1** In 22:71 the Sanhedrin was convinced that it had heard enough from Jesus and could dispense with witnesses to support the charges. At this place Luke does not specify whether that happened in order to condemn Jesus to death or to accuse him before Pilate.[27] The reader also remembers 22:1-6 and the intention to do away with Jesus. If along with the Jewish authorities Luke

mentions Pilate, whom he ordinarily wants to protect, it is because he is compelled to do so by tradition and memory.

Whether canonical (the four Gospels) or noncanonical (*Gospel of Peter* and *Acts of Pilate*), all the accounts of the passion that more or less vigorously underscore Jewish responsibility nevertheless keep the presence of the Roman governor.[28] Furthermore, among the rare episodes of the life of Jesus mentioned in the epistles is his appearance before Pilate:[29] "I charge you," writes the disciple of Paul, "in the presence of God who gives life to all things and in the presence of Christ who testified a good confession of faith before Pontius Pilate . . ." (1 Tim 6:13).[30] Thus, here in Luke 23 a mention of Pilate was simply unavoidable.

Furthermore, the name of the governor was not unknown to the attentive reader of the Third Gospel. Indeed, in the synchronism Luke establishes at the beginning of the Gospel, he adds the following clarification to the mention of the emperor Tiberius: "when Pontius Pilate was governor of Judea" (3:1).[31] The readers also realize that at this precise moment the trial swings from the Jewish side to the Roman side; yet they also note the discretion of the evangelist, who does not

25 See C. F. Evans, 840–42; Bovon, *Last Days*, 44–46. Garnsey ("Jurisdiction") shows that the right of capital punishment was granted to governors of a province since the beginning of the principate— indeed, even as early as the end of the republic, and not for the first time in the third century C.E.

26 See Ernst, 623. Bock (2:1807–8) is of the opinion that the three charges mentioned by the Jewish authorities in v. 2 come from historical memory, because they explain the crucifixion well.

27 The official residence of the Roman governor was in Caesarea. When he went up to Jerusalem, it was probably to reside on the western hill in what had been Herod's palace. It was certainly there, perhaps outdoors, that he dispensed justice. Some scholars think, on the contrary, that the trial of Jesus before Pilate took place in or before the fortress Antonia, located in the northwest corner of the temple area; see Plummer, 519–20; Blinzler, *Prozess*, 183–86; C. F. Evans, 844; Bovon, *Last Days*, 57–58.

28 Bammel ("Trial," 433–34, 446) is right to introduce into the discussion the *Testimonium Flavianum* (the controversial passage of the historian Josephus), the *Gospel of Peter*, and the *Acts of Pilate*.

29 In 1 Thess 2:15 Paul mentions only the responsibility of the Jews in the death of Christ. Mentioning the "prophets" alongside the "Lord Jesus" proves that the apostle takes his inspiration from the Deuteronomistic tradition of the nation of Israel that attacks God's messengers. Nowhere, however, does Paul deny that the Romans participated in condemning Jesus.

30 Thus, the author of 1 Timothy knows a tradition such as that of the Gospel of John, which describes a Jesus who is more active and confessional than in the Synoptic tradition. I understand ἐπὶ Ποντίου Πιλάτου in the precise sense of an appearance before a judicial body and not in the general sense of "at the time when Pontius Pilate was governor." See Schneider, *Passion Jesu*, 83 n. 1. The author of 1 Timothy knows precisely the names of the governor (Pontius is the family name, Pilate's *gens*). In the passion narrative, the Gospels are satisfied with ὁ Πιλᾶτος ("Pilate"), but in the synchronism of 3:1 Luke mentions "Pontius Pilate."

31 See Finegan, *Überlieferung*, 26.

call attention to the fact that from this point on Jesus is appearing before the judicial body of the occupying power.

On the other hand, to speak again of the Jewish authorities, Luke does not hesitate to exaggerate. "The entire multitude" arose as one man to take Jesus to Pilate (the expression ἄπαν τὸ πλῆθος αὐτῶν is an awkward description of the honored members of the Sanhedrin).[32] Luke gives in to polemics when he makes use of a popular expression. During the passion narrative, Luke uses various verbs to describe the movements that the opponents force Jesus to perform.[33] Here, as in 22:54, he uses the simple ἄγω ("to lead," "to conduct").

It has been rightly observed that there is a hiatus at the crucial moment of the transition from the Jewish trial to the Roman trial. The Gospels do not explain why Jesus' authority, debated in a Jewish context, was finally abolished by a Roman sentence.[34] They remain vague or quiet on this point.[35]

■ **2** Curiously, Mark mentions no Jewish charge against Jesus before Pilate. Luke is astonished at that omission and makes explicit what seems to him to be indispensable. As a matter of fact, every Roman trial begins with a presentation of the complaints made.[36] Without relying on a particular tradition, Luke composes v. 2 in his own way. Everything there is redactional. Nevertheless, the evangelist tries not to invent things but to gather here the charges made against Jesus as he has found them scattered in the sources and traditions available to him.

Several scholars claim that Luke does not simply list one after another the three complaints about which he reports.[37] In their view, he first lists the primary and general accusation (leading the people astray), which he then illustrates with two particular cases (refusal to pay taxes and messianic claim). It seems to me, however, that the three complaints are of equal importance (the three present participles emphasize the duration and the current interest of the threats Jesus poses).[38] Before we analyze the contents of these accusations, we must note the following points: In an appropriate way Luke uses the verb κατηγορέω ("to accuse"), and there is clearly ample evidence for its legal use.[39] It suggests the contempt the Jewish authorities have for Jesus by omitting the defendant's name and by pointing the finger at him and using the scornful τοῦτον ("this individual"). Even if it corresponds to an awkward habit of Luke, ἤρξαντο ("they began") is not a bad choice, since Luke will take over the flood of criticism at v. 5. The verb εὑρίσκω ("to find") is not surprising in a criminal context: the Jews mean to say that Jesus was caught in the act (Luke will use this same verb in Acts (e.g., 23:29; 24:5) when speaking of the accusation against the Christians).

32 Codex Bezae (D = 05) offers ἀναστάντες ἤγαγον ("rising up, they led"). It thus omits the expression "the entire multitude of them" and relates the participle in number to the implied subject and the principal verb. The manuscript from Tbilissi Θ = 038 also has the plural ἀναστάντες, but it keeps the expression "the entire multitude of them"; see the apparatus of Nestle-Aland (27th ed.) at this place; and Swanson, *Manuscripts*, 384.

33 Except for the simple ἄγω, Luke uses the compound verbs εἰσάγω ("to introduce," "to bring," "to cause to enter," 22:54) and ἀπάγω ("to lead away," "to involve," 22:66).

34 See C. F. Evans (840–41), who imagines that initially two independent traditions circulated, one evoking Jesus' appearance before the Jewish authority, the other recalling the trial of Jesus before the Roman authority.

35 Once again, it is John who makes the best effort to explain. He has the Jewish accusers say that they had lost the right of capital punishment (John 18:31).

36 See Kastner (*Pilatus*, 65), who cites Cicero *Pro Roscio Amerino* 20: Nocens nisi accusatus fuerit condemnari non potest, "And the guilty man, if he is not accused, cannot be convicted"; A. N. Sherwin-White, *Roman Society and Roman Law in the New Testament* (1963; reprinted Grand Rapids: Baker, 1978) 24–25.

37 Grundmann, 422; Schneider, 2:472. In "Political Charge," 407–8, Schneider bases his view on a certain use of καί . . . καί (see BDF §444.3) and on the priority given in vv. 5 and 14 to leading the people astray. See also Radl, "Sonderüberlieferungen," 132.

38 See Kastner, *Pilatus*, 65–67.

39 On κατηγορέω (followed by the genitive), see BAGD, s.v.; and Moulton-Milligan, *Vocabulary*, s.v. Acts 24:2 has a very similar formula: ἤρξατο κατηγορεῖν ὁ Τέρτυλλος ("Tertullus began his accusation").

The first charge: Jesus corrupts the people. The verb διαστρέφω is both strong and imprecise. Literally, it means "to twist," "to disconnect," and figuratively "to disfigure," "to pervert."[40] In 9:41 Luke put the participle of this verb along with ἄπιστος ("unbelieving") in Jesus' mouth to designate this "perverted" generation. In my opinion, if we think of ἐπιστρέφω to express returning to God, then διαστρέφω must mean distancing from God. In the eyes of the Jewish leaders, Jesus leads people away from the path to God and corrupts them. But since they are speaking to the Romans, the verb takes on a different, an ethical and political, coloring. Corrupting the people has dangerous social implications. It causes disorders and leads people to oppose the occupying power. It is no accident that Luke chooses ἔθνος ("nation") here instead of λαός to designate the "people."[41] It puts him on the side of the Roman hearer and designates the Jewish "nation." Luke himself does not accept the accusation. Quite to the contrary, for him the goal of the ministry of Jesus was to reestablish the people and to return this "perverted" (διεστραμμένη, 9:41) generation to God. Thus, it must have been costly to write what for him is slanderous.[42]

The second charge confirms the implications of the first accusation. The reality is that Jesus incites people to refuse to pay taxes.[43] It was in that day a sensitive issue. All the revolutionary movements against Rome saw in each census and each levy of taxes an intolerable expression of occupying oppression. For these insurrectionists, to restore Israel's independence was to reestablish God's right and to purify the promised land. In Jesus' day this Zealot opinion was not shared by the Pharisees and Sadducees, who drew a distinction between religious and political obligations. In Luke's day, after the Jewish revolt had been crushed, after the destruction of Jerusalem and its temple, as well as the end of Masada, it was no longer an issue.

The Lukan Jesus—and probably also the historical Jesus—had required "give to Caesar what is Caesar's and to God what is God's" (20:25). Even if, as we have seen, this requirement could seem to be ambiguous and prone to contradictory interpretations, Luke's interpretation of it separates the domains. The Christians pay taxes, even to the Romans, without damaging God whom they venerate. In Luke's eyes this second charge, like the first one, is false.[44]

It is the third grievance that catches Pilate's attention. It involves the personal identity of the one whom the accusers regard as an agitator. They say he claims (note the reflexive pronoun ἑαυτόν, "himself") to be χριστὸν βασιλέα. The expression can be understood in two ways. Written with a small letter, χριστόν is an adjective and means "anointed." Jesus proclaims himself to be Israel's "anointed king." In this case the accusers presuppose that Pilate is familiar with the royal customs of the Jews. Written with a capital letter, Χριστόν is a substantive, and even a proper name, "Christ." He claims to be "Christ King." I hold this second solution, since it would be more understandable for Pilate.[45] What matters, moreover, is not the first term "Christ" (Χριστόν) but the next one, "king" (βασιλέα).[46] Indeed, any monarchy represented a sensitive point for Roman authority.

---

40 Delebecque (*Évangile*, 141) translated as *fourvoyer*, "to mislead," "to lead astray."

41 Very many manuscripts have "the nation" and not "our nation"; see the apparatus of Nestle-Aland (27th ed.) on the text.

42 Heil ("Reader-Response") is of the opinion that there are several cases of dramatic irony in Jesus' trial before Pilate. He notes in particular that, on a certain level, the charge of corrupting the nation proves to be right: Jesus wants to lead the people astray from their bad shepherds in order to bring them back to God (176–77).

43 Delebecque (*Évangile*, 141) observes that the verb δίδωμι ("to give," translated as "to pay") is a present "infinitive, which means the *current* refusal to pay taxes."

44 There were several Greek terms to designate the various kinds of duties and taxes (see Rom 13:7). As he had done in 20:22, Luke here uses φόρος to indicate the tribute due the emperor. It is, moreover, the entire expression of 20:22 (ἔξεστιν ἡμᾶς Καίσαρι φόρον δοῦναι ἢ οὔ; "Are we permitted to pay tribute to Caesar or not?") that is the pattern for the redactional formulation of 23:2; see the commentary above on 20:22.

45 Plummer (520) chooses "Messias, a king."

46 Plummer (520) justifiably observes: "They [the Jewish authorities] add βασιλέα ['king'] that Pilate may know the political significance of Χριστός (Schanz)."

Furthermore, the Senate could play with the term in its own interest. Sometimes it sought to win the support of a *rex socius*, an allied king; other times it refused the title of "king" to a man who let himself get too ambitious. Although the Romans denied the title *rex* to their own leaders (they hated any submission to a king since they achieved independence from the Etruscan yoke), they tolerated it when the eastern part of the empire, not having a better term, used the Greek word βασιλεύς for the "emperor." According to Luke, the Jewish authorities, who wanted to misunderstand Jesus' injunction about the taxes, also distorted his messianic identity. Admittedly, the joyful crowd with the branches called Jesus "king" (βασιλεύς, 19:38), but the narrative and scriptural contexts prevented seeing any threat to the Romans in this modest procession.[47] Words can be unfaithful companions. For Luke, Jesus is indeed the Messiah of Israel, as the book of Acts often demonstrates. Yet his kingship, which comes from the resurrection beyond the cross, is of a different order than the political, and it rules over a territory that is different from the acres of this earth. In my opinion, Luke affirms the Johannine definition of Jesus' kingship (John 18:33-38). Thus, he can only reject the third charge and oppose what he regards as slander. In his view, Jesus did not claim the political kingship over Israel.[48]

■ **3** Luke preserves the short conversation between Pilate and Jesus that Mark transmits to him.[49] The Christian tradition collected by Mark is sensitive to nuances: it puts in Pilate's mouth an expression of political content, "king of the Jews," and not of religious meaning such as "king of Israel."[50] It chooses this expression based on the *titulus*, the historical memory of which had lasted through the years.[51]

As he had done before the Sanhedrin (22:70b), Jesus avoids Pilate's question. His reply, "you say it" (σὺ λέγεις), is capable of three different interpretations: (a) you say it, and I do not accept your opinion; (b) you say it, and I do accept your opinion; (c) you say it, and I refuse to express an opinion.[52] In any event, Jesus hesitates. The hostility present discourages him from engaging in a conversation that would be a trap. Furthermore, what Pilate says is ambiguous. On the one hand, it is false (Jesus is not a political king); on the other, the assertion is right (Jesus is authorized by God; the resurrection will establish him as Messiah and Lord, Acts 2:36).[53]

■ **4** Pilate must already be so familiar with Christianity that he is immediately satisfied with Jesus' answer and regards the defendant as innocent.[54] Luke is happy to find this tradition about a Pilate who whitewashes Jesus. It encourages him beyond the Christian readers to lead the pagan readers to recognize that the church, unlike the Jewish revolutionary movements, poses no danger to Roman power.[55] We read here the first of the three declarations of innocence (see below, 23:14 and 22).[56]

---

47 See the commentary above on 19:38.

48 For Luke, as for Mark and the Synoptic tradition, the Jewish authorities shift the accent from the religious to the political, but they do not act, for hypocritically they change neither the topic nor the complaint. The distinction between religion and politics was not yet complete. See Lagrange, 576; Bammel, "Trial," 417–18.

49 Tannehill (332) notes correctly that there is a caesura between v. 3 and v. 4.

50 For Mark's interpretation, see Gnilka, *Markus*, 2:299–300; for that of Matthew, see Luz, *Matthew 21–28*, 494–95.

51 See Mark 15:26 par. Matt 27:37 par. Luke 23:38 par. John 19:19; Bovon *Last Days*, 26–27. Ernst (622) points out the relationship between Pilate's question and the *titulus*.

52 See Irmscher ("Σὺ λέγεις") who presents an invaluable history of interpretation and concludes convincingly: Jesus' answer goes in the direction of a yes, but it expects of the recipient that he understand the speaker's hidden meaning. Also Aletti (*Art de raconter*, 163–64): Jesus' initially ambiguous answer finally has a positive meaning. It also goes without saying that one can take Jesus' reply as a question. The same uncertainty prevails about the meaning, which can correspond to irony, surprise, or a real question.

53 Delebecque (*Évangile*, 141) notes rightly that "twice the sense relates to the initial σύ ['you']."

54 On Luke's apologetic effort, see C. F. Evans, 843; Schneider, 2:473; and Radl, "Sonderüberlieferungen," 134. On vv. 2-3, Goulder (*New Paradigm*, 2:756) speaks of "Luke's sensitive political antennae."

55 Schlatter (439) observes that this is the only sentence Pilate addresses to Jesus.

56 Cyril of Alexandria (*Serm. Luc.* 151; see Payne Smith, *Cyril*, 2:711) notes and underscores this triple assertion of Pilate. Like many other Christian

In the Synoptic tradition the crowd intervened later, after the Barabbas episode (Mark 15:8, 11 par. Matt 27:17, 20). Luke, who had employed an ambiguous expression in v. 1, explicitly mentions in v. 4 the "crowd" along with the "chief priests."[57] He thus confers a public dimension on the trial. Moreover, in so doing he is not wrong. A Roman trial takes place by day, and it is open to the public. Luke thus imagines that the people followed their leaders and took part in the debate.[58]

■ **5** According to Luke, the opponents do not give up.[59] They redouble their efforts: ἐπισχύω means "to gather forces," "to seize the upper hand," "to press," "to insist." The imperfect underscores this recovery and confirms the adversaries' insistence.[60]

In other words, Luke repeats here the first complaint advanced by the Jewish authorities in v. 2. He asserts that, according to them, Jesus "agitates the people." To express himself he does not use a verb of his own choosing; as on other occasions, he takes one from Mark, but from a different context (in Mark the verb ἀνασείω appears at the end of the Barabbas episode, Mark 15:11). The verb ἀνασείω offers a different connotation from the verb διαστρέφω in v. 2. It suggests shock, agitation, insurrection. I translate it as "to agitate."

What causes the agitation is the teaching of Jesus. The reader still feels here the grip of Luke. Above all, Jesus' ministry consisted of teaching (διδάσκων), admittedly accompanied by mighty deeds.[61] Instead of the contents of Jesus' teaching to which v. 2 referred, here we have the success and the extent of Jesus' ministry. The perspective is Lukan, and it emphasizes the characteristics that the evangelist confers on Jesus' mission: the ministry begins in Galilee and ends here in Jerusalem. As some have remarked, it is an itinerant ministry, and it corresponds to a journey.[62] It is important to note the relationship between "from" (ἀπό) and "unto" (ἕως) This ministry encompasses the entire country. After the ascension, the nations will be reached by Christian missionaries. The word "Judea" probably does not have the limited sense of the territory around Jerusalem; as in 4:44 it has the broader sense of "land of the Jews." The accent is on "all" (ὅλης).[63] In fact, according to the evangelist, the followers and the opponents agree on the nature (a teaching), the extent (all Palestine), and the stages (Galilee, journey, Jerusalem) of Jesus' ministry. Their opinions diverge completely about its meaning. For the opponents it is negative: he agitates and perverts the people. For the evangelist and his fellow believers it is positive: Jesus brings the people together and rebuilds them.[64]

---

authors, the patriarch of Alexandria vigorously attacks the Jewish leaders. In his eyes their only goal is to kill the one who wants to lead them to life. Lagrange (575) and Bock (2:1806) are of the opinion that Luke concentrates on Jesus' innocence; see also Grundmann, 421.

57   The attitude of Roman jurists vis-à-vis the *vox populi* is ambiguous. On the one hand, they resist any popular pressure. On the other, they think the voice of the crowd can express the truth. Colin ("Procès") believes that the crowd played a decisive role and did so legitimately. He undoubtedly goes too far; see Bovon, *Last Days*, 50.

58   Two more details about v. 4: αἴτιον can be a neuter adjective (Pilate did not find anything "culpable" in Jesus) or a neuter substantive, the equivalent of αἰτία (Pilate found in Jesus no "charge," no "offense," no "crime"). If one chooses the second solution, the language is more legal than in the first. I prefer the first one, because the sense of the substantive τὸ αἴτιον is more often the "cause," the "principle" than the "complaint" or the "crime." In Acts Luke uses the substantive αἰτία with the

meaning of "cause," "reason," "charge," "complaint." In addition, from Pilate's lips ὁ ἄνθρωπος οὗτος ("this man") is more respectful than οὗτος ("this one," "this individual"), pronounced by the Jewish leaders.

59   According to Plummer (521), they think Pilate is taking things too lightly.

60   On ἐπισχύω, a *hapax legomenon* in the New Testament, see Alexandre, s.v.; and Plummer (521), who notes the intransitive sense given the verb here and calls attention to 1 Macc 6:6.

61   On the teaching Jesus, see Bovon, *Luke the Theologian*, 204–5.

62   See Robinson (*Way of the Lord*, 43–56), who presents a meticulous and convincing interpretation of this verse from Luke's editorial perspective. He emphasizes the dynamic character of Jesus' ministry.

63   The preposition κατά, followed by the genitive, has the meaning here of "throughout," "through"; see Acts 9:31; 10:37.

64   The Venerable Bede (*In Luc.* 6.1279–80), who recognizes this agreement and this disagreement, notes with acuteness that this *crimen*, a "guilty act"

History of Interpretation

The state of the manuscripts is important for the special-ist in textual criticism, but it also supplies information to the historian of interpretation. The history of the text and the history of interpretation come together.[65] The Old Latin witnesses, various Vulgate manuscripts, and, according to Epiphanius, Marcion himself[66] speak of a more extensive attack in v. 2. Not only does Jesus corrupt the people; he also reduces the Law and the Prophets to nothing. This additional criticism corresponds to what is said about the Christians in Acts of the Apostles (6:13; 18:13; 21:28, mentioning the temple and omitting the prophets). It is a criticism that the Lukan Paul rejects (Acts 24:14). The variant may owe its origin to the influ-ence of these passages. It may also have been added by Marcion (in this case Marcion, hostile to the Law and the Prophets, would have accepted the charge). Once more in v. 2, again according to Epiphanius, after the charge about taxes Marcion raised a further complaint: Jesus led astray the women and children. A similar accusation, not necessarily connected with Marcion and his disciples,[67] was made in the second century about the Christian missionaries. In any case, the variant shows a concern to introduce back into the life of Jesus the things for which his disciples were later reproached. Two Old Latin manu-scripts[68] are also familiar with this additional complaint, but they include it later, at the end of v. 5: Jesus would alienate the Jews' children and wives, who—a detail missing from Marcion's variant of v. 2—would not be baptized as the Jews were, nor would they be purified.[69] This reading is appropriate in the second century and makes sense not only in the context of Marcionism but also, more generally, in the context of conflicts among Jews, Christians, and Jewish-Christians over the rites of purification.[70]

In his *Adversus Marcionem* Tertullian refers to another variant of his opponent. According to Marcion, Pilate's question was not "Are you the king of the Jews?" but "Are you the Christ?"[71] Here again one can see that Marcion composed the accusations so that from his point of view they are legitimate. The passage of *Adversus Marcionem* also shows Tertullian's own interpretation. The African thinks that it makes sense that the Jews denounced Jesus to the Romans because he had claimed the title "Christ king." It also brings "you say it" closer to "it is you who say that I am" in the preceding pericope, Jesus' trial before the Sanhedrin (22:70b).[72] In both cases Tertul-lian understands Jesus' answer to be a positive response. If the Lord does not say more here, it is because he does not want to give the impression that he is afraid of the Romans. Finally, according to a system of prophecies and fulfillments that Marcion rejected, Tertullian affirms that Jesus' trial before Pilate represents the fulfillment of two Old Testament oracles, Isa 3:13-14 (the Lord in

---

for the Jews, is a *virtus*, a work of virtue, for the Christians. He then connects v. 5 to Acts 10:37-38.

65   On the variants I will discuss, see Lagrange, 577; Metzger, *Commentary* (2d ed.), 152; Parker, *Living Text*, 160.

66   See Harnack, *Marcion*, 235*.

67   See Adolf Harnack, *The Mission and Expansion of Christianity in the First Three Centuries* (2d ed.; trans. James Moffatt; 2 vols.; Theological Translation Library 19–20; New York: Putnam, 1908) 2:64–84; Pierre de Labriolle, *La réaction païenne: Étude sur la polémique antichrétienne du premier au IVᵉ siècle* (1934; reprinted Paris: Cerf, 2005) 284–87.

68   They are MSS e (fifth century, preserved in Trent, Dublin, Rome, and London) and—with a few differ-ences—c (twelfth–thirteenth centuries, preserved in Paris).

69   This is what MS e says; MS c uses the singular and explains that it is Jesus who is not baptized and who does not purify himself. It is more likely speaking of Jewish ritual baths and Jewish rules of purification than of Christian baptisms.

70   See François Bovon, "Fragment Oxyrhynchus 840, Fragment of a Lost Gospel, Witness of an Early Christian Controversy over Purity," *JBL* 119 (2000) 705–28.

71   See Harnack, *Marcion*, 235*; Tsutui, "Evangeliums Marcions," 125; Tertullian *Adv. Marc.* 4.42.1 (SC 456:510 n. 2).

72   One finds this bringing together of the two state-ments also in the Venerable Bede *In Luc.* 6.1255–57.

judgment)[73] and Ps 2:1-2 (the kings and leaders are united against the Lord and his anointed).[74]

Moving forward several centuries, we come to Bonaventure, who describes Jesus' appearance before Pilate in a lapidary formula. It consists of four elements, "a dishonest accusation, a correct interrogation, a legitimate excuse, and an inappropriate increase of the accusation."[75] Bonaventure thus summarizes vv. 2, 3a, 3b, and 5. When he repeats these points, the medieval theologian cites numerous Hebrew Bible antecedents and parallels from the Gospels. Thus, in his eyes Scripture explains Scripture. If Pilate holds to only the third reproach the Jews direct against Jesus, it is because he knows that the other two are false. The *Glossa ordinaria*,[76] which Bonaventure quotes here, had already said, following the Venerable Bede (*In Luc.* 6.1257–64), that Pilate asked only about things he did not yet know. In the theologian's opinion, the increased intensity of the accusations in v. 5 is especially inappropriate, because Jesus did not try to agitate the people or to get them to break the law; he wanted to lead them to repentance and to praise (Bonaventure *Comm. Luc.* 23.2–6).[77]

In the sixteenth century Erasmus makes some grammatical remarks in his *Annotationes*. He notices the presence of the definite article before the word "king" when Pilate says it (v. 3), and he gives it a demonstrative sense: "this king," that is to say, the single, unique person promised to the Jews. He is also of the opinion that the verb ἀνασείω ("to agitate") in v. 5 indicates not a single

action but a continuous movement.[78] In his *Paraphrasis* (458), the humanist cites the contrast that the Christians had been making for centuries between the Sanhedrin's malice and Pilate's honesty. Then, in a clear way, he explains Jesus' answer as follows: The Lord could not deny that he was king, but neither could he admit it without qualification, because his kingdom was of another kind. Since the governor was ignorant of the Law and the Prophets, he could not understand the "evangelical" character of this kingdom. Erasmus skillfully portrays Pilate as one who does not understand Jesus' answer but recognizes the malice of the Jews.

Along with literary (a tendency to harmonize the Synoptic data in their chronology) and historical (Pilate has only the "knowledge" of the main affairs in the legal sense of the *cognitio*) observations, John Calvin meditates on the enigmatic confrontation between the human judge and the Son of God, "a strange and deformed spectacle." He understands it theologically and makes several efforts to express its significance. He notes that this confrontation represented a "benefit" for the believers, who are called "we,"[79] because God's tribunal, which he skillfully contrasts with any human court, is "terrible." For its threat to be removed, Christ is indispensable. How does he release us from it? First of all, he must be declared innocent:[80] Pilate's words are more than an opinion; they are a confession. Then he who is innocent must be condemned so that we can benefit from divine forgiveness. Such is "God's providence."[81] Finally, Calvin

---

73   Tertullian seems to be the only one who relates this biblical passage to the passion of Jesus. I do not see whether in Tertullian's Bible the Lord judges or is judged.

74   The commentary of Ambrose concentrates on Jesus' silence before Pilate (found here in Matthew and Mark but not in Luke!): Jesus gives up his own salvation in order to obtain the salvation of all. The bishop of Milan also analyzes the ambiguous attitude of Pilate, who on the one hand exonerates Jesus and on the other condemns him (to accomplish the mystery: *crucifixit mysterio*, "he crucifies by reason of the mystery"); see Ambrose *Exp. Luc.* 10.97–98.

75   Bonaventure *Comm. Luc.* 23.1 (Bernardini, 566): *accusatio improba, inquisitio recta, exusatio iusta, accusationis aggravatio importuna.*

76   *Glossa ordinaria* on Luke 23:3 (*PL* 114:343–44).

77   Bernardini, 566–67.

78   Erasmus, *Annotationes*, 214. In addition, he thinks that the manuscripts vary in v. 1. Some carry the singular ἤγαγεν ("he led"), others the plural ἤγαγον ("they led").

79   Calvin's commentary is an engaged commentary, designed for believing readers with whom he maintains a conversation by resorting to the first person plural.

80   Calvin explains Jesus' answer, calling it "ambiguous" and "mediocre." The answer is positive, because Jesus acknowledges that he is king, but it is discreet, because it is not good for Jesus to defend himself.

81   Calvin, *Harmony,* 3:179–81, 183–84. Here the first formulation of the theological meaning of the trial: "The Son of God wished to stand bound before an earthly judge and there submit to the death sentence, that we might no doubt that we are freed of guilt and free to approach to the heavenly throne

comments on Christ's silence. He "said nothing . . . in order to open our mouths by his silence." Thanks to him we can now call God "Abba, Father" (Rom 8:15). Furthermore, although Christ was silent then, he is not silent now, since he is our intercessor with the Father (another allusion to Romans 8).

Conclusion

Faithful to Christian tradition and its sources, Luke does not eliminate Jesus' appearance before Pilate. In his eyes the Roman governor did not admit the political character of Jesus' ministry. In the evangelist's eyes and, he hopes, in the eyes of his readers, especially his Gentile readers, neither Jesus nor his followers represent a danger to the social order. The Christian message is on another level.

While he eventually yields to the pressure of the Jewish authorities and the crowd, Pilate initially looks for ways out of the situation. The declaration of Jesus' innocence (v. 4) is one of them. Turning the prisoner over to Herod (vv. 6-7) is another.

Luke is historian enough to yield to the weight of the facts: Jesus underwent a Roman punishment pronounced by a Roman court. He is also theologian enough[82] to feel the paradox of what is happening—the judge of the living and the dead is being tried before a penal court—and to recognize its necessity from the perspective of the divine economy. The Son of Man is delivered for the redemption of human beings.

---

of God" (179). On pp. 183–84 he comes back to this central point.

82 Aletti (*Art de raconter*, 155–76) is more interested in the significance than in the unfolding of the facts. It is his view that Matthew and Mark base their description of Jesus' suffering on the psalms of lament, while Luke is inspired by the psalms of trust. The evangelist proceeds discreetly without imposing a pattern of biblical reading. He is also reserved in his account of the events. He lets them speak for themselves and does not explicitly indicate their meaning.

Jesus before Herod (23:6-12)

Bibliography

Bickerman, E. J., "Utilitas Crucis: Observations sur les récits du procès de Jésus dans les évangiles canoniques," *RHR* 112 (1935) 169–241.

Bielinski, Krzysztof, *Jesus vor Herodes in Lukas 23,6-12: Eine narrativ-sozialgeschichtliche Untersuchung* (SBB 50; Stuttgart: Katholisches Bibelwerk, 2003).

Blinzler, Josef, "Herodes und der Tod Jesu," *Klerusblatt* 37 (1957) 118–21.

Idem, *Prozess*, 205–19, 284–300.

Bornhäuser, Karl, "Die Beteiligung des Herodes am Prozesse Jesu," *NKZ* 40 (1929) 714–18.

Borse, Udo, "Die geschichtliche Absicherung (Lk 23,5-16) des christologischen Psalmwortes (Ps 2,1s. LXX) und seiner Auslegung (Apg 4,25-28)," *SNTU* 26 (2001) 129–38.

Brandon, *Trial*, 120–22.

Brown, *Death of the Messiah,* 1:760–86.

Büchele, Anton, *Der Tod Jesu im Lukasevangelium: Eine redaktionsgeschichtliche Untersuchung zu Lk 24* (FTS 26; Frankfurt: Knecht, 1978) 25–41.

Buck, Erwin, "The Function of the Pericope 'Jesus before Herod' in the Passion Narrative of Luke," in Wilfrid Haubeck and Michael Bachmann, eds., *Wort in der Zeit: Neutestamentliche Studien. Festgabe für Karl Heinrich Rengstorf* (Leiden: Brill, 1980) 165–78.

Corbin, Michel, "Jésus devant Hérode: Lecture de Luc 23,6-12," *Christus* 25 (1978) 190–97.

Delbrueck, Richard, "Antiquarisches zu den Verspottungen Jesu," *ZNW* 41 (1942) 124–45.

Dibelius, Martin, "Herodes und Pilatus," *ZNW* 16 (1915) 113–26; reprinted in idem, *Botschaft und Geschichte: Gesammelte Aufsätze* (2 vols.; Tübingen: Mohr, 1953, 1956) 1:278–92.

Hoehner, Harold W., *Herod Antipas* (SNTSMS 17; Cambridge: Cambridge University Press, 1972).

Idem, "Why Did Pilate Hand Jesus Over to Antipas?" in Ernst Bammel, ed., *The Trial of Jesus: Cambridge Studies in Honour of C. F. D. Moule* (SBT 2/13; Naperville, Ill.: Allenson, 1970) 84–90.

Joüon, Paul, "Luc 23, 11: ἐσθῆτα λαμπράν," *RSR* 26 (1936) 80–85.

Klein, Hans, "Die lukanisch-johanneische Passionstradition," *ZNW* 67 (1976) 155–86.

Manus, Chris U., "The Universalism of Luke and the Motif of Reconciliation in Luke 23:6-12," *ATJ* 16 (1987) 121–35.

Matera, "Jesus before Pilate."

Müller, Karlheinz, "Jesus vor Herodes: Eine redaktionsgeschichtliche Untersuchung zu Lk 23, 6-12," in Gerhard Dautzenberg et al., eds., *Zur Geschichte des Urchristentums* (Festschrift Rudolf Schnackenburg; QD 87; Freiburg: Herder, 1979) 111–41.

Omerzu, Heike, "Das traditionsgeschichtliche Verhältnis der Begegnungen von Jesus mit Herodes Antipas und Paulus mit Agrippa II," *SNTU* 28 (2003) 121–45.

Parker, Pierson, "Herod Antipas and the Death of Jesus," in E. P. Sanders, ed., *Jesus, the Gospels, and the Church: Essays in Honor of William R. Farmer* (Macon, Ga.: Mercer University Press, 1987) 197–208.

Radl, *Paulus und Jesus*, 46–49, 65, 217.

Schütz, Frieder, *Der leidende Christus: Die angefochtene Gemeinde und das Christuskerygma der lukanischen Schriften* (BWANT 89; Stuttgart: Kohlhammer, 1969) 128–29.

Sherwin-White, *Roman Society*, 28–31, 123, 136–38.

Soards, Marion L., "Herod Antipas' Hearing in Luke 23:8," *BiTr* 37 (1986) 146–47.

Idem, "The Silence of Jesus before Herod: An Interpretive Suggestion," *ABR* 33 (1985) 41–45.

Idem, "Tradition, Composition, and Theology in Luke's Account of Jesus before Herod Antipas," *Bib* 66 (1985) 344–64.

Streeter, B. H., "On the Trial of Our Lord before Herod—A Suggestion," in W. Sanday, ed., *Studies in the Synoptic Problem* (Oxford: Clarendon Press, 1911) 228–31.

Tyson, Joseph B., "Jesus and Herod Antipas," *JBL* 79 (1960) 239–46.

Untergassmair, Franz Georg, "Zur Problematik der lukanischen Passionsgeschichte: Jesus vor Herodes (Lk 23, 6-12)," in Knut Backhaus und Franz Georg Untergassmair, eds., *Schrift und Tradition: Festschrift für Josef Ernst zum 70. Geburtstag* (Paderborn: Schöningh, 1996) 273–92.

Verrall, A. W., "Christ before Herod (Luke xxiii 1-16)," *JTS* 10 (1908–9) 321–53.

6 And when Pilate heard this, he inquired[a] whether the man was a Galilean,[b] 7/ and when he learned that he had come out of[c] Herod's area of authority, he turned him over[d] to Herod, who was himself in Jerusalem in these days. 8/ And when Herod saw Jesus, he was very happy, because he had been wanting to see him for a long time because of what he had heard about him; he also was hoping[e] to see him work a sign.[f] 9/ So he asked him many questions,[g] but he gave no answer. 10/ The chief priests and the scribes stood there, vehemently accusing him. 11/ Herod also, after he regarded him as of no account and, along with his soldiers, ridiculed him, dressed him in bright clothes and sent him back to Pilate. 12/ On this day Herod and Pilate became friends with one another; indeed, previously they had lived with hatred for one another.[h]

a Literally: "he questioned."
b Or: "was Galilean."
c Literally: "was."
d Or: "sent him."
e Or: "and he hoped."
f Literally: "a sign worked by him."
g Literally: "He thus questioned him in many words."
h Literally: "indeed, they existed previously in hatred for one another."

The episode in which Jesus appears before Herod Antipas[1] represents an interlude. At the end, in v. 11, the situation is the same as it was at the beginning, in v. 5. Jesus again finds himself in the hands of an embarrassed Pilate.[2] Yet history is never repeated in exactly the same way. There are three new elements in the story: Jesus comes back to Pilate ridiculed and honored, dressed ostentatiously (v. 11); Herod and Pilate have been reconciled (v. 12); as a result, Pilate no longer has (v. 12) the way of evading the situation he had at the beginning (vv. 6-7). Paradoxically, the incident thus seems useless and, at the same time, full of meaning.

Analysis

Of what does the incident consist? Of Pilate's active and reflective initiative (vv. 6-7); of Herod's action that satis-

fies his own desire and does not do what the Roman governor wants (vv. 8-9); of the ill-tempered presence of the chief priests and scribes (v. 10); of a surprising decision of the Jewish prince (v. 11); and, concluding the incident, of the transformation of a human relationship (v. 12).[3]

Some commentators have wanted to see here a composition in the form of a chiasm: the two authorities, Pilate and Herod, initially rivals (vv. 6-7a), are reconciled at the end (v. 12). In the middle of the first part Jesus is sent to Herod (v. 7b); in the middle of the last part Jesus is returned to Pilate (v. 11b). The second part, with Herod's desire (vv. 8-9), is opposite the penultimate part, with Herod's contempt (v. 11a). The accusation of the chief priests and the scribes stands in the middle of the composition (v. 10).[4] In my opinion, this view of the text overestimates the importance of v. 10 and neglects the movement of the text.[5]

1 Soards ("Tradition," 344) correctly thinks that vv. 6-12 constitute a self-contained literary unit. He enumerates the five questions that exegetes have raised in connection with this passage: (a) Why does Pilate send Jesus to Herod? (b) Why does Jesus remain silent? (c) Why does Herod ridicule Jesus? (d) Why does Herod put a robe on Jesus? (e) Why do Herod and Pilate become friends? He presents a detailed analysis of the text and concludes that Luke was very active in creating the literary character of the text, with Mark contributing only a light influence (in vv. 9 and 11) and some influence from another tradition (vv. 7b, 9a, and 12b). What Luke wanted to underscore, according to Soards, was Jesus' innocence.

2 Buck ("Function," 165): "It does not appear to advance the overall plot to any noticeable degree. . . ."

3 Bock (2:1817) divides the episode into four consecutive parts: Pilate sends Jesus to Herod (vv. 6-7); Herod questions Jesus, who remains silent (vv. 8-9); Jesus is accused and ridiculed (vv. 10-11); Herod and Pilate are reconciled (v. 12).

4 See Meynet, *Évangile*, 1:213, 2:226–27; idem, *Guide*, 107–8 (I do not understand why Meynet calls this unit "The Interrogation by Pilate"). See also Bossuyt and Radermakers, 2:492–93.

5 The diagram of Manus ("Universalism," 123) may put too much emphasis on reconciliation, but it has the merit of calling attention to the similarity

Another approach seems to me to be more interesting. Like any trial, that of Jesus refers to facts, but it also includes situations, characters, and feelings. These elements go beyond the case at hand. Life is such that the charge against Jesus affects Pilate, Herod, and the Jewish authorities *beyond* the trial itself, whose unfolding is not merely judicial. Pilate's program deviates from legal procedure just as that of Herod goes its own way. To be sure, Jesus' trial will end in a judgment against him, but that will not happen without altering relationships, revealing personalities, changing intentions. When Pilate improvises a procedure or when Herod takes advantage of a situation, they are not interested in advancing Jesus' lost cause; they are concerned about their own interests.

In order to understand a text, it is customary for scholars to compare it with other, similar texts. Staying with Luke's two-volume work, some have compared Luke 23:6-12 with Acts 4:25-28, the beginning of the prayer the early Christians offer when the apostles Peter and John are released from prison.[6] After an invocation, this prayer quotes vv. 1-2 of Psalm 2, which mention a coalition of kings and political leaders against the Lord and his anointed. The prayer continues with an application to the recent situation: "Yes, Herod and Pontius Pilate, along with the nations and the peoples of Israel, have gathered together in this city against Jesus, your holy servant, whom you have anointed. Thus they have done everything your hand and your will have ordained." While the other canonical Gospels know nothing about Jesus' appearance before Herod, Luke bears witness to it a second time here in Acts. The parallels are impressive.

The relationship between Pilate and Herod is explicitly mentioned; the two men met in the city of Jerusalem, and together they dealt with Jesus. It should thus be acknowledged that in both places Luke referred to the same situation and the same facts. There are, however, also differences between the two passages. In the Gospel we have a narrative, in Acts a liturgical prayer quoted by the narrator. In the Gospel—the difference is significant—the intentions of Pilate and Herod diverge and—at this time—they do not come together in a judgment against Jesus.[7] Finally, there is in Luke 23:6-12 neither a biblical quotation nor a theological reflection, while in Acts Psalm 2 nourishes the narrative memory, and the prayer shows the divine hand behind human actions. While Luke 23:6-12 stays with the innocence of Jesus, Acts 4:25-28 differs by emphasizing the judgment against him. To make sense of these similarities and differences, I make use of the distinction between tradition and redaction. In Acts 4, Luke takes over a liturgical tradition that he respects and scarcely changes. In Luke 23, he follows his own special source, which he strongly reworks.[8]

It is necessary to compare Luke 23:6-12 with another passage of the Acts of the Apostles, the trial of Paul.[9] Indeed, we know that for reasons of literary symmetry and theological ethics Luke likes to see parallels.[10] For the evangelist, it is important that the fate of the Christians resemble that of Christ. As Stephen dies in a spirit similar to that of Jesus (Acts 7:60), so Paul stands before the Roman and Jewish authorities as Jesus had done. In chaps. 25 and 26 of Acts, Paul is accused by the Jewish authorities and confronted by the Roman governor.

---

between the beginning and the end (Pilate) and centering the episode on Herod (vv. 8-11).

6   It is primarily Dibelius ("Herodes") who brings these two passages together, applies form criticism to them, and concludes that, while Pilate moved from the Gospel narrative to the credo, Herod went the opposite way, from the liturgy to the Gospel narrative. See also Borse, "Absicherung," 130–32; Neyrey (*Passion*, 78–79, summarized and critiqued by Bock, 2:1814–15) gives eight reasons why our pericope depends on Mark and the scriptural prophecies, among them Ps 2:1-2.

7   Müller ("Herodes," 131) is of the opinion that Herod performs here the function of a legal advisor and not that of a judge. The legal vocabulary of vv. 7, 9, and 11 does not give me that impression.

8   On the connections between Luke 23 and Acts 4, see Fitzmyer, 2:1478–79; Matera, "Jesus before Pilate," 541–46.

9   I am thinking of Acts 25–26, with Paul's appearance before Festus and then before Herod Agrippa II and his wife, Bernice. Yet one can also think of the scene in which the apostle faces Felix, then the same Felix accompanied by his wife, Drusilla, who was Jewish (Acts 24). Omerzu ("Verhältnis") thinks that in 23:6-12 Luke is inspired not by Acts 4 but by Acts 25–26.

10 See Radl, *Paulus und Jesus*, 169–221; Omerzu, "Verhältnis" (a bibliography on these parallels, 121 n. 1).

Faced with a difficult situation, Festus takes advantage of the visit of Herod Agrippa II to turn the case over to him. The Jewish king expresses his desire to hear the defendant. The rest of the interview leads Agrippa and his wife, Bernice, to share the opinion of Festus: nothing in Paul's conduct is deserving of death. The alleged culprit is innocent.

The similarities between the accounts in Acts and the Gospel are obvious. When he created these parallels, Luke did his work well. Yet here too there is no lack of differences. The episode takes place in Caesarea and not in Jerusalem; Paul defends himself vigorously, while Jesus maintains his silence; the friendship between the Roman governor and the Jewish king is established at the beginning and is not forged at the end of the hearing. Agrippa wants to hear Paul, while Antipas wanted to see Jesus. If the relationship between tradition and redaction made it possible to explain the connections between Acts 4 and Luke 23, here it is Luke's literary composition that makes understandable the connections between Luke 23 and Acts 25–26. The evangelist is concerned to make the fate of Jesus the Master and that of his disciple, Paul, as parallel as possible. In all probability the literary movement flows from the disciple to the Master. When he creates the Gospel episode, Luke is already thinking of Paul's appearance, which he will portray in his second work.

Luke's intertextuality does not stop there. Indeed, Herod Antipas appears on several occasions in the Third Gospel,[11] particularly in 9:7-9. In this passage, which he shares with Mark, the evangelist added one particular note to the episode. He is the only one who said that Herod Antipas wanted to meet Jesus: καὶ ἐζήτει ἰδεῖν αὐτόν ("and he sought to see him," 9:9). When he wrote these words, undoubtedly Luke was already thinking of Jesus' trial and he had in mind the tradition his own special material had given him. Thus, Herod's wish was going to be carried out.

Is there also a connection between 13:1-3 and 23:6-12? Since Luke mentions in chap. 13 a massacre that Pilate perpetrated on Galileans,[12] some exegetes have imagined—without any basis in the text—that Herod took umbrage that the Roman governor may have interfered not only in Jewish but also in Galilean matters.[13] They then see in this incident the origin of the hostility between Herod and Pilate that is mentioned 23:12. Since Luke does not connect these two texts, it is better to abandon this conclusion, which has more historical fiction than scholarly inquiry about it.[14]

The comparison must go beyond Luke's two-volume work. What is the situation with the other Gospels? Apparently there is nothing there, since neither Mark nor Matthew is aware of the episode. This observation, however, is not the last word on the matter. The appearance before Herod and the mocking scene with which it ends are reminiscent of Jesus' appearance before Pilate and of the derision following the Barabbas episode in the narratives of Mark and Matthew. The elements one finds here and there correspond exactly to the elements Luke omitted from Jesus' appearance before Pilate (23:1-5). The points of contact are the following: a high-ranking authority questions Jesus;[15] the latter keeps silent and refuses to answer; instead of making a concrete decision, the high-ranking person expresses his feelings; the mocking that follows involves soldiers; and it includes clothing Jesus in a spectacular robe.[16]

There are, of course, differences. Here there are

---

11 On Herod Antipas in the Gospel of Luke, see Dibelius, "Herodes," 123; Untergassmair, "Problematik," 282–83.

12 See vol. 2 of this commentary, on 13:1-2.

13 See Hoehner, *Antipas*, 172–83.

14 C. F. Evans (851) and Wiefel (390) observe that the episode of Luke 23:6-12 is lacking in concrete elements and that those that are present were brought from elsewhere.

15 Even if he advocates the curious opinion that Luke draws on Matthew, Goulder (*New Paradigm*, 2:758) has imagined that in the original tradition the judge did not have a proper name. On the next page (759), the British exegete makes a series of judicious philological comments.

16 Note the following comparisons: the verb ἐπερωτάω (v. 9; Mark 15:2); the expressions οὐδὲν ἀπεκρίνατο (v. 9) and οὐκέτι οὐδὲν ἀπεκρίθη (Mark 15:5); σὺν τοῖς στρατεύμασιν αὐτοῦ (v. 11) and οἱ στρατιῶται (Mark 15:16); the verb ἐμπαίζω (v. 11; Mark 15:20).

Herod's soldiers; there Pilate's. Here the garment is white or at least glittering; there it is purple. The crown of thorns and the reed as a scepter are missing here, while they are present there.[17] Here the insulting language is implied; there it is explicit. Here the scene is narrated briefly; there it is more expansively shown. How shall we explain these similarities and these singularities? Some people think that Luke created his Herod scene by drawing from other episodes of his Gospel (9:7-9) and from Mark (15:4-5, 16-20). I think instead that Luke follows here his own source, which was familiar with an appearance of Jesus before Herod. This episode was based on a tradition that also lies behind Jesus' appearance before Pilate and behind the mocking episode. Jesus appeared before an authority whose identity was of little importance but whose political power was of great importance. Mark used this tradition to describe what happened with Pilate, and Luke's special source drew on this tradition to tell what happened before Herod. One can thus understand why Luke omitted certain Markan elements when he rewrote Jesus' appearance before Pilate. He wanted to avoid any repetition with the following episode, the appearance before Herod.

In order to understand why Luke has two more appearances after the trial before the Sanhedrin (22:66-71), we must understand the influence of Psalm 2 as well as the references to Pilate and Herod in primitive Christianity.[18] It is not so much a historical recollection that explains the presence of Herod (in that case it would be difficult to see why Mark and Matthew would not have known about it or would have forgotten it) as it is the pressure of Scripture. In order to accept the horror of the death of the Messiah, one had to believe in the intervention of God's mysterious plan (see Acts 4:28), and in order to dare to recognize it, one had to appeal to Scripture, in particular to Psalm 2.[19]

It is not Luke, however, who first did this exegetical work.[20] He did not construct all the parts of the episode beginning with the Scripture and odds and ends of Gospel narratives. He labors under the weight of a tradition found in the prayer of the Jerusalem community quoted in Acts 4, then in Ignatius of Antioch, Justin Martyr, Tertullian, the *Acts of Thomas*, the *Didascalia apostolorum*, and especially in the *Gospel of Peter*.[21] This Gospel fragment starts without an introduction[22] in the following way: "But of the Jews none washed their hands, neither Herod nor any one of his judges. And as they would not wash, Pilate arose. And then Herod the king commanded that the Lord should be marched off, saying to them, 'What I have commanded you to do to him, do ye.'" The account continues with the request of Joseph of Arimathea to Pilate (before the crucifixion) for permission to bury the Lord later. The governor then sends a missive to Herod in order to get Jesus' body from him for Joseph. Herod answers favorably, not without saying that even without the measure taken by the governor he would have given him a decent burial.[23] I think that the *Gospel of Peter* was independent of the canonical Gospels but that it shares

17 On these emblems, see Delbrueck, "Antiquarisches," 137–42; Brown, *Death of the Messiah*, 1:774–75. See also the variant reading of Luke 23:37, which probably was contaminated by the parallels of Mark 15:17 par. Matt 27:29 par. John 19:2, 5.

18 Acts 4:25-27; Ignatius *Smyrn.* 1.2; Justin *1 Apol.* 40; *Dial.* 103.4; Tertullian *Adv. Marc.* 4.42.2–3; *Acts Thom.* 32.3; *Did. Apost.* 21 §5.19; *Gos. Pet.* 1–5; see Wiefel, 389; Ernst, 624; Bock 2:1817.

19 Some have also suggested the legal requirement in the Law of Moses (Deut 19:15) according to which at least two witnesses are needed to establish the guilt of a criminal. See Grundmann, 424; C. A. Evans, 333; Ernst, 624.

20 Klein ("Passionstradition") is of the opinion that behind Luke's original copy and that of John there is a primitive layer based not on Mark but on Mark's original. He examines vv. 5-16 (and not only 6-12)

from the perspective of this hypothesis (156–62). He concludes that, while the episode of Jesus before Herod is editorial, it contains traditional elements, some of which unquestionably have parallels in the Gospel of John (esp. in vv. 13 and 14).

21 See n. 18 above.

22 It is a fragment discovered at the end of the nineteenth century in Akhmîm in Upper Egypt. On this passage of the *Gospel of Peter,* see Schneemelcher, *New Testament Apocrypha,* 1:223.

23 A fragment of papyrus published at the end of the twentieth century, *P.Oxy.* 2949, dating from the end of the second or the beginning of the third century, contains a text that corresponds, not without variants, to vv. 3-5 of the fragment from Akhmîm. See Dieter Lührmann, "POx 2949: EvPt 3–5 in einer Handschrift des 2./3. Jahrhunderts," *ZNW* 72 (1981) 216–26.

a tradition with Luke and his special source, which contains the collaboration of the Roman governor and the Jewish sovereign. The *Gospel of Peter* goes beyond even the Gospel of Luke in putting the main responsibility for condemning Jesus on Herod's shoulders.

To conclude this analysis I would like to object to two opinions that are often combined in German-language exegesis.[24] Scholars who hold these opinions, representatives of what is known as redaction criticism, resist the hypothesis of a source in addition to Mark in the passion narrative with a vigor I have difficulty understanding.[25] In my opinion, the material unique to Mark in both the passion narrative and the travel narrative is so ample and so characteristic that it compels another source in addition to Mark and Q.[26] Elsewhere I have explained the Lukan use of this document in chaps. 22–24 of the Gospel. There the evangelist makes use of his method of alternating blocks of material.[27] For example: From Jesus' arrest to the appearance before Pilate he follows and adapts Mark (22:47—23:5); from the appearance before Herod to the crucifixion (23:6-43) he again takes up and reworks his own special material.

These same exegetes insist on the Lukan character of almost every verse of our pericope.[28] They are certainly right to do so, and our interpretations of the details will confirm their judgment. But adding up all the Lukanisms does not explain the presence of a tradition that describes Jesus' appearance before Herod and for which there is so much evidence at the end of the first century. Luke did not invent the episode,[29] because not all of the patristic witnesses depend on him.[30] He copies an episode contained in his own special source by adapting it to his vocabulary and style. Even though I tend to prefer this hypothesis, that does not mean that I support the historicity of the episode.[31] That there was a tradition bearing witness to the collaboration of Pilate and Herod as well as Jesus' appearance before both of these authorities does not yet mean that we must assume that these episodes are historical.[32] I believe, rather, that the simple historical tradition began to be enriched and duplicated when the Scripture, and especially Psalm 2, made it possible for the early Christians to give meaning, and a providential meaning, to what at the first profane glance appeared to be completely senseless. Moreover, this hermeneutical work began very early. As early as 1 Cor 2:7-8 Paul says that not one, but several human authorities condemned the Son of God. Note the plural "rulers of this world": "None of the rulers of this age understood

24 See, e.g., Müller, "Herodes"; and Untergassmair, "Problematik."

25 Müller ("Herodes," 112) writes without sufficient justification: "Above all, however, Luke attaches importance to a scene, which adds an appearance of Jesus before Herod's tribunal, even though the pre-Lukan tradition gives no evidence of knowing it."

26 Fortunately, I am not the only person who defends the hypothesis of a special source. I can refer to two lists of advocates of this hypothesis; see Bovon, "Lukan Story of the Passion," 90–91; Müller, "Herodes," 112 n. 12, 113 n. 13; see esp. Grundmann, 421, 423; Ernst, 621.

27 Bovon, "Lukan Story of the Passion," 92–98.

28 In their eyes the only exceptions are the terms that Luke takes over from Mark when he uses Jesus' silence before Pilate to describe his silence before Herod and when he describes the insults from Herod's rabble using the mocking of Pilate's soldiers.

29 Those who see Luke as the single author of the episode often regard the episode as unhistorical; see C. F. Evans, 849 n. *s*.

30 Schneider (2:474) thinks that Luke introduced here a special tradition (*Sonderüberlieferung*).

31 Two scholars have tried with erudition to defend the historicity of the event: Blinzler (*Prozess*, 205–19) and Hoehner (*Antipas*, 224–50). The defenders of the episode's authenticity sometimes ask how the information could have gotten to the evangelist. Two channels are then mentioned: either Joanna, the wife of Chuza, Herod's steward (8:3), or Manaen, Herod's friend from childhood (Acts 13:1); see Hoehner, *Antipas*, 231–32; Plummer, 522; Sabourin, 360. Parker ("Herod") thinks that historically the three allied authorities, Herod Antipas, Pilate, and the Sanhedrin, conspired to eliminate Jesus and that the initiative fell to Herod Antipas, whose role was much more important than the Gospels let us imagine. C. F. Evans (849–51) emphasizes the reasons for questioning the historicity of the episode.

32 Brandon (*Trial*, 120) notes: "But if such a notable incident had happened, why is it not mentioned in any of the other Gospels?" The remark is valid, even though he neglects the *Gospel of Peter*.

God's wisdom; for if they had, they would not have crucified the Lord of glory" (*NRSV*).[33]

Commentary

■ **6-7** The words "Galilee" (v. 5) and "Galilean" (v. 6) fix a logical sequence from one episode to the other, a sequence that is all the more necessary since Luke changes sources here. Indeed, he moves from Mark to his own source. In editing v. 5, he intentionally mentioned Galilee in order to facilitate this transition. In Jesus' day, as also at the time of Luke, Galilee in particular raises the idea of Jewish resistance against Rome. Since he did not want to upset the Roman governor with the simple mention of Galilee,[34] Luke underscores his conviction that neither Jesus nor the religious movement he launched represented a political danger. Pilate can send Jesus to Herod without fear.

The evangelist tends to repeat a word he likes. The simple verb ἐρωτάω ("to interrogate," "to ask," v. 3) closely follows here the meaning of ἐπερωτάω (which I translate in v. 6 as "inquire"), which is used again in v. 9 and had been used already in 22:64.

Luke locates the action on the legal level. The verb ἐπιγινώσκω ("to learn") indicates a knowing that is

the fruit of an investigation, a *cognitio*, of the judge.[35] By saying that in Pilate's view Jesus is under Herod's authority[36] Luke is suggesting that at that time one judged on the basis of the defendant's residence (*forum domicilii*) and not the place of the crime (*forum delicti*). He must be mistaken, however, because there is only late evidence for such usage, and it does not apply to the penal procedure followed by a governor of a province, imperial or procuratorial, concerning a *peregrinus* (that is, someone who is not a Roman citizen).[37]

There are several ways of understanding the verb ἀναπέμπω. Should we take it with the common meaning of "to send" or with the legal meaning of "to refer" to another authority? Since Luke makes a point of putting the episode in a legal framework, we must understand the verb in its technical sense. Is it also necessary to emphasize the prefix ἀνα- of this compound verb and to think of a specific direction: "to turn over to a higher authority"? That is unlikely, since Luke does not understand Herod to be a higher judge than Pilate.[38] I thus retain the simple legal sense of "to refer," "to turn over."[39]

If Herod is in Jerusalem[40] "in these days," it is that these days, as the readers know (22:1, 7), are the days of the feast of the Passover. The prince is in the city as a pilgrim.[41] Josephus speaks of a similar case (*Ant.* 18.5.3

---

33 On 1 Cor 2:7-9, see Wolfgang Schrage, *Der erste Brief an die Korinther* (EKKNT 7/1; Neukirchen-Vluyn: Neukirchener Verlag, 1991) 250–56.

34 Since Luke likes to use the present participle (e.g., 2:46-47), it is necessary to note here the aorist, which implies an anteriority: Pilate reacts after he had heard the matter. The aorist participle is also frequent in Luke (e.g., 6:49; 7:3, 9, 29). Numerous manuscripts specify that it is rightly the word "Galilee" that Pilate heard; see the apparatus of Nestle-Aland (27th ed.) on this text.

35 Delebecque (*Évangile*, 142) correctly thinks that Luke is drawing a distinction between "the meaning of the simple verb and that of the compound verb." It was something Pilate learned or discovered during the investigation. On the Lukan character of this verb and its participle, see Untergassmair, "Problematik," 280; Bock, 2:1818 n. 1.

36 Luke uses the term ἐξουσία ("authority," "power") elsewhere (4:6; 20:2 [twice]; 22:53; Acts 26:18), but never in a precise legal sense as here. In this point the evangelist probably depends on his special source, contra Untergassmair, "Problematik," 280.

37 See Bovon, *Last Days*, 47–48; Hoehner, "Why," 86–87; C. F. Evans, 849–85.

38 If the ἀνα- adds a nuance, it is rather that of a return (see Phlm 12): Pilate sends the Galilean back to the master of Galilee.

39 On the verb ἀναπέμπω, see Plummer, 522; Bickerman, "Utilitas," 206; Grundmann, 424; C. F. Evans, 851; Bock, 2:1818; Moulton-Milligan, *Vocabulary*, s.v. Hoehner ("Why," 86) thinks, probably incorrectly, that the verb does not have its legal sense here.

40 Luke or his source uses here the Greek form Ἱεροσόλυμα and not the Semitic form Ἱερουσαλήμ. On these two forms, see vol. 2 of this commentary, on 13:22.

41 Several people are of the opinion that Herod lodged in Jerusalem in the palace located on the western side of the hill, the palace formerly occupied by the Hasmoneans; see Lagrange, 579; Benoit, *Passion and Resurrection*, 144; Sabourin, 360. I think it is more likely that it was used as a residence by the Roman governor, unless each one of them occupied a wing of the palace!

§122):[42] Herod Antipas, the sovereign, and Vitellius, the governor of Syria, go up to Jerusalem together on the occasion of a religious festival.[43]

■ **8** Cleverly the author—Luke or before him the author of the special source—changes the register and moves from the domain of the law to that of social, almost mundane, relationships. Whereas Pilate did his work against his will, Herod thinks with all his heart of his leisure.

The vocabulary, syntax, and style of this passage are characteristic of Luke or his special source. The ἰδών ("having seen," "after having seen") is reminiscent of the threefold ἰδών of the parable of the Good Samaritan (10:31, 32, 33),[44] the ἐξ ἱκανῶν χρόνων ("for a long time")[45] of the parable of the murderous winegrowers (20:9). The periphrastic construction ἦν . . . θέλων ("he wanted"),[46] as well as the substantive infinitive with the preposition διά: διὰ τὸ ἀκούειν ("because of what he had heard"),[47] are Lukan style.[48]

The text refers to a former incident,[49] Herod's puzzlement about Jesus during the latter's ministry in Galilee (9:7-9). Luke had added a personal touch to this episode of the threefold tradition, the words "and he sought to see him," thus anticipating the future appearance. The evangelist specifies Herod's motivation here. The tetrarch of Galilee hopes[50] that Jesus will work a miraculous "sign" (σημεῖον). This verse can be read with a feeling of contempt toward Herod for simply being eager to see a miracle. One can also read it more seriously when one remembers that a sign from heaven validated the authority of one sent by God. The apostle Paul, who knows whereof he speaks, characterizes the Jews as a people who demand "signs" (the same word, σημεῖα, in the plural, 1 Cor 1:22). If the Lukan Jesus has already refused to give any sign other than that of Jonah (11:29) to those who demanded one of him (11:16), it is because such a request did not come from faith. The same thing happens here. Herod hopes for a proof that would relieve him of the risk of personal engagement and faith.[51] He wanted what he "had heard" (ἀκούειν) "about him" (περὶ αὐτοῦ)[52] to be directly available to him (ἰδεῖν, "to

---

42 See Hoehner, "Why," 86. In a passage of the *War of the Jews* (*Bell.* 1.20.4 §399) this same Josephus relates that forty years earlier the Roman governor of Syria, Varro, advised the procurators of Judea not to undertake anything without consulting the king, Herod the Great; see Joüon, "Luc 23, 11," 83.

43 According to Tannehill (333), exegetes have offered three different explanations why Pilate sent Jesus to Herod: (a) Pilate is trying to get out of an embarrassing case; (b) Pilate is not turning Jesus over to Herod; he is simply asking for his opinion; (c) Pilate wants to make a gesture to Herod without asking so much for his opinion. For Schneider (2:474), the main function of the scene is to declare Jesus innocent.

44 The verb "to see" appears three times in v. 8; see C. F. Evans, 852; Delebecque, *Évangile*, 142.

45 The text is uncertain here. Alexandrinus (A = 02) and the majority of the Byzantine manuscripts have ἦν γὰρ θέλων ἐξ ἱκανοῦ ("because he wanted for a long time"). The Athos manuscript (Ψ = 044) and other witnesses have ἦν γὰρ ἐξ ἱκανοῦ χρόνου θέλων ("because he wanted for a long time"); see the apparatus of Nestle-Aland (27th ed.); and Swanson, *Manuscripts*, 387. Luke likes to use ἱκανός with the meaning of "large," "long," or of "many" (see Acts 8:11); Lagrange, 579. As for χρόνος ("time"), he uses it in the singular as well as in the plural; see, e.g., 8:27 (singular) and 8:29 (plural). See Müller, "Herodes," 115.

46 See Acts 1:10; Ernst Haenchen, *The Acts of the Apostles: A Commentary* (Philadelphia: Westminster Press, 1971) 149 n. 7.

47 See 2:4; BDF §402 (1). Many manuscripts specify that Herod heard "much" of Jesus' speaking. They add πολλά after ἀκούειν; see the apparatus of Nestle-Aland (27th ed.).

48 Luke does not like to use the verb χαίρω ("to be delighted") to mean bad or negative joy. He used it in 22:5 following Mark 14:11. If he uses it here too with a negative connotation, it may be under the influence of his special material. Nowhere else does he use the adverb λίαν ("extremely," "very"), which he associates with it. The expression χαίρω λίαν ("to be very happy") is common in Greek, much like our "enchanted." We find it twice in the Johannine epistles (2 John 4; 3 John 3).

49 The procedure is not unusual in Luke; 22:35-38 refers back to 10:4.

50 The verb ἐλπίζω ("to hope") appears five times in Luke-Acts, generally in a profane or even a negative sense, e.g., Acts 24:26: "At the same time (Felix) was hoping that Paul would give him money." See Spicq, *Lexicon*, 1:480–92.

51 See vol. 2 of this commentary, on 11:29-32.

52 Soards ("Hearing") compares six English translations of the expression διὰ τὸ ἀκούειν περὶ αὐτοῦ and suggests translating it as "because of what he had heard about him."

see") in the form of an additional proof, a sign worked "by him" ($\dot{\epsilon}\pi\,'\,\alpha\dot{\upsilon}\tau o\hat{\upsilon}$).[53]

■ **9-10** If the question of the hoped-for sign belongs to Lukan redaction, the following question comes from the tradition of the special source. There is, indeed, a tension between v. 8 and vv. 9-10. Verses 9-10 take us back to the situation of the trial that v. 8 had abandoned. The defender and his accusers are standing before the judge.

As in Mark's parallel account (15:2-5), the judge—here Herod, there Pilate—receives no answer from the accused.[54] This silence of Jesus is a way of recalling his innocence, his nobility of heart, his courage in the face of adversity, and his personal responsibility for his own fate.[55] And yet here, as there, neither the accusers nor the accusations are missing.[56] Here the chief priests and the scribes accuse him with loud cries; there it is: "see all the charges they bring against you" (Mark 15:4). The adverb $\epsilon\dot{\upsilon}\tau\acute{o}\nu\omega\varsigma$ ("with vigor," "with vehemence"—$\acute{o}$ $\tau\acute{o}\nu o\varsigma$ means the "cord," the "strap," the "muscle," then the "tension," the "effort," the "intensity," the "vigor," the

"energy") appears infrequently in the New Testament. We meet it a second time from the same author in Acts 18:28, in a context of controversy. There it is Paul who vigorously argues with his adversaries. He shows them in the Scriptures that Jesus is the Christ. Here Jesus' opponents, equally vehemently, refuse to recognize this same messiahship of the Nazarene. The opponents are "the chief priests and the scribes"[57] who have followed him vindictively since the beginning of the passion narrative (22:2).[58]

■ **11** Herod reacts. According to tradition, he is disappointed by Jesus' silence, and, according to the redaction, he is disappointed by Jesus' refusal to work a miracle.[59] Is he disappointed as a dissatisfied judge or as an offended sovereign? Is the framework still judicial, or is it again princely? If we look at the parallel in Acts in which the governor Festus invites the king, Herod Agrippa II, to form an opinion, we must reject the alternative. The power of the prince is such that sometimes he can give an audience the character of a trial, sometimes the aspect of

---

53   See Bock, 2:1819.

54   The Syriac version known as the Curetonian adds at the end of v. 9, after it has mentioned Jesus' silence: "as if he were not there"; see *NTG*, 207; I thank Chip Coakley who has helped me on this point.

55   On the silence, see Sir 20:1 ("There is a reproof which is not timely; and there is a man who keeps silent but is wise"); Dan (Greek) 13:34-41 (wrongly accused, Susanna maintains her silence); and Isa 53:7. Josephus (*Ant.* 15.7.5 §§234–35) tells how Mariamme, the wife of Herod the Great, reacted when he condemned her to death: she kept silent, thus showing the nobility of her character. See the opinion of Bonaventure below in the section "History of Interpretation." Soards ("Silence") presents the various interpretations of Jesus' silence given in the modern period: (a) the theological interpretation (a refusal to submit to arbitration with Herod); (b) the biblical interpretation (fulfillment of prophecies); (c) the comparative interpretation (silence in the Mithra liturgy); (d) the form-critical interpretation (the situation of the church, not only of Jesus). He himself suggests using Luke to explain Luke, explaining v. 9 with 22:37, which quotes Isa 53:12. Luke had to be thinking of Isa 53:7, the silence of the Suffering Servant. Buck ("Function," 173–75) emphasizes the example Jesus gives here to the Christians of the early church. He refers in particular to the story of Peter and Herod Agrippa in Acts 12.

56   Grammarians are interested in the form $\epsilon\dot{\iota}\sigma\tau\acute{\eta}\kappa\epsilon\iota\sigma\alpha\nu$. It is the pluperfect of the verb $\ddot{\iota}\sigma\tau\alpha\mu\alpha\iota$ ("to hold fast," "to remain"); see Plummer, 522.

57   See 22:2; see also 22:4 (chief priests and officers); 22:52 (chief priests, officers of the temple, and elders); 22:66 (assembly of the elders of the people, chief priests, and scribes).

58   The famous Syriac Sinai manuscript discovered by the sisters Agnes Smith Lewis and Margaret Dunlop Gibson often reflects a very old state of the text; it does not have vv. 10-12. Yet in spite of Julius Wellhausen (*Das Evangelium Lucae* [Berlin: Reimer, 1904] 131–32), who prefers the logic of the short text, we must be dealing with an omission. Indeed, these verses appear in all the Greek manuscripts as well as in the manuscripts of all the versions, including the Syriac, with the exception of the Sinai manuscript. See Dibelius ("Herodes," 121–23), who thinks that the text was shortened because it was considered to be uninteresting or repetitive (a repetition of the material given by Matthew and Mark about Pilate). I am not convinced by this argument, but I admit that the reasons for the omission escape me.

59   Tannehill (334) rightly calls attention to the expression $\kappa\alpha\dot{\iota}$ $\acute{o}$ $\dot{H}\rho\acute{\omega}\delta\eta\varsigma$. It should be translated as "also Herod" or "Herod, he also."

an invitation. Nevertheless, while Herod does not formally condemn Jesus, he does react against him vehemently. Moreover, the syntax is jolting in keeping with the mood of the prince (the two participles, ἐμπαίξας περιβαλών ("having ridiculed after having thrown around") are juxtaposed without being coordinated and strike against one another). The participle ἐξουθενήσας ("after he regarded him as of no account") is a strong expression. It contains the word "nothing" (οὐθέν) and implies that Herod thinks that Jesus is a being without any value, a good-for-nothing. While this verb expresses an opinion, the verb ἐμπαίζω ("to toy with," "to have fun at the expense of," "to ridicule") takes us into the field of action. Herod gives free reign to his feeling in the form of mocking. Contrary to the proverb that affirms that ridicule does not kill, there are words, insults, or ridiculing comments that wound as much as blows do.[60]

Then a gesture is indicated that, in the spirit of Luke, must correspond to the mocking described by the aorist participles ἐξουθενήσας ("after he regarded him as of no account") and ἐμπαίξας ("had ridiculed him"). The Hellenist Edouard Delebecque is of the opinion that "the second aorist participle [παριβαλών] is subordinated to the first [ἐμπαίξας] by juxtaposition; the first expresses

time, the second the aspect (the absence of duration). Herod and his guards[61] mock Jesus 'by covering him,' that is, 'by the fact that they cover him.'"[62] I do not think that is right, because on the level of the meaning and the action I bring the two participles together, ἐξουθενήσας and ἐμπαίξας, and I regard the third, περιβαλών ("after having covered") as a subsequent action, which prepares the return to Pilate.[63]

While the clothes worn today by Westerners are cut to fit the various parts of the body, in the ancient world the clothing retained the form given by the loom on which it was produced. It was about drapery. If the cloak was of wool, the tunic was usually of linen. They resembled one another structurally by their rectangular form. Whereas the tunic was sewn, however, the cloak was not. Workers and peasants usually wore only the tunic. To general amazement, the early Spartans and strict philosophers were satisfied with the cloak alone. Unlike the cloak of the Greeks, the Roman toga, which originally had been rectangular, early on was rounded on one of its sides.

Herod puts a festive garment on Jesus.[64] The participle περιβαλών is appropriate for the act of putting on a cloak, that is, the external garment that goes on top. The word ἐσθής is a general term.[65] It can refer to all

---

60 To be convinced, it is enough to see the film *Ridicule* by Patrice Leconte (1996). At the court of the king of France the words had the destructive power of weapons.

61 Verrall ("Christ") reconstructs the scene in an ingenious way. He brings the expression σὺν τοῖς στρατεύμασιν closer to the subject of Herod and imagines that Herod's back was protected by his guards. Creed (282) thinks that this assumption is too subtle and that we must associate the soldiers themselves with the mocking.

62 Delebecque, *Évangile*, 142.

63 My position corresponds to that of Joüon ("Luc 23, 11," 82–83), who writes: "We believe, on the contrary, that the purpose of putting on white clothing is not to cause the mocking, but to prepare for returning Jesus to Pilate."

64 The two studies that are most useful here are Joüon, "Luc 23, 11," and Delbrueck, "Antiquarisches." Joüon shows that the verb περιβάλλω ("to throw around") is appropriate only for an outer garment, a cloak (in antiquity, among both Greeks and Jews, the cloak is "a simple rectangular piece of fabric," 80 n. 2). The general word ἐσθής ("garment")

could designate the cloak or the tunic, but the verb περιβάλλω, as well as the entire scene, suggests the cloak alone. Joüon even wonders whether the fact that Luke does not use the precise word ἱμάτιον ("coat") does not mean that he is talking about a "special garment," "for example, a kind of scarf" (81). Bornhäuser ("Beteiligung") concedes that the middle form would be more appropriate than the active περιβαλών, but he supposes that the verb has an intransitive sense here and imagines that it is Herod who puts the showy garment on himself and accompanies Jesus to Pilate. This hypothesis is improbable.

65 See 2 Macc 8:35 (τὴν δοξικὴν . . . ἐσθῆτα); 2 Macc 11:8 (ἐν λευκῇ ἐσθῆτι); Acts 12:21 (ἐσθῆτα βασιλικήν); see also what Josephus says (*Ant.* 8.7.3 §186) about Solomon's royal robes; Polybius (*Historiae* 10.4.8) says that the *toga candida*, the "white toga," is the garment appropriate for a candidate for a public function; in its proper sense the word *candidatus* designates the candidate who is wearing the white toga. See Wiefel, 391 n. 10.

of a person's clothing. At that time, the tunic (the short χιτών or the long στολή of the Greeks) was worn as an undergarment, and the draped cloak (the civilian ἱμάτιον or the military χλαμύς for the Greeks, the toga for the Romans) as an outer garment. It can also designate only the cloak. Furthermore, one must also distinguish between the civilian dress and the military uniform, everyday clothing and ceremonial costumes, the profane and the sacred, the Greek and the Roman, western and eastern, male and female fashion.[66] The adjective λαμπρά facilitates the decision. It means "bright," "a white brightness," and leans toward ostentation.[67] The ἐσθὴς λαμπρά thus means a ceremonial cloak. To understand what is happening, we must turn to the parallel scene (omitted by Luke) in which Pilate's soldiers mock Jesus. There they force a purple robe on him.[68] They make fun of the one who is accused of regarding himself as a king. (For the Romans and the Greeks, purple was the mark of royal and imperial dignity). Herod and his rabble of soldiers organize a game of mocking and masquerade that has the same sense but within a Jewish framework. The white, shining wool cloak was reserved for the past, present, or coming king of Israel. The two mocking scenes, doubtless coming from a single tradition, conveyed the same message: Jesus' opponents, whether Pilate the Roman or Herod the Jew, ridiculed Jesus' messianic kingship. Although they still do not condemn him to death, they both refuse to believe him. Herod sends Jesus back to Pilate. The repetition of the verb ἀνέπεμψεν ("he sent," "he returned," vv. 7, 11) shows cruelly that Jesus has become a plaything of the princes of this world. Does each one not play him off against the other?

■ **12** In this playfulness (there is the idea of play in the verb ἐμπαίζω, "to ridicule," v. 11), the two get along wonderfully well. Luke does not tell us why the two men previously could not stand each other,[69] nor does he tell us how he knows about it.[70] What counts in his eyes is that on this occasion they became friends. Influenced as he is by Greek culture, Luke likes the vocabulary of friendship.[71] Does he necessarily apply it to a reality he deplores? Or is it necessary, as some think, to see a positive sense behind this malignant alliance?[72] Various thoughtful theologians have referred to the important text in Ephesians, which celebrates the reconciliation between Jews and pagans that the redemptive death of Christ brought about (Eph 2:11-22). Do we read here a discreet allusion to this victory over hatred and the reconciliation of the nations? What immediately follows

---

66 See Léon Heuzey (*Histoire du costume antique d'après des études sur le modèle vivant* [Paris: Champion, 1922]), from whom I derive much information. See also Edgar Haulotte, *Symbolique du vêtement selon la Bible* (Théologie [P] 65; Paris: Aubier, 1966).

67 Plummer (523) and Lagrange (580) think that the adjective indicates the quality and not the color of the garment; on the contrary, Schlatter (440) is of the opinion that the bright whiteness of the clothing testifies to both Jesus' innocence and to his messiahship. Joüon ("Luc 23, 11," 81–83) and Untergassmair ("Problematik," 287–88) also insist that Jesus' innocence is expressed this way. By contrast, I follow Joüon in noting that, according to Josephus (*Ant.* 14.9.4 §172), the accused were to appear before the Sanhedrin in black garments.

68 Mark 15:17-20a par. Matt 27:28-31a par. John 19:1-3. The Peshitta speaks in v. 11 about "clothing of scarlet" (Joüon, "Luc 23, 11," 80, 82 n. 8). It must be a question of trying to make the scene more like that of the mocking inflicted by Pilate's soldiers in the other Gospels.

69 Luke is the only New Testament author who resorted to the verb προϋπάρχω (only twice, here and in Acts 8:9). When an author employed this

verb, he expressed his intention to write carefully. The verb is a good choice, because it indicates an earlier reality. Depending on its context, it is translated as "to exist before," "to precede." As v. 12b says, formerly the hatred had been dominant between Pilate and Herod. Philo of Alexandria (*Leg. Gaj.* 299–305) reports a confrontation between Pilate and the Jewish people, who were defended by the four sons of Herod the Great, one of whom was Herod Antipas.

70 See the analysis above.

71 See Ann Graham Brock, "The Significance of φιλέω and φίλος in the Tradition of Jesus' Sayings and in the Early Church," *HTR* 90 (1997) 393–409.

72 See Schweizer, 234; Talbert, *Reading*, 217; Manus, "Universalism." This latter author, who is current with the particularly European and American exegesis, reads the text from the perspective of an African theology. In his opinion, Luke's theology contains the idea of a natural revelation (see Acts 14:15-17; 17:24-26) and, in the form of reconciliation, christologically goes beyond the Roman and Jewish religions represented here by Pilate and Herod.

(Pilate's cowardice and Herod's disappearance) leads us to answer no. What follows after that (the declaration of his innocence, then the crucifixion and resurrection) encourages us to answer yes.

As he had brought the two authorities together in the same city (v. 7), Luke brings them together here on the same day (v. 12) and emphasizes the mutual character ($\mu\epsilon\tau$ $\dot{\alpha}\lambda\lambda\dot{\eta}\lambda\omega\nu$, "with one another") of their unexpected friendship.

History of Interpretation

After recalling the appearance before Pilate,[73] Tertullian expresses the opinion that sending Jesus to Herod (v. 7) was a gift (*Adv. Marc.* 4.42.3). If that is true, it is because Hosea had prophesied it: "And in chains they will lead him to the king as a present" (Hos 10:6 LXX and Old Latin version; *Et vinctum eum ducent xenium regi* is Tertullian's Latin text of Hos 10:6). The African continues his interpretation, connecting Gospel facts with biblical oracles: the silence of Jesus (v. 9), who knows when to speak and when to keep silent, verifies the statement of Isa 53:7, the silence of the servant of God. The polemic against Marcion is implied here, but it is real in its indication of correspondences between the Old and New Testaments that were rejected by the opponent (4.42.3).

Ambrose of Milan, a hundred and fifty years later, was also interested in this silence.[74] If Jesus remained silent and refused to give a sign, it was for two reasons: "Because of the cruelty of the person (namely, Herod), he did not deserve to see divine things, and also because the Lord avoided putting himself forward." The white robe covering Jesus (v. 11) represents the immaculate character of the passion, as the two magistrates, Pilate and Herod, represent the Gentiles and the Jews. If they then become friends (v. 12), it is to anticipate the reconciliation in Christ. That Pilate precedes Herod, signifies that the Gentiles will believe first and will favor the conversion of Israel. Without saying it, Ambrose begins his reflections with the Epistle to the Romans (11:7-32). As one can see, the connection that certain modern interpreters establish between the friendship of the two judges and the reconciliation in Christ was already established in Christian antiquity, for Ambrose was not the first person to meditate on this effect of the presence of Jesus. Cyril of Jerusalem, his contemporary, takes his interpretation in the same direction (*Hom. Cat.* 13.14).[75] In his thirteenth catechetical homily, the bishop of Jerusalem says that "it is appropriate that he who was to restore peace between heaven and earth would first establish peace between the men who condemned him." He is thinking of Ephesians 2 and, moreover, quotes the book of Job (The Lord "who reconciles[76] the hearts of the princes of this world," Job 12:24 LXX). Later in the West, the Venerable Bede would offer briefly a similar interpretation (*In Luc.* 6.1335–41).

One can read the most developed and most interesting interpretation in Bonaventure (*Comm. Luc.* 23.8–15).[77] Thinking logically, as usual, he is of the opinion that vv. 6-12 present four elements: Pilate's sly caution, Herod's guilty curiosity, the dishonesty of the accusing crowd, and the *stoliditas principis vilipendentis*, "the unreasonableness of the prince who condemns as despicable." In a subtle way he thinks that Pilate certainly resorts to a subterfuge, but that he does not do so without a legal basis. Quoting Rom 13:1 (every authority has been ordained by God), Bonaventure thinks that Pilate turned Jesus over to the right authority. Then, quoting Luke 16:8 (the children of this age are more clever than the children of light), it is his view that Pilate acted cleverly. *Unde apparet, quod Pilatus fecit caute, fecit etiam iuste* ("It follows that Pilate acted prudently but that he also acted legally"). As he regularly does, the medieval theologian supports his interpretation with a salvo of biblical quotations. He does this in particular in connection with Herod's impatient pleasure, which he contrasts with the

---

73   In the middle of the second century Justin (*Dial.* 103.4) knew the episode, which he summarizes: $\chi\alpha\rho\iota\zeta\dot{o}\mu\epsilon\nu\circ\varsigma$ $\delta\epsilon\delta\epsilon\mu\dot{\epsilon}\nu\circ\nu$ $\tau\dot{o}\nu$ $\dot{\mathrm{I}}\eta\sigma\circ\hat{\upsilon}\nu$ $\ddot{\epsilon}\pi\epsilon\mu\psi\epsilon$ ("to do him a favor he sent Jesus to him in chains"). Justin also speaks of it in his *First Apology* (40.6).

74   The interpretation of Luke 23:6-12 is in Ambrose *Exp. Luc.* 10.99–101 and 103. The quotation comes from §99.

75   See Just, *Luke*, 354. Plummer (523) provides the opinion of another fourth-century author, Ephraem the Syrian.

76   The verb in the LXX is $\delta\iota\alpha\lambda\lambda\dot{\alpha}\sigma\sigma\omega$. Cyril understands it to mean "to reconcile," but it initially means "to exchange."

77   Bernardini, 567–69.

joy of Abraham (John 8:56), of Job (Job 23:3), and of Jesus' contemporaries (Luke 10:23-24). All wanted to see the Lord, but Herod did it in a bad spirit: *Non sic Herodes, sed ex curiositate* ("It was not that way with Herod, but he did it from curiosity"). Let us not forget that in the Middle Ages, although it was not a capital sin, curiosity was more strongly condemned than it is today.[78] Bonaventure, quite energetic at this passage, then distinguishes between "seeing" and "hearing." Herod would have done better had he listened to the word rather than seeking a miraculous sign: *non sicut studiosus, sed sicut curiosus* (he was not "like a studious person but like a curious one"). Is it not normal that one gives no answer to a person who has such bad intentions? Jesus' silence was justified. And Bonaventure lays out a series of biblical examples of justified silences. In connection with the charges made by the chief priests and the scribes (v. 10), which constitute the third element of the pericope, Bonaventure sees, in spite of the Vulgate's *constanter*, "steadfastly, with perseverance," not a sign of "constancy" (*constantia*) but one of "obstinacy" (*pertinacia*). In his eyes, Herod follows here in the line of Cain, Pharaoh, Jannes and Jambres (2 Tim 3:8), all persecutors, all imitators of the dragon (Rev 12:10). Finally, the fourth element, the insults inflicted. They were made because Jesus had disappointed Herod by not performing a miracle, by giving no answer, by refusing to defend himself. Thus, Jesus was humiliated three times during his trial: by the malice of the Jews (22:63-65), by the arrogance of Herod (here), and by the ignorance of the soldiers (John 19:1-3). Concerning the clothing designed to make Jesus look ridiculous, the white garment on the part of Herod and the purple robe on the part of Pilate, Bonaventure comments that "our priest will have worn the sacerdotal vestments dur-

ing his passion." And he enumerates all the garments a priest wore in the Middle Ages. Finally, he takes from the sudden friendship between Herod and Pilate a negative sense (the alliance of the persecutors) and a positive sense (the reconciliation of opposing persons). On this subject he quotes the *Glossa ordinaria*, which in turn quotes the Venerable Bede in a passage to which I have already referred (see above).[79]

Conclusion

Historically there were only two trial appearances of Jesus, one before the Jewish authorities (22:66-71 par.; see already 1 Thess 2:15), the other before the Roman power (23:1-5; see also 1 Tim 6:13). At an early date Christian reflection based on Scripture (Ps 2:1-2) added a redundant digression (23:6-12; see Acts 4:25-28; see also *Gos. Pet.* 1–3). Luke integrated this episode into Jesus' trial before Pilate (23:1-25 par.).

In this form, according to Luke, the incident offers Pilate a delay, the Jewish authorities a new occasion to resist, Herod a hope for a divine sign, and Jesus the chance to express his courage in the face of death with his silence.

By referring to the sign and mentioning the ultimate reconciliation of the hostile princes, the evangelist grafts to the story thinly veiled religious connotations. The readers realize that only faith and not sight makes it possible to lay hold of the identity and the work of Jesus Christ. They understand that, even if the Christian religion often brings forces together against itself that previously were divided, it also bears witness to a reconciliation brought about by the one who wears the messianic cloak not simply as an object of derision.

---

78 Bonaventure is aware of the reminiscence in v. 8 of Luke 9:9 (the desire to see Jesus).

79 For the sixteenth century, see Erasmus, *Annotationes*, 214 (grammatical remarks and explanation of the vocabulary); idem, *Paraphrasis*, 459–60 (here more explanatory than narrative). Luther (*Evangelien-Auslegung*, 1189–90) attacks Herod: "ein grundböser Bube," "ein grosser Heuchler," "ein böses und doch sehr listiges thier" ("a basically malicious kid," "a large hypocrite," "a malicious and yet very cunning animal"). One does not answer such people, and, referring to Psalm 2, Luther says

that princes in dispute themselves often intend to persecute. Calvin (*Harmony*, 3:181–82) offers a historical explanation. Like Bonaventure, who is not quoted, he draws a contrast between the desire to see and the absence of the desire to hear. Herod is an example of what "the flesh" desires: a desire focused on God's visible works that refuses to pay attention to the invisible God. The prince of Galilee "shut out the grace of God." God had hardened his heart with such a scene, "because he was not worthy to see one spark of the heavenly glory in Christ."

The Final Appearance
(23:13-25)
Bibliography

Bajsic, Alois, "Pilatus, Jesus und Barabbas," *Bib* 48 (1967) 7–28.

Bammel, "Trial," 415–51.

Bartsch, Hans-Werner, "Wer verurteilte Jesus zum Tode?" *NovT* 7 (1964–65) 210–16.

Blinzler, Josef, "Der Entscheid des Pilatus: Exekutionsbefehl oder Todesurteil?" *MThZ* 5 (1954) 171–84.

Idem, *Prozess*, 249–62, 308–14.

Brandon, S. G. F., *Jesus and the Zealots: A Study of the Political Factor in Primitive Christianity* (New York: Scribner, 1967) 4–5.

Idem, *Trial*, 107–39.

Brawley, Robert L., *Text to Text Pours Forth Speech: Voices of Scripture in Luke-Acts* (Indiana Studies in Biblical Literature; Bloomington: Indiana University Press, 1995) 42–60.

Caillemer, E., "ἀνάκρισις," in Charles Daremberg and Edmond Saglio, eds., *Dictionnaire des antiquités grecques et romaines* (3d ed.; Paris: Hachette, 1881) 261–64.

Carroll, J. T., "Luke's Crucifixion Scene," in Dennis D. Sylva, ed., *Reimaging the Death of the Lukan Jesus* (Athenäums Monografien: Theologie 73; Frankfurt: Hain, 1990) 108–24, 194–203.

Carter, Warren, *Pontius Pilate: Portraits of a Roman Governor* (Collegeville, Minn.: Liturgical Press, 2003).

Cassidy, Richard J., "Luke's Audience, the Chief Priests and the Motive for Jesus' Death," in idem and Philip J. Scharper, eds., *Political Issues in Luke-Acts* (Maryknoll, N.Y.: Orbis, 1983) 146–67.

Chavel, Charles B., "The Releasing of a Prisoner on the Eve of Passover in Ancient Jerusalem," *JBL* 60 (1941) 272–78.

Chico Cano, Manuel, "Der Prozess Jesu: Eine literarkritische und redaktionsgeschichtliche Untersuchung zu Lk 23,1-25" (diss., Münster i. W., 1984).

Cohen, Haim, *The Trial and Death of Jesus* (New York: Harper & Row, 1971).

Colin, Jean, *Les villes libres de l'Orient gréco-romain et l'envoi au supplice par acclamations populaires* (Latomus 82; Brussels-Berchem: Latomus, 1965).

Costen, James Hutten, "Doing the Right Thing: Isaiah 53:1-12, Luke 23:13-25," *Journal of the Interdenominational Theological Center* 24 (1996–97) 207–13.

Davies, Stevan L., "Who Is Called Bar Abbas," *NTS* 27 (1980–81) 260–62.

Derrett, J. Duncan M., "The Trial of Jesus and the Doctrine of Redemption," in idem, *Law in the New Testament* (London: Darton, Longman & Todd, 1970) 389–460.

Finegan, *Überlieferung*, 29–30.

Ford, J. Massyngberde, "'Crucify Him, Crucify Him' and the Temple Scroll," *ExpT* 87 (1975–76) 275–78.

Foulon-Piganiol, C. L., "Le rôle du peuple dans le procès de Jésus: Une hypothèse juridique et théologique," *NRTh* 98 (1976) 627–37.

George, "Sens."

Herranz Marco, Mariano, "Un problema de crítica histórica en el relato de la pasión: La liberación de Barrabás," *EstBib* 30 (1971) 137–60.

Juster, Jean, *Les Juifs dans l'empire romain: Leur condition juridique, économique et sociale* (2 vols.; Paris: Paul Geuthner, 1914).

Karris, Robert J., *Luke, Artist and Theologian: Luke's Passion Account as Literature* (New York: Paulist, 1985) 79–92.

Kodell, Jerome, "Luke's Use of Laos, 'People,' Especially in the Jerusalem Narrative (Lk 19:28—24:53)," *CBQ* 31 (1969) 327–43.

Lemonon, Jean-Pierre, *Pilate et le gouvernement de la Judée: Texte et monuments* (EtB; Paris: Gabalda, 1981) 191–95.

Lietzmann, "Prozess Jesu."

Lohfink, Gerhard, *Die Sammlung Israels: Eine Untersuchung zur lukanischen Ekklesiologie* (SANT 39; Munich: Kösel, 1975) 42–43.

Lohse, *Geschichte*, 89–93.

Maccoby, H. Z., "Jesus and Barabbas," *NTS* 16 (1969–70) 55–60.

Matera, "Jesus before Pilate."

Mayer-Maly, Theo, "Das Auftreten der Menge im Prozess Jesu und in den ältesten Christenprozessen," *Österreichisches Archiv für Kirchenrecht* 6 (1955) 321–45.

Merkel, Johannes, "Die Begnadigung am Passahfeste," *ZNW* 6 (1905) 293–316.

Merritt, Robert L., "Jesus Barabbas and the Paschal Pardon," *JBL* 104 (1985) 57–68.

Neyrey, *Passion*, 80–84.

Popkes, *Christus traditus*, 13–55, 82–104, 122–24, 153–89, 217–19.

Rau, Gottfried, "Das Volk in der lukanischen Passionsgeschichte: Eine Konjektur zu Lc 23,13," *ZNW* 56 (1965) 41–51.

Rigg, Horace Abram, "Barabbas," *JBL* 64 (1945) 417–56.

Rilliet, Frédéric, "Barabbas: quel père, quel fils?" in *Figures du Nouveau Testament chez les Pères* (CBiPa 3; Strasbourg: Centre d'analyse et de documentation patristiques, 1991) 209–32.

Schniewind, *Parallelperikopen*, 62–77.

Schulte, F. W. C., "Bar-Abbas een bijnaam," *NThS* 3 (1920) 114–18.

Sherwin-White, *Roman Society*, 24–28.

273

Sloyan, Gerard Stephen, *Jesus on Trial: The Development of the Passion Narratives and Their Historical and Ecumenical Implications* (Philadelphia: Fortress Press, 1973) 68.

Taylor, *Passion Narrative*, 84–89.

Trilling, Wolfgang, *Fragen zur Geschichtlichkeit Jesu* (Düsseldorf: Patmos, 1966) 130–41.

Unnik, W. C. van, "Levensmogelijkheid of doodvonnis," in A. J. Bronkhorst et al., eds., *Woorden gaan leven: Opstellen van en over Willem Cornelis van Unnik (1910–1978)* (Kampen: Kok, 1979) 127–32.

Vicent Cernuda, "Barrabás."

Winter, Paul, "Marginal Notes on the Trial of Jesus," *ZNW* 50 (1959) 14–33, 221–51.

Idem, *On the Trial*, 94, 131–43.

13 **Pilate, who had called together the chief priests, the leaders, and the people, 14/ said to them, "You have brought this man to me as someone who had corrupted the people, and behold, after I have examined him in your presence, I did not find that this man was guilty of any of the things of which you accused him; 15/ nor did Herod, for he sent him back to us; and behold, nothing he has done is deserving of death. 16/ Thus after I have punished him, I will release him."[a]**

18 **But they all shouted together these words: "Get rid of that one, and release Barabbas to us!" 19/ This one had been thrown into prison following an uprising in the city and a murder. 20/ Again Pilate declared to them that he wanted to release Jesus. 21/ But they cried out all the more saying, "Crucify, crucify him!" 22/ But he said to them a third time, "What evil did this one do? I have found nothing in him deserving of death. So after I have punished him, I will release him." 23/ But they insisted with loud voices, asking that he be crucified. And their voices prevailed.**

24 **Pilate then determined that their demand had to be accepted. 25/ So he released the one who had been thrown into prison because of insurrection and murder and whom they had asked for. But he delivered Jesus to their will.**

a On the absence of v. 17 in the original text of the Gospel, see the commentary below on v. 17. The text of v. 17 is as follows: "Because he was compelled to release someone to them on the occasion of the festival."

The plot (22:2-6) led to the arrest (22:47-53) and the appearance before the Sanhedrin (22:66-71). Once it had become a legal matter, it continued before Pilate (23:1-5) before moving on to Herod (23:6-12). Now here it is again before Pilate (23:13-25).[1] Although Jesus remained active from the fomenting of the plot until his arrest, now he becomes the object of a development whose subject he had been to that point.[2] We would be mistaken, however, to see him as passive, because his active will is unyielding in supporting a fate that increasingly is against him. In spite of the comfort he gives by his last comments (22:15-38), he has to watch while his

1 Following Neyrey (*Passion*, 81) and Sherwin-White (*Roman Society*, 24–28), Bock (2:1823) notes that Pilate's efforts follow well the possible course of a trial according to Roman law (the seven stages here are arrest, charges brought, examination, sentence, complementary verdict, request for acquittal, warning).

2 See Bovon, "Lukan Story of the Passion," 76.

main disciple collapses (22:54-62). From now on it is the opponents who surround him. Their social superiority—they are portrayed as the political and religious authorities of the country—gives them immediate power. Of course, this power is limited: on the one hand, by the people who instill fear in these leaders (22:2) and, on the other, by the Roman governor, whose presence reminds them that they are not masters alongside God. Pilate's threefold declaration of Jesus' innocence (23:4, 14, 22) momentarily compensates for Peter's threefold denial (22:54-62). Unfortunately, this antithetic parallel becomes a simple parallel, since Pilate is not able to enforce his opinion (23:24). The people themselves, thus far always favorable to Jesus, suddenly line up on the side of the opponents (23:13). The signs of repentance, which the narrative lays out along the way like white stones (23:27, 35, 48), do not make one forget the twofold cry, "Crucify, crucify him!" (23:21). Abandoned by his own people, Jesus is abandoned by all.[3]

Synchronic Analysis

Verses 13-25 of chap. 23 form a unit. Pilate, who received the request in v. 1 and who tried to dodge the issue in vv. 6-7, now takes things in hand. If in v. 1 "Pilate" was the last word in the sentence and was in the accusative, here (v. 13) as in vv. 6 and 24, he is at the beginning of the sentence and in the nominative. As the end of the pericope indicates, however, this activity of the governor, which gave way to Herod's advantage, ends up collapsing to the advantage of Jesus' Jewish opponents—to quote the evangelist, to the advantage of "their will" (v. 25). The name of Pilate, who is so active and resigned, frames the literary unit and establishes its limits (v. 13 and vv. 24-25).

This unit has its own movement and coherence. It unfolds like a tragedy in miniature. It begins (vv. 13-16) with the main character summarizing the situation and indicating his intention; in the second part (vv. 18-23)[4] the summoned conversation partners react and express their opposition at the top of their voices; in the third part the one who has the main role abandons his project and submits to them (note the twofold description of this abduction: τὸ αἴτημα αὐτῶν ("their request") is granted, and Jesus is delivered τῷ θελήματι αὐτῶν ("to their will," vv. 24-25).[5] The drama contrasts opposing desires, wills, and narrative programs. Voices and cries respond to one another. As in the theater, there are words before there are acts. Pilate's εἶπεν ("he says," v. 14) and the "strong voices" (v. 23) of the opponents confront one another. Between these words Jesus' silence is so discreet that one could say that it is not mentioned. Thus, the missing answer (v. 9) still attracts attention. Yet all of this is not theater; it is a trial. Does a trial not consist of words and deliberations that result in acts?

Pilate's comments and the words of the leaders of Israel are on different levels. Pilate speaks (εἶπεν, "he says," v. 14), while his conversation partners shout (ἀνέκραγον, "they shouted," v. 18).[6] The governor expresses himself carefully, his opposite number

---

3 Goulder (*New Paradigm*, 2:761) is of the opinion that in this passage the Lukan tendencies are present throughout and the linguistic characteristics are Lukan. The British exegete provides the philological details and the statistics relating to the vocabulary used in these verses (761–62).

4 On v. 17, which does not belong to the original text of Luke, see the commentary below.

5 My division into three parts corresponds to that of Sabourin (361) and Bock (2:1823). Goulder (*New Paradigm*, 2:760–64) takes vv. 13-32 together. He regards vv. 13-16 as a preface and vv. 27-32 as an appendix. Ernst (626–27) thinks that vv. 1-25 form a unit. He is not wrong: in my judgment, vv. 13-25 constitute a small unit within the larger vv. 1-25. As is his custom, Meynet (*Évangile*, 2:225–26) is of the opinion that the construction of vv. 13-25 is

concentric. Each of the two parts, vv. 14b-16 and vv. 18b-25, has a sentence of introduction, vv. 13-14a and v. 18a. As I say below in n. 47, he is wrong to put v. 17 in the middle of the composition, since in the almost unanimous view of the exegetes this verse was not part of the original text of Luke. The central themes of this unit would be the parody of the Passover, the incriminating and carried out subversion, and the perversion of justice. See also Meynet, *Guide*, 105–7.

6 The meaning of ἐπιφωνῶ in v. 21 is also "to call while shouting," "to cry out all the more." See the commentary below on v. 21.

brusquely and with imperatives ($\alpha\hat{\iota}\rho\epsilon$, "eliminate"; $\sigma\tau\alpha\acute{\upsilon}\rho o\upsilon$, "crucify"). The voice of reason tries in vain to silence that of unreason. In Acts Luke will say that this unreason was born of ignorance (Acts 3:17; 13:27). He also implies that Satan had insinuated himself into the heart of Judas (Luke 22:3). Thus, the human voices represent only the surface of things. As in any tragedy, the divine plan is realized through human beings and even through demonic powers (Acts 2:23; 4:28). It is less a matter of the guilt of the actors than of collective fate. The fault is projected onto the figure of the one who is silent. It is stated by the opponents at the beginning (v. 2), then repeated indirectly (v. 14), and finally directly by the violent shouts (vv. 18, 20). Pilate, followed by Herod, does not cease saying the truth, however, and proclaiming Jesus' innocence (vv. 14-15, 20, 22).

The guilt attributed to Jesus is even precisely stated; it is fundamental. Politically, it represents an attack against the authority of Israel's leaders and against Roman power. Religiously, it corresponds to corrupting the people; it leads them astray from God's ways. The narrator then tries to add his voice to the voices of the actors of the drama. One can hear him saying in v. 19 that Barabbas himself was guilty of this capital sin, since he had taken part in acts of terror during a rebellion in the holy city. In v. 25 Luke raises his voice again to repeat his view. The blindness, he suggests, is so complete that the innocent one will be declared guilty and the guilty one will be released.

Diachronic Analysis

Three textual elements stand out here in opening a synopsis of this passage. First, in Mark and Matthew there is no parallel to Luke's vv. 13-16. Second, in Luke there is no immediate parallel to vv. 6-11 of Mark 15 (par. Matt 27:15-20). Third, the Gospels come closer together only for the final dialogue between the Jews and the governor, a dialogue that ends with Pilate's sentence (vv. 18-25). How shall we explain this textual reality?[7] If one thinks, as many exegetes do, that the evangelist uses only Mark, one will attribute vv. 13-16 to Lukan redaction. These verses initially recall the details of what happened. They describe the role of the Jewish leaders who brought Jesus and accused him; then they mention the role of Pilate, who, although he thought Jesus was innocent, still consulted Herod Antipas. They are completed finally by the brief statement of Pilate's intention: after a warning he will release Jesus. Luke wrote this paragraph to summarize the situation and to ensure a transition. According to these exegetes, Mark 15:6-11 did not disappear from the Third Gospel. Luke, who does not like it when Mark digresses,[8] moves these verses and rewrites them. Their contents, about Barabbas, appear in the comment of the narrator (v. 19), who feels he must describe in greater detail the identity of the imprisoned terrorist. In spite of their characteristics, vv. 18-25 are only a Lukan rewriting that abridges their Markan parallel.[9]

Such a hypothesis has a number of weaknesses. Why does Luke have to write such a long transition (vv. 13-16)? Why does he get entangled without explanation in the Barabbas episode, while Mark makes it so logically understandable?[10] Why does he omit the important expression "king of the Jews," which is so significant on Pilate's lips (Mark 15:9, 12)? Why does he replace a judicious imperative aorist ($\sigma\tau\alpha\acute{\upsilon}\rho\omega\sigma o\nu$, "crucify," with point action) with an awkward imperative present ($\sigma\tau\alpha\acute{\upsilon}\rho o\upsilon$, with continuous action)? One finds too many special

---

7   On the literary character and the historical value of the Lukan account, see Brandon, *Trial*, 116–25. Luke depends on Mark and probably on independent information coming from the Jerusalem church and the house of Herod. Luke, who writes for pagan, Greek-speaking readers, has a rational and theological view of Jesus' trial. He wants to rewrite Mark, omitting the charge that Jesus attacked the temple and adding the scene in which Jesus appeared before Herod. In his eyes it is the trial before Pilate, and not that before the Sanhedrin, that is the more decisive. Brandon summarizes it thus (122): "It is a contest over the fate of Jesus waged by Pilate on one side, and the Jewish leaders and people on the other."

8   One will remember that Luke omits the Markan digression about the death of John the Baptist (Mark 6:17-29).

9   The position I have presented here, which is not mine, corresponds, for example, to that of Schneider, 2:476. Matera ("Jesus before Pilate") also comes to the conclusion that a second source alongside Mark is not needed to explain the genesis of Luke 23:13-25. In his opinion, it is enough to note the extent of Luke's redactional work.

10   Lagrange writes (582): "What interests Luke,

features in the Lukan account of the passion for one to be satisfied with only a single source. According to my hypothesis,[11] Luke has another source, and he skillfully alternates the accounts from his sources. Of necessity, the two sources have much in common (historical memories, biblical references, liturgical requirements, and theological coherence). In my understanding, Luke, who reworked Mark until Pilate's first interrogation, follows his own source from the episode with Herod until the crucifixion (v. 43). Arguments in support of this opinion include the following: In vv. 13-16 one hears not only Luke's voice but also that of the author of the special material. The charges made against Jesus in v. 14 correspond to those of v. 2; they have no equivalent in Mark and must come from Luke's second source.[12] One finds Pilate's threefold declaration of Jesus' innocence only in Luke and John.[13] Since Mark has no knowledge of it, it too must correspond to material of the special source. Luke's presentation of the case of Barabbas and the use he makes of it are not to be explained by a rewriting of Mark; these elements have rather a literary dependence on another document. In Luke, releasing a prisoner does not correspond to a religious custom; it is an expression of popular pressure. Certainly, the language is that of Luke, but it is also that of the author of the special material. This one—one must remember—readily makes use of a vocabulary that exceeds elementary words. That is what one sees here. The summons (v. 13), the declarations of innocence (vv. 4, 14, 22), the intention to release him (vv. 16, 20), the shouts of the crowd (v. 23), and Pilate's final abdication (vv. 24-25) are expressed in precise and elegant terms. Some are characteristic of Luke, but others come from the author of the special material. I think of him when I read $\pi\alpha\mu\pi\lambda\eta\vartheta\epsilon\acute{\iota}$ ("all together,"

v. 18), unique in its adverbial form; the abstract $\tau\grave{o}$ $\alpha\breve{\iota}\tau\eta\mu\alpha$ $\alpha\grave{\upsilon}\tau\tilde{\omega}\nu$ ("their request," v. 24); and the verbs that echo one another: $\pi\rho o\sigma\phi\omega\nu\acute{\epsilon}\omega$ ("to declare," v. 20) and $\grave{\epsilon}\pi\iota\phi\omega\nu\acute{\epsilon}\omega$ ("to shout," v. 21).[14]

John the evangelist is also aware of Jesus' trial before Pilate. As we have seen, he deploys it in a sequence of concentric scenes. While the Fourth Gospel's reference to the Passover privilege is reminiscent of the Gospel of Mark, the repeated declarations of innocence as well as the absence of mocking at the end of the hearing and before the crucifixion recall Luke. Some of John's details, such as the verb $\alpha\breve{\iota}\rho\omega$ (John 19:15; see v. 18), the repeated "crucify, crucify" (John 19:6; see v. 21), or Pilate's decisive act (John 19:16; see v. 25), the preference for Barabbas (John 18:40; see v. 18) also suggest that the evangelists have one or more traditions in common that are independent of Mark.[15]

Pilate also appears in the *Gospel of Peter*, where he even seems to be subject to Herod's authority. It is this collaboration between the two men, which, as we have seen,[16] makes it possible to establish connections between the Gospel of Luke and the fragment of Akhmîm. Pilate's other character traits and actions have no special relationship with the Third Gospel. That Pilate appears to regard Jesus as innocent is common to all the Gospels. That Joseph of Arimathea asks Pilate for the body of Jesus is another common element. That Pilate posts guards near the tomb of Jesus and that he speaks with them after the experience of the resurrection brings it closer to the Gospel of Matthew.[17] At the end of these intertextual comparisons, I will say—what is not surprising—that the closest parallels to Luke 23:1-25 are in the Acts of the Apostles (2:23; 3:13-15; 4:10; 4:27-28; 10:39; 13:27-29).[18]

---

instead of a custom or the intervention of the members of the Sanhedrin, is the odious comparison between Jesus and Barabbas."

11 See Bovon, "Lukan Story of the Passion."

12 In the source they may have appeared where we read them (v. 14), at the time of the second audience before Pilate. In reediting Mark, Luke anticipates them by mentioning them on the occasion of the first audience before Pilate (v. 2).

13 See the commentary above on 23:4.

14 Grundmann (421–28), who favors a special tradition (*Sonderüberlieferung*), calls attention to the opin-

ion of some scholars who support this hypothesis. Since then, Ernst (626–27) shares this opinion.

15 See Schniewind, *Parallelperikopen*, 62–77.

16 See above, Analysis of 23:6-12.

17 See *Gos. Pet.* 1–49. Luke should also be compared with the *Acts of Pilate* and the *Book of the Cock* translated in *Écrits apocryphes chrétiens* 2:261–97 and 153–203. On the *Acts of Pilate*, see initially Plummer, 527.

18 See C. A. Evans, 33.

At the end of this analysis it is by no means illegitimate to raise the question of the historicity of the events reported by an evangelist who aspires to strengthen the message he is proclaiming with historical reports (see 1:1-4). These days the moderate historian's approach[19] is based on Mark, much as Luke is. Initially, therefore, one must question Mark.[20] Yet Luke is probably based on another source. How much can the historian trust Luke's special source? The qualities of this author revealed in his document are, in my opinion, more literary than historical. In the section before us he also is familiar with the Barabbas episode, but it is his original idea that in releasing the prisoner Pilate was not following custom but yielding to popular pressure. It is difficult to say if he is right, since the question of the historicity of the Passover privilege is hotly debated.[21]

If the hypothesis of a second source is accepted, it must also be recognized that the Barabbas incident is doubly attested, which increases its historical probability. Nevertheless, I am of the opinion that historically there was only one appearance of Jesus before Pilate following an arrest by the Jewish authorities and a confrontation with the priests and the scribes. It is far from certain that there was a hearing presided over by Herod and a second appearance before Pilate as described by the special source that Luke likes and edits. The role of the people is also a matter of controversy. Current exegesis tends to minimize it and to put the burden on the Jewish lead-

---

19   Lietzmann ("Prozess Jesu," 251 in the collection) writes: "For the passion narrative we have only a single primary source, the Gospel of Mark." I give up listing the authors of the many recent books on the historical Jesus. For me it is enough to refer to the already old but balanced pages of Trilling, *Fragen*, 130–41.

20   See Bovon, *Last Days*, 3–24, esp. 7–8.

21   See Plummer (525), who refers to Titus Livius (*Ab urbe condita* 5.13.7), who alludes to the first *Lectisternium*, the Roman festival, during which prisoners were released. Schneider (2:476) thinks it is possible that on the Jewish side an annual amnesty occurred at the time of the Passover feast. Bock (2:1833, 1953–54) finally accepts the historicity of the custom and this incident. Many studies examine this Passover privilege. Since the specified custom is not explicitly mentioned by Luke, I can simply mention the ones that were accessible to me: Finegan (*Überlieferung*, 29–30) thinks that Luke skillfully connects the Barabbas episode to the trial before Pilate that precedes it. By doing this, he avoids mentioning the practice. Chavel ("Releasing") begins by calling attention to the Greek and Roman precedents and parallels advanced by the scholars (the Athenian festivals of *Panathenea* and *Thesmophomoria* and the Roman festival of *Lectisternium*). Then he points out a Jewish witness of the release of prisoners on the occasion of the Passover (*m. Pesaḥ.* 8.6). As a matter of fact, Merkel ("Begnadigung") had already called attention to this rabbinic text, but he did not think it was convincing. By contrast, Rigg ("Barabbas") is of the opinion that there was no custom of a Passover amnesty and that there was no person distinct from Jesus whose name was Barabbas. It is Jesus whom one initially judged as Jesus Barabbas, Jesus Son of the Father. Pilate released him. Later Jesus was accused of being Jesus the Christ, and Pilate condemned him for high treason. It was only later that the tradition made a distinction between two different persons. Rigg himself recognizes (453) that his thesis is fanciful. Maccoby ("Jesus and Barabbas") advocates a very similar thesis: The crowd called for the release of Jesus the Teacher (BarRabba[n]), and the chief priests procured this man's death. Winter (*On the Trial*, 131–43) rejects the validity of the rabbinic text *m. Pesaḥ.* 8.6 as evidence for the Passover privilege. There were indeed two different men, both of them prisoners, and both of them called Jesus. The purpose of Pilate's question was to distinguish one Jesus from the other. This historical reality was then modified by the Christian authors. There was no traditional Passover privilege. Merritt ("Pardon") answers the arguments of Rigg and Maccoby, and adds to the list of possible antecedents or parallels to the custom of the Passover privilege. He calls special attention to Babylonian, Greek, and Roman examples of amnesty. Vicent Cernuda ("Barrabás") offers an unusual historical reconstruction. He thinks that Barabbas was a famous charioteer and that those who were calling for his release were his fans at the hippodrome. Pilate made the mistake of believing that these people were in disagreement with the chief priests and of confusing Jesus' trial with the Passover privilege. The Barabbas partisans had been indoctrinated. They knew that releasing Barabbas would mean Jesus' crucifixion.

ers and the Roman governor. The Gospels unanimously agree, however, that there was a resounding *vox populi.* Is that only because of the Christian effort to place the responsibility on the Jews? In view of the freedom a magistrate in the emperor's service had while following the *cognitio extra ordinem*, it is not impossible that the governor was sensitive to popular opinion. Nor is it impossible that the crowd has changed its colors. While as a whole they were favorable toward Jesus, it may be that they became disappointed and decided to give up on him. By "people" I am thinking in all probability of part of the population of Jerusalem. Admittedly, Luke the evangelist describes the fate of the people during the passion of Jesus freely and artistically. He sees them continually attached to Jesus until the appearance before Pilate and after Jesus is condemned to death. Yet he states precisely (v. 13) that the people are present and active at the crucial moment when it is a question of persuading the governor. Furthermore, this destiny of the people recalls that of Peter and satisfies a theological requirement (cross and resurrection make conversion possible). Nevertheless, it may be that this description also has a historical basis. That does not justify, however, Christian acrimony or hostile feelings toward the Jews in general.

Commentary

■ **13** While the Jewish authorities took the initiative in the first appearance, here it is the Roman governor who summons the people.[22] The first situation corresponds to the beginning of a trial in the ancient world in which the process of justice begins when a complaint is made. The second takes place when a procedure has already begun.[23] While the first phase of the trial concerned the Jewish authorities,[24] the second involves the people as well.[25] Luke, and probably the special source before him, wants to say that at the critical moment Jesus was abandoned by everybody, including the people.[26] The evangelist was careful to bring the people gradually closer to the center of the action (see the imprecise "the multitude of them" in v. 1 and "the crowds" in v. 4). In v. 18 the people are there en masse ($\pi\alpha\mu\pi\lambda\eta\vartheta\epsilon\acute{\iota}$, "all together") to shout.

While the chief priests are mentioned constantly during the trial, the same is not true of the other attackers: the scribes in 22:2 at the time of the plotting; the officers in 22:52 at the arrest; probably the elders and the scribes in 22:66 at the time of the trial before the Sanhedrin; here the leaders and the people. It is difficult to see why

---

22 Lagrange (580) writes in connection with Pilate's summons to assemble: "A sentence had to be delivered." Plummer (524) calls attention to 9:1 ($\sigma\upsilon\gamma\kappa\alpha\lambda o\hat{\upsilon}\mu\alpha\iota$).

23 See Sherwin-White, *Roman Society*, 26.

24 Cassidy ("Chief Priests") analyzes precisely what Luke says about the chief priests and what this sacerdotal group represented then. In those days the chief priests were not beloved by the people, who accused the priests of not being the legitimate descendants of the sacerdotal line and for dishonestly exploiting the situation to their advantage. The chief priests bore a grudge against Jesus for criticizing them when he drove the traders out of the temple and for telling the parable of the murderous winegrowers.

25 Rau's hypotheses ("Volk") is ingenious. It builds on an intuition of Winter (*On the Trial*, 201 n. 23). To eliminate the surprise of seeing the people gathered, Rau suggests changing the accusitive $\kappa\alpha\grave{\iota}$ $\tau\grave{o}\nu$ $\lambda\alpha\acute{o}\nu$ ("and the people") to a genitive $\tau o\hat{\upsilon}$ $\lambda\alpha o\hat{\upsilon}$ ("of the people"). Thus, the people disappear from the scene and only "the chief priests and the leaders of the people" are convened. Against this hypoth-

esis one must call attention to the $\tau o\grave{\upsilon}\varsigma$ $\ddot{o}\chi\lambda o\upsilon\varsigma$ ("the crowds") of v. 4 and the $\pi\alpha\mu\pi\lambda\eta\vartheta\epsilon\acute{\iota}$ ("all together") of v. 18. See Schneider 2:477.

26 Ernst (627) is of the opinion that by adding the people here Luke wants to contrast all Jews, who demanded Jesus' condemnation, with the Romans, who declared him to be innocent. See also Kodell ("Laos"), who analyzes the use of $\lambda\alpha\acute{o}\varsigma$ ("people") in Luke's work. The evangelist tries to minimize the responsibility of the people that the tradition transmitted to him. He understands this term in the context of salvation history. Here the people are responsible, but through ignorance, and later they will repent. See further Tannehill (335–36), who thinks that $\lambda\alpha\acute{o}\varsigma$ here and in general in Luke is not the crowd but the people of Israel. These people, usually favorable to Jesus, are guilty here, but after having sinned they will change. Their attitude is like that of Peter. See finally Aletti (*Art de raconter*, 166), who has written in connection with v. 13: "Jesus' fate becomes everyone's business."

these opponents vary so. Perhaps it is because they have different tasks. The officers, for example, provide a valid service at the arrest.[27]

■ **14** At the beginning of the new hearing, the Lukan Pilate pauses[28] for a moment to take stock.[29] He summarizes vv. 1-5 in an elegant and balanced manner,[30] takes up again in particular the accusation made by the Jewish authorities while no longer using the pejorative τοῦτον ("this one"), and replaces it with the neutral τὸν ἄνθρωπον τοῦτον ("this man"). He keeps only the most serious grievance, leading the people astray. He chooses ἀποστρέφω ("to lead astray," "to corrupt") over the stronger διαστρέφω ("to pervert," v. 2). He speaks of λαός ("people"), where the plaintiffs speak of the "nation," because in Pilate's eyes it is a problem of internal and social politics.[31] For the second time (see v. 4 above) he affirms Jesus' innocence.[32] He states explicitly[33] that he bases his opinion on an investigation (ἀνακρίνω, "to carry out the inquiry" or "to carry out the examination," is the verb used for investigations or inquiries; here it has a legal sense).[34]

■ **15** This verse recalls the appearance before Herod and summarizes vv. 6-12. How should we understand the words ἀλλ᾽ οὐδὲ Ἡρῴδης? As "but Herod also not," which puts the Jewish prince and the Roman governor on the same level? Or as "not even Herod," which makes Herod an expert in Jewish matters.[35] I hold to this second translation, since the appearance before Herod implied a geographical closeness between the judge and the defendant and a religious closeness with the Jewish authorities. The narrator goes straight to the heart of the matter and does not tell us how Herod communicated his opinion to Pilate; what is essential is that Herod shares Pilate's opinion.[36] We do not know what would have happened—from a legal and practical point of view—had Herod had a different opinion. The agreement of the two men is not surprising. On the narrative level, the text sets the political authorities so skillfully over against the religious authorities that the readers can visualize the two fronts. On the historical level, the text reflects a reality. Since the days of Herod the Great, his family always sought to align its opinion with that of the

---

27 Aletti (*Art de raconter*, 173–75) is of the opinion that, after the drama, Jesus' adversaries will be divided into two groups. One, the chief priests, will maintain their opposition. The other, the people, will realize their mistake and will repent. The coherence of the narrative lies not in the unremitting opposition but in the process of verification.

28 Luke frequently uses πρός followed by the accusative instead of the dative after the *verba dicendi*. It is a sign of the progressive disaffection with the dative.

29 The important thing for Goulder (*New Paradigm*, 2:760) is that Pilate summons the plaintiffs and takes up the trial again.

30 See C. F. Evans (853), who notes the reversed repetition. The you–me–this man of the beginning becomes at the end I–you–this man.

31 See Delebecque, *Évangile*, 142.

32 The manuscripts are undecided between οὐθέν and its synonym οὐδέν ("nothing"); see the apparatus of Nestle-Aland (27th ed.) on this text. Οὐθέν is a more recent form. See Zorell, *Lexicon*, s.v. οὐδείς, NB (= nota bene). Bailly (s.v. οὐδείς, οὐδεμία, οὐδέν) writes: "Instead of οὐδείς, οὐδέν, οὐδενός, from 378 BCE on the forms οὐθείς, οὐθέν, οὐθενός appear, and from 330 BCE on the latter dominate. At the time of the Atticists there is a

return to the old form." One will notice that Pilate immediately (v. 15) says, Οὐδὲν ἄξιον θανάτου ("nothing . . . worthy of death"). It may be that, used alone, οὐθέν (v. 14) is emphatic: "Not the least grievance." Several manuscripts omit the preposition κατά, making αὐτοῦ depend directly on the verb κατηγορεῖτε. This is correct, and it does not change the sense. See BAGD, s.v.

33 Note both appearances of ἰδού in vv. 14 and 15. Repeated, they especially heighten the drama; see C. F. Evans, 854.

34 On ἀνακρίνω, which is used also in Acts 4:9; 12:19; and 24:8, see Caillemer, "ἀνάκρισις." Lagrange (581) notes the emphatic ἐγώ: Pilate himself carried out the investigation. See also Plummer, 524; C. F. Evans, 854.

35 See Creed, 282–83; C. F. Evans, 854; see before them Erasmus, *Paraphrasis*, 460.

36 It is to be supposed that, if Herod returned Jesus to Pilate, he regards him as innocent; see Creed, 283. It is also to be understood that ἡμᾶς ("us") is a *pluralis majestatis*, not very frequent in ancient Greek. We may have here a copy of the Latin *nos* in the mouth of the high functionary.

Romans, thus lining up on the side of the stronger. The presence for the third time of the verb ἀναπέμπω (with the same form, the aorist, and the same person, third person singular) underscores Jesus' humiliation, sent from one authority to another, from Charybdis to Scylla (vv. 7, 11, and 15). (The legal sense of "to turn over," "to send" is quite appropriate for the first two cases. It is also appropriate in the third case, but the nuance of returning must be added, "to return," "to send back," a nuance that the prefix ἀνα- can contain.)[37] Luke emphasizes that a governor expresses himself carefully. The reader has noted the elegance of v. 14. In v. 15 in particular one admires the choice sequence of words (the subject of the sentence, "nothing he has done," is formed by οὐδέν at the beginning and πεπραγμένον at the end)[38] and the classic use of the dative with the perfect passive, while everyday usage in Luke's day favored the preposition ὑπό ("by") followed by the genitive.[39] What is essential here, as in vv. 4 and 22, is οὐδὲν ἄξιον θανάτου ("nothing deserving of death"). Such is the truth that Luke, the Christian, attributes to the Roman authority at the time of Jesus and that he wants to see the Roman authorities affirm in his own day.

■ **16** Παιδεύσας: The verb παιδεύω means "to educate," "to inform," "to teach," "to form," "to draw up," sometimes "to correct" and "to punish."[40] It is to be taken here with the meaning of "to inflict a punishment," but since Pilate thinks that Jesus is innocent, the action of the verb is less a punishment than a warning.[41] Luke does not state exactly what the nature of this warning is. It can be a warning in the form of a verbal threat, but it can also be physical punishment in the form of lashing. In this case, the verb παιδεύω would be a euphemism.[42] One readily thinks of such physical punishment because of the parallels. It really should be more precise, because the Romans distinguished among various forms of corporal punishment: the *verberatio*, the *flagellatio*, the *fustigatio*. If we are to see the verb as a euphemism, it would be a question of the *fustigatio*, a whip lashing that the Romans administered as a preventive measure and regarded as a warning.[43]

Οὖν ("therefore") gives the impression that Pilate, who has formed an opinion, actually passes judgment here, a judgment of acquittal. The verb ἀπολύω ("to release") will return as an option that, as everyone knows, will not be realized (see vv. 20 and 22). It is Barabbas who will benefit from it (see vv. 18 and 25).[44]

■ **17** The *textus receptus*, that is, the Greek text of the New Testament that prevailed from the time of the Renaissance until the nineteenth century, contains after v. 16 the following sentence: "because it was his duty to release someone to them at the festival" (ἀνάγκην δὲ εἶχεν ἀπολύειν αὐτοῖς κατὰ ἑορτὴν ἕνα). The editors then allotted the designation v. 17 to these words, which they regarded as an integral part of the Third Gospel. The development of textual criticism, particularly the discovery and the value in the nineteenth and twentieth centuries of the old uncials such as the Vaticanus (B = 03) and Alexandrinus (A = 02), as well as valuable papyri such as the Bodmer Papyrus XIV–XV (𝔓[75]), called into question the authenticity of this sentence. Today v. 17 tends to disappear from the editions and translations of the New Testament. There are three reasons for this critical decision: (a) It is easy to understand why the sentence would have been added, since without it the reader has difficulty understanding the sudden appear-

---

37 Verse 15 has two well-attested variants in which Pilate expresses himself in the first person singular and obviously says something other than "because he sent him back to us." According to one, Pilate says, "because I sent you (plural) back to him," according to the other, "because he sent him back to you (plural)." See the apparatus of Nestle-Aland (27th ed.) on this text for the details of the manuscripts and the versions; see also Plummer, 524; Bock, 2:1834.

38 The verb πράσσω ("to do," "to accomplish," "to work with") belongs to the Lukan vocabulary; see, in addition to a concordance, C. F. Evans, 854.

39 See BDF §191; Delebecque, *Évangile*, 143.

40 See LSJ, s.v.

41 See Plummer, 525. Schneider (2:477) is of the opinion that the action he envisages corresponds to a punishment and a warning.

42 See Lagrange, 581.

43 See ibid.; Sherwin-White, *Roman Society*, 27–28; Bock 2:1828; Bovon, *Last Days*, 51.

44 The verb ἀπολύω ("release") appears in a variant of 22:68; see p. 244 n. 39 above on 22:66-71. The verb is present also in v. 17, which I regard below as a gloss.

ance of Barabbas in v. 18. (b) In addition to the numerous and important manuscripts that are unaware of it, Codez Bezae (D = 05) along with the Syriac Siniatic and Curétonian translations copy the verse at the end of v. 19, an instability that makes one think that a gloss was introduced into the text here or there.[45] (c) Although the language of this verse differs little from that of Luke,[46] its contents are taken from parallel passages from the other Gospels (Matt 27:15 par. Mark 15:6 par. John 18:39). In summary, I regard v. 17 as an explanatory gloss and think that in Luke's original text the cries of the crowd (v. 18) responded to Pilate's decision (v. 16).[47]

■ **18-19** The reaction is immediate and loud.[48] In ἀνα-κράζω the readers will have to hear in the cry (κράζω) either the loudness or the nature of the answer (depending on the two connotations the prefix ἀνα- can have).[49] The author specifies that it is a unanimous reaction: The adverb παμπληθεί, a *hapax legomenon* in the New Testament, is affected.[50] It is appropriate for the careful language of the special source. The plaintiffs voice their demand. They take up again the scornful "this one" (τοῦτον) and want him to disappear. The Greek αἶρε ("eliminate") is both vulgar and violent. The crowd in

Jerusalem will use the same imperative about Paul when it wants to see him disappear: Αἶρε αὐτόν (Acts 21:36) "to death," literally, "take him away!"[51] The modern reader should not hear these cries and these words as reliable recordings. Let us not forget that they come from the pen of a Christian author who is distancing himself from Judaism and wants to defame it.

Following the special source, which likes the names of people,[52] Luke mentions here a man named Barabbas, whom he describes. As usual, either the evangelist does not know or fails to give the etymology of the name,[53] but he indicates his crimes precisely, even powerfully. Barabbas had done everything he needed to do to raise the ire of the Roman occupiers. He took part in a revolution (στάσις, "insurrection," "uprising"),[54] and he did so in the capital, Jerusalem, which obviously makes it more serious. His participation in the rebellion caused blood to be shed (ὁ φόνος, the "homicide," the "murder," the "assassination"). Arrested in circumstances Luke does not mention, he ends up in prison. The text is well written. With a verb of movement, βάλλω ("to throw"), the author uses the preposition ἐν with the dative, which expresses the absence of movement.[55] It is not

---

45 A minuscule manuscript, 892, has v. 17 only as a marginal note; see the apparatus of Nestle-Aland (27th ed.) here.

46 Several exegetes have emphasized that the expression ἀνάγκην . . . εἶχεν, literally "had the need," with the sense "had the obligation, duty," corresponded to Luke's language; see 14:18.

47 See Lagrange, 581–82; Bock, 2:1834–35. It is at the very least curious that a modern exegete tries to rehabilitate v. 17 and even to make it the center of a decisive chiasm; see Meynet, *Évangile*, 2:225; and idem, *Guide*, 106.

48 The δέ of v. 18 is adversative; see Lagrange, 582: "The δέ is in opposition to Pilate's proposal. It would not make sense after v. 17." C. A. Evans (333) writes: "The people are not interested in Jesus, the man of peace. They want the release of Barabbas, a man of violence."

49 Luke prefers here the second aorist, ἀνέκραγον, which is the only form of the verb ἀνακράζω used in classical Greek; the first aorist, ἀνέκραξαν, prevailed in the Koine. The manuscripts waver between the two forms; see Plummer, 525.

50 On the adverb παμπληθεί (one also finds the spelling πανπληθεί), see C. F. Evans, 855.

51 See also Acts 8:33; 22:22; John 19:15; *Mart. Pol.* 3.2; Delebecque, *Évangile*, 143; Ernst, 628.

52 See, e.g., Zacchaeus in 19:2 and Cleopas in 24:18. On this point the special source is different from Mark who leaves so much of the world in anonymity.

53 Written Barabbas, the name means "son of the father"; written Barrabas or Barraban, it means "son of our teacher." Matthew, who appears to know more than the others, puts the given name "Jesus" on him. One thus sees how confusion was possible. Some exegetes have even surmised that Pilate's question did not pose an alternative but was trying to clarify the identities. See C. F. Evans, 855–56, and n. 21 above.

54 The word στάσις initially means the "upright position," the "state," the "status," the "existence," or the "condition." Then it means, as here, "sedition," the "rebellion," the "movement of revolt," the "tumult," the "dispute," or the "controversy"; see Zorell, *Lexicon*, s.v.; BAGD, s.v.; Plummer, 525–26; C. F. Evans, 857.

55 See Delebecque, *Évangile*, 143.

an awkwardness; on the contrary it is an elegant way to indicate the result, the imprisonment.[56] Thus, Barabbas languishes "in prison" (ἐν τῇ φυλακῇ).[57]

■ **20** When he hears these cries, Pilate has to raise his voice. The verb προσφωνέω ("to utter acclamations," "to hail," "to declare") reflects this reality better than would the simple verb "say." He repeats that his will is to release Jesus.[58] The presence of the same verb ἀπολύω ("to release") as well as the sequence of the two following sentences, each of which ends with a proper name (v. 18 and v. 20), clearly underscores the antagonism of the two ideas, that of the Jewish authorities and that of the Roman authority. Herod is forgotten; the parenthesis of vv. 6-12 is indeed closed.

■ **21** The voice of the accusers drowns out Pilate's voice; ἐπιφωνέω ("to exclaim," "to shout more and more")[59] indicates the louder noise. With its prefix ἐπι-, ἐπε-φώνουν may also indicate a gradation compared to ἀνέκραγον ("they shouted," v. 18); thus my translation "But they cried out all the more." A double imperative (v. 21) carries more force than a simple imperative (v. 18).[60] The verb "to crucify" is more concrete and more violent than the verb "to remove," or "to eliminate."[61]

The imperative σταύρου deserves an explanation. While Mark (15:14) and John (19:15), who tell of the same cry, correctly use the aorist imperative σταύρωσον (the aorist indicates a single point action), Luke, or the special source before him, curiously resorts to the present imperative active σταύρου, which normally expresses continuous or repeated action.[62] Matthew also chooses an aorist imperative, but he retains the third person passive: σταυρωθήτω ("let him be crucified," 27:22). Luke probably wants to emphasize that the shouting was persistent.

■ **22** As far as the content is concerned, the Lukan Pilate adds nothing to his earlier remarks.[63] At the most, he expresses his surprise, perhaps his irritation,[64] with a rhetorical question.[65] He repeats his intention to release Jesus with a warning. The evangelist wants to make clear that, when he gives in, Pilate says "for the third time" (τρίτον) that Jesus is innocent. In the ancient world, popular stories often took place in three steps, as one sees in Luke in the parable of the murderous winegrowers (20:12) or that of the pounds (19:11-27, without the use of the adverb), or in Mark in the story of Gethsemane (14:41). When one has come to three, all sides of a question have been settled.[66]

■ **23** The Barabbas episode ends as it began, with yelling (see v. 18). Twice (v. 23) Luke uses—intentionally—the word "voice" (φωνή) and puts it in the plural. The first

---

56   The periphrastic construction with the aorist participle is unusual; see Plummer, 526.

57   On the various attempts to rebel against the Roman occupiers, most of which began in Galilee, see Prigent, *Fin de Jérusalem*; Horsley and Hanson, *Bandits*. More generally on hostility toward Rome in the empire, especially in the eastern provinces, see Harald Fuchs, *Der geistige Widerstand gegen Rom in der antiken Welt* (Berlin: de Gruyter, 1938).

58   I can say "declared again" because of πάλιν ("again"), and I can speak of his "will" because of the present participle θέλων ("wanting," "who wanted"). Ernst (628) notes that at this moment Pilate exchanges his function as judge for that of the defense attorney. Brandon (*Trial*, 124) thinks that Luke has changed the trial into a confrontation between Pilate and the Jews in which the fate of Jesus is at stake.

59   See Lagrange, 583.

60   The same is true of the double vocatives one sometimes meets in Lukan passages, e.g., 10:41 ("Martha, Martha") and 22:31 ("Simon, Simon").

61   Delebecque (*Évangile*, 143) feels a crescendo building from ἀπολύω ("to release," v. 18), and ending in σταυρόω ("to crucify," v. 21), by way of ἀναιρέω ("to eliminate," 22:2), and αἴρω ("to eliminate," v. 18).

62   "One does not see why Luke has written the present imperative σταύρου instead of σταύρωσον (aorist)," writes Lagrange (583). The present imperative middle σταύρου is hardly likely here; contra Fitzmyer, 2:1491.

63   These are vv. 4 and 14–15. The last sentence of v. 22 is identical with that of v. 16, and some elements (the verb "to find" and the adjective "guilty") appear in three places.

64   Delebecque (*Évangile*, 143) writes: "Luke uses γάρ in a question in a classical way: the particle shows the surprise and even the indignation."

65   Pilate speaks of Jesus here as the accusers do, calling him οὗτος. One can imagine, however, that it has no pejorative connotation, since its purpose here is to distinguish "this one" from "that one," Barabbas.

66   On the rule of three, see Jeremias, *Parables*, 92–93.

time he adds that they are "big," that is to say "loud,"[67] the second time that they are victorious, they prevail over the opposing opinions (κατίσχυον, "succeeded," "had their way").[68] Indeed, the evangelist has said consistently that the conflict was a battle of words. The reader may remember that in the middle of the episode Luke set Pilate's προσφωνέω against the ἐπιφωνέω of the attackers (vv. 20-21).[69]

The verb ἐπίκειμαι, literally, "to be placed on," has the sense here of "to urge," "to insist," "to persist in." The Jewish leaders, accompanied by the people, insist strongly: "they persisted in asking" (αἰτέω is more here than "to demand")[70] that he should be crucified. Readers will notice the two imperfects (ἐπέκειντο[71] and κατίσχυον) that emphasize the persistence of Jesus' opponents. They also note that it is these people and not Pilate who first speak of crucifixion. Furthermore, the governor does not himself say the word "cross" or the verb "to crucify."[72] The author's intention is clear.

■ **24-25** In v. 23 the opponent was the dominant subject. Here it is Pilate who makes the decisions (he appears to be the master of the situation).[73] He decides to let the opponents have their way, himself becoming subordinate to them. In this decisive sentence the Lukan Pilate shows himself to be who he truly is. He is the governor; it is he who holds the reins of power. Rome's institutional power exists, but he decides to submit to the wish of the Jewish leaders.[74] It is Pilate who in his person disgraces his function. "That their demand had to be accepted" sounds like the negative copy of the Mount of Olives episode in which Jesus finally wished that the Father's will be fulfilled (22:42). Yet on another level, a theological level or the level of God's economy, it is the holy will of God that is done through this perverted human will (see Acts 2:23; 4:27-28). Moreover, the term "will" comes up in relation to the opponents at the end of the sentence.[75] Indeed, Pilate delivers Jesus "to their will," "to their pleasure" (τῷ θελήματι αὐτῶν). Before that, and contrary to his plan, Pilate offers to deliver Barabbas, whose name is not mentioned. He releases the one who is a revolutionary murderer and not the one he wanted to free.[76] He releases—the wording is precisely

---

67 See the expression in the singular 4:33; 8:28; 17:15; Acts 7:57; 8:7; 14:10; 16:28; 26:24. With reference to the verb ἐπίκειμαι ("to press closely," "to persist in"), Plummer (526) refers here to Josephus *Ant.* 18.6.6 §184 and 20.5.3 §110.

68 Intransitive in the language of the New Testament, the verb κατισχύω, which Luke used in 21:36, means "to dominate," "to be strong," "to become strong," or "to be robust." Followed by the genitive, always intransitive, it signifies "to prevail," "to override." In the imperfect it has here the meaning of "to assert oneself"; see Zorell, *Lexicon*, s.v.; Lagrange, 583.

69 C. F. Evans (858) writes on v. 23: "The language here is strongly expressive of the power of mob clamour to pervert justice." Josephus (*Bell.* 2.9.2–3 §§169–74; *Ant.* 18.3.1 §§55–59) notes the role of the crowd in other incidents involving Pilate; the Jewish historian tells of another public trial, *Bell.* 2.10.5 §§199–203; see Bock, 2:1827. Schlatter (442–43) calls attention to other parallels in Josephus to details of Luke.

70 The verb αἰτέω appears relatively frequently in Luke's writings (see 1:63; 11:9, 12-13; 12:48; here 23:23, 25; 23:52; it appears ten times in Acts); see Walter Radl, "αἰτέω, etc.," *EDNT* 1 (1990) 43.

71 See 1 Cor 9:16: "This is a necessity that is laid on (ἐπίκειται) me."

72 We must remember the cruelty and infamy of crucifixion, never imposed on a Roman citizen. We must also remember Cicero's opinion, which was shared by many people: "May the word 'cross' itself be remote not only from the bodies of the Roman citizens but also from their thoughts, their eyes, and their ears" (*Pro Rabirio* 5.16).

73 The verb ἐπικρίνω means "to confirm by his judgment," "to approve"; see 2 Macc 4:47; *3 Macc.* 4:2. On the one hand, there is irony, because far from confirming his earlier opinion, Pilate is crippled. On the other, there is tragedy, because Pilate confirms the opposite opinion, approving those of whom he disapproves. But the verb is used in Greek also for a decision or a final sentence, and that is what it is here. Lagrange (583) speaks here of "a positive and sovereign act."

74 At the end of the trial the noun αἴτημα ("demand," v. 24) and the verb αἰτέω ("to ask," vv. 23 and 25) direct the action, just as the verb κατηγορέω ("to accuse") did (23:2, 10, 14) at the beginning of the trial.

75 On the term "will," used in 12:47 and 22:42, see Delebecque, *Évangile*, 85.

76 Luke intentionally uses the verb (ἀπολύω "release," v. 25) about the release of Barabbas that Pilate had

that of v. 19—"the one who had been thrown into prison" (this time it is the movement in the accusative with the preposition εἰς that is emphasized).[77] As is stated in v. 19, he was in prison because of his participation in the "insurrection" (στάσις) and "murder" (φόνος). Instead of saying simply that Pilate released Barabbas, Luke says that the opposite of justice is here and that, according to him, the danger to Rome comes from people like Barabbas, not from people like Jesus. The verb "to deliver" (παραδίδωμι)[78] underscores the Roman judge's abdication in favor of the Jewish authorities. The latter govern a nation that nevertheless is subject to the occupying power. The word has a double meaning, however, and it also retains the positive connotation of the evangelical tradition. In Luke's day the creedal formulas like to use this verb to refer to the transmission of the gospel (see 1 Cor 15:3) or to speak of the passion of Jesus Christ (see Rom 4:25).[79] The use of this verb may have been inspired by the LXX, especially by Isa 53:6, 12.[80]

History of Interpretation

Tertullian summarizes the content of our pericope in one sentence: "Barabbas, a man of most criminal conduct, is released as though a good man: while Christ, most righteous, is demanded for death as though a murderer" (*Adv. Marc.* 4.42.4).[81] This paradox that is present in the text is recalled here. In the course of the history of interpretation it will be explained repeatedly.[82]

Origen enriches the exegesis of our verses in a number of ways. In his interpretation of Leviticus 16 (*Hom. Lev.* 10.2),[83] the institution of the scapegoat, he opposes a literal interpretation and refuses to allow Christians to practice the fasting of the Jewish Day of Atonement. In reality, the biblical text mentions two goats, one is sacrificed and becomes the share of the Lord, the other is not sacrificed and is driven alive into the desert, bearing the sins of the people. Since Moses was a prophet, his instructions must be understood typologically. To Origen, the two goats suggest Barabbas and Christ. Since the two animals filled a liturgical function and participated in the atonement, Barabbas loses his negative character. Once he is released, he realizes the fate of the goat sent into the desert, who is laden with the sins of the people. Burdened with sins, he is still alive, but if he is released and liberated, he is free in the way of the humanity that is set free by Christ. Christ himself fulfills the figure of the other goat, the one who remains a captive and is offered as an atoning sacrifice. It is he who "effects the true atonement for the people who believe in him." Thus, the fate of the goats is neither parallel nor complementary. It presupposes an exchange (the one who is sacrificed permits the other to survive) for which Origen finds justification in the contrast between Barabbas and Jesus.[84]

---

used three times to say that he intended to release Jesus (vv. 16, 20, 22).

77   Verse 25, τὸν . . . βεβλημένον εἰς φυλακήν· The same expression is used about John the Baptist in John 3:24; the same use of βάλλω is in Luke 16:20.

78   On παραδίδωμι, see Sabourin, 363; Popkes, *Christus traditus*, 153–89. Luke has already used the verb about the passion in a slightly different way. In 9:44 Jesus is generally delivered to human beings; in 18:32 he is delivered to the Gentiles; in 20:20 he is in danger of being delivered to the governor; see below, 24:7 and 20.

79   On the meaning of v. 25, see Wiefel, 393: Very Lukan, the phrase becomes part of the apologetics of the third evangelist.

80   See Sabourin, 363.

81   Trans. Evans, *Tertullian*, 2:501.

82   See Bonaventure (*Comm. Luc.* 23.23 [Bernardini, 570]), who writes a thousand years later: "This

was the greatest impiety: to give life to a destroyer (murderer) and to take the life of the source of all life" (Et haec fit summa impietas, vitam reddere destructori, et auferre vitam fonti totius vitae). And four centuries after Bonaventure, John Calvin (*Harmony*, 3:183) comments: "Both must have been seized with an amazing kind of frenzy not satisfied with plotting the death of an innocent man unless, in their hatred for him, they also released a robber." These writers show theological sensitivity, but it is accompanied by hostility toward the Jewish authorities, whose attitude they explain in part by attributing it to the intervention of Satan.

83   Trans. and ed. Marcel Borret (SC 287; Paris: Cerf, 1981) 134–35. For this reference I am indebted to Just, *Luke*, 355, 356.

84   Origen continues the allegory by seeing Pilate as the one who leads the living goat into the desert. He also plays on the idea that the goat, once

In *Contra Celsum* (8.42), the same theologian rejects an argument of his opponent.[85] It is wrong to say, as did the pagan philosopher Celsus, that Jesus' opponents have not been punished for their crime. The fall of Jerusalem shortly thereafter[86] is enough to contradict him.

In the fourth century, Ambrose of Milan meditated on this episode. He associates Pilate with the future judges of Christians: Jesus' passion prefigures that of the martyrs.[87] Then he establishes a connection between Barabbas and Satan that will become part of the tradition. If Barabbas means "son of the father," then, on the basis of John 8:44 ("Your father is the devil"), he is the son of the devil.[88] He meditates on the paradoxical or antithetical relationship between the facts and their true meaning. If the Jews are guilty in his eyes, "they still portend the glorious outcome: because by inflicting wounds on him they crown him; by mocking him they adore him" (*Exp. Luc.* 10.101–6; quotation from 105).

Frédéric Rilliet has studied the history of exegesis of the scene that contrasts Jesus and Barabbas.[89] He notes how the Christians who are hostile to the Jews think it is absurd to prefer a criminal to the author of salvation. Jacob of Sarug, a Syrian preacher who was active at the end of the fifth century and the beginning of the sixth, uses the image of the physician: "insane patients who were jealous of the doctor because he had made their wounds disappear."[90] Following other Greek and Syrian fathers, the bishop of Sarug compares the confrontation between Jesus and Barabbas to the episode of the golden calf. Here as there the sin of idolatry manifests itself.[91] Jacob of Sarug is original in associating Barabbas with Adam. Is not the name of the criminal "son of the father"? In this case the Father is God (see the Lukan genealogy where Adam is designated as "son of God" [3:38]).[92]

The commentary by the Venerable Bede manifests great wealth here (*In Luc.* 6.1342–1433). It contains an attack against the *Acts of Pilate*, mentions the pillar of flagellation in the Church of Mount Zion in Jerusalem, affirms that crucifixion is always cruel because it draws out the agony, and teaches the lesson from ecclesiastical history that the Christian martyrs have always conformed to the passion of Christ. He also develops reflections, both exegetical (Pilate had three reasons for wanting to release Jesus[93]) and theological (he expresses with dignity the exchange that takes place [6.1377–85]).

Bonaventure describes the sentence of Jesus in four ways, corresponding to four aspects of the text.[94] It

---

washed, becomes as pure as the governor after he has washed his hands.

85 I also have this reference from Just, *Luke*, 355, 356–57.

86 By emphasizing this brief time, relatively speaking, Origen rhetorically connects the fall of Jerusalem to Jesus' execution.

87 Cyril of Jerusalem (*Hom. Cat.* 13.3) compares Jesus' fate with that of others who were crucified. Yet in his view the comparison is not justified, for the others who have been crucified in history have paid for their own faults, while Christ died for the sins of others; see Just, *Luke*, 355–56.

88 One finds the argument also in Hilary of Poitiers *Comm. Matt.* 33.2 (ed. Jean Doignon; SC 258; Paris: Cerf, 1979) 248–50. 2 Thessalonians 2:3 likewise plays a role in the argument.

89 Rilliet, "Barabbas."

90 James of Sarug, "Homélie en prose sur le vendredi de la Passion," 31 in idem, *Six homélies festales en prose: édition critique du texte syriaque, introduction et traduction française* (ed. Frédéric Rilliet; PO 43/4; Turnhout: Brepols, 1986) 626–29.

91 James of Sarug, "Homélie sur la crucifixion," in Paul Bedjan, ed., *Homiliae selectae Mar Jacobi Sarugennsis, with Additional Material by Sebastian P. Brock* (Piscataway, N.J.: Gorgias Press, 2006) 537–38. I am grateful to Brent Landau for facilitating for me the understanding of this passage.

92 Jerome has two meanings for the name of the brigand. In *De nominibus hebraicis* (*PL* 23:884, 889–90) he thinks that Barabban in Matthew (the equivalent of Barraban) in Aramaic or Syriac but not in Hebrew means "son of our teacher," while the Barabba (the equivalent of Barabbas) of John is to be explained as the "son of the Father." In his *Comm. Matt.* 4 on Matt 27:16 (ed. Émile Bonnard; [SC 259; Paris: Cerf, 1979] 278–80) Jerome claims that the *Gospel of the Hebrews* translates the name as "son of their teacher."

93 Pilate thought that Jesus was innocent; he took into consideration Herod's opinion; he respected the Passover privilege.

94 Bonaventure *Comm. Luc.* 23.17–29 (Bernardini, 569–72). The quotations come from paragraphs 24 and 25.

was unjust because justice was violated. It was ungodly because the Passover privilege was misused. It was extorted because the judge's will was forced. Finally, it was distorted because it contradicted right reason. The medieval theologian was most interested in the figure and the role of Pilate. In his opinion, the governor first complies with Roman law by summoning the parties before he pronounces sentence. He again conforms to it by himself affirming Jesus' innocence and allowing Herod to confirm it. In total, he tries to save Jesus' life in seven different ways. Nevertheless he ends up pronouncing such an unfair death sentence. Thus, his will was divided, and, according to the Vulgate, that is what the book of Proverbs says: *Vult et non vult piger*, "the lazy man wants and at the same time does not want" (Prov 13:4).

From the beginning Christians have discovered God's life-giving will behind the homicidal will of human beings. The idea that God is active behind the actors of the drama has been present since the patristic age. Bonaventure recalls: "This did not happen outside of God's plan" (Sed hoc non fuit sine divina dispositione). Erasmus agrees: "So it is seen by the divine plan that Jesus, the source and origin of all glory, would be so despised to the point . . ." (Sic visum est consilio divino, ut Jesus omnis gloriae fons et auctor, ad hoc veniret contemtus . . .). This providential character, which on the surface appears to be a fatal miscarriage of justice or a satanic perversion, is part of the entire Christian heritage (see also Erasmus, *Paraphrasis*, 460). The Reformation will accept it with theocentric confidence.

Indeed, Luther warned his hearers and readers:[95] the trial before Pilate teaches Christians what is the world and what is the kingdom of the devil. The devil manages to manipulate the Jews, who still are the disciples nearest to God and his beloved people. As the host and hostess of an inn, the devil and the world (*die Welt* is feminine in German) set themselves up as enemies of the Creator.

But God reacts against this defeat of reason (an interesting use of the term *Vernunft*, "reason") and uses these events to develop the gospel. This divine operation offers believers a real consolation when they mourn the death of Christ. In this episode good and evil, sin and the gospel face one another.

Calvin, a theologian of the decree of God, also defends this exegetical legacy.[96] Satan's activity does not escape God's control, and it corresponds to God's plan. The articulation of good and evil that characterizes the passion of Christ has its parallel in the anthropology of the believers. They may be horrified that they take part in the crucifixion of Jesus. Shame may overcome them, yet when they look to God and his work they are filled with assurance, the assurance of faith.

> Meanwhile we must consider God's purpose, by which Christ came to be crucified as the basest of men. Indeed the Jews rage against him with blinded fury, but since God had ordained him to be the sacrificial outcast (κάθαρμα) for the expiation of the world's sins, he suffered him to be placed lower than a robber and a murderer. That God's Son was brought down to that level is a fact no one will really consider without the utmost horror and displeasure with himself and detestation for his own sins. Yet here also emerges great ground for confidence, that Christ plunged into the depths of disgrace precisely to win, by his abasement, an ascent for us into the heavenly glory. Thus he was reckoned worse than a thief, to bring us into the company of angels.[97]

Moving to an author of the seventeenth century, with Grotius we enter the modern period.[98] His remarks cover the areas of history, of law, of textual criticism or of literature. The surprising ἄρχοντες of v. 13 must be the elders of the people. The verb ἀποστρέφω ("to

---

95   Luther, *Evangelien-Auslegung*, 1190–92.
96   Calvin, *Harmony*, 3:182–86. A lawyer by training, the Geneva reformer criticized the use of the Passover privilege. It is "an example brought in without sense or reason" (184), because justice knows no exception and the magistrates have received the sword from God himself (Calvin is thinking of Rom 13:1-7). He also explains why, as the deputy of the emperor, the governor has the right of *coertio*. Pilate wants to use it here in flogging Jesus. If he were to do so, however, he would act unjustly, since Jesus is innocent. Yet the punishment would certainly be less cruel than that of crucifixion.
97   Ibid., 3:183–84.
98   Grotius, *Annotationes*, 915–16.

corrupt, lead astray," v. 14) must be explained: Jesus had caused the people to abandon the allegiance they owed the Roman Empire. The verb ἀνακρίνω ("to examine, conduct an investigation" v. 14) is judicial language. The expression ἀλλ᾽ οὐδὲ Ἡρῴδης (v. 15), understood to mean "not even Herod," emphasizes that in religious matters the Jewish prince was more reliable than the Roman governor. In addition, in v. 15 we must read the third person singular, according to Grotius, instead of following the Syriac version familiar to him and reading the first person singular. In v. 16 the verb παιδεύω means "to chastise." This punishment was inflicted on those persons who tried to introduce a new religion. The verb ἐπικρίνω (v. 24) means "to issue a ruling during the trial" (*judicando decernere*).

Conclusion

According to the Lukan plot, Pilate did not initiate the trial of Jesus; he was forced to get involved (vv. 1-5). Then, convinced of Jesus' innocence, he tried to get a second opinion from Herod (vv. 6-12). Supported by Herod in his conviction, he wanted to release Jesus (vv. 13-16). The court of the people and especially their leaders demanded that Pilate release[99] an enemy of the Romans, probably a supporter of Jewish independence. At first, the governor did not give in (vv. 18-20).[100] The unanimous cries of hostility shattered if not his certainty then at least his political acumen and—why not—his comfort (vv. 21-23). He then took the fatal decision to deliver Jesus to them (vv. 24-25).[101]

While Luke did not explicitly say it here,[102] Christian exegetes have thought that the persons in the drama, both Jesus' opponents and his weak supporters, did not act voluntarily. Superhuman forces took part in the action. The devil set things in motion, and God accomplished his purpose.[103] Thus, the decision to condemn Jesus was a disaster only from a certain point of view. *Sub specie aeternitatis* it was the will of God.[104]

The human drama, however, did not show nor does it reflect a conflict between the devil and God. The interpretation of the passion Luke gives elsewhere in the work, especially in Acts,[105] shows that the evangelist is in accord with the Christian interpreters of his work. God, who refuses to save the world by means of violence,[106] does not oppose Satan in a metaphysical struggle, because he wants to be—this is the secret of his plan—a God who suffers and who incites Satan to do his regular work. In order to win, he accepts defeat. He goes as far as he can go on the path of nonresistance. On the human level, the Jewish leaders and the people of Israel thought they were free; on the divine level, Satan and his minions think they are free. In reality, they are in the service of the God of love, who because of their mediation wants to give freedom through the arrest of Jesus and to grant life through the death of the Son on the cross.

---

99 Bock (2:1826) notes that Pilate makes three successive efforts: he declares Jesus' innocence (v. 4); he sends him to Herod (vv. 6-12); he wants to inflict a warning, then release him (vv. 13-25). For its part, this third effort becomes concrete in three efforts to release Jesus (vv. 16, 20, and 22).

100 Tannehill (337) is of the opinion that there is a confrontation here between two opposing political attitudes: that of violence, embodied by Barabbas, and that of peace, represented by Jesus. The choice of Barabbas instead of Jesus is a political choice.

101 Schneider (2:478) thinks that Luke's intention in this passage is less to acquit Pilate than it is to make the Jews responsible. Luke composes this accusation in an apologetic effort to convince the Romans. Talbert (*Reading*, 212–18) emphasizes the example Jesus gives to Christians. Luke's suffering Christ is the model for the Christian martyrs.

102 According to George ("Sens," 196), Luke shows that things happen but does not explain why they happen.

103 Bossuyt and Radermakers (2:495) rightly emphasize this aspect; see also Trilling, *Fragen*, 141; George, "Sens," 188–89.

104 Tannehill (338) writes: "This drama includes an ironic twist: human rejection becomes the means by which God's saving purpose for both Jews and Gentiles is realized." George ("Sens," 201–11) emphasizes the role that, according to Luke, the death of Jesus plays in God's plan.

105 See Luke 9:51; 12:50; 18:31; 22:19, 22, 37; Acts 2:23; 4:28; 13:29.

106 I am inspired here by the beautiful farewell lecture of Henry Mottu, "Le Dieu proche et le Dieu des lointains, un itinéraire théologique," *Cahiers de l'Institut Romand de Pastorale* 49 (2004) 9–23, esp. 15–16.

What Christian readers over the centuries have not seen, however, and what Luke himself may not even have noticed, are the pernicious social and personal consequences of such a theological construction. In spite of the will of God realized through the actions of the human agents in the drama, Christians have often stayed on the historical level of the concrete evidence, seeing only the enemies of Christ rather than remaining silent before the mystery. Thus, over the centuries the spectacle of the passion has led to waves of anti-Semitism, even while it has inspired legitimate movements of self-criticism and worship.

On the Way to the Cross
and At the Cross (23:26-43)
Bibliography

Aletti, *Art de raconter*, 155–76.

Altheim, Franz, and Ruth Stiel, "Aramäische Herrenworte," in *Die Araber in der alten Welt* (5 vols.; Berlin: de Gruyter, 1969) 2:361–67.

Amedick, Rita, "'Iesus Nazarenus Rex Iudaiorum': Hellenistische Königsikonographie und das Neue Testament," in Annette Weissenrieder, Friederike Wendt, and Petra von Gemünden, eds., *Picturing the New Testament: Studies in Ancient Visual Images* (WUNT 2/193; Tübingen: Mohr Siebeck, 2005) 53–66.

Aus, Roger David, *Samuel, Saul, and Jesus: Three Early Palestinian Jewish Christian Gospel Haggadoth* (South Florida Studies in the History of Judaism 105; Atlanta: Scholars Press, 1994) 158–73.

Berger, Klaus, *Die Amen-Worte Jesu: Eine Untersuchung zum Problem der Legitimation in apokalyptischer Rede* (BZNW 39; Berlin: de Gruyter, 1970) 87.

Berlingieri, Giovanni, *Il lieto annuncio della nascita e del concepimento del precursore di Gesù (Lc 1,5–23.24–25) nel quadro dell'opera Lucana: Uno studio tradizionale e redazionale* (AnGr 258; Rome: Pontificia Università gregoriana, 1991).

Blinzler, *Prozess*, 263–81.

Blum, Matthias, *Denn sie wissen nicht, was sie tun: Zur Rezeption der Fürbitte Jesu am Kreuz (Lk 23, 34a) in der antiken jüdisch-christlichen Kontroverse* (NTAbh n.F. 46; Münster i. W.: Aschendorff, 2004).

Bovon, François, "Lukan Story of the Passion."

Idem, "Les sentences propres à Luc dans l'évangile selon Thomas," in Louis Painchaud and Paul-Hubert Poirer, eds., *Colloque International: L'évangile selon Thomas et les textes de Nag Hammadi* (BCNH 8; Quebec: Presses de l'Université Laval, 2007) 43–58.

Bultmann, *History*, 37, 115–16.

Carroll, J. T., "Luke's Crucifixion Scene," in Dennis D. Sylva, ed., *Reimaging the Death of the Lukan Jesus* (Athenäums Monografien: Theologie 73; Frankfurt: Hain, 1990) 108–24, 194–203.

Conzelmann, *Theology*, 88–90.

Cothenet, Édouard, "Paradis," *DBSup* 6 (1960) 1177–1220.

Crowder, Stephanie R. Buckhanon, *Simon of Cyrene: A Case of Roman Conscription* (StBL 46; New York: P. Lang, 2002).

Crowe, Jerome, "The Laos at the Cross: Luke's Crucifixion Scene," in Aelred Lacomara, ed., *The Language of the Cross* (Chicago: Franciscan Herald Press, 1977) 75–101.

Dammers, A. H., "Studies in Texts: Luke xxiii, 34a," *Theol* 52 (1949) 138–39.

Daube, David, "'For They Know Not What They Do': Luke 23, 34," *StPatr* 4 (TU 79; Berlin: Akademie-Verlag, 1961) 58–70.

Delobel, Joël, "Luke 23:34a: A Perpetual Text-Critical Crux?" in William L. Petersen et al., eds., *Sayings of Jesus: Canonical and Non-Canonical. Essays in Honour of Tjitze Baarda* (NovTSup 89; Leiden: Brill, 1997) 25–36.

Idem, "The Sayings of Jesus in the Textual Tradition: Variant Readings in the Greek Manuscripts of the Gospels," in idem, ed., *Logia: Les Paroles de Jésus—The Sayings of Jesus: Mémorial Joseph Coppens* (Leuven: Leuven University Press, 1982) 431–57.

Delorme, "Procès."

Démann, Paul, "'Père, pardonnez-leur' (Lc 23,34)," *CSion* 5 (1951) 321–36.

Derrett, J. Duncan M., "The Two Malefactors (Lk xxiii 33, 39–43)," in idem, *Studies in the New Testament* (6 vols.; Leiden: Brill, 1977–95) 3:200–214.

Dibelius, *Tradition*, 178–217.

Dupont, Jacques, *Les Béatitudes* (3 vols.; EtB; Paris: Gabalda, 1969–73) 3:133–45.

Ehman, "Luke 23:1-49."

Feuillet, André, "Souffrance et confiance en Dieu: Commentaire du Psaume xxii," *NRTh* 70 (1948) 137–49.

Fitzmyer, Joseph A., "Crucifixion in Ancient Palestine, Qumran Literature, and the New Testament," *CBQ* 40 (1978) 493–513.

Flusser, David, "'Sie wissen nicht, was sie tun?' Geschichte eines Herrenwortes," in Paul-Gerhard Müller and Werner Stenger, eds., *Kontinuität und Einheit für Franz Mussner* (Freiburg: Herder, 1981) 393–410.

Fusco, Vittorio, "La Morte del Messia," in Associazione biblica italiana, ed., *Gesù e la sua Morte* (Brescia: Paideia, 1984) 51–73.

García Pérez, José Miguel, "El relato del Buen Ladron," *EstBib* 44 (1986) 263–304.

Garland, David E., *One Hundred Years of Study on the Passion Narratives* (NABPR Bibliographic Series 3; Macon, Ga.: Mercer University Press, 1989).

George, "Sens."

Gese, Hartmut, "Psalm 22 und das Neue Testament," *ZThK* 65 (1968) 1–22.

Giblin, *Destruction*, 93–104.

Giesen, Heinz, "'Noch heute wirst du mit mir im Paradies sein' (Lk 23,43): Zur individuellen Eschatologie im lukanischen Doppelwerk," in Christoph Gregor Müller, ed., *Licht zur Erleuchtung der Heiden und Herrlichkeit für dein Volk Israel: Studien zum lukanischen Doppelwerk [Josef Zmijewski zur Vollendung seines 65. Lebensjahres am 23. Dezember 2005]* (BBB 151; Hamburg: Philo, 2005) 151–77.

Green, Joel B., "The Demise of the Temple as Cultural Center in Luke-Acts: An Exploration of the Rending of the Temple Veil," *RB* 101 (1994) 495–515.

Grelot, Pierre, "'Aujourd'hui tu seras avec moi dans le Paradis' (Luc, XXIII, 43)," *RB* 74 (1967) 194–214.

Hachlili, Rachel, and Ann E. Killebrew, "Jewish Funerary Customs during the Second Temple Period, in the Light of the Excavations at the Jericho Necropolis," *PEQ* 115 (1983) 115–26.

Heffernan, Thomas J., *Sacred Biography: Saints and Their Biographers in the Middle Ages* (New York: Oxford University Press, 1992) 80–87.

Hengel, Martin, *The Atonement: The Origins of the Doctrine in the New Testament* (trans. John Bowden; Philadelphia: Fortress Press, 1981) 65–75.

Idem, *Crucifixion in the Ancient World and the Folly of the Message of the Cross* (trans. John Bowden; Philadelphia: Fortress Press, 1977).

Henry, D. M., "'Father, Forgive Them; for They Know Not What They Do' (Luke xxiii. 34)," *ExpT* 30 (1918–19) 87.

Jeremias, Joachim, "παράδοσις," *TDNT* 5 (1967) 765–73.

Karavidopoulos, John D., "Τὸ πάθος τοῦ δούλου τοῦ ἐπὶ τοῦ σταυροῦ κατὰ διήγησιν τοῦ εὐαγγελιστοῦ Λουκᾶ (23, 33-49)," *DBM* 1 (1972) 189–211.

Käser, Walter, "Exegetische und theologische Erwägungen zur Seligpreisung der Kinderlosen Lc 23:29b," *ZNW* 54 (1963) 240–54.

Kellermann, Ulrich, "Elia als Seelenführer der Verstorbenen oder Elia-Typologie in Lk 23,34: 'Heute wirst du mit mir im Paradies sein,'" *BN* 83 (1996) 35–53.

Kloppenborg, John S., "Exitus clari viri: The Death of Jesus in Luke," *TJT* 8 (1992) 106–20.

Kuhn, Heinz-Wolfgang, "Jesus als Gekreuzigter in der frühchristlichen Verkündigung bis zur Mitte des 2. Jahrhunderts," *ZThK* 72 (1975) 1–46.

Lange, Joachim, "Zur Ausgestaltung der Szene vom Sterben Jesu in den synoptischen Evangelien," in Helmut Merklein and Joachim Lange, eds., *Biblische Randbemerkungen: Schülerfestschrift für Rudolf Schnackenburg zum 60. Geburtstag* (2d ed.; Würzburg: Echter, 1974) 50–55.

Leloir, L., "Hodie, mecum eris in Paradiso (Lc., XXIII, 43)," *RDN* 13 (1959) 471–83.

Liberto, David, "To Fear or Not to Fear? Christ as Sophos in Luke's Passion Narrative," *ExpT* 114 (2003) 219–23.

Lindars, Barnabas, *New Testament Apologetic: The Doctrinal Significance of Old Testament Quotations* (Philadelphia: Westminster, 1961) 88–93.

Linnemann, *Studien*, 136–70.

Luter, A. Boyd, "Women Disciples and the Great Commission," *Trinity Journal* 16 (1995) 171–85.

MacDonald, Dennis R., "The Breasts of Hecuba and Those of the Daughters of Jerusalem: Luke's Transvaluation of a Famous Iliadic Scene," in Jo-Ann Brant et al., eds., *Ancient Fiction: The Matrix of Early Christian and Jewish Narrative* (SBL Symposium Series 32; Atlanta: Society of Biblical Literature, 2005) 239–54.

MacRae, G. W., "With Me in Paradise," *Worship* 35 (1961) 235–40.

Malina, Bruce J., and Richard L. Rohrbaugh, *Social Science Commentary on the Synoptic Gospels* (Minneapolis: Fortress Press, 1992) 406–9.

Manicardi, Ermenegildo, "L'ultima parola di Gesú secondo Luca e il racconto della morte di Stefano in Atti," in Rinaldo Fabris, ed., *La Parola di Dio cresceva (At 12,24): scritti in onore di Carlo Maria Martini nel suo 70. compleanno* (SRivBib 33; Bologna: EDB, 1998) 251–70.

Matera, Frank J., "The Death of Jesus according to Luke: A Question of Sources," *CBQ* 47 (1985) 469–85.

McMahon, E. J., "The Death and Resurrection of Jesus in Luke 23:26—24:53: A Greimassian Analysis" (diss., Vanderbilt University, 1984).

Moffatt, James, "Exegetica: Luke xxiii. 34," *Exp* 8/7 (1914) 92–93.

Neyrey, "Absence."

Idem, "Jesus' Address to the Women of Jerusalem (Lk 23:27-31): A Prophetic Judgment Oracle," *NTS* 29 (1983) 74–86.

Idem, *Passion*, 108–55.

Pelletier, André, "La tradition synoptique du 'voile déchiré' à la lumière des réalités archéologiques," *RSR* 46 (1958) 161–80.

Idem, "Le 'voile' du temple de Jérusalem est-il devenu la 'portière' du temple d'Olympie?" *Syria* 32 (1955) 289–307.

Pitre, Brant James, "Blessing the Barren and Warning the Fecund: Jesus' Message for Women Concerning Pregnancy and Childbirth," *JSNT* 81 (2001) 59–80.

Prete, Benedetto, "Le preghiere di Gesù al Monte degli Ulivi e sulla Croce nel racconto lucano della passione," in Associazione biblica italiana, ed., *Gesù e la sua Morte* (Brescia: Paideia, 1984) 75–96.

Radl, Walter, "Der Tod Jesu in der Darstellung der Evangelien," *ThGl* 72 (1982) 432–44.

Rese, *Motive*, 200–202.

Reumann, John H., "Psalm 22 and the Cross," *Int* 28 (1974) 39–58.

Riesner, Rainer, "Golgota und die Archäologie," *BiKi* 40 (1985) 21–26.

Rigato, Maria-Luisa, *Il Titolo della Croce di Gesù: Confronto tra i Vangeli e la Tavoletta-reliquia della Basilica Eleniana a Roma* (Tesi gregoriana. Serie teologia 100; Rome: Pontificia università gregoriana, 2003).

Rinaldi, B., "Beate le sterili (Lc 23,29b): Riflessioni sull'ottava stazione della Via Crucis," *BeO* 15 (1973) 61–64.

Robbins, Vernon K., "The Crucifixion and the Speech of Jesus," *Forum* 4.1 (1988) 33–46.

Rosenblatt, "Crucifixion."

Russ, Rainer, "Das Vermächtnis des gekreuzigten Herrn: Jesu Letzte Worte im Evangelium nach Lukas (Bilder von Dieter Groß)," *BiKi* 50 (1995) 128–35.

Sauget, Joseph M., "Nouvelles homélies du Commentaire sur l'Évangile de s. Luc de Cyrille d'Alexandrie dans leur traduction syriaque," in *Symposium Syriacum 1972* (OrChrA 197; Rome: Pont. Institutum Orientalium Studiorum, 1974) 439–56.

Scheifler, José Ramón, "El salmo 22 y la crucifixión del Señor," *EstBib* 24 (1965) 5–83.

Schneider, Gerhard, *Parusiegleichnisse im Lukasevangelium* (SBS 74; Stuttgart: Katholisches Bibelwerk, 1975) 81–84.

Schniewind, *Parallelperikopen*, 77–85.

Smit Sibinga, J., "The Making of Luke 23:26-56: An Analysis of the Composition Technique in Luke's Crucifixion Narrative," *RB* 104 (1997) 378–404.

Simons, Jan Jozef, *Jerusalem in the Old Testament: Researches and Theories* (Leiden: Brill, 1952) 282–343.

Smith, R. H., "Paradise Today: Luke's Passion Narrative," *CThMi* 3 (1976) 323–36.

Soards, Marion L., "A Literary Analysis of the Origin and Purpose of Luke's Account of the Mockery of Jesus," *BZ* 31 (1987) 110–16.

Idem, "Tradition, Composition, and Theology in Jesus' Speech to the Daughters of Jerusalem," *Bib* 68 (1987) 221–44.

Sterling, "*Mors philosophi.*"

Stöhr, Martin, "Bist du nicht der Christus? Lukas 23,33-49: Sozialgeschichtliche Bibelauslegung," *JK* 60 (1999) 160–63.

Strobel, August, "Der Tod Jesu und das Sterben des Menschen nach Lk 23:39-43," in idem, ed., *Der Tod: Ungelöstes Rätsel oder überwundener Feind?* (Stuttgart: Calwer, 1974) 81–102.

Taylor, *Passion Narrative*, 89–99.

Trilling, Wolfgang, *Christusverkündigung in den synoptischen Evangelien: Beispiele gattungsgemässer Auslegung* (BiH 4: Munich: Kösel, 1969) 191–211.

Untergassmair, Franz Georg, "Der Spruch vom 'grünen und dürren Holz' (Lk 23,31)," *SNTU* 16 (1991) 55–87.

Walaskay, Paul W., "The Trial and Death of Jesus in the Gospel of Luke," *JBL* 94 (1975) 81–93.

Whitlark, Jason A., and Mikeal C. Parsons, "The 'Seven' Last Words: A Numerological Motivation for the Insertion of Luke 23.34a," *NTS* 52 (2006) 188–204.

Wilkinson, John, "The Seven Words from the Cross," *SJT* 17 (1964) 69–82.

Winter, Paul, "Lucan Sources," *ExpT* 68 (1957) 285.

Idem, *On the Trial*, 90–96.

Zehnle, Richard, "The Salvific Character of Jesus' Death in Lucan Soteriology," *TS* 30 (1969) 420–44.

---

26 And when they had led him away, they laid hands on a certain Simon of Cyrene who was coming from the field.[a] They laid the cross on his shoulders[b] to carry it behind Jesus. **27/** A large crowd of people followed him and women who bewailed and lamented him. **28/** Turning to them, Jesus said, "Daughters of Jerusalem, do not weep for me, but weep for yourselves and for your children. **29/** For behold, the days are coming in which they will say, 'Blessed are the barren and the wombs that did not bear and the breasts that have not fed.' **30/** Then they will begin to say to the mountains, 'Fall on us,' and to the hills, 'Cover us,' **31/** because if they do this when the wood is green,[c] what will happen when it is dry?" **32/** And two other criminals were brought to be put to death with him. **33/** When

a   Or: "from the country."
b   Literally: "on him."
c   Literally: "wet," "soft."

they came to the place called the Skull, they crucified him there, one of the malefactors on his right, the other on his left. 34/ Jesus said, "Father, forgive them, for they do not know what they are doing."[d] Then when they had divided his clothes, they cast lots. 35/ And the people stood and watched.[e] But the rulers scoffed at him, saying, "He saved others; if he indeed is[f] God's Messiah, the Chosen One, let him save himself." 36/ The soldiers also mocked him, approached and offered him vinegar, 37/ saying, "If you are the king of the Jews, save yourself." 38/ There was also a superscription above him: "This is the king of the Jews." 39/ One of the criminals hanging there insulted him, saying, "And you, are you not the Messiah? Save yourself and us with you!" 40/ The other replied by reproving him with the words, "Do you not even fear God? For you are subject to the same judgment. 41/ For we are deservedly getting the punishment for what we have done,[g] but this one has done nothing wrong." 42/ Then he said,[h] "Jesus, remember me when you come into your kingdom." 43/ Jesus said to him, "Truly, I say to you, today you will be with me in paradise."

d   On the text-critical problem raised by this sentence, see the commentary below on v. 34.
e   Literally: "contemplating."
f   Literally: "if this one is."
g   Literally: "things worthy of what we have done."
h   The imperfect, rather than the aorist, is surprising. It indicates that the good thief repeats his request or emphasizes the wording.

Luke ended the previous scene by showing Pilate as he delivered Jesus (23:25). In the scene before us (vv. 26-43) he tells about the last moments of the condemned: his march to the cross, his crucifixion, and his last words. That may be the skeleton of the story, but it is not the body. There are indeed other characters: Simon of Cyrene, the women of Jerusalem, the two thieves, the authorities, the soldiers, and the people. And when Jesus speaks, it is not to gain attention but to challenge, to pray, and to promise, thus to get the other people involved.

To interrupt the narrative in v. 43, as I do here for practical reasons, marks a caesura that may well appear to be more important than it is. The Lukan story of the passion has its coherence and its unity. Jesus' death, the logical consequence of the conviction and execution of the sentence, accompanied by signs and followed by a statement (vv. 44-49), immediately follows the crucifixion. Thus, one might not hesitate to merge the two units, vv. 26-43 and vv. 44-49, into a single unit. One might even consider adding the burial (vv. 50-56).

Synchronic Analysis

Roland Meynet decides for the latter option and thinks that vv. 50-56, the deposition from the cross and the burial, should be included in the literary unit that begins in v. 26.[1] In his opinion, vv. 26-56, for which the entire Gospel offers several agreements and to which Holy Scripture offers a number of references,[2] are organized concentrically in seven brief passages. At the center of the chiasm Meynet puts the inscription on the cross, v. 38. Verses 47-56 correspond to vv. 26-32; in both places the crowd is mentioned beating their

1   See Roland Meynet, *Quelle est donc cette parole? Lecture "rhétorique" de l'évangile de Luc (1–9, 22–24)* (2 vols.; LD 99 A–B; Paris: Cerf, 1979) 1:186–88; idem, *Évangile*, 1:216–21, 2:230–34; idem, *Guide*, 111–19.
2   Among the intratextual agreements the author mentions Jesus' first word (2:49), the expectation of the kingdom of God (2:25, 38), the centurion of

Capernaum (7:1-10), and Stephen (Acts 6:8—7:4). Among the intertextual references are Psalms 21 (22); 68 (69); and 30 (31); see Meynet, *Parole*, 1:186. On the role of the scriptural references in the passion narrative, see Lohse, *Geschichte*, 93.

breast. Verses 33-34 and vv. 44-46, with their prayers and the reference to the Father, also correspond to one another. This is true even of vv. 35-37 and vv. 39-43, which speak of Christ and his kingdom. As for the *titulus*, located centrally in v. 38, it proclaims Jesus' true identity. Not only am I not certain how much attention Luke gives to the christological title "King of the Jews," I am also not convinced that the mocking (vv. 35-37) and the conversation with the two robbers (vv. 39-43) parallel one another.

Wolfgang Wiefel also pays careful attention to the Lukan composition. He believes that the crucifixion (vv. 33-49) is "the heart and high point of the passion narrative,"[3] preceded by the way to the cross (vv. 26-32) and followed by the burial (vv. 50-56). Rightly, he points out how important the number three is.[4] There are three sayings of Jesus in the central part (vv. 34, 43, 46); three successive mockings with their threefold invitation to save himself (vv. 35, 37, 39); three effects of Jesus—on the centurion (v. 47), the people (v. 48), and the acquaintances (v. 49). In contrast to Meynet, Wiefel assigns a central role to the episode of the two thieves. This last conversation confirms the parenetic character the evangelist gives his story.[5]

In spite of the unity and flow of the narrative,[6] I am struck by the *Episodenstil*, the stylistic recourse to successive episodes here in the passion narrative as well as in the rest of the Gospel. As a result of this procedure,

a number of minor figures appear: Simon of Cyrene (v. 26), the crowd, the women of Jerusalem (vv. 27-31),[7] the two robbers (vv. 32-33 and 39-43), the leaders of the people (v. 35) and the soldiers (vv. 36-37), later the centurion (v. 47), Joseph of Arimathea (vv. 50-54), and the women of Galilee (vv. 55-56). There are only a few episodes in which the focus is on Jesus, and even there he is not alone. He is in the company of his Father (v. 34 and v. 46). The presence of a number of friends and opponents has a twofold implication. It means, first of all, that Jesus' death, far from being an isolated event, involves the fate of many.

It also demonstrates that the many witnesses and architects of the cross do not remain indifferent. The intention of the author is that the readers should appropriate this twofold implication. Luke summons them to take advantage of the benefit of the passion and to engage in a process of repentance and joining.[8]

Diachronic Analysis

Readers will recall that from the various explanations of the origin of the passion narrative I have chosen the procedure of alternating sources. In my opinion, Luke alternates between Mark's Gospel and his own special source.[9] He does not favor one of his sources, scattering other elements throughout it, as, among many others, Gerhard Schneider thinks.[10] It is thus my opinion that in

3   Wiefel, 397: "Herzstück und Höhepunkt der Passionsgeschichte."

4   Tannehill (342, 346) is also struck by the importance here of the three mockings and the three reactions to the death of Jesus.

5   See Wiefel, 397.

6   See also Linnemann, *Studien*, 136–70; Karavidopoulos, "Πάθος"; Giblin, *Destruction*, 93–104; and Smit Sibinga ("Making," 378–79), summarized as follows: "Luke's composition method in the crucifixion narrative is shown to be strictly logical and highly disciplined: it is organized on the basis of the numbers of (a) verbal forms, (b) words and (c) syllables. As a result, internal proportions can be defined simply and precisely. There is, for instance, balance and symmetry; there is the use of the 'golden rule' and the theorem of Pythagoras. Certain phrases stand out in a special way (e.g., Luke 23:25[c], 29[b, d], 30[b, d], 44[b], 45[b]), and the same is

true of at least two brief passages (Luke 23:28[b]-31, 39-43). In short, while admiring Luke's literary art, one should also do justice to his superior craftsmanship and his intellectual abilities."

7   On vv. 27-31, see Rinaldi, "Beate"; Neyrey, "Women"; idem, *Passion*, 108–21; Soards, "Daughters"; Pitre, "Barren."

8   Dupont (*Béatitudes*, 3:133) is of the opinion that the evangelist constructed the passion narrative artistically: the promise made to the good thief lies between "two references to the attitude of the people" (vv. 35 and 48). I do not understand how Bossuyt and Radermakers (2:496) are able to define the last part of the passion as "a grand liturgical celebration."

9   See the diachronic analysis above on 22:7-14 and 23:13-25; also Bovon, "Lukan Story of the Passion."

10 See Schneider, 2:480, 482, 486. The perspectives of Walter Schmithals (*Das Evangelium nach Lukas*

chap. 23 Luke quotes and adapts his special source from vv. 6 to 43, while from v. 44 to v. 11 of chap. 24 he takes up and rewrites Mark.

Even though it resembles its Markan equivalent (15:20-21), v. 26 is differently formulated:[11] The coming crucifixion is not mentioned; Simon is not forced to carry the cross, but it is laid on him; his two sons, Alexander and Rufus, are not mentioned; he will carry (a different verb) the cross "behind Jesus," which Mark does not say. The only literal contact between Luke and Mark is the expression here "who was coming from the field" (ἐρχόμενον ἀπ' ἀγροῦ).[12]

Verses 27-31 are a good example of Luke's independence from Mark and his dependence on a particular source.[13] Walter Käser, who had tried to go back behind the special source, also suggests considering vv. 29-30 as an outgrowth of two statements from Jesus.[14] The first statement, taken from apocalyptic language, is an oracle of woe in the form of what I would call a calamity beatitude. The second phrase confirms the first by quoting, without explicitly acknowledging it, a passage from the prophet Hosea (Hos 10:8). The *Gospel of Thomas* also confirms the original independence of this addition. In logion 79, at the end of a brief dialogue, the author of the apocryphal statement quotes it as a negative counterpart to the beatitude "Blessed are those who have heard the word of the Father and have kept it in truth!" a statement that itself responds to praise of the mother of Jesus. As we know, Luke, too, knows this brief dialogue in the form of two beatitudes that correspond to each other, but

he also quotes it elsewhere by putting it in another context and omitting the beatitude of woe (Luke 11:27-28). The context of this negative beatitude appears to be no more original in the *Gos. Thom.* 79 than in Luke 23:27-31, for the apocryphal evangelist seems to have adapted the saying to the brief dialogue: He reduced to two terms (womb and breasts) the three terms present in Luke and probably in the tradition (barren, wombs, and breasts).[15] In conclusion, I regard the calamity beatitude as a floating saying that the authors of Luke's special source and the *Gospel of Thomas* used as they saw fit. In Luke's special source it is the evoking of the tragic fate of the daughters of Jerusalem and their children that, following the logic of a dark future, determined the inclusion of this somber beatitude. For good measure, one added a statement of despair from the prophet Hosea (v. 30). A formal indication of this progression is the doubled and awkward ὅτι, in v. 29 (translated as "for") and in v. 31 ("because"). Along with Käser and many who follow him, I imagine that at some level prior to the redaction of the special source v. 31 (with only a single ὅτι, "because") was immediately connected to v. 28.[16]

While Mark and Matthew provide the information later and with different words[17]—after the drink is offered, the crucifixion itself, casting lots for the garments, and the reference to the *titulus*—Luke, or rather the author of the special source, calls attention here to the presence of the robbers. In its vocabulary and style, v. 32 corresponds to v. 26 and brings to a conclusion a paragraph that refers to characters who are submissive

---

[ZBK.NT 3.1; Zurich: Theologischer Verlag, 1980] 223, 225, 227) and of Fitzmyer (2:1494, 1500, 1507, 1512) are no different.

11 Jeremias (*Sprache*, 304–5) indicates the details of v. 26 that he regards as redactional and those he names as traditional. The verb ἐπιλαμβάνομαι is part of the evangelist's favorite vocabulary, while καί ("and") at the beginning of a sentence and a καὶ ὡς ("and when") followed by the aorist indicative must be pre-Lukan.

12 There are two "minor agreements" between Matthew and Luke. Both evangelists begin with the same verb, ἀπάγω, in the same aorist form, and both omit the reference to Simon's two sons, Alexander and Rufus. In the two cases, they have reacted the same way, independently of one another. The names of the two sons must have

seemed anecdotal to them and unnecessary for those who never even knew they existed.

13 See already Plummer, 527.

14 Käser, "Seligpreisung."

15 The apocryphal Gospel is thinking of a woman or of all women with a womb (singular) and breasts (plural). The canonical Gospel has the plural twice. See Bovon, "Luc dans l'évangile selon Thomas."

16 Käser, "Seligpreisung," 242.

17 Mark 15:27 par. Matt 27:38; these two Gospels speak of λησταί ("thieves," "bandits"), Luke of κακοῦργοι ("evildoers," "robbers"); instead of "two," Luke says "the other two." Left is called ἐξ εὐωνύμων in Mark 15:27 par. Matt 27:38; it is called ἐξ ἀριστερῶν by Luke in v. 33.

(Jesus and Simon at the beginning, v. 26, the two robbers at the end, v. 32) and to witnesses who are active (the crowd and the women).

If vv. 26-32 recount briefly the way to the cross, vv. 33-34 also say succinctly that the people arrive at their destination, the place of the Skull. Luke's source is satisfied to mention the arrival of the procession, the Greek name of the place, the crucifixion of the three condemned men, a prayer of Jesus, and the distribution of the garments. The Semitic name of Golgotha does not appear, just as the name of Gethsemane was absent in chap. 22. The first drink—Luke mentions the second in v. 36—is omitted. The inscription on the cross will be cited later in v. 38. On the other hand, Jesus' prayer asking forgiveness for his executioners is found only in Luke.[18] Only the casting of lots for the garments (without being expressed in the same way) is like the other two Synoptic Gospels.[19] These numerous differences confirm the hypothesis that Luke quotes here his own special source and not Mark.

While Matthew follows Mark closely,[20] laying out the jeers of the passersby, the statement about the temple, and the ironic appeal to save himself that is taken up by the chief priests and the other people (Matt 27:38-43 par. Mark 15:27-32), Luke begins in a much more sober way and broadens the rest with different accents. Only the leaders mock, while the people watch. The reference to the temple is missing. The ironic invitation to save himself does indeed appear, but often in terms different from those of Mark. Luke's version continues where Mark's stops. The soldiers take over the insults and offer vinegar to the condemned man (vv. 36-37). Finally, the inscription is mentioned (v. 38).

What is true of the differences in content is even more true of the differences in vocabulary. In Luke, the people are standing there; in Mark, they are passing by. Here the people are watching; there the people insult him and shake their heads. The authorities scoff ($\dot{\epsilon}\kappa\mu\nu\kappa\tau\eta\rho\dot{\iota}\zeta\omega$) here; there the chief priests and scribes mock ($\dot{\epsilon}\mu\pi\alpha\dot{\iota}\zeta\omega$). Here God's Messiah is the Chosen One; there the Messiah is the king of Israel. These differences in form and content confirm for me that here, as throughout the passage 23:6-43, Luke stays with a source other than Mark, what I call his special source.[21] As the evangelist elsewhere did not take over Mark without revising him, here he did not slavishly draw on the special source. Some features that could well belong to Luke's redaction of the special source are the following: Luke loves the people of Israel ($\lambda\alpha\dot{o}\varsigma$) and tends to be considerate of them (here the people do not share in the insults). He quite readily emphasizes the responsibility of the leading authorities (see 22:2) and likes the term $\ddot{\alpha}\rho\chi o\nu\tau\epsilon\varsigma$ (see 14:1; 18:18; 23:13). Elsewhere (16:14) he uses the rare verb $\dot{\epsilon}\kappa\mu\nu\kappa\tau\eta\rho\dot{\iota}\zeta\omega$ in an editorial statement. Finally, that the Christ is God's "Chosen" is not foreign to his Christology (see $\dot{o}$ $\dot{\epsilon}\kappa\lambda\epsilon\lambda\epsilon\gamma\mu\acute{\epsilon}\nu o\varsigma$, "the Chosen," spoken by the divine voice at the transfiguration, 9:35).

While Mark and Matthew are satisfied to mention the two thieves crucified with Jesus and to note that they are both hostile (Mark 15:32b par. Matt 27:44), Luke transmits an episode that contrasts two opposing attitudes and includes a conversation among the three main characters (vv. 39-43). The basic differences in content (in Mark and Matthew there is no good thief and no conversation among those who are crucified) and form (the very word for "robber" is different here and there) are such that most people who think that Luke was dependant on Mark are forced to admit that he here uses a different

---

18 In Acts 7:60, Luke puts a similar prayer on Stephen's lips, but it is expressed in different words.

19 These differences are carefully examined by Benoit (*Passion and Resurrection*, 153–80) and Lohse (*Geschichte*, 87–97), but the objective of these authors is to arrive at a historical reconstruction.

20 The first evangelist adds a final insult in 27:43: "He put his trust in God, so now, if he wants him, let God deliver him, for he said: I am the Son of God."

21 For their part, Schmithals (225) and Schneider (2:482) think that from v. 33 through v. 38 Luke depends only on Mark 15:22-32. Fitzmyer (2:1500–1501) believes instead that Luke merges here

elements from Mark and from the special source. In my opinion, the evangelist does not like to mix sources; he prefers to alternate between them. One result of disregarding Mark this way is that Jesus' cry of abandonment (Mark 15:34-35) is missing in Luke. This does not mean that Luke tries to make Jesus a sage who stoically endures suffering and death; I reject here this thesis put forward by Neyrey ("Absence"), Sterling ("*Mors Philosophi*"), and Liberto ("Fear").

source.[22] We must assume, therefore, that here (23:39-43) Luke quotes and adapts his special source.

It is interesting to compare Luke 23:26-43 with passion narratives other than Mark and Matthew.[23] John, for example, ignores the character of Simon of Cyrene and emphasizes that Jesus carried his own cross (19:17). He does not hesitate to give the Hebrew name of Golgotha and to point out that there were other convicted men on both sides of Jesus (19:17-18). He also mentions the inscription and even makes of it a special episode (19:19-22). In addition, John develops the story of casting lots for the garments (19:23-24). He is the only one who locates Jesus' mother and the Beloved Disciple at the foot of the cross (19:25-27). He then creates another episode from the tradition about the vinegar (19:28-30a). After a final word from Jesus, John lets him bow his head and die (19:30b). As we have shown, the fourth evangelist is familiar with various traditional motifs that Mark and the special source also know, and he develops them in both narrative and dialogue, not without including some elements of his theology. We cannot say that the Lukan and Johannine versions of the facts are particularly close.

The *Gospel of Peter* (10–20) contains the following sequence: (a) two robbers were crucified alongside Jesus; (b) the *titulus* is mentioned, bearing the inscription "This is the king of Israel"; (c) the garments are divided; (d) the good thief speaks; (e) an additional punishment is inflicted on the good thief or on Jesus; (f) the darkness spreads over Judea, followed by a collective fear and a scriptural prediction; (g) vinegar is offered Jesus; (h) the narrator comments that the opponents have reached the full measure of their sins; (i) lamps are lit; (j) Jesus speaks a final word: "My power, O power, you have abandoned me"; (k) Jesus is carried away; (l) the temple veil is torn.

As this summary demonstrates, the *Gospel of Peter* contains some unique elements: in (a) Jesus' silence and the appearance that he is not suffering; in (e) if it is about the good thief, there is the punishment that the executioners add (in order to prolong his agony, they do not break his legs); in (h) the emphasis on the guilt of Jesus' opponents; in (i) the episode of the lighted lamps; in (j) the participial form of Jesus' last words; in (k) Jesus' departure as an abduction or an ascension. The *Gospel of Peter* shared other elements with the canonical Gospels. It is close to Luke, and only to Luke, in one particular point: the statement of one of the two robbers, "We have landed in suffering for the deeds of wickedness which we have committed, but this man, who has become the saviour of men, what wrong has he done you?" is very similar to Luke 23:40b-41.[24] Of course, it is not the same as Luke; the statement is spoken to the executioners and not to the evil robber, and, of course, the good robber exchanges no words with Jesus. Yet the closeness is noteworthy, just as was the agreement between Pilate and Herod at the beginning of Luke 23.[25] Without any literary dependence of one Gospel on another, traditional elements, which moved from one community to another, have been taken over from both sides, just as we have seen with Jesus' beatitude about barren women (v. 29), which is found in the *Gos. Thom.* 79.[26]

Another traditional element that was circulating was the repentance of a number of Jewish witnesses of the crucifixion. Luke may allude to it (in vv. 27-28, 48), and according to Jerome a Jewish-Christian Gospel, the *Gospel of the Hebrews*—confirmed by a medieval passion narrative—emphasizes this fruit of Jesus' prayer. Accordingly many Jews repent and are converted. And the text adds that a delay of forty years was granted the people of Israel (we are to understand it to mean between the death of Jesus and the fall of Jerusalem).[27]

In his *Dialogue with Trypho* (101.3), Justin Martyr shows that he is familiar with Luke or with the special source

---

22 Thus Schneider (2:482). Schmithals (226) attributes the episode not to a particular tradition but to Lukan redaction. According to him, Luke would have created the episode from Mark 15:32b.

23 See Brown, *Death of the Messiah*, 2:884–1349.

24 Trans. Christian Maurer and Wilhelm Schneemelcher in Schneemelcher, *New Testament Apocrypha*, 1:223.

25 Luke 23:6-12 and *Gos. Pet.* 1–2; see the analysis above of 23:6-12 and commentary on 23:12.

26 See earlier in this diachronic analysis.

27 See Jerome *Epist.* 120.8; *Historia passionis Domini*, f. 55[r]; Haymo of Halberstadt (rather Haymo of Auxerre) *Comm. Is.* 53:12; Aland, *Synopsis*, 484; A. F. J. Klijn, *Jewish-Christian Gospel Tradition* (VCSup 17; Leiden: Brill, 1992) 22–23, 129–31; Bovon, "Lukan Story of the Passion," 99.

by using the verb ϑεωρέω ("contemplate") and the form μυξωτῆρσιν (see ἐκμυκτηρίζω in 23:35) (see also Justin *1 Apol.* 38). The way the apologist presents Jesus' passion proves that there were many versions of this drama. Down to the time of Irenaeus of Lyon (about 180 C.E.) Christians believed that these stories were compatible and complemented one another.[28]

The variety is evident also in the transmission of one and the same version of the passion. If there are few other stories with so many textual variants, it is because it took time for the Lukan version of the passion to be stabilized. In the detailed exegesis I will be able to examine each of these variants; here I will simply mention the best known. Is Jesus' prayer for his oppressors (v.34a) original or was it later grafted onto the story? Was the statement of the bad thief (v. 39b) removed from the original text or added to it? How are we to explain the different formulations of the good thief's request (v. 42)? It is clear that the formation of the canon late in the second century gradually led to stabilizing the text of the Gospel. Yet this stabilization did not happen everywhere in the same way, and that resulted in the different main forms of the text, the so-called Egyptian, Western, and Byzantine texts.[29]

The question of the literary genre of this pericope[30] arises in two ways. First, as part of a larger whole, our pericope belongs to the genre of the passion narrative. This has been defined as the long history of the tragic end of a life consisting of the trial, the torments, and the agony that led to Easter morning. Designed as a memorial liturgy to be recited as part of a weekly or annual celebration,[31] this story focuses on the baffling fate of Jesus planned by God and is designed to gather the community, to recall the historical basis of its new faith, to underscore that Jesus' life unfolded according to plan by fulfilling the Scriptures of Israel, and to encourage the faithful to go a similar way in their own lives.

As such, any narrative of the passion of Jesus performs a function similar to the Passover reminder of the exodus for the Jewish people[32] and, for the Greeks, the recitations made at the Panhellenic festivals.[33] Jesus' fate (which fulfills God's plan), the fulfillment of the Scriptures, the historical narration, the encouragement to follow in Jesus' footsteps—all of these elements, characteristic of the genre, are found in the pericope examined here. Even if Martin Dibelius with sharp sensitivity has observed the orientation Luke gives the story—a hagiographic orientation that leads the narrative in the direction of martyrdom—we must be careful not to widen the gap between Luke and the parallel narratives and to neglect the other concerns such as the historical reference, the fulfillment of prophecy, and laying a doctrinal foundation.

Second, as is true of the entire passion narrative, our pericope is the result of a construction, the bringing together of individual memories, the creation of a necklace with multiple pearls. This finding becomes obvious when we examine the style of this passage. Luke, the author of the special source, and the oral tradition before them have composed a story by accumulating anecdotes. Each could have originated independently and must have been combined with the others to arrive at the present form. A Christian man remembered Simon

---

28 See Lee Martin McDonald and James A. Sanders, eds., *The Canon Debate* (Peabody, Mass.: Hendrickson, 2002) passim.

29 Whoever wants to address the text-critical problems of this pericope will make use of the following tools: the editions of Constantin Tischendorf (the eighth *editio major*), of Hermann von Soden, of B. F. Westcott and F. J. A. Hort, and of the American and British committees (abbreviated here as *NTG*); also the work of Reuben J. Swanson, *Manuscripts*; the manual of Bruce M. Metzger, *Textual Commentary* (2d ed.); and some of the commentaries, especially those of Fitzmyer (2:1493–1511) and Wiefel (396–97).

30 See Bultmann, *History*, 275–84; Dibelius, *Tradition*, 178–217; Bertram, *Leidensgeschichte*, 1–8, 96–102

(who understands the passion narrative as a cultic story of the primitive community); Senior, *Passion*, 119–38; Brown, *Death of the Messiah*, 2:905–7.

31 See Étienne Trocmé, *The Passion as Liturgy: A Study in the Origin of the Passion Narratives in the Four Gospels* (London: SCM, 1983) 77–82.

32 See Robert Martin-Achard, *Essai biblique sur les fêtes d'Israël* (Geneva: Labor et Fides, 1974) 29–51.

33 I take my inspiration here from Gregory Nagy, *The Best of the Acheans: Concepts of the Hero in Archaic Greek Poetry* (rev. ed.; Baltimore: Johns Hopkins University Press, 1999) 7–9, 115–21, 139–42; and idem, *Pindar's Homer: The Lyric Possession of an Epic Past* (Baltimore: Johns Hopkins University Press, 1990).

of Cyrene, Christian women the daughters of Jerusalem, and so on. Taken alone, these episodes direct one's attention to the people with whom Jesus deals: his opponents, his supporters, or his partners in suffering. To be more precise, I would say they emphasize the interactions that bind the people momentarily to Jesus before they do so permanently. These episodes do not function in isolation in exactly the way they do in the fabric of the entire narrative. In the Simon episode, "following Jesus" is in the air, since the Lukan version emphasizes that he is walking "behind Jesus" (v. 26).[34] In the episode of the daughters of Jerusalem, there is less hostility toward the inhabitants of Jerusalem and more respect before the omnipotence of the God who judges. As for the three mockings, they now serve to eliminate christological misunderstanding: the authority and power of Jesus, God's Messiah, are not for the purpose of evading suffering and easily defeating death. The conversation between the good thief and Jesus demonstrates that this authority and this power exist on another level and have a different goal. The entire episode is very important. It serves to describe repentance and faith in contrast to callousness and attachment to what is tangible, to define more precisely belonging to God and thus the identity of the people of God. It also opens the way for Christian mission and the book of Acts. Finally, it suggests a renewed perception of eschatology by including individual hope in a collective and cosmic context of the delayed kingdom of God.

Commentary

■ 26 The immediate move from the judgment (23:25) to the execution of the sentence (v. 26) corresponds on the narrative level to the rapid succession of the events on the historical level. The criminal procedure known as *extra ordinem*, of an administrative character, gave the governor of a procuratorial province the right to enforce immediately the judgment he had just made.[35] The conjunction ὡς, followed by the indicative aorist, indicates a temporal priority, and the prefix ἀπο- in the form ἀπάγω marks the separation: "And when they had led him away. . . ."[36] The verb ἐπιλαμβάνομαι denotes a brisk action: "to seize," "to catch," "to surprise."[37] It is normally followed by the genitive rather than, as here, by the accusative.[38] Once they had Simon in their hands, the anonymous subjects of the action put the cross on his shoulders. The typically Greek construction puts the direct object, "the cross," first and then the verb, "to carry." There is a dual intention and a dual action: they lay the cross on him so that he will carry it. The infinitive of purpose φέρειν could be preceded by τοῦ or by εἰς τό.[39] Luke does not explain, any more than the other Gospels, why they had to make use of Simon of Cyrene's service. It is likely that he assumes that Jesus has been weakened by the bad treatment he has received (22:63-65).

We must respect the haziness that comes from the absence of an explicit subject. Although historically it was Pilate and his soldiers who had Jesus' fate in their hands,[40] according to Luke it had to be the same people who had brought Jesus to Pilate, since Pilate had finally delivered him to their mercy (23:25, with the same impreciseness). Luke has mentioned in 22:2, 52, 66, 71 and 23:13 who Jesus' opponents were, Israel's religious and political authorities, to whom he adds as a rare exception, the people (23:13, 18), who will soon repent (23:27, 48). In spite of what some authors think,[41] Luke is not thinking primarily of the Romans; as we know, he wants to spare them.[42] Admittedly, he does not deny that

34   The author of the Gospel of John has a different concern. Because of his anti-Docetism, he emphasizes the reality of suffering and cannot stand the idea that someone other than Jesus carries the cross (John 19:17). Thus, in his work Simon of Cyrene has disappeared.
35   See Bovon, *Last Days*, 44–50.
36   See Zorell, *Lexicon*, s.v. ὡς, IV.1.a. Codex Vaticanus (B = 03) has retained the imperfect καὶ ὡς ἀπῆγον, which must be translated "as they were leading him away."

37   See Delebecque, *Évangile*, 144. Luke likes to use this verb; see, e.g., 9:47 and Acts 16:19.
38   The variant that puts Simon of Cyrene in the genitive is well attested and conforms to the most common usage of the object of the verb. It does not affect the meaning. On this variant, see Fitzmyer, 2:1497.
39   It might also have a final ἵνα as in Mark 15:21.
40   See Bovon, *Last Days*, 25–27, 44–50.
41   For example, Lagrange, 584; and Wiefel, 394.
42   With Fitzmyer, 2:1496.

it was Pilate's decision (23:25), or that the punishment is Roman, or that the soldiers who undoubtedly are Roman (v. 36) take part. His primary concern is to leave the question vague.

The right to impress people has been a matter of study, but Luke does not speak to this legal question.[43] It seems that a person sentenced to death was not required to carry the entire cross but only the *patibulum*, the transverse, horizontal part of the cross.[44] The justices also wanted the people to see the guilty man walk to his punishment.[45] If one accepts that the trial before Pilate took place at Herod's palace on the western hill and not in the Tower of Antonia on the Temple Mount, the distance was not great to the place of the Skull, which along with many people I locate at the site of the Church of the Holy Sepulchre, a place that in those days was outside the walls.[46] It is possible that the procession did not go directly from one place to another but made a detour through the city. This is the route Pierre Benoit, who is quite knowledgeable of the topography of Jerusalem, proposes: "He would

have left Herod's palace, the present-day 'Tower of David', taken the present 'David Street' as far as the three parallel 'souks', followed these northwards and ended up at the gate which now stands in the Alexander Hospice. Going out by this gate, he would have been close to Calvary."[47] This assumed course is different from, even almost directly opposite of, today's Via Dolorosa, which dates back only to a medieval tradition.

Among the inhabitants of Jerusalem were a number of Diaspora Jews who had settled in the holy city.[48] This was the case with Simon, whose origin in Cyrene had not been forgotten.[49] It also served to distinguish him from other Simons. The area of Cyrene corresponds to modern Libya and was known for having a large Jewish minority.[50] That he is coming from the field or the country (the expression ἀπ᾽ ἀγροῦ, literally, "from the field," is frequently used to say "from the country")[51] is not initially surprising. It is the Lukan chronology, making this the day of the Passover, that shocks some people,[52] since what is forbidden on the Sabbath also refers to festi-

---

43 Mark and Matthew use the technical verb "to requisition," "to commandeer" (ἀγγαρεύω, a verb of Persian origin that has passed over into Greek, Latin, and even French [*angarie*]); see Spicq (*Lexicon,* 1:23–25) and Crowder (*Simon of Cyrene,* 46–50, 69–77), who think it was probably the Romans who commandeered Simon and that they chose him because he came from far away and may have had a dark skin.

44 On the *patibulum* and crucifixion in general, see Blinzler, *Prozess,* 265 n. 13; and Hengel, *Crucifixion.* Commentators frequently quote a passage from Plutarch (*De sera num. vind.* 9, *Mor.* 554B), which states that "each criminal carries his own cross" (ἕκαστος τῶν κακούργων ἐκφέρει τὸν ἑαυτοῦ σταυρόν); see Fitzmyer, 2:1497.

45 We are indebted to Plautus (frg. *Carbonaria,* 2) for the statement "Patibulum ferat per urbem" ("Let him carry his cross through the city.") For this reference I thank Benoit (*Passion and Resurrection,* 164 n. 1), who also calls attention to Josephus *Ant.* 20.6.3 §136.

46 Benoit, *Passion and Resurrection,* 165 n. 1.

47 Ibid., 165.

48 In Acts 6:9 Luke confirms that Jews from Cyrene were living in Jerusalem. He also mentions their presence in Antioch of Syria (Acts 11:20), even naming a certain Lucius ὁ Κυρηναῖος ("the Cyrenian," Acts 13:1): "Now there were at Antioch,

in the church at that place, prophets and teachers: Barnabas, Symeon, who was called Niger, Lucius of Cyrene, Manaen, a childhood friend of Herod the tetrarch, and Saul." Finally, he includes in the list of nations "Libya of Cyrene" (Acts 2:10: "of Phrygia and Pamphylia, of Egypt and the Cyrenian Libya, of Rome, those who were living here"). Edicts that shed light on the application of Roman criminal law in the provinces have been discovered in the area of Cyrene; see Fernand de Visscher, *Les édits d'Auguste découverts à Cyrène* (1940; reprinted Osnabrück: Zeller, 1965); Bovon, *Last Days,* 45–48.

49 It was the feast of the Passover, and many Diaspora Jews had made the pilgrimage to Jerusalem. Simon could have been one of them. That "of Cyrene" was attached to his name, however, leads one to think that he now lives in or near the capital (the words ἀπ᾽ ἀγροῦ, "from the fields," suggest that he has a farm or that he works as a farmer).

50 On Cyrenia, see Plummer, 527; Hans Volkmann, "Kyrene (Κυρήνη)," in Konrat Ziegler and Walther Sontheimer, eds., *Der Kleine Pauly: Lexikon der Antike* (Munich: Deutscher Taschenbuch Verlag, 1979) 3:410–11. There is an exegetical tradition that makes Simon a Gentile; see Bonaventure *Comm. Luc.* 23.30 (Bernardini, 572).

51 Alexandre, s.v.

52 See Fitzmyer, 2:1497.

vals. Thus, on those days one should not walk more than a certain number of steps. Instead of clinging to this anomaly, if indeed there is an anomaly (Simon may have limited his walk to what was permitted), it is better to note that Luke does not worry about such complications; he prefers to emphasize a different aspect. Following the Synoptic tradition, he interprets Simon as an example of a disciple. In keeping with a statement of Jesus (9:23; 14:27), he takes up the cross and follows Jesus.[53] Luke, or the author of the special source, emphasizes this comparison, adding what is not found in Mark 15:21 and Matt 27:32, the words ὄπισθεν τοῦ Ἰησοῦ ("behind Jesus").[54]

■ **27** The verb that opens this verse, ἀκολουθέω ("to follow"), appears in 9:23 in connection with bearing the cross. The name used for the crowd following Jesus is λαός ("people"), a term Luke almost always uses in a good sense, often even to speak of the "people of God."[55] It follows that, in spite of the hostile context, the readers expect something positive.[56] This "large crowd of people"—notice the hyperbole that reduces the opponents to the minority—is also, according to Luke, made up of women. Today this formula is surprising, but in those days a meeting was made up only of men.[57] Luke wants to

say that all the people, men and women, followed Jesus. Even if the feminine pronoun (αἵ, "who") agrees with the nearest antecedent, the women, is it possible that the men were also included in the lament? There are two reasons for rejecting this hypothesis: (a) the custom of the day was that mourners were women and not a mixture of the two genders; (b) Jesus' response is directed only to the "daughters of Jerusalem" (v. 28).

It is probably wrong to say that the rabbinic tradition, based on Deut 21:22-23, forbids mourning people condemned to death.[58] It speaks of the custom. *Sifre Deuteronomy* 308 says, "When a man is crucified, his father weeps and his mother prostrates herself before him. The father says 'Woe is me!' The mother says, 'Woe is me!' But does the lament concern only the one who goes out to be condemned?"[59] Here in v. 27 the women undoubtedly beat their breasts;[60] that is the visible part of their action. They lament;[61] that is the audible part of their action. Even if Luke suggests that these acts were spontaneous, they were no less ritualized. Their ritualization, which can still be seen today in the Near East, does not minimize their sincerity.[62] Nothing in Luke suggests, as an author might do,[63] that these women were protesting

---

53   Ambrose of Milan (*Exp. Luc.* 10.107) and then the Venerable Bede (*In Luc.* 6.1437–43) have regard for this aspect.

54   In a hymnic text, 1 Pet 2:21 celebrates the Christ who died so that believers could follow in his footsteps. See also the *Glossa ordinaria*, Luke 23:26 (*PL* 114:346). On Simon as a model for the Christians, see Schneider, 2:481; Schmithals, 223–24; Sabourin, 364. See also Crowder, *Simon of Cyrene.*

55   See Crowe, "Laos."

56   Lucian of Samosata (*Peregr. Mort.* 34) alludes to the curious who follow the condemned persons walking to their crucifixion. On the basis of this passage, Erich Klostermann (*Das Lukasevangelium* [HNT 2.1; Tübingen: Mohr Siebeck, 1919] 227) concludes that here also it is more curiosity than pity that guides the crowd of Jerusalemites.

57   The Nestle-Aland text (27th ed.) has the genitive καὶ γυναικῶν: the large crowd is also composed of women. Some Greek manuscripts, including Codex Bezae (D = 05) and several Latin and Syriac witnesses show or presuppose the nominative καὶ γυναῖκες ("and women"). See the apparatus in Nestle on this text. This variant tries to improve an unusual expression, in spite of its logic.

58   Contra Schneider, 2:481; and Bossuyt and Rademakers, 2:497.

59   *Sifre: Tannaitic Commentary on the Book of Deuteronomy* (trans. Reuven Hammer; New Haven: Yale University Press, 1986) 313; Wiefel, 395.

60   The verb κόπτω means "to strike," "to beat," "to hammer," "to cut," "to annoy." In the middle voice it means "to hit oneself," especially "to hit oneself as an expression of pain," "to lament," "to bewail"; see Alexandre, s.v. Luke has already used it in 8:52. See vol. 1 of this commentary, 340, on 8:52-53; BAGD, s.v.

61   The verb θρηνέω signifies "to weep," "to lament," "to bewail." It has led to the French word *thrène,* which means "funereal mourning." We find it as early as Homer (e.g., *Od.* 24.61). In Sophocles (*Electra* 94) it implies a form of commiseration; see Zorell, *Lexicon,* s.v. Luke has used this verb already in 7:32; see BAGD, s.v.

62   Josephus (*Ant.* 6.14.8 §377) makes use of these two verbs when he tells about the mourning following Israel's defeat by the Philistines and the death of Saul and his three sons (1 Sam [LXX 1 Kgdms] 31:11-13); see Fitzmyer, 2:1497.

63   Josef Schmid, *Das Evangelium nach Lukas* (3d ed.; RNT; Regensburg: Pustet, 1955) 346.

against Jesus' sentence of death.[64] He is not indifferent to the fact that it is women who are in solidarity with Jesus. Nowhere in the Gospel are they hostile toward him.[65]

We do not know whether the author of the special source and, following him, Luke give an account here of a historical memory, but we must understand that it is not out of the question that a scriptural text, a prophecy of Zechariah, contributed to the redaction of this passage: "So that, when they look on me whom they have pierced, they shall mourn for him, as one mourns for an only son, and weep bitterly over him, as one weeps over a firstborn. On that day the mourning in Jerusalem will be as great as the mourning for Hadad-rimmon in the plain of Megiddo" (Zech 12:10-11).[66]

■ **28** Luke, or probably the author of the special source before him, likes to say that Jesus "turns to" his conversation partners before he speaks to them.[67] Since the formula does not appear in Acts, a book in which the Master is physically absent, it suggests a special and affectionate attention from the Lord.[68] In a chiastic sentence,[69] which underscores the polarity of "I" and "you," Jesus makes a recommendation[70] based on an implicit knowledge. It should be noted that the negative imperative in the present tense involves continuous rather than point action. The final reference to children even suggests a period

of more than a generation. Jesus encourages them to look at themselves, their destiny, and their descendants. His refusal to feel sorry about his own fate reflects the image that the first Christians, Luke in particular, had about the Master's personal ethics. The traditions conveyed both by the epistles and by the Gospels unanimously praise Jesus' self-denial and his love of others. One thinks of Phil 2:6-8 or Luke 22:27. By inviting the women of Jerusalem[71] to weep for themselves,[72] the Lukan Christ sends a double message. The first concerns the "daughters," the second "Jerusalem."[73] To be sure, he does not recommend using a double standard, as if he were inviting these women to adopt a selfish attitude. He encourages them to face the situation, their situation, to assume responsibility for themselves, as do the sick people who consult a physician or the disturbed people who turn to a therapist. Weeping is here the beginning of wisdom, of the fear of God; it is the first step in the process of conversion. To fear God is to think of the fate he has in store for his holy city. The implicit knowledge that Luke suggests here is the connection that the early Christians established between Jesus' death and the fall of Jerusalem.[74] This is the fourth time the Gospel of Luke has mentioned this terrible prospect: in 13:34-35 Jesus announced the fall of the temple;[75] in 19:41-44,

---

64 On the funeral dirges, see Margaret Alexiou, *The Ritual Lament in Greek Tradition* (2d ed.; Lanham, Md.: Rowman & Littlefield, 2002); Bertrand Bouvier, *Le mirologue de la Vierge: Chansons et poèmes grecs sur la passion du Christ* (BHRom 16; Geneva: Institut suisse de Rome, 1976); John Dominic Crossan, *The Birth of Christianity: Discovering What Happened Immediately after the Execution of Jesus* (San Francisco: HarperSanFrancisco, 1998) 517–73; Kimberley Christine Patton and John Stratton Hawley, eds., *Holy Tears: Weeping in the Religious Imagination* (Princeton: Princeton University Press, 2005).

65 See already Plummer, 528; and recently Bock, 2:1844–45.

66 On the role of Zech 12:10-11, see André Lacocque, *Zacharie 9–14* (CAT 11c; Neuchâtel: Delachaux et Niestlé, 1981) 181–92.

67 Luke applies here a favorite literary device: He connects the πρὸς αὐτάς ("to them") not only with στραφείς ("having turned") but also with εἶπεν ("he said"); see vol. 1 of this commentary, 33 n. 21, on 1:6. Some manuscripts have the reverse order of the words: ὁ Ἰησοῦς πρὸς αὐτάς; see the apparatus of Nestle-Aland (27th ed.) on this text.

68 In the Gospel, see 7:9, 44; 9:55; 10:23; 14:25; and 22:61.

69 A (Do not weep)—B (for me)—B´ (but for yourselves)—A´ (weep, and for your children).

70 It is difficult to say whether this is a recommendation or a command. The same imperative can perform both functions.

71 On the later legend of Veronica, see Plummer, 529; and Rainer Warland, "Veronika," *LThK* 10 (2001) 714–15.

72 Three times Codex Bezae (D = 05) omits the preposition ἐπί. Thus, it here regards the verb κλαίω ("to weep") as transitive (this usage is well attested; see Matt 2:18). In the first occurrence this manuscript adds grief to the tears: μηδὲ πενθεῖτε ("and do not mourn").

73 The anonymous Irish commentator of the late eighth century (*Comm. Luc.* 23:28 [CCSL 108C:94]) notes about v. 28: It is as if Jesus had said that his own torments would end today, while those of the women of Jerusalem would begin on that day.

74 See Kaestli, *L'eschatologie*, 42–43.

75 See vol. 2 of this commentary, on 13:34-35.

when approaching the holy city, he wept over it;[76] in 21:20-24 he predicted the siege and the fall.[77] In the latter two cases he mentioned how important knowledge of the coming things is and regretted ignorance about them. The book of Acts will pursue this reflection on the tangled relationship between the destinies of Jerusalem and Jesus (see Acts 1:8, 12; 2:5, 14; 10:37-41). The ignorance of the inhabitants of Jerusalem, in the sense of blindness, was certainly serious but not fatal. The message of the resurrection gave everyone a last chance to repent—according to Luke, that is the challenge the apostles address to Israel (see Acts 3:17; 13:27). Along with many other Christians, the evangelist Mark believed that the death of Jesus and the fall of Jerusalem belonged to the last events, the beginning of the end of the world (Mark 13). Luke's preference is to insist on including these events in God's plan, but his salvation history does not exclude painting with an eschatological brush. He simply refuses to give in to an excess of apocalyptic.[78]

The expression "daughters of Jerusalem" has its roots in the biblical tradition that speaks of the "daughter of Jerusalem" and the "daughter of Zion" to refer collectively to the people of Israel, the inhabitants of Jerusalem, or the holy city itself.[79] We find the plural expression addressed to the choir in the Song of Songs.[80] "Daughters of Jerusalem" refers no more to young girls than the expression "sons of Israel" designates children.

■ 29 The expression "behold, the days are coming" is apocalyptic and is rooted in the prophetic style. See in the LXX Jer 7:32; 9:24; 16:14; 19:6; 23:5, 7; 38:27 (MT 31:31). It introduces an oracle, often one of woe and

of punishment.[81] The use of the present tense underscores the inexorable character of this future. Without its being always stated, the action announced originates with God.[82] Here, as indeed sometimes is the case with Jeremiah, the future situation is complex and has two stages. In the second, explicitly stated stage, human beings respond to God's work, which takes place in the first stage, but this stage is presupposed but not expressed. Thus, Jer 7:32 LXX: "Therefore behold, the days are coming, says the Lord, and one will no longer say 'Altar of Tapheth' and 'Valley of the sons of Ennom,' but 'Valley of the slaughtered.'"[83] In our v. 29 as well, it is not the calamity that is named but the human reaction it causes. The same reaction is driven home three times by mentioning in succession the barren women, their wombs, and their breasts. They each express the same idea: after such a catastrophe it is better to have no children. This conviction has been expressed throughout the course of history and has even been shared in recent days after the genocides that decimated the Armenians, the Jews, or the Ugandans. While normally infertile women experience shame (see 1:25), in this exceptional time they will be praised as the only ones who are blessed.[84] They will neither have to inflict this spectacle on their children nor will they see them perish before their very eyes. The book of the prophet Isaiah, which already contains this idea, may have served as an inspiration or model: "Rejoice, you barren one, who no longer bears children, break out in song and shout, you who bring no more children into the world" (Isa 54:1).[85] The reader is reminded that the second apocalyptic

---

76   See the commentary above on 19:41–44.

77   See the commentary above on 21:20–24.

78   See Bovon, *Luke the Theologian*, 1–85.

79   See Isa 37:22; 52:2; 62:11; Zeph 3:14; Zech 9:9 (this verse is quoted in Matt 21:5 and John 12:15).

80   Cant 1:5; 2:7; 3:5, 10-11; 5:8, 16; 8:4. See C. F. Evans (862), who notes the possible connections between the Song of Songs and the cult of the god Tammuz, whose death is lamented by mourners.

81   See the great lament in the *Syriac Apocalypse of Baruch*, which is similar to our passage. Here is an excerpt: "Women, do not ask for children, because the barren ones will rejoice greatly, those who have no sons will think they are happy, and those who do have sons will groan. Why bring people to the world in pain (who must) later be buried in tears (*2 Bar.* 10:13-15).

82   The words Jesus speaks here are not to console the daughters of Jerusalem; see Senior, *Passion*, 121–23.

83   Note the similarity between the beginning of Jer 7:32 (διὰ τοῦτο ἰδοὺ ἡμέραι ἔρχονται, λέγει ὁ κύριος, καὶ οὐκ ἐροῦσιν ἔτι . . .) and that of Luke 23:29 (ὅτι ἰδοὺ ἔρχονται ἡμέραι ἐν αἷς ἐροῦσιν . . .).

84   Schmithals (224) and Wiefel (395) emphasize the paradoxical nature of the beatitude. On the literary genre of the beatitude, see vol. 1 of this commentary, 221–22, on 6:20-26. On this beatitude, see the diachronic analysis above.

85   On the connections between Isa 54:1 and Luke 23:29, see Nolland, 3:1137, who rightly points out a difference in their situations. In Isaiah the barren women can rejoice today because a happy future is on the horizon.

303

discourse that Luke puts in the mouth of Jesus contains an exclamation that recalls the oracle of Isaiah 54: "Woe to those who are pregnant and to those who are nursing children in those days!" (21:23).[86] There are also many parallels in the classical literature of antiquity.[87]

What is the catastrophe that is all the more menacing and frightening for not being explicitly stated? When one refers to the other three laments over Jerusalem—13:34-35; 19:41-44; and 21:20-24—it can only mean the fall of the holy city. As we have often seen (see 2:49),[88] Luke likes to maintain a certain haziness about the prophecies.[89]

■ **30** Since the verb ἄρχομαι is one of his favorites, Luke may have written or edited the beginning of the sentence himself. The oracle itself must have existed before him. But exactly who is it for? Neither the daughters of Jerusalem nor the women who will be barren in the future, but the people who have declared the beatitude of woe. The impersonal subject of ἐροῦσιν ("one will say") is still the subject of "one will begin to say" (ἄρξονται λέγειν). To designate who it is I would rather speak of a collective than of an impersonal subject. Without the author saying it, these people express themselves in a biblical manner. They borrow their tragic wish[90] from the prophet Hosea (Hos 10:8), whom they cite from memory according to the LXX. One notes a reversal in the order and some minor differences· καὶ ἐροῦσι τοῖς ὄρεσι, καλύψατε ἡμᾶς, καὶ τοῖς βουνοῖς, πέσατε ἐφ᾽ ἡμᾶς (Hos 10:8 LXX). In the words of the prophet, the sentence is taken from an oracle of judgment against the northern kingdom, which has been guilty of idolatry and injustice. Desiring misfortune is not unique to Hosea; it is a common attitude in apocalyptic literature (Hos 10:8 is quoted in Rev 6:16). Even violent death becomes the lesser evil. The normal attitude is to pray that the rocks not collapse on you. Here the order of the values is reversed so that one hopes for the opposite. In Semitic style the sentence uses the common method of *parallelismus membrorum*: May the mountains fall on us and the hills cover us.

Nothing in vv. 29-30 alludes to the passion of Christ or the fall of Jerusalem. It is possible, therefore, that this oracle of judgment was imported from another apocalyptic context to emphasize how serious the present situation is as well as what will come in the future. This adaptation could have been made during the oral transmission of the Lukan passion narrative or in the redaction of the special source. It was done in the context of the Greek language, since it is the LXX version that is quoted.

■ **31** The enigmatic sentence of v. 31 belongs to the genre of wisdom proverbs. By its very nature it differs, therefore, from the preceding apocalyptic words (vv. 29-30). As befits a proverbial sentence, it uses concrete terms and does so in pictorial images such as here the "green wood"[91] and the "dry wood." It is also appropriate that these concrete terms relate to everyday life, which easily communicates the message. Beyond vv. 29-30, the contrast that the statement expresses returns to the opposites of v. 28 between the fate of one person ("me")

---

86 Fitzmyer (2:1498) invites one to read all of Isa 54:1-10: the barren women can really rejoice, because ultimately God will comfort and overwhelm them. Should there be a note of hope in Luke 23:29? The use of the word "blessed" is not enough to awaken such hope.

87 The commentaries (see those by Plummer [529], Lagrange [586], and recently Bock [2:1846]) like to refer to Euripides *Andr.* 395; Euripides *Alc.* 882; Tacitus *Ann.* 2.75; Seneca the Elder *Contr.* 2.3.2; Apuleius *Apologia* 85.

88 See Bovon, *Révélations*, 65–74.

89 Three remarks here about the text of v. 29: (a) ἰδού ("behold") is omitted by good Greek, Latin, and Syriac witnesses; see the apparatus of Nestle-Aland (27th ed.) on the text. But we must retain the word because it is in keeping with the literary genre. (b)

Some witnesses reverse the order of the words and offer ἡμέραι ἔρχονται. The reading of Codex Bezae (D = 05) and a family of manuscripts (f^{13}), ἐλεύσονται ἡμέραι ("the days are coming"), leads me to keep Nestle-Aland's (27th ed.) order. (c) Instead of ἔθρεψαν ("fed"), the Byzantine text has retained ἐθήλασαν ("nursed," "breastfed"). This reading must be secondary, because it improves the style somewhat. See the list of witnesses in apparatus of Nestle-Aland (27th ed.) on the text.

90 See Tannehill (339), who notes the "mood of pathos" and the "sense of tragedy."

91 Literally, "the wet wood," thus the tender wood; see Alexandre, s.v. ὑγρός, ά, όν. On the LXX expression about Ezek 17:24, see n. 98 below.

and the fate of others ("you"). Beyond these certainties there are the uncertainties that come from the vague and general character of the verbs. What is the meaning of "they do this" and "what will happen"? The meaning of the preposition ἐν is also uncertain. I understand it in the instrumental sense of "with" or as relational, "with regard to,"[92] and perceive a Semitic original behind the Greek. Jesus, still young and alive, compares himself with the green wood; Jerusalem, ancient, dry, and hardened, with dry wood.[93] The collective subject of the first verb represents the human agents of history. It is they who are responsible for the death of Jesus. The indefinite character of the second refers to those who are responsible for the fall of Jerusalem. The human instrumentality does not exclude the divine intentionality.[94]

The reader should be aware that some exegetes explain this enigmatic-looking proverb differently. Bock presents five possible explanations, simply stated.[95] (a) If the Romans treat Jesus, who is innocent, this way, how will they treat those who are guilty? (b) If the Jews act this way toward the one who came to save them, what treatment will they in turn receive? (c) If the whole human race behaves this way when its sin is still in its early stages, what will happen when it reaches its high point? (d) If God did not spare Jesus, how will he spare the human beings who do not repent?[96] (e) The prov-erb speaks of the coming judgment without referring to future events or to specific persons.[97]

To solve the puzzle, people have turned to Scripture. They have appealed to Isa 10:16-19; Jer 11:16, 19; Ezek 17:24;[98] 21:3 (LXX 20:47); 24:9-10; Prov 11:31; and 1 Pet 4:17-18 for help. It is obvious that fire consumes wood and that dry wood burns better than green wood. It is also clear that God's judgment is easily compared with a destructive or purifying fire.[99] In addition, it is true that if the righteous will have their reward, the wicked will certainly not escape their punishment (that is the sense of Prov 11:31). Finally, it is certain that there is no exact equivalent in Israel's Scriptures. In rabbinic literature, however, one finds similar sentences.[100] In the *Seder Eliyahu Rabbah* 14 (F.65) we read: "If the fire consumes the green wood, what will the dry wood do?"[101] It may be, therefore, that we are dealing here in v. 31 with a proverb of Semitic origin that circulated in Israel and was translated into Greek and used by the early Christians. It is even possible that the historical Jesus used it before or during his passion.[102] The apophthegm that had begun in v. 27 ends here: An incident or a situation gives the main character an opportunity to express an intelligent opinion with impressive terms and thus to have the last word.[103]

---

92 On the meaning and use of the preposition ἐν, see BAGD, s.v.; and BDF §§218–20.

93 Tannehill (339) also is of this opinion.

94 The fourth hypothesis presented below emphasizes the divine intervention in history.

95 Bock, 2:1847. See before him Plummer (529–30), who gives a short list of explanations; see also Untergassmair, "Holz."

96 This explanation is often favored by the exegetes; see, e.g., Marshall, 865; and Fitzmyer, 2:1498–99.

97 This is the explanation of Nolland (3:1138).

98 Ezekiel 17:24 contrasts dry wood and green wood but from a different perspective. The LXX translates the "dry wood" as ξύλον ξηρόν and the "green wood" as ξύλον χλωρόν. The use of χλωρός, ά, όν, to speak of "green wood" is more natural in Greek than is the use of ὑγρός, ά, όν.

99 See the metaphorical connotations of fire offered concerning 12:49 ("I came to cast fire on the earth") and vol. 2 of this commentary, on 12:49.

100 It is said that when Rabbi Jose ben Jo'ezer was being led to his execution around 150 B.C.E. he said to his nephew: "If this [capital punishment] happens to those who do the will of God, what will happen to those who offend him?" (*Gen. Rab.* 65.18). This example is cited by Johannes Schneider, "ξύλον," *TDNT* 5 (1967) 38 n. 7; and Sabourin, 365.

101 Should this mean: What will become of the dry wood? For other rabbinic parallels, see Str-B 2:263–64.

102 I point out two variants in this v. 31, which hardly affect the meaning. The definite article τῷ before "green wood" is omitted by a number of important manuscripts, among them Codex Vaticanus (B = 03) and Codex Ephraem (C = 04). The 25th edition of Nestle also omits it from the text. Instead of γένηται, the aorist subjunctive functioning as a future, various manuscripts have the indicative future, γενήσεται, a more explicit reading, which, for that reason, must be secondary.

103 On the apophthegm in general and this one in particular, see Bultmann, *History*, 37, 55–69.

■ **32** The evangelist, or perhaps the author of the special source, wants to point out that before Jesus arrived at the place of the Skull he was accompanied by two other condemned men.[104] As a result, v. 32 echoes v. 26 (see the verbs ἀπάγω, "to lead away," in v. 26 and ἄγω, "to lead," in v. 32; being accompanied by Simon, then by one of the two robbers; the infinitive of purpose "to carry," and "to be put to death";[105] "behind Jesus" and "with him"). Thus, the ground is prepared for the description of the three crucifixions (v. 33) and the final conversation (vv. 39-43). The result finally is that Jesus' prophecy is fulfilled that he would be counted among the lawless (22:37, citing Isa 53:12). The reader notices, however, a slight awkwardness: by saying "two other criminals" the author gives the appearance that he is admitting Jesus' guilt. But in fact he recognizes that the innocent Jesus is recorded among the wicked. By choosing the term κακοῦργος (literally, "criminal"), the evangelist avoids the word used by Mark (15:27) and Matthew (27:38), λῃστής ("armed robber," "brigand"), which is used to refer to the Jewish rebels who resisted the Roman occupation of the country.[106] On every page Luke avoids any confusion between the Christian movement and the Jewish insurrection.[107] One sees that in 22:52.

■ **33** If the place is called "the Skull," it is not because Adam was buried there (a relationship between the place of Christ's death and Adam's resting place will not be established until later);[108] it is because of the shape of the hill or the mound. Father Vincent of the French École biblique et archéologique, who lived in Jerusalem, still heard an old Arab refer to the place (where today the holy sepulcher is still located) as the "*Râs,*" that is to say "Head."[109] There they crucified Jesus.[110]

Verse 33 does not repeat the awkwardness of v. 32. It speaks not of the three criminals but of Jesus and the criminals. By stating the position of each cross, the author prepares for the conversation that follows and above all, as in Matthew's great parable (Matt 25:33), he makes a distinction between good and evil. The left has already been given a negative and the right a positive connotation.[111] We imagine, therefore, that the good thief was crucified to the right of Jesus. That is, in any case, how the artists represent the scene. Without speaking of the left and the right, the Gospels of John and of Peter also state that the two thieves were crucified on each side of Jesus (John 19:18; *Gos. Peter* 10).[112]

■ **34** This verse poses one of the major textual problems of the Gospel of Luke.[113] The prayer of Jesus imploring his Father to forgive his executioners (v. 34a)—was it part of the original text of Luke, or was it added later? The age, the weight, and the quality of the manuscripts on the two sides are equal. In its original version,

---

104 The order of the words κακοῦργοι δύο is reversed in certain ancient manuscripts such as Alexandrinus (A = 02), Codex Ephraem (C = 04), and Codex Bezae (D = 05), as well as in the witnesses of the Byzantine text. Luke's custom is to put the cardinal numbers after the names. I retain the order of Nestle-Aland (27th ed.).

105 The verb ἀναιρέω ("to remove," "to eliminate," "to kill," "to put to death") is used with reference to Jesus in 22:2 and Acts 13:28 and several times in Acts about other people, including James, the son of Zebedee (Acts 12:2); see the analysis above on 22:1-6; BAGD, s.v.

106 On κακοῦργος, see BAGD, s.v.; on λῃστής, regularly used by Josephus to designate Jewish revolutionaries, see BAGD, s.v.; and Spicq, *Lexicon,* 2:389–95.

107 An eighth-century Latin manuscript, l, preserved in Berlin, provides the names of the two thieves. They are called Joathas and Maggatras. These names are surprising, for various parts of the Pilate cycle have circulated in Christianity the names Desmas and Gestas; see Plummer, 530, 534; Bovon et al., *Écrits apocryphes chrétiens,* 2:347.

108 See Plummer, 531; Réau, *Iconographie,* 2/2:488–91; BAGD, s.v. Γολγοθᾶ, ἡ.

109 Pierre Benoit, the former director of this school, provides this information (*Passion and Resurrection,* 169).

110 On the crucifixion itself, see Rosenblatt, "Crucifixion"; Winter, *On the Trial,* 90–96; Fitzmyer, "Crucifixion"; Hengel, *Crucifixion.*

111 See vol. 2 of this commentary, on 15:3-7.

112 To mark the arrival of the group at the place of the Skull, countless manuscripts prefer either ἀπῆλθον ("went away") or εἰσῆλθον ("arrived") over the simple verb ἦλθον that Nestle-Aland (27th ed.) has. Farther down, when mentioning the crucifixion, Codex Bezae (D = 05) and a Latin manuscript add an adverb ὁμοῦ ("together"). Still in v. 33 some manuscripts remind the reader that the criminals were two in number.

113 See Metzger, *Textual Commentary* (2d ed.), 154; Henry, "Forgive"; Dammers, "Studies"; Démann,

Sinaiticus (ℵ = 01) contains it, while the Bodmer Papyrus XIV–XV (p[75]) omits it. Vaticanus (B = 03) and Codex Bezae (D = 05) omit it in their original form, but it is attested by Tatian, Irenaeus, and Hegesippus around 170–180.[114] The external evidence is not enough to form an opinion; one must also make use of internal criticism. The vocabulary and style are consistent with those of Luke. The vocative πάτερ ("Father") is exactly what one finds in the prayer of Jesus in 10:21 and the way the Lukan version of the Lord's Prayer begins (11:2). The content of the prayer also obeys the requirement of the Sermon on the Plain to pray for one's enemies (6:28). That Jesus' opponents acted in ignorance corresponds to the opinion Luke attributes to Peter (Acts 3:17) and Paul (Acts 13:27) in Acts. The parallels between Jesus and Stephen also speak in favor of the primitive character of Jesus' prayer. The first martyr, whose fate Luke portrays in the image of that of his Master, prays for his executioners (Acts 7:60).[115] That the wording of Acts is different from that of the Gospel is not a counterargument; Luke avoids mechanical repetitions. Jason Whitlark and Mikael Parsons[116] have offered an ingenious explanation for what they regard as an addition: at the time when the four Gospels were canonized (in the second half of the second century), Christians wanted Christ to have spoken seven words from the cross, since seven was the sacred number representing totality. Thus, they imagined the seventh saying and inserted it at this place. I believe instead that the genuinely Lukan prayer of Jesus has been eliminated by many. Why? For reasons of logic and anti-Semitism. As we have seen, the fall of Jerusalem in 70 appeared to the Christians to be retribution for the death of Jesus. To transmit the prayer of Jesus was to admit that the Master was mistaken, since God had not forgiven. To remove this mark of charity was also to give free rein, as unfortunately many Christians in antiquity did, to hostility against the Jews. I retain, therefore, the prayer of Jesus in the text of the Gospel of Luke. The presence of this prayer confirms the saintliness that the author applies to Christ during his agony.[117]

Whether or not one accepts the prayer of Jesus at this point (v. 34a), the reference to casting lots for the garments (v. 34b) is curiously attached to what precedes it. To understand the importance of this act, found in the canonical Gospels and the *Gospel of Peter*, we must remember how important scriptural proof is in the eyes of Luke and the early Christians.[118] The evangelist, along with his co-religionists, was concerned to convince the Jews, the Greeks, and the Romans, as well as himself, that it was not abnormal to worship a crucified person as Lord. The biblical argument allowed for including the offensive, the paradoxical, and the inconceivable in God's plan. Psalm 21 (22), with its presentation of the suffering righteous, offered its services. Like the other evangelists, witnesses with him of the Christian tradition, Luke sketches Jesus' last moments using patterns taken from Scripture. That it was the custom of the executioners to divide the clothes of the condemned among themselves is not important.[119] The only thing that matters is the relationship of the passion to the Psalms and the Prophets. One also notes that Luke does not insist on saying "as it is written."[120] In his eyes, the words carry more weight if the agreement is implicit. The harmony is more convincing when it speaks for itself.[121]

"Père"; Daube, "They Know Not"; Flusser, "Sie wissen nicht"; Delobel, "Crux"; and especially Blum, *Denn sie wissen nicht*, 17–28.

114 Reading the critical apparatus is impressive; it leaves the exegete in a quandary. Even the scribes are uncertain. A first corrector of Sinaiticus (ℵ = 01), for example, eliminated the prayer, so a second one reintroduced it. The scribe of Codex Bezae (D = 05) does not know it; a corrector carefully inserts it.
115 "Lord, do not hold this sin against them" are the words placed on Stephen's lips.
116 Whitlark and Parsons, "The 'Seven' Last Words."
117 On the verb ἀφίημι and the idea of forgiveness in Luke, see vol. 1 of this commentary, 182–84, on 5:21-24 and the excursus on the forgiveness of sins, and 296–98, on 7:44-50.
118 See Feuillet, "Souffrance"; Lindars, *Apologetic*, 88–93; Scheifler, "Salmo," 22; Reumann, "Psalm 22."
119 On this question of social history, see Blinzler, *Prozess*, 271–72.
120 The evangelist John does not share Luke's discretion. He writes, "The soldiers said to one another: Let us not tear it, but draw lots to see who will get it, so that the Scripture might be fulfilled: They divided my garments, and they cast lots for my tunic" (John 19:24).
121 See the text of the LXX: διεμερίσαντο τὰ ἱμάτιά μου ἑαυτοῖς, καὶ ἐπὶ τὸν ἱματισμόν μου ἔβαλον

■ 35-37 Before listing the insults directed at Jesus, the evangelist continues his rehabilitation of the "people." While it was friendly to Jesus during his ministry in Galilee and on his trip to Jerusalem, the λαός collapsed during the appearance before Pilate (23:13, 18). After that it returned to its former behavior: As eyewitness, it followed the procession of the condemned men without any expression of hostility (v. 27), and in this moment (v. 35) it stands[122] and watches. It is my opinion that in Luke as in John ϑεωρέω defines an attitude, the attitude of people who are reflective while they are looking.[123] It is significant that the verb ϑεωρέω and the later verb ἐκμυκτηρίζω are read close to each other in Ps 21 (22):8.[124]

In the first mocking scene, 22:63-65, Jesus' opponents accused him of being a false prophet. Here, in the second, they believe they can prove that he usurps the title of messianic king. Relying on Israel's old ideology[125]—which, without making a distinction between religion and politics, conceived of its leaders, judges, or kings as liberators—first the "authorities," the ἄρχοντες, then the "soldiers," the στρατιῶται, and finally the evil robber challenge Jesus and ironically call on him to continue his work of "salvation." The readers cannot fail to

see that this is a wretched quarrel in the eyes of the evangelist, because for each category he uses a strong verb: ἐκμυκτηρίζω ("to sneer") for the leaders, ἐμπαίζω ("to mock") for the soldiers, and βλασφημέω ("to insult") for the robber.[126]

This virulent criticism reminds one on the literary level of Jesus' temptations in the desert.[127] There the devil also raised the argument three times. He also based his statement on Jesus' pretended messiahship and used the same type of hypothetical proposition (see 4:3 and 9: "If you are the Son of God"). In the temptations, the Lukan Jesus responded by making use of Scripture. Here too he accepts the challenge, but in a different way: first by remaining silent, then by promising the good thief a place with him in paradise.[128]

On the historical and doctrinal level the passage is important in the framework of the dispute between the Christians and the Jews at the end of the first century C.E. Since the text puts us on the side of the Christians, Luke initially suggests that the Jews and the Romans did not understand Jesus' true identity. They ignored it because they saw only the gap between the fate of the crucified man and his previous claims (his divine mission). The text then suggests that, in the eyes of the Christians, the

---

κλῆρον (Ps 21 [22]:19). There are some variant readings in the transmission of the Lukan text. Indeed, some scribes have tried to align the statement of the Gospel more fully with the text of the psalm. They were also concerned to reconcile the Lukan version with those of Matthew and Mark (Matt 27:35; Mark 15:24).

122 Although the form εἰστήκει is the third person singular pluperfect of the intransitive verb ἵσταμαι, it has the sense of an imperfect. Indeed, the perfect ἕστηκα has the meaning of "I stand"; see Zorell, *Lexicon*, s.v. ἵστημι, II; and BDF §341. Although Luke likes to use this verb both in the Gospel and in Acts, this is the only time he uses the pluperfect. The verb can have the nuance of "to stand there without falling," "to stand with perseverance," "not to be resigned."

123 See 10:18 and vol. 2 of this commentary, on 10:17-19. Unlike Bultmann (*John*, 69 n. 2), I do not think we should regard the verbs of seeing as synonyms. Sabourin (366) notes that the people stand here "in respectful silence." Schmithals (226) rightly thinks the people are on Jesus' side.

124 In the psalm the same people are watching and

mocking. Luke is careful to make a distinction between them.

125 See Albrecht Alt, *Essays on Old Testament History and Religion* (trans. R. A. Wilson; Oxford: Blackwell, 1966) 239–59.

126 On ἐκμυκτηρίζω, see 16:14, and vol. 2 of this commentary on 16:14-15; on ἐμπαίζω, see 22:63, and the commentary above on 22:63-65; on βλασφημέω, which can mean "to insult" and not necessarily "to blaspheme," see 12:10, and vol. 2 of this commentary on that verse. On these verbs, see Plummer, 532.

127 See Bossuyt and Radermakers, 2:499; and Tannehill, 342–43.

128 One should not push too far the parallelism between the two scenes, for the christological titles, even if close, are not identical ("Son of God" in chap. 4; "Messiah" and "King" in chap. 23). In chap. 4 Jesus enters the debate; in chap. 23 he does not directly participate. Finally, in chap. 23 the first two opponents do not speak directly to Jesus (they use the third person singular), while in chap. 4 the devil challenges Jesus three times.

death of Jesus is not an affront to his messiahship. Of course, the title Messiah[129] does deserve to be defined. Luke illustrates the definition throughout his entire two-volume work. It includes the divine election (here ὁ ἐκλεκτός, "the chosen one"),[130] qualification (the Holy Spirit and the divine voice at baptism, 3:22), the power to heal (4:39) and to forgive (5:20-26) as part of a work of salvation that does not become entangled in political power (Jesus resists the temptation of absolute power over the nations 4:5-8). Jesus' authority (4:31-32 and 20:1-8) nevertheless exists, but it is consistent with service (22:27) and transcends death. Luke 24:46 will explain that the Scriptures predict not the impossible program of the opponents but God's plan, which includes the passion and resurrection. Acts 26:23 speaks of the suffering Messiah. Verses 35-37 and in a larger sense the passion narrative have this double dimension: They express—*via negationis*—the identity the Christians attribute to Jesus and formulate the reproaches to be directed at those who have misunderstood him.

Some additional remarks:[131]

(a) The motif contained in the words "he saved others, let him save himself," also found in the Gospels of Mark and Matthew (Mark 15:31-32 par. Matt 27:42), is known in the popular literature, and one finds parallels in the sources of antiquity.[132]

(b) Luke gives no information about the identity of the soldiers. Historically they must have been Roman soldiers. Luke does not deny that, but neither does he affirm it.[133]

(c) These men offer Jesus ὄξος ("vinegar"). Originally it could have been a gesture of compassion. To give the victim some relief the soldiers offer a few swallows of their drink, their *posca*, a refreshing drink that is a mixture of vinegar and water. A hymn from Qumran (1QH 4.9–11) also contains the motif: The "interpreters of lies" have taken the liquor of knowledge from the mouth of the thirsty and have "given them vinegar to drink."[134]

■ **38** According to Luke, the inscription on the cross[135] says the truth, but if it is misunderstood then it contradicts the truth.[136] The evangelist believes that Jesus is indeed the Messiah of Israel and that he deserves the title King (see 19:38). But as was the case with the term Messiah, the title must be defined. As the reign of God is different from the kingdoms of this world, Christ is a king whose nature differs from that of earthly monarchs. Luke would agree with the distinction the evangelist John makes on this subject (John 18:33-38). Historically, the inscription on the cross is one of the most solid data for the passion of Jesus: Its content is almost identical in the four Gospels, and the custom of giving a sum-

129 The title "Messiah (or Anointed) of God" appears only here in the New Testament. It is rare in the Old Testament (in the LXX Lev 21:12 and 2 Sam [2 Kgdms] 23:1; more common is the title "Messiah [or Anointed] of the Lord").
130 See BAGD, s.v. This entry refers to parallel texts, in particular in *Ethiopic Enoch* (*1 Enoch* 39:6-7; 40:5; 45:3-5; 49:2-4) and to various modern studies. See also 9:35, where Jesus is called the ἐκλελεγμένος ("the chosen"); see vol. 1 of this commentary, 379–80, on 9:34-35. According to Lagrange (589), the adjective "chosen" explains the title "Messiah."
131 I add a textual note: the text of vv. 35-37 is unstable, although that does not substantially change the meaning; see the apparatus of Nestle-Aland (27th ed.) on this verse.
132 It is enough to think of Ps 21 (22):7-9 or Wis 2:12-24.
133 By following his own source, Luke has neglected the episode reported by Mark according to which the soldiers draped Jesus in purple and placed a crown

of thorns on his head (Mark 15:16-20). Common to both accounts is the title "King of the Jews" in the mouth of the soldiers (Mark 15:18; Luke 23:37).
134 See André Dupont-Sommer and Marc Philonenko, eds., with the collaboration of Daniel A. Bertrand, *La Bible: Écrits intertestamentaires* (Paris: Gallimard, 1987) 246; see also Sabourin, 367.
135 Numerous manuscripts are influenced by the Gospel parallels and report, as does John 19:20, that the sign was written in Greek, Latin, and Hebrew. There are also minor variants in the content of the inscription. The title "King of the Jews," however, is amazingly constant. See Nestle-Aland (27th ed.) on this verse.
136 Several interpreters, including Schneider (2:484), are of the opinion that, because of the literary context in which it stands, the inscription is part of the mocking. I think instead that Luke does not deprive the sign of its seriousness.

mary of the charge, the *causa poenae*, is attested in Latin sources.[137]

■ **39-41** If, moreover, the episodes of the passion focus on Jesus, who reflects the attention onto other people, the opposite is happening here. We are witnessing a scene that is unique in the Gospels.[138] Jesus is present, but he is silent and inactive. It is the others who compare their opinions about him.[139]

That one or both malefactors turn to Jesus is a traditional fact found in the Synoptic Gospels and the *Gospel of Peter*. The content of the insults, however, is unique to Luke and owes its wording to the context in which the episode is placed. The bad thief[140] takes over the christological affirmation[141] and the "save yourself" from the previous scene (v. 37; see also v. 35). Wisely, the author adapts the sentence and adds "and us with you" (v. 39).[142]

The good thief[143] rebukes[144] his companion. His reply contains three elements: an appeal to the fear of God in the biblical tradition (see Prov 1:7),[145] an affirmation of their common[146] guilt, and an exception for Jesus, who has been unjustly treated. In the good thief's opinion, by submitting to their "condemnation" ($\kappa\rho\acute{\iota}\mu\alpha$) the robbers should accept that they have done wrong[147] and suffer a just condemnation ($\delta\iota\kappa\alpha\acute{\iota}\omega\varsigma$, "rightly," and $\check{\alpha}\xi\iota\alpha$, "worthy," that is to say, a punishment that corresponds to what they have done). To acknowledge one's guilt and to fear God are, in the eyes of the writer of this episode, an act of repentance and the beginning of conversion. Such a move, such action, is possible—this is the implicit message—until the last hour of one's life. The rich people in the parables of Luke 12:16-21 and 16:19-31 were not able to decide in time.

Jesus has done nothing $\check{\alpha}\tau\sigma\pi\sigma\nu$, literally, "out of place."[148] The adjective is usually understood in a negative sense: "incoherent," "absurd," "evil," "bad." It emphasizes both the strange and the reprehensible aspects of the implied actions. Luke uses $\check{\alpha}\tau\sigma\pi\sigma\varsigma$ twice

---

137 See Bovon, *Last Days*, 26–27. In fact, the sign was usually hung around the neck of the condemned person or carried by a servant who walked ahead of him on the way to the execution. In Jesus' case the *titulus* shows that Jesus was condemned by Pilate, no doubt because Pilate thought he had laid claim to kingship in Israel. Rigato (*Titolo*) has devoted an entire monograph to this sign.

138 Strobel ("Tod," 88–92) rightly contrasts the attitude of the two robbers. The first follows a natural inclination. He knows that death awaits everyone. He can only put his hope in a *deus ex machina*. He will miss his death as he has missed his life. The second also accepts death, but he faces God. On the scene of the two criminals, see Derrett ("Malefactors"), who evokes Gen 40:14 ("But remember me when it is well with you; please do me the kindness to make mention of me to Pharaoh, and so get me out of this place" [*NRSV*]) and the haggadah of Joseph, the son of Jacob.

139 As a related text one can think of no better than 9:18-22, where Jesus asks the disciples about himself. Like the good thief, Peter confesses Jesus as the Messiah. In this earlier passage it is Jesus himself who announces the connection that must be established between messiahship and passion.

140 The precise term $\kappa\rho\epsilon\mu\alpha\sigma\vartheta\acute{\epsilon}\nu\tau\omega\nu$ ("hanged") that is to say, "crucified," is omitted by Codez Bezae (D = 05) and various Bohairic manuscripts; see the apparatus of Nestle-Aland (27th ed.) on this verse.

141 The wording of this beginning is somewhat different from that of v. 37. Instead of a hypothetical proposition, the text presents an interrogative clause, the rhetorical question: "And you, are you not the Messiah?" A number of manuscripts, however, have $\epsilon\grave{\iota}$ ("if") instead of $\sigma\grave{\upsilon}\chi\acute{\iota}$ ("not?").

142 Codex Bezae (D = 05) and an ancient Latin manuscript (e, from the fifth century) omit the words of the wicked thief. They are content to say that this man insulted Jesus.

143 The term $\acute{o}$ $\check{\epsilon}\tau\epsilon\rho\sigma\varsigma$ is correct, since the meaning of this word is "the other one of the two."

144 The verb $\grave{\epsilon}\pi\iota\tau\iota\mu\acute{\alpha}\omega$ in the sense of "to blame," "to reprimand," "to reproach," is well established in the Synoptic tradition, in the Third Gospel in particular. Usually, of course, it is Jesus who is the subject (see, e.g., 4:39, 41).

145 Plummer (534) correctly notes that the negation $\sigma\grave{\upsilon}\delta\acute{\epsilon}$ can go neither with $\sigma\acute{\upsilon}$ ("you") nor with $\tau\grave{\sigma}\nu$ $\vartheta\epsilon\acute{\sigma}\nu$ ("God") but only with the verb $\varphi\sigma\beta\hat{\eta}$ ("you fear"): "Do you not even fear?"

146 At the end of v. 40 many manuscripts prefer "we are" to "you are"; see the apparatus in Nestle-Aland (27th ed.) on this verse.

147 It is the actions that count, not the intentions. Note the use of the verb $\pi\rho\acute{\alpha}\sigma\sigma\omega$ ("do") twice in v. 41.

148 Codex Bezae (D = 05) prefers the reading $\pi\sigma\nu\eta\rho\acute{\sigma}\nu$ ("evil," "bad").

in Acts.[149] In Acts 25:5, on the lips of Festus, the adjective designates something "irregular." In 28:6, in spite of the expectations of the people, nothing "unusual," "amiss" happens to Paul, who is bitten by a snake when gathering firewood.[150]

■ **42-43** What began surprisingly as a conversation about Jesus ends as a well-structured apophthegm. To a request inspired by the setting of death (v. 42), Jesus responds with a sure and victorious promise (v. 43).[151] What I said in the introduction to explain the many textual variants is confirmed here. While saying essentially the same thing, the text varies from one manuscript to another. These fluctuations reflect differences in a number of tellings. Although they appear to be insignificant, the link is important. Is the reading εἰς τὴν βασιλείαν σου or ἐν τῇ βασιλείᾳ σου? In the first instance the good thief, as a good believer, awaits the apocalyptic enthronement of the Messiah. In the second he expects Jesus to come with royal power. Simply put, here it is a matter of the kingdom, there of the reign; here of a future that can last, there of an immediate future. I propose to keep the first reading retained in the Nestle-Aland text (27th ed.), because following the second, admittedly more difficult, text would mean keeping the entire sentence as the *textus receptus* has it, especially the "And he said to Jesus, remember me, Lord . . . ," which is clearly secondary to "And he said, Jesus, remember me . . . ." To be precise, I must say that the difference in meaning as I have presented it is not certain, because in that day the preposition ἐν ("in") in contrast to classical usage, can accompany the verbs of movement,[152] while εἰς ("in"), followed by the accusative (with the gradual loss of affection for the dative) will eventually express standing. Thus, ὅταν

ἔλθῃς ἐν τῇ βασιλείᾳ σου does not necessarily mean, "When you come arrayed in royal power." It can also have the same meaning as the variant ὅταν ἔλθῃς εἰς τὴν βασιλείαν σου, "when you come into your kingdom." Similarly, ἔρχομαι means not only "to come"; it can also mean "to go."[153]

But back to the beginning! The good thief "was saying." In Greek the imperfect may be endowed with several nuances.[154] I retain here the duration or the repetition, in a word the persistence of the good thief. He is not lacking in impudence. In all of the Gospels he is one of the few who dare to speak to Christ, calling him by his name, "Jesus" (see 4:34; 8:28; 17:13; 18:38; Mark 1:24; 5:7; 10:47). The "remember" he demands is obviously not passive. It signifies a privileged intervention. We remember that disasters befell Israel when the new pharaoh did not know Joseph and did not remember him (Exod 1:8). We also recall that God's memory is the best guarantee of protection and salvation.[155] The theme of kingship is omnipresent in the entire crucifixion scene, but it is less a question of the kingdom of God than of Jesus' kingly power, his right, legitimate or usurped, to be called "Messiah" and "king" (vv. 35, 37, 38, 39). According to Luke, the good thief acknowledges Jesus' royal messiahship but realizes that it is not for today and that it is not separate from death. He will be only too happy if on the other side of his suffering Jesus does not forget him.

The response of the Lukan Jesus is solemn: Ἀμήν σοι λέγω, "In truth, I say to you." It is also charged with authority: Jesus believes that he is entitled to speak and to promise. The answer also highlights the adverb σήμερον, "today." While Jesus refused to respond to the scoffers who put themselves on the material level

149 See also 2 Thess 3:2, the only other appearance in the New Testament.
150 As we have seen in n. 32 above, the statement of the good thief (vv. 40-41) has an equivalent in *Gos. Pet.* 13.
151 On the promise made to the good thief, see MacRae, "Paradise"; Grelot, "Aujourd'hui"; Strobel, "Tod", 88–99; Garciá Pérez, "Buen Ladrón"; Kellermann, "Elia."
152 Garciá Pérez ("Buen Ladrón," 276–80) makes this point clearly. He is of the opinion that the Greek wording of the episode of the good thief reveals an Aramaic influence, that the conversation in it is

not a haggadic development of Mark 15:32b but the fruit of an ancient tradition.
153 Garciá Pérez ("Buen Ladrón," 272–76) gives good examples here.
154 See BDF §§ 325–34.
155 See Robert Martin-Achard (*La mort en face selon la Bible hébraïque* [Essais bibliques 15; Geneva: Labor et Fides, 1988] 31–36, 83–84), who says more, however, about God's power over death than about the memory in which God preserves his people.

of human temporality (vv. 35-38), he does agree to speak on the level of his transcendent messianic lordship. He does not wait for an indefinitely postponed enthronement, because the radius of his power is already extended.[156] Had the "today" of the messianic enthronement (Ps 2:7, quoted by Luke in Acts 13:33)[157] not already taken place at the beginning of Jesus' ministry in the synagogue of Nazareth (4:21)? Does not the "today" of God's Word (Ps 94 [95]:7), which Hebrews will make its own (Heb 3:7—4:13), reach the dying good thief not only *in extremis* but also *in primis*?[158]

There is no more reassuring divine promise than "you will be with me." "Being with" is a constant of biblical fidelity, whether it is God's presence with his own or the people in the company of their Lord.[159] Immanuel, "God with us"! Luke treasures such expressions and makes use of them.[160] He may be so subtle that he promises the dying person who is anxious about the beyond that he will be "with him," while to those who are struggling on earth, he will be "with them" (see Christ's appearance to Paul by night in Acts 18:10). In any case, in this text, which is so close to the resurrection of Jesus, the text of the Gospel confers on the Messiah the gifts and the powers reserved to God. In v. 42 the βασιλεία had been given to Christ, and the one who says he "will be with me" is the second κύριος, the Son and not the Father.

There remains the question of "paradise."[161] The term,[162] from Persia, designates first of all a part of domesticated nature, a garden or a park where the king or another lord can rest or go hunting. The term and the reality it covers were taken over by the Jewish representatives of apocalyptic (see *1 Enoch* 60:8). There it may be the semantic equivalent of the kingdom of God or the eschatological feast, but it may also designate the happy abode of the righteous dead, who are awaiting the final resurrection.[163] Ancient Judaism, whether apocalyptic or Pharisaic, was not able to harmonize the views about the afterlife and the end of time.[164] Luke's two-volume work shares this uncertainty. Luke speaks both about the resurrection of the dead, innocent and guilty, preceding the last judgment (Acts 4:2; 17:32) and about the resurrection only of the righteous, which seems to be a final, happy condition (Luke 14:14). It also takes up the hope of the early Christians in the cosmic coming of God's kingdom, and it also knows how to portray the future so that it is personally imminent for each person. It is

---

156 Dupont (*Béatitudes*, 3:133–35) thinks that the mocking of Jesus represents a threefold challenge to which his action in favor of the good thief is a response.

157 See the "Western" variant of 3:22: The divine voice at baptism speaks nothing other than the quotation from Ps 2:7.

158 Altheim and Stiel ("Herrenworte," 361–63) sense that there is tension between "today" and the time of "paradise." They think they can solve it by using an Aramaic substrate. The equivalent of "today," *yaumānā*, can also mean "on this day." This expression was mistranslated.

159 See Dieter Vetter, *Jahwes Mit-Sein: Ein Ausdruck des Segens* (AzTh 1.45; Stuttgart: Calwer, 1971).

160 Aus (*Samuel*, 158–73) believes that he can detect here the influence of 1 Samuel 28–31, esp. 28:19, on the death of Saul and his sons. The dead Samuel, when invoked by Saul, announces to the king his imminent death along with that of his sons. Then he and his sons will be "with" the prophet in the abode of the dead. A Jewish tradition located this place under God's throne. Like the good thief, Saul acknowledges his fault, as he shares with him the status of murderer.

161 In vv. 42-43, Codex Bezae (D = 05) has a very different text from the other manuscripts: "After he turned to the Lord, he said: Remember me on the day of your arrival. In response, Jesus said to the one who had scolded him: Take courage. Today you will be with me in paradise." See Hans-Werner Bartsch, *Codex Bezae versus Codex Sinaiticus im Lukasevangelium* (Hildesheim: George Olms, 1984) 200. Why does this manuscript, slightly corrected at this place, believe that the good thief rebuked Jesus?

162 On the word "paradise," see esp. Jeremias, "παράδεισος"; MacRae, "Paradise"; Grelot, "Aujourd'hui"; García Pérez, "Buen Ladrón."

163 See *1 Enoch* 25:4-5; *4 Esdras* 7:36; 8:52; *Apoc. Abr.* 21:6-7; see also Horst Balz, "παράδεισος," etc. *EDNT* 3 (1993) 17–18; Dupont-Sommer and Philonenko, *Écrits intertestamentaires*, 1879 (the thematic index refers to many texts; see n. 134 above).

164 See Grelot, "Aujourd'hui," 195–96; George W. E. Nickelsburg, *Resurrection, Immortality, and Eternal Life in Intertestamental Judaism and Early Christianity* (Expanded ed.; HTS 56; Cambridge, Mass.: Harvard University Press, 2006).

sensitive to the fate of everybody, not only in the framework of the eschatological kingdom but also in that of personal death. It does not appear to be bothered by putting Jesus and the thief in paradise "today," even though God will not raise him, Jesus, until the "third day."[165] If we want to be consistent with Luke, which I think I can and should do, I think that Luke, as he had done with Lazarus (16:22), locates the righteous in a place of happiness between their death and the final resurrection. The "bosom of Abraham" is one way of speaking about it; "paradise" is another. There are great scholars, such as Jacques Dupont and Gerhard Schneider, who disapprove of explaining Luke this way,[166] but they are attacking a construction that resembles medieval elaborations.[167] In my opinion, while Luke does use images such as that of paradise, he gives them not a topographical or chronological objectivity but evocative and kerygmatic power. The verbal figures are less representative and more promise and commitment. They assure the believers that they will be with God beyond death.

History of Interpretation

Christian antiquity gave great importance to the Lukan passage examined here, so much so that many of the witnesses have survived. A number of them manifest a chris-tological density; unfortunately, they have an equally passionate polemic against the Jews. The hermeneutical effort I propose is that I will not silence the theological depth of these texts, nor will I pursue the anti-Semitic hostility.

Around 150 C.E., Justin Martyr is one of the oldest witnesses to the passion of Jesus. In his *Dialogue with Trypho* (101.5) he mentions the memoirs of the apostles, that is, the Gospels, and he refers to the mocking by using an expression inspired by the Lukan verb ἐκμυκτηρίζω ("to scoff," 23:35).[168] A little later he cites Jesus' last prayer ("Father, into your hands I commit my spirit") that Luke is the only one to transmit (*Dial.* 105.5). In emphasizing the fate of Christ, however, the apologist quotes his sources freely—sources that may include extra-canonical data—rather than defending the intangible character of the Gospels.[169]

Conflicting data keep us from determining whether Marcion had eliminated from his Gospel the casting of lots for Jesus' garments (v. 34b).[170] Tertullian, who says it was omitted, emphasizes the correlation between the prophecy (Ps 21 [22]:19) and its fulfillment at the foot of the cross. In his rhetorical way of arguing, he exclaims: "The garments of Christ, that is the entire psalm!" (*Adv. Marc.* 4.42.4). In addition, the African underscores the companionship of the criminals. In his opinion, their

---

165 Kellermann ("Elia") believes that the parallels to v. 43 thus far advanced by scholars are unconvincing. In his opinion, Luke establishes a typological relationship between Jesus and Elijah. Indeed, in Israel Elijah represents the comforter in all circumstances and the guide of the souls of the dead.

166 Dupont, *Évangiles synoptiques,* 2:1066–75; Schneider, *Parusiegleichnisse,* 81–82.

167 See Jacques Le Goff, *The Birth of Purgatory* (trans. Arthur Goldhammer; Chicago: University of Chicago Press, 1984).

168 It is the formula τοῖς μυξωτῆρσιν . . . διαρρι-νοῦντες ("to move the nostrils . . . to snivel"). The passage also draws on Matt 27:39, referring to the head wagging of the spectators. See also Justin Martyr *1 Apol.* 38.6–8.

169 At the same time, the disciples of Basilides were teaching that Simon of Cyrene not only carried the cross but was crucified in place of Jesus. He took on the features of Jesus, and Jesus took his. In spite of Irenaeus (*Adv. haer.* 1.24.4), this appears not to have been the doctrine of Basilides himself.

Photius (*Bibl.* 114) attributes to Leucius Charinus (who he thinks is the author of the *Peregrinationes Apostolorum,* thus the apocryphal *Acts of the Apostles*) the following doctrine: "It was not Christ who was crucified but another in his place, and that is why he mocks those who thought they had crucified him." See Plummer, 528; Ekkehard Mühlenberg, "Basilides," *TRE* 5 (1980) 296–301, esp. 299.

170 Tertullian (*Adv. Marc.* 4.42.4) says yes; Epiphanius (*Schol.* 71) says no. See Harnack (*Marcion,* 236*), who thinks that Marcion had removed all of vv. 35–43 (except for an allusion to v. 35); and Tsutsui, "Evangelium Marcions," 125–26. In addition, Epiphanius (*Schol.* 72) says that Marcion had removed the promise made to the good thief; cf. Plummer, 536; Harnack, *Marcion,* 236*, and Tsutsui, "Evangelium Marcions," 126. See the next section, p. 335 n. 116.

presence justifies Jesus' prediction taken from Scripture (Isa 53:12): "And he was reckoned with the lawless men" (Luke 22:37).[171]

A *catena* fragment attributed to Apollinaris of Laodicea,[172] a fourth-century author, speaks of a contradiction between Matthew and Luke. It harmonizes the data by saying that Matthew has simplified while Luke was more precise: By accepting his punishment, Luke's good thief has learned not to blaspheme anymore, while in Apollinaris's day there are people who deny the faith after having confessed. Previously, Origen had extended to all believers the promise made to the good thief (*Hom. Lev.* 9.5).[173] He wisely notes—many will follow him on this point—that the promise is all the stronger, since the gates of paradise had been locked behind Adam. Only Christ was able to set aside the vigilant sentinel who, armed with his flaming sword, was guarding the access to paradise.

Two fourth-century poets speak about the crucifixion. In his *Hymn on Paradise* (8.1), Ephraem the Syrian rejoices over Jesus' response to the good thief and wishes ardently that he too could be received into the divine garden.[174] Later he follows the fate of Adam (I assume he is thinking of the entire human race), who once in contact with the cross may return to Eden (12.10).[175] As for Prudentius, he derived a similar message from the water flowing from the wounds of Jesus and from the words spoken to the good thief: "Both sides of Christ are pierced; water and blood flow from them. The blood is the victory, the water is baptism. On the two crosses close at hand, on either side of Jesus, are two very different bandits. The one denies the divinity of Christ, the other wins the crown" (*Dittochaeon* 42). As one sees, the analogy applies to the good thief but not to the bad.[176] We may mention here that early Christian iconography liked to contrast the two trees, the tree of death and the tree of life. One serves as a gallows for Judas or Adam; the other bears the Christ, who blesses.[177]

Cyril of Jerusalem (*Hom. cat.* 13.31) establishes a contrast between the two powers of the tree: one destroys Adam and the other permits the return to paradise. As for the future promised the good thief, it is expressed in terms not of departure but of arrival: "Today you will be with me in paradise." For his part, Jerome believes that the good thief was the first to regain paradise, because he believed without seeing. In his view, the cross is the key to paradise.[178] Maximus of Turin (*Sermo* 74), referring to 1 Cor 1:23-24, believes that the cross was not a scandal for the good thief as it was for many people. In spite of the condemnation weighing on Jesus, the criminal does not believe that Jesus is guilty, and he realizes that the beatings were on behalf of guilty humanity. Thus, the

---

171 The *Second Treatise of the Great Seth* (NHC VII, 2; 56.3–19) is familiar with the passion narrative of the Gospels but interprets it in the manner of the disciples of Basilides: it is Simon of Cyrene (Matt 27:32 par. Mark 15:21 par. Luke 23:26) who carries the cross on his shoulders and doubtless dies in Jesus' place. For his part, Christ is on high rejoicing and laughing at the ignorance of those who deceived themselves about him.

172 Fragment 17 in Reuss, *Lukas-Kommentare*, 9.

173 It is Just (*Luke*, 357–67) who has drawn my attention to this text as well as to the following texts of Ephraem, Athanasius, Prudentius, Jerome, Maximus of Turin, Cyril of Jerusalem, Chrysostom, Augustine, and Leo the Great.

174 Ephraem the Syrian *Hymn on Paradise* 8.1 (Brock, 131).

175 Brock, 164. Amazingly, Ephraem seems to say that Adam the sinner became like the fig tree, which bore only leaves and in contact with the cross was covered with glory. In his *Commentary on the Diatessaron* (20.26) Ephraem connects the water that flowed

together with the blood from the wounds of the crucified Jesus (John 19:34) with the forgiveness granted to the good thief. Prudentius has the same comparison (*Dittochaeon* 42).

176 In his hymn *The Cathemerinon* (10.157–60) Prudentius writes:
We follow, Redeemer, your orders,
When you triumph over the somber death,
To the thief and friend of the cross
You say he is to walk in your footsteps.

177 See Réau, *Iconographie* 2.1:85. On the fifth-century plaque of the ivory casket in the British Museum, the tree of death stands to the left of the cross, the symbol of life. Judas hanged himself on the one, while Christ is triumphant on the other. Luz (*Matthew 21–28*, 323) contains a reproduction of this plaque.

178 Jerome *Homilia in Lucam, de Lazaro et divite* (PLS 2:181–82).

bishop of Turin contrasted the robber with Judas in an original way. In several of his festal letters Athanasius of Alexandria finds that in Christ death has died and life has been offered to mortals.[179] John Chrysostom is struck by the suddenness. As at Adam's creation, what God says happens immediately, so the words of Christ addressed to the good thief are also realized immediately.[180] This finding allows the Golden Mouth to approach the Son of the Father in their divine fellowship. In several sermons Augustine reflects on the cross. In *Sermo* 382.2, he meditates on Christ's prayer for his enemies that they can become his friends. This prayer is "for us," "in us," and "through us." This provocative affirmation remains enigmatic when he comments on it, saying "for us" means that Christ is the "Chief Priest," "in us" that he is our "head," and "through us" that he is our "God." In *Sermo* 317.1–5, he describes Stephen as the one who truly imitates Christ in agony, because the first martyr also forgives his enemies.

In his *Explanation of the Gospel according to Saint Luke*, Ambrose of Milan has left us a commentary on the Third Gospel in homiletic form. On 23:26-43 he lays emphasis on the cross as a trophy and speaks of a triumphant gallows (*Exp. Luc.* 10.107–24). In doing so he proclaims the soteriological value of the death of Christ, the second Adam (10.110).[181] If I understand correctly, he takes risks by allegorically bringing Simon together with the human nature of Christ and Jesus with his divine nature. In so doing, he tries to reconcile the Gospels of Luke and John (10.107).[182] Doctrinally speaking, he walks on dangerous ground when he limits the death of Christ to his humanity and later on says that the divinity of the Son left him at the moment of his death, which in his opinion could only have been the death of a human being.[183] He

is also somewhat confused when he attributes a universal scope ("Here flourishes the beauty of the redeemed peoples" [10.111]) to the inscription on the cross that is centered on Israel. Finally, he impresses me with his piety when he exclaims: "Yes, that Christ would die for me in his passion so that after his passion he can be raised" (10.116), and notes that the good thief asks for less than he receives: "The Lord always gives more than we ask for" (10.121).

The collection of sermons dedicated to the Gospel of Luke from Cyril of Alexandria (first half of the fifth century) today includes three sermons on our passage. *Sermo* 152[184] does not surprise the reader: it insists that the Jews are guilty and regards their misfortunes as the result of their opposition to Jesus. He ponders the paradox of the cross, where death itself has been defeated by death. He relates the lifting up on the cross to the words of Jesus preserved in the Gospel of John: "And I, when I am lifted up from the earth will draw all people to myself" (John 12:32). He harmonizes Luke and John on the role of Simon of Cyrene (by saying that his services had to be used only halfway). In Isaac, who carries the wood for his imminent sacrifice, he sees a type of Christ. He ignores neither the tears of the women nor Jesus' observations about them (vv. 28-29). He understands the green wood as Christ himself, who bears leaves and fruit, and the dry wood as sterile Israel. In *Sermo* 153[185] Cyril emphasizes the profound mystery of the cross by citing Rom 11:33. He contrasts Adam and Christ, then analyzes the mocking, wondering why the Jews killed him if they did not regard him as the heir (an allusion to the parable of the murderous winegrowers, 20:9-19). Finally, he emphasizes the scriptural proofs and the allegorical identity of the two thieves, the Jews and the Christians.[186] *Sermo* 154,

---

179 Athanasius of Alexandria, Fourth Festal Letter 3 (3); Sixth Festal Letter 4 (10); 9 (21); Thirteenth Festal Letter 6 (23)–7 (27); Second Festal Letter 7 (15); Atanasio di Alessandria, *Lettere festali, Anonimo, Indice delle Lettere festali* (ed. and trans. Alberto Camplani; Letture cristiane del primo millenio 34; Milan: Paoline, 2003) 246, 288, 292, 398, 390, 449.
180 John Chrysostom *De Christo precibus contra Anomeos IX, In quatriduanum Lazarum* 2.9.2 (*PG* 48.782–83).
181 In §114 he says that he learned from the Hebrews that the place of the Skull also contained Adam's tomb. See the comment from Gabriel Tissot in SC 52bis, 194 n. 2.
182 Ambrose thinks that Simon of Cyrene was not a Jew but a foreigner (*alienigena atque peregrinus*). Ingeniously, he relates Simon's behavior to Jesus' statement about bearing the cross (Luke 9:23).
183 See Tissot's anxious comment in SC 52bis, 198 n. 1.
184 Payne Smith, *Cyril*, 2:713–17; see the Greek frgs. 358–60 edited by Reuss, *Lukas-Kommentare*, 222–23.
185 Payne Smith, *Cyril*, 2:718–21; see the Greek frgs. 361–63 edited by Reuss, *Lukas-Kommentare*, 223–24.
186 On the end of *Sermo* 153, see Payne Smith, *Cyril*, 2:721 n. g.

in Syriac, was recently discovered by Joseph Sauget, and various Greek fragments have been restored by Michel Aubineau,[187] but to my knowledge they have not yet been published.

In the middle of the fifth century, Leo the Great classically contrasted the criminals, one of whom represents the believers and the other the reprobates. The cross serves as the criterion for distinguishing between them, and the passion contains the mystery of salvation (*Sermo* 55 [42].1). In another sermon (53 [40].1) he underscores the authority and the power of the one who has lost everything. The promise Jesus gives the good thief, he says,[188] comes less from the wood of the cross than from the throne of power.[189]

In reading some of the medieval exegetes, including the Venerable Bede in the eighth-century and the *Glossa ordinaria*,[190] three concerns strike the reader: (a) The desire to collect and transmit the best of the patristic, especially Latin, interpretations, thus the quotations primarily from Ambrose, Jerome, and Augustine. This effort is especially evident in the writings of the Venerable Bede (*In Luc.* 6.1434–1715).[191] (b) The concern of these authors to harmonize what appears to them to be the contradictions among the Gospels. How are we to reconcile the Synoptics, who include Simon of Cyrene, with John, who ignores him? How can we harmonize Luke, who distinguishes between the attitudes of the two criminals, with Matthew and Mark, who mix them? Bonaventure is particularly concerned about this issue

(*Comm. Luc.* 23.30–52).[192] (c) The concern to establish the unanimity of the two Testaments by citing the Old Testament extensively to confirm the truth of the New. Here again it is Bonaventure who is a master in this latter exercise (ibid.).

The *Paraphrasis* of Erasmus (see 461–63) is now available in English translation accompanied by valuable annotations.[193] Readers will see the humanist follow the thread of the story, avoiding the allegory but not the devotion. They will come across some curious opinions there, such as this twofold view attributed to Erasmus in connection with v. 28: Jesus wanted to have a glorious death, and the death of an innocent person need not be lamented. Finally, they will notice that Erasmus meditates long on v. 34a, Jesus' intercession for his enemies.[194]

The cross plays such a prominent role in the theology of Luther that it is not surprising that the reformer often spoke about the passion narratives.[195] Concerning Simon (v. 26), "an image of all Christians," Luther underscores first of all that he carried the cross of Christ and not the punishment all sinners deserve. Second, the cross was imposed on him, and it does not correspond to those burdens that monks and nuns freely accept in an unnecessary concern about asceticism. In the third place, we must not confuse Simon with Jesus. Jesus alone is the true victim who atones for the sins of the world.[196] Concerning the tears of the daughters of Jerusalem (vv. 27-31), Luther explains that, far from crying about Jesus, we must instead rejoice over an agony that rec-

---

187 See Sauget, "Nouvelles homélies"; Michel Aubineau, "Les 'catenae in Lucam' de J. Reuss et Cyrille d'Alexandrie," *ByZ* 80 (1987) 29–47, esp. 41.

188 Later (*Sermo* 53 [40].3) Leo describes the death of Christ as the sacrifice of the true paschal lamb.

189 The exchange of words between the good thief and Jesus (vv. 42-43) inspired numerous preachers of antiquity; see Hermann Josef Sieben, *Kirchenväterhomilien zum Neuen Testament: Ein Repertorium der Textausgaben und Übersetzungen, mit einem Anhang der Kirchenväterkommentare* (IP 22; Steenbrugis: In Abbatia S. Petri; The Hague: Nijhoff, 1991) 84–85.

190 See *Glossa ordinaria* Luke 23:26-43 (*PL* 114:346–48).

191 Usually Bede does not mark his quotations as such.

192 Bernardini, 572–81.

193 Phillips, *Paraphrase*, 214–21.

194 In the *Annotationes* (215–16) Erasmus pays special attention to the inscription on the cross in three languages and to the promise made to the good

thief. Then, as some do, he refuses to connect the adverb "today" with the previous words, "Truly, I say to you." He says that this interpretation tries to evade the question and to avoid a contradiction between the immediate presence of the good thief in paradise and the descent of his body into the tomb and his soul into the realm of death. In addition, Erasmus claims that the word "paradise" designates simply a state of repose and of delight.

195 Concerning the crucifixion, see Luther, *Evangelien-Auslegung*, 1201–33; Mülhaupt, 5:7–167.

196 Luther, *Evangelien-Auslegung*, 1202–5 (the short quotation comes from 1202). Later (ibid., 1208) Luther develops the thesis according to which the Christ on the cross represents not only the victim but also the chief priest; the cross serves as the altar for this sacrifice.

onciles human beings with God and weep for our sins, asking for forgiveness.[197] If Jesus prays for his enemies (v. 34), it is because in so doing he fulfills his priestly function. It is legitimate only if the priest is ordained by God, and it is fulfilled only if he accompanies his sacrifice with prayer. Following the Scripture, Luther makes a distinction between voluntary sins and sins committed in ignorance, and he thinks that Jesus prayed for forgiveness only for the first category.[198] After reflecting on the inscription on the cross, casting lots for the garments, and the mocking to which Jesus submitted,[199] he speaks of the criminals crucified beside Jesus. He believes that the good thief was able to come to a clear faith, a faith he confessed after he heard Jesus' prayer. If he came to believe, it was not without the help of the Holy Spirit or the influence of the biblical readings of the prophets, which he must have heard sometime in the temple (of course, without understanding them!). Luther believes—an original thesis—that what the good thief said must have comforted Jesus just as the angel in the garden on the Mount of Olives must have encouraged him. As for the good thief himself, he is the first to reap the fruit of Jesus' answered prayer: the Father has forgiven. The thief has become a different person. From being a sinner he has become pious and holy, thanks to the atonement of Christ.[200]

The Christians of all centuries and all nations have meditated on Christ's death, his last words, his last encounters. I have quoted Luther, as I have before me Calvin[201] because of my denominational affiliation. It would be fitting—and I would like to have the time to do it—to complete the tableau with interpretations from the Russian Orthodox, the Catholics of Latin America, the Christians of Asia.

Conclusion

To tell about Jesus' way to the cross and his last moments, Luke trusts his special material. He relates how Simon of Cyrene was commandeered and became a model of the disciple who follows in the footsteps of his master. He alludes to the sadness of the Jewish people of Jerusalem and especially to that of the women who wept for Jesus, but he nevertheless transmits a threatening apophthegm with an apocalyptic character: Worse than the death of Jesus is the divine punishment that will strike those who are responsible for this conviction. Crucified between two thieves, Jesus still intercedes with his Father, asking that these guilty people be acquitted. In tension with each other, both perspectives, sadness and guilt, open the door for the apostolic preaching that, along with the good news of the resurrection, will proclaim a final opportunity for repentance. Aware of the messianic title that is applied to the condemned man, the actors and the spectators of the drama ironically encourage Jesus to use the power associated with the title to escape from the cross. Christ shows that his power exists, but that he uses it differently. It includes suffering and death and offers the promise of a happy future to those who turn to him and trust him. In this moment Jesus is less alone and finds a certain consolation in this criminal.

---

197 Ibid., 1205–6. These pages also contain a strong criticism of the Jews.
198 Ibid., 1209–11.
199 Ibid., 1211–14, 1217–18.
200 Ibid., 1218–20.
201 Calvin, *Harmony*, 3:186–205. I also have in my hands the learned comments of Grotius (*Annotationes*, 916–23) and Bengel (*Gnomon*, 1:522–26).

Death and Burial (23:44-56a)

Bibliography

Aletti, *Art de raconter*, 155–76.

Bahat, Dan, "Does the Holy Sepulchre Church Mark the Burial of Jesus?" *BARev* 12, no. 3 (1986) 26–45.

Barkay, Gabriel, "The Garden Tomb: Was Jesus Buried Here?" *BARev* 12, no. 2 (1986) 40–57.

Benoit, *Passion and Resurrection*, 181–230.

Bligh, John, "Christ's Death Cry," *HeyJ* 1 (1960) 142–46.

Blinzler, Josef, "Die Grablegung Christi in historischer Sicht," in Édouard Dhanis, ed., *Resurrexit: Actes du Symposium international sur la résurrection de Jésus* (Vatican City: Libreria editrice vaticana, 1974) 56–107.

Idem, *Prozess*, 282–308.

Idem, "Zur Auslegung der Evangelienberichte über Jesu Begräbnis," *MThZ* 3 (1952) 403–14.

Boman, Thorleif, "Das letzte Wort Jesu," *StTh* 17 (1963) 103–19.

Bons, Eberhard, "Das Sterbewort Jesu nach Lk 23,46," *BZ* 38 (1994) 93–101.

Bornhäuser, Karl, "Kreuzabnahme," *NKZ* 42 (1931) 38–56.

Bovon, *Luke the Theologian*, 80–81, 187–88, 294–95, 517–18.

Brändle, Max, "Die synoptischen Grabeserzählungen," *Orientierung* 31 (1967) 179–84.

Braun, François-Marie, "La sépulture de Jésus," *RB* 45 (1936) 34–52, 184–200, 346–63.

Briend, Jacques, "La sépulture d'un crucifié," *BTS* 133 (1971) 6–10.

Broer, Ingo, *Die Urgemeinde und das Grab Jesu: Eine Analyse der Grablegungsgeschichte im Neuen Testament* (StANT 31; Munich: Kösel, 1972) 138–200.

Brown, Raymond E., "The Burial of Jesus (Mark 15:42-47)," *CBQ* 50 (1988) 233–45.

Idem, *Death of the Messiah*, 2:1201–83.

Bulst, W., "Untersuchungen zum Begräbnis Christi," *MThZ* 3 (1952) 244–55.

Burkitt, F. C., "A Note on Lk. xxiii 51 in the Dura Fragment," *JTS* 36 (1935) 258–59.

Celada, B., "El Velo del Templo," *CB* 15 (1958) 109–12.

Chafins, Timothy L., "Women and Angels . . . When They Speak, It's Time to Listen! A Study of the Structure of Luke 23:50—24:12," *AThJ* 21 (1990) 11–17.

Chenderlin, Fritz, "Distributed Observances of the Passover: A Preliminary Test of the Hypothesis," *Bib* 57 (1976) 1–24.

Clarke, W. K. Lowther, "St. Luke and the Pseudepigrapha: Two Parallels," *JTS* 15 (1913–14) 597–99.

Cousin, Hugues, "Sépulture criminelle et sépulture prophétique," *RB* 81 (1974) 375–93.

Daube, *Rabbinic Judaism*, 23–26.

Demel, Sabine, "Jesu Umgang mit Frauen nach dem Lukasevangelium," *BN* 57 (1991) 52–95, esp. 82–86.

Dhanis, Édouard, "L'ensevelissement de Jésus et la visite au tombeau dans l'évangile de saint Marc (xv,40—xvi, 8)," *Greg* 39 (1958) 367–410.

Ehman, "Luke: 23:1-49."

Evans, L. E. Cox, "The Holy Sepulchre," *PEQ* 100 (1968) 112–36.

Feldkämper, *Der betende Jesus*, 251–84.

Finegan, *Überlieferung*, 34–35.

Gaechter, Paul, "Zum Begräbnis Jesu," *ZKTh* 75 (1953) 220–25.

Goulder, M. D., "Mark xvi. 1-8 and Parallels," *NTS* 24 (1977–78) 235–40.

Grández, Rufino Maria, "Crítica textual de Luc 23:45a: καὶ ἐσκοτίσθη ὁ ἥλιος," *ScrVict* 44 (1997) 5–20.

Idem, "Las tinieblas en la muerte de Jesús: Historia de la exegesis de Lc 23, 44-45a," *EstBib* 47 (1989) 177–223.

Grass, Hans, *Ostergeschehen und Osterberichte* (4th ed.; Göttingen: Vandenhoeck & Ruprecht, 1970) 173–86.

Green, Joel B., "The Death of Jesus and the Rending of the Temple Veil (Luke 23:44-49): A Window into Luke's Understanding of Jesus and the Temple," in Eugene H. Lovering, Jr., ed., *SBLSP 1991* (Atlanta: Scholars Press, 1991) 543–57.

Idem, "Demise."

Hachlili, Rachel, and Ann E. Killebrew, "Jewish Funerary Customs during the Second Temple Period, in Light of the Excavations at the Jericho Necropolis," *PEQ* 115 (1983) 115–26.

Hanson, R. P. C., "Does δίκαιος in Luke xxiii.47 Explode the Proto-Luke Hypothesis," *Hermathena* 60 (1942) 74–78.

Harris, J. Rendel, "The Origin of a Famous Lucan Gloss," *ExpT* 35 (1923–24) 7–10.

Heeren, A. van der, "In narrationem evangelicam de sepultura Christi," *CBrug* 19 (1914) 435–39.

Holzmeister, Urban, "Die Finsternis beim Tode Jesu," *Bib* 22 (1941) 404–11.

Jackson, Clyo, "Joseph of Arimathea," *JR* 16 (1936) 332–40.

Jonge, Marinus de, "De berichten over het scheuren van het voorhangsel bij Jezus' dood in de synoptische evangeliën," *NedThT* 21 (1966–67) 90–114.

Karris, Robert J., "Luke 23:47 and the Lukan View of Jesus' Death," *JBL* 105 (1986) 65–74.

Kennard, J. Spencer, Jr., "The Burial of Jesus," *JBL* 74 (1955) 227–38.

Kenyon, Kathleen M., *Jerusalem: Excavating 3000 Years of History* (New York: McGraw-Hill, 1967) 146–54.

Kilpatrick, G. D., "A Theme of the Lucan Passion Story and Luke xxiii.47," *JTS* 43 (1942) 34–36.

Kloppenborg, "Exitus."

Klumbies, Paul-Gerhard, "Das Sterben Jesu als Schauspiel nach Lk 23:44-49," *BZ* 47 (2003) 186–205.

Lamarche, Paul, "La mort du Christ et le voile du temple selon Marc," *NRTh* 96 (1974) 583–99.

Légasse, Simon, "Les voiles du Temple de Jérusalem: Essai de parcours historique," *RB* 87 (1980) 560–89.

Léon-Dufour, Xavier, "Le dernier cri de Jésus," *Études* 348 (1978) 667–82.

Liberto, "Fear."

Liebowitz, Harold, "Jewish Burial Practices in the Roman Period," *MKQ* 22 (1981–82) 107–17.

Lindeskog, Gösta, "The Veil of the Temple," in Seminarium neotestamenticum Upsaliense, ed., *In Honorem Antonii Fridrichsen, sexagenarii* (ConNT 11; Lund: Gleerup, 1947) 132–37.

Lubich, Chiara, "Unity and Jesus Crucified and Forsaken: Foundation of a Spirituality of Communion," *ER* 55 (2003) 87–95.

MacAdam, Henry Innes, "σκότος ἐγένετο: Luke 3:1; 23:44 and Four First Century Solar Eclipses at Antioch," *IBSt* 21 (1999) 2–39.

Mailhet, J., "L'ensevelissement de Jésus," *L'Année théologique* 9 (1948) 21–43.

Manicardi, "Parola."

Masson, Charles, "L'ensevelissement de Jésus (Marc xv, 42-47)," *RThPh* 31 (1943) 192–203; reprinted in idem, *Vers les sources d'eau vive: Études d'exégèse et de théologie du Nouveau Testament* (Lausanne: Payot, 1961) 102–13.

Matera, Frank, "The Death of Jesus according to Luke: A Question of Sources," *CBQ* 47 (1985) 469–85.

McBirnie, William Steuart, *The Search for the Authentic Tomb of Jesus* (Montrose, CA: Acclaimed Books, 1975).

McMahon, E. J., "The Death and Resurrection of Jesus in Luke 23:26—24:53: A Greimassian Analysis" (diss., Vanderbilt University, 1984).

Mercurio, Roger, "A Baptismal Motif in the Gospel Narratives of the Burial," *CBQ* 21 (1959) 39–54.

Michel, Otto, "Jüdische Bestattung und urchristliche Ostergeschichte," *Judaica* 16 (1960) 1–5.

Müller, Christoph G., "Josef von Arimathäa und die Grablegung Jesu (Lk 23,50-56)," in idem, ed., *"Licht zur Erleuchtung der Heiden und Herrlichkeit für*

dein Volk Israel": Studien zum lukanischen Doppelwerk* (BBB 151; Hamburg: Philo, 2005) 179–98.

O'Rahilly, Alfred, "The Burial of Christ," *IER* 58 (1941) 302–16, 493–503; 59 (1942) 150–71.

Pelletier, "Tradition."

Pesch, Rudolf, "Der Schluss der vormarkinischen Passionsgeschichte und des Markusevangeliums: Mk 15,42—16,8," in Maurits Sabbe, ed., *L'Évangile selon Marc: Tradition et rédaction* (BEThL 34; Leuven: Leuven University Press, 1974) 365–409.

Pobee, John, "The Cry of the Centurion—A Cry of Defeat," in Ernst Bammel, ed., *The Trial of Jesus: Cambridge Studies in Honour of C. F. D. Moule* (SBT 13; Naperville, Ill.: Allenson, 1970) 91–102.

Prete, "Preghiere."

Radl, Walter, "Der Tod Jesu in der Darstellung der Evangelien," *ThGl* 72 (1982) 432–44.

Rese, *Motive*, 200–202.

Rice, George E., "Western Non-Interpolations: A Defense of the Apostolate," in Charles H. Talbert, ed., *Luke-Acts: New Perspectives from the Society of Biblical Literature Seminar* (New York: Crossroad, 1984) 1–16.

Riggs, Christina, *The Beautiful Burial in Roman Egypt: Art, Identity, and Funerary Religion* (Oxford: Oxford University Press, 2005).

Russ, "Vermächtnis."

Sawyer, John F. A., "Why Is a Solar Eclipse Mentioned in the Passion Narrative (Luke xxiii. 44-45)?" *JTS* 23 (1972) 124–28.

Schreiber, Johannes, "Die Bestattung Jesu: Redaktionsgeschichtliche Beobachtungen zu Mk 15, 42-47 par," *ZNW* 72 (1981) 141–77.

Schwemer, Anna-Maria, "Jesu letze Worte am Kreuz (Mk 15,34; Lk 23,46; Joh 19,28ff)," *ThBei* 29 (1998) 5–29.

Smit Sibinga, J., "The Making of Luke 23:26-56: An Analysis of the Composition Technique in Luke's Crucifixion Narrative," *RB* 104 (1997) 378–404.

Simons, Jan Jozef, *Jerusalem in the Old Testament: Researches and Theories* (Leiden: Brill, 1952) 282–343.

Smith, Robert Houston, "The Tomb of Jesus," *BA* 30 (1967) 74–90.

Sterling, "*Mors philosophi*."

Sylva, Dennis D., "The Temple Curtain and Jesus' Death in the Gospel of Luke," *JBL* 105 (1986) 239–50.

Taylor, *Passion Narrative*, 91–103.

Trilling, *Christusverkündigung*, 191–211.

Vincent, Louis-Hugues, "Garden Tomb: Histoire d'un mythe," *RB* 34 (1925) 401–31.

Wilkinson, "Words."

Winkel, Johannes, "Das Begräbnis und das leere Grab Jesu in den Evangelien," in Rainer Reuter and Wolfgang Schenk, eds., *Semiotica Biblica: Eine Freundesgabe für Erhardt Güttgemanns* (Theos 31; Hamburg: Kovac, 1999) 7–21.

Yates, Thomas, "The Words from the Cross, VII: 'And When Jesus Had Cried with a Loud Voice,

He Said, Father into Thy Hands I Commend My Spirit' (Luke xxiii. 46)," *ExpT* 41 (1929–30) 427–29.

Zehnle, "Death."

---

44 It was already about noon[a] and darkness covered the entire land until three o'clock in the afternoon,[b] 45/ the sun had disappeared. As for the veil of the temple, it was torn in the middle. 46/ Then raising his voice, Jesus said with a loud voice, "Father, into your hands I commit my spirit." When he had said these words, he expired. 47/ When the centurion saw what had happened, he glorified God, saying, "Truly, this man was just." 48/ All the crowds that had gathered to see this spectacle contemplated what was happening.[c] Then they returned home, beating their breasts. 49/ All who knew him stood at a distance and the women who had accompanied him from Galilee were also there to see it all.[d]

50 And behold, there was a man named Joseph, who was a member of the Sanhedrin,[e] a good and righteous man—51/ this one had not agreed to their plan or their action—from Arimathea, a city of the Jews. He was waiting for the kingdom of God. 52/ Going to Pilate, this one asked for the body of Jesus. 53/ Taking it down, he wrapped it in linen and laid it in a tomb carved from stone where no one had lain before. 54/ The day was a Friday, and the Sabbath was breaking. 55/ The women who had come with Jesus[f] from Galilee, having accompanied him, saw the tomb and how his body had been placed. 56/ After they returned, they prepared spices and ointments.

a   Literally: "the sixth hour."
b   Literally: "until the ninth hour."
c   I divided the sentence and made of a participle ("beholding") a main verb ("contemplated").
d   Literally: "it."
e   Literally: "counselor."
f   Literally: "with him."

Two extraordinary signs, the night in broad daylight and the tearing of the veil of the temple, open the way for a last word and the last breath of Jesus. Two human appearances, that of the centurion and that of the crowd, then react positively to events. Two groups in the background, Jesus' relatives and the women who came with him from Galilee, witness the outcome. Finally, two last and necessary episodes take place: Joseph of Arimathea buries Jesus, and the group of women prepares the spices. Thus ends a life, without death being the last word. In fact, the last sentence of chap. 23 forms a unity with the first one of chap. 24. The $\mu\acute{\varepsilon}\nu$ ("on the one hand"), which is next to the Sabbath (23:56b), expects the $\delta\acute{\varepsilon}$ ("on the other hand"), which accompanies the dawning of the next day (24:1). Bridging Saturday, the Sabbath day, Good Friday and Easter were and remain inseparable.[1]

---

1   It is better to end the pericope at 23:56a. On the passage from one day to the next, see Plummer, 543.

Analysis

Many things have happened thus far on this Friday morning (the beginning of the day is mentioned in 22:66): the gathering of the Sanhedrin, the hearing before Pilate, the transfer to Herod, the return to Pilate, the Barabbas episode, Jesus' sentence, the way of the cross, the crucifixion, the episode with the good thief (22:66—23:43). The narrator determines the hour here: the sixth hour, thus the middle of the day, roughly noon (v. 44). Suddenly a darkness lasting three hours falls over the land (vv. 44-45a), and the curtain of the temple is torn (v. 45b). After a final prayer, Jesus dies at the ninth hour, about three o'clock in the afternoon. As the crucifixion required only a few words (23:33), death also requires only a few ("when he had said these words, he expired," v. 46b). The rest of the passage deals with what surrounds the drama: what precedes it, accompanies it, follows it, is a witness to it, or interprets it. Everything revolves around the death of the innocent man, but this central event, out of respect, or from feelings, or from caution, remains only a point, but certainly a focal point. The same was true for the crucifixion in 23:33; it was quietly mentioned in the midst of the episodes surrounding it. This took place during the second half of the morning, while the death occurs during the first part of the afternoon. The chronological structure makes clear the narrative structure.

Luke does not create the story of this martyrdom out of whole cloth. Following the principle of alternating sources (which is my hypothesis),[2] he returns here to the Gospel of Mark. With no other formal changes, he makes mention of the three hours of darkness (v. 44 par. Mark 15:33) but inserts here as the second sign the episode of the torn veil, which Mark has somewhat later (15:38). Of the two episodes Mark locates in the interval, Luke omits the first because it embarrasses him theologically (the cry of abandonment, Mark 15:34-35), and, following his other source, the special source (Luke 23:36), he has already moved past the second episode (the vinegar, Mark 15:36). He explains, however, Jesus' last exclama-tion (v. 46), the content of which Mark omitted or merely thought was an inarticulate cry (Mark 15:37), by putting in Jesus' mouth a prayer of trust taken from a psalm (Ps 30 [31]:6). In the following verse he continues his rereading and calls attention to the presence and the reaction of the centurion (v. 47). For some reason, which I will try to explain,[3] he changes the confession. In Luke the centurion calls Jesus "just" ($\delta i \kappa \alpha \iota o \varsigma$, v. 47), while in Mark he does not hesitate to say "Son of God" or "a son of God" (Mark 15:39). Luke, who likes the following expression (see, e.g., 5:26), says explicitly that the centurion wanted to "glorify God." For some reason, which we will try to identify, the evangelist goes on to describe the presence of the crowds that, in view of the spectacle, beat their breasts (v. 48). Since the vocabulary, the syntax, and the style of this sentence are strongly redactional, it is Luke alone who is responsible for this statement, which he has derived from no source. The situation is different in v. 49; here Mark has provided the various elements (15:40-41): the presence of the women, their Galilean origin, their keeping their distance, and their intention to see what is happening. For some reason, which must be explained, Luke does not list the names of the Galilean women or indicate the services they performed for Jesus. Luke—and he is the only Synoptic evangelist to do so—adds a masculine counterpart, men who knew Jesus.

Still following Mark, Luke then has the episode of Joseph of Arimathea. Reading the hagiographic literature, especially the various recensions of the same martyrdom,[4] makes it easy to compare and understand the different forms of the burial. All three Synoptic Gospels bear witness to the role of Joseph of Arimathea, his successful intervention with Pilate, the shroud in which Jesus' body is wrapped, and the burial in a tomb of stone. Luke also shares with Mark, his source here, Joseph's function as a "member of the Sanhedrin" ($\beta o \upsilon \lambda \epsilon \upsilon \tau \eta \varsigma$) and his piety as one who is waiting for the coming of the kingdom of God. Nevertheless, he omits some of the material in his source: the courage Joseph needed to go to Pilate, Pilate's surprise at how rapidly the crucified one had died and his confirmation of the death from the

---

2   See Bovon, "Lukan Story of the Passion," 88–97.
3   See the commentary below on v. 47.
4   See François Bovon, "The Dossier on Saint Stephen, First Martyr," *HTR* 96 (2003) 279–315.

centurion, Joseph's purchase of the shroud, and the rolling of the stone to seal the tomb. Only a single narrative element is unique to Luke: the fact that Joseph was not part of the Sanhedrin's decision (v. 51a). Worth noting among the minor agreements that Luke shares with Matthew are the preference for the verb προσέρχομαι ("go to," v. 52 par. Matt 27:58), the absence of hesitation on Pilate's part in turning over the victim's body (v. 52 par. Matt 27:58), the omission of Joseph's purchase of the shroud, the choice of the verb ἐντυλίσσω ("to wrap"), which may be more appropriate than Mark's ἐνειλῶ ("to roll up"). Since I do not think Luke borrowed from Matthew,[5] I explain these agreements as the same stylistic reactions and/or as coming from a living oral tradition. I conclude this Synoptic comparison by saying that Luke once again uses his source, in this circumstance Mark, in a way that is both faithful and free.

Extending the comparison beyond the Synoptic Gospels is worthwhile. If we reread the Gospel of John[6] with Luke's Gospel in mind, we note that John does not have the three hours of darkness and the cry of abandonment (Mark 15:34-35 par. Matt 27:46-47). Jesus speaks two different last words ("I thirst" and "it is finished"; John 19:28, 30). The centurion is absent, but the mother and the beloved disciple are present (John 19:26-27). The company of women is present; unlike in Luke but as in Mark and Matthew, the fourth evangelist mentions their names (John 19:25). John includes the blow with the spear, missing from the Synoptic Gospels (John 19:31-37). Along with the Synoptics, John includes the role of Joseph of Arimathea (John 19:38-42) and, as in Matt 27:57, includes that he is a disciple of Jesus (John 19:38). He includes the help that Nicodemus gives Joseph (John 19:39), which is absent in the Synoptics, and mentions the one hundred pounds of a mixture of myrrh and aloes (John 19:39). John says that the tomb was new (John 19:41), as do Luke (v. 53) and Matthew (27:60). He indicates the day (that of "preparation," "Friday," παρασκευή, 19:42),[7] as do Luke and Mark (v. 54; Mark

15:42). Finally, compared with Luke (v. 56), John does not mention the preparation of the spices by the women. Each Gospel medium thus has a particular version of a common narrative, following a process that excludes neither borrowing nor further developments.

The *Gospel of Peter*, whose autonomy and age I appreciate,[8] also offers material for comparison and reflection. In this long fragment, in which Joseph of Arimathea is also present and active, Joseph anticipates the event. Said to be a friend both of Pilate and of the Lord (the name given to Jesus in this document), Joseph goes to Pilate and asks for the body of the Lord so he can guarantee that it will be buried. He does this while Jesus is still alive and when Herod is about to condemn him, more precisely, to deliver him to the people. Here I will skip the walk to the cross and the crucifixion, discussed above, and will come to the deposition from the cross and the burial. The *Gospel of Peter* mentions the darkness that covers all of Judea, the people's fear of death after sunset, the explanation of the law that gives meaning to this fear, and the offer of the vinegar. The noncanonical document emphasizes the sin of Jesus' opponents, which has reached its climax; mentions passersby strolling with lamps; records a final word of Jesus that is closer to Mark and Matthew than to Luke or John and yet is independent of them ("My power, O power, thou hast forsaken me"; *Gos. Pet.* 19); gives an ambiguous statement about the death of the Lord ("And having said this he was taken up"; *Gos. Pet.* 19); and finally notes the tearing of the temple veil. The deposition from the cross (reference is made to the nails that are torn out) coincides with the return of the sun and the observation that it was not yet past the ninth hour, then about three o'clock in the afternoon. Here is what follows: "The Jews rejoiced and gave his body to Joseph that he might bury it, since he had seen all the good that he (= Jesus) had done. And he took the Lord, washed him, wrapped him in linen and brought him into his own sepulcher, called Joseph's Garden" (*Gos. Pet.* 23–24). The story continues

---

5   My opinion differs here from that of Goulder, *New Paradigm*, 2:769–73.

6   See in particular Benoit, *Passion and Resurrection*, 181–230; Brown, *Death of the Messiah*, 2:1031–1313.

7   Remember the double meaning of παρασκευή, "preparation" of the Sabbath and "preparation" of the Passover. In John the two overlap, since there

Jesus died on a Friday, which is also the eve of the major Jewish holiday (see John 19:31).

8   See Bovon, *Last Days*, 15–18. I cite the translation of Christian Maurer in Schneemelcher, *New Testament Apocrypha*, 1:223–26.

by saying that the Jews realized—it is not said explicitly that they repented—that they had sinned and that their punishment, the destruction of Jerusalem, was imminent (*Gos. Pet.* 25). Surprising is the following, in which a disciple—it must be Peter—explains this circumstance: "But I mourned with my fellows, and being wounded in heart we hid ourselves, for we were sought after as evildoers and as persons who wanted to set fire to the Temple. Because of all these things we were fasting and sat mourning and weeping night and day until the Sabbath" (*Gos. Pet.* 26–27). While in the previous material the *Gospel of Peter* emphasized the role of Herod and the good thief, much as Luke has done, here he is like Luke only in one specific point. Even if the wording is different, the *Gospel of Peter*, like Luke, mentions the discreet presence of disciples near the cross. The text continues with the positioning of guards to watch the tomb.

According to a number of patristic and medieval witnesses, a lost Jewish-Christian Gospel dating from the second century contained information that complemented the Gospel of Luke.[9] As we have seen in connection with v. 27[10] and were able to repeat with v. 48,[11] this document spoke of the repentance of a number of eyewitnesses of the crucifixion and of their conversion to Christianity.[12] Thus, the text had the same sense as the *Gos. Pet.* 25. In addition, this lost Gospel believed that what was split in two was not the temple veil but a large block of stone. Jerome (in two places—*Comm. Matt.* 27.51 and *Epist.* 120.8.2) and the medieval report entitled *Historia passionis Domini*[13] convey the information using the

same term: *superliminare templi*, "a lintel of the temple." The testimony of the *Historia* adds that the Jewish historian Josephus reports the same information, and it adds the following: "Terrifying (*horribles*) voices would then be lifted up, shouting: 'Let us get away from these seats!'"[14]

About the middle of the second century Justin Martyr, himself an author of a harmony of the Gospels that has been lost, reported various memories of the passion in the works that have been preserved. In particular, he writes in his *Dialogue with Trypho*: "For when he breathed his last on the cross, he said: 'Father, into your hands I commit my spirit,' which I learned again this time from the memoirs," that is to say, from the recollections of the apostles, a designation he chose when speaking of the Gospels (105.5).

The similarity and the variety of recollections of the passion go through late antiquity: As we know, in the second century Tatian wrote his *Diatessaron*, probably based on the harmony put together by his master, Justin Martyr. The Greek original of the work has disappeared with the exception of a fragment, a fragment that relates specifically to our passage:

. . . [of Zebe]dee and Salome and the women who had come with him from Galilee to see the crucified one. It was the [Day] of Preparation. The Sabbath began. In the evening, after t[he P]rep[a]ra[tion], which is the day before the Sabbath, there appeared a man, a member of the Sanhedrin, who was from Erinmathea, a city of Judas. His name was Jo[seph],

---

9 See Bovon, "Lukan Story of the Passion," 99–100.
10 See the analysis above on 23:27.
11 See the Latin text in Aland, *Synopsis*, 484.
12 The Syriac version of the Gospel of Luke edited by Cureton has at the end of v. 48 a development translated by Harris ("Gloss," 8), which corrects Cureton's translation: "and saying, Woe to us! What has befallen us? Woe to us from our sins." This development roughly corresponds to the one found in a Latin manuscript from the eighth–ninth centuries, g¹, which is also added to the end of v. 48: "They say: 'Woe to us, what is happening to us today occurs because of our sins. Indeed, Jerusalem's desolation is at hand.'" (The manuscript reads "Woe to you," but changing it is justified.) Harris ("Gloss") finds the traces of this development in the *Doctrina Addai*, 27–28, in the commentary on the *Diatessaron* from

Ephraem the Syrian, in Syrian authors, and above all in *Gos. Pet.* 25 and concludes that Tatian's *Diatessaron* must be the source of this passage. According to apparatus of Nestle-Aland (27th ed.) on this text, the Syriac translation of Sinai is familiar with this same development. See William L. Petersen, *Tatian's Diatessaron: Its Creation, Dissemination, Significance, and History in Scholarship* (VCSup 25; Leiden: Brill, 1994) 414–20.
13 See the Latin text in Aland, *Synopsis*, 489.
14 The *Letter of Barnabas* (7.3) indicates that, on the basis of Lev 23:29, the temple priests were given an inspired interpretation of the vinegar and gall that Jesus drank on the cross. Was this revelation one of the positive responses to the passion of Christ? It is more likely that it coincided chronologically with the redaction of Lev 23:29.

he was a g[oo]d and ju[st] disciple of Je[sus], but he was hiding for fear of the Jews, and he was waiting for the Kingdom of God. He himself did not take part in their plan.

With the help of the Greek wording given in Aland's *Synopsis*, the reader will see how much this fragment borrows from the Gospel of Luke.[15]

The Christian apocryphal literature contains other stories, perhaps of a more recent date, which may rely on old information. It is not impossible that in its various forms the first part of the *Acts of Pilate*, which also circulated under the titles the *Gospel of Nicodemus*,[16] and the *Book of the Cock*, and which was kept in Ethiopia, preserve ancient traditions as well, especially Jewish-Christian traditions.[17]

Commentary

■ **44** The Lukan Christ had predicted that an hour of darkness was imminent (22:53).[18] This hour has come.[19] The natural darkness confirms here in a supernatural way the blackness that is taking place on the plane of history. The Jewish reader remembers the darkness that accompanies the theophanies as well as the eschatological events marking the Day of Yahweh, in particular as the *Dies irae*. The Greek or Roman readers remember cosmic outbursts or signs from heaven, $\tau\acute{\epsilon}\rho\alpha\tau\alpha$ or *prodigia*, which underscore the importance of the death of princes, heroes, or even gods.[20]

The expression $\dot{\epsilon}\varphi'\,\ddot{o}\lambda\eta\nu\,\tau\grave{\eta}\nu\,\gamma\grave{\eta}\nu$ is ambiguous. It can mean "over the whole country" or "over the whole earth." *Gospel of Peter* 15 reflects a tradition that limits the darkness to Judea. Luke's two-volume work, whose universalistic ambition is well known, automatically retains the basic meaning of "earth" ($\gamma\grave{\eta}$) that embraces the entire earth. "You will be my witnesses . . . unto the ends of the earth" (Acts 1:8).[21] Thus, I retain here the second meaning.

■ **45** As in the story of the Mount of Olives (22:39-46),[22] Luke confirms here his doctrinal sensitivity by omitting the cry of abandonment (Mark 15:34-36). He admits neither that God has abandoned his Son nor that the Son expressed a feeling of loneliness. Contra Jerome H. Neyrey and Gregory E. Sterling,[23] this theological attitude does not mean that the evangelist eliminates the rigors of the death and increases the courage of the martyr. As in the story of the Garden of Olives, Jesus actually suffers, but he also actually believes. As for God, he is neither cruel nor indifferent. He pursues his plan, a plan to which the Son has agreed. As the angel had come to strengthen the stricken Christ, the darkness signifies the divine agreement and even participation in the

---

15 See Aland, *Synopsis*, 490–91; see also Petersen, *Diatessaron*, 196–203 (n. 12 above).

16 See Schneemelcher, *New Testament Apocrypha*, 1:505–21.

17 See ibid., 1:501–5.

18 On the darkness episode, see in chronological order Clarke ("Parallels"), who connects *2 Enoch* 67:1-3 and 68:1, 5-7 with Luke 23:44, 47-48, 52; Holzmeister ("Finsternis"), who tests the historicity and thinks that God can make use of the most diverse means; Sawyer ("Eclipse"), who will be discussed below (on n. 34); Grández, who offers a valuable history of the interpretation of the Good Friday darkness, which he himself understands as a reflection of divine reality ("Tinieblas"), and who is interested in the textual question posed by v. 45a and decides for the *textus receptus* $\kappa\alpha\grave{\iota}\,\dot{\epsilon}\sigma\kappa\sigma\tau\acute{\iota}\sigma\vartheta\eta$ $\dot{o}\,\ddot{\eta}\lambda\iota\sigma\varsigma$ ("and the sun was darkened") ("Crítica"); and MacAdam ("$\sigma\kappa\acute{o}\tau\sigma\varsigma$"), whom I present below (on n. 35).

19 The Byzantine text reads $\ddot{\eta}\nu\,\delta\acute{\epsilon}$ ("but it was") rather than $\kappa\alpha\grave{\iota}\,\ddot{\eta}\nu$ ("and it was"), which is a bit more elegant and thus more suspect. Moreover, a number of witnesses omit $\ddot{\eta}\delta\eta$ ("already"), which is far from indispensable when we remember how many events have already taken place on this day.

20 See Isa 13:10; Jer 4:23; Xavier Léon-Dufour, ed., *Dictionary of Biblical Theology* (2d ed.; New York: Seabury, 1973) s.v. "Light and Dark"; Plutarch *Def. Orac.* 17, *Mor.* 419A–E; Pierre Grimal, *The Dictionary of Classical Mythology* (trans. A. R. Maxwell-Hyslop; Oxford: Blackwell, 1987) s.v., "Pan."

21 Comparing the Third Gospel to Mark 15:33, one notes the addition of $\dot{\omega}\sigma\epsilon\acute{\iota}$ ("about") to the indication of the time. This is Luke's usage; see Henry J. Cadbury, *The Style and Literary Method of Luke* (Cambridge, Mass.: Harvard University Press, 1920) 129. Luke prefers here the parataxis ($\kappa\alpha\grave{\iota}\,\ddot{\eta}\nu$ . . . $\kappa\alpha\grave{\iota}\,\sigma\kappa\acute{o}\tau\sigma\varsigma\,\dot{\epsilon}\gamma\acute{\epsilon}\nu\epsilon\tau\sigma$, "And it was . . . and darkness covered") to Mark's syntax in 15:33, which uses a genitive absolute before the main clause.

22 See the commentary above on 22:43-44.

23 Neyrey, "Absence"; Sterling, *"Mors Philosophi."*

drama. In the Garden of Olives Jesus had finally faced the matter in faith. He prays with the same faith at the time of his death, calling God his Father and entrusting his life to him (v. 46). Paradoxically, the darkness reveals God, certainly here a *deus absconditus*, a hidden God. It also indicates that the death that is happening leads to life, that the darkness in the tunnel precedes the light of the resurrection.

Since Luke wants to skip the cry of abandonment (Mark 15:34-36) and to put the tearing of the veil (Mark 15:38) before the death of Jesus (Mark 15:37), he has to make a transition by repeating in his own words the reality of the first cosmic sign: "the sun had disappeared" (τοῦ ἡλίου ἐκλιπόντος, v. 45a). The verb ἐκλείπω is commonly used in Greek to designate an eclipse.[24] Does this suggest that Luke is thinking of an eclipse? Yet a solar eclipse cannot happen with a full moon, and Passover takes place on the full moon. Is Luke confused? Or does he remember the total solar eclipse of November 24 in 29 c.e.,[25] recalled by the eclipses of 49 (partial), of 59

(total), and 80 (partial)?[26] That raises a lot of questions about three words. Luke is more interested in salvation history than in astronomy. He is more attentive to God's intervention than to the natural defects of the stars. In his opinion, this is a cosmic sign that underscores the importance of the death of Israel's Messiah (more than the meaning that remains enigmatic until Easter and even beyond).

As the day is broken into two parts (it reappears in all clarity three hours later),[27] the curtain of the temple in Jerusalem is torn[28] in the same moment.[29] Luke accepts Mark's information here, his source in this passage. How does he understand this sign that neither he nor the second evangelist interprets? The scholars themselves have no problem suggesting the meaning:[30] It is a prelude to the destruction of the temple, which entails the end of the sacrificial cult, the end of divine revelation, the end of immediate and henceforth access to God, and the end of the separation between Israel and the nations.[31] A preliminary question arises: Since there were two veils, of

24 Instead of the text I retain, following Nestle-Aland (27th ed.), the witnesses of the Byzantine text and perhaps Marcion, according to Epiphanius, and also Origen, according to certain Latin manuscripts, have καὶ ἐσκοτίσθη ὁ ἥλιος ("and the sun was darkened"); see the apparatus of Nestle-Aland (27th ed.); and Grández, "Crítica." Along with various Vulgate manuscripts, an important ninth-century Greek manuscript (33), held in the Bibliothèque Nationale in Paris, omits the beginning of v. 45 and comes immediately to the temple veil.

25 This eclipse was visible in Syria and Asia Minor. It lasted only a minute and a half, not three hours. Sawyer ("Eclipse") is of the opinion that what may have been the personal memory of this eclipse influenced Luke and made the redaction of v. 45a easier.

26 See MacAdam ("σκότος"), who goes in the same direction as Sawyer (see preceding note). He adds the other three eclipses of the first century c.e. and thinks that the total solar eclipse of the year 29 c.e. provided for Luke a "cosmic model" to explain the Christian tradition about the hours of darkness on Good Friday.

27 *Gospel of Peter* 22 explicitly mentions the return of the sun: "Then the sun shone, and it was found that it was the ninth hour."

28 Beginning with Elisha weeping at the departure of Elijah and tearing his clothes into two pieces (2 Kgs

[LXX 4 Kgdms] 2:12), Daube (*Rabbinic Judaism*, 23–26) recalls the ritual of lamentation that consists of cutting one's garment in two. Parallel to that is the complete tearing of the temple veil as "a sign of deepest sorrow" (24).

29 One speaks of the "veil" of the temple, but καταπέτασμα means "curtain," suggesting a fabric of a certain thickness and weight. Codex Bezae (D = 05) ignores the tearing of the curtain here. It mentions it at the end of v. 46, following a different word order; see the apparatus of Nestle-Aland (27th ed.) on the text.

30 Sylva ("Curtain") presents a tableau of different interpretations. He chiefly adds a new explanation: for Luke the tearing of the curtain shows at that moment the communion between God and Jesus. Green ("Veil") thinks that for Luke the episode marks the removal of social and ethnic barriers between the nations. In his article "Demise," Green attempts to link the tearing of the curtain with the Lukan theology of the temple: the episode announces not the future destruction of the sacred edifice but the end of its cultural and religious hegemony.

31 See a brief presentation of the various patristic interpretations from the pen of Pelletier, "Tradition," 161–65.

which one is he speaking?[32] Is the evangelist thinking of the veil that marked the entrance to the sanctuary, itself called the Holy Place, to which access was forbidden to everyone—Gentiles and Jews, men and women—except for the priests? Or is he thinking of the veil forbidden to everyone, including the priests, except for the high priest who once a year on the great Day of Atonement had access to the holiest part of the temple, the Holy of Holies?[33] Before I respond to the question, we must recall the symbolic value attached to the veil. Philo and Josephus give a Jewish interpretation of the outer veil:[34] It is of a cosmic order. The Letter to the Hebrews offers a Christian interpretation of the interior veil:[35] It has a christological character. I certainly respect the absence of a Lukan interpretation of the sign, but I would suggest that we see in it a symbol of the death of Jesus, who by giving his life makes available access to God. Hebrews 10:19-20 set me on the way to this understanding. Thus, I think that Luke[36] envisages the second veil, the one that provided access to the Holy of Holies.[37] I also think that the location of the episode—before rather than after Jesus' death—comes from Luke's desire to connect the two signs closely, the disappearance of the sun and the tearing of the veil.

■ **46** Luke likes biblical expressions that contain etymological figures:[38] "raising his voice, with a loud voice" (καὶ φωνήσας φωνῇ μεγάλῃ). This is, according to Luke, the introduction to Jesus' last words. There is one grammatical question left without a definite answer: Does the aorist participle φωνήσας designate a previous act ("after he had raised his voice, with a loud voice") or does it coincide with the main action without indicating time ("raising his voice, with a loud voice")?[39] Just as the cry of abandonment according to Mark represents a quotation from Ps 21 (22):2, so Jesus' prayer in Luke corresponds to Ps 30 (31):6 in the LXX.[40] Psalm 30 (31) represents both a call for help and an expression of great confidence. Like the Psalmist, the Jesus of Luke places his spirit into God's hands, because he knows that God is stronger than the enemies and than death itself. To emphasize the relationship between the one who is praying and his God, the evangelist adds to the quotation from the psalm the vocative πάτερ ("Father"). This appeal addressed to the "Father" consistently heads the

---

32   The distinction between these two veils or curtains is mentioned already in the book of Exodus (26:31-37; 36:35-38; 40:21-28).

33   According to Pelletier ("Tradition," 161–65), the Christian writers of antiquity were divided on this question.

34   Philo (*Vit. Mos.* 2.86–88) makes a distinction between the "curtain" (καταπέτασμα) sealing the Holy Place and the "veil" barring the Holy of Holies. The symbolic interpretation he gives applies to both veils as well as to other curtains of the temple. See also Josephus *Bell.* 5.5.4–5 §§210–21; *Ep. Arist.* 7.86; Sir 50:5; and *3 Enoch* 45:1.

35   Hebrews 10:19–20: "We have, brothers, boldness to enter the sanctuary by the blood of Jesus. We have a new and living way that he inaugurated through the veil, that is, though his humanity."

36   On the tearing of the veil, see Pelletier, "Tradition"; Légasse, "Voiles"; Lamarche, "Voile"; Lindeskog, "Veil"; Celada, "Velo"; Daube, *Rabbinic Judaism*, 23–26; Sylva, "Curtain"; Green, "Veil"; idem, "Demise." As we have seen, the last three articles examine in particular the Lukan interpretation of the veil and its tearing.

37   Opinions remain divided on this subject. Pelletier ("Tradition," 165–66) is certain that it is the exte-

rior curtain; Lindeskog ("Veil," 132) has no doubt that it is the inner curtain; on this subject, see Sylva, "Curtain," 239 n. 2.

38   See Acts 16:28 ἐφώνησεν δὲ μεγάλῃ φωνῇ ("But Paul cried with a loud voice").

39   Like most of the people I consulted, Plummer (538) and Delebecque (*Évangile*, 145) choose the latter. The question lies again at the end of the verse: What is the significance of εἰπών? Has Jesus finished the statement before he dies, or does he die while he is saying it? In the view of the philologist Bertrand Bouvier, the aorist always indicates priority, no matter how small. For him, Jesus made the statement, then gave up the spirit.

40   Luke changes the text of the LXX on only one point. He prefers the present παρατίθεμαι ("I commit"), which is obviously just happening, to the future of the LXX, παραθήσομαι ("I will commit"). While Codez Bezae (D = 05), the minuscule family *f*¹, and some other Greek manuscripts, have the active παρατίθημι ("I lay down"), the Byzantine text of the Gospel brings back the LXX quotation and writes the future παραθήσομαι ("I will commit").

prayers of Jesus in the Third Gospel (see 10:21; 22:42; 23:34; also 11:2).

What Jesus, according to the psalm, commits to God is his "spirit" ($\pi\nu\epsilon\hat{u}\mu\alpha$). The root of this word is found in the subsequent verb "he expired" ($\dot{\epsilon}\xi\dot{\epsilon}\pi\nu\epsilon\upsilon\sigma\epsilon\nu$). The "spirit" ($\pi\nu\epsilon\hat{u}\mu\alpha$) designates not only part of the person but the breath of life, which thus constitutes the whole person.

By concluding the execution this way, the evangelist points out discreetly that, although mistreated by human beings, Jesus nevertheless retains control of his destiny. As in the story of the mocking and the episode of the two thieves, Jesus certainly does not have the power to avoid death, but he is able to face it before it overcomes him.[41]

■ **47** Luke believes that the first onlooker to admire the courage of the condemned man was an officer (he must be seen as a Roman, thus a Gentile).[42] In this way he demonstrates his concern that the gospel be open to the nations.

Here again Luke avoids a foreign word,[43] the Latinism $\kappa\epsilon\nu\tau\upsilon\rho\acute{\iota}\omega\nu$ (for *centurio;* Mark 15:39). He chooses the Greek equivalent $\dot{\epsilon}\kappa\alpha\tau\omega\nu\tau\acute{\alpha}\rho\chi\eta\varsigma$ ("leader of one hundred") and rewrites the entire sentence. He ignores

the reminder of Jesus' death (Mark 15:39), which would have amounted to a repetition and speaks modestly of "what had happened." Like many God-fearers mentioned in Luke-Acts, this officer recognizes God's majesty and providence. Luke likes to say what Mark has not yet expressed—namely, that the centurion is giving glory to God.[44] This officer acknowledges the mysterious plan of Israel's Lord, who accepted the unjust death of his Messiah. He expresses the other side of the coin, the quality of this human being. To affirm the intensity of his conviction, he uses the adverb "really," "truly" ($\check{o}\nu\tau\omega\varsigma$). What Jesus really was, was that he was "righteous" ($\delta\acute{\iota}\kappa\alpha\iota\sigma\varsigma$).[45]

There are two possible translations and interpretations of this adjective. One of them places Jesus' righteousness in the biblical tradition of the צְדָקָה of moral uprightness, of religious authenticity, of belonging to God's people as part of the covenant. In this translation of "just" Jesus represents the "suffering righteous man" of the Psalms and of Deutero-Isaiah. The other prefers to stay in the secular framework of Jesus' trial. When the centurion declares Jesus to be "righteous" ($\delta\acute{\iota}\kappa\alpha\iota\sigma\varsigma$) he is doing nothing more than declaring that the accused is innocent. By repeating Pilate's affirmations, the

---

41 On the last word of Jesus according to Luke, see in particular in chronological order: Yates ("Words"), who perceives here a tone of victory; Wilkinson ("Words"), who recalls that this last word of Jesus is the prayer a Jewish child spoke before going to sleep; Rese (*Motive*, 200–201), who prefers not to talk about a quotation since there is no introduction but still remarks that Luke is referring to the Scriptures here; Feldkämper (*Der betende Jesus*, 268–84), who emphasizes that Jesus submits to the will and the affection of his Father; Prete ("Preghiere," 94–96), who for two reasons thinks that Luke has substituted Ps 30 (31):6 for Ps 21 (22):2 ([a] his pagan listeners were likely to believe that Jesus really had been abandoned by God; [b] Psalm 30 [31] corresponds better to Luke's Christology); Bons ("Sterbewort"), who regards the motif of hope as the main reason for the substitution; Russ ("Vermächtnis"), who concludes from this prayer that Jesus leaves this life in peace and gives back all that he has received; Manicardi ("Parola"), who compares the last moments of Jesus and Stephen, emphasizing the verb $\varphi\omega\nu\epsilon\omega$ ("to lift the voice") and pointing out that Jesus does not beg; Liberto ("Fear"), who thinks that, by showing Jesus as pray-

ing this way, Luke describes what must be the right attitude toward death. On the one hand, Luke competes with the Greeks by showing that his hero does not fear death. On the other, he criticizes them by reminding them of the importance of the fear of God.

42 Codex Bezae offers a different beginning of the verse. It omits the centurion's look but calls attention to what he exclaims ($\vartheta\omega\nu\acute{\eta}\sigma\alpha\varsigma$).

43 In omitting the cry of abandonment, Luke eliminates at the same time a $\lambda\acute{\epsilon}\xi\iota\varsigma$ $\beta\alpha\rho\beta\alpha\rho\iota\kappa\acute{\eta}$: "Eloi, Eloi, lama sabaqthani?" which means "My God, my God, why have you forsaken me?" (Mark 15:34). See Henry J. Cadbury, *The Style and Literary Method of Luke* (1920; HTS 6; reprinted New York: Kraus Reprint, 1969) 154–58.

44 Many manuscripts, especially those that transcribe the Byzantine text, prefer the aorist $\dot{\epsilon}\delta\acute{o}\xi\alpha\sigma\epsilon\nu$ ("he glorified") to the imperfect $\dot{\epsilon}\delta\acute{o}\xi\alpha\zeta\epsilon\nu$ ("he was glorifying").

45 The article by Pobee ("Cry") deals with Mark's version of the centurion's exclamation.

centurion affirms that Jesus was "innocent" and that as a result he was the victim of a miscarriage of justice.[46] Before one chooses, one must answer a related question. Why did Luke avoid the strong christological answer that Mark and, following him, Matthew transmit? I believe that Luke wants to wait until Easter and the emergence of the apostolic proclamation before he allows a man, especially a Gentile, to confess a faith that is not Jewish but Christian. Finally, I retain the meaning of "righteous," because it fits the immediate context. The centurion can hardly praise God for the innocence of the crucified man; he does so because of Jesus' righteousness. In addition, the theme of righteousness corresponds to Luke's theological intention as it is expressed precisely in the chapters of the passion (e.g., 22:27, 51, 61; 23:28, 31, 34a, 41, 43).[47] Furthermore, the meaning of "righteous" includes the sense of "innocent."[48]

■ **48** Much as Matthew does (27:54), Luke takes the centurion out of the splendid isolation in which Mark leaves him, adding all the spectators who are energetically on Jesus' side. Suddenly Jesus has no more enemies. All who are present beat their breasts before going home, that is, before they leave the place of the Skull located outside the city walls and go back into the city. As Tertullian would say later about the victims of persecution, the church blossomed because of the blood of the martyrs (*Apol.* 50.13: *semen est sanguis Christianorum*).[49]

The vocabulary that Luke chooses for this redactional verse is significant. The people observe or contemplate ($\vartheta \epsilon \omega \rho \acute{\eta} \sigma \alpha \nu \tau \epsilon \varsigma$) what is there to be observed or con-templated ($\epsilon \pi \grave{\iota} \tau \grave{\eta} \nu \vartheta \epsilon \omega \rho \acute{\iota} \alpha \nu \tau \alpha \acute{\upsilon} \tau \eta \nu$).[50] According to Luke, this attention is the beginning of an awareness (of their personal responsibility and the injustice done collectively by the authorities), a regret that leads to repentance and will be expressed by the beating of breasts in guilt. The redactional v. 48 refers to vv. 27 and 35, which are also very Lukan. Yet he goes beyond them and generalizes the sadness and penitence. In v. 27 only the women were grieving; their sadness was directed to the Jesus for whom they wept. In v. 35 the people certainly were affected, but in that case Luke mentions only the watchful attention. Here in v. 48 the crowds observe what is happening, and all of them beat their breasts.[51] The choice of the verb is not unimportant: $\tau \acute{\upsilon} \pi \tau o \nu \epsilon \varsigma \tau \grave{\alpha} \sigma \tau \acute{\eta} \vartheta \eta$ ("beating their breasts"), the spectators begin not a process of mourning as the women had done ($\epsilon \kappa \acute{o} \pi \tau o \nu \tau o \kappa \alpha \grave{\iota} \epsilon \vartheta \rho \acute{\eta} \nu o \upsilon \nu \alpha \grave{\upsilon} \tau \acute{o} \nu$, "bewailed and lamented him," v. 27) but a movement of repentance. Here Jesus' death brings the consciences to a confession of sin, while there it moved the hearts to the sadness of mourning.

■ **49** In this verse, which he takes from Mark with no changes, Luke first includes those he calls "all who knew him" ($\pi \acute{\alpha} \nu \tau \epsilon \varsigma o \acute{\iota} \gamma \nu \omega \sigma \tau o \grave{\iota} \alpha \grave{\upsilon} \tau \hat{\omega}$). Just as he had not specifically mentioned the apostles in the prologue of his Gospel (1:2),[52] here he calls them neither disciples nor apostles. Why? It may be that he does not dare to contradict Mark (14:50) and the oral tradition, which speak of the flight of all the disciples.[53] Perhaps he is ashamed for them that these friends of Jesus are not only not more active but also "keep their distance." When he spoke of

---

46   It is Kilpatrick ("Theme") who has proposed the meaning of "innocent." He has been contradicted by Hanson ("Proto–Luke"). As Karris shows at the beginning of his article ("Death"), the translation "innocent" has become popular.

47   Karris ("Death") also resolutely opts for this sense of "righteous."

48   One remembers that Luke wants to highlight Jesus' innocence in the eyes of the Roman governor, Pilate (see 23:4, 14-15, 22).

49   Talbert (*Reading*, 221–25) offers valuable parallels to the Lukan passion of Jesus in the classic Jewish and Christian literature.

50   According to Ernst (639), the crowd witnessed the crucifixion as a passion play. He adds: "The beginnings of the passion plays are obvious here." In an important article, Klumbies ("Schauspiel") is interested in the term $\vartheta \epsilon \omega \rho \acute{\iota} \alpha$, used by Luke in v. 48.

He notes that for the Greeks of the ancient world the term designates the fact of seeing and giving the meaning of what is seen. Such an understanding appears also in Jewish authors of the day who wrote in Greek, as in *Ep. Arist.* 83–91 in its description of the temple. Klumbies goes even further and expresses the opinion that Luke describes Christ's passion as a theatrical play, turning Mark's mythological presentation into a logical performance marked by a "mythical correctness" (196).

51   Codex Bezae (D = 05) and a Latin manuscript, c, in a slightly different form add the foreheads to the breasts: $\kappa \alpha \grave{\iota} \tau \grave{\alpha} \mu \acute{\epsilon} \tau \omega \pi \alpha$ ("and the foreheads"); see the apparatus in Nestle-Aland (27th ed.) on the passage.

52   See vol. 1 of this commentary, 20–21, on 1:2.

53   It will be remembered that in 22:47-53 Luke omits this detail.

Peter's denial, which was deserving of criticism, Luke used the same adverb: Peter accompanied him, but "at a distance" (μακρόθεν). We have the same adverb here in composite form: "from a distance" (ἀπὸ μακρόθεν). Perhaps Luke also suggests that these men—the masculine form must be taken seriously, since it will be followed by the feminine to describe the women from Galilee—must wait for the resurrection of Christ and the descent of the Holy Spirit to become authorized witnesses. The adjective "all" (πάντες) is important: No one is omitted in this summons; all can become confirmed disciples. Luke is not thinking here of Judas, whose sad end he lets Peter tell in Acts 1:16-20. While Luke likes to use the neuter in Acts,[54] he does use the masculine γνωστός one other time. In the story of the twelve-year-old Jesus, he reports that Mary and Joseph sought the child "among their relatives and acquaintances" (2:44).[55] Grammatically a γνωστός is initially someone who "can be known," then who "is known." But as the knowledge is soon reciprocal, these men who were known to Jesus also knew him well.[56] As 2:44 shows, the γνωστοί are not relatives.[57]

It is Mark who tells Luke that these women are from Galilee. This is convenient for the evangelist, since he distinguishes between two groups: the "daughters of Jerusalem" (23:27-31) and the "women . . . from . . . Galilee . . ." (v. 49). Those from Jerusalem are associated with the Judaism that will witness the punishment of Jerusalem; those from Galilee with the Judaism that will witness the resurrection (see 23:55b—24:8). Since Luke likes to use compound verbs, he does not hesitate to formulate a pleonasm: "to accompany with" (συνακολουθέω) translated as "to accompany."[58] These women whom Luke has mentioned—their existence, their names, the benefit they have derived from their contact with Jesus, and the services they have rendered to the Master and his disciples (8:1-3)—form in his eyes the counterpart of the group of male disciples (v. 49a). Since the evangelist has expressed reservations about the latter (they keep their distance), will he do the same about the former? Their intention is certainly noble. They want to be witnesses; they would like to verify the facts.[59] Later, in v. 55, the evangelist will say that the women from Galilee want to know where the tomb is and how the body of Jesus was placed there. That is again to their credit. Yet they are not prepared to receive the stunning surprise of the empty tomb, since they have to prepare spices and perfumes for their part in the burial of Jesus.[60]

■ **50-51** The presentation of Joseph of Arimathea corresponds to Luke's style. The use of "man" (ἀνήρ), "by name" (ὀνόματι) and "being" (ὑπάρχων, translated as "who was") belong to the evangelist's literary habits.[61] These terms are not in the Markan parallel. The emphasis on the moral qualities of the benefactor is also typical of Luke's thought.[62] Joseph is "good" (ἀγαθός), as is

---

54 See, e.g., Acts 2:14: "Understand what is happening" (τοῦτο ὑμῖν γνωστὸν ἔστω).

55 See vol. 1 of this commentary, 111, on 2:43-45.

56 See Zorell, *Lexicon*, s.v.

57 The Gospel of John uses the term twice in connection with the trial of Jesus: Peter's companion, who accompanies the apostle into the court, is known to the high priest (John 18:15-16).

58 On συνακολουθέω, see BAGD, s.v. See also the occurrences in Josephus cited by Schlatter, 451. In v. 55 Luke will use another compound verb, κατακολουθέω, but about the women who follow Joseph of Arimathea. In the prologue, 1:3, the evangelist has used the verb παρακολουθέω ("to follow," "to inquire"); see vol. 1 of this commentary, 21–23, on 1:3.

59 The form ὁρῶσαι is a present participle feminine nominative plural. The verb ὁράω, which can express active or passive seeing, expresses here the desire to see, thus the active seeing. The present participle emphasizes the duration of this contemplation. See Zorell, *Lexicon*, s.v.

60 There are some minor variants in vv. 49-51 that do not change the meaning; see the apparatus in Nestle-Aland (27th ed.) on this passage. The principal one concerns the participle of the verb συγκατατίθημι; see n. 65 below.

61 See 5:12 and Acts 10:1, e.g., for ἀνήρ; 1:5 and Acts 5:34 for ὀνόματι; and 9:48 and Acts 22:3 for ὑπάρχων. See Cadbury, *Style*, 155.

62 Goulder (*New Paradigm*, 2:771) writes that "Joseph is loaded with Lucan virtue." Mark also emphasizes Joseph's qualities. He calls him εὐσχήμων ("distinguished," "eminent"). Luke, who uses this adjective in Acts 13:50 and 17:12, avoids it here, because in this context he evokes social and not moral qualities. See Fitzmyer, 2:1524–26; Spicq, *Lexicon*, 2:139–42. For his part, Matthew thinks that this man is "rich" and a disciple of Jesus (Matt 27:57).

Barnabas (Acts 11:24), and "righteous" (δίκαιος) as is the aged Simeon (2:25). His pre-Christian virtue predisposes him to be interested in Christ and the gospel. Like those whom the evangelist regards as the future of the church, he is waiting for the kingdom of God, a statement Luke takes from Mark with gratitude.[63]

Joseph is—Mark whispers the term to Luke—a βουλευτής, a member of a βουλή, a "council," probably the Sanhedrin. Without being very specific,[64] Luke indicates that Joseph, the βουλευτής, was associated[65] neither with their βουλή nor with their πρᾶξις. What does he mean by these terms? Does the term βουλή designate here the will, the intention, the project, or the decision of the council? Luke may understand the word here in a negative sense and be thinking of the plot mentioned in 22:1-6 and of the disastrous meeting of the council reported in 22:66-71. As far as the πρᾶξις is concerned, it designates not a particular action but a realization of a plan that includes Jesus' arrest, his hearing, his transfer to Pilate, and his execution (22:47—23:46). Here it has a negative connotation.[66] In his two-volume work Luke contrasts the destructive human decisions with God's plan (the same term βουλή)[67] and the sinful deeds

with the great works of the Lord (for which he uses not πρᾶξις but πράγματα ["events," 1:1], μεγάλα ["great things," 1:49], μεγαλεῖα ["great works," Acts 2:11],[68] or ἔργον ["work," Acts 5:38]). The opinion expressed by Gamaliel in Acts 5:38-39 represents indeed that of Luke himself. He distinguishes between human action and divine action; in the end God's action will prevail.

The evangelist provides one last bit of information about Joseph: he comes from Arimathea, which, he explains, is "a city of the Jews." What does he mean by this added information that is not in his source, Mark? First of all, that Joseph is Jewish, then that the city is located in Judea.[69] As is confirmed with other indications, when Luke expresses himself this way[70] he reveals that he is a Gentile, or at least that it is his intention to speak to the Gentiles.

Thus far the city of Arimathea has not been identified with certainty. Scholars have proposed identifying it with Ramathaim-zophim, the birthplace of Samuel (1 Sam 1:1), mentioned as Ramathaim or Rathamin in 1 Macc 11:34 and Ramathain by Josephus (*Ant.* 13.4.9 §127).[71] This city is located in Ephraim, about thirty kilometers northwest of Jerusalem as the crow flies, northeast of

---

63 Simeon (2:25) was waiting for the consolation of Israel just as Anna's hearers (2:38) were waiting for Jerusalem's deliverance (in both cases the same verb, προσδέχομαι ("to wait for," "to expect"), is used as here in 23:51). On the kingdom of God, see the brief excursus in vol. 2 of this commentary at 13:18.

64 Was Joseph of Arimathea present or not in the morning meeting of the Sanhedrin (22:66-71)?

65 The verb συγκατατίθημι ("to deposit together"), a *hapax legomenon* in the New Testament, in the middle voice in which it almost always appears, means "to consent to," "to agree with," "to give one's vote." It is used in the LXX in Exod 23:32: Israel will consent to no covenant with its opponents nor with their gods. Nestle-Aland's apparatus on the text (27th ed.) has with the negation the perfect participle συγκατατεθειμένος, whose meaning is well suited: "Who has not given his agreement." The variant συγκατατιθέμενος is a present participle, is consistent with the imperfect ἦν ("was") and emphasizes duration. Both readings are well attested; see the apparatus in Nestle-Aland (27th ed.) on the text.

66 It is especially the plural that is used in a nega-

tive sense. Nevertheless, Polybius (2.7.9) uses the singular this way; see Plummer, 541, and BAGD, s.v. πρᾶξις 4b.

67 See 7:30; Acts 2:23; 4:28; 5:38-39; 13:36; see Jacques Dupont (*Le discours de Milet: Testament pastoral de Saint Paul [Actes 20, 18-36* [LD 32; Paris: Cerf, 1962] 119–25), who speaks of "deliberate will" and of "plan."

68 See Gerhard Lohfink, *The Work of God Goes On* (trans. Linda M. Maloney with the assistance of Bonnie Bowman Thurston; Philadelphia: Fortress, 1987).

69 See John 1:19; 11:19, 31, 33, 36, 45, 54, where the words οἱ Ἰουδαῖοι clearly designate the inhabitants of Judea, the Judeans. Like the evangelist John, Luke sometimes uses the term οἱ Ἰουδαῖοι to designate Judeans as opposed to Galileans or Samaritans, sometimes to indicate the Jews as opposed to Gentiles.

70 One may compare the expression "city of the Jews" with the one we encounter in Acts 10:39: "in the territory of the Jews and Jerusalem."

71 Fitzmyer, 2:1526.

Lydda and southeast of Antipatris. Eusebius mentions it under the name of Remphis or Remfthis.[72] Some have also suggested Ramah (Matt 2:18) and Ramallah, fifteen kilometers north of Jerusalem.[73] It is probable that Joseph's ancestors lived in Ramathaim and/or that he himself had been born there. That he has a tomb in Jerusalem suggests that he lives permanently in the capital.[74]

■ **52-53** The parenthesis (v. 51a), the repetition of "this one" (οὗτος, vv. 51, v. 52), the relative clause (v. 51b), as well as the subsequent parataxis (καὶ . . . καὶ . . . καί, vv. 53-54) make this passage one of the most awkward Luke has written.[75] By trying to say too much, the evangelist says it badly. He wants to introduce Joseph socially and religiously and at the same time list his deeds. Unlike Mark (15:43-44), he does not make the request to the governor a separate episode. He does not say—he merely lets it be understood—that the request was granted,[76] and, omitting the governor's surprise[77] and the purchase of the shroud (Mark 15:44-46a), he goes to what in his view is essential,[78] the dual protection offered the corpse.[79] It is wrapped in a shroud[80] and laid in the tomb. It must be remembered here how important burial was in antiquity for the Jews as well as for the Greeks and the Romans. The burial represents the final honor paid to someone who had at one time been a living person, and,

at the same time, it protected the survivors from possible reprisals if the funeral customs were not respected. Funeral ceremonies were usually a family affair. What must have caused the episode to be remembered is that it was precisely a third person rather than a member of the family of Jesus or one of his close disciples who took care of Jesus. Simon of Cyrene, the good thief, and Joseph of Arimathea form a new group of confederates and friends of Jesus against the hostility of the fellow countrymen and Jewish co-religionists, the terror of the disciples who keep their distance, and the indifference of the family of Jesus. In Luke, only the women from Galilee escape this verdict, for in their way they work with Joseph of Arimathea (vv. 55-56).

Was it customary that the friends and relatives of a man condemned to death should ask the legal authorities for the body after the execution? The answer is yes. Such a request was necessary because, according to Roman law, people condemned to death were not to be buried.[81] Along with this legitimate concern for a decent burial[82] there was the duty in Judaism to obey the Mosaic command not to let the sun go down on an unburied person who has been hanged (Deut 21:22-23).[83]

Was it customary to wrap a corpse in a shroud? Again the answer is yes, and philologists and historians can pro-

72 Called Rentis today; Eusebius of Caesarea *Onomasticon* 44ʳ, lines 27–29 [Greek] and 146, lines 27–29 [Latin] (GCS; *Eusebius Werke,* 3:144–45); see Fitzmyer, 2:1526.

73 See F.-M. Abel, *Géographie de la Palestine* (2 vols.; Paris: Gabalda, 1967) 2:428–29; K. Elliger, "Rama," *BHH* 3 (1966) 1548–49 (see also the map in vol. 4). Following Lagrange (596), Benoit writes without giving details or references: "Arimathaea is usually identified as the Arab village of Rentis, to the west of Aboud. Other sites have been suggested by scholars, but Rentis remains the most probable" (*Passion and Resurrection,* 213 n. 1]).

74 His case parallels that of Simon of Cyrene (23:26); see the commentary above on 23:26.

75 See C. F. Evans, 880.

76 A Latin manuscript of the twelfth–thirteenth centuries, c, feels this defect and completes the text: "Now when Pilate had heard that he had died, he praised the Lord and gave the body to Joseph."

77 Unlike in the *Gospel of Peter* (3–5), Joseph makes his request to the governor after the death of Jesus.

78 Luke follows Mark for the deposition and uses the

79 same verb καθαιρέω (aorist καθεῖλον), which means "to take [something or someone] down," "to deposit," then "to demolish," "to destroy."

79 The Markan parallel (15:45) does not hesitate to speak about the πτῶμα ("cadaver"). Luke is satisfied with σῶμα ("body"), knowing that σῶμα can designate the "dead body." That is even its original meaning in Homer; see 17:37; and vol. 2 of this commentary on 17:37.

80 On ἐντυλίσσω, see the analysis above on this section; Blinzler, *Prozess,* 290–93; and BAGD, s.v.

81 See Blinzler, *Prozess,* 282–89; Winkel ("Begräbnis," 7) offers a valuable vocabulary list of terms relating to the burial and the tomb of Jesus.

82 On the text of the Mishna, see n. 95 below; and Rachel Hachlili, *Jewish Funerary Customs, Practices, and Rites in the Second Temple Period* (JSJSup 94; Leiden: Brill, 2005).

83 On the role of Deut 21:22-23 in connection with the passion of Christ, see Blinzler, *Prozess,* 284–86. The Jewish historian Josephus says that, in the Jewish war, the Jews respect the dead at this point and "pay so much regard to obsequies that even those found

vide parallels.[84] The word used here by Luke is σινδών, a term that designates a fabric of cotton or linen, a fine cloth, light and of good quality.[85] It can refer to a piece of clothing—for example, a robe[86]—a sail, a sheet, or a shroud. The three Synoptics choose this word to refer to the shroud of Christ.[87] Mark says that it had to be purchased, and Matthew, that it was of excellent quality. They confirm what the word itself already suggests. A Christian interest is expressed here: the concern to honor Jesus.[88]

It may well be that the remains of the historical Jesus ended without a shroud in a common grave (see Acts 13:27-29). Yet the unexpected appearance of Joseph of Arimathea, neither a disciple nor a relative, makes him a legitimate candidate for historicity.[89] Was it common that he had a tomb in anticipation of his own burial? Here again the answer is positive, and the many tombs from the first century of the Common Era that can still be seen in Jerusalem today are evidence of this concern that one have a dignified and respectable final abode.[90] That some of them have remained unfinished may be an indication that men or women who were rich enough died before completing their own tomb.[91]

While Mark 15:46 speaks of a "monument," "sepulcher" (μνημεῖον), here as in 24:1 Luke prefers the term for "a monument erected in someone's honor," "sepulcher," "tomb" (μνῆμα). Since the two terms can be synonymous and Luke uses the former term two verses later (v. 55) and several times in chap. 24 (24:2, 9, 12, 22, 24), he changes the words for the sake of variety. Even if the adjective λαξευτός ("cut from stone" or "cut in the stone") is a *hapax legomenon* in the New Testament, it is not surprising, because it is used in the LXX and the version of Aquila, as well as by Jewish writers.[92] The term probably indicates that the tomb was made of stones that were not only taken from their quarries and sawed

---

guilty and crucified are taken down and buried before sunset" (*Bell.* 4.5.2 §317; trans. G. A. Williamson). See Benoit, *Passion and Resurrection*, 228.

84 See Blinzler, *Prozess*, 290–93.

85 One likes to say of such cloth that it came from India or Egypt; see Zorell, *Lexicon*, s.v.

86 Thus the garment, mentioned twice, of the young man in Mark 14:51-52, who eventually fled naked,but in Mark is it a robe or a loincloth?

87 On σινδών as a shroud, see Fitzmyer, 2:1527; BAGD, s.v. In the report of the resurrection of Lazarus the word σινδών ("shroud") does not appear. There it is a question of κειρίαι ("bandages") and a σουδάριον, a "face-cloth." In the Easter story John again uses the term σουδάριον ("face-cloth," "cloth") and also mentions ὀθόνια ("cloths" or "strips").

88 Fitzmyer (2:1527–29) introduces the shroud of Turin, which many regard as the shroud of Christ (see the display of the transparent photographs in the Church of Saint-Sulpice in Paris in the summer of 2005). The carbon 14 test that Fitzmyer calls for has been done. It indicates with 95 percent certainty that the relic dates from the Middle Ages (between 1260 and 1390). See P. E. Damon et al., "Radiocarbon Dating of the Shroud of Turin," *Nature* 337 (1989) 611–15. Several persons have tried to cast doubt on these results.

89 His generous act is reminiscent of that of Barnabas, who sold a field and laid the money at the feet of the apostles (Acts 4:36-37). On the historicity of the common tomb or the tomb of Joseph of Arimathea, see Bovon, *Last Days*, 56; and below at the end of the commentary on v. 56.

90 See André Parrot, *Golgotha and the Church of the Holy Sepulchre* (trans. Edwin Hudson; SBA 6; London: SCM, 1957) 84–122; Jack Finegan, *The Archaeology of the New Testament*, vol. 1: *The Life of Jesus and the Beginning of the Early Church* (Princeton: Princeton University Press, 1969) 191–96; Yigael Yadin, ed., *Jerusalem Revealed: Archaeology in the Holy City, 1968–1974* (Jerusalem: Israel Exploration Society, 1975) 63–74; Fitzmyer, 2:1529; Max Küchler, *Jerusalem: Ein Handbuch und Studienreiseführer zur Heiligen Stadt* (OLB 4/2; Göttingen: Vandenhoeck & Ruprecht, 2007) 698–730.

91 Benoit (*Passion and Resurrection*, 214–15), who knows this area, says that everywhere in Palestine there are tombs carved in the rock, as Mark 15:46 says; that in Jerusalem it was easy to carve a funeral chamber; that some but not all tombs were closed by a rolling stone (such as the tomb of Helen of Adiabene called "tomb of the kings"; see Küchler, *Jerusalem*, 985–95); and that the Holy Sepulchre actually preserves the original place of the tomb of Jesus, which was destroyed by a mad caliph; see Küchler, *Jerusalem*, 415–81.

92 The adjective, which is not classical, is used once in the LXX (Deut 4:49), four times in the version of Aquila (Num 21:20; 23:14; Deut 24:1; Josh 13:20) and once in that of Theodotion (Judg 7:11). The verb λαξεύω appears several times in the LXX. As Plummer (542) writes: "Verb and adjective seem

but that they also were carefully cut (Mark 15:46 and Matt 27:60 use the verb λατομῶ, "to cut the stones," to describe the making of the tomb).[93]

The end of v. 53 presents a paradox.[94] According to the Mishna, executed criminals certainly should be buried, but not in the company of those who died honorably, since their remains could contaminate the surrounding graves.[95] Here, however, Luke emphasizes—as, moreover, John also does (John 19:41)—that the tomb was new. Since no one else had been buried in the tomb (caves with several vaults were frequent), Jesus will not contaminate anyone, just as he also will not be defiled by the presence of common dead persons.[96]

■ **54** Luke provides here a new chronological reference (see 22:1, 7, 66): The burial takes place on a Friday, at the end, one can say, of a long day. The Jews called this day παρασκευή ("preparation"), because it was the eve of a Sabbath.[97]

Furthermore, the Sabbath is also mentioned. Unfortunately, the verb that defines it, ἐπιφώσκω, is ambiguous.

Etymologically, the verb suggests that the day, the arrival of the "light" (φῶς), is imminent.[98] But for the Jews the day begins in the evening. It may be that ἐπιφώσκω has lost its etymological meaning "to begin to dawn" and no longer mentions daybreak.[99] A final, perhaps too subtle, possibility is that the Jews calculated, and still calculate, the beginning of the Sabbath at the appearance of a first star, thus at the appearance of a source of "light" (φῶς),[100] which would correspond to the moment described by the evangelist, the evening.[101]

■ **55-56a** The women[102] continue their movement. While Jesus was living, they followed him from Galilee to Jerusalem; by following Joseph,[103] they accompany the dead Jesus from the cross to the grave. To avoid any misunderstanding, Luke identifies them: they are the women mentioned in v. 49 who had come with him[104] from Galilee. Luke still does not give us their names (he will do that in 24:10).

Even if it is Mark who dictates this presence of the women, the way it is presented here corresponds to

---

to belong to the important class of words which became current through having been needed to express Jewish ideas and customs." The adjective λαξευτός comes from the verb λαξεύω, which etymologically is constructed from λᾶας or λᾶς, the "stone," and ξέω ("to scrape," "to plane," "to engrave," "to make an incision in," "to carve").

93 One thinks of the French word *latomies* borrowed from the Greek, the prisons made of quarries such as those in Syracuse.

94 Note the triple negation: οὐκ . . . οὐδείς οὔπω. Luke is emphatic.

95 The Mishna (*Sanh.* 6.5–6) says that there were two burial vaults for people condemned to death, one for those strangled and beheaded, the other for those stoned and burned. Do these stipulations reflect a historical reality, and were they applied in Jesus' day?

96 While various Greek manuscripts are influenced by Matt 27:60 and add the rolling of the stone, Codex Bezae (D = 05) and several other witnesses have submitted to this influence, but they add a detail that may be reminiscent of Homer (*Od.* 9.240–42): The stone was so heavy that twenty people (in Homer twenty-two chariots) were barely able to move it; see Plummer, 542. For the other variants that have little importance, see the apparatus in Nestle-Aland (27th ed.) on the text.

97 To be precise, the term also can mean the day of

preparation for the Passover, but if we stay with Luke's admittedly sometimes awkward chronology, παρασκευή must be translated here as "Friday."

98 Matthew 28:1 uses this verb to speak of the dawning of Easter morning.

99 On the verb, see C. F. Evans, 884; BAGD, s.v.

100 I add: Were candles lit at the beginning of the Sabbath as is done today?

101 The other two Synoptic evangelists also provide a chronological indication, but they do so at the beginning and not at the end of the episode of Joseph of Arimathea (Mark 15:42; Matt 27:57). Both mention the evening.

102 The definite article is missing in many Greek manuscripts. Codex Bezae (D = 05), several Old Latin witnesses, and some Vulgate manuscripts limit the number of women to "two." On the other minor variants of v. 55, see the apparatus of Nestle-Aland (27th ed.) on the text.

103 On κατακολουθέω, see Acts 16:17 (the slave girl with the spirit of a python walked after Paul, thus following him) and several times in the LXX, including 1 Macc 6:23. One could also imagine that κατά implies descent: the latter would then correspond to an underground tomb. See n. 58 above.

104 The form συνεληλυθυῖαι is the feminine perfect participle nominative plural of the verb συνέρχομαι.

Luke's style. The evangelist does not take over from Mark the verb θεωρέω, which he had used in v. 48 with reference to all the spectators. To avoid repetition he chooses θεῶμαι here. I understand this verb as well as θεωρέω in v. 48 as indicating not a simple look but an exact observing or a sustained contemplating. For Christian witness it is important to cover the entire life of Jesus—the ministry, the passion, the death, and the resurrection. But when Luke insists here so much on this activity one could suspect him of wanting to compensate for what is here a deficient witness.

The evangelist, who must consider μνημεῖον here in v. 55 and μνῆμα in v. 53 as equivalents, says that the women look first at the sepulcher itself and then at what it contains. This focus includes the position of the body, not only its location (καὶ ὡς ἐτέθη τὸ σῶμα αὐτοῦ, "and how his body[105] had been placed").

After the women of Galilee had satisfied their legitimate curiosity, they returned to the city to prepare[106] the spices and ointments. Unlike the Egyptians, the Israelites did not embalm their dead. Thus, the spices and ointments were added to the corpse so that as much as possible their scent might overcome the odor of the decomposition and perhaps even slow the pace of decay. The stone that the women think they will have to push or roll (cf. 24:2) not only protects the remains from thieves and animals; it also keeps disagreeable people away (see John 11:39).

The "herbs" are spices made from plants. They can stay dry or be mixed with oils or salves.[107] On visiting the marketplaces of the Middle East it is clear what loving attention the inhabitants of these countries give to spices and perfumes. Luke does indicate the kind and identity of the selected spices.[108] Yet he adds the reference to "ointments." In Greek a μύρον is an "ointment" that can be perfumed. It was a μύρον with which the sinful woman anointed the feet of Jesus (7:38).[109] In that day one anointed the dead as well as the living.[110]

Luke says that the women themselves have prepared these substances, while Mark 16:1 says that they bought them. The time of these preparations also varies. Luke still locates the action on Friday; Mark puts it on the day after the Sabbath, thus on Easter. It is not uncommon for minor variants, which do not affect the general sense, to appear in the various recensions of the same story of martyrdom.

According to Luke, between the preparation and the intended use of the spices and ointments lies the Sabbath, which requires rest (v. 56b).[111]

Exegesis takes place in dialogue with history and theology. On the historical level, the scene we have analyzed has been subjected to a firestorm of criticism. Some have proposed that persons condemned to death ended up in a common grave, while others have trusted the unanimity of the Gospels—Synoptic, Johannine, and even apocryphal. Still others, applying the rules of the history of literary genres, have located the roots of the pericope in the life of a church that remembers its sacred origins. For my part I put myself in the last group of scholars and am inclined to acknowledge that Jesus was buried and

---

105 On σῶμα in the sense of "dead body," "corpse," see n. 79 above.

106 On the verb ἑτοιμάζω ("to prepare") to which Luke often gives a religious significance, see vol. 1 of this commentary, 102–3, on 2:31. A text of the Mishna (*Sabb.* 23.5) permits everything to be done on the Sabbath that is necessary for a burial, in particular washing and anointing the body of the deceased. Fitzmyer (2:1530) rightly wonders whether those provisions already had the force of law before 70 C.E.

107 Mark 16:1 explains that the women wanted to anoint Jesus with the spices.

108 On the spices in antiquity, especially in Israel, see Wilhelm Michaelis, "μύρον κτλ.," *TDNT* 4 (1967) 800–801; idem, "σμυρνίζω," *TDNT* 7 (1971) 458–59; Str-B 2:53; Susan Ashbrook Harvey, *Scenting Salva-*

tion: Ancient Christianity and the Olfactory Imagination (Berkeley, Calif.: University of California Press, 2006).

109 See vol. 1 of this commentary, 294–95, on 7:38.

110 By and large, the Gospel of John (19:39–40) confirms the narrative of the Synoptics. It adds to the spices, however, a mixture of myrrh and aloes weighing about one hundred pounds (according to Benoit, *Passion and Resurrection*, 224), provided by an additional character, Nicodemus. This must be a legendary development.

111 On the burial of Jesus, see Blinzler, *Prozess*, 282–308; Benoit, *Passion and Resurrection*, 203–30; Brown, *Death of the Messiah*, 2:1201–83.

that the early Christians sought to create the memory of his burial. Relevant here is a passage from Acts where Luke cites a less visual kerygmatic tradition than that of the Gospels. According to Acts 13:27-29, it was the Jews hostile to Jesus and not a friendly Joseph of Arimathea who buried the crucified one.[112] This tradition must be older and historically more reliable than the data of the Gospels.

The historical question has theological implications. One of the earliest creeds speaks not only of Jesus' death but also of his burial. The placing of the body in the tomb is the signature to the crucifixion. It is here an argument against any form of Docetism. Thus a passage of the fragment quoted by the apostle Paul: "Christ died for our sins according to the scriptures. He was buried" (1 Cor 15:3b-4a). The story about Joseph of Arimathea serves less as a defense of the incarnation against Docetism than as an apology for the resurrection. If the first Christians wanted to use the empty tomb as an argument, it obviously had to be able to be identified and located. The function that the Gospels of Matthew and Peter assign to the guards accentuates this apologetic effect.[113]

History of Interpretation

Like the entire passion, the death and burial of Jesus have captured the attention of all Christian centuries. Exegetes and spiritual teachers, the authors of passions and the composers of music, have expressed their reaction to the cross and the tomb by reading conjointly the four canonical witnesses.[114] Such consideration to the harmony of the Gospels, however, has not kept people from giving special attention to the Lukan version of the passion of Jesus.[115] From the mass of materials, the following pages will offer only a selection of authors. First I will offer some exegetical works and sermons that embrace the entirety of our passage and then examine some particular aspects, such as the three hours of darkness, the tearing of the curtain, and the centurion's confession, before turning to the last words of Jesus—words that only Luke remembers: "Father, into your hands I commit my spirit" (v. 46).

In his opposition to Marcion, Tertullian (early third century) defends the convergence of the Hebrew Scriptures and the Gospel story. Jesus' fate, dividing the garments,[116] and the piercing of the hands and feet correspond to the Psalms,[117] while the darkness was predicted by Isaiah and Amos.[118] These agreements, which filled Marcion with horror, permitted Tertullian to see the movement of the sun as an affirmation of the cosmic lordship of Christ, for if Christ really were separate from the Creator, the elements would have rejoiced at his defeat. Tertullian takes the last word of Jesus as an argument for the incarnation: it is the flesh that returns the spirit. According to Marcion, mocked by his opponent because of the death of Jesus, the only thing left behind when Jesus died was the ghost of a ghost (*Adv. Marc.* 4.42.4–8).

Ambrose of Milan (late fourth century) sees the cross as a trophy: "On the triumphant gallows" hang "the spoils taken from the age" (*Exp. Luc.* 10.109). This objective aspect of a universal soteriology does not hinder the intimacy of a subjective piety: "Yes, that

---

112 On the historical problems posed by the burial of Jesus, see the bibliographical citations in n. 111.

113 On the Lukan account of the passion and the meaning the evangelist gives to the death of Jesus, see the special bibliographies for Luke 23:44-56a and Luke 23:26-43. See in particular Trilling, *Christusverkündigung*, 191–211; Zehnle, "Death"; Bovon, "Salut"; George, "Sens"; Untergassmair, "Sinndeutung"; Fusco, "Morte"; Radl, "Tod"; Matera, "Death"; Aletti, *Art de raconter*, 155–76; Senior, *Passion*; Carroll, "Crucifixion"; Sylva, *Reimaging*; Kloppenborg, "Exitus"; Smit Sibinga, "Making"; Ehman, "Luke 23:1-49"; Sterling, "*Mors Philosophi*"; Lubich, "Unity"; Taylor, *Passion Narrative;* Büchele, *Tod Jesu;* Franz Georg Untergassmair, *Kreuzweg und Kreuzigung Jesu: Ein Beitrag zur lukanischen Redaktionsgeschichte*

und zur Frage nach der lukanischen "Kreuzestheologie" (Paderborner theologische Studien 10; Paderborn: Schöningh, 1980).

114 See Luz, *Matthew 21–28*, 305–28.

115 See the Polish composer Krzysztof Penderecki, *Passio et mors domini nostri Jesu Christi secundum Lucam* (1966).

116 While Tertullian (*Adv. Marc.* 4.42.4) thinks that Marcion omitted the casting of lots for the garments, Epiphanius says the opposite. It is difficult to explain this contradiction; see the note in René Braun in *Tertullien, Contre Marcion* IV (SC 456:513 n. 7). See the previous section, n. 170.

117 Tertullian refers to Ps 21 (22):19, 17, 8-9.

118 The citations from Isa 50:3 and esp. Amos 8:9 soon become standard in this context.

Christ died for me in his passion to be resurrected after his passion" (10.116). The historical recollection does not exclude the allegorical interpretation. When in his agony Jesus drinks the vinegar, he takes into himself "the evil of the immortality spoiled by Adam" (10.124). When he commits his spirit, he does not lose it; like all things entrusted to him he will regain it (10.126). As the three hours of darkness and the tearing of the temple veil show, this is a great mystery in apocalyptic dimensions (10.126–28). The bishop of Milan emphasizes the uniqueness of each evangelist: Matthew and Mark bear witness to "My God, my God, why have you abandoned me?" John notes that the mother of Jesus and the beloved disciple are nearby. Luke tells of the forgiveness offered the good thief. In speaking of Jesus' "priestly intercession," Ambrose believes that the reception given the thief was the result of Jesus' prayer for his enemies who do not know what they do (10.129–31).[119]

The Venerable Bede (end of the eighth century)[120] wrote a running and balanced commentary on all the verses of our passage (*In Luc.* 6.1716–1884). The darkness at the hour of the crucifixion shows that the Lord died for the sins of Adam, who had been surprised by God in the garden during the afternoon. The tearing of the temple veil represents the transfer of all the mysteries of the law to the multitude of the nations. When he prays to the "Father," Jesus manifests himself as the "Son of God." The centurion's confession prefigures the church's faith. That the spectators beat their breasts can be understood in at least two ways: either because they had demanded the death of the one they had loved during his lifetime, or because they had seen the glory he showed during his death. What strikes the Venerable Bede is the diversity of reactions from the crowd. That the friends of Jesus keep their distance from him is a fulfillment of Psalm 87 (88):19 (God has kept the psalmist's friends away). According to the Vulgate, Joseph of Arimathea was a decurion, whose administrative function the Venerable Bede explains. If his dignity is great in the world, it is even greater before God. To explain the shroud he quotes—as was his custom, without saying so—one of his predecessors, Jerome, who comments on the Gospel of Matthew. The old doctor's authority does not prohibit other interpretations, such as that Jesus' tomb was different from that of other human beings in order to indicate that his work of salvation is different from their weakness and that he will be raised from the dead. And Bede emphasizes—an often repeated thesis— the analogy between Jesus' natural and supernatural birth and his human and special death. After he has explained the days of preparation and the Sabbath, not without referring to the ages of the world, Bede mentions the preparations of the women. Overall, the venerable exegete respects both the literal meaning and the historicity of the passion as well as its figurative and spiritual meaning.

The *Glossa ordinaria* presents the medieval exegesis in compact form and synthesizes many previous interpretations.[121] Whole sentences of Ambrose or the Venerable Bede pass before the reader's eyes, but some notations seem to be original. On the role of Joseph of Arimathea the author points out—is he the only person or the first person to say it?—that Joseph's intervention was providential. For if the apostles had buried Jesus themselves, it would have appeared that the body had not been buried; it had simply disappeared.

Like Bede, Bonaventure analyzes all the elements of the text and compares it with other Gospels to remove

---

119 The recently discovered, probably abbreviated Syriac translation of the end of Cyril of Alexandria's sermons on Luke has not yet been published. Some Greek fragments, however, extracted from the catenae, could be attributed to them; see above, p. 316 n. 187, on 23:26-43; Fragments 2.109 and 110 in Reuss, *Lukas-Kommentare*, 272–73; Payne-Smith, *Cyril*, 2:722–23.

120 Just (*Luke*, 367–73) offers various exegetical extracts in translation from Ephraem the Syrian, from Cyril of Alexandria, from Ambrose of Milan, from Cyril of Jerusalem, from Maximus of Turin, and from Origen. The passages quoted from the sermons of Maximus of Turin are especially interesting. One finds parallels there between the birth and the death of Jesus, between the Virgin Mary and Joseph of Arimathea (*Sermo* 39.1 and *Sermo* 78.2). We learn there that the remains were placed in the tomb of another person in order to indicate that Jesus' death atoned for the sins of others. The body of Jesus stayed in the tomb for only a short time, which means that its sojourn there was more like sleep than death (*Sermo* 39.3).

121 *Glossa ordinaria* Luke 23:44-56 (*PL* 114:348–50).

the contradictions in the details (*Comm. Luc.* 23.54–72).[122] He believes that the darkness was not a natural phenomenon and that the torn veil represents the revelation of the Scriptures to the pagan nations. In order to reconcile Matthew, John, and Luke and to value the three final sayings of Jesus that they transmit, Bonaventure claims that Jesus uttered three final cries. The famous passage in Hebrews (5:7, 9-10) supports Luke's view: With his last breath Jesus uttered a prayer. Mary was present at both ends of her son's life. If at his birth she gave birth in joy, at his death she gave birth in pain. The simplicity of the shroud has inspired the modesty of ecclesiastical garments. On the moral and spiritual level it is also a sign of innocence. These examples may suffice.

The Renaissance does not substantially change the interpretation of our passage. In his *Paraphrasis,* Erasmus of Rotterdam expresses the opinion that the darkness at the time of the death of the one who was the light of the world bears witness to the shock of all nature against this crime. He also sees in the tearing of the veil the announcement of the end of the Jewish cult, since the cross as a sacrifice is sufficient for all time. The last word, "Father, I commit my spirit into your hands" (v. 46), shows that, unlike other human beings, Jesus died not of necessity but by an act of his will.[123] About the confession of the centurion, Erasmus anticipates G. D. Kilpatrick by insisting on Jesus' innocence, and he provides further evidence of his hostility toward the Jews. By declaring Jesus innocent, he condemns those who had unjustly declared him to be guilty. Like many people before him in the Middle Ages, Erasmus believed that those who beat their chests did so for various reasons, some out of respect for Jesus, others from fear of punishment. The

paragraphs on the initiative of Joseph of Arimathea, the burial of Jesus, and the preparations of the women correspond to the genre and the title of the entire work: It is a paraphrase. Yet one remark deserves attention. Having accomplished his task on Friday, Jesus could spend the Sabbath resting in his tomb.[124]

Among the commentaries of the Reformation,[125] that of Calvin distinguishes itself for his clarity, his concern for the literal sense and the harmonization of Scripture, his historical precision, and his theological dimension.[126] Calvin accepts that on the cross "the weakness of the flesh obscured for a short time the glory of the Godhead." Yet "in the disgrace of shame and contempt" God has "raised some portents of the glory to come," such as, "the sun's eclipse, the earthquake, the cloven rock, the tearing of the veil." The darkness, which had to be limited to Judea, also had another function, to awaken the Jewish people and to invite them "to consider his [God's] amazing purpose in the death of Christ." The soteriology forces Calvin to admit that Jesus had to suffer on the cross not only physically because of human cruelty but also spiritually because of the divine condemnation. The Gospel of Luke can complement, even correct the picture, because it "records the words of the second call," helping us understand that Jesus' faith ultimately was not shaken. Jesus refuses to speak to men. "He took his words direct to God and entrusted his testimony of confidence into his very bosom." In doing so, Jesus "gathered up, as it were, all the souls of the faithful in a bundle, to keep them safe with his own." After a few conventional remarks about the torn veil, the exclamation of the centurion, and the reaction of the crowds, Calvin underscores the role of the Galilean women: "Not with-

122 Bonaventure *Comm. Luc.* 23.54–72 (Bernardini, 581–87). The commentary of Bruno of Segni (*Comm. Luc.* 2.48 [*PL* 165:445]) refers essentially to the one that this author has devoted to the Gospel of Matthew.

123 See the comments by Phillips in *Paraphrase,* 222 n. 53.

124 Desiderius Erasmus of Rotterdam, *Paraphrasis,* 463–65; see also idem, *Annotationes,* 216, containing several text-critical and philological observations. See Phillips, *Paraphrase,* 221–26.

125 See Luther, *Evangelien-Auslegung,* 1221–24, 1229–31. For the reformer, the horrible darkness is unnatural and represents a new world. When he pronounces

Ps 30 (31):6, Jesus is taking leave. He does it for our sake so that we can see the heart of God. Now we must repent. The death of Jesus causes agitation and fear among his opponents, consolation and courage among his supporters. As for the burial, it shows Joseph's qualities in contrast to the mediocrity of the apostles during these hours. Finally, Luther emphasizes the various "fruits" of the passion of Jesus, such as the good thief and Joseph of Arimathea.

126 Calvin, *Harmony,* 3:206–18. The quotations come in a sequence from pp. 206, 207, 209–10, 214, and 215.

out reason, however, do the evangelists give first place to the women, as worthy to be put before the men." God is behind the testimony of these women. Calvin concludes the explanation of chap. 23 by saying that the burial of Christ is "a transitional passage from the ignomy of the cross to the glory of the resurrection."[127]

If we want to observe the impact of certain verses on Christian civilization, we can draw on the works of Pierre de Labriolle and Rufino M. Grández dealing with the three hours of darkness (vv. 44-45a). This darkness and the mention of a solar eclipse by a pagan author Phlegon have occupied the spirits since the second century.[128] Some pagan opponents of Christianity appear to reduce the hours of darkness to an ordinary eclipse, while a Pseudo-Origen and Julius Africanus have defended the miracle of the darkness. Later Tertullian, Origen, and Eusebius used the darkness to include the Gospel story in the universal chronology.[129] Some ecclesiastical writers, such as Cyprian (*Test.* 2.23),[130] have drawn on biblical prophecies, for example, Amos 8:9-10 and Jer 15:9, to proclaim the event. These references, found even before Cyprian, quickly became traditional. Dionysius the Areopagite (late fifth century) plays an important

role in this history of interpretation.[131] He believes that there is no need to rely on Gentile authors. Since as a universal cause Christ was able to achieve such a miracle, a natural explanation is not necessary. The exegetes of the scholastic period, such as Albert the Great, adopted this interpretation (*Evang. Luc.* 23.45).[132] Between the sixteenth and twentieth centuries, the hypothesis of an eclipse reappears, but some refer to it as supernatural. At the end of the sixteenth century John Maldonat devoted no fewer than four pages of his commentary on Matthew to this theme.[133] With the emergence of the historical consciousness and modern scholarship, criticisms began to appear, and there was an increase in academic discussions. In 1720, for example, Augustin Calmet published in Paris a *Dissertation sur les ténèbres arrivées à la mort de Jesus-Christ.* For his part, Ernst Renan in his *Vie de Jésus*[134] evades the problem of the three hours of darkness and prefers to occupy himself with the psychology of the one who is dying.

A remarkable article by André Pelletier makes it possible to understand the hesitations of the first Christian centuries concerning the tearing of the temple veil (v. 45b).[135] One sees two different orientations. One of

---

127 I have before me the *Annotationes* of Hugo Grotius (913–25). I read there, among other things, philological and exegetical comments on the future παραθήσομαι (v. 46), the reading he preferred, giving it a present sense, or on the verb ἐπιφώσκω (v. 54), which evokes here the moon and the stars, which become bright, and not the rising sun. I also have access to Bengel's exegetical and theological notes in his *Gnomon* (G) 1.413–14. If the Father receives the spirit of Jesus, he writes on v. 46, so Jesus welcomes the spirit of the believer. As for the crowds mentioned in v. 48 who had been manipulated to shout "crucify!" they change their attitude and their state of mind. That is a preparation for Pentecost. Finally, by placing Jesus' body in his own tomb, Joseph of Arimathea (v. 53) prefigures the believers who die with their Lord and are buried with him. And as Jesus will remain in the tomb only a short time, so too will the believer. God is the God of the living.

128 Pierre de Labriolle, *La réaction païenne: Étude sur la polémique antichrétienne du Iᵉ au VIᵉ siècle* (1934; reprinted Paris: Cerf, 2005) 204–20; Grández, "Tinieblas." Maurice Goguel (*Jesus and the Origins of Christianity*, vol. 1: *The Life of Jesus* [trans. Olive Wyon; New York: Harper, 1960] 91–93) thought he

could demonstrate that a Samaritan named Thallus who lived in Rome in the middle of the first century C.E. already engaged in a polemic against the Christians about the darkness during the crucifixion. Yet the first real evidence about the polemic dates from the third century.

129 Pseudo-Origen *Comm. Matt.* (*PG* 17:309); the fragment of Julius Africanus is preserved by George Syncellus and published in *PG* 10:88–89; Tertullian *Apol.* 5–6; Origen *Cels.* 2.33, 59; Eusebius *Chronicon (anni 32)* (*Eusebius Werke* 7, GCS 47:174–76); Plummer, 537.

130 See also Eusebius *Dem. evang.* 10.6.6–8; 10.8.8, 15–16 (*Eusebius Werke* 6, GCS 23:468–74).

131 Dionysius the Areopagite *Theologia mystica, Epistula* 7.2 (*PG* 3:1081).

132 Albert the Great *Evang. Luc.* 23.45 (733).

133 Juan de Maldonado, *Commentarii in quatuor evangelistas*, vol. 2 (ed. Franz Sausen; Paris/Louvain, 1841) 403–7.

134 Renan (*Life*, 367) writes: "The sky was dark; and the earth, as in all the environs of Jerusalem, dry and gloomy."

135 Pelletier, "Tradition."

them links the theme of knowing to what is ultimately an unveiling or a disclosure. For Augustine, the episode makes manifest the grace of Christ the Mediator: "Earlier this reality was present among the people . . . but it was in a latent state; now it is perceivable to all nations as an openly visible space."[136] The other major line of interpretation connects the desecration of the rituals with what is primarily a tearing. The event is a sign that the ceremonies of the temple are abrogated. Thus, Theodoret of Cyrus interprets the episode as the desecration of the Holy of Holies: "The tearing of the curtain shows concretely that the grace that was located there simply abandoned the sanctuary, and what once was available only to the one high priest has become secular."[137]

These two interpretations can be combined. Thus Sedulius, a Christian poet of the fourth century, writes in his *Paschale Carmen*: "Like a little boy in tears, the glorious temple sees the collapse of the pinnacle of the other temple that is greater than it is. It bares its wounded breast to show that from now on its secret mysteries can be revealed to future generations, since the Law of Moses, long hidden under the veil, is opened to us by the coming of Christ."[138]

The first interpretation can also be subdivided, according to whether the authors regard the first or the second veil as an object of divine intervention. If it is the first curtain, the veil that covers the access to the temple itself, the revelation given by the tear is only partial. One must wait for the eschatological tear of the second veil that covers the entrance to the Holy of Holies to see no longer as in a mirror but face to face.[139] If it is the second

veil that is torn, then, as a fragment attributed to Chrysostom says, "everything that one was forbidden to see in the *adyton* becomes visible to the whole world."[140]

As one can imagine, the two major interpretations, the revelation and the abrogation, each involved a great deal of hostility toward the Jews. Chrysostom or one of his successors says, "That way God shows that all the mysteries of the Jews are profane and that their shame will be made manifest to the whole world."[141] Fifteen centuries later it would be the perpetrators of such interpretations who would bear the shame.

In his *Sacred Biography*, Thomas J. Heffernan mentions and analyzes the role that Jesus' last words (v. 46) played in the lives of the saints of the Middle Ages.[142] Like Luke, who modeled Stephen's martyrdom after the passion of Christ, the medieval biographers attributed to the saints when telling of their deaths characteristics and words that the Gospels report about Jesus. Thus, Walter Daniel relates about the abbot Aelred (twelfth century) that when he died he said, "Into your hands I commit my spirit."[143] In this regard, Heffernan points out several medieval interpretations of the last words of Jesus according to Luke. The reader will realize that the word "spirit" (*spiritus*) was likely to have various nuances. For some, it was the individual breath of life given to all creatures. For others, it was the spirit of God himself, which, according to Gen 2:7, he gave to Adam and only to the human race.[144] Regardless of the interpretation given, the medieval exegetes sometimes give it trinitarian connotations: Does not the Spirit connect the Father with the Son?

136 Et tunc ergo . . . erat in populo Dei, sed . . . inerat latens; nunc autem . . . in omnibus gentibus tanquam area cernitur patens (Augustine of Hippo *Liber de peccato originali* 25 (*PL* 44:400).

137 Theodoret of Cyrus *In Danielem* 9.27 (*PG* 81:1481); see Pelletier, "Tradition," 162–63.

138 Sedulius, *Paschale Carmen* 5.270–75 (CSEL 10:134); see Pelletier, "Tradition," 165.

139 See Origen's interpretation, *Comm. Matt. Ser. 138* (*Origenes Werke* 11, GCS 38:285–86).

140 *Symbolorum . . . in Mattheum*, vol. 1 (ed. P. Poussines; Toulouse, 1646) on Matt 27:45-53; see Pelletier, "Tradition," 162. Since I did not have access to this edition of P. Poussines, I am relying on the work of Pelletier.

141 *Symbolorum . . . in Mattheum*, vol. 1 (ed. P. Poussines;

Toulouse, 1646) on Matt 27:45-53; see Pelletier, "Tradition," 163.

142 Thomas J. Heffernan, *Sacred Biography: Saints and Their Biographers in the Middle Ages* (New York: Oxford University Press, 1988) 74–87. I thank Beverly Kienzle, who gave me this reference.

143 *Vita sancti Aelredi*, 56–57; see Walter Daniel, *The Life of Aelred of Rievaulx* (trans. and notes by F. M. Powicke; introduction by Marsha Dutton; Cistercian Fathers Series 57; Kalamazoo, Mich.: Cistercian Publications, 1994) 137–38.

144 I adapt Heffernan (*Sacred Biography*, 83–85) to my way of looking at the data, who is not very clear on the matter.

Historians of art and, more modestly, museum visitors know that there are two main types of the crucifixion. One of them, which could be called eastern, has only the cross of Jesus Christ surrounded by his mother and the beloved disciple. The one that could be called western depicts in historical and narrative manner a large stage including the three crosses and all the characters associated with these tragic hours.[145] This second type corresponds to Luke's intentions. On the centurion (v. 47), however, artists, and especially their patrons, prefer the version of Matthew and Mark. They retain the expression "Truly, this was the Son of God," rather than the Lukan expression, "This man was truly righteous." The same is true of the grisaille fabric from Bayonne (fifteenth century) preserved in the Louvre. The phylactery attached to the centurion contains, as expected, the title in Latin "Son of God."[146] In fact, in conformity with the principle of Gospel harmony, a number of exegetes, preachers, and theologians make the same choice. In his explanation of Luke, Ambrose already says: "Finally, here is the centurion himself who calls him the Son of God whom he himself had crucified" (*Exp. Luc.* 10.128).

The exegete who is interested in the history of the influence (*Wirkungsgeschichte*) of the deposition from the cross and the burial will also turn to art. The manuals of Louis Réau and Gertrud Schiller and the *Lexikon zur christlichen Ikonographie* edited by Engelbert Kirschbaum[147] and the final volume of Ulrich Luz's Matthew commentary make it possible for one to become familiar

with these interpretations.[148] The collection of Arthur A. Just[149] offers the possibility of following the patristic interpretation of these episodes (vv. 48-56a).

Conclusion

It was not without reason that Martin Dibelius compared the Lukan version of the passion of Jesus with a martyrdom narrative.[150] Indeed, the narration tends to make visible, even spectacular, the successive episodes. The martyr himself faces his fate with admirable courage. The readers or listeners are challenged, and the invitation they receive leads them on the way of imitation. It would be a mistake, however, to take this comparison so far that the Master's courage would become that of a hero and his attitude would be closer to that of the Stoic view of Socrates than to that of the Suffering Servant of Isaiah,[151] because according to Luke Jesus' humanity remains entire. Just as fear came over him on the Mount of Olives, here Jesus can do nothing except pray (v. 46). While he does not mention, as he does in Matthew and Mark, that he feels abandoned, Jesus lives through what he had predicted (22:53), the hours of darkness, and he does not escape death.[152]

If the elements of the darkness and temple veil confirm the dramatic character of the present hour, the attitude of the people, changed by the extent of Jesus' agony and death, testifies not only to the exemplary character but also to the redemptive nature of the passion.[153]

---

145 See Réau (*Iconographie,* 2.2:492–93), who offers even more subdivisions; see also Schiller (*Iconography,* 2:88–164); and Engelbert Kirschbaum, ed., *Lexikon der christlichen Ikonographie* (8 vols.; Rome: Herder, 1968–76) 2:562–90, 600–642.

146 Réau (*Iconographie,* 2.2:497) has little interest in this person but says that this was the content of the phylactery on the centurion on the main altar of Conrad of Soest in Niederwildungen (1404).

147 Réau, *Iconographie,* 2.2:513–28; Schiller, *Iconography,* 2:164–84; Kirschbaum, *Lexikon* (see n. 145 above), 590–95, 192–96.

148 Luz, *Matthew 21–28,* 515–21, 527–30, 531–33, 537, 545–50, 554–59, 581–83.

149 Just, *Luke,* 370–73.

150 Dibelius, *Tradition,* 201–3.

151 I am opposing here a tendency of contemporary Lukan research influenced by the work of Neyrey, "Absence"; Kloppenborg, "Exitus"; and Sterling, "*Mors Pholosophi.*"

152 See the remarkable doctoral dissertation by Claire Clivaz published as *L'ange et la sueur de sang.* See above, p. 211 n. 124, on 22:39-46.

153 See Bovon, "Salut."

The Empty Tomb and the Fullness of the Message (23:56b—24:12)

Bibliography

Akaabiam, Terwase H., *The Proclamation of the Good News: A Study of Lk 24 in Tiv Context* (EHS.T 673; Frankfurt a. M./New York: Lang, 1999).

Baldensperger, Guillaume, "Le tombeau vide," *RHPhR* 12 (1932) 413–43; 13 (1933) 105–44; 14 (1937) 97–125.

Bedenbender, Andreas, "Geschlechtertausch und Geschlechtsverlust (Lk 24,10 und Pred 7,27): Zur Funktion der Attribute 'männlich' und 'weiblich' im Lukasevangelium und im Prediger Salomo," *TeKo* 21 (1998) 17–34.

Benoit, *Passion and Resurrection*, 231–61.

Bickermann, Elias, "Das leere Grab," *ZNW* 23 (1924) 281–92.

Bode, Edward Lynn, *The First Easter Morning: The Gospel Accounts of the Women's Visit to the Tomb of Jesus* (AnBib 45; Rome: Biblical Institute Press, 1970) 105–26.

Brändle, Max, "Auferstehung Jesu nach Lukas," *Orientierung* 24 (1960) 84–89.

Brock, *Mary Magdalene*, 19–40.

Campenhausen, Hans von, *Der Ablauf der Osterereignisse und das leere Grab* (2d ed.; SHAW.PH 2; Heidelberg: Winter, 1958).

Chafins, T. L., "Women and Angels . . . When They Speak, It's Time to Listen! A Study of the Structure of Luke 23:50—24:12," *AThJ* 21 (1990) 11–17.

Craig, William Lane, "The Disciples' Inspection of the Empty Tomb (Lk 24,12-24/Jn 20,2-10)," in Adelbert Denaux, ed., *John and the Synoptics* (BEThL 101; Leuven: Leuven University Press, 1992) 614–19.

Idem, "The Historicity of the Empty Tomb of Jesus," *NTS* 31 (1985) 39–67.

Curtis, K. Peter G., "Luke xxiv.12 and John xx.3-10," *JTS* 22 (1971) 512–15.

Dauer, Anton, "Lk 24,12: Ein Produkt lukanischer Redaktion," in Frans van Segbroeck et al., eds., *The Four Gospels, 1992: Festschrift Frans Neirynck* (3 vols.; BEThL 100; Leuven: Leuven University Press, 1992) 2:1697–1716.

Idem, "Zur Authentizität von Lk 24,12," *EThL* 70 (1994) 294–318.

DeGuglielmo, Antonine, "Emmaus," *CBQ* 3 (1941) 293–301.

Dhanis, Édouard, ed., *Resurrexit: Actes du symposium international sur la résurrection de Jésus* (Rome: Libreria editrice vaticana, 1974).

Dillon, Richard J., *From Eye-Witnesses to Ministers of the Word: Tradition and Composition in Luke 24* (AnBib 82; Rome: Biblical Institute Press, 1978) 1–68.

Dupont, Jacques, "Les discours de Pierre dans les Actes et le chapitre XXIV de l'Évangile de Luc," in Frans Neirynck, ed., *L'Évangile de Luc—The Gospel of Luke* (2d ed.; BEThL 32; Leuven: Leuven University Press/Peeters, 1989) 329–71; reprinted in idem, *Nouvelles études*, 58–111.

Dussaut, Louis, "Le triptyque des apparitions en Luc 24 (analyse structurelle)," *RB* 94 (1987) 161–213.

Eckardt, A. Roy, "Why Do You Search among the Dead?" *Encounter* 51 (1990) 1–17.

Ehrman, *Corruption*, 212–17.

Engelbrecht, J., "The Empty Tomb (Lk 24:1-12) in Historical Perspective," *Neot* 23 (1989) 235–49.

Ernst, Josef, "Schriftauslegung und Auferstehungsglaube bei Lukas," *ThGl* 60 (1970) 360–74; reprinted in idem, *Schriftauslegung: Beiträge zur Hermeneutik des Neuen Testaments und im Neuen Testament* (Munich: Schönigh, 1972) 177–92.

Gaechter, Paul, "Die Engelerscheinungen in den Auferstehungsberichten," *ZKTh* 89 (1967) 191–202.

Gerits, H., "Le message pascal au tombeau (Lc 24,1-12): La résurrection selon la présentation théologique de Luc," *EstTeol* 8, no. 15 (1981) 3–63.

Gollwitzer, Helmut, *Jesu Tod und Auferstehung nach dem Bericht des Lukas* (6th ed.; KT 44; Munich: Kaiser, 1979).

Grass, *Ostergeschehen*, 15–23, 32–35.

Hengel, Martin, "Maria Magdalena und die Frauen als Zeugen," in Otto Betz et al. (eds.), *Abraham unser Vater: Juden und Christen im Gespräch über die Bibel: Festschrift für Otto Michel zum 60. Geburtstag* (Arbeiten zur Geschichte des Spätjudentums und Urchirstentums 5; Leiden: Brill, 1963) 243–56.

Hodges, Zane C., "The Women and the Empty Tomb," *Biblia Sacra* 123 (1966) 301–9.

Hoffmann, Paul, "Der garstige breite Graben: Zu den Anfängen der historisch-kritischen Osterdiskussion," in idem, *Tradition und Situation: Studien zur Jesusüberlieferung in der Logienquelle und den synoptischen Evangelien* (NTAbh n.F. 28; Münster: Aschendorff, 1995) 341–72.

Ilan, Tal, *Jewish Women in Greco-Roman Palestine: An Inquiry into Image and Status* (Peabody, Mass.: Hendrickson, 1996) 163–66.

Jeremias, Joachim, *Heiligengräber in Jesu Umwelt (Mt 23,29; Lk 11,47): Eine Untersuchung zur Volksreligion der Zeit Jesu* (Göttingen: Vandenhoeck & Ruprecht, 1958).

Johnson, Luke Timothy, "Luke 24:1-11: The Not-So-Empty Tomb," *Int* 46 (1992) 57–61.

Kremer, Jacob, "Zur Diskussion über das 'leere Grab,'" in Édouard Dhanis, ed., *Resurrexit: Actes du symposium international sur la résurrection de Jésus* (Rome: Libreria editrice vaticana, 1974) 137–68.

341

LaVerdiere, Eugene A., "The Passion and Resurrection of Jesus according to St. Luke," *ChiSt* 25 (1986) 35–50.

Léon-Dufour, Xavier, *Résurrection de Jésus et message pascal* (Parole de Dieu; Paris: Seuil, 1971) 173–245.

Mainville, Odette, "De Jésus à l'Église: Étude rédactionnelle de Luc 24," *NTS* 51 (2005) 192–211.

Meynet, *Évangile*, 1:222–25; 2:235–36, 243–44.

Idem, *Jésus passe: Testament, jugement, exécution et résurrection du Seigneur Jésus dans les évangiles synoptiques* (Rhétorique Biblique 3; Rome: Pontificia Università Gregoriana, 1999).

Idem, *Quelle est donc cette parole?: Lecture rhétorique de l'Évangile de Luc (1–9, 22–24)* (2 vols.; LD 99; Paris: Cerf, 1979) 1:188–91; vol. 2, plate 14 and D4.

Muddiman, John, "A Note on Reading Luke xxiv.12," *EThL* 48 (1972) 542–48.

Nauck, Wolfgang, "Die Bedeutung des leeren Grabes für den Glauben an den Auferstandenen," *ZNW* 47 (1956) 243–67.

Neirynck, Frans, "*ANATEIΛANTOΣ TOY HΛIOY* (Mc 16,2)," *EThL* 54 (1978) 70–103; reprinted in idem, *Evangelica: Gospel Studies = Evangelica: Études d'évangile: Collected Essays* (ed. Frans van Segbroeck; 3 vols.; BEThL 60, 99, 150; Leuven: Peeters, 1982) 2:181–214.

Idem, "*AΠHΛΘEN ΠPOΣ EAYTON*: Lc 24,12 et Jn 20,10," *EThL* 54 (1978) 104–18; reprinted in idem, *Evangelica*, 1:441–55.

Idem, "Lc xxiv.12: Les témoins du texte occidental," in T. Baarda et al., eds., *Miscellanea Neotestamentica: Studia ad Novum Testamentum Praesertim Pertinentia* (NovTSup 47–48; Leiden: Brill, 1978) 45–60; reprinted in idem, *Evangelica*, 2:313–28.

Idem, "Luke 24,12: An Anti-Docetic Interpolation?" in Adelbert Denaux, ed., *New Testament Textual Criticism and Exegesis: Festschrift J. Delobel* (BEThL 161; Leuven: Peeters, 2002) 145–58.

Idem, "Lc 24,36-43. Un récit lucanien," in *À cause de l'Évangile: Études sur les Synoptiques et les Actes. Offertes au P. Jacques Dupont, O.S.B. à l'occasion de son 70e anniversaire* (LD 123; Paris: Cerf, 1985) 655–80.

Idem, "Once More Luke 24,12," *EThL* 70 (1970) 319–40.

Idem, "παρακύψας βλέπει: Lc 24,12 et Jn 20,5," *EThL* 53 (1977) 113–52; reprinted in idem, *Evangelica*, 2:401–40.

Idem, "Le récit du tombeau vide dans l'évangile de Luc (24,1-12)," *OLP* 6/7 (1975–76) 427–41; reprinted in idem, *Evangelica*, 2:297–312.

Idem, "A Supplementary Note on Lk 24,12," *EThL* 72 (1996) 425–30, reprinted in idem, *Evangelica* 3:572–78.

Idem, "The Uncorrected Historic Present in Lk xxiv.12," *EThL* 48 (1972) 548–53; reprinted in idem, *Evangelica*, 2:329–34.

Osborne, Grant R., *The Resurrection Narratives: A Redactional Study* (Grand Rapids: Baker, 1984) 99–146.

Parrot, *Holy Sepulchre*, 49–59.

Parsons, Mikeal C., "A Christological Tendency in 𝔓75," *JBL* 105 (1986) 463–79.

Perkins, Pheme, *Resurrection: New Testament Witness and Contemporary Reflection* (Garden City, N.Y.: Doubleday, 1984) 113–94.

Plevnik, Joseph, "'The Eleven and Those with Them' according to Luke," *CBQ* 40 (1978) 205–11.

Idem, "The Eyewitnesses of the Risen Jesus in Luke 24," *CBQ* 49 (1987) 90–103.

Prete, Benedetto, "L'annunzio dell'evento pasquale nella formulazione di Luca 24,5-7," *SacDoc* 16 (1971) 485–523; reprinted in idem, *L'opera di Luca: Contenuti e prospettive* (Turin: Leumann, Elle di ci, 1986) 281–306.

Rigato, M.-L., "Remember, Then They Remembered: Lk 24.6-8," in Gerald O'Collins and Gilberto Marconi, eds., *Luke and Acts* (trans. Matthew J. O'Connell; New York: Paulist, 1993) 269–80.

Ross, J. M., "The Genuineness of Luke 24:12," *ExpT* 98 (1986–87) 107–8.

Sabugal, Santos, "La Resurrección de Jesús en el Evangelio de Lucas (Lc 24,1-49)," *RevAg* 33 (1992) 463–94.

Schenke, Ludger, *Auferstehungsverkündigung und leeres Grab: Eine traditionsgeschichtliche Untersuchung von Mk 16,1-8* (SBS 33; Stuttgart: Katholisches Bibelwerk, 1968).

Schubert, Paul, "The Structure and Significance of Luke 24," in Walther Eltester, ed., *Neutestamentliche Studien für Rudolf Bultmann: zu seinem Geburtstag am 20. August 1954* (BZNW 21; Berlin: Töpelmann, 1954) 165–86.

Seim, Turid Karlsen, "Conflicting Voices, Irony, and Reiteration: An Exploration of the Narrational Structure of Luke 24.1-35 and Its Theological Implications," in Ismo Dunderberg et al., eds., *Fair Play: Diversity and Conflicts in Early Christianity: Essays in Honour of Heikki Räisänen* (NovTSup 103; Leiden/Boston: Brill, 2002) 151–64.

Shellard, Barbara, "The Relationship of Luke and John: A Fresh Look at an Old Problem," *JTS* 46 (1995) 70–98.

Sleczka, Reinhard, "'Nonsense' (Lk 24.11): Dogmatische Beobachtungen zu dem historischen Buch von Gerd Lüdemann, 'Die Auferstehung Jesu. Historie. Erfahrung. Theologie,'" *KD* 40 (1994) 170–81.

Swanson, *Manuscripts*, 405–9.

Tilborg, Sjef van, and Patrick Chatelion Counet, *Jesus' Appearances and Disappearances in Luke 24* (Biblical Interpretation Series 45; Leiden: Brill, 2000) 23–51.

Wallace, Robert W., *"Ορθρος,"* *TAPA* 119 (1989) 201–7.

23:56b   **They rested on the Sabbath according to the commandment. 24:1/ But on the first day of the week,[a] early in the morning,[b] they went to the tomb with the spices they had prepared. 2/ But they found the stone rolled away from the tomb. 3/ When they had entered, they did not find the body of the Lord Jesus. 4/ And it happened that while they were troubled about it, behold, two men stood before them in dazzling apparel. 5/ While they were seized with fear with their faces bowed to the ground, the men said, "Why do you seek the Living among the dead? 6/ He is not here but is risen.[c] Remember what he said to you while he was still[d] in Galilee. 7/ He said[e] that the Son of Man must be delivered into the hands of sinful men, be crucified, and rise again on the third day." 8/ And they remembered his words. 9/ When they had returned from the tomb, they told all of this to the Eleven and to all the others. 10/ This was[f] Mary Magdalene, Joanna, Mary the mother of James,[g] and the other women with them. They said this to the apostles. 11/ And these words appeared to them to be nonsense, and they did not believe the women.[h] 12/ But Peter rose and ran to the tomb and when he had stooped to look he saw only the linen cloths. He then returned home,[i] amazed at what had happened.**

a   Literally: "of the Sabbaths."

b   Literally: "while the dawn was deep."

c   Literally: "he has been resurrected."

d   I am adding this necessary adverb in French and English.

e   Literally: "saying."

f   Literally: "they were."

g   Literally: "Mary of James."

h   Literally: "them."

i   The expression also suggests that he returned to himself.

Chapter 24 of the Gospel constitutes the second wing of a diptych: it represents the victory of life over the power of death (chaps. 22–23). More broadly, it serves as a transition between the first and the second of Luke's books, concluding the life of Jesus and preparing the beginnings of the church.[1]

Synchronic Analysis

Exegetes have suggested various plans of this chapter. Paul Schubert has discerned three principal parts: the empty tomb, the Emmaus meeting, and the appearance to the disciples, followed by the ascension. For him, the story

---

1   Akaabiam (*Proclamation*, 14–20) offers a variety of contemporary views on Luke 24.

culminates in the manifestation of Christ to explain the Scriptures and to underscore the fulfillment of the prophecies.[2] Grant R. Osborne emphasizes the linear development of the story:[3] Each section summarizes the details of the previous section while adding a new element. He also notes the soteriological characteristic of the chapter, the ecclesiological repercussions of the events, the role of the witnesses, and the central place occupied by Jerusalem. He distinguishes four parts: the empty tomb (23:54—24:12), the appearance in Emmaus (24:13-35), the appearance to the Eleven (24:36-49), and the ascension (24:50-53). Finally, he subdivides each part. The subdivisions he sees in the empty tomb episode are as follows: the movement of the women (23:54—24:1); the opening of the tomb (24:2-3); the angelic message (24:4-8); the report of the women (24:9-11); and Peter's reaction (24:12).

Odette Mainville affirms the unity of the chapter and the progression of the story.[4] Thematically she discloses a continuing theological dimension, an ethical scope, and a missionary verve. Formally, she identifies six successive units: (1) the revelation at the tomb (24:1-11); (2) Peter's run to the tomb (24:12); (3) the instruction of the Emmaus disciples (24:13-32); (4) the authentication of the Emmaus disciples (24:33-35); (5) the mission of the disciples (24:36-49); (6) the blessing and the departure (24:50-53). Using the image of a mosaic, the Quebec exegete believes that the entire unit forms a bridge between the message of Jesus and the kerygma of the apostles.

Advocates of formal analyses have been concerned to regard the chapter as a whole and, not without hesitations and disputes, have suggested several schematizations of its various parts.[5] Louis Dussaut, for example, divides the chapter into three parts (24:1-12; 24:13-33a; 24:33b-53), each of which is centered on an appearance and has a concentric structure.[6] He adds that Luke 24

also contains what he calls four "biographical kerygmata" (passages relating to Christ, 24:6b-8; 24:19b-21; 24:25-27; 24:44-48). These testimonies also have a literary function: They serve as pillars that support the three concentric symmetries. The author of this study conceives of the pericope of the empty tomb (24:1-12) in the following way. After the introduction (vv. 1-2), the body of the episode is divided into two parts: the entry to the tomb (vv. 3-8) and the return along with the message to the community (vv. 9-11). The literary unit ends with Peter's visit to the tomb, which serves as a conclusion (v. 12). The call to remember (vv. 6b-8), the first "biographical kerygma," is the center of the section.

In my view, the Christian message proclaimed by Peter in the Acts of the Apostles invites us to understand Luke 24 as the counterpart of chaps. 22–23. Indeed, the contrasting pattern (*Kontrastschema*) that is the focus of the christological sermons (see, e.g., Acts 4:10) explains that the "resurrection" part (Luke 24) corresponds to the "passion" part (Luke 22–23). In addition, Luke 24 has its own process and coherence. If the proponents of formal analyses have difficulty agreeing, it is because Luke organizes disparate materials. Whenever they agree, it is because they have found a redactor's victorious will. In my opinion, here in Luke 24 Luke tries to structure in an elegant way the memories he has received and adapted. The empty tomb prepares for the meeting with the living Christ. The Emmaus disciples meet the Risen One and recognize him. In the appearance to the Eleven there is a demonstration of the resurrection, a theological interpretation with the help of the Scriptures, and a missionary command added to a recognition. The ground is well prepared for the Christian proclamation to take flight. Thus, Jesus Christ can leave the stage, which he does in the final episode, the ascension.

---

2   Schubert, "Structure"; see Bovon, *Luke the Theologian*, 89, 92–94. Sabugal ("Resurrección") emphasizes the unity of Luke 24 and demonstrates its coherent structure.

3   Osborne, *Resurrection Narratives*, 99–146. Akaabiam (*Proclamation*, 20–26) also underscores what he calls the dialectical movement and dynamic nature of Luke 24.

4   Mainville, "De Jésus à l'Église."

5   See Aletti, *Art de raconter*, 177–98; Meynet, *Parole*, 1:188–91, and vol. 2, plate 14; idem, *Évangile,* 1:235–

44; 2:223–37. According to Meynet "this sequence includes two sub-sequences consisting of three and five passages surrounding a central sub-sequence, the story of the Emmaus pilgrims, in which it is possible to recognize three passages" (*Évangile,* 1:235). The author emphasizes the chiastic structure of the chapter, whose center he sees in v. 23 (Jesus lives). Dussaut ("Triptyque," 162 n. 3) calls attention to additional literature.

6   Dussaut, "Triptyque."

Staying with Luke 23:56b—24:12, I propose the following structuration. Luke 23:56b—24:1 serves as an introduction in two periods, in two days: on the Sabbath (v. 56b) and on the first day of the week (v. 1). Logically, the first is characterized by rest and the second by activity. Note the contrast μέν (v. 56b)—δέ (v. 1), "on the one hand," "on the other" (translated as "they rested," "but they"). After this introduction, after these preparations, in vv. 2-3 Luke cleverly contrasts what the women find (and did not expect to find), the open tomb, and what they do not find (and expected to find), the body of Jesus. The contrast between "they found" (εὗρον) and "they did not find" (οὐχ εὗρον) is striking. As surprising as they may be, however, these two incidents are still part of the preliminaries. The essential part of the story begins in v. 4 in the manner of the LXX with the words "and it came to pass, as . . . ." (καὶ ἐγένετο ἐν τῷ . . .).[7] The women are confused (v. 4a, following their double surprise) when two "men," two angels, come to them (v. 4b). This new contrast, between the visitors and their conversation partners, continues in v. 5, the real literary and thematic heart of the unit. While the women are anxious and bow down (v. 5a), the two beings clothed in light say, "Why do you seek the Living among the dead?" (v. 5b). The question is first followed by a brief explanation ("He is not here but is risen," v. 6a) then by a long injunction (to remember what Jesus had said earlier in Galilee. The injunction takes the form of a christological and prophetic reminder, vv. 6b-7). Luke then mentions that the call to remember has been heard (v. 8). He certainly does not go so far as to say in particular what the modern reader[8] wants to know—whether this memory was associated with the belief in the resurrection of Jesus. Entering the tomb and staying there briefly are echoed by leaving the realm of the dead and returning to the land of the living. Doubtless the women return to Jerusalem (though the starting point, ἀπὸ τοῦ μνημείου, "from the tomb," is indicated, the destination remains implicit), and although Luke is not more specific, they tell "all of this" to the Eleven and their companions (v. 9). Suddenly the evangelist takes pride in being precise and provides a list of the women who unintentionally have become witnesses (v. 10a). A curious repetition of v. 9b (v. 10b) leads to the obvious disbelief of the "apostles" (vv. 10b-11). Unless v. 12 is a tiny independent entity,[9] the unit ends without any apparent logic with Peter's lightning visit to the empty tomb (v. 12).

Thus, Luke 23:56b—24:12 has the characteristics of a complete whole and the movement of a narrative. It progresses through three stages: the preliminaries, presented in contrasting form, 23:56b—24:3; the meeting, vv. 4-8; and the results, vv. 9-12, also characterized by an opposition.

Diachronic Analysis

Luke does not compose the final chapter of his Gospel with empty hands. According to my hypothesis,[10] since the beginning of the passion narrative he has alternated between two sources, the Gospel of Mark and his own special source. He continues to do that here in chap. 24. In the first report, that of the empty tomb,[11] he rewrites Mark before turning to his own source for what follows.

The evangelist's fidelity to his source is especially evident at the beginning. In the central part Luke certainly does not neglect to mention Galilee, but he undertakes a daring reversal. Instead of being the place where one will meet the Risen One in the future (Mark 16:7), Galilee becomes the place of the earlier christological teaching (vv. 6b-7).[12] The end of the episode also changes from one evangelist to another. In Mark 16:8, the women leap from the tomb, flee, and are silent, overcome by fear. In Luke they hurry to share the news with the Eleven and their companions. This step meets with misunderstanding (v. 11). In an exceptional literary element, Peter hurries to the tomb, finds the wrappings lying there,

---

7   See vol. 1 of this commentary, 4–5 and 33–34, the introduction and the commentary on 1:5.

8   For example, Plevnik, "Eyewitnesses," 91–94.

9   Dauer ("Authentizität") argues that v. 12 is an interpolation based on John 20:3-10.

10   Bovon, "Lukan Story of the Passion."

11   I think that Luke knew neither the Matthean nor the Johannine version of the episode (Matt 28:1-8 and John 20:1-10). On the episode of Peter at the tomb see the commentary below on v. 12.

12   Conzelmann (*Theology*, 93–94, 202) has noted the importance of this change. On its meaning see the commentary below on vv. 6b-8.

and leaves in amazement (v. 12). All of these details are absent from Mark. Must they simply be attributed to the editorial imagination of Luke, or does the evangelist again draw here on an independent tradition or his own source? In reality we must approach each element independently. Peter's presence at the tomb (v. 12), missing from Mark and Matthew, is attested also in the Gospel of John. The two Gospels even agree in several specific points (Peter's presence, the running to the tomb, the use of the participle παρακύψας, "stooping," the historical present "he sees" [βλέπει] and contemplating the "linen cloths" [ὀθόνια]). It is certain that Luke does not depend on John, but in my opinion the Fourth Gospel also does not draw directly from Luke. Nor do I see v. 12 as a later gloss inspired by John 20.[13] In my view, the two evangelists know a tradition that, as is often the case,[14] contains various concrete and significant details: the movement of Peter, who bends forward or stoops to see, and the presence of the funereal cloths. I think, therefore, that Luke knows Peter's presence at the tomb from a tradition that may have been included in his own special material. The story of the Emmaus disciples shows that Luke is aware of an appearance of Christ to the same apostle Peter (24:34). It is not clear, however, that these two Petrine elements, empty tomb and appearance, were together in the tradition, for the apostle is called Peter in v. 12 and Simon in v. 34. What is surprising is that Luke, who is so careful to emphasize Peter's apostolic privilege and authority, did not take this occasion to tell in detail these two experiences of the apostle.

The other puzzling element is the list of the women present at the tomb. Mark provides such a list, but he does so at the beginning of the story (16:1). Luke wants to provide it later and inserts in Mark's list elements from his own list, either from his special source or from an independent tradition. This list is different from that of Mark and is similar to the one that Luke presented in his account in Galilee (8:2-3). Joanna appears here and in chap. 8 and is absent from Mark's list. The agreement

is not complete, however, because Susanna (8:2) does not appear here, and Mary the mother of James is absent from 8:2. The difference does not bother Luke, however, since he adds here (v. 10) a general formula: "and the other women with them." There (in 8:2) he has "and many others." Mark has no such all-encompassing formula. The reference to "Mary of James" must come from Mark. Luke 24:10 (see 8:2), Mark 16:1, as well as all the Gospels, including the *Gospel of Peter*, connect the name of Mary Magdalene with the events of Easter (see Matt 28:1; John 20:11-18; *Gos. Pet.* 50).

Here, finally, are the major differences between this passage in Luke and his primary source, Mark, as noted by J. Engelbrecht.[15] While three women are present at the tomb in Mark, there are more of them in Luke. The women, who in Mark are concerned about opening the tomb, do not worry about it in Luke. In Luke the women enter the tomb on their own initiative, while in Mark it is the young man, that is, the angel, who invites them. While Mark mentions only one "young man," Luke—as, by the way, John also (John 20:12)—speaks of "two men in dazzling apparel." The angelic message is different, as I have said, from all of the other evangelists.[16] Unlike the silence in which Mark keeps the women, Luke remembers their words and their message. The third evangelist ignores the women's fear as they leave the tomb, while fear is the final word in Mark. Luke mentions the negative reaction of the hearers (v. 11) and reports Peter's visit to the tomb, two elements that, as we have seen, are absent from Mark.

In summary, Luke knows and uses Mark here. He also uses other memories that are either independent or part of his special source. If he draws on his own material at the end of the episode, he does it all the more so because it will connect him firmly with the Emmaus pericope (24:13-35).

The tradition of the empty tomb, first attested in Mark, then in the two other Synoptics and in the Gospels of John and of Peter (John 20:1-10; *Gos. Pet.* 37–40), is

---

13 See n. 9 above.
14 See Christine M. Thomas, *The Acts of Peter, Gospel Literature, and the Ancient Novel: Rewriting the Past* (Oxford: Oxford University Press, 2003) 61–64, 70–71.
15 Engelbrecht, "Empty Tomb," 235–36.

16 Like Mark, Matthew knows the command to go to Galilee (Matt 28:7). He even repeats the content a little later (Matt 28:10), while Luke avoids it at all costs.

doubtless old, and it may well have been told independently.[17] It must, however, face two objections. Why is Paul not aware of it in his chapter on the resurrection where he invokes only the appearances? In addition, how are we to reconcile the tradition of the empty tomb and the role of Joseph of Arimathea in the burial with the statement in Acts that it was the opponents of Jesus who buried the crucified one (Acts 13:29-30)?

Concerning the first question, it is not enough to appeal to the kerygmatic formula quoted by Paul and the proposition it contains: "He was buried" (1 Cor 15:4).[18] Indeed, there is no positive counterpart to this proposition, such as: "On the third day he came forth from the tomb." Furthermore, since Paul stresses the discontinuity between the physical body and the resurrected body (1 Cor 15:35-49), the affirmation that Christ is risen does not *ipso facto* mean that Jesus' mortal remains disappeared because of the resurrection. What is true for the apostle, however, may not be true for the bearers of the tradition that the apostle passes on, or for other traditions, since for many Christians (who emphasize the bodily resurrection of Jesus as Luke 24:36-43 shows) there is no return to life without either an unchanging identity or the transformation of the body of the deceased.[19] Thus, it is possible that the authors of the early tradition quoted by Paul in 1 Cor 15:3b-5 did believe that in the Easter resurrection Jesus' body came out of the tomb and was changed. Since this is not explicitly stated in the passage, however, the text of 1 Cor 15:4 does not really furnish an argument in favor of the empty tomb.

On the second question, it is curious that, after he essentially makes use of the Markan version of Jesus' burial and the empty tomb, in Acts Luke takes over a different version of the facts without correcting them. There it is the inhabitants of Jerusalem and the Jewish authorities (Acts 13:27) who "took him down from the tree and laid him in a tomb" (Acts 13:29).[20] I imagine that Luke has tolerated this tension because he regarded the traditional formulation of Acts as vague and general enough that it could coexist several pages removed from the precise description at the end of the Gospel.[21]

The question of the historicity of the resurrection of Jesus and in particular that of the empty tomb have been hotly debated since the Enlightenment.[22] In the twentieth century, great historians such as Hans von Campenhausen have given a positive answer to the question of the empty tomb.[23] Since the Second Vatican Council, however, the argument of the empty tomb no longer serves as proof of the resurrection of Jesus.[24] Many exegetes do not even raise the question of the historicity of the report.[25]

The Church of the Holy Sepulchre, which is still standing, was probably built over what was once the venerated tomb of Jesus. There is a clue: in the fourth century this building was erected on the location of the second-century temple built by the emperor Hadrian in honor of Jupiter Capitoline in a controversial move to eradicate the memory of the tomb of Jesus and the veneration with which it was associated.[26] Accordingly, the historians know where Jesus may well have been buried, but they cannot say either that Jesus' body had disap-

---

17 Rudolf Bultmann (*History*, 284–87) and Martin Dibelius (*Tradition*, 189–91) concede the independent nature of the story of the empty tomb. Contrary to what I think, they, Bultmann more than Dibelius, believe that this is a recent legend. But I doubt that the sociological root of this story, its *Sitz im Leben*, was a liturgical celebration that took place at the tomb of Jesus. This hypothesis, developed by Wolfgang Nauck ("Bedeutung") and Ludger Schenke (*Auferstehungsverkündigung*), is improbable, because such a ceremony seems to be anachronistic in the first century of the Common Era.
18 See Kremer, "Diskussion," 141–45.
19 See the case of Lazarus (John 11) and Kremer ("Diskussion," 143–45).
20 See C. K. Barrett, *A Critical and Exegetical Commentary on the Acts of the Apostles* (2 vols.; Edinburgh: T&T Clark, 1994, 1998) 1:641–42.
21 One should not forget that in the following account about the Emmaus disciples Luke summarizes precisely the episode of the women's visit to the tomb (24:22-23). On the parallel (24:24) to Peter's visit to the tomb, see the commentary below on v. 24.
22 See Hoffmann, "Graben"; and below, the end of "History of Interpretation."
23 Von Campenhausen, *Ablauf*, 50–51.
24 See Kremer, "Diskussion," 137. The entire collection *Resurrexit* (ed. Dhanis) demonstrates the change.
25 See, e.g., C. A. Evans, 346–48; Meynet, *Évangile*, 2:235–37.
26 Parrot, *Holy Sepulchre*, 49–59; Max Küchler, *Jerusalem: Ein Handbuch und Studienreiseführer zur*

peared or even that it disappeared because of the resurrection. Such an affirmation comes not from knowledge but from faith. As far as the identity of the persons who buried Jesus is concerned, as well as the kind of tomb in which Jesus' body was laid, these questions are certainly a matter of historical research, but since there is no reliable evidence, they cannot be answered definitively. It is probable that Jesus was buried in the pit reserved for those who were condemned to death. It is far from certain that such a place had been carved into the rock and that there was a round stone to seal the entrance. A new, easily identifiable tomb corresponds too well to an apologetic Christian elaboration.[27]

Commentary

■ **23:56b—24:1** In v. 54 of chap. 23 Luke noted the transition from Friday to Saturday, the Sabbath. On that day (it must still have been Friday) the women had prepared the spices and ointments. As is proper—one respects the law

at both ends of the Gospel (see 1:6, 8-9, 59; 2:21-24, 41; 4:16)—the women keep the Sabbath.[28] As we have seen,[29] the δέ in v. 1 corresponds to the μέν in v. 56b, marking a contrast: activity replaces rest.[30] At daybreak[31] they go to the tomb.[32] Following Mark, Luke explains that this is the first day of the week.[33] They bring what they have prepared.[34] The end of the verse varies in the manuscripts; several add the presence of some other women. Others expand this reading and, influenced by Mark 16:3, mention the anxious question of the visitors to the tomb.[35]

■ **2** Unlike in Mark 16:3-4, neither the fear of the women who cannot roll the stone away nor the miracle of the open tomb attracts Luke's attention. The author simply says without emotion that Jesus' friends find the stone already rolled away. Probably the evangelist does not want to distract from what is essential, the message of the angels. As for the verb ἀποκυλίω ("to roll," "to roll away"), Luke takes it from Mark 16:3-4, where, by the way, it is repeated.[36]

heiligen Stadt (OLB 4.2; Göttingen: Vandenhoeck & Ruprecht, 2007) 409–10, 415–81. See n. 36 below.

27 Even a systematic theologian such as Hans Grass (*Ostergeschehen*, 32–51 [on Luke] and 85–93 [concluding the study of the canonical Gospels]) remains concerned about the historical question, and for a theological reason. Unlike von Campenhausen (*Ablauf*, 50–51), he comes to the conclusion (51) that Luke's stories are not helpful on the historical question of the Easter events.

28 Curiously, Codex Bezae (D = 05) omits the words κατὰ τὴν ἐντολήν, "according to the commandment." On the Sabbath observance, see Fitzmyer, 2:1543.

29 See above, end of Synchronic Analysis; see also Lagrange, 599.

30 There is a contradiction between Mark and Luke about the time when the women purchased or prepared the spices. In one of them it is done *after* the Sabbath (Mark 16:1); in the other *before* (Luke 23:56a), but only shortly before (Luke 23:54).

31 On ὄρθρος ("daybreak"), see BAGD, s.v. In Acts 5:21 Luke uses the expression ὑπὸ τὸν ὄρθρον instead of the genitive. On the genitive to mark the time or date, see BDF §186 (2). Grammatically, βαθέως may be the genitive of the adjective, or the adverb. With Plummer (547) and Lagrange (599) I take it as an adjective. The expression ὄρθρος

βαθύς is common; see the examples provided by Plummer, 547.

32 In chaps. 23–24 Luke usually uses the term μνημεῖον to designate the tomb (23:55; 24:2, 9, 12, 22, 24). A few times, however (23:53 and 24:1), he uses μνῆμα, since he regards the two terms as synonyms. The scribes share this view. Accordingly, the variations between the two terms in the same passage are frequent.

33 To designate Sunday as Mark does, Luke uses the cardinal number (μία) rather than the ordinal (πρώτη). It is a Semitism; see Plummer (547), who refers to Gen 1:5 LXX. Concerning the day, as a purist Luke prefers the dative to Mark's genitive.

34 On the importance Luke gives to the verb ἑτοιμάζω, see vol. 1 of this commentary, 102–3, on 2:31.

35 See the apparatus of Nestle-Aland (27th ed.) on the passage. Codex Bezae (D = 05) omits the term "spices."

36 Scholars such as Lagrange (599) and Benoit (*Passion and Resurrection*, 253–55), who have lived in Jerusalem for a long time, provide valuable information about ancient graves and funeral rites. See also Joachim Jeremias, *Jerusalem in the Time of Jesus: An Investigation into Economic and Social Conditions during the New Testament Period* (trans. F. H. Cave and C. H. Cave; Philadelphia: Fortress, 1975) 43; and Fitzmyer, 2:1544; see n. 26 above. From the anthro-

■ **3** The word σῶμα can have the meaning of "dead body" without being the exact synonym of πτῶμα.[37] Luke solemnly proclaims Jesus here as "Lord": τοῦ κυρίου Ἰησοῦ. This use of the title, which anticipates the Christian confession after Easter and Pentecost (see Acts 2:36), already appears here and there in the Gospel as if Luke is preparing the way.[38] I note that some manuscripts do not have the name "Jesus" and that Codex Bezae (D = 05) and various Old Latin witnesses omit the entire expression τοῦ κυρίου Ἰησοῦ ("of the Lord Jesus"). This is one of the short readings of Codex Bezae that are especially numerous in Luke 24 (see vv. 3, 6, 12, 36, 40, 51, 52) and that B. F. Westcott and F. J. A. Hort late in the nineteenth century regarded as authentic and, in a complicated way, called *Western non-interpolations*.[39] The discovery in the middle of the twentieth century of the Bodmer Papyrus XIV–XV (𝔓[75]), which attests the long text, dealt a severe blow to the hypothesis of the British scholars.[40] I retain the three words τοῦ κυρίου Ἰησοῦ here, thus the long text.

■ **4** The words "and it happened" (καὶ ἐγένετο) serve as a marker and signal the beginning of the main action.[41] The verb ἀπορέω, used primarily in the middle ἀπορούμαι, appears only one other time in Luke's work, in Acts 25:20, about the difficulty of Festus (see also John 13:22; Gal 4:20; 2 Cor 4:8). But Luke knows how to use the feminine noun ἀπορία, which defines the condition of one who does not understand,[42] such as the people who are confronted with the eschatological signs (21:25). Such a perplexity occurs in the circumstances in which God's plan is perceived but not yet evident. It is in such a liminal situation that the women find themselves.[43]

Καὶ ἰδού ("and see," translated as "behold") sets a new marker. The main action begins. When he speaks of "men" in dazzling clothing, here as elsewhere Luke is referring to messengers of God.[44] They stand facing them (αὐταῖς). Their clothing is not simply white or bright; it is also glistening, as lightning (ἀστράπτουσα).[45] This description removes any ambiguity. These two creatures belong to the divine world, and their intervention will also be as rapid as lightning (ἀστραπή).[46]

■ **5** The women then understand what is happening.[47] In their uncertainty, but not abandoning the legitimate fear

---

pological point of view, the book of van Tilborg and Counet (*Jesus' Appearances*) discusses funeral rites at length.

37 See Luke 17:37 and vol. 2 of this commentary on 17:37.

38 See the exclamation of surprise when Elizabeth receives Mary, 1:43. On the title κύριος ("Lord") in Luke, see Bovon, *Luke the Theologian*, 214–18.

39 Westcott and Hort, *New Testament*, vol. 1: *Text*, 176.

40 See Parsons, "Tendency."

41 On the various constructions with καὶ ἐγένετο ("and it happened") see vol. 1 of this commentary, 163, on 5:1.

42 See Zorell, *Lexicon*, s.v.

43 On the verb ἀπορέω and the substantive ἀπορία, see BAGD, s.v. A number of manuscripts have the compact διαπορεῖσθαι in the middle, others have the active διαπορεῖν. This verb, whose meaning is hardly different from the simple verb, perhaps emphasizes how long the women's anxious uncertainty lasted. See Swanson, *Manuscripts*, 406.

44 See Acts 1:10; 10:30 (Acts 10:3, which speaks of an angel of God, confirms the identity of the "man" of Acts 10:30 as an angel). On angels in general, see C. A. Gieschen, *Angelomorphic Christology: Antecedents and Early Evidence* (AGJU 42; Leiden: Brill, 1998) 26–48. On the angels in Luke-Acts, see Ingo Broer,

"ἄγγελος," etc., *EDNT* 1 (1990) 13–16; Crispin H. T. Fletcher-Louis, *Luke-Acts: Angels, Christology and Soteriology* (WUNT 2/94; Tübingen: Mohr Siebeck, 1997) 1–32.

45 The angels at the ascension are clothed thus: ἐν ἐσθήσεσι λευκαῖς ("in white [or shining] garments," Acts 1:10).

46 The only other New Testament use of ἀστράπτω ("to cast lightning" or "to shine like lightning") is in Luke 17:24 in the literal sense in an apocalyptic context: "For as the lightning flashes from one end of heaven to the other, so will the Son of Man be in his day." See vol. 2 of this commentary on 17:24.

47 On the Lukan scope of vv. 5-7, see Prete, *Opera*, 281–306. Seim ("Conflicting Voices") is of the opinion that even if the women are prominent in Luke 24, they will nevertheless be silenced, especially in the book of Acts. She also sees the irony in the message of the angels; in her view it does not lead the women to faith. In chap. 24 Luke brings together discordant voices into a continuous narrative. The readers of this story have the disadvantage of arriving too late but the advantage that they know more than the disciples did then.

of God, they throw themselves to the ground in an act of veneration.[48]

The angelic message has a number of dimensions. It begins with a question, but it is a question that can be read in two ways depending on whether one understands τί in the first sense as the question "what?" ("what are you looking for?") or in the later sense of "why?" ("why are you seeking?").[49] I read it as "why?" because in the other case a "whom" (in the accusative masculine τίνα) would have been more appropriate than a neuter "what?" (τί). This "why?" introduces a rhetorical question and means: In fact, you are on the wrong way. You should not look for him "among the dead." A few chapters earlier Luke had said that God was not the God of the dead but of the living (20:38).[50] Even earlier, he let Jesus say: "Let the dead bury their dead" (9:60).[51] In the eyes of the angels that is what the women are doing: They are concerned about the dead. And the angels are right. But are the visitors wrong in what they are doing? Yes, in the view of the heavenly messengers. And they invite the women to make a cognitive or hermeneutical leap. They should stop looking among the dead and start looking among the living. The implication is that they will find "the Living One" (τὸν ζῶντα).

The behavior of the grieving women is described not as a simple coming (v. 1) or an entering (v. 3) but as a search: "you seek" (ζητεῖτε, v. 5). The angels' use of this verb runs slightly contrary to the narrative logic, but it corresponds to a deeper semantic logic.[52] The reader of the Gospel knows the importance of the verb "to seek." Jesus has said that whoever seeks, finds (11:9).[53] If one "seeks" a dead man to apply spices, is one not caught in the quotidian world, the world of obituaries and the number of victims?

How then are we to understand the words τὸν ζῶντα—as a participle, "the one who is living," or as a title, "the Living One"? Some biblical and patristic parallels[54] invite us to see it as a title in the way that some Christians sing "O Risen One." Mark admittedly tells of Jesus' resurrection in the parallel passage (Mark 16:6), but he does not use the vocabulary of life. It is Luke who is responsible for this theological and eschatological sense of life. The verb "to be alive" (ζάω), used to define the condition of the one who is risen, appears a little later in the Gospel (24:23) and even later in Acts (Acts 1:3; 25:19).[55] This Lukan use corresponds to the Johannine concept of "eternal life."[56] Luke will also—something that is unique among the Synoptics and also brings him closer to John[57]—make use of the vocabulary of glory. Has not the Risen One, according to Luke 24:26, entered "into his glory"?

■ **6a** After the editorial rhetorical question comes a traditional affirmation that combines the empty tomb ("he is not here") with the resurrection ("but he is risen").[58] Luke keeps Mark's affirmation and simply changes the wording in order to reach a climax "he is risen"

---

48   This act is accepted here, as is Peter's act before Jesus (5:8). By contrast, the *proskynēsis* of Cornelius before the apostle Peter (Acts 10:25-26) and the sacrifices that the people of Lystra want to offer Paul and Barnabas as gods (Acts 14:11-15) are not accepted. See also Rev 19:10 and 22:8-9, where even the angels appear to refuse this veneration; Bovon, *De Vocatione Gentium*, 199–202.

49   On τί, see Alexandre, s.v. τίς, τίς, τί and BAGD, s.v. τίς, τί.

50   See the commentary above on 20:38.

51   See vol. 2 of this commentary on 9:59-60.

52   Strictly speaking, they did not come to "seek" Jesus, because they knew where they could find him.

53   See vol. 2 of this commentary on 11:9-10.

54   The Gospels also speak of Jesus as "the Crucified" (Mark 16:6). In the *Acts of Peter* (31) Simon Magus claims for himself the title "the one who stands steadfast" (ὁ ἑστώς). Sabugal ("Resurrección") emphasizes the expression "the Living One."

55   On the vocabulary of "life," see Luise Schottroff, "ζῶ, etc.," *EDNT* 2 (1990)105–9; BAGD, s.v., ζάω and ζωή (these three articles contain references); and François Bovon, "Jésus-Christ, vie du monde," *Les Cahiers protestants*, n.s. no. 5 (October 1983) 12–20.

56   See Bultmann, *John*, 39–45, 152 n. 2, 182–87, 227 n. 1, 257–61, 321, 403–4, 494–95, 530, 605–6, 619, 699 n. 3.

57   On δόξα in Luke and John, see Harald Hegermann, "δόξα, etc." *EDNT* 1 (1990) 344–49; Spicq, *Lexicon*, 1:362–79; see also the work of Fletcher-Louis mentioned above in n. 44 and Fitzmyer, 1:789; 2:1566.

58   Verse 6a is missing in Codex Bezae (D = 05) and several Old Latin witnesses. It is one of the Western non-interpolations to which I referred earlier in the commentary on v. 3.

(ἠγέρθη).[59] The angels do not predict the resurrection of Jesus; they proclaim it and thus prepare the way for the later apostolic testimony. Yet before the apostles, whose institutional authority Luke appreciates, it is the women who are the first to know and also the first to testify to the good news (v. 9)—having the success with these gentlemen about which we already know (v. 11).[60]

■ **6b-8** In the second half of v. 6 Luke decisively departs from Mark. Does he follow his special source or his own theological imagination? It is difficult to say.[61] Even if the theme of remembering is not specifically Lukan, the motif of fulfilled prophecy is dear to the heart of the third evangelist.[62]

As in Mark, Galilee serves as a hinge,[63] but while in Mark it is open to the future of an imminent meeting,[64] in Luke it remains the place of prophetic teaching. In Luke's writing, the verb "to speak" (λαλέω) can serve to express an inspired word, the language of prophecy.[65] The present does not erase the past as current reality urges it to do; it fulfills the promises. Christian remembrance[66] is not nostalgia; neither does it create current events in a magical way. By respecting time and the times, past, present, and future, it understands the correspondences and the achievements. Luke recalls the predictions of the passion by using the past words of Jesus: the "Son of Man," the verb "must," the delivery, the dirty "hands" of the responsible persons, the death on the cross, and the resurrection on the third day.[67] Some scholars emphasize the differences;[68] I prefer to underscore the similarities between these vv. 6b-8 and the four continuous predictions of the passion in the Gospel of Luke: 9:22; 9:44; 17:25; 18:32-33.[69] It does not matter that the last two were made on the way to Jerusalem rather than in Galilee. What is important is that the first two were there and in the second Jesus even said: "Let these words into your ears" (9:44).[70] Although the rhythm of the recollection is threefold, in fact he refers to the four stages of Jesus' passion:[71] (a) the role of the Jewish authorities, (b) who deliver Jesus to the Romans, (c) who crucify Jesus, (d) the one whom God restores to life. The women had not closed their ears. They remember the premonitory words that Jesus had laid in their head and in their heart.[72]

59   When ἠγέρθη is placed at the end of the sentence, it receives the emphasis. One could understand this aorist passive as intransitive, but since Luke often attributes Jesus' resurrection to God (see, e.g., Acts 3:15; 4:10), it is best to retain the passive sense here, even if the translation is difficult; see Fitzmyer, 2:1545. On v. 6a, see C. F. Evans, 895–96; Ernst, 652.

60   See Brock, *Mary Magdalene*, 34–36.

61   See Fitzmyer (2:1540–43), who has two opinions and retains a Lukan redaction based solely on the Markan tradition; see also Neirynck, "Tombeau vide," 427–28, 437–38; Osborne, *Resurrection Narratives*, 105–11.

62   Schubert ("Structure") has rightly emphasized this point.

63   See Sean Freyne, "Galilee as Laboratory: Experiments for New Testament Historians and Theologians," *NTS* 53 (2007) 147–64.

64   See Willi Marxsen (*Mark the Evangelist: Studies on the Redaction History of the Gospel* [trans. James Boyce et al.; Nashville: Abingdon, 1969] 111–16), who is of the opinion that this meeting will be that of the parousia.

65   On λαλέω, see vol. 1 of this commentary, 356 n. 26, on 9:10-11.

66   On remembrance, see Pierre Bonnard, *Anamnesis: Recherches sur le Nouveau Testament* (Cahiers RThPh 3; Lausanne: Revue de théologie et de philosophie, 1980) 1–11.

67   On these predictions of the passion, see Lohse, *Geschichte*, 18–19.

68   See Bock, 2:1893–95.

69   See vol. 1 of this commentary, 363 and 387–93, on 9:22 and 9:43-44 and vol. 2 on 17:25 and 18:32-33.

70   See vol. 1 of this commentary, 393, on 9:43b-44.

71   See Bovon, *Last Days*, 7.

72   On the remembering of the women according to vv. 6-8, see Rigato, "Remember." Some authors, especially Gerhard Lohfink (*Die Himmelfahrt Jesu: Untersuchungen zu den Himmelfahrts- und Erhöhungstexten bei Lukas* [StANT 26; Munich: Kösel, 1971] 171–72, 253–54), are of the opinion that the disciples, men and women, did not come to Christian faith until after the appearances, at the end of chap. 24. Plevnik ("Eyewitnesses") tries to contradict them. In his view, the women at the empty tomb did indeed believe in the resurrection of Jesus. Sabugal ("Resurrección," 472–74) emphasizes the inner spiritual experience the women had there, while in his view Peter's experience as evidenced in v. 12 remained external.

■ **9-11** What matters is the "tomb" ($\mu\nu\eta\mu\epsilon\hat{\iota}o\nu$). Luke prefers to say that the women returned "from the tomb"[73] rather than that they went back into the city. In order to make that statement, he resorts again (see vv. 1-3) to a feminine participle ($\dot{\upsilon}\pi\sigma\sigma\tau\rho\dot{\epsilon}\psi\alpha\sigma\alpha\iota$, literally, "being returned," translated as "when they had returned"). As if he wanted to emphasize the women, he lists their names in v. 10. First there is Mary Magdalene, of whom Luke ignores or chooses to ignore the personal appearance she was granted (Matt 28:9-10 and John 20:11-18). If he maintains the presence of this one to whom he refuses greater honor, it is because the memory of the women followers of Jesus was inseparable from Easter morning. In any case, Mark puts her first in his list (Mark 16:1). That she is called "of Magdala" lets us presume that she is not married and that there is no husband to be named.[74] As in 8:2-3, he names her with Joanna, whose husband, Herod's steward, he no longer needs to mention.[75] Before he concludes by adding "and the other women with them," he mentions a third name, Mary of James (his mother, rather than his daughter or wife). This information corresponds to what Mark 16:1 says. Mark 15:40 had explained that Mary was the mother of James and Joses.[76] Luke, who thus far has not mentioned her, must take over Mark's view and assume that in 8:1-3 she was one of the "many others." The reader does not understand why the evangelist then neglects Salome (Mark 16:1) or why he puts Mary the mother of James in third place (in Mark she is second). These are not idle questions, because, as we have seen in 8:1-3,[77] some of these lists were official, such as those that list the men. Here,

in v. 10, the list interrupts the story.[78] In Mark, where it is placed at the beginning of the episode, the list has a more natural place (Mark 16:1). Thus, Luke sacrifices style in favor of the women's proclamation. Unlike Mark (16:8), Luke lets the women speak. He even mentions twice that they speak, even though he says it in a way that is grammatically awkward (vv. 9 and 10).[79] Luke is careful not to specify the content of this proclamation. He says once "all of this" (v. 9), then "this" (v. 10), then "these words" (v. 11). The first time he chooses the word "to announce, report" ($\dot{\alpha}\pi\alpha\gamma\gamma\dot{\epsilon}\lambda\lambda\omega$) in the aorist (point action) and the second time the word "to say" ($\lambda\dot{\epsilon}\gamma\omega$) in the imperfect (a time that suggests either the duration, the repetition, or the importance of the speaking).[80] As the content of the message Luke is probably thinking more of the sequence of the events than their significance. Yet this unfolding of events includes the assertion that Jesus is alive. The people who receive these words are designated with the expression "to the Eleven and to all the others" in v. 9 and as "the apostles" in v. 10. The first expression recalls the group's past spent with Jesus; the second anticipates the future of the church's organization.[81]

There are two ways to explain the failure of this testimony. According to the first, traditional way, the message of the resurrection was so revolting to human common sense that it could meet only with incomprehension.[82] According to the second way, a product of modern feminism, the evangelist, like Paul before him, did not want the truth of the gospel to be based on the testimony of women.[83] These two explanations are not mutually exclu-

73 Codex Bezae (D = 05) and some Old Latin manuscripts omit the three words $\dot{\alpha}\pi\dot{o}$ $\tau o\hat{\upsilon}$ $\mu\nu\eta\mu\epsilon\dot{\iota}o\upsilon$ ("from the tomb"). Indeed, these words are indispensable only from a certain point of view.

74 In recent years there has been no end to the literature on this woman. See earlier Bovon, *Révélations*, 215–30; more recently, Brock, *Mary Magdalene*.

75 See vol. 1 of this commentary, 301–2, on 8:1-3.

76 I follow here the opinion of Fitzmyer, 2:1546–47.

77 See vol. 1 of this commentary, 299–302 on 8:1-3.

78 The words $\hat{\eta}\sigma\alpha\nu$ $\delta\dot{\epsilon}$ ("they were"), which make of v. 10 an independent sentence, are missing from several manuscripts, especially from Codex Alexandrinus (A = 02) and Codex Bezae (D = 05).

79 Many manuscripts add in v. 10b the feminine plural relative pronoun $\alpha\ddot{\iota}$ ("who"), to introduce the verb $\ddot{\epsilon}\lambda\epsilon\gamma o\nu$ ("they said"). Without this pronoun the

sentence remains an independent main clause. In this case it would have to be provided with a particle. This must be a redactional awkwardness caused by Luke's desire to insert the list of the women in v. 10a.

80 See BDF §329.

81 Luke has used the title "apostles" several times already in the Gospel (6:13; 9:10; 17:5; 22:14), because, unlike Paul (1 Cor 9:1), he believes that it was necessary for an apostle to have been with Jesus during his earthly life; see Bovon, *Luke the Theologian*, 408–16 and passim.

82 See Schmithals, 232.

83 See already Lagrange, 601: "The contempt for an unusual report given by women is not surprising in the Orient, or less so than elsewhere." Luke Timothy Johnson, *The Gospel of Luke* (Sacra Pagina

sive. While Luke makes room for women in his work, especially in the Gospel, it is always among those who receive and hear.[84] It is true that they give their property and offer hospitality, but in Acts they have no apostolic responsibility and they do not proclaim the gospel. It is not surprising, therefore, that their words sound here to authorized ears as a "babbling," a "silliness," a "delusion" ($\lambda \hat{\eta} \rho o \varsigma$).[85] The word appears only here in Luke's work and in the New Testament. In medical language it can refer to the "delirium" that comes over some patients. One does not trust such talk: "and they did not believe them" ($\kappa \alpha \grave{\iota} \ \dot{\eta} \pi \acute{\iota} \sigma \tau o \upsilon \nu \ \alpha \dot{\upsilon} \tau \alpha \hat{\iota} \varsigma$, v. 11). That the Eleven, and following them Luke, disdained the testimony of the women does not mean that they were especially hostile. Jewish law and the Greek philosophers—that is, the ancient societies—were no different.[86] Not all Christians, however, shared this view. Some of them acknowledged the importance of the testimony of Mary Magdalene and the other women at the tomb.[87] The evangelists themselves, including Luke, do not deny their participation in the events. Luke, however, creates a crescendo that builds from the empty tomb, witnessed by the women, to the appearance to the eleven disciples, all males. He does so out of conviction but also for strategic reasons. Around 180 C.E. will Celsus, the adversary of the Christians, not accuse them of basing the truth of their doctrine on the weak shoulders of delirious women?[88]

■ **12** To confirm what we have just said, read on. Verse 12 should convince the readers that the fragile testimony of the women received a more reliable confirmation through a man—and through what man? The leader of the Twelve and the future spokesman of the church, Peter.[89] Mark, who is followed by Matthew on this point, once again is ignorant of such a development. It is true that this v. 12 is missing from Codex Bezae (D= 05) and from Old Latin witnesses. Earlier, many people regarded this absence as early and authentic,[90] but today it is thought to be an omission.[91] I share this opinion and believe that the verse is an integral part of the Third Gospel.[92] The reading of the fourth evangelist dem-

3; Collegeville, Minn.: Liturgical Press, 1991) 388: "There is a definite air of male superiority in this response."

84   Luke's idea of the role of women in the Christian community is debated; see in particular Brock, *Mary Magdalene*, 32–40; and Mitzi J. Smith, *The Literary Construction of the Other in the Acts of the Apostles: Charismatics, the Jews, and Women* (PTMS 154; Eugene, Ore.: Pickwick, 2011) 95–153. For a list of works that read Luke-Acts from a feminist perspective, see Bovon, *Luke the Theologian*, 639.

85   See Plummer, 550; Bock, 2:1898. The term appears in *4 Macc.* 5:11 and in Josephus *Bell.* 3.8.9 §405.

86   In that day Jewish law limited the rights of women without completely denying them; see Josephus *Ant.* 4.8.15 §219; the Mishna is aware of several cases in which the testimony of women can be accepted; see *m. Ketub.* 1.1–2.9; *m. Yeb.* 15.3–16.7; Ilan, *Jewish Women*, 163–66. On philosophical reservations about the word of women, see Plato *Leg.* 11.937A–D; R. J. Bonner, "Did Women Testify in Homicide Cases at Athens?" *Classical Philology* 1 (1906) 127–32.

87   It is probable that this participation of women was important in early Christianity and that these female voices were later silenced in the developing church; see Elisabeth Schüssler Fiorenza, *In Memory of Her: A Feminist Theological Reconstruction of Chris-*

tian Origins (New York: Crossroad, 1984) 80–84; Brock, *Mary Magdalene*, 161–71.

88   The testimony of Celsus has been preserved by his opponent, Origen, in *Cels.* 2.55; see Pierre de Labriolle, *La réaction païenne: Étude sur la polémique antichrétienne du Iᵉʳ au VIᵉ siècle* (1934; reprinted Paris: Cerf, 2005) 112–79. On the women, see also Renan, *Life*, 120.

89   This verse has instigated a great deal of work: in chronological order, see Curtis, "Luke XXIV. 12"; Muddiman, "Note"; Neirynck, "*ΠΑΡΑΚΥΨΑΣ*"; idem, "*ΑΠΗΛΘΕΝ*"; idem, "Texte occidental"; Dauer, "Produkt"; Neirynck, "Once More"; Ehrman, *Corruption*, 212–17; Dauer, "Authentizität"; Shellard, "Relationship," 93–96; Neirynck, "Supplementary"; idem, "Anti-Docetic."

90   This is one of the Western non-interpolations of Westcott and Hort; see the commentary above on v. 3 and n. 39. Even today, some scholars such as Dauer ("Authentizität") regard this verse as an interpolation created from John 20.

91   Shellard, "Relationship." In spite of his preference mentioned in the previous footnote, Dauer ("Authentizität," 297–304) states clearly the case for the authenticity. He lists equally clearly the arguments against the authenticity! (304–18).

92   This verse is contained not only in 𝔓⁷⁵, the famous Bodmer Papyrus XIV–XV, but in almost all Greek

onstrates that this was a very early development based on an ancient tradition. It is due to the presence at the right time and the right place of his leader, the beloved disciple. According to the rule of popular narratives, he did not hesitate to divide into two the male characters who come to the tomb. For the tradition preserved by Luke, however, Peter was the only one.[93] This tradition probably originated to complement or to counteract the tradition of Mary Magdalene at the tomb. As we will see, Luke is also concerned to mention an appearance of the Risen One to the first of the apostles (24:34), presumably to reject the appearance of the living Christ to Mary Magdalene (an appearance which, as we have seen, Luke may have ignored).

Then Peter[94] ran to the tomb. The style is Lukan; the ἀναστάς imitates the LXX.[95] The fact that he runs rather than walks suggests, following a biblical practice, that at this hour the God of Israel is doing something.[96] The verb παρακύπτω, which initially means "to stoop," "to look to the side," "to bend down to look," finally means simply "to look." Here the verb means that Peter bends or lowers his head to look.[97] He can look more easily into the tomb by bending over.[98] In the LXX—and more generally in the religious language of the Jews, the Greeks, and then the Christians—this verb can be associated with the viewing of revelations and mysteries. The First Epistle of Peter (1:12) uses it, for example, to express an attitude or an act of the angels, who bend down from heaven to look at the earth.[99] This religious tone is not absent from v. 12: Peter is about to observe a situation that is out of the ordinary.[100] In order to express that the mortal remains are gone, Luke reports that Peter sees the traces of the dead Jesus—only (μόνα) the bindings (τὰ ὀθόνια) in which the body was wrapped.[101] In order not to anticipate and minimize the effects of the later appearances, the evangelist does not yet say that Peter believes. The apostle is surprised, amazed, and wondering (it is difficult to grasp the nuances here of the verb θαυμάζω). This attitude, however, is already a mark of progress. The reluctant admiration of v. 12 follows the lack of faith (ἀπιστέω) of v. 11. Luke is not displeased that this progress takes place in the passage from the feminine (the visit of the women to the tomb) to the masculine (Peter's visit).

---

manuscripts as well. The vocabulary and the style of the verse also reflect Lukan usage. If there are some unexpected and non-Lukan aspects, they must come from the tradition used by the evangelist.

93   The specialists on the Fourth Gospel wonder whether John used the Gospel of Luke or an oral or written tradition. They also explain the inclusion of another disciple, doubtless the beloved disciple, along with Peter and the competition that ensued between them. See Raymond E. Brown, *An Introduction to the Gospel of John* (ed. Francis J. Moloney; New York: Doubleday, 2003) 94–104.

94   As we know, the apostle's name varies from one text to another. It can be Simon, Simon Peter, Cephas, or Peter. In v. 34 he will be called Simon; see vol. 1 of this commentary, 210–11, on 6:14-16.

95   See vol. 1 of this commentary, 57–58, on 1:39-40; Haenchen, *Acts*, 159 n. 2.

96   See vol. 1 of this commentary, 58 n. 26, on 1:39-40.

97   On the verb παρακύπτω, see Delebecque (*Évangile*, 148) and especially Neirynck ("ΠΑΡΑΚΥΨΑΣ"), who resolutely chooses the meaning "to look," forgetting too much the physical posture of the one who is looking. In the etymology of the verb there is certainly the idea of stooping. Luke uses other compound verbs, ἀνακύπτω in 13:11 and 21:28;

συγκύπτω in 13:11. See my article "La dame à sa fenêtre: Un cas d'intertextualité entre Eschyle et le livre des Juges," in Antje Kolde et al., eds., Κορυφαίῳ ἀνδρί: *Mélanges offerts à André Hurst* (Geneva: Droz, 2005) 587–94. In addition to the Gospel of John (where it is used twice, in John 20:5 for the beloved disciple and John 20:11 for Mary Magdalene) the *Gospel of Peter* (55–56) uses the verb twice in the context of the empty tomb.

98   See Lagrange, 602.

99   See also *1 Enoch* 9:1. This aspect is overlooked by many commentators.

100   See Paul J. Achtemeier, *1 Peter: A Commentary* (Hermeneia; Minneapolis: Fortress Press, 1996) 112; and Neirynck, "ΠΑΡΑΚΥΨΑΣ," 128–29.

101   One notes, as in John 20:5, the historical present, which is unusual in Luke; see Neirynck, "ΠΑΡΑΚΥΨΑΣ." To be debated, moreover, is whether ὀθόνιον means a cloth or a tapelike binding. Since John 20:5-6 draws a distinction between ὀθόνια and σουδάριον ("shroud" or "sweat cloth"), I propose to retain for ὀθόνια the meaning of "fabric" or "linen bands." I specify that in John 20:6 σουδάριον refers not to a large body shroud but to a small cloth, since it covers only the head. I would add that in the descent from the cross the body of Jesus is deposited into a σινδών, a "shroud" (Mark

One last expression still offers a difficulty: πρὸς ἑαυτόν.[102] Does Peter return (ἀπῆλθεν) "home" or does he come "to himself"?[103] Once again we should probably admire Luke's skill in suggesting both a literal and a figurative sense. Peter's movement may also be close to God's call to Abraham to לֶךְ־לְךָ, "go to yourself." The surprising wording of Gen 12:1 probably involves more than an effort of internalizing. What Abraham and—perhaps here—Peter must do is leave in order to achieve his identity and fulfill his destiny.[104] Peter did return home, as did the women (v. 9), but, like the prodigal son in the parable (15:17), he also came to himself.[105]

History of Interpretation

Since the history of the interpretation of the text took place for centuries in Christian circles, no one questioned the historicity of the episode. The principal source of concern was the attention given to the agreement among the Gospels. Who were these women who were present? When did all this happen? Did one or two angels appear? What was the message given to the women? Why does Luke not mention another disciple along with Peter as John does? During late antiquity and especially during the Middle Ages, another trend appears: that of allegorizing the stories, even one so wonderful and compelling as that of the empty tomb. The preparation of the spices becomes a spiritual

exercise, and the spices themselves become prayers or pious acts.

It is within the Christian society in France, England, and Germany that the major figures manifest themselves in the age of the Enlightenment. Doubts about the historicity of the empty tomb grow stronger and stronger. Then the theologians will attempt to limit the damage by making use of the tools of the historians.

To give an idea of the history of the interpretation of Luke 23:56b—24:12, from the sources that historical contingences have preserved, I will call attention to the testimonies of Tertullian, Ambrose, Cyril of Alexandria, the Venerable Bede, the anonymous Irish commentator, Bonaventure, Erasmus, Calvin, Bengel, Reimarus, and Strauss.

On the page that he devotes to the empty tomb (*Adv. Marc.* 4.45.1–2), Tertullian calls attention, arguing against Marcion, to the harmony between the Old and New Testaments. The person of Joseph of Arimathea, the *sepultor* of Christ, as well as the women with their pious tasks, have been prophetically announced in the Holy Scriptures. With reference to Mary Magdalene and her companions Tertullian cites Hos 5:15—6:2 (LXX: "They will seek my face, etc."), then Isa 57:2 (LXX: sepulcher will be removed), and Isa 27:11 (LXX: the presence of women). The African adds with finesse that, on arriving at the tomb, the women were torn between pain and hope. He goes on to say that the presence of the two

---

15:46; Matt 27:59; Luke 23:53). Among the various Gospel traditions there is, therefore, no uniformity of vocabulary or unanimity of representations; see Benoit, *Passion and Resurrection*, 253–56; Fitzmyer, 2:1547–48.

102 On this expression, about which much ink has been spilled, see Neirynck ("ΑΠΗΛΘΕΝ"), who, after examining the LXX and Josephus, retains the meaning of "returning home."

103 Some people, surprised by the unusual use in Luke of the preposition πρός ("to") after the verb ἀπέρχομαι ("to go away") have wanted to see a dependence on John 20:10. Others, influenced by the Vulgate's *secum mirans*, have attached πρὸς ἑαυτόν to the following verb, the participle θαυμάζων, in the opinion that Peter is intrigued or inwardly wondering. Still others, interested in Semitisms, have thought that πρὸς ἑαυτόν somewhat clumsily rendered the *dativus ethicus* of an Aramaic original. It would then have the meaning "for his part."

Neirynck ("ΑΠΗΛΘΕΝ") gives the reasons for all of these hypotheses. Personally, I maintain the grammatical link between ἀπέρχομαι and πρὸς ἑαυτόν, but, unlike Neirynck, I do not limit the meaning to the literal sense of returning "home."

104 See Marie Balmary, *Le sacrifice interdit: Freud et la Bible* (Paris: Grasset, 1986) 123–33. I note that the translation "to come to yourself" is controversial. The *dativus ethicus* may not indicate a direction. Moreover, Luke knows how to make his heroes practice an inner dialogue (12:17) and return to themselves (15:17). These attitudes are not far from μετάνοια ("repentance") and ἐπιστρέφω ("to be converted"); see vol. 2 of this commentary on 12:17 and on 15:17; Bovon, *Luke the Theologian*, 305–28, 540–43.

105 I observe that in v. 24 the Emmaus disciples mention a visit to the tomb following that of the women. Curiously, it concerns not only Peter, but several persons (see the commentary below on v. 24).

angels provided a valid witness and concludes that the incredulity of the Eleven was actually a good thing: it made possible the next episode, that of the Emmaus disciples, and the lesson of Christian hermeneutics that Christ gave from the Scriptures.

Ambrose of Milan (*Exp. Luc.* 10.144–67) begins by congratulating the women. The last to leave the tomb, they are the first to return to it. "In any case, they are there at the hour of the resurrection; and while the men fled, only they are warned by the angel not to be afraid. They call Peter; their zeal outstrips him, their faith follows him" (§145). He then turns to the problems that have caused confusion in Christian antiquity: the contradictory statements of the Gospels about the chronology and the persons. He spends time harmonizing these with exegetical manipulations that sometimes seem to be sleight of hand. To reduce the tensions, does he not imagine that there was a second Mary Magdalene?[106]

Cyril of Alexandria, or perhaps some other Greek Father, deals with the empty tomb and the Emmaus disciples.[107] The author is often content simply to tell the story, but he punctuates it with a few comments. The Word of God took the risk to become incarnate and in so doing became mortal. By the grace of God the death of Christ means at the same time the death of death. Thus, the Risen One, who regained the heavenly glory, opened the way for our own incorruptibility. It was appropriate that the angels were present at the resurrection, just as they were with the shepherds of Bethlehem on the occasion of the birth. The theologian is happy that the news of the resurrection was first announced to the women. Now they are free, and the curse hanging over them has been transformed into a blessing. When the apostles do not believe them, it is because they (the apostles) have not understood the Scriptures.

The Venerable Bede (*In Luc.* 6.1885–2010) also relates the facts, but he gives them at the same time a spiritual sense. He emphasizes the quest of the women who seek and find in the fervor of their affection. They are for us a mystical example of access to the altar of the Lord, represented here by the sepulcher, and of emerging from the darkness, which symbolizes the vices. After continuing this eucharistic allegory, Bede gives the spices a figurative meaning, understanding them as virtues and prayers, and the rolled-away stone as a symbol of exceeding the letter of the law. Bede goes even further and applies the command of the consoling and proclaiming angels to the Christians of his day, to "us"—the heavenly mysteries come near to us. Thus, with an allegorical exegesis the Venerable Bede several times justifies not only spiritual attitudes but also ecclesiastical practices.[108]

Bonaventure (*Comm. Luc.* 24.1–15)[109] remains true to himself. He divides the material into different units. The Gospel of Luke has four parts, because it deals in

---

106 In his work *Questions and Answers on the Gospels*, of which only fragments and a summary remain, Eusebius expresses the same hypothesis. See the summary, 2.7 (*PG* 22:947–48); and Claudio Zamagni, "Les Questions et réponses sur les évangiles d'Eusèbe de Césarée: Étude et édition du résumé grec" (diss., Lausanne-Paris, 2003) 59–62bis. The Greek catenae have preserved two fragments of Apollinaris of Laodicea on our passage. In the first, the theologian asks about the exact time that the women arrived at the tomb; in the second, he harmonizes the stories of the two evangelists whom he says he most trusts—Matthew, who speaks of one angel, and Luke, who mentions two; see Reuss, *Lukas-Kommentare*, 9–10, frgs. 18 and 19.

107 These pages are edited by Reuss (*Lukas-Kommentare*, 273–78 [frags. 2.112–15]) and translated by Payne-Smith (*Cyril*, 2:724–31). Their authenticity is not certain. Even if they are authentic, it is not clear that they were part of Cyril's commentary on Luke.

See the commentary above, on 23:26-43, p. 316 n. 187, and below, on 24:13-35, p. 377 n. 71.

108 The anonymous Irish commentator (*Comm. Luc.* 24, 1–11 [CCSL 108C:98–99]) is also resolutely allegorical. The arrival of the women at the sepulcher represents the churches' access to faith in Jesus Christ, died and resurrected. The spices symbolize the good works prepared under the old law and manifested under the new law; the rolled-away stone symbolizes abominable impiety, and so on. The Irish commentator also recalls and explains the literal sense of the story. It is the absence of the body in the tomb that astonishes Peter. The twofold connection to the literal and figurative sense is evident also in the *Glossa ordinaria*, Luke 23:56b—24:12 (*PL* 114:350–51), where one finds many of the observations of the Venerable Bede.

109 Bernardini, 587–91; Karris, *St. Bonaventure's Commentary*, 2189–2202.

succession with the incarnation, the ministry, the passion, and the resurrection. The resurrection itself is also organized into four sections: the revelation (vv. 1-12), the appearance (vv. 13-32), the certainty (vv. 33-47), and the distribution of this certainty (vv. 48-53). The revelation at the empty tomb deserves three explanations. The first relates to the occasion, which, of course, was the arrival of the women at the tomb. Yet this evidence does not resolve the disputed question about the time of the resurrection (Bonaventure concedes that there is a difference of opinion here: Did it happen during the night or at dawn?). This difference does not keep him from giving a figurative sense to the darkness from which the women are emerging. This darkness represents the obscurity of death and of the realm of death. The second explanation concerns the manner: Does the stone roll before or after the resurrection? Bonaventure, explicitly basing his view on the Venerable Bede, chooses the latter. Then he allegorizes the tomb to mean the Holy Scripture and the stone, the veil covering the Scripture. If I see correctly, the third explanation deals with the positive message of the angels. After he settles (thanks to an ingenious harmonization) the question of the number of angels, which differs from one Gospel to another, Bonaventure compares the joy of the moment with that of the birth, also proclaimed by angels (2:10). Then he underscores the fact that Jesus' destiny, including, of course, the resurrection, corresponded in all respects to the various predictions of the passion he had addressed to his disciples. For the theologian, the words of the angel are both a testimony and a demonstration. Since the women remember these prophecies, they are brought to faith. Then Bonaventure expressed the view that it was not without divine intention that the resurrection came to men through the mediation of women.[110] According to the medieval author, since sin and death entered the world through a woman, it is normal that the same thing happens with life and immortality. If, in addition, Mary Magdalene goes before the other women, it is because she loves Jesus more than the others, and this is true, of course, for four reasons! As for Peter, he was frozen in his stupor, because, according to John 20:9, he had not yet understood the Scriptures.[111]

In his *Paraphrasis* (465–67),[112] Erasmus points out that, although the women's preparations were pious, they were no less superfluous. After telling about the precautions that had been taken to ensure that the body was not stolen, he underscores the courage of the women who dared to enter the sepulcher. He then adds that the glittering allure of the angels declared the triumph of the resurrection. The following material appropriately wears the name of the entire work of Erasmus. It is a paraphrase of the story, although here and there the humanist slips in an interpretation. He is especially of the opinion that the angels' message was delivered calmly and pleasantly. He also concluded from the resurrection that the body could not have been in the sepulcher. If you have verified the announcement of the death of Jesus, do not hesitate, he charges, to believe in the fulfillment of the prophecy about the resurrection. Moreover, he believes that one can rely on Jesus' calculations that forewarned what was to happen. If he talked about the third day, it was because he had foreseen that he would die on the first day, lie in the tomb on the second, and rise from the dead on the third. Convinced as they were by the arguments of the angels and nourished in spirit by the revived memories, the women therefore had no more reason to stay at the empty tomb. Thus, they returned to those who had forgotten everything and had succumbed to despair. Then, moving from the narrative to the speculative, Erasmus takes up the traditional argument that woman was both the occasion of the fall and the source of redemption.[113] In order to explain why the Eleven rejected the testimony of the women, Erasmus uses an argument that goes back to Gregory the Great[114] and

---

110 Bonaventure is based explicitly on John Chrysostom. According to Robert Karris (*St. Bonaventure's Commentary*, 2199 n. 23), this is a passage from *Hom. Joh.* 85 (84).4 (*PG* 59:465).

111 See also Thomas Aquinas *Catena aurea*, 309–12; and Theophylactus *Enarr. Luc.* 24.4–12 (*PG* 123:1109–12).

112 See Phillips, *Paraphrase*, 226–30.

113 See the comments of Phillips (*Paraphrase*, 229 n. 12 and n. 10), who on this point calls attention to the predecessors of Erasmus and to the permanence of the verb *transfudere*, in order to express the idea since Ambrose of Milan that women have transmitted sin as well as grace.

114 Gregory the Great *Hom. Evang.* 29.1 (*PL* 76:1213).

runs throughout the Middle Ages (one finds it quoted in Bede *In Luc.* 6.1990–96). This refusal was not completely negative; it forced God to give more evidence of the resurrection, something that worked to the advantage of future generations, especially "ours." Nevertheless, the women's insistence did induce Peter to stand and form an opinion for himself. The empty tomb was not enough to cause him to believe; it merely succeeded in intriguing him and raising in his mind various possibilities. As one can see, Erasmus still participates in ancient and medieval exegesis. He still expresses no suspicion about the historicity of the resurrection. He does, however, trim the overgrown allegorical branches.[115]

Luther's passages, which I have before me and many of which are homiletic, show the same characteristics, although they demonstrate a more theological sensitivity.[116] Two points in particular are close to the reformer's heart: (a) the status of the women's faith—while they love Jesus, their faith is a childlike faith, since they have not yet met the Risen One;[117] and (b) the meaning of Christ's absence—when it is said that "Christ is not here," it also means for Luther that he is not where many believe they can contain him, in the piety of rites and ceremonies.[118]

Calvin is committed to the theological dimension of his exegesis (I offer here Calvin's exegesis as it is found in his *Harmony of the Gospels*).[119] He begins his analysis with the following doctrinal statement: "Now we come to the closing passage of our redemption." Believing in the resurrection, therefore, is essential to salvation (Calvin refers here to 1 Cor 15:14), for by his death and resurrec-

tion Jesus has acquired for us righteousness with God. Our feelings, what Calvin calls "our fleshly sense," would have rather had a different manifestation of our redemption. God wanted it differently, and he was right to do so, for he progressed gradually from the empty tomb to the appearances: "Gradually he brought them along, according to their own capacity, into fuller understanding." And Calvin values the providence, which gave the women courage when the men were half dead. By following this strategy "he honors them [the women] with exceptional distinction, taking the apostolic office away from the men. . . ." The reformer also exercises a Synoptic comparison and does more relativizing than harmonizing the differences among the Gospels. There is some diversity among them, but "in the actual events, they agree very well." Calvin believes that the Jews were unique among the peoples of antiquity in practicing legitimate funeral rites, because they were connected with the resurrection. After Jesus' resurrection, however, these rituals were no longer necessary. Curiously, Calvin avoids the difficulty[120] and is not bothered by the conflicting orders the angels give the women, depending on whether one reads Luke or Matthew and Mark.[121]

The criticism of Christianity began with a criticism of the hegemony of the church and the sovereignty of dogma; religion, God, and even Jesus were less subjects of criticism. English Deism, French philosophers, then German thinkers have claimed the triumph of reason over revelation. Since then the resurrection of Jesus has become a decisive issue.[122] As an example I present the intellectual attitude of Hermann Samuel Reimarus, the

---

115 In his *Annotationes* (216–17), Erasmus introduces the reader to the Greek text of the Gospel, which he quotes here and there and compares with the Vulgate. He also explains certain expressions such as ὄρϑρου βαϑέος (that is the orthography he uses), "at the break of day" (*diluculum*), which follows the crowing of the cock (*gallicinium*), which follows the silence of the night (*conticinium*); or παρακύψας, which he understands in the sense of "to look with his head bowed to the side." Finally, he calls attention to a few textual variants.

116 Luther, *Evangelien-Auslegung*, 1233–47.

117 Ibid., 1334–35.

118 Ibid., 1236.

119 Calvin, *Harmony*, 3:220–29. The quotations come successively from 221 (four times) and 223 (once).

120 Calvin (*Harmony*, 3:229) concludes his analysis by

expressing the opinion that Luke intentionally changes the order of the story, placing Peter's run to the tomb where he does. In his view that is not a bad thing. Luke follows a Hebrew custom: "it was regular for Hebrews to relate afterwards events they omitted at the right point." According to Calvin, in this point we must follow John's chronological order, which locates the run to the tomb earlier.

121 Bengel (*Gnomon* [G] 1:415) believes, as I do, that τὸν ζῶντα says more than that Jesus was alive again. He became "the Living One." He has "not merely returned to life, but is altogether the Living One." After quoting v. 12, Bengel moves from exegesis to prayer and to the confession of faith: "Lord Jesus, with my whole heart I believe that God raised you from the dead."

122 For this part I am greatly indebted to the article

author of the famous *Wolfenbüttel Fragments*,[123] published by Gotthold Ephraim Lessing posthumously in 1774 and 1777. It is significant that Reimarus did not want to publish his work during his lifetime.[124] He preferred to undertake the investigation for himself personally and for the private circle of his family and his enlightened friends. He worked on it until his death. The two thick volumes of the final version did not appear in their entirety until 1972.[125] The fragments published by Lessing are excerpts from an earlier, shorter version of the work.

Unlike the philosophers, Reimarus practices exegesis, textual criticism, and history. He reads the Bible as any other book of antiquity, and thus has an attitude that is obviously exceptional in that day. He is attentive to differences and contradictions among the Gospels. His criticism is more exegetical than is that of his English predecessors. In the fifth fragment "On the resurrection story," Reimarus casts doubt on the historicity of the episode of the guards at the tomb, which only Matthew mentions.[126] Then he turns to the empty tomb and the resurrection itself. It is true that all the Gospels proclaim it, but their testimony is so full of contradictions (Reimarus does not fail to enumerate and to analyze them) that they cannot be trusted. Thus, Reimarus opposes the contemporary attempts to harmonize them, a harmonization that was based on centuries of theological exegesis. He concludes his inquiry with the hypothesis that Jesus' body had been stolen. While the hypothesis is as old as the Gospel (see Matt 27:64), unlike the early Christians Reimarus has the audacity to stand on the side of the opponents of the evangelist.

David Friedrich Strauss published his *Leben Jesu* (*Life of Jesus*) in 1835.[127] He was twenty-five years old and was opposed to both the rationalists, whom he accused of being unable to explain the transition of the historical Jesus to the Christ of faith,[128] and the supernaturalists, who in his opinion made the mistake of taking the miracles at face value. Strauss chooses—he is not the first to introduce the notion—the term "myth" to explain the realities documented by the New Testament. By myth he means giving religious ideas a historical aspect. The life of Jesus, according to Strauss, had a historical basis. Jesus spent his childhood in Nazareth, was baptized by John, formed a circle of disciples, went around the country of the Jews proclaiming the kingdom and opposing the Pharisees, and ended his life on the cross. The disciples, however, moved by their religious faith, gave a mythical dimension to these historical memories: "This framework was surrounded with the most diverse and meaningful threads of pious reflections and fantasies by changing into facts, woven into the course of his life, all the ideas earliest Christianity had about its disappeared Master."[129]

On the Easter events Strauss takes up the arguments of Reimarus. First he tries to prove the legendary character of the episode of the guards at the tomb; then he emphasizes the contradictions of the Gospels about Easter morning and the empty tomb, contradictions that no harmonization can reconcile. He believes that none of the witnesses transmitted by the New Testament has the value of an eyewitness testimony, and this comment is equally true for the empty tomb and for the appearances of the Risen One. In conclusion, Strauss chooses

---

"Graben," by Hoffmann; he calls attention to the controversy in Great Britain in the middle of the eighteenth century in which, among others, Anthony Collins, Thomas Woolston, Peter Annet, Thomas Sherlocks, Gilbert West and Thomas Chubb were involved (348–51).

123 They appeared in the journal published by Lessing, *Zur Geschichte und Literatur: Aus den Schätzen der Herzoglichen Bibliothek zu Wolfenbüttel.* Another fragment appeared independently in 1778 with the title "Von dem Zwecke Jesu und seiner Jünger." See Gotthold Ephraim Lessing, ed., *Fragmente des Wolfenbüttelschen Unbekannten* (4th ed.; Berlin: Sander, 1835).

124 Reimarus gave his work the following title: "Apologie oder Schutzschrift für die vernünftigen Verehrer Gottes."

125 Hermann Samuel Reimarus, *Apologie oder Schutzschrift für die vernünftigen Verehrer Gottes* (ed. Gerhard Alexander; 2 vols.; Frankfurt a. M.: Insel, 1972).

126 Today we know that the guards are mentioned also in *Gos. Pet.* 28–49.

127 Here again I rely on the article by Hoffmann ("Graben"), esp. 361–72.

128 Strauss did not use this terminology yet. He accused them of being unable to explain how Jesus could have become the object of a cult.

129 See David Friedrich Strauss, *Das Leben Jesu kritisch bearbeitet* (2 vols.; Tübingen: Osiander, 1838, 1839) 71–72 and 74 [Strauss eliminated or moved the quotation from later editions. Thus, it does not appear in English translations]; see also Hoffmann, "Graben," 363.

neither the hypothesis that the body was stolen nor that of an apparent death. Jesus actually died on the cross. Only the religious beliefs of the early Christians, their sense of the Scriptures, and the enthusiasm of their piety made possible the construction of the resurrection of Jesus and its two narrative manifestations, the legend of the empty tomb and the stories of the appearances of the Risen One. It goes without saying that both Reimarus and Strauss have provoked intense reactions. Numerous theologians defended the historicity of the resurrection of Jesus and the authenticity of the stories that bear witness to it. Yet, since their time the intellectual and spiritual climate is no longer what it was in antiquity, the Middle Ages, and even in the Renaissance. It is no longer possible to read Luke 23:56b—24:12 without remembering the view of a Reimarus or a Strauss.

Conclusion

The story of the empty tomb fulfills for the New Testament the function that the crossing of the Red Sea occupied for the Old. This tradition is an important memorial for the Christian faith and illustrates the kerygma. Since the age of the Enlightenment and that of historicism the literary approaches have revealed the nature and the role of the founding narratives. Their historicity is less important than their kerygmatic scope. The historian and even today's believer may ignore the historical question without neglecting the value of the message.[130] The depictions of the story of the empty tomb, for example, by such artists as Piero della Francesca or Grünewald, show the decisive message of Jesus' resurrection. Further, the narrative of the empty tomb introduces the stories of the appearances.

As special Lukan features of the event we should note the audacity to declare that the irretrievably dead is alive and even to honor him with the title "the Living One"; the inversion of looking ahead (going to Galilee) into a retrospective memory (remembering Galilee), which determines that the facts agree with the expectations; and the verve of the apostle Peter in the tracks of Mary Magdalene and her companions.

---

130 Dillon (*Eye-Witnesses*) emphasizes the indispensable theological interpretation of the facts.

The Emmaus Disciples
(24:13-35)
Bibliography

Adams, J. E., "The Emmaus Story, Lk xxiv.13-35: A Suggestion," *ExpT* 17 (1905–6) 333–35.

Aletti, *Art de raconter*, 177–98.

Idem, "Luc 24,13-33: Signes, accomplissement et temps," *RSR* 75 (1987) 305–20.

Idem, *Quand Luc raconte: Le récit comme théologie* (Paris: Cerf, 1998) 220–23.

Annand, Rupert, "'He was seen of Cephas': A Suggestion about the First Resurrection Appearance to Peter," *SJT* 11 (1958) 180–87.

Arc, Jeanne d', "Catechesis on the Road to Emmaus," *LV* 32 (1977) 143–56.

Eadem, "Un grand jeu d'inclusions dans 'les pèlerins d'Emmaüs,'" *NRTh* 99 (1977) 62–76.

Eadem, "Le partage du pain à Emmaüs (Luc 24, 28-32)," *VSpir* 130 (1976) 896–909.

Eadem, *Les pèlerins d'Emmaüs* (LiBi 47; Paris: Cerf, 1977).

Arndt, William, "Ἄγει, Luke 24:21," *CTM* 14 (1943) 61.

Biemer, Günter, "Sonntag: Der Auferstehungstag der Woche (zu Lk 24,35ff)," *Diakonia* 28 (1997) 281–83.

Benoit, *Passion and Resurrection*, 263–82.

Betz, Hans Dieter, *Lukian von Samosata und das Neue Testament: Religionsgeschichtliche und paränetische Parallelen. Ein Beitrag zum Corpus Hellenisticum Novi Testamenti* (TU 76; Berlin: Akademie-Verlag, 1961) 124–30, 161–63, 169–71.

Idem, "The Origin and Nature of Christian Faith according to the Emmaus Legend (Luke 24:13-32)," *Int* 23 (1969) 32–46.

Billy, Dennis J., "The Road to Emmaus: The Journey of Discipleship," *Emmanuel* 107 (2001) 155–59.

Bokel, P., "Luc 24,25: Il leur ouvrit l'esprit à l'intelligence des Écritures," *BTS* 36 (1961) 2–3.

Bonus, Albert, "Emmaus Mistaken for a Person," *ExpT* 13 (1901–2) 561–62.

Borse, Udo, "Der Evangelist als Verfasser der Emmauserzählung," *SNTU* Serie A 12 (1987) 35–67.

Bowen, Clayton Raymond, "The Emmaus Disciples and the Purposes of Luke," *BW* 35 (1910) 234–45.

Broer, Ingo, "'Der Herr ist dem Simon erschienen' (Lk 24,34): Zur Entstehung des Osterglaubens," *SNTU* 13 (1988) 81–100.

Idem, "'Der Herr ist wahrhaft auferstanden' (Lk 24,34): Auferstehung Jesu und historisch-kritische Methode: Erwägungen zur Entstehung des Osterglauben," in Lorenz Oberlinner, ed., *Auferstehung Jesu—Auferstehung der Christen. Deutungen des Osterglaubens* (QD 105; Freiburg i. Br.: Herder, 1986) 39–62.

Brunck, George R., "The Concept of the Resurrection according to the Emmaus Account in Luke's Gospel" (dissertation, Union Theological Seminary, Richmond, VA, 1975).

Idem, "Journey to Emmaus and to Faith: An Illustration of Historical-Critical Method," in Willard M. Swartley, ed., *Essays on Biblical Interpretation: Anabaptist-Mennonite Perspectives* (Text-Reader Series 1; Elkhart, Ind.: Institute of Mennonite Studies, 1984) 203–22.

Brunot, Amédée, "Emmaüs, cité pascale de la fraction du pain," *BTS* 36 (1961) 4–11.

Certeau, Michel de, "Les pèlerins d'Emmaüs," *Christus* 13 (1957) 56–63.

Charlesworth, C. Evelyn, "The Unnamed Companion of Cleopas," *ExpT* 34 (1922–23) 233–34.

Chauvet, Louis-Marie, *Symbole et sacrement: Une relecture sacramentelle de l'existence chrétienne* (CFi 144; Paris: Cerf, 1987) 167–85.

Chinello, N. "I discepoli di Emmaus e l'Eucaristia," *PaVi* 16 (1971) 352–63.

Clancy, Finbarr G., "St. Augustine's Commentary on the Emmaus Scene in Luke's Gospel," *StPatr* 43, vol. 5 (2006) 51–58.

Combet-Galland, Corina, and Françoise Smyth-Florentin, "Le pain qui fait lever les Écritures. Emmaüs, Luc 24/13-35," *EThR* 68 (1993) 323–32.

Corley, Kathleen E., review of *The Ongoing Feast: Table Fellowship and Eschatology at Emmaus*, by Arthur A. Just, *JBL* 114 (1995) 338–40.

Correia, João Alberto S., "O caminho do reconhecimento e do anúncio: Lc 24,13-35 em perspectiva cristológica," *Theologica* 36 (2001) 359–402.

Crehan, Joseph H., "St. Peter's Journey to Emmaus," *CBQ* 15 (1953) 418–26.

Cummings, Charles, "A Tale of Two Travellers," *TBT* 21 (1983) 116–20.

Dagens, Claude, "Pour une lecture pascale des épreuves de la foi à la lumière de l'évangile d'Emmaüs," *EeV* 113 (2003) 3–7.

Dahl, Nils A., "The Crucified Messiah and the Endangered Promises," *Word and World* 3 (1983) 251–62.

DeGuglielmo, Antonine, "Emmaus," *CBQ* 3 (1941) 293–301.

DeLeers, Stephen V., "The Road to Emmaus," *TBT* 24 (1986) 100–107.

Delzant, Antoine, "Les disciples d'Emmaüs (Luc 24,13-35)," *RSR* 73 (1985) 177–85.

Derrett, J. Duncan M., "The Walk to Emmaus (Lk 24.13-35): The Lost Dimension," *EstBib* 54 (1996) 183–93.

Dillon, *Eye-Witnesses*, 69–155.

Dupont, Jacques, "Les disciples d'Emmaüs (Lc 24,13-35)," in Martin Benzerath et al., eds., *La Pâque du Christ: Mystère de salut. Mélanges offerts à F.-X.*

Durrwell pour son 70e anniversaire (LD 112; Paris: Cerf, 1982) 167–95; reprinted in Dupont, *Évangiles synoptiques,* 2:1153–81.

Idem, "The Meal at Emmaus," in Jean Delorme, ed., *The Eucharist in the New Testament: A Symposium* (Baltimore: Helicon, 1964) 105–21.

Idem, "Les pèlerins d'Emmaüs (Luc xxiv, 13-35)," in Romualdo María Díaz Carbonell, ed., *Miscellanea Biblica B. Ubach* (SDM 1; Montserrat: Abbatia Montisserrati, 1953) 349–74; reprinted in idem, *Évangiles synoptiques* 2.1128–52.

Dussaut, "Triptyque."

Dutheil, Michel, "Le pain partagé ou l'expérience pascale continuée," in *L'Eucharistie: parole nouvelle pour un monde nouveau* (Paris: Le Centurion, 1978) 15–47.

Ehrhardt, Arnold, "The Disciples of Emmaus," *NTS* 10 (1963–64) 182–201.

Idem, "Emmaus, Romulus and Apollonius," in Alfred Stuiber and Alfred Hermann, eds., *Mullus: Festschrift Theodor Klauser* (Münster i. W.: Aschendorff, 1964) 93–99.

Ehrlich, Michael, "The Identification of Emmaus with Abū Ġōš in the Crusader Period Reconsidered," *ZDPV* 112 (1996) 165–69.

Fendrich, Herbert, *Rembrandts Darstellungen des Emmausmahles* (Bochumer Schriften zur Kunstgeschichte 13; Frankfurt a. M.: Lang, 1990).

Feuillet, André, "L'apparition du Christ à Marie Madeleine Jean 20,11-18: Comparaison avec l'apparition aux disciples d'Emmaüs Luc 24,13-35," *EeV* 88 (1978) 193–204, 209–23.

Idem, "Les pèlerins d'Emmaüs (Lc 24,13-35)," *NV* 47 (1972) 89–98.

Idem, "La recherche du Christ dans la Nouvelle Alliance d'après la christophanie de Jean 20,11-18. Comparaison avec Cant. 3,1-4 et l'épisode des pèlerins d'Emmaüs," in *L'Homme devant Dieu: Mélanges offerts au père Henri de Lubac,* vol. 1 (Théologie 56; Paris: Aubier, 1963) 93–112.

Fianu, Emmanuel Kofi, "A Narrative-Critical and Theological Study of Luke 24,13-35," (Diss., Università Gregoriana, Rome, 2000).

Fiedler, Peter, "Die Gegenwart als österliche Zeit, erfahrbar im Gottesdienst: Die 'Emmausgeschichte' Lk 24,13-35," in Lorenz Oberlinner, ed., *Auferstehung Jesu—Auferstehung der Christen: Deutungen des Osterglaubens* (QD 105; Freiburg i. Br.: Herder, 1986) 124–44.

Figueras, Pau, "Quel est donc le chemin d'Emmaüs?" *NCI* 26 (1978) 132–34.

Forest, Jim, "In the Breaking of the Bread: Recognizing the Face of Jesus," *Sojourners* 14 (1985) 34–36.

Führmann-Eike, Monika, "Auf dem Weg nach Emmaus: Bibliodrama im Konfirmandenunter-

richt am Beispiel der 'Emmausjünger', Luk 24.13-35," *FoRe* 3 (1997) 34–38.

Gaide, Gilles, "Les apparitions du Christ ressuscité d'après s. Luc, Luc 24,13-48," *AsSeign* 24 (1969) 38–56.

Ghiberti, Giuseppe, "L'eucaristia in Lc 24e negli Atti degli Apostoli," *PSV* 7 (1983) 159–73.

Gibbs, James M., "Luke 24:13-33 and Acts 8:26-39: The Emmaus Incident and the Eunuch's Baptism as Parallel Stories," *BTF* 7 (1975) 17–30.

Gilbert, Maurice, "A Six-Day Retreat with the Disciples of Emmaus. Luke 24:13-35," in Pontificio Instituto biblico, ed., *Emmaus in Manresa: The Bible and the Exercise* (Gujarat/Rome: Gujarat Sahita Prakash, 1992) 10–24.

Gillièron, Bernard, *Un dimanche à Emmaüs: Quand le Vivant nous fait revivre* (Poliez-le-Grand: Moulin, 2005).

Idem, *Le repas d'Emmaüs: Quand les yeux s'ouvrent sur le Christ ressuscité* (Aubonne: Moulin, 1984).

Gillman, John, "The Emmaus Story in Luke-Acts Revisited," in Reimund Bieringer et al., eds., *Resurrection in the New Testament: Festschrift Jan Lambrecht* (BEThL 165; Leuven: Peeters, 2002) 165–88.

Goldberg, Gary J., "The Coincidences of the Emmaus Narrative of Luke and the Testimonium of Josephus," *JSPE* 13 (1995) 59–77.

Gordon, Edwin, "The Road to Emmaus," *HPR* 100 (2000) 25–32.

Graesslé, Isabelle, "De la conversation à la conversion: Actualité des chemins homilétiques," *RThPh* 129 (1997) 209–23.

Grappe, Christian, "Au croisement des lectures et aux origines du repas communautaire: Le récit des pèlerins d'Emmaüs, Luc 24,13-35," *EThR* 73 (1998) 491–501.

Grassi, Joseph A., "Emmaus Revisited (Luke 24,13-35 and Acts 8,26-39)," *CBQ* 26 (1964) 463–67.

Grünwaldt, Klaus, "Ökumenische Annäherung als Heimkehr: Zur päpstlichen Deutung der Emmaus-Geschichte," *DtPfrBl* 101 (2001) 123–24.

Guillaume, Jean-Marie, *Luc interprète des anciennes traditions sur la résurrection de Jésus* (Paris: Gabalda, 1979) 67–159.

Hall, I. H., "Luke xxiv.32 in Syriac," *Journal of the Society of Biblical Literature and Exegesis* 3 (1883) 153–54.

Hickling, Colin, "The Emmaus Story and Its Sequel," in Stephen Barton und Graham Stanton, eds., *Resurrection: Essays in Honour of Leslie Houlden* (London: SPCK, 1994) 21–23.

Hoffmann, "Graben."

Hölscher, Elisabeth, and Michael Klessmann, "Die Auferstehung einer Geschichte: Eine bibliodramatische Bearbeitung von Lk 24, 13-33," *EvTh* 54 (1994) 391–99.

Hoppe, Rudolf, "'Da gingen ihnen die Augen auf . . .': Die Emmausgeschichte als Schlüssel zur lukanischen Osterbotschaft," in P.-G. Müller, ed., *Das Zeugnis des Lukas* (Stuttgart: Katholisches Bibelwerk, 1985) 84–89.

Hornik, Heidi J., and Mikeal C. Parsons, "Caravaggio's London 'Supper at Emmaus': A Counter-Reformation Reading of Luke 24," *CScR* 28 (1999) 561–85.

Huffmann, Norman A., "Emmaus among the Resurrection Narratives," *JBL* 64 (1945) 205–26.

Hug, Joseph, *La finale de l'Évangile de Marc (Mc 16,9-20)* (EtB; Paris: Gabalda, 1978) 166–67 et passim.

Iersel, Bastiaan van, "Terug van Emmaus: Bijdragen tot een structurele tekstanalyse van Lc. 24,13-35," *TTh* 18 (1978) 294–323.

Jacobson, Howard, "A New Biblical Etymology," *VC* 53 (1999) 325.

Jockwig, Klemens, "Erfahrung und Vermittlung von Lebensbedeutsamkeit als Wesensmerkmal der Verkündigung: Homiletische Überlegungen zur Emmaus-Perikope (Lk 24,13-35)," *ThG(B)* 29 (1986) 119–25.

Johnson, Luke Timothy, "The Eucharist and the Identity of Jesus," *PrPe* 15 (2001) 230–35.

Just, Arthur A., *The Ongoing Feast: Table-fellowship and Eschatology at Emmaus* (Collegeville, Minn.: Liturgical Press, 1993).

Karris, Robert J., "Luke 24, 13-35," *Int* 41 (1987) 57–61.

Keller, Marie Noel, "A Road to Emmaus," *Way* 39 (1999) 39–47.

Koet, B.-J., "Some Traces of a Semantic Field of Interpretation in Luke 24.13-35," *Bijdragen* 46 (1985) 59–72.

Kremer, Jacob, "Die Bezeugung der Auferstehung Christi in Form von Geschichten: Zu Schwierigkeiten und Chancen heutigen Verstehens von Lk 24, 13-53," *GuL* 61 (1988) 172–87.

Lagrange, Marie-Joseph, "Origène, la critique textuelle et la tradition topographique," *RB* 4 (1895) 87–92.

Lash, Nicholas, *Theology on the Way to Emmaus* (London: SCM, 1986).

Leaney, A. R. C., "The Resurrection Narratives in Luke (xxiv.12-53)," *NTS* 2 (1955–56) 110–14.

Lee, G. M., "The Walk to Emmaus (Lk 24)," *ExpT* 77 (1966) 380–81.

Legrand, Lucien, "Christ the Fellow Traveller: The Emmaus Story in Lk 24.13-35," *ITS* 19 (1982) 33–34.

Liefeld, Walter L., "Exegetical Notes: Luke 24:13-35," *Trinity Journal* n.s. 2 (1981) 223–29.

Lindquist, J. E., "The Emmaus Story in St. Luke 24:13-35 as Early Catholic Liturgical Catechesis," in Martti Parvio et al., eds., *Ecclesia, Leiturgia, Ministerium: Studia in Honorem Toivo Harjunpää* (Helsinki: Loimaan Kirjapaino, 1977) 68–88.

Lombardi, Riccardo, "Emmaus: un'icona interpretative del rapporto catechesi-liturgia nell'itinerario di fede," *Lat* 52 (1986) 399–410.

Maas, Jacques, "'. . . puis il devient invisible et leur échappe': Les pèlerins d'Emmaüs," *SémBib* 111 (2003) 24–33.

Mackinlay, Shane, "Eyes Wide Shut: A Response to Jean-Luc Marion's Account of the Journey to Emmaus," *MoTh* 20 (2004) 447–56.

Mackowski, Robert M., "Where Is the Biblical Emmaus?" *ScEs* 32 (1980) 93–103.

Maggioni, Bruno, "I due discepoli di Emmaus (Lc 24, 13-35)," in *Initium sapientiae: scritti in onore di Franco Festorazzi suo 70. compleanno* (SRivBib 36; Bologna: EDB, 2000) 263–70.

Magne, Jean M., "Le pain de la multiplication des pains et des disciples d'Emmaüs comme preuve de l'origine gnostique des sacrements, de l'Église et du Sauveur," *StEv* 6 [TU 112] (1973) 341–47.

Mainville, Odette, "De Jésus prophète au Christ glorieux: Le récit d'Emmaüs comme lieu de passage identitaire et fonctionnel," in Emmanuelle Steffek and Yvan Bourquin, eds., *Raconter, Interpréter, Annoncer: Parcours de Nouveau Testament. Mélanges offerts à Daniel Marguerat* (MdB 47; Geneva: Labor et Fides, 2003) 160–68.

Manns, F. "Luc 24.32 et son contexte juif," *Anton* 60 (1985) 225–32.

Marion, Denis, "Luc 24, 13-35: Le repas d'Emmaüs. L'eucharistie, présence du ressuscité," *EeV.P* 110 (2000) 1–4.

Marion, Jean-Luc, "Ils le reconnurent et lui-même leur devint invisible," in Jean Duchesne et al., eds., *Demain l'Église* (Paris: Flammarion, 2001) 134–43.

Marsh, Clive, "Rembrandt Reads the Gospels: Form, Context and Theological Responsibility in New Testament Interpretation," *SJT* 50 (1997) 399–413.

Maxey, James, "The Road to Emmaus: Changing Expectations: A Narrative-Critical Study," *CThMi* 32 (2005) 112–23.

McBride, Denis, *Emmaus: The Gracious Visit of God according to Luke* (Dublin: Dominican Publications, 1991).

Mekkattukunnel, A. G., "Further Proof for the Unity of Luke-Acts," *BiBh* 29 (2003) 221–29.

Meynet, Roland, "Commençant à partir de Jérusalem, vous êtes les témoins de cela! L'annonce du kérygme aux nations en Lc 24. 33b-53," *StMiss* 51 (2002) 1–22.

Idem, "Comment établir un chiasme: À propos des 'pèlerins d'Emmaüs'," *NRTh* 100 (1978) 233–49.

Idem, *Évangile*, 1:232–35; 2:239–43.

Idem, *Guide*, 136–39.

Idem, *Parole*, 1:88–191; vol. 2, plate 14 and D 4.

Michael, J. H., "The Text of Luke 24:34," *ExpT* 60 (1949) 292.

Mottu, Henry, *Le geste prophétique: Pour une pratique protestante des sacrements* (Pratiques 17; Geneva: Labor et Fides, 1998) 14, 114–23.

Müller, H., "Menschen machen sich auf den Weg: Lk 24.13-35," *Diakonia* 35 (2004) 142–43.

Murphy, Richard T., "The Gospel for Easter Monday: The Story of Emmaus (Lk. 24:13-25)," *CBQ* 6 (1944) 131–41.

Nortjé, S. J., "On the Road to Emmaus: A Woman's Experience," in P. J. Hartin and J. H. Petzer, eds., *Text and Interpretation: New Approaches in the Criticism of the New Testament* (NTTS 15; Leiden: Brill, 1991) 271–80.

Ochs, R., "Die Emmaus-Erzählung: Beispielerzählung für das pastorale Handlungsmodell der Begleitung," *KatBl* 122 (1997) 107–9.

Okure, Teresa, "Von Bogota nach Hongkong—von Emmaus nach Sychar: Gedanken zu Lk 24 und Joh 4 aus afrikanischer Perspektive," *BK* 2 (1997) 74–79.

Orlett, Raymond, "An Influence of the Early Liturgy upon the Emmaus Account," *CBQ* 21 (1959) 212–19.

Overvoorde, Chris Stoffel, "Paintings of the Supper at Emmaus: Caravaggio and Rembrandt," *Christianity and the Arts* 8 (2001) 6–10.

Perrot, Charles, "Emmaüs ou la rencontre du Seigneur (Lc 24,13-35)," in Martin Benzerath et al., eds., *La Pâque du Christ, mystère de salut: Mélanges offerts au F.-X. Durrwell pour son 70e anniversaire* (LD 112; Paris: Cerf, 1982) 159–66.

Polaski, Sandra Hack, "Identifying the Unnamed Disciple: An Exercise in Reader-Response Criticism," *PRSt* 26 (1999) 193–202.

Pratscher, Wilhelm, "Predigt über Lk 24:13-31, gehalten in der evangelischen Hochschulgemeinde Wien im Wintersemester 1997/98," in James Alfred Loader und Hans Volker Kieweler, eds., *Vielseitigkeit des Alten Testaments: Festschrift für Georg Sauer* (Wiener Alttestamentliche Studien 1; New York: P. Lang, 1999) 465–70.

Prete, Benedetto, "Il racconto dei discepoli di Emmaus e le sue prospettive eucharistiche (Lc 24,13-35)," in *L'Eucharistia nella Comunità locale. XVIII Congresso Eucaristico Nazionale* (Udine: 1972) 47–70; reprinted in idem, *Opera*, 307–27.

Prétot, Michel, "'Ils le reconnurent à la fraction du pain': Le repas d'Emmaüs dans l'histoire de la tradition et son influence en théologie sacramentaire" (unpublished Diplomarbeit, Paris, 1988).

Prétot, Patrick, "Les yeux ouverts des pèlerins d'Emmaüs," *MD* 195 (1993) 7–48.

Radcliffe, Timothy, "Lk 24:13-35: The Emmaus Story, Necessity and Freedom," *NBl* 64 (1983) 483–93.

Ramaroson, Léonard, "La première question posée aux disciples d'Emmaüs en Lc 24,17," *ScEs* 47 (1995) 299–303.

Rasco, Emilio, "Lc 24,13-35: come riconoscere il Cristo dopo la Risurrezione, Theologica et historica," *Annali della Pontificia Facoltà teologica della Sardegna* 3 (1994) 111–26.

Read-Heimerdinger, Jenny, "Where Is Emmaus? Clues in the Text of Luke 24 in Codex Bezae," in D. G. K. Taylor, ed., *Studies in the Early Text of the Gospels and Acts: The Papers of the First Birmingham Colloquium on the Textual Criticism of the New Testament* (Text-Critical Studies 1; Atlanta: Society of Biblical Literature, 1999) 229–44.

Read-Heimerdinger, Jenny, and Josep Rius-Camps, "Emmaous or Oulammaous? Luke's Use of the Jewish Scriptures in the Text of Luke 24 in Codex Bezae," *RCatT* 27 (2002) 23–24.

Reece, Steve, "Seven Stades to Emmaus," *NTS* 48 (2002) 262–66.

Riesner, Rainer, "Wo lag das neutestamentliche Emmaus (Lukas 24,13)?" *Zeitschrift für Antikes Christentum* 11 (2007) 201–19.

Robinson, Bernard P., "The Place of the Emmaus Story in Luke Acts," *NTS* 30 (1984) 488–89.

Rosica, Thomas M., "In Search of Jesus: The Emmaus Lesson," *Church* [New York] 8 (1992) 21–25.

Idem, "The Road to Emmaus and the Road to Gaza: Luke 24:13-35 and Acts 8:26-40," *Worship* 68 (1994) 117–31.

Idem, "Two Journeys of Faith," *TBT* 31 (1993) 177–80.

Roth, Wolfgang, "Disclosure at Emmaus," *TBT* 31 (1993) 46–51.

Rousseau, François, "Un phénomène particulier d'inclusions dans Luc 24.13-35," *SR* 18 (1989) 67–79.

Rudrauf, Lucien, *Le repas d'Emmaüs: Étude d'un thème plastique et de ses variations en peinture et en sculpture* (2 vols.; Paris: Nouvelles Éditions latines, 1955–56).

Rusche, Helga, "Gastfreundschaft in Emmaus," *BiKi* 42 (1987) 65–67.

San Sylvester, Tung Kiem, "Experience of the Risen Lord in Luke 24:13-35," (Ph.D. dissertation extract, Urbaniana University, 1997).

Santaner, Marie-Abdon, *Quel homme suis-je? Du jardin d'Eden à la rencontre d'Emmaüs* (Paris: Médiaspaul, 1999).

Scheffler, Eben H., "Emmaus: A Historical Perspective (Lk 24:13-35)," *Neot* 23 (1989) 251–67.

Schnider, Franz, and Werner Stenger, "Beobachtungen zur Struktur der Emmausperikope (Lk 24, 13-35)," *BZ* n.s. 16 (1972) 94–114.

Schwarz, G., "οἱ δὲ ὀφθαλμοὶ αὐτῶν ἐκρατοῦντο? (Lukas 14, 16a)," *BN* 55 (1990) 16–17.

Schwemer, Anna Maria, "Der Auferstandene und die Emmausjünger," in Friedrich Avemarie and Hermann Lichtenberger, eds., *Auferstehung-Resurrection: The Fourth Durham-Tübingen Research Symposium* (WUNT 135; Tübingen: Mohr Siebeck, 2001) 95–117.

Shanks, Hershel, "Emmaus: Where Christ Appeared," *BARev* 34 (2008) 40–51.

Sidel, M., "'He Was Made Known to Them in the Breaking of the Bread': A Meditation on Luke 24:33-35," *PJT* 17 (1997) 98–99.

Smith, Robert H., "Did Not Our Hearts Burn Within Us?" *CThMi* 3 (1976) 323–36.

Thévenot, Xavier, "Emmaüs, une nouvelle Genèse? Une lecture psychanalytique de Genèse 2–3 et Luc 24,13-35," *MScRel* 37 (1980) 3–18.

Thiede, Carsten Peter, "À la recherche du miracle d'Emmaüs: Tradition littéraire et archéologie," *RRéf* 53 (2003–4) 15–29.

Idem, "Die Wiederentdeckung von Emmaus bei Jerusalem," *Zeitschrift für Antikes Christentum* 8 (2004) 593–99.

Tilborg, Sjef van. and P. C. Counet, *Jesus' Appearances*, 53–87.

Tremblay, Réal, "Le pain rompu à manger et le vin versé à boire, visage du crucifié ressuscité dans le temps de l'Église: Dans le sillage de Lc 24.13-35," *StMor* 38 (2000) 127–40.

Idem, "Pane e vino eucaristici, volto del risorto nella chiesa: nella scia di Lc 24, 13-35," *RdT* 41 (2000) 261–70.

Trudinger, Paul, "Two Lukan Gospel Stories Key to the Significance of the Dominical Sacraments in the Life of the Early Church," *DRev* 118 (2000) 17–26.

Vincent, Louis-Hugues, and Félix-Marie Abel, *Emmaüs, sa basilique et son histoire* (Paris: E. Leroux, 1932).

Wagner, Thomas, "Von Emmaus über Sodom und zurück," *Werkstatt Theologie* 10 (2003) 182–88.

Walther, O. Kenneth, "A Solemn One Way Trip Becomes a Joyous Round Trip: A Study of the Structure of Luke 24:13-35," *AThJ* 14 (1981) 60–67.

Wanke, Joachim, *Emmauserzählung: Eine Redaktionsgeschichtliche Untersuchung zu Lk 24.13-35* (EThSt 31; Leipzig: St. Benno, 1973).

Idem, "Wie sie ihn beim Brotbrechen erkannten: Zur Auslegung der Emmauserzählung Lk 24:13-35," *BZ* n.s. 18 (1974) 180–89.

Warma, Susanne J., "Christ, First Fruits, and the Resurrection: Observations on the Fruit Basket in Caravaggio's London 'Supper at Emmaus,'" *ZKW* 53 (1990) 584–86.

Weismann, F. J., "Kerygma y Eucaristía en Lucas 24,13-35," *Stromata* 43 (1987) 309–29.

Widengren, Geo, "Was Not Then Our Heart Burning in Us?" in Edgar C. Polomé, ed., *Essays in Memory of Karl Kerényi* (Journal of Indo-European Studies Monograph Series 4; Washington, D.C.: Journal of Indo-European Studies, Institute for the Study of Man, 1984) 116–22.

Williams, Frederick, "Archilochus and the Eunuch: the Persistence of a Narrative Pattern," *Classics Ireland* 1 (1994) 96–112.

Wojcik, Jan, *The Road to Emmaus: Reading Luke's Gospel* (West Lafayette, Ind.: Purdue University Press, 1989).

Wulf, F., "'Sie erkannten ihn beim Brechen des Brotes': Lk 24.35," *GuL* 37 (1964) 81–83.

Zwickel, Wolfgang, "Emmaus, ein neuer Versuch," *BN* 74 (1994) 33–36.

13 And behold, on the same day two of them were going to a village about sixty stadia from Jerusalem, whose name was Emmaus. 14/ And they were talking about everything that had happened. 15/ And it happened that while they were talking and discussing, Jesus himself came near and went with them. 16/ But their eyes were kept from recognizing him. 17/ He said to them, "What are you talking about as you are walking?" And they stood still, looking somber. 18/ One of them, named Cleopas, responded and said, "Are you the only one in Jerusalem who does not know what happened in the city in these days?" 19/ He said to them, "Which things?" They said, "The things about Jesus of Nazareth, who before God and all the people became a prophet[a] mighty in deed and word; 20/ how our chief priests and our leaders delivered him to be condemned to death and crucified him. 21/ But we were hoping he would be Israel's liberator, yet with all this, this is the third day since these events took place. 22/ Admittedly, some women among us astonished us. They came early to the tomb, 23/ and when they did not find his body, they came and said they had had an appearance of angels[b] who told them he was alive. 24/ Some of those with us went to the tomb and found the place as the women had said, but him they did not see." 25/ And he said to them, "O foolish and slow of heart to believe everything the prophets have declared! 26/ Was it not necessary that the Messiah should suffer these things and enter into his glory?" 27/ And beginning with Moses and all the prophets, he explained to them in all the Scriptures the things about himself. 28/ And as they approached the village where they were headed, he acted as if he were going farther. 29/ But they compelled him, saying, "Stay with us, because it is almost evening, and the day is about to end." And he went in to stay with them. 30/ And it happened, while he was at the table with them, he took the bread, blessed it, and when he had broken it he gave it to them. 31/ Then their eyes were opened, and they recognized him. But he vanished from their sight. 32/ They said to one another, "Did not our heart burn within us when he spoke to us on the road, when he opened the Scriptures to us?" 33/ At the same hour they got up and returned to Jerusalem. They found the Eleven and those who were with them. 34/ The latter said to them, "The Lord is risen indeed, and he has appeared to Simon."[c] 35/ But they explained what had happened to them on the way and how he had made himself known to them in the breaking of the bread.

a   Literally: "a man prophet."
b   Literally: "they had seen a vision of angels."
c   Or: "he appeared."

There is the structure of the Emmaus story; there is the movement of the text; and there is the context into which the narrative is inserted. There are also the many textual variants—sometimes the vocabulary is so Lukan, and at other times it is so original. There is the style characteristic of the special source. There are these connections between the text and the material of the story and the reader outside the text. There are the millions of readers who have left no traces and the thousands of the men and women who in their writings or their art have expressed their interpretation. Finally, there is this Jesus, who is present and absent at the time of the incident, in the story, and today.

Synchronic Analysis

Following the work of Jeanne d'Arc and Roland Meynet,[1] Louis Dussaut has carefully analyzed the composition of what he calls the second, central phase of the triptych that constitutes chap. 24 of the Gospel of Luke.[2] He even thinks that "this component offers one of the most prestigious, concentric symmetries of the Bible."[3] While there is no doubt about the beginning of the literary unit (v. 13), the end leaves the exegete uncertain about what to do with vv. 33-35. According to Dussaut, these transition verses introduce the next episode. Since they still deal with the two disciples, I connect them with the preceding verses while noting the reference to the apostle Peter. As he ran to the empty tomb at the end of the previous literary unit (v. 12), here he is granted an appearance of the Risen One (v. 34). Luke wants to see his authority cover the first two witnesses of the resurrection.

Although I do not look for chiasms everywhere, I do accept the concentric structure highlighted by the French researchers. A conclusion (vv. 33-35) does serve as a counterpart to an introduction (vv. 13-14). At the beginning, the two disciples are alone; at the end they are without Christ. In both places they reflect on their memories. In the introduction they are leaving Jerusalem; in the conclusion they return to it. The difference in their state of mind corresponds to this difference in their direction. Misunderstanding, despair, and isolation are replaced by recognition, hope, and community.[4] Along with Dussaut, I think that the conversation between the disciples and Jesus is the center of the pericope, which is bounded by the sudden appearance (v. 15b) and disappearance (v. 31c) of Jesus. Two passages (vv. 15-19a and vv. 28-32) surround the central part (vv. 19b-27). Each of them mentions walking ($\sigma \nu \mu \pi o \rho \epsilon \acute{\nu} o \mu \alpha \iota$, "going with," v. 15; $\pi o \rho \epsilon \acute{\nu} o \mu \alpha \iota$, "to go," v. 28; see v. 13) and uses the verb "to approach" ($\grave{\epsilon} \gamma \gamma \acute{\iota} \zeta \omega$: v. 15, for Jesus; v. 28, for the two disciples). The formula $\kappa \alpha \grave{\iota} \grave{\epsilon} \gamma \acute{\epsilon} \nu \epsilon \tau o$ appears here in v. 15 and there in v. 30; it is followed by an exchange of words (vv. 17-18) and preceded by a dialogue (v. 29). Jesus' sudden arrival, which the two disciples do not recognize (vv. 15-16), is answered by the abrupt disappearance of the one the men have recognized (vv. 30-31). There are other symmetries: the tense discussion between the disciples, who finally come to a halt (v. 17), and the pressing invitation to Jesus to stay with them (v. 29); the pretense of Jesus, who appears to know nothing (vv. 18-19a), and the pretense of the same Jesus that he is going to continue his journey (v. 28b). There is also a contrasting correspondence between the status of Jesus the traveler (v. 18b) and the desire to keep him with them (v. 29b). The central part, in particular, is structured logically: it has two summaries of speeches, that of the disciples (vv. 19b-24, which can be further subdivided), and that of Jesus (vv. 25-27). In the center of this center there is a reminder of the angel's statement that Jesus is alive (v. 23b). It is elegantly framed on either side by the references to the women and the tomb (vv. 22 and 24). When Jesus finally gives his version of the events he uses in reverse order (vv. 25-27) the words of the disciples (vv. 19b-21): the human lack of intelligence, the Messiah's suffering, the oracles of the prophets. Finally, inclusions emphasize the symmetries: the one concerning Jesus (v. 19b and v. 27d); the passion of Jesus (v. 20 and v. 26a); the expressed, then corrected, eschatological hope (v. 21ab and v. 25bc); the universal scope of the

---

1   See d'Arc, "Partage du pain"; eadem, *Pèlerins*; Meynet, "Chiasme"; idem, *Parole*, 1:188–91 and vol. 2, plate 14 and D4; idem, *Guide*, 136–39; idem, *Évangile*, vol. 1, section 4; 2.239–43.

2   See the synchronic analysis above of 23:56b—24:12.

3   Dussaut, "Triptyque," 170.

4   Here, as elsewhere in this exegesis of the Emmaus disciples, I draw on an unpublished work of Henry Mottu, for which I am very grateful. See also Dussaut, "Triptyque," 171.

particular event (vv. 19d and 21c facing vv. 25c and 27b-d); Israel's fate (v. 21a) and the Scriptures of this people (v. 27).

An extremely simple version of the outline is the following:

vv. 13-14 Introduction
    vv. 15-19a Frame
        vv. 19b-27 The disciples' dialogue (vv. 19b-24) and their dialogue with Jesus (vv. 25-27)
    vv. 28-32 Frame
vv. 33-35 Conclusion[5]

Jacques Dupont has correctly reminded us that the formal structure should not cause us to forget the movement, the dynamics of the story.[6] There is indeed a dramatic progression from the declaration of the women to the unseen presence of the Risen One to his appearance. It is not easy for a concentric symmetry to portray the long march and the moment of recognition.[7] There is indeed a scene of recognition whose tension comes from the difference between the readers, who know Jesus' identity, and the actors, who are walking in the dark. As Corina Combet-Galland and Françoise Smyth-Florentin have seen well, this founding narrative articulates an "afterward" and an "already": The two disciples discovered "afterward" that Jesus was "already there."[8] This unexpected discovery—and this is the paradox that gives life and tension to the story—comes at the end of a slow gestation. Echoing the work of a group on semiotics, Antoine Delzant rejects the monopoly of any methodology and lists the various criteria used to divide the text and to follow the narrative program or programs.[9] To identify the site one notices that there is a long road to Emmaus (fourteen verses) and a brief return to Jerusalem (three verses). Looking at the persons, one sees clearly that the disciples and Jesus have different plans before they converge. And when one looks for the global function of the story, Delzant suggests the distinction introduced by Tzvetan Todorov between the "narrative" logic that tells what is happening and the "ritual" logic that explains what it is about.[10] The Emmaus story belongs to this second type. It scarcely explains the sequence of the events, but it gives meaning to the events that are known. And it emphasizes the ἔδει ("it was necessary," v. 26), thus God's plan.

Jean-Noël Aletti, who also is sensitive to the formal aspects of the text, argues that Luke, who respects the rules of antiquity's rhetoric, chose to summarize his entire Gospel in the episode of the Emmaus disciples.[11] Indeed, the two disciples are able to collect in a few sentences the origin, the ministry, and the passion of one who has occupied center stage for more than twenty chapters. In what is said in summary and what is happening, the evangelist gives this pericope as well as all of chap. 24 the function of a conclusion.[12]

Diachronic Analysis

In its vocabulary, syntax, style, and content the Emmaus episode represents the work of the evangelist.[13] The terminology of walking (πορεύομαι, "to walk," "to be on the way," v. 13 and v. 28), the repeated use of "and it happened . . ." (καὶ ἐγένετο, v. 15 and v. 30), the periphrastic construction (ἦσαν πορευόμενοι, "they were on the way," v. 13), the references to other parts of the Gospel (Jesus' prophetic ministry, v. 19; the passion, v. 20; and the women at the tomb, vv. 22-23), the theology of God's plan (οὐχὶ . . . ἔδει, "should he not?" v. 26), as well as the agreement between scriptural prophecy and its fulfillment in history ("everything the prophets have declared," v. 25; "and beginning with Moses . . . ," v. 27).

5   Dussaut ("Triptyque," 192–93) gives a much more detailed version of the outline.

6   Dupont, "Disciples." Aletti (*Quand Luc raconte*, 222–23) is also of the opinion that Luke organizes the episodes in a dramatic ascent.

7   Combet-Galland and Smyth-Florentin ("Pain," 323) begin their article by calling attention to this contrast.

8   Ibid., 327.

9   Delzant, "Disciples."

10   Tzvetan Todorov, *The Poetics of Prose* (trans. Richard Howard; Ithaca, N.Y.: Cornell University Press, 1977) 119–42, esp. 130–33.

11   I refer here to Aletti, *Quand Luc raconte*, 221–23; but one must also mention his *Art de raconter*, 177–98; and idem, "Signes."

12   See also Schnider and Stenger, "Struktur."

13   See Wanke, *Emmauserzählung*, 23–126; Dillon, *Eye-Witnesses*, 69–155; Guillaume, *Luc interprète*, 67–159; Fitzmyer, 2:1555–56.

All of these elements correspond exactly to Luke's ways of believing, thinking, and writing.

There are two reasons, however, that speak against concluding that the evangelist invented this episode. The first comes from form criticism, the method that believes that the literary units are the written form of stories that first circulated orally. The story of the Emmaus meeting has the characteristics of this original oral literature. The story stands on its own; it is of limited size and involves only a few characters; in addition, it fulfills a function that goes beyond the episodic; when it is told, it nourishes the faith of the first communities.

Complementing form criticism, redaction criticism—that is to say, the study of the redactional effort of the evangelists—has shown that while Luke interprets the memories he has received in terms of his theology, he does not create completely new episodes. The evangelist is attached to the traditions he inherits from his community. Here he reworks one of them.

A second reason confirms the first. Even if it were Lukan, the episode of the Emmaus disciples does not come completely from its author.[14] In its vocabulary, and especially its style, the story shows that it earlier belonged to the special material. The full majesty and the slow progression of the narrative correspond to the literary habits of Luke's predecessor. The precision and even the vocabulary he chooses also betray what the author imposed on Luke: the disciples debate together what has happened (ὁμιλέω, v. 14; and συμβαίνω, v. 14, are not common in Luke-Acts); their eyes are prevented (literally, "restrained," ἐκρατοῦντο, v. 16) from recognizing the traveler who accompanies them. The unfruitful character of the words they exchange (ἀντιβάλλω, v. 17), the disappointment, which renders them immobile (σκυθρωποί, "looking somber," v. 17), and "to pretend" (προσποιοῦμαι, v. 28) are expressions of a high literary quality. Non-Lukan is the rhetorical exclamation "O foolish and slow of heart . . . ," (ὦ ἀνόητοι καὶ βραδεῖς

τῇ καρδίᾳ, v. 25), which is reminiscent of Paul's anger in Gal 3:1 (ὦ ἀνόητοι Γαλάται, "O foolish Galatians"). Characteristic, finally, of the special source is the concern to give names to the characters, here Cleopas (v. 18), Martha and Mary (10:38-39), Lazarus (16:20), and Zacchaeus (19:1).

Like many before me, among others Joachim Wanke, Gerd Petzke, Jean-Marie Guillaume, and Joseph A. Fitzmyer,[15] I think that Luke takes over and adapts a traditional story. In my opinion, it had already been written by the author of the special source. As always in such cases, one must ask how much is due to the final redaction, that of Luke. To answer the question, one must have points of comparison. The only one available to us is of limited interest. It is the summary of the episode as it appears in Mark's inauthentic conclusion (Mark 16:12-13): "After that he appeared in a different form to two of them as they were walking to the country. And they came back to tell the others; they did not believe them either." For the comparison to be useful, we must be certain that Mark 16:12-13 does not depend on Luke 24. That is not certain, however, since Mark's inauthentic conclusion specifically gathers recollections of the resurrection of Jesus, usually from the Gospels themselves. It may be, however, that the brief presentation of the Emmaus disciples is based not on Luke 24 but on a phase of the story older than the Lukan redaction. A detail of Mark 16:12, which does not correspond to Luke 24, suggests as much: Jesus' appearance takes place while the two disciples are going not to Emmaus but εἰς ἀγρόν ("to the field" or "into the country"). Thus, it is possible that we have here the summary of the oral phase of the episode or that of the redaction of the special source. In this case we would have access to the original structure or to an old form of the story. Essential to the story would be an appearance of Christ in a different form to two disciples on their way to the country. After their return they unsuccessfully tell the other disciples about their encounter. This brief

---

14   See Guillaume, *Luc interprète*, 71–73. This author analyzes the vocabulary of the pericope, which is not characteristic of Luke. He is of the opinion, in my view mistakenly, that this vocabulary comes not from a tradition Luke would have taken over but from the evangelist's knowledge of the Greek language. He describes the literary genres to which scholars have attributed the Emmaus episode: a

travel legend, a recognition scene, or an epiphany (90–92). For him it is primarily kerygmatic instruction. In his opinion the genre continues to be complex.

15   Schnider and Stenger, "Struktur," 100–112; Wanke, *Emmauserzählung*, 122–25; Petzke, *Sondergut*, 201–2; Guillaume, *Luc interprète*, 93–96; Fitzmyer, 2:1554–55.

summary confirms the presence of two disciples and the revelation that leads to the recognition. The appearance of the Risen One seems to have had difficulty in the early phase. The expression "in a different form" suggests as much. The narrative of Mark 16:12-13, like that of Luke 24, ends with an unsuccessful announcement. Although the incident exists in both versions of the story, the meeting of the Emmaus pilgrims with the other disciples is not essential to the story, and it may have been grafted on when the various appearance stories were connected and coordinated.

Moreover, I would attribute further redundancies to the account of the Lukan redaction. The historical recollection offered by the two disciples may not always have been as extensive as is thought today. From the narrative point of view, the only thing that mattered was their disappointed hopes. Similarly, the final speech of revelation did not necessarily include the scriptural demonstration so characteristic of Luke (vv. 25b-27; see below—in the appearance to the Eleven vv. 44-49 are also Lukan). These speculations must remain hypothetical as long as the exegete has no other Synoptic comparison. The traditional story remains inaccessible to us in its precise form.[16]

Commentary

■ **13** Luke connects the next episode, not without some awkwardness, to what has gone before. He forgets v. 12 and associates the two disciples with the group mentioned in vv. 9-11.[17] These two pilgrims are part of "all the others" and not the apostles, since Cleopas and probably the other disciple do not belong to the group of the Twelve. They may have been part of the Seventy that Luke alone mentions (10:1-20). Christian tradition has regarded the companion of Cleopas as a man.[18] Since he likes to present a man and a woman together (see 1:5-38; 15:3-10), the evangelist may well have imagined that the second person was a woman.[19]

The evangelist underscores that all the events he relates in chap. 24 take place on the same day ($\dot{\epsilon}\nu$ $\alpha\dot{\upsilon}\tau\hat{\eta}$ $\tau\hat{\eta}$ $\dot{\eta}\mu\dot{\epsilon}\rho\alpha$ means "on that day," "on the same day," v. 13). Following the concentric symmetry of the passage, vv. 13-14 are the counterpart of vv. 33-35 (the return of the disciples to Jerusalem).

There is some uncertainty among the manuscripts. Most of them fix the distance from Jerusalem to Emmaus at sixty stadia, about eleven kilometers.[20] A minority—but by no means minor manuscripts, since they include the Codex Sinaiticus ($\aleph$ = 01)—raise the number to 160 stadia, or thirty kilometers.[21] Since the plot anticipates a return to Jerusalem that night, the longer distance is unlikely (it is to be explained by the claim of a city at that distance in the fourth century, the century of the first pilgrimages). Luke seems sure of the distance. Contrary to his usual custom he does not say "about" ($\dot{\omega}\varsigma$).

Locating and identifying Emmaus has intrigued Christians since antiquity. Modern scholars have shared this curiosity. In the 1970s, forty scholarly studies on the subject had already appeared,[22] and a new group has been added to the list.[23] Let us begin by saying that the

---

16 See Wanke (*Emmauserzählung*, 114, 125), who refuses to describe the contours of this tradition but nevertheless says that it is rooted in liturgy. In his review of Wanke's work (*RSR* 64 [1976] 441), Xavier Léon–Dufour writes: "In this tradition, which the author along with Bultmann assumes is very old, one cannot determine the content of the text but only its core material."

17 See $\dot{\epsilon}\xi$ $\alpha\dot{\upsilon}\tau\hat{\omega}\nu$ ("of them").

18 Some have even wanted to identify him as Peter. See Fitzmyer (2:1563), who calls attention to this hypothesis before rejecting it. See nn. 62, 66, and 81. Bruno of Segni (*Comm. Luc.* 49 [*PL* 165:446]) is of the opinion that it is Luke himself. See the next note.

19 See Kathleen E. Corley's review of Just, *Ongoing Feast* (*JBL* 114 [1995] 340). Actually, the idea is

older; see Fitzmyer (2:1563), who indicates that many have wanted to see the wife of Cleopas in this person. He accepts this solution no more than the previous one.

20 A stadion measures 600 Greek feet and 625 Roman feet: "varying widely depending on the different foot sizes" (O. W. Reinmuth, "Stadion," *KP* 5 [1979] 336–37), the equivalent of 180–92 meters.

21 The text-critical question is examined by DeGuglielmo ("Emmaus"), who for external and internal reasons selects the number sixty. See also Fitzmyer, 2:1561.

22 See Wanke, *Emmauserzählung*, 37–42.

23 For more recent literature, see Zwickel, "Emmaus." See also Benoit, *Passion and Resurrection*, 273–76; Mackowski, "Emmaus"; Fitzmyer, 2:1561–62.

term Emmaus is derived from the Hebrew חמם or חמת and means "spring," "hot spring." Of course, various sites could bear this name.[24] There are primarily five places that have captured the attention of believers and scholars. We can dismiss Ammaus, Nicopolis in Greek, also known by the name Latrun, which is located on the road from Jerusalem to Tel Aviv. This is probably a "city," while Luke calls Emmaus a "village" (κώμη, v. 13).[25] If a Byzantine tradition going back to antiquity identifies this as the location,[26] it is because the place and probably the claims of the Christians of this city were important. It may be that this explains the change from 60 to 160 stadia in the manuscript tradition, since Ammaus-Nicopolis is about 30 kilometers from the holy city, about 160 stadia.[27] Medieval Latin pilgrims have proposed two other locations. The first is Abu Gosh, known in the Bible as Kiryat Yeʾarim, about 15 kilometers west of Jerusalem.[28] Then there is El Qoubeibeh, 14 kilometers northwest of the holy city. "The 'movement' of the medieval Emmaus [Abu Gosh] to the present site of the village of El-Qoubeibeh seems to have been motivated by security reasons."[29] Political and even practical reasons have also played a role. The absence of ancient traditions and archaeological evidence leads me to eliminate these two sites as well, especially since they seem never to have worn the name Ammaus or Emmaus. The fourth site, Mozah, located on a hill 6 kilometers west of the holy city,[30] is called Ammaus by the historian Josephus (Bell.

7.6.6 §217). "Its Arabic name, Koloniyeh, probably comes from the colony of Roman soldiers established by Vespasian after the capture of Jerusalem in the year 70 of our era."[31] The objection to Mozah is that this market town is too close to Jerusalem, the equivalent of 30 stadia.[32] We must therefore reject it also, unless the distance of 60 stadia represents a round trip, which is unlikely. In 1994 Wolfgang Zwickel proposed a fifth site, Bir el-Hammam, whose name suggests a hot spring and near which archaeological ruins have been found that come especially from the Hellenistic and Roman periods.[33] It is a village, and it is the right distance from Jerusalem (10 kilometers as the crow flies, 11 kilometers by road). These arguments do not appear to be enough, however, to gain the support of scholars and believers, who must, therefore, continue to be uncertain. Yet one thing now seems to be established: in antiquity, to speak of 30 stadia was to indicate about an hour's walk.[34] Thus, according to Luke, Emmaus was a two-hour walk from Jerusalem. Luke gives this detail because of his desire to locate the appearances of the Risen One in the holy city or its surroundings.[35] For the rest, it continues to be a mystery.

■ **14** The sentence is carefully crafted without being characteristically Lukan. I sense the hand of the author of the special source. The two disciples talk while they are walking. The logic of the narrative requires that they discuss what has happened.

■ **15-16** Something happens then that is important in

24 One finds the same in Greece, where many places are called Loutra or Therma because they have baths.

25 This city is mentioned in 1 Maccabees (3:40, 57; 4:3; 9:50), in Josephus (e.g., *Bell.* 1.11.2 §222), in rabbinic sources, and Pliny the Elder (*Nat. hist.* 5.15.70); see Fitzmyer, 2:1561. Vincent and Abel argue for this site in their impressive work, *Emmaus.* These two scholars are of the opinion that Emmaus was a village in Jesus' day after its decline as a city and before its renewed importance under the name Nicopolis.

26 See Figueras, "Chemin," 132.

27 It is even possible that the correction from 60 to 160 is the work of Origen, who visited Ammaus Nicopolis. See Lagrange, "Origène," 87–92; Benoit, *Passion and Resurrection,* 272–73.

28 On Abu Gosh, see Figueras, "Chemin," 132, 133–34.

29 Figueras, "Chemin," 134.

30 Mozah is attested under this name in Josh 18:26 and in both Talmuds.

31 Figueras, "Chemin," 132. This is the site chosen, with caution, by Benoit, *Passion and Resurrection,* 273–74; by Mackowski, "Emmaus"; and also Wilfried Eckey (*Das Lukasevangelium: Unter Berücksichtigung seiner Parallelen* [2 vols.; Neukirchen-Vluyn: Neukirchener Verlag, 2004] 2:975–76), who mentions several advocates of this hypothesis.

32 A manuscript of the text of Josephus *Bell.* 7.6.6 §217 indicates, probably under the influence of Luke 24:13, sixty stadia instead of thirty.

33 See Zwickel, "Emmaus."

34 See Christa Möller and Götz Schmitt, *Siedlungen Palästinas nach Flavius Josephus* (Beihefte zum Tübinger Atlas des Vorderen Orients, B 14; Wiesbaden: Reichert, 1976) 16.

35 Fitzmyer (2:1562) and Johnson (393) insist on this point.

the eyes of the author and his readers. The narrative tension comes from the fact that the characters in the story do not realize it. "And it happened" (καὶ ἐγένετο) marks the beginning of an action that will be decisive. Καὶ αὐτός, attracting the attention of the readers, underscores the importance of the person who suddenly accompanies the two disciples (a christological αὐτός).[36] The message to the women (vv. 5-7) turns out to be true: Jesus is alive. The verb "to talk" (ὁμιλέω) shows that this is a serious conversation (in Acts 20:11 the verb appears in a liturgical context and almost has the meaning of "to preach").[37] The verb συζητέω ("to endeavor together," "to discuss," even "to dispute") implies a difference here, if not to say a difference of opinion.[38] What is most important, however, is not what happens on the side of the disciples but that Jesus approaches them and goes on the way with them. The readers will recall how important the verb πορεύομαι ("to walk," "to be under way") has been in the previous chapters of the Gospel.[39] It expresses the determination of the one who is going up to Jerusalem to face his tragic fate. Here it is the disciples' turn to walk, but without knowing it they are not alone. The author wants to underscore the weakness of the pilgrims (their eyes "were kept from recognizing him," ἐκρατοῦντο τοῦ μὴ ἐπιγνῶναι αὐτόν) in order to prepare for the scene of recognition. According to the symmetry envisaged (recognition and disappearance), vv. 15-16 correspond to vv. 30-31. Luke is an advocate of "seeing" as much as of "hearing."[40] The eye represents intelligence here. The disciples see and thus should

understand (in reality, they do not understand; they do not seem surprised [v. 18] when Jesus speaks to them [v. 17]). The passive "they were forced" (ἐκρατοῦντο, translated in the context as "they were kept") is skillful: The author suggests both the human weakness and the divine strength, which prepares the denouement in advance. The evangelist will not fail to note that at the time of recognition "then their eyes were opened, and they recognized him" (v. 31).[41] The readers of antiquity—and perhaps those of today also!—will think of Odysseus from their high school or college classes. He remained incognito for a long time before he was recognized by his son Telemachos and his old nurse Eurycleia and was found out by his wife Penelope (Homer *Od.* 13.185–23.296).

■ **17-18** Here, according to Luke, are the first words the Risen One speaks. Yet since the speaker has not yet revealed himself, his words cause not the joy of reunion but a sad surprise. The two disciples do not understand how one cannot know about the recent events.[42] There is no malice, however, in Jesus' question, nor does it imply anything.[43] Still, the two disciples stop.[44] Luke adds that they remain standing "looking somber" (σκυθρωποί; the adjective, rare, is emphasized by its position at the end of the sentence). The meaning of this adjective, which refers to one's facial expression, vacillates among sadness, severity, sulking, weariness, a bad mood, perplexity, and anxiety. It is difficult to find the nuance intended here. What is certain is that the pilgrims express their disapproval in a nonverbal way. Following the concentric

---

36   See vol. 1 of this commentary, 168, on 5:1.
37   See Michael Lattke ("ὁμιλέω, etc." *EDNT* 2 [1991] 509–10), who emphasizes the communitarian dimension this verb introduces.
38   See Edvin Larsson, "συζητέω, etc." *EDNT* 3 (1993) 284.
39   On πορεύομαι, see vol. 2 of this commentary on 9:51.
40   See Stephen D. Moore, "The Gospel of the Look," in David Jobling and Stephen D. Moore, eds., *Poststructuralism as Exegesis* (Semeia 54; Atlanta: Scholars Press, 1992) 159–96.
41   This twofold sharing corresponds to the Platonic and later popular idea that seeing is possible when the eye casts rays of light from the inside and when the sun or some other source of light does the same; see the excursus on the eye as the light of the body in vol. 2 of this commentary on 11:34.

42   The author—I imagine it is more likely the author of the special source than of the Gospel—skillfully recalls the situation without repeating it: ἀντιβάλλω ("to exchange," "to talk about") takes over the idea of the tense conversation (vv. 14-15), and περιπατέω ("to walk"), that of the pathway (vv. 13, 15).
43   Luke often uses the plural οἱ λόγοι ("the words"— twelve times in the Gospel and nine times in Acts). He always takes seriously these words of the various characters and even gives them a certain solemnity.
44   The intransitive ἐστάθησαν, an aorist passive in form but with an active sense, signifies here that the disciples stopped and not that they stayed there or that they remained upright.

symmetry, this expression finds its positive counterpart in v. 29, in their enthusiasm to keep Jesus with them.

The story turns toward the dialogue (note ἀποκρι-θείς, "responded," v. 18). Cleopas does not beat around the bush: "are you the only one" (σὺ μόνος) is not without a touch of aggressiveness. In his view, Jesus' ignorance can only mean that he is a stranger passing through (παροικέω, which originally meant "to dwell nearby," in Luke's day designates the status of a foreigner, a new resident, or guest who is just passing through; the verb has no technical or legal meaning here).[45] The author creates a certain suspense with his vague description of Cleopas.[46] This process allows the debate to flare up again in v. 19. While there is a concentric symmetry, there is also an intentional imbalance between the slow conversation, charged with misunderstanding, and the sudden, concluding revelation (vv. 30-32).

A word about Cleopas and his name. The name is an abbreviated form of Cleopatros (the masculine Κλεό-πατρος existed as well as the feminine Κλεοπάτρα). The name has been compared with the Semitic Klopas, but in reality the two names have no relationship. Some have even identified the Cleopas of Luke with Clopas, the husband or the father of one of the three Marys, who, according to John 19:25, stood at the foot of the cross. If, moreover, that Mary was the sister of the Virgin, Cleopas would become Jesus' uncle![47]

■ **19-24** No sooner is he interrupted by a new question of Jesus—a question contained in a single word, the interrogative pronoun "which things?" (ποῖα)—than Cleopas, supported here by his companion,[48] finally expresses what is bothering them. First he tells in brief the outline of the Gospel of Luke as if it were stripped of its kerygmatic shell. On the factual level, he makes no mistakes. Jesus is indeed from Nazareth; he was a prophet in word and deed; he placed himself in the sight of God and presented himself to the people (v. 19). In short, that is what the evangelist had told up to the passion narrative. Without giving the reasons for this hostility, Luke con-

tinues with a severely condensed account of the passion (v. 20). Every word of this summary is found in chaps. 22–23.[49] Added to the factual objectivity is the subjectivity of the disappointed and confused companions. With great skill the evangelist recounts the devastating effect of a story deprived of its kerygmatic dimension. The hope is expressed in the imperfect (ἠλπίζομεν, "we were hoping"). It was legitimate, even if it was ambiguous. What kind of Israel's deliverance is meant? Deliverance from the Romans and political oppression or from sin and the inevitable death? Whatever it was, the hope was in the dim past: It is the third day already. The reader notes the irony this chronology evokes: Was not the third day the duration predicted by the Lukan Jesus in some of the announcements of his passion (9:22; 18:33)?

Cleopas continues his story from his own perspective, namely, that of the group of disciples who were impervious to the message of the women and the wisdom of the angels. In vv. 22-24, more talkative than ever, the obstinate unbeliever summarizes what the readers recently have come to discover: the episode of the women at the empty tomb, accurately summarized, and the journey of some men to the tomb. The summary of Peter's trip to the tomb is perfect in every way, with one exception. Why does the evangelist speak of the visitors in the plural (τινὲς τῶν σὺν ἡμῖν, "some of those with us")? Does he know that somebody was with Peter, as in John 20:3-10? I think it is more likely that Luke wants to remain vague. These are facts that change nothing about Jesus' tragic death. There is, however, a glimmer of hope in the background. Cleopas admits that neither the women nor the men have seen the dead Christ. Thus, the absence of Jesus' body intrigues the reader, who hears for the second time the angelic message: he is alive (v. 23, referring back to v. 5). As we have seen,[50] the concentric symmetry puts vv. 22-24 at the heart of the chiasm. The unsuccessful and successful visit of the women (vv. 22-23) corresponds to the unsuccessful and successful visit of the men (v. 24). The difference between the two is the

---

45 See LSJ, s.v.; BAGD, s.v.

46 Nevertheless, the content of the dramatic events that took place is not explained in v. 14, or in v. 15, or in v. 17, or in v. 18!

47 See Just, *Ongoing Feast*, 72–74.

48 See nn. 18–19 above.

49 For example, the "chief priests" and the "leaders,"

23:13. While all the words are found there, they are not necessarily used in the same way. In chaps. 22–23, the verb "to deliver" is used to speak of the transfer to the Jewish authorities rather than the sending to the ordeal.

50 See the synchronic analysis above.

fact that the women have seen the angels (ὀπτασία ἀγγέλων) and have heard their message "who said" (οἳ λέγουσιν): "he lives" (αὐτὸν ζῆν).

■ **25-27** The readers discover the sharp rebuke, but they do not know how Cleopas and the other disciple respond to Jesus' reprimand and criticism. The adjective "slow" (βραδεῖς) is probably one of the keys of the narrative. Things have lasted too long. The length of the sentence underscores their slowness in believing. The voice of the strange visitor does not blame his companions for not recognizing him. A resurrected body does not immediately resemble the human being whose existence it recreates. Nor does this voice express two other complaints. One is that they had not believed Jesus' predictions of his passion; the other that they were unable to discern the meaning of recent events. No, the accusation is about reading the Holy Scriptures. The two persons challenged are "senseless" (ἀνόητοι, literally "without intelligence") because they did not believe (τοῦ πιστεύειν) with a reasonable and not an absurd faith, because they were slow in heart (faith is not only intellectual; it is also emotional, personal, existential, holistic).

What follows is a condensation of Lukan theology: the articulation of a prophetic statement and a kerygmatic summary. What the prophets have proclaimed and predicted (λαλέω in the sense of pronouncing solemn words, here the oracles) is what they have just witnessed, the necessary (ἔδει) passion (παθεῖν) of the Messiah, as well as what they still must realize—Christ's entry into his glory. After having been focused on the disciples' groping, vv. 14-15 and vv. 19-24, all the attention turns to Jesus' explanation (v. 27). In its twofold structure of Law and Prophets the entire Scripture (and as if this were not enough, Jesus emphasizes "in all the scriptures," v. 27) is about him. The location of the words "the things about himself" (τὰ περὶ ἑαυτοῦ) at the end gives them a certain emphasis.[51] Note also the play of the prepositions: The two instances of ἀπό ("of," "from," translated "with" in v. 27) underscore the origin of "everything the prophets have declared" (v. 25) and ἐν ("in," v. 27) directs the attention to the content of the Scriptures. The connection between promise and fulfillment needs

an explanation, which, as the verb διερμήνευσεν shows, Jesus gives. This verb, which literally means "he translated," recognizes that there is a distance between the two realities that must be overcome (hence the prefix δια-, "through"); a translation, transferring, explanation, interpretation is required. Luke may know the verb from the Pauline tradition where glossolalia needs a translator-interpreter in order to become a source of edification (1 Cor 14:26-28). In a parallel way, the risen Christ avoids the ambiguity of the prophecies and their fulfillment and illuminates his own destiny in the light of the Scripture. For faith everything is clear: the Scripture and Jesus' fate. For doubt everything is obscure: the sense of Scripture and the sense of Jesus' destiny.

Now comes the suspense. The author does not say that Cleopas and the person with him understand the hermeneutics of the Risen One. Instead, he implies that they are still slow to believe. The disappointment of Jesus and the Gospel's readers with this lack of understanding is even more dramatic in the concentric symmetry in which the strong words of the Risen One (vv. 25-27) correspond to the hopeless words of the disciples (vv. 19b-21).

■ **28-29** Here is a transition that maintains the suspense and gives the sense that something else is about to happen. The two walkers near their goal, while the stranger acts as if he intends to go on. Thus, it seems that the hour of parting has come. The repetition of the verb πορεύομαι ("to go," "to be under way") is not accidental. Walking is a model of human life, as the life of faith, and it must come to an end, even if only provisionally. Life has its stages. For the second time (v. 28) Jesus "pretends" (vv. 17-19), but as he had "gone with them" (συνεπορεύετο αὐτοῖς, v. 15), in the end he will stop and "stay with them" (τοῦ μεῖναι σὺν αὐτοῖς, v. 29). The reason given is legitimate, even if it is not the primary reason: It is, of course, almost evening, but their desire to be with him increases. The pressing invitation for him to stay with them shows that his outburst had more shaken than offended them. The readers could well wonder whether the hermeneutical lecture had not borne fruit. The specific and rare verbs προσποιοῦμαι ("to pretend," "to act as if") and παραβιάζομαι ("to compel")[52] are

---

51   The participle ἀρξάμενος ("beginning") indicates that the movement goes from the promise to its fulfillment.

52   The verb προσποιοῦμαι is a Lukan and even New Testament *hapax legomenon* (it appears in John 8:6 in a variant reading with the meaning "to take note

symptoms of the elegant style characteristic of the special source.

■ **30-32** The final, decisive event takes place: "and it happened" (καὶ ἐγένετο), as in v. 15. In the evening, after walking the whole way, it is time to sit or lie and to share a meal.[53] It is also the Jewish custom to pronounce a benediction before the meal. As bread is the basis for a meal, "to take bread," as synecdoche, means "to take a meal." Although Jesus has been invited, he plays the role of the head of the house. It is he who pronounces the prayer and shares the bread. In several places in Acts, Luke uses the expression "to break bread" (see Acts 2:46; 20:7, 11; 27:35)[54] (in Acts 2:42 he even knows the technical expression κλάσις τοῦ ἄρτου, the "breaking of the bread"). In a sense, this meal is the first in the series scattered throughout the book of Acts. It also recalls the last meal taken shortly before Jesus' arrest and passion (22:14-20). The formula "he took the bread, blessed it, and when he had broken it he gave it to them" (λαβὼν τὸν ἄρτον εὐλόγησεν καὶ κλάσας ἐπεδίδου αὐτοῖς, v. 30b) recalls precisely "and after he had taken a loaf and had given thanks, he broke it and gave it to them" (λαβὼν ἄρτον εὐχαριστήσας ἔκλασεν καὶ ἔδωκεν αὐτοῖς, 22:19a).[55] Thus, Luke marks the rite that, next to baptism, characterized the liturgical life of the early Christians. This is a special meal, not an ordinary one, and biblical scholars are not wrong when they speak of the "eucharistic" framework of the revelation of the Risen One to the Emmaus disciples.[56] But the sacred moment that marks the breaking of the bread and the benediction or prayer of thanksgiving takes place during an actual meal.

Luke mentions no other action of Jesus. He had done everything possible. He has assured his disciples of his presence and has filled them with his word and his "sacrament." The sequence of events depends then on them.

Without recourse to the language of the miraculous, Luke mentions the recognition as something that is natural. To say that "their eyes were opened, and they recognized him" seems to be self-evident. Yet how many signs and words it took to get there: first the presence of Jesus, then the word, then the reminder of the Scriptures. It is only logical that Luke's Christian readers identified with the disciples of Emmaus. They too have heard the word, understood the Scriptures, participated in the Lord's Supper, and perceived his presence.

Let us talk about this presence. In the story it is real, but provisional. No sooner had they recognized that this figure is the Risen One than he becomes "invisible" (ἄφαντος). In life his presence is real but invisible. Modern theologians are not wrong when they speak of an absent presence.

Then everything is opened: first the eyes (v. 31) that the author had said were blind (v. 16); then the intelligence, of which sight was a symbolic image (vv. 31 and 35; see v. 45); then the heart, which had been slow and stupid (v. 32) but now is burning (v. 32); and finally the Scriptures explained by the Risen One (v. 32c).

Like John the evangelist, Luke walks a tightrope. He must affirm the continuity between the historical Jesus and the risen Christ (hence the recognition) while emphasizing the discontinuity introduced by the new status of the resurrection (hence the slowness in recognizing him and the possibility, unique to him, of disappearing just as easily as he had appeared). This difficulty is compounded by a danger. Luke must keep the Risen One from appearing to be a simple ghost. Overcoming this obstacle will be one of the functions of the next story, that of Jesus' appearance to the Eleven (vv. 36-49).

■ **33-35** The story does not end euphorically. On their return to Jerusalem[57] the two disciples have no time to tell about their amazing experience, because the Eleven,

---

of"); see BAGD, s.v. Luke uses the verb παραβιά-ζομαι in another case, in Acts 16:15, where in a similar situation Lydia urges Paul to come to stay at her house (the same verb μένω is in Luke 24:29). On this verb, see BAGD, s.v.

53   Given the author's assumptions, the meal here probably takes place in a dining room, a *triclinium*; see vol. 1 of this commentary, 293, on 7:36.

54   See Bovon, *Luke the Theologian*, 430–34, 560–62.

55   Luke's readers also remember the multiplying of the loaves. There also Jesus takes, blesses, breaks, and distributes the loaves (9:16).

56   It is especially, but by no means exclusively, Catholic exegetes who emphasize this eucharistic component; see d'Arc, "Partage du pain"; Fitzmyer, 2:1559–60.

57   The same day (see v. 33).

meeting together[58] and invested by Luke with an almost enervating authority, announce an appearance that must take precedence over all the others: "The Lord is risen indeed, and he has appeared to Simon,"[59] that is to say, to Simon Peter, thus to the leader of the apostles. This intervention is similar to and corresponds to the apostle's race that crowns the episode of the empty tomb, v. 12.

Verse 33 recalls the units of time and place that are so important for Luke. Jerusalem remains the center of salvation history, the passion and resurrection of Jesus; and the same day, the first day of the week, the first Sunday, remains the favorable time of salvation.

Verse 34 uses the traditional language of the resurrection (ἐγείρω, literally, "to awaken," then "to resuscitate," "to bring to life again" as it appears in the formulas of Acts 3:15 and 4:10, and in Rom 4:24; 1 Cor 15:4) and the appearances (ὤφθη, "he has appeared," as in 1 Cor 15:5). Paul knows of an appearance of the Risen One to Peter, but he calls him by his Aramaic surname, Cephas (1 Cor 15:5), while Luke gives him the name Simon, as he did at the beginning of his Gospel (4:38; 5:10; 6:14).

Verse 35 finally gives voice to the Emmaus disciples. They explain what had happened to them (the verb ἐξηγοῦμαι shows that their experience needs to be explained). The concept of the way recalls the importance of the verb "to walk," "to be underway" (πορεύομαι). The words "what had happened to them on the way" (τὰ ἐν τῇ ὁδῷ) sums up the encounter, the dia-logue, and its misunderstandings, as well as the interpretation of Scripture. They also involve the "breaking of bread," the liturgical, eucharistic context of the recognition (ἐγνώσθη is passive, but it must be given the value of an intransitive: "He had made himself known" or "recognized").

History of Interpretation

Tertullian's *Adversus Marcionem* (early third century) opens the way to one of the oldest interpretations[60] of the episode of the Emmaus disciples (4.43.3–5). Luke's text suits the African, because it allows him to show that Jesus Christ both before and after his resurrection is not a "new" Messiah, as Marcion would have it,[61] but the Messiah proclaimed by and in Israel's Scriptures. Even the disciples' slowness to believe is a blessing, because it gives the Risen One the chance to explain his identity.

A few years later, Origen was struck at first by the story itself, which serves as an argument for the historicity of the resurrection against the taunts of the pagan philosopher, Celsus (Origen *Cels.* 2.62).[62] Then v. 32 fascinates the Alexandrian. This burning of the heart is essential for Christian faith. It occurs when "a fire springs up from the words of the Holy Spirit and inflames the heart of the believers" (*Hom. Lev.* 9.9).[63] It appears also when Christ unlocks the seal of the Scripture (*Hom. Ex.* 12.4)[64] and reveals its meaning.[65]

---

58 They are accompanied by others; see "and those who were with them."

59 When Luke mentions here Simon instead of Peter, is it for local color or because of a tradition? At the apostle's visit to the tomb (v. 12), Luke speaks of Peter. In the farewell discourse (Luke 22), it is sometimes a question of Simon (v. 31), sometimes of Peter (v. 34).

60 Without explicitly mentioning the Emmaus disciples, Justin Martyr borrows some expressions from Luke 24:25-27 when he speaks of the appearances and the last teaching of the Risen One; see *1 Apol.* 50.12 and *Dial.* 53.5; 106.1. Irenaeus (*Adv. haer.* 3.14.3) mentions the disciples on the way who recognized the Lord in the breaking of bread. This statement appears at the end of events reported only by Luke and underscores that Christians would have to do without if they were to reject the Gospel of Luke. See also *Adv. haer.* 3.16.5; 4.26.1.

61 In v. 21 Marcion seems to have read ἐνομίζομεν ("we thought") rather than ἠλπίζομεν ("we hoped"), which Tertullian seems to allow (*nos autem putabamus*) in §3 and following (where he uses the verb *estimare*); see notes 1–2 from René Braun in *Tertullian, Contra Marcion*, vol. 4 (SC 456:522). See also Harnack, *Marcion*, 238*; and Tsutui, "Evangelium Marcions," 128.

62 Here, as in his commentary on John (1.5.7 and 1.8.10). Origen calls Cleopas's companion Simon. He is probably thinking of Simon Peter. See n. 18 above.

63 See Just, *Luke*, 382.

64 See ibid., 383.

65 A Greek fragment of Origen's *Hom. Lukas* has survived. It refers to the glory of the body of the Risen One, a glory that corresponds to that shown at the transfiguration; see Origen *Hom. Lukas*, frg. 255 (ed. Max Rauer, *Origenes Werke*, 9:335).

Curiously, the Greek and Latin Fathers, who are so sensitive about the themes of the resurrection, the proclamation of the word, and, as we shall see, of hospitality have paid no attention to the eucharistic character of the Emmaus scene.[66] The exception, and it is a major one, is Augustine. In his *Sermo* 235,[67] delivered in Hippo on the day after Easter sometime after 400, the bishop notes that the pericope for the day was the Emmaus episode,[68] while Matthew's story of the resurrection had been read on Easter itself. The preacher begins by reassuring his parishioners that the differences between the Gospels are not contradictions.[69] He then puts the presence of the risen Lord among his people at the heart of his sermon. He meditates on how this appearance took place and on the fact that he was "both visible and hidden." The disciples "were not kept from seeing him, but they were kept from recognizing him." The moment of recognition was "the breaking of the bread."[70] As in the subsequent centuries we Christians cannot see him directly, it is when "we break bread" that "we recognize the Lord." It follows that "God's absence is not an absence. Have

faith and he is with you, even when you do not see him." Look at the disciples, he says: "They had lost faith. They had lost hope. They were dead while walking with a living person, they walked dead while walking with life." They have made a decisive gesture: "They offered him hospitality." Like other preachers and theologians of late antiquity, Augustine urges his hearers to imitate the Emmaus disciples: "Remember the stranger if you want to recognize your Savior." If the Risen One then disappeared, it was to maintain the status of faith. "For if you believe only what you see, where is faith?" But he adds: "Seeing will be restored to us." The Risen One will return at the parousia: "Be assured, he will come."[71]

The Augustinian interpretation of the Emmaus disciples would not fall into oblivion. Passages of his work continued to be cited in later centuries, especially by the Venerable Bede and in the *Catena aurea*. He would also be quoted by Gregory the Great (late sixth century),[72] from whom a brief sermon has been preserved: Reflections on Christ *peregrinus*, "the stranger," "the traveler." The bishop of Rome begins by noting that

66 Ambrose (*Exp. Luc.* 10.167–68) goes directly from the empty tomb (Luke 23:56b—24:12) to the appearance to the Eleven (24:36-49) without mentioning the Emmaus disciples (24:13-35). Once, at the beginning of his citation of 24:35b-37 (*Exp. Luc.* 10.172), he mentions the breaking of the bread without explicitly referring to the episode. Then he alludes briefly to the episode when he compares the appearance to the Eleven with that to the two disciples (ibid., 173). Here, as also in *Exp. Luc.* 7.132 and *Apologia David altera* 7.43, he calls the companion of Cleopas Ammaon or Ammaus. Is that a mistaken reference to Simon (see n. 62 above) or confusion with the place-name Emmaus? Or is Ambrose following another tradition?

67 *PL* 38:1117–20); French translation by France Quéré, in *L'Évangile selon Luc commenté par les Pères* (Paris: Desclée, 1987) 156–59; see also what Augustine says of the Emmaus scene in his *De cons. Evang.* 25.70–73. See Clancy ("Augustine") who provides a summary of the exegesis of the bishop of Hippo without realizing how new the eucharistic interpretation was.

68 See Clancy ("Augustine," 51), who says that Luke's Emmaus episode was read in the church on the Monday or Tuesday after Easter. This liturgical tradition was maintained throughout the Middle Ages.

69 Augustine, whose text of Mark contained the ending regarded by most modern scholars as inauthentic, says to his hearers that the Second Gospel briefly alludes to the event of Emmaus (Mark 16:12-13).

70 In his *Epist.* 149.3.32 (*PL* 33.644), Augustine confirms that the breaking of bread is a sacrament; see Just, *Luke*, 382. See also Augustine *Sermo* 234 and *Sermo* 236.

71 References to other ancient authors include the following. In a fragment ascribed to Apollinaris of Laodicea (fourth century), the author says that the reference to time, "at the same hour," applies to the return to Jerusalem and not to the conversation with the Eleven, which took place on the fortieth day, the day of the ascension; see frg. 20 in Reuss, *Lukas-Kommentare*, 10. To my surprise, this fragment appears also in a sermon attributed to Cyril of Alexandria; see Payne Smith, *Cyril*, 2:727–28; see above, n. 107 on 23:56b—24:12. Just (*Luke*, 377–83) provides still other citations, especially Ephraem's *Hymn on Paradise* 15.4.

72 Gregory the Great *Hom. Ev.* (*PL* 76:1181–83).

Jesus appeared to the disciples in a form they could not recognize: "What the Lord has done externally, before the eyes of the body, is what he accomplished internally for his own before the eyes of the heart" (*Hoc ergo egit foris Dominus in oculis corporis quod apud ipsos agebatur intus in oculis cordis*). Gregory then emphasizes this presence–absence, which without a doubt is based on Augustine. The reaction of the disciples, he explains, was a result of love and doubt. Moreover, the disciples did not simply invite the traveler; they compelled him to remain with them. Thus, they did not simply listen; they also acted. Gregory then cites the passages of the New Testament that encourage the practice of hospitality: Heb 13:2; 1 Pet 4:9; and especially Matt 25:35 (unintentionally welcoming Christ). By receiving Christ, the believers are preparing to be received by him.

Around the year 700 the Venerable Bede summarized the results of patristic exegesis (*In Luc.* 6.2011–2167). Like many before him, he was interested in the facts and did not care to allegorize. He explains the length of a stadion and (incorrectly, as do modern scholars) identifies Emmaus with Nicopolis. He then explains the presence of the Risen One with his two disciples as the fulfillment of a promise ("For where two or three are gathered in my name, I am there in their midst," Matt 18:20). The disciples did not realize what they were saying by calling Jesus *peregrinus*, "stranger," because his resurrection had removed him from earthly realities. If they were sad, it was because they were accusing themselves of having hoped falsely. As many others have done,[73] Bede emphasized the lesson in biblical hermeneutics that the Risen One gives here. He states that the work of Christ cannot be explained solely with the help of Scripture, even if Moses and the prophets have proclaimed it. The two disciples finally recognized Christ only in the breaking of the bread. Bede also joins an exegetical tradition[74] when he connects v. 32 ("did not our heart burn?") with Luke 12:49 ("I came to cast fire on the earth"). This fire that comes to people is the Holy Spirit; it does away with desires and inflames the love of God.

A probably quite rare allegorizing of the Emmaus scene also comes from the early Middle Ages, around 780–785, in the writing of the anonymous Irish author.[75] The two disciples symbolize the Savior's double law, which extends from Jerusalem to the church of the Gentiles. That the church is separated from Jerusalem by the number sixty shows that belief in the Trinity does not yet exist and that perfect peace is not yet established. That the two disciples are conversing with each other must be understood in terms of the law, doubtless the double law of the old and the new economies, which in dialogue with itself proves that the truth is in search of the various figures, and so on.[76]

Brother Patrick, whose birth name is Michel Prétot, submitted in 1988 a master's thesis in theology to the Catholic Institute of Paris entitled *"Ils le reconnurent à la fraction du pain": Le repas d'Emmaüs dans l'histoire de la tradition et son influence en théologie sacramentaire.* ("They recognized him in the breaking of the bread": The meal at Emmaus in the history of tradition and its influence in sacramental theology). It is the only work on the history of interpretation of which I am aware, and it remains unpublished. Unfortunately, as is too often the case among Catholic theologians, he understands "tradition" to mean the Western and Latin tradition. Thus, he neglects the Orthodox and Eastern traditions. Yet this work has the threefold merit of analyzing the role of the pericope in liturgy, of following the history of interpreta-

---

73   See in the sixth century Caesarius of Arles *Sermo* 169.8 (CCSL 104:694–95); in the twelfth century Petrus Venerabilis *Contra Petrobrusianos* 34 (CCCM 10:27–28).

74   Ambrose already quoted v. 32 in the course of his spiritual explanation of Luke 12:49-50; see *Exp. Luc.* 7.132.

75   *Comm. Luc.* 24.13–35 (CCSL 108C:99–100).

76   The readers will discover details of medieval exegesis by reading the *Glossa Ordinaria* (*PL* 114:351–53) and the *Catena aurea* of Thomas Aquinas (312–15). They will realize that the works cited highlight primarily the literal and historical sense. Of course, the theological dimension is not despised in the episode, but it is not made conspicuous by the allegorical method. The *Catena aurea*, citing Theophylactus, thinks about the two walkers and concludes that they are still strangers to faith. When Jesus approaches them, he does so not merely spatially but also spiritually. He will ignite in them the faith they lacked. The "other form" of the Risen One, noted in Mark 16:12, is that of the spiritual body. Thus, the voice of Christ is more angelic than human. Quoting Augustine, the text adds: If Satan was able to blind the two pilgrims, God in his providence can give them sight.

tion, and of integrating it with Christian iconography. Here is what I regard as essential in the work:

Amalarius of Metz (first half of the ninth century), following Augustine, played an important role in connecting the Emmaus story with the Eucharist. It was a connection for which, as we have seen, there was little evidence in Christian antiquity.[77] While the author notes the relationship between Jesus' breaking of the bread and the act of the officiating priest, in general the medieval period does not use the Emmaus story in the controversies revolving around the real presence in the eucharistic meal. Is this because the eucharistic interpretation is almost completely missing in the patristic period?

It is remarkable that Christian iconography, following the exegesis of the Fathers, first remembered the meeting on the way.[78] This is what happened in Sant' Apollinare Nuovo in Ravenna (mosaic) in the second half of the sixth century, at the beginning of the eighth century in Santa Maria Antiqua in Rome (fresco), then in Sant' Angelo in Formis near Capua in Campania (fresco) in the second half of the eleventh century.[79] In this time the theme of the meal joined that of walking on the way. The sacramentary of Echternach (*Codex aureus Epternacensis*, between 1020 and 1030) shows the scene of the pilgrims and that of the meal side by side. In this last scene, which became common during the Romanesque period, there are several indications underscoring the eucharistic scope that the artists and their patrons attribute to the breaking of the bread. The table can look like an altar; a tablecloth can underscore the solemn character of the event; the bread itself can wear a cross on its surface.

In his commentary on the Gospel of Luke, Bonaventure devotes a number of pages to the Emmaus episode (*Comm. Luc.* 24.18–42).[80] He discerns three phases: (a) When he joins the two disciples on the way without letting them know who he is, the risen Christ presents himself in a different form (Mark 16:12 is cited here), but fundamentally he remains the same. For their part, the pilgrims display both their affection and their doubt. (b) When the group begins a discussion, the disciples express their disappointed hopes; if they are not able to believe the message of the women or to grasp the meaning of the Scriptures, it is because they are creatures too much under the influence of their senses. (c) When, finally, they invite their enigmatic companion, they exercise the virtue of hospitality. The Christ who makes himself known in the breaking of the bread prefers to reveal himself to those who act (inviting) rather than to those who are content to hear (listening to the explanation of the Scriptures). Referring to Gregory the Great, Bonaventure is also familiar with Bede's interpretation that Christ is known only in the church. He also knows that for some people the second pilgrim is none other than Luke himself, an opinion Bonaventure is reluctant to adopt.[81] The doctor knows many exegetical traditions: When he distinguishes between the physical presence (which disappears) and the spiritual presence (which remains), or when he affirms that hearts were inflamed by the fire of the Word nourished by the Spirit, he draws on the views of his predecessors. Among them are, of course, Augustine and Gregory the Great.[82]

I have worked through the *Paraphrasis* and the *Annota-*

---

77 It is now thought that there was only one person named Amalarius at that time. He was born in Metz, became bishop of Trier, later of Lyon—thus the various names that have been given him. Amalarius, *Missae expositionis geminus codex*, vol. 1, *De fractione oblatarum*, 3–10; see also *Liber officialis* 3.28.4 and 33.2 in Jean Michel Hanssens, ed., *Amalarii episopi opera liturgica omnia* (3 vols.; StT 138–140; Vatican City: Biblioteca apostolica vaticana, 1948–50) 1:263–64; 2:354, 365; Prétot, "Repas d'Emmaus," 129.

78 We should note, however, that, compared to another event, the presence of the women at the empty tomb, the incident is rarely represented prior to the ninth century.

79 See Prétot, "Repas d'Emmaüs, 41. See also the presentation and the lists of Réau, *Iconographie*

2.2:561–67. See finally Rainer Kahsnitz, Ursula Mende, and Elisabeth Rücker, *Das goldene Evangelienbuch von Echternach: Eine Prunkhandschrift des 11. Jahrhunderts* (Germanisches Nationalmuseum Nürnberg, Bibliothek) (Frankfurt a. M.: Fischer, 1982) plate 36 and p. 191; Anja Grebe, *Codex Aureus: Das goldene Evangelienbuch von Echternach* (Darmstadt: Wissenschaftliche Buchgesellschaft, 2007) 101; Janine Wettstein, *Sant' Angelo in Formis et la peinture médiévale en Campanie* (Travaux d'humanisme et Renaissance 42; Geneva: E. Droz, 1960).

80 Bernardini, 591–98; trans. Karris, *St. Bonaventure's Commentary*, 3:2203–26; Bonaventure integrates vv. 33-35 into the next pericope (vv. 33-47).

81 On the other identifications see above, nn. 18, 19, 62, and 66.

82 The commentary of Bruno of Segni is easily

tiones of Erasmus,[83] certain sermons of Luther,[84] and Calvin's *Gospel Harmony*.[85] Over all commentaries,[86] however, I prefer Rembrandt's successive attempts. Better than the oil paintings[87] I like the drawings and engravings.[88] There the artist tries to represent what cannot be pictured, the resurrection. He hesitates, trying something, then correcting or retracting it. Sometimes he shows the human but radiant face of the Risen One; sometimes he prefers to see him as disappearing; and sometimes he emphasizes the vivid, luminous streak Christ leaves when he departs. Never have I so keenly felt the truth of this presence–absence, this vanishing spiritual presence as I do with Rembrandt.

As we have seen in the exegesis of the preceding pericope, that of the empty tomb, the century of the Enlightenment (eighteenth century) and that of historicism (nineteenth century) have called into question the dogma of the resurrection.[89] There was no weakening in the attention given to the disciples of Emmaus, but what remains of the event is simply a lovely, pious story.[90]

The contemporary period has revived a double theological interest in the episode of the Emmaus pilgrims. With Jean-Luc Marion we are moving into the area of systematic theology.[91] Here is his argument: Faith does not fill the gaps in our intuition or our experience. Indeed, the Emmaus episode can say that faith channels the excess of our intuitions and criticizes the proliferation of our concepts. Thus, the disciples had a wealth of information about Jesus, such as historical memories and the report of the women. Yet they were unable to recognize the Living One who was facing them, because for them, within the limits of their understanding, Jesus was dead, just dead. Faith offered Cleopas and the other disciple the adequate concept that corresponded to their intuition. Christ, by becoming the master who taught, effected this transformation. The Gospel of John asserts that Jesus Christ, the divine Word, was the Father's exegete (ἐκεῖνος ἐξηγήσατο, "that one told" [or: explained]" John 1:18). The lesson of the lesson offered by the Son took place at the moment when the two disciples invited Jesus to stay with them. In this instant they were truly interested in him. For his part, in breaking the bread, the Risen One allowed them finally to see what they had been unable to contemplate. From that time on they could see reality from God's perspective. What remains unclear in this interpretation of Marion is the nature of this abundant content that is to be filtered. What is this abundance due to our intuitions and our concepts? Undoubtedly, the excess is concerned not with the revelation itself but with the historical events it has permeated and the intellectual constructs with which we try to understand.[92]

With Louis-Marie Chauvet we enter the area of sacramental theology.[93] This author bears witness to the considerable prestige that the Emmaus story enjoys in the twentieth century among liturgical specialists. He

---

accessible, *Comm. Luc.* 49 (*PL* 165:446–48). With sensitivity he insists on the role of memory: Jesus has not forgotten those who remember him.

83 Erasmus, *Paraphrasis*, 467–86; trans. Phillips, *Paraphrase*, 230–73. Erasmus is verbose when he presents the speech of the Risen One explaining the Scriptures. He takes the opportunity to define the links that in his view connect the Old and the New Testaments and to show how Jesus' life fulfills the prophecies; see the long n. 31 in Phillips, *Paraphrase*, 235–36. See also Erasmus, *Annotationes*, 217.

84 Luther, *Evangelien-Auslegung*, 1257–63; Mülhaupt, 5:288–90. Luther holds three particular points. The Emmaus story bears witness to the historicity of the meeting and thus of the resurrection. He then shows what is the power and what is the fruit of the resurrection. He finally realizes that the resurrection of Christ is made known through the word and is received by faith. See again Mülhaupt, 5:280–84, 308–12.

85 Calvin, *Harmony*, 3:230–40.

86 See also Grotius, *Annotationes*, 926–37; and Bengel (*Gnomon*, 1:531; *Gnomon* [G], 1:415–18), who comments primarily on vv. 33-34. The apostles' incredulity glorifies Christ's fidelity.

87 See Marsh, "Rembrandt." Three oil paintings are known (a fourth is probably not authentic).

88 On the drawings and engravings, see Rudrauf, *Repas d'Emmaüs;* and especially Fendrich, *Rembrandts Darstellungen*.

89 See Hoffmann, "Graben."

90 See Prétot, "Repas d'Emmaüs," 130.

91 Marion, "Ils le reconnurent."

92 The article by Marion has not gone without a response; see Mackinlay, "Eyes Wide Shut."

93 Chauvet, *Symbole et sacrement*, 167–85.

even accords such importance to the story that he sees it as a "womb (matrix) text" (*texte matriciel*). In his view, the story tells and thus explains how one becomes a believer, how the Risen One makes possible the passage of non-faith to faith in the shared meal. Chauvet believes that the absent Christ becomes present in his church, which Chauvet sees as the sacrament of the Living One who disappeared from the eyes of his disciples. In my opinion this author brings the church too close to Christ. Then, more concretely and closer to Luke 24, he shows that it is the eucharistic meal that makes the Risen One present and allows faith to be born. Chauvet neglects here neither the role of the testimony nor that of the Scriptures.

Conclusion

The story of the Emmaus disciples, along with those of the prodigal son and the Samaritan, is one of the jewels of Luke's special source. It combines suggestive details such as the number of "stadia" or the name of Cleopas with the strongest of themes: the eyes being struck by blindness and the Scriptures whose meaning is opened; the physical and yet spiritual journey; the hospitality of the one and the hospitality of the other; the presence that begins as an enigma and the following absence radiating meaning; the transformation of the disciples who come to Christian faith.

Bibliography

Albertz, Martin, "Zur Formgeschichte der Auferste-hungsberichte," *ZNW* 21 (1922) 259–69.

Allison, Dale C., *Resurrecting Jesus: The Earliest Christian Tradition and Its Interpreters* (New York: T&T Clark, 2005).

Alsup, John E., *The Post-Resurrection Appearance Stories of the Gospel Tradition: A History-of-Tradition Analysis* (CThM A, 5; Stuttgart: Calwer, 1975) 147–90.

Amphoux, Christian-Bernard, "Le chapitre 24 de Luc et l'origine de la tradition textuelle du Codex de Bèze (D.05 du NT)," *Filologia Neotestamentaria* 4 (1991) 21–48.

Asensio, Félix, "Trasfondo profético-evangélico del pasa exousia de la 'Gran Misión,'" *EstBib* 27 (1968) 27–48.

Atkins, Peter, "Luke's Ascension Location: A Note on Luke 24:50," *ExpT* 109 (1998) 205–6.

Bailey, John Amedee, *The Traditions Common to the Gospels of Luke and John* (NovTSup 7; Leiden: Brill, 1969) 85–102.

Basset, Jean-Claude, "Dernières paroles du ressuscité et mission de l'Église aujourd'hui (à propos de Mt 28, 18-20 et parallèles)," *RThPh* 114 (1982) 349–67.

Benoit, *Passion and Resurrection*, 313–21, 326–32.

Betori, Giuseppe, "Luke 24:47: Jerusalem and the Beginning of the Preaching to the Pagans in the Acts of the Apostles," in Gerald O'Collins and Gilberto Marconi, eds., *Luke and Acts* (trans. Matthew J. O'Connell; New York: Paulist, 1993) 103–20.

Bishop, Eric F. F., "With Saint Luke in Jerusalem from Easter Day till Pentecost," *ExpT* 56 (1944–45) 192–94, 200–223.

Black, C. Clifton, "Our Shepherd's Voice: Biblical Resources for the Easter Season," *QR* 14 (1994) 89–110.

Bockel, P., "Luc 24, 45: 'Il leur ouvrit l'esprit à l'intelligence des Écritures'," *BTS* 36 (1961) 2–3.

Boismard, Marie-Emile, "Le réalisme des récits évangéliques," *LV(L)* 107 (1972) 31–41.

Bovon, François, "Gespenst," in *Neues Bibel-Lexikon* 1 (1991) 830.

Idem, "Lukan Story of the Passion," 100–101.

Braun, François-Marie, *Jean le théologien* (3 vols.; EtB; Paris: Gabalda, 1959) 1:268–69, 280–82.

Brox, Norbert, *Zeuge und Märtyrer: Untersuchungen zur frühchristlichen Zeugnis-Terminologie* (StANT 5; Munich: Kösel, 1961) 43–69, 184–86.

Bultmann, Rudolf, and Dieter Lührmann, "ἐπιφαίνω, κτλ.," *TDNT* 9 (1974) 7–10.

Burchard, Christoph, *Der dreizehnte Zeuge: Traditions- und kompositionsgeschichtliche Untersuchungen zu Lukas' Darstellung der Frühzeit des Paulus* (FRLANT 103; Göttingen: Vandenhoeck & Ruprecht, 1970) 130–35.

Cattanéo, Enrico, *Trois homélies pseudo-chrysostomiennes sur la Pâque comme œuvre d'Apollinaire de Laodicée: Attribution et étude théologique* (ThH 58; Paris: Beauchesne, 1981) 39.

Cherubini, Beatrice, "'Mangiò pesce e miele': Un' antica tradizione sul Risorto" (Diss., Università di Roma Tre, 2005–6).

Chevallier, Max-Alain, "'Pentecôtes' lucaniennes et 'pentecôtes' johanniques," *RSR* 69 (1981) 301–13.

Clivaz, Claire, "'Incroyants de joie' (Lc 24,41): Point de vue, histoire et poétique," in *Regards croisés sur la Bible: Études sur le point de vue. Actes du IIIe colloque international du Réseau de recherche en narrativité biblique, Paris, 8–10 juin 2006* (LD; Paris: Cerf, 2007) 184–95.

Coleridge, Mark, "'You Are Witnesses' (Luke 24:48): Who Sees What in Luke?" *ABR* 45 (1997) 1–19.

Dauer, Anton, *Johannes und Lukas: Untersuchungen zu den johanneisch-lukanischen Parallelperikopen Joh 4, 46-54/Lk 7, 1-10 – Joh 12, 1-8/Lk 7, 36-50, 10, 38-42 – Joh 20, 19-29/Lk 24, 36-49/* (FB 50; Würzburg: Echter, 1984) 207–88.

Delling, Gerhard, "'Als er uns die Schrift aufschloss': Zur lukanischen Terminologie der Auslegung des Alten Testaments," in Horst Balz and Siegfried Schulz, eds., *Das Wort und die Wörter: Festschrift Gerhard Friedrich zum 65. Geburtstag* (Stuttgart: Kohlhammer, 1973) 75–84.

Dillon, Richard J., "Easter Revelation and Mission Program in Luke 24:46-48," in Daniel Durken, ed., *Sin, Salvation, and the Spirit: Commemorating the Fiftieth Year of the Liturgical Press* (Collegeville, Minn.: Liturgical Press, 1979) 240–70.

Idem, *Eye-Witnesses*, 157–220.

Dömer, Michael, *Das Heil Gottes: Studien zur Theologie des lukanischen Doppelwerks* (BBB 51; Cologne/Bonn: Hanstein, 1978) 99–106.

Duesberg, Hilaire, "He Opened Their Minds to Understand the Scriptures," *Concil* 30 (1968) 111–21.

Dumm, Demetrius R., "Luke 24:44-49 and Hospitality," in Daniel Durken, ed., *Sin, Salvation, and the Spirit: Commemorating the Fiftieth Year of the Liturgical Press* (Collegeville, Minn.: Liturgical Press, 1979) 231–39.

Dupont, Jacques, "Les discours de Pierre dans les Actes et le chapitre XXIV de l'évangile de Luc," in Frans Neirynck, ed., *L'Évangile de Luc—The Gospel of Luke* (2d ed.; BEThL 32; Leuven: University Press/Peeters, 1989) 239–84, 328–30; reprinted in Dupont, *Nouvelles études*, 58–111.

Idem, "La mission de Paul d'après Actes 26,16-23 et la mission des apôtres d'après Luc 24,44-49 et Actes 1,8," in M. D. Hooker and S. G. Wilson, eds., *Paul and Paulinism: Essays in Honour of C. K. Barrett* (London: SPCK, 1982) 290–301; reprinted in Dupont, *Nouvelles études*, 446–56.

Idem, "La portée christologique de l'évangélisation des nations d'après Luc 24,47," in Joachim Gnilka, ed., *Neues Testament und Kirche: Für Rudolf Schnackenburg* (Freiburg i. B.: Herder, 1974) 125–43; reprinted in Dupont, *Nouvelles études*, 37–57.

Eckstein, Hans-Joachim, "Bodily Resurrection in Luke," in Ted Peters et al., eds., *Resurrection: Theological and Scientific Assessments* (Grand Rapids: Eerdmans, 2002) 115–23.

Idem, "Die Wirklichkeit der Auferstehung Jesu: Lukas 24,34 als Beispiel früher formelhafter Zeugnisse," in idem and Michael Welker, eds., *Wie wirklich ist die Auferstehung? Biblische Zeugnisse und heutiges Erkennen* (Neukirchen-Vluyn: Neukirchener Verlag, 2002) 1–20.

Eggen, Wiel, "Witness God's Finger Lifting Evil: Mission of Dialogue in Luke 24:47-48," *Exchange* 28 (1999) 153–69.

Ernst, "Schriftauslegung."

Flusser, David, "'Wie in den Psalmen über mich geschrieben steht' (Lk 24,44)," *Jud* 48 (1992) 40–42.

Fuller, Reginald H., *The Formation of the Resurrection Narratives* (New York: Macmillan, 1971) 114–23.

George, Augustin, "L'intelligence des Écritures (Luc 24, 44-53)," *BVC* 18 (1957) 65–71.

Idem, "Les récits d'apparitions aux Onze à partir de Luc 24, 36-53," in Paul de Surgy et al., *La résurrection du Christ et l'exégèse moderne* (LD 50; Paris: Cerf, 1969) 75–104.

Grass, *Ostergeschehen*, 40–43.

Grasso, S., "Fattori ermeneutici per la codificazione delle parole del risorto all'interno del Vangelo lucano (24,36-43; 44-9)," in *San luca evangelista testimona della fede che unisce: Atti del congresso internazionale Padove 16–21 ottobre 2000* (3 vols.; Padove: Istituto per la storia ecclesiastica padovana, 2002-4) 1:299–313.

Guillaume, Jean-Marie, *Luc interprète des anciennes traditions sur la résurrection de Jésus* (EtB; Paris: Gabalda, 1979) 163–201.

Hartmann, Gert, "Die Vorlage der Osterberichte in Joh 20," *ZNW* 55 (1964) 197–220.

Hoffmann, Paul, "Auferstehung Jesu Christi," *TRE* 4 (1979) 478–513.

Hubbard, Benjamin J., "Commissioning Stories in Luke-Acts: A Study of Their Antecedents, Form and Content," *Semeia* 8 (1977) 103–26.

Hug, Joseph, *La finale de l'Évangile de Marc (Mc 16,9-20)* (EtB; Paris: Gabalda, 1978) 168–69.

Kilpatrick, G. D., "Luke 24:42-43," *NovT* 28 (1986) 306–8.

Kingsbury, Jack Dean, "Luke 24:44-49," *Int* 35 (1981) 170–74.

Köster, Helmut, *Synoptische Überlieferung bei den apostolischen Vätern* (TU 65, 5th series 10; Berlin: Akademie-Verlag, 1957) 44–56.

Kremer, Jacob, *Die Osterbotschaft der vier Evangelien: Versuch einer Auslegung der Berichte über das leere Grab und die Erscheinungen des Auferstandenen* (2d ed.; Stuttgart: Katholisches Bibelwerk, 1968) 72–86.

Idem, *Die Osterevangelien—Geschichten um Geschichte* (Stuttgart: Katholisches Bibelwerk, 1977) 136–52.

Kümmel, *Promise*, 105.

Leaney, A. R. C., "The Resurrection Narratives in Luke (xxiv.12-53)," *NTS* 2 (1955–56) 110–14.

Legrand, Lucien, "The Missionary Command of the Risen Christ: I. Mission and Resurrection," *ITS* 23 (1986) 290–309.

Léon-Dufour, *Résurrection*, 123–37, 199–207, 215–20, 279–80, 326.

Lods, Adolphe, *La croyance à la vie future et le culte des morts dans l'antiquité israélite* (Paris: Fischbacher, 1906) 227–64.

Luter, A. Boyd, "Women Disciples and the Great Commission," *Trinity Journal* 16 (1995) 171–85.

Mainville, Odette, and Daniel Marguerat, eds., *Résurrection: L'après-mort dans le monde ancien et le Nouveau Testament* (Geneva: Labor et Fides, 2001).

Manicardi, Ermenegildo, "La terza apparizione del Risorto nel Vangelo secondo Luca," *Rivista di teologia dell' evangelizzazione* 1 (1997) 5–27.

Martini, C. M., "L'apparizione agli Apostoli in Lc 36–43 nel complesso dell'opera lucana," in Édouard Dhanis, ed., *Resurrexit: Actes du Symposium international sur la résurrection de Jésus* (Rome: Libreria editrice vaticana, 1974) 230–45.

Mekkattukunnel, "Proof," 221–29.

Mierzwa, T., "Gesù risorto l'adempimento delle scritture e la pienezza escatologica: Analisi del brano Lc 24,44-49," *CoTh* 71A (2001) 53–66.

Milne, Douglas, "Luke's Great Commission," *VR* 51 (1988) 24–28.

Moore, Thomas S., "The Lucan Great Commission and the Isaianic Servant," *BSABR* 154 (1997) 47–60.

Neirynck, Frans, "Lc 24, 36-43, un récit lucanien," in *A cause de l'Evangile: Études sur les Synoptiques et les Actes, offertes au P. Jacques Dupont, O.S.B., à l'occasion de son 70e anniversaire* (LD 123; Paris: Cerf, 1985) 655–80.

Nellessen, Ernst, *Zeugnis für Jesus und das Wort: Exegetische Untersuchungen zum lukanischen Zeugnisbegriff* (BBB 43; Cologne/Bonn: Hanstein, 1976) 107–18.

Nestle, Eberhard, "The Honeycomb in Luke xxiv," *ExpT* 22 (1910–11) 567–68.

O'Collins, Gerald, "Did Jesus Eat the Fish (Luke 24:42-43)?" *Greg* 69 (1988) 65–76.

Orbe, Antonio, *Cristologia Gnóstica: Introdución a la soteriologia de los siglos II y III* (2 vols.; BAC 384–85; Madrid: La Editorial Católica, 1976) 1:383–87, 2:515–17.

Ordon, Hubert, "Ostatnie przemówienie zmartwychwstalego Chrystusa (Lk 24, 44-49) (The last speech of the risen Christ)," *RTK* 34 (1987) 87–100.

Pariseau, Claire, "Le kérygme de Lc 24, 46-48, synthèse des discours missionaires du livre des Actes" (Diss., Laval University, 1999).

Porsch, Felix, *Pneuma und Wort: Ein exegetischer Beitrag zur Pneumatologie des Johannesevangeliums* (FTS 16; Frankfurt: J. Knecht, 1974) 353–57.

Prast, Franz, *Presbyter und Evangelium in nachapostolischer Zeit: Die Abschiedsrede des Paulus in Milet (APG. 20,17-38) im Rahmen der lukanischen Konzeption der Evangeliumsverkündigung* (FB 29; Stuttgart: Katholisches Bibelwerk, 1979) 281–84.

Prete, Benedetto, "'Aprì loro la mente all'intelligenza delle scripture' (Lc 24,45)," *San Luca evangelista testimone della fede che unisce* 1 (2002) 461–75.

Prince, Deborah Thompson, "The 'Ghost' of Jesus: Luke 24 in Light of Ancient Narratives of Post-Mortem Apparitions," *JSNT* 29 (2007) 287–301.

Rigaux, *Dieu l'a ressuscité*, 258–63, 274–76.

Ringgren, Helmer, "Luke's Use of the Old Testament," *HTR* 79 (1986) 227–35.

Roloff, Jürgen, *Apostolat, Verkündigung, Kirche: Ursprung, Inhalt und Funktion des kirchlichen Apostelamtes nach Paulus, Lukas und den Pastoralbriefen* (Gütersloh: Mohn, 1965) 188–92.

Samain, Etienne, "La notion de APXH dans l'œuvre lucanienne," in Frans Neirynck, ed., *L'Évangile de Luc—The Gospel of Luke* (2d ed.; BEThL 32; Leuven: University Press/Peeters, 1989) 209–38, 327.

Schmidtke, Alfred, "Zum Hebräerevangelium," *ZNW* 35 (1936) 24–44, esp. 27–28.

Schmitt, Joseph, "Le récit de la résurrection dans l'évangile de Luc: Étude de critique littéraire," *RSR* 25 (1951) 119–37, 219–42.

Idem, "Résurrection de Jésus dans le kérygme, la tradition, la catéchèse," *DBSup* 10 (1985) 487–582.

Schneider, Gerhard, "Der Missionsauftrag Jesu in der Darstellung der Evangelien," in Karl Kertelge, ed., *Mission im Neuen Testament* (QD 93; Freiburg: Herder, 1982) 71–92; reprinted in Schneider, *Lukas*, 184–205.

Sieber, John H., "The Spirit as the 'Promise of My Father' in Luke 24: 49," in Daniel Durken, ed., *Sin, Salvation, and the Spirit: Commemorating the Fiftieth Year of the Liturgical Press* (Collegeville, MN: Liturgical Press, 1979) 271–78.

Thayil, P., "Witness Mandate of the Risen Jesus in Lk 24,48 and Acts 1,8: Its Theological and Juridical Implications" (Diss., Pontificia Università Gregoriana, 1993).

Vanni, Ugo, "Il crocifisso risorto di Tommaso (Gv 20, 24-29): Un'ipotesi di larvoro," *StPat* 50 (2003) 753–75.

van Tilborg and Counet, *Jesus' Appearances*, 89–127.

Varro, R., "Présence du Ressuscité et mission de l'Église (Lc 24,39,47)," *AmiCl* 80 (1970) 196–200.

Wright, Nicholas Thomas, *Christian Origins and the Question of God*, vol. 3, *The Resurrection of the Son of God* (Minneapolis: Fortress, 2003) 647–61.

36 **While they were saying this he stood in their midst and says to them, "Peace be with you." 37/ Filled with terror, they were frightened and thought they were seeing a spirit. 38/ And he said to them, "Why are you troubled and why are these discussions coming up in your hearts? 39/ See my hands and my feet; it is I myself. Touch me and see: a spirit has neither flesh nor bones, which, as you see, I have." 40/ And saying this, he showed them his hands and feet. 41/ And while for joy they still disbelieved and were stunned, he said to them, "Do you have anything to eat here?" 42/ They gave him a piece of broiled fish. 43/ And he took it and ate it in their presence.**

44 **Then he said to them, "These words are mine; I told you of them while I was still with you:[a] Everything written about me in the Law of Moses, the Prophets, and the Psalms must be**

a Literally: "These are my words that I spoke to you while I was still with you, that must be . . ."

fulfilled." 45/ Then he opened their minds to understand the Scriptures. 46/ And he said to them, "Thus it is written that the Christ had to suffer and to rise from the dead on the third day, 47/ and that repentance leading to the forgiveness of sins should be proclaimed in his name to all the nations, beginning in Jerusalem. 48/ You, you are the witnesses of these things. 49/ And behold, I will send the promise of my Father on you. As for you, stay in the city until you have been clothed with power from on high."[b]

b   The many textual problems posed by vv. 36-49 will be discussed during the course of the exegesis.

At the conclusion of the Gospel, before the farewell scene, Luke tells of a final meeting between the disciples and the risen Christ. He first underscores the real identity of the one who rises from the dead (vv. 36-43), and then mentions the Lord's last teaching (vv. 44-49).[1]

Analysis

The readers will recall the meeting of the two disciples from Emmaus and the eleven disciples gathered in Jerusalem (vv. 33-35). There the evangelist somehow established a transition between two originally independent stories. He added the memory of a third episode, that of an appearance of the Lord to Simon Peter. In v. 36 he unsparingly plunges the readers who have followed him thus far into the heart of the events, the moment when Jesus presents himself alive to the disciples engaged in conversation.

The literary unit (vv. 36-49) falls into two parts.[2] The first part, vv. 36-43, deals with the question of the identity of the person who manifests himself. By showing his hands and his feet and then offering to eat something, he is not only recognized for who he is; he is also accepted among the living. In a second part, vv. 44-49, he recalls and confirms his teaching. Each part suggests that the difficulty in communication comes more from the resistance of the hearers (v. 37; v. 41; v. 45) than from the particular status of the speaker, who is sure of his own concern (v. 36; v. 39; v. 43; v. 44; v. 49).

A number of exegetes have tried to connect the transition (vv. 33-35) and the ascension scene (vv. 50-53) to this appearance to the disciples (vv. 36-49).[3] There are structural reasons that speak in favor of this hypothesis. In this case the explanation of the Scriptures (vv. 44-47) forms the center of the literary unit, and the appearance of the Risen One (ἔστη ἐν μέσῳ αὐτῶν, "he stood in their midst," v. 36) corresponds to his disappearance (διέστη ἀπ' αὐτῶν, "he departed from them," v. 51). I have already explained why I linked vv. 33-35 to the preceding material. I may add here that the introduction of v. 50 as well as the change of locations it mentions (from Jerusalem to Bethany) implies a break after v. 49. Thus, I retain the unity of vv. 36-49 and the idea of a diptych. Verses 36-43 reveal the speaker's identity, and vv. 44-49 are heard as the last speech he delivers.

The evangelist provides each of the two panels with movement and order. In spite of the peace offered in greeting, the rapid appearance (v. 36) causes panic (v. 37). The unexpected visitor, who wonders and is perhaps irritated, asks a rhetorical question (v. 38) and in

1   See Benoit, *Passion and Resurrection*, 282–87; George, "Onze"; Léon-Dufour, *Résurrection*, 123–37, 199–207, 215–20; Rigaux, *Dieu l'a ressuscité*, 258–63, 274–76; Martini, "Apparizione"; Alsup, *Appearance Stories*, 147–90; Dillon, *Eye-Witnesses*, 157–220; Guillaume, *Luc interprète*, 163–201; Dauer, *Johannes und Lukas*, 207–88; Neirynck, "Récit lucanien"; Legrand, "Missionary Command." Dillon offers a selected bibliography in *Eye-Witnesses*, 257–59.

2   For Meynet (*Guide*, 122–25) the unit extends from v. 33b to v. 53. It is divided into five sections (vv. 33b-35; vv. 36-43; vv. 44-47a; vv. 47b-49; vv. 50-53) and forms a chiasm whose center is constituted by vv. 44-47a: "Jesus explains the Scriptures." See also Meynet, *Évangile*, 1:226–31; 2:237–39.

3   E.g., Meynet, *Guide*, 122–25; idem, *Évangile*, 1:231.

addition shows the visible parts of his body, thus explaining that this demonstration negates the incongruous theory that he is a ghost (vv. 39-40). Verse 41 contains a paradox that suggests that their belief is not yet complete. The joy of recognizing Jesus does not eliminate the difficulty of believing. The eating (vv. 41-43) will thus be necessary to convince the disciples completely (but this conclusion is still implicit).[4]

While many later noncanonical conversations with the Savior use the time of the resurrection to construct new doctrines,[5] Luke uses this time to confirm the validity of the teaching already given. Verse 44a is quite clear. The words Jesus will say ($o\hat{v}\tau oi$ oi $\lambda\acute{o}\gamma oi$ μov, "these words are mine") are those he had already spoken when he was still (he is no longer, or no longer in the same way) with them.

In the detailed commentary I will return to the range of this summary (v. 44b, vv. 46-49), which resembles the kerygmatic speeches in the Acts of the Apostles more than it does the words of Jesus in the Gospel. Suffice it to enumerate here the doctrinal content. The person and fate of Jesus ($\pi\epsilon\rho\grave{\iota}$ $\acute{\epsilon}\mu o\hat{v}$, "about me") make up the fulfillment of "all" (note the ambitious $\pi\acute{a}\nu\tau a$) of the Scriptures (v. 44b). The passion of the Messiah and his resurrection are indeed consistent with what is written (v. 46). The same is true of what has not yet taken place and will be told in the Acts of the Apostles (the universal proclamation, v. 47). We must add a third component to the facts that have just taken place and to the prophecies that have been proclaimed: their spokespersons. Verse 48 calls these people "witnesses" and identifies Jesus' hearers with "you," the disciples. As the prophecies have added a divine touch to the historical facts, the Holy Spirit (the term is not used, but the reality is shown) remains on these witnesses as a "power from on high" (v. 49).

Two arguments support the hypothesis that the evangelist made use of a tradition in the first part of the diptych (vv. 36-43):[6] the presence of non-Lukan expressions and the existence of parallels. In particular, John E. Alsup, Jean-Marie Guillaume, and Anton Dauer have examined the language of vv. 36-43.[7] Even if the Lukan characteristics are obvious,[8] there are several terms that would be unusual from the pen of the evangelist. It would be wrong to assume that exceptional circumstances require an exceptional vocabulary, since the narrator is concerned to emphasize that Christ's presence is completely normal. What is exceptional, the return of a corpse to life, is not told; it has already happened and is presupposed.

The formula that introduces v. 36b, "and he says to them" ($\kappa a\grave{\iota}$ $\lambda\acute{\epsilon}\gamma\epsilon\iota$ $a\grave{v}\tau o\hat{\iota}\varsigma$) with its historical present is foreign to Luke. While on one occasion (10:5), he uses the traditional Jewish greeting invoking "peace" ($\epsilon\grave{\iota}\rho\acute{\eta}\nu\eta$), the evangelist usually prefers the Greek salutation, "greeting," "hail" ($\chi a\hat{\iota}\rho\epsilon$, 1:28; see also Acts 15:23; 23:26). The use of $\pi\nu\epsilon\hat{v}\mu a$ to designate a "spirit" or a "ghost" is unique in Luke. The self-presentation "it is I myself" ($\acute{\epsilon}\gamma\acute{\omega}$ $\epsilon\grave{\iota}\mu\iota$ $a\grave{v}\tau\acute{o}\varsigma$) is also unique, because Luke uses $\acute{\epsilon}\gamma\acute{\omega}$ $\epsilon\grave{\iota}\mu\iota$ only to reveal the identities of people for whom he gives the name: Gabriel (1:19), Jesus (Acts 9:5), Saul the Jew = Paul (Acts 22:3). Both the content, which corresponds to a Jewish way of thinking, and the vocabulary of v. 39b (especially the verb $\psi\eta\lambda a\varphi\acute{a}\omega$, "to feel," "to touch," and the expression $\sigma\acute{a}\rho\kappa a$ $\kappa a\grave{\iota}$ $\acute{o}\sigma\tau\acute{\epsilon}a$, "flesh and bones") are foreign to Lukan concerns and ways of expression. Of course, the tension manifested in v. 41 may come from Luke, who refers to joy to excuse the disciples' slowness to believe conveyed by the tradition. In the same v. 41, the neuter adjective "edible," "to eat" ($\beta\rho\acute{\omega}\sigma\iota\mu ov$) is a *hapax legomenon* in the New Testa-

---

4   Guillaume (*Luc interprète*, 178) writes: "The emphasis on the physicality and the identity of the Risen One is obvious and is progressing."

5   See Schneemelcher, "Dialogues of the Redeemer," Introduction in Schneemelcher, *New Testament Apocrypha*, 1:228–31.

6   On Luke's probable use of a tradition, see George, "Onze," 93–104; Alsup, *Appearance Stories*, 147–90; Guillaume, *Luc interprète*, 170–201; Dauer, *Johannes und Lukas*, 202–88; Basset, "Dernière paroles"; Boismard, "Réalisme."

7   Alsup, *Appearance Stories*, 182–84; Guillaume, *Luc interprète*, 177–81; Dauer, *Johannes und Lukas*, 259–75.

8   The introduction as a genitive absolute (v. 36a), the expression of fear (v. 37), Jesus' question (v. 38), the reference to the disciples' disbelief and amazement (v. 41), and the way the intake of food is expressed (v. 43) correspond in their vocabulary and style to the evangelist's customs; see Dauer, *Johannes und Lukas*, 259–75.

ment (the New Testament knows βρῶμα and βρῶσις to designate "food" only rarely).[9] The same is true of the pair "grilled fish" (ἰχϑὺς ὀπτός).

By general agreement, however, vv. 44-49 carry the mark of the evangelist.[10] This statement is true for both the manner of expression and the themes.[11] Nevertheless, some elements of this last speech of Christ are not especially Lukan: principally the preaching of repentance and the forgiveness of sins as expressions of salvation. Since the traditional scene probably included more than a recognition, it is likely that in it the Risen One already charged his disciples to proclaim forgiveness. From this brief mandate entrusted to him Luke has made an ambitious theological program, the many components of which our commentary will analyze in detail.

The second reason that leads the exegete to see a tradition behind vv. 36-43, and even behind vv. 36-49, is that there are parallel accounts available. Of course, one should not confuse similar stories and related stories. Several modern authors have looked for parallel texts. While Greek and Roman writings offer few real similarities, certain theophanies and appearances of angels in the Hebrew Bible and the Jewish Pseudepigrapha reveal the existence of a literary genre to which the pericope of Luke 24:36-49 belongs. Since the appearance of the 1922 article by Martin Albertz,[12] we know that appearance stories must be divided into two groups. There are those that are limited to recognition (such as the story about the disciples of Emmaus) and those that include an apostolic appointment and a missionary mandate (such

as the story before us here). There is, of course, a difference between belonging to a literary genre and making use of a particular tradition. Yet the presence of related episodes in the Gospel of Matthew, in Mark's inauthentic conclusion, in the Gospel of John, and in a passage of Ignatius of Antioch leads to the hypothesis that there was one tradition used knowingly by several authors.

When the English-speaking theologians speak of the "great commission," they are thinking primarily of the end of the Gospel of Matthew (Matt 28:16-20).[13] Yet one must not forget the Gospel of Luke. Even if the place is different—Galilee in Matthew, Jerusalem in Luke—there are common elements in these two writings about the universal mission entrusted to the apostles: a gathering of the eleven disciples, a manifestation of the Risen One, a final address that contains a command to engage in universal mission, a doubt among the disciples. Although the language varies in its details, the structure of the episode is basically the same. Thus, Matthew and Luke have kept alive the memory of a final meeting of the apostles with the living Christ and a missionary command given solemnly on this occasion. The relationship goes no further, however.

Mark's late and inauthentic ending (16:14-18) is closer to Luke than to Matt 28:16-20. The passage is preceded by a reminder of the empty tomb (Mark 16:9-11) and the Emmaus disciples (Mark 16:12-13). It is followed by a reference to the ascension (Mark 16:19). Added to this structural relationship to Luke 24 is the same arrangement of the appearance to the Eleven: The meeting of

---

9   On βρῶμα ("nourishment," "food," "solid food"), often used in the plural, see John 4:34; Rom 14:15, 20; 1 Cor 3:2; Luke 3:11; 9:13 (seventeen times in the New Testament). On βρῶσις (the "act of eating," "nourishment"), see John 4:32; Rom 14:17 (absent from Luke-Acts; eleven times in the New Testament).

10   After concluding that vv. 36-43 reveal the presence of a tradition, Dauer (*Johannes und Lukas*, 275) affirms: "Numerous observations indicate, however, that this farewell discourse of Jesus is essentially a Lukan formation." Dillon (*Eye-Witnesses*, 167) emphasizes "the thoroughly *Lucan* character of this passage," which has become "a common place in studies of recent date." Both authors then cite the names of many scholars who share this view. See also George, "Onze," 79.

11   On a number of occasions Jacques Dupont, who is interested in Luke's editorial efforts, has emphasized the Lukan character of vv. 44-49; see his "Discours de Pierre"; idem, "Portée christologique"; idem, "Mission de Paul."

12   Albertz, "Formgeschichte."

13   On the literary genre of mission sending in the ancient Orient, the Bible, and Luke-Acts in particular, see Hubbard, "Commissioning Stories." The genre did indeed exist, but it has been applied with great flexibility. It was useful, because it was a way of expressing the unspeakable encounter between the divine and the human. See Basset, "Dernières paroles"; Schneider, "Missionsauftrag"; Legrand, "Missionary Command"; Milne, "Luke's Great Commission." On Matt 28:16-20 see Luz, *Matthew 21–28*, 614–36, with a rich bibliography.

the group is followed by the appearance of the Risen One, the disciples' doubt, the Master's rebuke, and the missionary command. There are, however, two major differences. Mark 16 emphasizes the group's resistance to faith, and Luke 24 uses eating to prove that the Risen One has returned to life. It is not clear whether the author of Mark's long ending knows the Gospel of Luke. It may be based, as is Matthew, on a similar tradition.[14] In no case does Luke depend on Mark 16:14-18, for these verses are too recent to have influenced him.

In comparing Luke 24:36-49 to the Gospel of John, we must refer to three passages.[15] The most obvious is John 20:19-23. Here the relationship goes beyond a similarity of structure to the statement itself. When the disciples have once been assembled, Jesus appears and "stood in the midst" (ἔστη εἰς τὸ μέσον, John 20:19), "stood in their midst" (ἔστη ἐν μέσῳ αὐτῶν, Luke 24:36); "and he says to them: peace be with you" (καὶ λέγει αὐτοῖς· εἰρήνη ὑμῖν, John 20:19), the same wording in Luke 24:36).[16] Without waiting, Jesus "shows" (ἔδειξεν, the same verb form in John and Luke) his disciples, "his hands and his side" (τὰς χεῖρας καὶ τὴν πλευράν, John 20:20), "his hands and his feet" (τὰς χεῖρας καὶ τοὺς πόδας, Luke 24:40; see already v. 39). Both Gospels then mention the disciples' joy (ἐχάρησαν, "they rejoiced," John 20:20; ἀπὸ τῆς χαρᾶς, "for joy," Luke 24:41). Then in both Gospels, of course with different words, the missionary command rings out (John 20:21; Luke 24:47-48). In both cases there is a reference to the Holy Spirit (conferred in John 20:22, promised in Luke 24:49) and to the forgiveness of sins (John 20:23; Luke 24:47). The many common themes and the relationship of the vocabularies lead to the following hypothesis: as elsewhere in the passion narrative and the story of the resurrection, Luke and John share here not only common memories but also a strong tradition. Of course, they make use of it freely, but they do so with the same respect.

The second Johannine passage confirms this hypothesis. The fourth evangelist is the only one who has presented the case of doubting Thomas, but in order to create a striking picture of the scene he emphasizes the tangible reality of the body of the Risen One and the possibility offered Thomas to ascertain this reality for himself (John 20:24-29).[17] The Gospel of Luke also emphasizes the body of the Risen One and the tangible proofs that are available (Luke 24:39-43). It is likely, therefore, that John transferred to the Thomas episode this demonstration that, as Luke suggests, originally was part of the appearance to the Eleven.

Finally, a generation after that of the fourth evangelist, the author of John 21 was also aware of the tradition about the appearance of the Risen One to the disciples, and he uses an aspect neglected by his predecessor to describe the manifestation of Christ on the shore of the Sea of Tiberias. Faced with the trouble the disciples have in recognizing him, Jesus asks if they have "something to eat" (τὶ προσφάγιον) to go with the bread, more specifically, fish (John 21:5, where Luke 24:41 has τὶ βρώσιμον, "something to eat"). Since they had caught nothing in their nets so far, the risen Lord offers them a miraculous catch of fish and then organizes a meal for them. In the same way that Luke speaks of the "broiled fish," the author of John 21 speaks of an ὀψάριον, etymologically "something cooked," to eat with the bread, then "fish" (John 21:9), as he has just mentioned the miraculous "fishes" (ἰχθύς in the genitive plural, John 21:6).

The Synoptic comparison not only turns out to be rich;[18] it also holds a surprise. In his letter to the Smyrnaeans, Ignatius of Antioch, who wrote early in the second century, says this about Jesus Christ:

For I know and believe that he was in the flesh even after the resurrection. And when he came to those with Peter he said to them: "Take, handle me and

---

14   See Hug, *Finale*, 168–69.

15   In dialogue with Dauer (*Johannes und Lukas*), Neirynck ("Récit lucanien") comes to the conclusion that John uses only Luke and that we should not imagine that there was an intermediate narrative. See also Bailey, *Traditions*, 85–102; Porsch, *Pneuma und Wort*, 353–57.

16   It is true that these words are missing from some manuscripts; on the textual problem see the commentary below on v. 36.

17   See Vanni ("Tommaso"), who observes the transition from the collective (the Eleven) to the individual (Thomas) and is of the opinion that in Luke it is Jesus Christ in general who is identified, while in John it is the Crucified One.

18   Léon-Dufour (*Résurrection*, 133–34) in the same way as Goulder (*New Paradigm*, 2:790–91) emphasizes the parallel between Luke 24:36-43 and Jesus' walking on the water (Mark 6:45-52 par.).

see that I am not a phantom without a body." And they immediately touched him and believed, being mingled both with his flesh and spirit. Therefore they despised even death, and were proved to be above death. And after his resurrection he ate and drank with them as a being of flesh, although he was united in spirit to the Father. (*Smyrn.* 3.1–3; trans. Lake, LCL)[19]

It has been suggested, incorrectly, that Ignatius repeated in his own way what he had read in the Gospels of Luke and John. Apart from the fact that the differences between this fragment and the canonical Gospels are too significant, two patristic witnesses, one Origen, the other Jerome, affirm that the statement of Jesus as Ignatius quotes it was part of a noncanonical book. According to Origen (*Princ.* 1, *prooemium* 8) it was the *Kerygma of Peter;* according to Jerome (*Comm. Is.* 18, *praefatio,* and *Vir. ill.* 16) it was the *Gospel of the Hebrews.* It may well be an *agraphon,* a free-floating sentence, since other ancient Christian authors know and quote it. It seems clear to me that Ignatius, just like Luke and the author of John 21, is aware of an appearance story that tells how the Risen One demonstrated the reality of his return to bodily life by taking and sharing food. Very quickly the argument for the bodily resurrection was combined with the liturgical affirmation of commensality. Indeed, the Acts of the Apostles insists on the latter aspect in 10:41 ("we who ate and drank with him after he rose from the dead") and probably also in 1:4, if one reads συναλιζό-μενος literally as "he who shared the salt," thus "ate" with them.

In summary, the evangelists and some of the ancient Christian writers know that in a final appearance Jesus charged his followers to spread the gospel among all nations. More precisely, some of them, including Luke and John, knew a story in which in this last conversation Christ also gave two proofs of his bodily resurrection, first by letting himself be seen and touched, then by consuming food, especially grilled fish.

This tradition and this story that contains it do not go back to the early years of Christianity. Indeed, it took some time for the mission to the Gentiles to be accepted by everyone, and the problem of the bodily reality of the resurrection first arose at the end of the first century. The Lukan construction of the conversion of the Roman officer Cornelius as an argument for the *vocatio gentium* comes from the years 80–90, and it is about the year 100 that the author of the Johannine epistles and Ignatius of Antioch emphasize the bodily reality of the resurrection of Jesus Christ. The idea that there was an ultimate limit to the appearances of the Risen One does not come from the earliest stage of Christianity. As we know, Paul is the earliest witness of this theological requirement of closure (1 Cor 15:8: ἔσχατον δὲ πάντων . . . , "last of all . . .").

Commentary

■ **36** The transition is brief and common; the time is given with a genitive absolute, a form Luke loves. Does the verb λαλέω have a particular nuance here? It can underscore either the vocal aspect of the conversation or the religious character of what was said.[20] Without feeling the need to name the subject of the action, namely, Jesus, Luke speaks of the sudden presence of the risen Lord in the midst of his own.[21] To do so he uses the verbal form ἔστη, which the LXX sometimes uses to indicate an angelic appearance.[22] Moreover, the evangelist himself, a short time earlier, used a compound form of this verb (ἐπέστησαν, "stood before," 24:4). As if guarding

19 On this passage from Ignatius, see Plummer, 560; Schmidtke, "Zum Hebräerevangelium"; Braun, *Jean le thélogien,* 1:268–69, 280–82; Köster, *Synoptische Überlieferung,* 50–56; Bovon, *Studies,* 100–101; Neirynck, "Récit lucanien," 672–77. I admire Grotius (*Annotationes,* 936), who quotes the passage of Ignatius and knows the opinions of Eusebius and Jerome.

20 On the religious use of the verb λαλέω, see vol. 1 of this commentary, 92–93 and 355–56, on 2:17-18 and 9:10-11.

21 Schweizer (249) describes Christ here as the one who comes to help.

22 For the use of ἔστη during the appearance of heavenly beings, see Num 22:24 LXX (appearance of an angel); Deut 31:15 LXX (appearance of the Lord). See also Tob 5:4 (Codex Sinaiticus): "Outside he found the angel Raphael standing (ἑστηκότα) before him, but he does not suspect it is an angel of God."

against an excessive rejection, the one who surprised them added the pronoun "to you," "with you" ($\dot{\nu}\mu\hat{\iota}\nu$) to the salutation "peace" ($\epsilon\dot{\iota}\rho\dot{\eta}\nu\eta$).[23]

Nestle-Aland's text (27th ed.) corresponds to most of the Greek manuscripts, beginning with the oldest, the Bodmer Papyrus XIV–XV ($\mathfrak{P}^{75}$), and the ancient versions. Is the weight of Codex Bezae (D = 05) and all or some Old Latin manuscripts as well as the parallel of John 20:19 enough to compel the short reading of this verse (without the words "and he says to them: Peace be with you")? That appears not to be the case, even if it is a venerable reading, going back to the second century and corresponding to Marcion's text. A long reading adding "it is I, fear not" after the peace greeting, is represented by a few Greek witnesses and some versions.[24] It should probably be rejected. It may be explained by the influence of Tatian's *Diatessaron*, which must have been inspired by Jesus walking on the water (John 6:20; see also Matt 14:27 and Mark 6:50, which, however, add beforehand "take heart"). What is certain is that in the second century the text of the Gospels has not yet achieved a canonical stability, a stability that, by the way, will never be perfect.[25]

■ **37** As is well known, the *numinous* causes terror. As the appearance of the angels to the women at the tomb creates fear (24:4-5), the appearance of the Risen One provokes panic. The disciples' anguish reaches an even higher level than that of the women. Indeed, Luke is not satisfied with the adjective "frightened" ($\dot{\epsilon}\mu\varphi o\beta o\varsigma$), which he had used in the episode of the empty tomb (24:5); he precedes it with the participle of an expressive verb $\pi\tau o\dot{\epsilon}\omega$, which means "be terrified."[26] The disciples' terror comes from how they regard the one who has burst into their midst. They think they are seeing a "spirit," a "ghost."[27] To put it bluntly, the biblical tradition forbids necromancy not because the dead do not show themselves but because, on the contrary, they do appear when they are invoked, and then they are all the more dangerous.[28] This explains the panic that seized the disciples. Codex Bezae (D = 05) is both right and wrong here. It is wrong because it changes the text (with this one exception, the Greek witnesses all have the word $\pi\nu\epsilon\hat{\upsilon}\mu\alpha$, "spirit" here). Yet it is right because the word in this passage designates a "ghost" ($\varphi\dot{\alpha}\nu\tau\alpha\sigma\mu\alpha$). Furthermore, Luke thinks the disciples are not satisfied merely to "see"—they focus their attention; they want to "observe," or even to "contemplate" ($\vartheta\epsilon\omega\rho\epsilon\hat{\iota}\nu$).[29] But— the evangelist clarifies—they were mistaken, because that is merely what they "thought" ($\dot{\epsilon}\delta\acute{o}\kappa o\nu\nu$), what they "believed" they contemplated. Their surmise was misleading.

■ **38** The style and content of this verse are Lukan and are reminiscent of the rhetorical questions that Jesus addressed to the Emmaus disciples (24:17, 25-26) and those that the angels posed to the women who came to the tomb (24:5). The reference to the disturbance

---

23 In contrast to Dillon (*Eye-Witnesses*, 187–93), I make no connection between Jesus' missionary discourse, with which he encourages the disciples to bless the house with peace (10:5), and the appearance of the Risen One to the apostles (24:36). L'Eplattenier (300) emphasizes the "full significance" of the word "peace" here. Has Jesus not just defeated the enemy, death? L'Eplattenier calls attention to 1:79.

24 For the details, see the apparatus of Nestle-Aland (27th ed.) on the text; and Metzger, *Textual Commentary* (2d ed.), 160.

25 One finds a good presentation of the textual problems of v. 36 in Guillaume, *Luc interprète*, 163–69; see also George, "Onze," 77; Rigaux, *Dieu l'a ressuscité*, 259; Dillon, *Eye-Witnesses*, 182–83. These authors also address other textual problems that are especially numerous in their verses. Commentators such as Fitzmyer (2:1573, 1575–77, 1583–84); Wiefel (413); and Eckey (984–85) also give them attention.

26 The Bodmer Papyrus ($\mathfrak{P}^{75}$) and Codex Vaticanus (B = 03), two of the earliest witnesses of the Gospel of Luke, use here a different, more expressive verb, $\vartheta\rho o\dot{\epsilon}\omega$, which is used three times in the New Testament and only in the passive with the meaning of "to be afraid," "to be alarmed" (e.g., Matt 24:6).

27 On the meaning of $\pi\nu\epsilon\hat{\upsilon}\mu\alpha$ here, see Nolland 3:1213; Sabourin (383), who refers to Acts 12:15 (Peter's "angel"); Acts 23:8-9 ("angel" or "spirit"); and Josephus *Ant.* 13.16.3 §416. Note Caird's caustic comment (261): "This means that to a Jew a disembodied spirit could only seem a ghost, not a living being, but a thin, unsubstantial carbon-copy which had somehow escaped from the filing system of death."

28 On necromancy in Israel and the ancient world, see Bovon, "Gespenst."

29 Luke likes this verb $\vartheta\epsilon\omega\rho\dot{\epsilon}\omega$ and uses it again in v. 39.

($\tau\alpha\rho\acute{\alpha}\sigma\sigma\omega$, "to disturb"), the hesitations ($\delta\iota\alpha\lambda o\gamma\iota\sigma$-$\mu\acute{o}\varsigma$, "dispute"),[30] and the "heart" ($\kappa\alpha\rho\delta\acute{\iota}\alpha$; see 24:25) correspond to the author's customs. Only the use of "to mount," "to come up" ($\grave{\alpha}\nu\alpha\beta\alpha\acute{\iota}\nu\omega$) in a figurative sense is not characteristic of Luke. Note also here as in v. 36 the use of the dative ($\alpha\grave{\upsilon}\tauo\hat{\iota}\varsigma$, "to them") after the verb "to say." It may be a vestige of the tradition that Luke used, since he often avoids the dative and prefers $\pi\rho\acute{o}\varsigma$ and the accusative after the *verba dicendi*.

■ **39** In the episode of the doubting Thomas, the fourth evangelist dots the "*i*." By looking and touching, the disciple wants to find the print of the nails (John 20:25). Without explicitly saying so, Luke wants to achieve the same result. The feet and hands must bear the marks that reveal an identity. The nurse Eurycleia recognizes Odysseus from a scar on his leg (Homer *Od.* 19.308–507). Otherwise, one must look at the face to recognize a person ($\acute{o}\tau\iota\ \grave{\epsilon}\gamma\acute{\omega}\ \epsilon\grave{\iota}\mu\iota\ \alpha\grave{\upsilon}\tau\acute{o}\varsigma$, "it is I"). One must still agree on the status of this "I." The tradition quoted by Luke rejects the idea that a person's remains survive after death in the form of a ghost, a $\pi\nu\epsilon\hat{\upsilon}\mu\alpha$ ("spirit," the same word as in v. 37). Nor does it accept that Jesus avoided martyrdom and simply continued to live. No, "it is I" designates the newness of the resurrection in the continuity of the person: in a word, the Christian mystery.

Verse 39 consists of two sentences in the imperative that overlap and complement each other.[31] The first speaks only of the look ($\acute{\iota}\delta\epsilon\tau\epsilon$, "see," "look"); the second adds the touch ($\psi\eta\lambda\alpha\phi\acute{\eta}\sigma\alpha\tau\acute{\epsilon}\ \mu\epsilon\ \kappa\alpha\grave{\iota}\ \acute{\iota}\delta\epsilon\tau\epsilon$, "touch me and see"). Obedience to the first command will lead to recognition; obedience to the second avoids misunderstanding. Indeed, these are the two sides of the same coin. It will be a twofold confirmation. What appears in tangible form cannot be a ghost; the marks he shows are intended to identify who he is.

Following the authors and bearers of the tradition, Luke acknowledges the corporeality of the resurrection. To be convincing, feet and hands must consist of bones

covered with flesh.[32] Yet Paul, Luke's mentor, thinks that "flesh and blood cannot inherit the kingdom of God" (1 Cor 15:50). But the apostle, who emphasizes the spiritual character of the resurrection, nevertheless believes that for the resurrection to be personal it must be bodily. It is this aspect of Paul's thought that Luke takes over; hence the famous expression "spiritual body" ($\sigma\hat{\omega}\mu\alpha$ $\pi\nu\epsilon\upsilon\mu\alpha\tau\iota\kappa\acute{o}\nu$, 1 Cor 15:44), which has the twofold advantage that it ensures the continuity of the person ($\sigma\hat{\omega}\mu\alpha$, "body") in the discontinuity of the nature ($\pi\nu\epsilon\upsilon$-$\mu\alpha\tau\iota\kappa\acute{o}\nu$, "spiritual"). This new dimension follows and at the same time sets itself against the historical human and contingent dimension of the "flesh" ($\sigma\acute{\alpha}\rho\xi$; see "in the flesh," Gal. 2:20). The tradition Luke is following corresponds to a trend that gains momentum late in the first century and, in the second and third centuries, asserts itself against those who reject the resurrection as well as against the supporters of a spiritual resurrection. As the resurrection is called bodily, it increasingly makes use of the vocabulary of the flesh.[33]

It may be, however, that Luke wanted to give a metaphorical note to the prosaic vocabulary of flesh and bones. A reader of the LXX, he remembers the vision of the dry bones (Ezekiel 37). In Luke's day no one in Alexandria or Ephesus took the prophet's description literally. One must understand these bones that have come together and the flesh that has been formed anew in a figurative and spiritual sense. It will be the same way in the Renaissance. When Luca Signorelli in Orvieto painted young and beautiful bodies gradually coming out of the tombs, he is thinking of a new life that includes the spirit. After the centuries of the Middle Ages, when the body was either hidden or its suffering was exhibited, the painter rejoices in physical beauty. Thus, it is the task of Christian faith to show that the living side of creation can enter the service of the still-hidden side of redemption. It is therefore possible—at least the way I read Luke—that the flesh and the bones

---

30   On the term $\delta\iota\alpha\lambda o\gamma\iota\sigma\mu\acute{o}\varsigma$ in Luke, see Johnson, 401; and vol. 1 of this commentary, 105, on 2:35b; 182 n. 30 on the excursus "The Forgiveness of Sins"; and 394 on 9:46.

31   On vv. 39-40, see Vanni, "Tommaso."

32   The expression "bones and flesh" is biblical: see Gen 29:14; Judg 9:2; 2 Sam [LXX 2 Kgdms] 5:1; Homer (*Od.* 11.219) also offers a parallel: in Hades

"no longer do the sinews hold the bones and the flesh" (trans. Albert Cook); see C. F. Evans, 919. Schlatter (462) refers to Josephus *Ant.* 12.4.9 §211; 15.7.5 §236; 19.7.1 §325.

33   See Schmithals, 236; Caroline Walker Bynum, *The Resurrection of the Body in Western Christianity, 200–1336* (New York: Columbia University Press, 1995) 1–71.

of the Risen One permit one not only to recognize the historical Jesus, the Christ of the past, but also to imagine the Christ of the future, the triumphant Risen One. To speak of such things human beings have no words and images apart from those of everyday life. The task is not easy, for even the most beautiful colors, such as those used, for example, by Mathias Grünewald in the Isenheim Altarpiece, may by their very excess have a negative effect.

■ **40** What the double imperative had demanded is realized in v. 40. While he is still talking, the Risen One shows[34] his wounds. Since the story could function without this explanation, it is not surprising that some scribes have thought that this sentence was not necessary. Some exegetes, who value what they complicatedly call the *Western non-interpolations*, that is, the short formulations of the so-called Western text, have thought that v. 40, as well as v. 36b, are interpolations taken from John's parallel account (John 20:19b-20a). Since the discovery of the Bodmer Papyrus XIV-XV ($\mathfrak{P}^{75}$), which contains v. 40 and v. 36b, the theory of an interpolation has lost its panache. Since the "Western" text corresponds to that of Marcion, it is probably dependent on him.

■ **41** We must first note a tension with v. 34, which puts the Easter message on the lips of the disciples. This tension between belief and disbelief exists because the stories Luke includes in this chapter originally were independent of one another. We then should note the paradox expressed by the genitive absolute: The disciples doubt and rejoice at the same time. Matthew is more rational; he says that, when they saw the Risen One, some worshiped him and others doubted (Matt 28:17). Here in Luke, for all of them it is difficult to believe and easy to rejoice. Claire Clivaz has shown that from Homer on in their poetic compositions the Greeks willingly acknowledged divided feelings.[35] In the Roman period, Greek, Roman, and Jewish historians were not reluctant to

include feelings in their works. The manuals of rhetoric even taught students how to do it. The manual of Eudemus arranges joy, astonishment, and disbelief in a definition of ἄγη, the "horrified surprise." As one can see, the feelings mentioned by Luke fit this definition. What Luke wants to express, in particular with the oxymoron "while for joy they still disbelieved," is the psychological, physical, and existential disruption caused by contact with the divine, more specifically, as the result of God's intervention, that is, Christ's resurrection.[36]

The feelings are then expressed in simple words and gestures. Jesus asks for something to eat—politely, he does not say "give me"; he says "do you have?"

■ **42** The disciples then offer him "a piece of broiled fish." To explain how fish could be on the menu in a city far from the ocean or a lake and without a river, sharp-minded exegetes (see n. 44 below) point out that salt was used to conserve food and that Zebedee's family may have sold its catch in a small shop in the capital! Of greater interest is the symbolic significance of the fish. It may permit the physical demonstration of the resurrection to move to the communal significance of the act. By eating fish, as the multitudes did with the multiplication of the loaves (9:13), Christ eats the same food as his disciples. Luke suggests here the commensality, the fellowship, and even the eucharistic liturgy.

A textual variant confirms this hypothesis, or at least demonstrates that there were many people during the first centuries of the Christian era who gave this episode a eucharistic dimension. Indeed, there are a number of manuscripts, versions, and patristic witnesses who add a honeycomb to the portion of fish. Now we know that in antiquity fish and honey often appeared on the communion tables along with bread and wine. Since honey was also regarded as paradisiacal food, we cannot rule out an eschatological connotation. Furthermore, is Jesus not risen?[37] The weight of this variant (actually, a principal

---

34 The oldest manuscripts have ἔδειξεν, the text retained by Nestle-Aland's 27th edition. Important witnesses such as Alexandrinus (A = 02), the Freer Codex (W = 032), Codex Koridethi (Θ = 038), an uncial manuscript from Athos (Ψ = 044), the minuscule family f^{13}, and countless manuscripts from the Byzantine period have the compound ἐπέδειξεν, "he showed openly."

35 Clivaz, "Incroyants." She refers to Eudemus Περὶ

λέξεων ῥητορικῶν, folio 3, line 33 (*Excerpta ex Eudemi codice Parisino, n. 2635*, ed. Benedikt Niese, *Philologus suppl.* 15 (1922) 145–60.

36 In this context we may waver on the meaning of the verb θαυμάζω. Are the disciples stupefied, dumbfounded (my translation), or do they marvel (translation of Delebecque, *Évangile*, 151)?

37 See Nestle, "Honeycomb"; and Kilpatrick ("Luke 24"), who asks whether a repetition is not responsi-

variant, μέρος καὶ ἀπὸ μελισσίου κηρίου, and a secondary variant, μέρος καὶ ἀπὸ μελισσίου κηρίον)[38] is such that an Italian scholar, Beatrice Cherubini, has written a prized scholarly thesis about it. Among the Greek uncial manuscripts, for the first variant I call attention from the sixth century in chronological order to N (= 022), E (= 07), Ψ (= 044), H (= 013), K (= 017), M (= 021), U (= 030), V (= 031), Δ (= 037), S (= 028), X (= 033) and Γ (= 036);[39] among the minuscules, to the two families *f*[1] and *f*[13] and to number 33.[40] Among the versions, most of the Old Latin manuscripts and the Vulgate, along with the Curetonian Syriac version, witness to one or the other form of the variant. Among the Christian authors are perhaps Tatian in his *Diatessaron*, then certainly *De resurrectione* 9.3 of Pseudo-Justin;[41] Tertullian *De corona* 14.4, Pseudo-Athanasius *Quaestiones in Scripturam sacram* (*PG* 28:725C and 728B); Cyril of Jerusalem *Catechetical Lectures on Baptism* 14.11 (*PG* 33:837, 840), Epiphanius *Panarion* 66.38—39.4; Gregory of Nyssa *De Tridui* (*PG* 46:628); Amphilochius *Contra haereticos* 27.1055 (*CCSG* 3:213), etc. These lists are impressive. They prove how vital the biblical writing was in its variety in the patristic era.

■ **43** In v. 43 we return to apologetic and to the physical demonstration of the resurrection, for Jesus takes the fish and eats it.[42] By saying that he did it "in their presence" (ἐνώπιον αὐτῶν) Luke emphasizes the argument for the resurrection. Of course, various exegetes remember that the LXX (and perhaps Luke) uses the preposition "before" (ἐνώπιον) in the sense of "together with" (σύν) and thus suggests a shared meal.[43] Relying on 13:26, I think the opposite—that ἐνώπιον is different from σύν and presents a Jesus who eats in the presence of his disciples. In that moment they precisely do not eat; they merely watch the demonstration.[44]

Luke does not yet ask the question, but it will be asked in the second century: Did the Risen One digest this food and, if so, how did he do it? The Christians will find the answer in the Jewish tradition that had to solve the same problem about the angels who had accepted the invitation of Abraham and Sarah (Gen 18:6-8). Instead of saying that Christ only pretended to eat, the ancient authors preferred to imagine that the resurrected or angelic bodies did indeed eat, but that they did not digest the food as did human bodies. They thought that

---

ble for the omission of the words "of a honeycomb": μερος ΚΑΙΑπομελισσιου κηριου ΚΑΙΛαβων.
As these authors have observed, in the Hellenistic Jewish romance *Joseph and Aseneth* 16–17, honey, of which a comb comes from paradise, is regarded as a food of immortality. See esp. Cherubini, "Mangiò pesce e miele."

38   In the first case, μελίσσιος, -ον is an adjective, "of bees," "of the bee hive"; in the second, τὸ μελίσσιον, "the swarm of bees," "the hive," is a noun. In the first case the Risen One receives "a piece of broiled fish and a piece of a honeycomb" (μέρος refers to the two pieces of food and ἀπό is superfluous); in the second, he receives "a piece of broiled fish and a honeycomb from a hive," which is more generous. Bertrand Bouvier helped me clarify this point.

39   Codex Koridethi (Θ = 038) has the second variant.

40   Did *f*[13] have the first (thus Cherubini) or the second variant (Nestle-Aland, 27th ed.)?

41   See Alberto D'Anna, *Pseudo-Gustino, Sulla rezurrezione: Discorso cristano del II secolo* (Letteratura cristiana antica; Brescia: Morcelliana, 2001) 48–49.

42   According to Luke, in this moment the disciples recognize the Risen One for who he is, but the evangelist does not bother to tell us. Martini ("Apparizione," 232) remembers that Joseph was recognized by his brothers (Gen 45:1-16 and Acts 7:13) and that Jesus was recognized by Paul (Acts 9:5) and emphasizes the notion of "recognition." He also points out that the appearance to the Eleven is remembered in Acts but that it has little in common with the mention of appearances or visions.

43   Throughout his entire monograph, but esp. on pp. 195 and 201–2, Dillon (*Eye-Witnesses*) refuses to see here an argument for the physical resurrection directed against Docetism and promotes more the idea of table fellowship between Jesus and his disciples. Dumm ("Hospitality") defends the same idea and emphasizes the hospitality offered and received. Most exegetes, however, hold that the principal sense of the episode was apologetic but retain a symbolic overture as a secondary meaning; see, e.g., Ernst, 666–68.

44   O'Collins ("Did Jesus Eat the Fish?") offers a number of answers to his question. He himself is reluctant to answer yes and refuses to read Luke "literalistically" (72)! Bishop ("With Saint Luke") thinks that the fish had been salted to conserve it and that it came from the fishery of the sons of Zebedee, who had an agent in Jerusalem!

a divine fire came down and consumed the food just as did the flames of the burnt offering.[45]

■ **44** In this moment the second part of the episode begins, the final speech of the Risen One.[46] Luke, a man of continuity, does not imagine a final revelation; he reiterates the teaching already given.[47] A long clause deals with the Scriptures. They are divided into three parts, and each of them contains prophecies that must be fulfilled. Two words placed at the end of the sentence are enough to indicate the contents: $\pi\epsilon\rho\grave{\iota}\ \grave{\epsilon}\mu o\hat{\upsilon}$ ("about me"). Of course, Luke does not say that all the stories and all the commandments of the Old Testament speak of Christ. Yet he dares to impose a christological reading on Israel's Scriptures. The $\pi\acute{\alpha}\nu\tau\alpha$ ("everything") confirms this ambition.

Four comments are still to be made: (a) This is the second time Luke underscores the christological character of the fulfillment of Scripture; see 24:27 ($\tau\grave{\alpha}\ \pi\epsilon\rho\grave{\iota}\ \grave{\epsilon}\alpha\upsilon\tau o\hat{\upsilon}$, "the things about himself").[48] (b) It is also the second time in a resurrection story that Luke directs the attention of the readers to the past; see 24:6. (c) This fulfillment is expressed in Lukan terms (see $\delta\epsilon\hat{\iota}$ ["must be"], the verb $\pi\lambda\eta\rho\acute{o}\omega$ ["to fulfill"], $\tau\grave{\alpha}\ \gamma\epsilon\gamma\rho\alpha\mu\mu\acute{\epsilon}\nu\alpha$

["what is written"]). (d) The only peculiarity of this passage is the division of the Scriptures into not merely two parts, Law and Prophets (see 24:27), but into three.[49] Luke is one of the first witnesses of this new division, and he chooses the Psalms as a witness of the writings being formed as Scripture. The speeches in Acts will draw their most important arguments from this collection. Let us say in conclusion that the evangelist was a skilled and experienced author, who can repeat himself (see 24:6-7; 24:25-27 and here, v. 44) without becoming monotonous.[50]

■ **45** Although the message remains the same—it even includes the various scattered announcements of the passion since the Galilean period—the understanding of the listeners must change.[51] The predictions of the passion had fallen in vain on the ears of the disciples. Luke 9:44-45 underscored the incomprehension that confronted the teaching of Jesus. For Luke neither the message of the women returning from the empty tomb, nor the words of the disciples who have come back from Emmaus, nor the proofs of the resurrection were enough to provide a key to interpreting the holy Scriptures.[52] That requires the spiritual intervention of the risen

---

45   See Tertullian *Adv. Marc.* 3.9; Harnack, *Marcion*, 125; Orbe, *Cristologia Gnóstica*, 1:383–87; 2:515–17; Bynum, *Resurrection of the Body* (see n. 33 above), 21–43.

46   See George, "Intelligence"; Dillon, *Eye-Witnesses*, 203–20; Dillon, "Easter Revelation," 243–56; Dumm, "Hospitality"; Kingsbury, "Luke 24"; Dupont, "Mission de Paul." Moore ("Great Commission") believes that Luke wrote this passage thinking of the servant in Isaiah; like Roland Meynet, Mierzwa ("Gesù") loves chiasms; Prete, "Intelligenza."

47   Black ("Voice," 99) suggests that the Risen One's explanations expanded the disciples' powers of perception.

48   Lagrange (613) writes: "Jesus reveals the divine plan. His words weld together in his person the past, that is, the Scriptures, with the future or the mission of the apostles."

49   In 1992 Flusser ("Psalmen") already noted that the text of Qumran 4QMMT (4Q 397–398) contains the same division of the Scriptures into three parts, with the Psalms as the third part. Flusser refuses to speak of an Essene influence on Luke and says that all three parts, the Law, the Prophets,

and the Psalms are "witnesses of salvation history" (41).

50   As others also do, Dömer (*Heil*, 99) parallels the introduction of v. 44 with the beginning of Deuteronomy in the LXX: $o\hat{\upsilon}\tau o\iota\ o\iota\ \lambda\acute{o}\gamma o\iota,\ o\grave{\upsilon}\varsigma\ \grave{\epsilon}\lambda\acute{\alpha}\lambda\eta\sigma\epsilon\nu\ M\omega\ddot{\upsilon}\sigma\hat{\eta}\varsigma\ \pi\alpha\nu\tau\grave{\iota}\ \Ì\sigma\rho\alpha\grave{\eta}\lambda\ \pi\acute{\epsilon}\rho\alpha\nu\ \tau o\hat{\upsilon}\ \Ì\rho\delta\acute{\alpha}\nu o\upsilon\ \grave{\epsilon}\nu\ \tau\hat{\eta}\ \grave{\epsilon}\rho\acute{\eta}\mu\omega$ (Deut 1:1). In my opinion this parallel is not necessary. Dupont ("Mission de Paul") is right that vv. 44-49 parallel Acts 1:8 and 26:16-23. "Luke applies to Paul's mission the same model that defines the mission of the twelve apostles" (297).

51   Bossuyt and Radermakers (2:527) remark with finesse: "Verse 45 is introduced by a conjunction [actually, an adverb] that marks a turning point: 'then' ($\tau\acute{o}\tau\epsilon$)."

52   See Ernst ("Schriftauslegung"), who is concerned to know how Luke speaks of the Scriptures and how he understands them in the light of Christ. The evangelist uses three procedures: scriptural proof, typology, and the promise–fulfillment scheme. Grasso ("Fattori," 305, 313) says that the Lukan pericope prepares in its own way the idea of a second Scripture, a New Testament. Read also Schneider's excursus "Verheißung und Erfüllung" (2:503–4).

Christ, since it is a matter of the transformation of the "mind" (νοῦς). Easter is the day of openings: opening the tomb (24:2), opening the eyes (24:31), opening the Scriptures (24:32), and here opening the mind (v. 45).[53] The process, however, is not merely intellectual. Here Luke uses "mind" (νοῦς) but he speaks also of the "heart" (καρδία, 24:25, 32). The transformation involves entire persons, especially their inner being. The episode could end here.

■ 46 If Luke gives the word again to the Risen One (note the repetition of in v. 44 and v. 46),[54] it is because he wants to describe in detail the essential parts of these prophecies. Moreover, the readers know them well, because they are related to the two main articles of the kerygma, the death and resurrection, which also constitute the core of the predictions of the passion (see 9:22, 44; 17:25; 18:32-33). Nor are the readers surprised by the wording, sometimes Lukan, sometimes traditional, of the central elements of the Christian faith. The death is defined here redactionally as a suffering[55] (see 24:26) and the return to life traditionally as a resurrection[56] on the third day (see 24:7).

What is surprising, however, is that the evangelist does not mention Jesus' ministry prior to the passion. Neither the mighty deeds nor the Messiah's teachings play a role here. Two explanations come to mind: (a) Luke is in the grip of a theological construction, attested by Paul, which focuses attention on the binomial cross–resurrection;

(b) Luke is about to turn the page and is already thinking ahead to the book of Acts. In this second book the apostles and the witnesses share Paul's predilection for a message centered on the death and resurrection (see the christological speeches of Acts). This orientation toward the future is no less paradoxical in verses that ostensibly refer to the past (v. 44).

■ 47 Luke loves to repeat basic truths, but he also knows how to vary the expressions. Here he even goes beyond variation to risk an expansion, adding what he had earlier refused. In a surprise he says that, in addition to their message, the Scriptures promise that this message will be spread abroad. As Jacques Dupont has correctly seen,[57] the spectrum covered by the Scriptures is expanded. It expands, according to Jesus, to include the church. The expression "thus it is written" (v. 46) includes the preaching of repentance and the offer of forgiveness. For two reasons Luke advances this thesis that he has suggested in his Gospel: faithfulness to the tradition he passes on and attention to the coming book of Acts (see Luke 1:77; 3:3-6; Acts 10:43).

As we have seen,[58] the wording of v. 47 contains elements that, coming from Luke, are surprising and must come from the tradition he uses. Nowhere else does Luke say that the "conversion" (μετάνοια) must be "proclaimed," and he does not emphasize the vocabulary of the "forgiveness of sins."[59] Characteristic of Luke are, however, the verb itself "proclaim" (κηρύσσω), the

---

53 On this theme of opening, see Delling, "Als er uns"; Prete, "Intelligenza," 467–71.

54 The πρὸς αὐτούς, which follows the verb in v. 44, is characteristic of the evangelist, and the dative αὐτοῖς, which follows in v. 46, may be an element of the tradition Luke used. Indeed, it is probable that the story of the appearance ended with a missionary command (see my comments above in the analysis).

55 In two different forms countless manuscripts like to recall the necessary character of the passion: they add καὶ οὕτως ἔδει ("and thus it was necessary"), following the formulation of 24:26; see the apparatus of Nestle-Aland (27th ed.) on the passage.

56 Luke clarifies here—something he does not always do—that this ἀναστῆναι, literally, "this fact of rising again," this "to resuscitate," is a resurrection "from the dead" (ἐκ νεκρῶν). This explanation is not indispensable: Codex Bezae (D = 05) and the Sahidic version do without it.

57 Dupont, "Portée christologique." The Belgian exegete rightly rejects the hypothesis of Wellhausen (141), who treats the infinitive κηρυχθῆναι as an imperative. Dupont notes that "the infinitive with the imperative meaning is always in the present tense" (127 n. 12). Referring to v. 44, Ernst ("Schriftauslegung," 371) speaks of a "visible historical expansion of the kerygma." In my opinion, the comment is especially true for v. 47. Legrand ("Missionary Command," 304) speaks in a broader perspective of vv. 44-49. Senior (Passion, 158): "In condensed form, Luke has summed up the entire Gospel and laid out the program for the Acts of the Apostles."

58 See the analysis above.

59 See Luke 1:77; 3:3; 5:20-24; 7:47-49; 11:4; 24:47; Acts 2:38; 3:19; 5:31; 10:43; 13:38; 22:16; 26:18. Tannehill (361) underscores that here Jesus gives a task to the disciples that previously John the Baptist

substantive "repentance," "conversion" ($\mu\epsilon\tau\acute{\alpha}\nu o\iota\alpha$), the specification "in his name" ($\dot{\epsilon}\pi\grave{\iota}\ \tau\hat{\omega}\ \dot{o}\nu\acute{o}\mu\alpha\tau\iota\ \alpha\dot{v}\tau o\hat{v}$), and especially the universal perspective "to all nations" ($\epsilon\dot{\iota}\varsigma\ \pi\acute{\alpha}\nu\tau\alpha\ \tau\grave{\alpha}\ \ddot{\epsilon}\vartheta\nu\eta$).[60]

The evangelist, who before all others will dare to add a second book to the life of Jesus told in the first, here prepares the ground for it. As everything converged and came to a head in Jerusalem (9:51, 53; 13:22; 17:11; 18:31; 19:28, 41, 45), everything will now begin in Jerusalem and go out from there (note $\dot{\alpha}\rho\xi\acute{\alpha}\mu\epsilon\nu o\iota\ \dot{\alpha}\pi\grave{o}$ Ἰερουσαλήμ, "beginning in Jerusalem"). It is possible that Luke is influenced here by Isaiah's oracle that makes Mount Zion in Jerusalem a point of convergence and departing (Isa 2:1-3).[61]

Although the words $\dot{\alpha}\rho\xi\acute{\alpha}\mu\epsilon\nu o\iota\ \dot{\alpha}\pi\grave{o}$ Ἰερουσαλήμ are easily explained theologically, one is embarrassed when it comes to integrating them into the sentence. First of all, into which sentence? Some exegetes make these words the conclusion of v. 47, a nominative absolute, a construction that sometimes in the late period fulfills the function of a genitive absolute. Luke, however, is not fond of this construction. Others relate the words to v. 48, thus to what follows. In this case the expression is awkward, because it encumbers the nominal phrase ($\dot{v}\mu\epsilon\hat{\iota}\varsigma\ \mu\acute{\alpha}\rho\tau\upsilon\rho\epsilon\varsigma\ \tau o\acute{v}\tau\omega\nu$, literally, "you, the witnesses of these things," translated "you, you are the witnesses of

these things"). Furthermore, the formula annoyed the copyists, because Nestle-Aland's critical apparatus (27th ed.) offers three variants: $\dot{\alpha}\rho\xi\acute{\alpha}\mu\epsilon\nu o\nu$, $\dot{\alpha}\rho\xi\alpha\mu\acute{\epsilon}\nu\omega\nu$, and $\dot{\alpha}\rho\xi\acute{\alpha}\mu\epsilon\nu o\varsigma$.[62] None of them really makes the reading easier, and none seems to be the best reading.

■ 48 The word $\mu\acute{\alpha}\rho\tau\upsilon\rho\epsilon\varsigma$ ("witnesses") refers the readers back to the prologue of the Gospel. There the generation of the apostles is called the generation of those who from the beginning have become $\alpha\dot{v}\tau\acute{o}\pi\tau\alpha\iota$, the "eyewitnesses," and the "servants" of the word ($\dot{v}\pi\eta\rho\acute{\epsilon}\tau\alpha\iota$, 1:2).[63] One point is clear: the $\mu\acute{\alpha}\rho\tau\upsilon\rho\epsilon\varsigma$ are not yet the martyrs of late antiquity. A second point is also clear: They are not passive eyewitnesses, because they have become what they are actively (by opting for a nominal sentence Luke avoids choosing between "becoming" and "being"). Third, the "things" of which they are witnesses are not all visible. Since the term "witnesses" reappears in Acts (see esp. 1:8; 5:32; 10:39; 13:31), this third point is indispensable. The witnesses are reliable, because they have a double allegiance: to history and to the truth. On the one hand, they knew the historical Jesus, before, during, and after his passion. On the other, they know the Christian kerygma and the meaning of the Scriptures. Fourth, as v. 49 notes, they need the Holy Spirit for their testimony to be effective.[64] Although it is not mentioned here, a fifth element appears elsewhere: according to

and he himself had carried out. The expression "in his name" ensures the continuity.

60   Along with others, Dömer (*Heil*, 105) is probably right when he says that Luke intentionally did not copy Mark 13:10 in 21:13 in order to include the mission command to all nations here in 24:47. On Luke's universalistic perspective, see Prast (*Presbyter*, 281–84), who agrees with Dömer (cited earlier in this note). Grasso notes ("Fattori," 307) that Luke repeats the most important part of v. 47 at the end of the Cornelius story in Acts 11:18.

61   See Bovon, *Studies*, 75–76.

62   See Samain, "Notion," 210–12; Betori ("Beginning") is of the opinion that there is some evidence that openness to Gentiles begins already at the outset of Acts.

63   The article by Coleridge ("Witnesses") represents a narrative analysis. On p. 16 the author finally comes to v. 48, which appears in the title of his article. Coleridge makes it the "climax of the disciples' epistemological journey" (18). Luke has prepared a "grammar of recognition" in four steps: (a) see-

ing without seeing; (b) hearing the explanations; (c) really seeing, that is to say, understanding; (d) becoming witnesses (18). Along with others, Grasso ("Fattori," 310) says that in Luke the disciples do not run away during the passion, because the evangelist needs them as witnesses.

64   On the Lukan idea of witness, see Brox, *Zeuge*, 43–69; Basset, "Dernières paroles," 361–63; Schneider, "Missionsauftrag," 186–90. Eggen ("Witness"), as he calls it on p. 167, criticizes the "common reading" of our passage. In his opinion this traditional interpretation has caused disasters in the mission fields. The author proposes to deconstruct this theological edifice. One of his results is to regard "all nations" as the margins of society. See also Grasso, "Fattori," 308–10; Bovon, *Luke the Theologian*, 416–19 (a critical presentation of the theses of six authors); and Mekkattukunnel, "Proof," 222–23.

Luke, the witnesses were chosen by Jesus (see Acts 1:2 where the election is mentioned).

■ **49** The christological "I" places a stamp on the pericope. It is present at the beginning in v. 44, referring back to the past ministry of the word, and it is present at the end in v. 49, announcing the future gift of the Holy Spirit.[65] Jesus' last statement in the Gospel looks forward to the beginning of Acts, namely, the story of Pentecost (Acts 2:1-4). This sentence will be repeated, according to a continuity and to variations that readers know and love, in the first chapter of Acts (1:4 and 8, where we find "the promise of the Father," the reception of a "power," waiting for the Spirit in Jerusalem, and the installation of the disciples as "witnesses").

One refers often to this scene as the appearance of the risen Lord to the Eleven. It is clear that, with the election of Matthias, the circle of the Twelve was reconstituted and, according to Luke, would serve as the basis for the church. It should be noted, however, that the evangelist is no narrow ecclesiologue who defends the hierarchy. Here he does not explicitly limit the appearance of the risen Lord to the Eleven. In v. 33 he speaks of a meeting of the Eleven and those who kept company with them. To this small world are added the two Emmaus disciples (still from v. 33). If we go back to the previous incident, we see that the women who returned from the tomb are still with the apostles (vv. 9-11). Even if he is thinking primarily of the Eleven, Luke does not exclude anyone from the scene.

Finally, it must be said that v. 49 has come to us in a sad condition. Almost every word has suffered abuse from the scribes and the centuries. In many cases these variants do not change the meaning,[66] but in one case the variant is interesting, because it changes the origin of the promise. Most witnesses speak of "the promise of my Father" ($\tau\grave{\eta}\nu$ $\dot{\epsilon}\pi\alpha\gamma\gamma\epsilon\lambda\acute{\iota}\alpha\nu$ $\tau o\hat{\upsilon}$ $\pi\alpha\tau\rho\acute{o}\varsigma$ $\mu o\upsilon$). Codex Bezae (D = 05) and a venerable Old Latin witness (e, from the fifth century) omit the mention of the Father, thus leading to the expression "my promise" ($\tau\grave{\eta}\nu$ $\dot{\epsilon}\pi\alpha\gamma\gamma\epsilon\lambda\acute{\iota}\alpha\nu$ $\mu o\upsilon$). I do not think this variant is earlier than the established text. There are two reasons for this variant. (a) First, a literary reason: playing on the word "promise," it recalls that the promise of the Holy Spirit was made by Jesus.[67] (b) A theological reason: in Acts Luke gives to understand that the Father uses the Son to distribute the Spirit, thus the expression "Spirit of Jesus" (Acts 16:7).

More important than these variants is the irruption here of the theme of the Holy Spirit. For Luke, in Israel's Scriptures the Spirit is promised; the gift of the Father is manifested in the Gospel, but its effects are reserved for the Son. For God's plan to be realized, this "power" ($\delta\acute{\upsilon}\nu\alpha\mu\iota\varsigma$, v. 49) must later be poured out in the church.[68] Luke understands the function of the Spirit first of all in a missionary sense: it is by this power (v. 49) that the message of conversion and forgiveness may be proclaimed and received (v. 47). It then will fulfill other functions in Acts, but these functions are not mentioned in the Gospel. Several times Luke has announced that this beneficent power will accompany the life of the disciples (see Luke 11:13; and, without the word being stated, Luke 21:15).

The evangelist likes to visualize the invisible. He demands that the disciples literally "sit" ($\kappa\alpha\theta\acute{\iota}\sigma\alpha\tau\epsilon$, v. 49, translated as "stay") and "wait" ($\pi\epsilon\rho\iota\mu\acute{\epsilon}\nu\epsilon\iota\nu$, Acts 1:4) "in the city" for the power that will come down "on them" ($\dot{\epsilon}\phi'\acute{\upsilon}\mu\hat{\alpha}\varsigma$, "on you," v. 49; and Acts 1:8), with which, literally, you will be "clothed" ($\dot{\epsilon}\nu\delta\acute{\upsilon}\sigma\eta\sigma\theta\epsilon$, v. 49). Using what one might call the hazy prophecy, Luke speaks in the Gospel of the "promise of my Father." In

---

65   On v. 49 and the gift of the Spirit in Luke, see Chevallier ("Pentecôtes"), who recognizes two important themes: (a) the decisive function of the Spirit in missionary activity; and (b) the eschatological offer of the Spirit to the entire people of God.

66   What difference does it make whether we should read $\kappa\alpha\grave{\iota}$ $\mathring{\iota}\delta o\grave{\upsilon}$ $\dot{\epsilon}\gamma\acute{\omega}$, $\kappa\alpha\grave{\iota}$ $\dot{\epsilon}\gamma\grave{\omega}$ $\mathring{\iota}\delta o\acute{\upsilon}$, or $\kappa\alpha\grave{\iota}$ $\dot{\epsilon}\gamma\acute{\omega}$? What difference does it make whether the manuscripts have $\dot{\alpha}\pi o\sigma\tau\acute{\epsilon}\lambda\lambda\omega$ or the compound $\dot{\epsilon}\xi\alpha\pi o\sigma\tau\acute{\epsilon}\lambda\lambda\omega$? What does it matter that numerous witnesses have the explanation "Jerusalem" after the words "in the city"? Why does it matter whether the order of the words is $\dot{\epsilon}\xi$ $\mathring{\upsilon}\psi o\upsilon\varsigma$ $\delta\acute{\upsilon}\nu\alpha\mu\iota\nu$, or $\delta\acute{\upsilon}\nu\alpha\mu\iota\nu$ $\dot{\epsilon}\xi$ $\mathring{\upsilon}\psi o\upsilon\varsigma$?

67   See the wording of Acts 1:4: "the promise of the Father, which, he said, you have heard from my mouth."

68   To indicate the divine origin of the Spirit, the text says that the power will come "from above." Grundmann (453) wisely reminds us of 1:78 ($\dot{\alpha}\nu\alpha\tau o\lambda\grave{\eta}$ $\dot{\epsilon}\xi$ $\mathring{\upsilon}\psi o\upsilon\varsigma$, "the sun rising from above").

Acts, closer to the realization, he does not hesitate to use along with this formula (Acts 1:4) the word "Holy Spirit" (Acts 1:8; see already Acts 1:5).[69]

History of Interpretation

As always,[70] Tertullian presents his interpretation in contrast to that of Marcion (*Adv. Marc.* 4.43.6–8). His explanation is simple: He rejoices over the words of Jesus and the bodily reality of the resurrection. By saying "Know that it is I" (v. 39), the Risen One evokes the memory of his disciples as a carnal being. Tertullian goes so far as to say: "But since they still did not believe him, he asked for food to show them that he even had teeth" (4.43.8). His presentation of Marcion is complex. To put it in simple terms, he acknowledges that the heretic, with a few exceptions, has not eliminated v. 39, but he reproaches him for having the Lukan text say the opposite of what it wants to say, namely, that Jesus said he was like a spirit and had no bones! Such an exegetical abuse is, according to Tertullian, as serious as leaving something out of the text.[71]

Origen's care in responding intelligently to the criticism of Celsus is impressive. The philosopher, it will be remembered, had placed a Jew in the first line of his anti-Christian front. It is the arguments of this Jew, who is hostile to the resurrection of Jesus, that the theologian attacks. Even if he refers to the appearance to the Eleven only two or three times, every line he writes deserves attention and admiration.[72] The reply, it must be said, had to respond to the high quality of the attack and was all the more important since it touched the heart of the entirely new Christian faith. Celsus's Jew requires an answer to the following question: "But we must examine this question whether anyone who really died ever rose again with the same body." He knows the argument that the Christians draw from the appearances. "Who saw this? . . . A hysterical female, as you say, and because she is not the only one recorded to have seen the risen Jesus, and as there are others as well, Celsus's Jew attacks these narratives too saying and perhaps some other one of those who were deluded by the same sorcery."[73]

In his response, even though he knows he must destroy the arguments of a pagan philosopher, Origen plays the game and responds to the Jew. He shares with him a critical opinion of various Greek myths. He then calls him to testify to the historicity of Jesus' crucifixion and burial, of which the Jews were indeed witnesses. He invokes the virtue of the disciples of Christ, who at risk to their lives defended the doctrine of the resurrection of Jesus. He then refers to the Old Testament stories, which the Jew certainly cannot dispute, of the resurrection of children by Elijah, then by Elisha (1 Kgs [LXX 3 Kgdms] 17:21-22 and 2 Kgs [LXX 4 Kgdms] 4:34-35). Jesus' resurrection surpasses these other episodes, because it was the work not of a prophet but of God, "his Father in heaven." Jesus' resurrection also produced immeasurably greater results than theirs. When the Jew curiously criticizes Jesus for not having "protected" himself, Origen says that, on the contrary, Jesus protected himself from evil by not sinning, but in another sense he did not protect himself and gave his life as a helpless

69   Kingsbury ("Luke 24") is of the opinion that, although the word is absent, the theme of vv. 36-49 is salvation.

70   In his *Dialogue with Trypho* (106.1), Justin tells of the meeting of Christ with his disciples after the resurrection. In so doing he uses one or two words of v. 36. At the same time the author of *Ep. apost.* 9–12 creates a harmony of the Gospels and in his way tells of the crucifixion, the resurrection, and the appearances of Jesus Christ. Written in the second half of the second century C.E., the *Acts of John* (62) tells that the brothers touched the feet of the apostle John and kissed his hands. Was the author under the influence of Luke 24:39-40?

71   See Harnack, *Marcion,* 239*, 305*; Tsutui, "Evangelium Marcions," 130–31; see also the comments by René Braun in *Tertullian, Contre Marcion,* vol. 4 (SC 456:525–27).

72   See principally Origen *Cels.* 2.54–63. The passages cited come sequentially from paragraphs 55 (twice) 58, 59, and 62. (Eng. trans. by Henry Chadwick in *Origen: Contra Celsum* [Cambridge: Cambridge University Press, 1980]).

73   See also *Cels.* 7.35. In his third-century treatise *Contra Christianos,* which, except for a few fragments, has been lost, Porphyry attacked the claim and even the story of the resurrection of Jesus. See the fragment preserved by Macarius Magnes in *Apocriticus* 2.14. See also Porphyry, trans. Adolf von Harnack, introduction by Detlef Weigt, *Gegen die Christen: Auszüge aus Makarios Magnes' "Apokritikos"* (Leipzig: Superbia, 2004) 40–41.

lamb. After that he was raised and "showed the marks of his punishment, and how his hands had been pierced." Jesus did not create an imaginary representation of these injuries. Origen then recalls the episode of Thomas and that of the Emmaus disciples. He finally concludes: "And although Celsus may wish to place what is told of Jesus, and of those who saw Him after his resurrection, on the same level with imaginary appearances of a different kind, and those who have invented such, yet to those who institute a candid and intelligent examination, the events will appear only the more miraculous."

In his homilies on the Third Gospel, Ambrose of Milan pays as much attention to the Gospels of Matthew and John as to that of Luke (*Exp. Luc.* 10.168–70). For him, as for Christian antiquity, the four Gospels speak with one voice. Thus, *Exp. Luc.* 10.168 treats of the appearance to Thomas, while the following paragraphs (169–70) deal with the one to the Eleven. Stressing the bodily reality of the Risen One, as Tertullian had done before him, the bishop of Milan tries to convince: "How indeed could there not have been a body, since it still had the marks of the wounds and the traces of the scars, which the Lord has shown to be touched?" (10.170).[74] He also meditates about the ability of the Risen One to pass through "impenetrable barriers" (prosaically, walls or closed doors) and reflects on the "coarse" body before and the "subtle" body after the resurrection. He concludes, as it happens, in a spiritual manner: Christ has carried away the traces of the crucifixion to heaven to present them to the Father and thus to display "the price of our liberation." In doing so he not only "strengthens the faith"; he also excites "devotion."[75]

Augustine of Hippo gave special attention to Luke 24:39-40. No fewer than eight of his sermons on this biblical passage have survived.[76] The Manichean past

of the bishop may well explain this interest. In arguing for the spiritual and not the bodily identity of the living Christ, the Manicheans, according to the argument Augustine reiterates to contradict them, repeat the error the apostles committed: "What ultimately the worst heretics thought of Christ, previously the disoriented disciples also believed."[77] Here, by way of example, is the argument of *Sermo* 237: Augustine begins with a frontal attack. The disciples were guilty of not believing, even though they saw the risen Christ. Following the callous disciples, the Manicheans are wrong to deny the physical presence of the Risen One. By regarding Jesus as a spirit they reject the incarnation and evacuate the entire mystery of redemption. Then, recounting the Lukan episode with increasing nervous tension, Augustine replies to the Manicheans, who boast of the superiority of the spirit over the flesh, that in faith they could defend a better cause and say less. The bishop then has no trouble remarking that the reprimand Jesus gave his gathered disciples on Easter is the best criticism of the Manichean position: "If the Lord has thus sent them away so that they come to believe, you must also be sent away."[78] After Augustine understands the cause and concedes that the disciples' attitude was human, he emphasizes that the Eleven did not stay there. Christ healed them as a physician. By showing them his scars, he healed the wounds of their hearts.[79] Inspired by John 1:14, he then develops a rich Christology.

From other sermons I have gleaned some additional elements: (a) Augustine adds the Priscillians to the Manicheans.[80] (b) He notes the joy of the Eleven, even while their confusion continues.[81] (c) He meditates on the words "while I was still with you." (d) In the mode of prayer he repeats the imperative *aperi* ("open"): "Come then, Lord, make the keys, open so that we can

---

74   The other quoted passages come from §§168, 169, and 170 (twice).

75   In quo non solum fidem firmat, sed etiam devotionem acuit.

76   Augustine of Hippo *Sermo* 116 (*PL* 38:657–61); *Sermo* 237 (*PL* 38:1122–24); *Sermo* 238 (*PL* 38:1125–26); *Sermo* 242 (*PL* 38:1138–43); *Sermo* 242A (*PLS* 2:478–80); *Sermo Mai* 86 (*PLS* 2:475–78); *Sermo Morin Guelferbytanus App.* 7 (*PLS* 2:653–57); *Sermo Morin* 17 (*PLS* 2:704–8); see Hermann Josef Sieben, *Kirchenväterhomilien zum Neuen Testament: Ein Repertorium der Textausgaben und Übersetzungen, mit*

einem Anhang der Kirchenväterkommentare (IP 22; The Hague: Nijhoff, 1991) 85–86.

77   Quod postea crediderunt de Christo pessimi haeretici, prius hoc crediderunt titubantes apostoli (*Sermo* 237.1 [*PL* 38:1122]).

78   Si Dominus sic eos dimisit, ut hoc putarent, dimittendus es et tu (*Sermo* 237.3 [*PL* 38:1123]).

79   *Sermo* 237.3 (*PL* 38:1124).

80   *Sermo* 238.2 (*PL* 38:1125).

81   *Sermo* 116.3 (*PL* 38:658).

understand!"[82] (e) He is sensitive to the necessity for the passion and the resurrection.[83] (f) The biblical passage helps him not only affirm an orthodox Christology but also remember the universality of the church (v. 47), undoubtedly against the Donatists, whom he blames for their provincialism.[84] He also notes a difference between the origins and today; back then the disciples saw Christ but did not see the church. They believed in it. Today we see the church, but we no longer see Christ. We believe in him.[85] (g) Augustine reflects on the nature of the resurrected bodies.[86] (h) He does not forget the "promise of my Father" (v. 49), which he sees as fulfilled on the day of Pentecost.[87]

By way of comparison, it is interesting to note the points that at the same time Peter Chrysologus emphasizes when he preaches on the same biblical passage.[88] This preacher is pleased to comment that the peace offered by the Risen One in v. 36 is doubly welcome. Did the death of Jesus not coincide with a chaos of the natural elements and with the disorder that invaded the heart of the disciples? Then he takes time to describe the "I" who is presented (along with some Old Latin witnesses and the Vulgate, in v. 36 the preacher reads the addition "For me I am God, because of you, a man. I am not a spirit appearing to be a carnal image, but the incarnate truth itself").[89] Peter, John, and the other disciples no longer have to be afraid, because the "I" that has returned from the realm of the dead, Christ, is alive. Peter Chrysologus then explains the disciples' misunderstanding (v. 37). It is that the Risen One had come through closed doors. If one does not believe in

the divine capacity and one stays with human nature, there is only one possible explanation: the disciples were wrong not to believe in the "solidity of the body" and to think that the soul had been content to return only in the form of a "carnal image."[90] It is Christ, the risen man, who by his divine power will calm the disciples whose thoughts then correctly rise, because they rise toward the mystery of God. They really do need to see, to touch with their fingers, until they can come to the truth. And, finally, commenting on the joy mixed with doubt (v. 41), he excuses the disciples. He says that it is never easy to believe in miracles, in such an unusual reality. He concludes: "Therefore God give us to understand and thanks to him to grasp that by ourselves we are not capable."[91] Even though it is not polemical, this sermon still defends the disciples by refuting some arguments against the bodily resurrection of Jesus.

On the side of Greek patristics, I will call attention to a few fragments of the commentary on Luke by Cyril of Alexandria.[92] Here a new, truly curious argument appears. The knowledge of hearts, a divine privilege that the Son shares with the Father (v. 38), shows the disciples the continuity of Jesus' person: the Risen One is the Crucified One. This is, according to Cyril, a very strong signal that is given. Less surprising is the assurance with which Cyril maintains the unity of the person of Christ. Even after the resurrection there dwells in him the human being that the disciples are invited to touch, cohabiting with the divine. Finally, polemically, the bishop of Alexandria opposes those who, based on 1 Cor 15:44 ("sown a physical body, raised a spiritual body"),

---

82 *Sermo* 116.5 (*PL* 38:659).
83 Ibid.
84 *Sermo* 238.3 (*PL* 38:1126).
85 Ibid.
86 He does it especially in *Sermo* 242.3–11 (*PL* 38:1140–43).
87 *Sermo Mai* 86.2–3 (*PLS* 2:477).
88 Peter Chrysologus *Sermo* 81 (CCSL 24A:498–503).
89 Ego sum. Nolite timere. Ego sum per me deus, propter vos homo. Ego sum non spiritus in figura carnis, sed ipsa veritas in carne" (ibid., 81.3 [CCSL 24A:499]).
90 Ibid., 81.4 (CCSL 24A:500).
91 "Deus ergo, quod per nos non possumus, ipse nos capere per se et sentire concedat (*Sermo* 81.7 [CCSL 24A:503]).
92 One can read them in *PG* 72:945–49; and in Reuss, *Lukas-Kommentare*, 276–78 (frgs. 2.119–25). The last fragment begins the same way here and there, but it differs then from one edition to the next. The frg 2.120 in Reuss is two lines shorter than the text reproduced in *PG*. Just (*Luke*, 385–86) gives the English translation of frg. 119 (the end of which is missing in Reuss). Sauget ("Nouvelles homélies," 450–52) has found a homily in a Syriac manuscript of Damascus (Syrian Orthodox Patriarchate, 12 [20]) that seems to combine homilies 155 and 156 (the last two of Cyril's commentaries, lost except for a few fragments, mentioned above); see above, p. 316 n. 187 on 23:26–43.

reject the bodily character of the resurrection. What Paul means by physical is not the human body but the fleshly desires. It is they that have no part in the resurrection. Cyril is happy about the proofs, convincing in his view, which demonstrate that the body that has suffered is the body that is raised. Finally, he thinks that the issue of the digestion of what Jesus ate (based on Matt 15:17 par. Mark 7:18-19) is unworthy of belief.[93]

Interested readers have access to medieval exegesis by reading the commentaries of the Venerable Bede (*In Luc.* 6.2168–2392) or Bonaventure (*Comm. Luc.* 24.46–62).[94] For the Byzantine world there are Theophylactus and Zigabenus in Migne's *Patrologia graeca*.[95] The *Paraphrasis* of Erasmus, written in Latin, is now available in English.[96] The Humanist emphasizes that the Lord calms the disciples before he shows them his hands and feet, and only after this demonstration does he give them a lesson in biblical hermeneutics. Here are a few opinions of the preacher, Luther: We must distinguish between the miraculous appearance, vv. 36-43, and the following instruction, vv. 44-49. The weakness of the apostles stands in contrast to the power of the gospel. Since the Risen One continues to be a human body, he does not stop being weak in this world. Christ is not always manifest, since even the disciples themselves are mistaken.[97]

In his *Harmony of the Gospels,* Calvin does more explaining than preaching.[98] He compares Luke with John and Mark's inauthentic conclusion. He asserts that the disciples saw the Risen One twice in Jerusalem before going to Galilee, where they met him for a third time (he relies on the reference to a "third time" in John 21:14).

He especially agrees with those he calls "our companions" to say that the corporeality of the Risen One, strongly emphasized in Luke 24, contradicts transubstantiation. "They [Calvin's Catholic opponents] wish Christ's body to be there, where it has no sign of body. It will follow on these lines that it has changed its nature, and has ceased to be what it was, ceased to exist in the way Christ proves it to be a real body." Calvin is also of the opinion that the risen Lord kept his scars as an act of charity for his disciples, even though his resurrected body did not need them. "It has been foolish, old women's nonsense to imagine that he is still marked with his scars when he comes to judge the world."

Conclusion

In this passage Luke tells how the risen Jesus demonstrated his true identity. Christ was always the same, even though he had passed through death and reached the divine glory. Thus, the evangelist makes the unforeseeable appear in the normal and the normal appear in the unforeseeable.

To this last appearance he adds a final teaching of Jesus. This teaching also leads to a paradox, for Luke, who emphasizes the biblical roots of the words of Christ and the harmony between the words spoken after and before the resurrection, presents something new. It is the mission given the disciples to preach to all nations. These circumstances leave the disciples as well in a paradoxical, or at least ambivalent, situation: joy overflows, but it lives with doubt.

93 I offer here fragment 119 according to Reuss; see Payne Smith, *Cyril,* 2:728–29. Just (*Luke,* 384–90) also cites various patristic commentaries.
94 Bernardini, 598–603; Karris, *St. Bonaventure's Commentary,* 3:2229–45.
95 Theophylactus *Enarr. Luc.* 24.36–49 (*PG* 123:1119–24) and Euthymius Zigabenus *Comm. Luc.* 24.36–49 (*PG* 129:1099–1102).
96 Erasmus, *Paraphrasis,* 486–88; Phillips, *Paraphrase,* 274–78.
97 Luther, *Evangelien-Auslegung,* 1263–73.
98 Calvin, *Harmony,* 3:

The Harmony of Farewell
(24:50-53)
Bibliography

Amphoux, Christian-Bernard, "Le chapitre 24 de Luc et l'origine de la tradition textuelle du Codex de Bèze (D.05 du NT)," *Filologia Neotestamentaria* 4 (1991) 21–48.

Argyle, A. W., "The Ascension," *ExpT* 66 (1954–55) 240–42.

Atkins, Peter, "Luke's Ascension Location: A Note on Luke 24:50," *ExpT* 109 (1998) 205–6.

Aubineau, Michel, "Sévère d'Antioche, Homélie cathédrale XXIV, In Ascensionem: Un fragment syriaque identifié (CPG 7037) et deux fragments grecs retrouvés," *RSLR* 24 (1988) 81–92.

Bacon, B. W., "The Ascension in Luke and Acts," *Exp* 7 (1909) 245–61.

Baird, William, "Ascension and Resurrection: An Intersection of Luke and Paul," in W. Eugene March, ed., *Texts and Testaments: Critical Essays on the Bible and Early Church Fathers. A Volume in Honor of Stuart Dickson Currie* (San Antonio: Trinity University Press, 1980) 3–18.

Benoit, Pierre, "Ascension," *RB* 56 (1949) 161–203; reprinted in idem, *Exégèse et Théologie,* 1:363–411.

Bertram, Georg, "Die Himmelfahrt Jesu vom Kreuz aus und der Glaube an seine Auferstehung," in *Festgabe für Adolf Deissmann zum 60. Geburtstag* (Tübingen: Mohr Siebeck, 1927) 187–217.

Bock, Emil, "Von der Himmelfahrt im Alten und Neuen Testament," *Christengemeinschaft* 4 (1927) 45–50.

Bouwman, Gilbert, "Die Erhöhung Jesu in der lukanischen Theologie," *BZ* 14 (1970) 257–63.

Bovon, François, "Himmelfahrt Christi," *EKL* 2 (1989) 522–23.

Idem, *Luke the Theologian*, 190–98.

Cabié, Robert, *La Pentecôte: L'évolution de la Cinquantaine pascale au cours des cinq premiers siècles* (Tournai: Desclée, 1965) 35–57, 117–78, 190–97.

Clarke, W. K. Lowther, "St. Luke and the Pseudepigrapha: Two Parallels," *JTS* 15 (1914) 597–99.

Creed, J. M., "The Text and Interpretation of Acts i 1-2," *JTS* 35 (1934) 176–82.

Daniélou, Jean, "Les Psaumes dans la liturgie de l'Ascension," *MD* 21 (1950) 40–55.

Davies, J. G., *He Ascended into Heaven: A Study in the History of Doctrine* (New York: Association Press, 1958) 168–84.

Idem, "The Prefigurement of the Ascension in the Third Gospel," *JTS* 6 (1955) 229–33.

Dillon, *Eye-Witnesses*, 220–25.

Doeve, J. W., "De hemelvaart in het Evangelie naar Lucas," *HeB* 20 (1961) 75–79.

Dömer, *Heil*, 106–9.

Donne, Brian K., *Christ Ascended: A Study in the Significance of the Ascension of Jesus Christ in the New Testament* (Exeter: Paternoster, 1983).

Dupont, Jacques, "*ΑΝΕΛΗΜΦΘΗ*" (Act. 1.2)," *NTS* 8 (1961–62) 154–57; reprinted in idem, *Études sur les Actes des apôtres* (Paris: Cerf, 1967) 477–80.

Enslin, Morton S., "The Ascension Story," *JBL* 47 (1928) 60–73.

Epp, Eldon Jay, "The Ascension in the Textual Tradition of Luke-Acts," in Eldon Jay Epp and Gordon D. Fee, eds., *New Testament Textual Criticism: Its Significance for Exegesis, Essays in Honour of Bruce M. Metzger* (New York: Oxford University Press, 1981) 131–45.

Fitzmyer, Joseph A., "The Ascension of Christ and Pentecost," *TS* 45 (1984) 409–40.

Franklin, Eric, "The Ascension and the Eschatology of Luke-Acts," *SJT* 23 (1970) 191–200.

Fridrichsen, Anton, "Die Himmelfahrt bei Lukas," *ThBl* 6 (1927) 337–41.

Friedrich, Gerhard, "Lk 9,51 und die Entrückungschristologie des Lukas," in Paul Hoffmann, ed., *Orientierung an Jesus: Zur Theologie der Synoptiker. Für Josef Schmid* (Freiburg i. B.: Herder, 1973) 70–74.

Fuller, George C., "The Life of Jesus, after the Ascension (Luke 24:50-53; Acts 1:9-11)," *WThJ* 56 (1994) 391–98.

Goudoever, Jan van, *Biblical Calendars* (Leiden: Brill, 1959) 195–205.

Graefe, Ferdinand, "Der Schluss des Lukasevangeliums und der Anfang der Apostelgeschichte: Eine textkritische Studie, zugleich ein Beitrag zur Italaforschung," *ThStK* 61 (1888) 522–41.

Grässer, Erich, "Die Parusieerwartung in der Apostelgeschichte," in Jacob Kremer, ed., *Les Actes des Apôtres: Traditions, rédaction, théologie* (28th Journées bibliques de Louvain, 1977; BEThL 48; Gembloux: Duculot, 1979) 99–127.

Idem, *Das Problem der Parusieverzögerung in den synoptischen Evangelien und in der Apostelgeschichte* (3d ed.; BZNW 22; Berlin: de Gruyter, 1977) 204–7.

Guillaume, *Luc interprète*, 203–74.

Hahn, Ferdinand, "Die Himmelfahrt Jesu: Ein Gespräch mit Gerhard Lohfink," *Bib* 55 (1974) 418–26.

Haroutunian, Joseph, "The Doctrine of the Ascension: A Study of the New Testament Teaching," *Int* 10 (1956) 270–81.

Holzmeister, U., "Der Tag der Himmelfahrt des Herrn," *ZKTh* 55 (1931) 44–82.

Houlden, Leslie, "Beyond Belief: Preaching the Ascension (II)," *Theol* 94 (1991) 173–80.

Hug, *Finale*, 128–53.

Jansen, John F., "The Ascension, the Church, and Theology," *ThTo* 16 (1959) 17–29.

Kaylor, Robert David, "The Ascension Motif in Luke-Acts, the Epistle to the Hebrews, and the Fourth Gospel" (Diss., Duke University, 1964).

Kellermann, Ulrich, "Zu den Elia-Motiven in den Himmelfahrtsgeschichte des Lukas," in Peter Mommer and Winfried Thiel, eds., *Altes Testament: Forschung und Wirkung: Festschrift für Henning Graf Reventlow* (Frankfurt: Lang, 1994) 123–37.

Kern, Walter, "Das Fortgehen Jesu und das Kommen des Geistes oder Christi Himmelfahrt," *GuL* 41 (1968) 85–90.

Kretschmar, Georg, "Himmelfahrt und Pfingsten," *ZKG* 66 (1954–55) 209–53.

Küchler, Max, *Jerusalem: Ein Handbuch und Studienreiseführer zur heiligen Stadt* (OLB 4.2; Göttingen: Vandenhoeck & Ruprecht, 2007) 876–904.

Larrañaga, Victoriano, *L'Ascension de Notre-Seigneur dans le Nouveau Testament* (trans. G. Cazaux; Rome: Institut Biblique Pontifical, 1938).

LaVerdiere, Eugene A., "The Ascension of the Risen Lord," *TBT* 95 (1978) 1553–59.

Leaney, A. R. C., "Why There Were Forty Days between the Resurrection and the Ascension in Acts 1, 3," *StEv* 4 [TU 102] (1968) 417–19.

Lohfink, *Himmelfahrt*, 147–76.

Idem, "'Was steht ihr da und schauet' (Apg 1, 11): Die 'Himmelfahrt Jesu' im lukanischen Geschichtswerk," *BiKi* 20 (1965) 43–48.

Maile, John F., "The Ascension in Luke-Acts," *TynB* 37 (1986) 29–59.

Mann, C. S., "The New Testament and the Lord's Ascension," *CQR* 158 (1957) 462–65.

Marion, Jean-Luc, *Prolégomènes à la charité* (Essais; Paris: Éditions de la Différence, 1986) 153–62.

Marrevee, William H., *The Ascension of Christ in the Works of St. Augustine* (Ottawa: University of Ottawa Press, 1967).

Mekkattukunnel, Andrews George, *The Priestly Blessing of the Risen Christ: An Exegetico-Theological Analysis of Luke 24, 50-53* (EHS.T 714; Bern: Lang, 2001).

Menoud, Philippe H., "'During Forty Days' (Acts 1.3)," in idem, *Jesus Christ and the Faith: A Collection of Studies* (trans. Eunice M. Paul; PTMS 18; Pittsburgh: Pickwick, 1978) 167–79.

Idem, "Observations on the Ascension in Luke-Acts," in idem, *Jesus Christ and the Faith: A Collection of Studies* (trans. Eunice M. Paul; PTMS 18; Pittsburgh: Pickwick, 1978) 107–20.

Metzger, Bruce M., "The Meaning of Christ's Ascension," *ChrTo* 10 (1966) 863–64.

Meynet, Roland, "La preghiera nel Vangelo di Luca," *CivCatt* 149 (1998) 379–92.

Michaelis, Wilhelm, *Die Erscheinungen des Auferstandenen* (Basel: Heinrich Majer, 1944) 89–91.

Idem, "Zur Überlieferung der Himmelfahrtgeschichte," *ThBl* 4 (1925) 101–9.

Miquel, Pierre, "Le mystère de l'Ascension," *QLP* 40 (1959) 105–26.

Morgan, R., "The Ending of Luke's Gospel," *ExpT* 113 (2001) 65.

Moule, C. F. D., "The Ascension: Acts 1,9," *ExpT* 68 (1957) 205–9.

Mussies, Gerard, "Variation in the Book of Acts," *Filología Neotestamentaria* 4 (1991) 165–82.

Odasso, G., "L'ascensione nell'evangelo di Luca," *BeO* 13 (1971) 107–18.

Palatty, Paul, "The Ascension of Christ in Luke-Acts (An Exegetical-Critical Study of Lk 24,50-53 and Acts 1,2-3, 9-11)," *BiBh* 12 (1986) 100–117, 166–81.

Parsons, Mikeal Carl, *The Departure of Jesus in Luke-Acts: The Ascension Narratives in Context* (JSNTSup 21; Sheffield: JSOT Press, 1987).

Idem, "Narrative Closure and Openness in the Plot of the Third Gospel: The Sense of an Ending in Luke 24:50-53," in Kent Harold Richards, ed., *SBLSP* 1986 (Atlanta: Scholars Press, 1986) 201–23.

Idem, "The Text of Acts Reconsidered," *CBQ* 50 (1988) 58–71.

Pesch, Rudolf, "Der Anfang der Apostelgeschichte: Apg 1,1-11," *EKKNTV* 3 (1971) 7–35.

Playoust, Catherine Anne, "Lifted Up From the Earth: The Ascension of Jesus and the Heavenly Ascents of Early Christians" (Diss., Harvard University, 2006).

Plooij, Daniel, *The Ascension in the "Western" Textual Tradition* (MNAW 1.67.2; Amsterdam: Koninklijke Akademie van Wetenschappen, 1929) 39–58.

Roscher, Wilhelm Heinrich, *Die Tessarakontaden und die Tessarakontadenlehren der Griechen und anderer Völker: Ein Vergleich zur vergleichenden Religionswissenschaft, Volkskunde und Zahlenmystik sowie zur Geschichte der Medizin und Biologie* (Leipzig: Teubner, 1909).

Schille, Gottfried, "Die Himmelfahrt," *ZNW* 57 (1966) 183–99.

Schlier, Heinrich, "Jesu Himmelfahrt nach den lukanischen Schriften," *GuL* 34 (1961) 91–99; reprinted in idem, *Besinnung auf das Neue Testament* (Exegetische Aufsätze und Vorträge 2; Freiburg: Herder, 1964) 227–41.

Schnider, Franz, "Die Himmelfahrt Jesu—Ende oder Anfang? Zum Verständnis des lukanischen Doppelwerkes," in Paul-Gerhard Müller and Werner Stenger, eds., *Kontinuität und Einheit: Für Franz Mussner* (Freiburg i. B.: Herder, 1981) 158–72.

Schrade, Hubert, "Zur Ikonographie der Himmelfahrt Christi," in *Vorträge der Bibliothek Warburg 1928/29* (Leipzig: Teubner, 1930) 66–190.

Stempvoort, P. A. van, "The Interpretation of the Ascension in Luke and Acts," *NTS* 5 (1958–59) 30–42.

Stockhausen, Carol L., "Luke's Stories of the Ascension: The Background and Function of a Dual Narrative," *Proceedings: Eastern Great Lakes and Midwest Biblical Societies* 10 (1990) 251–63.

Taylor, *Passion Narrative*, 114–15.

van Tilborg and Counet, *Jesus' Appearances*, 89–127.

Toon, Peter, *The Ascension of Our Lord* (Nashville: Nelson, 1984).

Torgovnick, Marianna, *Closure in the Novel* (Princeton: Princeton University Press, 1981).

Weinert, "Temple," 85–89.

Weinert, Franz-Rudolf, *Christi Himmelfahrt: Neutestamentliches Fest im Spiegel alttestamentlicher Psalmen. Zur Entstehung des römischen Himmelfahrtsoffiziums* (Dissertationen theologische Reihe 25; St. Ottilien: EOS Verlag, 1987).

Wilcke, Karin, *Christi Himmelfahrt: Ihre Darstellung in der europäischen Literatur von der Spätantike bis zum ausgehenden Mittelalter* (Beiträge zur älteren Literaturgeschichte; Heidelberg: Winter, 1991).

Wilson, Stephen G., "The Ascension: A Critique and an Interpretation," *ZNW* 59 (1968) 269–81.

Wind, Renate, "Der Gott, der bei uns ist, ist der Gott, der uns verläßt: Sozialgeschichtliche Bibelauslegung zu Lukas 24, 50-53," *JK* 58 (1997) 224–27.

Woolsey, Theodore Dwight, "The End of Luke's Gospel and the Beginning of the Acts: Two Studies," *BSac* 39 (1882) 593–619.

Wulf, Friedrich, "'Und sie kehrten mit grosser Freude nach Jerusalem zurück' (Lk 24, 52)," *GuL* 27 (1954) 81–83.

Zwiep, A. W., *The Ascension of the Messiah in Lukan Christology* (NovTSup 87; Leiden: Brill, 1997).

Idem, "The Text of the Ascension Narratives (Luke 24.50-53; Acts 1.1-2, 9-11)," *NTS* 42 (1996) 219–44.

50	**He led them out as far as the vicinity of Bethany, then, having lifted up his hands,[a] he blessed them. 51/ While he was blessing them, it happened that he left them and was carried up into heaven.**
52	**And they, after they had prostrated themselves before him, returned to Jerusalem filled with great joy.[b] 53/ They were continually in the temple compound[c] blessing God.**

a   One could also translate it as "arms."
b   Literally: "with great joy" (I added "filled").
c   Literally: "in the temple" in the larger sense.

The final verses of the Gospel are so closely related to the previous story that many exegetes believe that they form the conclusion of the appearance to the Eleven (24:36-49).[1] What makes it difficult for me to accept this solution is the change of location with which the evangelist makes the event of the ascension autonomous and thus gives it a special significance.

Analysis

In spite of its brevity, this concluding story clarifies several points and reports various events:

(a)   Jesus leads the group of disciples to Bethany (v. 50a);

(b)   he blesses them (v. 50b);

(c)   during this benediction he leaves them (v. 51);

(d)   after the disciples have knelt before him, they return to Jerusalem (v. 52);

(e)   they live on, praising God in the temple (v. 53).

The episode's structure is parallel rather than concentric. Parts (a) and (d) both refer to a change of location; parts (b) and (e) to a blessing at the place. The central part (c) combines the two aspects and speaks of blessing and change of location.[2] It is important to note right

---

1   See, e.g., Schmithals, 235–38.
2   See Odasso, "Ascensione," 110.

away that the acting persons change in the course of the events. While Christ conducts the action at the beginning (he is the subject of the verbs in the first two verses, vv. 50-51), it is the disciples who act at the end (they become the subject of the verbs in the last two sentences, vv. 52-53). In short, the literary unit alternates between movement and stability and lets the actions of one be followed by those of the others. When one looks at Jesus,[3] his destiny and his destination are clear and come together harmoniously. He goes to Bethany at the head of the group, after which he blesses those who are his. After he has blessed them, he leaves them and goes to heaven. When we look at the others, the disciples, their destiny and their destination are no less precise. As soon as Christ leaves them for another destination, they have no choice but to turn around and go back to Jerusalem from which the Master had led them. Thus, they go separate ways. Three expressions (to bow down, to feel great joy, and to bless, vv. 52-53), however, prevent the conclusion that could be drawn and keep one from speaking of a sad farewell or a painful separation.[4]

Thus ends the Gospel of Luke. As we know, this Gospel represents only the first part of a diptych. Following the "first volume" (Acts 1:1), from the pen of the same author and dedicated to the same Theophilus (Luke 1:3; Acts 1:1), is a second volume, the Acts of the Apostles. This second book opens, however, with a description that in many ways seems to overlap with the end of the Gospel. The ascension is mentioned there at the end of v. 2 and is then told again in vv. 9-11. The disciples' return to Jerusalem is mentioned in v. 12 in language very similar to Luke 24:52. Are these repetitions amazing? Some authors have thought so and have resorted

to the hypothesis of an interpolation.[5] Since Luke 24:49 predicts the fulfillment of the Father's promise and this is recalled in Acts 1:8, they have suggested that the original Luke-Acts formed a single book with Acts 1:6 following Luke 24:49 without a break and that the book was then cut in half when the first part joined the corpus of the Gospels in the process of canonization. They have added that vv. 50-53 of Luke 24 and vv. 1-5 of Acts 1 were then drafted to serve as the necessary conclusion to the Gospel and the necessary beginning of Acts. Three arguments militate against this hypothesis. (a) There is no manuscript evidence for it, since none provides a version of a book of Luke-Acts. (b) Placed back to back Luke and Acts exceed the conventional length of a book of antiquity, a length determined by practical requirements. When ancient authors wanted to compose works exceeding this standard length, they subdivided their work into two or more "books." That is exactly what Luke does here. His work will have two volumes (Acts 1:1 speaks precisely of the "first book"). (c) As the commentry will demonstrate, Luke 24:50-53 is, in the final analysis, a passage with Lukan features and not the work of a glossator.

More important than these arguments is the following observation. Luke, who values the divisions, those of the times of salvation history as well as those parts of his literary work, also knows to ensure continuity. He knows the art of transitions and how to cross thresholds easily. As an experienced author, however, he also knows how to keep these transitions from being unwieldy and repetitious. He likes to vary the presentations of the same truths or the same events.[6] This is exactly what he does in Luke 24 and Acts 1.

---

3   Although I cannot explain it, I note that there are no proper names in this last pericope. Jesus is the implied subject of the verbs where he is designated by the personal pronoun αὐτός ("he," "him," "the"). The disciples are always designated by the plural of the same pronoun (three times in the accusative, once in the genitive, once in the nominative). The last mention of Jesus goes back to v. 19, that of Peter and the disciples to vv. 33-35.

4   On this story, see especially Fridrichsen, "Himmelfahrt"; Larrañaga, *Ascension*; Schlier, *Himmelfahrt*; Lohfink, *Himmelfahrt;* Fitzmyer, "Ascension"; Maile, "Ascension"; Parsons, *Departure;* Zwiep, *Ascension*; Bovon, *Luke the Theologian*, 190–98. On the

homiletic problems posed by this text, see Houlden, "Preaching."

5   See, e.g., Menoud ("Observations"), who follows Kirsopp Lake and H. Sahlin. He writes: "If the addition is removed, Luke's work is restored to its original unity and clarity; the conversation of Jesus with his disciples, interrupted in Luke 24.49, continues naturally in Acts 1.6" (111). The ascension has the advantage of being mentioned only once, and the cumbersome "forty days" disappear. A few years later Menoud ("Forty Days") changed his mind and abandoned his hypothesis.

6   See Mussies, "Variation." The word "variation" appears as early as 1927 in the writing of Fridrich-

Some critics have responded by pointing to two incontrovertible realities: (a) the textual instability of both Luke 24:50-53 and Acts 1:1-5; and (b) the stylistic awkwardness of the beginning of Acts. It is true that the textual variations may reflect the chaotic origin of a passage, but it is also true that the beginning and the end of a work are frequently the object of manipulation just as much as the extremities of a manuscript. As we shall see, in the case of Luke 24 and Acts 1, doctrinal requirements have amplified this risk. One can note the following stylistic blunder: In Greek the particle $\mu\acute{\epsilon}\nu$ (Acts 1:1) normally should be followed by $\delta\acute{\epsilon}$. Yet there is no $\delta\acute{\epsilon}$ after this initial $\mu\acute{\epsilon}\nu$.[7] It is not my responsibility to comment on the book of Acts. For me it is enough to admit that, as it sometimes happens, Luke was somewhat confused at the beginning of his second book by wanting to say too much. This defect should not obscure merit, however: While he correctly summarizes his first "book" ("everything Jesus did and taught . . . ," Acts 1:1), the evangelist prefers to let the Risen One present the contents of the second: "But you will receive power when the Holy Spirit has come upon you; you will be my witnesses in Jerusalem, in all Judea and Samaria, and to the ends of the earth" (Acts 1:8).[8] The syntactic break, the absence of $\delta\acute{\epsilon}$, is the price Luke pays to justify the existence of a book of Acts—a work he is the first to risk writing—and to affirm theologically the content of this second volume.

The beginning of Acts has other difficulties as well. Among those that are important for understanding the end of the Gospel, it is important to note the strange mention of the ascension (Acts 1:2) before the appearances (Acts 1:3). Grammatical succession—this is my explanation—does not necessarily imply a chronological succession of the events.[9] Among the many matters Luke wants to settle in this beginning of Acts is also the problem of the delay of the parousia. He deals with it in vv. 6-8, offering the gift of the Spirit and the missionary task as positive substitutes for a fruitless expectation of Christ's return.[10] The solution of the problem appears again in v. 11 of this same chapter 1 of Acts. The question of the delay of the parousia is not important, the author suggests, only the assurance that it will happen.

For someone who is explaining the end of the Gospel, the most interesting parallel is the account of the ascension contained in the book of Acts.[11] While no other evangelist—indeed no other New Testament author—describes the ascension, Luke allows himself the luxury of telling it twice. When one reads these stories, one realizes that they are about the same event. It takes place near Jerusalem; Jesus is taken up into heaven in the sight of his disciples; then they return to the holy city. Thus, in both descriptions (Luke 24:50-53 and Acts 1:9-12) it must be one and the same event. As we have seen, however, Luke cannot repeat himself without making changes. He designates the location in two different ways. In Luke 24:50 he directs attention to Bethany, and in Acts 1:12 to the Mount of Olives. Although he pays no attention to chronology in Luke 24 (the readers always think they are following the events of an endless Easter day), Luke explains in Acts 1:3 that forty days have elapsed. While Christ faces the disciples in Luke 24 to bless them, in Acts 1 he turns his back without a gesture of comfort. Whereas in the Gospel the blessing maintains the link between the one who leaves and those who stay behind (hence their joy), in Acts Christ is taken abruptly from the disciples, who are so disconcerted that it takes two angels to help them recover. They do so without sparing the disciples. As we can see, Luke knows how to vary things. Our detailed exegesis will show that the wording in the Gospel is appropriate as a conclusion[12]

---

sen ("Himmelfahrt," 338). Parsons (*Departure*, 191–99) and Stockhausen ("Dual Narration") have been interested in the phenomena of repetition and redundancy.

7   The absence of a $\delta\acute{\epsilon}$ corresponding to a $\mu\acute{\epsilon}\nu$ is not as unusual as one likes to say. There are even examples in Luke-Acts: Luke 3:18; Acts 3:13, 21; 21:39; see Menoud, "Observations," 109–10.

8   See Conzelmann, *Theology*, 152, 182–84.

9   See how the TOB (*Traduction Œcuménique de la Bible*) renders the aorist $\pi\alpha\rho\acute{\epsilon}\sigma\tau\eta\sigma\epsilon\nu$: "C'est à eux qu'il s'était présenté. . . ." The *NRSV* offers: "After

his suffering he presented himself alive to them . . ." (Acts 1:3).

10   See in this regard the brilliant pages of Grässer, *Parusieverzögerung*, 204–7.

11   Remember also that the Gospel prepares for the ascension by referring to the $\dot{\alpha}\nu\acute{\alpha}\lambda\eta\mu\psi\iota\varsigma$, the "taking up," 9:51, and to the entry into Jerusalem (19:29-40); see Davies, "Prefiguration"; Atkins, "Location."

12   In his dissertation, Parsons (*Departure*, 65–113) has carefully examined how literary works end. He is attentive to the notion of closure and the function

and that of Acts as an introduction. It will also highlight the christological orientation of Luke 24 (the end of the life of Jesus) and the ecclesiological orientation of Acts 1 (the beginning of the church's mission). Finally, it will suggest that Luke 24 offers protection and Acts 1 involves people in responsibility.[13]

Luke has indicated that Jesus' resurrection meant not simply a return to human life but also entrance into divine glory (24:26). Now that he has come to the end of his hero's life, he must describe this exaltation. Indeed, such glorifications were not foreign to ancient beliefs. Luke's Bible gives a brief description of Enoch's removal ("And Enoch was well-pleasing to God, and was not found, because God translated him," Gen 5:24 LXX) and a somewhat longer description of Elijah's ascension in his chariot of fire (2 Kgs [LXX 4 Kgdms] 2:1-18).[14] Such a blessed fate is also reserved in the postbiblical, apocalyptic literature for Esdras, Baruch, and perhaps Moses.[15] The Greek and Latin worlds are also aware of such removals. The most famous are those of Heracles and Romulus.[16] These stories are different from the heavenly journeys of a seer who is called to receive a revelation, since he then returned to earth. Nor are they to be confused with references to the departure of heavenly messengers, since once their divine mission was accomplished they had to return. They also are not to be likened to the journey of the soul, which, according to various beliefs in Greece and Rome, reached the heights when, at the death of the body, it is separated from its fleshly envelope. Luke has emphasized the bodily reality of the Risen One. To tell removal stories the ancients readily made use of the same narrative scheme and a conventional vocabulary. They spoke of removal, of strong wind, of a heavenly chariot, of a cloud, of divine confirmation in the form of signs, and of human veneration as a response.[17]

Luke tries to follow this model in the narrative of Acts,[18] but it is not the one he retains in Luke 24. At the end of the Gospel Luke presents the Risen One in the way the Bible describes a patriarch at the end of his life. Faced with his "children," Christ blesses them before the final separation. He is the master of his feelings, and he communicates to his own the spiritual benefits they will need to survive. Here it is not a question of sudden removal but of separation. The disciples' response is more like the reaction of people who have received blessings than that of people who have witnessed a violent removal. Yet Luke must adapt the scheme to the christological reality of the resurrection. To do this he states (v. 51) that the separation ($\delta\iota\dot{\epsilon}\sigma\tau\eta$ $\dot{\alpha}\pi$' $\alpha\dot{\upsilon}\tau\hat{\omega}\nu$, "he left them") takes place with an ascension ($\kappa\alpha\grave{\iota}$ $\dot{\alpha}\nu\epsilon\varphi\acute{\epsilon}\rho\epsilon\tau o$ $\epsilon\grave{\iota}\varsigma$ $\tau\grave{o}\nu$ $o\dot{\upsilon}\rho\alpha\nu\acute{o}\nu$, "and was carried up into heaven").[19]

---

of these findings to the beginnings, the plot, and the narrator's point of view.

13 Several authors emphasize the complementarity of the two accounts; see Fridrichsen, "Himmelfahrt"; Lohfink, *Himmelfahrt;* Dömer, *Heil,* 106–9; Schnider, "Himmelfahrt."

14 On the influence of the biblical story of Elijah and the Jewish traditions about him, see Kellermann, "Zu den Elia-Motiven." Kellermann thinks that Luke applied to Jesus the Jewish hope of Elijah *redivivus* but corrects it with the doctrine of the servant of God. See also Zwiep, *Ascension,* 58–63, 116, 194.

15 See *4 Esdras* 14:1-50 (vv. 48b-50, missing in the Latin version, exist especially in the Syriac version) and *2 Baruch* 76; Lohfink, *Himmelfahrt,* 59–61. It is not impossible that legends have developed about the ascension of Moses; see Larrañaga, *Ascension,* 36, 97–98; see below on the contribution of iconography in the history of interpretation. Lohfink (*Himmelfahrt,* 61–69) advises against reading Josephus *Ant.* 4.8.47 §§315–26 in this sense. Tob 12:20-22 should be mentioned: the angel Raphael,

who assumed human form to help Tobit and his son Tobias, ultimately returns to God.

16 On Heracles, see Pierre Grimal, *The Dictionary of Classical Mythology* (trans. A. R. Maxwell-Hyslop; Oxford: Blackwell, 1987) 207. On Romulus, see Titus Livius *Ab urbe condita* 1.16; Plutarch *Vitae, Romulus,* 27–28; *Vitae, Numa,* 2. On Augustus, see Dio Cassius *Hist. rom.* 56.46.2; Lohfink, *Himmelfahrt,* 34–37.

17 It is Lohfink (*Himmelfahrt*) who has studied these models most carefully; see my summary in *Luke the Theologian,* 192–98; see also Larrañaga, *Ascension,* 83–97, and Palatty, "Ascension" (first article).

18 Zwiep (*Ascension*) interprets not only the two ascension stories but also Luke 9:51 and Acts 3:19-21 from the category of removal, what he calls "the rapture Christology."

19 Lohfink (*Himmelfahrt,* 147–62) draws a clear distinction between the identity and the function of the two stories; see Maile, "Ascension," 40–44.

The New Testament and the earliest Christian literature (roughly up to Justin and Irenaeus) know and confess an Easter exaltation of Christ, but with few exceptions they know nothing of an ascension story certified by witnesses. There are three exceptions, however, in addition to Luke-Acts. Early in the second century the *Epistle of Barnabas* invited people to celebrate Sunday, regarded as the eighth day, for the twofold reason that on this day Jesus "arose from the dead, and appeared, and ascended into heaven" (ἀνέστη ἐκ νεκρῶν καὶ φανερωθεὶς ἀνέβη εἰς οὐρανούς).[20] The *Gospel of Peter* contains an extraordinary story of the resurrection, which amazed the guards at the tomb. Accompanied by two angels and followed by the cross, Christ comes triumphantly from the tomb. Here resurrection and exaltation occur together.[21] Finally, there is what we read in Mark's inauthentic conclusion from the end of the second century. After a series of appearances culminating in a final speech to the Eleven, the Risen One is taken away thus: "So the Lord Jesus, after he had spoken to them, was taken up into heaven and sat at God's right hand. For their part, they went everywhere preaching. The Lord was working with them and confirmed the word by the signs that accompanied it" (Mark 16:19-20).[22]

Gerhard Lohfink has defended the thesis that Luke was the first and for a long time the only person who "historicized" the Easter exaltation (invisible and believed reality) into an event at which witnesses were present (visible and attested reality).[23]

Personally, I defend the following four theses:

(a) One should not overdo the distinction between the exaltation and the ascension.[24] Many ancient Christian writers speak of the ascension of the Risen One without caring whether this reality was merely believed or also seen.[25]

(b) Following a tendency that is his, Luke likes to visualize what it is he is thinking. Thus, he is happy to "historicize" or "narrativize" the ascension of the Risen One at the end of a series of appearances. But he is no slave of his own descriptions. He is careful not to make such ways of speaking too much a part of the narration (see the absence of the "forty days" in Luke 24 and its presence in Acts 1).

(c) Luke is not the only one who "historicizes" the inexpressible Easter exaltation. In addition to the "exceptions" mentioned above, there are others whose dates are difficult to fix (I am thinking here of the ascension stories in the noncanonical literature, in particular of the writings of Nag Hammadi).[26]

---

20 See *Barn.* 15.9 in Pierre Prigent, *Epître de Barnabé: Introduction, traduction et notes* (Greek text, Robert A. Kraft) (SC 172; Paris: Cerf, 1971) 188–89. For the English translation, see Bart Ehrman in LCL 25 (Cambridge, Mass.: Harvard University Press, 2003) 71.

21 See *Gos. Pet.* 9.34—10.42 and the comments of Maria Grazia Mara in her *Évangile de Pierre: introduction, texte critique, traduction, commentaire et index* (SC 201; Paris: Cerf, 1973) 57–59, 171–90. The vocabulary of the ascension appears often in the literature of antiquity when one speaks of the return to life from the realm of the dead. See *T. Benj.* 9:5; "The Story of King Abgar," Eusebius *Hist. eccl.* 1.13.20; *Doctrina Addai* 9; *Acts Thom.* 156; for other examples, see Lohfink, *Himmelfahrt*, 106.

22 According to Hug (*Finale*, 128–53), the Gospel of Luke and Mark's inauthentic ending separate the ascension and the resurrection, but otherwise the two texts have nothing in common. Mark 16:19 is inspired by its predecessor, Elijah (see 2 Kgs [LXX 4 Kgdms] 2:11; Sir 48:9; and esp. 1 Macc 2:58). On Enoch, see Sir 49:14.

23 See Lohfink, *Himmelfahrt*, 242–83, and my summary of chapter 6 in *Luke the Theologian*, 196. Fitzmyer ("Ascension," 424–25) shares Lohfink's opinion.

24 See Davies, *He Ascended;* Bouwman, "Erhöhung"; Fitzmyer, "Ascension," 420; Maile, "Ascension," 48.

25 See already in the New Testament John 13:3; Eph 1:20; 1 Tim 3:16.

26 See the variant contained in Mark 16:3 in the Latin manuscript of Bobbio (k), preserved in Turin and dating from the fourth or fifth century; see the apparatus of Nestle-Aland (27th ed.) on the text; and Lohfink, *Himmelfahrt*, 128–29. This variant speaks of the darkness at the moment when the women arrive at the tomb, of the descent of the angels from heaven, then of their return to heaven accompanied by the Risen One, and finally of the return of the light. The scenario is reminiscent of the *Gospel of Peter*, except that it is here the women and not the guards who witness the events. See Mara, *Évangile de Pierre*, 181 (see n. 19 above). On Nag Hammadi, see below, in the History of Interpretation.

(d) The Lukan "historicization" was probably not the first; it is probable, at least for Acts 1, that Luke had predecessors.[27] One of them, who is detected in Acts 1, had to draw on the stories of Enoch and Elijah as the Bible and the Jewish traditions had transmitted them to him. The best parallel to Acts 1:9-11 appears to be a passage of *Slavonic Enoch* (*2 Enoch*).[28] Another predecessor, the author of the special source, is hidden behind the short story of Luke 24:50-53. He drafted this farewell of Jesus by drawing on the farewell scenes of the patriarchs in Genesis and the blessings of Israel's priests. He must know the book of Sirach and the description of the high priest Simon contained in chap. 50.[29] In this chapter, which is also the last of the book (before a final hymn), Simon is magnified and his glory is emphasized: "When he went up to the holy altar, he filled the enclosure of the sanctuary with glory" (Sir 50:11). His priestly role evidently included a blessing, so he "lifted up his hands over the whole congregation of the sons of Israel to give with his lips the blessing of the Lord" (Sir 50:20). He is surrounded by priests as Jesus is by his disciples (Sir 50:12). The people, represented in Luke by the disciples, prostrated themselves (Sir 50:17 and 21).[30] As one can see, I understand the ascension neither as a late legend nor as an eyewitness account, nor as an invention of Luke without a traditional basis.

It is time to address the textual problems raised by this last pericope of the Gospel.[31] There are a number of them, but they are of varying importance. In v. 50 ἔξω ("outside") is redundant after the verb ἐξάγω ("to lead out"), and it shocked the purist scribes. We should probably keep it. Whether we choose πρός ("in the direction of") or εἰς ("to, toward") does not affect the meaning. Most surprising is the presence of ἕως ("until"), attested by all the manuscripts, which, together with ἔξω and πρός, constitutes an awkward expression. But as the only person in the New Testament to do so, Luke sometimes uses ἕως with a preposition or an adverb (see Acts 17:14; 21:5; 26:11).[32]

In v. 51, διέστη ("he left" [them]), is very well attested. Although the scribe of Codex Bezae (D = 05) preferred ἀπέστη ("he withdrew" [from them]), there is little difference in meaning. Διέστη may underscore the widening distance between Jesus, who goes no farther, and the disciples, who prepare to go on their way, while ἀπέστη expresses the separation that takes place between them.

The most interesting variant concerns the ascension itself. The vast majority of manuscripts, beginning with the oldest, the Bodmer Papyrus XIV–XV (𝔓[75]), contain the words καὶ ἀνεφέρετο εἰς τὸν οὐρανόν ("and was carried up into heaven"). Some important witnesses of the Western text, Codex Bezae (D = 05), most or all Old Latin witnesses (it), and the Syriac Sinaitic (sy[s]), accompanied on this point by the original hand of the Greek Codex Sinaiticus (ℵ = 01*), omit the words. Should we keep them in the text of Luke or not? This question has generated intense controversy. Nestle's twenty-fifth edition had relegated this expression to the apparatus. The twenty-seventh rehabilitated it because of the influence of the recently discovered Bodmer Papyrus XIV–XV (𝔓[75]). If we put this mention of the ascension in the text, we must explain its disappearance in the Western text. To provide that explanation we must consider other Western variants in Luke 24 (the ones scholars have called the "Western non-interpolations").[33] Daniel Plooij and Eldon Jay Epp have shown that the Western text has its coherence.[34] It seems to have changed the end of the Gospel and the beginning of Acts in one specific sense by eliminating as much as possible the visible and material

---

27 See Hahn, "Himmelfahrt."
28 *2 Enoch* 67–68; see Clarke, "Pseudepigrapha"; Lohfink, *Himmelfahrt*, 56–57.
29 See Lohfink, *Himmelfahrt*, 167–69.
30 See James L. Crenshaw, "Sirach," in *The New Interpreter's Bible* (Nashville: Abingdon, 1997) 5:858–62.
31 See Enslin, "Ascension"; Plooij, *Ascension;* Creed, "Text"; Larrañaga, *Ascension*, 43–50 and 131–213; Dömer, *Heil*, 107; Guillaume, *Luc interprète*, 224–28; Epp, "Ascension"; Hans-Werner Bartsch, ed., *Codex Bezae versus Codex Sinaiticus im Lukasevangelium* (Hildesheim: Olms, 1984) 210–11; Fitzmyer, "Ascen-

sion," 416–17; Maile, "Ascension," 30–35; Parsons, *Departure*, 29–52; Parsons, "Text"; Amphoux, "Chapitre 24"; Swanson, *Manuscripts*, 419–20; Zwiep, "Text."
32 Dömer, *Heil*, 107.
33 On the Western non–interpolations, see Westcott and Hort, *New Testament*, 2:175–77.
34 Plooij, *Ascension;* Epp, "Ascension."

character of the ascension. What these scholars perhaps have not said enough is that in this way the witnesses of the Western text defended an archaic concept of the exaltation that had been that of the first Christians. Personally, I maintain the long text of the Gospel and include the expression καὶ ἀνεφέρετο εἰς τὸν οὐρανόν ("and was carried up into heaven") in Luke's text.

This situation is repeated in v. 52, where the same witnesses, except for the original hand of the Greek Sinaiticus (ℵ = 01*), omit the participial προσκυνή-σαντες αὐτόν ("after they had prostrated themselves before him"). The absence of these words is to be explained in the same way as was the omission of the ascension in the previous verse. These scribes are concerned to minimize as much as possible the presence and the activity of human beings at the elevation of Christ.

The other variants are less important. When the first hand of Vaticanus (B* = 03*) omits the adjective μεγάλης ("great") and the first hand of Alexandrinus (A* = 02*) omits the words ἐν τῷ ἱερῷ ("in the temple compound"), these must be careless mistakes and not the preservation of an earlier text. The penultimate variant may serve as a model case. The Egyptian text has the words εὐλογοῦντες τὸν θεόν ("blessing God"); the Western text, αἰνοῦντες τὸν θεόν ("praising God"). The Byzantine text, more recent and not wanting to lose the past treasures, combines the two forms of the text and retains αἰνοῦντες καὶ εὐλογοῦντες τὸν θεόν ("praising and blessing God"). Finally, from habit, numerous scribes added ἀμήν at the end of their copy in order to express the sacred character of the text.

Commentary

■ **50** The Gospel and Acts do not contradict each other about the location of the ascension. Both locations are east of Jerusalem, not far from the city. Indeed, Bethany (Luke 24:50) is at the eastern foot of the Mount of Olives (Acts 1:12). Luke is simply concerned to use different expressions.[35]

Why did they leave Jerusalem to separate? In its own way the narrative of Acts provides the reason. The parousia will take place as did the ascension, simply in reverse order (Acts 1:11). An old biblical tradition associated this final coming of the Lord with the Mount of Olives (Zech 14:4; Ezek 11:23). For the anticipated ordinance to take place, the departure had to occur at the same place, outside the city on the east side.

The evangelist does not seem to feel a contradiction about the date of the event, yet there is tension. In the Gospel, the ascension seems to take place on the day of Easter and not, as required by Acts, forty days later (Acts 1:3). This period certainly has symbolic value. It is a period set aside, in this case for a final teaching about the kingdom of God (Acts 1:3).[36] It is also a limited time, so the "heretics" with their pretensions to final revelations will not interfere. It has also been said, correctly, that in Acts Luke does not explicitly fix the date of the ascension on the fortieth day.[37] Yet Luke's casualness is surprising.

When, according to Luke, Jesus blessed his disciples, he entered a long biblical tradition. First, there is God, who blessed Adam and Eve at the time of their creation (Gen 1:28), Noah and his family after the flood (Gen 9:1), then Abraham and his descendants at the time of his departure (Gen 12:1-3). Then there are the fathers who, relying on God, bless their children. Even when the patriarchal narratives tell of usurped (Genesis 27) or manipulated (Genesis 48) blessings, they rely on the following conviction: "The blessing of an aging father was both effective and irrevocable in the Old Testament and in other documents of the ancient Orient."[38]

---

35 See Atkins, "Location." At the beginning of Jesus' entry into Jerusalem (19:29), Luke mentions Bethany and the Mount of Olives together.

36 This is the understanding of Tertullian (*Apol.* 21.23), the only Christian writer before the fourth century to speak of the forty days.

37 See Menoud, "Forty Days," 171–72. Because of the "forty days" of Acts 1:3, several authors think that Luke 24:50-53 represents not the final ascension but the conclusion of an appearance scene. Acts 1 recalls other appearances and the ultimate ascension. See, with differences, Bacon, "Ascension"; Michaelis, "Überlieferung"; Benoit, "Ascension." In an opposite sense, see Fridrichsen ("Himmelfahrt") as early as 1927. On the "forty days," see also Enslin, "Ascension"; Maile, "Ascension," 48–54; and especially Roscher, *Tessarakontaden.*

38 Footnote in the TOB (*Traduction Œcuménique de la Bible*) on Gen 27:33.

To take a famous example, Deuteronomy 33 quotes at length the final blessing of Moses. According to Luke, therefore, before his last departure Jesus associates himself with this tradition and performs this ancestral gesture.

God's blessing was also mediated in ways other than through the hands of old men; it was also transmitted through the priests. The book of Numbers cites the famous blessing that Moses formulated for Aaron and his sons, which they were to use to bless Israel (Num 6:22-27). This is the cultic framework of the blessing of the high priest Simon (Sirach 50), whose influence on Luke 24 I noted above.[39] That hands are lifted up,[40] that words are spoken, that those blessed fall down with gratitude, all of these also speak in favor of the priestly character of Jesus' act. Even if he does not develop this component as does the author of the Epistle to the Hebrews,[41] the evangelist nevertheless confers on Christ here a liturgical function.[42] Without deciding for either model, Luke gives his readers to understand that Jesus blesses his "descendants" as a patriarch and blesses the gathered assembly as a priest.

As the raising up of the hands indicates, the blessing is more than a word. It is a performative act that communicates God's kindness and protection and, at the time of departure or separation, ensures continuity and faithfulness. The words pronounced on this occasion carry the weight of oaths. As Jean-Luc Marion writes: "When he blesses, Christ lets himself be recognized as the gift of the presence."[43] Thus, in our passage there is a paradox of withdrawal and gift, of absence and presence. As the philosopher perceives, the paradox of Emmaus is repeated here.[44]

Luke knows that the disciples' blessing will be spread to their own disciples and that from the people of Israel it will overflow to all nations. Does he not refer in Acts 3:25-26 to the promise given to Abraham when he puts the following words on Peter's lips? "You are the sons of the prophets and of the covenant God made with your fathers when he said to Abraham: 'In your descendents all the families of the earth will be blessed.' It is for you that God first raised up, then sent his Servant to bless you by turning each of you from his misdeeds." The end of this quotation reminds one of what in view of the importance of grace should not be forgotten. The blessing neither infantilizes nor does it relieve one of responsibility.[45] The believers know that God puts them at the crossroads: "See, I am setting before you today a blessing and a curse: the blessing, if you obey the commandments of the Lord your God that I am commanding you today; and the curse, if you do not obey the commandments of the Lord your God . . ." (Deut 11:26-28 NRSV).[46]

■ 51 The typically Lukan expression "and it happened that" (καὶ ἐγένετο) followed by ἐν τῷ and an infinitive, serves as a marker. An important event will take place.[47] Two verbs will describe it. The first marks the distance that happens between "him" and "them"; the second, the rising into heaven. In the book of Acts (1:2, 11, 22), as in the hymn of 1 Tim 3:16, and in Mark's inauthentic ending (16:19), "to remove," "to lift up" (ἀναλαμβάνω)

---

39 See above in the analysis, thesis (d).

40 In the episode of Jesus and the children, Mark 10:16 and Matt 19:15 mention that Jesus laid his hands on them (τιθεὶς or ἐπιτιθεὶς τὰς χεῖρας). Luke 18:15-17 omits this detail. At the beginning of the Sermon on the Plain, Luke says that Jesus lifted up his eyes (6:20; the same aorist participle ἐπάρας is used as here in v. 50).

41 See Heb 2:17; 3:1; 4:14-16; 5:5-10; 6:20; 7:26-28; 8:1; 9:11-14; 10:21.

42 See Odasso, "Ascensione," 118; and esp. Mekkattukunnel, *Priestly Blessing*, who insists on this aspect. His emphasis is probably exaggerated, as Morgan ("Ending") has correctly seen in his criticism. In my opinion, Luke conceives of Jesus here as Israel's eschatological priest and not as the initiator of the priesthood of the Christian churches.

43 Marion, *Prolégomènes*, 159.

44 Ibid., 160–61.

45 Wind ("Gott") is of the opinion that the ascension stories encourage Christians to live in the world as Dietrich Bonhoeffer has suggested: as adults who are aware of God's absence. She writes: "The underlying theme of the story of the 'ascension' is rather the contradictory unity of utopia and reality, of the necessity of living in a historically conditioned world and the simultaneous unavailability of the messianic vision of the Kingdom of God" (226).

46 See Hermann Wolfgang Beyer, "εὐλογέω κτλ.," *TDNT* 2 (1964) 754–65; Mekkattukunnel, *Priestly Blessing*, 61–91; 155–230.

47 See vol. 1 of this commentary, 167, on Luke 5:1.

with the passive serves to describe the ascension. For the sake of variety, Luke uses here a less common verb, "to carry away," "to raise" (ἀναφέρω) also in the passive.[48] I note, however, that Mark and Matthew use this verb in its active form to describe how Jesus leads his three disciples up the high mountain of the transfiguration (καὶ ἀναφέρει αὐτοὺς εἰς ὄρος ὑψηλόν, "and led them up a high mountain," Mark 9:2; Matt 17:1). Gerhard Lohfink finds the same usage of "to lead up" (ἀναφέρω) accompanied by the expression "into heaven" (εἰς τὸν οὐρανόν) in profane literature in Plutarch, Antoninus Liberalis, and in the scholia of the *Argonautica* of Apollonius of Rhodes.[49]

The book of Acts will confirm this earthly absence of the Risen One because of the ascension. In addition to chap. 1 of Acts and especially the second story of the ascension, we should note this significant statement attributed to Peter, the spokesman of the apostles: "So the times of refreshing given by the Lord will come, when he will send the Christ who has been appointed for you, Jesus, whom heaven must receive[50] until the times of restitution of all things of which God has spoken by the mouth of his holy prophets of the past" (Acts 3:20-21). As Calvin would later observe,[51] Luke emphasizes the absence of Christ on earth.[52] In Acts 1:9-11 he manages to repeat that, at the ascension, Jesus, withdrawn from the earth, has ascended "into heaven (εἰς τὸν οὐρανόν)."[53]

■ **52** It is natural that those who receive a blessing react to it.[54] The stories of blessing gladly include this aspect, as one notes in Sirach 50: "Then all the people together immediately fell to the ground on their faces to worship their Lord, the Almighty, the Most High God" (Sir 50:17). By contrast, however, in this passage, the disciples do not prostrate[55] themselves here before God as do the faithful who have received the blessing of a priest but, Luke writes, before Christ himself: "after they had prostrated themselves before him" (προσκυνήσαντες αὐτόν), Jesus has crossed the barrier that separates human beings from God.[56] After the resurrection he can receive divine honors. Unlike Matthew,[57] Luke, who is careful to pay attention to the stages, has thus far not said that human beings worship Christ. At the time of the ascension he does so without hesitation. Let us remember that on the day of Jesus' birth the shepherds returned "glorifying and praising" not the newborn child but "God" (2:20).

The verb προσκυνέω describes an attitude more than words would suggest. It is the gesture of one who bows to the ground, the expected reaction of one who is before a deity or who encounters a king. The word is used by the Greeks to refer to the worship they offer their gods. *Proskynēsis* was also part of the protocol at the court of the king of Persia and of the kingdoms of the ancient Near East.[58] Thus, the term belongs to the vocabulary of the temple and the palace, of religion and the court.

---

48 On the vocabulary of the ascension, see Lohfink, *Himmelfahrt*, 41–42, 170–71, 187–207; and Zwiep, *Ascension*, 80–117.

49 Plutarch *Vitae, Numa* 2.3; Antoninus Liberalis 25; the scholia of the *Argonautica* of Apollonius of Rhodes (edited Heinrich Keil) 4.57; see also Dio Cassius *Hist. rom.* 56.46.2; Lohfink, *Himmelfahrt*, 42 n. 72.

50 Must we not understand δέξασθαι in the sense of "retain" as well as "receive"?

51 Calvin, *Harmony*, 3:257.

52 On the departure and the absence of Christ according to Luke, see Houlden, "Preaching," 177–79.

53 Two other times the expression εἰς τὸν οὐρανόν indicates the direction in which the disciples are looking. See Fuller, "After the Ascension," 392.

54 On this verse, see Wulf, "Freude."

55 See J. M. Nützel, "προσκυνέω, etc.," *EDNT* 3 (1993) 173–75; and vol. 1 of this commentary, 144 n. 41, on 4:7.

56 It was the same in Rome in the framework of the imperial cult. Only after his death and apotheosis could the title *divus* ("divine") be applied without reservation to the sovereign; see S. R. F. Price, *Rituals and Power: The Roman Imperial Cult in Asia Minor* (Cambridge: Cambridge University Press, 1998) 75.

57 See the three uses of προσκυνέω ("to prostrate oneself") in the story of the magi in Matt 2:2, 8, 11; and *Mart. Pol.* 17.3: τοῦτον (scil. τὸν Χριστόν) μὲν γὰρ υἱὸν ὄντα τοῦ θεοῦ προσκυνοῦμεν, "for we adore him (i.e. Christ) because he is the Son of God."

58 We do not know whether the Greek verb designated first the human attitude before the gods or that of the subjects before their sovereign. On another point, however, we are more assured: *Proskynēsis* is not limited to a simple bending of the upper body; as is confirmed by the frequent presence of the verb "to fall," it implied kneeling and even prostrating oneself. It is also certain that the verb then came to be used figuratively and in some cases lost its power

The religion of Israel and, after it, the Christian religion, have chosen this gesture to express the human reaction to God and to Christ.

On returning to Jerusalem, the disciples return to daily life and find again their responsibilities. Jerusalem is where in Acts Luke has them do their missionary work. In naming the capital, Luke sometimes uses the sacred form and sometimes the secular, hellenized form. Here he chooses the religious and Semitic form: Ἰερουσα-λήμ.[59] The disciples' concrete life was marked by faith. Instead of immediately mentioning their daily work, the evangelist emphasizes their religious attitude in the temple, "they were blessing God" (εὐλογοῦντες τὸν θεόν, v. 53).

That "great joy" is mentioned here is only partly a surprise.[60] Of course, any separation causes great sadness, but here the one who leaves is also the one who remains (there is the same idea at the end of Matthew: "And I am with you all the days until the end of time," Matt 28:20). His presence–absence causes joyfulness.

Formally, the reader recognizes that the author attempts to develop an *inclusio* here. The Gospel started in Jerusalem, and it ends in Jerusalem. The great joy at the ascension (v. 52) parallels the great joy of Christmas (2:10). The temple provides the setting for the action here (v. 53) and there (1:9, 21; 2:27, 46).[61]

■ **53** Luke holds firmly to the Jewish roots of the Christian church. But even though the first witnesses of Christ are Jews, they do not engage, as some have done, in adventurous revolts. They are pious, and they frequent the temple, not the military camps. When the evangelist speaks of the ἱερόν and not the ναός (the space of

Zechariah, 1:9, 21), Luke indicates that these men and women are laypeople who stand in the "sacred space," not members of the clergy who enter the actual building. To this distinction Acts adds another change. Chapter 1 of the book, which tells of the establishing of the first Christian community, reports that the apostles and disciples of Jesus Christ, men and women, meet regularly[62] in a different area, the upper room. The reader then understands if not the double allegiance (to Christianity and to Judaism) at least the development Luke is hoping for Judaism. The temple is no longer the only religious option. It is no longer the place of sacrifice; it is now the place of prayer (Acts 3:1), and its surroundings will witness the missionary proclamation (Acts 3:12-26). God's future, which involves the future of his people, is to move from one time to another, from a sacred space to the whole world, from Jerusalem to the ends of the earth. That they are "continually"[63] in the temple is, of course, a figure of speech.

History of Interpretation

This is a long, tortuous, and impassioned story. Until the year 150, Christians for the most part confess their faith in the resurrection and exaltation of Jesus, which, in their view, constitute a whole.[64] Some, however, gradually grant the ascension a certain autonomy from the resurrection without showing any dependence on Luke-Acts (they say nothing about the forty days) (see John 20:17; Mark 16:19; Aristides *Apology* 2.8). One perceives an influence of Luke 24 and Acts 1 only with Justin Martyr[65] and especially since Irenaeus. In *1 Apol.* 50, Justin

and simply became a sign of respect or a salutation; see Heinrich Greeven, "προσκυνέω κτλ.," *TDNT* 6 (1968) 758–66.

59 See vol. 1 of this commentary, 99–100, esp. n. 23, on 2:22-24, and 213 n. 9, on 6:17-19.

60 On joy in Luke, see Bovon, *Luke the Theologian*, 457 n. 118; and vol. 1 of this commentary, 88, on 2:10. On the joy here in v. 52, see Wulf, "Freude."

61 A number of authors have noted these formal aspects. See, e.g., Guillaume, *Luc interprète*, 206; Nolland, 3:1229.

62 The apostles and the disciples are staying (καταμένοντες, "remaining," Acts 1:13) in the upper room and are "diligent," "constant" (προσκαρτεροῦντες, Acts 1:14) in prayer.

63 On διὰ παντός ("continually," "all the time"), see BAGD, s.v. διά, A II, 1, a.

64 See Lohfink, *Himmelfahrt*, 98–109; Larrañaga, *Ascension*, 492–512.

65 Lohfink (*Himmelfahrt*, 109) writes: "Almost everywhere there are credo-like formulations in Justin, the ascension is also named—see *Apologia* 1.21; 31; 42; 45; 46; 54; *Dialogus* 17.1; 32.3; 34.2; 36.5; 38.1; 39.7; 63.1; 82.1; 85.1, 2; 108.2; 126.1; 132.1—and in almost all of these examples it is clearly separate from the resurrection." See also Larrañaga, *Ascension*, 12–14, 492–93.

shows his dependence on Luke-Acts. He understands Jesus' ascension as a visible event and associates it with the subsequent gift of the Holy Spirit.[66] In chap. 21 of this same *Apology*, he says that he wants to oppose the unbelief of the pagans and also to denigrate their pagan myths as well as their pretended exaltations into heaven. Irenaeus, who explicitly refers to the Gospels and to Acts, alludes to Jesus' resurrection and his ascension confirmed by the eyewitness testimony of the apostles.[67]

We must wait for Tertullian, however, to have a reference to the forty days: "However, he passed forty days with some of his disciples in Galilee, a province of Judaea, teaching them what they were to teach. Then, when they had been ordained for the office of preaching throughout the world, a cloud enveloped him and he was taken up into heaven, a story that is much truer than the one which, among you, people like Proculus are wont to swear as true about Romulus" (*Apol.* 21.23).[68] As one can see, Tertullian is thinking of the narrative in Acts. He is, moreover, neither the first nor the last who frees the Christian affirmation of the exaltation of Christ from the suspicion of plagiarism. Justin preceded

him, and after him Origen and then Augustine (*Civ.* 3.15) take up the argument. They will say that it is the pagan stories that are false. In their eyes, Christian truth is ensured not only by the eyewitness testimony of the apostles but also—a provocative argument—by the moral value of these witnesses who have been willing to suffer for their faith as well as by the miracles that continue to occur. They had to respond to the allegations of a Celsus (Origen *Cels.* 3.22–36) or a Porphyrius[69] that reduced the resurrection or the ascension of the Lord to the level of pagan deifications or apotheoses.[70]

While it is not possible to specify the exact connections between these texts and the Lukan stories of the ascension, it is appropriate to note here a few narrative texts: *Gos. Pet.* 38–42 and 56 and the variant of Mark 16:3 (manuscript k);[71] *T. Adam* 3, in which Christ predicts his future;[72] *Asc. Isa.* 3:13-18; 9:12-18; 10:8-15; 11:25-35;[73] *Ep. apost.* 51 (62);[74] the *Acts of Pilate* or the *Gospel of Nicodemus* 16;[75] *Gospel of Mary* 9.5;[76] the *Apocryphon of James* 2.8-39; 7.35—8.4; 10.6-38; 14.19—16:39;[77] the *Apocryphon of John* 2.3 (pp. 1, 11–12 of NHC II, 1);[78] the *Epistle of Peter to Philip*, the *Sophia Jesu Christi* and the

66 See Lohfink, *Himmelfahrt*, 109–10.

67 Irenaeus *Adv. haer.* 1.10.1; 2.32.3; 3.10.6; 12.1, 5; 16.8; 17.2; 5.31.2; *Epideixis* (= *Demonstration of the Apostolic Preaching*) 41; 83; 84; see Lohfink, *Himmelfahrt*, 110–11.

68 English translation, FC 10; see Larrañaga, *Ascension*, 14–15.

69 See Larrañaga, *Ascension*, 16–17.

70 See Augustine *Sermo* 242 (*PL* 38:1140). Fragment 65, p. 86 in Adolf von Harnack, ed., *Porpyrius, "Gegen die Christen", 15 Bücher. Zeugnisse, Fragmente und Referate* (APAW, 1916, Philosophisch–historische Klasse 1; Berlin: Verlag der Königlichen Akademie der Wissenschaften, 1916), is from the work of Porphyrius against the Christians preserved by Anastasius Sinaita, *Hodegos* 3 (*PG* 89:233). It is summarized by Pierre de Labriolle (*La réaction païenne* [1934; reprinted Paris: Cerf, 2005] 271): "And why did he not ascend with a great spectacle in the midst of a vast concourse of Jews and Greeks from all nations, since that is the way he will come down at the parousia?" Porphyrius, as he is available to us in the fragment, is not very clear. He wonders why Jesus did not organize a great assembly on Mount Zion, even though the ascension takes place on the Mount of Olives. Then he alludes to an event that resembles the parousia (see Acts 1:11) but speaks of

a descent from heaven when we expect him to mention an ascension.

71 See n. 24 above.

72 See Lohfink, *Himmelfahrt*, 126.

73 See C. Detlef G. Müller in Schneemelcher, *New Testament Apocrypha*, 2:608, 615, 617, 619; Playout, "Lifted Up," 159–80.

74 See J.-N. Perès, "Épître des apôtres," in Bovon et al., *Écrits apocryphes chrétiens*, 1:392; C. Detlef G. Müller in Schneemelcher, *New Testament Apocrypha*, 1:278.

75 See Rémi Gounelle and Zbigniew Izydorczyk, *L'Évangile de Nicodème ou Les Actes faits sous Ponce Pilate, suivi de la lettre de Pilate à l'empereur Claude* (Apocryphes 9; Turnhout: Brepols, 1997) 179; Felix Scheidweiler in Schneemelcher, *New Testament Apocrypha*, 1:519–20.

76 See Françoise Morard, "Évangile selon Marie," in Bovon et al., *Écrits apocryphes chrétiens*, 2:17; James M. Robinson, ed., *The Nag Hammadi Library in English* (3d. ed.; New York: HarperCollins, 1988) 526.

77 This is NHC I, 2. See Playout, "Lifted Up," 103–19.

78 This text is known in various manuscripts: NHC II, 1; III, 1; IV, 1 and BG 8502 [Berlin Gnostic Codex], which represent a long version and a short version. I accept the division of the text proposed by Karen L. King, *The Secret Revelation of John* (Cambridge,

Pistis Sophia.[79] All of these texts mention or narrate an ascension of the Savior and share some Lukan convictions. There must be a distinction, for example, between ascension and Easter. For the most part it was viewed as a historical event with some eyewitnesses. In addition, the ascension is taken into the creed and thus becomes dogma.[80]

Three events will change the situation: the gradual canonization of the Gospel of Luke, the slower canonization of Acts, and then the establishment of the feast of the ascension. The canonization of Luke's work meant reading the texts in worship, the need to explain them, the duty to keep them as texts for preaching.[81] The feast of the ascension was not born without difficulty.[82] In the second century, when it began to be celebrated everywhere, Easter was not the festival of a single Sunday but of a longer period of celebrations. There were fifty days of Easter.[83] During this period the Christian mystery was celebrated in all its breadth: from the resurrection of Jesus to the gift of the Spirit, from Easter to Pentecost.

Then both ends of the celebration, the days of Easter and Pentecost, were especially solemn. In Syria and Palestine the feast of the ascension coincided with that of Pentecost[84] (sometimes the accent of Sunday morning was on the gift of the Holy Spirit and of Sunday afternoon on the ascension; this comes from the pilgrimage of Aetheria to the Holy Land [*Itinerarium* 43]). The canonization of Acts disturbed this scheme and required that the feast be held on Thursday, ten days before Pentecost. The change did not take place without the gnashing of teeth,[85] and there are numerous traces of resistance.[86]

These new realities, Luke-Acts as an important part of sacred Scripture and the feast of the Ascension as a date in the liturgical year,[87] which have either willingly or by force come together, account for the presence of commentaries, first patristic then Byzantine and medieval, as well as many sermons. Curiously, we have only a few commentaries from Christian antiquity. Ambrose, moreover, who is more a homiletician than an exegete, is not interested in the ascension,[88] and the conclusion of Cyril's

---

Mass.: Harvard University Press, 2006). The passage in question is attested in both versions.

79 The *Epistle of Peter to Philip* (NHC VII, 2) 138.3–10 and 139.4–9; *Sophia Jesu Christi* according to BG 8502.3, pp. 126–27; *Pistis Sophia* IV, 136 and 141 (book IV seems to be an independent work that is older than the other three books); I, 3–4.6 and 11–16. Irenaeus (*Adv. haer.* 1.3.2; 1.30.14) attacks a view of the ascension he considers heretical: After Easter, the Risen One still shared the life of his disciples for eighteen months.

80 Heinrich Denzinger, *Enchiridion symbolorum definitionum et declarationum de rebus fidei et morum* (31st ed.; ed. Karl Rahner; Freiburg i. B.: Herder, 1957) 2. Adolf von Harnack, *Das apostolische Glaubensbekenntnis: Ein geschichtlicher Bericht nebst einem Nachwort* (16th ed.; Berlin: Haack, 1892) 22, 25–26; Larrañaga, *Ascension*, 48–50; Lohfink, *Himmelfahrt*, 109.

81 To my knowledge, the canonization of Luke-Acts, as such, has not been studied in recent years, in spite of the many new books on the canon; see Andrew F. Gregory, *The Reception of Luke and Acts in the Period before Irenaeus: Looking for Luke in the Second Century* (WUNT 2/168; Tübingen: Mohr Siebeck, 2003) 52–53 and 204–5; and François Bovon, "The Reception and Use of the Gospel of Luke in the Second Century," in Craig G. Bartholomew et al., eds., *Reading Luke: Interpretation, Reflection, Forma-*

tion (Scripture and Hermeneutics Series 6; Grand Rapids: Zondervan, 2005) 379–400.

82 See Kretschmar, "Himmelfahrt"; Cabié, *Pentecôte*, 181–97. One finds a discussion of Kretschmar's theses in Lohfink, *Himmelfahrt*, 137–46; see esp. Weinert, *Himmelfahrt*.

83 See Odo Casel, *La fête de Pâques dans l'Église des Pères* (trans. Jean-Charles Didier; LO 37; Paris: Cerf, 1963) 11–87 (originally: "Art und Sinn der ältesten christlichen Osterfeier," *JLW* 14 [1938] 1–78); Cabié, *Pentecôte*, 35–76.

84 See Kretschmar, "Himmelfahrt," 209–13.

85 Kretschmar ("Himmelfahrt," 212) writes: "Indeed, one is almost tempted to say that the general acceptance of the Lukan time-frame destroyed the general age of joy."

86 See Miquel, "Mystère."

87 On the feast of the Ascension, see Weinert, *Himmelfahrt;* and Wilcke, *Himmelfahrt.* The earliest witnesses for the existence of the feast of the Ascension, a feast that must have appeared in the second half of the fourth century, are *Const. Ap.* 5.20.1–4; Gregory of Nyssa *Hom. in Ascensionem* (*PG* 46:689–93), controversial testimony; John Chrysostom *Hom. de sacra Pentecoste* 2.1 (*PG* 50:463–70); idem, *Hom. in Ascensionem* (*PG* 50:441–52); Weinert, *Himmelfahrt*, 13–22.

88 Ambrose (*Exp. Luc.* 10.179–81) goes directly from the appearances to the gift of the Holy Spirit and

commentary is not yet available.[89] It is the Venerable Bede who, at the gateway to the Middle Ages, offers us the more substantial commentary (*In Luc.* 6.2393–2469). He gives the etymology of Bethany, the "house of obedience," the obedience of the disciples, which brings them the blessing. With regard to the Mount of Olives, he refers to Jesus, the Anointed of the Lord. This one came down (in his incarnation) because of the disobedience of sinners, and he returns to heaven (in his ascension) because of the obedience of the faithful. It makes sense, Bede explains, that a church would be established on the slope of the Mount of Olives.[90] He compares the blessing received then by the apostles and the one enjoyed now by the faithful. He concludes that Luke, well represented by the *vitulus*, the sacrificial calf, has sketched the priestly character of Christ better than the other evangelists. Did he not conclude his Gospel at the place where he began it with Zechariah, in the temple? Today, however, praise and the blessing of God (Luke 24) have replaced bloody sacrifices (Luke 1).

The homiletics of the fifth and sixth centuries are represented on the Latin side by Leo the Great and on the Greek side by Severus of Antioch.[91] In *Sermo* 73, which the bishop of Rome preaches on the fortieth day after Easter, it is the day of the ascension.[92] As is his custom, he actualizes the ascension of Christ by telescoping the past and the present with his beloved *hodie*, "today."[93] He indicates that the forty days were needed to accumulate evidence of the resurrection that was all the more necessary since doubt had invaded the hearts of the disciples. The result was that when the Lord departed it was joy and not sadness that filled them. He concludes in a final paragraph with an idea that appears in both East and West and makes its way through the centuries: "Thus the ascension of Christ is our own exaltation, and there where the glory of the head precedes, the hope of the body is also called" (Leo the Great *Sermo* 60 [73]. 4). This event corrects the evils of the fall and is due to the presence in the exalted Christ of the humanity he has assumed.[94]

Early in the sixth century, Severus of Antioch preached several times on the day of the ascension.[95]

tries to harmonize the contradictions of the Gospels. Paragraphs 182–84 appear to be a postscript in which Ambrose tries to reconcile the command to go to Galilee (Matthew and Mark) with the one to stay in Jerusalem (Luke and John).

89 Sauget ("Nouvelles homélies") presents well the complex situation of this work whose two principal Syriac manuscripts are mutilated, and he reports on the discovery he made in Damascus; see above, p. 316 n. 187 on 23:26-43 and p. 400 n. 92 on 24:36-49. A Greek fragment has been preserved (frg. 125; Reuss, *Lukas-Kommentar*, 278): agreeing with dogma, it says that at his ascension the Risen One took his own fleshly humanity with him. In this manner he opened the way for humans.

90 The same themes surface in Bede's Homily on the Gospels 2.15 (CCSL 122:280–89). This homily has been translated into English by Lawrence T. Martin and David Hurst, *Bede the Venerable, Homilies on the Gospels*, Book 2, *Lent to the Dedication of the Church* (Kalamazoo, Mich.: Cistercian Publications, 1991) 135–48.

91 On the Syriac side, see James of Sarug, "Homélie sur l'Ascension" in Paul Bedjan, ed., *S. Martyrii qui et Sahdona, quae supersunt omnia* (Paris: O. Harrassowitz, 1902) 808–32; English introduction and translation by Thomas Kollamparampil, *Jacob of Serugh: Selected Festal Homilies* (Rome: Centre for Indian and Inter-Religious Studies, 1997) 329–52. I am grateful to Susan Ashbrook Harvey who called this homily to my attention.

92 Leo the Great *Sermo* 60 (73), ed. Antoine Chavasse and trans. René Dolle (SC 74bis: 268–75).

93 See the note by René Dolle in SC 74bis, 268 n. 4.

94 See also the second sermon dedicated by Leo the Great to the ascension: *Sermo* 61 (74) (SC 74bis: 274–87), where the same themes are presented. There he develops in particular a christological reflection and thinks that after the ascension the believers can depend more on the Son's divinity than on his humanity. This is a unique trait, since other preachers, for example, Augustine (*Sermo* 242.4.6 [*PL* 38:1140–41]) show their orthodoxy by emphasizing that Christ went to heaven taking with him his humanity. Leo does not deny that, but he accents here the divinity of Christ. On the ascension in Augustine's work, see Marrevee, *Ascension*.

95 Homily 24 is dated precisely on Thursday, May 16, 513. It is the article "Sévère" by Michel Aubineau that has drawn my attention to these homilies. On Severus of Antioch, see Berthold Altaner and Alfred Stuiber, *Patrologie: Leben, Schriften und Lehre der Kirchenväter* (8th ed.; Freiburg i. B.: Herder, 1978) 505–7.

Three of these sermons, delivered in Greek but preserved in Syriac, have survived.[96] More important than the biblical text of Luke and Acts[97] is, as in Leo the Great, the "today" of the festival. And more important than the story is the christological truth that must be defended against the heretics, Nestorians or Arians. In this regard, the three convictions Severus shares with a large Christian tradition are decisive here. According to the first, the Son returned to the heights equipped with his bodily humanity (we know that in Severus the divine and the human are united in Christ). According to the second, if Christ was carried up into heaven it was not because he needed it; it happened on our behalf according to God's plan (it was the same with the ascension as with the incarnation, the baptism, the crucifixion, or the resurrection). According to the third, the ascension includes the faithful in its movement.[98] As with Leo the Great, Severus emphasizes the participation of Christians in the exaltation of Christ, a theme neglected in the modern era.[99]

The influence of the Gospels on the Qur'an should not be neglected. Of course, Islam does not believe that Jesus was crucified, but it does admit his ascension. The holy book says: "No indeed, Allah raised him up to Himself. Allah is all-mighty, all-wise" (Qur'an Sura 4.156 [or 158]).[100]

Late antiquity provides a different kind of reception. Here there are the first artistic representations of the ascension. The oldest, dating probably from the fifth century, is an ivory plaque in the Munich museum.[101] It shows Jesus striding up a mountain with a scroll in his left hand and his right hand grasped by the hand of God. The image is a Christian adaptation of the Jewish representation of Moses climbing Sinai to receive the law. This relationship suggests that, along with Enoch and Elijah, Moses was one of the models for Christ's ascension.[102] I am not going to examine here more works of art representing the ascension. Suffice it to say that at this time the art of the East emphasized the divinity of Christ, while the art of the West emphasized his humanity.[103] I will simply call attention to the original creation of Cranach the Elder.[104] In two wood carvings of 1521, which are part of the *Passional Christi und Antichristi*, the artist contrasts Christ's ascension with the fall of the Antichrist. At the ascension he notes the tracks Jesus left at the time of his ascension, tracks that were shown to the pilgrims to the Mount of Olives. He also lets it be understood that the believers, following the implied command of the angel (Acts 1:11), are to stop looking into the sky and are to engage in the daily life of Christian witness. For Cranach, Luther's friend, this place of life is the Wartburg castle, which he painted in the background. As disciples

96 The homilies involved are 24, 47, and 71 (the third is ed. and trans. by Maurice Brière; the two others by Brière and François Graffin; PO 37:134–45; 35:304–15; 12:12–70).

97 In fact, it is Phil 2:6-11 that guides Severus in his homily 71.

98 See homily 24 (134–35); homily 47 (312–15); homily 71 (52–54).

99 It is a curious allegory that he develops in homily 24 (139) from the grilled fish: the fish evokes the moisture of human nature that Christ came to save, and the fire that grills the fish is the divine nature of the Son who became incarnate. Interesting is a moral exhortation: in homily 71 (67–68) he invites the believers to look up to heaven and to Christ instead of at the circus sports and their combats between humans and beasts. Of note finally is the praise Severus addresses to the emperor Anastasius, who, at the instigation of his wife, Ariane, had given the church a purple robe (homily 24, 142–45).

100 See Henri Michaud, *Jésus selon le Coran* (CTh 46; Neuchâtel: Delachaux et Niestlé, 1960) 63, 72–73.

101 Kretschmar ("Himmelfahrt") reproduces this picture between pages 224 and 225. On dating it in the fifth rather than the fourth century, see Lohfink, *Himmelfahrt*, 13.

102 See Kretschmar, "Himmelfahrt," 218–221; Schrade, "Ikonographie," 89–125. Schrade compares the Munich plate with representations of the Roman apotheosis. He notes their similarities and differences, but, if I see correctly, he neglects the parallel with Moses.

103 See Réau, *Iconographie*, 2:2, 582–90, esp. 584.

104 On this work of Cranach, see Peter Parshall, "The Vision of the Apocalypse in the Sixteenth and Seventeenth Centuries," in Frances Carey, ed., *The Apocalypse and the Shape of Things to Come* (Toronto: University of Toronto Press, 1999) 143–44. I am indebted to Ermanno Genre of the Facoltà Valdese di teologia in Rome for this reference to Cranach. On the footprints, see Küchler, *Jerusalem*, 876–97, 900.

of Jesus the artist draws contemporaries, dressed in the fashion of the sixteenth century.

Returning to the text, in the Middle Ages in the West[105] and the Byzantine period,[106] the exegesis of Bonaventure and that of Theophylactus are comparable. Although their languages are different, their spiritual intention is similar. Bonaventure relates the ascension to the Psalms, which, according to him, have predicted it (Ps 46 [47]:6 and Ps 67 [68]:19) (*Comm. Luc.* 24.63–66).[107] He is not without knowledge of the liturgy of the ascension in which the Psalms are abundantly quoted.[108] In the same way as Bede, he gives the etymology of Bethany, and, based on the beginning of Acts, he gives the date of Luke 24:50-51 as the fortieth day after Easter. He is of the opinion that the disciples' joy comes from the victorious ascension of Christ. Once again as with Bede, he sees the temple, as well as the transition from one priesthood to another, at the beginning and the end of the Gospel. Theophylactus (*Enarr. Luc.* 24), who also follows Acts and dates Luke's ascension on the fortieth day, thinks that the blessing helps the disciples wait for the Spirit and teaches us to bless and to entrust to God those we leave behind when we go on a journey.[109] He says that Elijah's exaltation into heaven is only symbolic language, but that of the Savior is real. He was accompanied by his human flesh with which he demonstrated that he was compatible with the Father. Thanks to Christ, human and divine, human nature is venerated by the entire angelic world at the time of the ascension. Even though the disciples have not yet received the Spirit, they act in a spiritual way. May we, he says, do the same today.

At the end of the Middle Ages, Erasmus, anticipating Lohfink, believed that when Jesus blesses he follows the example of the patriarchs and Moses (*Paraphrasis,* 488).[110] Luther avoids the criticisms of the ancients and outmaneuvers the suspicions of the moderns: One must believe in one's heart. Sensitive to the ubiquity of Christ, the reformer believes that even if the Lord leaves, he is nevertheless close to us. Furthermore, if he leaves, it is only to serve us better. He comes down to us in the preaching, and we ascend to him in faith.[111] To our surprise, Calvin, who in his doctrine of the Lord's Supper maintains his Lord at the right hand of the Father,[112] in his *Harmony of the Gospel* does not use Luke 24:50-53 to strengthen his so Lukan position.[113] He prefers to focus on other points. He notes artfully that Bethany, after having been associated with the passion, is here at the ascension. He underscores that when Christ left he let himself be seen by no one except the apostles. He develops a brief theology of blessing (reserved for God, its sole author, it was entrusted to the priests of the Old Testament, then to Christ, the true Melchizedek). Finally, he reflects on *proskynēsis,* which he understands as worship. If Luke is so brief on the activity of the disciples in the ten days between the ascension and Pentecost, it is

---

105 See, e.g., the *Glossa ordinaria*, Luke 24:50-53 (*PL* 114:355–56); and Albertus Magnus *Evang. Luc.* 24.50–53 (775–77).

106 At that time the *proskynēsis* is not reserved to God alone. At the Council of Nicaea II (787) at the end of the iconoclastic crisis, the council fathers distinguish between worship (λατρεία), reserved for God in his essence, and veneration (προσκύνησις), which is offered especially to icons; see Lampe, s.v. λατρεία B9 and προσκύνησις 3k.

107 Bernardini, 603–4; Eng. trans. Karris, *St. Bonaventure's Commentary*, 3:2245–49.

108 See Weinert (*Himmelfahrt*, 33–231), who reviews the psalms for the feast of the ascension, especially in the Roman tradition.

109 *PG* 123: 1125. See also the few explanations of Euthymius Zigabenus *Comm. Luc.* 24:50-53 (*PG* 129:1101). The latter is interested in the date (forty days after the resurrection), the means of transportation (the cloud mentioned in Acts), the joy (because of the resurrection and the promise of the Holy Spirit), the location (Bethany and the Mount of Olives are understood as a whole), and the continuous presence in the temple (i.e., only during religious services).

110 Trans. Phillips, *Paraphrase*, 278.

111 Luther, *Evangelien-Auslegung*, 1308–10.

112 John Calvin, *Institutes* 4.17.26–27: "The body with which Christ rose is declared, not by Aristotle, but by the Holy Spirit, to be finite, and to be contained in heaven until the last day." Then: "What? Does not the very name of ascension, so often repeated, intimate removal from one place to another? . . . Was he not carried up while the disciples looked on? Do not the Evangelists clearly relate that he was carried into heaven?" See John Calvin, *The Institutes of the Christian Religion* (trans. Henry Beveridge; Grand Rapids: Eerdmans, 1989) 579–80.

113 Calvin, *Harmony,*

because he already thinks he will "continue his history" in the book of Acts.

In the seventeenth century Grotius explains that Jesus' raised hands here are not a simple gesture of prayer (he refers to his commentary on 18:13; raised hands and raised eyes are equal) but a rite of blessing.[114] He refers to Isaac (Genesis 27) and to Jacob (Genesis 48). He then cites appropriately the case of Aaron in Lev 9:22 according to the LXX: "Aaron lifted up his hands on the people and blessed them" (ἐξάρας Ἀαρὼν τὰς χεῖρας ἐπὶ τὸν λαὸν εὐλόγησεν αὐτούς). He is of the opinion that the bishops have appropriated the gesture and that they do it at the beginning and the end of meetings. On the subject of worship (v. 52), Grotius notes finally that the disciples had never previously gone that far.

In the first half of the eighteenth century, Bengel bore witness to a traditional interpretation that is neglected in the modern era. He indicates this interpretation in one sentence, the last of a short prayer to Christ: "Where you are, there I will come."[115] Jesus' ascension is to be accompanied by the ascension of the believers.

When Bengel, the Pietist theologian, wrote his *Gnomon*, the age of the Enlightenment had begun and powerful minds had begun to doubt.[116] Some English deists,[117] the German Hermann Samuel Reimarus, whom Lessing posthumously published, the Frenchman Jean Meslier, whose testament hostile to Christianity Voltaire would circulate,[118] felt incapable of believing the dogma of the ascension, whose materiality is offensive to reason. It is, furthermore, not difficult at all for them to show that the biblical sources on which the dogma is based are contradictory and unreliable. Reimarus notes in particular that the only two evangelists who were disciples of Jesus, Matthew and John, are precisely those who do not tell the story of the ascension.[119] Victoriano Larrañaga has the credit for reporting about these two centuries of doubt and apologies.

There were people who claimed that fraud had occurred. According to Karl Friedrich Bahrdt, Jesus only appeared to die, and he left his disciples on the Mount of Olives when a cloud covered the area. Karl Heinrich Georg Venturini also believed that Jesus had not died on the cross. The ascension scene is based on a misunderstanding; it was only a scene of farewell. In 1805 a society based in The Hague launched a competition in defense of the Christian religion. Since no work was judged to demonstrate sufficiently the historical value of the ascension, the contest was renewed, and in 1809 the prize was awarded to the study of Wessel Albert van Hengel. For this work, judged to be "worthy of all praise," which defends the historicity of the ascension and rejects the idea of fraud, the author won a gold medal.[120]

Heinrich E. G. Paulus and Friedrich Schleiermacher then tried to give a naturalistic explanation to the mysteries of the resurrection and the ascension.[121] It is the patristic period that has transformed the ascension into a crude miracle of farewell followed by a spiritual exaltation. One sees then the establishment of the distinction on which the nineteenth and twentieth centuries both insist between the exaltation of Easter in which the first

114 Grotius, *Annotationes*, 941–42; In Lev 9:22 LXX Grotius reads ἐπάρας, not ἐξάρας.

115 Bengel, *Gnomon* (G), 1:420.

116 For the following pages I am indebted to Larrañaga, *Ascension*, 18–129.

117 See above, "History of Interpretation," on 23:56b—24:12 (on the resurrection).

118 See Voltaire, "Extrait des sentiments de Jean Meslier (1762)," in *Les œuvres complètes de Voltaire*, 56A (Oxford: Oxford University Press, 2001) 85–160, esp. 116–17; Larrañaga, *Ascension*, 20–22.

119 Gotthold Ephraim Lessing, ed., *Fragmente des Wolfenbüttelschen Ungenannten* (4th ed.; Berlin: Reimer, 1835) 384–85; Larrañaga, *Ascension*, 18–20.

120 Karl Friedrich Bahrdt, *Ausführung des Plans und Zwecks Jesu: In Briefen an Wahrheit suchende Leser* (12 vols.; Berlin: August Mylius, 1784–93) 10:205–18; 11:37–45; Karl Heinrich Georg Venturini, *Natürliche Geschichte des grossen Propheten von Nazareth* (4 vols.; Bethlehem/Kopenhagen: Schubothe, 1800–1806) 4:169–390. For a presentation of the contest and bibliographical references, see Larrañaga, *Ascension*, 24–27.

121 Heinrich E. G. Paulus, *Das Leben Jesu als Grundlage einer reinen Geschichte des Urchristentums* 1.2 (Heidelberg: Winter, 1828) 318–44 (Paulus believes that Jesus was exalted, but he refuses to admit that it was visible); Friedrich E. Schleiermacher, *The Life of Jesus* (trans. S. Maclean Gilmour; Philadelphia: Fortress Press, 1975) 431–65 (Schleiermacher speaks of a second human life of Jesus after the resurrection).

Christians believed and the visible ascension of which the apostles were eyewitnesses (see above, the beginning of the "History of Interpretation").

This naturalistic construction would be demolished by David Friedrich Strauss, who will put the explanation of a myth in its place. The theory, which originated with Karl von Hase,[122] "describes the myth of the ascension as something foreign to the apostolic sources that was created by the Christian community."[123]

Adolf von Harnack emphasized the close links that originally existed in the faith of the early Christians between the resurrection and the ascension. In the early days these two doctrines represented two sides of the same coin. In the beginning the ascension was a confessed exaltation. Gradually a distinction was made between it and the resurrection. The later insistence on the bodily character of Jesus' resurrection led people to make a distinction between the two events. Nevertheless, the ascension is not yet a visible phenomenon, and it takes place at Easter. With the forty days, chronology interfered a third time.[124] We should not forget that text-critical problems and assumptions about possible interpolations have played a role in these controversies on the origin and meaning of the ascension. Harnack refused to believe in an interpolation early in Acts, an interpolation that would have included the myth of the ascension.[125] He believed that Luke's position in his first volume corresponds to the second degree of the tradition, but in writing Acts the evangelist followed a later legend that takes place in a tertiary tradition.[126]

Those who want to follow the views of the exegetes and historians of early Christianity during the period of the history-of-religions school, form criticism, and redaction criticism can refer to the works of Larrañaga, Lohfink, and Zwiep.[127]

Conclusion

Scholars have understood Luke 24:50-53 variously as the eyewitness account of Jesus' ascension, as the report of the last appearance of the Risen One, as a legend related to the appearances, as a legend of the exaltation, or as a literary creation of the evangelist.[128] While I recognize Luke's editorial work, I see this passage as the literary fixing of a tradition, as a legend in the etymological sense of the term. This tradition was a reminder of the ascen-

---

122 Karl D. F. von Hase, *Das Leben Jesu* (Leipzig: Johann Friedrich Leich, 1829) 204. David Friedrich Strauss, *Das Leben Jesu kritisch bearbeitet*, vol. 2 (3d ed.; Tübingen: Osiander, 1839) 642–60, 696–717, esp. 707–17. (In both cases the English translation is based on later German editions.)

123 Larrañaga, *Ascension*, 33.

124 Adolf Harnack was interested in the problem of the ascension his entire life. He deals with it as early as 1878 in the second edition of the *Patrum Apostolicorum opera* 1.3, edited by Oscar von Gebhardt and Harnack (Leipzig: Hinrichs, 1878) 137–39. For a presentation and other references, see Larrañaga, *Ascension*, 48–50, 64–74; see also Lohfink, *Himmelfahrt*, 19–20; see, finally, below, n. 124.

125 Larrañaga, *Ascension*, 43–50, 60–64. According to this hypothesis, Acts 1:3-13 would constitute the interpolation. Thus, this hypothesis is different from the one noted above (see the beginning of the analysis of this section) according to which Luke 24:50–53 and Acts 1:1-5 constitute the interpolation.

126 Adolf Harnack, *The Acts of the Apostles* (trans. J. R. Wilkinson; New York: Putnam's Sons, 1909) 157–61. In an appendix to the *Bibliothek der Symbole und Glaubensregeln der alten Kirche*, edited by August Hahn and G. Ludwig Hahn (3d ed.; Breslau: Morgenstern, 1897) 382, Harnack notes that the author of the *Ascension of Isaiah* (9:16) and, according to Irenaeus (*Adv. haer.* 1.3.2 and 30.14), the Valentinians and the Ophites believed that Jesus' ascension took place eighteen months after Easter.

127 Larrañaga, *Ascension*, 83–129; Lohfink, *Himmelfahrt*, 13–31; Zwiep, *Ascension*, 1–35.

128 See Bovon, *Luke the Theologian*, 192. I am surprised that, from the formal and phenomenological point of view, few exegetes have compared the Lukan stories of Jesus' ascension with the stories of the assumption of Mary and Mohammed's journey to heaven. On the assumption of the Virgin, see Stephen J. Shoemaker, *Ancient Traditions of the Virgin Mary's Dormition and Assumption* (Oxford Early Christian Studies; Oxford: Oxford University Press, 2002); on the heavenly journey of the prophet, see Etienne Renaud, "Le récit du mi'râj . . . ," in Claude Kappler et al., *Apocalypses et voyages dans l'au-delà* (Paris: Cerf, 1987) 267–90; and, in the same volume, Angelo M. Piemontese, "Le voyage de Mahomet au paradis et en enfer . . . ," 293–320.

sion of Jesus at the end of his appearances and before the in-breaking of the Holy Spirit at Pentecost. This story served to confirm the belief of the early Christians in the exaltation of Jesus at Easter. By incorporating it from his special source,[129] the evangelist has reinforced the connections he felt were necessary between the resurrection of Christ and salvation history.[130] He who had suffered as God's servant was now reinstated and glorified.[131] He would now remain with the Father,[132] not to ignore the plight of human beings, especially that of his church, but to grant responsibility to each individual and to await the missionary engagement of the witnesses.[133]

As for me, having arrived at the end of this commentary, I repeat with Ambrose of Milan, "Would to God that with the end of the Gospel our speech will also come to an end!"[134]

---

129 See above, thesis (d) in the analysis.

130 This is one of the theses successfully defended by Lohfink (*Himmelfahrt*, 255); see also Zwiep, *Ascension*, 196

131 Davies (*He Ascended*, 60–68, 169–70) emphasizes this point.

132 Ibid., 179. Davies underscores this aspect.

133 See Maile ("Ascension," 54–59), who highlights the importance of the ascension for the disciples; and Schnider ("Himmelfahrt," 167–72), who shows that the ascension introduces the time of mission and invites the disciples not to remain inactive.

134 Atque utinam cum evangelii fine noster quoque sermo claudatur (Ambrose *Exp. Luc.* 10.181).

429

440

444

Designer's Notes

In the design of the visual aspects of *Hermeneia*, consideration has been given to relating the form to the content by symbolic means.

The letters of the logotype *Hermeneia* are a fusion of forms alluding simultaneously to Hebrew (dotted vowel markings) and Greek (geometric round shapes) letter forms. In their modern treatment they remind us of the electronic age as well, the vantage point from which this investigation of the past begins.

The Lion of Judah used as visual identification for the series is based on the Seal of Shema. The version for *Hermeneia* is again a fusion of Hebrew calligraphic forms, especially the legs of the lion, and Greek elements characterized by the geometric. In the sequence of arcs, which can be understood as scroll-like images, the first is the lion's mouth. It is reasserted and accelerated in the whorl and returns in the aggressively arched tail: tradition is passed from one age to the next, rediscovered and re-formed.

"Who is worthy to open the scroll and break its seals. . . ."

Then one of the elders said to me

"weep not; lo, the Lion of the tribe of David,
the Root of David, has conquered,
so that he can open the scroll and
its seven seals."

Rev. 5:2, 5

To celebrate the signal achievement in biblical scholarship which *Hermeneia* represents, the entire series will by its color constitute a signal on the theologian's bookshelf: the Old Testament will be bound in yellow and the New Testament in red, traceable to a commonly used color coding for synagogue and church in medieval painting; in pure color terms, varying degrees of intensity of the warm segment of the color spectrum. The colors interpenetrate when the binding color for the Old Testament is used to imprint volumes from the New and vice versa.

Wherever possible, a photograph of the oldest extant manuscript, or a historically significant document pertaining to the biblical sources, will be displayed on the end papers of each volume to give a feel for the tangible reality and beauty of the source material.

The title-page motifs are expressive derivations from the Hermeneia logotype, repeated seven times to form a matrix and debossed on the cover of each volume. These sifted-out elements will be seen to be in their exact positions within the parent matrix.

Horizontal markings at gradated levels on the spine will assist in grouping the volumes according to these conventional categories.

The type has been set with unjustified right margins so as to preserve the internal consistency of word spacing. This is a major factor in both legibility and aesthetic quality; the resultant uneven line endings are only slight impairments to legibility by comparison. In this respect the type resembles the handwritten manuscripts where the quality of the calligraphic writing is dependent on establishing and holding to integral spacing patterns.

All of the type faces in common use today have been designed between AD 1500 and the present. For the biblical text a face was chosen which does not arbitrarily date the text, but rather one which is uncompromisingly modern and unembellished so that its feel is of the universal. The type style is Univers 65 by Adrian Frutiger.

The expository texts and footnotes are set in Baskerville, chosen for its compatibility with the many brief Greek and Hebrew insertions. The double-column format and the shorter line length facilitate speed reading and the wide margins to the left of footnotes provide for the scholar's own notations.

Kenneth Hiebert

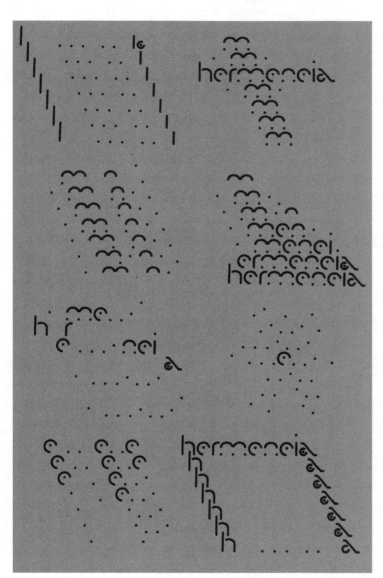

Category of biblical writing,
key symbolic characteristic,
and volumes so identified.

1
Law
(boundaries described)
  Genesis
  Exodus
  Leviticus
  Numbers
  Deuteronomy

2
History
(trek through time and space)
  Joshua
  Judges
  Ruth
  1 Samuel
  2 Samuel
  1 Kings
  2 Kings
  1 Chronicles
  2 Chronicles
  Ezra
  Nehemiah
  Esther

3
Poetry
(lyric emotional expression)
  Job
  Psalms
  Proverbs
  Ecclesiastes
  Song of Songs

4
Prophets
(inspired seers)
  Isaiah
  Jeremiah
  Lamentations
  Ezekiel
  Daniel
  Hosea
  Joel
  Amos
  Obadiah
  Jonah
  Micah
  Nahum
  Habakkuk
  Zephaniah
  Haggai
  Zechariah
  Malachi

5
New Testament Narrative
(focus on One)
  Matthew
  Mark
  Luke
  John
  Acts

6
Epistles
(directed instruction)
  Romans
  1 Corinthians
  2 Corinthians
  Galatians
  Ephesians
  Philippians
  Colossians
  1 Thessalonians
  2 Thessalonians
  1 Timothy
  2 Timothy
  Titus
  Philemon
  Hebrews
  James
  1 Peter
  2 Peter
  1 John
  2 John
  3 John
  Jude

7
Apocalypse
(vision of the future)
  Revelation

8
Extracanonical Writings
(peripheral records)

ΑΠΟΤΟΥΓΕΝΗΜΑΤΟCΤΗCΑΜΠΕΛΟΥ
ΕΩCΟΤΟΥΕΛΘΗΗΒΑCΙΛΕΙΑΤΟΥ ΘΥ

ϹϞϚ : ΚΑΙΛΑΒωΝ ΑΡΤΟΝ ΕΥΧΑΡΙCΤΗCΑC ΕΚΛΑCΕΝ
ϹϞΖ : ΚΑΙΕΔωΚΕΝΑΥΤΟΙCΛΕΓωΝ ΤΟΥΤΟCΤΙΝ
ϹϞΗ ΤΟCωΜΑΜΟΥ ΠΛΗΝΙΔΟΥΗΧΕΙΡΤΟΥ
ΠΑΡΑΔΙΔΟΝΤΟCΜΕΜΕΤΕΜΟΥΕΠΙΤΡΑΠΕΖΗC
ΟΤΙΜΕΝΟΥΙΟCΤΟΥ ΑΝΘΡωΠΟΥ ΚΑΤΑΤΟ
ωΡΙCΜΕΝΟΝΠΟΡΕΥΕΤΑΙΠΛΗΝΟΥΑΙΕΚΕΙΝω
ϹϞΘ : ΔΙΟΥΠΑΡΑΔΙΔΟΤΑΙ : ΑΥΤΟΙΔΕΗΡΞΑΝΤΟ
ϹΥΝΖΗΤΕΙΝΠΡΟCΕΑΥΤΟΥCΤΙCΑΡΑΕΙΗΟΜΕΛΛω
ΤΟΥΤΟΠΡΑCCΕΙΝ ΕΓΕΝΕΤΟΔΕ ΚΑΙ
ΦΙΛΟΝΙΚΕΙΑ ΕΝΑΥΤΟΙCΤΟΤΙCΑΝΤω
ΜΕΙΖωΝ ΟΔΕΕΙΠΕΝΑΥΤΟΙC
ΟΙΒΑCΙΛΕΙCΤωΝΕΘΝωΝ ΚΥΡΙΕΥΟΥCΙΝ
ΑΥΤωΝ ΚΑΙΟΙΕΞΟΥCΙΑΖΟΝΤΕCΑΥΤωΝ
ΕΥΕΡΓΕΤΑΙΚΑΛΟΥΝΤΑΙ
ΥΜΕΙCΔΕ ΟΥΧΟΥΤωC ΑΛΛΟΜΕΙΖωΝ
ΕΝΥΜΕΙΝ ΓΕΙΝΕCΘωωCΟΜΕΙΚΡΟΤΕΡΟC
ΚΑΙΟΗΓΟΥΜΕΝΟC ωCΟΔΙΑΚΟΝΟC
ϹΟΑ : ΜΑΛΛΟΝΗ ΟΔΑΝΑΚΕΙΜΕΝΟC ΕΓωΓΑΡ
ΕΝΜΕCωΥΜωΝ ΗΛΘΟΝ ΟΥΧωCΟΑΝΑΚΕΙΜΕΝΟC
ΑΛΛωCΟΔΙΑΚΟΝωΝ ΚΑΙΥΜΕΙCΗΥΖΕΩCΤΕ
ΕΝΤΗΔΙΑΚΟΝΙΑ ΜΟΥ ωCΟΔΙΑΚΟΝωΝ
ΟΙΔΙΑΜΕΜΕΝΗΚΟΤΕCΜΕΤΕΜΟΥ ΕΝΤΟΙC
ΠΕΙΡΑCΜΟΙCΜΟΥ ΚΑΓωΔΙΑΤΙΘΕΜΕΥΜΕΙΝ
ΚΑΘωCΔΙΕΘΕΤΟ ΜΟΙΟΠΑΤΗΡ ΒΑCΙΛΕΙΑΝΙΝΑ
ΕCΘΗΤΕ ΚΑΙΠΕΙΝΗΤΑΙΕΠΙΤΗCΤΡΑΠΕΖΗCΜΟΥ
ϹΟΒ : ΕΝΤΗΒΑCΙΛΕΙΑ ΚΑΙΚΑΘΗCΕCΘΕΕΠΙ ΙΒ
ΘΡΟΝΟΥC ΚΡΕΙΝΟΝΤΕC ΤΑC ΙΒ ΦΥΛΑC
ϹΟΓ : ΤΟΥΙCΡΑΗΛ : ΕΙΠΕΝΔΕΟ ΚΕ CΙΜωΝ
CΙΜωΝ ΙΔΟΥΟCΑΤΑΝΑCΕΞ ΗΤΗCΑΤΟ ΥΜΑC
ΤΟΥCΙΝΙΑCΑΙωCΟΤΟΝCΙΤΟΝ ΕΓωΔΕ
ΕΔΕΗΘΗΝΠΕΡΙCΟΥ ΙΝΑΜΗΕΚΛΙΠΗ